The Western Heritage

The Western Heritage

Donald Kagan / **Steven Ozment** / **Frank M. Turner**

YALE UNIVERSITY   HARVARD UNIVERSITY   YALE UNIVERSITY

Third Edition

Macmillan Publishing Company

New York

NOTE:
The dates cited for monarchs and popes are generally the years of their reign rather than of their births and deaths.

MACMILLAN PUBLISHING COMPANY
866 Third Avenue, New York, New York 10022

Collier Macmillan Canada, Inc.

Library of Congress Cataloging-in-Publication Data

Kagan, Donald.
  The Western heritage.

  Includes bibliographies and index.
  1. Civilization, Occidental. I. Ozment, Steven E.
II. Turner, Frank M. (Frank Miller),
III. Title.
CB245.K28 1987   909′.09821   86-5225
ISBN 0-02-363200-3

Printing: 3 4 5 6 7 8   Year: 8 9 0 1 2 3 4 5 6

THIS THIRD EDITION of *The Western Heritage,* while retaining the fundamental character, structure, and outlook of its earlier versions, has made several significant changes in response to needs expressed by readers and to important trends in the teaching of the history of western civilization in colleges and universities. Since the second edition we have further condensed the narrative and reduced the number of chapters dedicated to the ancient world. We have incorporated substantial coverage of the Byzantine Empire in Chapter Six. Colonial Latin America and its struggle for independence from Spain and Portugal are examined in depth in Chapters Ten, Sixteen, and Twenty. In addition to these changes, we have updated the material on the post-World War II era.

We have also tried to improve the style and organization wherever we saw the need. Once again, we have sought fresh historical documents and illustrations, changing about a third of each. The text is now divided into six sections. Each part is introduced with a brief essay, which gives an overview of major trends, influences, and events in each era.

Taking note of the continuing interest in social history among both professors and students, we have added new sections throughout the work dealing with that aspect of the human experience from ancient times to our own era. We believe that this new material adds depth, perspective, and interest by telling more about the private lives and concerns of men and women; at the same time, we hope that our account of larger events and institutions gives meaning to the experiences of individuals. This new emphasis will also be found in many of the new documents and illustrations. Notably, the full-color section from the second edition has been transformed into a pictorial essay entitled "Cities and Their People." We have also revised the bibliographies at the end of each chapter, referring to important new works while retaining the most important ones previously included.

This revision has gained much from the advice and teaching experience of our colleagues across the country, many of whom sent us advice and suggestions. We read and considered them all with care and made many changes and corrections as a result. We are especially grateful to the following readers who were good enough to criticize and evaluate the previous edition and early drafts of our revision:

Preface

David Applebaum, *Glassboro State College*
William Arnett, *West Virginia University*
Marc Baer, *Hope College*
James Barringer, *Hillsborough Community College*
Paul Chardoul, *Grand Rapids Junior College*
Walter Fraser, *Georgia Southern College*
W. Kent Hackman, *University of Idaho*
Louise Hoffman, *Pennsylvania State University—Capitol Campus*
Frayda Hoffnung, *California State University—Long Beach*
John Kesler, *Lakeland Community College*
Theodore Koditschek, *University of California—Irvine*
R. Michael Mase, *Golden West College*
Dean O'Donnell, *Virginia Polytechnic Institute*
Ann Quartararo, *United States Naval Academy*
Roger Schlosser, *Grand Rapids Junior College*

We benefitted greatly from their work, and we hope that this edition reflects their contributions.

The third edition is accompanied by several ancillaries designed to assist both the instructor and the student. Perry Rogers of the Ohio State University has authored the Instructor's Manual; the Study Guide was written by Anthony Brescia of Nassau Community College. Delta Software, in conjunction with Macmillan Publishing Company and the authors, is producing a computerized testing disk. Twenty-four color transparencies of maps from the text are also available.

Our intention in producing this revision has been to provide a text that is clear, informative, interesting, and easy to teach. Just as the revision of a textbook is a joint effort between authors and readers, so the use of a textbook is a joint effort between teachers and students—a relationship that we hope this volume will enhance and enliven.

D.K.
S.O.
F.M.T.

New Haven and Cambridge

Contents

Europe in Transition, 1300–1750

9 The Late Middle Ages and the Renaissance: Decline and Renewal (1300–1527)

10 The Age of Reformation

11 The Age of Religious Wars 405

29 Europe in the Era of the Superpowers

30 Twentieth-Century States of Mind

Documents

Maps

Illustrations in Color: Cities and Their People

Some Prominent Emperors, Kings, and Popes

ROMAN EMPIRE

Augustus	27 B.C.–A.D. 14	Trajan	98–117	Severus Alexander	222–235
Tiberius	14– 37	Hadrian	117–138	Philip the Arab	244–249
Caligula	37– 41	Antoninus Pius	138–161	Decius	249–251
Claudius	41– 54	Marcus Aurelius	161–180	Valerian	253–260
Nero	54– 68	Commodus	180–193	Gallienus	260–268
Vespasian	69– 79	Septimius Severus	193–211	Aurelian	270–275
Titus	79– 81	Caracalla	211–217	Diocletian	284–286
Domitian	81– 96	Elagabalus	218–222		

WEST		EAST		WEST		EAST	
Maximian	286–305	Diocletian	284–305	Gratian	375–383		
Constantius	305–306	Galerius	305–311	Valentinian II	383–392		
		Maximius	308–313	Theodosius	394–395	Theodosius	379–395
		Licinius	308–324	Honorius	395–423	Arcadius	393–408
Constantine	308–337	Constantine	324–337			Theodosius II	408–450
Maxentius	307–312			Valentinian III	425–455	Marcian	450–457
Constantine II	337–340					Leo	457–474
Constans	337–350			Romulus	475–476	Zeno	474–491
Constantius II	351–361	Constantius II	337–361			Anastasius	491–518
Julian	360–363	Julian	361–363			Justin	518–527
Jovian	363–364	Jovian	363–364			Justinian	527–565
Valentinian	364–375	Valens	364–378				

CAROLINGIAN KINGDOM

Pepin, Mayor of the Palace	680–714	Charlemagne and Carloman, Joint Kings	768–771
Charles Martel, Mayor of the Palace	715–741	Charlemagne, King	771–814
Pepin the Short, Mayor of the Palace	741–751	Charlemagne, Emperor	800–814
Pepin the Short, King	751–768	Louis the Pious, Emperor	814–840

WEST FRANKS

Charles the Bald	840–877
Louis II the Stammerer	877–879
Louis III	879–882
Carloman	879–884

LOTHARINGIA

Lothar	840–855
Louis II	855–875
Charles	855–863
Lothar II	855–869

EAST FRANKS

Louis the German	840–876
Carloman	876–880
Louis	876–882
Charles the Fat	884–887

HOLY ROMAN EMPIRE

SAXONS

Henry the Fowler	919–936
Otto I	962–973
Otto II	973–983
Otto III	983–1002

SALIANS

Conrad II	1024–1039
Henry III	1039–1056
Henry IV	1056–1106
Henry V	1106–1125
Lothar II	1125–1137

HOHENSTAUFENS

Frederick I Barbarossa	1152–1190
Henry IV	1190–1197
Philip of Swabia	1198–1208
Otto IV (Welf)	1198–1215
Frederick II	1215–1250
Conrad IV	1250–1254

LUXEMBURG, HAPSBURG, AND OTHER DYNASTIES

Rudolf of Hapsburg	1273–1291
Adolph of Nassau	1292–1298
Albert of Austria	1298–1308
Henry VII of Luxemburg	1308–1313
Ludwig IV of Bavaria	1314–1347
Charles IV	1347–1378
Wenceslas	1378–1400
Rupert	1400–1410
Sigismund	1410–1437

HAPSBURGS

Frederick III	1440–1493
Maximilian I	1493–1519
Charles V	1519–1556
Ferdinand I	1556–1564
Maximilian II	1564–1576
Rudolf II	1576–1612
Matthias	1612–1619
Ferdinand II	1619–1637
Ferdinand III	1637–1657
Leopold I	1658–1705
Joseph I	1705–1711
Charles VI	1711–1740
Charles VII	1742–1745
Francis I	1745–1765
Joseph II	1765–1790
Leopold II	1790–1792
Francis II	1792–1806

THE PAPACY

Leo I	440– 461	Innocent III	1198–1216	Julius II	1503–1513	Pius IX	1846–1878
Gregory I	590– 604	Gregory IX	1227–1241	Leo X	1513–1521	Leo XIII	1878–1903
Nicholas I	858– 867	Boniface VIII	1294–1303	Adrian VI	1522–1523	Pius X	1903–1914
Silvester II	999–1003	John XXII	1316–1334	Clement VII	1523–1534	Benedict XV	1914–1922
Leo IX	1049–1054	Gregory XI	1370–1378	Paul III	1534–1549	Pius XI	1922–1939
Nicholas II	1058–1061	Martin V	1417–1431	Paul IV	1555–1559	Pius XII	1939–1958
Gregory VII	1073–1085	Eugenius IV	1431–1447	Pius V	1566–1572	John XXIII	1958–1963
Urban II	1088–1099	Nicholas V	1447–1455	Gregory XIII	1572–1585	Paul VI	1963–1978
Paschal II	1099–1118	Pius II	1458–1464	Pius VII	1800–1823	John Paul I	1978
Alexander III	1159–1181	Alexander VI	1492–1503	Gregory XVI	1831–1846	John Paul II	1978–

ENGLAND

ANGLO-SAXONS

Alfred the Great	871– 900
Ethelred the Unready	978–1016
Canute (*Danish*)	1016–1035
Harold I	1035–1040
Hardicanute	1040–1042
Edward the Confessor	1042–1066
Harold II	1066

NORMANS

William the Conqueror	1066–1087
William II	1087–1100
Henry I	1100–1135
Stephen	1135–1154

ANGEVINS

Henry II	1154–1189
Richard I	1189–1199
John	1199–1216
Henry III	1216–1272
Edward I	1272–1307
Edward II	1307–1327
Edward III	1327–1377
Richard II	1377–1399

HOUSES OF LANCASTER AND YORK

Henry IV	1399–1413
Henry V	1413–1422
Henry VI	1422–1461
Edward IV	1461–1483
Edward V	1483
Richard III	1483–1485

TUDORS

Henry VII	1485–1509
Henry VIII	1509–1547
Edward VI	1547–1553
Mary I	1553–1558
Elizabeth I	1558–1603

STUARTS

James I	1603–1625
Charles I	1625–1649
Charles II	1660–1685
James II	1685–1688
William III and Mary II	1689–1694
William III alone	1694–1702
Anne	1702–1714

HANOVERIANS (from 1917, WINDSORS)

George I	1714–1727
George II	1727–1760
George III	1760–1820
George IV	1820–1830
William IV	1830–1837
Victoria	1837–1901
Edward VII	1901–1910
George V	1910–1936
Edward VIII	1936
George VI	1936–1952
Elizabeth II	1952–

FRANCE

CAPETIANS

Hugh Capet	987– 996
Robert II the Pious	996–1031
Henry I	1031–1060
Philip I	1060–1108
Louis VI	1108–1137
Louis VII	1137–1180
Philip II Augustus	1180–1223
Louis VIII	1223–1226
Louis IX	1226–1270
Philip III	1270–1285
Philip IV	1285–1314
Louis X	1314–1316
Philip V	1316–1322
Charles IV	1322–1328

VALOIS

Philip VI	1328–1350
John	1350–1364
Charles V	1364–1380
Charles VI	1380–1422
Charles VII	1422–1461
Louis XI	1461–1483
Charles VIII	1483–1498
Louis XII	1498–1515
Francis I	1515–1547
Henry II	1547–1559
Francis II	1559–1560
Charles IX	1560–1574
Henry III	1574–1589

BOURBONS

Henry IV	1589–1610
Louis XIII	1610–1643
Louis XIV	1643–1715
Louis XV	1715–1774
Louis XVI	1774–1792

POST 1792

Napoleon I, Emperor	1804–1814
Louis XVIII (*Bourbon*)	1814–1824
Charles X (*Bourbon*)	1824–1830
Louis Philippe (*Bourbon-Orléans*)	1830–1848
Napoleon III, Emperor	1851–1870

ITALY

Victor Emmanuel II	1861–1878	Victor Emmanuel II	1900–1946
Humbert I	1878–1900	Humbert II	1946

SPAIN

		HAPSBURGS		BOURBONS			
Ferdinand and	1479–1516						
Isabella	1479–1504	Philip I	1504–1506	Philip V	1700–1746	Ferdinand VII (restored)	
		Charles I (Holy Roman Emperor as Charles V)		Ferdinand VI	1746–1759		1814–1833
				Charles III	1759–1788	Isabella II	1833–1868
			1506–1556	Charles IV	1788–1808	Amadeo	1870–1873
		Philip II	1556–1598	Ferdinand VII	1808	Alfonso XII	1874–1885
		Philip III	1598–1621	Joseph Bonaparte		Alfonso XIII	1886–1931
		Philip IV	1621–1665		1808–1813	Juan Carlos I	1975–
		Charles II	1665–1700				

AUSTRIA AND AUSTRIA-HUNGARY

(Until 1806 all except Maria Theresa were also Holy Roman Emperors.)

Maximilian I, Archduke		Maximilian II	1564–1576	Leopold I	1658–1705	Leopold II	1790–1792
	1493–1519	Rudolf II	1576–1612	Joseph I	1705–1711	Francis II	1792–1835
Charles I (Emperor as		Matthias	1612–1619	Charles VI	1711–1740	Ferdinand I	1835–1848
Charles V)	1519–1556	Ferdinand II	1619–1637	Maria Theresa	1740–1780	Francis Joseph	1848–1916
Ferdinand I	1556–1564	Ferdinand III	1637–1657	Joseph II	1780–1790	Charles I	1916–1918

PRUSSIA AND GERMANY

HOHENZOLLERNS

Frederick William the		Frederick II the Great	1740–1786	William I	1861–1888
Great Elector	1640–1688	Frederick William II	1786–1797	Frederick III	1888
Frederick I	1701–1713	Frederick William III	1797–1840	William II	1888–1918
Frederick William I	1713–1740	Frederick William IV	1840–1861		

RUSSIA

		ROMANOVS			
Ivan III	1462–1505				
Basil III	1505–1533				
Ivan IV the Terrible	1533–1584	Michael	1613–1645	Elizabeth	1741–1762
Theodore I	1584–1598	Alexius	1645–1676	Peter III	1762
Boris Godunov	1598–1605	Theodore III	1676–1682	Catherine II the Great	1762–1796
Theodore II	1605	Ivan IV and Peter I	1682–1689	Paul	1796–1801
Basil IV	1606–1610	Peter I the Great alone		Alexander I	1801–1825
			1689–1725	Nicholas I	1825–1855
		Catherine I	1725–1727	Alexander II	1855–1881
		Peter II	1727–1730	Alexander III	1881–1894
		Anna	1730–1740	Nicholas II	1894–1917
		Ivan VI	1740–1741		

The Foundations of Western Civilization in the Ancient World

The roots of Western civilization may be found in the experience and culture of the Greeks, but Greek civilization itself was richly nourished by older, magnificent civilizations to the south and east, especially in Mesopotamia and Egypt. In the valley of the Tigris and Euphrates rivers (Mesopotamia) and soon after in the valley of the Nile in Egypt, human beings moved from a life in agricultural villages, using tools of wood, bone, shell, and stone, into a much richer and more varied social organization that we call *civilization*. The use of irrigation in the rich alluvial soil vastly increased the supply of food, thereby permitting a growth in population and even a surplus to support specialists: artisans, merchants, priests, and soldiers. For the first time, people lived in cities, complex centers of government, religion, metallurgy and advanced crafts, and commerce. The need for organizing this new and varied activity and for keeping records led to the invention of writing. The wealth acquired through more effective agriculture, better tools, the specialization of function, commerce, and conquest permitted the development of unprecedented skills. Great advances took place in the arts and the sciences, in literature, and in the development of complex religious ideas and organizations.

The new style of life required firm, efficient management and soon produced governments that were centralized and powerful. The kings' power rested on their capacity to manage the economy and to collect taxes. This capacity, in turn, permitted them to train and support armies, which imposed control over their subjects and also engaged in wars of expansion against their neighbors. The rulers' legitimacy was guaranteed by religion, for in Mesopotamia the kings were accepted as the representatives of the gods, and in Egypt they were themselves regarded as divine. The resulting combination of political, military, economic, and religious power produced societies that were rigidly divided into social classes: slaves, free commoners, priests, and aristocrats, as well as the divine or semidivine monarchs. There was almost no social mobility and little individual freedom; only a handful of people took part in government. The great power controlled by these rulers led the stronger of them to dominate kingdoms and empires that grew ever larger and more powerful.

The struggle between great empires sometimes permitted smaller city-states and kingdoms to survive and flourish in the spaces between them. Among these, two were especially important for the civilization that would some day arise in the West. The cities of Phoenicia, in what is now Lebanon, produced great sailors and traders who came into early and frequent contact with the Greeks. Through the Phoenicians, among other Eastern peoples, the Greeks learned the art of writing and were powerfully influenced by the art, technology, and mythology of the earlier cultures. Absorbed, transformed, and transmitted by the Greeks, the civilizations of Mesopotamia and Egypt, very indirectly, became part of the Western heritage. Neighbors of the Phoenicians, called Hebrews or Israelites, would have a more direct influence on the civilization of the West. They conceived a religion based on belief in a single all-powerful God who ruled over all peoples and the entire universe and made strong ethical demands on human beings. This religion of the Jews, as they came to be called from the name of their kingdom of Judah, became the basis of two later religions of great importance: Christianity and Islam.

Greek civilization arose after the destruction of the Bronze Age cultures on Crete and the Greek mainland before 1000 B.C. It took a turn sharply different from its predecessors in Egypt and western Asia. It was based on the independent existence of hundreds of city-states called *poleis* that retained their autonomy for hundreds of years before being incorporated into larger units. These cities attained a degree of self-government, broad political participation, and individual freedom never achieved before that time. They also introduced a new way of thinking that looked on the world as the product of natural forces to be understood by means of the senses and human reason, unaided by reference to supernatural forces. The result was the invention of science and philosophy as we know them. This approach led the Greeks to focus their attention on the life of human beings on earth, and a humanistic concern about accurate and realistic depiction of people came to characterize their art. In the same way their literature placed humankind at the center of its concerns, adapting and inventing a great variety of literary genres, from epic, lyric, and dramatic poetry, to history, philosophy, rhetoric, and fiction in prose. The Greeks' way of thinking, their forms of art and literature, and their commitment to self-government and political freedom became and have remained central to Western civilization.

The Greeks also developed ways of fighting on land and sea that enabled them to plant cities from Spain to the Black Sea and to defeat repeated attacks by the vast and powerful Persian Empire. At last, continued quarrels and wars between the *poleis* so weakened the Greeks that they fell under the control of their Macedonian cousins to the north. Alexander the Great of Macedon, using Greek troops as well as his own, swiftly conquered the Persian Empire, establishing Greek and Macedonian rule over the lands that had made up the great Eastern empires. After his death in 323 B.C. this vast territory was divided among his successors to form three great kingdoms. We call the new world that resulted and the culture that grew up in it *Hellenistic,* for it was different from the earlier culture of the independent *poleis* that we call *Hellenic.* Hellenistic culture was a mixture of Greek elements combined with some from the native peoples. It was without the particularism of the Hellenic world, and anyone speaking Greek could move comfortably from city to city and find a familiar and common culture. This was the world that succumbed to the Roman conquest in the last two centuries before the Christian era.

The Romans were tough farmers who began as inhabitants of a small town on the Tiber river in west-central Italy. After deposing their king in about 500 B.C., they invented a republican constitution and a code of law that provided a solid foundation for a stable and effective political order. Constantly at war with their neighbors, the Romans achieved military discipline and skills that allowed them to fight off attacks and to gain control of most of Italy by about 270 B.C. They developed an ingenious organization of the conquered lands whereby the conquered peoples came to be allies and even fellow citizens rather than subjects. In this way Rome expanded its military resources as well as its control when it gained new territory, and it acquired an army whose numbers could not be matched. From 264 until well into the first century B.C., the Romans extended their conquests overseas until they had conquered the Carthaginians in the west and defeated all the great Hellenistic powers, dominating the shores of the Mediterranean and lands well beyond. The Romans were fine engineers and road builders, but in art, literature, and philosophy they had barely made a start when they came into contact with the advanced Greek civilization of the Hellenistic world. In these areas the Romans became eager students, and as the Roman poet Horace put it, "Captive Greece took Rome captive." The Romans took the Greek poets and prose writers as their models, but in time they adapted them to suit their own experience and cast of mind. Educated Romans came to be bilingual, and Roman culture passed on the legacy of the Greeks both directly and indirectly, transformed by passing through Roman hands.

The conquest of most of the known world created many problems for a republican constitution designed to govern only a small collection of farmers. Competition for eminence, power, and wealth within the Roman aristocracy led to struggles and civil wars that ravaged Italy and the empire as well. Finally, Gaius Julius Caesar defeated his opponents, put an end to the republic, and established himself as dictator for life. Rumor had it that he meant to be installed as king. An aristocratic plot put an end to these plans, but from the civil wars that followed Caesar's assassination in 44 B.C., his nephew Octavian, later called Augustus, emerged as the commander of all of Rome's armed forces and as the effective ruler of the Roman Empire. His new constitution tried to conceal the death of the republic and its replacement by what was really an imperial monarchy, but it is correct to place the birth of the Roman Empire at the time of Augustus' victory at Actium in 31 B.C. Augustus' disguised monarchy flourished for almost two centuries, but after the death of the emperor Marcus Aurelius in 180 A.D., Rome's decline became obvious. Pressure from barbarian tribes on the frontiers, economic troubles at home, weak and incompetent emperors, and civil wars—all strained Rome's resources, human and material. By the fifth century A.D., the Roman Empire in the west had collapsed and was shared out among different Germanic tribes, although the eastern portion of the empire, with its capital at Constantinople, survived for a thousand years more. Before Rome's fall the empire had abandoned paganism and had adopted Christianity as its official religion. The heritage that the ancient world passed on to its medieval successor in western Europe was a combination of cultural traditions including those coming from Egypt, Mesopotamia, Israel, Greece, Rome, and the German tribes that destroyed the Roman Empire.

16

An eighth-century B.C. *alabaster relief of Gilgamesh, the god-like hero of an ancient Sumerian epic poem. The sculpture was found in the ruins of the palace of the Assyrian king Sargon II and is now in the Louvre.* [EPA]

HISTORY, IN ITS TWO SENSES—as the events of the past that make up the human experience on earth and as the written record of those events—is a subject of inescapable interest and importance. We are naturally interested in how we came to be what we are and in how the world we live in came to be what it is. In addition, we need to know the record of the past and to try to understand the people and forces that shaped it; whatever changes in the human condition may have occurred since the emergence of our species, the study of human experience through history remains the best aid to understanding present human behavior. We must, therefore, examine the life of people on this planet from the earliest times.

Early Human Beings and Their Culture

Scientists estimate that the earth may be as many as six billion years old, that creatures very much like humans may have appeared three to five million years ago, and that our own species of human being goes back at least fifty thousand years. Humans are different from other animals in that they are capable of producing and passing on a culture. Culture may be defined as the ways of living built up by a group and passed on from one generation to another. It may include behavior, material things, ideas, institutions, and beliefs. The source of humanity's creation of material culture is the hands. We can touch the balls of our fingers with the ball of the thumb, and so we can hold and make tools. The source of our ability to create ideas and institutions is in our capacity to speak, and this is what allows us to transmit our culture to future generations. Whether our ability to make a material culture is more important than our ability to speak, and therefore to think abstractly, is an interesting question, but clearly both abilities are needed for the development of human culture.

The anthropologist designates early human cultures by their tools. The earliest period is the Paleolithic (from Greek, ''old stone'') Age. In this immensely long period (from perhaps 600,000 to 10,000 B.C.), people were hunters, fishers, and gatherers, but not producers, of food. They learned to make and use tools of stone and of perishable materials like wood, to make and control fire, and to pass on what they learned in language. In the regions where civilization ultimately was born, people de-

1

The World Before the West

6

*The
Foundations of
Western
Civilization in
the Ancient
World*

pended on nature for their food and were very vulnerable to attacks from wild beasts and to natural disasters. Because their lives were often "solitary, poor, nasty, brutish, and short," as Thomas Hobbes put it, their responses to troubles and dangers were filled with fear. Their minds endowed all the objects they met with life or spirit, and they tried their best to put themselves in the right relationship to all these forces. They trusted magic, incantations, and ritual. Evidence of this Paleolithic culture has been excavated or found in caves in widely scattered areas of Europe, Asia, and Africa.

The style of life and the level of technology of the Paleolithic period could support only a sparsely settled society. If hunters were too numerous, game would not suffice. In Paleolithic times, people were subject to the same natural and ecological constraints that today maintain a balance between wolves and deer in Alaska.

But human life in the Paleolithic Age easily lent itself to division of labor by sex. The men engaged in hunting, fishing, making tools and weapons, and fighting against other families, clans, and tribes. The women, less mobile because of frequent childbearing, smaller in stature, and less strong and swift than the men, gathered nuts, berries, and wild grains; wove

Paleolithic cave painting of bulls and horses from the Dordogne valley of southern France. The animals, which were hunted by prehistoric humans, are depicted with remarkable realism. [Ronald Sheridan's Photo Library]

baskets; and made clothing. Women gathering food probably discovered how to plant and care for seeds. This knowledge eventually made possible the Age of Agriculture—the Neolithic Revolution.

Of early Paleolithic societies only a few developed into Neolithic or New Stone Age agricultural societies, and anthropologists disagree on why that revolutionary development occurred. In many areas, right into our own time, some isolated portions of humankind have been content to continue to live in the "Stone Age" unless compelled by more advanced cultures to change; why toil in fields, on a South Sea island, if fruit, vegetables, and fish are plentiful and free, the weather is wonderful, and there's a party on the beach? The reasons for the shift to agriculture by late Paleolithic groups are unclear. In the past, some scientists thought that climatic change—a drop in temperature and rainfall—forced people to be inventive and to seek new ways of acquiring food, but newer evidence suggests that there was little climatic variation in Neolithic times. Other theories focus on the human element: a possible growth in population, an increased sense of territoriality, and a resulting interference with the pursuit of herds for hunting.

However it happened, some ten thousand years ago parts of what we now call the Middle East began to shift from a hunter–gatherer culture to a settled agricultural one. People began to use precisely carved stone tools, so we call this period the Neolithic (from Greek, "new stone") Age. Animals as well as food crops were domesticated. The important invention of pottery made it possible to store surplus liquids, just as the invention of baskets had earlier made it possible to store dry foods. Cloth came to be made from flax and wool. Crops required constant care from planting to harvest, so the Neolithic people built permanent buildings, usually in clusters near the best fields.

The agricultural revolution may not have produced an immediate population explosion. Anthropologists suggest that village living produced a much greater incidence of disease, there being no provision for the disposal of human and animal waste. The Neolithic villages also provided attractive targets for raiders. Still, agriculture provided a steadier source of food and a greater production of food in a given area. It thus provided the basis for a denser population over time. It was a major step in human control of nature, and it was a vital precondition for the emergence of civilization. The earliest Neolithic societies appeared in the Near East about 8000 B.C., in India about 3600 B.C., and in China about 4000 B.C. The Neolithic revolution in the Near East and India was based on wheat and in China, on millet and rice; in Meso-America, several millennia later, it would be based on corn.

Neolithic villages and their culture, gradually growing from and replacing Paleolithic culture, could be located in almost any kind of terrain. But about four thousand years before the Christian era, people began to move in large numbers into the river-watered lowlands of Mesopotamia and Egypt. This shift evolved into a new style of life: an urban society and civilization. The shift was accompanied by the gradual introduction of new technologies and by the invention of writing.

Again, we do not know why people first chose to live in cities, with their inherent disadvantages: overcrowding, epidemics, wide separation from sources of food and raw materials, and the concentration of wealth that permitted organized warfare. Perhaps cities were created because, to quote the Greek philosopher Aristotle, "Man is by nature a political animal"; perhaps they arose merely because they offered more possibilities for amusement, occupational choice, and enrichment than had the Neolithic villages. In any event, by about 3000 B.C., when the invention of writing gave birth to history, urban life was established in the valleys of the Tigris and Euphrates rivers in Mesopotamia (modern Iraq) and of the Nile in Egypt. Somewhat later, urban life arose in the Indus valley of India and the Yellow River basin of China. The development of urban centers by no means meant the disappearance of numerous outlying peasant agricultural villages. Nevertheless, with the coming of cities, writing, and metals, humankind had attained civilization.

Early Civilizations to About 1000 B.C.

Civilization, then, is a form of human culture in which many people live in urban centers, have mastered the art of smelting metals, and have developed a method of writing. The rich alluvial plains where civilization began made possible the production of unprecedented surpluses of food—but only if there was an intelligent management of the water supply. Proper

Neolithic pots found in what is today Israel. The invention of pottery made it possible to store surplus liquids, such as water and cooking oil, just as the invention of baskets had earlier made it possible to store dry foods. [Ronald Sheridan's Photo Library]

flood control and irrigation called for the control of the river by some strong authority capable of managing the distribution of water. This control and management required careful observation and record keeping. The first use of writing may have been to record the behavior of the river and the astronomical events that gave clues about it. It was also used by the powerful individuals (the kings) who dominated the life of the river valleys to record their possessions, by priests to record omens, by merchants and artisans to record business transactions, and by others to record acts of the government, laws, and different kinds of literature.

This widely varied use of writing reflects the complex culture of the urban centers in the river valleys. Commerce was important enough to support a merchant class. Someone discovered how to smelt tin and copper to make a stronger and more useful material—bronze—which replaced stone in the making of tools and weapons; the importance of this technological development is reflected in the

7

term *Bronze Age*. The great need for record keeping created a class of scribes, because the picture writing and complicated scripts of these cultures took many years to learn and could not be mastered by many. To deal with the gods, great temples were built, and many priests worked in them. The collection of all these people into cities gave the settlements an entirely new character. Unlike Neolithic villages, they were communities established for purposes other than agriculture. The city was an administrative, religious, manufacturing, entertainment, and commercial center.

The logic of nature pointed in the direction of the unification of an entire river valley. Central control would put the river's water to the most efficient use, and the absence of central control would lead to warfare, chaos, and destruction. As a result, these civilizations produced unified kingdoms under powerful monarchs who came to be identified with divinity. The typical king in a river-valley civilization was regarded either as a god or as the delegate of a god. Around him developed a rigid class structure. Beneath the monarch was a class of hereditary military aristocrats and a powerful priesthood. Below them were several kinds of freemen, mostly peasants, and at the bottom were many slaves. Most of the land was owned or controlled by the king, the nobility, and the priests. These were traditional, conservative cultures of numerous peasant villages and urban centers of administration, commerce, and religious and military activity. Cultural patterns took form early and then changed only slowly and grudgingly.

MAP 1-1 *Two ancient river valley civilizations: While Egypt early was united into a single state, Mesopotamia was long divided into a number of city states.*

THE ANCIENT NEAR EAST

Mesopotamian Civilization

The first civilization appears to have arisen in the valley of the Tigris and Euphrates rivers, Mesopotamia (the land "between the rivers" from the Greek). Its founders seem to have been a people called Sumerians, who controlled the southern part of the valley (Sumer) close to the head of the Persian Gulf by the dawn of history, around 3000 B.C. (see Map 1.1). At first, city-states about one hundred square miles in size dotted the landscape. Ur, Erech, Lagash, and Eridu are examples of such cities that archaeologists have revealed to us. Quarrels over water rights and frontiers led to incessant fighting, and in time, stronger towns conquered weaker ones and expanded to form larger units, usually kingdoms. While the Sumerians were fighting with their neighbors and among themselves for supremacy in the south, a people from the Arabian Desert on the west called Semites had been moving into

The Reforms of a Sumerian King

Urukagina ruled the Sumerian city-state of Lagash from about 2415 to 2400 B.C. The following selections describe reforms that he claimed to have enacted, in the process revealing some of the social and economic problems of the time.

Formerly, from days of yore, from (the day) the seed (of man) came forth, the man in charge of the boatmen seized the boats. The head shepherd seized the donkeys. The head shepherd seized the sheep. The man in charge of the fisheries seized the fisheries. The barley rations of the guda-priests were measured out (to their disadvantage) in the Ashte (presumably the storehouse of the ensi*). The shepherds of the wool-bearing sheep had to pay silver (to the* ensi*) for (the shearing of) the white sheep. The man in charge of field surveyors, the head* gala*, the* agrig*, the man in charge of brewing, (and) all of the* ugula*'s had to pay silver for the shearing of the gaba-lambs. The oxen of the gods plowed the onion patches of the* ensi*, (and) the onion (and) cucumber fields of the* ensi *were located in the god's best fields. The* birra-*donkeys (and) the prize oxen of the* sanga*'s were bundled off (presumably as taxes for the* ensi*). The attendants of the* ensi *divided the barley of the* sanga*'s (to the disadvantage of the* sanga*'s). The wearing apparel (here follows a list of fifteen objects, principally garments, most of which are unidentifiable) of the* sanga*'s were carried off as a tax (to the palace of the* ensi*). The* sanga *(in charge) of the food (supplies) felled the trees in the garden of the indigent mother and bundled off the fruit.*

. . . .

These were the (social) practices of former days.

(But) when Ningirsu, the foremost warrior of Enlil, gave the kingship of Lagash to Urukagina, (and) his (Ningirsu's) hand had grasped him out of the multitude (literally, "36,000 men"); then he (Ningirsu) enjoined upon (literally, "set up for") him the (divine) decrees of former days.

He (Urukagina) held close to the word which his king (Ningirsu) spoke to him. He banned (literally, "threw off") the man in charge of the boatmen from (seizing) the boats. He banned the head shepherds from (seizing) the donkeys and sheep. He banned the man in charge of the fisheries from (seizing) the fisheries. He banned the man in charge of the storehouse from (measuring out) the barley ration of the guda-priests. He banned the bailiff from (receiving) the silver (paid for the shearing) of the white sheep and of the gaba-lambs. He banned the bailiffs from the tax of (that is, levied on) the sanga*'s which (used to be) carried off (to the palace).*

He made Ningirsu king of the houses of the ensi *(and) of the field of the* ensi*. He made Bau queen of the houses of the (palace) harem (and) of the fields of the (palace) harem. He made Shulshaggana king of the houses of the (palace) nursery (and) of the fields of the (palace) nursery. From the borders of Ningirsu to the sea, there was no tax collector.*

Trans. by S. N. Kramer, *The Sumerians* (Chicago: University of Chicago Press, 1963), pp. 317–319.

Mesopotamia north of Sumer. Their language and society were different from those of the Sumerians, but they soon absorbed Sumerian culture and established their own kingdom, with its capital at Akkad, near a later city known to us as Babylon. The most famous Akkadian king was Sargon, who conquered Sumer and extended his empire in every direction. Legends grew up around his name, and he is said to have conquered the "cedar forests" of Lebanon, far to the west near the coast of the Mediterranean Sea. He ruled about 2340 B.C. and established a family, or dynasty, of Semitic kings that ruled Sumer and Akkad for two centuries.

External attack and internal weakness destroyed Akkad. About 2125 B.C. the city of Ur in Sumer revolted and became the dominant power, and this Third Dynasty of Ur established a large empire of its own. About 2000 B.C., however, it was swept aside by another Semitic invasion, which ended Sumerian rule forever. Thereafter Semites ruled Mesopotamia, but the foundations of their culture were Sumerian. The Semites changed much of what they inherited; but in law, government, religion, art, science, and all other areas of culture, their debt to the Sumerians was enormous.

The fall of the Third Dynasty of Ur (ca. 2100–2000 B.C.) put an end to the Sumerians as an identifiable group. The Sumerian language survived only in writing, as a kind of sacred language known only to priests and scribes, preserving the cultural heritage of Sumer. For about a century after the fall of Ur, dynastic chaos reigned, but about 1900 B.C. a Semitic people called the Amorites gained control of the region, establishing their capital at Babylon. The high point of this Amorite, or Old Babylonian, dynasty came more than a hundred years later under its most famous king, Hammurabi (ca. 1792–1750 B.C.). He is best known for the law code connected with his name. Codes of law existed as early as the Sumerian period, and Hammurabi's plainly owed much to earlier models, but it is the fullest and best-preserved legal code we have from ancient Mesopotamia. The code reveals a society strictly divided in class: there were nobles, commoners, and slaves, and the law did not treat them equally. In general, punishments were harsh, literally applying the principle "an eye for an eye, a tooth for a tooth." The prologue to the code makes it clear that law and justice came from the gods through the king.

About 1600 B.C. the Babylonian kingdom fell apart under the impact of invasions from the north and east by the Hittites and the Kassites. The Hittites were only a raiding party who plundered what they could and then withdrew to their home in Asia Minor. The Kassites stayed and ruled Mesopotamia for five centuries.

GOVERNMENT. From the earliest historical records it is clear that the Sumerians were ruled by monarchs in some form. Some scholars have thought they could detect a "primitive democracy" in early Sumer, but the evidence, which is poetic and hard to interpret, shows no more than a limited check on royal power even in early times. The first historical city-states had kings or priest-kings who led the army, administered the economy, and served as judges and as intermediaries between their people and the gods. At first, the kings were thought of as favorites and representatives of the gods; later, on some occasions and for relatively short periods, they instituted cults that worshiped them as divine. This union of church and state (to use modern terminology) in the person of the king reflected the centralization of power typical of Mesopotamian life. The economy was managed from the center by priests and king and was planned very carefully. Each year the land was surveyed, fields were assigned to specific farmers, and the amount of seed to be used was designated. The government estimated the size of the crop and planned its distribution even before it was planted.

This process required a large and competent

KEY EVENTS AND PEOPLE IN MESOPOTAMIAN HISTORY

Sumerians arrive	ca. 3500 B.C.
Sumerian city-states early dynastic period	ca. 2800–2340 B.C.
Sargon establishes Semitic dynasty at Akkad	ca. 2340 B.C.
Third Dynasty of Ur	ca. 2125–2027 B.C.
Amorites at Babylon	ca. 1900 B.C.
Reign of Hammurabi	1792–1750 B.C.
Invasion by Hittites and Kassites	ca. 1600 B.C.

staff, the ability to observe and record natural phenomena, a good knowledge of mathematics, and, for all of this, a system of writing. The Sumerians invented the writing system known as *cuneiform* (from the Latin *cuneus*, "wedge") because of the wedge-shaped stylus with which they wrote on clay tablets; the writing also came to be used in beautifully cut characters in stone. Sumerians also began the development of a sophisticated system of mathematics. The calendar they invented had twelve lunar months. To make it agree with the solar year and to make possible accurate designation of the seasons, they introduced a thirteenth month about every three years.

RELIGION. The Sumerians and their Semitic successors believed in gods in the shape of humans who were usually identified with some natural phenomenon. They were pictured as frivolous, quarrelsome, selfish, and often childish, differing from humans only in their greater power and their immortality. They each appear to have begun as local deities. The people of Mesopotamia had a vague and gloomy picture of the afterworld. Their religion dealt with problems of this world, and they used prayer, sacrifice, and magic to achieve their ends. Expert knowledge was required to reach the perfection in wisdom and ritual needed to influence the gods, so the priesthood flourished. A high percentage of the cuneiform writing we now have is devoted to religious texts: prayers, incantations, curses, and omens. It was important to discover the will and intentions of the gods, and the Sumerians sought hints in several places. The movements of the heavenly bodies were an obvious evidence of divine action, so astrology was born. They also sought to discover the divine will by examining the entrails of sacrificial animals for abnormalities. All of this religious activity required armies of scribes to keep great quantities of records, as well as learned priests to interpret them.

Religion, in the form of myth, played a large part in the literature and art of Mesopotamia. In poetic language, the Sumerians and their successors told tales of the creation of the world, of a great flood that almost destroyed human life, of an island paradise from which the god Enki was expelled for eating forbidden plants, of a hero named Gilgamesh who performed many great feats in his travels, and many more.

Religion was also the inspiration for the

A clay model of a liver inscribed with omens and magical texts. Such model livers were used to help predict events and determine the will of the gods. [Courtesy of the Trustees of the British Museum]

most interesting architectural achievement in Mesopotamia: the ziggurat. The ziggurat was an artificial stepped mound surmounted by a temple. Neighbors and successors of the Sumerians adopted the style, and the eroded remains of many of these monumental structures, some partly restored, still dot the Iraqi landscape.

SOCIETY. We have a very full and detailed picture of the way people in ancient Mesopotamia conducted their lives and of the social conditions in which they lived during the reign of Hammurabi. More than fifty royal letters, many business contracts, and especially the Code of Hammurabi are the sources of our knowledge. We find that society was legally divided into three classes: nobles, commoners, and slaves. Punishment for crimes committed against freemen was harsher than for those against slaves, and crimes committed against nobles were more serious than those against commoners.

11

Hammurabi Creates a Code of Law in Mesopotamia

Hammurabi's Babylonian empire stretched from the Persian Gulf to the Mediterranean Sea. Building on earlier laws, Hammurabi compiled one of the great ancient codes. It was discovered about seventy-five years ago in what is now Iran. Hammurabi, like other rulers before and after, represented himself and his laws as under the protection and sponsorship of all the right gods. Property was at least as sacred as persons, and the eye-for-an-eye approach characterizes the code. Here are a few examples from it.

LAWS

If a son has struck his father, they shall cut off his hand.

If a seignior has destroyed the eye of a member of the aristocracy, they shall destroy his eye.

If he has broken another seignior's bone, they shall break his bone.

If he has destroyed the eye of a commoner or broken the bone of a commoner, he shall pay one mina of silver.

If he has destroyed the eye of a seignior's slave or broken the bone of a seignior's slave, he shall pay one-half his value.

If a seignior has knocked out a tooth of a seignior of his own rank, they shall knock out his tooth.

If he has knocked out a commoner's tooth, he shall pay one-third mina of silver. . . .

EPILOGUE

I, Hammurabi, the perfect king,
was not careless (or) neglectful of the black-headed (people),
whom Enlil had presented to me,
(and) whose shepherding Marduk had committed to me;
I sought out peaceful regions for them;
I overcame grievous difficulties; . . .
With the mighty weapon which Zababa and Inanna entrusted to me,
with the insight that Enki allotted to me,
with the ability that Marduk gave me,
I rooted out the enemy above and below;
I made an end of war;
I promoted the welfare of the land;
I made the peoples rest in friendly habitations; . . .
The great gods called me,
so I became the beneficent shepherd whose scepter is righteous. . . .

James B. Pritchard, *Ancient Near Eastern Texts*, 3rd ed. (Princeton: Princeton University Press, 1969), pp. 164–180.

Slaves were chiefly captives from wars, although some native Babylonians might be enslaved for committing certain crimes, such as kicking one's mother or striking an elder brother. Parents could sell their children into slavery or pledge themselves and their entire family as surety for a debt. In case of default, they would all become slaves of the creditor for a stated period of time. Some slaves worked for the king and the state, others for the temple and the priests, and still others for private citizens. Their tasks varied accordingly. Most of the temple slaves appear to have been women, who were probably used to spin and weave and grind flour. The royal slaves did the heavy work of building palaces, canals, and fortifications. Private owners used their slaves chiefly as domestic servants. Some female slaves were used as concubines. Laws against fugitive slaves or slaves who denied their masters were harsh, but in some respects, Mesopotamian slavery appears enlightened compared to other slave systems in history. Slaves could engage in business and, with certain restrictions, hold property. They could marry free men or women, and the resulting children would be free. A slave who acquired the necessary wealth could buy his or her own freedom. Children of a slave by the master might be allowed to share in his property after his death.

The code of Hammurabi. In the relief at the top, Hammurabi (ca. 1792–1750 B.C.) receives the law, which is inscribed below, from the sun god. [The Oriental Institute, University of Chicago]

Nevertheless, slaves, of course, were property, were subject to the will of their masters, and had little legal protection.

The Code of Hammurabi consists of 282 sections, and we may learn something of the society it governed by noticing where it placed the greatest emphasis. The second largest category deals with land tenure, as is not surprising in a society based so heavily on agriculture, but right behind this category comes the category relating to commerce. This position reveals how important and sophisticated trade and commercial life had become, for much is said about debts, rates of interest, security, and default. There are also sections dealing with the regulation of builders, surgeons, and other professionals, but the largest category relates to the family and its maintenance and protection.

Marriages were arranged by the parents, and the betrothal was followed by the signing of a marriage contract. The husband-to-be made a bridal payment, and the father of the bride-to-be agreed to a dowry for his daughter. Marriage was originally monogamous, but if the

A Sumerian husband and wife (ca. 2600 B.C.). The statuette seems to convey a sense of real affection and dependence. [The Oriental Institute, University of Chicago]

14

*The
Foundations of
Western
Civilization in
the Ancient
World*

wife were ill for a long time or childless, the husband could take a second wife. Extramarital relations between the husband and concubines, female slaves, and prostitutes were common and acceptable. The wife did not have similar privileges. She was, in fact, the legal property of her husband in theory, but in practice, she seems to have been treated as an individual with rights protected by the law. Divorce was relatively easy and not entirely inequitable. Women divorced by their husbands without good cause received their dowry back. A woman seeking divorce could also recover her dowry if her husband could not convict her of wrongdoing. On the other hand, a woman's place was thought distinctly to be in the home. One law states that if a wife "has made up her mind to leave in order to engage in business, thus neglecting her house and humiliating her husband, he may divorce her without compensation."

Egyptian Civilization

While a great civilization arose in the valley of the Tigris and Euphrates, another, no less important, emerged in Egypt. The center of Egyptian civilization was the Nile River. From its source in central Africa the Nile runs north some 4,000 miles to the Mediterranean, with long navigable stretches broken by several cataracts. Ancient Egypt included the 750 miles of the valley from the First Cataract to the sea and was shaped like a funnel with two distinct parts. Upper (southern) Egypt was the stem, consisting of the narrow valley of the Nile. The broad, triangular delta, which branches out about 150 miles from the sea, was Lower Egypt (see Map 1.1). The Nile alone made life possible in the almost rainless desert that surrounded it. Each year the river flooded and covered the land, and when it receded, it left a fertile mud that could produce two crops a year. The construction and maintenance of irrigation ditches to preserve the river's water, with careful planning and organization of planting and harvesting, produced agricultural prosperity unmatched in the ancient world.

The Nile also served as a highway connecting the long, narrow country and encouraging its unification. Upper and Lower Egypt were, in fact, already united into a single kingdom at the beginning of our historical record, about 3100 B.C. Nature helped protect and isolate the ancient Egyptians from outsiders. The cataracts, the sea, and the desert made it difficult for foreigners to reach Egypt for either friendly or hostile purposes. Egypt knew far more peace and security than Mesopotamia. This security, along with the sunny, predictable climate, gave Egyptian civilization a more optimistic outlook than the civilizations of the Tigris–Euphrates, which were always in fear of assault from storm, flood, earthquake, and hostile neighbors.

The more than three-thousand-year span of ancient Egyptian history is traditionally divided into thirty-one royal dynasties, from the first, founded by Menes, the unifier of Upper and Lower Egypt, to the last, established by Alexander the Great, who conquered Egypt (as we shall see in Chapter 3) in 332 B.C. The dynasties are conventionally arranged into periods (see table). The unification of Egypt was vital, for even more than in Mesopotamia, the entire river valley required the central control of irrigation. By the time of the Third Dynasty, the king had achieved full supremacy and had imposed internal peace and order, and his kingdom enjoyed great prosperity. The capital was at Memphis in Upper Egypt, just above the delta. The king was no mere representative of the gods but a god himself. The land was his own personal possession, and the people were his servants.

Nothing better illustrates the extent of royal power than the three great pyramids built as tombs by the kings of the Fourth Dynasty. The largest, that of Khufu, was originally 481 feet high and 756 feet long on each side; it was made up of 2,300,000 stone blocks averaging 2.5 tons each. It was said by the much later Greek historian Herodotus to have taken 100,000 men twenty years to build. The pyramids are remarkable not only for the technical skill that was needed to build them but even more for what they tell us of the royal power. They give evidence that the Egyptian kings had enormous wealth, the power to concentrate so much effort on a personal project, and the confidence to undertake one of such a long duration. There were earlier pyramids and many were built later, but those of the Fourth Dynasty were never surpassed.

THE OLD KINGDOM. In the Old Kingdom royal power was absolute. The pharaoh, as he was later called (the term originally meant "great house" or "palace"), governed his kingdom through his family and appointed officials removable at his pleasure. The peasants were carefully regulated, their movement was lim-

The great pyramids of Egypt. These colossal tombs are at Giza, near Cairo. From left to right, they are the tombs of Menkaure, Khafre, and Khufu, three pharaohs of the Fourth Dynasty (ca. 2620–2480 B.C.). The smaller tombs in the foreground may have been those of the pharaohs' wives and courtiers. [Egyptian Museum]

ited, and they were taxed heavily, perhaps as much as one fifth of what they produced. Luxury accompanied the king in life and death, and he was raised to a remote and exalted level by his people. Such power and eminence cannot be sustained long by force alone. The Egyptians worked for the king and obeyed him because he was a living god on whom their life, safety, and prosperity depended. He was the direct source of law and justice, so no law codes were needed.

In such a world, government was merely one aspect of religion, and religion dominated Egyptian life. The gods of Egypt had many forms: animals, humans, and natural forces. In time, Re, the sun god, came to have a special dominant place, but for centuries there seems to have been little clarity or order in the Egyptian pantheon. Unlike the Mesopotamians, the Egyptians had a rather clear idea of an afterlife. They took great care to bury their dead properly and supplied the grave with things that the departed would need for a pleasant life after death. The king and some nobles had their bodies preserved as mummies. Their tombs were beautifully decorated with paintings; food was provided at burial and even after. Some royal tombs were provided with full-sized ships for the voyage to heaven. At first, only kings were thought to achieve eternal life;

then nobles were included; finally, all Egyptians could hope for immortality. The dead had to be properly embalmed, and the proper spells had to be written and spoken. Later on, a moral test was added.

The Egyptians developed a system of writing not much later than the Sumerians. Though the idea may have come from Mesopotamia, the script was independent. It began as picture writing and later combined pictographs with sound signs to produce a difficult and compli-

PERIODS IN ANCIENT EGYPTIAN HISTORY (DYNASTIES IN ROMAN NUMERALS)		
Early Dynastic Period (I–II)	ca.	3100–2700 B.C.
Old Kingdom (III–VI)		2700–2200 B.C.
First Intermediate Period (VII–X)		2200–2052 B.C.
Middle Kingdom (XI–XII)		2052–1786 B.C.
Second Intermediate Period (XIII–XVII)		1786–1575 B.C.
Hyksos invasion	ca.	1700 B.C.
New Kingdom (or Empire) (XVIII–XX)		1575–1087 B.C.
Post-Empire (XXI–XXXI)		1087–30 B.C.

cated script that the Greeks called *hieroglyph* ("sacred carvings"). Though much of what we have is preserved on wall paintings and carvings, most of Egyptian writing was done with pen and ink on a fine paper made from the papyrus reed found in the delta. Egyptian literature was more limited in depth and imagination than the Mesopotamian writings. Hymns, myths, magical formulas, tales of travel, and "wisdom literature," or bits of advice to help one get on well in the world, have been preserved. But nothing as serious and probing as the story of Gilgamesh was produced in the happier and simpler world of Egypt.

THE MIDDLE KINGDOM. The power of the kings of the Old Kingdom waned as priests and nobles gained more independence and influence. The governors of the regions of Egypt called *nomes* gained hereditary claim to their offices, and their families acquired large estates. About 2200 B.C. the Old Kingdom collapsed and gave way to the decentralization and disorder of the First Intermediate Period (ca. 2200–2052 B.C.). Finally, the nomarchs (governors) of Thebes in Upper Egypt gained control of the country and established the Middle Kingdom, about 2052 B.C. The rulers of the Twelfth Dynasty restored the pharaoh's power over the whole of Egypt, though they could not completely control the nobles who ruled the nomes. Still, they brought order, peace, and prosperity to a troubled land. They encouraged trade and extended Egyptian power and influence northward toward Palestine and southward toward Ethiopia. Though they moved the capital back to the more defensible site at Memphis, they gave great prominence to Amon, a god especially connected with Thebes. He became identified with Re, emerging as Amon-Re, the main god of Egypt. The kings of this period seem to have emphasized their role in doing justice. In their statues they are often shown as burdened with care, presumably concern for their people. Tales of the period place great emphasis on the king as interested in right and in the welfare of his people. Much later, in the New Kingdom, ethical concerns appeared, as they had in the law codes of Mesopotamia, but the divine status of the kings gave them a novel place in religion as well.

THE NEW KINGDOM (THE EMPIRE). The Middle Kingdom disintegrated in the Thirteenth Dynasty with the resurgence of the power of the local nobility. About 1700 B.C. Egypt suffered an invasion. Tradition speaks of a people called the Hyksos who came from the east and conquered the Nile Delta. They seem to have been a collection of Semitic peoples from the area of Palestine and Syria at the eastern end of the Mediterranean. Egyptian nationalism reasserted itself about 1575 B.C.,

when a dynasty from Thebes drove out the Hyksos and reunited the kingdom. In reaction to the humiliation of the Second Intermediate Period, the pharaohs of the Eighteenth Dynasty, the most prominent of whom was Thutmose III (1490–1436 B.C.), created an absolute government based on a powerful army and an Egyptian empire extending far beyond the Nile valley (see Map 1.2).

From the Hyksos the Egyptians learned new

MAP 1-2 *About* 1400 B.C. *the Near East was divided among four empires. Egypt went south to Nubia and north through Palestine and Phoenicia. Kassites ruled in Mesopotamia, Hittites in Asia Minor, and Mitanni in Assyrian lands. In the Aegean the Mycenaean kingdoms were at their height.*

THE NEAR EAST AND GREECE ABOUT 1400 B.C.

18

*The
Foundations of
Western
Civilization in
the Ancient
World*

A wall painting depicting agricultural labor, ca. 1425 B.C. from the tomb of Menna, a noble of Thebes. As Menna watches from the upper left, his peasants harvest grain, herd cattle, and punish an unsatisfactory worker. [Peter Clayton]

The great hall of the Temple of Amon at Karnak, near Thebes. Embellished by pharaoh after pharaoh, Karnak was for centuries the largest, richest, and most magnificent temple in Egypt.

military techniques and obtained new weapons. To these they added determination, a fighting spirit, and an increasingly military society. They pushed the southern frontier back a long way and extended Egyptian power farther into Palestine and Syria and beyond to the upper Euphrates River. They were not checked until they came into conflict with the powerful Hittite empire of Asia Minor. Both powers were weakened by the struggle, and though Egypt survived, it again became the victim of foreign invasion and rule, as one foreign empire after another took possession of the ancient kingdom.

The Eighteenth Dynasty, however, witnessed an interesting religious change. One of the results of the successful imperial ventures of the Egyptian pharaohs was the growth in power of the priests of Amon and the threat it posed to the position of the king. When young Amenhotep IV (1367–1350 B.C.) came to the throne before the middle of the fourteenth century B.C., he apparently determined to resist the priesthood of Amon. He was supported by his family and advisers and ultimately made a clean break with the worship of Amon-Re. He moved his capital from Thebes, the center of Amon worship, and built an entirely new city about three hundred miles to the north at a place now called El Amarna. Its god was Aton, the physical disk of the sun, and the new city was called Akhtaton. The king changed his own name to Akhnaton, "It pleases Aton." The new god was different from any that had come before him, for he was believed to be universal, not merely Egyptian. Unlike the other gods, he had no cult statue but was represented in painting and relief sculpture as the sun disk.

The universal claims for Aton led to religious intolerance of the worshipers of the other gods. Their temples were shut down and the name of Amon-Re was chiseled from monuments on which it was carved. The old priests, of course, were deprived of their posts and privileges, and the people who served the pharaoh and his god were new, sometimes even foreign. The new religion, moreover, was more remote than the old. Only the pharaoh and his family worshiped Aton directly, and the people wor-

This unflattering portrayal of Akhnaton, the revolutionary pharaoh, is characteristic of the unusually realistic art of his reign (1367–1350 B.C.). [Egyptian Museum]

20

*The
Foundations of
Western
Civilization in
the Ancient
World*

Akhnaton Intones New Hymns to Aton, the One God

These hymns were composed in the reign of Amenhotep IV (1367–1350 B.C.), or Akhnaton, as he called himself after instituting a religious revolution in Egypt.

Thou makest the Nile in the Nether World,
Thou bringest it as thou desirest,
To preserve alive the people of Egypt
For thou hast made them for thyself,
Thou lord of them all, who weariest thyself
*   for them;*
Thou lord of every land, who risest for them.
Thou Sun of day, great in glory,
All the distant highland countries,
Thou makest also their life,
Thou didst set a Nile in the sky.
When it falleth for them,
It maketh waves upon the mountains,
Like the great green sea,
Watering their fields in their towns.

How benevolent are thy designs, O lord of
*   eternity!*
There is a Nile in the sky for the strangers
And for the antelopes of all the highlands
*   that go about upon their feet.*
But the Nile, it cometh from the Nether
*   World for Egypt.*

Thou didst make the distant sky in order to
*   rise therein,*
In order to behold all that thou hast made,
While thou wast yet alone
Shining in thy form as living Aton,
Dawning, glittering, going afar and
*   returning.*
Thou makest millions of forms
Through thyself alone;
Cities, villages, and fields, highways and
*   rivers.*
All eyes see thee before them,
For thou art Aton of the day over the earth,
When thou hast gone away,
And all men, whose faces thou hast fashioned
In order that thou mightest no longer see
*   thyself alone,*
[Have fallen asleep, so that not] one [seeth]
*   that which thou hast made,*
Yet art thou still in my heart.

REVELATION TO THE KING

There is no other that knoweth thee
Save thy son Akhnaton.
Thou hast made him wise
In thy designs and in thy might.

UNIVERSAL MAINTENANCE

The world subsists in thy hand,
Even as thou hast made them.
When thou hast risen they live,
When thou settest they die;
For thou art length of life of thyself,
Men live through thee.

The eyes of men see beauty
Until thou settest.
All labour is put away
When thou settest in the west.
When thou risest again
[Thou] makest [every hand] to flourish for the
*   king*
And [prosperity] is in every foot,
Since thou didst establish the world,
And raise them up for thy son,
Who came forth from thy flesh,
The king of Upper and Lower Egypt,
Living in Truth, Lord of the Two Lands,
Nefer-khepru-Re, Wan-Re [Akhnaton],
Son of Re, living in Truth, lord of diadems,
Akhnaton, whose life is long;
[And for] the chief royal wife, his beloved,
Mistress of the Two Lands, Nefer-nefru-Aton,
*   Nofretete,*
Living and flourishing for ever and ever.

James H. Breasted, *The Dawn of Conscience* (New York: Charles Scribners' Sons, 1933, 1961), p. 137.

shiped the pharaoh. Akhnaton's interest in religious reform apparently led him to ignore foreign affairs, which proved disastrous. The Asian possessions of Egypt fell away, and this imperial decline and its economic consequences presumably caused further hostility to the new religion. When the king died, a strong counterrevolution swept away the work of his lifetime. His chosen successor was soon put aside and replaced by Tutankhamon (1347–1339 B.C.), the young husband of one of the daughters of Akhnaton and his beautiful wife, Nefertiti. The new pharaoh restored the old religion and wiped out as much as he could of the memory of the worship of Aton. He restored Amon to the center of the Egyptian pantheon, abandoned El Amarna, and returned the capital to Thebes. There he and his successors built his magnificent tomb, which remained remarkably intact until its discovery in 1922. The end of the El Amarna age restored power to the priests of Amon and to the military officers. A general named Horemhab became king (1335–1308? B.C.), restored order, and recovered much of the lost empire. He referred to Akhnaton as "the criminal of Akhtaton" and erased his name from the records. Akhnaton's city and memory disappeared for over three thousand years, to be rediscovered only by chance about a century ago.

For the rest of its independent history, Egypt returned to its traditional culture, but its mood was more gloomy. The Book of the Dead, a product of this late period, was a collection of spells whereby the dead could get safely to the next world without being destroyed by a hideous monster. Egypt itself would soon be devoured by powerful empires no less menacing.

Ancient Near Eastern Empires

In the time of the Eighteenth Dynasty in Egypt, new groups of peoples had established themselves in the Near East: the Kassites in Babylonia, the Hittites in Asia Minor, and the Mitannians in northern Mesopotamia. They all spoke languages in the Indo-European group, which includes Greek, Latin, Sanskrit, Persian, Celtic, and the Germanic languages and is thought to have originated in the Ukraine (now the southwestern Soviet Union) or to the east of it. The Kassites and Mitannians were warrior peoples who ruled as a minority over more civilized folk and absorbed their culture without

A Hittite war chariot. The Hittites were among the first to use iron weapons and war horns. Here, a pair of eighth-century B.C. Hittite warriors trample the defeated enemy.

changing it. The Hittites arrived in Asia Minor about 2000 B.C., and by about 1500 B.C. they had established a strong, centralized government with a capital at Hattusas (near Ankara, the capital of modern Turkey). Between 1400 and 1200 B.C. they contested Egypt's control of Palestine and Syria and were strong enough to achieve a dynastic marriage with the daughter of the powerful Nineteenth Dynasty pharaoh, Ramses II, about 1265 B.C. By 1200 B.C. the Hittite kingdom was gone, swept away by the arrival of new, mysterious Indo-Europeans. However, Neo-Hittite centers flourished in Asia Minor and Mesopotamia for a few centuries longer.

In most respects the Hittites reflected the influence of the dominant Mesopotamian culture of the region, but their government resembled more closely what we know of other Indo-European cultures. Their kings did not claim to be divine or even to be the chosen representatives of the gods. In the early period the king's power was checked by a council of nobles, and the assembled army had to ratify his succession to the throne. The Hittites appear to have been responsible for a great technological advance, the smelting of iron. They also played an im-

21

portant role in transmitting the ancient cultures of Mesopotamia and Egypt to the Greeks, who lived on their frontiers.

The fall of the Hittites was followed shortly by the formation of empires that dominated the Near East's ancient civilizations and even extended them to new areas. The first of these empires was established by the Assyrians, whose homeland was in the valleys and hills of northern Mesopotamia on and to the east of the Tigris River. They had a series of capitals, of which the great city of Nineveh is perhaps best known (modern Mosul, Iraq). They spoke a Semitic language and, from early times, were a part of the culture of Mesopotamia. Akkadians, Sumerians, Amorites, and Mitannians had dominated Assyria in turn. The Hittites' defeat of Mitanni liberated the Assyrians and prepared the way for their greatness from earlier than 1000 B.C. By 665 B.C. they had come to control everything from the southern frontier of Egypt, through Palestine, Syria, and much of Asia Minor, down to the Persian Gulf in the southeast. They succeeded in part because they made use of iron weapons. Because iron was more common than copper and tin, it was possible for them to arm more men more cheaply. The Assyrians were also fierce, well disciplined, and cruel. Their cruelty was calculated, at least in part, to terrorize real and potential enemies, for the Assyrians boasted of their brutality.

Unlike earlier empires, the Assyrian Empire systematically and profitably exploited the area it held. The Assyrians used different methods of control, ranging from the mere collection of tribute, to the stationing of garrisons in conquered territory, to removing entire populations from their homelands and scattering them elsewhere, as they did to the people of the kingdom of Israel. Because of their military and administrative skills, they were able to hold vast areas even as they absorbed the teachings of the older cultures under their sway.

As these two reliefs from royal palaces show, the Assyrians boasted about their cruelty. The Assyrian kings used a policy of calculated terror to hold their empire together and to discourage revolt by subject peoples and attack by foreign foes. Above, the decapitated heads of enemies are being carefully counted by royal scribes as part of the spoils of victory. Below, the army of Ashurbanipal sacks the city of Hamanu in Syria. [Werner Forman]

In addition to maintaining their own empire, the Assyrians had to serve as a buffer of the civilized Middle East against the barbarians on its frontiers. In the seventh century B.C. the task of fighting off the barbarians so drained the overextended Assyrians that the empire fell because of internal revolution. A new dynasty in Babylon joined with the rising kingdom of Media to the east (in modern Iran) to defeat the Assyrians and destroy Nineveh in 612 B.C. The successor kingdoms, the Chaldean or Neo-Babylonian and the Median, did not last long; they were swallowed, by 539 B.C., by yet another great eastern empire, that of the Persians. We shall return to the Persians in Chapter 2.

KEY EVENTS IN THE HISTORY OF ANCIENT NEAR EASTERN EMPIRES	
Hittite Empire	ca. 1400–1200 B.C.
Rise of Assyrian power	ca. 1100 B.C.
Assyrian conquest of Palestine–Syria	732–722 B.C.
Assyrian conquest of Egypt	671 B.C.
Destruction of Assyrian capital at Nineveh	612 B.C.
Neo-Babylonian (Chaldean) Empire	612–539 B.C.

Palestine

None of the powerful kingdoms we have described has had as much influence on the future of Western civilization as the small stretch of land on the eastern shore of the Mediterranean between Syria and Egypt, the land called Palestine for much of its history. The three great religions of the modern world outside the Far East—Judaism, Christianity, and Islam—trace their origins, at least in part, to the people who arrived there a little before 1200 B.C. and the book that recounts their experiences, the Old Testament of the Bible.

Canaanites and Phoenicians

Before the Israelites arrived in their promised land, it was inhabited by groups of people speaking a Semitic language called Canaanite.

A Phoenician ship from a sarcophagus found in Beirut, Lebanon. [Roger Wood]

The Canaanites lived in walled cities and carried on a version of Mesopotamian culture that included the worship of many gods. The arrival of the Israelites probably forced them northward to settle among similar people who inhabited the coastal land of Phoenicia. The Phoenicians were an important commercial people from a very early time. They seem to have developed a simplified system of writing that lacked only vowel signs to be a true alphabet. They founded colonies as far west as Spain, though their most famous was Carthage, near modern Tunis in north Africa. Sitting astride all trade routes, the Phoenician cities were important sites for the transmission of culture and knowledge from east to west.

The Israelites

The history of the Israelites must be pieced together from various sources. They are mentioned only rarely in the records of their neighbors, so we must rely chiefly on their own account, the Old Testament. It is not intended as a history in our sense but is a complicated collection of historical narrative, wisdom literature, poetry, law, and religious witness. Scholars of an earlier time tended to discard it as a source for historians, but the most recent trend is to take it seriously while using it with caution.

We need not reject the tradition that the patriarch Abraham came from Ur in Mesopotamia about 1900 B.C., and wandered west to tend his flocks in the land of the Canaanites. Some of his people settled there and others wandered into Egypt, perhaps with the Hyksos. By the thirteenth century B.C., led by Moses, they had left Egypt and wandered in the desert until they reached Canaan. They established a united kingdom that reached its peak under David and Solomon in the tenth century B.C. The sons of Solomon could not maintain the unity of the kingdom, and it split into two parts: Israel in the north and Judah, with its capital at Jerusalem, in the south. The rise of the great empires brought disaster to the Israelites. The northern kingdom fell to the Assyrians in 722 B.C., and its people were scattered and lost forever. These were the "ten lost tribes." Only the kingdom of Judah remained, and hereafter we may call the Israelites Jews.

In 586 B.C. Judah was defeated by the Babylonian king Nebuchadnezzar II. He destroyed the great temple built by Solomon and took thousands of hostages off to Babylon. When

Two seals of Hebrew officials from the late seventh or eighth centuries B.C. *The top seal is inscribed "Belonging to Migneyaw, the Servant of Yahweh." The bottom seal, which is inscribed with an heraldic emblem, a fighting cock, belonged to Ya'azanyahu, a high royal official.* [*Bruce Zuckerman, West Semitic Research Project*]

MAP 1-3 *The Hebrews established a
unified kingdom in Palestine under
Kings David and Solomon in the tenth
century* B.C. *After the death of Solomon,
however, the kingdom was divided into
two parts—Israel in the north and
Judah, with its capital Jerusalem, in
the south. North of Israel were the great
commercial cities of Phoenicia.*

ANCIENT PALESTINE

THE ISRAELITES		
Reign of King David	ca. 1000–961	B.C.
Reign of King Solomon	ca. 961–922	B.C.
Assyrian conquest of Israel (northern kingdom)	722	B.C.
Destruction of Jerusalem; fall of Judah (southern kingdom); Babylonian Captivity	586	B.C.
Restoration of temple; return of exiles	539	B.C.

The Second Isaiah Defines Hebrew Monotheism

The strongest statement of Hebrew monotheism is found in these words of the anonymous prophet whom we call the Second Isaiah. He wrote during the Hebrew exile in Babylonia, 597–539 B.C.

42

⁵Thus says God, the LORD,
  who created the heavens and stretched them out,
  who spread forth the earth and what comes from it,
  who gives breath to the people upon it and spirit
  to those who walk in it:
⁶''I am the LORD, I have called you in righteousness,
  I have taken you by the hand and kept you;
I have given you as a covenant to the people,
  a light to the nations,
⁷ to open the eyes that are blind,
to bring out the prisoners from the dungeon,
  from the prison those who sit in darkness.
⁸I am the LORD, that is my name;
  my glory I give to no other,
  nor my praise to graven images.
⁹Behold, the former things have come to pass,
  and new things I now declare;
before they spring forth I tell you of them.''

44

⁶Thus says the LORD, the King of Israel and
  his Redeemer, the LORD of hosts:
''I am the first and I am the last; besides me
  there is no god.
⁷Who is like me? Let him proclaim it,
  let him declare and set it forth before me.
Who has announced of old the things to come?
  Let them tell us what is yet to be.
⁸Fear not, nor be afraid;
  have I not told you from of old and
    declared it?
  And you are my witnesses!
Is there a God besides me?
  There is no Rock; I know not any.''

49

²²Thus says the Lord GOD:
  ''Behold, I will lift up my hand to the
    nations,
  and raise my signal to the peoples;
  and they shall bring your sons in their
    bosom,
  and your daughters shall be carried on
    their shoulders.
²³Kings shall be your foster fathers,
  and their queens your nursing mothers.
With their faces to the ground they shall bow
    down to you,
  and lick the dust of your feet.
Then you will know that I am the LORD;
  those who wait for me shall not be put to
    shame.''

²⁴Can the prey be taken from the mighty, or
    the captives of a tyrant be rescued?
²⁵Surely, thus says the LORD:
''Even the captives of the mighty shall be
    taken,
  and the prey of the tyrant be rescued,
for I will contend with those who contend
    with you
  and I will save your children.
²⁶I will make your oppressors eat their own
    flesh,
  and they shall be drunk with their own
    blood as with wine.
Then all flesh shall know
  that I am the LORD your Savior,
  and your Redeemer, the Mighty One of
    Jacob.''

Revised Standard Version of the Bible (New York: Division of Christian Education, National Council of Churches, 1952).

the Persians defeated Babylonia, they ended this Babylonian Captivity of the Jews and allowed them to return to their homeland. After that, the area of the old kingdom of the Jews in Palestine was dominated by foreign peoples for some twenty-five hundred years until the establishment of the State of Israel in A.D. 1948.

Religion

The fate of this small nation would be of little interest were it not for its unique religious achievement. The great contribution of the Jews is the idea of monotheism, the existence of one universal God, the creator and ruler of the universe. This idea may be as old as Moses, as the Jewish tradition asserts, but it certainly dates as far back as the prophets of the eighth century B.C. The Jewish God is neither a natural force nor like human beings or any other creatures; He is so elevated that those who believe in Him may not picture Him in any form. The faith of the Jews is given special strength by their belief that God made a covenant with Abraham that his progeny would be a chosen people who would be rewarded for following God's commandments and the law He revealed to Moses.

A novelty of Jewish religious thought is the powerful ethical element it introduced. God is a severe but just judge. Ritual and sacrifice are not enough to achieve His approval. People must be righteous, and God Himself appears to be bound to act righteously. The Jewish prophetic tradition was a powerful ethical force. The prophets constantly criticized any falling away from the law and the path of righteousness. The prophets placed God in history, blaming the misfortunes of the Jews on God's righteous and necessary intervention to punish them for their misdeeds, but the prophets also promised the redemption of the Jews if they repented. The prophetic tradition expected the redemption to come in the form of a Messiah who would restore the house of David. The Christians eventually seized on this tradition and believed that Jesus of Nazareth was that Messiah.

Jewish religious ideas influenced the future development of the West, both directly and indirectly. The Jews' belief in an all-powerful creator, righteous Himself and demanding righteousness and obedience from humankind, a universal God who is the father and ruler of all peoples, is a critical part of the Western heritage.

General Outlook of Near Eastern Cultures

Our very brief account of the history of the ancient Near East so far reveals that the various peoples and cultures were different in many ways, yet the distance between all of them and the emerging culture of the Greeks, to whom we shall turn our attention in Chapter 2, is striking. We can see this distance best by comparing the approach of the other cultures to several fundamental human problems with the way some Greeks treated the same problems. The great questions are these: What is the relationship of humans to nature? to the gods? to other humans? These questions involve attitudes toward religion, philosophy, science, law, justice, politics, and government in general.

For the peoples of the Near East there was no simple separation between humans and nature or even between animate creatures and inanimate objects. Humanity was part of a natural continuum, and all things partook of life and spirit. These peoples imagined the universe to be dominated by gods more or less in the shape of humans, and the world they ruled was irregular and unpredictable, subject to divine whims. The gods were capricious because nature seemed capricious.

One Egyptian text speaks of humans as "the cattle of god." The Babylonian story of creation makes it clear that humanity's function is merely to serve the gods. The creator Marduk says,

> I will create Lullu "man" be his name,
> I will form Lullu, man.
> Let him be burdened with the toil of the gods,
>   that they may freely breathe.[1]

In a world ruled by powerful deities of this kind, human existence was precarious. Even disasters that we would think human in origin they saw as the product of divine will. So a Babylonian text depicts the destruction of the city of Ur by invading Elamites as the work of the gods, carried out by the storm god Enlil:

> Enlil called the storm.
>   The people mourn.
> Exhilarating winds he took from the land.
>   The people mourn.

[1]Henri Frankfort et al., *Before Philosophy* (Baltimore: Penguin, 1949), p. 197.

Good winds he took away from Sumer.
  The people mourn.
He summoned evil winds.
  The people mourn.
Entrusted them to Kingaluda, tender of storms.
He called the storm that will annihilate the land.
  The people mourn.
He called disastrous winds.
  The people mourn.
Enlil—choosing Gibil as his helper—
Called the (great) hurricane of heaven.
  The people mourn.[2]

The helpless position of humankind in the face of irrational divine powers is clearly shown in both the Egyptian and the Babylonian versions of the story of the flood. In one Egyptian tale, Re, the god who had created humans, decided to destroy them because of some unnamed evil that the god had suffered. He sent the goddess Sekhmet to accomplish the deed, and she was in the midst of her task, enjoying the work and wading in a sea of blood, when Re changed his mind. Instead of ordering a halt, he poured seven thousand barrels of blood-colored beer in Sekhmet's path. She quickly became drunk, stopped the slaughter, and preserved humanity. In the Babylonian story, the motive for the destruction of humanity is more obvious: "In those days the world teemed, the people multiplied, the world bellowed like a wild bull, and the great god was aroused by the clamour. Enlil heard the clamour and he said to the gods in council, 'The uproar of mankind is intolerable and sleep is no longer possible by reason of the babel.' So the gods in their hearts were moved to let loose the deluge."[3] The gods repented to a degree and decided to save one family, Utnapishtim and his wife, but they seem to have chosen him whimsically, for no particular reason.

In such a universe humans could not hope to understand nature, much less control it. At best, they could try by magic to use some mysterious forces against others. An example of this device is provided by a Mesopotamian incantation to break a sorcerer's spell. The sufferer tried to use the magical powers inherent in ordinary salt to fight the witchcraft, addressing the salt as follows:

O Salt, created in a clean place,
For food of gods did Enlil destine thee.

Without thee no meal is set out in Ekur,
Without thee god, king, lord, and prince do not
  smell incense.
I am so-and-so, the son of so-and-so,
Held captive by enchantment,
Held in fever by bewitchment.
O Salt, break my enchantment! Loose my spell!
Take from me the bewitchment!—and as my
  Creator
I shall extol thee.[4]

Human relationships to the gods were equally humble. There was no doubt that they could destroy humankind and might do so at any time for no good reason. Humans could—and, indeed, had to—try to win the gods over by prayers and sacrifices, but there was no guarantee of success. The gods were bound by no laws and no morality. The best behavior and the greatest devotion to the cult of the gods were no defense against the divine and cosmic irrationality.

In the earliest civilizations, human relations were guided by laws, often set down in written codes. The basic question about law concerned its legitimacy: Why, apart from the lawgiver's power to coerce obedience, should anyone obey the law? For the Egyptians the answer was simple: the law came from the king and the king was a god. For the Mesopotamians the answer was almost the same: they believed that the king was a representative of god, so that the laws he set forth were equally divine. The prologue to the most famous legal document in antiquity, the Code of Hammurabi, makes this plain,

I am the king who is preeminent among kings;
my words are choice; my ability has no equal.
By the order of Shamash, the great judge of
  heaven and earth,
may my justice prevail in the land;
by the word of Marduk, my lord,
may my statutes have no one to rescind them. . . .[5]

The Hebrews introduced some important new ideas. Their unique God was capable of great anger and destruction, but He was open to persuasion and subject to morality. He was therefore more predictable and comforting, for all the terror of His wrath. The biblical version of the flood story, for instance, reveals the great

[2]Frankfort et al., p. 154.
[3]*The Epic of Gilgamesh,* trans. by N. K. Sandars (Baltimore: Penguin, 1960), p. 105.

[4]Frankfort et al., p. 143.
[5]James B. Pritchard, *Ancient Near Eastern Texts,* 2nd ed. (Princeton: Princeton University Press, 1955), pp. 164–180.

difference between the Hebrew God and the Babylonian deities. The Hebrew God was powerful and wrathful, but He was not arbitrary. He chose to destroy His creatures for their moral failures: for the reason that "the wickedness of man was great in the earth, and that every imagination of the thought of His heart was evil continually . . . the earth was corrupt in God's sight and the earth was filled with violence."[6] When He repented and wanted to save someone, He chose Noah because "Noah was a righteous man, blameless in his generation."[7]

That God was bound by His own definition of righteousness is neatly shown in the biblical story of Sodom and Gomorrah. He had chosen to destroy these wicked cities but felt obliged first to inform Abraham because of God's covenant with him.[8] In this passage Abraham calls on his Lord to abide by His own moral principles, and the Lord sees Abraham's point. In such a world there is the possibility of order in the universe and on this earth. There is also the possibility of justice among human beings, for the Hebrew God had provided His people with law. Through his prophet Moses, He had provided humans with regulations that would enable them to live in peace and justice. If they would abide by the law and live upright lives, they and their descendants could expect happy and prosperous lives. This idea was quite different from the uncertainty of the Babylonian view, but like it and its Egyptian partner, it left no doubt of the centrality of the divine. Cosmic order, human survival, and justice were all dependent on God.

Toward the Greeks and Western Thought

Different approaches and answers to many of the same concerns were offered by ancient Greek thought. Calling attention, even this early, to some of those differences will help to point up the distinctive outlook of the Greeks and of the later cultures of Western civilization that have drawn heavily on it.

Greek ideas had much in common with the ideas of earlier peoples. The gods of the Greeks had most of the characteristics of the Mesopotamian deities; magic and incantations played a part in their lives; and their law was usually connected with divinity. Many, if not most, Greeks in the ancient world must have lived their lives with notions not very different from those held by other peoples. But the surprising thing is that some Greeks developed ideas that were strikingly different and, in so doing, set a part of humankind on an entirely new path. As early as the sixth century B.C. some Greeks living in the Ionian cities of Asia Minor raised some questions and suggested some answers about nature that produced an intellectual revolution. In speculating about the nature of the world and its origin, they made guesses that were completely naturalistic and made no reference to supernatural powers. One historian of Greek thought put the case particularly well:

In one of the Babylonian legends it says: "All the lands were sea . . . Marduk bound a rush mat upon the face of the waters, he made dirt and piled it beside the rush mat." What Thales did was to leave Marduk out. He, too, said that everything was once water. But he thought that earth and everything else had been formed out of water by a natural process, like the silting up of the Delta of the Nile. . . . It is an admirable beginning, the whole point of which is that it gathers together into a coherent picture a number of observed facts without letting Marduk in.[9]

Thales was the first Greek philosopher. His putting of the question of the world's origin in a naturalistic form as early as the sixth century B.C. may have been the beginning of the unreservedly rational investigation of the universe, and so the beginning of both philosophy and science.

The same relentlessly rational approach was used even in regard to the gods themselves. In the same century as Thales, Xenophanes of Colophon expressed the opinion that humans think that the gods were born and have clothes, voices, and bodies like themselves. If oxen, horses, and lions had hands and could paint like humans, they would paint gods in their own image; the oxen would draw gods like oxen and the horses like horses. Thus black people believed in flat-nosed, black-faced gods, and the Thracians in gods with blue eyes and red hair.[10] In the fifth century B.C. Protagoras of Abdera went so far in the direction of agnosticism as to say, "About the gods I

---

[6]Genesis 6:5–11.
[7]Genesis 6:9.
[8]Genesis 18:20–33.

[9]Benjamin Farrington, *Greek Science* (London: Penguin, 1953), p. 37.
[10]Frankfort et al., pp. 14–16.

30

*The
Foundations of
Western
Civilization in
the Ancient
World*

can have no knowledge either that they are or that they are not or what is their nature."[11] This rationalistic, skeptical way of thinking carried over into practical matters as well. The school of medicine led by Hippocrates of Cos (about 400 B.C.) attempted to understand, diagnose, and cure disease without any attention to supernatural forces or beings. One of the Hippocratics wrote of the mysterious disease epilepsy: "It seems to me that the disease is no more divine than any other. It has a natural cause, just as other diseases have. Men think it divine merely because they do not understand it. But if they called everything divine which they do not understand, why, there would be no end of divine things."[12] By the fifth century B.C., too, it was possible for the historian Thucydides to analyze and explain the behavior of humans in society completely in terms of human nature and chance, leaving no place for the gods or supernatural forces.

The same absence of divine or supernatural forces characterized Greek views of law and justice. Most Greeks, of course, liked to think in a vague way that law came ultimately from the gods. In practice, however, and especially in the democratic states, they knew very well that laws were made by humans and should be obeyed because they represented the expressed consent of the citizens. Law, according to the fourth century B.C. statesman Demosthenes, is "a general covenant of the whole State, in accordance with which all men in that State ought to regulate their lives."[13]

The statement of these ideas, so different from any that came before the Greeks, opens the discussion of most of the issues that appear in the long history of Western civilization and that remain major concerns in the modern world: What is the nature of the universe and how can it be controlled? Are there divine powers, and if so, what is humanity's relationship to them? Are law and justice human, divine, or both? What is the place in human society of freedom, obedience, and reverence? These and many other problems were either invented or intensified by the Greeks. We now need to see whether there was something special in the Greeks' experience that made them raise these questions in the way that they did.

[11]Hermann Diels, *Fragmente der Vorsokratiker,* 5th ed., ed. by Walter Kranz (Berlin: Weidmann, 1934–1938), Frg. 4.

[12]Diels, Frgs. 14–16.

[13]*Against Aristogeiton,* 16.

Suggested Readings

W. F. ALBRIGHT, *From the Stone Age to Christianity* (1957). An original and interesting interpretive study.

W. F. ALBRIGHT, *Archaeology of Palestine* (1960). A study of the physical remains by a great scholar.

CYRIL ALDRED, *Akhenaten, Pharaoh of Egypt: A New Study* (1968). A judicious and critical biography of the enigmatic pharaoh.

J. H. BREASTED, *Ancient Egyptian Religion* (1961). An illuminating study by one of the great Egyptologists.

V. GORDON CHILDE, *What Happened in History* (1946). A pioneering study of human prehistory and history before the Greeks from an anthropological point of view.

HENRI FRANKFORT, *Ancient Egyptian Religion: An Interpretation* (1948). A brief but masterful attempt to explore the religious conceptual world of ancient Egyptians in intelligible and interesting terms.

HENRI FRANKFORT, *Birth of Civilization in the Near East* (1968). A good brief study of the transition to civilization.

HENRI FRANKFORT et al., *Before Philosophy* (1949). A brilliant examination of the mind of the ancients from the Stone Age to the Greeks.

ALAN GARDINER, *Egypt of the Pharaohs* (1961). A sound narrative history.

O. R. GURNEY, *The Hittites* (1954). A good general survey.

W. W. HALLO and W. K. SIMPSON, *The Ancient Near East: A History* (1971). A fine survey of Egyptian and Mesopotamian history.

JACQUETTA HAWKES, *Prehistory and the Beginning of Civilization* (1963).

THORKILD JACOBSEN, *The Treasures of Darkness: A History of Mesopotamian Religion* (1976). A superb and sensitive re-creation of the spiritual life of Mesopotamian peoples from the fourth to the first millennia B.C.

D. C. JOHNSON and M. R. EDEY, *Lucy: The Beginnings of Mankind* (1981).

SAMUEL N. KRAMER, *The Sumerians: Their History, Culture and Character* (1963). A readable general account of Sumerian history.

S. MOSCATI, *Ancient Semitic Civilizations* (1960). A general survey of the ancient Semites.

A. T. OLMSTEAD, *History of Assyria* (1923). A good narrative account.

H. M. ORLINSKY, *Ancient Israel* (1960). Chiefly a political survey.

JAMES B. PRITCHARD (Ed.), *Ancient Near Eastern Texts Relating to the Old Testament* (1969). A good collection of documents in translation with useful introductory material.

CHARLES L. REDMAN, *The Rise of Civilization* (1978). An attempt to use the evidence provided by anthropology, archaeology, and the physical sciences to illuminate the development of early urban society.

G. ROUX, *Ancient Iraq* (1964). A good recent account of ancient Mesopotamia.

SAMUEL SANDMEL, *The Hebrew Scriptures* (1963). An examination of the Bible's value as history and literature.

K. C. SEELE, *When Egypt Ruled the East* (1965). A study of Egypt in its imperial period.

ROLAND DE VAUX, *Ancient Israel: Its Life and Institutions* (1961). A fine account of social institutions.

JOHN A. WILSON, *Culture of Ancient Egypt* (1956). A fascinating interpretation of the civilization of ancient Egypt.

The "Trojan Horse," as depicted on a seventh-century B.C. Greek vase. Note the wheels on the horse and the Greek soldiers holding weapons and armor who are hiding inside it. [German Archaeological Institute of Athens]

ABOUT 2000 B.C. Greek-speaking peoples settled the lands surrounding the Aegean Sea and established a style of life and formed a set of ideas, values, and institutions that spread far beyond the Aegean corner of the Mediterranean Sea. Preserved and adapted by the Romans, Greek culture powerfully influenced the society of western Europe in the Middle Ages and dominated the Byzantine Empire in the same period. The civilization emerging from this experience spread across Europe and in time crossed the Atlantic to the Western Hemisphere.

At some time in their history, the Greeks of the ancient world founded cities on every shore of the Mediterranean Sea, and pushing on through the Dardanelles, they placed many settlements on the coasts of the Black Sea in southern Russia and as far east as the approaches to the Caucasus Mountains. The center of Greek life, however, has always been the Aegean Sea and the islands in and around it. This location at the eastern end of the Mediterranean very early put the Greeks in touch with the more advanced and earlier civilizations of the Near East: Egypt, Asia Minor, Syria–Palestine, and the rich culture of Mesopotamia. A character in one of Plato's dialogues says, "Whatever the Greeks have acquired from foreigners they have, in the end, turned into something finer."[1] This proud statement indicates at least that the Greeks were aware of how much they had learned from other civilizations.

2
The Rise of Greek Civilization

The Bronze Age on Crete and on the Mainland to About 1150 B.C.

The Minoans

One source of Greek civilization was the culture of the large island of Crete in the Mediterranean. With Greece to the north, Egypt to the south, and Asia to the east, Crete was a cultural bridge between the older civilizations and the new one of the Greeks. The Bronze Age came to Crete not long after 3000 B.C., and in the third and second millennia B.C. a civilization arose that powerfully influenced the islands of the Aegean and the mainland of Greece. This civilization has been given the name *Minoan,* after Minos, the legendary king of Crete.

[1] *Epinomis,* 987 d.

A Minoan goddess brandishing snakes with a lion perched on her head. The statuette was found in the ruins of the palace at Cnossus on Crete and is about a foot high. [Giraudon/Art Resource]

On the basis of pottery styles and the excavated levels where the pottery and other artifacts are found, scholars have divided the Bronze Age on Crete into three major divisions with some subdivisions. Dates for Bronze Age settlements on the Greek mainland, for which the term *Helladic* is used, are derived from the same chronological scheme.

During the Middle and Late Minoan periods in the cities of eastern and central Crete, a civilization developed that was new and unique in its character and its beauty. Its most striking feature is presented by the palaces uncovered at such sites as Phaestus, Haghia Triada, and, most important, Cnossus. These palaces were built around a central court with a labyrinth of rooms surrounding it. Some sections of the palace at Cnossus were as much as four stories high. The basement contained many storage rooms for oil and grain, apparently paid as taxes to the king. The main and upper floors contained living quarters as well as workshops for making pottery and jewelry. There were sitting rooms and even bathrooms, to which water was piped through excellent plumbing. The ceilings were supported by lovely columns, which tapered downward, and many of the walls carried murals showing landscapes and seascapes, festivals, and sports. The palace design and the paintings show the influence of Syria, Asia Minor, and Egypt, but the style and quality are unique to Crete.

Along with palaces, paintings, pottery, jewelry, and other valuable objects, writing of three distinct kinds was found, and one of these proved to be an early form of Greek. The script was written on clay tablets like those found in Mesopotamia. They were preserved accidentally, being hardened in a great fire that destroyed the palace. They reveal an organization centered on the palace, in which the king ruled and was served by an extensive bureaucracy that kept remarkably detailed records. This sort of organization is typical of what we find in the Near East but nothing like what we will see among the Greeks; yet the inventories were written in a form of Greek. Why should Minoans, who were not Greek, write in a language not their own? This question raises the larger one of what the relationship was between Crete and the Greek mainland in the Bronze Age and leads us to an examination of mainland, or Helladic, culture.

The Mycenaeans

In the third millennium B.C. most of the Greek mainland, including many of the sites of later Greek cities, was settled by people who used metal, built some impressive houses, and traded with Crete and the islands of the Aegean. The names they gave to places, names that were sometimes preserved by later invaders, make it clear that they were not Greeks and spoke a language that was not Indo-European.

Not long after the year 2000 B.C., many of the Early Helladic sites were destroyed by fire, some were abandoned, and still others appear to have yielded peacefully to an invading people. This invasion probably signaled the arrival of the Greeks.

The invaders succeeded in establishing control of the entire mainland, and the shaft graves cut into the rock at the royal palace-fortress of Mycenae show that they prospered and sometimes became very rich. At Mycenae and all over Greece, there was a smooth transition between the Middle and Late Helladic periods. At Mycenae the richest finds come from the period after 1600 B.C. The city's wealth and power reached their peak during this time, and the culture of the whole mainland during the Late Helladic period goes by the name *Mycenaean*.

The excavation of Mycenaean sites reveals a culture influenced by, but very different from, the Minoan culture. Mycenae and Pylos, like Cnossus, were built some distance from the sea. It is plain, however, that defense against attack was foremost in the minds of the founders. Both cities were built on hills in a position commanding the neighboring territory. The Mycenaean people were warriors, as their art, architecture, and weapons reveal. The success of their campaigns and the defense of their territory required strong central authority, and all available evidence shows that the kings provided it. Their palaces, in which the royal family and its retainers lived, were located within the walls; most of the population lived outside the walls. The palace walls were usually covered with paintings, like those on Crete, but instead of peaceful scenery and games, the Mycenaean murals depicted scenes of war and boar hunting.

About 1500 B.C. the already impressive shaft graves were abandoned in favor of *tholos* tombs. They were large, beehivelike chambers cut into the hillside, built of enormous, well-cut, and fitted stones, and approached by an unroofed passage (*dromos*) cut horizontally into the side of the hill. The lintel block alone of one of these tombs weighs over a hundred tons. Only a strong king whose wealth was great, whose power was unquestioned, and who commanded the labor of many men could undertake such a project. His wealth came from plundering raids, piracy, and trade. Some of this trade went westward to Italy and Sicily, but most of it was with the islands of the Aegean, the coastal towns of Asia Minor, and

The Lion Gate to the citadel of Mycenae. It dates from the 13th century B.C. and is so massive that later Greeks believed it to be the work of giants. [Alison Frantz]

PERIODS OF THE AEGEAN BRONZE AGE	
Early Minoan, 2900–2100 B.C.	Early Helladic, 2900–1900 B.C.
Middle Minoan, 2100–1575 B.C.	Middle Helladic, 1900–1580 B.C.
Late Minoan, 1575–1150 B.C.	Late Helladic, 1580–1150 B.C.
Late Minoan I, 1575–1500 B.C.	Late Helladic I, 1580–1500 B.C.
Late Minoan II, 1500–1400 B.C.	Late Helladic II, 1500–1425 B.C.
Late Minoan III, 1400–1150 B.C.	Late Helladic III, 1425–1150 B.C.

A Linear B tablet from Pylos, dated about 1200 B.C. First discovered in the late 19th century, Linear B was only deciphered in 1952 by a brilliant young Englishman, Michael Ventris, who demonstrated that it was an early Greek dialect. This tablet is part of a palace inventory listing vases. It survived because it was baked when the palace at Pylos was destroyed by invaders. [TAP - Art Reference Bureau/Athens Museum]

the cities of Syria, Egypt, and Crete. The Mycenaeans sent pottery, olive oil, and animal hides in exchange for jewels and other luxuries.

Tablets containing Mycenaean writing have been found all over the mainland; the largest and most useful collection was found at Pylos. These tablets, written in a script called by the excavators *Linear B,* reveal a world very similar to the one shown by the records at Cnossus. The king, whose title was *wanax,* held a royal domain, appointed officials, commanded servants, and kept a close record of what he owned and what was owed to him. This evidence confirms all the rest: the Mycenaean world was made up of a number of independent, powerful, and well-organized monarchies.

Although their dating is still controversial, the Linear B tablets at Cnossus seem to belong to Late Minoan III, so that the great "palace period" at Cnossus came after an invasion by Mycenaeans in 1400 B.C. These Greek invaders inhabited a flourishing Crete until the end of the Bronze Age, and there is good reason to believe that at the height of Mycenaean power (1400–1200 B.C.), Crete was part of the Mycenaean world.

These were prosperous and active years for the Mycenaeans. Their cities were enlarged, their trade grew, and they even established commercial colonies in the east. They are mentioned in the archives of the Hittite kings of Asia Minor. They are named as marauders of the Nile Delta in the Egyptian records, and sometime about 1250 B.C. they probably sacked the city of Troy on the coast of northwestern Asia Minor, giving rise to the epic poems of Homer, the *Iliad* and the *Odyssey* (see Map 2.1). Around the year 1200 B.C., however, the Mycenaean world showed signs of great trouble, and by 1100 B.C. it was gone: its

palaces were destroyed, many of its cities abandoned, and its art, its pattern of life, its system of writing buried and forgotten. How was the Mycenaean world destroyed?

Modern scholars have suggested theories explaining the destruction of Mycenaean civilization by means of a natural disaster. Some believe that the destruction of Cnossus and the Minoan culture was caused about 1400 B.C. by the volcanic explosion of the Aegean island of Thera (modern Santorini), which blackened and poisoned the air for many miles around and sent a monstrous tidal wave to destroy the great palace civilization. Others think that the explosion took place about 1200 B.C. and caused the destruction of Bronze Age culture throughout the Aegean. This explanation has the convenient consequence of ending the Minoan and the Mycenaean civilizations with one blow, but the evidence does not support it. The Mycenaean towns were not destroyed at one time; many fell around 1200 B.C., but some flourished for another century, and the Athens of the period was never destroyed or abandoned.

No theory of natural disaster holds, and we are left to seek less dramatic explanations. One suggestion is that piratical sea-raiders may have been responsible for the destruction of Pylos and, perhaps, other sites on the mainland. The Greeks themselves believed in a legend that told of the Dorians, a rude people from the north who spoke a Greek dialect different from that of the Mycenaean peoples. The Dorians joined with one of the Greek tribes, the Heraclidae, in an attack on the southern Greek peninsula of Peloponnesus, which was repulsed. One hundred years later they returned and gained full control. This legend of "the return of the Heraclidae" has been identified by modern historians with the Do-

THE AEGEAN AREA IN THE BRONZE AGE

MAP 2-1 *The Bronze Age in the Aegean area lasted from about 1900 to about 1100 B.C. Its culture on Crete is called Minoan and was at its height about 1900–1400 B.C. Bronze Age Helladic culture on the mainland flourished from about 1600 to 1200 B.C.*

rian invasion, the incursion from the north into Greece by a less civilized Greek people speaking the Dorian dialect.

Archaeology has failed to provide material support for a single Dorian invasion or a series of them. In the present state of the evidence, certainty is impossible, but the chances are good that the end of the Bronze Age in the Aegean came about gradually over the century between 1200 B.C. and 1100 B.C. as a result of internal conflict among the Mycenaean kings and because of continuous pressure from outsiders, who raided, infiltrated, and eventually dominated Greece and its neighboring islands.

Cnossus, Mycenae, and Pylos were abandoned, their secrets to be kept for over three thousand years.

The Greek "Middle Ages" to About 750 B.C.

The immediate effects of the Dorian invasion were disastrous for the inhabitants of the Mycenaean world. The palaces and the kings and bureaucrats who managed them were destroyed. The wealth and organization that had supported the artists and the merchants were

An eighth-century B.C. bronze statuette of a lyre player, found on Crete. [Heraklion Archaelogical Museum]

likewise swept away by a barbarous people who did not have the knowledge or social organization to maintain them. Many villages were abandoned and never resettled. Some of their inhabitants probably turned to a nomadic life, and many perished.

Another result of the invasion was the spread of the Greek people eastward from the mainland to the Aegean islands and the coast of Asia Minor. The Dorians themselves, after occupying most of the Peloponnesus, swept across the Aegean to occupy the southern islands and the southern part of the Anatolian coast.

These migrations made the Aegean a Greek lake, but trade with the old civilizations of the Near East was virtually ended by the fall of the advanced Minoan and Mycenaean civilizations, nor was there much trade between different parts of Greece. The Greeks were forced to turn inward, and each community was left largely to its own devices. This happened at a time when the Near East was also in disarray, and no great power arose to impose its ways and its will on the helpless people who lived about the Aegean. These circumstances allowed the Greeks time to recover from their disaster and to create their unique style of life.

This period in Greek history is dark, for our knowledge of it rests on very limited sources. Writing disappeared after the fall of Mycenae, and no new script appeared until after 750 B.C. so we have no contemporary author to shed light on this period. Excavation reveals no architecture, sculpture, or painting until after 750 B.C.

The Age of Homer

For a picture of society in these "dark ages," the best source is Homer. His epic poems, the *Iliad* and the *Odyssey*, tell of the heroes who captured Troy, men of the Mycenaean age, but the world described in those poems clearly is a different one. Homer's heroes are not buried in *tholos* tombs but are cremated; they worship gods in temples, whereas the Mycenaeans had no temples; they have chariots but do not know their proper use in warfare. The poems of Homer are the result of an oral tradition that went back into the Mycenaean age. Through the centuries bards sang tales of the heroes who fought at Troy, using verse arranged in rhythmic formulas to aid the memory. In this way some very old material was preserved until the poems were finally written, no sooner

Odysseus Addresses Nobles and Commoners: Homeric Society

The *Iliad* was probably composed about 750 B.C. In this passage Odysseus is trying to stop the Greeks at Troy from fleeing to their ships and returning to their homes. The difference in his treatment of nobles and commoners is striking.

Whenever he found one that was a captain and a man of mark, he stood by his side, and refrained him with gentle words: "Good sir, it is not seemly to affright thee like a coward, but do thou sit thyself and make all thy folk sit down. For thou knowest not yet clearly what is the purpose of Atreus' son; now is he but making trial, and soon he will afflict the sons of the Achaians. And heard we not all of us what he spake in the council? Beware lest in his anger he evilly entreat the sons of the Achaians. For proud is the soul of heaven-fostered kings; because their honour is of Zeus, and the god of counsel loveth them."

But whatever man of the people he saw and found him shouting, him he drave with his sceptre and chode him with loud words: "Good sir, sit still and hearken to the words of others that are thy betters; but thou art no warrior, and a weakling, never reckoned whether in battle or in council. In no wise can we Achaians all be kings here. A multitude of masters is no good thing; let there be one master, one king, to whom the son of crooked-counselling Kronos hath granted it. . . ."

Homer, *The Iliad*, trans. by A. Lang, W. Leaf, and E. Myers (New York: Random House, n.d.), pp. 24–25.

than the eighth century B.C., but the society these old oral poems describe seems to be that of the tenth and ninth centuries B.C.

In the Homeric poems the power of the kings is much smaller than that of the Mycenaean rulers. The ability of the kings to make important decisions was limited by the need to consult the council of nobles. The nobles felt free to discuss matters in vigorous language and in opposition to the king's wishes. In the *Iliad*, Achilles does not hesitate to address Agamemnon, the "most kingly" commander of the Trojan expedition, in these words: "thou with face of dog and heart of deer . . . folk devouring king." Such language may have been impolite, but it was not treasonous. The king, on the other hand, was free to ignore the council's advice, but it was risky to do so.

The right to speak in council was limited to noblemen, but the common people could not be ignored. If a king planned a war or a major change of policy during a campaign, he would not fail to call the common soldiers to an assembly, where they could listen and express their feelings by acclamation, even though they could not take part in the debate. The evidence of Homer shows that even in these early times the Greeks, unlike their predecessors and contemporaries, practiced some forms of limited constitutional government.

Homeric society, nevertheless, was sharply divided into classes, the most important division being the one between nobles and commoners. We do not know the origin of the distinction, but we cannot doubt that at this time Greek society was aristocratic. Birth determined noble status, and wealth usually accompanied it. Below the nobles were the peasants, the landless laborers, and the slaves. We cannot tell whether the peasants owned the land they worked outright and so were free to sell it or if they worked a hereditary plot that belonged to their clan and was therefore not theirs to dispose of as they chose. It is clear, however, that the peasants worked hard to make a living.

Far worse was the condition of the hired agricultural laborer. The slave, at least, was attached to a family household and so was protected and fed. In a world where membership in a settled group gave the only security, the free laborers were desperately vulnerable.

Slaves were few in number and were mostly women, who served as maids and concubines. Some male slaves worked as shepherds. Few, if any, worked in agriculture, which depended on free labor throughout Greek history.

The Homeric poems hold up a mirror to this society, and they reflect an aristocratic code of values that powerfully influenced all future Greek thought. In classical times Homer was the schoolbook of the Greeks. They memorized his text, settled diplomatic disputes by citing passages in it, and emulated the behavior and cherished the values they found in it. Those values were physical prowess, courage; fierce protection of one's family, friends, and property; and above all, one's personal honor and reputation. Returning home after his wanderings, Odysseus ruthlessly kills all the suitors of his wife because they have used up all his wealth, wooed his wife, scorned his son, and so dishonored him. Speed of foot, strength, and, most of all, excellence at fighting in battle are what make a man great, yet Achilles leaves the battle and allows his fellow Greeks to be slain and almost defeated because Agamemnon has wounded his honor by taking away his battle prize. He returns not out of a sense of duty to the army but because his dear friend Patroclus has been killed. In each case the hero seeks to display the highest virtue of Homeric society, *arētē*—manliness, courage in the most general sense, and the excellence proper to a hero.

This quality was best revealed in a contest, or *agon.* Homeric battles are not primarily group combats but a series of individual contests between great champions. One of the prime forms of entertainment is the athletic contest, and the funeral of Patroclus is celebrated by such a contest. The central ethical idea in Homer can be found in the instructions that the father of Achilles gives to his son when he sends him off to fight at Troy: "Always be the best and distinguished above others." The father of another Homeric hero has given his son exactly the same orders and has added to them the injunction "do not bring shame on the family of your fathers who were by far the best in Ephyre and in wide Lycia." Here in a nutshell we have the chief values of the aristocrats of Homer's world: to vie for individual supremacy in *arētē* and to defend and increase the honor of the family. They would remain prominent aristocratic values long after Homeric society was only a memory.

The *Polis*

The characteristic Greek institution was the *polis.* The attempt to translate that word as "city-state" is misleading, for it says both too much and too little. All Greek *poleis* began as little more than agricultural villages or towns, and many stayed that way, so the word *city* is inappropriate. All of them were states, in the sense of being independent political units, but they were much more than that. The *polis* was thought of as a community of relatives; all its citizens, who were theoretically descended from a common ancestor, belonged to subgroups, such as fighting brotherhoods (*phratries*), clans, and tribes, and worshiped the gods in common ceremonies.

Aristotle argued that the *polis* was a natural growth and that the human being was by nature "an animal who lives in a *polis.*" Humans alone have the power of speech and from it derive the ability to distinguish good from bad and right from wrong, "and the sharing of these things is what makes a household and a *polis.*" Humans, therefore, who are incapable of sharing these things or who are so self-sufficient that they have no need of them are not humans at all, but either wild beasts or gods. Without law and justice human beings are the worst and most dangerous of the animals. With them humans can be the best, and justice exists only in the *polis.* These high claims were made in the fourth century B.C., hundreds of years after the *polis* came into existence, but they accurately reflect an attitude that was present from the first.

Development of the **Polis**

Originally the word *polis* referred only to a citadel, an elevated, defensible rock to which the farmers of the neighboring area could retreat in case of attack. The Acropolis in Athens and the hill called Acrocorinth in Corinth are examples. For some time such high places and the adjacent farms comprised the *polis.* The towns grew gradually and without planning, as the narrowness and the winding, disorderly character of their streets show. For centuries they had no city walls. Unlike the city-states of the Near East, they were not placed for commercial convenience on rivers or the sea, nor did they grow up around a temple to serve the needs of priests and to benefit from the needs of worshipers. The availability of farmland and of a natural fortress determined their location. They were placed either well inland or far enough away from the sea to avoid piratical raids. Only later and gradually did the *agora* appear. It grew to be not only a marketplace but also a civic center and the heart of the Greeks' remarkable social life, which was distinguished by conversation and argument carried on in the open air.

Some *poleis* probably came into existence early in the eighth century B.C. The institution was certainly common by the middle of the century, for all the colonies that were established by the Greeks in the years after 750 B.C. took the form of the *polis*. Once the new institution had been fully established, true monarchy disappeared. Vestigial kings survived in some places, but they were almost always only ceremonial figures without power. The original form of the *polis* was an aristocratic republic dominated by the nobility through its council of nobles and its monopoly of the magistracies.

The Hoplite Phalanx

A new military technique was crucial to the development of the *polis*. In earlier times the brunt of the fighting had been carried on by small troops of cavalry and individual "champions" who first threw their spears and then came to close quarters with swords. Toward the end of the eighth century B.C., however, the hoplite phalanx came into being. It remained the basis of Greek warfare thereafter.

The hoplite was a heavily armed infantryman who fought with a sword and a pike about nine feet long. These soldiers were formed into a phalanx in close order, usually at least eight ranks deep. So long as the hoplites fought bravely and held their ground, there would be few casualties and no defeat, but if they gave way, the result was usually a rout. All depended on the discipline, strength, and courage of the individual soldier. At its best the phalanx could withstand cavalry charges and defeat infantries not as well protected or disciplined. Until defeated by the Roman legion, it was the dominant military force in the eastern Mediterranean.

The usual hoplite battle in Greece was between the armies of two *poleis* quarreling over a piece of land. One army invaded the territory of the other at a time when the crops were almost ready for harvest. The defending army had no choice but to protect its fields. If the army was beaten, its fields were captured or destroyed and its people might starve. In every way the phalanx was a communal effort that relied not on the extraordinary actions of the individual but on the courage of a considerable portion of the citizens. The phalanx and the *polis* arose together, and both heralded the decline of the kings. The phalanx, however, was not made up only of aristocrats. Most of the hoplites were farmers working relatively small holdings. The immediate beneficiaries of the royal decline were the aristocrats, but because the existence of the *polis* depended on the small farmers, their wishes could not for long be wholly ignored. The rise of the hoplite phalanx created a bond between the aristocrats and the peasants who fought in it, and this bond helps explain why class conflicts were muted for some time. It also guaranteed, however, that the aristocrats, who dominated at first, would not always be unchallenged.

The hoplite phalanx. This vase is the earliest surviving depiction of the close-order, heavily armed infantry that the Greeks adopted in the late eighth century B.C. Note the large shields, plumed helmets, body armor, raised spears, and the close order of the soldiers. The music of their flutist helped the soldiers to march in step. [Hirmer Fotoarchive, Munich]

Importance of the Polis

The Greeks looked to the *polis* for peace, order, prosperity, and honor in their lifetime. They counted on it to preserve their memory and to honor their descendants after death. Some of them came to see it not only as a ruler, but as the molder of its citizens. It is easy to understand the pride and scorn that underlie the comparison made by the poet Phocylides between the Greek state and the capital of the great and powerful Assyrian Empire: "A little *polis* living orderly in a high place is stronger than a block-headed Nineveh."

Expansion of the Greek World

From the middle of the eighth century B.C. until well into the sixth, the Greeks vastly expanded the territory they controlled, their wealth, and their contacts with other peoples in a burst of colonizing activity that placed *poleis* from Spain to the Black Sea. A century earlier a few Greeks had established trading posts in Syria. There they had learned new techniques in the arts and crafts and much more from the older civilizations of the Near East. About 750 B.C. they borrowed a writing system from one of the Semitic scripts and added vowels to create the first true alphabet. The new Greek alphabet was easier to learn than any earlier writing system and made possible the widely literate society of classical Greece.

Syria and its neighboring territory were too strong to penetrate, so the Greeks settled the southern coast of Macedonia and the Chalcidic peninsula (see Map 2.2). These regions were sparsely settled, and the natives were not well enough organized to resist the Greek colonists. Southern Italy and eastern Sicily were even more inviting areas. Before long there were so many Greek colonies in Italy and Sicily that the Romans called the whole region *Magna Graecia* ("Great Greece"). The Greeks also put colonies in Spain and southern France. In the seventh century B.C. Greek colonists settled the coasts of the northeastern Mediterranean, the Black Sea, and the straits connecting them. About the same time they established settlements on the eastern part of the northern African coast. The Greeks now had outposts throughout the Mediterranean world.

The Greeks did not lightly leave home to join a colony. The voyage by sea was dangerous

PHOENICIAN AND GREEK

MAP 2-2 *Most of the coast line of the Mediterranean and Black Seas was populated by Greek or Phoenician colonies. The Phoenicians were a commercial people who planted their colonies in North Africa, Spain, Sicily, and Sardinia chiefly in the ninth century B.C. The height of Greek colonization came later, between about 750 and 550 B.C.*

and uncomfortable, and at the end of it were uncertainty and danger. Only powerful pressures like overpopulation and land hunger drove thousands of Greeks from their homes to found new *poleis*. The Greek word for "colony" was *apoikia*, literally, "away home." The colony, though sponsored by the mother city, was established for the good of the colonists rather than for the benefit of those who sent it out. The colony often copied the constitution from

COLONIZATION

home, worshiped the same gods at the same festivals in the same way, and carried on a busy trade with the mother city. Most colonies, though independent, were friendly with their mother cities. Each might ask the other for aid in time of trouble and expect to receive a friendly hearing, although neither was obliged to help.

Colonization had a powerful influence on Greek life. By relieving the pressure of a growing population, it was a safety valve that allowed the *poleis* to escape civil wars. By emphasizing the differences between the Greeks and the new peoples they met, colonization gave the Greeks a sense of cultural identity and fostered a Panhellenic ("all-Greek") spirit that led to the establishment of a number of common religious festivals. The most important

CHRONOLOGY OF THE RISE OF GREECE	
Minoan period	ca. 2900–1150 B.C.
Probable date of the arrival of the Greeks on the mainland	ca. 1900 B.C.
Mycenaean period	ca. 1600–1150 B.C.
Sack of Troy (?)	ca. 1250 B.C.
Destruction of Mycenaean centers in Greece	ca. 1200–1150 B.C.
Dark Ages	ca. 1100–750 B.C.
Major period of Greek colonization	ca. 750–500 B.C.
Probable date of Homer	ca. 725 B.C.
Probable date of Hesiod	ca. 700 B.C.
Major period of Greek tyranny	ca. 700–500 B.C.

The temple of Hera at Paestum in southern Italy (sixth century B.C.). It is considered the finest surviving example of Doric architecture. [Hirmer Fotoarchive, Munich]

ones were at Olympia, Delphi, Corinth, and Nemea.

Colonization also encouraged trade and industry. The influx of new wealth from abroad and the increased demand for goods from the homeland stimulated a more intensive use of the land and an emphasis on crops for export, chiefly the olive and the wine grape. The manufacture of pottery, tools, weapons, and fine artistic metalwork as well as perfumed oil, the soap of the ancient Mediterranean world, was likewise encouraged. New opportunities allowed some men, sometimes outside the nobility, to become wealthy and important. The newly enriched became a troublesome element in the aristocratic *poleis,* for they had an increasingly important part in the life of their states but were barred from political power, religious privileges, and social acceptance by the ruling aristocrats. These conditions soon created a crisis in many states.

The Tyrants
(About 700–500 B.C.)

The crisis produced by the new economic and social conditions usually led to or intensified factional divisions within the ruling aristocracy. In the years between 700 and 550 B.C., the result was often the establishment of a tyranny.

A tyrant was a monarch who had gained power in an unorthodox or unconstitutional but not necessarily wicked way and who exercised a strong one-man rule that might well be beneficent and popular.

The founding tyrant was usually a member of the ruling aristocracy who either had a personal grievance or led an unsuccessful faction. He often rose to power because of his military ability and support from the hoplites. He generally had the support of the politically powerless group of the newly wealthy and of the

Herodotus Relates the Tyranny of the Cypselids of Corinth

Herodotus (ca. 490–425 B.C.), "the father of history," was a Greek born in the city of Halicarnassus in Asia Minor. In this story he tells of the Cypselid tyrants of Corinth, who ruled from about 650 to about 585 B.C.

Having thus got the tyranny, he [Cypselus] showed himself a harsh ruler—many of the Corinthians he drove into banishment, many he deprived of their fortunes, and a still greater number of their lives. His reign lasted thirty years, and was prosperous to its close; insomuch that he left the government to Periander, his son. This prince at the beginning of his reign was of a milder temper than his father; but after he corresponded by means of messengers with Thrasybulus, tyrant of Miletus, he became even more sanguinary. On one occasion he sent a herald to ask Thrasybulus what mode of government it was safest to set up in order to rule with honour. Thrasybulus led the messenger without the city, and took him into a field of corn, through which he began to walk, while he asked him again and again concerning his coming from Corinth, ever as he went breaking off and throwing away all such ears of corn as overtopped the rest. In this way he went through the whole field, and destroyed all the best and richest part of the crop; then, without a word, he sent the messenger back. On the return of the man to Corinth, Periander was eager to know what Thrasybulus had counselled, but the messenger reported that he had said nothing; and he wondered that Periander had sent him to so strange a man, who seemed to have lost his senses, since he did nothing but destroy his own property. And upon this he told how Thrasybulus had behaved at the interview. Periander, perceiving what the action meant, and knowing that Thrasybulus advised the destruction of all the leading citizens, treated his subjects from this time forward with the very greatest cruelty.

Herodotus, *The Histories,* trans. by George Rawlinson (New York: Random House, 1942), p. 414.

poor peasants as well. When he took power, he often expelled many of his aristocratic opponents and divided at least some of their land among his supporters. He pleased his commercial and industrial supporters by destroying the privileges of the old aristocracy and by fostering trade and colonization.

The tyrants presided over a period of population growth that saw an increase especially in the number of city dwellers. They responded with a program of public works that included improvement of the drainage systems, care for the water supply, the construction and organization of marketplaces, the building and strengthening of city walls, and the erection of temples. They introduced new local festivals and elaborated the old ones. They were active in the patronage of the arts, supporting poets and artisans with gratifying results. All this activity contributed to the tyrant's popularity, to the prosperity of his city, and to his self-esteem.

In most cases the tyrant's rule was secured by a personal bodyguard and by mercenary soldiers. An armed citizenry, necessary for an aggressive foreign policy, would have been dangerous, so the tyrants usually pursued a program of peaceful alliances with other tyrants abroad and avoided war.

End of the Tyrants

By the end of the sixth century B.C. tyranny had disappeared from the Greek states and did not return again in the same form or for the same reasons. The last tyrants were universally hated for the cruelty and repression they employed. They left bitter memories in their own states and became objects of fear and hatred everywhere. Apart from the outrages committed by individual tyrants, there was something about the very concept of tyranny that was inimical to the idea of the *polis.* The notion of the *polis* as a community to which every member must be responsible, the connection of justice with that community, and the natural aristo-

46

*The
Foundations of
Western
Civilization in
the Ancient
World*

cratic hatred of monarchy all made tyranny seem alien and offensive. The rule of a tyrant, however beneficent, was arbitrary and unpredictable. Tyranny came into being in defiance of tradition and law and governed without either. Above all, the tyrant was not answerable in any way to his fellow citizens.

From a longer perspective, however, it is clear that the tyrants made important contributions to the development of Greek civilization. They put an end for a time to the crippling civil wars that threatened the survival of the aristocratic *poleis*. In general, they reduced the warfare between the states. They encouraged the economic changes that were necessary for the future prosperity of Greece. They increased the degree of communication with the rest of the Mediterranean world and made an enormous contribution to the cultivation of crafts and technology, as well as of the arts and literature. Most important of all, they broke the grip of the aristocracy and put the productive powers of the most active and talented of its citizens fully at the service of the *polis*.

This scene on an Attic jar from late in the sixth century B.C. shows how olives, one of Athens's most important crops, were harvested. [Courtesy of the Trustees of the British Museum]

Peasants and Aristocrats: Styles of Life in Archaic Greece

As the "dark ages" came to an end, the features that would distinguish Greek society thereafter took shape. The role of the artisan and the merchant grew more important as contact with the non-Hellenic world became easier, but the great majority of people continued to make their living from the land. Wealthy aristocrats with large estates, powerful households, families, and clans, however, led very different lives from those of the poorer peasants and the independent farmers who had smaller and less fertile fields.

Peasants rarely leave a record of their thoughts or activities, and we have no such record from ancient Greece. The poet Hesiod (ca. 700 B.C.), however, who presented himself as a small farmer was certainly no aristocrat. From his *Works and Days* we get some idea of the life of such a farmer. The crops included grain, chiefly barley but also wheat; grapes for the making of wine; olives for food, but chiefly for oil, used for cooking, lighting, and washing; green vegetables, especially the bean; and some fruit. Sheep and goats provided milk and cheese. The Homeric heroes had great herds of cattle and ate lots of meat, but by Hesiod's time land fertile enough to provide fodder for cattle was needed to grow grain. He and small farmers like him tasted meat chiefly from sacrificial animals at festivals.

These farmers worked hard to make their living. Although Hesiod had the help of oxen and mules and one or two hired helpers for occasional labor, his life was one of continuous toil. The hardest work came in October, at the start of the rainy season, the time for the first plowing. The plow was light and easily broken, and the work of forcing the iron tip into the earth was back-breaking, though Hesiod had a team of oxen to pull his plow. Not every farmer was so fortunate, and the cry of the crane that announced the time of year to plow "bites the heart of the man without oxen." Autumn and winter were the time for cutting wood, building wagons, and making tools. Late winter was the time to tend to the vines, May the time to harvest the grain, July to winnow and store it. Only at the height of summer's heat did Hesiod allow for rest, but when September came, it was time to harvest the grapes. No sooner was that task done than the cycle started again. The work went on under the burning sun and in the freezing cold. Hesiod wrote nothing of pleasure or entertainment. Less austere farmers than Hesiod gathered at the blacksmith's shop for warmth and companionship in winter, and even he must have taken part in religious rites and festivals that were accompanied by some kind of entertainment, but the life of the peasant farmers was hard and their pleasures few.

Most aristocrats were rich enough to employ many hired laborers, sometimes sharecroppers and sometimes even slaves, to work their extensive lands and were therefore able to enjoy leisure for other activities. The center of aristocratic social life was the drinking party, or *symposion*. This activity was not a mere drinking bout, meant to remove inhibitions and produce oblivion. The Greeks, in fact, almost always mixed their wine with water, and one of the goals of the participants was to drink as much as the others without becoming drunk. The *symposion* was a carefully organized occasion, with a "king" chosen to set the order of events and to determine that night's mixture of wine and water. Only men took part, and they ate and drank as they reclined on couches

---

Hesiod's Farmer's Almanac

Hesiod was a farmer and poet who lived in a village in Greece about 700 B.C. His poem *Works and Days* contains wisdom on several subjects, but its final section amounts to a farmer's almanac, taking readers through the year and advising them on just when each activity is demanded. Hesiod painted a picture of a very hard life for Greek farmers, allowing rest only in the passage that follows.

But when House-on-Back, the snail, crawls
　　from the ground up
the plants, escaping the Pleiades, it's no
　　longer time for vine-digging;
time rather to put an edge to your sickles,
　　and rout out your helpers.
Keep away from sitting in the shade or lying
　　in bed till the sun's up
in the time of the harvest, when the sunshine
　　scorches your skin dry.
This is the season to push your work and
　　bring home your harvest;
get up with the first light so you'll have
　　enough to live on.
Dawn takes away from work a third part of
　　the work's measure.
Dawn sets a man well along on his journey,
　　in his work also,
dawn, who when she shows, has numerous
　　people going their ways; dawn who puts
　　the yoke upon many oxen.
　　But when the artichoke is in flower, and
　　the clamorous cricket
sitting in his tree lets go his vociferous
　　singing, that issues

from the beating of his wings, in the
　　exhausting season of summer,
then is when goats are at their fattest, when
　　the wine tastes best,
women are most lascivious, but the men's
　　strength fails them
most, for the star Seirios shrivels them, knees
　　and heads alike,
and the skin is all dried out in the heat;
　　then, at that season,
one might have the shadow under the rock,
　　and the wine of Biblis,
a curd cake, and all the milk that the goats
　　can give you,
the meat of a heifer, bred in the woods, who
　　has never borne a calf,
and of baby kids also. Then, too, one can sit
　　in the shadow
and drink the bright-shining wine, his heart
　　satiated with eating
and face turned in the direction where
　　Zephyros blows briskly,
make three libations of water from a spring
　　that keeps running forever
and has no mud in it; and pour wine for the
　　fourth libation.

Works and Days, trans. by Richmond Lattimore, (Ann Arbor: 1959), University of Michigan Press, pp. 87, 89.

along the walls of the room. The sessions began with prayers and libations to the gods. Usually there were games, such as dice or *kottabos,* in which wine was flicked from the cups at different targets. Sometimes dancing girls or flute girls offered entertainment. Frequently the aristocratic participants provided their own amusements with songs, poetry, or even philosophical disputes. Characteristically these took the form of contests, with some kind of prize for the winner, for aristocratic values continued to emphasize competition and the need to excel, whatever the arena.

This aspect of aristocratic life appears in the athletic contests that became widespread early in the sixth century. The games included running events; the long jump; the discus and javelin throws; the *pentathlon,* which included all of these; boxing; wrestling; and the chariot race. Only the rich could afford to raise, train, and race horses, so the chariot race was a special preserve of aristocracy. Wrestling, however, was also especially favored by the nobility, and the *palaestra* where they practiced became an important social center for the aristocracy. The contrast between the hard, drab life of the peasants and the leisured and lively one of the aristocrats could hardly be greater.

An Athenian foot race ca. 530 B.C. *Athletics were an important part of Greek culture. The gods were honored with athletic games, and physical training was part of the essential education of all young men.* [*The Metropolitan Museum of Art, Rogers Fund,* 1914]

Sparta and Athens

Generalization about the *polis* becomes difficult not long after its appearance, for though the states had much in common, some of them developed in unique ways. Sparta and Athens, which became the two most powerful Greek states, had especially unusual histories.

Sparta

At first Sparta seems not to have been strikingly different from other *poleis,* but about 725 B.C. the pressure of population and land hunger led the Spartans to launch a war of conquest against their western neighbor, Messenia. The First Messenian War gave the Spartans as much land as they would ever need, and the reduction of the Messenians to the status of serfs, or Helots, meant that the Spartans need not even work the land that supported them. The turning point in Spartan history came with the Second Messenian War, a rebellion of the Helots, assisted by Argos and some other Peloponnesian cities, about 650 B.C. The war was long and bitter and at one point threatened the existence of Sparta. After the revolt had been put down, the Spartans were forced to reconsider their way of life. They could not expect to keep down the Helots, who outnumbered them perhaps ten to one, and still maintain the old free-and-easy habits typical of most Greeks. Faced with the choice of making drastic changes and sacrifices or abandoning their control of Messenia, the Spartans chose to introduce fundamental reforms that turned their city forever after into a military academy and camp.

The reforms are attributed to the legendary

Xenophon Tells How Lycurgus Encouraged Obedience at Sparta

Xenophon (ca. 430–354 B.C.) was an Athenian who was exiled and lived much of his life in the Peloponnesus. He was one of those rare foreigners who knew Sparta from his own observation.

We are all aware that there is no state in the world in which greater obedience is shown to magistrates, and to the laws themselves, than Sparta. But, for my part, I am disposed to think that Lycurgus could never have attempted to establish this healthy condition, until he had first secured the unanimity of the most powerful members of the state. I infer this for the following reasons. In other states the leaders in rank and influence do not even desire to be thought to fear the magistrates. Such a thing they would regard as in itself a symbol of servility. In Sparta, on the contrary, the stronger a man is the more readily does he bow before constituted authority. And indeed, they pride themselves on their humility, and on a prompt obedience, running, or at any rate not crawling with laggard step, at the word of command. Such an example of eager discipline, they are persuaded, set by themselves, will not fail to be followed by the rest. And this is precisely what has taken place. It is reasonable to suppose that it was these same noblest members of the state who combined to lay the foundation of the ephorate, after they had come to the conclusion themselves that of all the blessings which a state, or an army, or a household can enjoy, obedience is the greatest. Since, as they could not but reason, the greater the power with which men fence about authority, the greater the fascination it will exercise upon the mind of the citizen, to the enforcement of obedience.

Accordingly the ephors are competent to punish whomsoever they choose; they have power to exact fines on the spur of the moment; they have power to depose magistrates in mid career, nay, actually to imprison and bring them to trial on the capital charge. Entrusted with these vast powers, they do not, as do the rest of states, allow the magistrates elected to exercise authority as they like, right through the year of office; but, in the style rather of despotic monarchs, or presidents of the games, at the first symptom of an offense against the law they inflict chastisement without warning and without hesitation.

Xenophon, *Constitution of the Spartans,* trans. by H. G. Dakyns, in *The Greek Historians,* Vol. 2 (New York: Random House, 1942), p. 667.

figure Lycurgus. The new system that emerged late in the sixth century B.C. exerted control over each Spartan from birth, when officials of the state decided which infants were physically fit to survive. At the age of seven the Spartan boy was taken from his mother and turned over to young instructors who trained him in athletics and the military arts and taught him to endure privation, to bear physical pain, and to live off the country, by theft if necessary. At twenty the Spartan youth was enrolled in the army and lived in barracks with his companions until the age of thirty. Marriage was permitted, but a strange sort of marriage it was, for the Spartan male could visit his wife only infrequently and by stealth. At thirty he became a full citizen, an "equal." He took his meals at a public mess in the company of fifteen comrades. His food, a simple diet without much meat or wine, was provided by his own plot of land, which was worked by Helots. Military service was required until the age of sixty; only then could the Spartan retire to his home and family.

This educational program extended to the women, too. They were not given military training, but female infants were examined for fitness to survive in the same way as males. Girls were given gymnastic training, were permitted greater freedom of movement than among other Greeks, and were equally indoctrinated with the idea of service to Sparta. The

Tyrtaeus Describes Excellence: Code of the Citizen Soldier

The military organization of citizen soldiers for the defense of the *polis* and the idea of the *polis* itself, which permeated Greek political thought, found echoes in Greek lyric poetry. A major example is this poem by Tyrtaeus, a Spartan poet who wrote about 625 B.C. It gives important evidence on the nature of warfare in the phalanx and the values taught by the *polis*.

*I would not say anything for a man nor take account
of him
for any speed of his feet or wrestling skill he might
have,
not if he had the size of a Cyclops and strength to go
with it,
not if he could outrun Bóreas, the North Wind of
Thrace,
not if he were more handsome and gracefully formed
than Tithónos,
or had more riches than Midas had, or Kinyras too,
not if he were more of a king than Tantalid Pelops,
or had the power of speech and persuasion Adrastos
had,
not if he had all splendors except for a fighting spirit.
For no man ever proves himself a good man in war
unless he can endure to face the blood and the
slaughter,
go close against the enemy and fight with his
hands.
Here is courage, mankind's finest possession, here is
the noblest prize that a young man can endeavor to
win,
and it is a good thing his city and all the people share
with him
when a man plants his feet and stands in the
foremost spears
relentlessly, all thought of foul flight completely
forgotten,
and has well trained his heart to be steadfast and to
endure,
and with words encourages the man who is stationed
beside him.
Here is a man who proves himself to be valiant in
war.
With a sudden rush he turns to flight the rugged
battalions
of the enemy, and sustains the beating waves of
assault.*

*And he who so falls among the champions and loses
his sweet life,
so blessing with honor his city, his father, and all
his people,
with wounds in his chest, where the spear that he was
facing has transfixed
that massive guard of his shield, and gone through
his breastplate as well,
why, such a man is lamented alike by the young and
the elders,
and all his city goes into mourning and grieves for
his loss.
His tomb is pointed out with pride, and so are his
children,
and his children's children, and afterward all the
race that is his.
His shining glory is never forgotten, his name is
remembered,
and he becomes an immortal, though he lies under
the ground,
when one who was a brave man has been killed by
the furious War God
standing his ground and fighting hard for his
children and land.
But if he escapes the doom of death, the destroyer of
bodies,
and wins his battle, and bright renown for the work
of his spear,
all men give place to him alike, the youth and the
elders,
and much joy comes his way before he goes down to
the dead.
Aging he has reputation among his citizens. No one
tries to interfere with his honors or all he deserves;
all men withdraw before his presence, and yield their
seats to him,
and youth, and the men of his age, and even those
older than he.
Thus a man should endeavor to reach this high place
of courage
with all his heart, and, so trying, never be
backward in war.*

Greek Lyrics, trans. by Richmond Lattimore (Chicago: University of Chicago Press, 1949, 1950, 1955), pp. 14–15.

The oligarchic element was represented by a council of elders consisting of twenty-eight men over sixty, who were elected for life, and the kings. These elders had important judicial functions, sitting as a court in cases involving the kings. They also were consulted before any proposal was put before the assembly of Spartan citizens. In a traditional society like Sparta's, they must have had considerable influence.

The Spartan assembly consisted of all males over thirty. Theoretically they were the final authority, but because, in practice, debate was carried on by magistrates, elders, and kings alone, and because voting was usually by acclamation, the assembly's real function was to ratify decisions already taken or to decide between positions favored by the leading figures. In addition, Sparta had a unique institution, the board of ephors. This consisted of five men elected annually by the assembly. Originally they appear to have been intended to check the power of the kings, but gradually they acquired other important functions. They controlled foreign policy, oversaw the generalship of the kings on campaign, presided at the assembly, and guarded against rebellions by the Helots. The whole system was remarkable both for the way in which it combined participation by the citizenry with significant checks on its power and for its unmatched stability. Most Greeks admired the Spartan state for this quality and also for its ability to mold its citizens into a single pattern of men who subordinated themselves to an ideal. Many political philosophers, from Plato to modern times, have based utopian schemes on a version of the Spartan education and constitution.

By about 550 B.C. the Spartan system was well established, and its limitations were made plain. Suppression of the Helots required all the effort and energy that Sparta had. The Spartans could expand no further, but they could not allow unruly independent neighbors to cause unrest that might inflame the Helots. When the Spartans defeated Tegea, their northern neighbor, they imposed an unusual peace. Instead of taking away land and subjecting the defeated state, Sparta left the Tegeans their land and their freedom. In exchange they required the Tegeans to follow the Spartan lead in foreign affairs and to supply a fixed number of soldiers to Sparta on demand. This became the model for Spartan relations with the other states in the Peloponnesus, and soon Sparta was the leader of an alliance that included

A four-horse chariot racing at full speed. The chariot race was the main event at the Olympic Games, held every four years, and its winner was the most celebrated of the victors. Kings often sponsored drivers and sometimes raced themselves. [Courtesy of the Trustees of the British Museum]

entire system was designed to change the natural feelings of devotion to wife, children, and family into a more powerful commitment to the *polis*. Privacy, luxury, and even comfort were sacrificed to the purpose of producing soldiers whose physical powers, training, and discipline made them the best in the world. Nothing that might turn the mind away from duty was permitted. The very use of coins was forbidden lest it corrupt the desires of Spartans. Neither family nor money was allowed to interfere with the only ambition permitted to a Spartan male: to win glory and the respect of his peers by bravery in war.

SPARTAN GOVERNMENT. The Spartan constitution was mixed, containing elements of monarchy, oligarchy, and democracy. There were two kings, whose power was limited by law and also by the rivalry that usually existed between the two royal houses. The origins and explanation of this unusual dual kingship are unknown, but both kings ruled together in Sparta and exercised equal powers. Their functions were chiefly religious and military. A Spartan army rarely left home without a king in command.

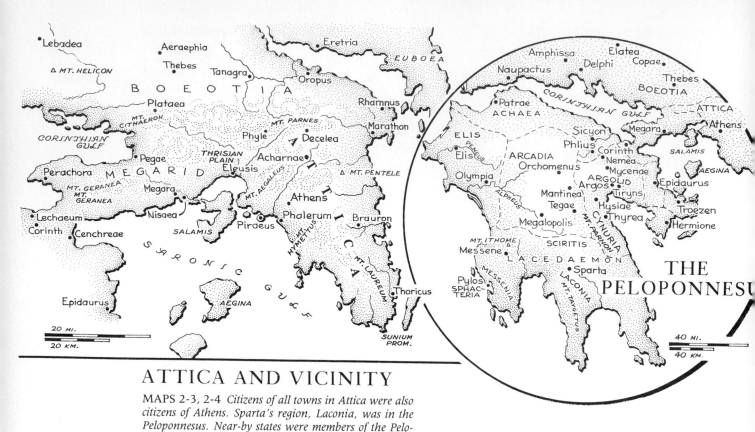

ATTICA AND VICINITY

MAPS 2-3, 2-4 *Citizens of all towns in Attica were also citizens of Athens. Sparta's region, Laconia, was in the Peloponnesus. Near-by states were members of the Peloponnesian League under Sparta's leadership.*

every Peloponnesian state but Argos; modern scholars have named this alliance the Peloponnesian League. It provided the Spartans with the security they needed, and it also made Sparta the most powerful *polis* in Hellenic history. By 500 B.C. Sparta and the league had given the Greeks a force capable of facing mighty threats from abroad.

Athens

Athens was slow to come into prominence and to join in the new activities that were changing the more advanced states, in part because Athens was not situated on the most favored trade routes of the eighth and seventh centuries B.C., in part because its large area (about one thousand square miles) allowed population growth without great pressure, and in part because the unification of the many villages and districts into a single *polis* was not completed until the seventh century B.C.

In the seventh century B.C. Athens was a typical aristocratic *polis*. The people were divided into four tribes and into a number of

clans and brotherhoods (phratries). The aristocrats held the most and best land and dominated religious and political life. There was no written law, and decisions were rendered by powerful nobles on the basis of tradition and, most likely, self-interest. The state was governed by the Areopagus, a council of nobles deriving its name from the hill where it held its sessions. Annually the council elected nine magistrates, who joined the Areopagus after their year in office. Because they served for only a year, were checked by their colleagues, and looked forward to a lifetime as members of the Areopagus after their terms were ended, it is plain that the aristocratic council was the true master of the state.

In the seventh century B.C. the peaceful life of Athens experienced some disturbances, which were caused in part by quarrels within the nobility and in part by the beginnings of an agrarian crisis. In 632 B.C. a nobleman named Cylon attempted a coup to establish himself as tyrant. He was thwarted, but the unrest continued.

In 621 B.C. a man named Draco was given

special authority to codify and publish laws for the first time. In later years the penalties were thought to be harsh, hence the saying that Draco's laws were written in blood. We still speak of unusually harsh penalties as Draconian. Draco's work was probably limited to laws concerning homicide and was aimed at ending blood feuds between clans, but the precedent was important. The publication of law strengthened the hand of the state against the local power of the nobles.

The root of Athens' troubles was agricultural. Many Athenians worked family farms, from which they obtained most of their living. It appears that they planted wheat, the staple crop, year after year without rotating fields or using sufficient fertilizer. In time this procedure exhausted the soil and led to bad crops. To survive, the farmer had to borrow from his wealthy neighbor to get through the year. In return he promised one sixth of the next year's crop. The arrangement was marked by the deposit of an inscribed stone on the entailed farm. Bad harvests persisted, and soon the debtor had to pledge his wife and children and himself as surety for the loans needed for survival. As bad times continued, many Athenians defaulted and were enslaved. Some were even sold abroad. Revolutionary pressures grew among the poor, who began to demand the abolition of debt and a redistribution of the land.

SOLON. The circumstances might easily have brought about class warfare and tyranny, but the remarkable conciliatory spirit of Athens intervened. In the year 594 B.C., as tradition has it, the Athenians elected Solon as the only archon, with extraordinary powers to legislate and revise the constitution. Immediately he attacked the agrarian problem by canceling current debts and forbidding future loans secured by the person of the borrower. He helped bring back many Athenians enslaved abroad as well as freeing those in Athens enslaved for debt. This program was called the "shaking off of burdens." It did not, however, solve the fundamental economic problem, and Solon did not redistribute the land. In the short run, therefore, he did not put an end to the economic crisis, but his other economic actions had profound success in the long run. He forbade the export of wheat and encouraged that of olive oil. This policy had the effect of making wheat more available in Attica and encouraging the cultivation of olive oil and wine as cash

KEY EVENTS IN THE EARLY HISTORY OF SPARTA AND ATHENS	
First Messenian War	ca. 725–710 B.C.
Second Messenian War	ca. 650–625 B.C.
Cylon tries to establish a tyranny at Athens	632 B.C.
Draco publishes legal code at Athens	621 B.C.
Solon institutes reforms at Athens	594 B.C.
Sparta defeats Tegea: Beginning of Peloponnesian League	ca. 560–550 B.C.
Pisistratus reigns as tyrant at Athens (main period)	546–527 B.C.
Hippias, son of Pisistratus, deposed as tyrant of Athens	510 B.C.
Clisthenes institutes reforms at Athens	ca. 508–501 B.C.

crops. By the fifth century B.C. this form of agriculture had become so profitable that much Athenian land was diverted from grain production to the cultivation of cash crops, and Athens became dependent on imported wheat. Solon also changed the Athenian standards of weights and measures to conform with those of Corinth and Euboea and the cities of the East. This change also encouraged commerce and turned Athens in the direction that would lead her to great prosperity in the fifth century. He also encouraged industry by offering citizenship to foreign artisans, and his success is reflected in the development of the outstanding Attic pottery of the sixth century. Solon also significantly changed the constitution. All male adults whose fathers were citizens were citizens, too, and to their number he added those immigrants who were offered citizenship. All these Athenian citizens were divided into four classes on the basis of wealth, measured by annual agricultural production. Men whose property produced 500 measures were called 500-measure men, and those producing 300 measures were called cavalry; these two classes alone could hold the archonship, the chief magistracy in Athens, and sit on the Areopagus. Producers of 200 measures were called owners of a team of oxen; these were allowed to serve as hoplites. They could be elected to the council of 400 chosen by all the citizens, 100 from each tribe. Solon seems to have meant this council to serve as a check on the Areopagus and to prepare any business that

Solon Discusses the Virtues of Good Government

The Athenians appointed Solon to revise their constitution in the year 594–593 B.C. He explained and defended his policies in excellent verse. In the following selection he made the most powerful claims for the benefits of a well-ordered city-state governed by good laws.

Thus the public Ruin invades the house of each citizen,
and the courtyard doors no longer have strength to keep it away,
but it overleaps the lofty wall, and though a man runs in
and tries to hide in chamber or closet, it ferrets him out.
So my spirit dictates to me: I must tell the Athenians
how many evils a city suffers from Bad Government,
and how Good Government displays all neatness and order,

and many times she must put shackles on the breakers of laws.
She levels rough places, stops Glut and Greed, takes the force from Violence;
she dries up the growing flowers of Despair as they grow;
she straightens out crooked judgments given, gentles the swollen
ambitions, and puts an end to acts of divisional strife;
she stills the gall of wearisome Hate, and under her influence
all life among mankind is harmonious and does well.

Greek Lyrics, trans. by Richmond Lattimore, (Chicago: University of Chicago Press, 1960), p. 21.

needed to be put before the assembly. The last class, producing less than 200 measures, were the *thetes.* They voted in the popular assembly for the archons and the council members and on any other business brought before them by the magistrates. They also sat on the new popular court established by Solon. At first, it must have had little power, for most cases continued to be heard in the country by local barons and in Athens by the aristocratic Areopagus. But the new court was recognized as a court of appeal, and by the fifth century B.C. almost all cases came before the popular courts.

PISISTRATUS. Solon's efforts to avoid factional strife failed. Within a few years contention reached such a degree that no archons could be chosen. Out of this turmoil emerged the first Athenian tyranny. Pisistratus, a nobleman, faction leader, and military hero, briefly seized power in 560 B.C. and again in 556 B.C., but each time his support was inadequate and he was driven out. At last, in 546 B.C. he came back at the head of a mercenary army from abroad and established a tyranny that lasted beyond his death, in 527 B.C., until the expulsion of his son Hippias in 510 B.C. In many respects Pisistratus resembled the other Greek tyrants. His rule rested on the force provided by mercenary soldiers. He engaged in great programs of public works, urban improvement, and religious piety. Temples were built and religious centers expanded and improved. New religious festivals were introduced, such as the one dedicated to Dionysus, the god of fertility, wine, and ecstatic religious worship imported from Phrygia in Asia Minor. Old ones, like the Great Panathenaic festival, were amplified and given greater public appeal. Poets and artists were supported to add cultural luster to the court of the tyrant.

Pisistratus aimed at increasing the power of the central government at the expense of the nobles. The festival of Dionysus and the Great Panathenaic festival helped fix attention on the capital city, as did the new temples and the reconstruction of the Agora as the center of public life. Circuit judges were sent out into the country to hear cases, another feature that weakened the power of the local barons. All this time Pisistratus made no formal change in the Solonian constitution. Assembly, councils,

and courts met; magistrates and councils were elected; Pisistratus merely saw to it that his supporters were chosen. The intended effect was to blunt the sharp edge of tyranny with the appearance of constitutional government, and it worked. The rule of Pisistratus was remembered as popular and mild. The unintended effect was to give the Athenians more experience in the procedures of self-government and a growing taste for it.

INVASION BY SPARTA. Pisistratus was succeeded by his oldest son, Hippias, who followed his father's ways at first. In 514 B.C., however, his brother Hipparchus was murdered as a result of a private quarrel. Hippias became nervous, suspicious, and harsh. At last one of the noble clans exiled by the sons of Pisistratus, the Alcmaeonids, won favor with the influential oracle at Delphi and used its support to persuade Sparta to attack the Athenian tyranny. Led by their ambitious king, Cleomenes I, the Spartans marched into Attica in 510 B.C. and deposed Hippias, who went into exile to the Persian court. The tyranny was over.

The Spartans must have hoped to leave Athens in friendly hands, and indeed Cleomenes' friend Isagoras held the leading position in Athens after the withdrawal of the Spartan army, but he was not unopposed. Clisthenes of the restored Alcmaeonid clan was his chief rival but lost out in the political struggle among the noble factions. Isagoras seems to have tried to restore a version of the pre-Solonian aristocratic state. As part of his plan he carried through a purification of the citizen lists, removing those who had been enfranchised by Solon or Pisistratus and any others thought to have a doubtful claim. Clisthenes then took an unprecedented action by turning to the people for political support and won it with a program of great popular appeal. In response Isagoras called in the Spartans again; Cleomenes arrived and allowed the expulsion from Athens of Clisthenes and a large number of his supporters. But the Athenian political consciousness, ignited by Solon and kept alive under Pisistratus, was fanned by the popular appeal of Clisthenes. The people would not hear of an aristocratic restoration and drove out the Spartans and Isagoras with them. Clisthenes and his allies returned, ready to put their program into effect.

CLISTHENES. A central aim of Clisthenes' reforms was to diminish the influence of traditional localities and regions in Athenian life, for these were an important source of power

56

*The
Foundations of
Western
Civilization in
the Ancient
World*

for the nobility and of factions in the state. He made the deme, the equivalent of a small town in the country or a ward in the city, the basic unit of civic life. It was a purely political unit that elected its own officers. Henceforth enrollment in the deme replaced enrollment in the phratry (where tradition and noble birth dominated) as evidence of Athenian citizenship.

Clisthenes immediately enrolled the disenfranchised who had supported him in the struggle with Isagoras. The demes, which ultimately reached about 175 in number, were divided into ten new tribes that replaced the traditional four. The composition of each tribe guaranteed that no region would dominate any of them. Because the tribes had common religious activities and fought as regimental units, the new organization would also increase devotion to the *polis* and diminish regional divisions and personal loyalty to local barons.

A new council of 500 was invented to replace the Solonian council of 400. Each tribe elected 50 councilors each year, and no one could serve more than twice. The council's main responsibility was to prepare legislation for discussion by the assembly, but it also had important financial duties and received foreign emissaries. Final authority in all things rested with the assembly composed of all adult male Athenian citizens. Debate was free and open; any Athenian could submit legislation, offer amendments, or argue the merits of any question. In practice political leaders did most of the talking, and we may imagine that in the early days the council had more authority than it did after the Athenians became more confident in their new self-government. It is fair to call Clisthenes the father of Athenian democracy. He did not alter the property qualifications of Solon, but his enlargement of the citizen rolls, his diminution of the power of the aristocrats, and his elevation of the role of the assembly, with its effective and manageable council, all give him a firm claim to that title.

As a result of the work of Solon, Pisistratus, and Clisthenes, Athens entered the fifth century B.C. well on the way to prosperity and democracy, much more centralized and united than it had been, and ready to take its place among the major states that would lead the defense of Greece against the dangers that lay ahead.

Aspects of Culture in Archaic Greece

Religion

Like most ancient peoples, the Greeks were polytheists, and religion played an important part in their lives. A great part of Greek art and literature was closely connected with religion,

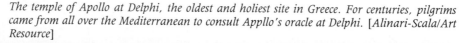

The temple of Apollo at Delphi, the oldest and holiest site in Greece. For centuries, pilgrims came from all over the Mediterranean to consult Appllo's oracle at Delphi. [*Alinari-Scala/Art Resource*]

as was the life of the *polis* in general. The Greek pantheon consisted of the twelve gods who lived on Mount Olympus: Zeus, the father of the gods; his wife, Hera; his brother, Poseidon, god of the seas and earthquakes; his sisters, Hestia, goddess of the hearth, and Demeter, goddess of agriculture and marriage; and his children—Aphrodite, goddess of love and beauty; Apollo, god of the sun, music, poetry, and prophecy; Ares, god of war; Artemis, goddess of the moon and the hunt; Athena, goddess of wisdom and the arts; Hephaestus, god of fire and metallurgy; and Hermes; messenger of the gods and connected with commerce and cunning.

On the one hand, these gods were seen as behaving very much as mortals behaved, with all the human foibles, except that they were superhuman in these as well as in their strength and immortality. On the other hand, Zeus, at least, was seen as being a source of human justice, and even the Olympians were understood to be subordinate to the Fates. Each *polis* had one of the Olympians as its guardian deity and worshiped the god in its own special way, but all the gods were Panhellenic. In the eighth and seventh centuries B.C. common shrines were established at Olympia for the worship of Zeus, at Delphi for Apollo, at the Isthmus of Corinth for Poseidon, and at Nemea once again for Zeus. Each held athletic contests in honor of its god, to which all Greeks were invited and for which a sacred truce was declared.

Besides the Olympians, the Greeks also worshiped countless lesser deities connected with local shrines and even heroes, humans real or legendary who had accomplished great deeds and had earned immortality and divine status. The worship of these deities was not a very emotional experience. It was a matter of offering prayer, libations, and gifts in return for protection and favors from the god during the lifetime of the worshiper. There was no hope of immortality for the average human and little moral teaching. Plato, in fact, at a later date, suggested that the poets be banned from the state because the tales they told of the gods were immoral and corrupting for humans. Most Greeks seem to have held to the commonsense notion that justice lay in paying one's debts; that civic virtue consisted of worshiping the state deities in the traditional way, performing required public services, and fighting in defense of the state; and that private morality meant to do good to one's friends and harm to one's enemies. In the sixth century B.C. the influence of the cult of Apollo at Delphi and of his oracle there became very great. The oracle was the most important of several that helped satisfy human craving for a clue to the future. The priests of Apollo preached moderation; their advice was exemplified in the two famous sayings identified with Apollo: ''Know thyself'' and ''Nothing in excess.'' Humans needed self-control (*sophrosynē*). Its opposite was arrogance (*hubris*), which was brought on by excessive wealth or good fortune. *Hubris* led to moral blindness and finally to divine vengeance. This theme of moderation and the dire consequences of its absence was central to Greek popular morality and appears frequently in Greek literature.

The somewhat cold religion of the Olympian

The god Dionysus dancing with two female followers. The vase was painted in the sixth century B.C. [*Bibliotheque Nationale, Paris*]

gods and of the cult of Apollo did little to attend to human fears, hopes, and passions. For these needs the Greeks turned to other deities and rites. Of these the most popular was Dionysus, a god of nature and fertility, of the grape vine and drunkenness and sexual abandon. In some of his rites the god was followed by maenads, female devotees who cavorted by night, ate raw flesh, and were reputed to tear to pieces any creature they came across.

Poetry

The great changes sweeping through the Greek world were also reflected in the poetry of the sixth century B.C. The lyric style, whether sung by a chorus or by one singer, predominated. Sappho of Lesbos, Anacreon of Teos, and Simonides of Cos composed personal poetry, often speaking of the pleasure and agony of love. Alcaeus of Mytilene, an aristo-

crat driven from his city by a tyrant, wrote bitter invective. Perhaps the most interesting poet of the century from a political point of view was Theognis of Megara. He was an aristocrat who lived through a tyranny, an unusually chaotic and violent democracy, and an oligarchy that restored order but ended the rule of the old aristocracy. Theognis was the spokesman for the old, defeated aristocracy of birth. He divided everyone into two classes, the noble and the base; the former were the good, the latter bad. Those nobly born must associate only with others like themselves if they were to preserve their virtue; if they mingled with the base, they became base. Those born base, on the other hand, could never become noble. Only nobles could aspire to virtue, and only nobles possessed the critical moral and intellectual qualities, respect or honor and judgment. These qualities could not be taught; they were innate. Even so they had to be carefully

---

Theognis of Megara Gives Advice to a Young Aristocrat

Theognis was born about 580 B.C. and lived to see his native city Megara torn by social upheaval and civil war. His poems present the political and ethical ideas of the Greek aristocracy.

Do not consort with bad men, but always hold to the good. Eat and drink with them, whose power is great, sit with them and please them. You will learn good from good men, but if you mingle with the bad you will lose such wisdom as you already have. Therefore consort with the good and one day you will say that I give good advice to my friends.

We seek thoroughbred rams, asses, and horses, Cyrnus, and a man wants offspring of good breeding. But in marriage a good man does not decline to marry the bad daughter of a bad father, if he gives him much wealth. Nor does the wife of a bad man refuse to be his bedfellow if he be rich, preferring wealth to goodness. For they value possessions and a good man marries a woman of bad stock and the bad a woman of good. Wealth mixes the breed. So do not wonder, son of Polypaus, that the race of your citizens is

obscured since bad things are mixed with good.

It is easier to beget and rear a man than to put good sense into him. No one has ever discovered a way to make a fool wise or a bad man good. If God had given the sons of Asclepius the knowledge to heal the evil nature and mischievous mind of man, great and frequent would be their pay. If thought could be made and put into a man, the son of a good man would never become bad, since he would obey good counsel. But you will never make the bad man good by teaching.

The best thing the gods give to men, Cyrnus, is judgment, judgment contains the ends of everything. O happy is the man who has it in his mind; it is much greater than destructive insolence and grievous satiety. There are no evils among mortals worse than these—for every evil, Cyrnus, comes out of them.

Trans. by Donald Kagan in *Sources in Greek Political Thought*, ed. by D. Kagan (New York: Free Press, 1965), pp. 39–40.

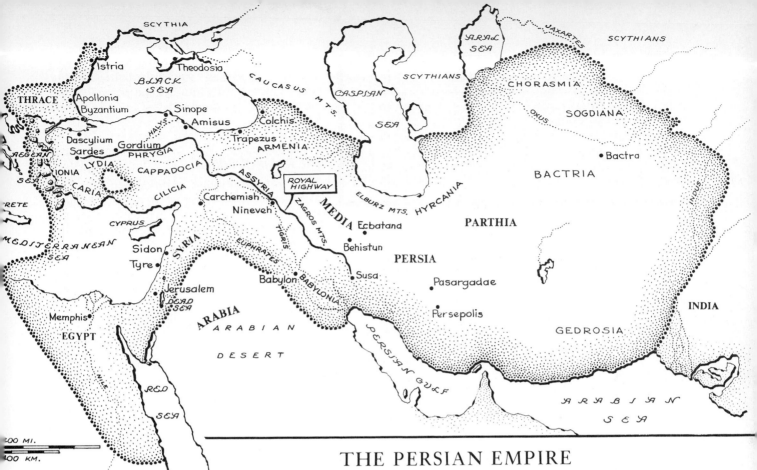

THE PERSIAN EMPIRE

MAP 2-5 *The empire created by Cyrus had fullest extent under Darius when Persia attacked Greece in 490 B.C. It reached from India to the Aegean—and even into Europe—including the lands formerly ruled by Egyptians, Hittites, Babylonians, and Assyrians.*

guarded against corruption by wealth or by mingling with the base. Intermarriage between the noble and the base was especially condemned. These were the ideas of the un-reconstructed nobility, whose power had been destroyed or reduced in most Greek states by this time. These ideas remained alive in aristocratic hearts throughout the next century and greatly influenced later thinkers, Plato, again, among them.

The Persian Wars

The Greeks' period of fortunate isolation and freedom at last came to an end. They had established colonies along most of the coast of Asia Minor from as early as the eleventh century B.C. The colonies maintained friendly relations with the mainland but developed a flour-

ishing economic and cultural life, independent of their mother cities and of their Oriental neighbors. In the middle of the sixth century B.C., however, these Greek cities of Asia Minor came under the control of Lydia and its king, Croesus (ca. 560–546 B.C.). The Lydian rule seems not to have been very harsh, but the Persian conquest of Lydia in 546 B.C. brought a subjugation that was less pleasant. The Persian Empire had been created in a single generation by Cyrus the Great. In 559 B.C. he came to the throne of Persia, then a small kingdom well to the east of the lower Mesopotamian valley; unified Persia under his rule; made an alliance with Babylonia; and led a successful rebellion toward the north against the Medes, who were the overlords of Persia (see Map 2.5). In succeeding years he expanded his empire in all directions, in the process defeating Croesus and occupying Lydia. Most of the Greek cities

byses, nor the civil war that followed it in 522–521 B.C. produced any disturbance in the Greek cities. Darius found Ionia perfectly obedient when he emerged as Great King in 521 B.C.

The Ionian Rebellion

The private troubles of the ambitious tyrant of Miletus, Aristagoras, started the rebellion. He had urged a Persian expedition against the island of Naxos; when it failed, he feared the consequences and organized the Ionian rebellion of 499 B.C. To gain support, he overthrew the tyrannies and proclaimed democratic constitutions. Then he turned to the mainland states for help. As the most powerful Greek state, Sparta was naturally the first stop, but the Spartans would have none of Aristagoras' promises of easy victory and great wealth. Sparta had no close ties with the Ionians and no national interest in the region, and the thought of leaving an undefended Sparta to the Helots while the army was far off for a long time was terrifying.

Aristagoras next sought help at Athens, and there the assembly agreed and voted to send a fleet of twenty ships to help the rebels. The Athenians were Ionians and had close ties of religion and tradition with the rebels. Besides, Hippias, the deposed tyrant of Athens, was an honored guest at the court of Darius, and the Great King (as the Persian rulers styled themselves) had already made it plain that he favored the tyrant's restoration. The Persians,

of Asia Minor sided with Croesus and resisted the Persians. By about 540 B.C., however, they had all been subdued. The western part of Asia Minor was divided into three provinces, each under its own satrap, or governor.

The Persians required their subjects to pay tribute and to serve in the Persian army. They ruled the Greek cities through local individuals, who governed their cities as "tyrants." The Ionians had been moving in the direction of democracy and were not pleased with monarchical rule, but most of the "tyrants" were not harsh, the Persian tribute was not excessive, and there was general prosperity. Neither the death of Cyrus fighting on a distant frontier in 530 B.C. nor the suicide of his successor, Cam-

Persian nobles paying homage to King Darius, from the treasury at Persepolis. Darius is seated on the throne; his son and successor Xerxes stands behind him. Darius and Xerxes are carved in larger scale to indicate their royal status. [Courtesy of the Oriental Institute, University of Chicago]

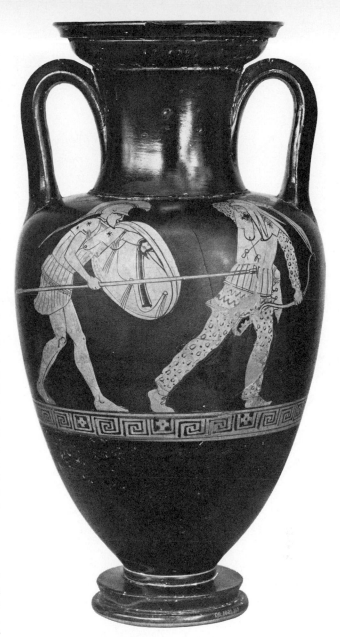

Greek hoplite attacking a Persian soldier. The contrast between the Greek's metal body armor, large shield, and long spear and the Persian's cloth and leather garments indicates one reason the Greeks won. This Attic vase was found on Rhodes and dates from ca. 475 B.C. [The Metropolitan Museum of Art, Rogers Fund, 1906]

moreover, controlled both sides of the Hellespont, the route to the grain fields beyond the Black Sea, which were increasingly vital to Athens. Perhaps some Athenians already feared that a Persian attempt to conquer the Greek mainland was only a matter of time. The Athenian expedition was strengthened by five ships from Eretria in Euboea, which participated out of gratitude for past favors.

In 498 B.C. the Athenians and their allies made a swift march and a surprise attack on Sardis, the old capital of Lydia and now the seat of the satrap, and burned it. This action caused the revolt to spread throughout the Greek cities of Asia Minor outside Ionia, but the Ionians could not follow it up. The Athenians withdrew and took no further part, and gradually the Persians imposed their will. In 495 B.C. they defeated the Ionian fleet at Lade, and in the next year they wiped out Miletus. Many of the men were killed, others were transported to the Persian Gulf, and the women and children were enslaved. The Ionian rebellion was over.

The War in Greece

In 490 B.C. the Persians launched an expedition directly across the Aegean to punish Eretria and Athens, to restore Hippias, and to gain control of the Aegean Sea (see Map 2.6). The force of infantry and cavalry under the command of Datis and Artaphernes landed first at Naxos and destroyed it for its successful resistance in 499 B.C. Then they destroyed Eretria and deported its people deep into the interior of Persia.

The Athenians chose to risk the fate of Eretria rather than submit to Persia and restore the hated tyranny. The resistance was led by Miltiades, an Athenian and an outstanding soldier who had fled from Persian service after earning the anger of Darius. His knowledge of the Persian army and his distaste for submission to Persia made him an ideal leader. He led the army to Marathon and won a decisive victory. The battle at Marathon (490 B.C.) was of

THE GREEK WARS AGAINST PERSIA	
Greek cities of Asia Minor conquered by Croesus of Lydia	ca. 560–546 B.C.
Cyrus of Persia conquers Lydia and gains control of Greek cities	546 B.C.
Greek cities rebel (Ionian rebellion)	499–494 B.C.
Battle of Marathon	490 B.C.
Xerxes' invasion of Greece	480–479 B.C.
Battles of Thermopylae, Artemisium, and Salamis	480 B.C.
Battles of Plataea and Mycale	479 B.C.

61

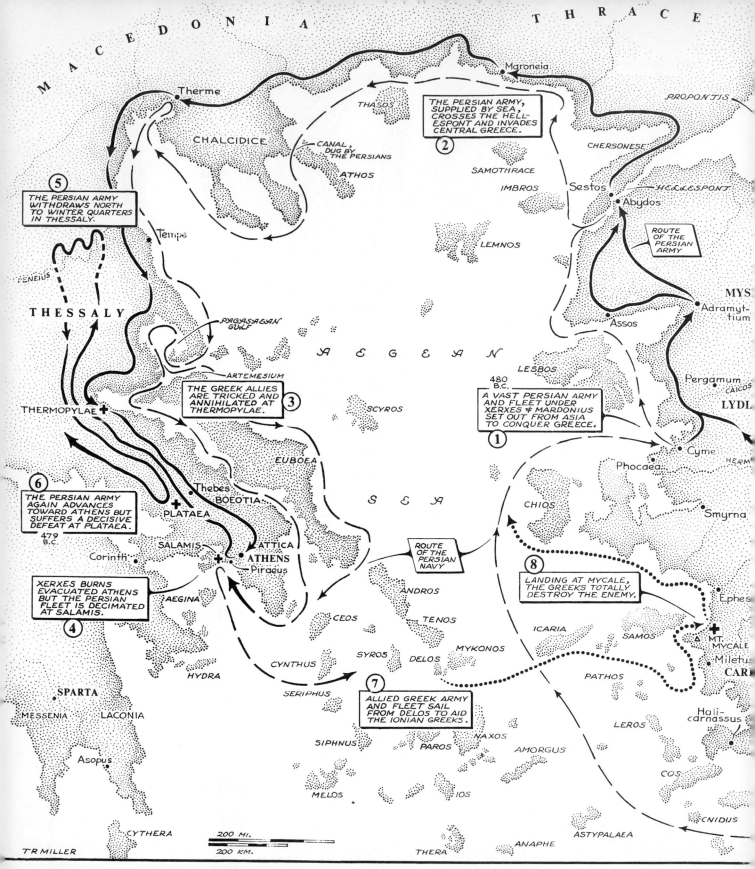

MACEDONIA ⋯⋯⋯⋯ THRACE

Therme

CHALCIDICE

CANAL, DUG BY THE PERSIANS

ATHOS

THASOS

Maroneia

PROPONTIS

CHERSONESE

SAMOTHRACE

IMBROS

Sestos

HELLESPONT

Abydos

LEMNOS

2 THE PERSIAN ARMY, SUPPLIED BY SEA, CROSSES THE HELL-ESPONT AND INVADES CENTRAL GREECE.

ROUTE OF THE PERSIAN ARMY

MYS

Adramyttium

5 THE PERSIAN ARMY WITHDRAWS NORTH TO WINTER QUARTERS IN THESSALY.

Tempe

Assos

PENEIUS

THESSALY

PAGASAEAN GULF

ARTEMESIUM

A E G E A N

LESBOS

480 B.C.

Pergamum

CAICOS

LYDI

3 THE GREEK ALLIES ARE TRICKED AND ANNIHILATED AT THERMOPYLAE.

SCYROS

1 A VAST PERSIAN ARMY AND FLEET UNDER XERXES & MARDONIUS SET OUT FROM ASIA TO CONQUER GREECE.

Cyme

HERM

THERMOPYLAE ✝

EUBOEA

Phocaea

Smyrna

6 THE PERSIAN ARMY AGAIN ADVANCES TOWARD ATHENS BUT SUFFERS A DECISIVE DEFEAT AT PLATAEA. 479 B.C.

Thebes

BOEOTIA

PLATAEA ✝

S E A

CHIOS

ROUTE OF THE PERSIAN NAVY

SALAMIS

ATTICA

ATHENS

Piraeus

8 LANDING AT MYCALE, THE GREEKS TOTALLY DESTROY THE ENEMY.

Corinth

4 XERXES BURNS EVACUATED ATHENS BUT THE PERSIAN FLEET IS DECIMATED AT SALAMIS.

AEGINA

ANDROS

Ephes

CEOS

TENOS

ICARIA

SAMOS

MT. MYCALE

Miletu

CAR

HYDRA

CYNTHUS

SYROS

DELOS

MYKONOS

PATHOS

LEROS

Hali-carnassus

SERIPHUS

SPARTA

MESSENIA

LACONIA

SIPHNUS

PAROS

NAXOS

AMORGUS

COS

Asopus

MELOS

IOS

7 ALLIED GREEK ARMY AND FLEET SAIL FROM DELOS TO AID THE IONIAN GREEKS.

CNIDUS

ASTYPALAEA

CYTHERA

200 MI.

200 KM.

THERA

ANAPHE

T.R. MILLER

THE PERSIAN INVASION OF GREECE

MAP 2-6 *This map traces the route taken by the Persian King Xerxes in his invasion of Greece in 480 B.C. The solid lines show movements of his army, the broken lines of his fleet.*

enormous importance to the future of Greek civilization. A Persian victory would have destroyed Athenian freedom, and the conquest of all the mainland Greeks would have followed. The greatest achievements of Greek culture, most of which lay in the future, would have been impossible under Persian rule. The Athenian victory, on the other hand, made a positive contribution to those achievements. It instilled in the Athenians a sense of confidence and pride in their *polis*, their unique form of government, and themselves.

For the Persians Marathon was only a small and temporary defeat, but it was annoying. Internal troubles, however, prevented swift revenge. In 481 B.C. Darius' successor, Xerxes, gathered an army of at least 150,000 men and a navy of more than six hundred ships for the conquest of Greece. The Greeks did not make good use of the delay, but Athens was an exception. Themistocles had become its leading politician, and he had always wanted to turn Athens into a naval power. The first step was to build a fortified port at Piraeus during his archonship in 493 B.C. A decade later the Athenians came upon a rich vein of silver in the state mines, and Themistocles persuaded them to use the profits to increase their fleet. By 480 B.C. Athens had over two hundred ships, the backbone of the navy that defeated the Persians.

As the Persian army gathered south of the Hellespont, only thirty-one Greek states out of hundreds were willing to fight. They were led by Sparta, Athens, Corinth, and Aegina. In the spring of 480 B.C. Xerxes launched his invasion. The Persian strategy was to march into Greece, destroy Athens, defeat the Greek army, and add the Greeks to the number of Persian subjects. The huge Persian army needed to keep in touch with the fleet for supplies. If the Greeks could defeat the Persian navy, the army could not remain in Greece long. Themistocles knew that the Aegean was subject to sudden devastating storms. His strategy was to delay the Persian army and then to bring on the kind of naval battle he might hope to win.

The Greek League, founded specifically to resist this Persian invasion, met at Corinth as the Persians were ready to cross the Hellespont. They chose Sparta as leader on land and sea and sent a force to Tempe to try to defend Thessaly. Tempe proved to be indefensible, so the Greeks retreated and took up new positions at Thermopylae (the "hot gates") on land and off Artemisium at sea. The opening between

the mountains and the sea at Thermopylae was so narrow that it might be held by a smaller army against a much larger one. The Spartans sent their king, Leonidas, with three hundred of their own citizens and enough allies to make a total of about nine thousand. The Greeks may have intended to hold only long enough to permit the Athenians to evacuate Athens, or to force a sea battle, or they may have hoped to hold Thermopylae until the Persians were dis-

A bronze helmet dedicated to Zeus by Miltiades to commemorate the Athenian victory over the Persians in 490 B.C. [*German Archaelogical Institute, Athens*]

These potsherds from fifth-century B.C. *Athens are inscribed with the names of two famous Athenian statesmen, Themistocles, son of Neocles, and Aristides, son of Lysimachus. At different times each man was banished from Athens for ten years.* [Agora Excavations, American School of Classical Studies at Athens]

couraged enough to withdraw. Perhaps they thought of all these possibilities, for they were not mutually contradictory.

Severe storms wrecked a large number of Persian ships while the Greek fleet waited safely in their protected harbor. Then Xerxes attacked Thermopylae, and for two days the Greeks butchered his best troops without serious loss to themselves. On the third day, however, a traitor showed the Persians a mountain trail that permitted them to come on the Greeks from behind. Many allies escaped, but Leonidas and his three hundred Spartans died to the last man. At about the same time the Greek and Persian fleets fought an indecisive battle, and the fall of Thermopylae forced the Greek navy to withdraw.

If an inscription discovered in 1959 is authentic, Themistocles had foreseen this possibility, and the Athenians had begun to evacuate their homeland and move to defend Salamis. The fate of Greece was decided in the narrow waters to the east of the island. Themistocles persuaded the reluctant Pelopon-

The Athenian Assembly Passes Themistocles' Emergency Decree

The following is a translation of a portion of the Themistocles decree.

The Gods

Resolved by the Council and the People

Themistocles, son of Neokles, of Phrearroi, made the motion:

To entrust the city to Athena the Mistress of Athens and to all the other Gods to guard and defend from the Barbarian for the sake of the land. The Athenians themselves and the foreigners who live in Athens are to send their children and women to safety in Troizen, their protector being Pittheus, the founding hero of the land. They are to send the old men and their movable possessions to safety on Salamis. The treasurers and priestesses are to remain on the acropolis guarding the property of the gods.

All the other Athenians and foreigners of military age are to embark on the 200 ships that are

ready and defend against the Barbarian for the sake of their own freedom and that of the rest of the Greeks along with the Lakedaimonians, the Korinthians, the Aiginetans, and all others who wish to share the danger. . . .

When the ships have been manned, with 100 of them they are to meet the enemy at Artemision in Euboia, and with the other 100 they are to lie off Salamis and the coast of Attica and keep guard over the land. In order that all Athenians may be united in their defense against the Barbarian those who have been sent into exile for ten years are to go to Salamis and to stay there until the People come to some decision about them, while those who have been deprived of citizen rights are to have their rights restored. . . .

Trans. by M. H. Jameson in "Waiting for the Barbarian," *Greece and Rome*, Second Series, Vol. 8 (Oxford: Clarendon Press, 1961), pp. 5–18.

nesians to stay by threatening to remove all the Athenians and settle anew in Italy; the Spartans knew that they and the other Greeks could not hope to win without the aid of the Athenians. The Greek ships were fewer, slower, and less maneuverable than those of the Persians, so the Greeks put soldiers on their ships and relied chiefly on hand-to-hand combat. The Persians lost more than half their ships and retreated to Asia with a good part of their army, but the danger was not over yet. The Persian general Mardonius spent the winter in central Greece, and in the spring he unsuccessfully tried to win the Athenians away from the Greek League. The Spartan regent, Pausanias, then led the largest Greek army up to that time to confront Mardonius in Boeotia. At Plataea, in the summer of 479 B.C., Mardonius died in battle and his army fled toward home.

Meanwhile the Ionian Greeks urged King Leotychidas, the Spartan commander of the fleet, to fight the Persian fleet at Samos. At Mycale, on the coast nearby, Leotychidas destroyed the Persian camp and its fleet offshore. The Persians fled the Aegean and Ionia. For the moment, at least, the Persian threat was gone.

Suggested Readings

A. ANDREWES, *Greek Tyrants* (1963). A clear and concise account of tyranny in early Greece.

A. ANDREWES, *The Greeks* (1967). A thoughtful general survey.

JOHN BOARDMAN, *The Greeks Overseas* (1964). A study of the relations between the Greeks and other peoples.

A. R. BURN, *The Lyric Age of Greece* (1960). A discussion of early Greece that uses the evidence of poetry and archaeology to fill out the sparse historical record.

J. B. BURY and R. MEIGGS, *A History of Greece,* 4th ed. (1975). A thorough and detailed one-volume narrative history.

E. R. DODDS, *The Greeks and the Irrational* (1955). An excellent account of the role of the supernatural in Greek life and thought.

V. EHRENBERG, *The Greek State* (1964). A good handbook of constitutional history.

V. EHRENBERG, *From Solon to Socrates* (1968). An interpretive history that makes good use of Greek literature to illuminate politics.

J. V. A. FINE, *The Ancient Greeks* (1983). An excellent survey that discusses historical problems and the evidence that gives rise to them.

M. I. FINLEY, *World of Odysseus,* rev. ed. (1965). A fascinating attempt to reconstruct Homeric society.

M. I. FINLEY, *Early Greece* (1970). A succinct interpretive study.

W. G. FORREST, *The Emergence of Greek Democracy* (1966). A lively interpretation of Greek social and political developments in the archaic period.

W. G. FORREST, *A History of Sparta,* 950–192 B.C. (1968). A brief but shrewd account.

P. GREEN, *Xerxes at Salamis* (1970). A lively and stimulating history of the Persian wars.

C. HIGNETT, *A History of the Athenian Constitution* (1952). A scholarly account, somewhat too skeptical of the ancient sources.

C. HIGNETT, *Xerxes' Invasion of Greece* (1963). A valuable account, but too critical of all sources other than Herodotus.

S. HOOD, *The Minoans* (1971). A sketch of Bronze Age civilization on Crete.

D. KAGAN, *The Great Dialogue: A History of Greek Political Thought from Homer to Polybius* (1965). A discussion of the relationship between the Greek historical experience and political theory.

G. S. KIRK, *The Songs of Homer* (1962). A discussion of the Homeric epics as oral poetry.

H. D. F. KITTO, *The Greeks* (1951). A personal and illuminating interpretation of Greek culture.

H. L. LORIMER, *Homer and the Monuments* (1950). A study of the relationship between the Homeric poems and the evidence of archaeology.

H. MICHELL, *Sparta* (1952). A study of Spartan institutions.

O. MURRAY, *Early Greece* (1980). A lively and imaginative account of the early history of Greece to the end of the Persian War.

A. T. OLMSTEAD, *History of the Persian Empire* (1960). A thorough survey.

D. L. PAGE, *History and the Homeric Iliad,* 2nd ed. (1966). A well-written and interesting, if debatable, attempt to place the Trojan War in a historical setting.

G. M. A. RICHTER, *Archaic Greek Art* (1949).

CARL ROEBUCK, *Ionian Trade and Colonization* (1959). An introduction to the history of the Greeks in the east.

B. SNELL, *Discovery of the Mind* (1960). An important study of Greek intellectual development.

A. M. SNODGRASS, *The Dark Age of Greece* (1972). A good examination of the archaeological evidence.

C. G. STARR, *Origins of Greek Civilization* 1100–650 B.C. (1961). An interesting interpretation based largely on archaeology and especially on pottery styles.

C. G. STARR, *The Economic and Social Growth of Early Greece,* 800–500 B.C. (1977).

EMILY VERMEULE, *Greece in the Bronze Age* (1972). A study of the Mycenaean period.

A. G. WOODHEAD, *Greeks in the West* (1962). An account of the Greek settlements in Italy and Sicily.

W. J. WOODHOUSE, *Solon the Liberator* (1965). A discussion of the great Athenian reformer.

Apollo, detail of a statue of the god found at the temple of Zeus at Olympia, ca. 460 B.C. *To the Greeks, Apollo was the radiant spirit of order, clarity, and reason.* [*Hirmer Fotoarchive, Munich*]

The Delian League

THE UNITY OF THE GREEKS had shown strain even in the life-and-death struggle against the Persians. Within two years of the Persian retreat it gave way almost completely and yielded to a division of the Greek world into two spheres of influence, dominated by Sparta and Athens. The need of the Ionian Greeks to obtain and defend their freedom from Persia and the desire of many Greeks to gain revenge and financial reparation for the Persian attack brought on the split.

Sparta had led the Greeks to victory, and it was natural to look to the Spartans to continue the campaign. But Sparta was ill suited to the task, which required a long-term commitment far from the Peloponnesus and continuous naval action.

The emergence of Athens as the leader of a Greek coalition against Persia was a natural development. Athens had become the leading naval power in Greece, and the same motives that had led her to support the Ionian revolt moved her to try to drive the Persians from the Aegean and the Hellespont. The Ionians were at least as eager for the Athenians to take the helm as the Athenians were to accept the responsibility and opportunity.

In the winter of 478–477 B.C. the islanders, the Greeks from the coast of Asia Minor, and some other Greek cities on the Aegean met with the Athenians on the sacred island of Delos and swore oaths of alliance. As a symbol that the alliance was meant to be permanent, they dropped lumps of iron into the sea; the alliance was to hold until these lumps of iron rose to the surface. The aims of this new Delian League were to free those Greeks who were under Persian rule, to protect all against a Persian return, and to obtain compensation from the Persians by attacking their lands and taking booty. League policy was determined by a vote of the assembly, in which each state, including Athens, had one vote. Athens, however, was clearly designated leader.

From the first the league was remarkably successful. The Persians were driven from Europe and the Hellespont, and the Aegean was cleared of pirates. Some states were forced into the league or were prevented from leaving. The members approved coercion because it was necessary for the common safety. In 467 B.C. a great victory over the Persians at the Eurymedon River in Asia Minor routed the Persians and added a number of cities to the league.

3

Classical and Hellenistic Greece

CLASSICAL GREECE

100 MI.

100 KM.

THE
ACROPOLIS AT ATHENS

MAPS 3-1, 3-2 *Greece in the classical period (ca. 480–338 B.C.) centered on the Aegean Sea. Although there were important Greek settlements in Italy, Sicily, and all around the Black Sea, the area shown in this general reference map embraced the vast majority of Greek states. The inset shows the location of the major monuments still visible on the Athenian Acropolis of the classical period.*

Cimon, son of Miltiades, the hero of Marathon, became the leading Athenian soldier and statesman soon after the Persian war. Themistocles appears to have been driven from power by a coalition of his enemies. Ironically the author of the Greek victory over Persia of 480 B.C. was exiled and ended his days at the court of the Persian king. Cimon, who was to dominate Athenian politics for almost two decades, pursued a policy of aggressive attacks on Persia and friendly relations with Sparta. In domestic affairs Cimon was conservative. He accepted the democratic constitution of Clisthenes, which appears to have become somewhat more limited after the Persian war. Defending this constitution and this foreign policy, Cimon led the Athenians and the Delian League to victory after victory, and his own popularity grew with success.

The First Peloponnesian War

In 465 B.C. the island of Thasos rebelled from the league, and Cimon put it down after a siege of more than two years. The revolt of Thasos had an important influence on the development of the Delian League, on Athenian politics, and on relations between Athens and Sparta. It is the first recorded instance in which Athenian interests alone seemed to determine league policy, a significant step in the evolution of the Delian League into the Athenian Empire. When Cimon returned to Athens from Thasos, he was charged with taking bribes not to conquer Macedonia, although that was not part of his assignment, but he was acquitted. The trial was only a device by which his political opponents tried to reduce his influence. Their program at home was to undo the gains made by the Areopagus and to bring about further changes in the direction of democracy; abroad, the enemies of Cimon wanted to break with Sparta and to contest its claim to leadership over the Greeks. They intended at least to establish the independence of Athens and its

70

*The
Foundations of
Western
Civilization in
the Ancient
World*

Athens Takes the Lead

After the defeat of the Persians at Plataea and Mycale in 479 B.C., many Greek states wanted to continue the war against Persia. At first, the Spartans continued to provide the leadership, sending their general Pausanias to conduct the campaign. Very soon, however, the Greeks rejected him and turned to the Athenians. In the following selection, Plutarch tells us how this came about.

. . . Well disposed as the Hellenes were toward the Athenians on account of the justice of Aristides and the reasonableness of Cimon, they were made to long for their supremacy still more by the rapacity of Pausanias and his severity. The commanders of the allies ever met with angry harshness at the hands of Pausanias, and the common men he punished with stripes, or by compelling them to stand all day long with an iron anchor on their shoulders. No one could get bedding or fodder or go down to a spring for water before the Spartans, nay, their servants armed with goads would drive away such as approached. On these grounds Aristides once had it in mind to chide and admonish him, but Pausanias scowled, said he was busy, and would not listen.

Subsequently the captains and generals of the Hellenes, and especially the Chians, Samians, and Lesbians, came to Aristides and tried to persuade him to assume the leadership and bring over to his support the allies, who had long wanted to be rid of the Spartans and to range themselves anew on the side of the Athenians. He replied that he saw the urgency and the justice of what they proposed, but that to establish Athenian confidence in them some overt act was needed, the doing of which would make it impossible for the multitude to change their allegiance back again. So Uliades the Samian and Antagoras the Chian conspired together, and ran down the trireme of Pausanias off Byzantium, closing in on both sides of it as it was putting out before the line. When Pausanias saw what they had done, he sprang up and wrathfully threatened to show the world in a little while that these men had run down not so much his ship as their own native cities; but they bade him be gone, and be grateful to that fortune which fought in his favour at Plataea; it was because the Hellenes still stood in awe of this, they said, that they did not punish him as he deserved. And finally they went off and joined the Athenians.

Plutarch, *Aristides* 23, trans. by Bernadotte Perrin (London and New York: Loeb Classical Library, William Heinemann, 1928).

alliance. The head of this faction was Ephialtes. His supporter, and the man chosen to be the public prosecutor of Cimon, was Pericles, a member of a distinguished Athenian family. He was still a young man, and his defeat in court did not do lasting damage to his career.

When the Thasians began their rebellion, they asked Sparta to invade Athens the next spring, and the ephors agreed. An earthquake, accompanied by a rebellion of the Helots that threatened the survival of Sparta, prevented the invasion. The Spartans asked their allies, the Athenians among them, for help. In Athens Ephialtes urged the Athenians "not to help or restore a city that was a rival to Athens but to let Sparta lie low and be trampled underfoot," but Cimon persuaded them to send help. The results were disastrous. The Spartans sent the Athenian troops home for fear of "the boldness and revolutionary spirit of the Athenians." While Cimon was in the Peloponnesus, helping the Spartans, Ephialtes stripped the Areopagus of almost all its power. In the spring of 461 B.C. Cimon was ostracized, and Athens made an alliance with Argos, Sparta's traditional enemy. Almost overnight Cimon's domestic and foreign policies had been overturned.

The new regime at Athens was confident and ambitious. When Megara, getting the worst of a border dispute with Corinth, withdrew from the Peloponnesian League, the Athenians accepted the Megarians as allies. This alliance gave Athens a great strategic advantage, for Megara barred the way from the Peloponnesus to Athens. It also brought on the First Peloponnesian War, for Sparta resented the defection of Megara to Athens. The early years of the war brought Athens great success. The Athenians conquered Aegina and gained control of Boeotia. At one moment Athens was supreme and invulnerable, controlling the states on her borders and dominating the sea (see Map 3.1.).

About 455 B.C., however, the tide turned. A disastrous defeat struck an Athenian fleet that had gone to aid an Egyptian rebellion against Persia. The great loss of men, ships, and prestige caused rebellions in the empire, forcing Athens to make a truce in Greece in order to subdue her allies in the Aegean. In 449 B.C. the Athenians ended the war against Persia. In 446 B.C. the war on the Greek mainland broke out again. Rebellions in Boeotia and Megara removed Athens' land defenses and brought a Spartan invasion. Rather than fight, Pericles, the commander of the Athenian army, agreed to a peace of thirty years by the terms of which he abandoned all Athenian possessions on the continent. In return, the Spartans gave formal recognition of the Athenian Empire. From then on Greece was divided into two power blocs: Sparta and its alliance on the mainland and Athens ruling her empire in the Aegean.

The Athenian Empire

After the Egyptian disaster the Athenians moved the Delian League's treasury to Athens and began to keep one sixtieth of the annual revenues for themselves. Because of the peace with Persia there seemed no further reason for the allies to pay tribute, so the Athenians were compelled to find a new justification for their empire. They called for a Panhellenic congress to meet at Athens to discuss rebuilding the temples destroyed by the Persians and to consider how to maintain freedom of the seas. When Spartan reluctance to participate prevented the congress, Athens felt free to continue to collect funds from the allies, both to maintain her navy and to rebuild the Athenian temples. Athenian propaganda suggested that henceforth the allies would be treated as colonies and Athens as their mother city, the whole to be held together by good feeling and common religious observances.

There is little reason, however, to believe that the allies were taken in or truly content

KEY EVENTS IN ATHENIAN HISTORY BETWEEN THE PERSIAN WAR AND THE GREAT PELOPONNESIAN WAR	
Delian League founded	478–477 B.C.
Cimon leading politician	ca. 474–462 B.C.
Victory over Persians at Eurymedon River	467 B.C.
Rebellion of Thasos	465–463 B.C.
Ephialtes murdered; Pericles rises to leadership	462 B.C.
Cimon ostracized	461 B.C.
Reform of Areopagus	461 B.C.
First Peloponnesian War begins	ca. 460 B.C.
Athens defeated in Egypt; crisis in the Delian League	454 B.C.
Peace with Persia	449 B.C.
Thirty Years' Peace ends First Peloponnesian War	445 B.C.

with their lot. Nothing could cloak the fact that Athens was becoming the master and her allies mere subjects. By 445 B.C. only Chios, Lesbos, and Samos were autonomous and provided ships. All the other states paid tribute. The change from alliance to empire came about because of the pressure of war and rebellion and in large measure because the allies were unwilling to see to their own defense. Although the empire was not universally unpopular and had many friends among the lower classes and the democratic politicians, it came to be seen more and more as a tyranny. But the Athenians had come to depend on the empire for their prosperity and security. The Thirty Years' Peace of 445 B.C. had recognized their empire, and the Athenians were determined to defend it at any cost.

Athenian Democracy

Even as the Athenians were tightening their control over their allies at home, they were evolving the freest government the world had ever seen. This extension of the Athenian democracy took place chiefly under the guidance of Pericles, who succeeded to the leadership of the democratic faction after the assassination of Ephialtes in 462 B.C. Legislation was passed making the hoplite class eligible for the archonship, and in practice no one was thereaf-

71

72

*The
Foundations of
Western
Civilization in
the Ancient
World*

ter prevented from serving on the basis of property class. Pericles himself proposed the law introducing pay for jury members, opening that important duty to the poor. Circuit judges were reintroduced, a policy making swift impartial justice available even to the poorest residents in the countryside. Finally, Pericles himself introduced a bill limiting citizenship to those who had two citizen parents. From a modern perspective this measure might be seen as a step away from democracy, and, in fact, it would have barred Cimon and one of Pericles' ancestors. In Greek terms, however, it was quite natural. Democracy was defined in terms of those who held citizenship, and because citizenship had become a valuable commodity, the decision to limit it must have won a large majority. Participation in government in all the Greek states was also denied to slaves, resident aliens, and women.

Within the citizen body, however, the extent of the democracy was remarkable. Every decision of the state had to be approved by the popular assembly, a collection of the people, not their representatives. Every judicial decision was subject to appeal to a popular court of not fewer than 51 and as many as 1,501 citizens, chosen from an annual panel of jurors widely representative of the Athenian population. Most officials were selected by lot without regard to class. The main elected officials, such as the generals and the imperial treasurers, were generally nobles and almost always rich men, but the people were free to choose otherwise. All public officials were subject to scrutiny before taking office, could be called to account and removed from office during their tenure, and were held to compulsory examination and accounting at the end of their term. There was no standing army, no police force, open or secret, and no way to coerce the people. If Pericles was elected to the generalship fifteen years in a row and thirty times in all, it was not because he was a dictator but because he was a persuasive speaker, a skillful politician, a respected general, an acknowledged patriot, and a man patently incorruptible. When he lost the people's confidence, they did not hesitate to depose him from office. In 443 B.C., however, he stood at the height of his power. He had been persuaded by the defeat of the Athenian fleet in the Egyptian campaign and the failure of Athens' continental campaigns that its future lay in a conservative policy of retaining the empire in the Aegean and living at peace with the Spartans. It was in this

MAP 3-3 *The Empire at its fullest extent shortly before 450 B.C. We see Athens and the independent states that provided manned ships for the imperial fleet but paid no tribute, dependent states who paid tribute, and states allied to but not actually in the Empire.*

An Athenian tribute list. In 454 B.C., the Athenians moved the treasury of the Delian League to Athens and began to keep one-sixtieth of the allies' annual contribution for themselves. On stones like this, which were displayed on the Acropolis, they recorded the annual assessment of each ally. This stone records the assessment for 432–431 B.C., the first year of the Peloponnesian War. [TAP—Art Reference Bureau]

THE ATHENIAN EMPIRE
ABOUT 450 B.C.

Map legend:
- INDEPENDENT MEMBERS
- DEPENDENT MEMBERS
- ALLIES

The Delian League Becomes the Athenian Empire

In the years following its foundation in the winter of 478–444 B.C., the Delian League gradually underwent changes that finally justified calling it the Athenian Empire. In the following selection, the historian Thucydides explains why the organization changed its character.

The causes which led to the defections of the allies were of different kinds, the principal being their neglect to pay the tribute or to furnish ships, and, in some cases, failure of military service. For the Athenians were exacting and oppressive, using coercive measures towards men who were neither willing nor accustomed to work hard. And for various reasons they soon began to prove less agreeable leaders than at first. They no longer fought upon an equality with the rest of the confederates, and they had no difficulty in reducing them when they revolted. Now the allies brought all this upon themselves; for the majority of them disliked military service and absence from home, and so they agreed to contribute a regular sum of money instead of ships. Whereby the Athenian navy was proportionally increased, while they themselves were always untrained and unprepared for war when they revolted.

Thucydides, *The Peloponnesian War*, trans. by Benjamin Jowett, Vol. 2, ed. by F. R. B. Godolphin in *The Greek Historians*, (New York: Random House, 1942), p. 609.

74

*The
Foundations of
Western
Civilization in
the Ancient
World*

Pericles on Athenian Democracy

Pericles (ca. 495–429 B.C.) delivered this speech after the first campaigning season of the Great Peloponnesian War, probably late in the winter of 431 B.C. It is the most famous statement of the ideals of the Athenian imperial democracy.

Our constitution does not copy the laws of neighbouring states; we are rather a pattern to others than imitators ourselves. Its administration favours the many instead of the few; this is why it is called a democracy. If we look to the laws, they afford equal justice to all in their private differences; if to social standing, advancement in public life falls to reputation for capacity, class considerations not being allowed to interfere with merit; nor again does poverty bar the way, if a man is able to serve the state, he is not hindered by the obscurity of his condition. The freedom which we enjoy in our government extends also to our ordinary life. There, far from exercising a jealous surveillance over each other, we do not feel called upon to be angry with our neighbour for doing what he likes, or even to indulge in those injurious looks which cannot fail to be offensive, although they inflict no positive penalty.

But all this ease in our private relations does not make us lawless as citizens. . . . Our public men have, besides politics, their private affairs to attend to, and our ordinary citizens, though occupied with the pursuits of industry, are still fair judges of public matters; for, unlike any other nation, regarding him who takes no part in these duties not as unambitious but as useless, we Athenians are able to judge at all events if we cannot originate, and instead of looking on discussion as a stumbling-block in the way of action, we think it an indispensable preliminary to any wise action at all. . . .

In short, I say that as a city we are the school of Hellas; while I doubt if the world can produce a man, who where he has only himself to depend upon, is equal to so many emergencies, and graced by so happy a versatility as the Athenian.

Thucydides, *The Peloponnesian War,* trans. by Richard Crawley (New York: Random House, 1951), pp. 104–106.

direction that he led Athens' imperial democracy in the years after the First Peloponnesian War.

The Women of Athens

Greek society, like most all over the world throughout history, was dominated by men. This was true of the democratic city of Athens in the great days of Pericles, in the fifth century B.C., no less than in other Greek cities, but just what was the position of women in classical Athens has been the subject of much controversy. The bulk of the evidence, coming from the law, from philosophical and moral writings, and from information about the conditions of daily life and the organization of society shows that women were excluded from most aspects of public life. They could not vote, take part in the political assemblies, hold public office, or take any direct part in politics at all. This was especially important in one of the few places in the ancient world where male citizens of all classes had these public responsibilities and opportunities.

The same sources show that in the private aspects of life women were always under the control of a male guardian: a father, a husband, or, failing these, an appropriate male relative. Women married young, usually between the ages of twelve and eighteen, whereas their husbands were typically over thirty, so in a way, they were always in a relationship like that of a daughter to a father. Marriages were arranged; the woman normally had no choice of husband, and her dowry was controlled by a male relative. Divorce was difficult for a woman to obtain, for she needed the approval of a male relative who was then willing to serve as her guardian after the dissolution of the marriage. In case of divorce, the dowry re-

The porch of the maidens on the Erechtheum on the Athenian Acropolis near the Parthenon. Built between 421 and 409 B.C., the Erechtheum housed the shrines of three different gods. In place of the usual fluted columns, the porch uses the statues of young girls taking part in a religious festival. [*Greek National Tourist Office*]

turned with the woman but was controlled by her father or the appropriate male relative.

The main function and responsibility of a respectable Athenian woman of a citizen family was to produce male heirs for the household (*oikos*) of her husband. If, however, her father's *oikos* lacked a male heir, the daughter became an *epikleros*, the "heiress" to the family property. In that case, she was required by law to marry the next of kin on her father's side in order to produce the desired male offspring. In the Athenian way of thinking, women were "lent" by one household to another for purposes of bearing and raising a male heir to continue the existence of the *oikos*.

Because the pure and legitimate lineage of the offspring was important, women were carefully segregated from men outside the family and were confined to the women's quarters in the house. Men might seek sexual gratification outside the house with prostitutes of high or low style, frequently recruited from abroad, but respectable women stayed home to raise the children, cook, weave cloth, and oversee the management of the household. The only public function of women was an important one in the various rituals and festivals of the state religion. Apart from these activities, Athenian women were expected to remain home out of sight, quiet and unnoticed. Pericles told the widows and mothers of the Athenian men who died in the first year of the Peloponnesian

76

*The
Foundations of
Western
Civilization in
the Ancient
World*

War only this: "Your great glory is not to fall short of your natural character, and the greatest glory of women is to be least talked about by men, whether for good or bad."

The picture derived from these sources is largely accurate, but it does not fit well with what we learn from the evidence of the pictorial art, the tragedy and comedy, and the mythology of the Athenians, which often shows women as central characters and powerful figures in both the public and the private spheres. The Clytemnestra in Aeschylus' tragedy *Agamemnon* arranges the murder of her royal husband and establishes the tyranny of her lover, whom she dominates. The terrifying and powerful Medea negotiates with kings. We are left with an apparent contradiction clearly revealed by a famous speech in Euripides' tragedy *Medea*. (See the accompanying document.)

The picture that Medea paints of women subjected to men accords well with much of the evidence, but we must take note of the fact that the woman who complains of women's lot is the powerful central figure in a tragedy bearing her name, produced at state expense before most of the Athenian population, and written by a man who was one of Athens' greatest poets and dramatists. She is a cause of terror to the audience and, at the same time, an object of their pity and sympathy as a victim of injustice. She is anything but the creature "least talked about by men, whether for good or for bad." There is reason to believe that the role played by Athenian women may have been more complex than their legal status might suggest.

Medea Bemoans the Condition of Women

In 431 B.C. Euripides (ca. 485–406 B.C.) presented his play *Medea* at the Dionysiac festival in Athens. The heroine is a foreign woman and has unusual powers, but in the speech that follows, she describes the fate of women in terms that appear to give an accurate account of the condition of women in fifth-century Athens.

*Of all things which are living and can form a
   judgment
We women are the most unfortunate
   creatures.
Firstly, with an excess of wealth it is required
For us to buy a husband and take for our
   bodies
A master; for not to take one is even worse.
And now the question is serious whether we
   take
A good or bad one; for there is no easy escape
For a woman, nor can she say no to her
   marriage.
She arrives among new modes of behavior
   and manners,
And needs prophetic power, unless she has
   learned at home,
How best to manage him who shares the bed
   with her.
And if we work out all this well and
   carefully,*

*And the husband lives with us and lightly
   bears his yoke,
Then life is enviable. If not, I'd rather die.
A man, when he's tired of the company in
   his home,
Goes out of the house and puts an end to his
   boredom
And turns to a friend or companion of his
   own age.
But we are forced to keep our eyes on one
   alone.
What they say of us is that we have a
   peaceful time
Living at home, while they do the fighting in
   war.
How wrong they are! I would very much
   rather stand
Three times in the front of battle than bear
   one child.*

Euripides, *Medea* in *Four Tragedies*, trans. by Rex Warner, (Chicago: University of Chicago Press, 1955), pp. 66–67.

The Great Peloponnesian War and Its Aftermath

In the decade after the Thirty Years' Peace of 445 B.C., the willingness of each side to respect the new arrangements was tested and not found wanting.

About 435 B.C., however, a dispute arose in a remote and unimportant part of the Greek world, plunging the Greeks into a long and disastrous war that shook the foundations of their civilization. Civil war broke out at Epidamnus, a Corcyraean colony on the Adriatic, causing a quarrel between Corcyra and her mother city and traditional enemy, Corinth.

Corinth's threat to the Corcyraean fleet, second in size only to Athens', led the Athenians to make an alliance with the previously neutral Corcyra. Athens could not run the risk of having Corcyra's navy fall under Corinthian control, thus changing the balance of power at sea and seriously threatening Athenian security. That alliance angered Corinth and led to a series of crises in the years 433–432 B.C. that threatened to bring the Athenian Empire into conflict with the Peloponnesian League.

In the summer of 432 B.C. the Spartans met to consider the grievances of their allies. They were persuaded by their allies, and chiefly the Corinthians, that Athens was an insatiably aggressive power that aimed at enslaving all the Greeks, and they voted for war. The treaty of 445 B.C. specifically provided that all differences be submitted to arbitration, and Athens repeatedly offered to arbitrate any question. Pericles insisted, however, that the Athenians refuse to yield to threats or commands and that they uphold the treaty and the arbitration clause. Sparta refused to arbitrate, and in the spring of 431 her army marched into Attica, the Athenian homeland.

The Spartan strategy was traditional: to invade the enemy's country and threaten the crops, forcing the enemy to defend them in a hoplite battle. Such a battle the Spartans were sure to win because they had the better army and they outnumbered the Athenians at least two to one. Any ordinary *polis* would have yielded or fought and lost, but Athens had an enormous navy, an annual income from the empire, a vast reserve fund, and long walls that connected the fortified city with the fortified port of Piraeus.

The Athenians' strategy was to allow devastation of the land to prove that Athens was in-

THE GREAT PELOPONNESIAN WAR	
Civil war at Epidamnus	435 B.C.
Sparta declares war on Athens	432 B.C.
Peloponnesian invasion of Athens	431 B.C.
Peace of Nicias	421 B.C.
Athenian invasion of Sicily	415–413 B.C.
Battle of Aegospotami	405 B.C.
Athens surrenders	404 B.C.

vulnerable. At the same time the Athenians launched seaborne raids on the Peloponnesian coast to show that the allies of Sparta could be hurt. Pericles expected that within a year or two, three at most, the Peloponnesians would become discouraged and make peace, having learned their lesson. If the Peloponnesians held out, Athenian resources were inadequate to continue for more than four or five years without raising the tribute in the empire and running an unacceptable risk of rebellion. The plan required restraint and the leadership only a Pericles could provide.

The first year of the war went as planned, with no result. In the second year a terrible plague broke out in Athens (it eventually killed a third of the population), and the demoralized Athenians removed Pericles from office and fined him heavily. They asked for peace, but the angry Spartans refused. In 429 B.C. the Athenians, recognizing their error and their need for his leadership, returned Pericles to office, but he died before the year was over. His strategy had gone wrong and all he had worked for was in danger.

After Pericles' death there was no one in Athens with his ability to dominate the scene and hold the Athenians to a consistent policy. Two factions vied for influence: one, led by Nicias, wanted to continue the defensive policy, and the other, led by Cleon, preferred a more aggressive strategy. In 425 B.C. the aggressive faction was able to win a victory that changed the course of the war. Four hundred Spartans surrendered, and Sparta offered peace at once to get them back. The great victory and the prestige it brought Athens made it safe to raise the imperial tribute, without which Athens could not continue to fight. And the Athenians wanted to continue, for the Spartan

78

*The
Foundations of
Western
Civilization in
the Ancient
World*

Thucydides Describes the Moral Degeneration Caused by the Great Plague at Athens

In the second year of the Great Peloponnesian War (430 B.C.), a terrible plague broke out in Athens that ultimately carried off a third of the population. Thucydides described the effects on Athenian society caused by this experience:

The bodies of dying men lay one upon another, and half-dead creatures reeled about the streets and gathered round all the fountains in their longing for water. The sacred places also in which they had quartered themselves were full of corpses of persons that had died there, just as they were; for as the disaster passed all bounds, men, not knowing what was to become of them, became utterly careless of everything, whether sacred or profane. All the burial rites before in use were entirely upset and they buried the bodies as best they could. Many from want of the proper appliances, through so many of their friends having died already, had recourse to the most shameless sepultures: sometimes getting the start of those who had raised a pile, they threw their own dead body upon the stranger's pyre and ignited it; sometimes they tossed the corpse which they were carrying on the top of another that was burning, and so went off.

Nor was this the only form of lawless extravagance which owed its origin to the plague. Men now coolly ventured on what they had formerly done in a corner, and not just as they pleased, seeing the rapid transitions produced by persons in prosperity suddenly dying and those who before had nothing succeeding to their property. So they resolved to spend quickly and enjoy themselves, regarding their lives and riches as alike things of a day. Perseverance in what men called honour was popular with none, it was so uncertain whether they would be spared to attain the object; but it was settled that present enjoyment, and all that contributed to it, was both honourable and useful. Fear of gods or law of man there was none to restrain them. As for the first, they judged it to be just the same whether they worshipped them or not, as they saw all alike perishing; and for the last, no one expected to live to be brought to trial for his offences, but each felt that a far severer sentence had been already passed upon them all and hung over their heads, and before this fell it was only reasonable to enjoy life a little.

Thucydides, *The Peloponnesian War*, trans. by Richard Crawley (New York: Random House, 1951), pp. 112–113.

peace offer gave no adequate guarantee of Athenian security.

In 424 B.C. the Athenians undertook a more aggressive policy: they sought to make Athens safe by conquering Megara and Boeotia. Both attempts failed, and defeat helped discredit the aggressive policy, leading to a truce in 423 B.C. Meanwhile, Sparta's ablest general, Brasidas, took a small army to Thrace and Macedonia. He captured Amphipolis, the most important Athenian colony in the region. Thucydides, the historian of the Great Peloponnesian War, was in charge of the Athenian fleet in those waters and was held responsible for the city's loss. He was exiled and was thereby given the time and opportunity to write his history. In 422 B.C. Cleon led an expedition to undo the work of

Brasidas. At Amphipolis both he and Brasidas died in battle. The removal of these two leaders of the aggressive factions in their respective cities paved the way for peace. The Peace of Nicias, named for its chief negotiator, was ratified in the spring of 421 B.C.

The peace was for fifty years and guaranteed the status quo with a few exceptions. Neither side carried out all its commitments, and several of Sparta's allies refused to ratify the peace. Corinth urged the Argives to form a new alliance as a separate force and encouraged the war party in Sparta. In Athens Alcibiades emerged as the new leader of the aggressive faction and was able to bring about an alliance with Argos.

In 415 B.C. Alcibiades persuaded the Atheni-

Greek fighting Greek: the siege of a Greek city in Asia Minor during the Great Peloponnesian War. [Michael Holford]

ans to attack Sicily to bring it under Athenian control. The undertaking was ambitious and unnecessary, but if it had succeeded, it would have deprived the Peloponnesians of all hope of western support in future wars and would have provided Athens with plenty of money for both military and domestic uses.

In 413 B.C. the entire expedition was destroyed. The Athenians lost some two hundred ships, about forty-five hundred of their own men, and almost ten times as many allies. It was a disaster perhaps greater than the defeat of the Athenian fleet in the Egyptian campaign some forty years earlier. It shook Athenian prestige, reduced the power of Athens, provoked rebellions, and brought the wealth and power of Persia into the war on Sparta's side.

It is remarkable that the Athenians were able to continue fighting in spite of the disaster. They survived a brief oligarchic coup in 411 B.C. and won several important victories at sea as the war shifted to the Aegean. As their allies rebelled, however, and were sustained by fleets paid for by Persia, the Athenians saw their financial resources shrink and finally disappear. When their fleet was caught napping at Aegospotami in 405 B.C., they could not build another. The Spartans, under Lysander, a clever and ambitious general who was responsible for obtaining Persian support, cut off the food supply through the Hellespont, and the Athenians were starved into submission. In 404 B.C. they surrendered unconditionally; the city walls were dismantled, Athens was permitted no fleet, and the empire was gone. The Great Peloponnesian War was over.

The Hegemony of Sparta

The collapse of the Athenian Empire created a vacuum of power in the Aegean and opened the way for Spartan leadership, or hegemony. Fulfilling the contract that had brought them the funds to win the war, the Spartans handed the Greek cities of Asia Minor back to Persia. Under the leadership of Lysander the Spartans went on to make a complete mockery of their promise to free the Greeks by stepping into the imperial role of Athens in the cities along the European coast and the islands of the Aegean. In most of the cities Lysander installed a board of ten local oligarchs loyal to him and supported them with a Spartan garrison. Tribute brought in an annual revenue almost as great as that the Athenians had collected.

Limited population, the Helot problem, and traditional conservatism all made Sparta less than an ideal state to rule a maritime empire. Some of Sparta's allies, especially Thebes and Corinth, were alienated by the increasing arro-

79

80 *The trireme was the dominant Greek warship in the fifth and fourth centuries* B.C. *Its superior speed and maneuverability swept the seas of competition. Previous naval warfare had relied on grappling and boarding, which made naval battles resemble land battles. The trireme, however, rammed the enemy at great speed with a metal prow, like a torpedo. The side view drawing (top) shows only the top of three rows of oarsmen. The cross section drawings from the front (left) show how the oars and rowers were arranged and how the oars struck the water and managed not to run afoul of one another. The two views of a trireme model from the front and top (right) show the positions of the three tiers of rowers.* [*Line drawings: J. D. Morrison and R. T. Williams:* Greek Oared Ships, 900–322 B.C. (*Cambridge University Press, 1968*), *plates 25 and 31. Photographs: J. S. Morrison, Cambridge University*]

Scale 1:180
Height of deck above waterline: 8 ft
Draught: 3 ft 9 ins
Length: 115 ft
(Breadth of Hull amidships: 12 ft)
Overall breadth including
outriggers: 16.ft)

Waterline

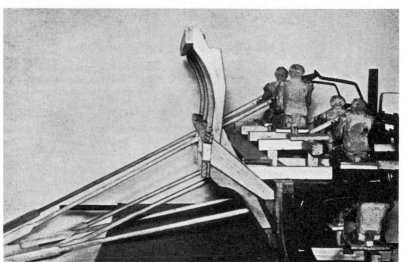

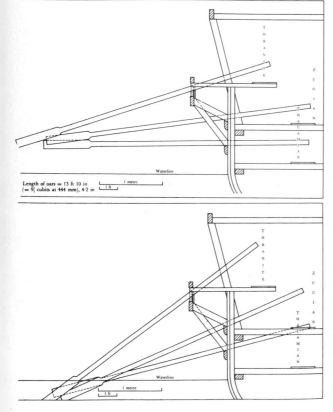

Length of oars = 13 ft 10 in
(= 9¼ cubits at 444 mm), 4·2 m

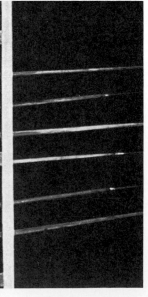

gance of Sparta's policies. In 404 B.C. Lysander installed an oligarchic government in Athens whose outrageous behavior earned them the title "Thirty Tyrants." Democratic exiles took refuge in Thebes and Corinth and created an army to challenge the oligarchy. Sparta's conservative king, Pausanias, replaced Lysander, arranging a peaceful settlement and ultimately the restoration of democracy. Thereafter Athenian foreign policy remained under Spartan control, but otherwise Athens was free.

In 405 B.C. Darius II of Persia died and was succeeded by Artaxerxes II. His younger brother, Cyrus, contested his rule and received Spartan help in recruiting a Greek mercenary army to help him win the throne. They marched inland as far as Mesopotamia, where they defeated the Persians at Cunaxa in 401 B.C., but Cyrus was killed. The Greeks were able to march back to the Black Sea and safety; their success revealed the potential weakness of the Persian Empire.

The Greeks of Asia Minor had supported Cyrus and were now afraid of Artaxerxes' revenge. The Spartans accepted their request for aid and sent an army into Asia, attracted by the prospect of prestige, power, and money. In 396 B.C. the command was given to Sparta's new king, Agesilaus. His personality and policy dominated Sparta throughout its period of hegemony and until his death in 360 B.C. Hampered by his lameness and his disputed claim to the throne, he seems to have compensated for both by always advocating aggressive policies and providing himself with opportunities to display his bravery in battle.

Agesilaus collected much booty and frightened the Persians. They sent a messenger with money and promises of further support to friendly factions in all the likely states. By 395 B.C. Thebes was able to organize an alliance that included Argos, Corinth, and a resurgent Athens. The result was the Corinthian War (395–387 B.C.), which put an end to Sparta's Asian adventure. In 394 the Persian fleet destroyed Sparta's maritime empire. Meanwhile the Athenians took advantage of events to rebuild their walls, to enlarge their navy, and even to recover some of their lost empire in the Aegean. The war ended when the exhausted Greek states accepted a peace dictated by the Great King of Persia.

The Persians, frightened by the recovery of Athens, turned the management of Greece over to Sparta. Agesilaus broke up all alliances except the Peloponnesian League. He inter-

THE SPARTAN AND THEBAN HEGEMONIES	
Thirty Tyrants rule at Athens	404–403 B.C.
Expedition of Cyrus, rebellious prince of Persia: Battle of Cunaxa	401 B.C.
Spartan War against Persia	400–387 B.C.
Reign of Agesilaus at Sparta	398–360 B.C.
Corinthian War	395–387 B.C.
Sparta seizes Thebes	382 B.C.
Second Athenian Confederation founded	378 B.C.
Thebans defeat Sparta at Leuctra; end of Spartan hegemony	371 B.C.
Battle of Mantinea; end of Theban hegemony	362 B.C.

fered with the autonomy of other *poleis* by using the Spartan army, or the threat of its use, to put friends in power within them. Sparta reached a new level of lawless arrogance in 382 B.C., when it seized Thebes during peacetime without warning or pretext. In 379 a Spartan army made a similar attempt on Athens. That action persuaded the Athenians to join with Thebes, which had rebelled from Sparta a few months earlier, to wage war on the Spartans. In 371 B.C. the Thebans, led by their great generals Pelopidas and Epaminondas, defeated the Spartans at Leuctra. The Thebans encouraged the Arcadian cities of the central Peloponnesus to form a federal league, freed the Helots, and helped them found a city of their own. They deprived Sparta of much of its farmland and of the people who worked it and hemmed it in with hostile neighbors. Sparta's population had shrunk so that it could put fewer than two thousand men into the field at Leuctra. Sparta's aggressive policies had led to ruin. The Theban victory brought the end of Sparta as a power of the first rank.

The Hegemony of Thebes; The Second Athenian Empire

Victorious Thebes had a democratic constitution, control over Boeotia, and two outstanding and popular generals. These were the basis for Theban power after Leuctra. Pelopidas died in a successful attempt to gain control of Thessaly. Epaminondas consolidated his work, and Thebes was soon dominant over all Greece

81

Xenophon Recounts How Greece Brought Itself to Chaos

Confusion in Greece in the fourth century B.C. reached a climax with the inconclusive battle of Mantinea in 362. The Theban leader Epaminondas was killed, and no other city or person emerged to provide the needed general leadership for Greece. Xenophon, a contemporary, pointed out the resulting near chaos in Greek affairs—tempting ground for the soon-to-appear conquering Macedonians under their king Philip.

The effective result of these achievements was the very opposite of that which the world at large anticipated. Here, where well-nigh the whole of Hellas was met together in one field, and the combatants stood rank against rank confronted, there was no one who doubted that, in the event of battle, the conquerors this day would rule; and that those who lost would be their subjects. But god so ordered it that both belligerents alike set up trophies as claiming victory, and neither interfered with the other in the act. Both parties alike gave back their enemy's dead under a truce, and in right of victory; both alike, in symbol of defeat, under a truce took back their dead. And though both claimed to have won the day, neither could show that he had thereby gained any accession of territory, or state, or empire, or was better situated than before the battle. Uncertainty and confusion, indeed, had gained ground, being tenfold greater throughout the length and breadth of Hellas after the battle than before.

Xenophon, *Hellenica*, trans. by H. G. Dakyns in *The Greek Historians*, ed. by F. R. B. Godolphin (New York: Random House, 1942), p. 221.

north of Athens and the Corinthian Gulf. The Thebans challenged the reborn Athenian Empire in the Aegean. All this activity provoked resistance, and by 362 B.C. Thebes faced a Peloponnesian coalition as well as Athens. Epaminondas once again led a victorious Boeotian army into the Peloponnesus at Mantinea but he died in the fight, and the loss of its two greater leaders ended Thebes' dominance.

Athens had organized the Second Athenian Confederation in 378 B.C. It was aimed at resisting Spartan aggression in the Aegean, and its constitution was careful to avoid the abuses of the Delian League. But the Athenians soon began to repeat those abuses, although this time they did not have the power to put down resistance. When the collapse of Sparta and Thebes and the restraint of Persia removed any reason for voluntary membership, Athens' allies revolted. By 355 B.C. Athens had had to abandon most of the empire. After two centuries of almost continuous warfare, the Greeks returned to the chaotic disorganization of the time before the founding of the Peloponnesian League.

The Culture of Classical Greece

The repulse of the Persian invasion released a flood of creative activity in Greece rarely, if ever, matched anywhere at any time. The century and a half between the Persian retreat and the conquest of Greece by Philip of Macedon (479–338 B.C.) produced achievements of such quality as to justify that era's designation as the Classical Period. Ironically we often use the term *classical* to suggest calm and serenity, but the word that best describes the common element present in Greek life, thought, art, and literature in this period is *tension*. It was a time in which conflict among the *poleis* continued and intensified as Athens and Sparta gathered most of them into two competing and menacing blocs. The victory over the Persians brought a sense of exultation in the capacity of humans to accomplish great things and of confidence in the divine justice that brought arrogant pride low. But these feelings conflicted with a sense of unease as the Greeks recognized that the fate

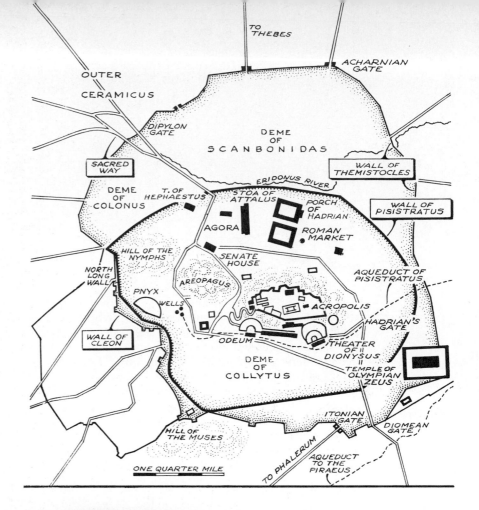

MAP 3-4 *This sketch locates some of the major features of the ancient city of Athens that have been excavated and are visible today. It includes monuments ranging in age from the earliest times to the period of the Roman Empire. The geographical relation of the Acropolis to the rest of the city is apparent, as is that of the Agora, the Areopagus (where the early council of aristocrats met), and the Pnyx (site of assembly for the larger, more democratic meetings of the entire people).*

This vase painting, ca. 470 B.C., depicts instruction in music and grammar in an Attic school. For the Greeks, music was always intimately bound up with literature, drama, and the dance. [State Museums, Berlin]

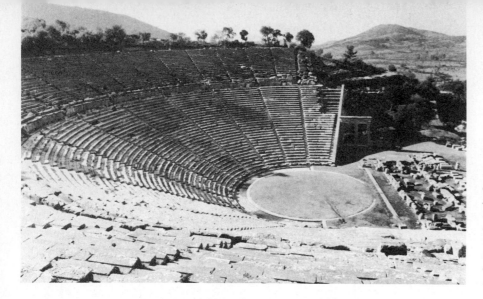

The theater at Epidaurus. Epidaurus, a city in the eastern Peloponnesus, was the site of a famous sanctuary to Asclepius, the god of healing. Thousands of the sick and crippled went there to be cured. The religious festivals held there included theatrical performances and athletic contests that drew vast crowds. [Alison Frantz]

that had met Xerxes awaited all those who reached too far. Another source of tension was the conflict between the soaring hopes and achievements of individuals and the claims and limits put on them by their fellow citizens in the *polis*. These forces were at work throughout Greece, but we know them best and they had the most spectacular results in Athens in its Golden Age, the time between the Persian and the Peloponnesian wars.

Attic Tragedy

Nothing reflects these concerns better than the appearance of Attic tragedy as a major form of Greek poetry in the fifth century B.C. The tragedies were presented as part of public religious observations in honor of the god Dionysus. The whole affair was very much a civic occasion. Each poet who wished to compete submitted his work to the archon. Each offered three tragedies, which might or might not have a common subject, and a satyr play (a comic choral dialogue with Dionysus) to close. The three best competitors were each awarded three actors and a chorus. The actors were paid by the state, and the chorus was provided by a wealthy citizen selected by the state to perform this service as *choregos*, for the Athenians had no direct taxation to support such activities. Most of the tragedies were performed in the theater of Dionysus on the south side of the Acropolis, and as many as thirty thousand Athenians could attend. Prizes and honors were awarded to the author, the actor, and the *choregos* voted best by a jury of Athenians chosen by lot. On rare occasions the subject of the play might be a contemporary or historical event, but almost always it was chosen from

mythology. Before Euripides it always dealt solemnly with serious questions of religion, politics, ethics, morality, or some combination of these.

Architecture and Sculpture

The great architectural achievements of Periclean Athens, just as much as Athenian tragedy, illustrate the magnificent results of the union and tension between religious and civic responsibilities on the one hand and the transcendent genius of the individual artist on the other. Beginning in 448 B.C. and continuing down to the outbreak of the Great Peloponnesian War, Pericles undertook a great building program on the Acropolis. The funds were provided by the income from the empire. The buildings were temples to honor the city's gods and a fitting gateway to the temples. Pericles' main purpose seems to have been to represent visually the greatness and power of Athens, but in such a way as to emphasize her intellectual and artistic achievement, her civilization rather than her military and naval power. It was as though these buildings were tangible proof of Pericles' claim that Athens was "the school of Hellas," that is, the intellectual center of all Greece.

Philosophy

Tragedy, architecture, and sculpture are all indications of the fifth century's extraordinary emphasis on human beings: their capacities, their limits, their nature, their place in the universe. The same concern is clear in the development of philosophy. Parmenides of Elea and his pupil Zeno, to be sure, carried on the theoretical debate about the nature of the cosmos.

In opposition to Heraclitus, they argued that change was only an illusion of the senses. Reason and reflection showed that reality was fixed and unchanging because it seemed evident that nothing could be created out of nothingness. Such fundamental speculations were carried forward by Empedocles of Acragas, who spoke of four basic elements: fire, water, earth, and air. Like Parmenides he thought that reality was permanent but not immobile, for the four elements were moved by two primary forces, Love and Strife, or, as we might be inclined to say, attraction and repulsion.

This theory is clearly a step on the road to the atomic theory of Leucippus of Miletus and Democritus of Abdera. They believed that the world consisted of innumerable tiny, solid particles that could not be divided or modified and that moved about in the void. The size of the atoms and the arrangement in which they were joined with others produced the secondary qualities that the senses could perceive, such as color and shape. These qualities, unlike the atoms themselves, which were natural, were merely conventional. Anaxagoras of Clazomenae, an older contemporary and a friend of Pericles, had previously spoken of tiny fundamental particles called *seeds,* which were put together on a rational basis by a force called *nous,* or "mind." Thus Anaxagoras suggested a distinction between matter and mind. The atomists, however, regarded "soul," or mind, as material and believed that everything was guided by purely physical laws. In the arguments of Anaxagoras and the atomists we have the beginning of the philosophical debate between materialism and idealism that has continued through the ages.

These discussions interested very few, and, in fact, most Greeks were suspicious of such speculations. A far more influential debate was begun by a group of professional teachers who emerged in the mid-fifth century B.C. and whom the Greeks called *Sophists.* They traveled about and received pay for teaching practical techniques such as rhetoric, a valuable skill in democracies like Athens. Others claimed to teach wisdom and even virtue. They did not speculate about the physical universe but applied reasoned analysis to human beliefs and institutions. This human focus was characteristic of fifth-century thought, as was the central problem that the Sophists considered: they discovered the tension and even the contradiction between nature and custom, or law. The more traditional among them argued that law itself

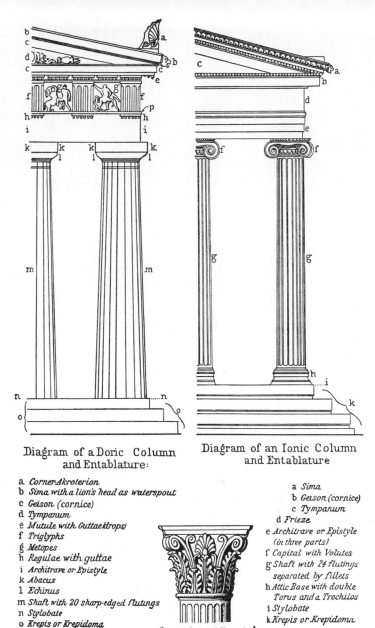

Diagram of a Doric Column and Entablature:

a *Corner Akroterion*
b *Sima with a lion's head as waterspout*
c *Geison (cornice)*
d *Tympanum*
e *Mutule with Guttae (drops)*
f *Triglyphs*
g *Metopes*
h *Regulae with guttae*
i *Architrave or Epistyle*
k *Abacus*
l *Echinus*
m *Shaft with 20 sharp-edged flutings*
n *Stylobate*
o *Krepis or Krepidoma*
p *Taenia*

Diagram of an Ionic Column and Entablature

a *Sima*
b *Geison (cornice)*
c *Tympanum*
d *Frieze*
e *Architrave or Epistyle (in three parts)*
f *Capital with Volutes*
g *Shaft with 24 flutings separated by fillets*
h *Attic Base with double Torus and a Trochilos*
i *Stylobate*
k *Krepis or Krepidoma*

Corinthian Capital

The three orders of Greek architecture: Doric, Ionic, and Corinthian. These three orders have enormously influenced Western architecture.

was in accord with nature, and this view fortified the traditional beliefs of the *polis.*

Others argued, however, that laws were merely conventional and not in accord with nature. The law was not of divine origin but merely the result of an agreement among peo-

85

(*Above*) *The Acropolis was both the religious and civic center of Athens. In its final form it is the work of Pericles and his successors in the late fifth century* B.C. *This photograph shows the Parthenon and to its left the Erechtheum.* [*Greek National Tourist Office*]

The temple of Victory on the Athenian Acropolis. This small temple was built in the Ionic order about 423 B.C. [*Greek National Tourist Office*]

ple. It could not pretend to be a positive moral force but merely had the negative function of preventing people from harming each other. The most extreme Sophists argued that law was contrary to nature, a trick whereby the weak control the strong. Critias, an Athenian oligarch and one of the more extreme Sophists, went so far as to say that the gods themselves had been invented by some clever person to deter people from doing what they wished. Such ideas attacked the theoretical foundations of the *polis* and helped provoke the philosophical responses of Plato and Aristotle in the next century.

Plato Reports the Claims of the Sophist Protagoras

Plato (ca. 429–347 B.C.) remains to many the greatest of the ancient philosophers. Protagoras, the famous Sophist from Leontini in Sicily, came to Athens in 427 B.C. and created great excitement. In the following passage from the dialogue *Protagoras*, Plato's spokesman, Socrates, introduces a young man who wishes to benefit from Protagoras' skills.

When we were all seated, Protagoras said: Now that the company are assembled, Socrates, tell me about the young man of whom you were just now speaking.

I replied: I will begin again at the same point, Protagoras, and tell you once more the purport of my visit: this is my friend Hippocrates, who is desirous of making your acquaintance; he would like to know what will happen to him if he associates with you. I have no more to say.

Protagoras answered: Young man, if you associate with me, on the very first day you will return home a better man than you came and better on the second day than on the first, and better every day than you were on the day before.

When I heard this, I said: Protagoras, I do not at all wonder at hearing you say this; even at your age, and with all your wisdom, if any one were to teach you what you did not know before, you would become better no doubt: but please to answer in a different way—I will explain how by an example. Let me suppose that Hippocrates, instead of desiring your acquaintance, wished to become acquainted with the young man Zeuxippus of Heraclea, who has lately been in Athens, and he had come to him as he has come to you, and had heard him say, as he has heard you say, that every day he would grow and become better if he associated with him: and then suppose that he were to ask

him, "In what shall I become better, and in what shall I grow?" Zeuxippus would answer, "In painting." And suppose that he went to Orthagoas the Theban, and heard him say the same thing, and asked him, "In what shall I become better day by day?" he would reply, "In flute-playing." Now I want you to make the same sort of answer to this young man and to me, who am asking questions on his account. When you say that on the first day on which he associates with you he will return home a better man, and on every day will grow in like manner,—in what, Protagoras, will he be better? and about what?

When Protagoras head me say this, he replied: You ask questions fairly, and I like to answer a question which is fairly put. If Hippocrates comes to me he will not experience the sort of drudgery with which other Sophists are in the habit of insulting their pupils; who, when they have just escaped from the arts, are taken and driven back into them by these teachers, and made to learn calculation, and astronomy, and geometry, and music (he gave a look at Hippias as he said this); but if he comes to me, he will learn that which he comes to learn. And this is prudence in affairs private as well as public; he will learn to order his own house in the best manner, and he will be able to speak and act for the best in the affairs of the state.

Plato, *Protagoras*, trans. by Benjamin Jowett in *The Dialogues of Plato*, Vol. 1 (New York: Random House, 1937), pp. 88–89.

88

The
Foundations of
Western
Civilization in
the Ancient
World

History

The fifth century produced the first prose literature in the form of history. Herodotus, born shortly before the Persian wars, deserves his title of "the father of history," for his account of the Persian wars goes far beyond all previous chronicles, genealogies, and geographical studies and attempts to explain human actions and to draw instruction from them. Although his work was completed about 425 B.C. and shows a few traces of Sophist influence, its spirit is that of an earlier time. Herodotus accepted the evidence of legends and oracles, although not uncritically, and often explained human events in terms of divine intervention. Human arrogance and divine vengeance are key forces that help explain the defeat of Croesus by Cyrus as well as Xerxes' defeat by the Greeks. Yet the *History* is typical of its time in celebrating the crucial role of human intelligence as revealed by Miltiades at Marathon and Themistocles at Salamis. Nor was Herodotus unaware of the importance of institutions. There is no mistaking his pride in the superiority of the Greek *polis* and the discipline it inspired in its citizen soldiers and his pride in the superiority of the Greeks' voluntary obedience to law over the Persians' fear of punishment.

Thucydides, the historian of the Peloponnesian War, was born about 460 B.C. and died a few years after the end of the Great Peloponnesian War. He was very much a product of the late fifth century, reflecting the influence of the scientific attitude of the Hippocratic school of medicine as well as the secular, human-centered skeptical rationalism of the Sophists. Hippocrates of Cos was a contemporary of Thucydides who was part of a school of medical writers and practitioners. They did important pioneer work in medicine and scientific theory, placing great emphasis on the need to combine careful and accurate observation with reason to make possible the understanding, prognosis, treatment, and cure of a disease. In the same way Thucydides took great pains to achieve factual accuracy and tried to use his evidence to discover meaningful patterns of human behavior. He believed that human nature was essentially unchanging, so that a wise person equipped with the understanding provided by history might accurately foresee events and thus help to guide them. He believed, however, that only a few had the ability to understand history and to put its lessons to good use. He thought that even the wisest could be foiled by the intervention of chance, which played a great role in human affairs. Thucydides focused his interest on politics, and in that area his assumptions about human nature do not seem unwarranted. His work has proved to be, as he hoped, "a possession forever." Its description of the terrible civil war between the two basic kinds of *polis* is a final and fitting example of the tension that was the source of both the greatness and the decline of classical Greece.

The Fourth Century B.C.

Historians often speak of the Peloponnesian War as the crisis of the *polis* and of the fourth century as the period of its decline. But the Greeks of the fourth century B.C. did not know that their traditional way of life was on the verge of destruction. Thinkers could not avoid recognizing that they lived in a time of troubles, but they responded in different ways. Some looked to the past and tried to shore up the weakened structure of the *polis;* others tended toward despair and looked for new solutions; and still others averted their gaze from the public arena altogether. All of these responses are apparent in the literature, philosophy, and art of the period.

Drama

The tendency of some to avert their gaze from the life of the *polis* and to turn inward to everyday life, the family, and their own individuality is apparent in the poetry of the fourth century B.C. Tragedy proved to be a form whose originality was confined to the fifth century. No tragedies written in the fourth century have been preserved, and it was common to revive the great plays of the previous century. Some of the late plays of Euripides, in fact, seem less like the tragedies of Aeschylus and Sophocles than forerunners of later forms such as the New Comedy. Plays of Euripides like *Helena, Andromeda,* and *Iphigenia in Tauris* are more like fairy tales, tales of adventure, or love stories than tragedies. Euripides was less interested in cosmic confrontations of conflicting principles than in the psychology and behaviour of individual human beings. His plays, which rarely won first prize when first produced for Dionysian festival competitions, became increasingly popular in the fourth century and after.

Comedy was introduced into the Dionysian festival early in the fifth century B.C. Such poets as Cratinus, Eupolis, and the great master of the genre called Old Comedy, Aristophanes (ca. 450–ca. 385 B.C.), the only one from whom we have complete plays, wrote political comedies filled with scathing invective and satire against such contemporary figures as Pericles, Cleon, Socrates, and Euripides. The fourth century, however, produced what is called Middle Comedy, which turned away from political subjects and personal invective toward a comic-realistic depiction of daily life, plots of intrigue, and mild satire of domestic situations. Significantly the role of the chorus, which in some way represented the *polis,* was very much diminished. These trends all continued and were carried even further in the New Comedy, whose leading playwright, Menander (342–291 B.C.), completely abandoned mythological subjects in favor of domestic tragicomedy. His gentle satire of the foibles of ordinary people and his tales of lovers temporarily thwarted before a happy and proper ending would not be unfamiliar to viewers of modern situation comedies.

Sculpture

The same movement away from the grand, the ideal, and the general and toward the ordinary, the real, and the individual is apparent in the development of Greek sculpture. To see these developments, one has only to compare the statue of the *Striding God of Artemisium* (ca. 460 B.C.), thought to be either Zeus on the

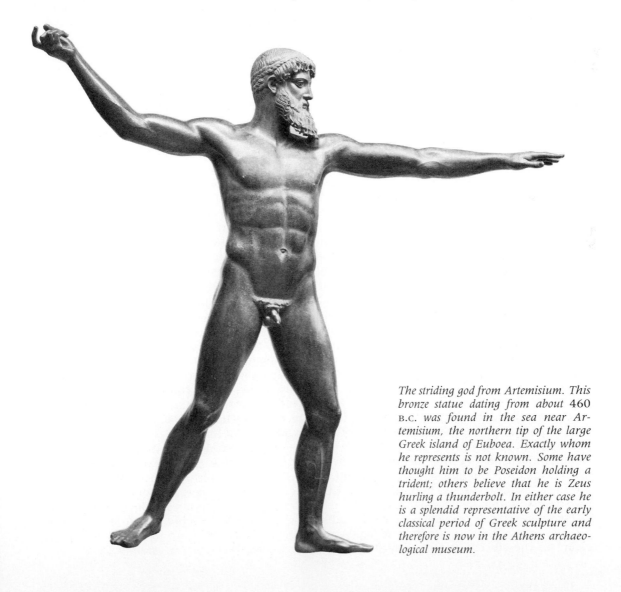

The striding god from Artemisium. This bronze statue dating from about 460 B.C. was found in the sea near Artemisium, the northern tip of the large Greek island of Euboea. Exactly whom he represents is not known. Some have thought him to be Poseidon holding a trident; others believe that he is Zeus hurling a thunderbolt. In either case he is a splendid representative of the early classical period of Greek sculpture and therefore is now in the Athens archaeological museum.

point of releasing a thunderbolt or Poseidon about to throw his trident, or the *Doryphoros* of Polycleitus (ca. 450–440 B.C.) with the *Hermes* of Praxiteles (ca. 340–330 B.C.) or the *Apoxyomenos* attributed to Lysippus (ca. 330 B.C.).

Philosophy

SOCRATES. Probably the most complicated response to the crisis of the *polis* may be found in the life and teachings of Socrates (469–399 B.C.). Because he wrote nothing, our knowledge of him comes chiefly from his disciples Plato and Xenophon and from later tradition. Although as a young man he was interested in speculations about the physical world, he later turned to the investigation of ethics and morality; as Cicero put it, he brought philosophy down from the heavens. He was committed to the search for truth and for the knowledge about human affairs that he believed could be discovered by reason. His method was to go among men, particularly those reputed to know something, like craftsmen, poets, and politicians, to question and cross-examine them. The result was always the same: those he questioned might have technical information and skills but seldom had any knowledge of the fundamental principles of human behavior. It is understandable that Athenians so exposed should be angry with their examiner, and it is not surprising that they thought Socrates was undermining the beliefs and values of the *polis*. Socrates' unconcealed contempt for democracy, which seemingly relied on ignorant amateurs to make important political decisions without any certain knowledge, created further hostility. Moreover, his insistence on the primacy of his own individualism and his determination to pursue philosophy even against the wishes of his fellow citizens reinforced this hostility and the prejudice that went with it.

But Socrates, unlike the Sophists, did not accept pay for his teaching; he professed ignorance and denied that he taught at all. His individualism, moreover, was unlike the worldly hedonism of some of the Sophists. It was not wealth or pleasure or power that he urged people to seek, but "the greatest improvement of the soul." He differed also from the more radical Sophists in that he denied that the *polis* and its laws were merely conventional. He thought, on the contrary, that they had a legitimate claim on the citizen, and he proved it in the most convincing fashion. In 399 B.C. he was condemned to death by an Athenian jury on the charges of bring new gods into the city and of corrupting the youth. His dialectical inquiries had angered many important people, and his criticism of democracy must have been viewed with suspicion, especially as Critias and Charmides, who were members of the Thirty Tyrants, and the traitor Alcibiades had been among his disciples. He was given a chance to escape, but in Plato's *Crito* we are told of his refusal because of his veneration of the laws. Socrates' career set the stage for later responses to the travail of the *polis*; he recognized its difficulties and criticized its shortcomings, and he turned away from an active political life, but he did not abandon the idea of the *polis*. He fought as a soldier in its defense, obeyed its laws, and sought to put its values on a sound foundation by reason.

THE CYNICS. One branch of Socratic thought—the concern with personal morality and one's own soul, the disdain of worldly pleasure and wealth, and the withdrawal from political life—was developed and then distorted almost beyond recognition by the Cynic school. Antisthenes (ca. 455–ca. 360 B.C.), a follower of Socrates, is said to have been its founder, but its most famous exemplar was Diogenes of Sinope (ca. 400–ca. 325 B.C.). Socrates disparaged wealth and worldly comfort, so Diogenes wore rags and lived in a tub. He performed shameful acts in public and made his living by begging, in order to show his rejection of convention. He believed that happiness lay in satisfying natural needs in the simplest and most direct way. Because actions to this end, being natural, could not be indecent, they could and should be done publicly.

Socrates questioned the theoretical basis for popular religious beliefs; the Cynics ridiculed all religious observances. As Plato said, Diogenes was Socrates gone mad. Beyond that, the way of the Cynics contradicted important Socratic beliefs. Socrates, unlike traditional aristocrats like Theognis, believed that virtue was a matter not of birth but of knowledge and that people do wrong only through ignorance of what is virtuous. The Cynics, on the contrary, believed that "Virtue is an affair of deeds and does not need a store of words and learning,"[1] Wisdom and happiness come from pursuing the proper style of life, not from philosophy.

[1] Diogenes Laertius, *Life of Antisthenes*.

They moved even further from Socrates by abandoning the concept of the *polis* entirely. When Diogenes was asked about his citizenship, he answered that he was *kosmopolites*, a citizen of the world. The Cynics plainly had turned away from the past, and their views anticipated those of the Hellenistic Age.

PLATO. (429–347 B.C.) was by far the most important of Socrates' associates and is a perfect example of the pupil who becomes greater than his master. He was the first systematic philosopher and therefore the first to place political ideas in their full philosophical context. He was also a writer of genius, leaving us twenty-six philosophical discussions, almost all in the form of dialogues, which somehow make the examination of difficult and complicated philosophical problems seem dramatic and entertaining. Plato came from a noble Athenian family and looked forward to an active political career until he was discouraged by the excesses of the Thirty Tyrants and the execution of Socrates by the restored democracy. Twice he made trips to Sicily in the hope of producing a model state at Syracuse under the tyrants Dionysius I and II, but without success. In 386 B.C. he founded the Academy, a center of philosophical investigation and a school for training statesmen and citizens that had a powerful impact on Greek thought and lasted until it was closed by the Emperor Justinian in the sixth century A.D.

Like Socrates, Plato firmly believed in the *polis* and its values. Its virtues were order, harmony, and justice, and one of its main objects was to produce good people. Like his master, and unlike the radical Sophists, Plato thought that the *polis* was in accord with nature. He accepted Socrates' doctrine of the identity of virtue and knowledge and made it plain what that knowledge was: *epistēmē*, science, a body of true and unchanging wisdom open to only a few philosophers, whose training, character, and intellect allowed them to see reality. Only such people were qualified to rule; they themselves would prefer the life of pure contemplation but would accept their responsibility and take their turn as philosopher kings. The training of such men required a specialization of function and a subordination of the individual to the community even greater than that at Sparta. This specialization would lead to Plato's definition of justice: that each man should do only that one thing to which his nature is best suited. Plato saw quite well that the *polis* of his day suffered from terrible internal stress, class struggle, and factional divisions. His solution, however, was not that of some Greeks, that is, conquest and resulting economic prosperity. For Plato the answer was in moral and political reform. The way to harmony was to destroy the causes of strife: private property, the family—anything, in short, that stood between the individual citizen and devotion to the *polis*.

Concern for the redemption of the *polis* was at the heart of Plato's system of philosophy. He began by asking the traditional questions: What is a good man, and how is he made? The goodness of a human being belonged to moral philosophy, and when it became a function of the state, it became political philosophy. Because goodness depended on knowledge of the good, it required a theory of knowledge and an investigation of what the knowledge was that was required for goodness. The answer must be metaphysical and so required a full examination of metaphysics. Even when the philosopher knew the good, however, the question remained how the state could bring its citizens to the necessary comprehension of that knowledge. The answer required a theory of education. Even purely logical and metaphysical questions, therefore, were subordinate to the overriding political questions. In this way Plato's need to find a satisfactory foundation for the beleaguered *polis* contributed to the birth of systematic philosophy.

ARISTOTLE. Aristotle (384–322 B.C.) was a pupil of Plato's and owed much to the thought of his master, but his very different experience and cast of mind led him in some new directions. He was born at Stagirus in the Chalcidice, the son of the court doctor of neighboring Macedon. As a young man he went to Athens to study at the Academy, where he stayed until Plato's death. Then he joined a Platonic colony at Assos in Asia Minor, and from there he moved to Mytilene. In both places he carried on research in marine biology, and biological interests played a large part in all his thoughts. In 342 B.C. Philip, the king of Macedon, appointed him tutor to his son, the young Alexander (see the following section). In 336 he returned to Athens, where he founded his own school, the Lyceum, or the Peripatos, as it was also called from the covered walk within it. In later years its members were called *Peripatetics*. On the death of Alexander in 323 B.C., the Athenians rebelled from Macedo-

Aristotle (383–322 B.C.). This is believed to be an ancient copy of an actual portrait of the philosopher. [Kunsthistorische Museum, Vienna]

nian rule, and Aristotle found it wise to leave. He died at Chalcis in Euboea in the following year.

The Lyceum was a very different place from the Academy. Its members took little interest in mathematics and were concerned with gathering, ordering, and analyzing all human knowledge. Aristotle wrote dialogues on the Platonic model, but none survive. He and his students also prepared many collections of information to serve as the basis for scientific works, but of these only the *Constitution of the Athenians,* one of 158 constitutional treatises, remains. Almost all of what we possess is in the form of philosophical and scientific studies, whose loose organization and style suggest that they were lecture notes. The range of subjects treated is astonishing, including logic, physics, astronomy, biology, ethics, rhetoric, literary criticism, and politics. In each field the method is the same. Aristotle began with observation of the empirical evidence, which in some cases was physical and in others was common opinion. To this body of information he applied reason and discovered inconsistencies or difficulties. To deal with these, he introduced metaphysical principles to explain the problems or to reconcile the inconsistencies. His view on all subjects, like Plato's, was teleological; that is, both Plato and Aristotle recognized purposes apart from and greater than the will of the individual human being. Plato's purposes, however, were contained in ideas, or forms, transcendental concepts outside the experience of most people, whereas for Aristotle the purposes of most things were easily inferred by observation of their behavior in the world. Aristotle's most striking characteristics are his moderation and his common sense. His epistemology finds room for both reason and experience; his metaphysics gives meaning and reality to both mind and body; his ethics aims at the good life, which is the contemplative life, but recognizes the necessity for moderate wealth, comfort, and pleasure.

All these qualities are evident in Aristotle's political thought. Like Plato he opposed the Sophists' assertion that the *polis* was contrary to nature and the result of mere convention. His response was to apply the teleology he saw in all nature to politics as well. In his view matter existed to achieve an end, and it developed until it achieved its form, which was its end. There was constant development from matter to form, from potential to actual. Therefore human primitive instincts could be seen as the matter out of which the human's potential as a political being could be realized. The *polis* made individuals self-sufficient and allowed the full realization of their potentiality. It was therefore natural. It was also the highest point in the evolution of the social institutions that serve the human need to continue the species—marriage, household, village, and finally, *polis.* For Aristotle the purpose of the *polis* was neither economic nor military but moral. "The end of the state is the good life" (*Politics* 1280b), the life lived "for the sake of noble actions" (1281a), a life of virtue and morality.

Characteristically Aristotle was less interested in the best state—the utopia that required philosophers to rule it—than in the best state practically possible, one that would combine justice with stability. The constitution for that state he called *politeia,* not the best constitution, but the next best, the one most suited to and most possible for most states. Its quality was moderation, and it naturally gave power to neither the rich nor the poor, but to the middle class, which must also be the most numerous. The middle class possessed many virtues: because of its moderate wealth it was free of the arrogance of the rich and the malice of the poor. For this reason it was the most stable class. The stability of the constitution also came from its being a mixed constitution, blending in some way the laws of democracy and of oligarchy. Aristotle's scheme was unique because of its realism and the breadth of its vision. All the political thinkers of the fourth century B.C. recognized that the *polis* was in danger, and all hoped to save it. All recognized the economic and social troubles that threatened it. Isocrates, a contemporary of Plato and Aristotle, urged a program of imperial conquest as a cure for poverty and revolution. Plato saw the folly of solving a political and moral problem by purely economic means and resorted to the creation of utopias. Aristotle combined the practical analysis of political and economic realities with the moral and political purposes of the traditional defenders of the *polis*. The result was a passionate confidence in the virtues of moderation and of the middle class and the proposal of a constitution that would give it power. It is ironic that the ablest defense of the *polis* came soon before its demise.

Emergence of the Hellenistic World

The term *Hellenistic* was coined in the nineteenth century to describe the period of three centuries during which Greek culture spread far from its homeland to Egypt and far into Asia. The new civilization formed in this expansion was a mixture of Greek and Oriental elements, although the degree of mixture varied from time to time and place to place. The Hellenistic world was larger than the world of classical Greece, and its major political units were much larger than the city-states, though these persisted in different forms. The new political and cultural order had its roots in the rise to power of a Macedonian dynasty that conquered Greece and the Persian Empire in the space of two generations.

The Macedonian Conquest

The quarrels among the Greeks brought on defeat and conquest by a new power that suddenly rose to eminence in the fourth century B.C., the kingdom of Macedon. The Macedonians inhabited the land to the north of Thessaly,

and through the centuries they had unknowingly served the vital purpose of protecting the Greek states from barbarian tribes further to the north. By Greek standards Macedon was a backward, semibarbaric land. It had no *poleis* and was ruled loosely by a king in a rather Homeric fashion. He was chosen partly on the basis of descent, but the acclamation of the army gathered in assembly was required to make him legitimate. Quarrels between pretenders to the throne and even murder to achieve it were not uncommon. A council of nobles checked the royal power and could reject a weak or incompetent king. Hampered by constant wars with the barbarians, internal strife, loose organization, and lack of money, Macedon played no great part in Greek affairs up to the fourth century B.C. The Macedonians were of the same stock as the Greeks and spoke a Greek dialect, and the nobles, at least, thought of themselves as Greeks. The kings claimed descent from Heracles and the royal house of Argos. They tried to bring Greek culture into their court and won acceptance at the Olympic games. If a king could be found with the ability to unify this nation, it was bound to play a greater part in Greek affairs.

PHILIP OF MACEDON. That king was Philip II (359–336 B.C.), who, while still under thirty, took advantage of his appointment as regent to overthrow his infant nephew and make himself king. Like many of his predecessors, he admired Greek culture. Between 367 and 364 B.C. he had been a hostage in Thebes, where he learned much about Greek politics and warfare under the tutelage of Epaminon-

THE RISE OF MACEDON	
Reign of Philip II	359–336 B.C.
Battle of Chaeronea; Philip conquers Greece	338 B.C.
Founding of League of Corinth	338 B.C.
Reign of Alexander III, the Great	336–323 B.C.
Alexander invades Asia	334 B.C.
Battle of Issus	333 B.C.
Battle of Gaugamela	331 B.C.
Fall of Persepolis	330 B.C.
Alexander reaches Indus Valley	327 B.C.
Death of Alexander	323 B.C.

94

*The
Foundations of
Western
Civilization in
the Ancient
World*

das. His natural talents for war and diplomacy and his boundless ambition made him the ablest king in Macedonian history. Using both diplomatic and military means, he was able to pacify the tribes on his frontiers and make his own hold on the throne firmer. Then he began to undermine Athenian control of the northern Aegean. He took Amphipolis, which gave him control of the Strymon valley and of the gold and silver mines of Mount Pangaeus. The income allowed him to found new cities, to bribe politicians in foreign towns, and to reorganize his army into the finest fighting force in the world.

THE MACEDONIAN ARMY. Philip put to good use what he had learned in Thebes and combined it with the advantages afforded by Macedonian society and tradition. His genius created a versatile and powerful army. The infantry was drawn from Macedonian farmers as well as from the hill people, who so frequently proved rebellious. In time these were integrated to form a loyal and effective national army. The infantry was armed with pikes that were thirteen feet long instead of the usual nine. They stood in a more open formation, which depended less on the weight of the charge than on the skillful use of the weapon. This tactic was effective because the phalanx was meant not to be the decisive force but merely to hold the enemy until the winning blow was struck by a massed cavalry charge on the flank or into a gap. The cavalry was made up of Macedonian nobles and clan leaders, who were called Companions and who lived closely with the king and developed a special loyalty to him. In addition Philip employed mercenaries who knew the latest tactics used by mobile light-armed Greek troops as well as the most sophisticated siege machinery known to the Greeks. The native Macedonian army might be as large as forty thousand men and could be expanded by drafts from the allies and by mercenaries.

THE INVASION OF GREECE. So armed, Philip turned south toward central Greece. Since 355 B.C. the Phocians had been fighting against Thebes and Thessaly. Philip gladly accepted the request of the Thessalians to be their general, defeated Phocis, and treacherously took control of Thessaly. Swiftly he turned northward again to Thrace and gained domination over the northern Aegean coast and the European side of the straits to the Black Sea. This conquest threatened the vital interests of Athens, which still had a formidable fleet of three hundred ships.

The Athens of 350 B.C. was not the Athens of Pericles. It had neither imperial revenue nor allies to share the burden of war on land or sea, and its own population was smaller than in the fifth century. The Athenians, therefore, were reluctant to go on expeditions themselves or even to send out mercenary armies under Athenian generals, for they must be paid out of taxes or contributions from Athenian citizens.

The leading spokesman against these tendencies and the cautious foreign policy that went with them was Demosthenes (384–322 B.C.), one of the greatest orators in Greek history. He was convinced that Philip was a dangerous enemy to Athens and the other Greeks and spent most of his career urging the Athenians to resist Philip's encroachments. He was right, for beginning in 349 B.C., Philip attacked several cities in northern and central Greece and firmly planted Macedonian power in those regions. The king of "barbarian" Macedon was elected president of the Pythian Games at Delphi, and the Athenians were forced to concur in the election.

In these difficult times it was Athens' misfortune not to have the kind of political leadership that Cimon or Pericles had offered a century earlier, which allowed for a consistent foreign policy. Many, perhaps most, Athenians accepted Demosthenes' view of Philip, but few were willing to run the risks and make the sacrifices necessary to stop his advance. Others, like Eubulus, an outstanding financial official and conservative political leader, favored a cautious policy of cooperation with Philip in the hope that his aims were limited and no real threat to Athens. Isocrates (436–338 B.C.), the head of an important rhetorical and philosophical school in Athens, looked to Philip to provide the unity and leadership needed for the Panhellenic campaign against Persia that he and other orators had been urging for some years. Isocrates saw the conquest of Asia Minor as the solution to the economic, social, and political problems that had brought poverty and civil war to the Greek cities ever since the Peloponnesian War. Finally, there seem to have been some Athenians who were in the pay of Philip, for he used money lavishly to win support in all of the cities.

The years between 346 B.C. and 340 B.C. were spent in diplomatic maneuvering, each side trying to win strategically useful allies. At

Demosthenes Denounces Philip of Macedon

Demosthenes (384–322 B.C.) was an Athenian statesman who urged his fellow citizens and other Greeks to resist the advance of Philip of Macedon (ca. 359–317 B.C.). The following is from the speech we call the First Philippic, delivered probably in 351 B.C.

Do not imagine, that his empire is everlastingly secured to him as a god. There are those who hate and fear and envy him, Athenians, even among those that seem most friendly; and all feelings that are in other men belong, we may assume, to his confederates. But now they are cowed, having no refuge through your tardiness and indolence, which I say you must abandon forthwith. For you see, Athenians, the case, to what pitch of arrogance the man has advanced, who leaves you not even the choice of action or inaction, but threatens and uses (they say) outrageous language, and, unable to rest in possession of his conquests, continually widens their circle, and whilst we dally and delay, throws his net all around us. When then, Athenians, when will ye act as becomes you? In what event? In that of necessity, I suppose. And how should we regard the events happening now? Methinks, to freemen the strongest necessity is the disgrace of their condition. Or tell me, do ye like walking about and asking one another:—is there any news? Why, could there be greater news than a man of Macedonia subduing Athenians, and directing the affairs of Greece? Is Philip dead? No, but he is sick. And what matters it to you? Should anything befall this man, you will soon create another Philip, if you attend to business thus. For even he has been exalted not so much by his own strength, as by our negligence.

Demosthenes, *The Olynthiac and Other Public Orations of Demosthenes*, trans. by C. R. Kennedy (London: George Bell and Sons, 1903), pp. 62–63.

last, Philip attacked Perinthus and Byzantium, the life line of Athenian commerce, and in 340 he besieged both cities and declared war. The Athenian fleet saved both, so in the following year Philip marched into Greece. Demosthenes performed wonders in rallying the Athenians and winning Thebes over to the Athenian side, but in 338 Philip defeated the allied forces at Chaeronea in Boeotia in a great battle whose decisive blow was a cavalry charge led by the eighteen-year-old son of Philip, Alexander.

THE MACEDONIAN GOVERNMENT OF GREECE. The Macedonian settlement of Greek affairs was not as harsh as many had feared, although in some cities the friends of Macedon came to power and killed or exiled their enemies. Demosthenes continued to be free to engage in politics, and Athens was not attacked on the condition that it give up what was left of its empire and follow the lead of Macedon. The rest of Greece was arranged in such a way as to remove all dangers to Philip's rule. To guarantee his security, Philip placed garrisons at Thebes, Chalcis, and Corinth; these came to be known as the fetters of Greece. In 338 B.C. Philip called a meeting of the Greek states to form the federal League of Corinth. The constitution provided for autonomy, freedom from tribute and garrisons, and suppression of piracy and civil war. The league delegates would make foreign policy, in theory without consulting their home governments or Philip. All this was a facade; not only was Philip of Macedon president of the league, he was its ruler. The defeat at Chaeronea was the end of Greek freedom and autonomy. Though its form and internal life continued for some time, the *polis* had lost control of its own affairs and the special conditions that had made it unique.

Philip's choice of Corinth as the seat of his new confederacy was not made out of convenience or by accident. It was at Corinth that the Greeks had gathered to resist a Persian invasion almost 150 years earlier, and it was there in 337 B.C. that Philip announced his intention to invade Persia in a war of liberation and revenge as leader of the new league. In the spring of 336 B.C., as he prepared to begin the campaign, Philip was assassinated.

In 1977 a mound was excavated at the Mac-

96

*The
Foundations of
Western
Civilization in
the Ancient
World*

Democracy crowns the people of Athens in this carving from 336 B.C. By that date Athens had already been forced to accept the hegemony of Philip of Macedon, and the era of the independent, democratic city-state was ending. [American School of Classical Studies, Athens]

edonian village of Vergina. The extraordinarily rich finds and associated buildings have led many scholars to conclude that this is the royal tomb of Philip II. If they are right, and the evidence seems persuasive, Philip richly deserved so distinguished a resting place. He found Macedon a disunited kingdom of semibarbarians, despised and exploited by the Greeks; at his death Macedon was a united kingdom, master and leader of the Greeks, rich, powerful, and ready to undertake the invasion of Asia. The completion of this task was left to Philip's first son, Alexander III (356–323 B.C.), later called Alexander the Great, who came to the throne at the age of twenty.

Alexander the Great

THE CONQUEST OF PERSIA AND BE-YOND. Along with his throne, the young king inherited his father's plan to invade Persia. The idea was daring, for Persia's empire was vast and its resources were enormous, but the usurper Cyrus and his Greek mercenaries had shown its vulnerability by penetrating deep into the Persian Empire at the beginning of the fourth century B.C. Its size and disparate nature also made it hard to control and exploit. There were always troubles on some of its far-flung frontiers and intrigues within the royal palace. Throughout the fourth century B.C. the Persian king called on Greek mercenaries to put down trouble. In 336 B.C. Persia was ruled by a new and inexperienced king, Darius III, but it remained formidable because of its huge army, its great wealth, and a navy that ruled the sea.

In 334 B.C. Alexander crossed the Hellespont into Asia. His army consisted of about thirty thousand infantry and five thousand cavalry; he had no navy and little money. These facts determined his early strategy: he must seek quick and decisive battles to gain money and supplies from the conquered territory. He must move along the coast so as to neutralize the Persian navy by depriving it of ports. Memnon, the commander of the Persian navy, recommended the perfect strategy against this plan: to retreat, to scorch the earth and deprive Alex-

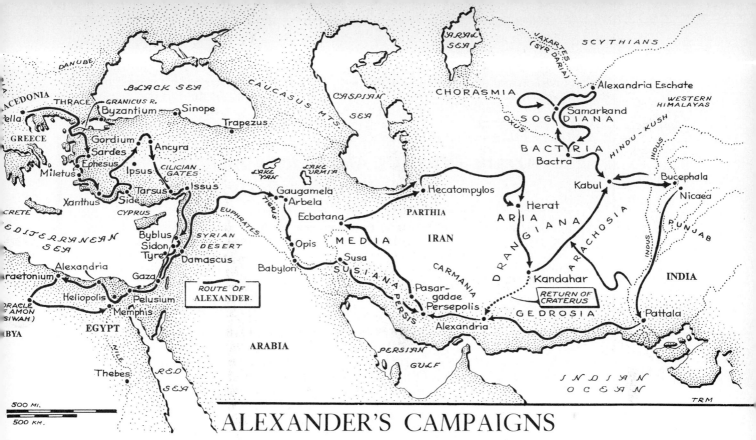

ALEXANDER'S CAMPAIGNS

MAP 3-5 *The route taken by Alexander the Great in his conquest of the Persian Empire, 334–323 B.C. Starting from the Macedonian capital at Pella, he reached the Indus valley before being turned back by his own restive troops. He died of fever in Mesopotamia.*

ander of supplies, to avoid battles, to use guerrilla tactics, and to stir up rebellion in Greece, but he was ignored. The Persians preferred to stand and fight; their pride and courage were greater than their wisdom.

Alexander met the Persian forces of Asia Minor at the Granicus River, where he won a smashing victory in characteristic style (see Map 3.5). He led a cavalry charge across the river into the teeth of the enemy on the opposite bank, almost losing his life in the process and winning the devotion of his soldiers. That victory left the coast of Asia Minor open, and Alexander captured the coastal cities, thus denying them to the Persian fleet.

In 333 B.C. Alexander marched inland to Syria, where he met the main Persian army under King Darius at Issus. Alexander himself led the cavalry charge that broke the Persian line and sent Darius fleeing into central Asia Minor. He continued along the coast and captured previously impregnable Tyre after a long and ingenious siege, putting an end to the threat of the Persian navy. He took Egypt with

little trouble and was greeted as liberator, pharaoh, and son of Re (an Egyptian god whose Greek equivalent was Zeus). At Tyre, Darius sent Alexander a peace offer, yielding his entire empire west of the Euphrates River and his daughter in exchange for an alliance and an end to the invasion. But Alexander aimed at conquering the whole empire and probably whatever lay beyond that.

In the spring of 331 B.C. Alexander marched into Mesopotamia. At Gaugamela, near the ancient Assyrian city of Nineveh, he met Darius, ready for a last stand. Once again Alexander's tactical genius and personal leadership carried the day. The Persians were broken and Darius fled once more. Alexander entered Babylon, again hailed as liberator and king. In January of 330 B.C. he came to Persepolis, the Persian capital, which held splendid palaces and the royal treasury. This bonanza ended his financial troubles and put a vast sum of money into circulation, with economic consequences that lasted for centuries. After a stay of several months Alexander burned Persepolis to dram-

97

atize the completion of Hellenic revenge for the Persian invasion and the destruction of the native Persian dynasty.

The new regime could not be secure while Darius lived, so Alexander pursued him eastward. Just south of the Caspian Sea he came

---

Arrian Describes Alexander's Actions at a Tragic Drinking Party

Arrian lived in the second century A.D., almost five hundred years after Alexander the Great, but his *Anabasis* is the best ancient source of information about Alexander's career. In 328 B.C. Alexander's expedition had reached Samarkand. By now he had adopted a number of Persian customs and had begun to reduce the distinction between Macedonians and Persians. The older Macedonians, in particular, were resentful, and in the following passage is described a drinking bout in which a quarrel arose between Alexander and one of the most distinguished Macedonian veterans.

When the drinking-party on this occasion had already gone on too long (for Alexander had now made innovations even in regard to drinking, by imitating too much the custom of foreigners), and in the midst of the carouse a discussion had arisen about the Dioscuri, how their procreation had been taken away from Tyndareus and ascribed to Zeus, some of those present, in order to flatter Alexander, maintained that Polydeuces and Castor were in no way worthy to compare with him and his exploits. Such men have always destroyed and will never cease to ruin the interests of those who happen to be reigning. In their carousal they did not even abstain from comparing him with Heracles, saying that envy stood in the way of the living receiving the honours due to them from their associates. It was well known that Clitus had long been vexed at Alexander for the change in his style of living in excessive imitation of foreign customs, and at those who flattered him with their speech. At that time also, being heated with wine, he would not permit them either to insult the deity or, by depreciating the deeds of the ancient heroes, to confer upon Alexander this gratification which deserved no thanks. He affirmed Alexander's deeds were neither in fact at all so great or marvellous as they represented in their laudation; nor had he achieved them by himself, but for the most part they were the deeds of the Macedonians. The delivery of this speech annoyed Alexander; and I do not commend it, for I think, in such a drunken bout, it would have been sufficient if, so far as he was personally concerned,

he had kept silence, and not committed the error of indulging in the same flattery as the others. But when some even mentioned Philip's actions without exercising a just judgment, declaring that he had performed nothing great or marvellous, they herein gratified Alexander; but Clitus being then no longer able to contain himself, began to put Philip's achievements in the first rank, and to depreciate Alexander and his performances. Clitus being now quite intoxicated, made other depreciatory remarks and even vehemently reviled him, because after all he had saved his life, when the cavalry battle had been fought with the Persians at the Granicus. Then indeed, arrogantly stretching out his right hand, he said, "This hand, O Alexander, preserved you on that occasion." Alexander could now no longer endure the drunken insolence of Clitus; but jumped up against him in a great rage. He was however restrained by his boon companions. As Clitus did not desist from his insulting remarks, Alexander shouted out a summons for his shield-bearing guards to attend him; but when no one obeyed him, he said that he was reduced to the same position as Darius, when he was led about under arrest by Bessus and his adherents, and that he now possessed the mere name of king. Then his companions were no longer able to restrain him; for according to some he leaped up and snatched a javelin from one of his confidential body-guards; according to others, a long pike from one of his ordinary guards, with which he struck Clitus and killed him.

Arrian, *The Anabasis of Alexander*, trans. by E. J. Chinnock in *The Greek Historians*, Vol. 2, ed. by F. R. B. Godolphin (New York: Random House, 1942), pp. 507–508.

upon the corpse of Darius, killed by his relative Bessus. The Persian nobles around Darius had lost faith in him and had joined in the plot. The murder removed Darius from Alexander's path, but now he had to catch Bessus, who proclaimed himself successor to Darius. The pursuit of Bessus (who was soon caught), a great curiosity, and a longing to go as far as he could and see the most distant places took Alexander to the frontier of India.

Near Samarkand, in the land of the Scythians, he founded the city of Alexandria Eschate ("Furthest Alexandria"), one of the many cities bearing his name that he founded as he traveled. As part of his grand scheme of amalgamation and conquest, he married the Bactrian princess Roxane and enrolled thirty thousand young Bactrians into his army. These were to be trained and sent back to the center of the empire for use later.

In 327 B.C. Alexander took his army through the Khyber Pass in an attempt to conquer the lands around the Indus River (modern Pakistan). He reduced its king, Porus, to vassalage but pushed on in the hope of reaching the river called Ocean that the Greeks believed encircled the world. Finally, his weary men refused to go on. By the spring of 324 B.C. the army was back at the Persian Gulf and celebrated in the Macedonian style, with a wild spree of drinking.

A gold medallion bearing a portrait of Alexander the Great (356–323 B.C.). [State Museums, Berlin]

THE DEATH OF ALEXANDER AND ITS AFTERMATH. Alexander was filled with plans for the future: for the consolidation and organization of his empire; for geographical exploration; for building new cities, roads, and harbors; perhaps even for further conquests in the west. There is even some evidence that he asked to be deified and worshiped as a god, although we cannot be sure if he really did so or what he had in mind if he did. In June of 323 B.C. he was overcome by a fever and died in Babylon at the age of thirty-three. His memory has never faded, and he soon became the subject of myth, legend, and romance. From the beginning, estimates of him have varied. Some have seen in him a man of grand and noble vision who transcended the narrow limits of Greek and Macedonian ethnocentrism and aimed at the brotherhood of humankind in a great world state. Others have seen him as a calculating despot, given to drunken brawls, brutality, and murder.

The truth is probably in between. Alexander was one of the greatest generals the world has seen; he never lost a battle or failed in a siege, and with a modest army he conquered a vast empire. He had rare organizational talents, and his plan for creating a multinational empire was the only intelligent way of proceeding. He established many new cities—seventy, according to tradition—mostly along trade routes. These cities had the effect of encouraging commerce and prosperity as well as of introducing Hellenic civilization into new areas. It is hard to know if the vast new empire could have been held together, but Alexander's death proved that only he had a chance to succeed.

Nobody was prepared for Alexander's sudden death in 323 B.C., and affairs were further complicated by a weak succession: Roxane's unborn child and Alexander's weak-minded half-brother. His able and loyal Macedonian generals at first hoped to preserve the empire for the Macedonian royal house, and to this end they appointed themselves governors of the various provinces of the empire. However, the conflicting ambitions of these strong-willed men led to prolonged warfare among various combinations of them, in which three of the original number were killed, and all of the direct members of the Macedonian royal house

100

The
Foundations of
Western
Civilization in
the Ancient
World

were either executed or murdered. With the murder of Roxane and her son in 310 B.C., there was no longer any focus for the enormous empire, and in 306 and 305 the surviving governors proclaimed themselves kings of their various holdings.

Three of these Macedonian generals founded dynasties of significance in the spread of Hellenistic culture:

Ptolemy I, 367?–283 B.C.; founder of the Thirty-first Dynasty in Egypt, the Ptolemies, of whom Cleopatra, who died in 30 B.C., was the last.

Seleucus I, 358?–280 B.C.; founder of the Seleucid dynasty in Mesopotamia.

Antigonus I, 382–301 B.C.; founder of the Antigonid dynasty in Asia Minor and Macedon.

For the first seventy-five years or so after the death of Alexander, the world ruled by his successors enjoyed considerable prosperity. The vast sums of money that he and they put into circulation greatly increased the level of economic activity. The opportunities for service and profit in the east attracted many Greeks and relieved their native cities of some of the pressure of the poor. The opening of vast new territories to Greek trade, the increased demand for Greek products, and the new availability of things wanted by the Greeks, as well as the conscious policies of the Hellenistic kings, all helped the growth of commerce. The new prosperity, however, was not evenly distributed. The urban Greeks, the Macedonians, and the hellenized natives who made up the upper and middle classes lived lives of comfort and even luxury, but the rural native peasants did not. During prosperous times these distinctions were bearable, although even then there was tension between the two groups. After a while, however, the costs of continuing wars, inflation, and a gradual lessening of the positive effects of the introduction of Persian wealth all led to economic crisis. The kings bore down heavily on the middle classes, who, however, were skilled at avoiding their responsibilities. The pressure on the peasants and the city laborers became great, too, and they responded by slowing down their work and even by striking. In Greece economic pressures brought clashes between rich and poor, demands for the abolition of debt and the redistribution of land, and even, on occasion, civil war.

These internal divisions, along with the international wars, weakened the capacity of the Hellenistic kingdoms to resist outside attack, and by the middle of the second century B.C. they were all gone, except for Egypt. The two centuries between Alexander and the Roman conquest, however, were of great and lasting importance. They saw the formation into a single political, economic, and cultural unit of the entire eastern Mediterranean coast and of Greece, Egypt, Mesopotamia, and the old Persian Empire. The period also saw the creation of a new culture that took root, at least in the urban portions of that vast area, one that deserves to be differentiated from the earlier one of the Greek city-states: Hellenistic culture.

Hellenistic Culture

The career of Alexander the Great marked a significant turning point in the thought of the Greeks as it was represented in literature, philosophy, religion, and art. His conquests and the establishment of the successor kingdoms put an end once and for all to the central role of the *polis* in Greek life and thought. Scholars disagree about the end of the *polis*. Some deny that Philip's victory at Chaeronea put an end to its existence; they point to the continuance of *poleis* throughout the Hellenistic period and even see a continuation of them in the Roman *municipia*, but these are only a shadow of the vital reality that had been the true *polis*.

Deprived of control of their foreign affairs, their important internal arrangements determined by a foreign monarch, the postclassical cities lost the kind of political freedom that was basic to the old outlook. They were cities, perhaps—in a sense, even city-states—but not *poleis*. As time passed, they changed from sovereign states to municipal towns merged in military empires. Never again in antiquity would there be either a serious attack on or a defense of the *polis*, for its importance was gone. For the most part, the Greeks after Alexander turned away from political solutions for their problems and sought instead personal responses to their hopes and fears, particularly in religion, philosophy, and magic. The confident, sometimes arrogant, humanism of the fifth century B.C. gave way to a kind of resignation to fate, a recognition of helplessness before forces too great for humans to manage.

Philosophy

These developments are noticeable in the changes that overtook the established schools of philosophy as well as in the emergence of two new and influential groups of philosophers, the Epicureans and the Stoics. Athens' position as the center of philosophical studies was reinforced, for the Academy and the Lyceum continued in operation, and the new schools were also located in Athens. The Lyceum turned gradually away from the universal investigations of its founder, Aristotle, even from his scientific interests, to become a center chiefly of literary and especially historical studies.

The Academy turned even further away from its tradition. It adopted the systematic Skepticism of Pyrrho of Elis, and under the leadership of Arcesilaus and Carneades, the Skeptics of the Academy became skilled at pointing out fallacies and weaknesses in the philosophies of the rival schools. They thought that nothing could be known and so consoled themselves and their followers by suggesting that nothing mattered. It was easy for them, therefore, to accept conventional morality and the world as it was. The Cynics, of course, continued to denounce convention and to advocate the crude life in accordance with nature, which some of them practiced publicly to the shock and outrage of respectable citizens. Neither of these views had much appeal to the middle-class city dweller of the third century B.C., who sought some basis for choosing a way of life now that the *polis* no longer provided one ready-made.

Epicurus of Athens (342–271 B.C.) *taught that the goal of philosophy was not knowledge, but happiness, which could be achieved through a reasonable and moderate way of life.* [Metropolitan Museum, Roger Fund, 1911]

THE EPICUREANS. Epicurus of Athens (342–271 B.C.) formulated a new teaching, which was embodied in the school he founded in his native city in 306. His philosophy conformed to the new mood in that its goal was not knowledge but human happiness, which he believed could be achieved if one followed a style of life based on reason. He took sense perception to be the basis of all human knowledge. The reality and reliability of sense perception rested on the acceptance of the physical universe described by the atomists, Democritus and Leucippus, in which atoms were continually falling through the void and giving off images that were in direct contact with the senses. These falling atoms could swerve in an arbitrary, unpredictable way to produce the combinations seen in the world; Epicurus thereby removed an element of determinism that existed in the Democritean system. When a person died, the atoms that composed the body dispersed so that the person

had no further existence or perception and therefore nothing to fear after death. Epicurus believed that the gods existed but that they took no interest in human affairs. This belief amounted to a practical atheism, and Epicureans were often thought to be atheists.

The purpose of Epicurean physics was to liberate people from their fear of death, of the gods, and of all nonmaterial or supernatural powers. Epicurean ethics were hedonistic, that is, based on the acceptance of pleasure as true happiness. But pleasure for Epicurus was chiefly negative: the absence of pain and trouble. The goal of the Epicureans was *ataraxia,* the condition of being undisturbed, without trouble, pain, or responsibility. Ideally a man should have enough means to allow him to withdraw from the world and avoid business

102

*The
Foundations of
Western
Civilization in
the Ancient
World*

and public life; Epicurus even advised against marriage and children. He preached a life of genteel, restrained selfishness, which might appeal to intellectual men of means, but it was not calculated to be widely attractive.

THE STOICS. Soon after Epicurus began teaching in his garden in Athens, Zeno of Citium in Cyprus (335–263 B.C.) established the Stoic school, which derived its name from the *Stoa Poikile,* or Painted Portico, in the Athenian Agora, where Zeno and his disciples walked and talked beginning about 300 B.C. From then until about the middle of the second century B.C., Zeno and his successors preached a philosophy that owed a good deal to Socrates, by way of the Cynics, and was fed also by a stream of Eastern thought. Zeno, of course, came from Phoenician Cyprus; Chrysippus, one of his successors, came from Cilicia; and other early Stoics came from such places as Carthage, Tarsus, and Babylon.

Like the Epicureans, the Stoics sought the happiness of the individual. Quite unlike them, the Stoics held a philosophy almost indistinguishable from religion. They believed that humans must live in harmony within themselves and in harmony with nature; for the Stoics god and nature were the same. The guiding principle in nature was divine reason (Logos), or fire. Every human had a spark of this divinity, and after death it returned to the eternal divine spirit. From time to time the world was destroyed by fire, from which a new world arose. The aim of humans, and the definition of human happiness, was the virtuous life, life lived in accordance with natural law, "when all actions promote the harmony of the spirit dwelling in the individual man with the will of him who orders the universe."[2] To live such a life required the knowledge possessed only by the wise, who knew what was good, what was evil, and what was neither, but "indifferent." Good and evil were dispositions of the mind or soul: prudence, justice, courage, temperance, and so on were good, whereas folly, injustice, cowardice, and the like were evil. Life, health, pleasure, beauty, strength, wealth, and so on were neutral, morally indifferent, for they did not contribute either to happiness or to misery. Human misery came from an irrational mental contraction, from passion, which was a disease of the soul. The wise sought freedom from passion (*apatheia*), because passion arose from things that were morally indifferent.

Politically the Stoics fit well into the new world. They thought of it as a single *polis* in which all people were children of god. Although they did not forbid political activity, and many Stoics took part in political life, withdrawal was obviously preferable because the usual subjects of political argument were indifferent. Because the Stoics aimed at inner harmony of the individual, their aim was a life lived in accordance with the divine will, their attitude fatalistic, and their goal a form of apathy, they fit in well with the reality of post-Alexandrian life. In fact, the spread of Stoicism made simpler the task of creating a new political system that relied not on the active participation of the governed, but merely on their docile submission.

Literature

The literature of the Hellenistic period reflects the new intellectual currents and, even more, the new conditions of literary life and the new institutions created in that period. The center of literary production in the third and second centuries B.C. was the new city of Alexandria in Egypt. There the Ptolemies, the kings of Egypt during that time, founded the museum, a great research institute where scientists and scholars were supported by royal funds, and the library, which contained almost half a million volumes, or papyrus scrolls. In the library were the works making up the great body of past Greek literature of every kind, a great deal of which has since been lost. The Alexandrian scholars saw to it that what they judged to be the best works were copied; they edited and criticized these works from the point of view of language, form, and content and wrote biographies of their authors. Much of their work was valuable and is responsible for the preservation of most of ancient literature. Some of it is dry, petty, quarrelsome, and simply foolish. At its best, however, it is full of learning and perception.

The scholarly atmosphere of Alexandria naturally gave rise to work in the field of history and its ancillary discipline, chronology. Eratosthenes (ca. 275–195 B.C.) established a chronology of important events dating from the Trojan War, and others undertook similar tasks. Contemporaries of Alexander, such as Ptolemy I, Aristobulus, and Nearchus, wrote what were apparently sober and essentially

[2]Diogenes Laertius, *Life of Zeno* 88.

factual accounts of his career. Most of the work done by Hellenistic historians is known to us only in fragments cited by later writers, but it seems in general to have emphasized sensational and biographical detail rather than the rigorous impersonal analysis of a Thucydides.

Architecture and Sculpture

The opportunities open to architects and sculptors were greatly increased by the advent of the Hellenistic monarchies. There was plenty of money, the royal need for conspicuous display, the need to build and beautify new cities, and a growing demand from the well-to-do for objects of art. The new cities were usually laid out on the gridiron plan introduced in the fifth century by Hippodamus of Miletus. Temples were built on the classical model, and the covered portico, or *stoa*, became a very popular addition to the *agoras* of the Hellenistic towns.

Sculpture reflected the cosmopolitan nature of the Hellenistic world, for leading sculptors accepted commissions wherever they were attractive, and the result was a certain uniformity of style, although Alexandria, Rhodes, and the

The drunken old woman. A Roman copy of a second century B.C. bronze. It is marked by a stark realism very different from the classic serenity of the fifth-century B.C. Apollo pictured at the beginning of the chapter. [State Museum of Antiquities and Sculpture, Munich]

A Roman copy of one of the masterpieces of Hellenistic sculpture, the Laocoon. *In the* Iliad, *Laocoon was a priest who warned the Trojans not to take the wooden horse within their city. This sculpture depicts his punishment: Great serpents sent by the goddess Athena, who was on the side of the Greeks, devoured Laocoon and his sons before the horrified people of Troy. [German Archaelogical Institute, Rome]*

kingdom of Pergamum in Asia Minor developed their own characteristic styles. For the most part Hellenistic sculpture carried forward the tendencies of the fourth century B.C., moving away from the balanced tension and idealism of the fifth century toward a sentimental, emotional, and realistic mode. These qualities are readily apparent in the marble statue called the *Laocoon* which was carved at Rhodes in the second century B.C. and afterwards taken to Rome, and one of a drunken old woman in bronze cast in the second century B.C.

103

Mathematics and Science

Among the most spectacular and remarkable intellectual developments of the Hellenistic age were those that came in mathematics and science. The burst of activity in these subjects drew from several sources. The stimulation and organization provided by the work of Plato and Aristotle should not be ignored. To these was added the impetus provided by Alexander's interest in science, evidenced by the scientists he took with him on his expedition and the aid he gave them in collecting data. The expansion of Greek horizons geographically and the consequent contact with the knowledge of Egypt and Babylonia were also helpful. Finally, the patronage of the Ptolemies and the opportunity for many scientists to work with one another at the museum at Alexandria provided a unique opportunity for scientific work. It is not too much to say that the work done by the Alexandrians formed the greater part of the scientific knowledge available to the Western world until the scientific revolution of the sixteenth and seventeenth centuries A.D.

Euclid's *Elements* (written early in the third century B.C.) remained the textbook of plane and solid geometry until just recently. Archimedes of Syracuse (ca. 287–212 B.C.) made further progress in geometry, as well as establishing the theory of the lever in mechanics and inventing hydrostatics. The advances in mathematics, when added to the availability of Babylonian astronomical tables, allowed great progress in the field of astronomy. As early as the fourth century Heraclides of Pontus (ca. 390–310 B.C.) had argued that Mercury and Venus circulate around the sun and not the Earth, and he appears to have made other suggestions leading in the direction of a heliocentric theory of the universe. Most scholars, however, give credit for that theory to Aristarchus of Samos (ca. 310–230 B.C.), who asserted that the sun, along with the other fixed stars, did not move and that the Earth revolved around the sun in a circular orbit and rotated on its axis while

---

Plutarch Cites Archimedes and Hellenistic Science

Archimedes (ca. 287–211 B.C.) was one of the great mathematicians and physicists of antiquity. He was a native of Syracuse in Sicily and a friend of its king. Plutarch discusses him in the following selection and reveals much about the ancient attitude toward applied science.

Archimedes, however, in writing to King Hiero, whose friend and near relation he was, had stated that given the force, any given weight might be moved, and even boasted, we are told, relying on the strength of demonstration, that if there were another earth, by going into it he could remove this. Hiero being struck with amazement at this, and entreating him to make good this problem by actual experiment, and show some great weight moved by a small engine, he fixed accordingly upon a ship of burden out of the king's arsenal, which could not be drawn out of the dock without great labour and many men; and, loading her with many passengers and a full freight, sitting himself the while

far off, with no great endeavor, but only holding the head of the pulley in his hand and drawing the cords by degrees. . . . Yet Archimedes possessed so high a spirit, so profound a soul, and such treasures of scientific knowledge, that though these inventions had now obtained him the renown of more than human sagacity, he yet would not deign to leave behind him any commentary or writing on such subjects; but, repudiating as sordid and ignoble the whole trade of engineering, and every sort of art that lends itself to mere use and profit, he placed his whole affection and ambition in those purer speculations where there can be no reference to the vulgar needs of life. . . .

Plutarch, ''Marcellus,'' in *Lives of the Noble Grecians and Romans,* trans. by John Dryden, rev. by A. H. Clough (New York: Random House, n.d.), pp. 376–378.

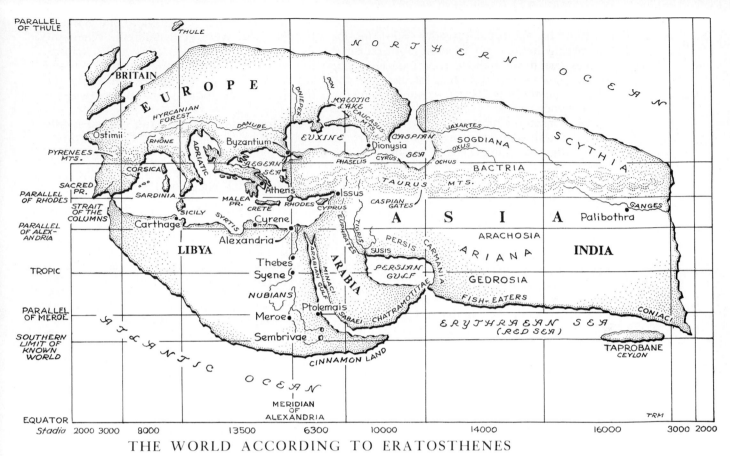

PARALLEL
OF THULE

PARALLEL
OF RHODES

PARALLEL
OF ALEX-
ANDRIA

TROPIC

PARALLEL
OF MEROE

SOUTHERN
LIMIT OF
KNOWN
WORLD

EQUATOR

THE WORLD ACCORDING TO ERATOSTHENES

MAP 3-6 *Eratosthenes of Alexandria (ca. 275–195 B.C.) was a Hellenistic geographer. His map, reconstructed here, was remarkably accurate for its time. The world was divided by lines of "latitude" and "longitude," thus anticipating our global divisions.*

doing so. The heliocentric theory ran contrary not only to the traditional view codified by Aristotle but to what seemed to be common sense. Besides, Hellenistic technology was not up to proving the theory, and, of course, the planetary orbits are not circular. The heliocentric theory did not, therefore, take hold. Hipparchus of Nicaea (born ca. 190 B.C.) constructed a model of the universe on the geocentric theory, employing an ingenious and complicated model that did a very good job of accounting for the movements of the sun, the moon, and the planets. Ptolemy of Alexandria (second century A.D.) adopted Hipparchus' system with a few improvements, and it remained dominant until the work of Copernicus, in the sixteenth century A.D.

Hellenistic scientists made progress in mapping the earth as well as the sky. Eratosthenes of Cyrene (ca. 275–195 B.C.) was able to calculate the circumference of the earth within about two hundred miles and wrote a treatise on geography based on mathematical and physical reasoning and the reports of travelers. In spite of the new data that were available to later geographers, Eratosthenes' map (see Map 3.6) was in many ways more accurate than the one that was constructed by Ptolemy and that became standard in the Middle Ages.

The Hellenistic Age made little contribution to the life sciences. Biology, zoology, and even medicine made little progress. Even the sciences that had such impressive achievements to show in the third century B.C. made little progress thereafter. In fact, to some extent, there was a retreat from science. Astrology and magic became the subjects of great interest as scientific advance lagged. The question has

105

106

*The
Foundations of
Western
Civilization in
the Ancient
World*

often been asked why science did not progress further in the ancient world: Why, for instance, was there no scientific and industrial revolution in the Hellenistic period? Many answers have been suggested, for example, the lack of an adequate base in technology and the absence of refined instruments of observation and measurement. Another explanation offered is that the deterrent effect of slavery on invention, the sharp class distinctions in ancient society, and the contemptuous attitude of the upper classes toward work separated the intellectual scientist from the practical application of any discoveries. All of these conditions may have played some role, but the wrong question seems to have been asked. To ask it in the usual way is to assume that anyone understands why the scientific and industrial revolutions took place when and where they did, but that assumption is unfounded. Perhaps when historians have solved the modern problem, they may more successfully approach the ancient one.

The Achievement of the Hellenistic Age

The Hellenistic Age speaks to us less fully and vividly than that of classical Greece or of the Roman Republic and Empire, chiefly because it had no historian to compare with Herodotus and Thucydides or Livy and Tacitus. We lack the continuous, rich, lively, and meaningful narrative without which it is difficult to get a clear picture. This deficiency should not obscure the great importance of the achievements of the age. The literature, art, scholarship, and science of the period deserve attention in their own right, but in addition the Hellenistic Age performed a vital civilizing function. It spread the Greek culture over a remarkably wide area and made a significant and lasting impression on much of it. Greek culture also adjusted to its new surroundings to a degree, unifying and simplifying its cultural cargo so as to make it more accessible to outsiders. The various Greek dialects gave way to a version of the Attic tongue, the *koinē* or common language. In the same way, the scholarship of Alexandria established canons of literary excellence and the scholarly tools with which to make the great treasures of Greek culture understandable to later generations. The syncretism of thought and belief introduced in this period also made

understanding and accord more likely among peoples who were very different. When the Romans came into contact with Hellenism, they were powerfully impressed by it, and when they conquered the Hellenistic world, they became, as Horace said, captives of its culture.

To Rome and the Romans we must now turn.

Suggested Readings

E. BARKER, *Political Philosophy of Plato and Aristotle* (1959). A sober and reliable account.

H. I. BELL, *Egypt from Alexander the Great to the Arab Conquest* (1948).

MAX CARY, *History of the Greek World from 323 to 146 B.C.* (1968). The major part is devoted to political history.

G. CAWKWELL, *Philip of Macedon* (1978). A brief but learned account of Philip's career.

W. R. CONNOR, *The New Politicians of Fifth-Century Athens* (1971). A study on changes in political style and their significance for Athenian society.

J. K. DAVIES, *Democracy and Classical Greece* (1978). Emphasizes archaeological evidence and social history.

V. EHRENBERG, *The People of Aristophanes* (1962). A study of Athenian society as revealed by the comedies of Aristophanes.

J. R. ELLIS, *Philip II and Macedonian Imperialism* (1976). A study of the career of the founder of Macedonian power.

J. FERGUSON, *The Heritage of Hellenism* (1973). A good survey.

W. S. FERGUSON, *Hellenistic Athens* (1970). Reprint of an old but still valuable study.

J. R. LANE FOX, *Alexander the Great* (1973). An imaginative account that does more justice to the Persian side of the problem than is usual.

A. FRENCH, *The Growth of the Athenian Economy* (1964). An interesting examination of economic developments in Athenian history.

M. GRANT, *From Alexander to Cleopatra* (1982). A general account of the Hellenistic period.

PETER GREEN, *Alexander the Great* (1972). A lively biography.

W. K. C. GUTHRIE, *The Sophists* (1971). A fine volume in an excellent history of Greek philosophy.

N. G. L. HAMMOND AND G. T. GRIFFITH, *A History of Macedonia*, Vol. 2, 550–336 B.C. (1979). A thorough account of Macedonian history that focuses on the careers of Philip and Alexander.

C. M. HAVELOCK, *Hellenistic Art* (1971). A fine interpretive study.

W. JAEGER, *Demosthenes* (1938). A good biography of the Athenian statesman.

A. H. M. JONES, *The Greek City from Alexander to*

Justinian (1940). A fine study of the significance and spread of urban life.

D. KAGAN, *The Outbreak of the Peloponnesian War* (1969). A study of the period from the foundation of the Delian League to the coming of the Peloponnesian War that argues that war could have been avoided.

D. KAGAN, *The Archidamian War* (1974). A history of the first ten years of the Peloponnesian War.

D. KAGAN, *The Peace of Nicias and the Sicilian Expedition* (1981). A history of the middle period of the Peloponnesian War.

H. D. F. KITTO, *Greek Tragedy* (1966). A good introduction.

B. M. W. KNOX, *The Heroic Temper: Studies in Sophoclean Tragedy* (1964). A brilliant analysis of tragic heroism.

J. A. O. LARSEN, *Greek Federal States* (1968). Emphasis on the federal movements of the Hellenistic era.

G. E. R. LLOYD, *Greek Science After Aristotle* (1974).

A. A. LONG, *Hellenistic Philosophy: Stoics, Epicureans, Sceptics* (1974).

R. MEIGGS, *The Athenian Empire* (1972). A fine study of the rise and fall of the empire, making excellent use of inscriptions.

J. J. POLLITT, *Art and Experience in Classical Greece* (1972). A scholarly and entertaining study of the relationship between art and history in classical Greece with excellent illustrations.

M. I. ROSTOVTZEFF, *Social and Economic History of the Hellenistic World,* 3 vols. (1941). A masterpiece of synthesis by a great historian.

W. W. TARN, *Alexander the Great,* 2 vols. (1948). The first volume is a narrative account, the second a series of detailed studies.

W. W. TARN AND G. T. GRIFFITH, *Hellenistic Civilization* (1961). A survey of Hellenistic history and culture.

A. E. TAYLOR, *Socrates* (1953). A good, readable account.

V. TCHERIKOVER, *Hellenistic Civilization and the Jews* (1970). A fine study of the impact of Hellenism on the Jews.

F. W. WALBANK, *The Hellenistic World* (1981).

T. B. L. WEBSTER, *Hellenistic Poetry and Art* (1961). A clear survey.

A. E. ZIMMERN, *The Greek Commonwealth* (1961). A study of political, social, and economic conditions in fifth-century Athens.

The "Old Republican," a portrait bust of a Roman senator from ca. 75 B.C.

THE ACHIEVEMENT of the Romans was one of the most remarkable accomplishments in human history. The descendants of the inhabitants of a small village in central Italy ruled the entire Italian peninsula, then the entire Mediterranean coastline. They conquered most of the Near East and finally much of continental Europe. They ruled this vast empire under a single government that provided considerable peace and prosperity for centuries. At no time before the Romans or since has that area been united, and rarely, if ever, has it enjoyed a stable peace. But Rome's legacy was not merely military excellence and political organization. The Romans adopted and transformed the intellectual and cultural achievements of the Greeks and combined them with their own outlook and historical experience. They produced that Graeco-Roman tradition in literature, philosophy, and art that served as the core of learning for the Middle Ages and the inspiration for the new paths taken in the Renaissance. It remains at the heart of Western civilization to this day.

4

Rome: From Republic to Empire

Prehistoric Italy

The culture of Italy developed late. Paleolithic settlements gave way to the Neolithic mode of life only about 2500 B.C. The Bronze Age came about 1500 B.C., and about 1000 B.C. Italy began to be infiltrated by bands of new arrivals coming from across the Adriatic Sea and around its northern end. The invaders were warlike people who imposed their language and social organization on almost all of Italy. Their bronze work was better than their predecessors', and soon they made weapons, armor, and tools of iron. They cremated their dead and put the ashes in tombs stocked with weapons and armor. Before 800 B.C. people living in this style occupied the highland pastures of the Apennines. These tough mountain people—Umbrians, Sabines, Samnites, Latins, and others—spoke a set of closely related languages we call *Italic*.

They soon began to challenge the earlier settlers for control of the tempting western plains. Other peoples lived in Italy in the ninth century B.C., but the Italic speakers and three peoples who had not yet arrived—the Etruscans, the Greeks, and the Celts—would shape its future.

The Etruscans

The Etruscans exerted the most powerful external influence on the Romans. Their civilization arose in Etruria (now Tuscany), west of the Apennines between the Arno and Tiber rivers, about 800 B.C. (see Map 4.1). Their origin is far from clear, but their tomb architecture, resembling that of Asia Minor, and their practice of divining the future by inspecting the livers of sacrificial animals point to an eastern origin.

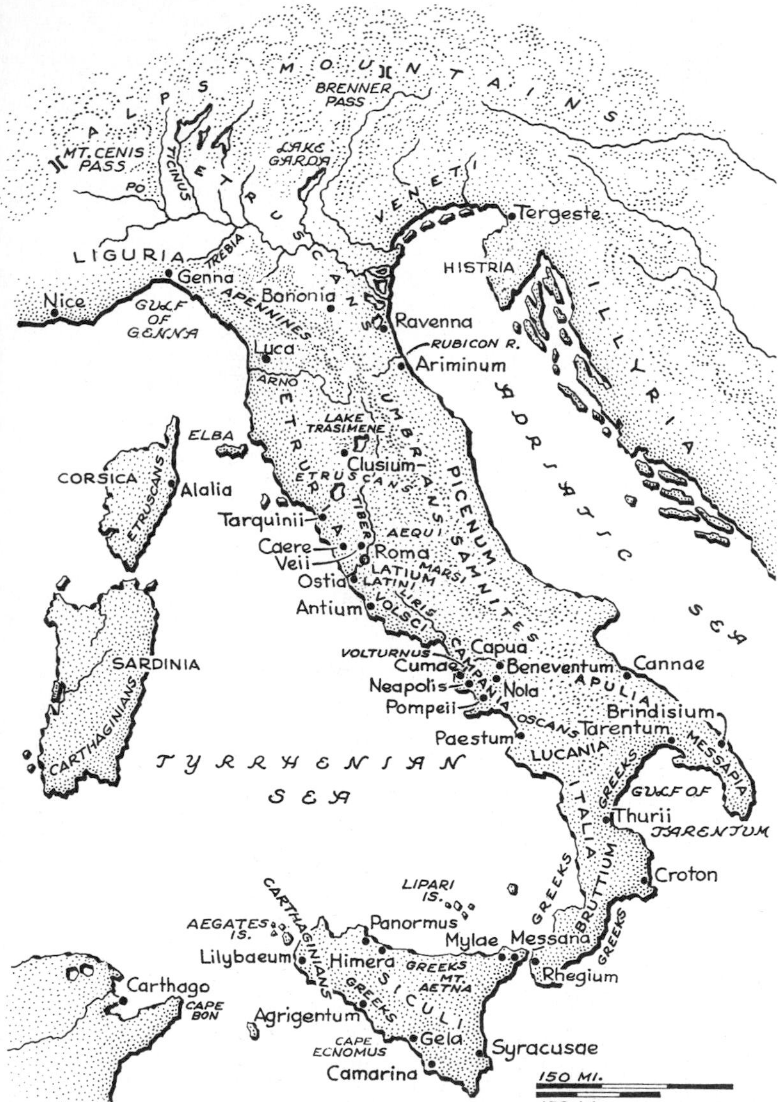

The Etruscans brought civilization with them. Their settlements were self-governing, fortified city-states, of which twelve formed a loose religious confederation. At first these cities were ruled by kings, but they were replaced by an aristocracy of the agrarian nobles, who ruled by means of a council and elected annual magistrates. The Etruscans were a military ruling class that dominated and exploited the native Italians, who worked their land and mines and served as infantry in their armies. This aristocracy accumulated considerable wealth through agriculture, industry, piracy, and a growing commerce with the Carthaginians and the Greeks.

The Etruscans' influence on the Romans was greatest in religion. They imagined a world filled with gods and spirits, many of them evil. To deal with such demons, the Etruscans evolved complicated rituals and powerful priesthoods. Divination by sacrifice and omens in nature helped discover the divine will, and careful attention to precise rituals directed by priests helped please the gods. After a while the Etruscans, influenced by the Greeks, worshiped gods in the shape of humans and built temples for them.

The Etruscan aristocracy remained aggressive and skillful in the use of horses and war chariots. In the seventh and sixth centuries B.C. they expanded their power in Italy and across the sea to Corsica and Elba. They conquered Latium (a region that included the small town of Rome) and Campania, where they became neighbors of the Greeks of Naples. In the north they got as far as the Po valley. These conquests were carried out by small bands led by Etruscan chieftains who did not work in concert and would not necessarily aid one another in distress. As a result, the conquests outside Etruria were not firmly based and did not last long. Etruscan power reached its height some time before 500 B.C. and then rapidly declined. About 400 B.C. the Celts broke into the Po valley, drove out the Etruscans, and settled their conquered land so firmly that the Romans thereafter called it Cisalpine Gaul (Gaul on this side of the Alps). Thereafter even Etruria lost its independence and was incorporated into Roman Italy. The Etruscan language was forgotten and Etruscan culture gradually became only a memory, but its influence on the Romans remained.

ANCIENT ITALY

MAP 4-1 *This map of the Italian peninsula and its neighbors in antiquity shows the major cities and towns, as well as a number of geographical regions and the locations of some of the Italic and non-Italic peoples of the area.*

Clay statue of Apollo from the Etruscan city of Veii in central Italy, ca. 500 B.C. It is evidence of the considerable influence of Greek culture on Etruscan civilization. [German Archaelogical Institute, Rome]

Royal Rome

Rome was an unimportant town in Latium until its conquest by the Etruscans, but its location gave it several advantages over its Latin neighbors. Its site was on the Tiber River, fifteen miles from its mouth, at the point where the hills on which Rome was situated made further navigation impossible. The island in the Tiber southwest of the Capitoline hill made the river fordable, so that Rome was naturally a center for communication and trade, both east–west and north–south.

Government

In the sixth century B.C. Rome came under Etruscan control. Led by their Etruscan kings, the Roman army, equipped and organized like the Greek phalanx, gained control of most of Latium. They achieved this success under an effective political and social order that gave extraordinary power to the ruling figures in both public and private life. To their kings the Romans gave the awesome power of *imperium*, the right to issue commands and to enforce them by fines, arrests, and corporal or even capital punishment. The kingship was elective and the office appears to have tended to remain in the same family. The Senate, however, had to approve the candidate, and the *imperium* was formally granted by a vote of the people in assembly. The basic character of Roman government was already clear: great power was granted to executive officers, but it had to be approved by the Senate and was derived ultimately from the people.

In theory and law the king was the commander of the army, the chief priest, and the supreme judge. He could make decisions in foreign affairs, call out the army, lead it in battle, and impose discipline on his troops, all by virtue of his *imperium*. In practice the royal power was much more limited. The second branch of the early Roman government was the Senate. Tradition says that Romulus, Rome's legendary first king, chose 100 of Rome's leading men to advise him. Later the number rose to 300, where it stayed through

Like the Egyptians, the Etruscans also believed that a person's spirit would continue to live well after death if a tomb were properly equipped. In this tomb, all the tools and utensils a person might need in the afterlife are carved on the walls. [Alinari/Art Resource]

most of the history of the republic. Ostensibly the Senate had neither executive nor legislative power; it met only when summoned by the king and then only to advise him. In reality its authority was great, for the senators, like the king, served for life. The Senate, therefore, had continuity and experience, and as it was composed of the most powerful men in the state, it could not lightly be ignored.

In early Rome citizenship required descent from Roman parents on both sides. All citizens were organized into the third branch of government, the curiate assembly made up of thirty groups. It met only when summoned by the king; he determined the agenda, made proposals, and recognized other speakers, if any. For the most part the assembly was called to listen and approve. Voting was not by head but by group; a majority within each group determined its vote, and the decisions were made by majority vote of the groups. Group voting was typical of all Roman assemblies in the future.

The Family

The center of Roman life was the family. At its head stood the father, whose power and authority within the family resembled those of the king within the state. Over his children he held broad powers analogous to *imperium* in the state, for he had the right to sell his children into slavery, and he even had the power of life and death over them. Over his wife he had less power; he could not sell his wife or kill her. As the king's power was more limited in practice than in theory so it was with the father. His power to dispose of his children was limited by consultation with the family, by public opinion, and, most of all, by tradition. The wife could not be divorced except for stated serious offenses, and even then she had to be convicted by a court made up of her male blood relatives. The Roman woman had a respected position and the main responsibility for managing the household. The father was the chief priest of the family. He led it in daily prayers to the dead that reflected the ancestor worship central to the Roman family and state.

Clientage

Clientage was one of Rome's most important institutions. The client was "an inferior entrusted, by custom or by himself, to the protection of a stranger more powerful than he, and rendering certain services and observances in return for this protection."[1] The Romans spoke of a client as being in the *fides,* or trust, of his patron, so that the relationship always had moral implications. The patron provided his client with protection, both physical and legal; he gave him economic assistance in the form of a land grant, the opportunity to work as a tenant farmer or a laborer on the patron's land, or simply handouts. In return the client would fight for his patron, work his land, and support him politically. These mutual obligations were enforced by public opinion and tradition. When early custom was codified in the mid-fifth century B.C., one of the twelve tablets of laws announced: "Let the patron who has defrauded his client be accursed." In the early history of Rome, patrons were rich and powerful whereas clients were poor and weak, but as time passed it was not uncommon for rich and powerful members of the upper classes to become clients of even more powerful men, chiefly for political purposes. Because the client–patron relationship was hereditary and was sanctioned by religion and custom, it was to play a very important part in the life of the Roman Republic.

Patricians and Plebeians

In the royal period, Roman society was divided in two by a class distinction based on

[1]E. Badian, *Foreign Clientelae* (264–70 B.C.) (Oxford, 1958), p. 1.

A patrician with portraits of his ancestors. Roman patricians took great pride in their lineage and would not marry outside their own group. [German Archaelogical Institute, Rome]

birth. The upper class was composed of the patricians, the wealthy men who held a monopoly of power and influence. They alone could conduct the religious ceremonies in the state, sit in the Senate, or hold office, and they formed a closed caste by forbidding marriage outside their own group. The plebeians must originally have been the poor and dependent men who were small farmers, laborers, and artisans, the clients of the nobility. As Rome and her population grew in various ways, families that were rich but outside the charmed circle gained citizenship. From very early times, therefore, there were rich plebeians, and incompetence and bad luck must have produced some poor patricians. The line between the classes and the monopoly of privileges remained firm, nevertheless, and the struggle of the plebeians to gain equality occupied more than two centuries of republican history.

The Republic and Its Constitution

Roman tradition tells us that the republic replaced the monarchy at Rome suddenly in 509 B.C. as the result of a revolution sparked by the outrageous behavior of the last kings and led by the noble families.

The Consuls

The Roman constitution was an unwritten accumulation of laws and customs that had won respect and the force of law over time.

The lictors, such as those pictured here, attended the chief Roman magistrates when they appeared in public. Note that one lictor carries an axe, while two others bear a bundle of wooden staffs. This symbolizes the power and the limits on the power of Roman magistrates to inflict corporal punishment on Roman citizens. Within the boundaries of the city of Rome, no citizen could be punished without a trial. To symbolize this the lictors in Rome carried bound-up staffs. Outside of the city, however, magistrates had the authority as commanders of the army to put anyone to death without a trial. This power was symbolized by their lictors bearing an axe. [Alinari/Art Resource]

The Romans were a conservative people, so they were never willing to deprive their chief magistrates of the great powers exercised by the monarchs. They elected two patricians to the office of consul and endowed them with *imperium.* They were assisted by two financial officials called *quaestors,* whose number ultimately reached eight. Like the kings, the consuls led the army, had religious duties, and served as judges. They retained the visible symbols of royalty—the purple robe, the ivory chair, and the *lictors* (minor officials) bearing rods and axe who accompanied them—but their power was limited legally and institutionally as well as by custom.

The vast power of the consulship was granted not for life but only for a year. Each consul could prevent any action by his colleague by simply saying no to his proposal, and the religious powers of the consuls were shared with others. Even the *imperium* was limited, for though the consuls had full powers of life and death while leading an army, within the sacred boundary of the city of Rome the citizens had the right to appeal to the popular assembly all cases involving capital punishment. Besides, after their one year in office, the consuls would spend the rest of their lives as members of the Senate. It was a most reckless consul who failed to ask the advice of the Senate or who failed to follow it when there was general agreement.

The many checks on consular action tended to prevent initiative, swift action, and change, but this was just what a conservative, traditional, aristocratic republic wanted. Only in the military sphere did divided counsel and a short term of office create important problems. The Romans tried to get around the difficulties by sending only one consul into the field or, when this was impossible, allowing the consuls sole command on alternate days. In really serious crises, the consuls, with the advice of the Senate, could appoint a single man, the *dictator,* to the command and could retire in his favor. The *dictator's* term of office was limited to six months, but his own *imperium* was valid both inside and outside the city without appeal. These devices worked well enough in the early years of the republic, when Rome's battles were near home, but longer wars and more sophisticated opponents revealed the system's weaknesses and required significant changes.

Long campaigns prompted the invention of the proconsulship in 325 B.C., whereby the term of a consul serving in the field was ex-

Polybius Summarizes the Roman Constitution

Polybius (ca. 203–120 B.C.) was a Greek from the city of Megalopolis, an important member of the Achaean League. As a hostage in Rome he became a friend of influential Romans and later wrote a history of Rome's conquest of the Mediterranean lands. He praised the Roman constitution as an excellent example of a "mixed constitution" and as a major source of Roman success.

As for the Roman constitution, it had three elements, each of them possessing sovereign powers: and their respective share of power in the whole state had been regulated with such a scrupulous regard to equality and equilibrium, that no one could say for certain, not even a native, whether the constitution as a whole were an aristocracy or democracy or despotism. . . .

. . . .

The result of this power of the several estates for mutual help or harm is a union sufficiently firm for all emergencies, and a constitution than which it is impossible to find a better. For whenever any danger from without compels them to unite and work together, the strength which is developed by the State is so extraordinary, that everything required is unfailingly carried out by the eager rivalry shown by all classes to devote their whole minds to the need of the hour, and to secure that any determination come to should not fail for want of promptitude; while each individual works, privately and publicly alike, for the accomplishment of the business in hand. Accordingly, the peculiar constitution of the State makes it irresistible, and certain of obtaining whatever it determines to attempt. . . . For when any one of the three classes becomes puffed up, and manifests an inclination to be contentious and unduly encroaching, the mutual interdependency of all the three, and the possibility of the pretensions of any one being checked and thwarted by the others, must plainly check this tendency: and so the proper equilibrium is maintained by the impulsiveness of the one part being checked by its fear of the other. . . .

Polybius, *Histories*, Vol. 1, trans. by E. S. Shuckburgh (Bloomington: Indiana University Press, 1962), pp. 468, 473–474.

tended. This innovation contained the seeds of many troubles for the constitution.

The introduction of the office of *praetor* also helped provide commanders for Rome's many campaigns. The basic function of the praetors was judicial, but they also had *imperium* and served as generals. By the end of the republic, there were eight praetors, whose annual terms, like the consuls', could be extended for military commands when necessary.

At first, the consuls classified the citizens according to age and property, the bases of citizenship and assignment in the army. After the middle of the fifth century B.C., two censors were elected to perform this duty. They conducted a census and drew up the citizen rolls, but this was no job for clerks. The classification fixed taxation and status, so that the censors had to be men of reputation, former consuls. The censors soon acquired additional powers. By the fourth century they compiled the roll of senators and could strike senators from that roll not only for financial reasons but for moral reasons as well. As the prestige of the office grew, it came to be considered the ultimate prize of a Roman political career.

The Senate and the Assembly

The end of the monarchy increased the influence and power of the Senate. It became the single continuous deliberative body in the Roman state. Its members were leading patricians, often leaders of clans and patrons of many clients. The Senate soon gained control of finances and of foreign policy. Its formal advice was not lightly ignored either by magistrates or by popular assemblies.

The most important assembly in the early republic was the centuriate assembly. In a sense, it was the Roman army acting in a political capacity, and its basic unit was the century, theoretically 100 fighting men classified according to their weapons, armor, and equipment. Because each man equipped himself, this meant that the organization was by classes according to wealth.

The assembly met on the Campus Martius, the drill field of the Roman army, convened by a military trumpet. Voting was by century and proceeded in order of classification from the cavalry down. The assembly elected the consuls and several other magistrates, voted on bills put before it, made decisions of war and peace, and also served as the court of appeal against decisions of the magistrates affecting the life or property of a citizen. In theory it had final authority, but the Senate exercised great, if informal, influence.

The Struggle of the Orders

The laws and constitution of the early republic clearly reflected the class structure of the Roman state, for they gave to the patricians almost a monopoly of power and privilege. Plebeians were barred from public office, from priesthoods, and from other public religious offices. They could not serve as judges, they could not even know the law, for there was no published legal code. The only law was traditional practice, and that existed only in the minds and actions of patrician magistrates. Plebeians were subject to the *imperium* but could not exercise its power. They were not allowed to marry patricians. When Rome acquired new land by conquest, patrician magistrates distributed it in a way that favored patricians. The patricians dominated the assemblies and the

Senate. The plebeians undertook a campaign to achieve political, legal, and social equality, and this attempt, which succeeded after two centuries of intermittent effort, is called the *struggle of the orders*.

The most important source of plebeian success was the need for their military service. Rome was at war almost constantly, and the patricians were forced to call on the plebeians to defend the state. According to tradition, the plebeians, angered by patrician resistance to their demands, withdrew from the city and camped on the Sacred Mount. There they formed a plebeian tribal assembly and elected plebeian tribunes to protect them from the arbitrary power of the magistrates. They declared the tribune inviolate and sacrosanct, and anyone laying violent hands on him was accursed and liable to death without trial. By extension of his right to protect the plebeians, the tribune gained the power to veto any action of a magistrate or any bill in a Roman assembly or the Senate. The plebeian assembly voted by tribe, and a vote of the assembly was binding on plebeians. They tried to make their decisions binding on all Romans but could not do so until 287 B.C.

The next step was for the plebeians to obtain access to the laws, and by 450 B.C. the Twelve Tables codified early Roman custom in all its harshness and simplicity. In 445 B.C. plebeians gained the right to marry patricians. The main prize was consulship. The patricians did not yield easily, but at last, in 367 B.C., the Licinian–Sextian Laws provided that at least one consul could be a plebeian. Before long plebeians held other offices, even the dictatorship and the censorship. In 300 B.C. they were admitted to the most important priesthoods, the last religious barrier to equality. In 287 B.C. the plebeians completed their triumph. They once again withdrew from the city and secured the passage of a law whereby decisions of the plebeian assembly bound all Romans and did not require the approval of the Senate.

It might seem that the Roman aristocracy had given way under the pressure of the lower class, but the victory of the plebeians did not bring democracy. An aristocracy based strictly on birth had given way to an aristocracy more subtle, but no less restricted, based on a combination of wealth and birth. The significant distinction was no longer between patrician and plebeian but between the *nobiles*—a relatively small group of wealthy and powerful families, both patrician and plebeian, whose members

THE RISE OF THE PLEBEIANS TO EQUALITY IN ROME

Kings expelled; republic founded	509 B.C.
Laws of the Twelve Tables published	450–449 B.C.
Plebeians gain right of marriage with patricians	445 B.C.
Licinian–Sextian Laws open consulship to plebeians	367 B.C.
Plebeians attain chief priesthoods	300 B.C.
Laws passed by Plebeian Assembly made binding on all Romans	287 B.C.

attained the highest offices in the state—and everyone else. The absence of the secret ballot in the assemblies enabled the *nobiles* to control most decisions and elections by a combination of intimidation and bribery. The leading families, although in constant competition with one another for office, power, and prestige, often combined in marriage and less formal alliances to keep the political plums within their own group. In the century from 233 to 133 B.C., for instance, twenty-six families provided 80 per cent of the consuls and only ten families accounted for almost 50 per cent. These same families dominated the Senate, whose power became ever greater. It remained the only continuous deliberative body in the state, and the pressure of warfare gave it experience in handling public business. Rome's success brought the Senate prestige, increased control of policy, and confidence in its capacity to rule. The end of the struggle of the orders brought domestic peace under a republican constitution dominated by a capable, if narrow, senatorial aristocracy. This outcome satisfied most Romans outside the ruling group because Rome conquered Italy and brought many benefits to its citizens.

The Conquest of Italy

Not long after the fall of the monarchy in 509 B.C., a coalition of Romans, Latins, and Italian Greeks defeated the Etruscans and drove them out of Latium for good. Throughout the fifth century B.C., the powerful Etruscan city of Veii, only twelve miles north of the Tiber River, raided Roman territory. After a hard struggle and a long siege, the Romans took it in 392 B.C., more than doubling the size of Rome. Roman policy toward defeated enemies used both the carrot and the stick. When they made friendly alliances with some, they gained new soldiers for their army. When they treated others more harshly by annexing their land, they achieved a similar end, for service in the Roman army was based on property, and the distribution to poor Romans of conquered land made soldiers of previously useless men. It also gave the poor a stake in Rome and reduced the pressure against its aristocratic regime. The long siege of Veii kept soldiers from their farms during the campaign. From that time on the Romans paid their soldiers, thus giving their army greater flexibility and a more professional quality.

ROMAN EXPANSION IN ITALY	
Fall of Veii; Etruscans defeated	392 B.C.
Gauls burn Rome	387 B.C.
Latin League defeated	338 B.C.
Battle of Sentinum; Samnites and allies defeated	295 B.C.
Pyrrhus driven from Italy	275 B.C.
Rome rules Italy south of the Po River	265 B.C.

Gallic Invasion of Italy and Roman Reaction

At the beginning of the fourth century B.C. the Romans were the chief power in central Italy, but a disaster struck. In 387 B.C. the Gauls, barbaric Celtic tribes from across the Alps, defeated the Roman army and captured, looted, and burned Rome. The Gauls sought plunder, not conquest, so they extorted a ransom from the Romans and returned to their homes in the north. Rome's power appeared to have been wiped out. When the Gauls left, some of Rome's allies and old enemies tried to take advantage of its weakness, but by about 350 B.C. the Romans had recovered their leadership of central Italy and were more dominant than ever. Their success in turning back new Gallic raids added still more to their power and prestige. As the Romans tightened their grip on Latium, the Latins became resentful. In 340 B.C. they demanded independence from Rome or full equality, and when the Romans refused, they launched a war of independence that lasted until 338. The victorious Romans dissolved the Latin League, and their treatment of the defeated opponents provided a model for the settlement of Italy.

Roman Policy Toward the Conquered

The Romans did not destroy any of the Latin cities or their people, nor did they treat them all alike. Some in the vicinity of Rome received full Roman citizenship; others farther away gained municipal status, which gave them the private rights of intermarriage and commerce with Romans but not the public rights of voting and holding office in Rome. They retained the rights of local self-government and could obtain full Roman citizenship if they moved to Rome. They followed Rome in foreign policy and provided soldiers to serve in the Roman legions.

117

Still other states became allies of Rome on the basis of treaties, which differed from city to city. Some were given the private rights of intermarriage and commerce with Romans and some were not; the allied states were always forbidden to exercise these rights with one another. Some, but not all, were allowed local autonomy. Land was taken from some but not from others, nor was the percentage always the same. All the allies supplied troops to the army, in which they fought in auxiliary battalions under Roman officers, but they did not pay taxes to Rome.

On some of the conquered land the Romans placed colonies, permanent settlements of veteran soldiers in the territory of recently defeated enemies. The colonists retained their Roman citizenship and enjoyed home rule, and in return for the land they had been given, they served as a kind of permanent garrison to deter or suppress rebellion. These colonies were usually connected to Rome by a network of military roads built as straight as possible and so durable that some are used even today. They guaranteed that a Roman army could swiftly reinforce an embattled colony or put down an uprising in any weather.

The Roman settlement of Latium reveals even more clearly than before the principles by which Rome was able to conquer and dominate Italy for many centuries. The excellent army and the diplomatic skill that allowed Rome to separate its enemies help to explain its conquests. The reputation for harsh punish-

The Via Latina was part of the network of military roads that tied all Italy to Rome. These roads enabled Roman legions to move swiftly to enforce their control of Italy. The Via Latina dates from the fourth century B.C. [Fototeca Unione]

Livy Describes Rome's Treatment of the Italians

Livy (59 B.C.–A.D. 17) wrote a history of Rome from its origins until his own time. The following passage describes the different kinds of treatment Rome gave to the defeated Latin cities after their revolt in the years 340–338 B.C.

The principal members of the senate applauded the consul's statement on the business on the whole; but said that, as the states were differently circumstanced, their plan might be readily adjusted and determined according to the desert of each, if they should put the question regarding each state specifically. The question was therefore so put regarding each separately and a decree passed. To the people of Lanuvium the right of citizenship was granted, and the exercise of their religious rights was restored to them with this provision, that the temple and grove of Juno Sospita should be common between the Lanuvian burghers and the Roman people. The peoples of Aricia, Nomentum, and Pedum were admitted into the number of citizens on the same terms as the Lanuvians. To the Tusculans the rights of citizenship which they already possessed were continued; no public penalty was imposed and the crime of rebellion was visited on its few instigators. On the people of Velitrae, Roman citizens of long standing, measures of great severity were inflicted because they had so often rebelled; their walls were razed, and their senate deported and ordered to dwell on the other side of the Tiber; any individual who should be caught on the hither side of the river should be fined one thousand asses, and the person who had apprehended him should not discharge his prisoner from confinement until the money was paid down. Into the lands of the senators colonists were sent; by their addition Velitrae recovered its former populous appearance.

Livy, *History of Rome*, Vol. 1, trans. by D. Spillan et al. (New York: American Book Company, n.d.), p. 561.

ment of rebels and the sure promise that such punishment would be delivered, made unmistakably clear by the presence of colonies and military roads, help to account for the slowness to revolt. But the positive side, represented by Rome's organization of the defeated states, is at least as important. The Romans did not regard the status given each newly conquered city as permanent. They held out to loyal allies the prospect of improving their status, even of achieving the ultimate prize, full Roman citizenship. In so doing, the Romans gave their allies a stake in Rome's future and success and a sense of being colleagues, though subordinate ones, rather than subjects. The result, in general, was that most of Rome's allies remained loyal even when put to the severest test.

Defeat of the Samnites

The next great challenge to Roman arms came in a series of wars with a tough mountain people of the southern Appenines, the Sam-nites. Some of Rome's allies rebelled, and soon the Etruscans and Gauls joined in the war against Rome. But most of the allies remained loyal. In 295 B.C., at Sentinum, the Romans defeated an Italian coalition, and by 280 they were masters of central Italy. Their power extended from the Po valley south to Apulia and Lucania.

The victory over the Samnites brought the Romans into direct contact with the Greek cities of southern Italy. Roman intervention in a quarrel between Greek cities brought them face to face with Pyrrhus, king of Epirus. Pyrrhus, probably the best general of his time, commanded a well-disciplined and experienced mercenary army, which he hired out for profit, and a new weapon: twenty war elephants. He defeated the Romans twice but suffered many casualties. When one of his officers rejoiced at the victory, Pyrrhus told him, "If we win one more battle against the Romans we shall be completely ruined." This "Pyrrhic" victory led him to withdraw to Sicily in 275 B.C. The Greek cities that had hired him were

Pyrrhus, king of Epirus (295–272 B.C.), in what is today Albania. Pyrrhus was one of the greatest generals of his time, but his victories against the Romans were too costly to be sustained. [Alinari/Art Resource]

forced to join the Roman confederation. By 265 B.C. Rome ruled all Italy as far north as the Po River, an area of 47,200 square miles. The year after the defeat of Pyrrhus, Ptolemy Philadelphus, king of Egypt, sent a message of congratulation to establish friendly relations with Rome. This act recognized Rome's new status as a power in the Hellenistic world.

Rome and Carthage

Rome's acquisition of coastal territory and her expansion to the toe of the Italian boot brought her face to face with the great naval power of the western Mediterranean, Carthage (see Map 4.2). Late in the ninth century B.C. the Phoenician city of Tyre had planted a colony on the coast of northern Africa near modern Tunis, calling it the New City, or Carthage. In the sixth century B.C. the conquest of Phoenicia by the Assyrians and the Persians made Carthage independent and free to exploit its very advantageous situation. The city was located on a defensible site and commanded an excellent harbor that encouraged commerce. The coastal

plain grew abundant grain, fruits, and vegetables. An inland plain allowed sheep herding. The Phoenician settlers conquered the native inhabitants and used them to work the land. Beginning in the sixth century B.C. the Carthaginians expanded their domain to include the coast of northern Africa west beyond the Straits of Gibraltar and eastward into Libya. Overseas they came to control the southern part of Spain, Sardinia, Corsica, Malta, the Balearic Islands, and western Sicily. The people of these territories, though originally allies, were all reduced to subjection like the natives of the Carthaginian home territory, and they all served in the Carthaginian army or navy and paid tribute. Carthage also profited greatly from the mines of Spain and from an absolute monopoly of trade imposed on the western Mediterranean.

Early relations between Rome and Carthage had been few but not unfriendly. Because Rome was neither a commercial nor a naval state and Carthage had no designs on central Italy, there was no reason for conflict. But an attack by Hiero, tyrant of Syracuse, on the Sicilian city of Messana just across from Italy caused trouble. Messana was held by a group of Italian mercenary soldiers who called themselves *Mamertines,* the sons of the war god Mars. Some years earlier they had seized the city, killed the men, taken the women, and launched a career of piracy, extortion, and attacks on their neighbors. When Hiero defeated the Mamertines, some of them called on the Cathaginians to help save their city. Carthage agreed and sent a garrison, for the Carthaginians wanted to prevent Syracuse from dominating the straits. One Mamertine faction, however, fearing that Carthage might take undue advantage of the opportunity, asked Rome for help.

In 264 B.C. the request came to the Senate, where it was debated at length, and rightly so, for the issue was momentous. The Punic garrison (the Romans called the Carthaginians *Phoenicians;* in Latin the word is *Poeni* or *Puni,* hence the adjective *Punic*) was in place at Messana. The Romans knew that intervention would not be against Syracuse but against the mighty empire of Carthage, a powerful state that was getting too close to Italy. Unless Rome intervened, Carthage would gain control of all Sicily and the straits. The assembly voted to protect the Mamertines, sent an army to Messana, and expelled the Punic garrison. The First Punic War was on.

THE WESTERN MEDITERRANEAN
AREA DURING THE RISE OF ROME

MAP 4-2 *This map covers the theater of the conflicts between the growing Roman dominions and those of Carthage in the third century B.C. The Carthaginian empire stretched westward from the city (in modern Tunisia) along the North African coast and into southern Spain.*

The First Punic War (264–241 B.C.)

The war in Sicily soon settled into a stalemate. At last the Romans built a fleet to cut off supplies to the besieged Carthaginian cities at the western end of Sicily. When Carthage sent its own fleet to raise the siege, the Romans destroyed it. In 241 B.C. Carthage signed a treaty giving up Sicily and the islands between Italy and Sicily and agreed to pay a war indemnity in ten annual installments, to keep its ships out of Italian waters, and not to recruit mercenaries in Italy. Neither side was to attack the allies of the other. Rome had earned Sicily, and Carthage could well afford the indemnity. The peace reflected reality without undue harshness. It left Carthage most of its empire and its self-respect and created no obvious grounds for future conflict. If the treaty had been carried out in good faith, it might have brought lasting peace.

The treaty did not bring peace to Carthage, even for the moment. A rebellion broke out among the Carthaginian mercenaries, newly recruited from Sicily and demanding their pay. In 238 B.C., while Carthage was still in danger, Rome seized Sardinia and Corsica and de-

manded that Carthage pay an additional indemnity. This was a harsh and cynical action by the Romans; even the historian Polybius, a great champion of Rome, could find no justification for it. The Romans were moved, no doubt, by the fear of giving Carthage a base so near Italy, but their action was unwise. It undid the calming effects of the peace of 241

THE PUNIC WARS	
First Punic War	264–241 B.C.
Rome seizes Sardinia and Corsica	238 B.C.
Hannibal takes command of Punic army in Spain	221 B.C.
Second Punic War	218–202 B.C.
Battle of Cannae	216 B.C.
Scipio takes New Carthage	209 B.C.
Battle of Zama	202 B.C.
Third Punic War	149–146 B.C.
Destruction of Carthage	146 B.C.

122

*The
Foundations of
Western
Civilization in
the Ancient
World*

B.C. and angered the Carthaginians without preventing them from recovering their strength to seek vengeance in the future.

The Roman conquest of territory overseas presented a new problem. Instead of following the policy they had pursued in Italy, the Romans made Sicily a province and Sardinia and Corsica another. It became common to extend the term of the governors of these provinces beyond a year. The governors were unchecked by colleagues and exercised full *imperium*. New magistracies, in effect, were thus created free of the limits put on the power of officials in Rome. The new populations were neither Roman citizens nor allies; they were subjects who did not serve in the army but paid tribute instead. The old practice of extending citizenship and, with it, loyalty to Rome stopped at the borders of Italy. Rome collected the new taxes by ''farming'' them out at auction to the highest bidder. At first, the tax collectors were natives from the same province, later Roman allies, and finally Roman citizens below senatorial rank who became powerful and wealthy by squeezing the provincials hard. These innovations were the basis for Rome's imperial organization in the future; in time they strained the constitution and traditions of Rome to such a degree as to threaten the existence of the republic.

After the First Punic War, campaigns against the Gauls and across the Adriatic distracted Rome. Meanwhile Hamilcar Barca was leading Carthage on the road to recovery. Hamilcar sought to compensate for losses elsewhere by building a Punic empire in Spain. As governor of Spain from 237 B.C. until his death in 229 B.C., he improved the ports and their commerce, exploited the mines, gained control of the hinterland, won over many of the conquered tribes, and built a strong and disciplined army.

Hamilcar's successor, his son-in-law Hasdrubal, pursued the same policies. His success alarmed the Romans, and they imposed a treaty in which he promised not to take an army north across the Ebro River in Spain, although Punic expansion in Spain was well south of that river at the time of the treaty. Even though the agreement preserved the appearance of Rome's giving orders to an inferior, the treaty gave equal benefits to both sides: if the Carthaginians agreed to accept the limit of the Ebro on their expansion in Spain, the Romans would not interfere with that expansion.

The Second Punic War (218–202 B.C.)

On Hasdrubal's assassination in 221 B.C. the army chose as his successor Hannibal, son of Hamilcar Barca, still a young man of twenty-five. He quickly consolidated and extended the Punic Empire in Spain. A few years before his accession Rome had received an offer from the people of the Spanish town of Saguntum, about one hundred miles south of the Ebro, to become the friends of Rome. The Romans accepted, thereby accepting the responsibilities of friendship with a foreign state. The Roman association with Saguntum may not have violated the letter of the Ebro treaty, but it certainly was contrary to its spirit. At first, Hannibal was careful to avoid interfering with the friends of Rome, but the Saguntines, confident of Rome's protection, began to interfere with some of the Spanish tribes allied with Hannibal.

Finally, the Romans sent an embassy to Hannibal warning him to let Saguntum alone and repeating the injunction not to cross the Ebro. The Romans probably expected Hannibal to yield as his predecessors had, but they misjudged their man. Hannibal ignored Rome's warning, besieged Saguntum, and took the town.

On hearing of Saguntum's fall, the Romans sent an ultimatum to Carthage demanding the surrender of Hannibal. Carthage refused, and Rome declared war in 218 B.C. Rome's policy between the wars had been the worst possible combination of approaches. Rome had insulted and injured Carthage by the annexation of Sardinia in 238 B.C. and had repeatedly provoked and insulted Carthage by interventions in Spain. But Roman policy took no measures to prevent the construction of a powerful and dangerous Punic Empire or even to build defenses against a Punic attack from Spain. Hannibal saw to it that the Romans paid the price for their blunders. By September of 218 B.C. he was across the Alps. His army was weary, bedraggled, and greatly reduced, but he was in Italy and among the friendly Gauls.

Hannibal defeated the Romans at the Ticinus River and crushed the joint consular armies at the Trebia River. In 217 B.C. he outmaneuvered and trapped another army at Lake Trasimene. Hannibal's first victory brought him reinforcements of fifty thousand Gauls, and his second confirmed that his superior generalship could defeat the Roman army. The key to success, however, would be defection by Rome's allies. Hannibal released Italian prisoners without harm or ransom and moved his army south of Rome to encourage rebellion. But the allies remained firm, perhaps because Hannibal was accompanied by the hated Gauls, perhaps because they were not convinced yet of Rome's ultimate defeat, and perhaps even out of loyalty to Rome.

Sobered by their defeats, the Romans elected Quintus Fabius Maximus dictator. He understood that Hannibal could not be beaten by the usual tactics and that the Roman army, decimated and demoralized, needed time to recover. His strategy was to avoid battle while following and harassing Hannibal's army. When the Roman army had recovered and Fabius could fight Hannibal on favorable ground, only then would the Romans fight.

In 216 B.C. Hannibal marched to Cannae in Apulia to tempt the Romans into another open fight. The Romans could not allow him to ravage the country freely, so they sent off an army of some eighty thousand men to meet him. Almost the entire Roman army was killed or captured. It was the worst defeat in Roman history; Rome's prestige was shattered, and most of her allies in southern Italy as well as Syracuse in Sicily now went over to Hannibal. In 215 B.C. Philip V, king of Macedon, made an alliance with Hannibal and launched a war to recover his influence on the Adriatic. For more than a decade no Roman army would dare face Hannibal in the open field, and he was free to roam over all Italy and do as he pleased.

Hannibal had neither the numbers nor the supplies to besiege such walled cities as Rome and the major allies, nor did he have the equipment to take them by assault. To win the war in Spain, the Romans appointed Publius Cornelius Scipio (237–183 B.C.), later called Africanus, to the command in Spain with proconsular *imperium*. This was such a breach of tradition as to be almost unconstitutional, for

The Origins of the Hannibalic War

The Second Punic War was often called the Hannibalic War after the brilliant Carthaginian general who launched it. The Roman historian Livy wrote some two centuries after the event, and his account of its origin presents what had become an orthodox Roman view.

I may be permitted to premise at this division of my work, what most historians have professed at the beginning of their whole undertaking; that I am about to relate the most memorable of all wars that were ever waged: the war which the Carthaginians, under the conduct of Hannibal, maintained with the Roman people. For never did any states and nations more efficient in their resources engage in contest; nor had they themselves at any other period so great a degree of power and energy. They brought into action too no arts of war unknown to each other, but those which had been tried in the first Punic war; and so various was the fortune of the conflict, and so doubtful the victory, that they who conquered were more exposed to danger. The hatred with which they fought also was almost greater than their resources; the Romans being indignant that the conquered aggressively took up arms against their victors; the Carthaginians, because

they considered that in their subjection it had been lorded over them with haughtiness and avarice. There is besides a story, that Hannibal, when about nine years old, while he boyishly coaxed his father Hamilcar that he might be taken to Spain, (at the time when the African war was completed, and he was employed in sacrificing previously to transporting his army thither,) was conducted to the altar; and, having laid his hand on the offerings, was bound by an oath to prove himself, as soon as he could, an enemy to the Roman people. The loss of Sicily and Sardinia grieved the high spirit of Hamilcar: for he deemed that Sicily had been given up through a premature despair of their affairs; and that Sardinia, during the disturbances in Africa, had been treacherously taken by the Romans, while, in addition, the payment of a tribute had been imposed.

Livy, 21. 1–18, trans. by D. Spiller and C. Edmonds.

A war elephant, such as Hannibal brought over the Alps into Italy. Fighting elephants were the heavy tanks of ancient warfare. [Ronald Sheridan's Photo Library]

(Below) Scipio Africanus, who conquered Spain and decisively defeated Hannibal at Zama in 202 B.C. [Alinari/ Art Resource]

Scipio was not yet twenty-five and had held no high office. But he was a general almost as talented as Hannibal. In 209 B.C. he captured New Carthage, the main Punic base in Spain. His skillful and tactful treatment of the native Iberians won them away from the enemy and over to his own army. Within a few years young Scipio had conquered all Spain and had deprived Hannibal of hope of help from that region.

In 204 B.C. Scipio landed in Africa, defeated the Carthaginians, and forced them to accept a peace whose main clause was the withdrawal of Hannibal and his army from Italy. Hannibal had won every battle but lost the war, for he had not counted on the determination of Rome and the loyalty of her allies. Hannibal's return inspired Carthage to break the peace and to risk all in battle. In 202 B.C. Scipio and Hannibal faced each other at the battle of Zama. The generalship of Scipio and the desertion of Hannibal's mercenaries gave the victory to Rome. The new peace terms reduced Carthage to the status of a dependent ally to Rome. The Second Punic War ended the Carthaginian command of the western Mediterranean and Carthage's term as a great power. Rome ruled the seas and the entire Mediterranean coast from Italy westward.

The Republic's Conquest of the Hellenistic World

The East

By the middle of the third century B.C. the eastern Mediterranean had reached a condition of stability. It was based on a balance of power among the three great kingdoms, and even lesser states had an established place. That equilibrium was threatened by the activities of two aggressive monarchs, Philip V of Macedon (221–179 B.C.) and Antiochus III of the Seleucid kingdom (223–187 B.C.). Philip and Antiochus moved swiftly, the latter against Syria and Palestine, the former against cities in the Aegean, in the Hellespontine region, and on the coast of Asia Minor.

The threat that a more powerful Macedon might pose to Rome's friends and, perhaps, even to Italy was enough to persuade the Romans to intervene.

In 200 B.C. the Romans sent an ultimatum to Philip ordering him not to attack any Greek city and to pay reparations to Pergamum. These orders were meant to provoke, not avoid, war, and Philip refused to obey. Two years later the Romans sent out a talented young general, Flamininus, who demanded that Philip withdraw from Greece entirely. In 197 B.C., with Greek support, he defeated Philip in the hills of Cynoscephalae in Thessaly, bringing an end to the Second Macedonian War (the first had been fought while the Romans were still occupied with Carthage, from 215 to 205 B.C.). The Greek cities freed from Philip were made autonomous, and in 196 B.C. Flamininus proclaimed the freedom of the Greeks.

Soon after the Romans withdrew from Greece, they came into conflict with Antiochus, who was expanding his power in Asia and on the European side of the Hellespont. On the pretext of freeing the Greeks from Roman domination, he landed an army on the Greek mainland. The Romans routed Antiochus at Thermopylae and quickly drove him from Greece, and in 189 B.C. they crushed his army at Magnesia in Asia Minor. The peace of Apamia in the next year deprived Antiochus of his elephants and his navy and imposed a huge indemnity on him. Once again, the Romans took no territory for themselves and left a number of Greek cities in Asia free. They continued their policy of regarding Greece, and now Asia Minor, as a kind of protectorate in which they could intervene or not as they chose.

In 179 B.C. Perseus succeeded Philip V as king of Macedon. He tried to gain popularity in Greece by favoring the democratic and revolutionary forces in the cities. The Romans, troubled by this threat to stability, launched the Third Macedonian War (172–168 B.C.), and in 168 Aemilius Paullus defeated Perseus at Pydna. The peace imposed by the Romans reveals a change in policy and a growing harshness. It divided Macedon into four separate republics, whose citizens were forbidden to intermarry or even to do business across the new national boundaries.

The new policy reflected a change in Rome

ROMAN ENGAGEMENT OVERSEAS	
First Macedonian War	215–205 B.C.
Second Macedonian War	200–197 B.C.
Proclamation of Greek freedom by Flamininus at Corinth	196 B.C.
Battle of Magnesia; Antiochus defeated in Asia Minor	189 B.C.
Third Macedonian War	172–168 B.C.
Battle of Pydna	168 B.C.
Roman wars in Spain	154–133 B.C.
Numantia taken	134 B.C.

from the previous relatively gentle one to the stern and businesslike approach favored by the conservative censor Cato. The new harshness was applied to allies and bystanders as well as to defeated opponents. Leaders of anti-Roman factions in the Greek cities were punished severely.

When Aemilius Paullus returned from his victory, he celebrated a triumph that lasted three days, during which the spoils of war, royal prisoners, and great wealth were paraded through the streets of Rome behind the proud general. The public treasury benefited to such a degree that the direct property tax on Roman citizens was abolished. Part of the booty went to the general and part to his soldiers. New motives were thereby introduced into Roman foreign policy, or, perhaps, old motives were given new prominence. Foreign campaigns could bring profit to the state, rewards to the army, and wealth, fame, honor, and political power to the general.

The West

Harsh as the Romans had become toward the Greeks, they were even worse in their treatment of the people of the Iberian Peninsula, whom they considered barbarians. They committed dreadful atrocities, lied, cheated, and broke treaties in their effort to exploit and pacify the natives, who fought back fiercely in guerrilla style. From 154 to 133 B.C. the fighting waxed, and it became hard to recruit Roman soldiers to fight in the increasingly ugly war. At last, in 134, Scipio Aemilianus took the key city of Numantia by siege, burned it to the ground, and put an end to the war in Spain.

Roman treatment of Carthage was no better.

126

*The
Foundations of
Western
Civilization in
the Ancient
World*

Although Carthage lived up to its treaty with Rome faithfully and posed no threat, some Romans refused to abandon their hatred and fear of the traditional enemy. Cato is said to have ended all his speeches in the Senate with the same sentence: "Ceterum censeo delendam esse Carthaginem" ("Besides, I think that Carthage must be destroyed"). At last the

---

Plutarch Describes a Roman Triumph

In 168 B.C. L. Aemilius Paullus defeated King Perseus in the battle of Pydna, bringing an end to the Third Macedonian War. For his great achievement the Senate granted Paullus the right to celebrate a triumph, the great honorific procession granted only for extraordinary victories and eagerly sought by all Roman generals. Plutarch described the details of Paullus's triumph.

The people erected scaffolds in the forum, in the circuses, as they call their buildings for horse-races, and in all other parts of the city where they could best behold the show. The spectators were clad in white garments; all the temples were open, and full of garlands and perfumes; the ways were cleared and kept open by numerous officers, who drove back all who crowded into or ran across the main avenue. This triumph lasted three days. On the first, which was scarcely long enough for the sight, were to be seen the statues, pictures, and colossal images which were taken from the enemy, drawn upon two hundred and fifty chariots. On the second was carried in a great many wagons the finest and richest armour of the Macedonians, both of brass and steel, all newly polished and glittering; the pieces of which were piled up and arranged purposely with the greatest art, so as to seem to be tumbled in heaps carelessly and by chance: . . .

    .   .   .   .

On the third day, early in the morning, first came the trumpeters, who did not sound as they were wont in a procession or solemn entry, but such a charge as the Romans use when they encourage the soldiers to fight. Next followed young men wearing frocks with ornamented borders, who led to the sacrifice a hundred and twenty stalled oxen, with their horns gilded, and their heads adorned with ribbons and garlands; and with these were boys that carried basins for libation, of silver and gold.

    .   .   .   .

After his children and their attendants came Perseus himself, clad all in black, and wearing the boots of his country, and looking like one altogether stunned and deprived of reason, through the greatness of his misfortunes. Next followed a great company of his friends and familiars, whose countenances were disfigured with grief, and who let the spectators see, by their tears and their continual looking upon Perseus, that it was his fortune they so much lamented, and that they were regardless of their own.

    .   .   .   .

. . . After these were carried four hundred crowns, all made of gold, sent from the cities by their respective deputations to Æmilius, in honour of his victory. Then he himself came, seated on a chariot magnificently adorned (a man well worthy to be looked at, even without these ensigns of power), dressed in a robe of purple, interwoven with gold, and holding a laurel branch in his right hand. All the army, in like manner, with boughs of laurel in their hands, divided into their bands and companies, followed the chariot of their commander; some singing verses, according to the usual custom, mingled with raillery; others, songs of triumph and the praise of Æmilius's deeds; who, indeed, was admired and accounted happy by all men, and unenvied by every one that was good; except so far as it seems the province of some god to lessen that happiness which is too great and inordinate, and so to mingle the affairs of human life that no one should be entirely free and exempt from calamities; but, as we read in Homer, that those should think themselves truly blessed whom fortune has given an equal share of good and evil.

Plutarch, "Aemilius Paullus," in *Lives of the Noble Grecians and Romans*, trans. by John Dryden, rev. by A. H. Clough (New York: Random House, n.d.), pp. 340–341.

Romans took advantage of a technical breach of the peace to destroy Carthage. In 146 B.C. Scipio Aemilianus took the city, plowed up its land, and put salt in the furrows as a symbol of the permanent abandonment of the site. The Romans incorporated it as the province of Africa, one of six Roman provinces, including Sicily, Sardinia–Corsica, Macedonia, Hither Spain, and Further Spain.

Civilization in the Early Roman Republic

Among the most important changes wrought by Roman expansion overseas were those in the Roman style of life and thought brought about by close and continued association with the Greeks of the Hellenistic world. Attitudes toward the Greeks themselves ranged from admiration for their culture and history to contempt for their constant squabbling, their commercial practices, and their weakness. Conservatives such as Cato might speak contemptuously of the Greeks as "Greeklings" (*Graeculi*), but even he learned Greek and absorbed Greek culture. Before long the education of the Roman upper classes was bilingual. In addition to the Twelve Tables young Roman nobles studied Greek rhetoric, literature, and sometimes philosophy. These studies even had an effect on education and the Latin language. As early as the third century B.C. Livius Andronicus, a liberated Greek slave, translated the *Odyssey* into Latin. It became a primer for young Romans and put Latin on the road to becoming a literary language.

The temple of Vesta, at Rome, first century B.C. Vesta was the Roman goddess of the hearth. Her cult included an eternal flame, which was tended by the famous Vestal Virgins. [Art Resource]

Religion

Roman religion was influenced by the Greeks almost from the beginning; the Romans identified their own gods with Greek equivalents and incorporated Greek mythology into their own. For the most part, however, Roman religious practice remained simple and Italian, until the third century B.C. brought important new influences from the east. In 205 the Senate approved the public worship of Cybele, the Great Mother goddess from Phrygia. Hers was a fertility cult accompanied by ecstatic, frenzied, and sensual rites that shocked and outraged conservative Romans to such a degree that they soon banned the cult to Romans. Similarly, the Senate banned the worship of Dionysus, or Bacchus, in 186 B.C. In the second century B.C. interest in Babylonian astrology also grew, and the Senate's attempt in 139 to expel the "Chaldaeans," as the astrologers were called, did not prevent the continued influence of their superstition.

Education

Human society depends on the passing on from generation to generation of the knowledge, skills, and values needed for life in any particular community. A system of education, whether formal or informal, is essential to each culture and reveals its character even as it tries to stamp that character on its children. The education provided in the early centuries of the Roman Republic reflected the limited, conservative, and practical nature of that community of plain farmers and soldiers. Education was entirely the responsibility of the family, the father teaching his own son at home. It is not clear whether in these early times girls received any education, though they certainly did later

127

128

*The
Foundations of
Western
Civilization in
the Ancient
World*

on. The boys learned to read, write, and calculate, and they learned the skills of farming. They memorized the laws of the Twelve Tables, Rome's earliest code of law; learned how to perform the usual religious rites; heard stories of the great deeds of early Roman history and particularly those of their ancestors; and engaged in the physical training appropriate for potential soldiers. This course of study was practical, vocational, and moral. It aimed at making the boys moral, pious, patriotic, law-abiding, and respectful of tradition.

In the third century B.C. the Romans came into contact with the Greeks of southern Italy, and this contact produced momentous changes in Roman education. Greek teachers came to Rome and introduced the study of language, literature, and philosophy, as well as the idea of a liberal education, or what the Romans called *humanitas,* the root of our concept of the humanities. The aim of education changed from the practical, vocational goals of earlier times to an emphasis on broad intellectual training, critical thinking, an interest in ideas, and the development of a well-rounded person.

The first need was to learn Greek, for Rome did not yet have a literature of its own. For this purpose schools were established where the teacher, called a *grammaticus,* taught his students the Greek language and its literature, especially the poets and particularly Homer. Hereafter educated Romans were expected to be bilingual. After the completion of this elementary education, Roman boys of the upper classes studied rhetoric, the art of speaking and writing well, with Greeks who were expert in those arts. For the Greeks rhetoric was a subject of less importance than philosophy, but the more practical Romans took to it avidly, for it was of great use in legal disputes and was becoming ever more valuable in political life. Some Romans, however, were powerfully attracted to Greek literature and philosophy. So important and powerful a Roman aristocrat as Scipio Aemilianus, the man who finally defeated and destroyed Carthage, surrounded himself and his friends with such Greek thinkers as the historian Polybius and the philosopher Panaetius. Other Romans, equally outstanding, such as Cato the Elder, were more conservative and opposed the new learning on

Cato Educates His Son

Marcus Porcius Cato (234–149 B.C.) was a remarkable Roman who rose from humble origins to the highest offices in the state. He stood as the firmest defender of the old Roman traditions at a time when Hellenic ideas were strongly influential. In the following passage Plutarch tells how Cato attended to his son's education.

. . . After the birth of his son, no business could be so urgent, unless it had a public character, as to prevent him from being present when his wife bathed and swaddled the babe. For the mother nursed it herself, and often gave suck also to the infants of her slaves, that so they might come to cherish a brotherly affection for her son. As soon as the boy showed signs of understanding, his father took him under his own charge and taught him to read, although he had an accomplished slave, Chilo by name, who was a schoolteacher, and taught many boys. Still, Cato thought it not right, as he tells us himself, that his son should be scolded by a slave, or have his *ears tweaked when he was slow to learn, still less that he should be indebted to his slave for such a priceless thing as education. He was therefore himself not only the boy's reading-teacher, but his tutor in law, and his athletic trainer, and he taught his son not merely to hurl the javelin and fight in armour and ride the horse, but also to box, to endure heat and cold, and to swim lustily through the eddies and billows of the Tiber. His History of Rome, as he tells us himself, he wrote out with his own hand and in large characters, that his son might have in his own home an aid to acquaintance with his country's ancient traditions.*

Plutarch, *Cato Major,* 20, trans. by Bernadotte Perrin (London and New York: Loeb Classical Library, William Heinemann, 1914).

the grounds that it would weaken Roman moral fiber; they were able on more than one occasion to pass laws expelling philosophers and teachers of rhetoric. But these attempts to go back to older ways failed. The new education suited the needs of the Romans of the second century B.C., who found themselves changing from a rural to an urban society, and who were being thrust into the sophisticated world of Hellenistic Greeks.

By the last century of the Roman Republic, the new Hellenized education had become dominant. Latin literature had come into being along with Latin translations of Greek poets, and these formed part of the course of study, but Roman gentlemen were expected to be bilingual, and Greek language and literature were still central to the curriculum. Many schools were established, and the number of educated people grew, extending beyond the senatorial class to the equestrians and outside Rome to the cities of Italy. Though the evidence is limited, we can be sure that girls of the upper classes were educated similarly to boys, at least through the earlier stages. They were probably taught by tutors at home rather than going to school, as was the increasing fashion among boys in the late republic. Young women did not study with philosophers and rhetoricians, for they were usually married by the age the men were pursuing their higher education. Still, some women found ways to continue their education. Some became prose writers and others poets. By the first century A.D. there were apparently enough learned women to provoke the complaints of a crotchety and conservative satirist:

Portrait bust of a Roman noblewoman from the first century B.C. Roman women had a respectable position and were responsible for managing their households. [M. B. Cookson]

Still more exasperating is the woman who begs as soon as she sits down to dinner, to discourse on poets and poetry, comparing Virgil with Homer; professors, critics, lawyers, auctioneers—even another woman—can't get a word in. She rattles on at such a rate that you'd think that all the pots and pans in the kitchen were crashing to the floor or that every bell in town was clanging. All by herself she makes as much noise as some primitive tribe chasing away an eclipse. She should learn the philosopher's lesson: "moderation is necessary even for intellectuals." And, if she still wants to appear educated and eloquent, let her dress as a man, sacrifice to men's gods and bathe in the men's baths. Wives shouldn't try to be public speakers; they shouldn't use rhetorical devices; they shouldn't read all the classics— there should be some things women don't understand. I myself cannot understand a woman who can quote the rules of grammar and never make a mistake and cites obscure, long-forgotten poets—as if men cared about such things. If she has to correct somebody let her correct her girl friends and leave her husband alone.[2]

In the late republic, Roman education, though still entirely private, became more formal and organized. From the ages of seven to twelve, boys went to elementary school accompanied by a Greek slave called a *paedagogus* (whence our term *pedagogue*) who looked after his physical well-being and his manners, and who improved his ability in Greek conversa-

[2]Juvenal, *Satires* 6.434–456, trans. by Roger Killian, Richard Lynch, Robert J. Rowland, and John Sims, cited by Sarah B. Pomeroy in *Goddesses, Whores, Wives, and Slaves* (New York: Schocken Books, 1975), p. 172.

130

*The
Foundations of
Western
Civilization in
the Ancient
World*

The temple of Fortuna Virilis in Rome, late second century B.C. The Romans modified Greek architecture with local Italian traditions. The Ionic order here is Greek, but the temple stands on a high podium in the Etruscan manner. Moreover, only the six columns at the front of the temple are free standing in the Greek style. The others are built into the walls, a favorite Roman practice. [*Chauffourier, Rome/Art Resource*]

tion. At school the boy learned to read and write, using a wax tablet and a stylus, and to do simple arithmetic with the aid of an abacus and pebbles *(calculi)*. Discipline was harsh and corporal punishment frequent. From twelve to sixteen, boys went to a higher school, where the *grammaticus* undertook to provide a liberal education, using Greek and Latin literature as his subject matter. In addition, he taught dialectic, arithmetic, geometry, astronomy, and music. Sometimes he included the elements of rhetoric, especially for those boys who would not go on to a higher education.

At sixteen, some boys went on to advanced study in rhetoric. The instructors were usually Greek, and they trained their charges by study of models of fine speech of the past and by having them write, memorize, and declaim speeches suitable for different occasions. Sometimes the serious student attached himself to some famous public speaker and followed him about to learn what he could.

Sometimes a rich and ambitious Roman would support a Greek philosopher in his own home so that his son could converse with him and acquire the learning and polish thought necessary for the fully cultured gentleman. Some, like the great orator Cicero, undertook what we might call postgraduate study by traveling abroad to study with great teachers of rhetoric and philosophy in the Greek world. One consequence of this whole style of education was to broaden the Romans' understanding through the careful study of a foreign language and culture and to make them a part of the older and wider culture of the Hellenistic world, a world that they had come to dominate and needed to understand.

Roman Imperialism

Rome's expansion in Italy and overseas was accomplished without a grand general plan.

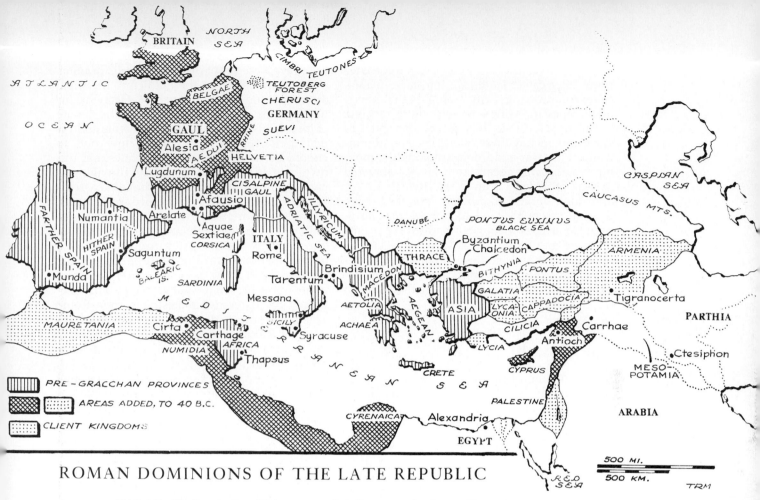

ROMAN DOMINIONS OF THE LATE REPUBLIC

MAP 4-3 *The Roman Republic's conquest of Mediterranean lands—and beyond—until the death of Julius Caesar is shown here. Areas conquered before Tiberius Gracchus (ca. 133 B.C.) are distinguished from later ones and from client areas owing allegiance to Rome.*

The new territories were acquired as a result of wars that the Romans believed were either defensive or preventive. Their foreign policy was aimed at providing security for Rome on Rome's terms, but these terms were often unacceptable to other nations and led to continued conflict. Whether intended or not, Rome's expansion brought the Romans an empire and, with it, power, wealth, and responsibilities. The republican constitution that had served Rome well during its years as a city-state and that had been well adapted to the mastery of Italy would be severely tested by the need to govern an empire beyond the seas. Roman society and the Roman character had maintained their integrity through the period of expansion in Italy. But these would be tested by the temptations and strains presented by the wealth and the complicated problems presented by an overseas empire.

The Aftermath of Conquest

War and expansion changed the economic, social, and political life of Italy. Before the Punic wars most Italians owned their own farms, which provided most of the family's needs. Some families owned larger holdings, but their lands chiefly grew grain, and they used the labor of clients, tenants, and hired workers rather than slaves. Fourteen years of fighting in the Second Punic War did terrible damage to much Italian farmland. Many veterans returning from the wars found it impossible or unprofitable to go back to their farms. Some moved to Rome, where they could find work as occasional laborers, but most stayed in the country to work as tenant farmers or hired hands. No longer landowners, they were no longer eligible for the army. Often the land they abandoned was gathered into large par-

131

132

*The
Foundations of
Western
Civilization in
the Ancient
World*

cels by the wealthy. They converted these large units, later called *latifundia,* into large plantations for growing cash crops—grain, olives, and grapes for wine—or into cattle ranches.

The upper classes had plenty of capital to stock and operate these estates because of profits from the war and from exploiting the provinces. Land was cheap, and slaves conquered in war provided cheap labor. By fair means and foul, large landholders obtained large quantities of public land and forced small farmers from it. These changes separated the people of Rome and Italy more sharply into rich and poor, landed and landless, privileged and deprived. The result was political, social, and ultimately constitutional conflict that threatened the existence of the republic.

The Gracchi

By the middle of the second century B.C. the problems caused by Rome's rapid expansion troubled perceptive Roman nobles. The fall in status of peasant farmers made it harder to recruit soldiers and came to present a political threat as well. The patron's traditional control over his clients was weakened by their flight from their land. Even those former landowners who worked on the land of their patrons as tenants or hired hands were less reliable. The introduction of the secret ballot in the 130s made them even more independent.

In 133 B.C. Tiberius Gracchus tried to solve these problems. He became tribune for 133 B.C. on a program of land reform; some of the most powerful members of the Roman aristocracy helped him draft the bill. They meant it to be a moderate attempt at solving Rome's problems. The bill's target was public land that had been acquired and held illegally, some of it for many years. The bill allowed holders of this land to retain as many as 300 acres in clear title as private property, but the state would reclaim anything over that. The recovered land would be redistributed in small lots to the poor, who would pay a small rent to the state and could not sell what they had received.

The bill aroused great hostility. Many senators held vast estates and would be hurt by its passage. Others thought it would be a bad precedent to allow any interference with property rights, even ones so dubious as those pertaining to illegally held public land. Still others feared the political gains that Tiberius and his associates would make if the beneficiaries of their law were properly grateful to its drafters.

When Tiberius put the bill before the tribal assembly, one of the tribunes, M. Octavius, interposed his veto. Tiberius went to the Senate to discuss his proposal, but the senators continued their opposition. Tiberius now had to choose between dropping the matter and undertaking a revolutionary course. Unwilling to give up, he put his bill before the tribal assembly again. Again Octavius vetoed, so Tiberius, strongly supported by the people, had Octavius removed from office, violating the constitution. The assembly's removal of a magistrate implied a fundamental shift of power from the Senate to the people. If the assembly could pass laws opposed by the Senate and vetoed by a tribune, if they could remove magistrates, then Rome would become a democracy like Athens instead of a traditional oligarchy. At this point many of Tiberius' powerful senatorial allies deserted him.

Tiberius proposed a second bill, harsher than the first and more appealing to the people, for he had given up hope of conciliating the Senate. This bill, which passed the assembly, provided for a commission to carry it out. When King Attalus of Pergamum died and left his kingdom to Rome, Tiberius proposed to use the Pergamene revenue to finance the commission. This proposal challenged the Senate's control both of finances and of foreign affairs. Hereafter there could be no compromise: either Tiberius or the Roman constitution must go under.

Tiberius understood the danger that he would face if he stepped down from the tribunate, so he announced his candidacy for a second successive term, another blow at tradition. His opponents feared that he might go on to hold office indefinitely, to dominate Rome in what appeared to them a demagogic tyranny. They concentrated their fire on the constitutional issue, the deposition of the tribune. They appear to have had some success, for many of Tiberius' supporters did not come out to vote. At the elections a riot broke out, and a mob of senators and their clients killed Tiberius and some three hundred of his followers and threw their bodies into the Tiber River. The Senate had put down the threat to its rule, but at the price of the first internal bloodshed in Roman political history.

The tribunate of Tiberius Gracchus brought a permanent change to Roman politics. Heretofore Roman political struggles had generally been struggles for honor and reputation between great families or coalitions of such families. Fundamental issues were rarely at stake. The revolutionary proposals of Tiberius, however, and the senatorial resort to bloodshed created a new situation. Tiberius' use of the tribunate to challenge senatorial rule encouraged imitation in spite of his failure. From then on, Romans could pursue a political career that was not based solely on influence within the aristocracy; pressure from the people might be an effective substitute. In the last century of the republic such politicians were called *populares,* whereas those who supported the traditional role of the Senate were called *optimates* ("the best men").

These groups were not political parties with formal programs and party discipline, but they were more than merely vehicles for the politi- cal ambitions of unorthodox politicians. Fundamental questions such as land reform, the treatment of the Italian allies, the power of the assemblies versus the power of the Senate, and other problems divided the Roman people, from the time of the Gracchi brothers to the fall of the republic. Some popular leaders, of course, were cynical self-seekers who used the issues only for their own ambitions. Some few may have been sincere advocates of a principled position. Most, no doubt, were a mixture of the two, like most politicians in most times.

The tribunate of Gaius Gracchus (brother of Tiberius) was much more dangerous than that of Tiberius because all the tribunes of 123 B.C. were his supporters, so there could be no veto, and a recent law permitted the reelection of tribunes. Gaius developed a program of such

---

The Murder of Tiberius Gracchus

In 133 B.C. the attempt of the tribune Tiberius Gracchus to introduce a limited redistri- bution of the land provoked violent resistance. As Plutarch told the story, Tiberius' enemies interpreted an innocent gesture by him as a request to be made king.

This news created general confusion in the sena- tors, and Nasica at once called upon the consul to punish this tyrant, and defend the govern- ment. The consul mildly replied, that he would not be the first to do any violence; and as he would not suffer any freeman to be put to death, before sentence had lawfully passed upon him, so neither would he allow any measure to be carried into effect, if by persuasion or compul- sion on the part of Tiberius the people had been induced to pass an unlawful vote. But Nasica, rising from his seat, "Since the consul," said he, "regards not the safety of the common- wealth, let everyone who will defend the laws, follow me." He then, casting the skirt of his gown over his head, hastened to the capitol; those who bore him company, wrapped their gowns also about their arms, and forced their way after him. And as they were persons of the greatest authority in the city, the common people did not venture to obstruct their passing, but were rather so eager to clear the way for them, that they tumbled over one another in haste. The attendants they brought with them had fur- nished themselves with clubs and staves from their houses, and they themselves picked up the feet and other fragments of stools and chairs, which were broken by the hasty flight of the common people. Thus armed, they made to- wards Tiberius, knocking down those whom they found in front of him, and those were soon wholly dispersed and many of them slain. Tibe- rius tried to save himself by flight. As he was running, he was stopped by one who caught hold of him by the gown; but he threw it off, and fled in his under-garment only. And stum- bling over those who before had been knocked down, as he was endeavouring to get up again, Publius Satureius, a tribune, one of his col- leagues, was observed to give him the first fatal stroke, by hitting him upon the head with the foot of a stool. The second blow was claimed, as though it had been a deed to be proud of, by Lucius Rufus. And of the rest there fell above three hundred killed by clubs and staves only, none by an iron weapon.

This, we are told, was the first sedition amongst the Romans, since the abrogation of kingly government, that ended in the effusion of blood.

Plutarch, *Tiberius Gracchus,* trans. by John Dryden.

134

*The
Foundations of
Western
Civilization in
the Ancient
World*

breadth as to appeal to a variety of groups. First, he revived the agrarian commission, which had been allowed to lapse. Because there was not enough good public land left to meet the demand, he proposed to establish new colonies: two in Italy and one on the old site of Carthage. Among other popular acts, he put through a law stabilizing the price of grain in Rome, which involved building granaries to guarantee an adequate supply.

Gaius broke new ground in appealing to the equestrian order in his struggle against the Senate. The equestrians (so called because they served in the Roman cavalry) were neither peasants nor senators. A highly visible minority of them were businessmen who supplied goods and services to the Roman state and collected its taxes. Almost continuous warfare and the need for tax collection in the provinces had made many of them rich. Most of the time these wealthy men had the same outlook as the Senate; generally they used their profits to purchase land and to try to reach senatorial rank themselves. Still they had a special interest in Roman expansion and in the exploitation of the provinces; toward the latter part of the second century B.C., they came to have a clear sense of group interest and to exert political influence.

In 129 B.C. Pergamum became the new province of Asia. Gaius put through a law turning over to the equestrian order the privilege of collecting its revenue. He also barred senators from serving as jurors on the courts that tried provincial governors charged with extortion. The combination was a wonderful gift for wealthy equestrian businessmen, who were now free to squeeze profits out of the rich province of Asia without much fear of interference from the governors. The results for Roman provincial administration were bad, but the immediate political consequences for Gaius were excellent. The equestrians were now given reality as a class, as a political unit that might be set against the Senate, and they might be formed into a coalition to serve Gaius' purposes.

Gaius easily won reelection as tribune for 122 B.C. He aimed at giving citizenship to the Italians, both to solve the problem that their dissatisfaction presented and to add them to his political coalition. But the common people did not want to share the advantages of Roman citizenship, and the Senate seized on this proposal as a way of driving a wedge between Gaius and his supporters.

The Romans did not reelect Gaius for 121 B.C., and he stood naked before his enemies. A hostile consul provoked an incident that led to violence. The Senate invented an extreme decree ordering the consuls to see to it that no harm came to the republic; in effect, this decree established martial law. Gaius was hunted down and killed, and a senatorial court condemned and put to death without trial some three thousand of his followers.

Marius and Sulla

For the moment the senatorial oligarchy had fought off the challenge to its traditional position. Before long it faced more serious dangers arising from troubles abroad. The first grew out of a dispute over the succession to the throne of Numidia, a client kingdom of Rome's near Carthage. The victory of Jugurtha, who became king of Numidia, and his massacre of Roman and Italian businessmen in Numidia gained Roman attention. Although the Senate was reluctant to become involved, pressure from the equestrians and the people forced the declaration of what became known as the Jugurthine War in 111 B.C.

As the war dragged on, the people, sometimes with good reason, suspected the Senate of taking bribes from Jugurtha. They elected C. Marius (157–86 B.C.) to the consulship for 107, and the assembly, usurping the role of the Senate, assigned him to the province of Numidia. This action was significant in several ways: Marius was a *novus homo*, a "new man," that is, the first in the history of his family to reach the consulship. Although a wealthy equestrian, he had been born in the town of Arpinum and was outside the closed circle of the old Roman aristocracy. His earlier career had won him a reputation as an outstanding soldier and something of a political maverick.

Marius quickly defeated Jugurtha, but Jugurtha escaped and guerrilla warfare continued. Finally Marius' subordinate, L. Cornelius Sulla (138–78 B.C.), trapped Jugurtha and brought the war to an end. Marius celebrated the victory, but Sulla, an ambitious but impoverished descendant of an old Roman family, resented being cheated of the credit he thought he deserved. Soon rumors circulated crediting Sulla with the victory and diminishing Marius' role. Thus were the seeds planted for a personal rivalry and a mutual hostility that would last until Marius' death.

While the Romans were fighting Jugurtha, a far greater danger threatened Rome from the north. In 105 B.C. two barbaric tribes, the Cimbri and the Teutones, had come down the Rhone valley and crushed a Roman army at Arausio (Orange). To meet the danger, the Romans elected Marius to his second consulship when these tribes threatened again. From 104 he served five consecutive terms until 100 B.C., when the crisis was over.

While the barbarians were occupied elsewhere, Marius used the time to make important changes in the army. He began using volunteers for the army, mostly the dispossessed farmers and rural proletarians whose problems had not been solved by the Gracchi. They enlisted for a long term of service and looked on the army not as an unwelcome duty but as an opportunity and a career. They became semi-professional clients of their general and sought guaranteed food, clothing, shelter, and booty from victories. They came to expect a piece of land as a form of mustering-out pay or veteran's bonus when they retired. Volunteers were most likely to enlist with a man who was a capable soldier and influential enough to obtain what he needed for them. They looked to him rather than to the state for their rewards. He, on the other hand, had to obtain these favors from the Senate if he was to maintain his power and reputation. Marius' innovation created both the opportunity and the necessity for military leaders to gain enough power to challenge civilian authority. The promise of rewards won these leaders the personal loyalty of their troops, and that loyalty allowed them to frighten the Senate into granting their demands.

The War Against the Italian Allies (90–88 B.C.)

For a decade Rome avoided serious troubles, but in that time the Senate took no action to deal with Italian discontent. The Italians were excluded from the land bill for Marius' veterans, and their discontent was serious enough to cause the Senate to expel all Italians from

Sallust Describes the New Model Army of Marius

Sallust (86–ca. 34 B.C.) wrote a number of historical monographs. In the one describing Rome's war against Jugurtha, king of Numidia in North Africa, he told the story of the important changes in army recruitment introduced by Marius. With the aid of the new troops Marius was able to win the war against Jugurtha in the years 107–105 B.C.

Marius, who as I said before, had been made consul with great eagerness on the part of the populace, began, though he had always been hostile to the patricians, to inveigh against them, after the people gave him the province of Numidia, with great frequency and violence. . . . He also enlisted all the bravest men from Latium, most of whom were known to him by actual service, some few only by report, and induced, by earnest solicitation, even discharged veterans to accompany him. Nor did the senate, though adverse to him, dare to refuse him anything; the additions to the legions they had voted even with eagerness, because military service was thought to be unpopular with the multitude, and Marius seemed likely to lose either the means of warfare, or the favour of the people. But such expectations were entertained in vain, so ardent was the desire of going with Marius that had seized on almost all. Every one cherished the fancy that he should return home laden with spoil, crowned with victory, or attended with some similar good fortune. Marius himself, too, had excited them in no small degree by a speech. . . .

. . . .

He himself, in the mean time, proceeded to enlist soldiers, not after the ancient method, or from the classes, but taking all that were willing to join him, and the greater part from the lowest ranks.

Sallust; *Jugurtha*, trans. by J. S. Watson (London: Bohn Classical Library, 1852), pp. 171, 172, 181.

136

*The
Foundations of
Western
Civilization in
the Ancient
World*

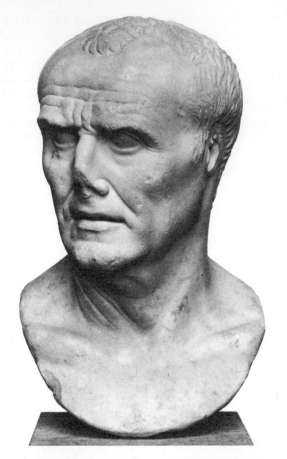

*Marius (157–86 B.C.), top, and Sulla (138–78 B.C.).
Their bloody struggle for power marked the beginning of
the end of the Roman Republic. [Hartwig Koppermann]*

Rome in 95 B.C. Four years later the tribune M. Livius Drusus put forward a bill to enfranchise the Italians. Drusus seems to have been a sincere aristocratic reformer, but he was assassinated in 90 B.C. In frustration the Italians revolted and established a separate confederation with its own capital and its own coinage.

Employing the traditional device of divide and conquer, the Romans immediately offered citizenship to those cities that remained loyal and soon made the same offer to the rebels if they laid down their arms. Even then, hard fighting was needed to put down the uprising, but by 88 B.C. the war against the allies was over. All the Italians became Roman citizens with the protections that citizenship offered, but they retained local self-government and a dedication to their own municipalities that made Italy flourish. The passage of time blurred the distinction between Romans and Italians and forged them into a single nation.

Sulla and His Dictatorship

During the war against the allies Sulla had performed well, and he was elected consul for 88 B.C. and was given command of the war against Mithridates, who was leading a major rebellion in Asia. At this point the seventy-year-old Marius emerged from obscurity and sought the command for himself. With popular and equestrian support, he got the assembly to transfer the command to him. Sulla, defending the rights of the Senate and his own interests, marched his army against Rome. This was the first time a Roman general had used his army against fellow citizens. Marius and his friends fled, and Sulla regained the command. No sooner had he left again for Asia than Marius joined with the consul Cinna and reconquered Rome by force. He outlawed Sulla and launched a bloody massacre of the senatorial opposition. Marius died soon after his election to a seventh consulship, for 86 B.C. Cinna now was the chief man at Rome. Supported by Marius' men, he held the consulship from 87 to 84 B.C. His future depended on Sulla's fortunes in the east.

By 85 B.C. Sulla had driven Mithridates from Greece and had crossed over to Asia Minor.

Appian Describes Sulla's Proscriptions of His Opponents

In 83 B.C. Sulla triumphed over the friends of Marius in a civil war and became dictator. In the following selection Appian describes Sulla's treatment of his defeated opponents.

Sulla recounted Sulpicius' and Marius' insulting treatment of himself and without saying anything definite—he was unwilling to speak yet about such a move as he contemplated— wanted them [his soldiers] to be on the alert for action. They understood what he meant and, fearing they would miss the campaign, themselves made Sulla's desires explicit and urged him to take courage and lead them against Rome. He was delighted and forthwith ordered his six legions to march. . . .

So the political struggle progressed from strife and faction to murder, and from murder to regular wars and now for the first time an army of citizens invaded their native city as if it were hostile territory. Henceforth political conflicts continued to be settled by armies, and there were constant assaults on Rome and sieges and military operations. Nothing induced any sense of shame in the authors of violence, neither the laws nor the constitution nor patriotism. Then a vote was passed that Sulpicius, who was still tribune, and Marius, who had been six times consul, and Marius' son, Publius Cethegus, Junius Brutus, Gnaeus and Quintus Granius, Publius Albinovinus and Marcus Laetorius, and about a dozen others who had fled from Rome, were enemies of the republic, having caused sedition and made war on the consuls and promised freedom to slaves to incite them to revolt. Any person was authorized to kill them without penalty or produce them before the consuls, and their property was confiscated.

Appian, *Civil Wars*, trans. by Horace White (London and New York: William Heinemann and The Macmillan Company, 1913), pp. 175–177.

Eager to regain control of Rome, he negotiated a compromise peace. In 83 B.C. he returned to Italy and fought a civil war that lasted for more than a year. Sulla won and drove the followers of Marius from Italy. He now held all power and had himself appointed dictator, not in the traditional sense, but for the express purpose of reconstituting the state.

Sulla's first step was to wipe out the opposition. The names of those proscribed were posted in public. As outlaws they could be killed by anyone, and the killer received a reward. Sulla proscribed not only political opponents but his personal enemies and men whose only crime was having wealth and property. With the proceeds from the confiscations, Sulla rewarded his veterans, perhaps as many as 100,000 men, and thereby built a solid base of support.

Sulla had enough power and influence to make himself the permanent ruler of Rome, but he was traditional enough to want a restoration of senatorial government, reformed in such a way as to prevent the misfortunes of the past. To deal with the decimation of the Senate caused by the proscriptions and the civil war, he enrolled 300 new members, many of them from the equestrian order and the upper classes of the Italian cities. The office of tribune, used by the Gracchi to attack senatorial rule, was made into a political dead-end.

Sulla's most valuable reforms improved the quality of the courts and the entire legal system. He created new courts to deal with specified crimes, to bring the total number of courts to eight. As both judge and jurors were senators, these courts, too, enhanced senatorial power. These actions were the most permanent of Sulla's reforms, laying the foundation for Roman criminal law.

Sulla retired to a life of ease and luxury in 79 B.C. He could not, however, undo the effect of his own example, of a general using the loyalty of his own troops to take power and to massacre his opponents, as well as innocent men. These actions proved to be more significant than his constitutional arrangements.

Fall of the Republic

Pompey, Crassus, Caesar, and Cicero

Within a year of Sulla's death his constitution came under assault. To deal with an armed threat to its powers, the Senate violated the very procedures meant to defend them. It gave the command of the army to Pompey (106–48 B.C.), who was only twenty-eight and had never been elected to a magistracy. Then, when Sertorius, a Marian general, resisted senatorial control, the Senate appointed Pompey proconsul in Spain in 77 B.C., once again violating the constitution by ignoring Sulla's rigid rules for office holding, which had been meant to guarantee experienced, loyal, and safe commanders. In 71 B.C. Pompey returned to Rome with new glory, having put down the rebellion of Sertorius. In 73 B.C. the Senate made another extraordinary appointment to put down a great slave rebellion led by the gladiator Spartacus. Marcus Licinius Crassus, a rich and ambitious senator, received powers that gave him command of almost all Italy and, together

---

Plutarch Describes How Crassus Became a Millionaire

Marcus Licinius Crassus (ca. 112–53 B.C.) was a fine general, a powerful politician, and the richest man in Rome. There is no doubt that his wealth contributed greatly to his power. In the following selection Plutarch describes how Crassus acquired his riches.

Now the Romans say that the many virtues of Crassus were obscured by his sole vice of avarice, and it seems that the one vice which became stronger than all the others in him dimmed the rest. The chief proofs of his avarice were the way in which he acquired his property and the size of it. For at first he was not worth more than 300 talents; then, during his consulship, he dedicated the tenth part of his property to Hercules, feasted the people, and gave to every citizen enough to live on for three months; still, when he made an inventory of his property before his Parthian expedition, he found it to have a value of 7,100 talents.

Most of this, if one must tell the scandalous truth, he gathered by fire and war, making the public calamities his greatest source of revenue. For when Sulla seized Rome and sold the property of those put to death by him, regarding and calling it booty, and wishing to make as many influential men as he could partners in the crime, Crassus refused neither to accept nor buy such property. Moreover, observing how natural and familiar at Rome were the burning and col-lapse of buildings, because of their massiveness and their closeness to one another, he bought slaves who were builders and architects. Then, when he had more than 500 of these, he would buy houses that were on fire and those adjoining the ones on fire. The owners would let them go for small sums, because of their fear and uncertainty, so that the greatest part of Rome came into his hands. But though he had so many artisans, he never built any house but the one he lived in, and used to say that those that were addicted to building would undo themselves without the help of other enemies. And though he had many silver mines, and very valuable land with laborers on it, yet one might consider all this as nothing compared with the value of his slaves, such a great number and variety did he possess—readers, amanuenses, silversmiths, stewards and table-servants. He himself directed their training, and took part in teaching them himself, accounting it, in a word, the chief duty of a master to care for his slaves as the living tools of household management.

Plutarch, *Life of Crassus*, trans. by N. Lewis and M. Reinhold, in *Roman Civilization*, Vol. 1 (New York: Columbia University Press, 1955), pp. 458–459.

Pompey the Great (106–48 B.C.) [*Alinari/Art Resource*]

with the newly returned Pompey, crushed the rebellion in 71 B.C. Extraordinary commands of this sort proved to be the ruin of the republic.

Crassus and Pompey were ambitious men whom the Senate feared. Both demanded special honors and election to the consulship for the year 70 B.C. Pompey was legally ineligible because he had never gone through the strict course of offices prescribed in Sulla's constitution, and Crassus needed Pompey's help. They joined forces, though they disliked and were jealous of one another. They gained popular support by promising to restore the full powers of the tribunes, which Sulla had curtailed, and they gained equestrian backing by promising to restore equestrians to the extortion court juries. They both won election and repealed most of Sulla's constitution, opening the way for further attacks on senatorial control and for collaboration between ambitious generals and demagogic tribunes.

In 67 B.C. a special law gave Pompey *imperium* for three years over the entire Mediterranean and fifty miles in from the coast, as well as the power to raise great quantities of troops and money to rid the area of pirates. The assembly passed the law over senatorial opposition, and in three months Pompey cleared the seas of piracy. Meanwhile a new war had broken out with Mithridates, and in 66 B.C. the assembly transferred the command to Pompey, giving him unprecedented powers. He held *imperium* over all Asia, with the right to make war and peace at will, and his *imperium* was superior to that of any proconsul in the field.

Once again Pompey justified his appointment. He defeated Mithridates and drove him to suicide. By 62 B.C. he had extended Rome's frontier to the Euphrates River and had organized the territories of Asia so well that his arrangements remained the basis of Roman rule well into the imperial period. When he returned to Rome in 62 B.C., he had more power, prestige, and popular support than any Roman in history. The Senate and his personal enemies had reason to fear that he might emulate Sulla and establish his own rule.

Rome had not been quiet in Pompey's absence. Crassus was the foremost among those who had reason to fear Pompey's return. Although rich and influential, he did not have

THE FALL OF THE ROMAN REPUBLIC

Tribunate of Tiberius Gracchus	133 B.C.
Tribunate of Gaius Gracchus	123–122 B.C.
Jugurthine War	111–105 B.C.
Consecutive consulships of Marius	104–100 B.C.
War against the Italian allies	90–88 B.C.
Sulla's march on Rome	88 B.C.
Sulla assumes dictatorship	82 B.C.
Crassus crushes rebellion of Spartacus	71 B.C.
Pompey defeats Sertorius in Spain	71 B.C.
Consulship of Crassus and Pompey	70 B.C.
Formation of First Triumvirate	60 B.C.
Caesar in Gaul	58–50 B.C.
Crassus killed in Battle of Carrhae	53 B.C.
Caesar crosses Rubicon; civil war begins	49 B.C.
Pompey defeated at Pharsalus; killed in Egypt	48 B.C.
Caesar's dictatorship	46–44 B.C.
End of civil war	45 B.C.
Formation of Second Triumvirate	43 B.C.
Triumvirs defeat Brutus and Cassius at Philippi	42 B.C.
Octavian and Agrippa defeat Anthony at Actium	31 B.C.

the confidence of the Senate, a firm political base of his own, or the kind of military glory needed to rival Pompey. During the 60s, therefore, he allied himself with various popular leaders. The ablest of these men was Gaius Julius Caesar (100–44 B.C.), a descendant of an old patrician family that claimed descent from the kings and even from the goddess Venus, but one that was politically obscure. In spite of this noble lineage, Caesar was connected to the popular party through his aunt, who was the wife of Marius, and through his own wife, Cornelia, the daughter of Cinna. Caesar was an ambitious and determined young politician whose daring and whose rhetorical skill made him a valuable ally in winning the discontented of every class to the cause of the *populares*. Though Crassus was very much the senior partner, each needed the other to achieve what both wanted: significant military commands whereby they might build a reputa-

tion, a political following, and a military force to compete with Pompey's.

The chief opposition to Crassus' candidates for the consulship for 63 B.C. came from Cicero (106–43 B.C.), a "new man" from Marius' home town of Arpinum. He had made a spectacular name as the leading lawyer in Rome. Cicero, though he came from outside the senatorial aristocracy, was no *popularis*. His program was to preserve the republic against demagogues and ambitious generals by making the government more liberal. He wanted to unite the stable elements of the state—the Senate and the equestrians—in a harmony of the orders. This program did not appeal to the senatorial oligarchy, but the Senate preferred him to Catiline, a dangerous and popular politician thought to be linked with Crassus. Cicero and Antonius were elected consuls for 63 B.C., Catiline running third.

Cicero soon learned of a plot hatched by

Plutarch Tells of the Luxury Practiced by Rome's Most Famous Epicure

The wealth produced by Rome's conquests introduced considerable luxury into the lives of the upper classes. Lucius Licinius Lucullus (ca. 117–56 B.C.) was a general who served with considerable success in Asia Minor. In 63 B.C. he retired to private life and devoted himself to the art of elegant living.

And, indeed, Lucullus' life, like the Old Comedy, presents us at the beginning with political acts and military commands, and at the end with drinking bouts and banquets, and what were practically orgies, and torch races, and all manner of frivolity. For I count as frivolity his sumptuous buildings, porticoes, and baths, still more his paintings and statues, and all his enthusiasm for these arts, which he collected at vast expense, lavishly pouring out on them the vast and splendid wealth which he acquired in his campaigns. Even now, with all the advance of luxury, the Lucullan gardens are counted the most costly of the imperial gardens. When Tubero the Stoic saw Lucullus' works on the seashore and near Naples, where he suspended hills over vast tunnels, encircling his residences

with moats of sea water and with streams for breeding fish, and built villas into the sea, he called him Xerxes in a toga. . . .

Lucullus' daily dinners were ostentatiously extravagant—not only their purple coverlets, beakers adorned with precious stones, choruses, and dramatic recitations, but also their display of all sorts of meats and daintily prepared dishes—making him an object of envy to the vulgar. . . . Once when he dined alone, he became angry because only one modest course had been prepared, and called the slave in charge. When the latter said that he did not think that there would be need of anything expensive since there were no guests, Lucullus said, "What, do you not know that today Lucullus dines with Lucullus?"

Plutarch, *Life of Lucullus*, trans. by N. Lewis and M. Reinhold, in *Roman Civilization*, Vol. 1 (New York: Columbia University Press, 1955), pp. 459–460.

Catiline. Catiline had run in the previous election on a platform of cancellation of debts, which appealed to discontented elements in general but especially to the heavily indebted nobles and their many clients. Made desperate by defeat, Catiline planned to stir up rebellions around Italy, to cause confusion in the city, and to take it by force. Quick action by Cicero defeated Catiline.

Formation of the First Triumvirate

Toward the end of 62 B.C. Pompey landed at Brundisium and, to general surprise, disbanded his army, celebrated a great triumph, and returned to private life. He had delayed his return in the hope of finding Italy in such a state as to justify his keeping the army and dominating the scene. Cicero's quick suppression of Catiline prevented his plan. Pompey, therefore, had either to act illegally or to lay down his arms. Because he had not thought of monarchy or revolution but merely wanted to be recognized and treated as the greatest Roman, he chose the latter course. He had achieved amazing things for Rome and simply wanted the Senate to approve his excellent arrangements in the east and to make land allotments to his veterans. His demands were far from unreasonable, and a prudent Senate would have granted them and would have tried to employ his power in defense of the constitution. But the Senate was jealous and fearful of overmighty individuals and refused his requests. In this way Pompey was driven to an alliance with his natural enemies, Crassus and Caesar, because all three found the Senate standing in the way of what they wanted.

In 60 B.C. Caesar returned to Rome from his governorship of Spain. He wanted the privilege of celebrating a triumph, the great victory procession that the Senate granted certain generals to honor especially great achievements, and of running for consul, but the law did not allow him to do both, requiring him to stay outside the city with his army but demanding that he canvass for votes personally within the city. He asked for a special dispensation, but the Senate refused. Caesar then performed a political miracle: he reconciled Crassus with Pompey and gained the support of both for his own ambitions. So was born the First Triumvirate, an informal agreement among three Roman politicians, each seeking his private goals, that further undermined the future of the republic.

Though he was forced to forgo his triumph, Caesar's efforts were rewarded with election to the consulship for 59 B.C. His colleague was M. Calpernius Bibulus, the son-in-law of Cato and a conservative hostile to Caesar and the other *populares.* Caesar did not hesitate to override his colleague. The triumvirs' program was quickly enacted. Caesar got the extraordinary command that would give him a chance to earn the glory and power with which to rival Pompey: the governorship of Illyricum and Gaul for five years. A land bill settled Pompey's veterans comfortably, and his eastern settlement was ratified. Crassus, much of whose influence came from his position as champion of the equestrians, won for them a great windfall by having the government renegotiate a tax contract in their favor. To guarantee themselves against any reversal of these actions, the triumvirs continued their informal but effective collaboration, arranging for the election of friendly consuls and the departure of potential opponents.

Caesar was now free to seek the military suc-

A triumph of Roman engineering, the Pont du Gard in southern France. The Romans were able to supply enormous quantities of fresh water to their cities. This aqueduct, built in the first century A.D., brought water to the city of Nimes. [Michael Holford]

Caesar Tells What Persuaded Him to Cross the Rubicon

Julius Caesar competed with Pompey for the leading position in the Roman state. Complicated maneuvers failed to produce a compromise. In the following selection Caesar gives his side of the story of the beginning of the Roman civil war. Note that Caesar writes about himself in the third person.

These things being made known to Caesar, he harangued his soldiers; he reminded them "of the wrongs done to him at all times by his enemies, and complained that Pompey had been alienated from him and led astray by them through envy and a malicious opposition to his glory, though he had always favored and promoted Pompey's honor and dignity. He complained that an innovation had been introduced into the republic, that the intercession of the tribunes, which had been restored a few years before by Sulla, was branded as a crime, and suppressed by force of arms; that Sulla, who had stripped the tribunes of every other power, had, nevertheless, left the privilege of intercession unrestrained; that Pompey, who pretended to restore what they had lost, had taken away the privileges which they formerly had; that whenever the senate decreed, 'that the magistrates should take care that the republic sustained no injury' (by which words and decree the Roman people were obliged to repair to arms), it was only when pernicious laws were proposed; when the tribunes attempted violent measures; when the people seceded, and possessed themselves of the temples and eminences of the city; (and these instances of former times, he showed them were expiated by the fate of Saturninus and the Gracchi): that nothing of this kind was attempted now, nor even thought of: that no law was promulgated, no intrigue with the people going forward, no secession made; he exhorted them to defend from the malice of his enemies the reputation and honor of that general under whose command they had for nine years most successfully supported the state; fought many successful battles, and subdued all Gaul and Germany." The soldiers of the thirteenth legion, which was present (for in the beginning of the disturbances he had called it out, his other legions not having yet arrived), all cry out that they are ready to defend their general, and the tribunes of the commons, from all injuries.

Having made himself acquainted with the disposition of his soldiers, Caesar set off with that legion to Ariminum, and there met the tribunes, who had fled to him for protection.

Julius Caesar, *Commentaries,* trans. by W. A. McDevitte and W. S. Bosh (New York: Harper and Brothers, 1887), pp. 249–250.

cess he craved. His province included Cisalpine Gaul in the Po valley, by now occupied by many Italian settlers as well as Gauls, and Narbonese Gaul beyond the Alps, modern Provence.

Relying first on the excellent quality of his army and the experience of his officers, then on his own growing military ability, Caesar made great progress. By 56 B.C. he had conquered most of Gaul, but he had not yet consolidated his victories firmly. He therefore sought an extension of his command, but quarrels between Crassus and Pompey so weakened the Triumvirate that the Senate was prepared to order Caesar's recall. To prevent the dissolution of his base of power, Caesar persuaded Crassus and Pompey to meet with him at Luca in northern Italy to renew the coalition. They agreed that Caesar would get another five-year command in Gaul, and Crassus and Pompey would be consuls again in 55 B.C. After that they would each receive an army and a five-year command. Caesar was free to return to Gaul and finish the job. The capture of Alesia in 50 B.C. marked the end of the serious Gallic resistance and of Gallic liberty. For Caesar it brought the wealth, fame, and military power he wanted. He commanded thirteen loyal legions, a match for his enemies as well as for his allies.

By the time Caesar was ready to return to Rome, the Triumvirate had dissolved and a crisis was at hand. At Carrhae, in 53 B.C., Crassus died trying to conquer the Parthians, successors to the Persian Empire. His death broke one link between Pompey and Caesar. The death of Caesar's daughter Julia, who had been Pompey's wife, dissolved another. As Caesar's star rose, Pompey became jealous and fearful. He did not leave Rome but governed his province through a subordinate. In the late 50s political rioting at Rome caused the Senate to appoint Pompey sole consul. This grant of unprecedented power and responsibility brought Pompey closer to the senatorial aristocracy in mutual fear of and hostility to Caesar. The Senate wanted to bring Caesar back to Rome as a private citizen after his proconsular command expired. He would then be open to attack for past illegalities. Caesar tried to avoid the trap by asking permission to stand for the consulship in absentia.

Early in January of 49 B.C. the more extreme faction in the Senate had its way and ordered Pompey to defend the state and Caesar to lay down his command by a specified day. For

---

Suetonius Describes Caesar's Dictatorship

Suetonius (ca. A.D. 69–ca. 140) wrote a series of biographies of the emperors from Julius Caesar to Domitian. In the following selection he describes some of Caesar's actions during his dictatorship in the years 46–44 B.C.

His other words and actions, however, so far outweigh all his good qualities, that it is thought he abused his power, and was justly cut off. For he not only obtained excessive honours, such as the consulship every year, the dictatorship for life, and the censorship, but also the title of emperor, and the surname of Father of His Country, besides having his statue amongst the kings, and a lofty couch in the theatre. He even suffered some honours to be decreed to him, which were unbefitting the most exalted of mankind; such as a gilded chair of state in the senate-house and on his tribunal, a consecrated chariot, and banners in the Circensian procession, temples, altars, statues among the gods, a bed of state in the temples, a priest, and a college of priests dedicated to himself, like those of Pan; and that one of the months should be called by his name. There were, indeed, no honours which he did not either assume himself, or grant to others, at his will and pleasure. In his third and fourth consulship, he used only the title of the office, being content with the power of dictator, which was conferred upon him with the consulship; and in both years he substituted other consuls in his room, during the last three months; so that in the intervals he held no assemblies of the people, for the election of magistrates, excepting only tribunes and ediles of the people; and appointed officers, under the name of præfects, instead of the prætors, to administer the affairs of the city during his absence. The office of consul having become vacant, by the sudden death of one of the consuls the day before the calends of January [the 1st Jan.], he conferred it on a person who requested it of him, for a few hours. Assuming the same licence, and regardless of the customs of his country, he appointed magistrates to hold their offices for terms of years. He granted the insignia of the consular dignity to ten persons of prætorian rank. He admitted into the senate some men who had been made free of the city, and even natives of Gaul, who were semi-barbarians. He likewise appointed to the management of the mint, and the public revenue of the state, some servants of his own household; and entrusted the command of three legions, which he left at Alexandria, to an old catamite of his, the son of his freed-man Rufinus.

He was guilty of the same extravagance in the language he publicly used, as Titus Ampius informs us; according to whom he said, "The republic is nothing but a name, without substance or reality. Sulla was an ignorant fellow to abdicate the dictatorship. Men ought to consider what is becoming when they talk with me, and look upon what I say as a law."

Suetonius, *The Lives of the Twelve Caesars*, trans. by Alexander Thompson, rev. by T. Forster (London: George Bell and Sons, 1903) pp. 45–47.

Caesar this meant exile or death, so he ordered his legions to cross the Rubicon River, the boundary of his province. This action was the first act of the civil war. In 45 B.C. he defeated the last of the enemy forces under Pompey's sons at Munda in Spain. The war was over, and Caesar, in Shakespeare's words, bestrode "the narrow world like a Colossus."

From the beginning of the civil war until his death in 44 B.C., Caesar spent less than a year and a half in Rome, and many of his actions were attempts to deal with immediate problems between campaigns. His innovations generally sought to make rational and orderly what was traditional and chaotic. An excellent example is Caesar's reform of the calendar. By 46 B.C. it was eighty days ahead of the proper season because the official year was lunar, containing only 355 days. Using the best scientific advice, Caesar instituted a new calendar, which, with minor changes by Pope Gregory XIII in the sixteenth century, is the one in use today. Another general tendency of his reforms in the political area was the elevation of the role of Italians and even provincials at the expense of the old Roman families, most of whom were his political enemies. He raised the number of senators to 900 and filled the Senate's depleted ranks with Italians and even Gauls. He was free with grants of Roman citizenship, giving the franchise to Cisalpine Gaul as a whole and to many individuals of various regions.

Caesar made few changes in the government of Rome. The Senate continued to play its role, in theory, but its increased size, its packing with supporters of Caesar, and his own monopoly of military power made the whole thing a sham. He treated the Senate as his creature and sometimes with disdain. His legal position rested on a number of powers. In 46 B.C. he was appointed dictator for ten years and in the next year for life. He also held the consulship, the immunity of a tribune (although, being a patrician, he had never been a tribune), the chief priesthood of the state, and a new position, prefect of morals, which gave him the censorial power. Usurping the elective power of the assemblies, he even named the magistrates for the next few years, because he expected to be away in the east.

The enemies of Caesar were quick to seize on every pretext to accuse Caesar of aiming at monarchy. A senatorial conspiracy gathered strength under the leadership of Gaius Cassius Longinus and Marcus Junius Brutus and included some sixty senators in all. On March 15, 44 B.C., Caesar entered the Senate, characteristically without a bodyguard, and was stabbed to death. The assassins regarded themselves as heroic tyrannicides and did not have a clear plan of action after the tyrant was dead. No doubt they simply expected the republic to be restored in the old way, but things had gone too far for that. There followed instead thirteen years of more civil war, at the end of which the republic received its final burial.

The Second Triumvirate and the Emergence of Octavian

Caesar had had legions of followers, and he had a capable successor in Mark Antony. But the dictator had named his eighteen-year-old grandnephew, Gaius Octavius (63 B.C.–A.D. 14), as his heir and had left him three quarters of his vast wealth. To everyone's surprise, the sickly and inexperienced young man come to Rome to claim his legacy, gathered an army, won the support of many of Caesar's veterans, and became a figure of importance—the future Augustus.

At first, the Senate tried to use Octavius against Antony, but when the conservatives rejected his request for the consulship, Octavius broke with them. Following Sulla's grim precedent, he took his army and marched on Rome. There he finally assumed his adopted name, C. Julius Caesar Octavianus. Modern historians refer to him at this stage in his career as Octavian, although he insisted on being called Caesar. In August of 43 B.C. he became consul and declared the assassins of Caesar outlaws. As Brutus and Cassius had an army of their own, Octavian sought help on the Caesarean side. He made a pact with Mark Antony and M. Aemilius Lepidus, a Caesarean governor of the western provinces. They took control of Rome and had themselves appointed "Triumvirs to put the republic in order," with great powers. This was the Second Triumvirate, and unlike the first, it was legally empowered to rule almost dictatorially.

The need to pay their troops, their own greed, and the passion that always emerges in civil wars led the triumvirs to start a wave of proscriptions that outdid even those of Sulla. In 42 B.C. the triumviral army defeated Brutus and Cassius at Philippi in Macedonia, and the last hope of republican restoration died with the tyrannicides. Each of the triumvirs received a command. The junior partner, Lepidus, was given Africa, Antony took the rich and inviting east, and Octavian got the west and the many troubles that went with it. He had to fight a war against Sextus, the son of Pompey, who held Sicily. He also had to settle 100,000 veterans in Italy, confiscating much property and making many enemies. Helped by his friend Agrippa, he defeated Sextus Pompey in 36 B.C. Among his close associates was Maecenas, who served him as adviser and diplomatic agent. Maecenas helped manage the delicate relations with Antony and Lepidus, but perhaps equally important was his role as a patron of the arts. Among his clients were Vergil and Horace, both of whom did important work for Octavian, painting him as a restorer of traditional Roman values, as a man of ancient Roman lineage and of traditional Roman virtues, and as the culmination of Roman destiny. More and more he was identified with Italy and the west as well as with order, justice, and virtue.

Meanwhile Antony was in the east, chiefly at Alexandria with Cleopatra, the queen of Egypt. In 36 B.C. he attacked Parthia, with disastrous results. Octavian had promised to send troops to support Antony's Parthian campaign but never sent them. Antony was forced to depend on the east for support, and to some considerable degree this meant Cleopatra. Octavian clearly understood the advantage of representing himself as the champion of the west, Italy, and Rome, while representing Antony as the man of the east, the dupe of Cleopatra, her tool in establishing Alexandria as the center of an empire and herself as its ruler. Such propaganda made it easier for Caesareans to abandon their veteran leader in favor of the young heir of Caesar. It did not help Antony's cause that he agreed to a public festival at Alexandria in 34 B.C., where he and Cleopatra sat on golden thrones. She was proclaimed "Queen of Kings," her son by Julius Caesar was named "King of Kings," and parts of the Roman Empire were doled out to her various children.

By 32 B.C. all pretense of cooperation came to an end. Octavian and Antony each tried to put the best face on what was essentially a struggle for power. Lepidus had been put aside some years earlier. Antony sought senatorial support and promised to restore the republican constitution. Octavian seized and published what was alleged to be the will of Antony, revealing his gifts of provinces to the children of Cleopatra, thereby causing the conflict in terms of east against west, Rome against Alexandria.

Profile of Brutus, one of Caesar's assassins, on a silver coin. The reverse shows a cap of liberty between two daggers and reads "Ides of March." [H. Roger Viollet]

MAP 4-4

THE TRANSITION FROM

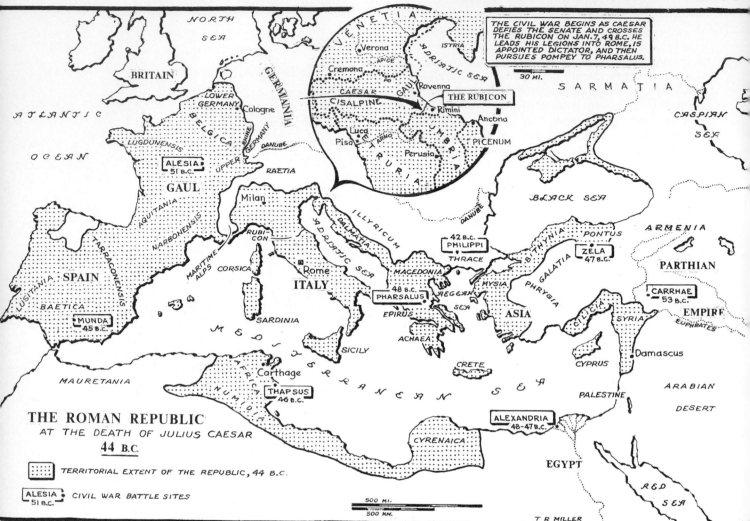

THE CIVIL WAR BEGINS AS CAESAR DEFIES THE SENATE AND CROSSES THE RUBICON ON JAN. 7, 49 B.C. HE LEADS HIS LEGIONS INTO ROME, IS APPOINTED DICTATOR, AND THEN PURSUES POMPEY TO PHARSALUS.

THE ROMAN REPUBLIC
AT THE DEATH OF JULIUS CAESAR
44 B.C.

TERRITORIAL EXTENT OF THE REPUBLIC, 44 B.C.

ALESIA 51 B.C. • CIVIL WAR BATTLE SITES

500 MI.
500 KM.

T R MILLER

By the time of Julius Caesar's dictatorship, Rome had grown from a small city-state in central Italy to the head of a vast Mediterranean Empire. The conquest of this territory posed many problems for the Republic that it could not ultimately solve. Commands in the provinces came to be sources of profit and prestige for the Roman nobility, and politics in the late Republic often consisted of quarrels over desired provincial assignments. At last, a quarrel between Julius Caesar and Pompey, on behalf of the Senate, led to a civil war that destroyed the Republic. This map shows the extent of the territory controlled by republican Rome at the time of Caesar's death. The insert indicates Caesar's route as he returned from his province, Gaul, to challenge Pompey and the Senate in January, 49 B.C. By crossing the Rubicon River, the border of his province, Caesar violated the law forbidding a proconsul from bringing his army into Italy and made the difficult and irrevocable choice for civil war rather than risk condemnation by a hostile Senate.

The reign of Augustus (31 B.C.–A.D. 14) produced a transition from an imperial aristocratic republic dominated by a narrow class of nobles to an autocratic empire. Augustus cloaked himself with republican titles and powers and ostensibly shared the government with the Senate, but he himself controlled the army on which all real power rested. This map shows the extent of the Roman Empire at the death of Augustus and how it had grown in the course of his reign. His most important gain came at the very beginning of his rule, when the victory over Cleopatra gave him Egypt, which he treated as a private possession and which provided him with vast wealth independent of senatorial control. By the end of his life he was the unquestioned ruler of Rome, secure enough to pass the Empire on to his chosen successor, Tiberius. Thereafter the cloak of republicanism was soon shed and the monarchical nature of imperial rule was entirely clear.

146

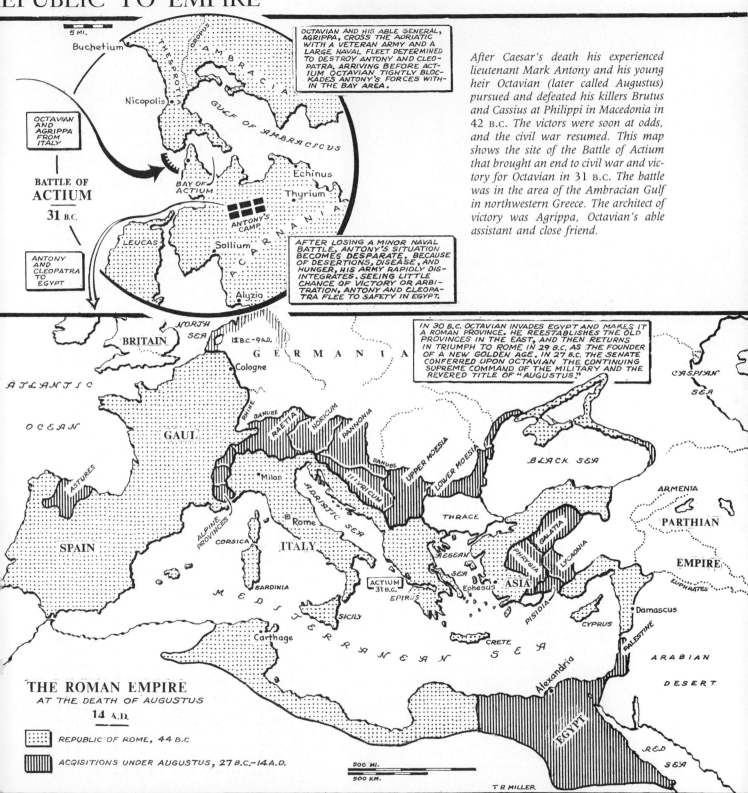

5 MI.

Buchetium

OCTAVIAN AND HIS ABLE GENERAL, AGRIPPA, CROSS THE ADRIATIC WITH A VETERAN ARMY AND A LARGE NAVAL FLEET DETERMINED TO DESTROY ANTONY AND CLEOPATRA. ARRIVING BEFORE ACTIUM OCTAVIAN TIGHTLY BLOCKADES ANTONY'S FORCES WITHIN THE BAY AREA.

Nicopolis

OCTAVIAN AND AGRIPPA FROM ITALY

BATTLE OF ACTIUM

31 B.C.

ANTONY AND CLEOPATRA TO EGYPT

BAY OF ACTIUM

Echinus

Thyrium

ANTONY'S CAMP

LEUCAS

Sollium

Alyzia

AFTER LOSING A MINOR NAVAL BATTLE, ANTONY'S SITUATION BECOMES DESPARATE, BECAUSE OF DESERTIONS, DISEASE, AND HUNGER, HIS ARMY RAPIDLY DISINTEGRATES. SEEING LITTLE CHANCE OF VICTORY OR ARBITRATION, ANTONY AND CLEOPATRA FLEE TO SAFETY IN EGYPT.

After Caesar's death his experienced lieutenant Mark Antony and his young heir Octavian (later called Augustus) pursued and defeated his killers Brutus and Cassius at Philippi in Macedonia in 42 B.C. The victors were soon at odds, and the civil war resumed. This map shows the site of the Battle of Actium that brought an end to civil war and victory for Octavian in 31 B.C. The battle was in the area of the Ambracian Gulf in northwestern Greece. The architect of victory was Agrippa, Octavian's able assistant and close friend.

IN 30 B.C. OCTAVIAN INVADES EGYPT AND MAKES IT A ROMAN PROVINCE. HE REESTABLISHES THE OLD PROVINCES IN THE EAST, AND THEN RETURNS IN TRIUMPH TO ROME IN 29 B.C. AS THE FOUNDER OF A NEW GOLDEN AGE. IN 27 B.C. THE SENATE CONFERRED UPON OCTAVIAN THE CONTINUING SUPREME COMMAND OF THE MILITARY AND THE REVERED TITLE OF "AUGUSTUS."

THE ROMAN EMPIRE
AT THE DEATH OF AUGUSTUS
14 A.D.

REPUBLIC OF ROME, 44 B.C.

ACQUISITIONS UNDER AUGUSTUS, 27 B.C.–14 A.D.

500 MI.

500 KM.

T R MILLER

147

Roman bust of Cleopatra, the last Ptolemaic ruler of Egypt. Her ambition to create a great Hellenistic empire in the East was shattered at the battle of Actium in 31 B.C. [Courtesy of the Trustees of the British Museum]

In 31 B.C. the matter was settled at Actium in western Greece. Agrippa, Octavian's best general, cut off the enemy by land and sea, forcing and winning a naval battle. Antony and Cleopatra escaped to Egypt, but Octavian pursued them to Alexandria, where both committed suicide. The civil wars were over, and at the age of thirty-two Octavian was absolute master of the Mediterranean world. His power was enormous, but so too was the task before him. He had to restore peace, prosperity, and confidence, and all of these required the establishment of a constitution that would reflect the new realities without offending unduly the traditional republican prejudices that still had so firm a grip on Rome and Italy.

Suggested Readings

F. E. ADCOCK, *The Roman Art of War Under the Republic* (1940).

E. BADIAN, *Foreign Clientelae* (1958). A brilliant study of the Roman idea of a client–patron relationship extended to foreign affairs.

E. BADIAN, *Roman Imperialism in the Late Republic*, 2nd ed. (1968).

A. H. BERNSTEIN, *Tiberius Sempronius Gracchus: Tradition and Apostasy* (1978). A new interpretation of Tiberius' place in Roman politics.

R. BLOCH, *Origins of Rome* (1960). A good account of the most generally accepted point of view.

P. A. BRUNT, *Social Conflicts in the Roman Republic* (1971).

B. CAVEN, *The Punic Wars* (1980).

T. CORNELL AND J. MATTHEWS, *Atlas of the Roman World* (1982). Much more than the title indicates, this book presents a comprehensive view of the Roman world in its physical and cultural setting.

D. C. EARL, *The Moral and Political Tradition of Rome* (1967).

R. M. ERRINGTON, *The Dawn of Empire: Rome's Rise to Power* (1972). An account of Rome's conquest of the Mediterranean.

M. GELZER, *Caesar: Politician and Statesman*, trans. by P. Needham (1968). The best biography of Caesar.

E. GJERSTAD, *Legends and Facts of Early Roman History* (1962). An unorthodox but interesting account of early Rome.

E. S. GRUEN, *The Last Generation of the Roman Republic* (1973). An interesting but controversial interpretation of the fall of the republic.

W. V. HARRIS, *War and Imperialism in Republican Rome, 327–70 B.C.* (1975). An analysis of Roman attitudes and intentions concerning imperial expansion and war.

L. P. HOMO, *Primitive Italy and the Beginning of Roman Imperialism* (1967). A study of early Roman relations with the peoples of Italy.

F. B. MARSH, *A History of the Roman World from 146 to 30 B.C.*, 3rd ed., rev. by H. H. Scullard (1963). An excellent narrative account.

C. NICOLET, *The World of the Citizen in Republican Rome* (1980).

M. PALLOTTINO, *The Etruscans*, 6th ed. (1974). Makes especially good use of archaeological evidence.

E. T. SALMON, *Roman Colonization Under the Republic* (1970).

H. H. SCULLARD, *A History of the Roman World 753–146 B.C.*, 4th ed. (1980). An unusually fine narrative history with useful critical notes.

H. H. SCULLARD, *From the Gracchi to Nero*, 5th ed. (1982). A work of the same character and quality.

A. N. SHERWIN-WHITE, *Roman Citizenship* (1939). A useful study of the Roman franchise and its extension to other peoples.

R. E. SMITH, *Cicero the Statesman* (1966). A sound biography.

D. STOCKTON, *Cicero: A Political Biography* (1971). A readable and interesting study.

D. STOCKTON, *The Gracchi* (1979). An interesting analytical narrative.

L. R. TAYLOR, *Party Policies in the Age of Caesar* (1949). A fascinating analysis of Roman political practices.

B. H. WARMINGTON, *Carthage* (1960). A good survey.

G. WILLIAMS, *The Nature of Roman Poetry* (1970). An unusually graceful and perceptive literary study.

Marcus Aurelius (A.D. 161–180), *one of the five ''good emperors,'' under whose rule the Roman Empire reached its peak stability and prosperity. This bronze is the only Roman equestrian statue that has survived. It stands in Rome's Piazza del Campidaglio on a marble base designed during the Renaissance by Michelangelo.*

The Augustan Principate

IF THE PROBLEMS FACING OCTAVIAN after the Battle of Actium were great, so too were his resources for addressing them. He was the master of a vast military force, the only one in the Roman world, and he had loyal and capable assistants. Of enormous importance was the great, seemingly inexhaustible treasury of Egypt, which Octavian treated as his personal property. Perhaps his most valuable asset, however, was the great eagerness of the people of Italy for an end to civil war and a return to peace, order, and prosperity. In exchange for these most of them were prepared to accept a considerable abandonment of republican practices and to give significant power to an able ruler. Even the resistance of the old Roman families was greatly reduced, for a remarkable number of their members had perished in the civil wars from 49 to 31 B.C. Yet the memory of Julius Caesar's fate was still clear in Octavian's mind, and its lesson was that it was dangerous to flaunt unprecedented powers and to disregard all republican traditions.

Octavian's constitutional solution proved to be successful and lasting, subtle and effective. It was not created at a single stroke but developed gradually as Octavian tried new devices to fit his perception of changing conditions. Behind all the republican trappings and the apparent sharing of authority with the Senate, the government of Octavian, like that of his successors, was a monarchy. All real power, both civil and military, lay with the ruler, whether he was called by the unofficial title of "first citizen" (*princeps*), like Octavian, the founder of the regime, or "emperor" (*imperator*), like those who followed. During the civil war Octavian's powers came from his triumviral status, whose dubious legality and unrepublican character were an embarrassment. From 31 B.C. on, he held the consulship each year, but this circumstance was not strictly legal or very satisfactory either. On January 13, 27 B.C., he put forward a new plan in dramatic style, coming before the Senate to give up all his powers and provinces. In what was surely a rehearsed response, the Senate begged him to reconsider, and at last he agreed to accept the provinces of Spain, Gaul, and Syria with proconsular power for military command and to retain the consulship in Rome. The other provinces would be governed by the Senate as before. Because his were the border provinces and contained twenty of the twenty-six le-

5

The Roman Empire

152

*The
Foundation of
Western
Civilization in
the Ancient
World*

gions, his true power was undiminished, but the Senate responded with almost hysterical gratitude, voting him many honors. Among them was the semireligious title "Augustus," which carried implications of veneration, majesty, and holiness. From this time on, historians speak of Rome's first emperor as Augustus and of his regime as the Principate. This would have pleased him, for it helps conceal the novel, unrepublican nature of the regime and the naked power on which it rested.

Emperor Augustus (27 B.C.–A.D. 14). *This statue, now in the Vatican, stood in the villa of Augustus's wife Livia. The figures on the elaborate breastplate are all of symbolic significance. At the top, for example, Dawn in her chariot brings in a new day under the protective mantle of the sky god; in the center Tiberius, Augustus's future successor, accepts the return of captured Roman army standards from a barbarian prince; and at the bottom, Mother Earth offers a horn of plenty.* [*Copyright by Leonard von Matt*]

In 23 B.C. Augustus resigned his consulship and held that office only rarely thereafter. Instead he was voted two powers that were to be the base of his rule thenceforth, the proconsular *imperium maius* and the tribunician power. The former made his proconsular power greater than that of any other proconsul and permitted him to exercise it even within the city of Rome. The latter gave him the right to conduct public business in the assemblies and the Senate, the power of the veto, the tribunician sacrosanctity, and a connection with the popular tradition. Thereafter there were minor changes in Augustus' position, but his powers were chiefly those conferred by the settlement of 23 B.C..

Administration

Augustus made important changes in the government of Rome, Italy, and the provinces. Most of these had the effect of reducing inefficiency and corruption, eliminating the danger to peace and order from ambitious individuals, and reducing the distinction between Romans and Italians, senators and equestrians. The assemblies lost their significance as a working part of the constitution, and the Senate took on most of the functions of the assemblies. Augustus purged the old Senate of undesirable members and fixed its number at 600. He recruited its members from wealthy men of good character, who entered after serving as lesser magistrates. Augustus controlled the elections and saw to it that promising young men, whatever their origin, served the state as administrators and provincial governors. In this way equestrians and Italians who had no connection with the Roman aristocracy entered the Senate in great numbers. For all his power Augustus was careful always to treat the Senate with respect and honor.

Among his many other talents Augustus had a genius for practical administration. He divided Rome into regions and wards with elected local officials. He gave the city, with its rickety wooden tenements, its first public fire department and rudimentary police force. Grain distribution to the poor was carefully controlled and limited, and organizations were created for providing an adequate water supply. The Augustan period was one of great prosperity, based on the wealth Augustus had brought in by the conquest of Egypt, on the great increase in commerce and industry made possible by general peace and a vast program of public works, and on a strong return to successful small farming on the part of Augustus' resettled veterans.

The union of political and military power in the hands of the *princeps* made it possible for him to install rational, efficient, and stable government in the provinces for the first time. The emperor, in effect, chose the governors, removed the incompetent or rapacious, and allowed the effective ones to keep their provinces for longer periods of time. At the same time he provided for much greater local autonomy, giving considerable responsibility to the upper classes in the provincial cities and towns and to the tribal leaders in less civilized areas.

The Army and Defense

The main external problem facing Augustus— and one that haunted all his successors—was the northern frontier. Rome needed to pacify the regions to the north and the northeast of Italy and to find defensible frontiers against the recurring waves of barbarians. Augustus' plan was to push forward into central Europe to create the shortest possible defensive line. The eastern part of the plan succeeded, and the campaign in the west started well. In A.D. 9, however, a revolt broke out led by the German tribal leader Herrmann, or Arminius, as the Romans called him. He ambushed and destroyed three Roman legions under the general Varus as they marched through the Teutoburg Forest. The aged Augustus abandoned the campaign, leaving a problem of border defense that caused great trouble for his successors.

Under Augustus, the armed forces achieved true professional status. Enlistment, chiefly by Italians, was for twenty years, but the pay was relatively good and there were occasional bonuses and the promise of a pension on retirement in the form of money or a plot of land. Together with the auxiliaries from the provinces, these forces formed a frontier army of about 300,000 men. In normal times this number was barely enough to hold the line. The Roman army permanently based in the provinces played a vital role in bringing Roman culture to the natives. The soldiers spread their language and customs, often marrying local women and settling down in the area of their service. They attracted merchants, who often became the nuclei of new towns and cities that became centers of Roman civilization. As time

The Secret of Rome's Military Success: Training

Vegetius was a Roman military writer of the fourth and fifth centuries A.D. His military handbook had great influence on European armies from the Renaissance on. In the following passage, he emphasizes the crucial role of training in the achievements of the Roman army.

In every battle victory is granted not by mere numbers and innate courage but by skill and training. For we see that the Roman people owed the conquest of the world to no other cause than military training, discipline in their camps, and practice in warfare. What chance would the small number of Romans have had against the multitude of Gauls? How could they have ventured, with their small stature, against the tall Germans? It is clear that the Spaniards excelled our men not only in numbers but also in physical strength. We have always been inferior to the Africans in the use of deception and in *wealth. And no one doubts that we were surpassed by the Greeks in skills and intelligence. But against all these we prevailed by skillful selection of recruits, by teaching, as I have said, the principles of war, by hardening them in daily exercise, by acquainting them beforehand through field maneuvers with everything that can happen in the line of march and in battles, and by severe punishment for indolence. For knowledge of military science nourishes boldness in combat. No one fears to do what he is confident he has learned well. . . .*

Vegetius, *Military Science,* trans. by N. Lewis and M. Reinhold, in *Roman Civilization,* Vol. 2 (New York: Columbia University Press, 1955), p. 497.

Roman soldiers building a fort on the Danube. Along the Rhine and Danube frontier, the Roman army built many forts, which often became the nuclei of new cities. (Art Resource)

behavior had become public knowledge. He worked at restoring the dignity of formal Roman religion, building many temples, reviving old cults, and reorganizing and invigorating the priestly colleges, and he banned the worship of newly introduced foreign gods. Augustus himself occupied some of the traditional priesthoods, and writers whom he patronized, such as Vergil, pointed out his family's legendary connection with Venus. During his lifetime he did not accept divine honors, though he was deified after his death, and as with Julius Caesar, a state cult was dedicated to his worship.

Civilization of the Ciceronian and Augustan Ages

The high point of Roman culture came in the last century of the republic and during the principate of Augustus. Both periods reflected the dominant influence of Greek culture, especially in its Hellenistic mode. The education of Romans of the upper classes was in Greek rhetoric, philosophy, and literature, which also served as the models for Roman writers and artists. Yet in spirit and sometimes in form, the art and writing of both periods show uniquely Roman qualities, though each in different ways.

The Late Republic

CICERO. The towering literary figure of the late republic was Cicero. He is most famous for his orations delivered in the law courts and in the Senate. Together with a considerable body of his private letters, these orations provide us with a clearer and fuller insight into his mind than into that of any other figure in antiquity. We see the political life of his period largely through his eyes. He also wrote treatises on rhetoric, ethics, and politics that put Greek philosophical ideas into Latin terminology and at the same time changed them to suit Roman conditions and values. Cicero's own views combined the teachings of the Academy, the Stoa, and other Greek schools to provide support for his moderate and conservative practicality. He believed in a world governed by divine and natural law that human reason could perceive and human institutions reflect. He looked to law, custom, and tradition to produce both stability and liberty. His literary

passed, the provincials on the frontiers became Roman citizens and helped strengthen Rome's defenses against the barbarians outside.

Religion and Morality

A century of political strife and civil war had undermined many of the foundations of traditional Roman society. Augustus thought it desirable to try to repair the damage, and he undertook a program aimed at preserving and restoring the traditional values of the family and religion in Rome and Italy. He introduced laws curbing adultery and divorce and encouraging early marriage and the procreation of legitimate children. He set an example of austere behavior in his own household and even banished his daughter, Julia, whose immoral

The Emperor Augustus Writes His Testament

Emperor Augustus wrote a record of his achievements to be read, engraved, and placed outside his mausoleum after his death. The following selections are from that document.

13. The temple of Janus Quirinus, which our ancestors desired to be closed whenever peace with victory was secured by sea and by land throughout the entire empire of the Roman people, and which before I was born is recorded to have been closed only twice since the founding of the city, was during my principate three times ordered by the senate to be closed.

. . . .

34. In my sixth and seventh consulships, after I had put an end to the civil wars, having attained supreme power by universal consent, I transferred the state from my own power to the control of the Roman senate and people. For this service of mine I received the title of Augustus by decree of the senate, and the doorposts of my house were publicly decked with laurels, the civic crown was affixed over my doorway, and a golden shield was set up in the Julian senate house, which, as the inscription on this shield testifies, the Roman senate and people gave me in recognition of my valor, clemency, justice, and devotion. After that time I excelled all in authority, but I possessed no more power than the others who were my colleagues in each magistracy.

35. When I held my thirteenth consulship, the senate, the equestrian order, and the entire Roman people gave me the title of ''father of the country'' and decreed that this title should be inscribed in the vestibule of my house, in the Julian senate house, and in the Augustan Forum on the pedestal of the chariot which was set up in my honor by decree of the senate. At the time I wrote this document I was in my seventy-sixth year.

Augustus, *Res Gestae*, trans. by N. Lewis and M. Reinhold, in *Roman Civilization*, Vol. 2 (New York: Columbia University Press, 1955), pp. 13, 19.

Cicero (106–43 B.C.) was the most important writer of the late Republic. [EPA]

style, as well as his values and ideas, was an important legacy for the Middle Ages and, reinterpreted, for the Renaissance.

HISTORY. The last century of the republic produced some historical writing, much of which is lost to us. Sallust (86–35 B.C.) wrote a history of the years 78–67 B.C., but only a few fragments remain to remind us of his reputation as the greatest of republican historians. His surviving work consists of two pamphlets on the Jugurthine War and on the Catilinarian conspiracy of 63 B.C. They reveal his Caesarean and antisenatorial prejudices and the stylistic influence of Thucydides.

Julius Caesar wrote important treatises on the Gallic and civil wars. They are not fully rounded historical accounts but chiefly military narratives written from Caesar's point of view and with propagandist intent. Their objective

156

*The
Foundation of
Western
Civilization in
the Ancient
World*

manner (Caesar always referred to himself in the third person) and their direct, simple, and vigorous style make them persuasive even today, and they must have been most effective with their immediate audience.

LAW. The period from the Gracchi to the fall of the republic was important in the development of Roman law. Before that time Roman law was essentially national and had developed chiefly by means of juridical decisions, case by case, but contact with foreign peoples and the influence of Greek ideas forced a change. From the last century of the republic on, the edicts of the praetors, which interpreted and even changed and added to existing law, had increasing importance in developing the Roman legal code. Quite early the edicts of the magistrates who dealt with foreigners developed the idea of the *jus gentium,* or law of peoples, as opposed to that arising strictly from the experience of the Romans. In the first century B.C. the influence of Greek thought made the idea of *jus gentium* identical with that of the *jus naturale,* or natural law, taught by the Stoics. It was this view of a world ruled by divine reason that Cicero enshrined in his treatise on the laws, *De Legibus.*

POETRY. The time of Cicero was also the period of two of Rome's greatest poets, Lucretius and Catullus, each representing a different aspect of Rome's poetic tradition. The Hellenistic poets and literary theorists saw two functions for the poet, as entertainer and as teacher. They thought the best poet combined both roles, and the Romans adopted the same view. When Naevius and Ennius wrote epics on Roman history, they combined historical and moral instruction with pleasure. Lucretius (ca. 99–ca. 55 B.C.) pursued a similar path in his epic poem *De Rerum Natura (On the Nature of the World).* In it he set forth the scientific and philosophical ideas of Epicurus and Democritus with the zeal of a missionary trying to save society from fear and superstition. He knew that his doctrine might be bitter medicine to the reader: "That is why I have tried to administer it to you in the dulcet strain of poesy, coated with the sweet honey of the Muses."[1]

Catullus (ca. 84–ca. 54 B.C.) was a poet of a thoroughly different kind. He wrote poems that were personal, even autobiographical. In imitation of the Alexandrians he wrote short poems filled with learned allusions to mythology, but he far surpassed his models in intensity of feeling. He wrote of the joys and pains of love, he hurled invective at important contemporaries like Julius Caesar, and he amused himself in witty poetic exchanges with others. He offered no moral lessons and was not interested in Rome's glorious history and in contemporary politics. In a sense he is an example of the proud, independent, pleasure-seeking nobleman who characterized part of the aristocracy at the end of the republic.

The Age of Augustus

The spirit of the Augustan Age, the Golden Age of Roman literature, was quite different, reflecting the new conditions of society. The old aristocratic order, with its system of independent nobles following their own particular interests, was gone. So was the world of poets of the lower orders, receiving patronage from any of a number of individual aristocrats. Augustus replaced the complexity of republican patronage with a simple scheme in which all patronage flowed from the *princeps,* usually through his chief cultural adviser, Maecenas. The major poets of this time, Vergil and Horace, had lost their property during the civil wars. The patronage of the *princeps* allowed them the leisure and the security to write poetry and at the same time made them dependent on him and limited their freedom of expression. They wrote on subjects that were useful for his policies and that glorified him and his family, but they were not mere propagandists. It seems evident that for the most part they were persuaded of the virtues of Augustus and his reign and sang its praises with some degree of sincerity. Because they were poets of genius, they were also able to maintain a measure of independence in their work.

VERGIL. Vergil (70–19 B.C.) was the most important of the Augustan poets. His first important works, the *Eclogues* or *Bucolics,* are pastoral idylls in a somewhat artificial mode. The subject of the *Georgics,* however, was suggested to Vergil by Maecenas. The model here was the early Greek poet Hesiod's *Works and Days,* but the mood and purpose of Vergil's poem are far different. It is, to be sure, a didactic account of the agricultural life, but it is also a paean to the beauties of nature and a hymn to the cults, traditions, and greatness of Italy. All this, of course, served the purpose of glorifying Augus-

---

[1]I, Lucretius, *De Rerum Natura,* lines 93lff.

tus' resettlement of the veterans of the civil wars on Italian farms and his elevation of Italy to special status in the empire. Vergil's greatest work is the *Aeneid*, a long national epic that succeeded in placing the history of Rome in the great tradition of the Greeks and the Trojan War. Its hero, the Trojan warrior Aeneas, personifies the ideal Roman qualities of duty, responsibility, serious purpose, and patriotism. As the Romans' equivalent of Homer, Vergil glorified not the personal honor and excellence of the Greek epic heroes but the civic greatness represented by Augustus and the peace and prosperity that he and the Julian family had given to imperial Rome.

HORACE. Horace (65–8 B.C.) was the son of a freed man and fought on the republican side until its defeat at Philippi. He was won over to the Augustan cause by the patronage of Maecenas and by the attractions of the Augustan reforms. His *Satires* are genial and humorous. His great skills as a lyric poet are best revealed in his *Odes*, which are ingenious in their adaptation of Greek meters to the requirements of Latin verse. Two of the *Odes* are directly in praise of Augustus, and many of them glorify the new Augustan order, the imperial family, and the empire.

OVID. The darker side of Augustan influence on the arts is revealed by the career of Ovid (43 B.C.–A.D. 18). He wrote light and entertaining love elegies that reveal the sophistication and the loose sexual code of a notorious sector of the Roman aristocracy. Their values and way of life were contrary to the seriousness and family-centered life Augustus was trying to foster. Ovid's *Ars Amatoria*, a poetic textbook on the art of seduction, angered Augustus and was partly responsible for the poet's exile in A.D. 8 to Tomi on the Black Sea. Ovid tried to recover favor, especially with his *Fasti*, a poetic treatment of Roman religious festivals, but to no avail. His most popular work is the *Metamorphoses*, a kind of mythological epic that turns Greek myths into charming stories in a graceful and lively style. Ovid's fame did not fade with his exile and death, but his fate was an effective warning to later poets.

HISTORY. The achievements of Augustus and his emphasis on tradition and on the continuity of his regime with the glorious history of Rome encouraged both historical and antiquarian prose works. A number of Augustan writers wrote scholarly treatises on history and geography in Greek. By far the most important and influential prose writer of the time, how-

---

Vergil on the Destiny of Rome

Vergil (70–19 B.C.) was the leading poet of the Augustan Age. His great epic, the *Aeneid*, is full of praise for Augustus, his family, his ancestors, and the settlement of the Roman world he achieved. The *Aeneid* was written in the last decade of Vergil's life.

Now fix your sight, and stand intent, to see
Your Roman race, and Julian progeny.
There mighty Caesar waits his vital hour,
Impatient for the world, and grasps his
     promised power.
But next behold the youth of form divine—
Caesar himself, exalted in his line—
Augustus, promised oft, and long foretold,
Sent to the realm that Saturn ruled of old;
Born to restore a better age of gold.
Africa and India shall his power obey;
He shall extend his propagated sway
Beyond the solar year, without the starry
     way. . . .

.   .   .   .
Let others better mould the running mass
Of metals, and inform the breathing brass,
And soften into flesh, a marble face;
Plead better at the bar; describe the skies,
And when the stars descend, and when they
     rise.
But Rome! 'tis thine alone, with awful sway,
To rule mankind, and make the world obey,
Disposing peace and war, thy own majestic
     way:
To tame the proud, the fettered slave to
     free;—
These are imperial arts, and worthy thee.

John Dryden, *The Works of Vergil* (New York: American Book Exchange, 1881), pp. 262–265.

The Gemma Augustea. This carved onyx from the first century glorifies the Emperor Augustus, who is shown on the upper left crowned with the laurels of victory and triumph. His wife Livia sitting beside him is arrayed as the goddess Roma. On the right, her son, the future emperor Tiberius, is portrayed descending from a triumphal chariot. Below the imperial family, Roman soldiers display prisoners of war and erect emblems of victory. [Kunsthistorisches Museum, Vienna]

ever, was Livy (59 B.C.–A.D. 17), an Italian from Padua. His *History of Rome* was written in Latin and treated the period from the legendary origins of Rome until 9 B.C. Only a fourth of his work is extant; of the rest we have only pitifully brief summaries. He based his history on earlier accounts, chiefly the Roman annalists, and made no effort at original research. His great achievement was in telling the story of Rome in a continuous and impressive narrative. Its purpose was moral, setting up historical models as examples of good and bad behavior, and, above all, patriotic. He glorified Rome's greatness and connected it with Rome's past, just as Augustus tried to do.

ARCHITECTURE AND SCULPTURE. The visual arts revealed the same tendencies as other aspects of Roman life under Augustus. Augustus was the great patron of the visual arts as he was of literature. He embarked on a building program that beautified Rome, glori-

fied his reign, and contributed to the general prosperity and his own popularity. He filled the Campus Martius with beautiful new buildings, theaters, baths, and basilicas; the Roman Forum was rebuilt; and Augustus built a forum of his own. At its heart was the temple of Mars the Avenger to commemorate Augustus' victory and the greatness of his ancestors. On Rome's Palatine hill he built a splendid temple to his patron god, Apollo. This was one of the many temples he constructed in pursuit of his religious policy.

Most of the building was influenced by the Greek classical style, which aimed at serenity and the ideal type. The same features were visible in the portrait sculpture of Augustus and his family. The greatest monument of the age is the Altar of Peace *(Ara Pacis)* dedicated in 9 B.C. Set originally in an open space in the Campus Martius, its walls still carry a relief. Part of it shows a procession in which Augustus and his family appear to move forward, followed in order by the magistrates, the Senate, and the people of Rome. There is no better symbol of the new order.

Life in Imperial Rome: The Apartment House

The civilization of the Roman Empire depended on the vitality of its cities, of which no more than three or four had a population of more than 75,000, the typical city having about 20,000 inhabitants. The population of Rome, however, was certainly greater than 500,000, and some scholars think it was more than a million. People coming to it for the first time found it overwhelming and were either thrilled or horrified by its size, bustle, and noise. The rich lived in elegant homes called *domus*, single-storied houses with plenty of space, an open central courtyard, and several rooms designed for specific and different purposes, such as dining, sitting, or sleeping, in privacy and relative quiet. Though only a small portion of Rome's population lived in them, these houses took up as much as a third of the city's space. Public space for temples, markets, baths, gymnasiums, theaters, forums, and governmental buildings took up another quarter of Rome's territory.

This left less than half of Rome's area to house the mass of its inhabitants. Inevitably, as the population grew, it was squeezed into mul-

Juvenal on Life in Rome

The satirical poet Juvenal lived and worked in Rome in the late first and early second centuries A.D. His poems present a vivid picture of the material and cultural world of the Romans of his time. In the following passages, he tells of the discomforts and dangers of life in the city, both indoors and out.

Who, in Praeneste's cool, or the wooded
   Volsinian uplands,
Who, on Tivoli's heights, or a small town like
   Gabii, say,
Fears the collapse of his house? But Rome is
   supported on pipestems,
Matchsticks; it's cheaper, so, for the landlord
   to shore up his ruins,
Patch up the old cracked walls, and notify all
   the tenants
They can sleep secure, though the beams are
   in ruins above them.
No, the place to live is out there, where no
   cry of Fire!
Sounds the alarm of the night, with a
   neighbor yelling for water,
Moving his chattels and goods, and the whole
   third story is smoking.
This you'll never know: for if the ground
   floor is scared first,
You are the last to burn, up there where the
   eaves of the attic

Keep off the rain, and the doves are brooding
   over their nest eggs.

.   .   .   .

Look at other things, the various dangers of
   nighttime.
How high it is to the cornice that breaks, and
   a chunk beats my brains out,
Or some slob heaves a jar, broken or cracked,
   from a window.
Bang! It comes down with a crash and proves
   its weight on the sidewalk.
You are a thoughtless fool, unmindful of
   sudden disaster,
If you don't make your will before you go out
   to have dinner.
There are as many deaths in the night as
   there are open windows
Where you pass by; if you're wise, you will
   pray, in your wretched devotions,
People may be content with no more than
   emptying slop jars.

Juvenal, *Satires*, trans. by Rolfe Humphries (Bloomington: Indiana University Press, 1958), pp. 40, 43.

tiple dwellings that grew increasingly tall. Most Romans during the imperial period lived in apartment buildings called *insulae* ("islands") that rose to a height of five or six stories and sometimes even more. The most famous of them, the Insula of Febiala, seems to have "towered above the Rome of the Antonines like a skyscraper."[2] These buildings were divided into separate apartments (*cenicula*) of undifferentiated rooms, the same plan on each floor. The apartments were cramped and uncomfortable. They had neither central heating nor an open fireplace; heat and fire for cooking came from small, portable stoves or braziers. The apartments were hot in summer, cold in winter, and stuffy and smoky when the stoves were lit. There was no plumbing, so tenants needed to go into the streets to wells or fountains for water and to public baths and latrines, or to less well-regulated places, to perform some natural functions. The higher up one lived, the more difficult these trips, so chamber pots and commodes were kept in the rooms. These receptacles were emptied into vats on the staircase landings or in the alleys outside, or on occasion, the contents, and even the containers, were tossed out the window. Roman satirists complained of the discomforts and dangers of walking the streets beneath such windows, and Roman law tried to find ways to assign responsibility for the injuries done to dignity and person.

In spite of these difficulties, the attractions of the city and the shortage of space caused rents to rise, making life in these buildings expensive

[2]J. Carcopino, *Daily Life in Ancient Rome* (New Haven, Conn.: 1940), p. 26.

Ruins of apartment houses in Ostia, the port of Rome. Built of brick and concrete, such tenements were originally several stories high. [Art Resource]

as well as uncomfortable. It was also dangerous. The houses were lightly built of concrete and brick, far too high for the limited area of their foundations, so they often collapsed. Laws limiting the height of buildings were not always obeyed and did not, in any case, always prevent disaster. The satirist Juvenal did not exaggerate much when he wrote, "We inhabit a city held up chiefly by slats, for that is how the landlord patches up the cracks in the old wall, telling the tenants to sleep peacefully under the ruin that hangs over their heads." Even more serious was the threat of fire. The floors were supported by wooden beams, and the rooms were lit by torches, candles, and oil lamps and heated by braziers. Fires broke out easily and, without running water, were not easily put out; once started, they usually led to disaster.

When we consider the character of these apartments and compare them with the attractive public places in the city, we can easily understand why the people of Rome spent most of their time out of doors.

Peace and Prosperity: Imperial Rome A.D. 14–180

The central problem for Augustus' successors was the position of the ruler and his relationship to the ruled. Augustus tried to cloak the monarchical nature of his government, but his successors soon abandoned all pretense. The ruler came to be called *imperator*—from which comes our word *emperor*—as well as *Caesar*. The latter title signified connection with the imperial house, and the former indicated the military power on which everything was based. Because Augustus was ostensibly only the "first citizen" of a restored republic and his powers were theoretically voted him by the Senate and the people, he could not legally name his successor. In fact, he plainly designated his heirs by favors lavished on them and by giving them a share in the imperial power and responsibility. Tiberius (emperor A.D. 14–37),[3] his immediate successor, was at first embarrassed by the ambiguity of his new role, but soon the monarchical and hereditary nature of the regime became patent. Gaius (Caligula, A.D. 37–41), Claudius (A.D. 41–54), and Nero (A.D. 54–68) were all descended from either Augustus or his wife, Livia, and all were elevated because of that fact. In A.D. 41 the naked military basis of imperial rule was revealed when the Praetorian Guard dragged the lame, stammering, and frightened Claudius from behind a curtain and made him emperor. In A.D. 68 the frontier legions learned what the historian Tacitus called "the secret of Empire . . . that an emperor could be made elsewhere than at Rome." Nero's incompetence and unpopularity, and especially his inability to control his armies, led to a serious rebellion in Gaul in A.D. 68. The year 69 saw four different emperors assume power in quick succession as different Roman armies took turns placing their commanders on the throne.

Vespasian (A.D. 69–79) emerged victorious from the chaos, and his sons, Titus (A.D. 79–

160

---

[3]Dates for emperors give the years of each reign.

Nero (A.D. 54–68) *was the last descendant of Augustus's family to become emperor. His incompetent rule ended in rebellion and civil war.* [Alinari/SCALA]

81) and Domitian (A.D. 81–96), carried forward his line, the Flavian dynasty. Vespasian was the first emperor who did not come from the old Roman nobility. He was a tough soldier who came from the Italian middle class. A good administrator and a hard-headed realist of rough wit, he resisted all attempts by flatterers to find noble ancestors for him. On his deathbed he is said to have ridiculed the practice of deifying emperors by saying, ''Alas, I think I am becoming a god.''

The assassination of Domitian put an end to the Flavian dynasty. Because Domitian had no close relative who had been designated as successor, the Senate put Nerva (A.D. 96–98) on the throne to avoid chaos. He was the first of the five ''good emperors,'' who included Trajan (A.D. 98–117), Hadrian (A.D. 117–138), Antoninus Pius (A.D. 138–161), and Marcus Aurelius (A.D. 161–180). Until Marcus Aurelius none of these emperors had sons, so they each followed the example set by Nerva of adopting an able senator and establishing him as successor. This rare solution to the problem of monarchical succession was, therefore, only a historical accident. The result, nonetheless, was almost a century of peaceful succession and competent rule, which ended when Marcus Aurelius allowed his incompetent son, Commodus (A.D. 180–192), to succeed him, with unfortunate results.

The genius of the Augustan settlement lay in its capacity to enlist the active cooperation of the upper classes and their effective organ, the Senate. The election of magistrates was taken from the assemblies and given to the Senate; it became the major center for legislation; and it exercised important judicial functions. This semblance of power persuaded some contemporaries and even some modern scholars that Augustus had established a ''dyarchy,'' a system of joint rule by *princeps* and Senate. This was never true, and the hollowness of the senatorial role became more apparent as time passed. Some emperors, like Vespasian, took pains to maintain, increase, and display the prestige and dignity of the Senate; others, like Caligula, Nero, and Domitian, degraded the Senate and paraded their own despotic power, but from the first its powers were illusory. Magisterial elections were, in fact, controlled by the emperors, and the Senate's legislative function quickly degenerated into mere assent to what was put before it by the emperor or his representatives. The true function of the Senate was to be a legislative and administrative extension of the emperor's rule.

There was, of course, some real opposition

161

WALL OF
ANTONINUS

WALL OF
HADRIAN

NORTH

SEA

HIBERNIA

BRITAIN

ATLANTIC

ELBE

ODER

VISTULA

RHINE

Cologne

GERMANIA
(INF.)

GERMANIA

OCEAN

SEINE

LUGDUNENSIS

LOIRE

GAUL

AQUITANIA

GERMANIA (SUP.)

RAETIA

DANUBE

NOR-
ICUM

DACIA

SARMA

DNIEPER

DNIESTER

PRUTH

NARBONENSIS

CISALPINE
GAUL

PO

(SUP.)

PANNONIA
(INF.)

DUERO

TARRACONENSIS

EBRO

RHÔNE

DALMATIA

(SUP.)

(INF.)

DANUBE

MOESIA

BLAC

CORSICA

ITALY

Rome

Apollonia

THRACE

Byzantium

LUSITANIA

SPAIN

BALEARIC IS.

SARDINIA

MACEDONIA

BITH

BAETICA

M   E   D   I

SICILY

ILLYRIA

GREECE

ASIA

ACHAEA

PISID

LYC

MAURETANIA

Carthage

T   E   R   R   A

CRETE

N   E   A   N

S   E   A

A   F   R   I   C   A

N   U   M   I   D   I   A

A   F   R   I   C   A

CYRENAICA

LIBYA

EG

	14 A.D. – DEATH OF AUGUSTUS
	14–98 A.D. – ACQUISITIONS, AUGUSTUS TO TRAJAN
	98–117 A.D. – ACQUISITIONS DURING THE REIGN OF TRAJAN

T R MILLER

PROVINCES OF
THE ROMAN EMPIRE TO A.D. 117

162

MAJOR
ROADS
OF THE
ROMAN EMPIRE

to the imperial rule. It sometimes took the form of plots against the life of the emperor. Plots and the suspicion of plots led to repression, the use of spies and paid informers, book burning, and executions. The opposition consisted chiefly of senators who looked back to republican liberty for their class and who found justification in the Greek and Roman traditions of tyrannicide as well as in the precepts of Stoicism. Plots and repression were most common under Nero and Domitian. From Nerva to Marcus Aurelius, however, the emperors, without yielding any power, again learned to enlist the cooperation of the upper class by courteous and modest deportment.

The Administration of the Empire

The provinces flourished economically and generally accepted Roman rule easily (see Map 5.1). In the eastern provinces the emperor was worshiped as a god, and even in Italy most emperors were deified after their death as long as the imperial cult established by Augustus continued. Imperial policy was for the most part a happy combination of an attempt to unify the empire and its various peoples with a respect for local customs and differences. Roman citizenship was spread ever more widely, and by A.D. 212 almost every inhabitant of the empire was a citizen. Latin became the language of the western provinces, and although the east remained essentially Greek in language and culture, even it adopted many aspects of Roman life. The spread of *Romanitas*, or Roman-ness, was more than nominal, for senators and even emperors began to be drawn from provincial families.

The army played an important role in the spread of Roman culture and the spiritual unification of the empire. The legionaries married

MAPS 5-1, 5-2 *The growth of the Empire to its greatest extent is here shown in three states—at the death of Augustus in* A.D. *14, at the death of Nerva in 98, and at the death of Trajan in 117. The division into provinces is also indicated. The inset outlines the main roads that tied the far-flung empire together.*

163

164

*The
Foundation of
Western
Civilization in
the Ancient
World*

local women and frequently settled in the province of their service when their term was over.

From an administrative and cultural standpoint the empire was a collection of cities and towns and had little to do with the countryside. Roman policy during the Principate was to raise urban centers to the status of Roman municipalities with the rights and privileges attached to them. A typical municipal charter left much responsibility in the hands of local councils and magistrates elected from the local aristocracy. Moreover, the holding of a magistracy, and later a seat on the council, carried Roman citizenship with it. Therefore the Romans enlisted the upper classes of the provinces in their own government, spread Roman law and culture, and won the loyalty of the influential people.

There were exceptions to this picture of success. The Jews found their religion incompatible with Roman demands and experienced savage repression of their rebellions in A.D. 66–70, 115–117, and 132–135. In Egypt the

---

Daily Life in a Roman Provincial Town: Graffiti from Pompeii

On the walls of the houses of Pompeii, buried and preserved by the eruption of Mount Vesuvius in A.D. 79, are many scribblings that give us an idea of what the life of ordinary people was like.

I

Twenty pairs of gladiators of Decimus Lucretius Satrius Valens, lifetime flamen *of Nero son of Caesar Augustus, and ten pairs of gladiators of Decimus Lucretius Valens, his son, will fight at Pompeii on April 8, 9, 10, 11, 12. There will be a full card of wild beast combats, and awnings [for the spectators]. Aemilius Celer [painted this sign], all alone in the moonlight.*

II

Market days: Saturday in Pompeii, Sunday in Nuceria, Monday in Atella, Tuesday in Nola, Wednesday in Cumae, Thursday in Puteoli, Friday in Rome.

III

Pleasure says: "You can get a drink here for an as *[a few cents], a better drink for two, Falernian for four."*

IV

A copper pot is missing from this shop. 65 sesterces reward if anybody brings it back, 20 sesterces if he reveals the thief so we can get our property back.

V

The weaver Successus loves the inkeeper's slave girl, Iris by name. She doesn't care for him, but he begs her to take pity on him. Written by his rival. So long.

[Answer by the rival:] Just because you're bursting with envy, don't pick on a handsomer man, a lady-killer and a gallant.

[Answer by the first writer:] There's nothing more to say or write. You love Iris, who doesn't care for you.

VI

Take your lewd looks and flirting eyes off another man's wife, and show some decency on your face!

VII

Anybody in love, come here. I want to break Venus' ribs with a club and cripple the goddess' loins. If she can pierce my tender breast, why can't I break her head with a club?

VIII

I write at Love's dictation and Cupid's instruction;

But damn it! I don't want to be a god without you.

IX

[A prostitute's sign:] I am yours for 2 asses cash.

N. Lewis and M. Reinhold, *Roman Civilization*, Vol. 2 (New York: Columbia University Press, 1955), pp. 359–360.

The ruins of Pompeii, an Italian provincial town on the Bay of Naples that was buried by volcanic ash from Mount Vesuvius in A.D. 79. Like many provincial centers during the early empire, Pompeii was a pleasant, prosperous town with elegant public buildings and comfortable houses. [*Fotocielo*]

Romans exploited the peasants ruthlessly and did not pursue a policy of urbanization.

As the efficiency of the bureaucracy grew, so did the number and scope of its functions and therefore its size. The emperors came to take a broader view of their responsibilities for the welfare of their subjects than before. Nerva conceived and Trajan introduced the *alimenta*, a program of public assistance on behalf of the children of indigent parents. More and more the emperors intervened when municipalities got into difficulties, usually financial, sending imperial troubleshooters to deal with problems. The importance and autonomy of the municipalities shrank as the central administration took a greater part in local affairs. The provincial aristocracy came to regard public service in their own cities as a burden rather than an opportunity; the price paid for the increased efficiency offered by centralized control was the loss of the vitality of the cities throughout the empire.

Augustus' successors, for the most part, accepted his conservative and defensive foreign policy. Trajan was the first emperor to take the offensive in a sustained way. Between A.D. 101 and 106 he crossed the Danube and, after hard fighting, established the new province of Dacia between the Danube and the Carpathian Mountains. He was tempted, no doubt, by its important gold mines, but he probably was also pursuing a new general strategy: to defend the empire more aggressively by driving wedges into the territory of

165

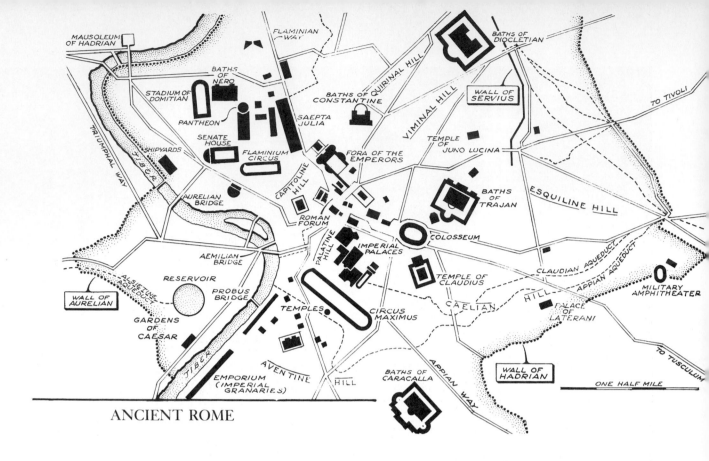

ANCIENT ROME

The Philanthropy of Herodes Atticus

The second century was a time of prosperity in the Roman Empire, when wealthy men often engaged in great philanthropic gestures to demonstrate their magnanimity and dedication to civic improvement. In the following passage, we read of the deeds of Herodes Atticus, an Athenian who reached the highest offices of the Roman Empire.

No man used his wealth to better purpose. . . . The sources of his wealth were many and derived from several families, but the greatest were the fortunes that came from his father [Atticus] and his mother. . . . This Atticus [the father] was also distinguished for his lordly spirit. As an instance, at a time when his son Herodes was overseer of the free cities of Asia, he observed that Troy was ill supplied with baths and that the inhabitants drew muddy water from their wells and had to dig cisterns to catch rain water. Accordingly, he wrote to the Emperor Hadrian to ask him not to allow an ancient city, conveniently near the sea, to perish from lack of water, but to bestow 3,000,000 drachmas upon them for a water supply, since he had already bestowed on mere villages many times that sum. The emperor approved of his advice in the letter as being in accordance with his own disposition and appointed Herodes himself to take charge of the water project. But when the outlay had reached the sum of 7,000,000 drachmas and the officials who governed Asia kept writing to the emperor that it was a scandal that the tribute of five hundred cities should be spent on the fountain of one city, the emperor expressed his disapproval of this to Atticus; whereupon Atticus replied in the most lordly fashion in the world, "Do not, O Emperor, allow yourself to be irritated over such trifles. The amount spent in excess of 3,000,000 I am presenting to my son, and my son will present it to the city."

Philostratus, *Lives of the Sophists*, trans. by N. Lewis and M. Reinhold, *Roman Civilization*, Vol. 2 (New York: Columbia University Press, 1955), p. 350.

MAP 5-3 *This is a sketch of the city of Rome during the late Empire. It indicates the seven hills on and around which the city was built, as well as the major walls, bridges, and other public sites and buildings. The Forum is between the Capitoline and Palatine hills.*

threatening barbarians. The same strategy dictated the invasion of the Parthian Empire in the east (A.D. 113–117). Trajan's early success was astonishing, and he established three new provinces in Armenia, Assyria, and Mesopotamia, but his lines were overextended. Rebellions sprang up, and the campaign crumbled.

Trajan was forced to retreat and died before getting back to Rome.

Hadrian returned to the traditional policy, keeping Dacia but abandoning the eastern provinces. Hadrian's reign marked an important shift in Rome's frontier policy. Heretofore, even under the successors of Augustus, Rome had been on the offensive against the barbarians. Although the Romans rarely gained new territory, they launched frequent attacks to chastise and pacify troublesome tribes. Hadrian hardened the Roman defenses, building a stone wall in the south of Scotland and a wooden one across the Rhine–Danube triangle. The Roman defense became rigid, and

---

Tacitus Gives a Provincial View of the Imperial Peace

Tacitus (A.D. 55–ca. 115) was a Roman senator. He is most famous as historian of Rome for the period A.D. 14–68, but the following selection comes from a eulogy for his father-in-law, Agricola. It gives an insight into the Roman Empire viewed critically.

The Britons, . . . convinced at length that a common danger must be averted by union, had, by embassies and treaties, summoned forth the whole strength of all their states. More than 30,000 armed men were now to be seen, and still there were pressing in all the youth of the country, with all whose old age was yet hale and vigorous, men renowned in war and bearing each decorations of his own. Meanwhile, among the many leaders, one superior to the rest in valour and in birth, Galgacus by name, is said to have thus harangued the multitude gathered around him and clamouring for battle:—

"Whenever I consider the origin of this war and the necessities of our position, I have a sure confidence that this day, and this union of yours, will be the beginning of freedom to the whole of Britain. To all of us slavery is a thing unknown; there are no lands beyond us, and even the sea is not safe, menaced as we are by a Roman fleet. And thus in war and battle, in which the brave find glory, even the coward will find safety. Former contests, in which, with varying fortune, the Romans were resisted, still

left in us a last hope of succour, inasmuch as being the most renowned nation of Britain, dwelling in the very heart of the country and out of sight of the shores of the conquered, we could keep even our eyes unpolluted by the contagion of slavery. To us who dwell on the uttermost confines of the earth and of freedom, this remote sanctuary of Britain's glory has up to this time been a defence. Now, however, the furthest limits of Britain are thrown open, and the unknown always passes for the marvellous. But there are no tribes beyond us, nothing indeed but waves and rocks, and the yet more terrible Romans, from whose oppression escape is vainly sought by obedience and submission. Robbers of the world, having by their universal plunder exhausted the land, they rifle the deep. If the enemy be rich, they are rapacious; if he be poor, they lust for dominion; neither the east nor the west has been able to satisfy them. Alone among men they covet with equal eagerness poverty and riches. To robbery, slaughter, plunder, they give the lying name of empire; they make a solitude and call it peace."

Tacitus, *Agricola,* in *Complete Works of Tacitus,* trans. by A. J. Church and W. Brodribb (New York: Random House, 1942), pp. 694–695.

Spoils from the temple in Jerusalem carried in triumphal procession by Roman troops. This relief from Titus's arch of victory in the Roman Forum celebrates his capture of Jerusalem after a two-year seige. The Jews found it difficult to reconcile their religion with Roman rule and frequently rebelled. [Art Resource]

initiative passed to the barbarians. Marcus Aurelius was compelled to spend most of his reign resisting dangerous attacks in the east and on the Danube frontier, and these attacks put enormous pressure on the human and financial resources of the empire.

This pressure took its toll only late in this period, which, in general, experienced considerable economic prosperity and growth. Internal peace and efficient administration benefited agriculture as well as trade and industry; farming and trade developed together as political conditions made it easier to sell farm products at a distance. This latter element encouraged the earlier tendency toward specialization of crops and the growth of large holdings. Small farms continued to exist, but the large

estate, managed by an absentee owner and growing cash crops, became the dominant form of agriculture. At first, these estates were worked chiefly by slaves, but in the first century this began to change. The end of wars of conquest made slaves less available and more expensive, for ancient societies never succeeded in breeding slaves. The tenant farmer, or *colonus*, became the mainstay of agricultural labor. Typically these sharecroppers paid rent in labor or in kind, though sometimes they made cash payments. Eventually their movement was restricted, and they were tied to the land they worked, much as were the manorial serfs of the Middle Ages. But the system was economically efficient and contributed to the general prosperity, whatever its social cost.

The Younger Pliny Describes the Growth of Tenant Farming

The reign of the Emperor Trajan (A.D. 98–117) has usually been considered near the peak of the Roman Empire's prosperity. The Younger Pliny (ca. A.D. 61–114), however, one of Trajan's associates, described conditions that showed that the growth of economic and social problems characteristic of the late empire had already begun in his own time. In the following letter to a friend, Pliny made it clear that tenant farming was characteristic of Roman agriculture and that tenants were not faring well.

Gaius Plinius to his dear Paulinus, greeting. . . . I am detained by the necessity of leasing my estates so as to set them in order for several years. In which connection I am obliged to adopt new arrangements. For in the last five-year period, despite large reductions [of rent], the arrears mounted. Hence several tenants no longer have any concern to reduce a debt which they despair of being able to pay off; they even seize and consume whatever is produced, acting like people who think they no longer have to be thrifty since *it is not their own property. The growing evils, therefore, have to be faced and relieved. There is one method of remedying them—to least not for a rent in money but on shares, and then to place some of my men to superintend the work and guard the produce. . . . It is true that this requires great integrity, keen eyes, and many hands. However, I must try the experiment and, as in a chronic disease, try and see what help a change may bring.*

Pliny, *Letters*, in N. Lewis and M. Reinhold, *Roman Civilization*, Vol. 2 (New York: Columbia University Press, 1955), p. 177.

The Culture of the Early Empire

LITERATURE. In Latin literature the years between the death of Augustus and the time of Marcus Aurelius are known as the Silver Age, and as the name implies, work of high quality was produced although probably not of so high a quality as in the Augustan era. In contrast to the hopeful, positive optimists of the Augustans, the writers of the Silver Age were gloomy, negative, and pessimistic. In the works of the former period, praise of the emperor, his achievements, and the world abounds; in the latter, criticism and satire lurk everywhere.

Some of the most important writers of the Silver Age came from the Stoic opposition and reflected its hostility to the growing power and personal excesses of the emperors.

The writers of the second century A.D. appear to have turned away from contemporary affairs and even recent history. Historical writing was about remote periods so that there was less danger of irritating imperial sensibilities. Scholarship was encouraged, but we hear little of poetry, especially any dealing with dangerous subjects.

In the third century A.D. romances written in Greek became popular and provide further evidence of the tendency of writers of the time to seek and provide escape from contemporary realities.

ARCHITECTURE. The prosperity and relative stability of the first two centuries of imperial Rome allowed for the full development of the Roman contribution to architecture. To the fundamental styles of buildings developed by the Greeks, the Romans added little; the great public bath and a new, free-standing kind of amphitheater were the main innovations.

The main contribution of the Romans lay in the great size of the structures they could build and in the advances in engineering that made these large structures possible. While keeping the basic post-and-lintel construction used by the Greeks, the Romans added to it the principle of the semicircular arch, borrowed from the Etruscans. They also made good use of concrete, a building material first used by the Hellenistic Greeks and fully developed by the Romans. The new principle, sometimes combined with the new material, allowed progress

Interior of the Pantheon, Rome. Built by the emperor Hadrian ca. A.D. 126, it is a great concrete drum with a cupola. Its design has inspired architects for centuries, including the dome of St. Peter's in Rome and Frank Lloyd Wright's Guggenheim Museum in New York. [Robert Frerck]

over the old style. The arch combined with the post and lintel produced the great Colosseum built by the Flavian emperors. When used internally in the form of vaults and domes, the arch permitted great buildings like the baths, of which the most famous and best preserved are those of the later emperors Caracalla and Diocletian.

One of Rome's most famous buildings, the Pantheon, begun by Augustus' friend Agrippa and rebuilt by Hadrian, is a good example of the combination of all these elements. Its portico of Corinthian columns is of Greek origin, but its rotunda of brick-faced concrete with its domed ceiling and relieving arches is thoroughly Roman. The new engineering also made possible the construction of more mundane but more useful structures like bridges and aqueducts.

SOCIETY. Seen from the harsh perspective of human history, the first two centuries of the Roman Empire deserve their reputation of a "golden age," but by the second century A.D., troubles had arisen, troubles that foreshadowed the difficult times ahead. The literary efforts of the time reveal a flight from the present and from reality and the public realm to the past, to romance, to private pursuits. Some of the same aspects may be seen in the more prosaic world of everyday life, especially in the decline of vitality in local government.

In the first century A.D. members of the upper classes vied with one another for election to municipal office and for the honor of doing service to their communities. By the second century A.D. much of their zeal had disappeared, and it became necessary for the emperors to intervene to correct abuses in local affairs

This sandstone relief from a Roman tomb in the Rhineland illustrates the comfortable life of the provincial upper classes in the first two centuries A.D. It shows a wealthy lady seated in a wicker chair. Her four slave girls attend her: one does her hair, while another holds up a mirror. The other two hold a perfume flask and a small pitcher.

The Roman Baths: Two Views

Public baths played an important part in the lives of the Romans of the imperial period. The finest architects built them, beautifully and expensively, for the citizens not only of Rome, but of most of the major cities in the empire. The baths served as vast community centers for social life and recreation. The first selection was written by Lucian, a writer of the second century A.D., who described the magnificence of the baths. The second selection presents a more jaundiced view of the people who used them. It was written by Lucius Annaeus Seneca (ca. 4 B.C.–A.D. 65), who was Nero's tutor and a leading Roman representative of the Stoic school of philosophy.

The building suits the magnitude of the site, accords well with the accepted idea of such an establishment, and shows regard for the principles of lighting. The entrance is high, with a flight of broad steps of which the tread is greater than the pitch, to make them easy to ascend. On entering, one is received into a public hall of good size, with ample accommodations for servants and attendants. On the left are the lounging rooms, also of just the right sort for a bath, attractive, brightly lighted retreats. Then, besides them, a hall, larger than need be for the purposes of a bath, but necessary for the reception of richer persons. Next, capacious locker rooms to undress in, on each side, with a very high and brilliantly lighted hall between them, in which are three swimming pools of cold water; it is finished in Laconian marble, and has two statues of white marble in the ancient style, one of Hygeia, the other of Aesculapius.

On leaving this hall, you come into another which is slightly warmed instead of meeting you at once with fierce heat; it is oblong, and has an apse on each side. Next to it, on the right, is a very bright hall, nicely fitted up for massage, which has on each side an entrance decorated with Phrygian marble, and receives those who come in from the exercising floor. Then near this is another hall, the most beautiful in the world, in which one can stand or sit with comfort, linger without danger, and stroll about with profit. It also is refulgent with Phrygian marble clear to the roof. Next comes the hot corridor, faced with Numidian marble. The hall beyond it is very beautiful, full of abundant light and aglow with color like that of purple hangings. It contains three hot tubs.

When you have bathed, you need not go back through the same rooms, but can go directly to the cold room through a slightly warmed chamber. Everywhere there is copious illumination and full indoor daylight. . . . Why should I go on to tell you of the exercising floor and of the cloak rooms? . . . Moreover, it is beautiful with all other marks of thoughtfulness—with two toilets, many exits, and two devices for telling time, a water clock that makes a bellowing sound and a sundial.

Lucian, *Hippias, or the Bath*, in N. Lewis and M. Reinhold, *Roman Civilization*, Vol. 2 (New York: Columbia University Press, 1955), pp. 227–228.

I live over a bathing establishment. Picture to yourself now the assortment of voices, the sound of which is enough to sicken one. When the stronger fellows are exercising and swinging heavy leaden weights in their hands, when they are working hard or pretending to be working hard, I hear their groans; and whenever they release their pent-up breath, I hear their hissing and jarring breathing. When I have to do with a lazy fellow who is content with a cheap rubdown, I hear the slap of the hand pummeling his shoulders, changing its sound according as the hand is laid on flat or curved. If now a professional ball player comes along and begins to keep score, I am done for. Add to this the arrest of a brawler or a thief, and the fellow who always likes to hear his own voice in the bath, and those who jump into the pool with a mighty splash as they strike the water. In addition to those whose voices are, if nothing else, natural, imagine the hair plucker keeping up a constant chatter in his thin and strident voice, to attract more attention, and never silent except when he is plucking armpits and making the customer yell instead of yelling himself. It disgusts me to enumerate the varied cries of the sausage dealer and confectioner and of all the peddlers of the cook shops, hawking their wares, each with his own peculiar intonation.

Seneca, *Moral Epistles*, in N. Lewis and M. Reinhold, *Roman Civilization*, Vol. 2 (New York: Columbia University Press, 1955), p. 228.

172

*The
Foundation of
Western
Civilization in
the Ancient
World*

A gladitorial show. This mosaic was found in Leptis Magna, a prosperous Roman city in North Africa, modern Libya. On the top we see the orchestra that played during the show. In the middle armed men duel with each other. At the bottom men hunt wild beasts, while leopards savage condemned criminals tied to stakes. [Roger Wood]

and even to force unwilling members of the ruling classes to accept public office. The reluctance to serve was caused largely by the imperial practice of holding magistrates and councilmen personally and collectively responsible for the revenues due. There were even some instances of magistrates' fleeing to avoid their office, a practice that became widespread in later centuries.

All of these difficulties reflected the presence of more basic problems. The prosperity brought by the end of civil war and the influx of wealth from the east, especially Egypt, could not sustain itself beyond the first half of the second century A.D. There also appears to have been a decline in population for reasons that remain mysterious. The cost of government kept rising as the emperors were required to maintain a costly standing army, to keep the people in Rome happy with "bread and circuses," to pay for an increasingly numerous bureaucracy, and, especially in the reign of Marcus Aurelius, to wage expensive wars to defend the frontiers against dangerous and determined barbarian enemies. The ever-increasing need for money compelled the emperors to raise taxes, to press hard on their subjects, and to bring on inflation by debasing the coinage. These were the elements that were to bring on the desperate crises that ultimately destroyed the empire, but under the able emperors, from Trajan to Marcus Aurelius, the Romans met the challenge successfully.

The Rise of Christianity

The story of how Christianity emerged, spread, survived, and ultimately conquered the Roman Empire is one of the most remarkable in history. Its origin among poor people from an unimportant and remote province of the empire gave little promise of what was to come. Christianity faced the hostility of the established religious institutions of its native Judaea and had to compete not only against the official cults of Rome and the highly sophisticated philosophies of the educated classes but even against other "mystery" religions like the cults of Mithra, Isis and Osiris, and many others. In

---

Seneca Describes Gladiatorial Shows at Rome

Roman society was never gentle, but by imperial times the public had become addicted to brutal public displays of violence in the form of combats involving gladiators. At first, gladiators were enslaved prisoners of war or condemned criminals, but later free men entered the combats, driven by poverty. They were all trained in schools by professional trainers. The following selection by Seneca gives an unfriendly account of the shows and of the spectators who watched them.

I chanced to stop in at a midday show, expecting fun, wit, and some relaxation, when men's eyes take respite from the slaughter of their fellow men. It was just the reverse. The preceding combats were merciful by comparison; now all trifling is put aside and it is pure murder. The men have no protective covering. Their entire bodies are exposed to the blows, and no blow is ever struck in vain. . . . In the morning men are thrown to the lions and the bears, at noon they are thrown to their spectators. The spectators call for the slayer to be thrown to those who in turn will slay him, and they detain the victor for an- *other butchering. The outcome for the combatants is death; the fight is waged with sword and fire. This goes on while the arena is free. "But one of them was a highway robber, he killed a man!" Because he killed he deserved to suffer this punishment, granted. . . . "Kill him! Lash him! Burn him! Why does he meet the sword so timidly? Why doesn't he kill boldly? Why doesn't he die game? Whip him to meet his wounds! Let them trade blow for blow, chests bare and within reach!" And when the show stops for intermission, "Let's have men killed meanwhile! Let's not have nothing going on!"*

Seneca, *Moral Epistles*, in N. Lewis and M. Reinhold, *Roman Civilization*, Vol. 2 (New York: Columbia University Press, 1955), p. 230.

174

*The
Foundation of
Western
Civilization in
the Ancient
World*

addition to all this, the Christians faced the opposition of the imperial government and even formal persecution, yet Christianity achieved toleration and finally exclusive command as the official religion of the empire.

Jesus of Nazareth

An attempt to understand this amazing outcome must begin with Jesus of Nazareth, though there are many problems in arriving at a clear picture of his life and teachings. Apart from the question of sectarian prejudices that might affect the historian's judgment, the sources present special difficulties. The most important evidence is in the Gospel accounts. All of them were written well after the death of Jesus; the earliest, by Mark, is dated about A.D. 70, and the latest, by John, about A.D. 100. They are not, moreover, attempts at simply describing the life of Jesus with historical accuracy; they are statements of faith by true believers. The authors of the Gospels believed that Jesus was the son of God and that he had come into the world to redeem humanity and to bring immortality to those who believed in him and followed his way; to the Gospel writers, Jesus' resurrection was striking proof of his teachings. At the same time, the Gospels regard Jesus as a figure in history, and they recount events in his life as well as his sayings. To distinguish historical fact from myth and religious doctrine is not easy, but there is agreement on some of the basic points.

Mark Describes the Resurrection of Jesus

Belief that Jesus rose from the dead after his Crucifixion (about A.D. 30) was and is central to traditional Christian doctrine. The record of the Resurrection in the Gospel of Mark, written a generation later (toward A.D. 70), is the earliest we have. The significance to most Christian groups revolves about the assurance given them that death and the grave are not final and that, instead, salvation for a future life is possible. The appeal of these views was to be nearly universal in the West during the Middle Ages. The church was commonly thought to be the means of implementing the promise of salvation; hence the enormous importance of the church's sacramental system, its rules, and its clergy.

And when evening had come, since it was the day of Preparation, that is, the day before the sabbath, Joseph of Arimathea, a respected member of the council, who was also himself looking for the kingdom of God, took courage and went to Pilate, and asked for the body of Jesus. And Pilate wondered if he were already dead; and summoning the centurion, he asked him whether he was already dead. And when he learned from the centurion that he was dead, he granted the body to Joseph. And he bought a linen shroud, and taking him down, wrapped him in the linen shroud, and laid him in a tomb which had been hewn out of the rock; and he rolled a stone against the door of the tomb. Mary Magdalene and Mary the mother of Jesus saw where he was laid.

And when the sabbath was past, Mary Magdalene, and Mary the mother of James, and Sa-lome, bought spices, so that they might go and anoint him. And very early on the first day of the week they went to the tomb when the sun had risen. And they were saying to one another, "Who will roll away the stone for us from the door of the tomb?" And looking up, they saw that the stone was rolled back; for it was very large. And entering the tomb, they saw a young man sitting on the right side, dressed in a white robe; and they were amazed. And he said to them, "Do not be amazed; you seek Jesus of Nazareth, who was crucified. He has risen, he is not here, see the place where they laid him. But go, tell his disciples and Peter that he is going before you to Galilee; there you will see him, as he told you." And they went out and fled from the tomb; for trembling and astonishment had come upon them; and they said nothing to any one, for they were afraid.

Gospel of Mark 15:42–47; 16:1–8, *Revised Standard Version of the Bible* (New York: Thomas Nelson and Sons, 1946, 1952).

Early Christian art showing Christ arrested by soldiers on the night before his crucifixion. Note that Christ is portrayed clean-shaven and dressed in the toga of a Roman aristocrat. [Hirmir Fotoarchiv]

There is no reason to doubt that Jesus was born in the province of Judaea in the time of Augustus and that he was a most effective teacher in the tradition of the prophets. This tradition promised the coming of a Messiah (in Greek, *christos*—so *Jesus Christ* means "Jesus the Messiah"), the redeemer who would make Israel triumph over its enemies and establish the kingdom of God on earth. In fact, Jesus seems to have insisted that the Messiah would not establish an earthly kingdom but would bring an end to the world as human beings knew it at the Day of Judgment. On that day God would reward the righteous with immortality and happiness in heaven and condemn the wicked to eternal suffering in hell. Until that day, which his followers believed would come very soon, Jesus taught the faithful to abandon sin and worldly concerns; to follow him and his way; to follow the moral code described in the Sermon on the Mount, which preached love, charity, and humility; and to believe in him and his divine mission.

Jesus had success and won a considerable following, especially among the poor. This success caused great suspicion among the upper classes. His novel message and his criticism of the current religious practices connected with the temple at Jerusalem and its priests provoked the hostility of the religious establishment. A misunderstanding of the movement made it easy to convince the Roman governor that Jesus and his followers might be dangerous revolutionaries. He was put to death in Jerusalem by the cruel and degrading device of crucifixion, probably in A.D. 30. His followers

175

believed that he was resurrected on the third day after his death, and that belief became a critical element in the religion that they propagated throughout the Roman Empire and beyond.

Although the new belief spread quickly to the Jewish communities of Syria and Asia Minor, there is reason to believe that it might have had only a short life as a despised Jewish heresy were it not for the conversion and career of Saint Paul.

Paul of Tarsus

Paul was born Saul, a citizen of the Cilician city of Tarsus in Asia Minor. Even though he had been trained in Hellenistic culture and was a Roman citizen, he was a zealous member of the Jewish sect known as the Pharisees, the group that was most strict in its insistence on adherence to the Jewish law. He took a vigorous part in the persecution of the early Christians until his own conversion outside Damascus about A.D. 35. The great problem facing the early Christians was their relationship to Judaism. If the new faith was a version of Judaism, then it must adhere to the Jewish law and seek converts only among Jews. James, called the brother of Jesus, was a conservative who held to that view, whereas the Hellenist Jews tended to see it as a new and universal religion. To force all converts to adhere to Jewish law would have been fatal to the growth of the new sect, for its many technicalities and dietary prohibitions were strange to gentiles, and the necessity of circumcision—a frightening, painful, and dangerous operation for adults— would have been a tremendous deterrent to conversion. Paul, converted and with his new name, supported the position of the Hellenists and soon won many converts among the gentiles. After some conflict within the sect, Paul won out, and the "apostle to the gentiles" deserves recognition as a crucial contributor to the success of Christianity.

Paul believed it important that the followers of Jesus be evangelists (messengers), to spread the gospel ("good news") of God's gracious gift, for he taught that Jesus would soon return for the Day of Judgment, and it was important that all who would should believe in him and accept his way. Faith in Jesus as the Christ was necessary but not sufficient for salvation, nor could good deeds alone achieve it. That final blessing of salvation was a gift of God's grace that would be granted to some but not to all.

Organization

Paul and the other apostles did their work well, and the new religion spread throughout the Roman Empire and even beyond its borders. It had its greatest success in the cities and for the most part among the poor and uneducated. The rites of the early communities appear to have been simple and few. Baptism by water removed original sin and permitted participation in the community and its activities. The central ritual was a common meal called the *agape* ("love feast"), followed by the ceremony of the *eucharist* ("thanksgiving"), a celebration of the Lord's Supper in which unleavened bread was eaten and unfermented wine was drunk. There were also prayers, hymns, and readings from the Gospels.

Not all the early Christians were poor, and it became customary for the rich to provide for the poor at the common meals. The sense of common love fostered in these ways focused the community's attention on the needs of the weak, the sick, the unfortunate, and the unprotected. This concern gave the early Christian communities a warmth and a human appeal that stood in marked contrast to the coldness and impersonality of the pagan cults. No less attractive were the promise of salvation, the importance to God of each individual human soul, and the spiritual equality of all in the new faith. As Paul put it, "There is neither Jew nor Greek, there is neither slave nor free, there is neither male nor female; for you are all one in Christ Jesus."[4]

The future of Christianity depended on its communities' finding an organization that would preserve unity within the group and help protect it against enemies outside. At first, the churches had little formal organization. Soon, it appears, affairs were placed in the hands of boards of *presbyters* ("elders") and *deacons* ("those who serve"). By the second century A.D., as their numbers grew, the Christians of each city tended to accept the authority and leadership of bishops (*episkopoi*, or "overseers"), who were elected by the congregation to lead them in worship and to supervise funds. As time passed, the bishops extended their authority over the Christian communities in outlying towns and the countryside. The power and almost monarchical authority of the bishops was soon enhanced by the doctrine of Apostolic Succession, which asserted that the

---

[4]Galatians 3:28. *Revised Standard Version of the Bible.*

powers that Jesus had given his original disciples were passed on from bishop to bishop by ordination.

The bishops kept in touch with one another, maintained communications between different Christian communities, and prevented doctrinal and sectarian splintering, which would have destroyed Christian unity. They maintained internal discipline and dealt with the civil authorities. After a time they began the practice of coming together in councils to settle difficult questions, to establish orthodox opinion, and even to expel as heretics those who would not accept it. It seems unlikely that Christianity could have survived the travails of its early years without such strong internal organization and government.

The Persecution of Christians

The new faith soon incurred the distrust of the pagan world and of the imperial government. At first Christians were thought of as a Jewish sect and were therefore protected by

A Roman painting on glass of Saints Peter and Paul. [*Metropolitan Museum of Art, Rogers Fund*, 1916]

Nero's Persecution of Christians

In the year A.D. 64 a terrible fire broke out in the city of Rome. The people blamed the Emperor Nero, and to divert suspicion from himself, he launched the first official prosecutions of Christians by the Roman government.

. . . All human efforts, all the lavish gifts of the emperor, and the propitiations of the gods, did not banish the sinister belief that the conflagration was the result of an order. Consequently, to get rid of the report, Nero fastened the guilt and inflicted the most exquisite tortures on a class hated for their abominations, called Christians by the populace. Christus, from whom the name had its origin, suffered the extreme penalty during the reign of Tiberius at the hands of one of our procurators, Pontius Pilatus, and a most mischievous superstition, thus checked for the moment, again broke out not only in Judaea, the first source of the evil, but even in Rome, where all things hideous and shameful from every part of the world find their centre and become popular. Accordingly, an arrest was first made of all who pleaded guilty; then, upon their information, an immense multitude was convicted, not so much of the crime of firing the city, as of hatred against mankind. Mockery of every sort was added to their deaths. Covered with the skins of beasts, they were torn by dogs and perished, or were nailed to crosses, or were doomed to the flames and burnt, to serve as a nightly illumination, when daylight had expired.

Nero offered his gardens for the spectacle, and was exhibiting a show in the circus, while he mingled with the people in the dress of a charioteer or stood aloft on a car. Hence, even for criminals who deserved extreme and exemplary punishment, there arose a feeling of compassion; for it was not, as it seemed, for the public good, but to glut one man's cruelty, that they were being destroyed.

Tacitus, *Annals*, 15. 44, trans. by A. J. Church and W. J. Brodribb.

Roman law. It soon became clear, however, that they were something quite different. They seemed both mysterious and dangerous. They denied the existence of the pagan gods and so were accused of atheism. Their refusal to worship the emperor was judged to be treason. Because they kept mostly to themselves, took no part in civic affairs, engaged in secret rites, and had an organized network of local associations, they were misunderstood and suspected. The love feasts were erroneously reported to be scenes of sexual scandal, and the alarming doctrine of the actual presence of Jesus' body in the eucharist was distorted into an accusation of cannibalism. The privacy and secrecy of Christian life and worship ran counter to a traditional Roman dislike of any private association, especially any of a religious nature, and the Christians thus earned the reputation of being "haters of humanity." Claudius expelled them from the city of Rome, and Nero tried to make them scapegoats for the great fire that struck the city in A.D. 64. By the end of the first century "the name alone"—that is, simple membership in the Christian community—was a crime.

But for the most part the Roman government did not take the initiative in attacking Christians in the first two centuries. When one of the emperor Trajan's governors sought instructions for dealing with the Christians, Trajan urged moderation: Christians were not to be sought out, anonymous accusations were to be disregarded, and anyone denounced could be acquitted merely by abjuring Christ and sacrificing to the emperor. Unfortunately no true Christian could meet the conditions, so there were some martyrdoms.

Most persecutions in this period, however, were instituted not by the government but by mob action. Though they lived quiet, inoffensive lives, some Christians must have seemed

---

Pliny and Trajan Discuss the Christians in the Empire

Pliny the Younger was the governor of the province of Bithynia in Asia Minor about A.D. 112. The following exchange between him and the Emperor Trajan is important evidence of imperial policy toward the Christians at the time.

TO THE EMPEROR TRAJAN

Having never been present at any trials of the Christians, I am unacquainted with the method and limits to be observed either in examining or punishing them.

. . . .

In the meanwhile, the method I have observed towards those who have been denounced to me as Christians is this: I interrogated them whether they were Christians; if they confessed it, I repeated the question twice again, adding the threat of capital punishment; if they still persevered, I ordered them to be executed. For whatever the nature of their creed might be, I could at least feel no doubt that contumacy and inflexible obstinacy deserved chastisement. There were others also possessed with the same infatuation, but being citizens of Rome, I directed them to be carried thither. . . .

TRAJAN TO PLINY

The method you have pursued, my dear Pliny, in sifting the cases of those denounced to you as Christians is extremely proper. It is not possible to lay down any general rule which can be applied as the fixed standard in all cases of this nature. No search should be made for these people, when they are denounced and found guilty they must be punished; with the restriction, however, that when the party denies himself to be a Christian, and shall give proof that he is not (that is, by adoring our Gods) he shall be pardoned on the ground of repentance, even though he may have formerly incurred suspicion. Informations without the accuser's name subscribed must not be admitted in evidence against anyone, as it is introducing a very dangerous precedent, and by no means agreeable to the spirit of the age.

Pliny the Younger, *Letters*, trans. by W. Melmoth, rev. by W. M. Hutchinson (London: William Heinemann, Ltd; Cambridge, Mass.: Harvard University Press, 1935), pp. 401, 403, 407.

unbearably smug and self-righteous. Unlike the tolerant, easygoing pagans, who were generally willing to accept the new gods of foreign people and add them to the pantheon, the Christians denied the reality of the pagan gods. They proclaimed the unique rightness of their own way and looked forward to their own salvation and the damnation of nonbelievers. It is not surprising, therefore, that pagans disliked these strange and unsocial people, tended to blame misfortunes on them, and, in extreme cases, turned to violence. But even this adversity had its uses. It weeded out the weaklings among the Christians, brought greater unity to those who remained faithful, and provided the church with martyrs around whom legends could grow that would inspire still greater devotion and dedication.

The Emergence of Catholicism

Division within the Christian church may have been an even greater threat to its existence than persecution from outside. The great majority of Christians never accepted complex, intellectualized opinions but held to what even then were traditional, simple, conservative beliefs. This body of majority opinion and the church that enshrined it came to be called *Catholic*, which means "universal." Its doctrines were deemed orthodox, whereas those holding contrary opinions were heretics.

The need to combat heretics, however, compelled the orthodox to formulate their own views more clearly and firmly. By the end of the second century A.D., an orthodox canon had been shaped that included the Old Testament, the Gospels, and the Epistles of Paul, among other writings. The process was not completed for at least two more centuries, but a vitally important start had been made. The orthodox declared the church itself to be the depository of Christian teaching and the bishops to be its receivers. They also drew up creeds, brief statements of faith to which true Christians should adhere. In the first century all that was required of one to be a Christian was to be baptized, to partake of the eucharist, and to call Jesus the Lord. By the end of the second century an orthodox Christian—that is, a member of the Catholic Church—was required to accept its creed, its canon of holy writings, and the authority of the bishops. The loose structure of the apostolic church had given way to an organized body with recognized leaders able to define its faith and to ex-

clude those who did not accept it. Whatever the shortcomings of this development, there can be little doubt that it provided the clarity, unity, and discipline needed for survival.

Rome As a Center of the Early Church

During this same period the church in the city of Rome came to have special prominence. As the center of communications and the capital of the empire, Rome had natural advantages. After the Roman destruction of Jerusalem in 135 A.D., no other city had any convincing claim to primacy in the church. Besides having the largest single congregation of Christians, Rome also benefited from the tradition that both Jesus' apostles Peter and Paul were martyred there. Peter, moreover,

The Catacomb of the Jordani in Rome. The early Christians built miles of tunnels, called catacombs, in Rome. They were used as underground cemeteries and as refuges from persecution. [Leonard von Matt.]

180

*The
Foundation of
Western
Civilization in
the Ancient
World*

was thought to be the first bishop of Rome, and the Gospel of Matthew (16:18) reported Jesus' statement to Peter: "Thou art Peter [in Greek, *Petros*] and upon this rock [in Greek, *petra*] I will build my church." Eastern Christians might later point out that Peter had been leader of the Christian community at Antioch before he went to Rome, but in the second century the church at Antioch, along with the other Christian churches of Asia Minor, was fading in influence, and by 200 A.D. Rome was the most important center of Christianity. Because of the city's early influence and because of the Petrine doctrine derived from the Gospel of Matthew, later bishops of Rome claimed supremacy in the Catholic Church, but as the era of the "good emperors" came to a close, this controversy was far in the future.

The Crisis of the Third Century

Dio Cassius, a historian of the third century A.D., wrote of the Roman Empire after the death of Marcus Aurelius as a decline from "a kingdom of gold into one of iron and rust," and though we have seen that the gold contained more than a little impurity, there is no reason to quarrel with Dio's assessment of his own time. Commodus (A.D. 180–192), the son of Marcus Aurelius, proved the wisdom of the "good emperors" in selecting their successors for their talents rather than for family ties, for Commodus was incompetent and autocratic. He reduced the respect in which the imperial office was held, and his assassination brought the return of civil war. Even an excellent emperor, however, would have had a difficult time as Rome's troubles, internal as well as external, grew.

Barbarian Invasions

The pressure on Rome's frontiers, already serious in the time of Marcus Aurelius, reached massive proportions in the third century. In the east the frontiers were threatened by a new power arising in the old Persian Empire. In the third century B.C. the Parthians had succeeded in making the Iranians independent of the Hellenistic kings and had established an empire of their own on the old foundations of the Persian Empire. Several Roman attempts to conquer them had failed, but as late as A.D. 198 the

Romans were able to reach and destroy the Parthian capital and bring at least northern Mesopotamia under their rule. In A.D. 224, however, a new Iranian dynasty, the Sassanians, seized control from the Parthians and brought new vitality to Persia. They soon recovered Mesopotamia and made raids deep into Roman provinces. In A.D. 260 they humiliated the Romans by actually taking the Emperor Valerian prisoner; he died in captivity.

On the western and northern frontiers the pressure came not from a well-organized rival empire but from an ever-increasing number of German tribes. Though they had been in contact with the Romans at least since the second century B.C., they had not been much affected by civilization. The men did no agricultural work, confining their activities to hunting, drinking, and fighting. They were organized on a family basis by clans, hundreds, and tribes led by chiefs, usually from a royal family, elected by the assembly of fighting men. The king was surrounded by a collection of warriors, whom the Romans called his *comitatus*. These tough barbarians were always eager for plunder and were much attracted by the civilized delights they knew existed beyond the frontier of the Rhine and the Danube rivers.

The most aggressive of the Germans in the third century A.D. were the Goths. Centuries earlier they had wandered from their ancestral home near the Baltic Sea into the area of southern Russia. In the 220s and 230s A.D. they began to put pressure on the Danube frontier, and by about A.D. 250 they were able to penetrate into the empire and overrun the Balkan provinces. The need to meet this threat and the one posed by the Persian Sassanids in the east made the Romans weaken their western frontiers, and other Germanic peoples—the Franks and the Alemanni—broke through in those regions. There was a considerable danger that Rome would be unable to meet this challenge.

Rome's perils were caused, no doubt, by the unprecedentedly numerous and simultaneous attacks against her, but Rome's internal weakness encouraged these attacks. The Roman army was not what it had been in its best days. By the second century A.D. it was made up mostly of romanized provincials. The pressure on the frontiers and epidemics of plague in the time of Marcus Aurelius forced the emperor to resort to the conscription of slaves, gladiators, barbarians, and brigands. Even more important, the Romans failed to respond to the new conditions of constant pressure on all the frontiers. A strong, mobile reserve that could meet a threat in one place without causing a weakness elsewhere might have helped, but no such unit was created.

Septimius Severus (emperor A.D. 193–211) and his successors played a crucial role in the transformation of the character of the Roman army. Septimius was a military usurper who owed everything to the support of his soldiers. He meant to establish a family dynasty, in contrast to the policy of the "good emperors" of the second century, and he was prepared to make Rome into an undisguised military monarchy. Septimius drew recruits for the army increasingly from peasants of the less civilized provinces, and the result was a barbarization of Rome's military forces.

Economic Difficulties

These changes were a response to the great financial needs caused by the barbarian attacks. Inflation had forced Commodus to raise the soldiers' pay, but the Severan emperors had to double it to keep up with prices, which increased the imperial budget by as much as 25 per cent. The emperors resorted to inventing new taxes, debasing the coinage, and even to selling the palace furniture, to raise money. Even then it was hard to recruit troops, and the new style of military life introduced by Septimius—with its laxer discipline, more pleasant duties, and greater opportunity for advance-

REIGNS OF SELECTED LATE EMPIRE RULERS (ALL DATES ARE A.D.)	
Commodus	180–192
Septimius Severus	193–211
Alexander Severus	222–235
Decius	249–251
Valerian	253–260
Gallienus	253–268
Claudius II Gothicus	268–270
Aurelian	270–275
Diocletian	284–305
Constantine	306–337
Constantine sole emperor	324–337
Constantius II	337–361
Julian the Apostate	361–363
Valentinian	364–375
Valens	364–378
Theodosius	379–395

ment, not only in the army but in Roman society—was needed to attract men into the army. The policy proved effective for a short time but could not prevent the chaos of the late third century.

The same forces that caused problems for the army did great damage to society at large. The shortage of workers reduced agricultural pro-

Roman tax collectors. The economic, military, and social problems of the third century forced the emperors to increase the burden of taxation, which fell with increasing severity on the middle and upper classes of the provinces. [Trier Museum]

182

*The
Foundation of
Western
Civilization in
the Ancient
World*

duction. As external threats distracted the emperors, they were less able to preserve domestic peace. Piracy, brigandage, and the neglect of roads and harbors all hampered trade. So, too, did the debasement of the coinage and the inflation in general. Imperial exactions and confiscations of the property of the rich removed badly needed capital from productive use. More and more the government was required to demand services that had been given gladly in the past. Because the empire lived hand-to-mouth, with no significant reserve fund and no system of credit financing, the emperors were led to compel the people to provide food, supplies, money, and labor. The upper classes in the cities were made to serve as administrators without pay and to meet deficits in revenue out of their own pockets. Sometimes these demands caused provincial rebellions, as in Egypt and Gaul. More typically they caused peasants and even town administrators to flee to escape their burdens. The result of all these difficulties was to weaken Rome's economic strength when it was most needed.

The Social Order

The new conditions caused important changes in the social order. The Senate and the traditional ruling class were decimated by direct attacks from hostile emperors and by economic losses. Their ranks were filled by men coming up through the army. The whole state began to take on an increasingly military appearance. Distinctions among the classes by dress had been traditional since the republic, but in the third and fourth centuries A.D. they developed to the point where the people's everyday clothing was a kind of uniform that precisely revealed their status. Titles were assigned to ranks in society as to ranks in the army, although they were more grandiloquent. The most important distinction was the one formally established by Septimius Severus, which drew a sharp line between the *honestiores* (senators, equestrians, the municipal aristocracy, and the soldiers) and the lower classes, or *humiliores*. Septimius gave the *honestiores* a privileged position before the law. They were given lighter punishments, could not be tortured, and alone had the right of appeal to the emperor.

As time passed, it became more difficult to move from the lower order to the higher, another example of the growing rigidity of the

late Roman Empire. Peasants were tied to their lands, artisans to their crafts, soldiers to the army, merchants and shipowners to the needs of the state, and citizens of the municipal upper class to the collection and payment of increasingly burdensome taxes. Freedom and private initiative gave way before the needs of the state and its ever-expanding control of its citizens.

Civil Disorder

Commodus was killed on the last day of A.D. 192, and the succeeding year was like the year 69: three emperors ruled in swift succession, Septimius Severus emerging, as we have seen, to establish firm rule and a dynasty. The death of Alexander Severus, the last of the dynasty, in A.D. 235 brought on a half century of internal anarchy and foreign invasion.

The empire seemed on the point of collapse, but the two conspirators who overthrew and then succeeded Gallienus were able soldiers. Claudius II Gothicus (A.D. 268–270) ånd Aurelian (A.D. 270–275) drove back the barbarians and stamped out internal disorder. The soldiers who followed Aurelian on the throne were good fighters and made significant changes in Rome's system of defense. They built heavy walls around Rome, Athens, and other cities that could resist barbarian attack. They drew back their best troops from the frontiers, relying chiefly on a newly organized heavy cavalry and a mobile army near the emperor's own residence. Hereafter the army was composed largely of mercenaries who came from among the least civilized provincials and even from among the Germans. The officers gave personal loyalty to the emperor rather than to the empire. These officers became a foreign, hereditary caste of aristocrats that increasingly supplied high administrators and even emperors. In effect, the Roman people hired an army of mercenaries, only technically Roman, to protect them.

The Fourth Century and Imperial Reorganization

The period from Diocletian (A.D. 284–305) to Constantine (A.D. 306–337) was one of reconstruction and reorganization after a time of civil war and turmoil. Diocletian was from Illyria (now Yugoslavia), a man of undistinguished birth who rose to the throne through the ranks of the army. He knew that he was not a great general and that the job of defending and governing the entire empire was too great for one man. He therefore decreed the introduction of the tetrarchy, the rule of the empire by four men with power divided on a territorial basis (see Map 5.4). Diocletian allotted the provinces of Thrace, Asia, and Egypt to himself. His co-emperor, Maximian, shared with him the title of Augustus and governed Italy, Africa, and Spain. In addition, two men were given the subordinate title of Caesar:

MAP 5-4 *Diocletian divided the sprawling empire into four prefectures for more effective government and defense. The inset map shows their boundaries, and the larger map gives some details of regions and provinces. The major division between East and West was along the broken line running south between Pannonia and Moesia.*

DIVISIONS OF THE ROMAN EMPIRE UNDER DIOCLETIAN

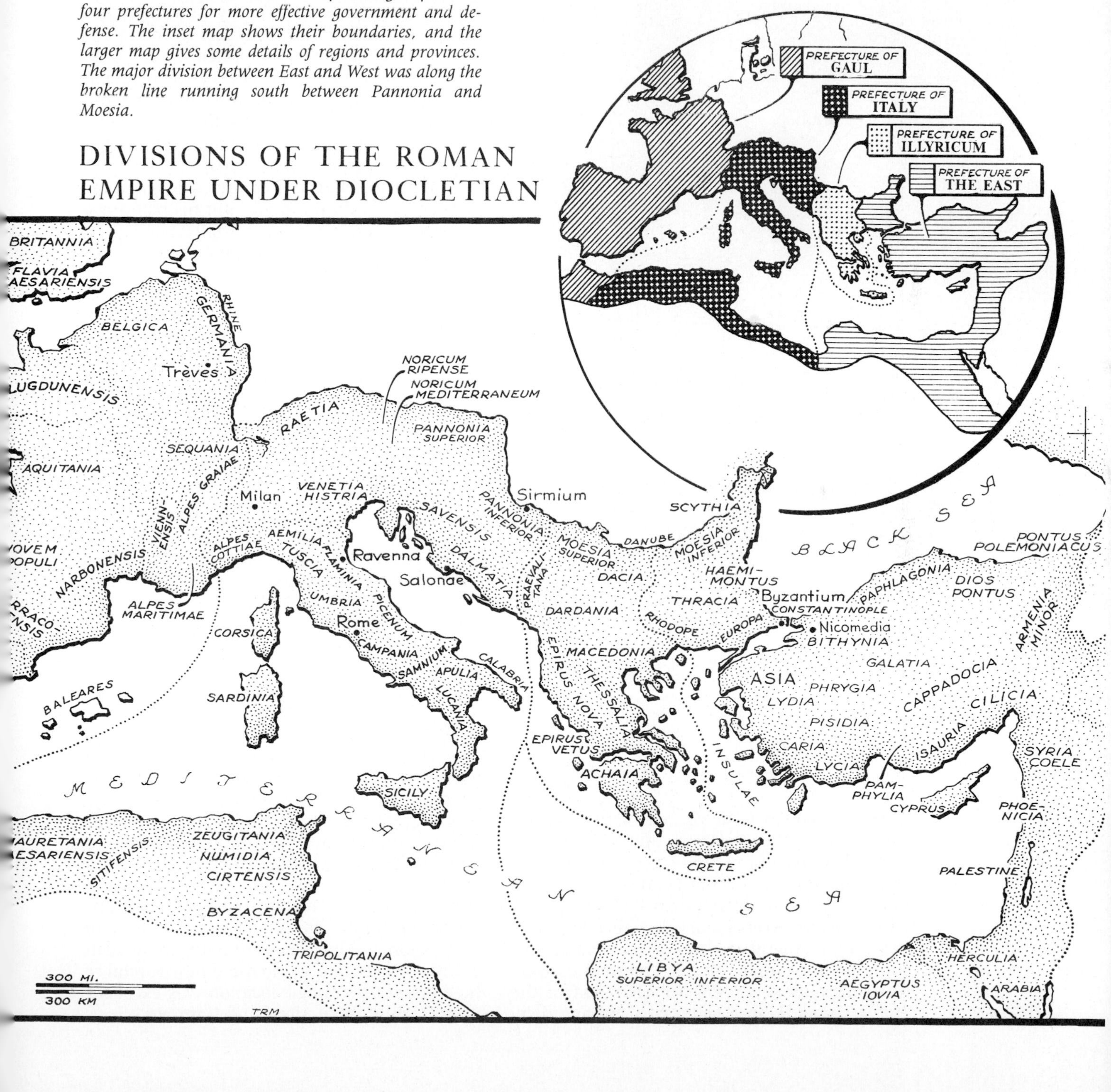

PREFECTURE OF GAUL
PREFECTURE OF ITALY
PREFECTURE OF ILLYRICUM
PREFECTURE OF THE EAST

The Tetrarchs. This porphyry sculpture on the corner of the church of San Marco in Venice depicts Emperor Diocletian (234–305) and his three imperial colleagues. They are in battle dress and clasp one another to express solidarity. This fourth-century sculpture was part of the booty brought back by the Venetians from their capture of Constantinople during the Fourth Crusade about nine hundred years later. [AHM]

marriages to daughters of the Augusti. It was a return, in a way, to the happy precedent of the "good emperors," who chose their successors from the ranks of the ablest men, and it seemed to promise orderly and peaceful transitions instead of assassinations, chaos, and civil war.

Each man established his residence and capital at a place convenient for frontier defense, and none chose Rome. The effective capital of Italy became the northern city of Milan. Diocletian beautified Rome by constructing his monumental baths, but he visited the city only once and made his own capital at Nicomedia in Bithynia. This was another step in the long leveling process that had reduced the eminence of Rome and Italy, and it was also evidence of the growing importance of the east.

In 305 Diocletian retired and compelled his co-emperor to do the same. But his plan for a smooth succession failed completely. In 310 there were five Augusti and no Caesars. Out of this chaos Constantine, son of Constantius, produced order. In 324 he defeated his last opponent and made himself sole emperor, uniting the empire once again; he reigned until 337. For the most part Constantine carried forward the policies of Diocletian. The one exception was his support of Christianity, which Diocletian had tried to suppress.

The development of the imperial office toward autocracy was carried to the extreme by Diocletian and Constantine. The emperor ruled by decree, consulting only a few high officials, whom he himself appointed. The Senate had no role whatever, and its dignity was further diminished by the elimination of all distinction between senator and equestrian.

The emperor was a remote figure surrounded by carefully chosen high officials. He lived in a great palace and was almost unapproachable. Those admitted to his presence had to prostrate themselves before him and kiss the hem of his robe, which was purple and had golden threads going through it. The emperor was addressed as *dominus* ("lord"), and his right to rule was not derived from the Roman people but from God. All this remoteness and ceremony had a double purpose: to enhance the dignity of the emperor and to safeguard him against assassination.

Constantine erected the new city of Constantinople on the site of ancient Byzantium on the Bosporus, which leads to both the Aegean and Black seas, and made it the new capital of the empire. Its strategic location was excellent for protecting the eastern and Danubian fron-

Galerius, who was in charge of the Danube frontier and the Balkans, and Constantius, who governed Britain and Gaul. This arrangement not only provided a good solution to the military problem but also provided for a peaceful succession. Diocletian was recognized as the senior Augustus, but each tetrarch was supreme in his own sphere. The Caesars were recognized as successors to each half of the empire, and their loyalty was enhanced by

184

Diocletian Attempts to Control Prices and Wages

Rome's troubles in the third century A.D. caused serious economic problems. Debased currency and vast government expenditures produced a runaway inflation. In an attempt to control it, Diocletian took the unprecedented step of issuing a decree that put ceilings on prices and wages throughout the empire in the year 301. In spite of the most drastic penalties prescribed by the decree, it was widely evaded. After a time its failure was acknowledged, and the decree was at last revoked.

. . . Who does not know that wherever the common safety requires our armies to be sent, the profiteers insolently and covertly attack the public welfare, not only in villages and towns, but on every road? They charge extortionate prices for merchandise, not just fourfold or eightfold, but on such a scale that human speech cannot find words to characterize their profit and their practices. Indeed, sometimes in a single retail sale a soldier is stripped of his donative and pay. Moreover, the contributions of the whole world for the support of the armies fall as profits into the hands of these plunderers, and our soldiers appear to bestow with their own hands the rewards of their military service and their veterans' bonuses upon the profiteers. The result is that the pillagers of the state itself seize day by day more than they know how to hold.

Aroused justly and rightfully by all the facts set forth above, and in response to the needs of mankind itself, which appears to be praying for release, we have decided that maximum prices of articles for sale must be established. We have not set down fixed prices, for we do not deem it just to do this, since many provinces occasionally enjoy the good fortune of welcome low prices and the privilege, as it were, of prosperity. Thus, when the pressure of high prices appears anywhere—may the gods avert such a calamity!—avarice . . . will be checked by the limits fixed in our statute and by the restraining curbs of the law.

It is our pleasure, therefore, that the prices listed in the subjoined schedule be held in observance in the whole of our Empire. And every person shall take note that the liberty to exceed them at will has been ended, but that the blessing of low prices has in no way been impaired in those places where supplies actually abound. . . . Moreover, this universal edict will serve as a necessary check upon buyers and sellers whose practice it is to visit ports and other provinces. For when they too know that in the pinch of scarcity there is no possibility of exceeding the prices fixed for commodities, they will take into account in their calculations at the time of sale the localities, the transportation costs, and all other factors. In this way they will make apparent the justice of our decision that those who transport merchandise may not sell at higher prices anywhere.

It is agreed that even in the time of our ancestors it was the practice in passing laws to restrain offenses by prescribing a penalty. For rarely is a situation beneficial to humanity accepted spontaneously; experience teaches that fear is the most effective regulator and guide for the performance of duty. Therefore it is our pleasure that anyone who resists the measures of this statute shall be subject to a capital penalty for daring to do so. And let no one consider the statute harsh, since there is at hand a ready protection from danger in the observance of moderation. . . . We therefore exhort the loyalty of all, so that a regulation instituted for the public good may be observed with willing obedience and due scruple, especially as it is seen that by a statute of this kind provision has been made, not for single municipalities and peoples and provinces but for the whole world. . . .

"Diocletian's Edict on Maximum Prices," from the *Corpus Inscriptionum Latinarum*, Vol. 3, in N. Lewis and M. Reinhold, *Roman Civilization*, Vol. 2 (New York: Columbia University Press, 1955), pp. 465–466.

tiers, and, surrounded on three sides by water, it was easily defended. This location also made it easier to carry forward the policies of fostering autocracy and Christianity. Rome was full of tradition, the center of senatorial and even republican memories and of pagan worship. Constantinople was free from both, and its dedication in A.D. 330 marked the beginning of a new era. Until its fall to the Turks in 1453, it served as the bastion of civilization, the preserver of classical culture, a bulwark against barbarian attack, and the greatest city in Christendom.

The autocratic rule of the emperors was carried out by a civilian bureaucracy, which was carefully separated from the military service to reduce the chances of rebellion by anyone combining the two kinds of power. Below the emperor's court the most important officials were the praetorian prefects, each of whom administered one of the four major areas into which the empire was divided: Gaul, Italy, Illyricum, and the Orient. The four prefectures were subdivided into twelve territorial units called *dioceses*, each under a vicar who was subordinate to the prefect. The dioceses were further divided into almost a hundred provinces, each under a provincial governor.

The operation of the entire system was supervised by a vast system of spies and secret police, without whom the increasingly rigid totalitarian organization could not be trusted to perform. In spite of these efforts, the system was filled with corruption and inefficiency.

The cost of maintaining a 400,000-man army as well as the vast civilian bureaucracy, the expensive imperial court, and the imperial taste for splendid buildings put a great strain on an already weak economy. Diocletian's attempts at establishing a uniform and reliable currency failed and merely led to increased inflation. To deal with it, he resorted to price control with his Edict of Maximum Prices in 301. For each product and each kind of labor, a maximum price was set, and violations were punishable by death. The edict failed despite the harshness of its provisions.

Peasants unable to pay their taxes and officials unable to collect them tried to escape, and Diocletian resorted to stern regimentation to keep all in their places and at the service of the government. The terror of the third century had turned many peasants into *coloni*, tenant farmers who fled for protection to the *villa* ("country estate") of a large and powerful landowner. They were tied to the land, as were their descendants, as the caste system hardened.

Division of the Empire

The peace and unity established by Constantine did not last long. His death was followed by a struggle for succession that was won by Constantius II (337–361), whose death, in turn, left the empire to his young cousin Julian (361–363), called by the Christians "the Apostate" because of his attempt to stamp out Christianity and restore paganism. Julian undertook a campaign against Persia with the aim of putting a Roman on the throne of the Sassanids and ending the Persian menace once and for all. He penetrated deep into Persia but was killed in battle. His death put an end to the expedition and to the pagan revival.

The Germans in the west took advantage of the eastern campaign to attack along the Rhine River and the upper Danube River, but even greater trouble was brewing along the middle and upper Danube (see Map 5.5). That territory was occupied by the eastern Goths, the Ostrogoths. They were being pushed hard by their western cousins, the Visigoths, who in turn had been driven from their home in the Ukraine by the fierce Huns, a nomadic people from central Asia. The Emperor Valentinian (364–375) saw that he could not defend the empire alone and appointed his brother Valens (364–378) as co-ruler. Valentinian made his own headquarters at Milan and spent the rest of his life fighting successfully against the Franks and the Alemanni in the west. Valens was given control of the east. The empire was once again divided in two. The two emperors maintained their own courts, and the two halves of the empire became increasingly separate and different. Latin was the language of the west and Greek of the east.

In 376 the hard-pressed Visigoths asked and received permission to enter the empire to escape the Huns. Contrary to the bargain, the Goths kept their weapons and began to plunder the Balkan provinces. Valens attacked the Goths and died, along with most of his army, at Adrianople in Thrace in 378. Theodosius (379–395), an able and experienced general, was named co-ruler in the east. By a combination of military and diplomatic skills Theodosius pacified the Goths, giving them land and a high degree of autonomy and enrolling many of them in his army. He made important military reforms, putting greater emphasis on the cav-

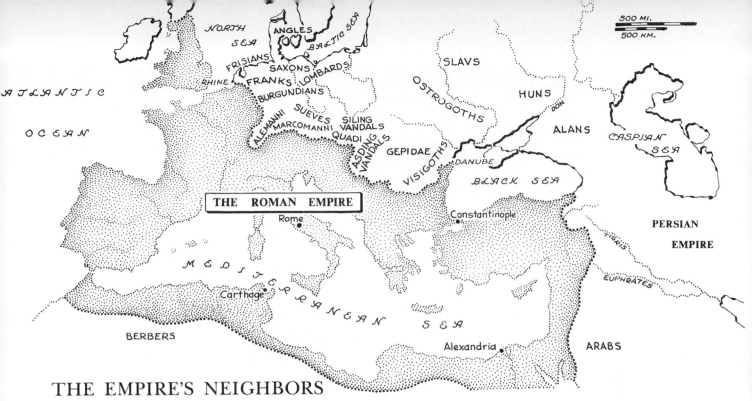

The map shows regions: NORTH SEA, ATLANTIC OCEAN, BALTIC SEA, ANGLES, FRISIANS, SAXONS, FRANKS, LOMBARDS, RHINE, BURGUNDIANS, ALEMANNI, SUEVES, MARCOMANNI, SILING VANDALS, QUADI, ASDING VANDALS, GEPIDAE, VISIGOTHS, DANUBE, SLAVS, OSTROGOTHS, HUNS, DON, ALANS, CASPIAN SEA, BLACK SEA, THE ROMAN EMPIRE, Rome, Constantinople, PERSIAN EMPIRE, TIGRIS, MEDITERRANEAN SEA, EUPHRATES, Carthage, BERBERS, Alexandria, ARABS, 500 MI., 500 KM.

THE EMPIRE'S NEIGHBORS

MAP 5-5 *In the fourth century the Roman Empire was nearly surrounded by ever more threatening neighbors. The map shows who these so-called barbarians were and where they lived before their armed contact with the Romans.*

Theodosius the Great (379–395), shown here at the chariot races in Constantinople. Theodosius was virtually the last emperor to control both the eastern and western halves of the empire. [Hirmer Verlag, Munich]

alry. Theodosius tried to unify the empire again, but his death in 395 left it divided and weak.

For the future the two parts of the empire went their separate and different ways. The west became increasingly rural as barbarian invasions continued and grew in intensity. The *villa*, a fortified country estate, became the basic unit of life. There, *coloni* gave their services to the local magnate in return for economic assistance and protection from both barbarians and imperial officials. Many cities shrank to no more than tiny walled fortresses ruled by military commanders and bishops. The upper classes moved to the country and asserted ever greater independence of imperial authority. The failure of the central authority to maintain the roads and the constant danger from robber bands sharply curtailed trade and communications, forcing greater self-reliance and a more primitive style of life. The new world emerging in the west by the fifth century and after was increasingly made up of isolated units of rural aristocrats and their dependent laborers. The only institution providing a high

187

degree of unity was the Christian Church. The pattern for the early Middle Ages in the west was already formed.

In the east the situation was quite different. Constantinople became the center of a vital and flourishing culture that we call *Byzantine* and that lasted until the fifteenth century. Be-cause of its defensible location, the skill of its emperors, and the firmness and strength of its base in Asia Minor, it was able to deflect and repulse barbarian attacks. A strong navy allowed commerce to flourish in the eastern Mediterranean and, in good times, far beyond. Cities continued to prosper and the emperors

---

The Empire Tries to Control Corruption in the Governmental Bureaucracy

As the role of the government in the lives of the people grew, so did the size of its bureaucracy. Our documents indicate that a significant amount of financial corruption existed among government officials, and its amount seems to have grown at least as fast as the size of the bureaucracy itself. In 438 the Emperor Theodosius II (A.D. 408–450) published his important code of Roman law, which included the following provisions aimed at suppressing corruption.

The rapacious hands of the functionaries shall immediately stop, they shall stop, I say; for, if after due warning they do not stop, they shall be cut off with the sword. The curtain of the judge['s chamber] shall not be venal; entrance shall not be purchased; his private chamber shall not be notorious for its bids; the very sight of the governor shall not be at a price. The ears of the judge shall be open equally to the poorest as well as to the rich. The introduction of persons inside shall be free from depredation by the one who is called the office head; the assistants of the said office heads shall employ no extortion on litigants; the intolerable onslaught of the centurions and other officials who demand small and large sums shall be crushed; and the unsated greed of those who deliver records to litigants shall be restrained. The ever-watchful diligence of the governor shall see that nothing is taken from a litigant by the aforesaid classes of men. And if they imagine they had to demand something in connection with civil cases, armed punishment will be at hand to cut off the heads and necks of the scoundrels, for all persons who have suffered extortion will be given an opportunity to provide information for an investigation by the governors. And if they dissemble, we open to all persons the right of complaint thereon before the comites *of the provinces—or before the Praetorian prefects, if they are closer at hand—* *so that we may be informed by their referrals and may produce punishments for such villainy.*

Theodosian Code I. xxxii. 1; A.D. 333

Through the fault of the procurators of the privy purse, of dyeworks, and of weaving establishments, our private substance is being diminished, the products manufactured in the weaving establishments are being ruined, and in the dyeworks the fraudulent admixture of impure dye produces blemishes. Such procurators shall abstain from the patronage whereby they obtain the aforementioned administrative positions, or, if they contravene this order, they shall be removed from the number of Roman citizens and beheaded.

Theodosian Code X. iv. 1; A.D. 313 or 326

If any person is harassed by an agent or procurator of our privy purse, he shall not hesitate to lodge a complaint concerning his chicanery and depredations. When such a charge is proved, we sanction that such person as dares to contrive anything against a provincial shall be publicly burned, since graver punishment should be fixed against those who are under our jurisdiction and ought to observe our mandates.

Theodosian Code, in N. Lewis and M. Reinhold, *Roman Civilization*, Vol. 2 (New York: Columbia University Press, 1955), pp. 484–485.

Ammianus Marcellinus Describes the People Called Huns

Ammianus Marcellinus was born about A.D. 330 in Syria, where Greek was the language of his well-to-do family. After a military career and considerable travel, he lived in Rome and wrote an encyclopedic Latin history of the empire, covering the years 96–378 and giving a special emphasis to the difficulties of the fourth century. Here he describes the Huns, one of the barbarous peoples pressing on the frontiers.

The people called Huns, barely mentioned in ancient records, live beyond the sea of Azof, on the border of the Frozen Ocean, and are a race savage beyond all parallel. At the very moment of birth the cheeks of their infant children are deeply marked by an iron, in order that the hair, instead of growing at the proper season on their faces, may be hindered by the scars; accordingly the Huns grow up without beards, and without any beauty. They all have closely knit and strong limbs and plump necks; they are of great size, and low legged, so that you might fancy them two-legged beasts or the stout figures which are hewn out in a rude manner with an ax on the posts at the end of bridges.

They are certainly in the shape of men, however uncouth, and are so hardy that they neither require fire nor well-flavored food, but live on the roots of such herbs as they get in the fields, or on the half-raw flesh of any animal, which they merely warm rapidly by placing it between their own thighs and the backs of their horses.

They never shelter themselves under roofed houses, but avoid them, as people ordinarily avoid sepulchers as things not fit for common use. Nor is there even to be found among them a cabin thatched with reeds; but they wander about, roaming over the mountains and the woods, and accustom themselves to bear frost and hunger and thirst from their very cradles. . . .

There is not a person in the whole nation who cannot remain on his horse day and night. On horseback they buy and sell, they take their meat and drink, and there they recline on the narrow neck of their steed, and yield to sleep so deep as to indulge in every variety of dream.

And when any deliberation is to take place on any weighty matter, they all hold their common council on horseback. They are not under kingly authority, but are contented with the irregular government of their chiefs, and under their lead they force their way through all obstacles. . . .

Ammianus Marcellinus, *Res Gestae,* trans. by C. D. Yonge (London: George Bell and Son, 1862), pp. 312–314.

made their will good over the nobles in the countryside. The civilization of the Byzantine Empire was a unique combination of classical culture, the Christian religion, Roman law, and eastern artistic influences. While the west was being overrun by barbarians, the Roman Empire, in altered form, persisted in the east. While Rome shrank to an insignificant ecclesiastical town, Constantinople flourished as the seat of empire, the "New Rome," and the Byzantines called themselves "Romans." When we contemplate the decline and fall of the Roman Empire in the fourth and fifth centuries, we are speaking only of the west. A form of classical culture persisted in the Byzantine east for a thousand years more.

The Triumph of Christianity

Religious Currents in the Empire

The rise of Christianity to dominance in the empire was closely connected with the political and cultural experience of the third and fourth centuries. Political chaos and decentralization had religious and cultural consequences. In some of the provinces, native languages replaced Latin and Greek, sometimes even for official purposes, and the classical tradition that had been the basis of imperial life became the exclusive possession of a small, educated aristocracy. In religion the public cults had grown up in an urban environment and were largely political in character. As the importance of the cities diminished, so did the significance of their gods. People might still take comfort in the worship of the friendly, intimate deities of family, field, hearth, storehouse, and craft, but these were too petty to serve their needs in a confused and frightening world. The only universal worship was of the emperor, but he was far off, and obeisance to his cult was more a political than a religious act.

In the troubled times of the fourth and fifth centuries people sought powerful, personal deities who would bring them safety and prosperity in this world and immortality in the next. Paganism was open and tolerant, and it was by no means unusual for people to worship new deities alongside the old and even to intertwine elements of several to form a new amalgam by the device called *syncretism*.

Manichaeism was an especially potent rival of Christianity. Named for its founder, Mani, a Persian who lived in the third century A.D., it contained aspects of various religious traditions, including Zoroastrianism from Persia and both Judaism and Christianity. The Manichaeans pictured a world in which light and darkness, good and evil, were constantly at war. Good was spiritual and evil was material; because human beings were made of matter, their bodies were a prison of evil and darkness, but they also contained an element of light and good. The "Father of Goodness" had sent Mani, among other prophets, to free humanity and gain its salvation. To achieve salvation, humans must want to reach the realm of light and to abandon all physical desires. Manichaeans led an ascetic life and practiced a simple worship guided by a well-organized

Marble relief depicting the sacrifice of a bull. Animal sacrifice was an integral part of the official Roman cults and continued until all pagan ritual was banned by the emperor Theodosius in A.D. 394. [*Vatican Museum*]

church. The movement reached its greatest strength in the fourth and fifth centuries, and some of its central ideas persisted into the Middle Ages.

Obviously Christianity had something in common with these cults and answered many of the same needs felt by their devotees. There can be no doubt that Christianity's success owed something to the same causes as accounted for the popularity of these other cults, and they are often spoken of as its rivals. None of them, however, attained Christianity's universality, and none appears to have given the early Christians and their leaders as much competition as the ancient philosophies or the state religion.

Imperial Persecution

By the third century Christianity had taken firm hold in the eastern provinces and in Italy, though it had not made much headway in the west. Christian apologists pointed out that the Christians were good citizens who differed from others only in not worshipping the public gods. Until the middle of the third century the emperors tacitly accepted this view, without granting official toleration. As times became bad and the Christians became more numerous and visible, that policy changed. Popular opinion blamed disasters, natural and military, on the Christians. About 250 the Emperor Decius (249–251) invoked the aid of the gods in his war against the Goths and required that all citizens worship the state gods publicly. True Christians could not obey, and Decius instituted a major persecution. Many Christians, even some bishops, yielded to threats and torture, but others held out and were killed. Valerian (253–260) resumed the persecutions, partly in order to confiscate the wealth of rich Christians. His successors, however, found other matters more pressing, and the persecution lapsed until the end of the century.

By the time of Diocletian the number of Christians had grown still greater and included some high state officials. At the same time hostility to the Christians grew on every level. Diocletian was not generous toward unorthodox intellectual or religious movements, and his own effort to bolster imperial power with the aura of divinity boded ill for the church, yet he did not attack the Christians for almost twenty years. In 303, however, he launched the most serious persecution inflicted on the Christians in the Roman Empire. He issued a series of

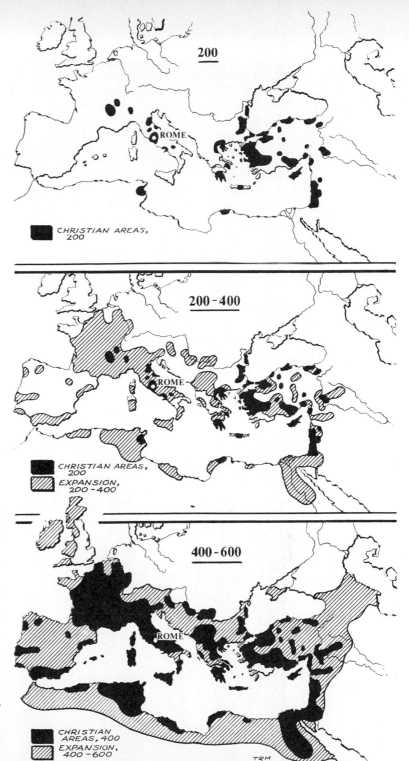

THE SPREAD OF CHRISTIANITY

MAP 5-6 *Christianity grew swiftly in the third, fourth, fifth, and sixth centuries—especially after the conversion of the emperors in the fourth century. By 600, on the eve of the birth of Mohammed's new Moslem religion, Christianity was dominant throughout the Mediterranean world and most of Western Europe.*

191

192

*The
Foundation of
Western
Civilization in
the Ancient
World*

edicts confiscating church property and destroying churches and their sacred books; he deprived upper-class Christians of public office and judicial rights, imprisoned clergy, enslaved Christians of the lower classes, and placed heavy fines on anyone refusing to sacrifice to the public gods. A final decree required public sacrifices and libations. The decrees were harsh, and there were many Christian martyrs, but enforcement was by no means uniform. The edict against the upper classes was the one most easily and widely enforced, but the persecution horrified many pagans, and the plight and the demeanor of the martyrs often aroused pity and sympathy. For these reasons, as well as the incapacity of any large ancient state to carry out a program of terror with the thoroughness of modern totalitarian governments, the Christians and their church survived to enjoy what they must have considered a miraculous change of fortune. In 311 Galerius, who had been one of the most vigorous perse-

cutors, was influenced, perhaps by his Christian wife, to issue an edict of toleration permitting Christian worship.

The victory of Constantine and his emergence as sole ruler of the empire changed the condition of Christianity from a precariously tolerated sect to the religion favored by the emperor and put it on the path to becoming the official and only legal religion in the empire.

Emergence of Christianity As the State Religion

The sons of Constantine continued to favor the new religion, but the succession of Julian the Apostate posed a new threat. He was a devotee of traditional classical pagan culture and, as a believer in Neoplatonism, an opponent of Christianity. Neoplatonism was a religious philosophy, or a philosophical religion, whose connection with Platonic teachings was dis-

The Neoplatonist philosopher Plotimus instructing his followers, from a third-century sarcophagus. [German Archaeological Institute, Rome]

tant. Its chief formulator was Plotinus (A.D. 205–270), who attempted to combine classical and rational philosophical speculation with the mystical spirit of his time. Plotinus' successors were bitter critics of Christianity, and Julian was influenced by their views. Though he refrained from persecution, he tried to undo the work of Constantine by withdrawing the privileges of the church, removing Christians from high offices, and attempting to introduce a new form of pagan worship. His reign, however, was short, and his work did not last.

In 394 Theodosius forbade the celebration of pagan cults and abolished the pagan religious calendar. At the death of Theodosius, Christianity was the official religion of the Roman Empire.

The establishment of Christianity as the state religion did not put an end to the troubles of the Christians and their church; instead it created new ones and complicated some that were old. The favored position of the church attracted converts for the wrong reasons and diluted the moral excellence and spiritual fervor of its adherents. The problem of the relationship between church and state arose, presenting the possibility that religion would become subordinate to the state, as it had been in the classical world and in earlier civilizations. In the east that is what happened to a considerable degree. In the west the weakness of the emperors prevented such a development and permitted church leaders to exercise remarkable independence. In 390 Ambrose, bishop of Milan, excommunicated Emperor Theodosius for a massacre he had carried out, and the emperor did humble penance. This act provided an important precedent for future assertions of the church's autonomy and authority, but it did not put an end to secular interference and influence in the church by any means.

Arianism and the Council of Nicaea

Internal divisions proved to be even more troubling as new heresies emerged. Because they threatened the unity of an empire that was now Christian, they took on a political character and inevitably involved the emperor and the powers of the state. Before long the world could view Christians persecuting other Christians with a zeal at least as great as had

---

The Council at Nicaea Creates the Test of Religious Orthodoxy

In A.D. 325 Emperor Constantine called a general council of leading Christians at Nicaea in Asia Minor in an attempt to end the quarreling over the question of the Trinity. The Nicene Creed was the result. Adherence to it became a test of orthodoxy, and those rejecting it were declared heretics.

We believe in one God, the Father Almighty, maker of all things visible and invisible; and in one Lord Jesus Christ, the Son of God, the only-begotten of his Father, of the substance of the Father, God of God, Light of Light; very God of very God, begotten not made, being of one substance with the Father, By whom all things were made, both which be in heaven and in earth. Who for us men and for our salvation came down [from heaven] and was incarnate and was made man. He suffered and the third day he rose again, and ascended into heaven. And he shall come again to judge both the quick and the dead. And [we believe] in the Holy Ghost. And whosoever shall say that there was time when the Son of God was not, or that before he was begotten he was not, or that he was made of things that were not, or that he is of a different substance or essence [from the Father] or that he is a creature, or subject to change or conversion— all that so say, the Catholic and Apostolic Church anathematizes them.

"The Nicene Creed," from *The Seven Ecumenical Councils*, Vol. 14, trans. by A. C. McGiffort and E. C. Richardson (New York: Library of the Nicene and Post-Nicene Fathers, 2nd Series, 1900), p. 3.

194

*The
Foundation of
Western
Civilization in
the Ancient
World*

been displayed against them by the most fanatical pagans.

Among the many controversial views that arose, the most important and the most threatening was Arianism, founded by a priest named Arius of Alexandria (ca. 280–336) in the fourth century. The issue creating difficulty was the relation of God the Father and God the Son. Arius argued that Jesus was a created being, unlike God the Father. He was, therefore, not made of the substance of God and was not eternal. "The Son has a beginning," he said, "but God is without beginning." For Arius, Jesus was neither fully man nor fully God but something in between. Arius' view did away with the mysterious concept of the Trinity, the difficult doctrine that God is three persons (the Father, the Son, and the Holy Spirit) and at the same time one in substance and essence. The Arian concept had the advantage of appearing to be simple, rational, and philosophically acceptable, but to its ablest opponent, Athanasius, it had serious shortcomings. Athanasius (ca. 293–373), later bishop of Alexandria, saw the Arian view as an impediment to any acceptable theory of salvation, to him the most important religious question. He adhered to the old Greek idea of salvation as involving the change of sinful mortality into divine immortality through the gift of "life." Only if Jesus were both fully human and fully God could the transformation of humanity to divinity have taken place in him and be transmitted by him to his disciples. "Christ was made man," he said, "that we might be made divine."

To deal with the growing controversy, Constantine called a council of Christian bishops at Nicaea, not far from Constantinople, in 325. For the emperor the question was essentially political, but for the disputants salvation was at stake. At Nicaea the view expounded by Athanasius won out, became orthodox, and was embodied in the Nicene Creed. But Arianism persisted and spread. Some later emperors were either Arians or sympathetic to that view. Some of the most successful missionaries to the barbarians were Arians, with the result that many of the German tribes that overran the empire were Arians. The Christian emperors hoped to bring unity to their increasingly decentralized realms by imposing the single religion, and over time it did prove to be a unifying force, but it also introduced new divisions where none had existed before.

Arts and Letters in the Late Empire

The art and literature of the late empire reflect the confluence of pagan and Christian ideas and traditions as well as the conflict between them. Much of the literature is of a polemical nature and much of the art is propaganda. At the same time, the great social changes that began to accelerate in the third century had parallel effects.

The salvation of the empire from the chaos of the third century was accomplished by a military revolution based on and led by provincials whose origins were in the lower classes. They brought with them the fresh winds of cultural change, which blew out not only the dust of classical culture but much of its substance as well. Yet the new ruling class was not interested in leveling; it wanted instead to establish itself as a new aristocracy. It thought of itself as effecting a great restoration rather than a revolution and sought to restore classical culture and absorb it. The confusion and uncertainty of the times were tempered in part, of course, by the comfort of Christianity, but the new ruling class sought order and stability—ethical, literary, and artistic—in the classical tradition as well.

The Preservation of Classical Culture

One of the main needs and accomplishments of this period was the preservation of classical culture and the discovery of ways to make it available and useful to the newly arrived ruling class. The great classical authors were reproduced in many copies, and their works were transferred from perishable and inconvenient papyrus rolls to sturdier codices, bound volumes that were as easy to use as modern books. Scholars also digested long works like Livy's *History of Rome* into shorter versions and wrote learned commentaries and compiled grammars. Original works by pagan writers of the late empire were neither numerous nor especially distinguished.

Christian Writers

Of Christian writings, on the other hand, the late empire saw a great outpouring. There were many examples of Christian apologetics in poetry as well as in prose, and there were sermons, hymns, and biblical commentaries. Christianity could also boast important scholars, Jerome (348–420), thoroughly trained in both the east and the west in classical Latin literature and rhetoric, produced a revised version of the Bible in Latin, commonly called the Vulgate, which became the Bible used by the Catholic church. Probably the most important eastern scholar was Eusebius of Caesarea (ca. 260–ca. 340). He wrote apologetics; an idealized biography of Constantine; and a valuable attempt to reconstruct the chronology of important events in the past. His most important contribution, however, was his *Ecclesiastical History,* an attempt to set forth the Christian view of history. He saw all of history as the working out of God's will. All of history, therefore, had a purpose and a direction, and Constantine's victory and the subsequent unity of empire and church were its culmination.

AUGUSTINE OF HIPPO. The closeness and also the complexity of the relationship between classical pagan culture and that of the

Late Roman art was a transition between classical and medieval, pagan and Christian. These reliefs from the arch of Constantine, which was built in A.D. 313, reveal the conflicting influences at work at the time. The circular medallion on the right depicts an emperor offering incense to Jupiter. The emperor is Hadrian, for whom the panel had originally been carved 200 years earlier. Although Constantine already sympathized with Christianity when the arch was built, he nonetheless incorporated this pagan religious scene in its structure. [EPA]

196

*The
Foundation of
Western
Civilization in
the Ancient
World*

Christianity of the late empire are nowhere better displayed than in the career and writings of Augustine (354–430), bishop of Hippo in north Africa. He was born at Carthage and was trained as a teacher of rhetoric. His father was a pagan, but his mother was a Christian and hers was ultimately the stronger influence. He passed through a number of intellectual way stations, skepticism and Neoplatonism among others, before his conversion to Christianity. His training and skill in pagan rhetoric and philosophy made him peerless among his contemporaries as a defender of Christianity and as a theologian. His greatest works are his *Confessions*, an autobiography describing the road to his conversion, and *The City of God.* The latter was a response to the pagan charge that Rome's sack by the Goths in 410 was caused by the abandonment of the old gods and the advent of Christianity. The optimistic view held by some Christians that God's will worked its way in history and was easily comprehensible needed further support in the face of this disaster. Augustine sought to separate the fate of Christianity from that of the Roman Empire. He contrasted the secular world, the City of Man, with the spiritual, the City of God. The former was selfish, the latter unselfish; the former evil, the latter good. Augustine argued that history was moving forward, in the spiritual sense, to the Day of Judgment but that there was no reason to expect improvement before then in the secular sphere. The fall of Rome was neither surprising nor important, for all states, even a Christian Rome, were part of the City of Man and therefore corrupt and mortal. Only the City of God was immortal, and it, consisting of all the saints on earth and in heaven, was untouched by earthly calamities.

Though the *Confessions* and *The City of God* are Augustine's most famous works, they emphasize only a part of his thought. His treatises *On the Trinity* and *On Christian Education* reveal the great skill with which he supported Christian belief with the learning, logic, and philosophy of the pagan classics. Augustine believed that faith is essential and primary, a thoroughly Christian view, but that it is not a substitute for reason, the foundation of classical thought. Instead, faith is the starting point for and liberator of human reason, which continues to be the means by which people can understand what is revealed by faith. His writings constantly reveal the presence of both Christian faith and pagan reason, as well as the tension between them, a legacy he left to the Middle Ages.

Problem of the Decline and Fall of the Empire in the West

Whether important to Augustine or not, the massive barbarian invasions of the fifth century put an end to effective imperial government in the west. For centuries people have speculated about the causes of the collapse of the ancient world. Every kind of reason has been put forward, and some suggestions seem to have nothing to do with reason at all. Soil exhaustion, plague, climatic change, and even poisoning caused by lead water pipes have been suggested as reasons for Rome's decline in population, vigor, and the capacity to defend itself. Some blame the institution of slavery and the failure to make advances in science and technology that they believe resulted from it. Others blame excessive government interference in the economic life of the empire, others the destruction of the urban middle class, the carrier of classical culture.

Perhaps a plausible explanation can be found that is more simple and obvious. It might begin with the observation that the growth of so mighty an empire as Rome's was by no means inevitable. Rome's greatness had come from conquests that provided the Romans with the means to expand still further, until there were not enough Romans to conquer and govern any more peoples and territory. When pressure from outsiders grew, the Romans lacked the resources to advance and defeat the enemy as in the past. The tenacity and success of their resistance for so long were remarkable. Without new conquests to provide the immense wealth needed for the defense and maintenance of internal prosperity, the Romans finally yielded to unprecedented onslaughts by fierce and numerous attackers.

To blame the ancients and the institution of slavery for the failure to produce an industrial and economic revolution like that of the later Western world, one capable of producing wealth without taking it from another, is to stand the problem on its head. No one yet has a satisfactory explanation for those revolutions, so it is improper to blame any institution or society for not achieving what has been achieved only once in human history, in what are still mysterious circumstances. Perhaps we would do well to think of the problem as Gibbon did:

The decline of Rome was the natural and inevitable effect of immoderate greatness. Prosperity ripened the principle of decay; the cause of the destruction multiplied with the extent of conquest; and, as soon as time or accident had removed the artificial supports, the stupendous fabric yielded to the pressure of its own weight. The story of the ruin is simple and obvious; and instead of inquiring why the Roman Empire was destroyed, we should rather be surprised that it had subsisted so long.[5]

[5]Edward Gibbon, *Decline and Fall of the Roman Empire*, 2nd ed., Vol. 4, ed. by J. B. Bury (London, 1909), pp. 173–174.

Suggested Readings

J. P. V. D. BALSDON, *Roman Women* (1962).

P. BROWN, *Augustine of Hippo* (1967). A splendid biography.

P. BROWN, *The World of Late Antiquity*, A.D. 150–750 (1971). A brilliant and readable essay.

J. BURCKHARDT, *The Age of Constantine the Great* (1956). A classic work by the Swiss cultural historian.

J. CARCOPINO, *Daily Life in Ancient Rome*, trans. by E. O. Lorimer (1940).

C. M. COCHRANE, *Christianity and Classical Culture* (1957). A study of intellectual change in the late empire.

S. DILL, *Roman Society in the Last Century of the Western Empire* (1958).

E. R. DODDS, *Pagan and Christian in an Age of Anxiety* (1965). An original and perceptive study.

E. GIBBON, *The History of the Decline and Fall of the Roman Empire*, 7 vols., ed. by J. B. Bury, 2nd ed. (1909–1914). One of the masterworks of the English language.

T. RICE HOLMES, *Architect of the Roman Empire*, 2 vols. (1928–1931). An account of Augustus' career in detail.

A. H. M. JONES, *The Later Roman Empire*, 3 vols. (1964). A comprehensive study of the period.

D. KAGAN (ED.), *The End of the Roman Empire: Decline or Transformation?*, 2nd. ed. (1978). A collection of essays discussing the problem of the decline and fall of the Roman Empire.

M. L. W. LAISTNER, *The Greater Roman Historians* (1963). Essays on the major Roman historical writers.

J. LEBRETON AND J. ZEILLER, *History of the Primitive Church*, 3 vols. (1962). From the Catholic viewpoint.

H. LIETZMANN, *History of the Early Church*, 2 vols. (1961). From the Protestant viewpoint.

F. LOT, *The End of the Ancient World and the Beginnings of the Middle Ages* (1961). A study that emphasizes gradual transition rather than abrupt change.

E. N. LUTTWAK, *The Grand Strategy of the Roman Empire* (1976). An original and fascinating analysis by a keen student of modern strategy.

R. MACMULLEN, *Enemies of the Roman Order* (1966). An original and revealing examination of opposition to the emperors.

R. MACMULLEN, *Paganism in the Roman Empire* (1981).

F. B. MARSH, *The Founding of the Roman Empire* (1959).

F. G. B. MILLAR, *The Roman Empire and Its Neighbors* (1968).

F. G. B. MILLAR, *The Emperor in the Roman World*, 31 B.C.–A.D. 337 (1977).

A. MOMIGLIANO (ED.), *The Conflict Between Paganism and Christianity* (1963). A valuable collection of essays.

H. M. D. PARKER, *A History of the Roman World from A.D. 138 to 337* (1969). A good survey.

M. I. ROSTOVTZEFF, *Social and Economic History of the Roman Empire*, 2nd. ed. (1957). A masterpiece whose main thesis has been much disputed.

E. T. SALMON, *A History of the Roman World, 30 B.C. to A.D. 138* (1968). A good survey.

C. G. STARR, *Civilization and the Caesars* (1965). A study of Roman culture in the Augustan period.

R. SYME, *The Roman Revolution* (1960). A brilliant study of Augustus, his supporters, and their rise to power.

L. R. TAYLOR, *The Divinity of the Roman Empire* (1931). A study of the imperial cult.

The Middle Ages, 476–1300

During the eight centuries between the fall of Rome and the beginning of the Renaissance, the major institutions of western European civilization acquired a definite shape. The many formative outside influences that had come upon the West from the Eastern or Byzantine Empire, the invading Germanic tribes, and the Muslim world during the early Middle Ages were folded into a distinctive civilization.

The Roman Catholic church emerged from the chaos of the Roman Empire's collapse as a major custodian of Western culture. Firmly based in the cities, yet centered in Rome, its broad network of loyal clergy made it the only Western institution capable of extending its influence over many diverse regions.

During the reign of the Carolingian rulers, who came to power in the seventh century, a modest revival of Western imperial pretensions occurred, assisted by the church. Particularly during the long reign of Charlemagne, Christian bishops and clergy became important allies in the organization of the Carolingian Empire, both in the countryside and in the towns.

New developments in farming increased the productivity of the rural manors, where 95 per cent of the population lived. By Charlemagne's time a better harness for oxen and ploughs that could cut deeply into the soil and furrow it improved yields. Rotation of crops among three fields kept land fertile and productive. These new techniques aided both population growth and cultural development.

Thanks to soaring mercantile activity in the twelfth and thirteenth centuries, towns and urban culture grew very rapidly. A new merchant class emerged in the towns and took its place alongside the nobility and the clergy. From the towns, the rulers increasingly drew lay servants and administrators, who formed a loyal bureaucracy and braintrust that made it possible for the rulers to challenge the nobility and the church successfully. This alliance between rulers and towns was an important factor in the rise of Europe's new secular monarchies and the creation of Europe's major nation-states.

Emperors and kings clashed repeatedly with popes during the twelfth and thirteenth centuries, when the Roman Catholic church was still a formidable political power. At the end of the Investiture Controversy in the twelfth century, a clear distinction was drawn between the spheres of ecclesiastical and secular authority. After 1300, monarchs progressively limited the church's influence over their political and economic affairs, restricting the church to an important but less threatening spiritual and cultural sphere of influence.

The Crusades to the Holy Land attested to the church's continuing popularity in the high Middle Ages, even though these ventures had acquired a mercenary character by the thirteenth century. In an increasingly materialistic age, the rise of the Dominican and Franciscan friars signaled a new spiritual revival among the clergy that also attracted large numbers of pious laity. Under the banner of apostolic poverty church reformers rallied until the Reformation.

This sixth-century ivory panel depicts the Byzantine emperor as the Champion of the Faith. For six centuries, from about 500 to 1100, Byzantium was the center of Christian civilization. [Giraudon, Art Resource]

THE EARLY MIDDLE AGES mark the birth of Europe. This was the period in which a distinctive western European culture began to emerge. In geography, government, religion, and language, western Europe became a land distinct from both the eastern or Byzantine world and the Arab or Muslim world. It was a period of recovery from the collapse of Roman civilization, a time of forced experimentation with new ideas and institutions. Western European culture, as we know it today, was born of a unique, inventive mix of surviving Graeco-Roman, new Germanic, and evolving Christian traditions.

The early Middle Ages have been called, and not with complete fairness, a "dark age." This is because they lost touch with classical, especially Greek, learning and science. In this period there were fierce invasions from the north and the east by peoples that the Romans somewhat arrogantly called barbarians, and to the south the Mediterranean was transformed by Arab dominance into an inhospitable "Muslim lake." Although western trade with the east was by no means completely cut off, western people became more isolated than they had been before. A Europe thus surrounded and assailed from north, east, and south understandably became somewhat insular and even stagnant. On the other hand, being forced to manage by itself, western Europe also learned to develop its native resources. The early Middle Ages were not without a modest renaissance of antiquity during the reign of Charlemagne. And the peculiar social and political forms of this period—manorialism and feudalism—proved to be not only successful ways to cope with unprecedented chaos on local levels but also a fertile seedbed for the growth of distinctive Western institutions.

On the Eve of the Frankish Ascendancy

Germanic and Arab Invasions

As we have already seen, by the late third century the Roman Empire had become too large for a single sovereign to govern. For this reason the Emperor Diocletian (284–305) permitted the evolution of a dual empire by establishing an eastern and a western half, each with its own emperor and, eventually, imperial bureaucracy. The Emperor Constantine the Great (306–337) briefly reunited the empire

6

The Early Middle Ages (476–1000): The Birth of Europe

by conquest and was sole emperor of the east and the west after 324. (The empire was redivided by his sons and subsequent successors.) In 330 Constantine created the city of Constantinople as the new administrative center of the empire and the imperial residence. Constantinople gradually became a "new Rome," replacing the old, whose internal political quarrels and geographical distance from new military fronts in Syria and along the Danube River made it less appealing. Rome and the western empire were actually on the wane in the late third and fourth centuries, well before the barbarian invasions in the west began. In 286 Milan had already replaced Rome as the imperial residence; in 402 the seat of western government was moved still again, to Ravenna. When the barbarian invasions began in the late fourth century, the west was in political disarray, and the imperial power and prestige had shifted decisively to Constantinople and the east.

GERMAN TRIBES AND THE WEST. The German tribes did not burst on the west all of a sudden. They were at first a token and benign

Coin of Alaric the Visigoth (ca 370–410).

presence. Before the great invasions from the north and the east, there had been a period of peaceful commingling of the Germanic and the Roman cultures. The Romans "imported" barbarians as domestics and soldiers before they came as conquerors. Barbarian soldiers rose to positions of high leadership and fame in Roman legions. In the late fourth century, however, this peaceful coexistence came to an end because of a great influx of Visigoths (west Goths) into the empire. They were stampeded there in 376 by the emergence of a new, violent people, the Huns, who migrated from the area of modern Mongolia. The Visigoths were a Christianized Germanic tribe who won from the eastern emperor Valens rights of settlement and material assistance within the empire in exchange for their defense of the frontier as *foederati*, special allies of the emperor. When in place of promised assistance the Visigoths received harsh treatment from their new allies, they rebelled, handily defeating Roman armies under Valens at the battle of Adrianople in 378.

After Adrianople the Romans passively permitted settlement after settlement of barbarians within the very heart of western Europe. Why was there so little resistance to the German tribes? The invaders found a badly overextended western empire physically weakened by decades of famine, pestilence, and overtaxation, and politically divided by ambitious military commanders. In the second half of the fourth century its will to resist had simply been sapped. The Roman Empire did not fall simply because of unprecedented moral decay and materialism, but because of a combination of political mismanagement, disease, and sheer poverty.

The late fourth and early fifth centuries saw the invasion of still other tribes: the Vandals, the Burgundians, and the Franks. In 410 Visigoths revolted under Alaric (ca. 370–410) and sacked the "eternal city" of Rome. From 451 to 453 Italy suffered the invasions of Attila the Hun (d. 453), who was known to contemporaries as the "scourge of God." In 455 the Vandals overran Rome.

By the mid-fifth century, power in western Europe had passed decisively from the hands of the Roman emperors to those of barbarian chieftains. In 476, the traditional date for the fall of the Roman Empire, the barbarian Odoacer (ca. 434–493) deposed and replaced the western emperor Romulus Augustulus and ruled as "king of the Romans." The eastern

203

*The Early
Middle Ages
(476–1000):
The Birth
of Europe*

Salvian the Priest Compares the Romans and the Barbarians

Salvian, a Christian priest writing around 440, found the barbarians morally superior to the Romans—indeed, truer to Roman virtues than the Romans themselves, whose failings are all the more serious because they, unlike the barbarians, had knowledge of Christianity.

In what respects can our customs be preferred to those of the Goths and Vandals, or even compared with them? And first, to speak of affection and mutual charity, . . . almost all barbarians, at least those who are of one race and kin, love each other, while the Romans persecute each other. . . . The many are oppressed by the few, who regard public exactions as their own peculiar right, who carry on private traffic under the guise of collecting the taxes. . . . So the poor are despoiled, the widows sigh, the orphans are oppressed, until many of them, born of families not obscure, and liberally educated, flee to our enemies that they may no longer suffer the oppression of public persecution. They doubtless seek Roman humanity among the barbarians, because they cannot bear barbarian inhumanity among the Romans. And although they differ from the people to whom they flee in manner and in language; although they are unlike as regards the fetid odor of the barbarians' bodies and garments, yet they would rather endure a foreign civilization among the barbarians than cruel injustice among the Romans.

It is urged that if we Romans are wicked and corrupt, that the barbarians commit the same sins. . . . There is, however, this difference, that if the barbarians commit the same crimes as we, yet we sin more grievously. . . . All the barbarians . . . are pagans or heretics. The Saxon race is cruel, the Franks are faithless . . . the Huns are unchaste,—in short there is vice in the life of all the barbarian peoples. But are their offenses as serious as [those of Christians]? Is the unchastity of the Hun so criminal as ours? Is the faithlessness of the Frank so blameworthy as ours?

Of God's Government, in James Harvey Robinson, *Readings in European History*, Vol. 1 (Boston: Athenaeum, 1904), pp. 28–30.

emperor, Zeno (emperor 474–491), recognized Odoacer's authority in the west, and Odoacer ceded to Zeno authority as sole emperor, being content to serve as his western viceroy. In a subsequent coup in 493 manipulated by Zeno, Theodoric (ca. 454–526), king of the Ostrogoths (east Goths), defeated Odoacer and thereafter ruled Italy with full acceptance by the Roman people and the Christian Church.

By the end of the fifth century the western empire was thoroughly overrun by barbarians. The Ostrogoths settled in Italy, the Franks in northern Gaul, the Burgundians in Provence, the Visigoths in southern Gaul and Spain, the Vandals in Africa and the Mediterranean, and the Angles and Saxons in England (see Map 6.1). Barbarians were now the western masters—but masters who were also willing to learn from the people they had conquered.

Western Europe was not transformed into a savage land. The military victories of the barbarians did not result in a great cultural defeat of the Roman Empire. The barbarians were militarily superior, but the Romans retained their cultural strength. Apart from Britain and northern Gaul, Roman language, law, and government continued to exist side by side with the new Germanic institutions. In Italy under Theodoric, Roman law gradually replaced tribal custom. Only the Vandals and the Anglo-Saxons refused to profess at least titular obedience to the emperor in Constantinople.

Behind this accommodation of cultures was the fact that the Visigoths, the Ostrogoths, and the Vandals entered the west as Christianized people. They professed, however, a religious creed that was considered heretical in the west. They were Arian Christians, that is, Christians who believed that Jesus Christ was not of one

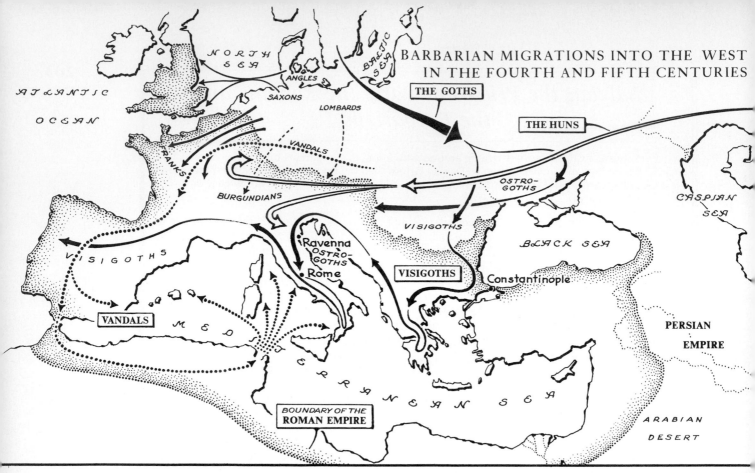

Map labels: NORTH SEA, BALTIC SEA, ATLANTIC OCEAN, ANGLES, SAXONS, LOMBARDS, THE GOTHS, THE HUNS, FRANKS, VANDALS, OSTRO-GOTHS, CASPIAN SEA, BURGUNDIANS, VISIGOTHS, VISIGOTHS, BLACK SEA, Ravenna, OSTRO-GOTHS, Rome, VISIGOTHS, Constantinople, PERSIAN EMPIRE, VANDALS, MEDITERRANEAN SEA, BOUNDARY OF THE ROMAN EMPIRE, ARABIAN DESERT

BARBARIAN MIGRATIONS INTO THE WEST IN THE FOURTH AND FIFTH CENTURIES

MAP 6-1 *The forceful intrusion of Germanic and non-Germanic barbarians into the Empire from the last quarter of the fourth century through the fifth century made for a constantly changing pattern of movement and relations. However, the map shows the major routes taken by the usually unwelcome newcomers and the areas most deeply affected by main groups.*

identical substance with God the Father—a point of view that had been condemned in 325 by the Council of Nicaea (see Chapter 5). Later, around 500, the Franks, under their strong king, Clovis, converted to the orthodox or "Catholic" form of Christianity supported by the bishops of Rome, and they helped conquer and convert the Goths and other barbarians in western Europe.

All things considered, rapprochement and a gradual interpenetration of two strong cultures—a creative tension—marked the period of the Germanic migrations. The stronger culture was the Roman, and it became dominant in a later fusion. Despite western military defeat, it can still be said that the Goths and the Franks became far more romanized than the Romans were germanized. Latin language, Nicene Christianity, and eventually Roman law and government were to triumph in the west during the Middle Ages.

The Byzantine Empire

As western Europe succumbed to the Germanic invasions, imperial power shifted to the Byzantine Empire, that is, the eastern part of the Roman Empire established in 330. Constantinople, created in 324 as the "new Rome," became the sole capital of the empire and remained such until the revival of the western empire in the eighth century by Charlemagne.

There are three distinct periods in the history of the Byzantine Empire: from the creation of Constantinople in 324 to the rise of Islam to dominance in the mid-seventh century; from 650 to the conquest of Asia Minor by the Turks in the 1070s *or*, as some prefer, to the fall of Constantinople to the western Crusaders in 1204; and finally, from 1070 or 1204 to the defeat of Constantinople by the Turks in 1453. Between 324 and 1453 the empire passed from an early period of expansion and splendor, to a time of contraction and splintering, to final catastrophic defeat.

In terms of territory, political power, and culture, the first period (324–650) was far and away the greatest. By the end of Justinian's reign (527–565), the Byzantines had spread an urban civilization around virtually the entire Mediterranean. In it they imaginatively integrated Christianity and Graeco-Roman culture. The empire at this time comprised a population in excess of 30 million. After the sixth century, the Arabs and the western Germanic tribes became the ascendant powers. They alternately invaded and conquered portions of the Byzantine Empire, shrinking it to Asia Minor and the Aegean islands. In the late sixth century migrating Slavs "barbarized" the Balkan peninsula. By the early seventh century Persians and Arabs had successively overrun Syria, Palestine, Egypt, and North Africa and had penetrated into Asia Minor.

A strong central government existed in Constantinople until the eleventh century. Much of its success was due to a large and growing voluntary army, in excess of a half million men by the end of the fourth century, by far the largest contingent of imperial servants. Although many of these soldiers lived in special camps, a substantial number were billeted in the cities.

MAP 6-2

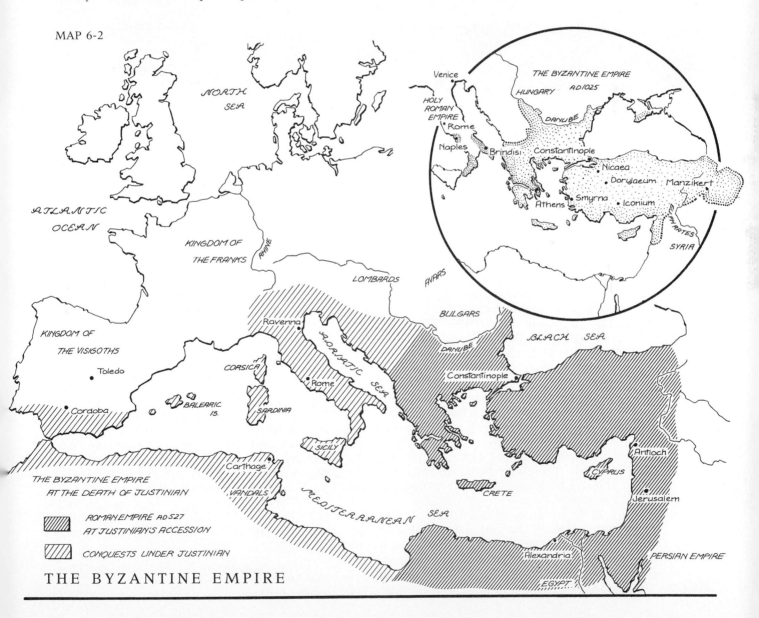

THE BYZANTINE EMPIRE

One of the most influential achievements of Byzantine art was the great church of Hagia Sophia (Holy Wisdom) built by the emperor Justinian between 532 and 537. Its great dome, 107 feet in diameter, and rich decoration of marbles and mosaics dazzled visitors to Constantinople for centuries. This mosaic from the south door of the Church shows two emperors, Justinian on the left and Constantine on the right, adoring the Virgin and Christ Child. Justinian holds his Church of Hagia Sophia, Constantine his city of Constantinople. [Hirmer Fotoarchiv]

In its heyday the empire *was* its cities. During Justinian's reign more than fifteen hundred cities existed. The largest, with perhaps 350,000 inhabitants, was Constantinople, the cultural crossroads of the Asian and European civilizations. The large provincial cities had populations of 50,000. Between the fourth and fifth centuries councils composed of local wealthy landowners, numbering around two hundred, governed the cities. Known as *decurions*, they made up the intellectual and economic elite of the empire. Heavily taxed, they were not always the emperor's most docile or loyal imperial servants. By the sixth century special governors and bishops, appointed from the landholding classes, replaced the decurion councils. They were better instruments of the emperor's will and helped to centralized imperial power.

A fifth-century statistical record gives us some sense of the size and splendor of Constantinople at its peak. According to the record, there were 5 imperial and 9 princely palaces; 8 public and 153 private baths; 4 public fora; 5 granaries; 2 theaters; a hippodrome; 322 streets; 4,388 substantial houses; 52 porticoes; 20 public and 120 private bakers; and 14 churches.[1] The most popular entertainments were the theater, frequently denounced by the clergy for nudity and immorality, and the races at the hippodrome. Numerous public taverns and baths existed, and evidence suggests laxity in sexual morality.

Since the fifth century the patriarch of Constantinople had crowned emperors in Constantinople. This practice reflected the close ties between the state and Christianity. In 380 Trinitarian Christianity was proclaimed the official religion of the eastern empire. All other religions and sects were denounced as "demented and insane."[2] Between the fourth and sixth centuries the patriarchs of Constantinople, Alexandria, Antioch, and Jerusalem acquired enormous wealth in the form of land and gold. The church, in turn, acted as the state's welfare agency, drawing on its generous

[1]Cyril Mango, *Byzantium: The Empire of New Rome* (New York: Charles Scribners Sons, 1980), p. 76.
[2]*Ibid.*, p. 88.

endowments from pious rich donors to aid the poor and needy. The prestige and comfort of the clergy swelled the clerical ranks.

Imperial policy was always to centralize and conform: "one God, one empire, one religion." To this end Justinian collated and revised Roman law, creating his famous Code in 533, the foundation of most subsequent European law. Religion also served imperial centralization. Orthodox Christianity was not, however, the only religion in the empire with a significant following. Nor did the rulers view religion as merely a political tool. At one time or another the Christian heresies of Arianism, Monophysitism, and Iconoclasm also received imperial support, and apparently because of genuine belief. Persecution and absorption into popular Christianity curtailed many pagan practices. The Jews, who lived in large numbers within the empire, had legal protection under Roman law as long as they did not proselytize among Christians, build new synagogues, or attempt to enter sensitive public offices or professions. Justinian, the emperor most intent on conformity, adopted a policy of Jewish conversion. The later emperors Heraclius (d. 641) and Leo III (717–740) ordered all Jews baptized and granted tax breaks to those who voluntarily complied. None of these efforts converted the Jews, however. Persecuted in the fifth century for proselytizing, Jews joined political revolts against the emperor in the sixth century.

Among the numerous Christian heresies, the most threatening to the empire was Monophysitism. The Monophysites taught that Jesus had only one nature, a composite divine-human nature, a point of doctrine fanatically held. The majority and orthodox view was that Jesus was of two separate natures, fully human and fully divine. The Monophysites gained a powerful ally in the person of the Empress Theodora, who disagreed on this sensitive point of Christological doctrine with her husband, Justinian, who remained strictly orthodox. Neither persecution nor compromise could break the Monophysites. In the sixth century they became a separate church, strong in the eastern provinces of the empire. Their persecution was costly to the empire in the seventh century, when Persians and Arabs laid siege to the eastern frontiers. Bitter about their treatment by the imperial government, the Monophysites apparently did little to resist.

As is clear from this discussion, the Byzantine world view was strongly biblical and theo-

The great mosque at Qairawan in modern Tunisia, eighth–ninth centuries. By the eighth century Islamic armies had conquered an empire that stretched from Spain to Persia. [Roger Wood]

logical. For the many who accepted official religion, Christian ascetic values and eschatological beliefs made the afterlife far more important than the present. Such a point of view tended to encourage political subservience and clearly aided political order as long as the emperor was perceived as holding the "true" religion.

Islam and Its Effects on East and West

A new drama began to unfold at this time, and it was to prove decisive for western Europe's future. In the south an enemy far more dangerous than the German tribes was on the march: the faith of Islam. During the lifetime of the prophet Muhammad (570–632) and thereafter, invading Arab armies absorbed the attention and resources of the emperors in

207

Constantinople, who found themselves in a life-and-death struggle.

In the early Middle Ages the Arabs were both open and cautious. During the ninth and tenth centuries they borrowed and integrated elements of Persian and Greek culture into their own. They also tolerated Jews and other religious minorities within their midst. However, they were also keen to protect the purity and integrity of Arab religion, language, and law from foreign corruption. With the passage of time—and increased conflict with the West—this protective instinct grew stronger. In the end, Arab culture did not creatively penetrate the West as did Germanic culture.

Muhammad had been raised an orphan by a family of modest means. He became a successful businessman, helped to this end by marriage to a wealthy widow in Mecca. When he was about forty, he had a religious experience in which he was called by God to preach against immorality and idolatry. His religion, Islam, means "submission to the will of Allah," and Muslims (Arabic for "true believers") are people who obey the will of Allah as revealed to Muhammad. This will is contained in the Koran (*Qur'an*, literally, "reciting" of God's will), a series of revelations received by Muhammad over a period of time and compiled by his successor. The Koran recognizes Jesus Christ as a prophet sent by God, but not one so great as Muhammad, and not God's coequal son as the Christians believe. Muhammad is the last in a line of God's prophets going back to Noah and Abraham, in this sense, "the Prophet."

Islam is uncompromisingly monotheistic. Among the things required of the faithful are prayer five times each day, generous almsgiving, fasting during the daylight hours for one month each year, and a pilgrimage to the holy city of Mecca, in what is now Saudi Arabia, at least once during one's lifetime. Muslims also permit polygamy (each man may have up to four wives) and forbid the eating of pork and the drinking of alcoholic beverages. Unlike Christianity, Islam makes no rigid distinction between the clergy and the laity. Another striking difference from Christianity, especially Western Christianity, is the complete unity of religion and politics.

Muhammad preached his message unsuccessfully for several years in what he considered "pagan" Mecca before fleeing the city in 622 for the neighboring and more receptive city of Medina. There many of his followers also migrated, making Medina the center of his movement. This flight, know to Muslims as the *Hegira*, became a key event in the history of Islam—the beginning of the new religion's political organization and geographical expansion and the starting point for its calendar. Muhammad and his followers were severely persecuted before becoming strong enough to fight back and win. Once established, Muhammad, supported by a great army of followers and able to impose his will, absolutely opposed any accommodation with pagans, and he converted fellow Arabs by holy war. He also turned sharply against Jews and Christians, having initially spoken well of them, because of their rejection of his message and authority. Mecca, a city of long association with Arab pagan rites, capitulated and became the center of Muslim activity and government. By its ability to define a common Arab culture and its willingness to impose it by force, Islam became a spiritual force capable of uniting the Arab tribes in a true Arab empire.

By the middle of the eighth century, Muslims had conquered the southern and eastern Mediterranean coastline (territories mostly still held by Islamic states today) and occupied parts of Spain, which they controlled or strongly influenced until the fifteenth century. In addition, their armies had pushed north and east through Mesopotamia and Persia and beyond (see Map 6.3). These conquests would not have been so rapid and thorough had the contemporary Byzantine and Persian empires not been exhausted by a long period of war. The Muslims struck at the conclusion of the successful campaign of Byzantine Emperor Heraclius (d. 641) against the Persian King Chosroes II. Most of the population in the conquered area was Semitic and more easily fired by hatred of the Byzantine Greek army of occupation than it was inspired to unity by a common Christian tradition. The Christian community was itself badly divided. The Egyptian (also known as *Coptic*) and Syrian churches were Monophysitic. Heraclius' efforts to impose Greek "orthodox" beliefs on these churches only increased the enmity between Greek and Semitic Christians, many of whom leaned toward Monophysitism. Many Egyptian and Syrian Christians may have looked on the Arabs as deliverers from the Byzantine conquerors.

Muslims tolerated conquered Christians, whether orthodox or Monophysite, provided they paid taxes, kept their distance, and made

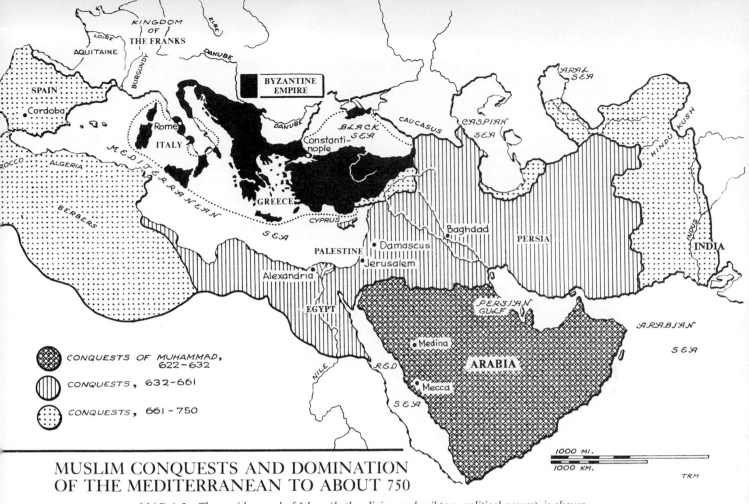

MUSLIM CONQUESTS AND DOMINATION OF THE MEDITERRANEAN TO ABOUT 750

MAP 6-3   *The rapid spread of Islam (both religion and military-political power) is shown here. From the West's viewpoint, the important fact was that in the 125 years after Muhammad's rise Muslims came to dominate Spain and all areas south and east of the Mediterranean.*

no efforts to proselytize Muslim communities. Anxious to maintain the purity of their religion and culture, the Arabs forbade mixed marriages. Special taxes on conquered peoples encouraged them to convert to Islam. After the middle of the eighth century, by which time the seat of Islam had been moved from Arabia to Damascus in Syria and from there to the brand-new city of Baghdad in Mesopotamia, the huge Muslim empire tended to break into separate states. These states often had their own caliphs (or rulers), each claiming to be the true successor of Muhammad.

Assaulted on both their eastern and their western frontiers and everywhere challenged in the Mediterranean, the Europeans developed a lasting fear and suspicion of the Muslims. In the east, during the reign of the Byzantine Leo III (717–740), the Arabs were stopped after a year's siege of Constantinople (717–

718). Leo and his successors in the Isaurian dynasty of Byzantine rulers created a successful defensive organization against the Arabs. It was so effective that it permitted the rulers of the following Macedonian dynasty (867–1057) to expand militarily and commercially into Muslim lands. Byzantine armies were also assisted by Muslim disunity. In 1071 the Seljuk Turks from central Asia, by way of Persia and Mesopotamia, overran Armenia at the eastern end of the empire in the first of a series of confrontations that would finally end with the fall of Constantinople in 1453 to the Seljuks' relatives, the Ottoman Turks. In 1096 the first Crusaders from western Europe arrived in Constantinople in the first of a series of moves to the east that ended with the capture of Constantinople in 1204 and the establishment of a half century of Latin or western rule over Byzantium.

209

As for the west's own dangers, the ruler of the Franks, Charles Martel, defeated a raiding party of Arabs on the western frontier of Europe at Poitiers (today in central France) in 732, a victory that ended any possible Arab effort to expand into western Europe by way of Spain. From the end of the seventh century to the middle of the eleventh century, the Mediterranean still remained something of a Muslim lake; although the trade of the western empire with the Orient was not cut off during these centuries, it was significantly decreased and was carried on in keen awareness of Muslim dominance.

When trade wanes, cities decline, and with them those centers for the exchange of goods and ideas that enable a society to look and live beyond itself. The Arab invasions and domination of the Mediterranean during a crucial part of the early Middle Ages created the essential conditions for the birth of western Europe as a distinctive cultural entity. Arab belligerency forced western Europeans to fall back on their own distinctive resources and to develop their peculiar Germanic and Graeco-Roman heritage into a unique culture. The Arabs accomplished this by diverting the attention and energies of the eastern empire at a time of Frankish and Lombard ascendancy (thereby preventing Byzantine expansion into the west)

and by greatly reducing western navigation of the Mediterranean (thereby closing off much eastern trade and cultural influence).

As western shipping was reduced in the Mediterranean, coastal urban centers declined. Populations that would otherwise have been engaged in trade-related work in the cities moved in great numbers into interior regions, there to work the farms of the great landholders. The latter needed their labor and welcomed the new emigrants, who were even more in need of the employment and protection that the landholders could provide. Ninety per cent of the population was peasants. There were free peasants, who owned their own land, and peasants who became "serfs" by surrendering their land to a more powerful landholder in exchange for assistance in time of dire need, like prolonged crop failure or foreign invasion. Basically serfdom was a status of servitude to an economically and politically stronger man, who provided land and dwelling in exchange for labor and goods. As the demand for agricultural products diminished in the great urban centers and as traffic between town and country was reduced, the farming belts became regionally insular and self-contained. Production and travel adjusted to local needs, and there was little incentive for bold experimentation and exploration. The domains of the great landholders became the basic social and political units of society, and

One of the reasons the Byzantines were able to repulse the Arab attack on Constantinople in 717–718 was a secret weapon: Greek fire, a highly inflammable mixture of petroleum, sulphur, and pitch that would burn even on water. In this fourteenth-century manuscript, the Byzantine navy is spraying Greek fire from a copper tube onto an enemy vessel. [Mas]

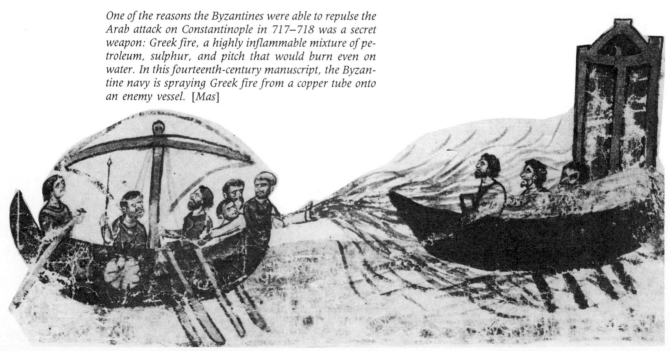

local barter economies sprang up within them. In these developments were sown the seeds of what would later come to be known as manorial and feudal society, the former an ordering of peasant society in which land and labor were divided among lords, peasants, and serfs for the profit and protection of all, the latter an ordering of aristocratic society in which a special class of warrior knights emerged as guarantors of order.

One institution remained firmly entrenched within the cities during the Arab invasions: the Christian Church. The church had long modeled its own structure on that of the imperial Roman administration. Like the latter, it was a centralized, hierarchical government with strategically placed "viceroys" (bishops) in European cities who looked for spiritual direction to their leader, the bishop of Rome. As the western empire crumbled and populations emigrated to the countryside after the barbarian and Arab invasions, local bishops and cathedral chapters filled the vacuum of authority left by the removal of Roman governors. The local cathedral became the center of urban life and the local bishop the highest authority for those who remained in the cities—just as in Rome, on a larger and more fateful scale, the pope took control of the city as the western emperors gradually departed and died out. Left to its own devices, western Europe soon discovered that the Christian Church was a rich repository of Roman administrative skills and classical culture.

The Developing Roman Church

The Christian Church had been graced with special privileges, great lands, and wealth by Emperor Constantine and his successors. In the first half of the fourth century, Christians gained legal standing and a favored status within the empire. In 391 Emperor Theodosius I (ca. 379–395), after whose death the empire would again be divided into eastern and western parts, raised Christianity to the official religion of the empire. Both Theodosius and his predecessors acted as much for political effect as out of religious conviction; in 313 Christians composed about one fifth of the population of the empire and were unquestionably the strongest of the competing religions. Mithraism, the religion popular among army officers and restricted to males, was its main rival.

Challenged to become a major political force, the church survived the period of Germanic and Arab invasions as a somewhat spiritually weakened and compromised institution; yet it was still a most potent civilizing and unifying force. It had a religious message of providential purpose and individual worth that could give solace and meaning to life at its worst. After the fall of Rome, this message was eloquently defined by Augustine (354–430) in his *City of God*, a favorite book of the Frankish king Charlemagne nearly four hundred years later. The western church also had a ritual of baptism and a creedal confession that united people beyond the traditional barriers of social class, education, and sex. After the Germanic and Arab invasions the church alone possessed an effective hierarchical administration, scattered throughout the old empire, staffed by the best-educated minds in Europe, and centered in emperorless Rome. The church also enjoyed the services of growing numbers of monks, who were not only loyal to its mission but also objects of great popular respect. Monastic culture proved again and again to be the peculiar strength of the church during the Middle Ages.

MONASTIC CULTURE. Monks were originally hermits, individuals who withdrew from society to pursue a more perfect way of life. They were inspired by the Christian ideal of a life of complete self-denial in imitation of Christ, who had denied himself even unto death. The popularity of monasticism began to grow as Roman persecution of Christians waned in the mid-third century. As the Romans stopped feeding Christians to the lions—indeed, as Christianity became the favored religion of the empire—monasticism replaced martyrdom as the most perfect way to imitate Christ and to confess one's faith. Embracing the biblical "counsels of perfection" (chastity, poverty, and obedience), the monastic life became the purest form of religious practice in the Middle Ages. Christians came to view monastic life as the superior Christian life, beyond the baptism and creedal confession that identified ordinary believers. This view evolved during the Middle Ages into a belief in the general superiority of the clergy and the mission of the church over the laity and the state—a belief that served the papacy in later confrontations with secular rulers.

Anthony of Egypt (ca. 251–356), the father of hermit monasticism, was inspired by Jesus' command to the rich young ruler: "If you will be perfect, sell all that you have, give it to the

monasticism. In southern Egypt in the first quarter of the fourth century, Pachomius (ca. 286–346) organized monks into a highly regimented common life. Hundreds shared a life together that was ordered and disciplined by a strict penal code and assigned manual labor. Such monastic communities grew to contain a thousand or more inhabitants, little "cities of God," separated from the collapsing Roman and the nominal Christian world. Basil the Great (329–379) popularized communal monasticism throughout the east, providing a rule that lessened the asceticism of Pachomius and directed monks beyond their enclaves of perfection into such social services as caring for orphans, widows, and the infirm in surrounding communities.

Athanasius (ca. 293–373) and Martin of Tours (ca. 315–ca. 399) introduced monasticism into the west, where the teaching of John Cassian (ca. 360–435) and Jerome (ca. 340–420) helped shape its basic values and practices. The great organizer of western monasticism was Benedict of Nursia (ca. 480–547). In 529 Benedict founded the mother monastery of the Benedictines at Monte Cassino in Italy, the foundation on which all western monasticism has been built. Benedict also wrote a sophisticated *Rule for Monasteries,* a comprehensive plan for every activity of the monks, even detailing how they were to sleep. The monastery was hierarchically organized and directed by an abbot, whose command was beyond question. Periods of devotion (about four hours each day were set aside for the "work of God," that is, regular prayers and liturgical activities) and study alternated with manual labor—a program that permitted not a moment's idleness and carefully promoted the religious, intellectual, and physical well-being of the cloistered. Each Benedictine monastery remained autonomous until the later Middle Ages, when the Benedictines became a unified order of the church.

THE DOCTRINE OF PAPAL PRIMACY. Constantine and his successors, especially the eastern emperors, ruled religious life with an

poor, and follow me'' (Matthew 19:21). Anthony went into the desert to pray and work, setting an example followed by hundreds in Egypt, Syria, and Palestine in the fourth and fifth centuries. This hermit monasticism was soon joined by the development of communal

213

*The Early
Middle Ages
(476–1000):
The Birth
of Europe*

The Benedictine Order Sets Its Requirements for Entrance

The religious life had great appeal in a time of political and social uncertainty. Entrance into a monastery was not, however, escapism. Much was demanded of the new monk, both during and after his probationary period, which is here described. Benedict's contribution was to prescribe a balanced blend of religious, physical, and intellectual activities within a well-structured community.

When anyone is newly come for the reformation of his life, let him not be granted an easy entrance; but, as the Apostle says, ''Test the spirits to see whether they are from God.'' If the newcomer, therefore, perseveres in his knocking, and if it is seen after four or five days that he bears patiently the harsh treatment offered him and the difficulty of admission, and that he persists in his petition, then let entrance be granted him, and let him stay in the guest house for a few days.

After that let him live in the novitiate, where the novices study, eat, and sleep. A senior shall be assigned to them who is skilled in winning souls, to watch over them with the utmost care. Let him examine whether the novice is truly seeking God, and whether he is zealous for the Work of God, for obedience and for humiliations. Let the novice be told all the hard and rugged ways by which the journey to God is made.

If he promises stability and perseverance, then at the end of two months let this Rule be read through to him, and let him be addressed thus: ''Here is the law under which you wish to fight. If you can observe it, enter; if you cannot, you are free to depart.'' If he still stands firm, let him be taken to the above-mentioned novitiate and again tested in all patience. And after the lapse of six months let the Rule be read to him, that he may know on what he is entering. And if he still remains firm, after four months let the same Rule be read to him again.

Then, having deliberated with himself, if he promises to keep it in its entirety and to observe everything that is commanded him, let him be received into the community. But let him understand that, according to the law of the rule, from that day forward he may not leave the monastery nor withdraw his neck from under the yoke of the Rule which he was free to refuse or to accept during that prolonged deliberation.

St. Benedict's Rule for Monasteries, trans. by Leonard J. Doyle (Collegeville, Minn.: Liturgical Press, 1948), Chap. 58, p. 79–80.

iron hand and consistently looked on the church as little more than a department of the state. Such political assumption of spiritual power involved the emperor directly in the church's affairs, even to the point of playing the theologian and imposing conciliar solutions on its doctrinal quarrels. State control of religion was the original Church–State relation in the west. The bishops of Rome never accepted such intervention and opposed it in every way they could. In the fifth and sixth centuries, taking advantage of imperial weakness and distraction, they developed for their own defense the weaponry of the doctrine of "papal primacy." This teaching raised the Roman pontiff to an unassailable supremacy within the church when it came to defining church doctrine; it also put him in a position to make important secular claims. The doctrine was destined to occasion repeated conflicts between church and state, pope and emperor, throughout the Middle Ages.

The notion of papal primacy was first conceived as a papal response to the decline of imperial Rome in favor of Milan and Ravenna and to the concurrent competitive claims of the patriarchs of the eastern church. The latter looked on the bishop of Rome as a peer, not as a superior, after imperial power was transferred to Constantinople. In 381 the ecumenical Council of Constantinople declared the bishop of Constantinople to be of first rank after the bishop of Rome "because Constantinople is the new Rome." In 451 the ecumenical Council of Chalcedon recognized Constantinople as having the same religious primacy in the east as Rome had traditionally possessed in the west. By the mid-sixth century the bishop of Constantinople regularly described himself in correspondence as a "universal" patriarch.

Roman pontiffs, understandably jealous of such claims and resentful of the ecclesiastical interference of eastern emperors, launched a counteroffensive. Pope Damasus I (366–384)[3] took the first of several major steps in the rise of the Roman church when he declared a Roman "apostolic" primacy. Pointing to Jesus' words to Peter in the Gospel of Matthew (16:18), the pope claimed to be in direct succession from Peter as the unique "rock" on which the Christian Church was built. Pope Leo I (440–461) took still another fateful step by assuming the title *pontifex maximus*—"supreme priest"—and he further proclaimed himself to be endowed with a "plentitude of power." During Leo's reign an imperial decree had already recognized his exclusive jurisdic-

[3]Papal dates give the years of each reign.

tion over the western church in 455. At the end of the fifth century Pope Gelasius I (492–496) proclaimed the authority of the clergy to be "more weighty" than the power of kings.

The western church was favored by events as well as ideology. It was the chief beneficiary of imperial adversity in the face of Germanic and Arab invasions. Islam may even be said to have "saved" the western church from eastern domination, and the emergent Lombards and Franks provided it with new political allies. The success of Arab armies ended eastern episcopal competition with Rome as the area of bishopric after bishopric fell to the Muslims in the east. The power of the exarch of Ravenna, who was the Byzantine emperor's regent in the west, was eclipsed by invading Lombards, who, thanks to Frankish prodding, became Nicene Christians loyal to Rome in the late seventh century. In an unprecedented act Pope Gregory I, "the Great" (590–604), negotiated an independent peace treaty with the Lombards that completely ignored the emperor and the imperial government in Ravenna, who were at the time too weak to offer resistance.

Augustine of Hippo Describes His Conversion to Christianity

Augustine of Hippo (354–430) frankly confessed his utter sinfulness and domination by lust until Christianity gave him the will to resist.

Who am I, and what am I? Is there any evil that is not found in my acts, or if not in my acts, in my words, or if not in my words, in my will? But you, O Lord, are good and merciful, and your right hand has had regard for the depth of my death, and from the very bottom of my heart it has emptied out an abyss of corruption. This was the sum of it: not to will what I willed and to will what you willed.

But throughout these long years where was my free will? Out of what deep and hidden pit was it called forth in a single moment, wherein to bend my neck to your mild yoke and my shoulders to your light burden, O Christ Jesus, "my helper and my redeemer"? How sweet did

it suddenly become to me to be free of the sweets of folly: things that I once feared to lose it was now joy to put away. You cast them forth from me, you the true and highest sweetness, you cast them forth, and in their stead you entered in, sweeter than every pleasure, but not to flesh and blood, brighter than every light, but deeper within me than any secret retreat, higher than every honor, but not to those who exalt themselves. Now was my mind free from the gnawing cares of favor-seeking, of striving for gain, of wallowing in the mire, and of scratching lust's itchy sore. I spoke like a child to you, my light, my wealth, my salvation, my Lord God.

The Confessions of St. Augustine, trans. by John K. Ryan (New York: Doubleday, 1960), pp. 205–206.

215

*The Early
Middle Ages
(476–1000):
The Birth
of Europe*

THE DIVISION OF CHRISTENDOM. The division of Christendom into eastern and western churches has its roots in the early Middle Ages. From the start there was the difference in language (Greek in the east, Latin in the west) and culture. Compared with their western counterparts, eastern Christians seemed to attribute less importance to life in this world. They were more concerned about questions affecting their eternal destiny. This concern made them more receptive than the western Christian to Oriental mysticism and theological ideas. It was, after all, a combination of Greek, Roman, and Oriental elements that formed Byzantine culture. The strong mystical orientation to the next world may also have caused the eastern church to submit more passively than western popes could ever do to royal intervention in church affairs.

As in the west, eastern church organization closely followed that of the secular state. A patriarch ruled over metropolitans and archbishops in the cities and provinces, and they, in turn, ruled over bishops, who stood as authorities over the local clergy. With the exception of the patriarch Michael Cerularius, who tried unsuccessfully to free the church from its traditional tight state control, the patriarchs were normally carefully regulated by the emperor.

Contrary to the evolving western tradition of universal clerical celibacy, which western monastic culture encouraged, the eastern church permitted the marriage of secular priests, while strictly forbidding bishops to marry. The eastern church also used leavened bread in the Eucharist, contrary to the western custom of using unleavened bread. Also unliked by the west was the tendency of the eastern church to compromise doctrinally with the politically powerful Arian and Monophysite Christians. In the background were also conflicting political claims over jurisdiction over the newly converted areas in the north Balkans.

Beyond these issues the major factors in the religious break between east and west revolved around questions of doctrinal authority. The eastern church put more stress on the authority of the Bible and of the ecumenical councils of the church than on the counsel and decrees of the bishop of Rome. The councils and Holy Scripture were the ultimate authorities in the definition of Christian doctrine. The claims of Roman popes to a special primacy of authority

---

Pope Gelasius I Declares the ''Weightiness'' of Priestly Authority

Some see this famous letter of Pope Gelasius to Emperor Anastasius I in 494 as an extreme statement of papal supremacy. Others believe it is a balanced, moderate statement that recognizes the independence of both temporal and spiritual power and seeks their close cooperation, not the domination of church over state.

There are two powers, august Emperor, by which this world is chiefly ruled, namely, the sacred authority of the priests and the royal power. Of these, that of the priests is the more weighty, since they have to render an account for even the kings of men in the divine judgment. You are also aware, dear son [emperor], that while you are permitted honorably to rule over humankind, yet in things divine you bow your head humbly before the leaders of the clergy and await from their hands the means of your salvation. In the reception and proper disposition of the heavenly mysteries you recognize that you should be subordinate rather than superior to the religious order, and that in these matters you depend on their judgment rather than wish to force them to follow your will. [And] if the ministers of religion, recognizing the supremacy granted you from heaven in matters affecting the public order, obey your laws, lest otherwise they obstruct the course of secular affairs . . . , with what readiness should you not yield them obedience to whom is assigned the dispensing of the sacred mysteries of religion?

James Harvey Robinson (Ed.), *Readings in European History*, Vol. 1 (Boston: Athenaeum, 1904), pp. 72–73.

This ninth-century Byzantine manuscript shows an iconoclast whiting out an image of Christ. The iconoclast controversy was an important stage in dividing Christendom into separate Latin and Greek branches. [Public Library, Moscow]

on the basis of the apostle Peter's commission from Jesus in Matthew 16:18 ("Thou art Peter, and upon this rock I will build my church") were completely unacceptable to the east, where the independence and autonomy of national churches held sway. As Steven Runciman summarized, "The Byzantine ideal was a series of autocephalous state churches, linked by intercommunion and the faith of seven councils."[4] This basic issue of authority in matters of faith lay behind the mutual excommunication of Pope Nicholas I and Patri-

arch Photius in the ninth century and that of Pope Leo IX and Patriarch Michael Cerularius in 1054.

A second major issue in the separation of the two churches was the western addition of the *filioque* clause to the Nicene–Constantino-politan Creed—an anti-Arian move that made the Holy Spirit proceed "also from the Son" (*filioque*) as well as from the Father. This addition made clear the western belief that Christ was "fully substantial with God the Father" and not a lesser being.

The final and most direct issue in the religious division of Christendom was the iconoclastic controversy of the first half of the eighth century. After 725 the eastern emperor, Leo III (717–740), attempted to force western popes to abolish the use of images in their churches. This stand met fierce official and popular resistance in the west, where images were greatly cherished. Emperor Leo punished the disobedient west by confiscating papal lands in Sicily and Calabria (in southern Italy) and placing them under the jurisdiction of the subservient patriarch of Constantinople. Because these territories provided essential papal revenues, the western church could not but view the emperor's action as a declaration of war. Later the empress Irene (mother of Constantine VI) made peace with the Roman church on this issue and restored the use of images at the sixth ecumenical council in Nicea in 787.

Leo's direct challenge of the pope came almost simultaneously with still another aggressive act against the western church: attacks by the heretofore docile Lombards of northern Italy. Assailed by both the emperor and the Lombards, the pope in Rome seemed surely doomed. But there has not been a more resilient and enterprising institution in Western history than the Roman papacy. Since the pontificate of Gregory the Great, Roman popes had eyed the Franks of northern Gaul as Europe's ascendant power and their surest protector. Imperial and Lombard aggression against the Roman pope in the first half of the eighth century provided the occasion for the most fruitful political alliance of the Middle Ages. In 754 Pope Stephen II (752–757) enlisted Pepin III and his Franks as defenders of the church against the Lombards and as a western counterweight to the eastern emperor. This marriage of religion and politics created a new western church and empire; it also determined much of the course of Western history into our times.

[4]*Byzantine Civilization* (London: A. and C. Black, 1933), p. 128.

The Kingdom of the Franks

Merovingians and Carolingians: From Clovis to Charlemagne

A warrior chieftain, Clovis (466?–511), a convert to Christianity around 496, made the Franks and their first ruling family, the Merovingians, a significant force in western Europe. Clovis and his successors subdued the pagan Burgundians and the Arian Visigoths and established within ancient Gaul the kingdom of the Franks. The Franks were a broad belt of people scattered throughout modern Belgium, the Netherlands, and western Germany, whose loyalties remained strictly tribal and local. The Merovingians attempted to govern this sprawling kingdom by pacts with landed nobility and by the creation of the royal office of count. The most persistent problem of medieval political history was the competing claims of the "one" and the "many"—on the one hand, the king, who struggled for a centralized government and transregional loyalty, and on the other, powerful local magnates, who strove to preserve their regional autonomy and traditions. The Merovingian counts were men without possessions to whom the king gave great lands in the expectation that they would be, as the landed aristocrats often were not, loyal officers of the kingdom. But like local aristocrats the Merovingian counts also let their immediate self-interests gain the upper hand. Once established in office for a period of time, they too became territorial rulers in their own right, with the result that the Frankish kingdom progressively fragmented into independent regions and tiny principalities. This centrifugal tendency was further assisted by the Frankish custom of dividing the kingdom equally among the king's legitimate male heirs.

Clovis Converts to Christianity

One of the attractions of Christianity in the late-ancient and early medieval world was its belief in a God providentially active in history who assisted those loyal to Him against their enemies. In the following account of Clovis's conversion, provided by the Christian Church historian Gregory of Tours, the Frankish king is said to have turned Christian because he believed that the Christian God had given him a military victory over a rival German tribe, the Alemanni.

Clovis took to wife Clotilde, daughter of the king of the Burgundians and a Christian. The queen unceasingly urged the king to acknowledge the true God, and forsake idols. But he could not in any wise be brought to believe until a war broke out with the Alemanni. . . . The two armies were in battle and there was great slaughter. Clovis' army was near to utter destruction. He saw the danger . . . and raised his eyes to heaven, saying: Jesus Christ, whom Clotilde declares to be the son of the living God, who it is said givest aid to the oppressed and victory to those who put their hope in thee, I beseech thy . . . aid. If thou shalt grant me victory over these enemies . . . I will believe in thee and be baptized in thy name. For I have called upon my gods, but . . . they are far removed from my
aid. So I believe that they have no power, for they do not succor those who serve them. Now I call upon thee, and I long to believe in thee. . . . When he had said these things, the Alemanni turned their backs and began to flee. When they saw that their king was killed, they submitted to the sway of Clovis, saying . . . Now we are thine.

After Clovis had forbidden further war and praised his soldiers, he told the queen how he had won the victory by calling on the name of Christ. Then the queen sent for the blessed Remigius, bishop of the city of Rheims, praying him to bring the gospel of salvation to the king. The priest, little by little and secretly, led him to believe in the true God . . . and to forsake idols, which could not help him nor anybody else.

James Harvey Robinson (Ed.), *Readings in European History*, Vol. 1 (Boston: Athenaeum, 1904), pp. 52–54.

Rather than purchasing allegiance and unity within the kingdom, the Merovingian largess simply occasioned the rise of competing magnates and petty tyrants, who became laws unto themselves within their regions. By the seventh century the Frankish king existed more in title than in effective executive power. Real power came to be concentrated in the office of the *mayor of the palace*, who was the spokesman at the king's court for the great landowners of the three regions into which the Frankish kingdom was divided: Neustria, Austrasia, and Burgundy. Through this office the Carolingian dynasty rose to power.

The Carolingians controlled the office of the mayor of the palace from the ascent to that post of Pepin I of Austrasia (d. 639) until 751, at which time the Carolingians, with the enterprising connivance of the pope, simply expropriated the Frankish crown. Pepin II (d. 714) ruled in fact if not in title over the Frankish

Carolingian cavalry, from a ninth-century Swiss manuscript. [*Mansell Collection*]

kingdom. His illegitimate son, Charles Martel ("the Hammer," d. 741), created a great cavalry by bestowing lands known as *benefices* or *fiefs* on powerful noblemen, who, in return, agreed to be ready to serve as the king's army. It was such an army that checked the Arab probings on the western front at Poitiers in 732—an important battle that helped to secure the borders of western Europe.

The fiefs so generously bestowed by Charles Martel to create his army came in large part from landed property that he usurped from the church. His alliance with the landed aristocracy in this grand manner permitted the Carolingians to have some measure of political success where the Merovingians had failed. The Carolingians created counts almost entirely out of the landed nobility from which the Carolingians themselves had risen. The Merovingians, in contrast, had tried to compete directly with these great aristocrats by raising landless men to power. By playing to strength rather than challenging it, the Carolingians strengthened themselves, at least for the short term. Because the church was by this time completely dependent of the protection of the Franks against the eastern emperor and the Lombards, it gave little thought at this time to the fact that its savior had been created in part with lands to which it held claim. Later the Franks partially compensated the church for these lands.

THE FRANKISH CHURCH. The church came to play a large and initially quite voluntary role in the Frankish government. By Carolingian times monasteries were a dominant force. Their intellectual achievements made them respected repositories of culture. Their religious teaching and example imposed order on surrounding populations. Their relics and rituals made them magical shrines to which pilgrims came in great numbers. And, thanks to their many gifts and internal discipline and industry, many had become very profitable farms and landed estates, their abbots rich and powerful magnates. Already in Merovingian times the higher clergy were employed in tandem with counts as royal agents. It was the policy of the Carolingians, perfected by Charles Martel and his successor, Pepin III ("the Short," d. 768), to use the church to pacify conquered neighboring tribes—Frisians, Thüringians, Bavarians, and especially the Franks' archenemies, the Saxons. Conversion to Nicene Christianity became an integral part of the successful annexation of conquered lands and people: the cavalry broke their bodies, while the clergy won their hearts and minds. The Anglo-Saxon missionary Saint Boniface (born Wynfrith; 680?–754) was the most important of the German clergy who served Carolingian kings in this way. Christian bishops in missionary districts and elsewhere became lords, appointed by and subject to the king—an ominous integration of secular and religious policy in which lay the seeds of the later Investiture Controversy of the eleventh and twelfth centuries.

The church served more than Carolingian territorial expansion. Pope Zacharias (741–752) also sanctioned Pepin the Short's termination of the vestigial Merovingian dynasty and supported the Carolingian accession to outright kingship of the Franks. With the pope's public blessing, Pepin was proclaimed king by the nobility in council in 751, while the last of the Merovingians, the puppet king Childeric III, was hustled off to a monastery and dynastic oblivion. According to legend, Saint Boniface first anointed Pepin, thereby investing Frankish rule from the very start with a certain sacral character.

Zacharias's successor, Pope Stephen II (752–757), did not let Pepin forget the favor of his predecessor. Driven from Rome in 753 by the Lombards, Pope Stephen appealed directly to Pepin to cast out the invaders and to guarantee papal claims to central Italy, which was dominated at this time by the eastern emperor. In 754 the Franks and the church formed an alliance against the Lombards and the eastern emperor. Carolingian kings became the protectors of the Catholic Church and thereby "kings by the grace of God." Pepin gained the title *patricius Romanorum*, "patrician of the Romans," a title first borne by the ruling families of Rome and heretofore applied to the representative of the eastern emperor. In 755 the Franks defeated the Lombards and gave the pope the lands surrounding Rome, an event that created what came to be known as the *Papal States*. The lands earlier appropriated by Charles Martel and parceled out to the Frankish nobility were never returned to the church, despite the appearance in this period of a most enterprising fraudulent document designed to win their return, the *Donation of Constantine* (written between 750 and 800), which, however, was never universally accepted in the west. This imperial parchment alleged that the Emperor Constantine had per-

sonally conveyed to the church his palace and "all provinces and districts of the city of Rome and Italy and of the regions of the West" as permanent possessions. It was believed by many to be a genuine document until definitely exposed as a forgery in the fifteenth century by the Humanist Lorenzo Valla.

The papacy had looked to the Franks for an ally strong enough to protect it from the eastern emperors. It is an irony of history that the church found in the Carolingian dynasty a western imperial government that drew almost as slight a boundary between State and Church, secular and religious policy, as did eastern emperors. Although eminently preferable to eastern domination, Carolingian patronage of the church proved in its own way to be no less dominating.

The Reign of Charlemagne (768–814)

Charlemagne continued the role of his father, Pepin the Short, as papal protector in Italy and his policy of territorial conquest in the north. After King Desiderius and the Lombards of northern Italy were decisively defeated in 774, Charlemagne took upon himself the title "King of the Lombards" in Pavia. He widened the frontiers of his kingdom further by

---

MAJOR POLITICAL AND RELIGIOUS DEVELOPMENTS OF THE EARLY MIDDLE AGES	
Emperor Constantine issues the Edict of Milan	313
Council of Nicaea defines Christian doctrine	325
Rome invaded by Visigoths under Alaric	410
St. Augustine writes *The City of God*	413–426
Council of Chalcedon further defined Christian doctrine	451
Europe invaded by the Huns under Attila	451–453
Barbarian Odoacer deposes western emperor and rules as king of the Romans	476
Theodoric establishes kingdom of Ostrogoths in Italy	488
Saint Benedict founds monastery at Monte Cassino	529
Justinian codifies Roman law	533
Muhammad's flight from Mecca (*Hegira*)	622
Charles Martel defeats Arabs at Poitiers	732
Pope Stephen II and Pepin III ally	754

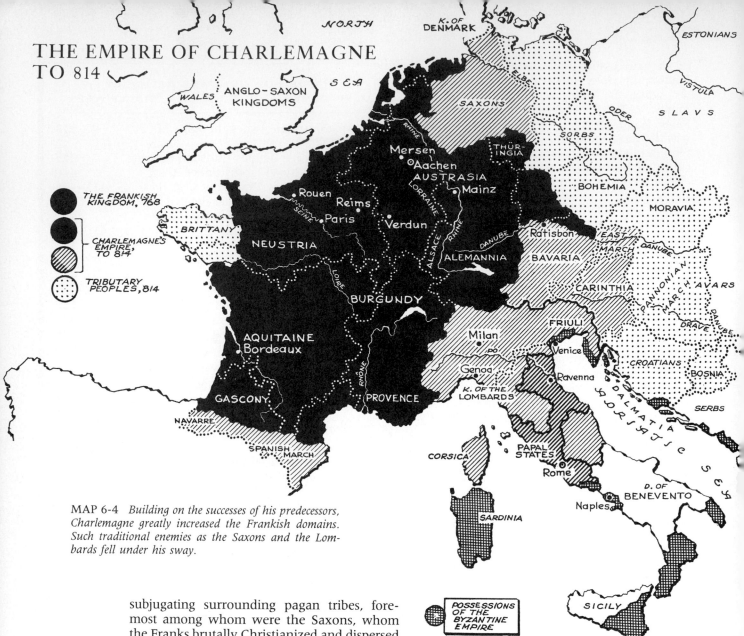

WALES   ANGLO-SAXON
         KINGDOMS

THE FRANKISH
KINGDOM, 768

CHARLEMAGNE'S
EMPIRE,
TO 814

TRIBUTARY
PEOPLES, 814

NORTH
SEA

K. OF
DENMARK

ESTONIANS

SAXONS

SLAVS

SORBS

THÜR-
INGIA

Mersen
Aachen
AUSTRASIA

BOHEMIA

MORAVIA

BRITTANY

Rouen   Reims
      Paris

Verdun

Mainz

Ratisbon

EAST
MARCH

NEUSTRIA

ALSACE

LORRAINE

DANUBE

ALEMANNIA   BAVARIA

AVARS

CARINTHIA

PANNONIAN MARCH

LOIRE

BURGUNDY

DANUBE
DRAVE
DANUBE

FRIULI

AQUITAINE
Bordeaux

RHÔNE

Milan
PO
K. OF THE
LOMBARDS
Genoa

Venice

CROATIANS

BOSNIA

DALMATIA

GASCONY

PROVENCE

Ravenna

ADRIATIC SEA

SERBS

NAVARRE

SPANISH
MARCH

CORSICA

PAPAL
STATES
Rome

D. OF
BENEVENTO

Naples

SARDINIA

POSSESSIONS
OF THE
BYZANTINE
EMPIRE

SICILY

MAP 6-4 *Building on the successes of his predecessors, Charlemagne greatly increased the Frankish domains. Such traditional enemies as the Saxons and the Lombards fell under his sway.*

subjugating surrounding pagan tribes, foremost among whom were the Saxons, whom the Franks brutally Christianized and dispersed in small groups throughout Frankish lands. The Avars (a tribe related to the Huns) were practically annihilated, so that the Danubian plains were brought into the Frankish orbit. The Arabs were chased beyond the Pyrenees. By the time of his death on January 28, 814, Charlemagne's kingdom embraced modern France, Belgium, Holland, Switzerland, almost the whole of western Germany, much of Italy, a portion of Spain, and the island of Corsica—an area approximately equal to that of the modern Common Market (see Map 6.4).

THE NEW EMPIRE.   Encouraged by his ambitious advisers, Charlemagne came to harbor imperial designs; he desired to be not only

king of the Germans but a universal emperor as well. He had his sacred palace city, Aachen (in French, Aix-la-Chapelle), constructed in conscious imitation of the courts of the ancient Roman and of the contemporary eastern emperors. Although permitted its distinctiveness, the church was looked after by Charlemagne with a paternalism almost as great as that of any eastern emperor. He used the church, above all, to promote social stability and hierarchical order throughout the kingdom—as an aid in the creation of a great Frankish Christian empire. Frankish Christians were ceremoniously baptized, professed the Nicene Creed (with the *filioque* clause), and learned in church to revere Charlemagne.

In the 790s the formation of a peculiar Carolingian Christendom was made clear by the royal issuance of the so-called *Libri Carolini*. In these documents Charlemagne attacked the second ecumenical Council of Nicaea, which had met in 787 to construct a new, approving, eastern position on the use of images in churches—actually a friendly gesture toward the west. The height of Charlemagne's imperial pretension was reached, however, on Christmas Day, 800, when Pope Leo II (795–816) crowned Charlemagne emperor. Only a short time before, Charlemagne had restored to power this contested pope, whom the Roman aristocracy had briefly imprisoned in 799 before his escape to Charlemagne. This fateful coronation was in part an effort by the pope to enhance the church's stature and to gain a certain leverage over this king who seemed to dominate everything in his path. It was no papal *coup d'etat*, however; Charlemagne's control over the church was as strong after as before the event. If the coronation benefited the church, as it certainly did, it also served Charlemagne's purposes. Before Christmas Day, 800, Charlemagne was a minor western potentate in the eyes of eastern emperors. After the coronation, eastern emperors reluctantly recognized his new imperial dignity, and Charlemagne even found it necessary to disclaim ambitions to rule as emperor over the east. Here began what would come to be known as the Holy Roman Empire, a revival, based in Germany, of the old Roman Empire in the west.

THE NEW EMPEROR. Charlemagne stood a majestic six feet three and one-half inches tall—a fact secured when his tomb was opened and exact measurements were taken in 1861. He was nomadic, ever ready for a hunt. Informal and gregarious, he insisted on the presence of friends even when he bathed and was widely known for his practical jokes, lusty good humor, and warm hospitality. Aachen was a festive palace city to which people and gifts came from all over the world. In 802

Emperor and pope: This ninth-century mosaic from the Cathedral of St. John Lateran in Rome depicts St. Peter giving spiritual authority to Pope Leo III and temporal power to the emperor Charlemagne. [*Vatican Library*]

Charlemagne even received from the caliph of Baghdad, Harun-al-Rashid, a white elephant, the transport of which across the Alps was as great a wonder as the creature itself.

Charlemagne had five official wives, possessed many mistresses and concubines, and sired numerous children. This connubial variety created special problems. His oldest son by his first marriage, Pepin, jealous of the attention shown by his father to the sons of his second wife and fearing the loss of paternal favor, joined with noble enemies in a conspiracy against his father. He ended his life in confinement in a monastery after the plot was exposed.

PROBLEMS OF GOVERNMENT. Charlemagne governed his kingdom through counts, of whom there were perhaps as many as 250. They were strategically located within the administrative districts into which the kingdom was divided. In Carolingian practice the count tended to be a local magnate, one who already possessed the armed might and the self-interest to enforce the will of a generous king. He had three main duties: to maintain a local army loyal to the king, to collect tribute and dues, and to administer justice throughout his district. This last responsibility he undertook through a district law court known as the *mallus*. The *mallus* assessed *wergeld*, or the compensation to be paid to an injured party in a feud, the most popular way of settling grievances and ending hostilities. In

---

The False Donation of Constantine

Among the ways in which Roman ecclesiasts fought to free the western church from political domination was to assert its own sovereign territorial and political rights. One of the most ambitious of such assertions was the so-called *Donation of Constantine* (eighth century), a fraudulent document claiming papal succession to much of the old Roman Empire.

The Emperor Caesar Flavius Constantinus in Christ Jesus . . . to the most Holy and blessed Father of fathers, Silvester, Bishop of the Roman city and Pope; and to all his successors, the pontiffs, who shall sit in the chair of blessed Peter to the end of time. . . . Grace, peace, love, joy, long-suffering, mercy . . . be with you all. . . . For we wish you to know . . . that we have forsaken the worship of idols . . . and have come to the pure Christian faith. . . .

To the holy apostles, my lords the most blessed Peter and Paul, and through them also to blessed Silvester, our father, supreme pontiff and universal pope of the city of Rome, and to the pontiffs, his successors, who to the end of the world shall sit in the seat of blessed Peter, we grant and by this present we convey our imperial Lateran palace, which is superior to and excels all palaces in the whole world; and further the diadem, which is the crown of our head; and the miter; as also the super-humeral, that is, the stole which usually surrounds our imperial neck; and the purple cloak and the scarlet tunic and all the imperial robes. . .

And we decree that those most reverend men, the clergy of various orders serving the same most holy Roman Church, shall have that eminence, distinction, power and precedence, with which our illustrious senate is gloriously adorned; that is, they shall be made patricians and consuls. And we ordain that they shall also be adorned with other imperial dignities. Also we decree that the clergy of the sacred Roman Church shall be adorned as are the imperial officers. . . .

We convey to the oft-mentioned and most blessed Silvester, universal pope, both our palace, as preferment, and likewise all provinces, palaces and districts of the city of Rome and Italy and of the regions of the West; and, bequeathing them to the power and sway of him and the pontiffs, his successors, we do determine and decree that the same be placed at his disposal, and do lawfully grant it as a permanent possession to the holy Roman Church.

Henry Bettenson (Ed.)., *Documents of the Christian Church* (New York: Oxford University Press, 1961), pp. 137–141.

223

*The Early
Middle Ages
(476—1000):
The Birth
of Europe*

*Charlemagne as law-giver, from a tenth-century French manuscript. [Bibliotheque Nationale,
Paris]*

very difficult cases where guilt or innocence
was unclear, recourse was often had to judicial
duels or to such "divine" judgments as the
length of time it took a defendant's hand to
heal after immersion in boiling water. In the
ordeal by water, another divine test when
human judgment was stymied, a defendant
was thrown with his hands and feet bound
into a river or pond that was first blessed by a
priest; if he floated, he was pronounced guilty,
because the pure water had obviously rejected
him; if, however, the water received him and
he sank, then he was deemed innocent.

As in Merovingian times, many counts used
their official position and new judicial powers
to their own advantage, becoming little despots
within their districts. As the strong were made
stronger, they became more independent. They
looked on the land grants with which they

were paid as hereditary possessions rather than
generous royal donations—a development
that began to fragment Charlemagne's kingdom. Charlemagne tried to oversee his overseers and improve local justice by creating special royal envoys known as *missi dominici*.
These were lay and clerical agents (counts and
archbishops and bishops) who made annual
visits to districts other than their own. But their
impact was only marginal. Permanent provincial governors, bearing the title of prefect,
duke, or margrave, were created in what was
still another attempt to supervise the counts
and organize the outlying regions of the kingdom. But as these governors became established in their areas, they proved no less cor-
ruptible than the others. Charlemagne never
solved the problem of a loyal bureaucracy. Ecclesiastical agents proved no better than secu-

The Duties of the Missi Dominici

Although they did not succeed in rendering universal justice, Charlemagne's special royal agents, the *missi dominici,* were an effort to implement Charlemagne's idea of what government should ideally do to gain respect and retain allegiance. The following is a general description of the *missi* and their duties from a capitulary (or Frankish legal ordinance) of 802.

The most serene and most Christian lord emperor Charles has chosen from his nobles the wisest and most prudent men, archbishops and some of the other bishops also, together with venerable abbots and pious laymen, and has sent them throughout his whole kingdom; through them he would have all persons live strictly in accordance with the law. Moreover, where anything which is not right and just has been enacted in the law, he has ordered them to inquire into this most diligently and to inform him of it; he desires, God granting, to reform it. . . . Let the missi *themselves make a diligent investigation whenever any man claims that an injustice has been done to him by any one, just as they desire to deserve the grace of omnipotent God and to keep their fidelity pledged to him, so that in all cases, everywhere, they shall, in accordance with the will and fear of God, administer the law fully and justly in the case of the holy churches of God and of the poor, of wards and widows, and of the whole people. And if there shall be anything . . . that they, together with the provincial counts, are not able of themselves to correct and to do justice concerning it, they shall, without any reservations, refer this, together with their reports, to the judgment of the emperor. The straight path of justice shall not be impeded by any one on account of flattery or gifts, or on account of any relationship, or from fear of the powerful.*

James Harvey Robinson (Ed.), *Readings in European History,* Vol. 1 (Boston: Athenaeum, 1904), pp. 139–140.

lar ones in this regard. Landowning bishops had not only the same responsibilities but also the same secular lifestyles and aspirations as the royal counts. Save for their attendance to the liturgy and to church prayers, they were largely indistinguishable from the lay nobility. Capitularies or royal decrees discouraged the more outrageous behavior of the clergy. But Charlemagne also sensed, rightly as the Gregorian reform of the eleventh century would prove, a danger to royal government in the emergence of a distinctive and reform-minded class of ecclesiastical landowners. Charlemagne purposefully treated his bishops as he treated his counts, that is, as vassals who served at the king's pleasure.

To be a Christian in this period was more a matter of ritual and doctrine, being baptized and reciting the Creed, than a prescribed ethical behavior and social service. For both the clergy and the laity it was a time when more primitive social goals were being contested. A legislative achievement of Charlemagne's reign, for example, was to give a free vassal the right to break his oath of loyalty to his lord if the lord tried to kill him, to reduce him to an unfree serf, to withhold promised protection in time of need, or to seduce his wife.

ALCUIN AND THE CAROLINGIAN RENAISSANCE. Charlemagne accumulated a great deal of wealth in the form of loot and land from conquered tribes. He used a substantial part of this booty to attract Europe's best scholars to Aachen, where they developed court culture and education. By making scholarship materially as well as intellectually rewarding, Charlemagne attracted such scholars as Theodulf of Orleans, Angilbert, his own biographer Einhard, and the renowned Anglo-Saxon master Alcuin of York (735–804), who, at almost fifty, became director of the king's palace school in 782. Alcuin brought classical and Christian learning to Aachen and was handsomely rewarded for his efforts with several monastic estates, including that of Saint Martin of Tours, the wealthiest in the kingdom.

Although Charlemagne also appreciated learning for its own sake, this grand palace school was not created simply for love of antiquity. Charlemagne intended it to upgrade the administrative skills of the clerics and officials who staffed the royal bureaucracy. By preparing the sons of the nobility to run the religious and secular offices of the realm, court scholarship served kingdom building. The school provided basic instruction in the seven liberal arts, with special concentration on grammar, logic, and mathematics, that is, training in reading, writing, speaking, and sound reasoning—the basic tools of bureaucracy. A clearer style of handwriting—the Carolingian minuscule—and accurate Latin appeared in the official documents. Lay literacy increased. Through personal correspondence and visitations Alcuin created a genuine, if limited, community of scholars and clerics at court and did much to infuse the highest administrative levels with a sense of comradeship and common purpose.

A modest renaissance or rebirth of antiquity occurred in the palace school as scholars col-

---

Einhard Describes His Admired Emperor, Charlemagne

We are fortunate to have an eye-witness account of Charlemagne by a court scholar, Einhard. Here are his remarks on the king's features, habits, and aspirations.

Charles was large and robust, of commanding stature and excellent proportions. . . . He took constant exercise in riding and hunting, which was natural for a Frank, since scarcely any nation can be found to equal them in these pursuits. He also delighted in the natural warm baths, frequently exercising himself by swimming, in which he was very skillful, no one being able to outstrip him. It was on account of the warm baths at Aix-la-Chapelle that he built his palace there and lived there constantly during the last years of his life and until his death. . . .

He wore the dress of his native country, that is, the Frankish. . . . He thoroughly disliked the dress of foreigners, however fine; and he never put it on except at Rome. . . .

In his eating and drinking he was temperate; more particularly so in his drinking, for he had the greatest abhorrence of drunkenness in anybody, but more especially in himself and his companions. . . . While he was dining he listened to music or reading. History and the deeds of men of old were most often read. He derived much pleasure from the works of St. Augustine, especially from his book called The City of God.

He was ready and fluent in speaking, and able to express himself with great clearness. He did not confine himself to his native tongue, but took pains to learn foreign languages, acquiring such knowledge of Latin that he could make an address in that language as well as in his own. Greek he could better understand than speak. Indeed, he was so polished in speech that he might have passed for a learned man.

He was an ardent admirer of the liberal arts, and greatly revered their professors, whom he promoted to high honors. In order to learn grammar, he attended the lectures of the aged Peter of Pisa, a deacon; and for other branches of knowledge he chose as his preceptor Alcuin, also a deacon,—a Saxon by race, from Britain, the most learned man of the day, with whom the king spent much time in learning rhetoric and logic, and more especially astronomy. He learned the art of determining the dates upon which the movable festivals of the Church fall, and with deep thought and skill most carefully calculated the courses of the planets.

Charles also tried to learn to write, and used to keep his tablets and writing book under the pillow of his couch, that when he had leisure he might practice his hand in forming letters; but he made little progress in this task, too long deferred and begun too late in life.

Life of Charlemagne, in James Harvey Robinson (Ed.), *Readings in European History,* Vol. 1 (Boston: Athenaeum, 1904), pp. 126–128.

Einhard, the chronicler of Charlemagne's reign. Einhard was among the many European scholars whom Charlemagne attracted to his court at Aachen. [Bibliotheque Nationale, Paris]

lected and preserved ancient manuscripts for a more curious posterity. Alcuin worked on a correct text of the Bible and made editions of the works of Gregory the Great and the monastic *Rule* of Saint Benedict. These scholarly activities aimed at concrete reforms and served official efforts to bring uniformity to church law and liturgy, to educate the clergy, and to improve moral life within the monasteries.

THE MANOR. The agrarian economy of the Middle Ages was organized and controlled through village farms known as *manors*. Here peasants labored as farmers in subordination to a lord, that is, a more powerful landowner who gave them land and tenements in exchange for their services and a portion of their crops. That part of the land farmed by the peasants for the lord was the *demesne*, on average about one quarter to one third of the arable land, and all crops grown there were harvested for the lord. The peasants were treated differently according to their personal status and the

size of their tenement, all in strict accordance with custom; indeed, a social hierarchy existed among the peasantry. When a *freeman*, that is, a peasant with his own modest allodial or hereditary property (property free from the claims of a feudal overlord) became a serf by surrendering this property to a greater landowner in exchange for his protection and assistance, the freeman received it back from the lord with a clear definition of economic and legal rights that protected the freeman's self-interest. Although the land was no longer his property, he had full possession and use of it, and the number of services and amount of goods to be supplied the lord were often carefully spelled out. On the other hand, peasants who entered the service of a lord without any real property to bargain with (perhaps some farm implements and a few animals) ended up as *unfree* serfs and were much more vulnerable to the lord's demands, often spending up to three days a week working the lord's fields. Truly impoverished peasants who lived and worked on the manor as serfs had the lowest status and were the least protected. Weak serfs often fled to a monastery rather than continue their servitude, and therefore this avenue of escape was eventually closed by law.

By the time of Charlemagne the moldboard plow and the three-field system of land cultivation were coming into use, developments that improved agricultural productivity. Unlike the older "scratch" plow, which crisscrossed the field with only slight penetration, the moldboard cut deep into the soil and turned it so that it formed a ridge, providing a natural drainage system to the field as well as permitting the deep planting of seeds. Unlike the earlier two-field system of crop rotation, which simply alternated fallow with planted fields each year, the three-field system increased the amount of cultivated land by leaving only one third fallow in a given year. It also better adjusted crops to seasons. In winter one field was planted with winter crops of wheat or rye; in the summer a second field was planted with summer crops of oats, barley, and lentils; and the third field was left fallow, to be planted in its turn with winter and summer crops.

Serfs were subject to so-called dues in kind: firewood for cutting the lord's wood, sheep for grazing their sheep on the lord's land, and the like. In this way the lord, by furnishing shacks and small plots of land from his vast domain, created an army of servants who provided him with everything from eggs to boots.

The discontent of the serfs is witnessed by the high number of recorded escapes. An astrological calendar from the period even marks the days most favorable for escaping. Escaped serfs roamed the land as beggars and vagabonds, searching for new and better masters.

RELIGION AND THE CLERGY. The lower clergy lived among and were drawn from the peasant class. They fared hardly better than peasants in Carolingian times. As owners of the churches on their lands, the lords had the right to raise chosen serfs to the post of parish priest, placing them in charge of the churches on the lords' estates. Although church law directed the lord to set a serf free before he entered the clergy, lords were reluctant to do this and risk thereby a possible later challenge to their jurisdiction over the ecclesiastical property with which the serf, as priest, was invested. Lords rather preferred a "serf priest," one who not only said the Mass on Sundays and holidays but who also continued to serve his lord during the week, waiting on the lord's table and tending his steeds. Like Charlemagne with his bishops, Frankish lords cultivated a docile parish clergy.

The ordinary people looked to religion for

In this eleventh-century manuscript, peasants harvest grain, trim vines, and plow fields behind yoked oxen.

comfort and consolation. They considered baptism and confession of the Creed a surety of future salvation. They baptized their children, attended mass, tried to learn the Lord's Prayer, and received extreme unction from the priest as death approached. This was all probably done with more awe and simple faith than understanding. Religious instruction in the meaning of Christian doctrine and practice remained at a bare minimum, and local priests on the manors were no better educated than their congregations. People understandably became particularly attached in this period to the more tangible veneration of relics and saints. Religious devotion to saints has been compared to secular subjection to powerful lords; both the saint and the lord were protectors whose honor the serfs were bound to defend and whose favor and help in time of need they hoped to receive. Veneration of saints also had strong points of contact with old tribal customs, from which the commoners were hardly detached, as Charlemagne's enforcement of laws against witchcraft, sorcery, and the ritual sacrifice of animals by monks makes all too clear. But religion also has an intrinsic appeal and special meaning to those who, like the masses of medieval men and women, find themselves burdened, fearful, and with little hope of material betterment this side of eternity. Charlemagne shared many of the religious beliefs of his ordinary subjects. He collected and venerated relics, made pilgrimages to Rome, frequented the church of Saint Mary in Aachen several times a day, and directed in his last will and testament that all but a fraction of his great treasure be spent to endow masses and prayers for his departed soul.

Breakup of the Carolingian Kingdom

In the last years of his life an ailing Charlemagne knew that his empire was ungovernable. The seeds of dissolution lay in regionalism, that is, the determination of each region, no matter how small, to look first—and often only—to its own self-interest. Despite his considerable skill and resolution, Charlemagne's realm became too fragmented among powerful regional magnates. Although they were his vassals, these same men were also landholders and lords in their own right. They knew that their sovereignty lessened as Charlemagne's increased and accordingly became reluctant royal servants. In feudal society a direct relationship existed between physical proximity to authority and loyalty to authority. Local people obeyed local lords more readily than they obeyed a glorious but distant king. Charlemagne had been forced to recognize and even to enhance the power of regional magnates in order to win needed financial and military support. But as in the Merovingian kingdom, so also in the Carolingian, the tail came increasingly to wag the dog. Charlemagne's major attempt to enforce subordination to royal dictates and a transregional discipline—through the institution of the *missi dominici*—proved ultimately unsuccessful.

LOUIS THE PIOUS. Carolingian kings did not give up easily. Charlemagne's only surviving son and successor was Louis the Pious (814–840), so-called because of his close alliance with the church and his promotion of puritanical reforms. Before his death Charlemagne secured the imperial succession for Louis by raising him to "co-emperor" in a grand public ceremony. After Charlemagne's death Louis no longer referred to himself as "king of the Franks." He bore instead the single title of *emperor*. The assumption of this title reflected not only Carolingian pretense to an imperial dynasty, but also Louis's determination to unify his kingdom and raise its people above mere regional and tribal loyalties. Unfortunately Louis's own fertility joined with Salic law and Frankish custom to prevent the attainment of this high goal.

Louis had three sons by his first wife. According to Salic, or Germanic, law, a ruler partitioned his kingdom equally among his surviving sons. (Salic law forbade women to inherit the throne.) Louis, who saw himself as an emperor and no mere German king, recognized that a tripartite kingdom would hardly be an empire and acted early in his reign, in the year 817, to break this legal tradition. This he did by making his eldest son, Lothar (d. 855), co-regent and sole imperial heir. To Lothar's brothers he gave important but much lesser appanages, or assigned hereditary lands; Pepin (d. 838) became king of Aquitaine, and Louis "the German" (d. 876) became king of Bavaria, over the eastern Franks.

In 823 Louis's second wife, Judith of Bavaria, bore him still a fourth son, Charles, later called "the Bald" (d. 877). Mindful of Frankish law and custom and determined that her son should receive more than just a nominal inheritance, the queen incited the brothers Pepin and Louis to war against Lothar, who fled for refute to the pope. More important, Judith was instrumental in persuading Louis to reverse his earlier decision and divide the kingdom equally among his four living sons. As their stepmother and the young Charles rose in their father's favor, the three brothers feared still further reversals, so they decided to act against their father. Supported by the pope, they joined forces and defeated their father in a battle near Colmar (833).

As the bestower of crowns on emperors, the pope had an important stake in the preservation of the revived western empire and the imperial title, both of which Louis's belated agreement to an equal partition of his kingdom threatened to undo. The pope condemned Louis and restored Lothar to his original inheritance. But Lothar's regained imperial dignity only stirred anew the resentments of his brothers, including his stepbrother, Charles, who resumed their war against him.

THE TREATY OF VERDUN AND ITS AFTERMATH. Peace finally came to the heirs of Louis the Pious in 843 in the Treaty of Verdun. But this agreement also brought about the disaster that Louis had originally feared: the great Carolingian empire was partitioned according to Frankish law into three equal parts, Pepin having died in 838. Lothar received a middle section, which came to be known as Lotharingia and embraced roughly modern Holland, Belgium, Switzerland, Alsace-Lorraine, and Italy. Charles the Bald received the western part of the kingdom, or roughly modern

The tenth-century crown of the Holy Roman Emperor reveals the close alliance between Church and throne. Not only is the crown surmounted by a cross, but it includes panels depicting the great kings of the Bible, David and Solomon. [Kunsthistorisches Museum, Vienna]

France. And Louis the German came into the eastern part, or roughly modern Germany (see Maps 6.5, 6.6). Although Lothar retained the imperial title, the universal empire of Charlemagne and Louis the Pious ceased to exist after

MAPS 6-5, 6-6 *The Treaty of Verdun divided the kingdom of Louis the Pious among his three feuding children: Charles the Bald, Lothar, and Louis the German. After Lothar' death in 855 the middle kingdom was so weakened by division among his three sons that Charles the Bald and Louis the German divided it between themselves in the Treaty of Mersen in 870.*

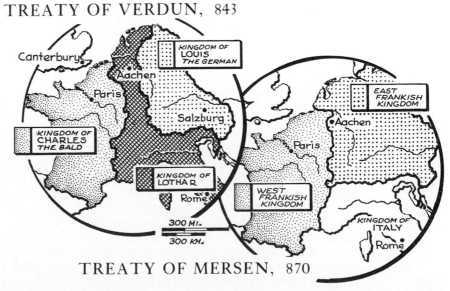

TREATY OF VERDUN, 843

TREATY OF MERSEN, 870

229

The Carolingian Dynasty (751–987)

Pepin III "the Short" becomes King of the Franks	751
Franks drive Lombards out of central Italy; creation of Papal States	755
Charlemagne rules as King of the Franks	768–814
Charlemagne defeats Lombards in northern Italy	774
Donation of Constantine protests Frankish domination of church	750–800
Pope Leo III crowns Charlemagne	800
Louis the Pious succeeds Charlemagne as "emperor"	814–840
Treaty of Verdun partitions the Carolingian Empire	843
Treaty of Mersen further divides Carolingian Empire	870
New invasions of Vikings, Muslims, and Magyars	875–950
Ottonian dynasty succeeds Carolingian in Germany	962
Capetian dynasty succeeds Carolingian in France	987

Verdun. Not until the sixteenth century, with the election in 1519 of Charles I of Spain as the Holy Roman Emperor Charles V, would the western world again see a kingdom so vast as Charlemagne's.

The Treaty of Verdun proved to be only the beginning of Carolingian fragmentation. When Lothar died in 855, his middle kingdom was divided equally among his three surviving sons, the eldest of whom, Louis II, retained Italy and the imperial title. This partition of the partition left the middle, or imperial, kingdom much smaller and weaker than those of Louis the German and Charles the Bald. In fact, it sealed the dissolution of the great empire of Charlemagne. Henceforth western Europe saw an eastern and a western Frankish kingdom—roughly Germany versus France—at war over the fractionalized middle kingdom, a contest that has continued into modern times.

In Italy the demise of the Carolingian emperors enhanced for the moment the power of the popes, who had long been adept at filling vacuums. The popes were now strong enough to excommunicate and override the wishes of weak emperors. Pope Nicholas I (858–867)

excommunicated Lothar II for divorcing his wife in a major church crackdown on the serial polygamy of the Germans. After the death of the childless emperor Louis II (875), Pope John VIII (872–882) installed Charles the Bald as emperor against the express last wishes of Louis II.

When Charles the Bald died in 877, both the papal and the imperial thrones suffered defeat. Each became a pawn in the hands of powerful Italian and German magnates, respectively. Neither pope nor emperor knew dignity and power again until a new western imperial dynasty—the Ottonians—attained dominance during the reign of Otto I (962–973). It is especially at this juncture in European history—the last quarter of the ninth and the first half of the tenth century—that one may speak with some justification of a "dark age." Simultaneously with the internal political breakdown of the empire and the papacy came new barbarian attacks, set off probably by overpopulation and famine in northern Europe. The late ninth and the tenth centuries saw successive waves of Normans (North-men), better known as Vikings, from Scandinavia; Magyars, or Hungarians, the great horsemen from the eastern plains; and Muslims from the south (see Map 6.7). In the 880s the Vikings penetrated to the imperial residence of Aachen and to Paris. Moving rapidly in ships and raiding coastal towns, they were almost impossible to defend against and kept western Europe on edge. The Franks built fortified towns and castles in strategic locations, which served as refuges. When they could, they bought off the invaders with outright grants of land (for example, Normandy) and payments of silver. In this period local populations became more dependent than ever before on local strongmen for life, limb, and livelihood. This brute fact of life provided the essential precondition for the maturation of feudal society.

Feudal Society

A chronic absence of effective central government and the constant threat of famine and war characterized the Middle Ages. *Feudal society* is a term used to describe the adjustment to this state of affairs as the weaker sought protection from the stronger. The term refers to the social, political, and economic system that emerged from repeated experience showing that only those who could guarantee immedi-

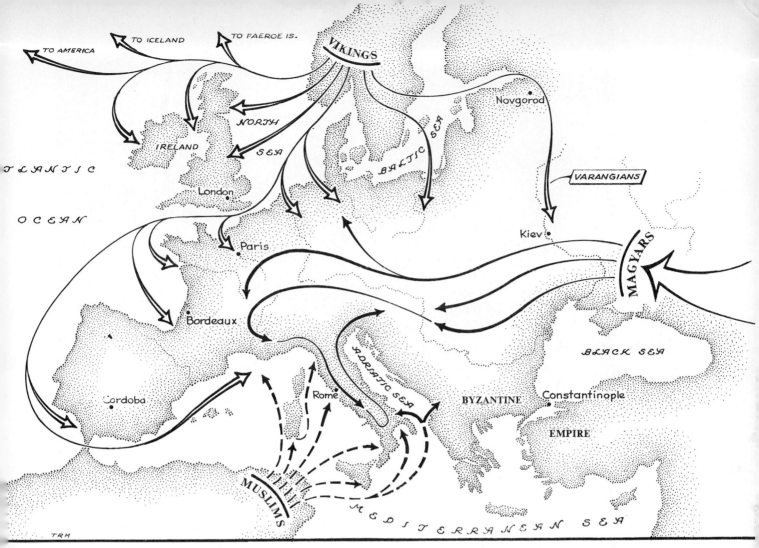

VIKING, MUSLIM, AND MAGYAR INVASIONS TO THE ELEVENTH CENTURY

MAP 6-7 *Western Europe was sorely beset by new waves of outsiders from the ninth to the eleventh century. From north, east, and south a stream of invading Vikings, Magyars, and Muslims brought the West at times to near collapse and of course gravely affected institutions within Europe.*

ate protection from rapine and starvation were true lords and masters. In a feudal society what people need most is the firm assurance that others can be depended on in time of dire need. Powerful individuals (princes or local lords) were recognized as personal superiors by lesser men who pledged themselves to them, promising faithful service. This network of relationships based on mutual loyalty enabled lords to acquire armies and to rule over territory without necessarily owning land or having a royal title to legitimate their rule. Large warrior groups of vassals sprang up, and they developed into a prominent professional mili-

tary class with its own code of knightly conduct. The extensive military organization was an adaptation to the absence of strong central government and a rural, noncommercial economy.

Origins

The main features of feudal government can be found in the divisions and conflicts of Merovingian society. In the sixth and seventh centuries there evolved the custom of individual freemen placing themselves under the protection of more powerful freemen. In this way the

231

A Viking longship. Huge and menacing, these ships struck terror into the coastal populations of Western Europe in the ninth and tenth centuries. [Giraudon]

latter built up armies and became local magnates, and the former solved the problem of simple survival. Freemen who so entrusted themselves to others were known as *ingenui in obsequio* ("freemen in a contractual relation of dependence"). Those who so gave themselves to the king were called *antrustiones*. All men of this type came to be described collectively as *vassi* ("those who serve"), from which evolved the term *vassalage*, meaning the placement of oneself in the personal service of another who promises protection in return.

Landed nobility, like kings, tried to acquire as many such vassals as they could, because military strength in the early Middle Ages lay in numbers. As it proved impossible to maintain these growing armies within the lord's own household, as was the original custom, or to support them by special monetary payments, the practice evolved of simply granting them land as a "tenement." Such land came to be known as a *benefice*, or a *fief*, and vassals were expected to dwell on it and maintain

their horses and other accouterments of war in good order. Originally vassals, therefore, were little more than gangs-in-waiting.

Vassalage and the Fief

Vassalage involved "fealty" to the lord. To swear fealty was to promise to refrain from any action that might in any way threaten the lord's well-being and to perform personal services for him on his request. Chief among the expected services was military duty as a mounted knight. This could involve a variety of activities: a short or long military expedition, escort duty, standing castle guard, and/or the placement of one's own fortress at the lord's disposal, if the vassal was of such stature as to have one. Continuous bargaining and bickering occurred over the terms of service. Limitations were placed on the number of days a lord could require services from a vassal. In France in the eleventh century about forty days of service a year were considered sufficient. It also became possible for vassals to buy their way out of military service by a monetary payment known as *scutage*. The lord, in turn, applied this payment to the hiring of mercenaries, who often proved more efficient than contract-conscious vassals. Beyond his military duty the vassal was also expected to give the lord advice when he requested it and to sit as a member of his court when the latter was in session.

Beginning with the reign of Louis the Pious (814–840), bishops and abbots swore fealty and received their offices from the king as a benefice. The king formally "invested" these clerics in their offices during a special ceremony in which he presented them with a ring and a staff, the symbols of high spiritual office. Louis's predecessors had earlier confiscated church lands with only modest and belated compensation to the church in the form of a tithe required of all Frankish inhabitants. Long a sore point with the church, the presumptuous practice of the lay investiture of the clergy provoked a serious confrontation of church and state in the eleventh and twelfth centuries, when reform-minded clergy rebelled against what they then believed to be involuntary clerical vassalage.

The lord's obligations to his vassals were very specific. He was, first of all, obligated to protect the vassal from physical harm and to stand as his advocate in public court. After fealty was sworn and homage paid, the lord provided for the vassal's physical maintenance by the bestowal of a benefice, or fief. The fief was simply the physical or material wherewithal to meet the vassal's military and other obligations. It could take the form of liquid wealth as well as the more common grant of real property. There were so-called money fiefs, which empowered a vassal to receive regular payments from the lord's treasury. Such fiefs were potentially quite devilish because they made it possible for one country to acquire vassals among the nobility of another. Normally the fief consisted of a landed estate of anywhere from a few to several thousand acres. But it could also take the form of a castle.

In Carolingian times a benefice, or fief, varied in size from one or more small villas to several *mansi*, which were agricultural holdings of

Bishop Fulbert Describes the Obligations of Vassal and Lord

Trust held the lord and vassal together. Their duties in this regard were carefully defined. Here are six general rules for vassal and lord, laid down by Bishop Fulbert of Chartres in a letter to William, Duke of Aquitaine, in 1020.

He who swears fealty to his lord ought always to have these six things in memory: what is harmless, safe, honorable, useful, easy, practicable. Harmless, that is to say, that he should not injure his lord in his body; safe, *that he should not injure him by betraying his secrets or the defenses upon which he relies for safety;* honorable, *that he should not injure him in his justice or in other matters that pertain to his honor;* useful, *that he should not injure him in his possessions;* easy *and* practicable, *that that good which his lord is able to do easily he make not difficult, nor that which is practicable he make not impossible to him.*

That the faithful vassal should avoid these injuries is certainly proper, but not for this alone does he deserve his holding; for it is not sufficient to abstain from evil, unless what is good is done also. It remains, therefore, that in the same six things mentioned above he should faithfully counsel and aid his lord, if he wishes to be looked upon as worthy of his benefice and to be safe concerning the fealty which he has sworn.

The lord also ought to act toward his faithful vassal reciprocally in all these things. And if he does not do this, he will be justly considered guilty of bad faith, just as the former, if he should be detected in avoiding or consenting to the avoidance of his duties, would be perfidious and perjured.

James Harvey Robinson (Ed.), *Readings in European History*, Vol. 1 (Boston: Athenaeum, 1904), p. 184.

The Franks Formalize the Entrance into Vassalage

Entrance into vassalage involved a formal and sacred ceremony in which the vassal pledged to serve and honor his lord and the lord to guard and protect his vassal from all his enemies. The following is a Frankish formula of commendation from the seventh century.

VASSAL:

To that magnificent Lord _____, I, _____, Since it is known familiarly to all how little I have whence to feed and clothe myself, I have therefore petitioned your Piety, and your good will has permitted me to hand myself over or commend myself to your guardianship, which I have thereupon done; that is to say, in this way, that you should aid and succor me as well with food as with clothing, according as I shall be able to serve you and deserve it.

And so long as I shall live I ought to provide service and honor to you, suitably to my free condition; and I shall not during my lifetime have the ability to withdraw from your power or guardianship, but must remain during the days of my life under your power or defense. Wherefore it is proper that if either of us shall wish to withdraw himself from these agreements, he shall pay _____ shillings to his companion, and this agreement shall remain unbroken. . . .

LORD:

It is right that those who offer to us unbroken fidelity should be protected by our aid. And since_____, a faithful one of ours, by the favor of God, coming here in our palace with his arms, has seen fit to swear trust and fidelity to us in our hand, therefore we herewith decree and command that for the future_____, above mentioned, be reckoned among the number of the antrustions [i.e., followers]. And if any one perchance should presume to kill him, let him know that he will be judged guilty of his weregild of six hundred shillings.

James Harvey Robinson (Ed.), *Readings in European History,* Vol. 1 (Boston: Athenaeum, 1904), pp. 175–176.

twenty-five to forty-eight acres. The king's vassals are known to have received benefices of at least thirty and as many as two hundred such holdings, truly a vast estate. Royal vassalage with a benefice understandably came to be widely sought by the highest classes of Carolingian society. As a royal policy, however, it proved deadly to the king in the long run. Although Carolingian kings jealously guarded their rights over property granted in benefice to vassals, resident vassals were still free to dispose of their benefices as they pleased. Vassals of the king, strengthened by his donations, in turn created their own vassals. These, in turn, created still further vassals of their own—vassals of vassals of vassals—in a reverse pyramiding effect that had fragmented land and authority from the highest to the lowest levels by the late ninth century.

Fragmentation and Divided Loyalty

In addition to the fragmentation brought about by the multiplication of vassalage, effective occupation of land led gradually to claims of hereditary possession. Hereditary possession became a legally recognized principle in the ninth century and laid the basis for claims to real ownership. Fiefs given as royal donations became hereditary possessions and, with the passage of time, in some instances even the real property of the possessor. Further, vassal engagements came to be multiplied in still another way as enterprising freemen sought to accumulate as much land as possible. One man actually became a vassal to several different lords. This development led in the ninth century to the concept of a "liege lord"—that one master whom the vassal must obey even to the harm of the others, should a direct conflict among them arise.

The problem of loyalty was reflected not only in the literature of the period, with its praise of the virtues of honor and fidelity, but also in the ceremonial development of the very act of "commendation" by which a freeman became a vassal. In the mid-eighth century an "oath of fealty" highlighted the ceremony. A vassal reinforced his promise of fidelity to the lord by swearing a special oath with his hand on a sacred relic or the Bible. In the tenth and eleventh centuries paying homage to the lord involved not only the swearing of such an oath but also the placement of the vassal's hands between the lord's and the sealing of the ceremony with a kiss.

As the centuries passed, personal loyalty and service became quite secondary to the acquisition of property. The fief overshadowed fealty; the benefice became more important than vassalage; freemen proved themselves prepared to swear allegiance to the highest bidder—developments that signaled the waning of feudal society.

Suggested Readings

MARC BLOCH, *Feudal Society*, Vols. 1 and 2, trans. by L. A. Manyon (1971). A classic on the topic and as an example of historical study.

PETER BROWN, *Augustine of Hippo: A Biography* (1967). Late antiquity seen through the biography of its greatest Christian thinker.

HENRY CHADWICK, *The Early Church* (1967). Among the best treatments of early Christianity.

R. H. C. DAVIS, *A History of Medieval Europe: From Constantine to St. Louis* (1972). Unsurpassed in clarity.

K. F. DREW (ED.), *The Barbarian Invasions: Catalyst of a New Order* (1970). Collection of essays that focuses the issues.

HEINRICH FICHTENAU, *The Carolingian Empire: The Age of Charlemagne*, trans. by Peter Munz (1964). Strongest on political history of the era.

F. L. GANSHOF, *Feudalism*, trans. by Philip Grierson (1964). The most profound brief analysis of the subject.

A. F. HAVIGHURST (ED.), *The Pirenne Thesis: Analysis, Criticism, and Revision* (1958). Excerpts from the scholarly debate over the extent of Western trade in the East during the early Middle Ages.

DAVID KNOWLES, *Christian Monasticism* (1969). Sweeping survey with helpful photographs.

M. L. W. LAISTNER, *Thought and Letters in Western Europe, 500 to 900* (1957). Among the best surveys of early medieval intellectual history.

JEAN LECLERCQ, *The Love of Learning and the Desire for God: A Study of Monastic Culture*, trans. by Catherine Misrahi (1962). Lucid, delightful, absorbing account of the ideals of monks.

J. LECLERCQ, F. VANDENBROUCKE, AND L. BOUYER, *The Spirituality of the Middle Ages* (1968). Perhaps the best survey of medieval Christianity, East and West, to the eve of the Protestant Reformation.

CYRIL MANGO, *Byzantium: The Empire of New Rome* (1980).

PETER MUNZ, *The Age of Charlemagne* (1971). Penetrating social history of the period.

HENRI PIRENNE, *A History of Europe, I: From the End of the Roman World in the West to the Beginnings of the Western States*, trans. by Bernhard Maill (1958). Comprehensive survey, with now-controversial views on the demise of Western trade and cities in the early Middle Ages.

STEVEN RUNCIMAN, *Byzantine Civilization* (1970). Succinct, comprehensive account by a master.

PETER SAWYER, *The Age of the Vikings* (1962). The best account.

R. W. SOUTHERN, *The Making of the Middle Ages* (1973). Originally published in 1953, but still a fresh account by an imaginative historian.

CARL STEPHENSON, *Medieval Feudalism* (1969). Excellent short summary and introduction.

A. A. VASILIEV, *History of the Byzantine Empire 324–1453* (1952). The most comprehensive treatment in English.

LYNN WHITE, JR., *Medieval Technology and Social Change* (1962). Often fascinating account of the way primitive technology changed life.

*Vassals paying homage to their lord. The word "vassal" means "one who serves." The
ceremony of homage symbolized the vassal's dependence on his lord and the lord's tie to his
vassal.* [Art Resource]

THE HIGH MIDDLE AGES marked a period of political expansion and consolidation and of intellectual flowering and synthesis. The noted medievalist Joseph Strayer called it the age that saw "the full development of all the potentialities of medieval civilization."[1] Some even argue that as far as the development of Western institutions is concerned, this was a more creative period than the later Italian Renaissance and the German Reformation.

The high Middle Ages saw the borders of western Europe largely secured against foreign invaders. Although there was intermittent Muslim aggression well into the sixteenth century, fear of assault from without diminished. A striking change occurred in the late eleventh century and the twelfth century. Western Europe, which had for so long been the prey of foreign powers, became through the Crusades and foreign trade the feared hunter within both the Eastern and the Arab worlds.

During the high Middle Ages "national" monarchies emerged in France, England, and Germany. Parliaments and popular assemblies representing the interests of the nobility, the clergy, and the townspeople also appeared at this time to secure local rights and customs against the claims of the developing nation-states. The foundations of modern representative institutions can be found in this period.

The high Middle Ages saw a revolution in agriculture that increased both food supplies and populations. This period witnessed a great revival of trade and commerce, the rise of towns, and the emergence of a "new-rich" merchant class, the ancestors of modern capitalists. Urban culture and education flourished through the recovery of the writings of the ancient Greek philosophers, which was made possible by the revival of Eastern trade and by way of Spanish contacts with Muslim intellectuals. Unlike the dabbling in antiquity during Carolingian times, the twelfth century enjoyed a true renaissance of classical learning.

The high Middle Ages were also the time when the Latin or Western church established itself as an authority independent of monarchical secular government, thereby sowing the seeds of the distinctive Western separation of Church and State. This occurred during the Investiture Struggle of the late eleventh century and the twelfth century. In this confrontation between popes and emperors a reformed

7

The High Middle Ages (1000–1300): Revival of Empire, Church, and Towns

[1] *Western History in the Middle Ages—A Short History* (New York: Appleton-Century-Crofts, 1955), pp. 9, 127.

papacy overcame its long subservience to the Carolingian and Ottonian kings. The papacy won out, however, by becoming itself a monarchy among the world's emerging monarchies, thereby preparing the way for still more dangerous confrontations between popes and emperors in the later Middle Ages. Some religious reformers would later see in the Gregorian papacy of the high Middle Ages the fall of the church from its spiritual mission as well as its declaration of independence from secular power.

The Emperor Otto II (913—983). The four tribute-bearing maidens symbolize his dominion over all of Western Europe. [Giraudon/Art Resource]

Otto I and the Revival of the Empire

The fortunes of both the old empire and the papacy began to revive after the dark period of the late ninth century and the early tenth century when the Saxon Henry I ("the Fowler," d. 936), the strongest of the German dukes, became the first non-Frankish king of Germany in 918. Henry rebuilt royal power by forcibly consolidating the duchies of Swabia, Bavaria, Saxony, Franconia, and Lotharingia. He secured imperial borders by checking the invasions of the Hungarians and the Danes. Although greatly reduced in size by comparison with Charlemagne's empire, Henry's German kingdom still placed his son and successor Otto I (936—973) in a strong territorial position.

The very able Otto maneuvered his own kin into positions of power in Bavaria, Swabia, and Franconia. He refused to treat each duchy as an independent hereditary dukedom, as was the trend among the nobility. He dealt with each as a subordinate member of a unified kingdom. In a truly imperial gesture in 951, Otto invaded Italy and proclaimed himself its king. In 955 he won his most magnificent victory when he defeated the Hungarians at Lechfeld, a feat comparable to Charles Martel's earlier victory over the Saracens at Poitiers in 732. The victory at Lechfeld secured German borders against new barbarian attack, further unified the German duchies, and earned Otto the well-deserved title "the Great."

As part of a careful rebuilding program, Otto, following the example of his predecessors, enlisted the church. Bishops and abbots, men who possessed a sense of universal empire yet did not marry and found competitive dynasties, were made royal princes and agents of the king. Because these clergy, as royal bureaucrats, received great land holdings and immunity from local counts and dukes, they also found such vassalage to the king very attractive. The medieval church did not become a great territorial power reluctantly. It appreciated the blessings of receiving, while teaching the blessedness of giving.

In 961 Otto, who had long aspired to the imperial crown, responded to a call for help from Pope John XII (955—964), who was at this time being bullied by an Italian enemy of the German king, Berengar of Friuli. In recompense for this rescue Pope John crowned Otto emperor on February 2, 962. At this time Otto also recognized the existence of the Papal States and proclaimed himself their special protector. The church was now more than ever under royal control. Its bishops and abbots were Otto's appointees and bureaucrats, and the pope reigned in Rome only by the power of the emperor's sword. Pope John belatedly recognized the royal web in which the church had become entangled. As a countermeasure he joined Italian opposition to the new emperor. This turnabout brought Otto's swift revenge. An ecclesiastical synod over which Otto personally presided deposed Pope John and proclaimed that henceforth no pope could take office without first swearing an oath of allegiance to the emperor. Under Otto I popes ruled at the emperor's pleasure.

Otto had shifted the royal focus from Germany to Italy. His successors—Otto II (973–983), Otto III (983–1002), and Henry II (1002–1024)—became so preoccupied with running the affairs of Italy that their German base began to disintegrate, sacrificed to imperial dreams. They might have learned a lesson from the contemporary Capetian kings, the successor dynasty to the Carolingians in France, who wisely mended local fences and concentrated their limited resources on securing a tight grip on their immediate royal domain, which was never neglected for the sake of foreign adventure. The Ottonians, in contrast, reached far beyond their grasp when they tried to subdue Italy. As the briefly revived empire began to crumble in the first quarter of the eleventh century, the church, long unhappy with Carolingian and Ottonian domination, prepared to declare its independence and exact its own vengeance.

The Reviving Catholic Church

The Cluny Reform Movement

During the late ninth and early tenth centuries the clergy had become tools of kings and magnates, and the papacy a toy of Italian nobles. The Ottonians made bishops their servile princes, and popes also served at their pleasure. A new day dawned for the church, however, thanks not only to the failing fortunes of the overextended empire but also to a new force for reform within the church itself. In a great monastery in Cluny in east-central France, a reform movement appeared that, by progressively winning the support of secular lords and German kings for monastic reform, gradually placed the church in a position to challenge political power over it at both episcopal and papal levels.

The reformers of Cluny were aided by widespread popular respect for the church. Most people admired clerics and monks. The church was medieval society's most democratic institution. In the Middle Ages any man could theoretically rise to the position of pope, and all were candidates for the church's grace and salvation. The church promised a better life to come to the great mass of ordinary people, who found the present one brutish and without hope. Since the fall of the Roman Empire popular support for the church had been especially inspired by the example of the monks. Monasteries provided an important alternative style of life for the religiously earnest in an age when most people had very few options. The tenth and eleventh centuries saw an unprecedented boom in their construction. Monks remained the least secularized and most spiritual of the church's clergy. Their cultural achievements were widely admired, their relics and rituals were considered magical, and their high religious ideals and sacrifices were imitated by the laity.

Cluny, the main source of the reform movement, was founded in 910 by William the Pious, duke of Aquitaine. It was a Benedictine monastery devoted to the strictest observance of Saint Benedict's *Rule for Monasteries*, with a special emphasis on liturgical purity. Although they were loosely organized and their demands not always consistent, the Cluny reformers were intent on maintaining a spiritual church. They absolutely rejected the subservience of the clergy, especially that of the German bishops, to royal authority. They taught that the pope in Rome was sole ruler over all the clergy. The Cluny reformers further resented the transgression of ascetic piety by "secular" parish clergy, who maintained concubines in a relationship akin to marriage. (Later a distinction would be formalized between the secular clergy who lived and ministered in the world [saeculum] and the regular clergy, monks and nuns withdrawn from the world and living according to a special rule [regula].)

The Cluny reformers resolved to free the clergy from both kings and "wives," to create an independent and chaste clergy. The church alone was to be the clergy's lord and spouse. The distinctive Western separation of Church

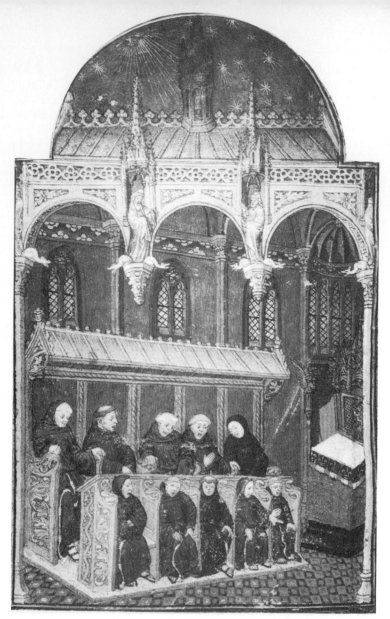

Benedictine monks at choir. The reform movement that began at the Benedictine monastery at Cluny in northern France in the tenth century spread throughout the Church and was ultimately responsible for the reassertion of papal authority. [*Trustees of the British Museum*]

enth century the Cluny reformers reached the summit when their reform program was embraced by the papacy itself.

In the late ninth and early tenth centuries the influence of this religious reform movement was demonstrated by the proclamation of the "Peace of God," a cooperative venture between the clergy and the higher nobility. This was a series of church decrees that attempted to lessen the endemic warfare of medieval society by threatening excommunication for all who, at any time, harmed such vulnerable groups as women, peasants, merchants, and clergy. The Peace of God was subsequently reinforced by proclamations of the "Truce of God," a church order that all men must abstain from every form of violence and warfare during a certain part of each week (eventually from Wednesday night to Monday morning) and in all holy seasons.

Popes devoted to reforms like those urged by Cluny came to power during the reign of Emperor Henry III (1039–1056). Pope Leo IX (1049–1054) promoted regional synods in opposition to simony (that is, the selling of spiritual things, such as church offices) and clerical concubinage. He also placed Cluniacs in key administrative posts in Rome. During the turbulent minority of Henry III's successor, Henry IV (1056–1106), reform popes began to assert themselves more openly. Pope Stephen IX (1057–1058) reigned without imperial ratification, contrary to the earlier declaration of Otto I. Pope Nicholas II (1059–1061) took the unprecedented step of establishing a College of Cardinals in 1059, and henceforth this body alone elected the pope. Only thirteen years earlier Henry III had deposed three schismatic popes, each a pawn of a Roman noble faction, and had installed a German bishop of his own choosing who ruled as Pope Clement II (1046–1047).

Such highhanded practices ended after 1059. With the creation of the College of Cardinals the popes declared their full independence of both local Italian and distant royal interference, although rulers continued to have considerable indirect influence on the election of popes. Pope Nicholas II also embraced Cluny's strictures against simony and clerical concubinage and even struck his own political alliances with the Normans in Sicily and with France and Tuscany. His successor, Pope Alexander II (1061–1073), was elected solely by the College of Cardinals, albeit not without a struggle.

and State and the celibacy of the Catholic clergy, both of which continue today, had their definitive origins in the Cluny reform movement.

Cluny rapidly became a center from which reformers were dispatched to monasteries throughout France and Italy. Under its aggressive abbots, especially Saint Odo (926–946), it grew to embrace almost fifteen hundred dependent cloisters, each devoted to monastic and church reform. In the last half of the elev-

240

The Peace and the Truce of God

The following proclamation of the Peace and the Truce of God occurred at the Council of Toulouse in the mid-eleventh century. It was designed to protect the property of the church and the persons of the clergy from the bullying of secular powers. In the "ordeal of cold water," mentioned at the conclusion, innocence or guilt was determined by whether a person sank (innocent) or floated (guilty) when thrown into a pool of blessed water—the belief being that blessed water would reject the guilty by divine intervention.

This Peace has been confirmed by the bishops, by the abbots, by the counts and viscounts and the other God-fearing nobles in this bishopric to the effect that in the future . . . no man may commit an act of violence in a church. . . . Furthermore, it is forbidden that any one attack the clergy, who do not bear arms, or the monks and religious persons, or do them any wrong; likewise it is forbidden to despoil or pillage the communities of canons, monks, and religious persons, the ecclesiastical lands . . . under the protection of the Church, or the clergy, who do not bear arms; and if any one shall do such a thing, let him pay a double composition [i.e., fine in compensation]. [Further] let no one burn or destroy the dwellings of the peasants and the clergy, the dove-cotes, and the granaries. Let no man dare to kill, to beat, or to wound a peasant or serf, or the wife of either, or to seize them and carry them off, except for misdemeanors which they have committed. . . . Let any one who has broken the peace, and has not paid his fines within a fortnight, make amends to him whom he has injured by paying a double amount. . . . The bishops . . . have [also] solemnly confirmed the Truce of God, which has been enjoined upon all Christians, from the setting of the sun of the fourth day of the week, that is to say, Wednesday, until the rising of the sun on Monday, the second day. . . . If any one during the Truce shall violate it, let him pay a double composition and subsequently undergo the ordeal of cold water.

James Harvey Robinson (Ed.), *Readings in European History*, Vol. 1 (Boston: Anthenaeum, 1904), pp. 230–231.

The Investiture Struggle: Gregory VII and Henry IV

It was Alexander's successor, Pope Gregory VII (1073–1085), a fierce advocate of Cluny's reforms who had entered the papal bureaucracy a quarter century earlier during the pontificate of Leo IX, who put the church's declaration of independence to the test. Cluniacs had repeatedly inveighed against simony. A case had been built up by Cardinal Humbert against the lay investiture of clergy as the supreme form of this evil practice. In 1075 Pope Gregory embraced these arguments and condemned under penalty of excommunication the lay investiture of clergy at any level. He had primarily in mind the emperor's well-established custom of installing bishops by presenting them with the ring and staff that symbolized episcopal office. After Gregory's ruling, bishops, no more than popes, were to enter their offices appearing to be the appointees of emperors. As popes were elected by the College of Cardinals and were not raised up by kings or nobles, so bishops would henceforth be installed in their offices by high ecclesiastical authority as empowered by the pope and none other.

Gregory's prohibition was a jolt to royal authority. Since the days of Otto I emperors had routinely passed out bishoprics to favored clergy. Bishops, who received royal estates, were the emperors' appointees and servants of the state. Henry IV's Carolingian and Ottonian predecessors had carefully nurtured the theocratic character of the empire in both concept and administrative bureaucracy. The church and religion were integral parts of government. Now Henry found himself ordered to secularize the empire by drawing a distinct line between the spheres of temporal and spiritual—royal and ecclesiastical—authority and jurisdiction.

Pope Gregory VII Asserts the Power of the Pope

Church reformers of the high Middle Ages vigorously asserted the power of the pope within the church and his rights against emperors and all others who might encroach on the papal sphere of jurisdiction. Here is a statement of the basic principles of the Gregorian reformers, known as the *Dictatus Papae* ("The Sayings of the Pope"), which is attributed to Pope Gregory VII (1073–1085).

That the Roman Church was founded by God alone.

That the Roman Pontiff alone is rightly to be called universal.

That the Pope may depose the absent.

That for him alone it is lawful to enact new laws according to the needs of the time, to assemble together new congregations, to make an abbey of a canonry; and . . . to divide a rich bishopric and unite the poor ones.

That he alone may use the imperial insignia.

That the Pope is the only one whose feet are to be kissed by all princes.

That his name alone is to be recited in churches.

That his title is unique in the world.

That he may depose emperors.

That he may transfer bishops, if necessary, from one See to another.

That no synod may be called a general one without his order.

That no chapter or book may be regarded as canonical without his authority.

That no sentence of his may be retracted by any one; and that he, alone of all, can retract it.

That he himself may be judged by no one.

That the Roman Church has never erred, nor ever, by the witness of Scripture, shall err to all eternity.

That the Pope may absolve subjects of unjust men from their fealty.

Church and State Through the Centuries: A Collection of Historic Documents, trans. and ed. by S. Z. Ehler and John B. Morrall (New York: Biblo and Tannen, 1967), pp. 43–44.

But if his key administrators were no longer to be his own carefully chosen and sworn servants, then was not his kingdom in jeopardy? Henry considered Gregory's action a direct challenge to his authority. The territorial princes, on the other hand, ever tending away from the center and eager to see the emperor weakened, were quick to see the advantages of Gregory's ruling: if the emperor did not have a bishop's ear, then a territorial prince might. In the hope of gaining an advantage over both the emperor and the clergy in their territory, the princes fully supported Gregory's edict.

The lines of battle were quickly drawn. Henry assembled his loyal German bishops at Worms in January 1076 and had them proclaim their independence from Gregory. Gregory promptly responded with the church's heavy artillery: he excommunicated Henry and absolved all Henry's subjects from loyalty to him. The German princes were delighted by this turn of events, and Henry found himself facing a general revolt led by the duchy of Saxony. He had no recourse but to come to terms with Gregory. In a famous scene Henry prostrated himself outside Gregory's castle retreat at Canossa on January 25, 1077. There he reportedly stood barefoot in the snow off and on for three days before the pope absolved his royal penitent. Papal power had, at this moment, reached its pinnacle. But heights are also for descending, and Gregory's grandeur, as he must surely have known when he pardoned Henry and restored him to power, was very soon to fade.

Henry regrouped his forces, regained much of his power within the empire, and soon acted as if the humiliation at Canossa had never occurred. In March 1080 Gregory excommunicated Henry once again, but this time such action was ineffectual. (Historically, repeated excommunications of the same individual have proved to have diminishing returns.) In 1084 Henry, absolutely dominant, installed his own antipope, Clement III, and forced Gregory into exile, where he died the following year. It

243

*The High
Middle Ages
(1000–1300):
Revival of
Empire,
Church, and
Towns*

Pope Gregory VII Describes in a Letter Henry IV's Penance at Canossa

Had Henry IV not succeeded in having the papal ban revoked, his powerful vassals in the empire were prepared to remove him from office. Both sides were aware of the high stakes; hence Henry's extreme penance to win absolution and the pope's long delay in granting it. Because it was against the church's own rule to refuse absolution to a sincere penitent, Henry had an advantage in the confrontation at Canossa. As Gregory himself pointed out, in the selection below, the longer forgiveness was withheld from the king, the more people suspected the pope of betraying his spiritual office.

Gregory . . . to all archbishops, bishops, dukes, counts, and other princes of the realm. . . .

Inasmuch as for love of justice you assumed common cause and danger with us in the struggle [with Henry] . . . we have taken care to inform you . . . how the king, humbled to penance, obtained the pardon of absolution. . . .

Before entering Italy, he sent to us suppliant legates, offering in all things to render satisfaction. . . . And he renewed his promise that, besides amending his ways of living, he would observe all obedience, if only he might deserve to obtain from us the favor of absolution and the apostolic benediction. When, after long postponing a decision, we . . . severely [took] him to task . . . he came at length of his own accord, with a few followers, showing nothing of hostility or boldness, to the town of Canossa where we were tarrying. And there, having laid aside all the belongings of royalty, wretchedly with bare feet and clad in wool, he continued for three days to stand before the gate of the castle. Nor did he desist from imploring with many tears the aid and consolation of the apostolic mercy until he had moved all . . . present . . . to such pity and depth of compassion that, interceding for him with many prayers and tears, all wondered at the unaccustomed hardness of our heart, while some actually cried out that we were exercising, not the dignity of apostolic severity, but the cruelty . . . of a tyrannical madness.

Finally, won by the persistence of his suit . . . we loosed the chain of anathema and . . . received him into the favor of communion and into the lap of the Holy Mother Church.

Frederic A. Ogg (Ed.), *A Source Book of Mediaeval History* (New York: American Book Company, 1908), pp. 275–276.

appeared as if the old practice of kings' controlling popes had been restored, and with a vengeance. Clement, however, was never recognized within the church, and the Gregorian party, which retained wide popular support, regained power during the pontificates of Victor III (1086–1087) and Urban II (1088–1099).

The settlement of the investiture controversy came in 1122 with the Concordat of Worms. Emperor Henry V (1106–1125), having early abandoned his predecessors' practice of nominating popes and raising up antipopes, formally renounced his power to invest bishops with ring and staff. In exchange Pope Calixtus II (1119–1124) recognized the emperor's right to be present and to invest bishops with fiefs before or after their investment with ring and staff by the church. The old Church–State "back scratching" in this way continued, but now on very different terms. The clergy received their offices and attendant religious powers solely from ecclesiastical authority and no longer from kings and emperors. Rulers continued to bestow lands and worldly goods on high clergy in the hope of influencing them; the Concordat of Worms made the clergy more independent but not necessarily less worldly.

The Gregorian party won the independence of the clergy at the price of encouraging the divisiveness of the feudal forces within the empire. The pope made himself strong by making imperial authority weak. In the end those who profited most from the investiture con-

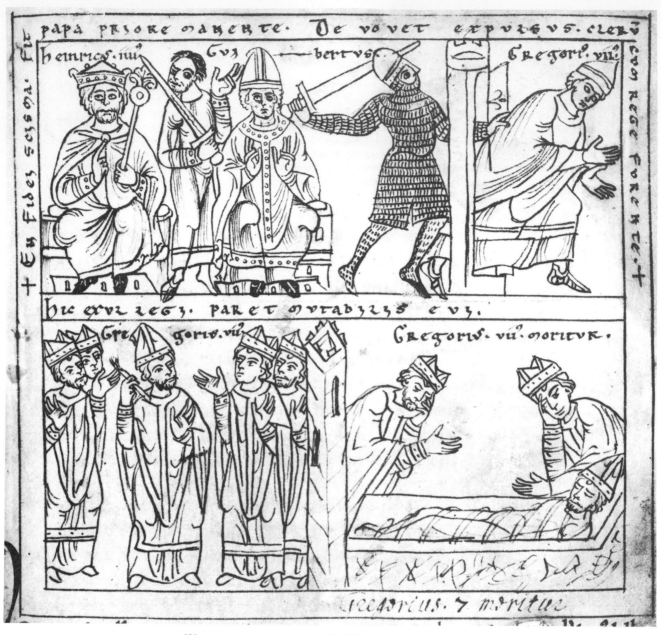

A twelfth-century German manuscript illustrating the struggle between Emperor Henry IV and Pope Gregory VII. In the top panel, Henry installs his puppet pope Clement III, and drives Gregory from Rome. Below, Gregory dies in exile. As can be seen, the sympathies of the artist, a monk, were with Gregory, not Henry. [University of Jena]

troversy were the local princes in Germany.

The new Gregorian fence between temporal and spiritual power did not prevent kings and popes from remaining good neighbors if each was willing. However, succeeding centuries demonstrated that royal and papal aspirations were too competitive for peaceful coexistence. The most bitter clash between Church and State was still to come. It would occur during the late thirteenth century and early fourteenth century in the confrontation between Pope Boniface VIII and King Philip IV of France.

Calixtus II and Henry V End the Investiture Controversy

The Concordat of Worms between Pope Calixtus II (1119–1124) and Emperor Henry V (1106–1125) on September 23, 1122, ended the investiture controversy. Calixtus acknowledged the emperor's right to be present as a judge and to bestow temporal rights and revenues (as distinct from ecclesiastical) on the candidate, and Henry acknowledged the exclusive right of the pope to invest clergy in their religious offices and further promised to restore previously usurped church possessions.

PRIVILEGE OF THE POPE:

I, Bishop Calixtus, servant of the servants of God, concede to you beloved son Henry—by the grace of God August Emperor of the Romans—that the election of those bishops and abbots in the German kingdom who belong to the kingdom [i.e., those in Germany, Italy, and Burgundy] shall take place in your presence without simony and without any violence; so that if any discord occurs between the parties concerned, you may—with the counsel or judgment of the metropolitan and the co-provincials—give your assent and assistance to the party which appears to have the better case. The candidate elected may receive the ''regalia'' [i.e., the temporal rights and revenues connected with the benefice] from you through the sceptre and he shall perform his lawful duties to you for them. But he who is elected in the other parts of the Empire shall, within six months, receive the ''regalia'' from you through the sceptre and shall perform his lawful duties for them, saving all things which are known as pertaining to the Church. If you complain to me in any of these matters and ask for help, I will furnish you the aid, if such is the duty of any office. I grant true peace to you and to all those who are or have been of your party during this discord.

PRIVILEGE OF THE EMPEROR:

In the name of Holy and Indivisible Trinity. I, Henry, by the grace of God August Emperor of the Romans, for the love of God and of the Holy Roman Church and of the lord Pope Calixtus and for the healing of my soul, do surrender to God, to the Holy Apostles of God, Peter and Paul, and to the Holy Roman Church all investiture through ring and staff; and do agree that in all churches throughout my kingdom and empire there shall be canonical elections and free consecration. I restore to the same Roman Church all the possessions and temporalities (''regalia'') which have been abstracted until the present day either in the lifetime of my father or in my own and which I hold; and I will faithfully aid in the restoration of those which I do not hold. The possessions also of all other churches and princes and of every one else, either cleric or layman, which had been lost in that war, I will restore, so far as I hold them, according to the counsel of the princes or according to justice; and I will faithfully aid in the restoration of those that I do not hold. And I grant a true peace to the lord Pope Calixtus and to the Holy Roman Church and to all who are or have been on its side. In matters where the Holy Roman Church would seek assistance I will faithfully grant it; and in those where she shall complain to me, I will duly grant justice to her.

Church and State Through the Centuries: A Collection of Historic Documents, trans. and ed. by S. Z. Ehler and John B. Morrall (New York: Biblo and Tannen, 1967), pp. 48–49.

The First Crusades

If an index of popular piety and support for the pope in the high Middle Ages is needed, the Crusades amply provide it. What the Cluny reform was to the clergy, the First Crusade to the Holy Land, proclaimed by Pope Urban II at the Council of Clermont in France in 1095, was to the laity: an outlet for the heightened religious zeal of what was Europe's most religious century before the Protestant Reformation. Actually there had been an earlier Crusade of

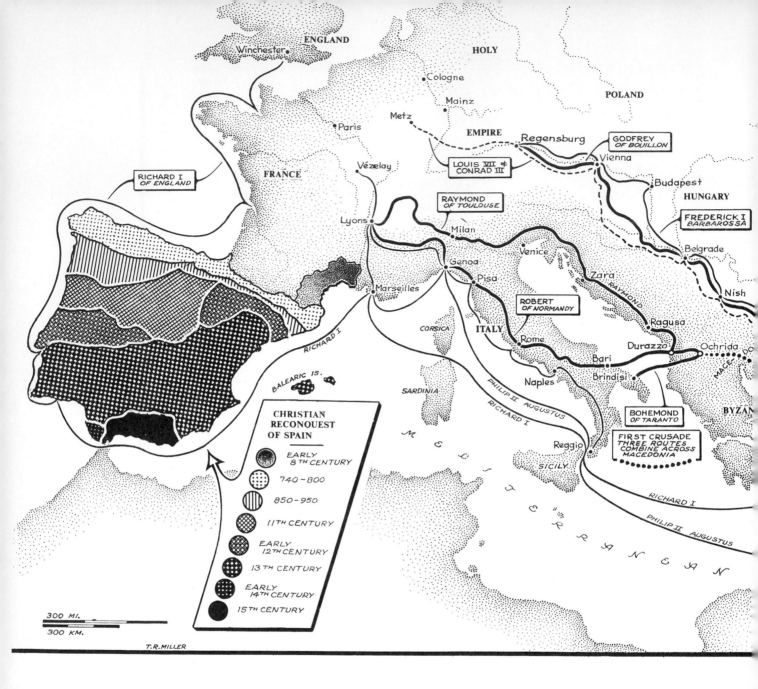

The map contains the following labels:

ENGLAND
Winchester

HOLY

Cologne
Mainz

POLAND

Metz

Paris

EMPIRE
Regensburg

GODFREY
OF BOUILLON

Vienna

FRANCE

Vézelay

LOUIS VII +
CONRAD III

Budapest

HUNGARY

RICHARD I
OF ENGLAND

RAYMOND
OF TOULOUSE

FREDERICK I
BARBAROSSA

Lyons

Milan

Belgrade

Venice

Genoa

Zara

Nish

RAYMOND

Marseilles

Pisa

Ragusa

RICHARD I

CORSICA

ITALY

ROBERT
OF NORMANDY

Durazzo

Ochrida

Rome

MACE-DO

Bari

BALEARIC IS.

Naples

Brindisi

BYZAN

SARDINIA

PHILIP II
AUGUSTUS

RICHARD I

BOHEMOND
OF TARANTO

**CHRISTIAN
RECONQUEST
OF SPAIN**

Reggio

FIRST CRUSADE
THREE ROUTES
COMBINE ACROSS
MACEDONIA

- EARLY
  8TH CENTURY
- 740–800
- 850–950
- 11TH CENTURY
- EARLY
  12TH CENTURY
- 13TH CENTURY
- EARLY
  14TH CENTURY
- 15TH CENTURY

SICILY

M E D I T E R R A N E A N

RICHARD I

PHILIP II
AUGUSTUS

300 MI.
300 KM.

T. R. MILLER

French knights, who, inspired by Pope Alexander II, attacked Muslims in Spain in 1064. Unlike the later Crusades, which were undertaken for patently mercenary as well as religious motives, the early Crusades were to a very high degree inspired by genuine religious piety and were carefully orchestrated by the revived papacy. Participants in the First Crusade to the Holy Land were promised a plenary indulgence should they die in battle, that is, a complete remission of any outstanding temporal punishment for unrepented mortal sins and hence release from suffering for them in purga-

tory. But this spiritual reward was only part of the crusading impulse. Other factors were the widespread popular respect for the reformed papacy and the existence of a nobility newly strengthened by the breakdown of imperial power and eager for military adventure. These elements combined to make the First Crusade a rousing success.

The Eastern emperor welcomed any aid against advancing Muslim armies. The Western Crusaders did not, however, assemble for the purpose of defending Europe's borders against aggression. They freely took the offensive to

THE EARLY CRUSADES

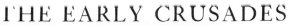

FIRST ___ ━━━━━━ ●●●●●●●● ▬▬▬▬▬ 1096 – 1099
SECOND ___ - - - - - - - - - - - 1147 – 1149
THIRD ___ ━━━━━━━━━━━━━━ 1189 – 1192

MAP 7-1 *Routes and several leaders of the crusades during the first century of the movement. Indicated names of the great nobles of the First Crusade do not exhaust the list. The even showier array of monarchs of the Second and Third still left the crusades, on balance, ineffective in achieving their ostensible goals.*

hardly considered them Christian brothers in a common cause. Nonetheless these fanatical Crusaders accomplished what no Eastern army had ever been able to do. They soundly defeated one Seljuk army after another in a steady advance toward Jerusalem, which fell to them on July 15, 1099.

The victorious Crusaders divided the conquered territory into the feudal states of Jerusalem, Edessa, and Antioch, which they allegedly held as fiefs from the pope. Godfrey of Bouillon, leader of the French-German army (and after him his brother Baldwin), ruled over the kingdom of Jerusalem. However, the Crusaders remained only small islands within a great sea of Muslims, who looked on the Western invaders as hardly more than savages. The conquerors built defensive fortifications and received assistance from the new religious-military orders of the Knights Hospitalers (founded in 1113) and the Knights Templars (founded ca. 1119). The Templars were orders of crack soldiers who took religious vows and dedicated themselves to protect pilgrims to the Holy Land against the infidel. But native persistence finally broke the Crusaders around mid-century, and the forty-odd-year Latin presence in the East began to crumble. Edessa fell to Muslim armies in 1144. A Second Crusade, preached by the eminent Bernard of Clairvaux (1091–1153), Christendom's most powerful monastic leader, attempted a rescue, but it met with dismal failure. In October 1187 Jerusalem itself was reconquered by Saladin (1138–1193), king of Egypt and Syria, and, save for a brief interlude in the thirteenth century, it remained thereafter in Islamic hands until modern times.

A Third Crusade in the twelfth century (1189–1192) attempted yet another rescue, enlisting as its leaders the most powerful Western rulers: Emperor Frederick Barbarossa; Richard the Lion-Hearted, king of England; and Philip Augustus, king of France. But the Third Crusade proved a tragicomic commentary on the passing of the original crusading spirit. Frederick Barbarossa accidentally drowned in the Saleph River while en route to

rescue the holy city of Jerusalem, which had been in non-Christian hands since the seventh century, from the Seljuk Turks. To this end three great armies—tens of thousands of Crusaders—gathered in France, Germany, and Italy. Following different routes, they reassembled in Constantinople in 1097. The convergence of these spirited soldiers on the Eastern capital was a cultural shock that only deepened Eastern antipathy toward the West. The weakened Eastern emperor, Alexis I, suspected their true motives, and the common people, who were forced to give them room and board,

the Holy Land. Richard the Lion-Hearted and Philip Augustus reached the outskirts of Jerusalem, but their intense personal rivalry shattered the Crusaders' unity and chances of victory. Philip Augustus returned to France and made war on English continental territories, and Richard fell captive to the Emperor Henry VI as he was returning to England. (Henry VI suspected Richard of plotting against him with Henry's mortal enemy, Henry the Lion, the duke of Saxony, who happened also to be Richard's brother-in-law.) The English were forced to pay a handsome ransom for their adventurous king's release. Popular resentment of taxes for this ransom became part of the background to the revolt against the English monarchy that led to the royal recognition of Magna Carta in 1215.

The long-term achievement of the first three Crusades had little to do with their original

A thirteenth-century depiction of Godfrey of Bouillon leading his knights on the First Crusade. [*Bibliotheque Nationale/Art Resource*]

Pope Eugenius III Promotes the Second Crusade

Full absolution and remission of all sins were just a part of the many benefits promised by the church to those who went on Crusades to the Holy Land. Here are the inducements offered by Pope Eugenius III (1145–1153) in 1146.

In virtue of the authority vested by God in us, we . . . have promised and granted to those who from a spirit of devotion have resolved to enter upon and accomplish this holy and necessary undertaking, that full remission of sins which our predecessor, Pope Urban, granted. We have also commanded that their wives and children, their property and possessions, shall be under the protection of the holy Church. . . . Moreover we ordain, by our apostolic authority, that until their return or death is fully proven, no lawsuit shall be instituted hereafter in regard to any property of which they were in peaceful possession when they took the cross.

Those who with pure hearts enter upon this sacred journey, and who are in debt, shall pay no interest. And if they, or others for them, are bound by oath or promise to pay interest, we free them by our apostolic authority. And after they have sought aid of their relatives, or of the lords of whom they hold their fiefs, if the latter are unable or unwilling to advance them money, we allow them freely to mortgage their lands and other possessions to churches, ecclesiastics, or other Christians, and their lords shall have no redress.

Following the example of our predecessor, and through the authority of omnipotent God and St. Peter, prince of the apostles, which is vested in us by God, we grant absolution and remission of sins, so that those who devoutly undertake and accomplish this holy journey, or who die by the way, shall obtain absolution for all their sins which they confess with humble and contrite heart, and shall receive from him who grants to each his due reward the prize of eternal life.

James Harvey Robinson (Ed.), *Readings in European History*, Vol. 1 (Boston: Anthenaeum, 1904), pp. 337–338.

purpose. Politically and religiously they were a failure, and the Holy Land reverted as firmly as ever to Muslim hands. These Crusades were more important for the way they stimulated Western trade with the East. The merchants of Venice, Pisa, and Genoa followed the Crusaders' cross to lucrative new markets. The need to resupply the new Christian settlements in the Near East not only reopened old trade routes that had long been closed by Arab domination of the Mediterranean but also established new ones. It is a commentary on both the degeneration of the original intent of the Crusades and their true historical importance that the Fourth Crusade became an enterprising commercial venture manipulated by the Venetians.

Trade and the Growth of Towns (1100–1300)

During the centuries following the collapse of the Roman Empire, western Europe became a closed and predominantly agricultural society, with small international commerce and even less urban culture. The great seaports of Italy were the exceptions. Venice, Pisa, and Genoa continued to trade actively with Constantinople and throughout the eastern Mediterranean, including Palestine, Syria, and Egypt, during the Middle Ages. The Venetians, Europe's most sober businessmen, jealously guarded their Eastern trade, attacking Western Christian competitors as quickly as Muslim predators. The latter were largely subdued by the success of the First Crusade, which proved a trade bonanza for Italian cities as the Mediterranean was opened to greater Western shipping. Venice, Pisa, and Genoa maintained major trading posts throughout the Mediterranean by the twelfth century. (See Map 7.2)

The Fourth Crusade

In an unintended chain reaction, Crusades created trade, which in turn gave rise to new towns and industry, which in turn brought about major social upheavals. The enterprising way in which the Venetians turned the Fourth Crusade to their own advantage reveals the interdependence of religion and business in the later Crusades. In 1202 Crusaders, some thirty thousand strong, arrived in Venice to set sail for Egypt. When they were unable to pay the price of transport, the Venetians negotiated as an alternative to payment the conquest of a rival Christian port city on the Adriatic: Zara.

Two views of Italian merchants at work: bargaining with customers (above) and recording the price of grain (below). [Art Resource]

To the shock of Pope Innocent III, the Crusaders obligingly subdued Zara. This proved to be only the beginning of the Crusaders' digression from their original goal. They further conquered Constantinople itself in support of disputed imperial claims made by the dethroned Greek prince Alexis. In July 1203 Constantinople fell, and by April 1204 it was completely in Western hands. Venice acquired thereby new lands and maritime rights that assured its domination of the eastern Mediterranean. During the decades of its occupation, Constantinople was the center for Western trade throughout the Near East.

The New Merchant Class

The Western commercial revival attendant on these events repopulated the old Roman urban centers and gave birth to new industries. Trade put both money and ideas into circulation. New riches, or the prospect of them, improved living conditions, raised hopes, and increased populations. In the twelfth century western Europe became a "boomtown." Among the most interesting creations were the traders themselves, who formed a new, distinctive social class. These prosperous merchants did not, as might first be suspected, spring from the landed nobility, although Venetian and Genoese traders began with the advantages of wealth. A goodly number of traders, however, were, to the contrary, poor, landless adventurers who had absolutely nothing to lose and everything to gain by the risks of foreign trade. For mutual protection they traveled together in great armed caravans, buying their products as cheaply as possible at the source and selling them as dearly as possible in Western marketplaces. They have been called the first Western capitalists, men inspired by profit and devoted to little more than amassing fortunes. But their very greed and daring laid the foundations for Western urban life as we have come to know it today.

Although in power, wealth, and privilege the great merchants were destined to join and eventually eclipse the landed aristocracy, they were initially misfits in traditional medieval society. They were freemen, often possessed of great wealth, yet they neither owned land nor tilled the soil. They did not value land and farming but were men of liquid wealth constantly on the move. Aristocrats and clergy looked down on them as degenerates, and the commoners viewed them with suspicion. They

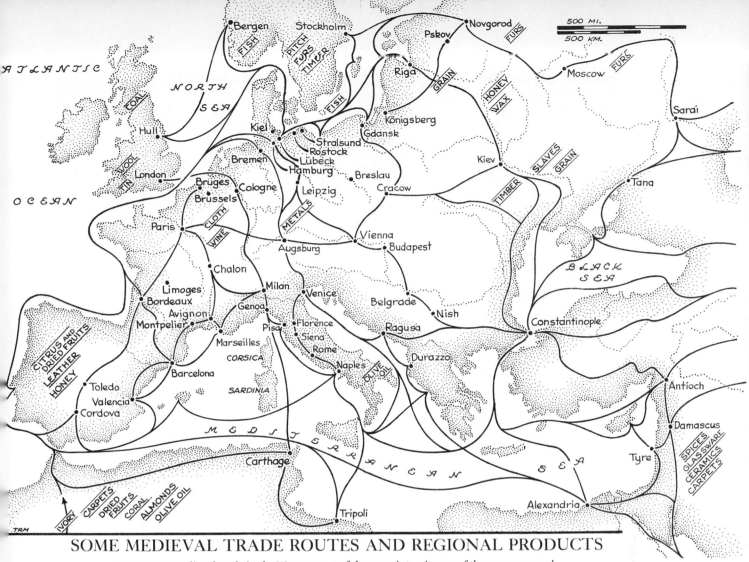

SOME MEDIEVAL TRADE ROUTES AND REGIONAL PRODUCTS

MAP 7-2 *Medieval trade in the West was not of the same intensity nor of the same geographical breadth in different periods. The map shows some of the channels that came to be used in interregional commerce. Labels tell part of what was carried in that commerce.*

were intruders within medieval society, a new breed who did not fit into the neat hierarchy of clergy, nobility, and serfs.

Merchants fanned out from the great Flemish and Italian trading centers: Bruges, Ghent, Venice, Pisa, Genoa, Florence. Wherever they settled in large numbers, they lobbied for the degree of freedom necessary for successful commerce, opposing tolls, tariffs, and other petty restrictions that discouraged the flow of trade. This activity brought them initially into conflict with the norms of static agricultural society. But as they demonstrated the many advantages of vigorous trade, the merchants progressively won their case. They not only remodeled city government to favor their new

industries and the free flow of trade but also imparted to cities an aura of importance unknown during previous centuries. By the late Middle Ages cities commonly saw themselves as miniature states, even self-contained Christendoms. "God has become a citizen of Bern," wrote a Bernese chronicler in the fourteenth century, "and who can fight against God?"

As they grew and became prosperous, medieval cities also became very jealous of their good fortune. They took every measure to protect skilled industries, to expand trade, and to prevent competition from the surrounding countryside. Government remained in the hands of the rich and the few—patricians, *grandi,* the "old rich"—although wealthy merchants, aspiring to the noble style of life, increasingly found their way into the inner circles of government, as money proved early that it could talk. By the thirteenth century city councils, operating on the basis of aristocratic constitutions and composed of patricians and wealthy merchants—the old rich *and* the new rich—internally controlled city life. These oligarchies were increasingly confronted by small artisans, who demanded improved living conditions and a role in making policy. Skilled artisans formed the far greater part of the new burgher class and organized to express their will through powerful corporations or craft guilds. These were exclusive organizations for the various skilled trades; they set standards, certified craftsmen, and in every way worked to enhance the economic well-being and political influence of their members (see Chapter 8, "Townspeople"). The high and late Middle Ages also saw a deepening conflict between craft masters, who were determined to keep their numbers at an absolute minimum, and journeymen, who found themselves frozen at the lower levels of their trade. The self-protectiveness and internal conflicts of medieval cities did not, however, prevent them from forming larger trade associations, such as the famous German Hanseatic League, or Hansa, which kept Baltic trade a German monopoly well into the fifteenth century.

Changes in Society

The rise of a merchant class was an important crack in the old social order. New-rich merchants, a class originally sprung from ordinary, landless people, broke into the aristocracy, and in doing so, they drew behind them the leadership of the new artisan class created by the urban industries that had grown up in the wake of the growth of trade. In the late Middle Ages the "middle classes" firmly established themselves and have been enlarging their numbers ever since.

Although from one perspective medieval towns were overly self-protective and "egoistic," they also became a force for innovation and change far beyond their walls. This fact is all the more remarkable when it is remembered that towns at this time contained hardly more than 5 per cent of the population. Townspeople became a major force in the breakup of feudal society, aiding both kings and the peasantry at the expense of the landed nobility. Generally speaking, towns and kings

Two Romanesque churches: ABOVE, *the Abbey of Germigny des Pres in northern France;* BELOW, *the interior of the Chapel of St. Michael in the Loire Valley. The architecture of the early Middle Ages is known as* Romanesque *because it was closely related to the style of the late Roman Empire. It is characterized by thick stone walls and rounded arches to support the roof. The few windows were often very small, often mere slits. This gives Romanesque buildings a fortresslike appearance.*

tended to ally themselves against the great feudal lords. A notable exception may be seen in England, where the towns joined the barons against the oppressive monarchy of King John (1199–1216) and became a part of the parliamentary opposition. Townspeople generally, however, found their autonomy better preserved by having one distant master rather than several nearer and factious overlords. Kings, in turn, courted the liquid wealth and the administrative skills of the town dwellers, who began to replace the clergy and the nobility in the royal bureaucracy. Urban money made it possible for kings to hire mercenary armies and thereby decrease their dependence on the noble cavalry—an important step in the consolidation of territories divided for centuries by feudal allegiances and customs.

From the burgher ranks kings drew the skilled lawyers who began the long process of replacing feudal custom with centralized Roman law, and towns also often had powerful militias that could be enlisted in royal service. Kings, in return, gave towns political recognition and guaranteed their constitutions against territorial magnates. This was more easily done in the stronger coastal towns than in interior areas, where urban life remained less vigorous and territorial power was on the rise. In France, towns became integrated into the royal government. In Germany and Austria, by contrast, towns fell under ever tighter control by territorial princes. In Italy towns uniquely grew to absorb their surrounding territory, becoming city-states.

Towns also aided the peasantry, to the detriment of the landed nobility. A popular maxim of the time in German cities was *"Stadtluft macht frei"*—"City air makes one free." Cities passed legislation making serfs who spent a year and a day within their walls free men. New urban industries provided lucky peasants vocations alternative to farming. The new money economy made it possible for serfs or their urban patrons to buy their freedom from

feudal services and rents as the latter became translatable into direct money payments. A serf or his patron could simply buy up the "contract." The growth of a free peasantry became especially evident in the thirteenth century.

All of this worked against the landed nobility. As urban trade and industries put more money into circulation, its value decreased (inflation). The great landowners, whose wealth was static, found themselves confronted, on the one hand, by serfs who longed to flee to the city and, on the other, by rising prices. They were losing their cheap labor supply and facing diminished productivity; at the same time they had to pay more for their accustomed style of life. The nobility were not disciplined people, and many fell prey to money-wise urban merchants, who beat them out of their landed wealth.

The new urban economy worked, then, to free both kings and peasants from dependence on feudal lords, although this was a long and complex process. As royal authority became centralized and kings were able to hire mercenary soldiers, the noble cavalry became militarily obsolescent, at most a minor part of the king's armed forces. And as towns and urban industries grew, attracting serfs from the farms, the nobility gradually lost its once all-powerful economic base. The long-term consequence was a strengthening of monarchy.

Medieval Universities and Scholasticism

Thanks to Spanish Muslim scholars, the logical works of Aristotle, the writings of Euclid and Ptolemy, the basic works of Greek physicians and Arab mathematicians, and the larger texts of Roman law became available to Western scholars in the early twelfth century. Muslim scholars preserved these works, translated portions of the Greek ones into Latin, and wrote extensive, thought-provoking commentaries on ancient texts. This renaissance of ancient knowledge, in turn, provided the occasion for the rise of universities.

Bologna and Paris

The first important Western university was in Bologna. It received its formal grant of rights and privileges from the emperor Frederick Barbarossa in 1158. University members, like clergy, were granted royal immunity from local jurisdiction and were viewed by local townspeople as a group apart. In Bologna we find the first formal organizations of students and professors and the first degree programs—the institutional foundations of the modern university. The "university" was at first simply a program of study that gave the student a license to teach others. Originally the term *university* meant no more than a group or corporation of individuals who were united by common self-interest and for mutual protection. As the local townspeople viewed both masters and students as foreigners without civil rights, such a union was necessary. It followed the model of a medieval trade guild. Bolognese students formed such a bloc in order to guarantee fair rents and prices from the townspeople and regular and high-quality teaching from their professors. Price gouging by townspeople was met with the threat to move the university to another town—a threat that could easily be carried out because the university at this time was not a great, fixed physical plant. Professors who failed to meet student expectations were boycotted. The mobility of the first universities gave them a unique independence.

Professors also formed protective associations and established procedures and standards for certification to teach within their ranks. The first academic degree was a certificate *(licentia docendi)* given by the professors' guild, which granted graduates in the liberal arts program or in the higher professional sciences of medicine, theology, and law "the right to teach anywhere" *(ius ubique docendi)*.

Bologna was distinguished as the center for the revival of Roman law. From the seventh to the eleventh centuries only the most rudimentary manuals of Roman law had survived and circulated. With the growth of trade and towns in the late eleventh century, Western scholars came into contact with the larger and more important parts of the Roman *Corpus Juris Civilis* of Justinian. The study and dissemination of this new material was directed by Irnerius (fl. early twelfth century). He and his students made authoritative commentaries or glosses on individual laws following their broad knowledge of the *Corpus Juris*. Around 1140 a monk named Gratian, also resident in Bologna, created the standard legal text in church or canon law, the *Concordance of Discordant Canons,* known more commonly as Gratian's *Decretum.*

As Bologna proved the model for southern

255

*The High
Middle Ages
(1000–1300):
Revival of
Empire,
Church, and
Towns*

The University of Bologna in central Italy was distinguished as the center for the revival of Roman law. This carving from the tomb of a professor of law shows students attending one of his lectures. [SCALA/Art Resource]

European universities and the study of law, Paris became the model for northern Europe and the study of theology. Oxford, Cambridge, and, much later, Heidelberg were among Paris's imitators. All these universities required a foundation in the liberal arts for further study in the higher sciences of medicine, theology, and law. The arts program consisted of the *trivium* (grammar, rhetoric, and logic) and the *quadrivium* (arithmetic, geometry, astronomy, and music).

Before the emergence of the universities, the liberal arts had been taught in the cathedral and monastery schools, that is, schools attached to cathedrals or monasteries for the purpose of training clergy. The most famous of the cathedral schools were those of Rheims and Chartres. Chartres won fame under the direction of such distinguished teachers as Saint Ivo and Saint Bernard of Chartres (not to be confused with Saint Bernard of Clairvaux), and Gerbert, who later became Pope Sylvester II (999–1003), guided Rheims to greatness in the last quarter of the tenth century. Gerbert was filled with enthusiasm for knowledge and promoted both logical and rhetorical studies. He did much to raise the study of logic to preeminence within the liberal arts, despite his personal belief in the greater relevance of rhetoric to the promotion of Christianity.

The University of Paris grew institutionally out of the cathedral school of Notre Dame, receiving its charter in 1200 from King Philip Augustus and Pope Innocent III. Papal sanction and regulations, among them the right of the faculty to strike, were issued in 1231 in the bull *Parens scientiarum* and gave the university freedom from local church control. At this time the University of Paris consisted of independent faculties of arts, canon law, medicine, and theology, with the masters of arts, who were grouped together in four national factions (French, Norman, English-German, and Picard), the dominant faculty.

At Paris the college system originated. At first, colleges were no more than hospices providing room and board for poor students. But the educational life of the university rapidly expanded into these fixed buildings and began to thrive on their sure endowments. In Paris the most famous college was the Sorbonne, founded around 1257 by Robert de Sorbon, chaplain to the king, for the purpose of educating advanced theological students. In Oxford and Cambridge the colleges became the basic unit of student life, indistinguishable from the university. By the fifteenth and sixteenth centuries colleges had tied the universities to physical plants and fixed foundations, restricting their previous autonomy and freedom of movement.

The Curriculum

Before the renaissance of the twelfth century the education available within the cathedral and monastic schools was quite limited. Students learned grammar, rhetoric, and elementary geometry and astronomy. They used the Latin grammars of Donatus and Priscian and studied Saint Augustine's *On Christian Doctrine,* Cassiodorus's *On Divine and Secular Learning,* and the various writings of Boethius (d. 524). Boethius was important for instruction in arithmetic and music and especially for the transmission of the small body of Aristotle's logical works known before the twelfth century. After the textual finds of the early twelfth century, Western scholars had the whole of Aristotle's logic, the astronomy of Ptolemy, the writings of Euclid, and many Latin classics. By the mid-thirteenth century the ethical, physical, and metaphysical writings of Aristotle were in circulation in the West.

Logic and dialectic rapidly triumphed in importance over the other arts. They were tools designed to discipline knowledge and thought. Even before the twelfth century, cathedral schools had directed students to Boethius's translation and commentary on Porphyry's *Introduction to Aristotle* and to his translation and commentaries on Aristotle's *Categories* and *On*

Interpretation. In the high Middle Ages the learning process was very basic. The student wrote commentaries on authoritative texts, especially those of Aristotle. His teachers did not encourage him to strive independently for undiscovered truth. He was taught rather to organize and harmonize the accepted truths of tradition. The basic assumption was that truth already existed; it was not something to be discovered but something at hand, requiring systematic organization and elucidation. Such conviction made logic and dialectic supreme within the liberal arts.

The Scholastic program of study, based on logic and dialectic, reigned supreme in all the faculties—in law and medicine as well as in philosophy and theology. Scholasticism was a peculiar method of study. The student read the traditional authorities in his field, formed short summaries of their teaching, disputed it by elaborating arguments pro and con, and then drew his own modest conclusions. The twelfth century saw the rise of the "summa," a summary of all that was known about a topic, and works whose purpose was to conciliate traditional authorities. In canon law there was Gratian's *Concordance of Discordant Canons.* In theology Peter Lombard's *Four Books of Sentences,* published around 1150, embraced traditional opinion on God, the creation, Christ, and the sacraments. It also enumerated the seven sacraments, which became traditional in the high Middle Ages (baptism, confirmation, penance, the Eucharist, extreme unction, holy orders, and marriage). Lombard's work evolved from Peter Abelard's *Sic et Non,* a juxtaposition of seemingly contradictory statements on the same subject by revered authorities. Lombard's *Sentences* became the standard theological textbook until the Protestant Reformation in the sixteenth century. In biblical studies the *Glossa Ordinaria* of Anselm of Laon (ca. 1120) and his disciples was the authoritative summary. In the thirteenth century came Saint Thomas Aquinas's magnificent *Summa Theologica,* an ambitious summary of the whole of theological knowledge from the Creation to the Last Day, which many consider the greatest theological work ever written.

Scholasticism had harsh critics even in the twelfth century. Such prominent men as John of Salisbury (ca. 1120–1180) and Saint Bernard of Clairvaux (1090–1153) rejected the dialectic of the logicians, which they found to be heartless and presumptuous. The later Humanist criticism of Scholastic learning as

The seven liberal arts of the medieval university curriculum: rhetoric, geometry, astronomy, music, natural and moral philosophy, and theology. At their feet sit the great teachers of antiquity: Cicero, Euclid, Ptolemey, Aristotle, Seneca, and Augustine. [*Art Resource*]

"useless" can be heard in their complaints. Although grammar and eloquence were eclipsed by dialectic and logic in medieval universities, professional rhetoricians, known as *dictatores*, retained their places within the universities and continued to give practical instruction in the composition of letters and official documents. These professional rhetoricians were the forerunners of the later Humanists, and their skills as secretaries were much in private demand in the high Middle Ages. The ability to persuade others by clear argument and eloquent prose and speech was the essence of successful government. A famous allegorical poem appeared in commentary on the domination of logic and dialectic within the universities. It was known as *The Battle of the Seven Arts* (1250). In the poem, which argues the rhetorician's position, vain logic is seen driving noble grammar into exile, where the latter patiently waits in confident expectation that a more enlightened age will demand its return.

Philosophy and Theology: Friends or Foes?

Scholastic thinkers in medieval universities quarreled over two basic problems: (1) the proper relation of philosophy, which was virtually identical with the writings of Aristotle, and theology (or of rational and revealed knowledge), and, to a lesser extent, (2) the status of so-called universal concepts.

The first problem arose from the fact that in Christian eyes there were manifestly heretical tenets in the corpus of Aristotle's writings, especially as his teaching was elaborated by the Muslim commentators. For example, Aristotle's belief in the eternality of the world called into question the Judeo-Christian teaching about the world's creation according to the

Bishop Stephen Complains About the New Scholastic Learning

Scholasticism involved an intellectual, learned approach to religion and its doctrines rather than simple, uncritical piety. Many saw in it a threat to the study of the Bible and the Church Fathers, as doctrines that should simply be believed and revered were rationally dissected for their logical meaning by allegedly presumptuous and none-too-well-trained youths. Here is a particularly graphic description of the threat, replete with classical allusion, as perceived by Stephen, Bishop of Tournai, in a letter to the pope written between 1192 and 1203.

The studies of sacred letters among us are fallen into the workshop of confusion, while both disciples applaud novelties alone and masters watch out for glory rather than learning. They everywhere compose new and recent summulae *[little summaries] and commentaries, by which they attract, detain, and deceive their hearers, as if the works of the holy fathers were not still sufficient, who, we read, expounded Holy Scripture in the same spirit in which we believe the apostles and prophets composed it. They prepare strange and exotic courses for their banquet, when at the nuptials of the son of the king of Taurus his own flesh and blood are killed and all prepared, and the wedding guests have only to take and eat what is set before them. Contrary to the sacred canons there is public disputation over the incomprehensible deity; concerning the incarnation of the Word, verbose flesh and blood irreverently litigate. The indivisible Trinity is cut up and wrangled over . . . so that now there are as many errors as doctors, as many scandals as classrooms, as many blasphemies as squares. . . . Faculties called liberal having lost their pristine liberty are sunk in such servitude that adolescents with long hair impudently usurp their professorships, and beardless youths sit in the seat of their seniors, and those who don't yet know how to be disciples strive to be named masters. And they write their* summulae *moistened with drool and dribble but unseasoned with the salt of philosophers. Omitting the rules of the arts and discarding the authentic books of the artificers, they seize the flies of empty words in their sophisms like the claws of spiders. Philosophy cries out that her garments are torn and disordered and, modestly concealing her nudity by a few specific tatters, neither is consulted nor consoles as of old. All these things, father, call for the hand of apostolic correction. . . .*

Lynn Thorndike, *University Records and Life in the Middle Ages* (New York: Octagon Books, 1971), pp. 22–24.

book of Genesis. Aristotelian teaching that intellect was one seemed to deny all individuality, Christian teaching about individual responsibility, and the personal immortality of the soul.

When theologians began to adopt the logic and the metaphysics of Aristotle, some critics saw a mortal threat to biblical and traditional authority. Berengar of Tours (d. 1088) applied logic to the sacrament of the Eucharist and came to question the church's teaching on transubstantiation. Peter Abelard (1079–1142) subjected the Trinity to logical examination. The curiosity of these new logicians shocked conservatives such as Lanfranc (d. 1089), the reformer of the Abbey of Bec, and especially the powerful Saint Bernard. The lat-

ter questioned whether the liberal arts course, dominated by Aristotelian logic, had become more a foe than an ally of theological study. A century of suspicion and criticism of Aristotle's influence on theological study culminated when the bishop of Paris condemned 219 philosophical propositions in 1277. This massive condemnation was directed against devotees of Aristotle, many of whom followed the Muslim authority Averroës (1126–1198), but it also caught in its net a few teachings of such orthodox Western theologians as Thomas Aquinas (d. 1274), who had tried to reconcile Aristotle with traditional Christian teaching.

After this condemnation philosophy never again had such importance within theology. William of Ockham (d. 1349), who represented conservative opinion in this controversy and may be seen as a watershed in the development of Scholasticism, strictly limited the ability of reason, assisted by logic and dialectic, to fathom the nature and decisions of God independently of divine revelation. Ockham taught that one must abandon all such efforts to penetrate the divine mind in essential theological matters and must be content with the Bible's teaching.

The Problem of Universals: Aquinas and Ockham

The classic Scholastic problem concerned the question whether or not universal concepts really exist apart from the human mind. Do words that signify a multitude of individual things, such as *man, dog,* and *chair,* refer to realities that have extramental existence? The question, perhaps strange at first to modern people, involved a very basic discussion of how one truly knows anything. Because individual physical things—a man, a dog, a chair—are

perishable, philosophical realists, who closely followed the views of Plato, believed that they could not be known by an immaterial and immortal soul. They reasoned that like can know and be known only by like. What is immaterial and immortal can know directly only immaterial and immortal things. Hence, these realists argued, there must be a transcendent world of being in which perfect, imperishable, immaterial models of individual things exist. It is because the human mind is privy to such a world that it can know immediately the world of physical things. These models, existing in a transcendent world of being, are the "universals," and according to the realists, they exist apart from the human mind. They are the original models of the individual things of the world, the ultimate principles of being and intelligibility. It is because individual things participate in universals that they both exist and can be known.

The moderate realists, who followed Aristotle more than Plato on this question, agreed that universals were really distinct from individual things. But they argued that such uni-

---

Thomas Aquinas Defines the Nature of Christian Theology

Although its premises and data came from divine revelation rather than from empirical observation, theology was considered a "science" in its own right in the Middle Ages, indeed, the "queen" of the sciences. Here Thomas Aquinas (ca. 1225–1274) defines Christian theology and explains its use of human reasoning to elucidate the truths of faith.

The premises of Christian theology are revealed truths, accepted on the word of the teacher who reveals them. Consequently its typical method is the appeal to authority. This does not impair its scientific dignity, for though to cite human authority is the poorest form of argument, the appeal to divine authority is the highest and most cogent.

Nevertheless, Christian theology also avails itself of human reasoning to illustrate the truths of faith, not to prove them. Grace does not scrap nature, but improves it; reason subserves faith,

and natural love runs through charity. Theology invokes great thinkers on matters where they are received authorities. . . . Theology treats them as sources of external evidence for its arguments. Its proper and indispensable court of appeal is to the authority of the canonical Scriptures. The writings of the Fathers of the Church are also proper sources, yet their authority is not final. Faith rests on divine revelation made through the prophets and apostles and set down in the canonical Scriptures, not on revelations, if there by any, made to other holy teachers.

From the *Summa Theologica,* Ia, i. 8, ad 2, in Thomas Gilby (Ed. and Trans.), *St. Thomas Aquinas: Theological Texts* (New York: Oxford University Press, 1955), pp. 22–23.

William of Ockham on Universals

William of Ockham (ca. 1300–1349) rejected any hint of the extramental existence of human concepts. Universals were only contents of the mind and verbal conventions.

We have to say that every universal is one singular thing. Therefore nothing is universal except by signification, that is, by being a sign of several things. . . . It must, however, be understood that there are two sorts of universal. There is one sort which is naturally universal; it is a sign naturally predicable of many things, in much the same way as smoke naturally signifies fire, or a groan the pain of a sick man, or laughter an inner joy. Such a universal is nothing other than a content of the mind; and therefore no substance outside the mind and no accident outside the mind is such a universal. . . . The other sort of universal is so by convention. In this way, an uttered word, which is really a single quality, is universal; for it is a conventional sign meant to signify many things. Therefore, just as the word is said to be common, so it can be said to be universal. But it is not so by nature, only by convention.

William of Ockham, *Summa Totius Logicae*, Ic, xiv, in *Ockham: Philosophical Writings*, ed. and trans. by Philotheus Boehner (New York: Nelson, 1962), pp. 33–34.

versals existed only *within* individual things as intrinsic qualities that gave them form and intelligibility. According to this point of view, championed by Thomas Aquinas, one came to know individual things by isolating and "abstracting" their intrinsic universal features. The universal, which is within individual things, is "extracted" from them by intellection and is lodged in the mind as a so-called intelligible species. It is by way of such abstracted universals in the mind that one knows the surrounding world.

Later the nominalists took the most radical position on the question of universals. They looked on universal concepts as simply "names" or "terms" created by the mind and existing only within the mind. William of Ockham was the most famous exponent of this point of view. As a general principle he believed that the simpler explanation was always the more convincing explanation. This was his famous "razor": "What can be explained by assuming fewer terms is vainly explained by assuming more." A special "world of being" and "intelligible species" were neither necessary nor helpful assumptions. Ockham felt that such speculations led only to greater confusion and skepticism. He taught that individual things were known directly and without mediation and that simple "intuitive knowledge" provided the foundation for the mind's formation of the universal concepts it used to aid its

recall and verbal communication. Universals were extrapolations from ordinary sensory experience and reflection, "conventions," naturally formed by the mind as essential aids to knowledge, but *really* existing only in the mind and in words.

Suggested Readings

JOHN W. BALDWIN, *The Scholastic Culture of the Middle Ages: 1000–1300* (1971). Best brief synthesis available.

M. W. BALDWIN (Ed.), *History of the Crusades*, I: *The First Hundred Years.* (1955). Basic historical narrative.

GEOFFREY BARRACLOUGH, *The Medieval Papacy* (1968). Brief, comprehensive survey, with pictures.

F. C. COPLESTON, *Aquinas* (1965). Best introduction to Aquinas's philosophy.

FREDERICK COPLESTON, *A History of Philosophy*, III/1: *Ockham to the Speculative Mystics* (1963). The best introduction to Ockham and his movement.

ETIENNE GILSON, *Heloise and Abelard* (1968). Analysis and defense of medieval scholarly values.

CHARLES H. HASKINS, *The Renaissance of the Twelfth Century* (1927). Still the standard account.

CHARLES H. HASKINS, *The Rise of Universities* (1972). A short, minor classic.

GORDON LEFF, *Paris and Oxford Universities in the Thirteenth and Fourteenth Centuries: An Instutitional and Intellectual History* (1968). Very good on Scholastic debates.

EMILE MÂLE, *The Gothic Image: Religious Art in France in the Thirteenth Century* (1913). A classic.

HANS EBERHARD MAYER, *The Crusades,* trans. by John Gilligham (1972). Extremely detailed, and best one-volume account.

ERWIN PANOFSKY, *Gothic Architecture and Scholasticism* (1951). A controversial classic.

HENRI PIRENNE, *Medieval Cities: Their Origins and the Revival of Trade,* trans. by Frank D. Halsey (1970). A minor classic.

HASTINGS RASHDALL, *The Universities of Europe in the Middle Ages,* Vols. 1–3 (1936). Dated but still standard comprehensive work.

FRITZ RÖRIG, *The Medieval Town,* trans. by D. J. A. Matthew (1971). Excellent on northern Europe.

BRIAN TIERNEY, *The Crisis of Church and State 1050–1300* (1964). Very useful collection of primary sources on key Church–State conflicts.

S. WILLIAMS (Ed.), *The Gregorian Epoch: Reformation, Revolution, Reaction* (1964). Variety of scholarly opinion on the significance of Pope Gregory's reign presented in debate form.

R. L. WOLFF AND H. W. HAZARD (Eds.), *History of the Crusades,* II: *The Later Crusades* 1189–1311 (1962).

A professor lecturing at the University of Paris. The University of Paris, which received a royal charter in 1200, was the most famous university in northern Europe. Its faculties of arts, theology, canon law, and medicine attracted students from all over Europe. [Giraudon/Art Resource]

The Order of Life

FOUR BASIC SOCIAL GROUPS were distinguished in the Middle Ages: those who fought (the landed nobility), those who prayed (the clergy), those who labored (the peasantry), and, after the revival of towns in the eleventh century, those who traded and manufactured (the townspeople). It would be false to view each of these groups as closed and homogeneous. Throughout medieval society, like tended to be attracted to like regardless of social grouping. Barons, archbishops, rich farmers, and successful merchants had far more in common with each other than they did with the middle and lower strata of their various professions.

Nobles

As a distinctive social group all noblemen did not begin simply as great men with large hereditary lands. Many rose from the ranks of feudal vassals or warrior knights. The successful vassal attained a special social and legal status based on his landed wealth (accumulated fiefs), his exercise of authority over others, and his distinctive social customs—all of which set him apart from others in medieval society. By the late Middle Ages there had evolved a distinguishable higher and lower nobility living in both town and country. The higher were the great landowners and territorial magnates; the lower were petty landlords, descendants from minor knights, new-rich merchants who could buy country estates, and wealthy farmers patiently risen from ancestral serfdom.

It was a special mark of the nobility that they lived on the labor of others. Basically lords of manors, the nobility of the early and high Middle Ages neither tilled the soil like the peasantry nor engaged in the commerce of merchants—activities considered beneath their dignity. The nobleman resided in a country mansion or, if he were particularly wealthy, a castle. He was drawn to the countryside as much by personal preference as by the fact that his fiefs were usually rural manors. Arms were his profession; the nobleman's sole occupation and reason for living was waging war. His fief provided the means to acquire the expensive military equipment that his rank required, and he maintained his enviable position as he had gained it, by fighting for his chief.

The nobility accordingly celebrated the physical strength, courage, and constant activity of warfare. Warring gave them both new

8

The High Middle Ages: Society and Politics

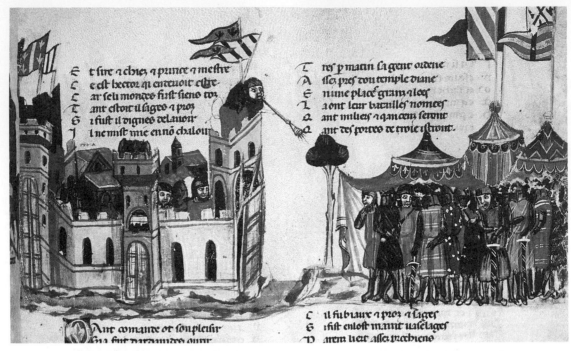

The siege of a city, from a twelfth-century French manuscript. The medieval nobility existed to wage war. Arms were the nobleman's profession, and warfare his means of acquiring riches and glory. (Art Resource)

riches and an opportunity to gain honor and glory. Knights were paid a share in the plunder of victory, and in time of war everything became fair game. Special war wagons, designed for the collection and transport of booty, followed them into battle. Periods of peace were greeted with great sadness, as they meant economic stagnation and boredom. Whereas the peasants and the townspeople counted peace the condition of their occupational success, the nobility despised it as unnatural to their profession. They looked down on the peasantry as cowards who ran and hid in time of war. Urban merchants, who amassed wealth by business methods strange to feudal society, were held in equal contempt, which increased as the affluence and political power of the townspeople grew. The nobility possessed as strong a sense of superiority over these "unwarlike" people as the clergy did over the general run of laity.

The nobleman nurtured his sense of distinctiveness within medieval society by the chivalric ritual of dubbing to knighthood, a ceremonial entrance into the noble class that became almost a religious sacrament. The ceremony was preceded by a bath of purification, confession, communion, and a prayer vigil. Thereafter the priest blessed the knight's standard, lance, and sword. As prayers were chanted, the priest girded the knight with his sword and presented him his shield, enlisting him as much in the defense of the church as in the service of his lord. Dubbing raised the nobleman to a state as sacred in his sphere as clerical ordination made the priest in his. This comparison is quite legitimate. The clergy and the nobility were medieval society's privileged estates. The appointment of noblemen to high ecclesiastical office and their eager participation in the church's Crusades had strong ideological and social underpinnings as well as economic and political motives.

In peacetime the nobility had two favorite amusements: hunting and tournaments. Because of the threat to towns and villages posed by wild animals, the great hunts actually aided the physical security of the ordinary people, while occupying the restless noblemen. However, where they could, noblemen progressively monopolized the rights to game, forbidding the common man from hunting in the "lord's" forests. This practice built resentment among common people to the level of revolt. Free game, fishing, and access to wood were basic demands in the petitions of grievance and the revolts of the peasantry throughout the high and later Middle Ages.

The pastime of tournaments also sowed seeds of social disruption, but more within the ranks of the nobility itself. Tournaments were designed not only to keep men fit for war, but also to provide the excitement of war without the useless maiming and killing of prized vassals. But as regions competed fiercely with one another for victory and glory, even mock battles with blunted weapons proved to be deadly. Tournaments tended to get out of hand, ending with bloodshed and animosity among the combatants. Remnants survive today in the intense regional rivalry of European soccer. The church came to oppose tournaments as occasions of pagan revelry and senseless violence. Kings and princes also turned against them as sources of division within their realms. Henry II of England proscribed them in the twelfth century. They did not end in France until the mid-sixteenth century, after Henry II of France received a mortal shaft through his visor during a tournament celebrating his daughter's marriage.

From the repeated assemblies in the courts of barons and kings, set codes of social conduct or "courtesy" developed in noble circles. With the French leading the way, mannered behavior and court etiquette became almost as important as battlefield expertise. Knights became literate gentlemen, and lyric poets sang and moralized at court. The cultivation of a code of behavior and a special literature to eulogize it was not unrelated to problems within the social life of the nobility. Noblemen were notorious philanderers; their illegitimate children mingled openly with their legitimate offspring in their houses. The advent of courtesy was in part an effort to reform this situation. Although the poetry of courtly love was sprinkled with frank eroticism and the beloved in these epics were married women pursued by those to whom they were not married, the love recommended by the poet was usually love at a distance, unconsummated by sexual intercourse. It was love without touching, a kind of sex without physical sex, and only as such was it considered ennobling. Court poets depicted those who did carnally consummate their illicit love as reaping at least as much suffering as joy from it.

In the twelfth century, knighthood was legally restricted to men of high birth. This circumscription of noble ranks came in reaction to the growing wealth, political power, and successful social climbing of the emergent urban patriciate. Kings remained free, however, to raise up knights at will and did not shrink from increasing royal revenues by selling noble titles to wealthy merchants. But the law was building fences—fortunately not without gates—between town and countryside in the high Middle Ages.

For their part, the merchants supported the passage of statutes prohibiting the nobility, who maintained houses and family businesses in the towns, from disrupting the merchants' carefully created monopolies by engaging in long-distance trade. Such jockeying to protect self-interests brought lawyers into a prominence that they have never lost in Western society.

Noblewomen watching a tournament. These mock battles were designed to provide the excitement of war without its mayhem. However, they tended to get out of hand, resulting in bloodshed and even death. [*University of Heidelberg*]

No medieval social group was absolutely uniform—not the nobility, the clergy, the townspeople, not even the peasantry. Not only was the nobility a class apart, it also had strong social divisions within its own ranks. Noblemen formed a broad social spectrum—from minor vassals without subordinate vassals to mighty barons, the principal vassals of a king or prince, who had many vassals of their own. Dignity and status within the nobility were directly related to the exercise of authority over others; a chief with many vassals obviously far excelled the small country nobleman who served another and was lord over none but himself.

Even among the domestic servants of the nobility, a broad social hierarchy developed in accordance with assigned manorial duties. Although they were peasants in the eyes of the law, the chief stewards charged to oversee the operation of the lord's manor and entrusted with the care and education of the noble children became powerful "lords" within their "domains." Some freemen found the status of the steward enviable enough to surrender their own freedom and become domestic servants in the hope of attaining it. In time the social superiority of the higher ranks of domestic servants won legal recognition as medieval law adjusted to acknowledge the privileges of wealth and power at whatever level they appeared.

In the late Middle Ages several factors forced the landed nobility into a steep economic and political decline from which it never recovered. These were the great population losses of the fourteenth century brought on by the great plague; the changes in military tactics occasioned by the use of infantry and heavy artillery during the Hundred Years' War; and the alliance of the wealthy towns with the king. Generally one can speak of a waning of the landed nobility after the fourteenth century. Thereafter the effective possession of land and wealth counted far more than parentage and family tree as qualification for entrance into the highest social class.

Clergy

Unlike the nobility and the peasantry, the clergy was an open estate. Although clerical ranks reflected the social classes from which the clergy came and a definite clerical hierarchy formed, one was still a cleric by religious training and ordination, not by the circumstances of birth or military prowess. There were two basic types of clerical vocation: the regular and the secular clergy. The former were the orders of monks, who lived according to a special ascetic rule *(regula)* in cloisters separated from the world. They were the spiritual elite among the clergy, and theirs was not a way of life lightly entered. Canon law required that one be at least twenty-one years of age before making a final profession of the monastic vows of poverty, chastity, and obedience. Their personal sacrifices and high religious ideals made the monks much respected in high medieval society. This popularity was a major factor in the success of the Cluny reform movement and of the Crusades of the eleventh and twelfth centuries. The Crusades became a way for the layman to participate in the admired life of asceticism and prayer. They were holy pilgrimages providing the opportunity to imitate the suffering of Jesus even unto death, just as the monks imitated his suffering and death by their retreat from the world and their severe self-denial.

Although many monks (and also nuns, who increasingly embraced the vows of poverty, obedience, and chastity without a clerical rank) secluded themselves altogether, the regular clergy were never completely cut off from the secular world. They maintained frequent contact with the laity through such charitable activities as feeding the destitute and tending the sick, through liberal arts instruction in monastic schools, through special pastoral commissions from the pope, and as supplemental preachers and confessors in parish churches during Lent and other peak religious seasons. It became the special mark of the Dominican and Franciscan friars to live a common life according to a special rule, and still to be active in worldly ministry. Some monks, because of their learning and rhetorical skills, even rose to prominence as secretaries and private confessors to kings and queens.

The secular clergy were those who lived and worked directly among the laity in the world *(saeculum)*. They formed a vast hierarchy. There were the high prelates—the wealthy cardinals, archbishops, and bishops, who were drawn almost exclusively from the nobility—the urban priests, the cathedral canons, and the court clerks; and, finally, the great mass of poor parish priests, who were neither financially nor intellectually very far above the common people they served (the basic educational requirement was an ability to say the Mass.) Until the Gregorian reform in the eleventh century began to reverse the trend, parish priests lived with women in a relationship akin to marriage, and their concubines and children were accepted within the communities they served. Because of their relative poverty, it was not unusual for priests to "moonlight" as teachers, artisans, or farmers, a practice also accepted and even admired by their parishioners.

One of the results of the Gregorian reform was the creation of new religious orders aspiring to live a life of poverty and self-sacrifice in imitation of Christ and the first apostles. The more important were the Canons Regular (founded 1050–1100), the Carthusians (founded 1084), the Cistercians (founded 1098), and the Praemonstratensians (founded 1121). Carthusians, Cistercians, and Praemonstratensians were extremely puritanical in their quest to recapture the purer religious life of the early church. The Cistercians were known as the white monks and the Praemonstratensians as the white order; both wore all-white attire—symbolic of apostolic purity. The Carthusians devoted themselves to long periods of silence and even self-flagellation in their quest for perfect conformity with Christ. The Canons Regular were independent groups of secular clergy and also earnest laity, who, in addition to services to souls in the world, also adopted the Rule of Saint Augustine, a monastic guide dating from around the year 500, and practiced the virtues of regular clerics. As there were monks who renounced exclusive withdrawal from the world, so were there priests who renounced exclusive involvement in it. By merging the life of the cloister with traditional clerical duties, the Canons Regular foreshadowed the mendicant friars of the thirteenth century, the Dominicans and the Franciscans, who combined the ascetic ideals of the cloister with a very active ministry in the world.

The monasteries and nunneries of the established orders recruited candidates from among the wealthiest social groups. Crowding in the convents and the absence of patronage were factors in the thirteenth-century growth of lay satellite convents known as *beguinages*, which housed large numbers of religiously earnest unmarried women from the upper and middle social strata. The city of Cologne established 100 such houses between 1250 and 1350, each containing eight to twelve women. A number of these convents, in Cologne and elsewhere, became heterodox in religious doctrine and practice, falling prey to heresy. Among the re-

Nuns at table. Communities of nuns became extremely numerous during the later Middle Ages. [*Alinari*]

sponsibilities of the new religious orders of Dominicans and Franciscans was the "regularization" of such convents.

There was a far greater proportion of clergy within medieval than within modern society. It has been estimated that 1.5 per cent of fourteenth-century Europe was in clerical garb.

267

The clergy were concentrated in urban areas, especially in towns with universities and cathedrals, where in addition to their studies they found work in a wide variety of religious services. In late-fourteenth-century England there was one cleric for every seventy laypeople, and in counties with a cathedral or a university the proportion rose to one cleric for every fifty laypeople.[1] In large university towns the clergy could exceed 10 per cent of the population. One of the most popular reforms of the Protestant Reformation in the sixteenth century, a uniquely urban movement, was a sharp reduction of the proportion of clergy in society. An early Protestant pamphleteer, Eberlin von Günzburg, for example, reflected a pervasive lay sentiment when he proposed that there be but one cleric for every three hundred laity.

Despite the moonlighting of poorer parish priests, the clergy as a whole, like the nobility, lived on the labor of others. Their income came from the regular collection of tithes and church taxes according to an elaborate system that evolved in the high and later Middle Ages. The church was, of course, a major landowner and regularly collected rents and fees. Monastic communities and high prelates amassed truly great fortunes; there was a popular saying that the granaries were always full in the monasteries. The immense secular power attached to high clerical posts can be seen in the intensity of the investiture struggle, when the loss of the right to present chosen clergy with the ring and staff of episcopal office seemed a direct threat to the emperor's control of his realm precisely because the bishops had become royal agents and were endowed to that purpose with royal lands that the emperor could ill afford to have slip from his control.

During the greater part of the Middle Ages the clergy were the "first estate," and theology was the queen of the sciences. How did the clergy come into such prominence? It was basically popular reverence for the clergy's role as mediator between God and humanity that made this superiority possible. The priest brought the very Son of God down to earth when he celebrated the sacrament of the Eucharist; his absolution released penitents from punishment for mortal sin. It was considered improper for mere laypeople to sit in judgment on such a priest. Theologians elaborated the distinction between the clergy and the laity

very much to the clergy's benefit. The belief in the superior status of the clergy underlay the evolution of clerical privileges and immunities in both person and property. As holy persons, the clergy could not be taxed by secular rulers without special permission from the proper ecclesiastical authorities. Clerical crimes were under the jurisdiction of special ecclesiastical courts, not the secular courts. Because churches and monasteries were deemed holy places, they, too, were free from secular taxation and legal jurisdiction. Hunted criminals, lay and clerical, regularly sought asylum within them, disrupting the normal processes of law and order. Ecclesiastical authorities were quick to threaten excommunication and interdict (the suspension of the church's sacraments, including Christian burial), which medieval towns feared almost as much as they did criminals, when this privilege of asylum was violated by city officials.

In the late Middle Ages townspeople came increasingly to resent the special immunities of the clergy. They complained that it was not proper for the clergy to have greater privileges yet far fewer responsibilities than all others who lived within the town walls. An early sixteenth-century lampoon reflected what had by then become a widespread sentiment:

> Priests, monks, and nuns
> Are but a burden to the earth.
> They have decided
> That they will not become citizens.
> That's why they're so greedy—
> They stand firm against our city
> And will swear no allegiance to it.
> And we hear their fine excuses:
> "It would cause us much toil and trouble
> Should we pledge our troth as burghers."[2]

Although the separation of Church and State and the distinction between the clergy and the laity have persisted into modern times, after the fifteenth century the clergy ceased to be the superior class they had been for so much of the Middle Ages. In both Protestant and Catholic lands governments progressively subjected them to the basic responsibilities of citizenship.

Peasants

The largest and lowest social group in medieval society was the one on whose labor the

---

[1] Denys Hay, *Europe in the Fourteenth and Fifteenth Centuries* (New York: Holt, Rinehart, 1966), pp. 58–59.

[2] Cited by S. Ozment, *The Reformation in the Cities* (New Haven, Conn.: Yale University Press, 1975), p. 36.

This aerial view of the fields surrounding a village in Leicestershire, England, where the medieval division of land has been preserved, reveals the relatively small plots farmed by medieval peasants. [Aerofilms, Ltd.]

welfare of all the others depended: the agrarian peasantry. They lived on and worked the manors of the nobility, the primitive cells of rural social life, and all were to one degree or another dependent on their lords and considered their property. The manor was originally a plot of land within a village, ranging from twelve to seventy-five acres in size, assigned to a certain member by a settled tribe or clan. This member and his family became lords of the land, and those who came to dwell there formed a smaller, self-sufficient community within a larger village community. In the early Middle Ages such a manor consisted of the dwellings of the lord and his family, the cottages of the peasant workers, agricultural sheds, and fields. The landowner or lord of the manor required a certain amount of produce (grain, eggs, and the like) and a certain number of services from the peasant families that came to dwell on and farm his land. The tenants were free to divide the labor as they wished, and what goods remained after the lord's levies were met were their own. A powerful lord might own many such manors, and kings later based their military and tax assessments on the number of manors owned by a vassal landlord.

There were both servile and free manors. The tenants of the latter had originally been freemen known as *coloni*, original inhabitants and petty landowners who swapped their small possessions for a guarantee of security from a more powerful lord, who came in this way to possess their land. Unlike the pure serfdom of the servile manors, whose tenants had no original claim to a part of the land, the tenancy obligations on free manors tended to be limited and their rights more carefully defined. Tenants of servile manors were by comparison far more vulnerable to the whims of their landlords. These two types of manor tended, however, to merge; the most common situation was the manor on which tenants of greater and lesser degrees of servitude dwelt together, their services to the lord defined by their personal status and local custom. In many regions free, self-governing peasant communities existed without any overlords and tenancy obligations.

Marc Bloch, the modern authority on manorial society, has vividly depicted the duties of tenancy:

> On certain days the tenant brings the lord's steward perhaps a few small silver coins or, more often, sheaves of grain harvested on his fields, chickens from his farmyard, cakes of wax from his beehives or from the swarms of the neighboring forest. At other times he works on the arable or the meadows of the demesne [the lord's plot of land in the manoral fields, between one third and one half of that available]. Or else we find him carting casks of wine or sacks of grain on behalf of the master to distant residences. His is the labour which repairs the walls or moats of the castle. If the master has guests the peasant strips his own bed to provide the necessary extra bed-clothes. When the hunting season comes round he feeds the pack. If war breaks out he does duty as a footsoldier or orderly, under the leadership of the reeve of the village.[3]

The lord also had the right to subject his tenants to exactions known as *banalities*. He could, for example, force them to breed their cows with his bull, and to pay for the privilege, as well as to grind their corn in his mill, bake their bread in his oven, make their wine in his

wine press, buy their beer from his brewery, and even surrender to him the tongues or other choice parts of all animals slaughtered on his lands. He had the right to levy small taxes at will.

Exploited as the serfs may appear to have been from a modern point of view, their status was far from chattel slavery. It was to the lord's advantage to keep his serfs healthy and happy; his welfare, like theirs, depended on a successful harvest. Serfs had their own dwellings and modest strips of land and lived by the produce of their own labor and organization. They were permitted to market for their own profit what surpluses might remain after the harvest. They were free to choose their spouses within the local village, although the lord's permission was required if a wife or husband was sought from another village. And serfs were able to pass their property (their dwellings and field strips) and worldly goods on to their children.

Peasants lived in mud huts with thatched roofs and, with the exception of the higher domestic servants, seldom ventured beyond their own villages. The local priest often was their window on the world, and church festivals were their major communal entertainment. Their religiosity was based in large part on the fact that the church was the only show in town, although their religious beliefs were by no means unambiguously Christian. Despite the social distinctions between free and servile serfs—and, within these groups, between those who owned ploughs and oxen and those who possessed only hoes—the common dependence on the soil forced close cooperation. As the ratio of seed to grain yield was consistently poor—about two bushels of seed were required to produce six to ten bushels of grain in good times—there was rarely an abundance of bread and ale, the staple peasant foods. There was no corn or potatoes in Europe until the sixteenth century. Pork was the major source of protein and every peasant household had its pigs. At slaughter time a family might also receive a little tough beef. But basically everyone depended on the grain crops. When they failed or fell short, the peasantry simply went hungry unless the lord had surplus stores that he was willing to share.

Two basic changes occurred in the evolution of the manor from the early to the later Middle Ages. The first was the fragmentation of the manor and the rise to dominance of the single-family unit. As the lords parceled out their land to new tenants, their own plots became pro-

[3] *Feudal Society*, trans. by L. A. Manyon (Chicago: University of Chicago Press 1968), p. 250.

A panorama of medieval society: above, soldiers, scholars, and merchants; below, peasants shown with two of the new tools which were developed between 1000 and 1200 A.D.: the large scythes with handgrips (left) made it much easier to harvest grain. The heavy plough (right) cut deeper into the soil, reducing ploughing time by half. [Bibliothèque Nationale, Paris]

A peasant sowing his field. About two bushels of seed were required to produce six to ten bushels of grain. Since medieval peasants depended on grain for most of their food, this poor yield meant that there was rarely abundant bread. [Trustees of the British Museum]

gressively smaller. The increase in tenants and the decrease in the lord's fields brought about a corresponding reduction in the labor services exacted from the tenants. In France, by the reign of Louis IX (1226–1270), only a few days a year were required, whereas in the time of Charlemagne peasants had worked the lord's fields several days a week. By the twelfth century the manor was hopelessly fragmented. As the single-family unit replaced the clan as the basic nuclear group, assessments of goods and services fell on individual fields and house-

A woodcut showing wild animals damaging peasant crops. One of the greatest problems for peasants was how to protect their crops from stags and deer. Forbidden by law from hunting them, the peasants built fences and used clubs to drive the animals away. [Deutsche Fotothek, Dresden]

Slaughter time on a medieval manor. Pork was the main source of protein for the peasantry and every household kept pigs. (Art Resource)

holds, no longer on manors as a whole. Family farms replaced manorial units. The peasants' carefully nurtured communal life made possible a family's retention of its land and dwelling after the death of the head of the household. In this way land and property remained in the possession of a single family from generation to generation.

The second change in the evolution of the manor was the translation of feudal dues into money payments, a change made possible by the revival of trade and the rise of the towns. This development, which was completed by the thirteenth century, permitted serfs to hold their land as rent-paying tenants and to overcome their servile status. Although tenants thereby gained greater freedom, they were not necessarily better off materially. Whereas servile workers had been able to count on the benevolent assistance of their landlords in hard times, rent-paying workers were left, by and large, to their own devices; their independence caused some landlords to treat them with indifference and even resentment.

Lands and properties that had been occupied by generations of peasants and were recognized as their own were always under the threat of the lord's claim to a prior right of inheritance and even outright usurpation. As their demesnes declined, the lords were increasingly tempted to encroach on such traditionally common lands. The peasantry fiercely resisted such efforts, instinctively clinging to the little they had. In many regions they successfully organized to win a role in the choice of petty rural officials. By the mid-fourteenth century a declining nobility in England and France, faced with the ravages of the great plague and the Hundred Years' War, attempted to turn back the historical clock by increasing taxes on the peasantry and passing laws to restrict their migration into the cities. The peasantry responded with armed revolts in the countryside. These revolts were rural equivalents of the organization of late medieval cities in sworn communes to protect their self-interests against territorial rulers. The revolts of the agrarian peasantry, like those of the urban proletariat, were brutally crushed. They stand out at the end of the Middle Ages as violent testimony to the breakup of medieval society. As growing national sentiment would break its political unity and heretical movements would end its nominal religious oneness, the revolts of the peasantry revealed the absence of medieval social unity.

Townspeople

In the eleventh century, towns and cities held only about 5 per cent of western Europe's population. Nonetheless one could find there the whole of medieval society: nobles visiting their townhouses, peasants living or working within the walls, resident monks and priests, university scholars, great merchants and poor journeymen, pilgrims en route to shrines, and beggars passing through. By modern comparison the great majority of medieval towns were merely small villages. Of some three thousand late medieval German towns, for example, twenty-eight hundred had populations under 1,000 and only fifteen had in excess of 10,000 inhabitants. Only London, Paris, and the great merchant capitals of Italy—Florence, Venice, and Naples—approached 100,000 by the fifteenth century.

The term *bourgeois* first appeared in the eleventh century to describe a new addition to the three traditional social ranks of knight (noble), cleric, and serf. The term initially designated the merchant groups, which formed new communities or "bourgs" as bases of operation in or around the old Roman towns that were governed by the landed nobility. These men, whose business was long-distance trade and commerce, were at first highly suspect within traditional medieval society. Clerics condemned the profits they gained from lending money as immoral usury, and noblemen viewed their fluid wealth and mobility as politically disruptive. The merchants, in turn, resented the laws and customs of feudal society that gave the nobility and the clergy special privileges. Town life was often disrupted because regional laws permitted the nobility and the clergy to live beyond the rules that governed the activities of everyone else.

Merchants especially wanted an end to the arbitrary tolls and tariffs imposed by regional magnates over the surrounding countryside. Such regulations hampered and could even bring to a standstill the flow of commerce on which both merchants and craftsmen in the growing urban export industries depended. The townspeople needed simple, uniform laws and a government sympathetic to their business interests; they wanted a government in which merchants and craftsmen had a major voice. That need created internal and external struggles with the old landed nobility. This basic conflict led towns in the high and late Middle Ages to form their own independent

The Rue du Matelas, a street in Rouen, Normandy, which was preserved intact from the Middle Ages to World War II. Note the narrowness of the street and the open sewer running down its center. The houses were built of rough cast stone, mud, and timber. [Roger-Viollet]

communes and to ally themselves with kings against the nobility—developments that bespoke the dissolution of feudal society.

Manorial society actually helped to create its urban challenger. Nobles longed for finished goods and the luxuries that came from faraway places. They urged their serfs to become skilled craftsmen. In return for a fixed rent and proper subservience, they granted charters conveying rights and privileges to those who would create towns on their land. By the eleventh century skilled serfs were beginning to pay their feudal dues in manufactured goods. Many serfs took their new skills to the growing urban centers, where they found greater freedom, as well as profits that could catapult an industrious craftsman into higher social ranks. As the migration of serfs to the towns accelerated, the lords offered them greater freedom and more favorable terms of tenure to keep them on the land. The twelfth and thirteenth centuries saw a mass "freeing" of serfs in the sense of a formal contractual fixing of rights and required services—a privilege heretofore known only by freemen. But serfs simply could not be kept down on the farm after they had seen the opportunities of town life. Rural society not only gave the towns their craftsmen and day laborers, but the first merchants themselves appear to have been wandering, enterprising serfs.

Despite unified resistance to external domination, the medieval town was not an internally harmonious social unit. It was a collection of many selfish, competitive communities. Only families of long standing and those who owned property had the full rights of citizenship and a say in the town's government. Workers in the same trade lived together on streets that bore their name, apparently doing so as much to monitor one another's business practices as to dwell among peers. Sumptuary laws regulated not only the dress but even the architecture of the residences of the various social groups. Merchant guilds appeared in the eleventh century and were followed in the twelfth by the craft guilds (organizations of drapers, haberdashers, furriers, hosiers, goldsmiths, and so on). These organizations existed solely to advance the business interests of their members and to advance their personal well-

being. They won favorable government policies and served as collection agencies for the unpaid accounts of individual members. The guilds also formed distinctive religious confraternities, close-knit associations that ministered to the needs of member families in both life and death.

The merchants and the stronger craft guilds quickly won a role in town government. "New-rich" patricians married into the old nobility and aped their social customs. Sharing the power of government in the city councils, the craft guilds used their position in the most selfish way to limit their membership, to regulate their own wages favorably, and to establish exacting standards of workmanship so that their products could not be copied by others (trademarks first appeared in the twelfth century). So rigid and exclusive did the dominant

275

A medieval apothecary weighing out his herbs. Apothecaries, like other merchants and craftsmen, were organized in their own guild. (Art Resource)

guilds become that they stifled their own creativity and inflamed the journeymen who were excluded from joining their ranks. In the fourteenth century unrepresented artisans and craftsmen, a true urban proletariat prevented by law from either forming their own guilds or entering the existing guilds, revolted in a number of places: Florence, Paris, and the cities of Flanders. Their main opponents were the merchant and craft guilds, which had themselves risen to prominence by opposing the antiquated laws and privileges of the old nobility.

A medieval shoemaker. Guilds of shoemakers date back to Ancient Rome. In the Middle Ages most people wore homemade clogs or wooden shoes. Leather shoes made to order by skilled craftsmen could be quite costly and elaborate in style and were mostly for the upper classes. [Vincent Virga Archives]

276

Medieval Women

The image and the reality of medieval women are two very different things. The image, both for contemporaries and for us today, was strongly influenced by male Christian clergy, whose ideal was the celibate life of chastity, poverty, and obedience. Drawing on classical medical, philosophical, and legal traditions that predated Christianity, as well as on ancient biblical theology, Christian theologians depicted women as physically, mentally, and morally weaker than men. On the basis of such assumptions medieval church and society sanctioned the coercive treatment of women, including corrective wife-beating. Christian clergy generally considered marriage a debased state by comparison with the religious life, and in their writings they praised virgins and celibate widows over wives. Women, as the Bible clearly taught, were the "weaker vessel." In marriage their role was to be subject and obedient to their husbands, who, as the stronger, had a duty to protect and discipline them.

This image of the medieval woman suggests that she had two basic options in life: to become either a subjugated housewife or a confined nun. In reality, the vast majority of medieval women were neither.

Both within and outside Christianity this image of women—not yet to speak of the reality of their lives—was contradicted. In chivalric romances and courtly love literature of the twelfth and thirteenth centuries, as in the contemporaneous cult of the Virgin Mary, women were presented as objects of service and devotion to be praised and admired, even put on pedestals and treated as superior to men. If the church shared traditional misogynist sentiments, it also condemned them, as in the case of the *Romance of the Rose* (late thirteenth century) and other popular "bawdy" literature. The learned churchman Peter Lombard (1100–1169) sanctioned an image of women that was often invoked in didactic Christian literature. Why, he asked, was Eve created from Adam's rib and not instead taken from his head or his feet? The answer was clear. God took Eve from Adam's side because he wanted woman neither to rule over nor to be enslaved by man, but to stand squarely at his side, as his companion and partner in mutual aid and trust. By so insisting on the spiritual equality of men and women and their shared responsibility to one another within marriage, the church also helped to raise the dignity of women.

A lady and her knight. The literature of chivalry and courtly love presented aristocratic women as objects of service and devotion, to be put on a pedestal by men. [University of Heidelberg]

Women also had basic rights under secular law that prevented them from being treated as mere chattel. All the major Germanic law codes recognized the economic freedom of women, that is, their right to inherit, administer, dispose of, and confer on their children family property and wealth. They could press charges in court against men for bodily injury and rape. Depending on the country in question, punishments for rape ranged from fines, flogging, and banishment to blinding, castration, and death.

The nunnery was an option for only a very small number of unmarried women from the uppermost classes. Entrance required a dowry *(dos)* and could be almost as expensive as a wedding, although usually it was less. Within the nunnery, a woman could rise to a position of leadership as abbess or mother superior and could exercise an organizational and administrative authority denied her in much of secular

The vast majority of medieval women were working peasants and townswomen. This fourteenth-century English manuscript shows women at their daily tasks: carrying jugs of fresh milk from the sheep pen, feeding chickens, and, most importantly, spinning and carding wool. [Trustees of the British Museum]

Townswomen at work in a medieval market. Although they practised virtually every "blue-collar" trade, medieval women were especially active in the food industry. (Art Resource)

life. However, the nunneries of the established religious orders were also under male supervision, so that even abbesses had finally to answer to higher male authority.

Nunneries also provided women an escape from the debilitating effects of multiple pregnancies. When, in the ninth century, under the influence of Christianity, the Carolingians made monogamous marriage their official policy (heretofore they had practiced polygyny and concubinage and had permitted divorce), it was both a boon and a burden to women. On the one hand, the selection of a wife now became a very special event. Wives gained greater dignity and legal security. On the other hand, a woman's labor as household manager and the bearer of children greatly increased. The aristocratic wife not only ran a large household but was also the agent of her husband during his absence. In addition to these responsibilities, one wife now had sole responsibility for the propagation of heirs. Such demands clearly took their toll. The mortality rates of Frankish women increased and their longevity decreased after the ninth century.

The Carolingian wife also became the sole object of her husband's wrath and displeasure. Under such conditions the cloister could serve as a welcome refuge to women. However, the number of women in cloisters was never very great. In late medieval England, for example, there are estimated to have been no more than thirty-five hundred.

The vast majority of medieval women were neither aristocratic housewives nor nuns, but working women. Every evidence suggests that they were respected and loved by their husbands, perhaps because they worked shoulder by shoulder and hour by hour with them. Between the ages of ten and fifteen, girls were apprenticed in a trade much as were boys, and they learned to be skilled workers. If they married, they either continued their particular trade, operating their bakeshops or dress shops next to their husbands' business, or they became assistants and partners in the shops of their husbands. Women appeared in virtually every "blue-collar" trade, from butchers to goldsmiths, although they were especially active in the food and clothing industries.

Women belonged to guilds, just like men, and they became craftmasters. In the later Middle Ages, townswomen increasingly had the opportunity to go to school and to gain vernacular literacy.

It is also true that women did not have as wide a range of vocations as men. They were excluded from the learned professions of scholarship, medicine, and law. They often found their freedom of movement within a profession more carefully regulated than a man's. Usually women performed the same work as men for a wage 25 per cent lower. And, as is still true today, they filled the ranks of domestic servants in disproportionate numbers. Still, women were as prominent and as creative a part of workaday medieval society as men.

Medieval Children

Historians have found much evidence to suggest that medieval parents remained emotionally distant from their children, showing them little interest and affection. Evidence of low parental regard for children comes from a variety of sources. First, the art and sculpture of the Middle Ages rarely portray children as distinct from adults; pictorially, children and adults look alike. Then, there was high infant and child mortality, which could only have made emotional investment in children risky. How could a medieval parent, knowing that a child had a 30–50 per cent chance of dying before age five, dare become too emotionally attached? Also, during the Middle Ages, children directly assumed adult responsibilities. The children of peasants became laborers in the fields alongside their parents as soon as they could physically manage the work. Urban artisans and burghers sent their children out of their homes to apprentice in various crafts and trades between the ages of eight and twelve. In many, perhaps most, instances a child was placed in the home of a known relative or friend, but often he or she ended up with a mere acquaintance, even a complete stranger. That children were expected to grow up fast in the Middle Ages is also suggested by the canonical ages for marriage: twelve for girls and fourteen for boys.

Infanticide is an even more striking indication of low esteem for children. The ancient Romans exposed unwanted children at birth. In this way they regulated family size, and the surviving children appear to have been given both attention and affection. The Germanic tribes of medieval Europe, by contrast, had large families but tended to neglect their children. Infanticide appears to have been directed primarily against girls. Early medieval penance books and church synods condemned the practice outright and also forbade parents to sleep with infants and small children, as this became an occasion and an excuse (alleged accidental suffocation) for killing them.

Also, among the German tribes one paid a much lower *wergild*, or fine, for injury to a child than for injury to an adult. The *wergild* for injuring a child was only one fifth that for injuring an adult. That paid for injury to a female child under fifteen was one half that for injury to a male child—a strong indication that female children were the least esteemed members of German tribal society. Mothers appear also to have nursed boys longer than they did girls, which favored boys' health and survival. However, a woman's *wergild* increased a full eightfold between infancy and her childbearing years, at which time she had obviously become highly prized.[4]

Despite such varied evidence of parental neglect of children, there is another side to the story. Since the early Middle Ages, physicians and theologians, at least, have clearly understood childhood to be a distinct and special stage of life. Isidore of Seville (560–636), the metropolitan of Seville and a leading intellectual authority throughout the Middle Ages, carefully distinguished six ages of life, the first four of which were infancy (between one and seven years of age), childhood (seven to fourteen), adolescence, and youth. According to the medical authorities, infancy proper extended from birth to anywhere between six months and two years (depending on the authority) and covered the period of speechlessness and suckling. The period thereafter, until age seven, was considered a higher level of infancy, marked by the beginning of a child's ability to speak and his or her weaning. At age seven, when a child could think and act decisively and speak clearly, childhood proper began. After this point, a child could be reasoned with, could profit from regular discipline, and could begin to train for a lifelong vocation. At seven a child was ready for schooling, private tutoring, or an apprenticeship in a chosen craft or trade. Until physical

[4]David Herlihy, "Medieval Children," in *Essays on Medieval Civilization*, ed. by B. K. Lackner and K. R. Phelp (University of Texas Press, 1978), pp. 109–131.

growth was completed, however—and that could extend to twenty-one years of age—a child or youth was legally under the guardianship of parents or a surrogate authority.

There is evidence that high infant and child mortality, rather than distancing parents from children, actually made them look on them as all the more precious. The medical authorities of the Middle Ages—Hippocrates, Galen, and Soranus of Ephesus—dealt at length with postnatal care and childhood diseases. Both in learned and popular medicine, sensible as well as fanciful cures can be found for the leading killers of children (diarrhea, worms, pneumonia, and fever). When infants and children died, medieval parents grieved as pitiably as modern parents do. In the art and literature of the Middle Ages, we find mothers baptizing dead infants and children or carrying them to pilgrim shrines in the hope of reviving them. There are also examples of mental illness and suicide brought on by the death of a child.[5]

We also find a variety of children's toys, even devices like walkers and potty chairs, clear evidence of special attention being paid to children. The medieval authorities on child rearing

[5]Klaus Arnold, *Kind und Gesellschaft im Mittelalter und Renaissance* (Paderborn, 1980), pp. 31, 37.

Parents bathing a child. High child mortality may have made medieval parents consider those children who survived even more precious. [Trustees of the British Museum]

Children watching a puppet show. [Trustees of the British Museum]

widely condemned child abuse and urged moderation in the disciplining of children. In church art and drama, parents were urged to love their children as Mary loved Jesus. By the high Middle Ages, if not earlier, children were widely viewed as special creatures with their own needs and possessed of their own rights.

England and France: Hastings (1066) to Bouvines (1214)

William the Conqueror

The most important change in English political life was occasioned in 1066 by the death of the childless Anglo-Saxon ruler Edward the Confessor, so-named because of his reputation for piety. Edward's mother was a Norman princess, and this fact gave the duke of Normandy a hereditary claim to the English throne. Before his death Edward, who was not a strong ruler, acknowledged this claim and even directed that his throne be given to William of Normandy (d. 1087). But the Anglo-Saxon assembly, which customarily bestowed

the royal power, had a mind of its own and vetoed Edward's last wishes. It chose instead Harold Godwinsson. This defiant action brought the swift conquest of England by the powerful Normans. William's forces defeated Harold's army at Hastings on October 14, 1066. Within weeks of the invasion William was crowned king of England in Westminster Abbey, both by right of heredity and by right of conquest.

Thereafter all of England became William's domain. Every landholder, whether large or small, was henceforth his vassal, holding land legally as a fief from the king. William organized his new English nation shrewdly. On the one hand, he established a strong monarchy whose power was not fragmented by independent territorial princes. On the other hand, he took care not to destroy Anglo-Saxon democratic traditions, which had been nurtured by Alfred the Great (871–899), who, although a strong and willful king, still cherished the advice of his councilors in the making of laws, and had been respected by Canute (1016–1035), the Dane who restored order and brought unity to England after the civil wars

William the Conqueror, on horseback, leads his Norman troops against the English at the Battle of Hastings (October 14, 1066). From the Bayeux Tapestry, about 1073–1083. [Musée de l'Évêché, Bayeux, France. Avec autorisation spéciale de la ville de Bayeux. Giraudon]

How William the Conqueror Won the Battle of Hastings

This account of the Battle of Hastings appears in the *Chronicle* of the kings of England, written by a Benedictine monk, William of Malmesbury, the son of a Norman father and an English mother. Although William wrote over a half century after the Battle of Hastings, his chronicle is our fullest account of these events.

The courageous leaders mutually prepared for battle, each according to his national custom. The English passed the night without sleep, in drinking and singing, and in the morning proceeded without delay against the enemy. All on foot, armed with battle-axes, and covering themselves in front by joining their shields, they formed an impenetrable body. . . . King Harold himself, on foot, stood with his brothers near the standard in order that, so long as all shared equal danger, none could think of retreating. . . .

The Normans passed the whole night in confessing their sins, and received the communion of the Lord's body in the morning. Their infantry, with bows and arrows, formed the vanguard, while their cavalry, divided into wings, was placed in the rear. The duke [of Normandy], with serene countenance, declaring aloud that God would favor his . . . side, called for his arms. . . . Then starting the song of Roland, in order that . . . the example of that

[early French war] hero might stimulate the soldiers, and calling on God for assistance, the battle commenced on both sides . . . neither side yielding ground during the greater part of the day.

Observing this, William gave a signal to his troops, that, pretending flight, they should withdraw from the field. By means of this device the solid phalanx of the English opened for the purpose of cutting down the fleeing enemy and thus brought upon itself swift destruction; for the Normans, facing about, attacked them, thus disordered, and compelled them to fly. . . . [The English were not] without their own revenge, for, by frequently making a stand, they slaughtered their pursuers in heaps. . . . [Such] alternating victory, first by one side and then by the other, continued as long as Harold lived to check the retreat; but when he fell, his brain pierced by an arrow, the flight of the English ceased not until night.

Frederic Austin Ogg (Ed.), *A Source Book of Mediaeval History: Documents Illustrative of European Life and Institutions from the German Invasions to the Renaissance* (New York: American Book Co., 1908), pp. 235–237.

that had engulfed the land during the reign of the incompetent Ethelred II (978–1016). The Norman king thoroughly subjected his noble vassals to the crown, yet he also consulted with them regularly about decisions of "state." The result was a unique blending of the "one" and the "many," a balance between monarchical and parliamentary elements that has ever since characterized English government.

For the purposes of administration and taxation William commissioned a county-by-county survey of his new realm, a detailed accounting known as the *Domesday Book* (1080–1086). The title of the book reflects the thoroughness of the survey: just as none would escape the doomsday judgment of God, so none was overlooked by William's assessors.

Henry II

William's son, Henry I (ruled 1100–1135), died without a male heir, throwing England into virtual anarchy until Henry II (1154–1189), son of the duke of Anjou and Matilda, daughter of Henry I, mounted the throne as head of the new Plantagenet dynasty. Under Henry II the English monarchy began to drift toward an oppressive rule. Henry brought to the throne greatly expanded French holdings, partly by inheritance from his father (Burgundy and Anjou) and partly by his marriage to Eleanor of Aquitaine (1122?–1204), a union that created the so-called Angevin or English-French empire. Eleanor married Henry while he was still the count of Anjou and not yet king of England. The marriage occurred only eight weeks after the annulment of Eleanor's fifteen-year marriage to the ascetic French king Louis VII in March 1152. Although the annulment was granted on grounds of consanguinity (blood relationship), the true reason for the dissolution of the marriage was Louis's suspicion of infidelity (according to rumor, Eleanor had been intimate with her cousin). The annulment was very costly to Louis, who lost Aquitaine together with his wife. Eleanor bore Henry eight children, five of them sons, among them the future kings Richard the Lion-Hearted and John. Not only did England, under Henry, come to control most of the coast of France, but Henry also conquered a part of Ireland and made the king of Scotland his vassal.

The French king, Louis VII, who had lost both his wife and considerable French land to Henry, saw a mortal threat to France in this English expansion. He responded by adopting what came to be a permanent French policy of containment and expulsion of the English from their continental holdings in France—a policy that was not finally successful until the mid-fifteenth century, when English power on the Continent collapsed at the conclusion of the Hundred Years' War.

Eleanor of Aquitaine and Court Culture

Eleanor of Aquitaine helped shape court culture and literature in France and England. After marrying Henry, she settled in Angers, the chief town of Anjou, where she sponsored troubadours and poets at her lively court. There the troubadour Bernart de Ventadorn composed in Eleanor's honor many of the most popular love songs of high medieval aristocratic society. Eleanor spent the years 1154–1170 as Henry's queen in England. She separated from him in 1170, partly because of his public philandering and cruel treatment, taking revenge by joining Louis VII in stirring Henry's three sons, who were unhappy with the terms of their inheritance, to rebellion against their father in 1173. During the last years of his life (1179–1189), Henry placed Eleanor under mild house arrest to prevent any further such mischief.

After her separation from Henry in 1170 Eleanor lived in Poitiers with her daughter Marie, the countess of Champagne, and the two made the court of Poitiers a famous center for the literature of courtly love. This literary

The effigy of Eleanor of Aquitaine, who had been queen of France as well as queen of England, is on her tomb at Fontevrault Abbey in France. [*The Granger Collection*]

genre, with its thinly veiled eroticism, has been viewed as an attack on medieval ascetic values. Be that as it may, it was certainly a commentary on contemporary problems within the domestic life of the aristocracy. The code of chivalry that guided the relations between lords and their vassals looked on the seduction of the wife of one's lord as the most heinous of offenses. In some areas such adultery was punished by castration and/or execution. The troubadours hardly promoted such promiscuity at court. They rather presented in a frank and entertaining way stories that satirized or depicted in tragic irony illicit carnal love, while glorifying the ennobling power of friendly or "courteous" love. The most famous courtly literature was Chrétien de Troyes's stories of King Arthur and the Knights of the Round Table, which contained the tragic story of Sir Lancelot's secret and illicit love for Arthur's wife, Guinevere.

Popular Rebellion and Magna Carta

As Henry II acquired new lands abroad, he became more autocratic at home, subjecting his vassals more than ever to the royal yoke.

He forced his will on the clergy in the Constitutions of Clarendon (1164), measures that placed limitations on judicial appeals to Rome, subjected the clergy to the civil courts, and gave the king control over the election of bishops. The result was strong political resistance from both the nobility and the clergy. The archbishop of Canterbury, Thomas à Becket (1118?–1170), once Henry's compliant chancellor, broke openly with the king and fled to Louis VII. Becket's subsequent assassination in 1170 and his canonization by Pope Alexander III in 1172 forced the king to retreat from his heavy-handed tactics, as popular resentment grew. (Two hundred years later Geoffrey Chaucer, writing in an age made cynical by the Black Death and the Hundred Years' War, had the pilgrims of his *Canterbury Tales* journey to the shrine of Thomas à Becket.)

English resistance to the king became outright rebellion under Henry's successors, the brothers Richard the Lion-Hearted (1189–1199) and John (1199–1216). Their burdensome taxation in support of unnecessary foreign Crusades and a failing war with France left the English people little alternative. Richard had to be ransomed at a high price from the Holy Roman Emperor Henry VI, who had taken him prisoner during his return from the ill-fated Third Crusade. In 1209 Pope Innocent III excommunicated King John and placed England under interdict. This humiliating experience saw the king of England declare his country a fief of the pope. But it was the defeat

Henry II of England with Archbishop Thomas à Becket of Canterbury. Becket's murder by courtiers of the king brought the wrath of the Church on Henry, who was forced to abandon his autocratic attempt to control the English Church. [Trustees of the British Museum]

The English Nobility Imposes Restraints on King John

The gradual building of a sound English constitutional system in the Middle Ages was in danger of going awry if a monarch overstepped the fine line dividing necessary strength from outright despotism. The danger became acute under the rule of King John. The English nobility, therefore, forced the king's recognition of Magna Carta (1215), which reaffirmed the traditional rights and personal liberties of free men against royal authority. The document has remained enshrined in English law.

A free man shall not be fined for a small offense, except in proportion to the gravity of the offense; and for a great offense he shall be fined in proportion to the magnitude of the offense, saving his freehold; and a merchant in the same way, saving his merchandise; and the villein shall be fined in the same way, saving his wainage, if he shall be at our [i.e., the king's] mercy; and none of the above fines shall be imposed except by the oaths of honest men of the neighborhood. . . .

No constable or other bailiff of ours [i.e., the king's] shall take anyone's grain or other chattels without immediately paying for them in money, unless he is able to obtain a postponement at the good will of the seller.

No constable shall require any knight to give money in place of his ward of a castle [i.e., standing guard] if he is willing to furnish that ward in his own person, or through another honest man if he himself is not able to do it for a reasonable cause; and if we shall lead or send him into the army he shall be free from ward in proportion to the amount of time which he has been in the army through us.

No sheriff or bailiff of ours [i.e., the king's], or any one else, shall take horses or wagons of any free man, for carrying purposes, except on the permission of that free man.

Neither we nor our bailiffs will take the wood of another man for castles, or for anything else which we are doing, except by the permission of him to whom the wood belongs. . . .

No free man shall be taken, or imprisoned, or dispossessed, or outlawed, or banished, or in any way injured, nor will we go upon him, nor send upon him, except by the legal judgment of his peers, or by the law of the land.

To no one will we sell, to no one will we deny or delay, right or justice.

James Harvey Robinson (Ed.), *Readings in European History,* Vol. 1 (Boston: Atheneaum, 1904), pp. 236–237.

---

of the English by the French at Bouvines in 1214 that proved the last straw. With the full support of the clergy and the townspeople, the English barons revolted against John. The popular rebellion ended with the king's grudging recognition of Magna Carta ("Great Charter") in 1215.

This monumental document was a victory of feudal over monarchical power in the sense that it secured the rights of the many—the nobility, the clergy, and the townspeople—over the autocratic king; it restored the internal balance of power that had been the English political experience since the Norman Conquest. The English people, at least the privileged English people, thereby preserved their right to be represented at the highest levels of government, especially in matters of taxation. The monarchy remained intact, however, and its legitimate powers and rights were duly recognized and preserved. This outcome contrasted with the experience on the Continent, where victorious nobility tended to humiliate kings and emperors and undo all efforts at centralization.

With a peculiar political genius the English consistently refused to tolerate either the absorption of the power of the monarchy by the nobility or the abridgment of the rights of the nobility by the monarchy. Although King John continued to resist the Great Charter in every way he could, his son Henry III formally ratified it, and it has ever since remained a cornerstone of English law.

Although Gothic architecture was adopted throughout medieval Europe (Gothic cathedrals were built in cities from Compostella in northern Spain to Cracow in Poland), it originated in France and enjoyed immense popularity there. Gothic was, in fact, often known in the Middle Ages as the "French style." Among the earliest examples of French Gothic architecture was the abbey church of Saint Denis near Paris, built by Abbot Suger between 1137–1144. This photograph shows the ribbed vaulting and pointed arches in the interior of the church. [Jean Roubier]

Beginning in the mid-twelfth century, the Gothic style evolved from romanesque architecture. Gothic at first meant "barbaric" and was applied to the new style by its critics. Its most distinctive visible features are its ribbed, criss-crossing vaulting, its pointed arches rather than rounded ones, and its frequent exterior buttresses. The result gives an essential impression of vertical lines. The vaulting and the extensive addition of "flying" buttresses made possible more height than the Romanesque style and sought. Because walls, therefore, did not have to carry all of a structure's weight, wide expanses of windows were possible—hence the extensive use of stained glass and the characteristic color that often floods Gothic cathedrals. Use of the windows to show stories from the Bible, saints' lives, and local events was similar to earlier use of mosaics.

This diagram show the typical vaulting, arches, and buttresses of a Gothic building. [World Architecture, Trewin Copplestone, General Editor (London: Hamlyn, 1963), p. 216.)

Two further examples of French Gothic: (left) Reims, where the kings of France were crowned, and (opposite) Chartres, one of the supreme masterpieces of medieval architecture. (Jean Roubier, Scala/Art Resource; Manley Photo/Shostal)

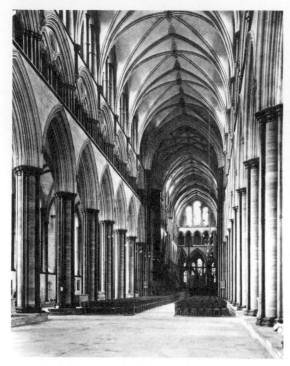

The interior of Salisbury cathedral, showing the vaulting and the pointed arches. [The National Monuments Record, London]

ABOVE: *The ability of Gothic architecture to achieve a light, airy effect and, as it were, to lift the viewer heavenward, is illustrated by the whole of Milan cathedral, of which this illustration shows only one detail. Begun in 1386, the cathedral was not completed until the nineteenth century. This is the main spire, built in 1750, as seen from the roof. [AHM]*

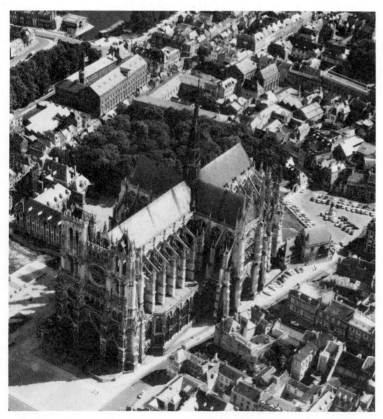

LEFT: *The cathedral at Amiens, France, is another splendid example of the thirteenth-century flowering of Gothic architecture. [Aerofilms Limited]*

Salisbury cathedral, built 1220–1265, an example of English Gothic. Note the flying buttresses, which permit greater height, and the soaring towers and spire. [British Tourist Authority, New York]

Philip II Augustus

During the century and a half between the Norman Conquest (1066) and Magna Carta (1215), a strong monarchy was never in question in England. The English struggle in the high Middle Ages was to secure the rights of the many, not the authority of the king. The French faced the reverse problem in this period. Powerful feudal princes dominated France for two centuries, from the beginning of the Capetian dynasty (987) until the reign of Philip II Augustus (1180–1223). During this period the Capetian kings wisely concentrated their limited resources on securing the royal domain, their uncontested territory round about Paris known as the Île-de-France. They did not rashly challenge the more powerful nobility. Aggressively exercising their feudal rights in this area, they secured absolute obedience and a solid base of power. By the time of Philip II, Paris had become the center of French government and culture, and the Capetian dynasty had become a secure hereditary monarchy. Thereafter the kings of France were in a position to impose their will on the French nobles, who were always in law, if not in political fact, the king's sworn vassals.

The Norman conquest of England helped stir France to unity and make it possible for the Capetian kings to establish a truly national monarchy. The duke of Normandy, who after 1066 was master of the whole of England, was also among the vassals of the French king in Paris. Capetian kings understandably watched with alarm as the power of their Norman vassal grew. Other powerful vassals of the king also watched with alarm. King Louis VI (1108–1137) entered an alliance with Flanders, which had traditionally been a Norman enemy. King Louis VII (1137–1180), assisted by a brilliant minister, Suger, the abbot of St. Denis and famous for his patronage of Gothic architecture, found allies in the great northern French cities and used their wealth to build a royal army. Philip II Augustus, Louis VII's successor, inherited financial resources and an administrative bureaucracy, which in his capable hands resisted the divisive French nobility and clergy and pressed the contest with the English king.

Philip Augustus faced, at the same time, an internal and an international struggle, and he was successful in both. His armies occupied all the English territories on the French coast, with the exception of Aquitaine. As the show-down with the English neared on the Continent, however, the Holy Roman Emperor Otto IV (1198–1215) entered the fray on the side of the English, and the French found themselves assailed from both east and west. But when the international armies finally clashed at Bouvines on July 27, 1214, in what became the first great European battle in history, the French won handily over the English and the Germans. This victory unified France around the monarchy and thereby laid the foundation for French ascendancy in the later Middle Ages. Philip Augustus also gained control of the lucrative urban industries of Flanders. The defeat so weakened Otto IV that he fell from power in Germany.

The Pontificate of Innocent III (1198–1215)

The New Papal Monarchy

Pope Innocent III, a papal monarch in the Gregorian tradition of papal independence from secular domination, proclaimed and practiced as none before him the doctrine of the plenitude of papal power. In a famous statement he likened the relationship of the pope to the emperor—or the Church to the State—to that of the sun to the moon. As the moon received its light from the sun, so the emperor received his brilliance (that is, his crown) from the hand of the pope—an allusion to the famous precedent set on Christmas Day, 800, when Pope Leo III crowned Charlemagne. Although this pretentious theory greatly exceeded Innocent's ability to practice it, he and his successors did not hesitate to act on their ambitions. When Philip II tried unlawfully to annul his marriage, Innocent placed France under interdict, suspending all church services save baptism and the last rites. And the same punishment befell England with even greater force when King John refused to accept Innocent's nominee to the archbishopric of Canterbury.

Innocent made the papacy a great secular power, with financial resources and a bureaucracy equal to those of contemporary monarchs. It was during his reign that the papacy transformed itself into that efficient ecclesiocommercial complex attacked by reformers throughout the later Middle Ages. Innocent consolidated and expanded ecclesiastical taxes on the laity, the chief of which at this time was

Pope Innocent III (1198–1215). Innocent made the papacy a great power, with financial resources and a bureaucracy equal to those of secular monarchies. [SCALA/Art Resource]

Innocent's predilection for power politics also expressed itself in his use of the Crusade, the traditional weapon of the church against Islam, to suppress internal dissent and heresy. The latter had grown under the influence of religious reform movements attempting, often naively, to disassociate the church from the growing materialism of the age and to keep it pure of political purpose. In 1209 he launched a Crusade against the Albigensians, or Cathars ("pure ones"), advocates of an ascetic, dualist religion who were concentrated in the area of Albi in Languedoc in southern France, but who also had adherents among the laity in Italy and Spain. The Albigensians opposed Christian teaching on several points. They denied the Old Testament and its God of wrath, as well as the Christian belief in God's incarnation in Jesus Christ, and many rejected human procreation either by extreme sexual asceticism or by the use of contraceptives (sponges and acidic ointments) and even abortion—this in the belief that to continue corporeal bodies was to prolong the imprisonment of one's immortal soul. They sought instead a pure and simple religious life, following the model of the apostles of Jesus in the New Testament. It was in opposition to such sects, who even challenged the propagation of the human species, that the church developed its social teachings on contraception and abortion.

The Crusades against the heretics were carried out by powerful noblemen from northern France. These great magnates, led by Simon de Montfort, were as much attracted by the great wealth of the area of Languedoc, among the richest regions of Europe at the time, as they were moved by Christian conscience to stamp out heresy. A succession of massacres occurred, ending with a Crusade led by King Louis VIII of France in 1225–1226, which completely destroyed the Albigensians as a political entity. Pope Gregory IX (1227–1241) introduced the Inquisition into the region to complete the work of the Crusaders. This institution, a formal tribunal for the detection and punishment of heresy, had been in use by the church since the mid-twelfth century as a way for bishops to maintain diocesan discipline. During Innocent's pontificate it became centralized in the papacy, and papal legates were dispatched to chosen regions to conduct the interrogations and subsequent trials and executions.

Peter's pence, long a levy on all but the poorest English houses, which became a lump-sum payment by the English crown in the twelfth century. He imposed an income tax of 2.5 per cent on the clergy. Annates (the payment of a portion or all of the first year's income received by the holder of a new benefice) and fees for the pallium (the symbol of episcopal office) became especially popular revenue-gathering devices employed by the pope. Innocent also reserved to the pope the absolution of many sins and religious crimes, forcing those desirous of pardons or exemptions to bargain directly with Rome. It was a measure of the degree to which the papacy had embraced the new money economy that Lombard merchants and bankers were employed by Rome to collect the growing papal revenues.

It was also during Innocent's pontificate that the Fourth Crusade to the Holy Land was launched (1202). Its stunning capture of Constantinople established Latin control of the Eastern Empire until 1261, when the Eastern emperor Michael Paleologus, assisted by the Genoese, who envied Venetian prosperity in the East, finally recaptured the city. Innocent was initially embarrassed by the fall of Constantinople to the Crusaders. But the papacy soon adjusted to this unforeseen turn of events and shared in the spoils. The Eastern base gave the Western church a unique opportunity. A confidant of Innocent's, Tommaso Morosini, became patriarch of Constantinople and launched a mission to win the Greeks and the Slavs back to the Roman church. The almost fifty-year occupation of Constantinople did nothing to heal the political and religious divi-

sions between East and West. To the contrary, it only intensified Eastern resentment of the West.

The Fourth Lateran Council

Under Innocent's direction the Fourth Lateran Council met in 1215 to establish hierarchical church discipline from pope to parish. This council was a landmark in ecclesiastical legislation. It gave the controversial theory of transubstantiation full dogmatic sanction, and the Catholic Church has ever since taught that the bread and wine of the Lord's Supper become the true body and blood of Christ on consecration by the priest. The council also made annual confession and Easter communion mandatory for every adult Christian. This latter legislation formalized the sacrament of pen-

---

Saint Francis of Assisi Sets Out His Religious Ideals

Saint Francis of Assisi (1182–1226) was the founder of the Franciscan Order of friars. Here are some of his religious principles as stated in the definitive Rule of the Order, approved by the pope in 1223; the rule especially stresses the ideal of living in poverty.

This is the rule and way of living of the Minorite brothers, namely, to observe the holy Gospel of our Lord Jesus Christ, living in obedience, without personal possessions, and in chastity. Brother Francis promises obedience and reverence to our lord Pope Honorius, and to his successors who canonically enter upon their office, and to the Roman Church. And the other brothers shall be bound to obey Brother Francis and his successors.

I firmly command all the brothers by no means to receive coin or money, of themselves or through an intervening person. But for the needs of the sick and for clothing the other brothers, the ministers alone and the guardians shall provide through spiritual friends, as it may seem to them that necessity demands, according to time, place, and the coldness of the temperature. This one thing being always borne in mind, that, as has been said, they receive neither coin nor money.

Those brothers to whom God has given the ability to labor shall do so faithfully and devoutly, but in such manner that idleness, the enemy of the soul, being averted, they may not extinguish the spirit of holy prayer and devotion, to which other temporal things should be subservient. As a reward, moreover, for their labor, they may receive for themselves and their brothers the necessities of life, but not coin or money; and this humbly, as becomes the servants of God and the followers of most holy poverty.

The brothers shall appropriate nothing to themselves, neither a house, nor a place, nor anything; but as pilgrims and strangers in this world, in poverty and humility serving God, they shall confidently go seeking for alms. Nor need they be ashamed, for the Lord made Himself poor for us in this world.

A Source Book of Mediaeval History, ed. by Frederic Austin Ogg (New York: Cooper Square Publishers, 1972), pp. 375–376.

ance as the church's key instrument of religious education and discipline in the later Middle Ages.

Franciscans and Dominicans

No action of Pope Innocent affected religious life more than his official sanction of the mendicant orders of the Franciscans and the Dominicans. Lay interest in religious devotion, especially among urban women, was particularly intense at the turn of the twelfth century. In addition to the heretical Albigensians, there were movements of Waldensians, Beguines, and Beghards, each of which stressed biblical simplicity in religion and aspired to a life of poverty in imitation of Christ. They were especially vocal in Italy and France. The heterodox teachings and critical frame of mind within these movements caused the pope deep concern that lay piety would turn against the church in militant fashion. The Franciscan and Dominican orders were a response to heterodox piety as well as an answer to lay criticism of the worldliness of the papal monarchy. Unlike other regular clergy, the friars went out into the world to preach the church's mission and to combat heresy, begging or working to support themselves.

The Franciscan Order was founded by Saint Francis of Assisi (1182–1226), the son of a rich Italian cloth merchant, who became disaffected with wealth and urged his followers to practice extreme poverty. Pope Innocent recognized the order in 1210 and its official rule was approved in 1223. The Dominican Order, the Order of Preachers, was founded by Saint Dominic (1170–1221), a well-educated Spanish cleric, and was sanctioned in 1216. Both orders received special privileges from the pope and were solely under his jurisdiction. This special relationship with Rome gave the friars an independence from local clerical authority that caused them to be resented by some secular clergy.

Pope Gregory IX (1227–1241) canonized Saint Francis only two years after his death. That was both a fitting honor for Francis and a stroke of genius on the part of the pope. By bringing the age's most popular religious figure, one who had even miraculously received the stigmata (bleeding wounds like those of the crucified Jesus), so emphatically within the confines of the church, he enhanced papal authority over lay piety.

Two years after the canonization Gregory

New religious orders were founded throughout the Middle Ages. Unlike the clergy of other orders, however, Franciscans (in dark robes) and Dominicans (in white) did not live in cloister, but went out into the world to combat heresy. [Bibliotheque Nationale]

canceled Saint Francis's own *Testament*, which had admonished a life of strictest poverty. The pope set it aside as an authoritative rule for Franciscans both because he found it to be an impractical guide for the order and because the nonconventual life of nomadic poverty urged by Francis on his followers conflicted with papal plans to enlist the order as an arm of church policy. A majority of Franciscans themselves, under the leadership of moderates like Saint Bonaventure, general of the order between 1257 and 1274, also came to doubt the wisdom of extreme asceticism. During the thirteenth century the order progressively complied with papal wishes. In the fourteenth century the Spiritual Franciscans, extreme followers of Saint Francis who considered him almost a new Messiah, were condemned, and absolute poverty was declared a fictitious ideal that not even Christ endorsed.

The Dominicans, a less factious order, combated doctrinal error through visitations and preaching. They conformed convents of Beguines to the church's teaching, led the church's campaign against heretics in southern France, and staffed the offices of the Inquisition after its centralization by Pope Gregory IX in 1223. Their leading theologian, Thomas Aquinas, was canonized in 1322, and his teaching has remained the most definitive statement of Catholic belief.

The Dominicans and the Franciscans strengthened the church among the laity. Through the institution of so-called Third Orders they provided ordinary men and women the opportunity to affiliate with the monastic life and pursue the high religious ideals of poverty, obedience, and chastity, while still remaining laymen and laywomen. Laity who joined such orders were known as *tertiaries*. Such organizations helped keep lay piety orthodox and within the church during a period of heightened religiosity.

The Hohenstaufen Empire (1152–1272)

During the twelfth and thirteenth centuries stable governments developed in both England and France. In England Magna Carta balanced the rights of the nobility against the authority of the kings, and in France the reign of Philip II Augustus secured the authority of the king over the competitive claims of the nobility. The experience within the Holy Roman Empire,

which embraced Germany, Burgundy, and northern Italy by the mid-thirteenth century, was a very different story. There, primarily because of the efforts of the Hohenstaufen dynasty to extend imperial power into southern Italy, disunity and blood feuding remained the order of the day for two centuries and left as a legacy the fragmentation of Germany until modern times.

Frederick I Barbarossa

The investiture struggle had earlier weakened imperial authority. After the Concordat of Worms the German princes held the dominant lay influence over episcopal appointments and within the rich ecclesiastical territories.

A new day seemed to dawn for imperial power, however, with the accession to the throne of Frederick I Barbarossa (1152–1190), the first of the Hohenstaufens, the successor dynasty within the empire to the Franks and the Ottonians. The Hohenstaufens not only reestablished imperial authority but also initiated a new phase in the contest between popes and emperors, one that was to prove even more deadly than the investiture struggle had been. Never have kings and popes despised and persecuted one another more than during the Hohenstaufen dynasty.

As Frederick I surveyed his empire, he saw powerful feudal princes in Germany and Lombardy and a pope in Rome who believed that the emperor was his creature. There existed, however, widespread disaffection with the incessant feudal strife of the princes and the turmoil caused by the theocratic pretensions of the papacy. Popular opinion was on the emperor's side. Thus Frederick had a foundation on which to rebuild imperial authority, and he was shrewd enough to take advantage of it. He championed Roman law, which was at the time enjoying a revival in Bologna under Irnerius. Roman law served Frederick on both his fronts: on the one hand, it enhanced centralized authority against the nobility; on the other, it stressed the secular foundation of imperial power against Roman election, and especially against the tradition of papal coronation of the emperor.

Switzerland became Frederick's base of operation. From there he attempted to hold the empire together by involking feudal bonds. He was relatively successful in Germany, thanks largely to the fall from power in 1180 and the exile to England of his strongest German rival,

The Emperor Fredrick I Barbarossa (1152–1190) submitting to Pope Alexander III (1159–1181) in 1177. [Art Resource]

Henry the Lion (d. 1195), the duke of Saxony. Although realistically acknowledging the power of the German duchies, Frederick never missed the opportunity to apprise each duchy of its prescribed duties as a fief of the king. If Frederick was not everywhere ruler in fact, he was clearly so in law, and no one was permitted to forget it. The same tactic had been successfully employed by the Capetian kings of France when they faced superior noble forces.

Italy proved to be the great obstacle to imperial plans. In 1155 Frederick restored Pope Adrian IV (1154–1159) to power in Rome after a religious revolutionary, Arnold of Brescia (d. 1155), had gained control of the city. For his efforts Frederick won a coveted papal coronation—and strictly on his terms, not on those of the pope. The door to Italy thereby opened. Having won recognition of his rights of jurisdiction in Burgundy in 1157, Frederick attempted to secure the same recognition in Italy. Resistance to him became fiercest in Lombardy. The Milanese balked at the implementation of these rights, which had been defined by the imperial Diet of Roncaglia, and refused to recognize Frederick's representatives within the city.

As this challenge to royal authority was occurring, one of Europe's most skilled lawyers, Cardinal Roland, was elected Pope Alexander III (1159–1181). While a cardinal he had ne- gotiated an alliance between the papacy and the Norman kingdom of Sicily in a clever effort to strengthen the papacy against imperial influence. Perceiving him to be a very capable foe, Frederick had opposed his election as pope and had even backed a schismatic pope against him in a futile effort to undo Alexander's election. Frederick now found himself at war with the pope, Milan, and Sicily. In 1167 the combined forces of the north Italian communes drove him back into Germany. The final blow to imperial plans in Italy came a decade later, in 1176, when Italian forces soundly defeated Frederick at Legnano. In the final Peace of Constance in 1183 Frederick recognized the claims of the Lombard cities to full rights of self-rule.

Henry VI and the Sicilian Connection

Frederick's reign ended with stalemate in Germany and defeat in Italy. At his death in 1190 he was not a ruler of the stature of the kings of England and France. After the Peace of Constance in 1183 he seems himself to have conceded as much, as he accepted the reality of the empire's indefinite division among the feudal princes of Germany. An opportunity both to solve his problem with Sicily, still a papal ally, and to form a new territorial base of power for future emperors opened when the

297

Norman ruler of the kingdom of Sicily, William II (1166–1189), sought an alliance with Frederick that would free him to pursue a scheme to conquer Constantinople. The alliance was sealed in 1186 by a most fateful marriage between Frederick's son, the future Henry VI (1190–1197), and Constance, heiress to the kingdom of Sicily. This alliance proved, however, to be only another well-laid political plan that went astray. The Sicilian connection became a fatal distraction for Hohenstaufen kings, leading them repeatedly to sacrifice their traditional territorial base in northern Europe to that temptress, imperialism. Equally ominous, this union of the empire with Sicily left Rome encircled, thereby ensuring the undying hostility of a papacy already thoroughly distrustful of the emperor. The marriage alliance with Sicily proved to be the first step in what soon became a fight to the death between pope and emperor.

When Henry VI came to rule in 1190, he faced a multitude of enemies: a hostile papacy, still smarting from the refusal of his father to recognize territorial claims within the Papal States; supremely independent German princes, led by the archbishop of Cologne; and an England whose adventurous king, Richard the Lion-Hearted, was encouraged to plot against Henry by the exiled duke of Saxony, Henry the Lion.

Into this divided kingdom a son, the future Frederick II, was born in 1194. To stabilize his monarchy, Henry campaigned vigorously for the recognition of the principle of hereditary succession; he wanted birth alone to secure the imperial throne uncontestably. He won a large number of German princes to this point of view by granting them full hereditary rights to their fiefs—an appropriate exchange. But the encircled papacy was not disposed to secure Hohenstaufen power by supporting a hereditary right to the imperial throne. The pope wanted, rather, to return to the period before 1152, when imperial power had been diffused among many princes. He accordingly joined dissident German princes against Henry.

Otto IV and the Welf Interregnum

Henry died in September 1197 and chaos proved his immediate heir. Between English intervention in its politics and the pope's deliberate efforts to sabotage the Hohenstaufen dynasty, Germany was thrown into anarchy and civil war. England gave financial support to anti-Hohenstaufen factions, and its candidate for the imperial throne, Otto of Brunswick of the rival Welf dynasty, the son of Henry the Lion, bested Philip of Swabia, Henry VI's brother. Otto was crowned Otto IV by his supporters in Aachen in 1198 and later won general recognition in Germany. With England supporting Otto, the French rushed in on the side of the fallen Hohenstaufen—the beginning of periodic French fishing in troubled German waters. Meanwhile Henry VI's four-year-old son, Frederick, was safely tucked away as a ward of Pope Innocent III (1198–1215), a shrewd pope determined to break imperial power and restore papal power in Italy and willing to play one German dynasty against the other to do so.

Hohenstaufen support remained alive in Germany, however, and Otto reigned over a very divided kingdom. In October 1209 Pope Innocent crowned him emperor, a recognition that enhanced his authority. But the pope quickly moved from benefactor to mortal enemy when, after his coronation, Otto proceeded to reconquer Sicily and once again to pursue an imperial policy that left Rome encircled. Within four months of his papal coronation Otto received a papal excommunication.

Frederick II

Pope Innocent, casting about for a counterweight to the treacherous Otto, joined the French, who had remained loyal to the Hohenstaufens against the English-Welf alliance. His new ally, Philip Augustus, impressed on Innocent the fact that a solution to their problems with Otto IV lay near at hand in Innocent's ward, Frederick of Sicily. Frederick, the son of the late Hohenstaufen Emperor Henry VI, was now of age and, unlike Otto, had an immediate hereditary claim to the imperial throne. In December 1212 the young Frederick, with papal, French, and German support, was crowned king of the Romans in Mainz. Within a year and a half Philip Augustus ended the Welf interregnum of Otto IV on the battlefield of Bouvines. Philip sent Frederick II Otto's fallen imperial banner from the battlefield, a bold gesture that suggests the extent to which Frederick's ascent to the throne was intended to be that of a French-papal puppet. In 1215 Frederick repeated his earlier crowning, this time in the imperial city of Aachen.

If Frederick had been intended by Innocent

A marble head of Emperor Frederick II (1215–1250), whose preoccupation with Italy and Sicily led to the collapse of imperial power in Germany. [German Archaelogical Institute, Rome]

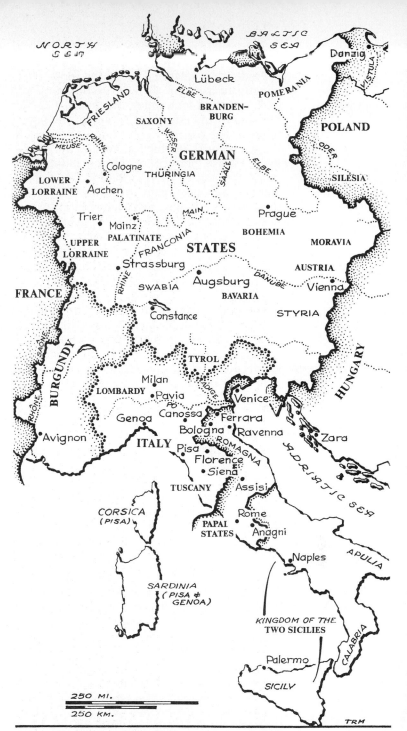

to be a puppet king, he soon disappointed any such hopes. His reign was an absolute disaster for Germany and may be credited with securing German fragmentation until modern times. Frederick was Sicilian and dreaded travel beyond the Alps. Only nine of his thirty-eight years as emperor were spent in Germany, and six of those were before 1218. Although Frederick continued to pursue royal policies in Germany through his representatives, he seemed to desire only one thing from the German princes, the imperial title for himself and his sons, and he was willing to give them what they wanted to secure it. His eager compliance with their demands laid the foundation for six centuries of German division. In 1220 he recognized the jurisdictional claims of the ecclesiastical princes of Germany, and in 1232 he extended the same recognition to the secular princes. The German princes had become too powerful to be denied. Thereafter they were undisputed lords over their territories. Frederick's concessions were tantamount to an abdication of imperial responsibility in Germany. They have been characterized as a German equivalent to Magna Carta in the sense that they secured the rights of the German nobility. Unlike Magna Carta, however, they did so without at the same time securing the rights of monarchy. Magna Carta placed the king and the nobility (parliament) in England in a creative tension; the reign of Frederick II simply made the German nobility petty kings.

GERMANY AND ITALY IN THE MIDDLE AGES

MAP 8-1 *Medieval Germany and Italy were divided lands. The Holy Roman Empire (Germany) embraced hundreds of independent territories that the emperor ruled only in name. The papacy controlled the Rome area and tried to enforce its will on Romagna. Under the Hohenstaufens (mid-12th to mid-13th century), internal German divisions and papal conflict reached new heights; German rulers sought to extend their power to southern Italy and Sicily.*

Frederick's relations with the pope were equally disastrous. He was excommunicated no fewer than four times, the first in 1227 for refusing to undertake a Crusade at the pope's request. The papacy came to view Frederick as the Anti-Christ, the biblical beast of the Apocalypse whose persecution of the faithful signaled the end of the world. The basis of the conflict lay once again in an imperial policy that encircled Rome. Although Frederick abandoned Germany, he was determined to control Lombardy. His efforts to establish a dominant Lombardy–Sicily axis in Italy brought his excommunication in 1238, an action that Frederick fiercely resisted as unwarranted papal interference in his secular rights as emperor.

The pope finally won the long struggle that ensued, although his victory proved in time to be a Pyrrhic one. In the contest with Frederick II, Pope Innocent IV (1243–1254) launched the church into European politics on a massive scale, and this wholesale secularization of the

papacy made the church highly vulnerable to the criticism of religious reformers and royal apologists. Innocent organized and led the German princes against Frederick, who—thanks to Frederick's grand concessions to them—had become a superior force and were in full control of Germany by the 1240s. German and Italian resistance kept Frederick completely on the defensive throughout his last years.

When Frederick died in 1250, the German monarchy died with him. The princes established an informal electoral college in 1257, which thereafter reigned supreme (it was formally recognized by the emperor in 1356). The "king of the Romans" became their puppet, this time with firmly attached strings; he was elected and did not rule by hereditary right. Between 1250 and 1272 the Hohenstaufen dynasty slowly faded into oblivion. It finally died altogether after the dual defeat of Frederick's illegitimate son Manfred in 1266

Frederick II Denounces the Pope

When Frederick II learned that he had once again been excommunicated by the pope, this time at the council of Lyons in 1245, he raged at the presumption of popes to depose kings—an ominous condemnation of the temporal power of popes that would be heard again and again in the later Middle Ages. The following report of Frederick's reaction comes from the *Greater Chronicle* of Matthew of Paris.

When the Emperor Frederick was made fully aware of all these proceedings [his excommunication at Lyons] he could not contain himself, but burst into a violent rage, and, darting a scowling look on those who sat around him, he thundered forth: "The Pope in his synod has disgraced me by depriving me of my crown. Whence arises such great audacity? Whence proceeds such rash presumption? Where are my chests which contain my treasures?" And on their being brought and unlocked before him, by his order, he said, "See if my crowns are lost now"; then finding one, he placed it on his head and, being thus crowned, he stood up, and, with threatening eyes and a dreadful voice, unrestrainable from passion, he said aloud, "I have not yet lost my crown, nor will I be deprived of it by any attacks of the Pope or the council, without a bloody struggle. Does his vulgar pride raise him to such heights as to enable him to hurl from the imperial dignity me, the chief prince of the world, than whom none is greater—yea, I who am without an equal . . .? In some things I was bound to obey, at least to respect, him [the pope]; but now I am released from all ties of affection and veneration, and also from the obligation of any kind of peace with him." From that time forth, therefore, Frederick, in order to injure the Pope more effectually . . . did all kinds of harm to his Holiness, to his money, as well as to his friends and relatives.*

Frederic Austin Ogg (Ed.), *A Source Book of Mediaeval History: Documents Illustrative of European Life and Institutions from the German Invasions to the Renaissance* (New York: American Book Co., 1908), pp. 408–409.

and his grandson Conradino in 1268 by Charles of Anjou, the adventurous brother of the sainted French King Louis IX.

The Hohenstaufen legacy was to make permanent the divisions within the empire. Independent princes now controlled Germany. Italy fell to local magnates. The connection between Germany and Sicily, established by Frederick I, was permanently broken. And the papal monarchy emerged as one of Europe's most formidable powers, soon to enter its most costly conflict with the French and the English.

Medieval Russia

Early in the ninth century missionaries from Byzantium had converted Russia to the Christianity of the Eastern Orthodox Church. This development meant that Russia would remain culturally separated from the Latin Christianity of western Europe. Between the late ninth century and the mid-thirteenth century the city of Kiev was the center of Russian political life. Although the city enjoyed fairly extensive trade relations with its neighbors, it failed to develop a political system that provided effective resistance to foreign domination. The external threat to Kievan Russia came from the east when the Mongols moved across the vast Eurasian plains and into Russia as Genghis Khan built his empire. By 1240 the Mongols had conquered most of Russia and had turned its various cities and their surrounding countryside into dependent principalities from which tribute could be exacted. The portion of the Mongol Empire to which Russia thus stood in the relationship of a vassal was called the *Golden Horde*. It included the steppe, in what is now south Russia, with its largely nomadic population. This vassal relationship encouraged an Eastern orientation on the part of the Russians for over two centuries, although the connection of the Russian church to the Byzantine Empire remained important. During this period there was no single central political authority in Russia. The land was divided into numerous appanages, or feudal principalities, each of which was militarily weak and subject in one degree or another to the Golden Horde.

The rise of Moscow as a relatively strong power eventually brought the appanage age of Russian history to an end. In the fourteenth century, under Grand Prince Ivan I, the city began to cooperate with its Mongol—or as the Russians called them, Tatar—overlords in the collection of tribute. Ivan kept much of this tribute for himself and was soon called Ivan Kalita, or John of the Moneybag. When Mongol authority began to weaken, the princes of Moscow, who had become increasingly wealthy, filled the political power vacuum in the territory near the city. The princes extended their authority and that of the city by purchasing some territory, colonizing other areas, and conquering new lands. This slow extension of the appanage, or principality, of Moscow is usually known as *gathering the Russian land*.

In 1380 Grand Prince Dmitry of Moscow defeated the Mongols in battle. The result was not militarily decisive, but Moscow had demonstrated that the Mongol armies were not invincible. Conflict with the Mongols continued for another century before they were driven out. During these years the princes of Moscow asserted their right to be regarded as the successors of the earlier Kievan rulers, and they also made Moscow the religious center of Russia.

France in the Thirteenth Century: The Reign of Louis IX

If Innocent III realized the fondest ambitions of medieval popes, Louis IX (1226–1270), the grandson of Philip Augustus, embodied the medieval view of the perfect ruler. His reign was a striking contrast to that of his contemporary, Frederick II of Germany. Coming to power in the wake of the French victory at Bouvines (1214), Louis inherited a unified and secure kingdom. Although he was also endowed with a moral character that far excelled that of his royal and papal contemporaries, he was also at times prey to naiveté. Not beset by the problems of sheer survival, and a reformer at heart, Louis found himself free to concentrate on what medieval people believed to be the business of civilization.

Magnanimity in politics is not always a sign of strength, and Louis could be very magnanimous. Although in a position to drive the English from their French possessions during negotiations for the Treaty of Paris (1259), he refused to take such advantage. Had he done so and ruthlessly confiscated English territories on the French coast, he might have lessened, if not averted altogether, the conflict of the Hun-

King Louis IX (1226–1270) giving justice. Louis, who was canonized in 1297, was the medieval ideal of a perfect ruler. [Giraudon/Art Resource]

dred Years' War. Instead he surrendered to Henry III disputed territory on the borders of Gascony and confirmed Henry's possession of the duchy of Aquitaine. Although he occasionally chastised popes for their crude ambitions, Louis remained neutral during the long struggle between Frederick II and the papacy, and his neutrality redounded very much to the pope's advantage. Louis also remained neutral when his brother, Charles of Anjou, intervened in Italy and Sicily against the Hohenstaufens. Urged on by the Welfs and the pope, Charles was crowned king of Sicily in Rome, and his subsequent defeat of the grandsons of Frederick II ended the Hohenstaufen dynasty. For

their assistance, both by action and by inaction, the Capetian kings of the thirteenth century became the objects of many papal favors.

Louis's greatest achievements lay at home. The efficient French bureaucracy, which his predecessors had used to exploit their subjects, became under Louis an instrument of order and fair play in local government. He sent forth royal commissioners *(enquêteurs),* reminiscent of Charlemagne's far less successful *missi dominici,* to monitor the royal officials responsible for local governmental administration (especially the *baillis* and *prévôts,* whose offices had been created by his predecessor, Philip Augustus) and to ensure that justice would truly be meted out to all. These royal ambassadors were received as genuine tribunes of the people. Louis further abolished private wars and serfdom within his royal domain, gave his subjects the judicial right of appeal from local to higher courts, and made the tax system, by medieval standards, more equitable. The French people came to associate their king with justice, and national feeling, the glue of nationhood, grew very strong during his reign.

Respected by the kings of Europe, Louis became an arbiter among the world's powers, having far greater moral authority than the pope. During his reign French society and culture became an example to all of Europe, a pattern that would continue into the modern period. Northern France became the showcase of monastic reform, chivalry, and Gothic art and architecture. Louis's reign also coincided with the golden age of Scholasticism, which saw the convergence of Europe's greatest thinkers on Paris, among them Saint Thomas Aquinas and Saint Bonaventure.

Louis's perfection remained, however, that of a medieval king. Like his father, Louis VIII (1223–1226), who had led the second Albigensian Crusade, Louis was something of a religious fanatic. He sponsored the French Inquisition. He led two French Crusades against the Arabs, which were inspired by the purest religious motives but proved to be personal disasters. During the first (1248–1254), Louis was captured and had to be ransomed out of Egypt. He died of a fever during the second in 1270. It was especially for this selfless, but also quite useless, service on behalf of the church that Louis later received the rare church honor of sainthood.

Suggested Readings

PHILIPPE ARIÈS, *Centuries of Childhood: A Social History of Family Life* (1962). Pioneer effort on the subject.

GEOFFREY BARRACLOUGH, *The Origins of Modern Germany* (1963). Penetrating political narrative.

MARC BLOCH, *French Rural Society*, trans. by J. Sondheimer (1966). A classic by a great modern historian.

ANDREAS CAPELLANUS, *The Art of Courtly Love*, trans. by J. J. Parry (1941). Documents from the court of Marie de Champagne.

M. CLAGETT, G. POST, AND R. REYNOLDS (Eds.), *Twelfth-Century Europe and the Foundations of Modern Society* (1966). Demanding but stimulating collection of essays.

R. H. C. DAVIS, *A History of Medieval Europe: From Constantine to St. Louis* (1972), Part 2.

GEORGES DUBY, *Rural Economy and Country Life in the Medieval West* (1968). Slice-of-life analysis.

GEORGES DUBY, *The Three Orders: Feudal Society Imagined*, trans. by Arthur Goldhammer (1981). Large, comprehensive, authoritative.

ROBERT FAWTIER, *The Capetian Kings of France: Monarchy and Nation 987–1328*, trans. by L. Butler and R. J. Adam (1972). Detailed, standard account.

E. H. KANTOROWICZ, *The King's Two Bodies* (1957). Controversial analysis of political concepts in the high Middle Ages.

R. S. LOOMIS (Ed.), *The Development of Arthurian Romance* (1963). Basic study.

ROBERT S. LOPEZ AND I. W. RAYMOND (Eds.), *Medieval Trade in the Mediterranean World* (1955). Illuminating collection of sources, concentrated on southern Europe.

P. MANDONNET, *St. Dominic and His Work* (1944). For the origins of the Dominican Order.

LLOYD DE MAUSE, (ED.), *The History of Childhood* (1974).

JOHN MOORMAN, *A History of the Franciscan Order* (1968). The best survey.

JOHN B. MORRALL, *Political Thought in Medieval Times* (1962). Readable and illuminating account.

JOHN T. NOONAN, *Contraception: A History of Its Treatment by the Catholic Theologians and Canonists* (1967). Fascinating account of medieval theological attitudes toward sexuality and sex-related problems.

CHARLES PETIT-DUTAILLIS, *The Feudal Monarchy in France and England from the Tenth to the Thirteenth Century*, trans. by E. D. Hunt (1964). Political narrative.

J. M. POWELL, *Innocent III: Vicar of Christ or Lord of the World* (1963). Excerpts from the scholarly debate over Innocent's reign.

EILEEN POWER, *Medieval Women* (1975). Seminal essays.

F. W. POWICKE, *The Thirteenth Century* (1962). Outstanding treatment of English political history.

SHULAMITH SHAHAR, *The Fourth Estate: A History of Women in the Middle Ages* (1983). Best survey.

R. W. SOUTHERN, *Medieval Humanism and Other Studies* (1970). Provocative and far-ranging essays on topics in intellectual history of high Middle Ages.

W. L. WAKEFIELD AND A. P. EVANS (Eds.), *Heresies of the High Middle Ages* (1969). A major document collection.

SUZANNE WEMPLE, *Women in Frankish Society: Marriage and the Cloister 500–900* (1981). What marriage and the cloister meant to medieval women.

Europe in Transition, 1300–1750

Between the early fourteenth and the mid-eighteenth centuries, Europe underwent far-reaching changes. These were years both of remarkable cultural and political construction and of massive physical suffering brought on by disease and war.

The era began with one of the greatest disasters in European history: a bubonic plague, known as the *Black Death,* that had killed an estimated two fifths of the population by the mid-fourteenth century. That event had been preceded by a century of sharp conflicts between the pope and the secular rulers. A hundred years of warfare between England and France followed the great demographic crisis. The emergence of strong, ruthless monarchies accompanied the decline in papal power during the later Middle Ages. Commanding greater economic and military resources, the new rulers steadily gained control over the church in their lands. By the fourteenth century, the nation-states of Europe were warring with one another, not with the armies of the pope.

Also in the fourteenth century the great cultural resurgence of Europe known as the *Renaissance* began. This was a rebirth of education and culture closely associated with the discovery of new Greek and Latin writings and with the rapid growth of colleges and universities throughout western Europe.

Interest in the past was not the only way in which Europeans extended their minds in directions previously uncharted. In the late fifteenth century voyages began to America, around Africa, and across the Indian Ocean to Asia. These voyages of discovery introduced Europeans to exotic cultures and non-Western values. Science was still another frontier. Beginning with Copernicus and culminating in Sir Isaac Newton, a new view of the universe emerged. The voyages of discovery and the scientific revolution gave Europeans both new confidence in the power of the human mind and a new perspective on their society.

In the sixteenth century a major religious revolt divided Europe spiritually and led to a restructuring of Christendom. The Protestant Reformation began in 1517 when an obscure German professor named Martin Luther challenged the religious teaching and authority of the papacy. Within a quarter century Europe was permanently divided between a growing variety of Protestant churches and the Roman Catholic church. For a century and a half the new religious differences also fueled political conflict. Religious warfare devastated France in the second half of the sixteenth century and wreaked havoc on Germany in the first half of the seventeenth.

By the middle of the seventeenth century most religious warfare had ended. The religious turmoil had strengthened the hand of the secular state. For many rulers and their subjects, political stability now became a higher value than religious allegiance. By the early eighteenth century, Europe's rulers, with the notable exception of the English monarchs, were imitating the French king, Louis XIV. Through efficient tax collectors, loyal administrators, and a powerful standing army, Louis subjected France

304

to his will, making it the model of the absolute state. By the second half of the seventeenth century the balance of power had shifted away from Spain to the strong monarchies of France, Austria, and Prussia and to the parliamentary monarchy of Great Britain. Also, for the first time, Russia emerged as a major European power.

With the end of religious conflict, energies were turned toward economic expansion. New, more efficient farming methods appeared, and nations took the first steps toward industrialization. In the New World, the colonies grew and were consolidated. By the eighteenth century competition over trade had replaced religion as the cause of war. The demand for political independence, most notably by the English colonies in America, now replaced the earlier demands for religious independence. A new age had dawned, one still believing in the power of God, but increasingly fascinated by human power.

Michelangelo's Pieta. *This was Michelangelo's first sculpture, done when he was only eighteen in 1493–1494. Michelangelo portrayed the Madonna on a larger scale than Christ to give the effect of a mother holding her young son. The statue is now in St. Peter's in Rome. (Art Resource)*

THE LATE MIDDLE AGES and the Renaissance marked a time of unprecedented calamity and of bold new beginnings. There was the Hundred Years' War between England and France (1337–1453), an exercise in seemingly willful self-destruction, which was made even more terrible in its later stages by the invention of gunpowder and heavy artillery. There was almost universal bubonic plague, known to contemporaries as the Black Death. Between 1348 and 1350 the plague killed as much as one third of the population in many regions and transformed many pious Christians into believers in the omnipotence of death. There was a schism within the church that lasted thirty-seven years (1378–1415) and saw, by 1409, the election of no fewer than three competing popes and colleges of cardinals. And there was the onslaught of the Turks, who in 1453 marched seemingly invincibly through Constantinople and toward the West. As their political and religious institutions buckled, as disease, bandits, and wolves ravaged their cities in the wake of war, and as Muslim armies gathered at their borders, Europeans beheld what seemed to be the imminent total collapse of Western civilization.

But if the late Middle Ages saw unprecedented chaos, it also witnessed a rebirth that would continue into the seventeenth century. Two modern Dutch scholars have employed the same word (*Herfsttij*, "harvesttide") with different connotations to describe the period, one interpreting the word as a "waning" or "decline" (Johan Huizinga), the other as a true "harvest" (Heiko Oberman). If something was dying away, some ripe fruit and seed grain were also being gathered in. The late Middle Ages were a creative breaking up.

It was in this period that such scholars as Marsilius of Padua, William of Ockham, and Lorenzo Valla produced lasting criticisms of medieval assumptions about the nature of God, humankind, and society. It was a period in which kings worked through parliaments and clergy through councils to place lasting limits on the pope's temporal power. The principle that a sovereign (in this case, the pope) is accountable to the body of which he or she is head was established. The arguments used by conciliarists (advocates of the judicial superiority of a church council over a pope) to establish papal accountability to the body of the faithful provided an example for the secular sphere, as sovereigns, who also had an independent tradition of ruler accountability in Roman law,

9

The Late Middle Ages and the Renaissance: Decline and Renewal (1300–1527)

were reminded of their responsibility to the body politic.

The late Middle Ages also saw an unprecedented scholarly renaissance, as Italian Humanists made a full recovery of classical knowledge and languages and set in motion educational reforms and cultural changes that would spread throughout Europe in the fifteenth and sixteenth centuries. In the process the Italian Humanists invented, for all practical purposes, critical historical scholarship and exploited a new fifteenth-century invention, the "divine art" of printing with movable type. It was in this period that the vernacular, the local language, began to take its place alongside Latin, the international language, as a widely used literary and political language. The independent nation-states of Europe progressively superseded the universal church as the community of highest allegiance, as patriotism and incipient nationalism became a major force. Nations henceforth "transcended" themselves not by journeys to Rome but by competitive voyages to the Far East and the Americas, as the age of global exploration opened.

A time of both waning and harvest, constriction (in the form of nationalism) and expansion (in the sense of world exploration), the late Middle Ages saw medieval culture grudgingly give way to the age of Renaissance and Reformation.

Political and Social Breakdown

The Hundred Years' War and the Rise of National Sentiment

CAUSES OF THE WAR. From May 1337 to October 1453 England and France periodically engaged in what was for both a futile and devastating war. The conflict was initiated by the English king Edward III (1327–1377), who held a strong claim to the French throne as the grandson of Philip the Fair (1285–1314). When Charles IV (1322–1328), the last of Philip the Fair's surviving sons, died, Edward, who was only fifteen at the time, asserted his right to Capetian succession. The French barons, however, were not willing to place an English king on the French throne. They chose instead the first cousin of Charles IV, Philip VI of Valois (1328–1350), the first of a new French dynasty that was to rule into the sixteenth century.

But there was much more to the Hundred Years' War than just a defense of Edward's prestige. In the background were other equally important factors that help to explain both Edward's success in gaining popular and parliamentary support after the war started and the determination of the English and the French people to endure the war to its bitter end. For one thing, the English king held Gascony, Anjou, Guyenne, and other French territories as fiefs from the French king. Thus he was, in law, a vassal of the French king—a circumstance that stretched back to the Norman Conquest. In May 1329 Edward journeyed to Amiens and, most perfunctorily, swore fealty to Philip VI. As Philip's vassal Edward was, theoretically if not in fact, committed to support policies detrimental to England, if his French lord so commanded. If such vassalage was intolerable to Edward, the English possession of French lands was even more repugnant to the French, especially inasmuch as the English presence remained a permanent threat to the royal policy of centralization.

Still another factor that fueled the conflict was French support of the Bruces of Scotland, strong opponents of the English overlordship of Scotland who had won a victory over the English in 1314. The French and the English were also at this time quarreling over Flanders, a French fief, yet also a country whose towns were completely dependent for their livelihood on imported English wool. Edward III and his successors manipulated this situation to English advantage throughout the conflict; by controlling the export of wool to Flanders, England influenced Flanders' foreign policy. Finally, there were decades of prejudice and animosity between the French and the English people, who constantly confronted one another on the high seas and in port towns. Taken together, these various factors made the Hundred Years' War a struggle to the death for national control and identity.

FRENCH WEAKNESS. Throughout the conflict France was the stronger on paper; it had three times the population of England, was far the wealthier, and fought on its own soil. Yet, for the greater part of the conflict, until after 1415, the major battles ended in often stunning English victories. France was not as strong as it appeared. It was, first of all, internally disunited by social conflict and the absence of a centralized system of taxation to fund the war. French kings raised funds by

309

*The Late
Middle Ages
and the
Renaissance:
Decline and
Renewal
(1300–1527)*

*Edward III paying homage to his feudal lord Philip VI of France. In law, the king of England
was a vassal of the king of France.* [*Snark/EPA*]

depreciating the currency, taxing the clergy,
and borrowing heavily from Italian bankers—
self-defeating practices that created a financial
crisis by mid-century. As a tool to provide him
money, the king raised up a representative
council of townsmen and noblemen that came
to be known in subsequent years as the *Estates
General.* It convened in 1355, and although it
levied taxes at the king's request, its members
also used the king's plight to enhance their
own regional rights and privileges. Just how
successful they were is indicated by the creation in this period of the Burgundian state, a
powerful new territory that became a thorn in
the sides of French kings throughout the fifteenth century. France, unlike England, was
still struggling in the fourteenth century to
make the transition from a fragmented feudal
society to a centralized "modern" state.

Beyond this struggle, there was the clear fact
of English military superiority, due to the
greater discipline of its infantry and the rapid-
fire and long-range capability of that ingen-
iously simple weapon, the English longbow,
which could shoot six arrows a minute with a
force sufficient to pierce an inch of wood or the
armor of a knight at two hundred yards. The

longbow scattered the French cavalry and
crossbowmen in one engagement after the
other. Only in the later stages of the war, with
the introduction of heavy artillery, did the
French alter their military tactics to advantage.

Finally, French weakness was related in no
small degree to the comparative mediocrity of
royal leadership during the Hundred Years'
War. English kings were far the shrewder. Historians have found it to be a telling commentary on the leadership ability of French kings in
this period that the most memorable military
leader on the French side in the popular imagination is Joan of Arc.

Progress of the War

The war had three major stages of development, each ending with a seemingly decisive
victory by one or the other side: (1) during the
reign of Edward III (d. 1377); (2) from Edward's death to the Treaty of Troyes (1420);
and (3) from the appearance of Joan of Arc
(1429) to the English retreat.

**THE CONFLICT DURING THE REIGN OF
EDWARD III.** Edward prepared for the first

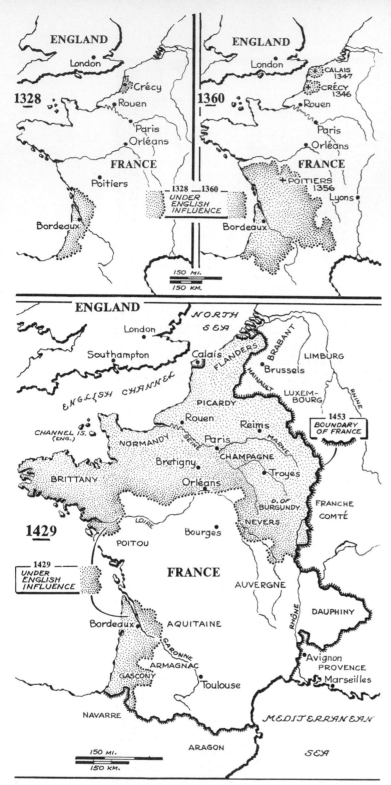

1328

1360

ENGLAND

London

Crécy

Rouen

Paris
Orléans

FRANCE

Poitiers

Bordeaux

ENGLAND

London

CALAIS
1347

CRÉCY
1346

Rouen

Paris
Orléans

FRANCE

POITIERS
1356

Lyons

Bordeaux

— 1328 — 1360
UNDER
ENGLISH
INFLUENCE

150 MI.
150 KM.

ENGLAND

London

NORTH
SEA

Southampton

Calais

FLANDERS

BRABANT

LIMBURG

Brussels

HAINAULT

LUXEM-
BOURG

RHINE

ENGLISH CHANNEL

CHANNEL IS.
(ENG.)

PICARDY

Rouen

SEINE

NORMANDY

Reims

Paris

MARNE

CHAMPAGNE

1453
BOUNDARY
OF FRANCE

BRITTANY

Bretigny

Orléans

Troyes

D. OF
BURGUNDY

FRANCHE
COMTÉ

1429

LOIRE

NEVERS

POITOU

Bourges

1429 —
UNDER
ENGLISH
INFLUENCE

FRANCE

AUVERGNE

DAUPHINY

Bordeaux

AQUITAINE

GARONNE

ARMAGNAC

GASCONY

Toulouse

RHÔNE

Avignon
PROVENCE

Marseilles

NAVARRE

MEDITERRANEAN

ARAGON

SEA

150 MI.
150 KM.

THE HUNDRED YEARS' WAR

MAP 9–1 *The Hundred Years' War went on intermittently from the late 1330s until 1453. These maps show the remarkable English territorial gains up to the sudden and decisive turning of the tide of battle in favor of the French by the forces of Joan of Arc in 1429.*

stage of the war by securing allies in the Netherlands and a personal pledge of support from the emperor Louis IV of Bavaria (1314–1347). By slapping an embargo on English wool to Flanders, Edward sparked urban rebellions by merchants and the trade guilds. Inspired by a rich merchant, Jacob van Artevelde, the Flemish cities, led by Ghent, revolted against the French. Having at first taken as neutral a stand as possible in the conflict, these cities, whose economies faced total collapse without imported English wool, signed a half-hearted alliance with England in January 1340, acknowledging Edward as king of France.

Edward defeated the French fleet in the first great battle of the war in the Bay of Sluys on June 23, 1340. But his subsequent effort to invade France by way of Flanders failed, largely because his allies proved undependable. As a stalemate developed, a truce was struck and was more or less observed until 1346. In that year Edward attacked Normandy and won a series of easy victories that were capped by that at Crécy in August. This was quickly followed by the seizure of Calais, which the English held thereafter for over two hundred years. Both sides employed scorched-earth tactics and completely devastated the areas of conflict.

Exhaustion and the onset of the Black Death forced a second truce in late 1347, and the war entered a lull until 1355. On September 19, 1356, the English won their greatest victory, near Poitiers, routing the noble cavalry and even taking the French king, John II the Good (1350–1364), captive back to England. After Poitiers there was a complete breakdown of political order in France. Disbanded soldiers from both sides became professional bandits, roaming the land, pillaging areas untouched by the war, and bringing disaster almost as great as the war itself.

Power in France lay with the privileged classes, who expressed their will through the representative assembly of the Estates General. Convened in 1355 by the faltering king so that revenues might be provided to continue the war, the Estates General, led by powerful merchants of Paris under Étienne Marcel, had demanded and received rights similar to those granted the English privileged classes in Magna Carta. The English Parliament, too, had grown out of councils convened by kings (John, 1199–1216, and Henry III, 1216–1272), which were widely representative of the English upper classes and were designed to provide the king an opportunity to discuss (and thereby to persuade those attending to adopt) the king's views on laws and taxes. During the reign of Edward I (1272–1307) these "parliaments" or "parleyings" with the king became a fixed political institution. Unlike the English Parliament, which represented the interests of a comparatively unified English nobility, the French Estates General was a many-tongued lobby, a forum for the diverse interests of the new-rich urban commercial and industrial classes, the territorial princes, and the clergy. Such a diverse body was no instrument for effective government.

The war also occasioned internal political policies that alienated and embittered the peasants. To secure their rights, the privileged classes bullied the French peasantry, who were forced to pay ever-increasing taxes and to repair without compensation the war-damaged properties of the nobility. The pressure became more than the peasantry could bear. Burdened by the Estates General, terrified by the Black Death, and emboldened by the cowardly retreat of the French cavalry at Poitiers, the peasantry exploded in several regions in a series of bloody uprisings known as the *Jacquerie*. The revolt was, however, put down by the nobility, who matched "Jacques Bonhomme," as the peasant revolutionary was popularly known, atrocity for atrocity.

On May 9, 1360, another milestone of the war was reached when England forced the Peace of Bretigny on the French. This agreement declared Edward's vassalage to the king of France ended and affirmed his sovereignty over English territories in France (including Gascony, Guyenne, Poitou, and Calais). France also pledged to pay a ransom of three million gold crowns to win King John the Good's release. In return, Edward renounced his claim to the French throne.

Such a partition of French territorial control was completely unrealistic, and sober observers on both sides knew it could not long continue. France became strong enough to strike back in the late 1360s, during the reign of John the Good's successor, Charles V (1364–1380). In 1369 Flanders came into the French fold when Charles's brother, Philip the Bold, who held the duchy of Burgundy as his appanage (landed inheritance), married the daughter of the count of Flanders. Backed by the Estates General and blessed with a brilliant military commander in Bertrand du Guesclin, the French launched a successful counteroffensive.

Edward I (1271–1307) presiding over parliament. It was during Edward's reign that parliament became a fixed political institution. [Royal Library, Windsor Castle, by gracious permission of HM the Queen]

By the time of Edward's death in 1377, the English had been beaten back to coastal enclaves and the territory of Bordeaux.

FRENCH DEFEAT AND THE TREATY OF TROYES. After Edward's death the English war effort lessened considerably, partly because of domestic problems within England. During the reign of Richard II (1377–1399), England had its own version of the *Jacquerie*. To counter the economic strain of the war with France and the ravages of the Black Death, Parliament had reduced the wages of peasants and artisans, imposed new tolls and taxes, and reasserted old domainal rights in an effort to keep the peasants bound to the land. Both the urban proletariat and the agrarian peasantry greatly resented these measures, which the king's uncle and regent, John of Gaunt, the duke of Lancaster, enforced. In June 1381 a great revolt of the unprivileged classes exploded under the leadership of John Ball, a

311

secular priest, and Wat Tyler, a journeyman. As in France, the revolt was short-lived, brutally crushed within the year. But it left the country divided for decades.

In 1396 France and England signed still another truce, this time backed up by the marriage of Richard II to the daughter of the French king, Charles VI (1380–1422). This truce lasted through the reign of Richard's successor, Henry IV of Lancaster (1399–1413). His successor, Henry V (1413–1422), reheated the war with France by taking advantage of the internal French turmoil created by the rise to power of the duchy of Burgundy. Charles VI had gone mad in the second half of his reign, and control of the French government had devolved on his brother, the duke of Orléans. Orléans struggled manfully but in vain to contain the aggressive duke of Burgundy, John the Fearless (1404–1419). Indeed, the latter succeeded in having Orléans assassinated in 1407. Thereafter civil war enveloped France; the count of Armagnac took up the royal banner, while John the Fearless found allies in the French cities.

With France so internally divided, Henry V struck hard in Normandy. John the Fearless and the Burgundians foolishly watched from the sidelines while Henry's army routed the numerically stronger but tactically less shrewd Armagnacs at Agincourt on October 25, 1415. In the years thereafter the Burgundians closed ranks behind the royal forces as they belatedly recognized that a divided France would remain an easy prey to the English. But this inchoate French unity, which promised to bring eventual victory, shattered in September 1419. In a belated reprisal for the assassination of the duke of Orléans twelve years earlier, soldiers of Charles VI stabbed John the Fearless to death only hours after the two men had quarreled. This shocking turn of events stampeded John's son, Philip the Good (1419–1467). He determined to avenge his father's death at any price, even if it meant giving the English control of France. The result was a Burgundian alliance with England.

With Burgundian support behind the English, France became Henry V's for the taking— at least in the short run. The Treaty of Troyes in 1420 disinherited the legitimate heir to the French throne, the dauphin (a title used by the king's oldest son), the future Charles VII, and made Henry V successor to the mad Charles VI. When Henry V and Charles VI died within months of one another in 1422, the infant Henry VI of England was proclaimed in Paris to be king of both France and England under the regency of the duke of Bedford. The dream of Edward III, the pretext for continuing the great war, was now, for the moment, realized: in 1422 an English king was the proclaimed ruler of France.

The dauphin went into retreat in Bourges, where, on the death of his father, he became Charles VII to most of the French, who ignored the Treaty of Troyes. Although some years were to pass before he was powerful enough to take his crown in fact, the French people would not deny the throne to a legitimate successor, regardless of the terms dictated by the Treaty of Troyes. National sentiment, spurred to unprecedented heights by Joan of Arc, soon brought the French people together as never before in a victorious coalition.

JOAN OF ARC AND THE WAR'S CONCLUSION. Joan of Arc (1412–1431), a peasant from Domrémy, presented herself to Charles VII in March 1429. When she declared that the King of Heaven had called her to deliver besieged Orléans from the English, Charles was understandably skeptical. But the dauphin and his advisers, in retreat from what seemed to be a completely hopeless war, were desperate men, willing to try anything to reverse French fortunes on the battlefield. Certainly the deliverance of Orléans, a city strategic to the control of the territory south of the Loire, would be a godsend. Charles's desperation overcame his skepticism, and he gave Joan his leave.

Circumstances worked perfectly to Joan's advantage. The English force was already exhausted by its six-month siege of Orléans and actually at the point of withdrawal when Joan arrived with fresh French troops. After the English were repulsed at Orléans, there followed a succession of French victories that were popularly attributed to Joan. Joan truly deserved much of the credit; not, however, because she was a military genius. She gave the French people and armies something military experts could not: a unique inspiration and an almost mystical confidence in themselves as a nation. Within a few months of the liberation of Orléans, Charles VII received his crown in Rheims and ended the nine-year "disinheritance" prescribed by the Treaty of Troyes.

Charles forgot his liberator as quickly as he had embraced her. Joan was captured by the Burgundians in May 1430, and although he was in a position to secure her release, the French king did little to help her. She was turned over to the Inquisition in English-held Rouen. The Burgundians and the English wanted Joan publicly discredited, believing this would also discredit her patron, Charles VII, and might demoralize French resistance. The skilled inquisitors broke the courageous "Maid of Orléans" in ten weeks of merciless interrogation, and she was executed as a relapsed heretic on May 30, 1431. Charles reopened Joan's trial at a later date, and she was finally declared innocent of all the charges against her on July 7, 1456, twenty-five years after her execution. In 1920 the church declared her a saint.

Joan of Arc (1412–1421). This painting in the National Archives in Paris is believed to be a contemporary portrait. [Giraudon]

Joan of Arc Refuses to Recant Her Beliefs

Joan of Arc, threatened with torture, refused to recant her beliefs and instead defended the instructions she had received from the voices that spoke to her. Here is a part of her self-defense from the contemporary trial record.

On Wednesday, May 9th of the same year [1431], Joan was brought into the great tower of the castle of Rouen before us the said judges and in the presence of the reverend father, lord abbot of St. Cormeille de Compiegne, of masters Jean de Châtillon and Guillaume Erart, doctors of sacred theology, of André Marguerie and Nicolas de Venderes, archdeacons of the church of Rouen, of William Haiton, bachelor of theology, Aubert Morel, licentiate in canon law; Nicolas Loiseleur, canon of the cathedral of Rouen, and master Jean Massieu.

And Joan was required and admonished to speak the truth on many different points contained in her trial which she had denied or to which she had given false replies, whereas we possessed certain information, proofs, and vehement presumptions upon them. Many of the points were read and explained to her, and she was told that if she did not confess them truthfully she would be put to the torture, the instruments of which were shown to her all ready in the tower. There were also present by our in- *struction men ready to put her to the torture in order to restore her to the way and knowledge of truth, and by this means to procure the salvation of her body and soul which by her lying inventions she exposed to such grave perils.*

To which the said Joan answered in this manner: "Truly if you were to tear me limb from limb and separate my soul from my body, I would not tell you anything more: and if I did say anything, I should afterwards declare that you had compelled me to say it by force." Then she said that on Holy Cross Day last she received comfort from St. Gabriel; she firmly believes it was St. Gabriel. She knew by her voices whether she should submit to the Church, since the clergy were pressing her hard to submit. Her voices told her that if she desired Our Lord to aid her she must wait upon Him in all her doings. She said that Our Lord has always been the master of her doings, and the Enemy never had power over them. She asked her voices if she would be burned and they answered that she must wait upon God, and He would aid her.

The Trial of Jeanne D'Arc, trans. by W. P. Barrett (New York: Gotham House, 1932), pp. 303–304.

THE HUNDRED YEARS' WAR (1337–1443)

English victory at Bay of Sluys	1340
English victory at Crécy and seizure of Calais	1346
Black Death strikes	1347
English victory at Poitiers	1356
Jacquerie disrupts France	1358
Peace of Bretigny recognizes English holdings in France	1360
English peasants revolt	1381
English victory at Agincourt	1415
Treaty of Troyes proclaims Henry VI ruler of both England and France	1422
Joan of Arc leads French to victory at Orléans	1429
Joan of Arc executed as a heretic	1431
War ends; English retain only coastal town of Calais	1453

Charles VII and Philip the Good made peace in 1435, and a unified France, now at peace with Burgundy, progressively forced the English back. By 1453, the date of the war's end, the English held only the coastal enclave of Calais.

During the Hundred Years' War there were sixty-eight years of at least nominal peace and forty-four of hot war. The political and social consequences were lasting. Although the war devastated France, it also awakened the giant of French nationalism and hastened the transition in France from a feudal monarchy to a centralized state. Burgundy became a major European political power. The seesawing allegiance of the Netherlands throughout the conflict encouraged the English to develop their own clothing industry and foreign markets. In both France and England the on-again, off-again war devastated the peasantry, who were forced to bear its burden in taxes and services. After the *Jacquerie* of 1358 France did not see another significant peasant uprising until the French Revolution in the eighteenth century.

The Black Death

PRECONDITIONS AND CAUSES. In the late Middle Ages nine tenths of the population were still farmers. The three-field system, in use in most areas since well before the fourteenth century, had increased the amount of arable land and thereby the food supply. The growth of cities and trade had also stimulated agricultural science and productivity. But as the food supply grew, so also did the population. It is estimated that Europe's population doubled between the years 1000 and 1300. By 1300 the balance between food supply and population was decisively tipped in favor of the latter. There were now more people than food to feed them or jobs to employ them, and the average European faced the probability of extreme hunger at least once during his or her expected thirty-five-year life span.

Famines followed the population explosion in the first half of the fourteenth century. Between 1315 and 1317 crop failures produced the greatest famine of the Middle Ages. Great suffering was inflicted on densely populated urban areas like the industrial towns of the Netherlands. Decades of overpopulation, economic depression, famine, and bad health progressively weakened Europe's population and made it highly vulnerable to a virulent bubonic plague that struck with full force in 1348. This Black Death, so called by contemporaries because of the way it discolored the body, followed the trade routes from Asia into Europe. Appearing in Sicily in late 1347, it entered Europe through the port cities of Venice, Genoa, and Pisa in 1348, and from there it swept rapidly through Spain and southern France and into northern Europe. Areas that lay outside the major trade routes, like Bohemia, appear to have remained virtually unaffected. By the end of the fourteenth century it is estimated that western Europe as a whole had lost as much as two fifths of its population, and a full recovery was not made until the sixteenth century. (See Map 9.2.)

POPULAR REMEDIES. In the Black Death people confronted a catastrophe against which they had neither understanding nor defense. Never have Western people stood so helpless against the inexplicable and the uncontrollable. Contemporary physicians did not know that the disease was transmitted by rat- or human-transported fleas, and hence the most rudimentary prophylaxis was lacking. Popular wisdom held that a corruption in the atmosphere caused the disease. Some blamed poisonous fumes released by earthquakes, and many adopted aromatic amulets as a remedy. According to the contemporary observations of Boccaccio, who recorded the varied reactions to the plague in the *Decameron* (1353), some sought a remedy in moderation and a temperate life; others gave themselves over entirely to

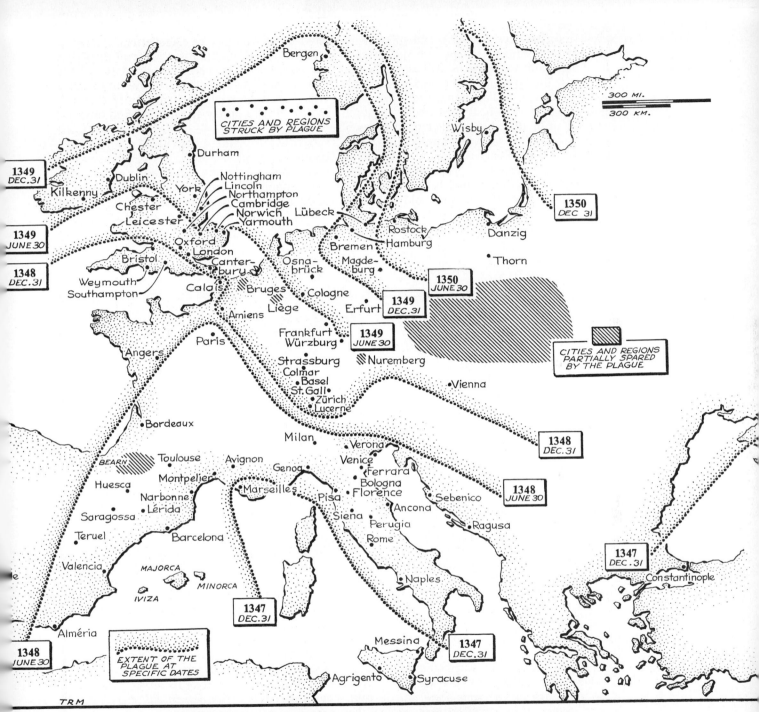

SPREAD OF THE BLACK DEATH

MAP 9–2 *Apparently introduced by sea-borne rats from Black Sea areas where plague-infested rodents have long been known, the Black Death brought huge human, social, and economic consequences. One of the lower estimates of Europeans dying is 25,000,000. The map charts its spread in the mid-fourteenth century. Generally following trade routes, the plague reached Scandinavia by 1350, and some believe it then went on to Iceland and even Greenland. Areas off the main trade routes were largely spared.*

their passions (sexual promiscuity among the stricken apparently ran high); and still others, "the most sound, perhaps, in judgment," chose flight and seclusion as the best medicine.

Among the most extreme social reactions were processions of flagellants. These were religious fanatics who beat their bodies in ritual penance until they bled, believing that such action would bring divine intervention. The Jews, who were hated by many because of centuries of Christian propaganda against them and because they had become society's moneylenders, a disreputable and resented profession but one of the few that Jews were allowed to practice, became scapegoats. Pog-

roms occurred in several cities, sometimes incited by the advent of flagellants. The terror created by the flagellants, whose dirty bodies may have actually served to transport the disease, became so socially disruptive and threatening even to established authority that the church finally outlawed such processions.

SOCIAL AND ECONOMIC CONSEQUENCES. Among the social and economic consequences of the plague were a shrunken labor supply and the devaluation of the estates of the nobility. Villages vanished in the wake of the plague. As the number of farm laborers decreased, their wages increased and those of

---

Boccaccio Describes the Ravages of the Black Death in Florence

The Black Death provided an excuse to the poet, Humanist, and storyteller Giovanni Boccaccio (1313–1375) to assemble his great collection of tales, the *Decameron*. Ten congenial men and women flee Florence to escape the plague and to while away the time telling stories. In one of the stories, Boccaccio embedded a fine clinical description of plague symptoms as seen in Florence in 1348 and of the powerlessness of physicians and the lack of remedies.

In Florence, despite all that human wisdom and forethought could devise to avert it, even as the cleansing of the city from many impurities by officials appointed for the purpose, the refusal of entrance to all sick folk, and the adoption of many precautions for the preservation of health; despite also humble supplications addressed to God, and often repeated both in public procession and otherwise, by the devout; towards the beginning of the spring of the said year [1348] the doleful effects of the pestilence began to be horribly apparent by symptoms that shewed as if miraculous.

Not such were these symptoms as in the East, where an issue of blood from the nose was a manifest sign of inevitable death; but in men and women alike it first betrayed itself by the emergence of certain tumours in the groin or the armpits, some of which grew as large as a common apple, others as an egg, some more, some less, which the common folk called gavoccioli. *From the two said parts of the body this deadly* gavocciolo *soon began to propagate and spread itself in all directions indifferently; after which the form of the malady began to change, black spots or livid making their appearance in many cases on the arm or the thigh or elsewhere, now few and large, now minute and numerous. And as the* gavocciolo *had been and still was an infallible token of approaching death, such also were these spots on whomsoever they shewed themselves. Which maladies seemed to set entirely at naught both the art of the physician and the virtues of physic; indeed, whether it was that the disorder was of a nature to defy such treatment, or that the physicians were at fault . . . and, being in ignorance of its source, failed to apply the proper remedies; in either case, not merely were those that recovered few, but almost all died within three days of the appearance of the said symptoms, sooner or later, and in most cases without any fever or other attendant malady.*

The Decameron of Giovanni Boccaccio, trans. by J. M. Rigg (New York: Dutton, 1930), p. 5.

skilled artisans soared. Many serfs now chose to commute their labor services by money payments, to abandon the farm altogether, and to pursue more interesting and rewarding jobs in skilled craft industries in the cities, an important new vocational option opened by the Black Death. Agricultural prices fell because of lowered demand, and the price of luxury and manufactured goods—the work of skilled artisans—rose. The noble landholders suffered the greatest decline in power from this new state of affairs. They were forced to pay more for finished products and for farm labor, and they received a smaller return on their agricultural produce. Everywhere their rents were in steady decline after the plague.

To recoup their losses, some landowners converted arable land to sheep pasture, substituting more profitable wool production for labor-intensive grain crops. Others abandoned the effort to farm their land and simply leased it to the highest bidder. Most ominously, legislation was sought to force peasants to stay on their farms and to freeze their wages at low levels, that is, to close off immediately the new economic opportunities opened for the peasantry by the demographic crisis. In France the direct tax on the peasantry, the *taille*, was increased, and opposition to it was prominent among the grievances behind the *Jacquerie*. A Statute of Laborers was passed by the English Parliament in 1351 that limited wages to preplague levels and restricted the ability of peasants to leave the land of their traditional masters. Opposition to such legislation was also a prominent factor in the English Peasants' Revolt of 1381.

Although the plague hit urban populations especially hard, the cities and their skilled industries came, in time, to prosper from it. Cities had always been careful to protect their interests; as they grew, they passed legislation to regulate competition from rural areas and to control immigration. After the plague their laws were progressively extended over the surrounding lands of nobles and feudal landlords, many of whom were peacefully integrated into urban life on terms very favorable to the cities.

The basic unit of urban industry was the master and his apprentices (usually one or two). Their numbers were purposely kept low and jealously guarded. As the craft of the skilled artisan was passed from master to apprentice only very slowly, the first wave of plague created a short supply of skilled labor almost overnight. But this short supply also

More than one European in three died of the Black Death. In some localities so many people died that the traditional rites of death were abandoned in favor of hurried mass burials in communal pits. [*Vincent Virga Archives*]

raised the prices of available manufactured and luxury items to new heights. Ironically the omnipresence of death whetted the appetite for the things that only skilled urban industries could produce. Expensive cloths and jewelry, furs from the north, and silks from the south were in great demand in the second half of the fourteenth century. Faced with life at its worst, people insisted on having the very best. The townspeople profited coming and going: as wealth poured into the cities and per capita income rose, the cost to urban dwellers of agricultural products from the countryside, which were now less in demand, actually declined.

The church also profited from the plague as gifts and bequests multiplied. Although the church, as a great landholder, also suffered losses, it had offsetting revenues from the vastly increased demand for religious services for the dead and the dying.

NEW CONFLICTS AND OPPORTUNITIES. By increasing the importance of skilled artisans, the plague contributed to new conflicts within the cities. The economic and political power of local artisans and trade guilds grew steadily in the late Middle Ages along with the demand for their goods and services. The merchant and patrician classes found it increasingly difficult to maintain their traditional dominance and grudgingly gave guild masters a voice in city government. As the guilds won political power, they encouraged restrictive

317

legislation to protect local industries. These restrictions, in turn, brought confrontations between master artisans, who wanted to keep their numbers low and expand their industries at a snail's pace, and the many journeymen, who were eager to rise to the rank of master. To the long-existing conflict between the guilds and the urban patriciate was now added a conflict within the guilds themselves.

Another indirect effect of the great plague was to assist monarchies in the development of centralized states. The plague caused the landed nobility to lose much of their economic power in the same period that the military superiority of paid professional armies over the traditional noble cavalry was being demonstrated by the Hundred Years' War. The plague also killed large numbers of clergy—perhaps one third of the German clergy fell victim to it as they heroically ministered to the sick and dying. This reduction in clerical ranks occurred in the same century in which the residence of the pope in Avignon (1309–1377) and the Schism (1378–1415) were undermining much of the church's popular support. After 1350 the two traditional "containers" of monarchy— the landed nobility and the church—were on the defensive, and to no small degree as a consequence of the plague. Kings took full advantage of the new situation, as they drew on growing national sentiment to centralize their governments and economies.

Ecclesiastical Breakdown and Revival: The Late Medieval Church

The Thirteenth-Century Papacy

At first glance the popes may appear to have been in a very favorable position in the latter half of the thirteenth century. Frederick II had been vanquished and imperial pressure on Rome had been removed. The French king, Louis IX, was an enthusiastic supporter of the church, as his two disastrous Crusades, which won him sainthood, testify. Although it lasted only seven years, a reunion of the Eastern church with Rome was proclaimed by the Council of Lyons in 1274, as the Western church took advantage of the Emperor Michael Palaeologus's request for aid against the Turks. Despite these positive events, the church was not really in as favorable a position as it appeared.

As early as the reign of Pope Innocent III (1198–1216), when papal power reached its height, there were ominous developments. Innocent had elaborated the doctrine of papal plenitude of power and on that authority had declared saints, disposed of benefices, and created a centralized papal monarchy with a clearly political mission. Innocent's transformation of the papacy into a great secular power had the consequence of weakening the church religiously as he sought to strengthen it politically. Thereafter the church as a papal monarchy and the church as the "body of the faithful" came increasingly to be differentiated; it was against the "papal church" and in the name of the "true Christian church" that both reformers and heretics raised their voices in protest until the Protestant Reformation.

What Innocent began, his successors perfected. Under Urban IV (1261–1264) the papacy established its own law court, the Rota Romana, which tightened and centralized the church's legal proceedings. The latter half of the thirteenth century saw an elaboration of the system of clerical taxation; what had begun in the twelfth century as an emergency measure to raise funds for the Crusades became a fixed institution. In the same period, papal power to determine appointments to many major and minor church offices—the so-called reservation of benefices—was greatly broadened. The thirteenth-century papacy became a powerful political institution governed by its own law and courts, serviced by an efficient international bureaucracy, and preoccupied with secular goals.

Papal centralization of the church tended to undermine both diocesan authority and popular support. Rome's interests, not local needs, came to control church appointments, policies, and discipline. Discontented lower clergy appealed to the higher authority of Rome against the disciplinary measures of local bishops. In the second half of the thirteenth century bishops and abbots protested such undercutting of their power. To its critics the church in Rome seemed hardly more than a legalized, fiscalized, bureaucratic institution. As early as the late twelfth century, heretical movements of Cathars and Waldensians had appealed to the biblical ideal of simplicity and separation from the world as opposed to a perceived materialism in official religion against which reformers loyal to the church, such as St. Francis of Assisi, would also protest.

The church of the thirteenth century was

being undermined by more than internal religious disunity. The demise of imperial power meant that the papacy in Rome was no longer the leader of antiimperial (Guelf, or propapal) sentiment in Italy. Instead of being the center of Italian resistance to the emperor, popes now found themselves on the defensive against their old allies. That was the ironic price paid by the papacy to vanquish the Hohenstaufens.

Rulers with a stake in Italian politics now directed the intrigue formerly aimed at the emperor toward dominating the college of cardinals. Charles of Anjou, king of Sicily, for example, managed to create a French-Sicilian faction within the college. Such efforts to control the decisions of the college led Pope Gregory X (1271–1276) to establish the so-called conclave of cardinals. This was the practice of sequestering the cardinals immediately on the death of the pope so that extraneous political influence on the election of new popes might be kept to a minimum. But the conclave proved to be of little avail, so politicized had the college of cardinals become.

In 1294 such a college, in frustration after a deadlock of over two years, chose a saintly but inept Calabrian hermit as Pope Celestine V. Celestine abdicated under suspicious circumstances after only a few weeks in office and also died under suspicious circumstances (his successor's critics later argued that he had been murdered to ensure the unity of the papal office). His tragicomic reign shocked a majority of the college into unified affirmative action. He was quickly replaced by his very opposite, Pope Boniface VIII (1294–1303), a nobleman and a skilled politician, whose pontificate, however, saw the beginning of the end of papal pretensions to great power status.

Boniface VIII and Philip the Fair

Boniface came to rule when England and France were maturing as nation-states. In England a long tradition of consultation between the king and powerful members of English society evolved into formal "parliaments" during the reigns of Henry III (1216–1272) and Edward I (1272–1307), and these Parliaments

Pope Boniface VIII (1294–1303) *who opposed the taxation of clergy by the kings of France and England and issued one of the strongest declarations of papal authority, the bull* Unam Sanctam. *The statue is in the Museo Civico, Bologna, Italy.* [Alinari/SCALA]

helped to create a unified kingdom. The reign of the French king Philip IV the Fair (1285–1314) saw France become an efficient, centralized monarchy. Philip was no Saint Louis, but a ruthless politician intent on ending England's continental holdings, controlling wealthy Flanders, and establishing French hegemony within the Holy Roman Empire. Boniface had the further misfortune of bringing to the papal throne memories of the way earlier popes had brought kings and emperors to their knees. Very painfully he was to discover that the papal monarchy of the early thirteenth century was no match for the new political powers of the late thirteenth century.

France and England were on the brink of all-out war when Boniface became pope (1294). Only Edward I's preoccupation with rebellion in Scotland, which the French encouraged, prevented a full-scale English invasion of France around the turn of the century—a turn of events that would have started the Hundred Years' War a half century earlier. As both countries mobilized for war, they used the pretext of preparing for a Crusade to tax the clergy heavily. In 1215 Pope Innocent III had decreed that the clergy were to pay no taxes to rulers without prior papal consent. Viewing English and French taxation of the clergy as an assault on traditional clerical rights, Boniface took a strong stand against it. On February 5, 1296, he issued a bull, *Clericis Laicos,* which forbade lay taxation of the clergy without prior papal approval and took back all previous papal dispensations in this regard.

In England Edward I retaliated by denying the clergy the right to be heard in royal court, in effect removing from them the protection of the king. But it was Philip the Fair who struck back with a vengeance. In August 1296 he forbade the exportation of money from France to Rome, thereby denying the papacy revenues without which it could not operate. Boniface had no choice but to come quickly to terms with Philip. He conceded Philip the right to tax the French clergy "during an emergency," and, not coincidentally, he canonized Louis IX in the same year.

Boniface was at this time also under siege by powerful Italian enemies, whom Philip did not fail to patronize. A noble family (the Colonnas), rivals of Boniface's family (the Gaetani) and radical followers of Saint Francis of Assisi (the Spiritual Franciscans), were at this time seeking to invalidate Boniface's election as pope on the grounds that Celestine V had re-signed the office under coercion. Charges of heresy, simony, and even the murder of Celestine, who had died shortly after his abdication, were hurled against Boniface.

In the year 1300 Boniface's fortunes appeared to revive. Tens of thousands of pilgrims flocked to Rome in that year for the Jubilee celebration. In a Jubilee year all Catholics who visited Rome and there fulfilled certain conditions received a special indulgence, or remission of their sins. Heady with this display of popular religiosity, Boniface reinserted himself into international politics. He championed Scottish resistance to England, for which he received a firm rebuke from an outraged Edward I and from Parliament.

But once again a confrontation with the king of France proved the more costly. Philip, seemingly spoiling for another fight with the pope, arrested Boniface's Parisian legate, Bernard Saisset, the bishop of Pamiers and also a powerful secular lord, whose independence Philip had opposed. Saisset was accused of heresy and treason and was tried and convicted in the king's court. Thereafter Philip demanded that Boniface recognize the process against Saisset, something that Boniface could do only if he was prepared to surrender his jurisdiction over the French episcopate. This challenge could not be sidestepped, and Boniface acted swiftly to champion Saisset as a defender of clerical political independence within France. He demanded Saisset's unconditional release, revoked all previous agreements with Philip in the matter of clerical taxation, and ordered the French bishops to convene in Rome within a year. A bull, *Ausculta Fili* ("Listen, My Son"), was sent to Philip in December 1301, pointedly informing him that "God has set popes over kings and kingdoms."

UNAM SANCTAM (1302). Philip unleashed a ruthless antipapal campaign. Two royal apologists, Pierre Dubois and John of Paris, refuted papal claims to the right to intervene in temporal matters. Increasingly placed on the defensive, Boniface made a last-ditch stand against state control of national churches when on November 18, 1302, he issued the bull *Unam Sanctam.* This famous statement of papal power declared that temporal authority was "subject" to the spiritual power of the church. On its face a bold assertion, *Unam Sanctam* was in truth the desperate act of a besieged papacy.

After *Unam Sanctam* the French and the

321

*The Late
Middle Ages
and the
Renaissance:
Decline and
Renewal
(1300–1527)*

Boniface VIII Reasserts the Church's Claim to Temporal Power

Defied by the French and the English, Pope Boniface VIII (1294–1303) boldly reasserted the temporal power of the church in the bull *Unam Sanctam* (November 1302). This document claimed that both spiritual and temporal power on earth were under the pope's jurisdiction, because, in the hierarchy of the universe, spiritual power both preceded and sat in judgment on temporal power.

We are taught by the words of the Gospel that in this church and in her power there are two swords, a spiritual one and a temporal one. . . . Certainly anyone who denies that the temporal sword is in the power of Peter has not paid heed to the words of the Lord when he said, "Put up thy sword into its sheath" (Matthew 26:52). Both then are in the power of the church, the material sword and the spiritual. But the one is exercised for the church, the other by the church, the one by the hand of the priest, the other by the hand of kings and soldiers, though at the will and suffrance of the authority subject to the spiritual power. . . . For, according to the blessed Dionysius, it is the law of divinity for the lowest to be led to the highest through intermediaries. In the order of the universe all things are not kept in order in the same fashion and immediately but the lowest are ordered by the intermediate and inferiors by superiors. But that the spiritual power excels any earthly one in dignity and nobility we ought the more openly to confess in proportion as spiritual things excel temporal ones. Moreover we clearly perceive this from the giving of tithes, from benediction and sanctification, from the acceptance of this power and from the very government of things. For, the truth bearing witness, the spiritual power has to institute the earthly power and to judge it if it has not been good. So it is verified the prophecy of Jeremiah (1:10) concerning the church and the power of the church, "Lo, I have set thee this day over the nations and over kingdoms."

Brian Tierney, *The Crisis of Church and State* 1050–1300 (Englewood Cliffs, N.J.: Prentice-Hall, 1964), pp. 188–189.

Colonnas moved against Boniface with force. Guillaume de Nogaret, Philip's chief minister, denounced Boniface to the French clergy as a common heretic and criminal. An army, led by Nogaret and Sciarra Colonna, surprised the pope in mid-August 1303 at his retreat in Anagni. Boniface was badly beaten up and almost executed before an aroused populace liberated and returned him safely to Rome. But the ordeal proved too much for the pope, who died a few months later, in October 1303.

Boniface's immediate successor, Benedict XI (1303–1304), excommunicated Nogaret for his deed, but there was to be no lasting papal retaliation. Benedict's successor, Clement V (1305–1314), was forced into French subservience. A former archbishop of Bordeaux, Clement declared that *Unam Sanctam* should not be understood as in any way diminishing French royal authority. He released Nogaret from excommunication and pliantly condemned the Knights Templars, whose treasure Philip thereafter forcibly expropriated. Clement established the papal court at Avignon, on the southeastern border of France, in 1309. The imperial city of Avignon, situated on land that belonged to the pope, maintained its independence from the king. In 1311 Clement made the city his permanent residence, both to escape a Rome ridden with strife after the confrontation between Boniface and Philip, and also to escape pressure from Philip. There the papacy was to remain until 1377.

After Boniface's humiliation popes never again so seriously threatened kings and emperors, despite continuing papal excommunications and political intrigue. In the future the relation between Church and State would tilt toward state control of religion within particular monarchies and the subordination of ecclesiastical authority to larger secular political purposes.

Palace of the popes in Avignon, France. In 1311 Clement V made the city his permanent residence, and the popes remained there until 1377.

Petrarch Describes the Papal Residence at Avignon

Petrarch, the father of Humanism, lived in Avignon and personally observed the papacy there over a long period of time. In this letter written between 1340 and 1353, he described with deep, pious outrage the ostentation and greed of the Avignon popes.

I am now living in [Avignon], in the Babylon of the West. . . . Here reign the successors of the poor fishermen of Galilee [who] have strangely forgotten their origin. I am astounded, as I recall their predecessors, to see these men loaded with gold and clad in purple, boasting of the spoils of princes and nations; to see luxurious palaces and heights crowned with fortifications, instead of a boat turned downwards for [their] shelter. We no longer find the simple nets which were once used to gain a frugal living from the lake of Galilee. . . . One is stupefied nowadays to hear the lying tongues, and to see worthless parchments turned by a leaden seal [i.e., official bulls of the pope] into nets which are used, in Christ's name, but by the arts of Belial [i.e., the devil], to catch hordes of unwary Christians. These fish, too, are dressed and laid on the burning coals of anxiety before they fill the insatiable maw of their captors.

Instead of holy solitude we find a criminal host and crowds . . . ; instead of sobriety, licentious banquets . . . ; instead of pious pilgrimages . . . foul sloth; instead of the bare feet of the apostles . . . horses decked in gold. . . . In short, we seem to be among the kings of the Persians or Parthians, before whom we must fall down and worship, and who cannot be approached except presents be offered.

James Harvey Robinson (Ed.), *Readings in European History*, Vol. 1 (Boston: Athenaeum, 1904), pp. 502–530.

323

*The Late
Middle Ages
and the
Renaissance:
Decline and
Renewal
(1300–1527)*

The Avignon Papacy (1309–1377)

The Avignon papacy was in appearance, although not always in actual fact, under strong French influence. During Clement V's pontificate the French came to dominate the college of cardinals. Clement also expanded papal taxes, especially the practice of collecting annates, the first year's revenue of a church office or benefice bestowed by the pope—a practice that contributed much to the Avignon papacy's reputation as being materialistic and politically motivated.

POPE JOHN XXII. Pope John XXII (1316–1334), the most powerful Avignon pope, tried to restore papal independence and return to Italy. This goal led him into war with the Visconti, the most powerful ruling family of Milan, and a costly contest with Emperor Louis IV, whose election as emperor in 1314 John had challenged in favor of the rival Habsburg candidate. The result was a minor replay of the confrontation between Philip the Fair and Boniface VIII. When John obstinately and without legal justification refused to recognize Louis's election, the emperor retaliated by declaring John deposed and setting in his place an antipope. As Philip the Fair had also done, Louis enlisted the support of the Spiritual Franciscans, whose views on absolute poverty John had condemned as heretical. Two outstanding pamphleteers wrote lasting tracts for the royal cause: William of Ockham, whom John excommunicated in 1328, and Marsilius of Padua (ca. 1290–1342/43), whose teaching John declared heretical in 1327.

MARSILIUS OF PADUA. In his *Defender of Peace* (1324), Marsilius of Padua stressed the independent origins and autonomy of secular government. Clergy were subjected to the strictest apostolic ideals and confined to purely spiritual functions, and all power of coercive judgment was denied the pope. Marsilius argued that spiritual crimes must await an eter-

---

Marsilius of Padua Denies Coercive Power to the Clergy

According to Marsilius, the Bible gave the pope no right to pronounce and execute sentences on any person. The clergy held a strictly moral and spiritual rule, their judgments to be executed only in the afterlife, not in the present one. Here, on earth, they should be obedient to secular authority. Marsilius argued this point by appealing to the example of Jesus.

We now wish . . . to adduce the truths of the holy Scripture . . . which explicitly command or counsel that neither the Roman bishop called pope, nor any other bishop or priest, or deacon, has or ought to have any rulership or coercive judgment or jurisdiction over any priest or non-priest, ruler, community, group, or individual of whatever condition. . . . Christ himself came into the world not to dominate men, nor to judge them [coercively] . . . not to wield temporal rule, but rather to be subject as regards the . . . present life; and moreover, he wanted to and did exclude himself, his apostles and disciples, and their successors, the bishops or priests, from all coercive authority or worldly rule, both by his
example and by his word of counsel or command. . . . When he was brought before Pontius Pilate . . . and accused of having called himself king of the Jews, and [Pilate] asked him whether he had said this . . . [his] reply included these words . . . "My kingdom is not of this world," that is, I have not come to reign by temporal rule or dominion, in the way . . . worldly kings reign. . . . This, then, is the kingdom concerning which he came to teach and order, a kingdom which consists in the acts whereby the eternal kingdom is attained, that is, the acts of faith and the other theological virtues; not however, by coercing anyone thereto.

Marsilius of Padua: The Defender of Peace: The Defensor Pacis, trans. by Alan Gewirth (New York: Harper, 1967), pp. 113–116.

nal punishment. Transgressions of divine law, over which the pope had jurisdiction, were to be punished in the next life, not in the present one, unless the secular ruler declared a divine law also a secular law. This assertion was a direct challenge of the power of the pope to excommunicate rulers and place countries under interdict. The *Defender of Peace* depicted the pope as a subordinate member of a society over which the emperor ruled supreme and in which temporal peace was the highest good.

John XXII made the papacy a sophisticated international agency and adroitly adjusted it to the growing European money economy. The more the Curia (or papal court) mastered the latter, however, the more vulnerable it became to criticism. Under John's successor, Benedict XII (1334–1342), the papacy became entrenched in Avignon. Seemingly forgetting Rome altogether, Benedict began construction of the great Palace of the Popes and attempted to reform both papal government and the religious life. His high-living French successor, Clement VI (1342–1352), placed papal policy in lockstep with the French. In this period the cardinals became barely more than lobbyists for policies favorable to their secular patrons.

NATIONAL OPPOSITION TO THE AVIGNON PAPACY. As Avignon's fiscal tentacles probed new areas, monarchies took strong action to protect their interests. The latter half of the fourteenth century saw legislation restricting papal jurisdiction and taxation in France, England, and Germany. In England, where the Avignon papacy was identified with the French enemy after the outbreak of the Hundred Years' War, statutes of *provisors* and *praemunire*, which restricted payments and appeals to Rome, were several times passed by Parliament between 1351 and 1393. In France ecclesiastical appointments and taxation were regulated by the so-called Gallican liberties. These national rights over religion had long been exercised in fact and were legally acknowledged by the church in the Pragmatic Sanction of Bourges in 1438. This agreement recognized the right of the French church to elect its own clergy without papal interference, prohibited the payment of annates to Rome, and limited the right of appeals from French courts to the Curia in Rome. In German and Swiss cities in the fourteenth and fifteenth centuries, local governments also took the initiative to limit and even to overturn traditional clerical privileges and immunities.

JOHN WYCLIFFE AND JOHN HUSS. The popular lay religious movements that most successfully assailed the late medieval church were the Lollards in England and the Hussites in Bohemia. Both John Wycliffe (d. 1384) and John Huss (d. 1415) would have disclaimed the extremists who revolted in their name, yet Wycliffe's writings gave at least a theoretical justification to the demands of the Lollards and Huss's writings to the programs of both moderate and extreme Hussites.

Wycliffe's work initially served the anticlerical policies of the English government. An Oxford theologian and a philosopher of high standing, Wycliffe became within England what William of Ockham and Marsilius of Padua had been at the Bavarian court of Emperor Louis IV: a major intellectual spokesman for the rights of royalty against the secular pretensions of popes. After 1350 English kings greatly reduced the power of the Avignon papacy to make ecclesiastical appointments and collect taxes within England, a position that Wycliffe strongly supported. His views on clerical poverty followed original Franciscan ideals and, more by accident than by design, gave justification to government restriction and even confiscation of church properties within England. Wycliffe argued that the clergy "ought to be content with food and clothing." He also maintained that personal merit, not rank and office, was the only basis of religious authority—a dangerous teaching because it raised allegedly pious laypeople above allegedly corrupt ecclesiasts, regardless of the latter's official stature. There was a threat in such teaching to secular as well as to ecclesiastical dominion and jurisdiction. At his posthumous condemnation by the pope, Wycliffe was accused of the ancient heresy of Donatism—the teaching that the efficacy of the church's sacraments did not lie in their sheer performance but also depended on the moral character of the clergy who administered them. Wycliffe also anticipated certain Protestant criticisms of the medieval church by challenging papal infallibility, the sale of indulgences, and the dogma of transubstantiation.

English advocates of Wycliffe's teaching were called *Lollards*. Like the Waldensians, they preached in the vernacular, disseminated translations of Holy Scripture, and championed clerical poverty. At first, they came from every social class, being especially prominent among the groups that had something tangible to gain from the confiscation of clerical properties (the nobility and the gentry) or that had suffered most under the current church system (the lower clergy and the poor people). After the English Peasants' Revolt of 1381, an uprising filled with egalitarian notions that could find support in Wycliffe's teaching, Lollardy was officially viewed as subversive. Opposed by an alliance of church and crown, it became a capital offense in England by 1401.

Heresy was not so easily harnessed in Bohemia, where it coalesced with a strong national movement. The University of Prague, founded in 1348, became the center for both Czech nationalism and a native religious reform movement. The latter began within the bounds of orthodoxy and was led by local intellectuals and preachers, the most famous of whom was John Huss, the rector of the university after 1403. The reformers supported vernacular translations of the Bible and were critical of traditional ceremonies and allegedly superstitious practices, particularly those relating to the sacrament of the Eucharist. They advocated lay communion with cup as well as bread (traditionally only the priest received communion with both cup and bread, the laity with bread only, a sign of the clergy's spiritual superiority over the laity), taught that bread and wine remained bread and wine after priestly consecration, and questioned the validity of sacraments performed by priests in mortal sin. Wycliffe's teaching appears to have influenced the movement very early. Regular traffic between England and Bohemia had existed for decades, ever since the marriage in 1381 of Anne of Bohemia to King Richard II. Czech students studied at Oxford, and many returned with copies of Wycliffe's writings.

Huss became the leader of the pro-Wycliffe faction at the University of Prague, and in 1410 his activities brought about his excommunication and the placement of Prague under papal interdict. In 1414 Huss won an audience with the newly assembled Council of Constance. He journeyed to the council eagerly, armed with a safe-conduct pass from Emperor Sigismund, and naively believing that he would convince his strongest critics of the truth of his teaching. Within weeks of his arrival in early November 1414, he was formally accused of heresy and imprisoned. He died at the stake on July 6, 1415, and was followed there less than a year later by his colleague Jerome of Prague. The reaction in Bohemia to the execution of these national heroes was fierce revolt as militant Hussites, the Taborites, set out to transform

A German portrayal of the burning of John Huss for heresy. His ashes were dumped into the Rhine to prevent their becoming relics. [Vincent Virga Archives]

Bohemia by force into a religious and social paradise under the military leadership of John Ziska. After a decade of belligerent protest, the Hussites won significant religious reforms and control over the Bohemian church from the Council of Basel.

The Great Schism (1378–1417) and the Conciliar Movement to 1449

URBAN VI AND CLEMENT VII. Pope Gregory XI (1370–1378) reestablished the papacy in Rome in January 1377, ending what had come to be known as the "Babylonian Captivity" of the church in Avignon, the reference being to the biblical bondage of the Israelites. The return to Rome proved to be short-lived, however. On Gregory's death on March 27, 1378, the cardinals, in Rome, elected an Italian archbishop as Pope Urban VI (1378–1389), who immediately proclaimed his intention to reform the Curia. This announcement came as an unexpected challenge to the cardinals, most of whom were French, and made them amenable to royal pressures to return the papacy to Avignon. The French king, Charles V, not wanting to surrender the benefits of a papacy located within the sphere of French influence, lent his support to a schism. Five months after Urban's election, on September 20, 1378, thirteen cardinals, all but one of whom was French, formed their own conclave and elected a cousin of the French king as Pope Clement VII (1378–1397). They insisted, probably with some truth, that they had voted for Urban in fear of their lives, surrounded by a Roman mob that demanded the election of an Italian pope. Be that as it may, thereafter the papacy became a "two-headed thing" and a scandal to Christendom. Allegiance to the two papal courts divided along political lines: England and its allies (the Holy Roman Empire, Hungary, Bohemia, and Poland) acknowledged Urban VI, whereas France and its orbit (Naples, Scotland, Castile, and Aragon) supported Clement VII. Only the Roman line of popes, however, came to be recognized as official in subsequent church history.

Two approaches were initially taken to end the schism. One tried to win the mutual cession of both popes, thereby clearing the way for a new election of a single pope. The other sought to secure the resignation of the one in favor of the other. Both proved completely fruitless, however. Each pope considered himself fully legitimate, and too much was at stake for a magnanimous concession on the part of either. There was one way left: the forced deposition of both popes by a special council of the church.

CONCILIAR THEORY OF CHURCH GOVERNMENT. Legally a church council could be convened only by a pope, and the competing popes were not inclined to summon a council for their own deposition. Also, the deposition of a legitimate pope against his will by a council of the church was as serious a matter as the forced dethronement of a legally recognized hereditary monarch by a representative body.

The correctness of a conciliar deposition of a pope was debated a full thirty years before any direct action was taken. Conciliar theorists, chief among whom were the masters of the University of Paris, Conrad of Gelnhausen, Henry of Langenstein, Jean Gerson, and Pierre d'Ailly, challenged the popes' identification of the church's welfare with their own and developed arguments in favor of a more representative government of the church; their goal was a church in which a representative council could effectively regulate the actions of the pope. Conciliarists defined the church as the whole body of the faithful, a body of which the elected head, the pope, was only one part, and a part whose sole purpose was to maintain the unity and well-being of the body as a whole—something that the schismatic popes were far from doing. The conciliarists further argued that a council of the church, as a Holy Spirit–inspired spokesman for a majority of the faithful, acted with greater authority than the pope alone. In the eyes of the pope(s) such a concept of the church threatened both its political and its religious unity.

THE COUNCIL OF PISA (1409–1410). On the basis of such arguments, cardinals representing both sides convened a council on their own authority in Pisa in 1409. There they deposed both the Roman and the Avignon popes and elected in their stead a new pope, Alexander V. To the council's consternation neither pope accepted its action, and after 1409 Christendom confronted the spectacle of three contending popes. Although the vast majority of Latin Christendom did at this time accept Alexander and his Pisan successor John XXIII (1410–1415), the popes of Rome and Avignon refused to step down.

THE COUNCIL OF CONSTANCE (1414–1417). This intolerable situation ended when the emperor Sigismund prevailed on John XXIII to summon a "legal" council of the church in Constance in 1414, a council also recognized by the Roman pope Gregory XII. Gregory, however, soon resigned his office, raising grave doubts forevermore about whether the council was truly convened with Rome's blessing and hence valid. In a famous declaration entitled *Haec Sancta*, the council fathers asserted their supremacy and proceeded to conduct the business of the church. In November 1417 the council successfully accomplished its main business when it elected a new pope, Martin V (1417–1431), after the

327

*The Late
Middle Ages
and the
Renaissance:
Decline and
Renewal
(1300–1527)*

The Chronicler Calls the Roll at the Council of Constance

The Council of Constance, in session for three years (1414–1417), not only drew many clergy and political representatives into its proceedings but also required a great variety of supporting personnel. Here is an inventory from the contemporary chronicle by Ulrich Richental.

Pope John XXIII came with 600 men.

Pope Martin, who was elected pope at Constance, came with 30 men.

5 patriarchs, with 118 men.

33 cardinals, with 3,056 men.

47 archbishops, with 4,700 men.

145 bishops, with 6,000 men.

93 suffragan bishops, with 360 men.

Some 500 spiritual lords, with 4,000 men.

24 auditors and secretaries, with 300 men.

37 scholars from the universities of all nations, with 2,000 men.

217 doctors of theology from the five nations, who walked in the processions, with 2,600 men.

361 doctors of both laws, with 1,260 men.

171 doctors of medicine, with 1,600 men.

1,400 masters of arts and licentiates, with 3,000 men.

5,300 simple priests and scholars, some by threes, some by twos, some alone.

The apothecaries who lived in huts, with 300 men. (16 of them were masters.)

72 goldsmiths, who lived in huts.

Over 1,400 merchants, shopkeepers, furriers, smiths, shoemakers, innkeepers, and handworkers, who lived in huts and rented houses and huts, with their servants.

24 rightful heralds of the King, with their squires.

1,700 trumpeters, fifers, fiddlers, and players of all kinds.

Over 700 harlots in brothels came, who hired their own houses, and some who lay in stables and wherever they could, beside the private ones whom I could not count.

In the train of the Pope were 24 secretaries with 200 men, 16 doorkeepers, 12 beadles who carried silver rods, 60 other beadles for the cardinals, auditors and auditors of the camera, and many old women who washed and mended the clothes of the Roman lords in private and public.

132 abbots, all named, with 2,000 men.

155 priors, all recorded with their names, with 1,600 men.

Our lord King, two queens, and 5 princely ladies.

39 dukes, 32 princely lords and counts, 141 counts, 71 barons, more than 1,500 knights, more than 20,000 noble squires.

Embassies from 83 kings of Asia, Africa, and Europe, with full powers; envoys from other lords without number, for they rode in and out every day. There were easily 5,000.

472 envoys from imperial cities.

352 envoys from baronial cities.

72,460 persons.

Richental's *Chronicle of the Council, Constance,* in *The Council of Constance,* ed., by J. H. Mundy and K. M. Woodey, trans. by Louise R. Roomis (New York: Columbia University Press, 1961), pp. 189–190.

three contending popes had either resigned (Gregory XIII) or were deposed (Benedict XIII and John XXIII). The council made provisions for regular meetings of church councils, scheduling a general council of the church for purposes of reform within five, then seven, and thereafter every ten years. Constance has remained, however, an illegitimate church council in official eyes; nor are the schismatic popes of Avignon and Pisa recognized as legitimate (for this reason, another pope could take the name John XXIII in 1958).

THE COUNCIL OF BASEL (1431–1449). Conciliar government of the church both peaked and declined during the Council of Basel. In 1432 the council invited the Hussites to send a delegation to Basel to make peace.

The Council of Constance Declares Conciliar Supremacy

The decree *Haec Sancta* (April 1415) asserted the supremacy of councils over popes in time of emergency in the church. This was the legal basis on which the Council of Constance proceeded to remove the contending popes from power and end the schism by electing a new pope, Martin V (1417–1431).

This holy Council of Constance . . . declares, first that it is lawfully assembled in the Holy Spirit, that it constitutes a General Council, representing the Catholic Church, and that therefore it has its authority immediately from Christ; and that all men, of every rank and condition, including the pope himself, are bound to obey it in matters concerning the Faith, the abolition of the schism, and the reformation of the Church of God in its head and its members. Secondly, it declares that anyone, of any rank and condition, who shall contumaciously refuse to obey the orders, decrees, statutes or instructions, made or to be made by this holy Council, or by any other lawfully assembled general council . . . shall, unless he comes to a right frame of mind, be subjected to fitting penance and punished appropriately: and, if need be, recourse shall be had to the other sanctions of the law.

From *Documents of the Christian Church*, ed. by Henry Bettenson (New York: Oxford University Press, 1961), pp. 192–193.

The Hussites presented a doctrinal statement known as the *Four Articles of Prague*, which served as a basis for the negotiations. This document contained requests for (1) giving the laity the Eucharist with cup as well as bread (hence their name *Utraquists*, from the Latin word meaning "both," and *Calixtines*, from the Latin word for "cup"); (2) free, itinerant preaching; (3) the exclusion of the clergy from holding secular offices and possessing property; and (4) just punishment of clergy who have committed mortal sins. In November 1433 an agreement was reached between the emperor, the council, and the Hussites. The Bohemian church received jurisdictional rights similar to those already secured by France and England. Three of the four Prague articles were conceded: communion with cup, free preaching by ordained clergy, and like punishment of clergy and laity for mortal sins. The church firmly retained the right to possess and dispose of property.

THE COUNCIL OF FERRARA–FLORENCE (1438–1439). The termination of the Hussite wars and the reform legislation curtailing the papal power of appointment and taxation were the high points of the Council of Basel. Heady with success, the Basel council seemed to its critics to assert its powers beyond the original intention of the decrees of Constance and in doing so undermined much internal and external support. Original supporters of the council, prominent among them the philosopher Nicholas of Cusa, turned their backs on the council when Pope Eugenius IV (1431–1447) ordered it to transfer to Ferrara in 1437. The pope had a golden opportunity to upstage the Council of Basel by negotiating a reunion with the Eastern church, which was bargaining for Western aid against new Turkish advances. A majority of Basel's members refused to transfer to Ferrara, and their defiance made Basel a schismatic council. Those in Basel watched while the reunion of the Eastern and Western churches was proclaimed in Florence, where the council of Ferrara had transferred because of plague, in 1439. This agreement, although short-lived, restored papal prestige and signaled the demise of the conciliar movement.

The notion of conciliar superiority suffered a mortal blow with the collapse of the Council of Basel in 1449. A decade later the papal bull *Execrabilis* (1460) condemned appeals to councils as "erroneous and abominable" and "completely null and void."

Although many who had worked for reform

now despaired of ever attaining it, the conciliar movement was not a total failure. It planted deep within the conscience of all Western peoples the conviction that the leader of an institution must be responsive to its members and that the head exists to lead and serve, not to bring disaster on, the body.

A second consequence of the conciliar movement was the devolving of religious responsibility on the laity. In the absence of papal leadership, secular control of national or territorial churches increased. Kings asserted power over the church in England and France. Magistrates and city councils reformed and regulated religious life in German, Swiss, and Italian cities. This development was not reversed by the powerful "restoration" popes of the high Renaissance. On the contrary, as the papacy became a limited territorial regime, national control of the church simply ran apace. Perceived as just one among several Italian states, the Papal States could be opposed as much on the grounds of "national" policy as for religious reasons.

Revival of Monarchy: Nation Building in the Fifteenth Century

After 1450 there was a progressive shift from divided feudal to unified national monarchies as "sovereign" rulers emerged. This is not to say that the dynastic and chivalric ideals of feudal monarchy did not continue. Territorial princes did not pass from the scene, and representative bodies persisted and in some areas even grew in influence. But in the late fifteenth and early sixteenth centuries the old problem of the one and the many was decided clearly in favor of the interests of monarchy.

The feudal monarchy of the high Middle Ages was characterized by the division of the basic powers of government between the king and his semiautonomous vassals. The nobility and the towns acted with varying degrees of unity and success through such evolving representative assemblies as the English Parliament, the French Estates General, and the Spanish Cortes to thwart the centralization of royal power. Because of the Hundred Years' War and the schism in the church, the nobility and the clergy were in decline in the late Middle Ages. The increasingly important towns began to ally with the king. Loyal, business-wise townspeo-

ple, not the nobility and the clergy, staffed the royal offices and became the king's lawyers, bookkeepers, military tacticians, and foreign diplomats. It was this new alliance between king and town that finally broke the bonds of feudal society and made possible the rise of sovereign states.

In a sovereign state the power of taxation, war making, and law enforcement is no longer the local right of semiautonomous vassals but is concentrated in the monarch and is exercised by his or her chosen agents. Taxes, wars, and laws become national rather than merely regional matters. Only as monarchs were able to act independently of the nobility and the representative assemblies could they overcome the decentralization that had been the basic obstacle to nation building. Ferdinand and Isabella rarely called the Cortes into session. The French Estates General did not meet at all from 1484 to 1560. Henry VII (1485–1509) of England managed to raise revenues without going begging to Parliament after Parliament voted him customs revenues for life in 1485. Monarchs were also assisted by brilliant theorists, from Marsilius of Padua in the fourteenth century to Machiavelli and Jean Bodin in the sixteenth, who eloquently argued the sovereign rights of monarchy.

The many were, of course, never totally subjugated to the one, and still today the cry of "states' rights" is very distinct. But in the last half of the fifteenth century, rulers increasingly demonstrated that the law was their creature. Civil servants whose vision was no longer merely local or regional filled royal offices. In Castile they were the *corregidores*, in England the justices of the peace, in France bailiffs operating through well-drilled lieutenants. These royal ministers and agents were not immune to becoming closely attached to the localities they administered in the ruler's name. And regions were able to secure congenial royal appointments. Throughout England local magnates served as representatives of the Tudors. Nonetheless these new executives were truly *royal* executives, bureaucrats whose outlook was "national" and whose loyalty was to the "state."

Monarchies also began to create standing national armies in the fifteenth century. As the noble cavalry receded and the infantry and the artillery became the backbone of the armies, mercenary soldiers were recruited from Switzerland and Germany to form the major part of the "king's army." Professional soldiers who fought for pay and booty proved far more efficient than feudal vassals who fought simply for honor's sake. Monarchs who failed to meet their payrolls, however, faced a new danger of mutiny and banditry on the part of alien troops.

The more expensive warfare of the fifteenth and sixteenth centuries increased the need to develop new national sources of royal income. The expansion of royal revenues was especially hampered by the stubborn belief among the highest classes that they were immune from government taxation. The nobility guarded their properties and traditional rights and despised taxation as an insult and a humiliation. Royal revenues accordingly grew at the expense of those least able to resist, and least able to pay. The monarchs had several options. As feudal lords they could collect rents from their royal domain. They could also levy national taxes on basic food and clothing, such as the *gabelle* or salt tax in France and the *alcabala* or 10 per cent sales tax on commercial transactions in Spain. The rulers could also levy direct taxes on the peasantry. This they did through agreeable representative assemblies of the privileged classes in which the peasantry did not sit. The *taille*, which the French kings independently determined from year to year after the Estates General was suspended in 1484, was such a tax. Sale of public offices and issuance of high-interest government bonds appeared in the fifteenth century as innovative fund-raising devices. But rulers did not levy taxes on the powerful nobility. They turned to rich nobles, as they did to the great bankers of Italy and Germany, for loans, bargaining with the privileged classes, who in many instances remained as much the kings' creditors and competitors as their subjects.

France

Charles VII (1422–1461) was a king made great by those who served him. His ministers created a professional army, which—thanks initially to the inspiration of Joan of Arc—drove the English out of France. And largely because of the enterprise of an independent merchant banker named Jacques Coeur, the French also developed a strong economy, diplomatic corps, and national administration during Charles VII's reign. These were the sturdy tools with which Charles's successor, the ruthless Louis XI (1461–1483), made France a great power.

There were two cornerstones of French nation-building in the fifteenth century. The first was the collapse of the English empire in France following the Hundred Years' War. The second was the defeat of Charles the Bold and the duchy of Burgundy. Perhaps Europe's strongest political power in the mid-fifteenth century, Burgundy aspired to dwarf both France and the Holy Roman Empire as the leader of a dominant middle kingdom. It might have succeeded in doing so had not the continental powers joined together in opposition. When Charles the Bold died in defeat in a battle at Nancy in 1477, the dream of Burgundian empire died with him. Louis XI and Habsburg Emperor Maximilian I divided the conquered Burgundian lands between them, with the treaty-wise Habsburgs getting the better part. The dissolution of Burgundy ended its constant intrigue against the French king and left Louis XI free to secure the monarchy. The newly acquired Burgundian lands and his own Angevin inheritance permitted the king to end his reign with a kingdom almost twice the size of that with which he had started. Louis successfully harnessed the nobility, expanded the trade and industry so carefully nurtured by Jacques Coeur, created a national postal system, and even established a lucrative silk industry at Lyons (later transferred to Tours).

A strong nation is a two-edged sword. It was because Louis's successors inherited such a secure and efficient government that France was able to pursue Italian conquests in the 1490s and to fight a long series of losing wars with the Habsburgs in the first half of the sixteenth century. By the mid-sixteenth century France was again a defeated nation and almost as divided internally as during the Hundred Years' War.

Spain

Spain, too, became a strong country in the late fifteenth century. Both Castile and Aragon had been poorly ruled and divided kingdoms in the mid-fifteenth century. The union of Isabella of Castile (1474–1504) and Ferdinand of Aragon (1479–1516) changed that situation. The two future sovereigns married in 1469, despite strong protests from neighboring Portugal and France, both of which foresaw the formidable European power such a union would create. Castile was by far the richer and more populous of the two, having an estimated five million inhabitants to Aragon's population of under one million. Castile was also distinguished by its lucrative sheep-farming industry, which was run by a government-backed organization called the *Mesta*, another example of developing centralized economic planning. Although the two kingdoms were dynastically united by the marriage of Ferdinand and Isabella in 1469, they remained constitutionally separated, as each retained its respective government agencies—separate laws, armies, coinage, and taxation—and cultural traditions.

Ferdinand and Isabella could do together what neither was able to accomplish alone: subdue their realms, secure their borders, and venture abroad militarily. Between 1482 and 1492 they conquered the Moors in Granada. Naples became a Spanish possession in 1504. By 1512 Ferdinand had secured his northern borders by conquering the kingdom of Navarre. Internally Ferdinand and Isabella won the allegiance of the Hermandad, a powerful league of cities and towns, which served them against stubborn landowners. Townspeople allied themselves with the crown and progressively replaced the nobility within the royal administration. The crown also extended its authority over the wealthy chivalric orders, a further circumscription of the power of the nobility.

Spain had long been remarkable among European lands as a place where three religions—Islam, Judaism, and Christianity—coexisted with a certain degree of toleration. This toleration was to end dramatically under Ferdinand and Isabella, who made Spain the prime example of state-controlled religion. Ferdinand and Isabella exercised almost total control over the Spanish church as they placed religion in the service of national unity. They appointed the higher clergy and the officers of the Inquisition. The Inquisition, run by Tomás de Torquemada (d. 1498), Isabella's confessor, was a key national agency established in 1479 to monitor the activity of converted Jews *(conversos)* and Muslims *(Moriscos)* in Spain. In 1492 the Jews were exiled and their properties were confiscated. In 1502 nonconverting Moors in Granada were driven into exile by Cardinal Francisco Jiménez de Cisneros (1437–1517), the great spiritual reformer and educator. Spanish spiritual life remained largely uniform and successfully controlled—a major reason for Spain's remaining a loyal Catholic country throughout the sixteenth century and providing a base of operation for the European Counter-Reformation.

Ferdinand (1479–1516) and Isabella (1474–1504), from the royal chapel in the Cathedral of Granada. Their marriage in 1469, which joined the kingdoms of Aragon and Castile, made Spain a united nation. [Robert Frerck]

Despite a certain internal narrowness, Ferdinand and Isabella were rulers with wide horizons. They contracted anti-French marriage alliances that came to determine a large part of European history in the sixteenth century. In 1496 their eldest daughter, Joanna, later known as "the Mad," married Archduke Philip, the son of Emperor Maximilian I. The fruit of this union, Charles I of Spain, the first ruler over a united Spain, came by his inheritance and election as emperor in 1519 to rule over a European kingdom almost equal in size to that of Charlemagne. A second daughter, Catherine of Aragon, wed Arthur, the son of the English King Henry VII, and after Arthur's premature death, she married his brother, the future King Henry VIII. The failure of this latter marriage became the key factor in the emergence of the Anglican church and the English Reformation.

The new Spanish power was also revealed in Ferdinand and Isabella's promotion of overseas exploration. Their patronage of the Genoese adventurer Christopher Columbus (1451–1506), who discovered the islands of the Caribbean while sailing west in search of a shorter route to the spice markets of the Far East, led to the creation of the Spanish empire in Mexico and Peru, whose gold and silver mines helped to make Spain Europe's dominant power in the sixteenth century.

England

The last half of the fifteenth century was a period of especially difficult political trial for the English. Following the Hundred Years' War, a defeated England was subjected to internal warfare between two rival branches of the royal family, the House of York and the House of Lancaster. This conflict, known to us today as the War of the Roses (as York's symbol, according to legend, was a white rose, and Lancaster's a red rose), kept England in turmoil from 1455 to 1485.

The Lancastrian monarchy of Henry VI (1422–1461) was consistently challenged by the duke of York and his supporters in the prosperous southern towns. In 1461 Edward IV (1461–1483), son of the duke of York, successfully seized power and instituted a strong-arm rule that lasted over twenty years, being only briefly interrupted in 1470–1471 by Henry VI's short-lived restoration. Edward, assisted by loyal and able ministers, effectively bent Parliament to his will. His brother and successor was Richard III (1483–1485). During the reign of the Tudors a tradition arose that painted Richard III as an unprincipled villain who murdered Edward's sons in the Tower of London to secure the throne. The best-known version of this characterization—unjust according to some—is found in Shakespeare's *Richard III*. Be that as it may, Richard's reign saw the growth of support for the exiled Lancastrian Henry Tudor. Henry returned to England to defeat Richard on Bosworth Field in August 1485.

Henry Tudor ruled as Henry VII (1485–1509), the first of the new Tudor dynasty that would dominate England throughout the sixteenth century. In order to bring the rival royal families together and to make the hereditary claim of his offspring to the throne uncontestable, Henry married Edward IV's daughter, Elizabeth of York. He succeeded in disciplining the English nobility through a special instrument of the royal will known as the *Court of Star Chamber*. Created in 1487 with the sanction of Parliament, this court enabled the king to act quickly and decisively against his opponents. Henry shrewdly construed legal precedents to the advantage of the crown, using

English law to further his own ends. He managed to confiscate noble lands and fortunes with such success that he governed without dependence on Parliament for royal funds, always a cornerstone of strong monarchy. In these ways Henry began to shape a monarchy that would develop into one of early modern Europe's most exemplary governments during the reign of his granddaughter, Elizabeth I.

The Holy Roman Empire

Germany and Italy were the striking exceptions to the steady development of centralized nation-states in the last half of the fifteenth century. Unlike England, France, and Spain, the empire saw the many thoroughly repulse the one. In Germany territorial rulers and cities resisted every effort at national consolidation and unity. As in Carolingian times rulers continued to partition their kingdoms, however small, among their sons, and by the late fifteenth century Germany was hopelessly divided into some three hundred autonomous political entities.

The princes and the cities did work together to create the machinery of law and order, if not of union, within the divided empire. An agreement reached between the emperor and the major German territorial rulers in 1356, known as the *Golden Bull*, established a seven-member electoral college consisting of the archbishops of Mainz, Trier, and Cologne; the duke of Saxony; the margrave of Brandenburg; the count Palatine; and the king of Bohemia. This group also functioned as an administrative body. They elected the emperor and, in cooperation with him, provided what transregional unity and administration existed. The figure of the emperor gave the empire a single ruler in law, if not in actual fact. As the conditions of his rule and the extent of his powers over his subjects, especially the seven electors, were renegotiated with every imperial election, the rights of the many (the princes) were always balanced against the power of the one (the emperor). In the fifteenth century an effort was made to control incessant feuding by the creation of an imperial diet (*Reichstag*). This was a national assembly of the seven electors, the nonelectoral princes, and the sixty-five imperial free cities. The cities were the weakest of the three bodies represented in the diet. During such an assembly in Worms in 1495, the members won from the emperor, Maximilian I (1493–1519), concessions that had been suc-

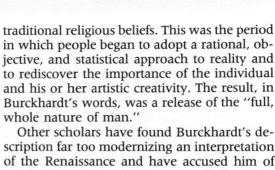

Emperor Maximilian (1493–1519) and his family, painted in 1515 by Bernard Strigel. Note the prominent Habsburg chin of the middle child. [Kunsthistoriches Museum, Vienna]

cessfully resisted by his predecessor, Frederick III (1440–1493). Led by Berthold of Henneberg, the archbishop of Mainz, the Diet of Worms secured an imperial ban on private warfare, a court of justice (the *Reichskammergericht*) to enforce internal peace, and an imperial Council of Regency (the *Reichsregiment*) to coordinate imperial and internal German policy. The latter was very grudgingly conceded by the emperor because it gave the princes a share in executive power.

Although important, these reforms were still a poor substitute for true national unity. In the sixteenth and seventeenth centuries the territorial princes became virtually sovereign rulers in their various domains. Such disunity aided religious dissent and conflict. It was in the cities and territories of still-feudal, fractionalized, backward Germany that the Protestant Reformation broke out in the sixteenth century.

The Renaissance in Italy (1375–1527)

In his famous study, *Civilization of the Renaissance in Italy* (1860), Jacob Burckhardt described the Renaissance as the prototype of the modern world. He believed that it was in fourteenth- and fifteenth-century Italy, through the revival of ancient learning, that new secular and scientific values first began to supplant traditional religious beliefs. This was the period in which people began to adopt a rational, objective, and statistical approach to reality and to rediscover the importance of the individual and his or her artistic creativity. The result, in Burckhardt's words, was a release of the "full, whole nature of man."

Other scholars have found Burckhardt's description far too modernizing an interpretation of the Renaissance and have accused him of overlooking the continuity between the Middle Ages and the Renaissance. His critics especially stress the still strongly Christian character of Humanism and the fact that earlier "renaissances," especially that of the twelfth century, also revived the ancient classics, professed interest in Latin language and Greek science, and appreciated the worth and creativity of individuals.

Despite the exaggeration and bias of Burckhardt's portrayal of the Renaissance, most scholars agree that the Renaissance was a time of transition from the medieval to the modern world. Medieval Europe, especially before the twelfth century, had been a fragmented feudal society with an agriculturally based economy, and its thought and culture were largely dominated by the church. Renaissance Europe, especially after the fourteenth century, was characterized by growing national consciousness and political centralization, an urban economy based on organized commerce and capitalism, and ever greater lay and secular control of thought and culture, including religion.

It was especially in Italy between the late fourteenth and the early sixteenth centuries, from roughly 1375 to 1527, the year of the infamous sack of Rome by imperial soldiers, that the distinctive features and achievements of the Renaissance, which also deeply influenced northern Europe (see Chapter 10), are most strikingly revealed.

The Italian City-State: Social Conflict and Despotism

Renaissance society was no simple cultural transformation. It first took distinctive shape within the cities of late medieval Italy. Italy had always had a cultural advantage over the rest of Europe because its geography made it the natural gateway between East and West. Venice, Genoa, and Pisa traded uninterruptedly with the Near East throughout the Middle Ages and maintained vibrant urban societies.

When commerce revived on a large scale in the eleventh century, Italian merchants quickly mastered the business skills of organization, bookkeeping, scouting new markets, and securing monopolies. During the thirteenth and fourteenth centuries trade-rich cities expanded to become powerful city-states, dominating the political and economic life of the surrounding countryside. By the fifteenth century the great Italian cities had become the bankers of much of Europe.

The growth of Italian cities and urban culture was assisted by the endemic warfare between the emperor and the pope and the Guelf (propapal) and Ghibelline (proimperial) factions that this warfare had created. Either of these might have successfully challenged the cities had they permitted the other to concentrate on it. They chose instead to weaken one

RENAISSANCE ITALY

MAP 9–3 *The city-states of Renaissance Italy were self-contained principalities whose internal strife was monitored by their despots and whose external aggression was long successfully controlled by treaty.*

An Italian bank in the late fourteenth century. By 1400, the great Italian cities had become the bankers of much of Europe. [Mansell Collection]

another and thus strengthened the merchant oligarchies of the cities. Unlike in northern Europe, where the cities tended to be dominated by kings and territorial princes, the great Italian cities were left free to expand into states. They became independent states, absorbing the surrounding countryside and assimilating the area's nobility in a unique urban meld of old and new rich. There were five such major, competitive states in Italy; the duchy of Milan; the republics of Florence and Venice; the Papal States; and the kingdom of Naples (see Map 9.3).

Social strife and competition for political power were so intense within the cities that, for sheer survival's sake, most evolved into despotisms by the fifteenth century. Venice was the notable exception to this rule. It was ruled by a successful merchant oligarchy with power located in a patrician senate of 300 members and a ruthless judicial body, the Council of Ten, that anticipated and suppressed rival groups. Elsewhere the new social classes and divisions within society produced by rapid urban growth fueled chronic, near-anarchic conflict.

Florence was the most striking example. There were four distinguishable social groups within the city. The first was the old rich, or *grandi*, the nobles and merchants who traditionally ruled the city. The second group was the emergent new-rich merchant class, capitalists and bankers known as the *popolo grosso*, or "fat people." They began to challenge the old rich for political power in the late thirteenth and early fourteenth centuries. Then there were the middle-burgher ranks of guildmasters, shopowners, and professionals, those smaller businessmen who, in Florence as elsewhere, tended to take the side of the new rich against the conservative policies of the old rich. Finally, there was the *popolo minuto*, the little people, the lower middle classes. In 1457 one third of the population of Florence, about thirty thousand people, were officially listed as paupers.

Florentine women at work. Needlework, spinning, and weaving took up much of a woman's time, and contributed to the elegance of dress for which both male and female Florentines were famed. [Alinari]

These social divisions produced conflict at every level of society, to which was added the ever-present fear of foreign intrigue. In 1378 feuding between the old and the new rich combined with the social pressures of the Black Death, which cut the city's population almost in half, and with the collapse of the banking houses of Bardi and Peruzzi, to ignite a great revolt by the poor. It was known as the

The Duomo, or Cathedral of Florence. One of the masterpieces of Renaissance architecture, it was begun in 1296 and completed in 1461. The famous campanile, or bell tower, which stands to one side of the front of the Cathedral, was begun by Giotto in 1334. [EPA]

Ciompi Revolt and established a chaotic four-year reign of power by the lower Florentine classes. True stability did not return to Florence until the ascent to power in 1434 of Cosimo de' Medici (1389–1464).

Cosimo de' Medici, the wealthiest Florentine and an astute statesman, controlled the city internally from behind the scenes, skillfully manipulating the constitution and influencing elections. Florence was governed by a council of six (later eight) members known as the *Signoria*. These men were chosen from the most powerful guilds—those representing the major clothing industries (cloth, wool, fur, and silk) and such other groups as bankers, judges, and doctors. Through his informal, cordial relations with the electoral committee, Cosimo was able to keep councillors loyal to him in the *Signoria*. As head of the Office of Public Debt, he was able to favor congenial factions. His grandson Lorenzo the Magnificent (1449–1492) ruled Florence in almost totalitarian fashion during the last quarter of the fifteenth century, having been made cautious by the assassination of his brother in 1478 by a rival Florentine family, the Pazzi, who plotted with the pope against Medici rule.

Despotism was less subtle elsewhere. In order to prevent internal social conflict and foreign intrigue from paralyzing their cities, the dominant groups cooperated to install a hired strongman, known as a *podestà*, for the purpose of maintaining law and order. He was given executive, military, and judicial authority, and his mandate was direct and simple: to permit, by whatever means required, the normal flow of business activity without which not the old rich, the new rich, or the poor of a city could long survive. Because these despots could not depend on the divided populace, they operated through mercenary armies, which they obtained through military brokers known as *condottieri*. It was a hazardous job. Despots were not only subject to dismissal by the oligarchies that hired them, but they were also popular objects of assassination attempts. However, the spoils of success were very great. In Milan it was as despots that the Visconti family came to power in 1278 and the Sforza family in 1450, both ruling without constitutional restraints or serious political competition. The latter produced one of Machiavelli's heroes, Ludovico il Moro.

Political turbulence and warfare gave birth to diplomacy, by which the various city-states were able to stay abreast of foreign military

A terra cotta bust of Lorenzo de' Medici by the sculptor Andrea del Verrocchio (ca. 1435–1488). [*National Gallery of Art, Washington; Samuel H. Kress Collection*]

developments and, if shrewd enough, to gain power and advantage short of actually going to war. Most city-states established resident embassies in the fifteenth century, and their ambassadors not only represented them in ceremonies and as negotiators but also became their watchful eyes and ears at rival courts.

Whether within the comparatively tranquil republic of Venice, the strong-arm democracy of Florence, or the undisguised despotism of Milan, the disciplined Italian city proved a most congenial climate for an unprecedented flowering of thought and culture. Italian Renaissance culture was promoted as vigorously by despots as by republicans and by secularized popes as enthusiastically as by the more spiritually minded. Such widespread support resulted from the fact that the main requirement for patronage of the arts and letters was the one thing that Italian cities of the high Renaissance had in abundance: great wealth.

Humanism

There are several schools of thought on the essence of Humanism. Those who follow the nineteenth-century historian Jacob Burckhardt, who saw the Italian Renaissance as the birth of modernity, view it as an unchristian philosophy that stressed the dignity of humankind and championed individualism and secular values. Others argue that Humanists were

337

*The Late
Middle Ages
and the
Renaissance:
Decline and
Renewal
(1300–1527)*

the very champions of authentic Catholic Christianity, who opposed the pagan teaching of Aristotle and the ineloquent Scholasticism that his writings nurtured. Still others see Humanism as a form of scholarship consciously designed to promote a sense of civic responsibility and political liberty. One of the most authoritative modern commentators, Paul O. Kristeller, has accused all these views of dealing more with the secondary effects than with the essence of Humanism. Humanism, he believes, was no particular philosophy or value system but simply an educational program concentrated on rhetoric and sound scholarship for their own sake.

There is truth in each of these definitions. Humanism was the scholarly study of the Latin and Greek classics and the ancient Church Fathers both for their own sake and in the hope of a rebirth of ancient norms and values. Humanists were advocates of the *studia humanitatis*, a liberal arts program of study that embraced grammar, rhetoric, poetry, history, politics, and moral philosophy. Not only were these subjects considered a joy in themselves, they were also seen as celebrating the dignity of humankind and preparing people for a life of virtuous action. The Florentine Leonardo Bruni (1374–1444) first gave the name *humanitas* ("humanity") to the learning that resulted from such scholarly pursuits. Bruni was a student of Manuel Chrysoloras, a Byzantine scholar who opened the world of Greek scholarship to a generation of young Italian Humanists when he taught at Florence between 1397 and 1403.

The first Humanists were orators and poets. They wrote original literature, in both the classical and the vernacular languages, inspired by and modeled on the newly discovered works of the ancients, and they taught rhetoric within the universities. When Humanists were not employed as teachers of rhetoric, their talents were sought as secretaries, speech writers, and diplomats in princely and papal courts.

The study of classical and Christian antiquity

Petrarch's Letter to Posterity

In old age Petrarch wrote a highly personal letter to posterity in which he summarized the lessons he had learned during his lifetime. The letter also summarizes the original values of Renaissance Humanists: their suspicion of purely materialistic pleasure, the importance they attached to friendship, and their utter devotion to and love of antiquity.

I have always possessed extreme contempt for wealth; not that riches are not desirable in themselves, but because I hate the anxiety and care which are invariably associated with them . . . I have, on the contrary, led a happier existence with plain living and ordinary fare. . . .

The pleasure of dining with one's friends is so great that nothing has ever given me more delight than their unexpected arrival, nor have I ever willingly sat down to table without a companion. . . .

The greatest kings of this age have loved and courted me. . . . I have fled, however, from many . . . to whom I was greatly attached; and such was my innate longing for liberty that I studiously avoided those whose very name seemed incompatible with the freedom I loved.

I possess a well-balanced rather than a keen intellect—one prone to all kinds of good and wholesome study, but especially to moral philosophy and the art of poetry. The latter I neglected as time went on, and took delight in sacred literature. . . . Among the many subjects that interested me, I dwelt especially upon antiquity, for our own age has always repelled me, so that, had it not been for the love of those dear to me, I should have preferred to have been born in any other period than our own. In order to forget my own time, I have constantly striven to place myself in spirit in other ages, and consequently I delighted in history. . . .

If only I have lived well, it matters little to me how I have talked. Mere elegance of language can produce at best but an empty fame.

Frederic A. Ogg (Ed.), *A Source Book of Mediaeval History* (New York: American Book Company, 1908), pp. 470–473.

Petrarch (1304–1374) is considered to be the father of humanism. [*Roger-Viollet*]

ther of Humanism. He left the legal profession to pursue his love of letters and poetry. Although most of his life was spent in and around Avignon, he became caught up in Cola di Rienzo's popular revolt and two-year reign (1347–1349) in Rome as "tribune" of the Roman people. He also served the Visconti family in Milan in his later years. Petrarch celebrated ancient Rome in his *Letters to the Ancient Dead,* fancied personal letters to Cicero, Livy, Vergil, and Horace. He also wrote a Latin epic poem (*Africa,* a poetic historical tribute to the Roman general Scipio Africanus) and a set of biographies of famous Romans (*Lives of Illustrious Men*). His critical textual studies, elitism, and contempt for the allegedly useless learning of the Scholastics were features that many later Humanists also shared. Petrarch's most famous contemporary work was a collection of highly introspective love sonnets to a certain Laura, a married woman whom he romantically admired from a safe distance. Classical and Christian values coexist, not always harmoniously, in his work, and this uneasy coexistence is

existed before the Italian Renaissance. There were recoveries of ancient civilization during the Carolingian renaissance of the ninth century, within the cathedral school of Chartres in the twelfth century, during the great Aristotelian revival in Paris in the thirteenth century, and among the Augustinians in the early fourteenth century. However, these precedents only partially compare with the grand achievements of the Italian Renaissance of the late Middle Ages. The latter was far more secular and lay-dominated, possessed much broader interests, was blessed with far more recovered manuscripts, and was endowed with far superior technical skills than had been the case in the earlier "rebirths" of antiquity. Unlike their Scholastic rivals, Humanists were less bound to recent tradition; their method was not to summarize and compare the views of recognized authorities on a text or question, but to go directly to the original source itself and draw their own conclusions. Avidly searching out manuscript collections, Italian Humanists made the full sources of Greek and Latin antiquity available to scholars during the fourteenth and fifteenth centuries. Mastery of Latin and Greek was the surgeon's tool of the Humanist. There is a kernel of truth—but only a kernel—in the arrogant boast of the Humanists that the period between themselves and classical civilization was a "dark middle age."

PETRARCH, DANTE, AND BOCCACCIO. Francesco Petrarch (1304–1374) was the fa-

Dante Aligheri (1265–1321). This drawing is considered the most authentic likeness of the poet. Dante's Divine Comedy *was one of the first works to appear in Italian. Its style so influenced subsequent writers that Dante has been called the creator of modern literary Italian.* [*National Library, Florence*]

true, too, of many later Humanists. Medieval Christian values can be seen in Petrarch's imagined dialogues with Saint Augustine and in tracts written to defend the personal immortality of the soul against the Aristotelians. Petrarch was, however, far more secular in orientation than his famous near contemporary Dante Alighieri (1265–1321), whose *Vita Nuova* and *Divine Comedy* form with Petrarch's sonnets the cornerstones of Italian vernacular literature. Petrarch's student and friend Giovanni Boccaccio (1313–1375), author of the *Decameron*, one hundred bawdy tales told by three men and seven women in a country retreat from the plague that ravaged Florence in 1348, was also a pioneer of Humanist studies. An avid collector of manuscripts, Boccaccio also assembled an encyclopedia of Greek and Roman mythology.

EDUCATIONAL REFORMS AND GOALS. The goal of Humanist studies was to be wise and to speak eloquently, both to know what is good and to practice virtue. Learning was not to remain abstract and unpracticed. "It is better to will the good than to know the truth," Petrarch had taught, and this became a motto of many later Humanists. Pietro Paolo Vergerio (1349–1420) left a classic summary of the Humanist concept of a liberal education:

We call those studies liberal which are worthy of a free man; those studies by which we attain and practice virtue and wisdom; that education which calls forth, trains, and develops those highest gifts of body and mind which ennoble men and which are rightly judged to rank next in dignity to virtue only, for to a vulgar temper, gain and pleasure are the one aim of existence, to a lofty nature, moral worth and fame.[1]

The ideal of a useful education and well-rounded people inspired far-reaching reforms in traditional education. Quintilian's *Education of the Orator*, the full text of which was discovered by Poggio Bracciolini (d. 1459) in 1416, became the basic classical guide for the Humanist revision of the traditional curriculum. The most influential Renaissance tract on education, Vergerio's *On the Morals That Befit a Free Man*, was written directly from classical models. Vittorino da Feltre (d. 1446) was a teacher who not only directed his students to a highly

disciplined reading of Pliny, Ptolemy, Terence, Plautus, Livy, and Plutarch but also combined vigorous physical exercise and games with intellectual pursuits. Another educator, Guarino da Verona (d. 1460), rector of the new University of Ferrara and a student of the Greek scholar Manuel Chrysoloras, streamlined the study of classical languages and gave it systematic form. Baldassare Castiglione's (1478–1529) famous *Book of the Courtier*, written for the cultured nobility at the court of Urbino, also embodied the highest ideals of Italian Humanism. It stressed the importance of integrating knowledge of language and history with athletic, military, and musical skills, as well as good manners and moral character.

Humanists were not bashful scholars. They delighted in going directly to primary sources. They refused to be slaves of tradition, satisfied, as they felt their Scholastic rivals to be, with the commentaries of the accepted masters. Such an attitude not only made Humanists innovative educators but also kept them constantly in search of new sources of information. Poggio Bracciolini and Francesco Filelfo (d. 1481) assembled magnificent manuscript collections.

THE FLORENTINE ACADEMY AND THE REVIVAL OF PLATONISM. Of all the important recoveries of the past made during the Italian Renaissance, none stands out more than the revival of Greek studies, especially the works of Plato, in fifteenth-century Florence. Many factors combined to bring this revival about. An important foundation was laid in 1397 when the city invited Manuel Chrysoloras to come from Constantinople and promote Greek learning. A half century later (1439), the ecumenical Council of Ferrara–Florence, having convened to negotiate the reunion of the Eastern and Western churches, opened the door for many Greek scholars and manuscripts to enter the West. After the fall of Constantinople to the Turks in 1453, Greek scholars fled to Florence for refuge. This was the background against which the Florentine Platonic Academy evolved under the patronage of Cosimo de' Medici and the supervision of Marsilio Ficino (1433–1499) and Pico della Mirandola (1463–1494).

Although the thinkers of the Renaissance were interested in every variety of ancient wisdom, they seemed to be especially attracted to the Platonic tradition and to those Church Fathers who tried to synthesize Platonic philoso-

---

[1]Cited by De Lamar Jensen, *Renaissance Europe: Age of Recovery and Reconciliation* (Lexington, Mass.: D. C. Health, 1981), p. 111.

phy and Christian teaching. The Florentine Academy, a small villa designed for comfortable discussion, became both a cultic and a scholarly center for the revival of Plato and the Neoplatonists: Plotinus, Proclus, Porphyry, and Dionysius the Areopagite. There Ficino edited and saw to the publication of the complete works of Plato.

The appeal of Platonism lay in its flattering view of human nature. Platonism distinguished between an eternal sphere of being and the perishable world in which humans actually lived. Human reason was believed to belong to the former, indeed, to have preexisted in this pristine world and to continue to commune with it, as the present knowledge of mathematical and moral truth bore witness. Strong Platonic influence can be seen in Pico's *Oration on the Dignity of Man*, perhaps the most famous Renaissance statement on the nature of humankind. Pico wrote the

Oration as an introduction to a pretentious collection of nine hundred theses, which were published in Rome in December 1486 and were intended to serve as the basis for a public debate on all of life's important topics. The *Oration* drew on Platonic teaching to depict man as the one creature in the world who possessed the freedom to be whatever he or she chose, able at will to rise to the height of angels or to descend to the level of pigs.

CRITICAL WORK OF THE HUMANISTS: LORENZO VALLA. Because they were guided by a scholarly ideal of philological accuracy and historical truthfulness, the Humanists could become critics of tradition even when that was not their intention. Dispassionate critical scholarship shook long-standing foundations, not the least of which were those of the medieval church.

The work of Lorenzo Valla (1406–1457),

Pico della Mirandola States the Renaissance Image of Man

One of the most eloquent descriptions of the Renaissance image of humankind comes from the Italian Humanist Pico della Mirandola (1463–1494). In his famed *Oration on the Dignity of Man* (ca. 1486), Pico described humans as free to become whatever they choose.

The best of artisans [God] ordained that that creature (man) to whom He had been able to give nothing proper to himself should have joint possession of whatever had been peculiar to each of the different kinds of being. He therefore took man as a creature of indeterminate nature and, assigning him a place in the middle of the world, addressed him thus: ''Neither a fixed abode nor a form that is thine alone nor any function peculiar to thyself have we given thee, Adam, to the end that according to thy longing and according to thy judgment thou mayest have and possess what abode, what form, and what functions thou thyself shalt desire. The nature of all other beings is limited and constrained within the bounds of laws prescribed by Us. Thou, constrained by no limits, in accordance with thine own free will, in whose hand We have placed thee, shall ordain for thyself the limits of thy nature. We have set thee at the world's center that thou mayest from thence more easily observe whatever is in the world. We have made thee neither of heaven nor of earth, neither mortal nor immortal, so that with freedom of choice and with honor, as though the maker and molder of thyself, thou mayest fashion thyself in whatever shape thou shalt prefer. Thou shalt have the power to degenerate into the lower forms of life, which are brutish. Thou shalt have the power, out of thy soul's judgment, to be reborn into the higher forms, which are divine.'' O supreme generosity of God the Father, O highest and most marvelous felicity of man! To him it is granted to have whatever he chooses, to be whatever he wills.

Giovanni Pico della Mirandola, *Oration on the Dignity of Man*, in *The Renaissance Philosophy of Man*, ed. by E. Cassirer et al. (Chicago: Phoenix Books, 1961), pp. 224–225.

author of the standard Renaissance text on Latin philology, the *Elegances of the Latin Language* (1444), reveals the explosive character of the new learning. Although a good Catholic, Valla became a hero to later Protestants. His popularity among Protestants stemmed from his defense of predestination against the advocates of free will, and especially from his exposé of the Donation of Constantine, a fraudulent document written in the eighth century alleging that the Emperor Constantine had given vast territories to the pope. The exposé of the Donation was not intended by Valla to have the devastating force that Protestants attributed to it. He only demonstrated in a careful, scholarly way what others had long suspected. Using the most rudimentary textual analysis and historical logic, Valla proved that the document was filled with such anachronistic terms as *fief* and made references that were meaningless in the fourth century. In the same dispassionate way Valla also pointed out errors in the Latin Vulgate, still the authorized version of the Bible for the Roman Catholic church.

Such discoveries did not make Valla any less loyal to the church, nor did they prevent his faithful fulfillment of the office of Apostolic Secretary in Rome under Pope Nicholas V. Nonetheless, historical criticism of this type served those less loyal to the medieval church, and it was no accident that young Humanists formed the first identifiable group of Martin Luther's supporters.

CIVIC HUMANISM. Italian Humanists were exponents of applied knowledge; their basic criticism of traditional education was that much of its learning was useless. Education, they believed, should promote individual virtue and public service. This ideal inspired what has been called *civic Humanism*, by which is meant examples of Humanist leadership of the political and cultural life, the most striking instance of which was to be found in the city of Florence. There three Humanists served as chancellors: Colluccio Salutati (1331–1406), Leonardo Bruni (ca. 1370–1444), and Poggio Bracciolini (1380–1459). Each used his rhetorical skills to rally the Florentines against the aggression of Naples and Milan. Bruni and Poggio also wrote adulatory histories of the city. Another accomplished Humanist scholar, Leon Battista Alberti (1402–1472), was a noted architect and builder in the city.

On the other hand, many Humanists became clubbish and snobbish, an intellectual elite

Madonna and Child *by Giotto. Most historians consider Giotto to be the herald of modern Western art. The people in his painting seem strikingly real and alive.* [*National Gallery of Art, Washington, D.C., Samuel H. Kress Collection*]

concerned only with pursuing narrow, antiquarian interests and writing pure, classical Latin in the quiet of their studies. It was in reaction against this elitist trend that the Humanist historians Niccolò Machiavelli (1469–1527) and Francesco Guicciardini (1483–1540) adopted the vernacular and made contemporary history their primary source and subject matter.

Renaissance Art

In Renaissance Italy, as in Reformation Europe, the values and interests of the laity were no longer subordinated to those of the clergy. In education, culture, and religion the laity assumed a leading role and established models for the clergy to imitate. This was a development due in part to the church's loss of its international power during the great crises of the late Middle Ages. But it was also encouraged by the rise of national sentiment, the creation of competent national bureaucracies staffed by the laity rather than clerics, and the rapid growth of lay education during the fourteenth

and fifteenth centuries. Medieval Christian values were adjusting to a more this-worldly spirit. Men and women began again to appreciate and even glorify the secular world, secular learning, and purely human pursuits as ends in themselves.

This new perspective on life is prominent in the painting and sculpture of the high Renaissance—the late fifteenth and early sixteenth centuries, when Renaissance art reached its full maturity. Whereas medieval art tended to be abstract and formulaic, Renaissance art was emphatically concerned with the observation of the natural world and the communication of human emotions. Renaissance artists also attempted to give their works a greater rational (chiefly mathematical) order, a symmetry and proportionality that did justice pictorially to their deeply held belief in the harmony of the universe. The interest of Renaissance artists in ancient Roman art was closely allied to an independent interest in humanity and nature.

Renaissance artists had the advantage of new technical skills developed during the fifteenth century. In addition to the availability of oil paints, two special techniques were perfected: that of using shading to enhance naturalness (chiaroscuro) and that of adjusting the size of figures so as to give the viewer a feeling of continuity with the painting (linear perspective). These techniques permitted the artist to "rationalize" space and paint a more natural world. The result was that, when compared with their flat Byzantine and Gothic counterparts, Renaissance paintings were filled with energy and life and stood out from the canvas in three dimensions.

The new direction was signaled by Giotto (1266–1336), the father of Renaissance painting. An admirer of St. Francis of Assisi, whose love of nature he shared, Giotto painted a more natural world than his Byzantine and Gothic predecessors. Though still filled with religious seriousness, his work was no longer so abstract and unnatural a depiction of the world. The painter Masaccio (1401–1428) and the sculptor Donatello (1386–1466) continued to portray the world around them more literally and

David, by Donatello (1386–1466). This was the first freestanding nude statue sculpted since ancient Rome. Compare Donatello's treatment of David as a young, somewhat delicate youth with Michelangelo's more heroic portrayal of the same theme on page 345. [SCALA]

343

*The Late
Middle Ages
and the
Renaissance:
Decline and
Renewal
(1300–1527)*

naturally. The heights were reached by the great masters of the high Renaissance: Leonardo da Vinci (1452–1519), Raphael (1483–1520), and Michelangelo Buonarroti (1475–1564).

LEONARDO DA VINCI. More than any other person in the period, Leonardo exhibited the Renaissance ideal of the universal person. He was a true master of many skills. One of the greatest painters of all time, he was also a military engineer for Ludovico il Moro in Milan, Cesare Borgia in Romagna, and the French king Francis I. Leonardo advocated scientific experimentation, dissected corpses to learn anatomy, and was an accomplished, self-

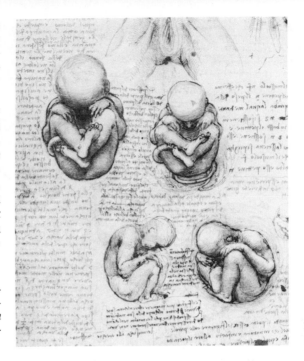

Leonardo da Vinci's drawing of the human fetus. Renaissance artists and scientists, in contrast to medieval artists, began to base their portrayal of the human body on the actual study of it. [The Royal Library, Windsor Castle, by gracious permission of HM the Queen]

A Contemporary Description of Leonardo

Giorgio Vasari (1512–1574), friend and biographer of the great Renaissance painters, sculptors, and architects, described Leonardo's versatility as actually a handicap, as it prevented him from dwelling on one pursuit sufficiently.

The richest gifts are occasionally seen to be showered, as by celestial influence, upon certain human beings; nay, they sometimes supernaturally and marvelously gather in a single person—beauty, grace, and talent united in such a manner that to whatever the man thus favored may turn himself, his every action is so divine as to leave all other men far behind. . . . This was . . . the case of Leonardo da Vinci . . . who had . . . so rare a gift of talent and ability that to whatever subject he turned his attention . . . he presently made himself absolute master of it. . . .

He would without doubt have made great progress in the learning and knowledge of the sciences had he not been so versatile and changeful. The instability of his character led him to undertake many things, which, having commenced, he afterwards abandoned. In arith-

metic, for example, he made such rapid progress in the short time he gave his attention to it, that he often confounded the master who was teaching him. . . . He also commenced the study of music and resolved to acquire the art of playing the lute . . . singing to the instrument most divinely. . . .

Being also an excellent geometrician, Leonardo not only worked in sculpture but also in architecture; likewise he prepared . . . designs for . . . entire buildings. . . . While only a youth, he first suggested the formation of a canal from Pisa to Florence by means of certain changes . . . in the river Arno. He made designs for mills, fulling machines, and other engines run by water. But as he had resolved to make painting his profession, he gave the greater part of his time to drawing from nature.

James Harvey Robinson (Ed.), *Readings in European History*, Vol. 1 (Boston: Athenaeum, 1904), pp. 535–536.

The Mona Lisa, *by Leonardo. This is perhaps the most famous painting in Western art. It reveals Leonardo's mastery at conveying inner moods through complex facial features.* [*Art Resource*]

so great that it tended to shorten his attention span, so that he was constantly moving from one activity to another. His great skill in conveying inner moods through complex facial features can be seen in the most famous of his paintings, the *Mona Lisa,* as well as in his self-portrait.

RAPHAEL. Raphael, an unusually sensitive man whose artistic career was cut short by his premature death at thirty-seven, was apparently loved by contemporaries as much for his person as for his work. He is famous for his tender madonnas, the best known of which graced the monastery of San Sisto in Piacenza and is now in Dresden. Art historians praise his fresco *The School of Athens,* a grandly conceived portrayal of the great masters of Western philosophy, as one of the most perfect examples of Renaissance technique. It depicts Plato and Aristotle surrounded by the great philosophers and scientists of antiquity, who are portrayed with features of Raphael's famous contemporaries, including Leonardo and Michelangelo.

MICHELANGELO. The melancholy genius Michelangelo also excelled in a variety of arts and crafts. His eighteen-foot godlike sculpture *David,* which long stood majestically in the great square of Florence, is a perfect example of the Renaissance artist's devotion to harmony, symmetry, and proportion, as well as his extreme glorification of the human form. Four different popes commissioned works by Michelangelo, the most famous of which are the frescoes for the Sistine Chapel, painted during

taught botanist. His inventive mind foresaw such modern machines as airplanes and submarines. Indeed, the variety of his interests was

Vasari Describes the Magic of Raphael's Personality

There was among his many extraordinary gifts one of such value and importance that I can never sufficiently admire it and always think thereof with astonishment. This was the power accorded him by heaven of bringing all who approached his presence into harmony, an effect . . . contrary to the nature of our artists. Yet all . . . became as of one mind once they began to labor in the society of Raphael, and they contin-

ued in such unity and concord that all harsh feelings and evil dispositions became subdued and disappeared at the sight of him. . . . This happened because all were surpassed by him in friendly courtesy as well as in art. All confessed the influence of his sweet and gracious nature. . . . Not only was he honored by men, but even by the very animals who would constantly follow his steps and always loved him.

James Harvey Robinson (Ed.), *Readings in European History,* Vol. 1 (Boston: Athenaeum, 1904), pp. 536–537.

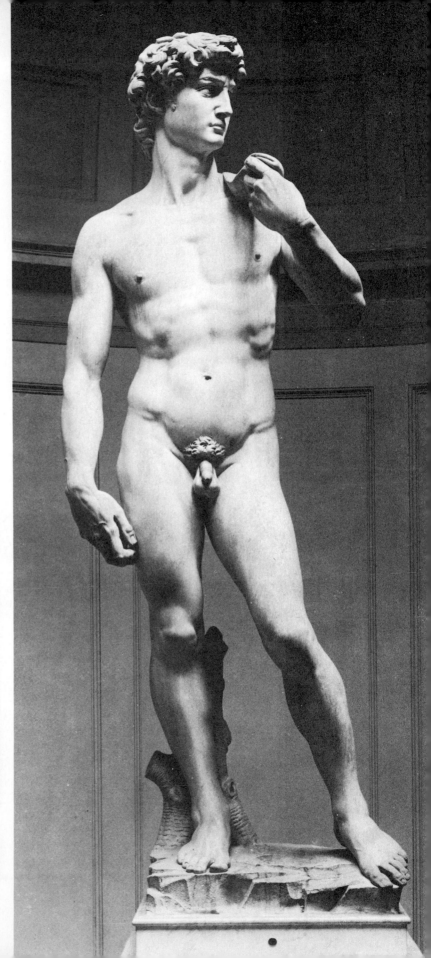

David, *by Michelangelo. Executed on a much larger scale than Donatello's, this statue has been one of the most popular sculptures in the world, since Michelangelo carved it between 1501 and 1504. Many consider it the symbol of the Italian Renaissance.* [Art Resource]

the pontificate of Pope Julius II (1503–1513), who also set Michelangelo to work on his own magnificent tomb. The Sistine frescoes originally covered 10,000 square feet and involved 343 figures, over half of which exceeded 10 feet in height. But it is their originality and perfection as works of art that impress most. This labor of love and piety, painted while Michelangelo was lying on his back or stooping, took four years to complete and left Michelangelo partially crippled. A man of incredible energy and endurance who lived to be ninety, Michelangelo insisted on doing almost everything himself and permitted his assistants only a few of the many chores involved.

Moses, *by Michelangelo. Originally intended for the tomb of Pope Julius II (1503–1513), this statue is now in the Church of St. Peter in Chains in Rome. The horns on Moses' head symbolize divine inspiration.* [Art Resource]

The Sistine Chapel in the Vatican, painted by Michelangelo during the pontificate of Julius II (1503–1513). The frescoes on the ceiling and the Last Judgement on the wall behind the altar are considered the supreme masterpiece of Renaissance painting. [Art Resource]

His later works are more complex and suggest deep personal changes within the artist himself. They mark, artistically and philosophically, the passing of high Renaissance painting and the advent of a new style known as *mannerism*, which reached its peak in the late sixteenth and early seventeenth centuries. A reaction against the simplicity and symmetry of high Renaissance art, which also found expression in music and literature, mannerism made room for the strange and even the abnormal and gave freer reign to the subjectivity of the artist. It derived its name from the fact that it permitted the artist to express his own individual perceptions and feelings, to paint, compose, or write in a "mannered" or "affected" way. Tintoretto (d. 1594) and especially El Greco (d. 1614) became its supreme representatives.

Michelangelo's Inability Ever to Be Satisfied with His Work

According to Vasari, Michelangelo was such an extreme perfectionist that he found fault in everything he did and frequently abandoned his sculptures and paintings before they were completed.

Michelangelo worked . . . almost every day at a group of four figures [in St. Peter's in Rome], but he broke up the block at last, either because it was found to have numerous veins, or was excessively hard and caused the chisel to strike fire, or because his judgment was so severe that he could never content himself with anything that he did. . . . Few of the works undertaken in his manhood were ever entirely completed, those finished being the productions of his youth. . . . He would himself often remark that if he were really permitted to satisfy himself in the works [he was commissioned] to produce, he would give little or nothing of it to public view. And the reason for this is obvious. He had advanced to such an extent of knowledge in art that the very slightest error could not exist in any figure without his immediate discovery; and having found such after the work had been given to view, he would never attempt to correct it, but would commence some other production, believing that a like failure would not happen again. This was, as he often declared, the reason why the number of pictures and statues finished by his hand was so small.

James Harvey Robinson (Ed.), *Readings in European History,* Vol. 1 (Boston: Athenaeum, 1904), pp. 540–541.

The Transport of the Body of St. Mark, *by Tintoretto (d. 1594). This was painted between 1562 and 1566 for the Doge of Venice (St. Mark is the patron saint of Venice). Tintoretto's paintings were immensely popular, and his influence helped to stimulate the painting of northern Europe in the late sixteenth and early seventeenth centuries. [Alinari]*

Italy's Political Decline: The French Invasions (1494–1527)

The Treaty of Lodi

As a land of autonomous city-states, Italy's peace and safety from foreign invasion, especially from invasion by the Turks, had always depended on internal cooperation. Such cooperation had been maintained during the last half of the fifteenth century, thanks to a carefully constructed political alliance known as the Treaty of Lodi (1454–1455). The terms of the treaty brought Milan and Naples, long traditional enemies, into alliance with Florence. These three stood together for decades against Venice, which was frequently joined by the Papal States to create an internal balance of power that also made possible a unified front against external enemies.

Around 1490, following the rise to power of the Milanese despot Ludovico il Moro, hostilities between Milan and Naples resumed. The peace made possible by the Treaty of Lodi ended in 1494 when Naples, supported by Florence and the Borgia Pope Alexander VI (1492–1503), prepared to attack Milan. Ludovico made what proved to be a fatal response to these new political alignments: he appealed for aid to the French. French kings had ruled Naples from 1266 to 1435, before they were driven out by Duke Alfonso of Sicily. Breaking a wise Italian rule, Ludovico invited the French to reenter Italy and revive their dynastic claim to Naples. In his haste to check his rival, Naples, Ludovico did not recognize sufficiently that France also had dynastic claims to Milan, nor did he foresee how insatiable the French appetite for Italian territory would become once French armies had crossed the Alps.

Charles VIII's March Through Italy

The French king Louis XI had resisted the temptation to invade Italy, while nonetheless keeping French dynastic claims in Italy alive. His successor, Charles VIII (1483–1498), an eager youth in his twenties, responded to Ludovico's call with lightning speed. Within five months he had crossed the Alps (August 1495) and raced as conqueror through Florence and the Papal States into Naples. As Charles approached Florence, the Florentine ruler, Piero de' Medici, who had allied with Naples against Milan, tried to placate the French king by handing over Pisa and other Florentine possessions. Such appeasement only brought about Piero's forced exile by a population that was revolutionized at this time by the radical preacher Girolamo Savonarola (1452–1498). Savonarola convinced a majority of the fearful Florentines that the French king's advent was a long-delayed and fully justified divine vengeance on their immorality.

Charles entered Florence without resistance and, thanks to Savonarola's flattery and the payment of a large ransom, spared the city a threatened destruction. Savonarola continued to rule Florence for four years after Charles's departure. The Florentines proved, however, not to be the stuff theocracies are made of. Savonarola's puritanism and antipapal policies made it impossible for him to survive indefinitely. This was especially true after the Italian cities reunited and the ouster of the French invader, whom Savonarola had praised as a godsend, became national policy. Savonarola was imprisoned and executed in May 1498.

Charles's lightning march through Italy also struck terror in non-Italian hearts. Ferdinand of Aragon, whose native land and self-interests as king of Sicily now became vulnerable to a French-Italian axis, took the initiative to create a counteralliance: the League of Venice, formed in March 1495, with Venice, the Papal States, and the Emperor Maximilian I joining Ferdinand against the French. The stage was set for a conflict between France and Spain that would not end until 1559.

Ludovico il Moro meanwhile recognized that he had sown the wind; having desired a French invasion only so long as it weakened his enemies, he now saw Milan threatened by the whirlwind of events that he had himself created. In reaction he joined the League of Venice, and this alliance was able to send Charles into retreat by May. Charles remained thereafter on the defensive until his death in April 1498.

Pope Alexander VI and the Borgia Family

The French returned to Italy under Charles's successor, Louis XII (1498–1515), this time assisted by a new Italian ally, the Borgia pope, Alexander VI (1492–1503). Alexander, probably the most corrupt pope who ever sat on the papal throne, openly promoted the political careers of the children he had had before he became pope, Cesare and Lucrezia, as he placed the efforts of the powerful Borgia family to secure a political base in Romagna in tandem with papal policy there.

In Romagna several principalities had fallen away from the church during the Avignon papacy, and Venice, the pope's ally within the League of Venice, continued to contest the Papal States for their loyalty. Seeing that a French alliance could give him the opportunity to reestablish control over the region, Alexander took steps to secure French favor. He annulled Louis XII's marriage to Charles VIII's sister so that Louis could marry Charles's widow, Anne of Brittany—a popular political move designed to keep Brittany French. The pope also bestowed a cardinal's hat on the

archbishop of Rouen, Louis's favorite cleric. But most important, Alexander agreed to abandon the League of Venice, a withdrawal of support that made the league too weak to resist a French reconquest of Milan. In exchange, Cesare Borgia received the sister of the king of Navarre, Charlotte d'Albret, in marriage, a union that greatly enhanced Borgia military strength. Cesare also received land grants from Louis XII and the promise of French military aid in Romagna.

All in all it was a scandalous tradeoff, but one that made it possible for both the French king and the pope to realize their ambitions

Isabella d'Este by the Venetian painter Titian (1477–1576). Titian was the most popular portrait painter of the age, patronized by the richest and most influential people in Europe. Isabella d'Este, the Duchess of Mantua, a small state in northern Italy, was one of the greatest patrons of the Renaissance. Her court was a major center for artists, musicians, and humanists. She also became the sister-in-law of Lucrezia Borgia, when Lucrezia married Isabella's brother Alfonso, Duke of Ferrara in 1502. [Kunsthistorisches Museum, Vienna]

within Italy. Louis successfully invaded Milan in August 1499. Ludovico il Moro, who had originally opened the Pandora's box of French invasion, spent his last years languishing in a French prison. In 1500 Louis and Ferdinand of Aragon divided Naples between them, while the pope and Cesare Borgia conquered the cities of Romagna without opposition. Alexander awarded his victorious son the title "duke of Romagna."

Pope Julius II

Cardinal Giuliano della Rovere, a strong opponent of the Borgia family, became Pope Julius II (1503–1513). He suppressed the Borgias and placed their newly conquered lands in Romagna under papal jurisdiction. Julius came to be known as the "warrior pope" because he brought the Renaissance papacy to a peak of military prowess and diplomatic intrigue. Shocked, as were other contemporaries by this thoroughly secular papacy, the Humanist Erasmus (1466?–1536), who had witnessed in disbelief a bullfight in the papal palace during a visit to Rome, wrote a popular anonymous satire entitled *Julius Excluded from Heaven*. This humorous account purported to describe the pope's unsuccessful efforts to convince Saint Peter that he was worthy of admission to heaven.

Assisted by his powerful allies, Pope Julius succeeded in driving the Venetians out of Romagna in 1509, thereby ending Venetian claims in the region and fully securing the Papal States. Having realized this long-sought papal goal, Julius turned to the second major undertaking of his pontificate: ridding Italy of his former ally, the French invader. Julius, Ferdinand of Aragon, and Venice formed a second Holy League in October 1511, and within a short period Emperor Maximilian I and the Swiss joined them. By 1512 the league had the French in full retreat, and they were soundly defeated by the Swiss in 1513 at Novara.

The French were nothing if not persistent. They invaded Italy still a third time under Louis's successor, Francis I (1515–1547). French armies massacred Swiss soldiers of the Holy League at Marignano in September 1515, revenging the earlier defeat at Novara. The victory won from the pope the Concordat of Bologna in August 1516, an agreement that gave the French king control over the French clergy in exchange for French recognition of the pope's superiority over church councils and his

Pope Julius II (1503–1513), by Raphael in about 1511.

right to collect annates in France. This was an important compromise that helped keep France Catholic after the outbreak of the Protestant Reformation. But the new French entry into Italy also led to the first of four major wars with Spain in the first half of the sixteenth century: the Habsburg–Valois wars, none of which France won.

Niccolò Machiavelli

The period of foreign invasions made a shambles of Italy. The same period that saw Italy's cultural peak in the work of Leonardo, Raphael, and Michelangelo also witnessed Italy's political tragedy. One who watched as French, Spanish, and German armies wreaked havoc on his country was Niccolò Machiavelli (1469–1527). The more he saw, the more convinced he became that Italian political unity and independence were ends that justified any means. A Humanist and a careful student of

349

Machiavelli Discusses the Most Important Trait for a Ruler

Machiavelli believed that the most important personality trait of a successful ruler was the ability to instill fear in his subjects.

Here the question arises; whether it is better to be loved than feared or feared than loved. The answer is that it would be desirable to be both but, since that is difficult, it is much safer to be feared than to be loved, if one must choose. For on men in general this observation may be made: they are ungrateful, fickle, and deceitful, eager to avoid dangers, and avid for gain, and while you are useful to them they are all with you, offering you their blood, their property, their lives, and their sons so long as danger is remote, as we noted above, but when it ap-

proaches they turn on you. Any prince, trusting only in their words and having no other preparations made, will fall to his ruin, for friendships that are bought at a price and not by greatness and nobility of soul are paid for indeed, but they are not owned and cannot be called upon in time of need. Men have less hesitation in offending a man who is loved than one who is feared, for love is held by a bond of obligation which, as men are wicked, is broken whenever personal advantage suggests it, but fear is accompanied by the dread of punishment which never relaxes.

Niccolò Machiavelli, *The Prince* (1513), trans. and ed. by Thomas G. Bergin (New York: Appleton-Century-Crofts, 1947), p. 48.

MAJOR POLITICAL EVENTS OF THE ITALIAN RENAISSANCE (1375–1527)

The Ciompi Revolt in Florence	1378–1382
Medici rule in Florence established by Cosimo de' Medici	1434
Treaty of Lodi allies Milan, Naples, and Florence (in effect until 1494)	1454–1455
Charles VIII of France invades Italy	1494
Savonarola controls Florence	1494–1498
League of Venice unites Venice, Milan, the Papal States, the Holy Roman Empire, and Spain against France	1495
Louis XII invades Milan (the second French invasion of Italy)	1499
The Borgias conquer Romagna	1500
The Holy League (Pope Julius II, Ferdinand of Aragon, Emperor Maximilian, and Venice) defeat the French	1512–1513
Machiavelli writes *The Prince*	1513
Francis I leads the third French invasion of Italy	1515
Concordat of Bologna between France and the papacy	1516
Sack of Rome by imperial soldiers	1527

ancient Rome, Machiavelli was impressed by the deliberate and heroic acts of ancient Roman rulers, what Renaissance people called *Virtù*. Stories of the unbounded patriotism and self-sacrifice of the old Roman citizenry were his favorites, and he lamented the absence of such traits among his compatriots. Machiavelli's romanticization of the ancient Romans caused his interpretation of both ancient and contemporary history to be somewhat exaggerated. His Florentine contemporary, Francesco Guicciardini, who was a more sober historian and was less given to idealizing antiquity, wrote truer chronicles of Florentine and Italian history.

The juxtaposition of what Machiavelli believed the ancient Romans had been with the failure of contemporary Romans to realize such high ideals made him the famous cynic we know in the popular epithet *Machiavellian*. Only an unscrupulous strongman, he concluded, using duplicity and terror, could impose order on so divided and selfish a people; the moral revival of the Italians required an unprincipled dictator.

It has been argued that Machiavelli wrote *The Prince* in 1513 as a cynical satire on the way rulers actually did behave and not as a serious recommendation of unprincipled despotic rule. To take his advocacy of tyranny literally, it is argued, contradicts both his earlier works and his own strong family tradition of republican service. But Machiavelli seems to have been in earnest when he advised rulers to discover the advantages of fraud and brutality. He apparently hoped to see a strong ruler emerge from the Medici family, which had captured the papacy in 1513 with the pontificate of Leo X (1513–1521). At the same time, the Medici family retained control over the powerful territorial state of Florence—a situation similar to that of Machiavelli's hero Cesare Borgia and his father Pope Alexander VI, who had earlier brought factious Romagna to heel by placing secular family goals and religious policy in tandem. *The Prince* was pointedly dedicated to Lorenzo de' Medici, duke of Urbino and grandson of Lorenzo the Magnificent.

Whatever Machiavelli's hopes may have been, the Medicis were not destined to be Italy's deliverers. The second Medici pope, Clement VII (1523–1534), watched helplessly as Rome was sacked by the army of Emperor Charles V in 1527, also the year of Machiavelli's death.

Suggested Readings

MARGARET ASTON, *The Fifteenth Century: The Prospect of Europe* (1968). Crisp social history, with pictures.

HANS BARON, *The Crisis of the Early Italian Renaissance,* Vols. 1 and 2 (1966). A major work, setting forth the civic dimension of Italian Humanism.

BERNARD BERENSON, *Italian Painters of the Renaissance* (1957).

JACOB BURCKHARDT, *The Civilization of the Renaissance in Italy* (1867). The old classic that still has as many defenders as detractors.

WALLACE K. FERGUSON, *Europe in Transition* 1300–1520 (1962). A major survey that deals with the transition from medieval to Renaissance society.

MYRON GILMORE, *The World of Humanism* 1453–1517 (1952). A comprehensive survey, especially strong in intellectual and cultural history.

J. R. HALE, *Renaissance Europe: The Individual and Society,* 1480–1520 (1971). Many-sided treatment of social history.

DENYS HAY, *Europe in the Fourteenth and Fifteenth Centuries* (1966). Many-sided treatment of political history.

DAVID HERLIHY, *The Family in Renaissance Italy* (1974).

JOHAN HUIZINGA, *The Waning of the Middle Ages: A Study of the Forms of Life, Thought, and Art in France and the Netherlands in the Dawn of the Renaissance* (1924). A classic study of "mentality" at the end of the Middle Ages.

DE LAMAR JENSEN, *Renaissance Europe: Age of Recovery and Reconciliation* (1981).

RUTH KELSO, *Doctrine of the Lady of the Renaissance* (1978).

PAUL O. KRISTELLER, *Renaissance Thought: The Classic, Scholastic, and Humanist Strains* (1961). A master shows the many sides of Renaissance thought.

HARRY A. MISKIMIN, *The Economy of Early Renaissance Europe* 1300–1460 (1969). Shows interaction of social, political, and economic change.

HEIKO A. OBERMAN, *The Harvest of Medieval Theology* (1963). A demanding synthesis and revision.

PETER PARTNER, *Renaissance Rome, 1500–1559: A Portrait of a Society* (1976). Detailed and comprehensive.

EDOUARD PERROY, *The Hundred Years' War,* trans. by W. B. Wells (1965). The most comprehensive one-volume account.

J. B. A. POCOCK, *The Machiavellian Moment: Florentine Political Thought and the Atlantic Republican Tradition* (1975). Traces the influence of Florentine political thought.

YVES RENOVARD, *The Avignon Papacy* 1305–1403, trans. by D. Bethell (1970). Standard narrative.

QUENTIN SKINNER, *The Foundations of Modern Political Thought I: The Renaissance* (1978). Broad survey, very comprehensive.

MATTHEW SPINKA, *John Huss's Concept of the Church* (1966).

J. W. THOMPSON, *Economic and Social History of Europe in the Later Middle Ages* 1300–1530 (1958). A bread-and-butter account.

BRIAN TIERNEY, *Foundations of the Conciliar Theory* (1955). Important study showing the origins of conciliar theory in canon law.

BRIAN TIERNEY, *The Crisis of Church and State* 1050–1300 (1964). Part IV provides the major documents in the clash between Boniface VIII and Philip the Fair.

WALTER ULLMANN, *Origins of the Great Schism* (1948). A basic study by a controversial interpreter of medieval political thought.

CHARLES T. WOOD, *Philip the Fair and Boniface VIII* (1967). Excerpts from the scholarly debate over the significance of this confrontation.

H. B. WORKMAN, *John Wyclif,* Vols. 1 and 2 (1926). Dated but still standard.

PHILIP ZIEGLER, *The Black Death* (1969). Highly readable journalistic account.

Luther and the Wittenberg reformers, painted about 1543 by Lucas Cranach the Younger (1515–1586). Luther stands to the left behind the dominating figure of the Elector John Frederick of Saxony (1532–1547). The electors of Saxony were the first princely patrons of the Reformation. Their support protected Luther from the hostility of pope and emperor. [Toledo Museum of Art; gift of Edward Drummond Libbey]

IN THE SECOND DECADE of the sixteenth century there began in Saxony in Germany a powerful religious movement that rapidly spread throughout northern Europe, deeply affecting society and politics as well as the spiritual lives of men and women. Attacking what they believed to be burdensome superstitions that robbed people of both their money and their peace of mind, Protestant reformers led a broad revolt against the medieval church. In a relatively short span of time hundreds of thousands of people from all social classes set aside the beliefs of centuries and adopted a more simplified religious practice.

The Protestant Reformation challenged aspects of the Renaissance, especially its tendency to follow classical sources in glorifying human nature and its loyalty to traditional religion. Protestants were more impressed by the human potential for evil than by the inclination to do good and encouraged parents, teachers, and magistrates to be firm disciplinarians. On the other hand, Protestants also embraced many Renaissance values, especially in the sphere of educational reform and particularly with regard to training in ancient languages. Like the Italian Humanists, the Protestant reformers studied ancient languages and went directly to the original sources; only for them this meant the study of the Hebrew and Greek Scriptures and the consequent challenge of traditional institutions on the authority of the Bible.

We are, however, getting well ahead of our story. The road to the Reformation was long in preparation. As the Protestant ethic influenced an entire age, it was also itself born out of changes in European society beyond those within the purely religious and ecclesiastical spheres.

For Europe the late fifteenth and the sixteenth centuries were a period of unprecedented territorial expansion and ideological experimentation. Permanent colonies were established within the Americas, and the exploitation of the New World's human and seemingly endless mineral resources was begun. The American gold and silver imported into Europe spurred scientific invention and a weapons industry and touched off an inflationary spiral that produced a revolution in prices by century's end. The new bullion also helped create international traffic in African slaves, who were needed in ever-increasing numbers to work the mines and the plantations of the

10

The Age of Reformation

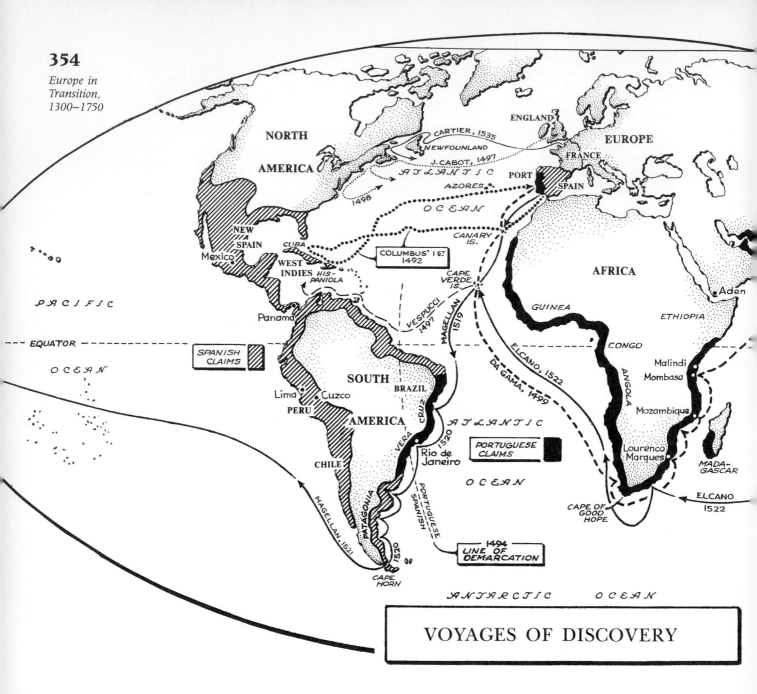

NORTH
AMERICA

CARTIER, 1535

NEWFOUNLAND

J. CABOT, 1497

ATLANTIC

ENGLAND

EUROPE

FRANCE

PORT

SPAIN

1498

AZORES

OCEAN

NEW
SPAIN

CUBA

CANARY
IS.

AFRICA

Aden

Mexico

WEST
INDIES

HIS-
PANIOLA

COLUMBUS' 1ST
1492

CAPE
VERDE
IS.

GUINEA

ETHIOPIA

PACIFIC

Panama

VESPUCCI,
1497

MAGELLAN
1519

DA GAMA, 1499

ELCANO, 1522

CONGO

Malindi

Mombasa

EQUATOR

SPANISH
CLAIMS

SOUTH

Lima

Cuzco

AMERICA

OCEAN

ANGOLA

Mozambique

PERU

BRAZIL

ATLANTIC

CHILE

VERA CRUZ 1520

Rio de
Janeiro

PORTUGUESE
CLAIMS

OCEAN

Lourenco
Marques

MADA-
GASCAR

MAGELLAN, 1521

PATAGONIA

PORTUGUESE
SPANISH

1494
LINE OF
DEMARCATION

CAPE OF
GOOD
HOPE

ELCANO
1522

1520

CAPE
HORN

ANTARCTIC   OCEAN

VOYAGES OF DISCOVERY

New World as replacements for faltering natives. This period further saw social engineering and political planning on a large scale as newly centralized governments were forced as never before to develop long-range economic policies, a practice that came to be known as *mercantilism.*

The late fifteenth and sixteenth centuries also marked the first wide-scale use of the printing press, an invention greatly assisted by the development of a process of cheap paper manufacture and publishers eager to exploit a fascinating new technology. Printing with movable type was invented by Johann Guttenberg (d. 1468) in the mid-fifteenth century in the German city of Mainz. Residential colleges and universities had greatly expanded in northern Europe during the fourteenth and fifteenth centuries, and there was a growing literate public in the cities eager to possess and read books. The new technology also made propaganda possible on a massive scale, as thousands of inexpensive pamphlets could now be rapidly produced and disseminated.

MAP 10–1   *The map dramatizes the expansion of the area of European interest in the fifteenth and sixteenth centuries. Not until today's ''space age'' has a comparable widening of horizons been possible.*

Hypothetical reconstruction of the printing press of Johannes Gutenberg of Mainz (in what is now West Germany). Between about 1435 and 1455, Gutenberg worked out the complete technology of making individual rectangular metal types, composing the type into pages held together by pressure, and printing from those on an adaptation of the wooden standing press with ink of lampblack mixed with oil varnish. This new technology for the first time made it possible to manufacture numerous identical copies of written works and was basic to the intellectual development of the West. [Gutenberg-Museum, Mainz]

Voyages of Discovery and of Empire and Changes in Society

Spices, Gold, and Silver

On the eve of the Reformation the geographical as well as the intellectual horizons of Western people were broadening. The fifteenth century saw the beginning of western Europe's global expansion and the transference of commercial supremacy from the Mediterranean and the Baltic to the Atlantic seaboard. Mercenary motives, reinforced by traditional missionary ideals, inspired Prince Henry the Navigator (1394–1460) to sponsor the Portuguese exploration of the African coast. His main object was the gold trade, which for centuries had been an Arab monopoly. By the last decades of the fifteenth century gold from Guinea was entering Europe by way of Portuguese ships calling at the port cities of Lisbon and Antwerp, rather than by Arab land routes. Antwerp became the financial center of Europe, a commercial crossroads where the enterprise and derring-do of the Portuguese and the Spanish met the capital funds of the German banking houses of Fugger and Welser.

The rush for gold quickly expanded into a rush for the spice markets of India. In the fifteenth century the diet of most Europeans was a dull combination of bread and gruel, cabbage, turnips, peas, lentils, and onions, together with what meat became available during seasonal periods of slaughter. Spices, especially pepper and cloves, were in great demand both to preserve and to enhance the taste of food. Bartholomew Dias (d. 1500) opened the Portuguese empire in the East

Detail of a portrait of Christopher Columbus by Sebastiano del Piombo (1485–1547). It shows Columbus, who died in 1506, late in life. [Metropolitan Museum of Art, New York; gift of J. Pierpont Morgan, 1900]

when he rounded the Cape of Good Hope at the tip of Africa in 1487. A decade later, in 1498, Vasco da Gama (d. 1524) reached the coast of India. When he returned to Portugal, he brought with him a cargo worth sixty times the cost of the voyage. In subsequent years the Portuguese established themselves firmly on the Malabar Coast with colonies in Goa and Calcutta and successfully challenged the Arabs and the Venetians for control of the European spice trade.

While the Portuguese concentrated on the Indian Ocean, the Spanish set sail across the Atlantic. They did so in the hope of establishing a shorter route to the rich spice markets of the East Indies. Rather than beating the Portuguese at their own game, however, Christopher Columbus (1451–1506) discovered the Americas instead.

Amerigo Vespucci (1451–1512) and Ferdinand Magellan (1480–1521) demonstrated that these new lands were not the outermost territory of the Far East, as Columbus died believing, but an entirely new continent that opened on the still greater Pacific Ocean. Magellan died in the Philippines.

The Spanish Empire in the New World

Columbus's voyage of 1492 marked, unknowingly to those who undertook and financed it, the beginning of more than three centuries of Spanish conquest, exploitation, and administration of a vast American empire. That imperial venture, which created the largest and longest lived of all the great mercantile trading blocs, produced important results for the cultures of both the European and the American continents. The gold and silver extracted from its American possessions financed Spain's major role in the religious and political conflicts of the age and contributed to European inflation in the sixteenth century. In large expanses of both South and North America, Spanish government set an imprint of Roman Catholicism, economic dependence, and hierarchical social structure that has endured to the present day. Spanish economic and social influences came to dominate because the early explorers conquered the existing Indian civilizations and imposed their own.

A Conquered World

Mistaking the islands where he landed for the East Indies, Columbus called the native peoples whom he encountered *Indians*. That name persisted even after it had become clear that a new continent had been discovered. These native peoples had migrated onto the American landmass many thousands of years before the European voyages of discovery. They had come from Asia, probably across the Bering Straits, and by 9000 B.C. lived in various kinds of communities all the way from Alaska to the southernmost sections of South America. In what is today considered Latin America, these Indian peoples had established very high civilizations by approximately A.D. 500. The most famous of these is the Mayan civilization centered in present-day Guatemala and the Yucatán peninsula of Mexico. The Mayans built large cities in which stood immense pyramids. They also achieved very considerable skills in mathematics and astronomy. This remarkable civilization fell into decay and dissolution around the year A.D. 1000 and was an extinguished civilization when the Spanish arrived.

The two major Indian peoples whom the Spanish explorers and conquerors encountered were the Aztecs in Mexico and the Incas in Peru. Both were relative newcomers to political power and had established themselves through the conquest of other Indian tribes. Both were very rich, and their conquest promised the greedy Spanish the possibility of large quantities of gold.

The forebears to the Aztecs whom the Spanish encountered in the early sixteenth century had arrived in the Valley of Mexico early in the twelfth century. They had been forced by other tribes to live on marginal land as a subservient people. Over the years, the Aztecs became highly skilled in military matters. In 1428, under the leadership of a new chief named

---

Columbus Reports His Discovery of the Entrance to Paradise

During his third voyage, Columbus reached the mouth of the Orinoco River in Venezuela. He believed he was in the East Indies, where, according to tradition, Adam and Eve had first trod the earth. Columbus believed that he had now come upon the very entrance into Paradise. In October 1498 he wrote of this discovery to his patrons, Ferdinand and Isabella, monarchs of Spain.

I have already described my ideas concerning this hemisphere and its form [he believed it to be pear-shaped]. I have no doubt that if I could pass below the equinoctial line, after reaching the highest point . . . I should find a much milder temperature and a variation in the stars and in the water. Not that I suppose that elevated point to be navigable, nor even that there is water there; indeed, I believe it is impossible to ascend to it, because I am convinced that it is the spot of the earthly paradise, whither none can go but by God's permission. . . .

I do not suppose that the earthly paradise is in the form of a rugged mountain, as the descriptions of it have made it appear, but that it is on the summit of the spot, which I have described as being in the form of the stalk of a pear. The approach to it . . . must be by constant and

gradual ascent, but I believe that . . . no one could ever reach the top. I think also that the water I have described may proceed from it, though it be far off, and that stopping at the place which I have just left, it forms this lake. There are great indications of this being the terrestrial paradise, for its site coincides with the opinion of the holy and wise theologians whom I have mentioned. Moreover, the other evidences agree . . . for I have never read or heard of fresh water coming in so large a quantity in close conjunction with the water of the sea. The idea is also corroborated by the blandness of the temperature. If the water of which I speak does not proceed from the earthly paradise, it seems to be a still greater wonder, for I do not believe that there is any river in the world so large or so deep.

The Renaissance and the Reformation 1300–1600, ed. by Donald Weinstein (New York: Free Press, 1965), pp. 138–139.

A sixteenth-century Aztec depiction of the Spanish conquest of Mexico.

Itzcoatl, they allied with two other tribes and rebelled against their rulers in Atzcapotzalco. That rebellion opened a period of Aztec conquest that reached its climax just after 1500. Their last ruler in this age of conquest was Montezuma. The Aztecs governed a large number of smaller tribes in a particularly harsh manner. Not surprisingly, they demanded payment of labor and tribute from the conquered tribes. However, they also demanded and received thousands of captives each year to be sacrificed to their gods. The Aztecs believed that the gods must literally be fed with human bodies to guarantee continuing sunshine and soil fertility. These policies meant that the Aztecs were surrounded by various "allied" tribes who felt no loyalty; rather, they felt a terror from which they wished to be liberated.

In 1519, Hernán Cortés landed on the coast of Mexico with a force of about six hundred men. He opened communication with tribes nearby and then with Montezuma. The Aztec chief lived in the capital city of Tenochtitlán (modern Mexico City), which was located on an island in the center of a lake and is said to have somewhat resembled Venice as a city built on water. Montezuma initially believed Cortés to be a god. Aztec religion contained the legend of a priest named Quetzalcoatl who had been driven away four centuries earlier and

had promised to return in the very year in which Cortés arrived. Montezuma initially attempted to appease Cortés with gifts of gold, which only whetted the appetites of the Spanish. After several weeks of negotiations and the forging of alliances with subject tribes, Cortés's forces marched on Tenochtitlán, conquered it, and imprisoned Montezuma, who later died under unexplained circumstances. The Aztecs—under a new leader, Cuauhtémoc—attempted to drive the Spanish out, but the Aztecs were eventually defeated by late 1521 after great loss of life. Cortés proclaimed the Aztec Empire to be New Spain.

The second great Indian civilization to experience Spanish conquest was that of the Incas. Located in the highlands of Peru, the Incas were simply the most recent Indian rulers of the region. Like the Aztecs, they had commenced their own conquests in the early fifteenth century. By the early sixteenth century, the Incas ruled several million Indians. They were not as numerous a people as the Aztecs, nor did they possess so large a military organization. Instead, they compelled conquered tribes to fight for them. They carried out this policy by richly rewarding successful warriors and by treating well the conquered tribes who aided them. They also required the conquered peoples to speak Quechua, their own unwritten language. They created a relatively large bureaucracy that helped them to make use of forced labor to build roads, to farm land, and to construct their great cities, such as Cuzco and Machu Picchu. By the time the Spanish arrived, the Incas, whose chief was Atahualpa, were engaged in civil war among their own political elite.

In 1531, largely inspired by Cortés's example in Mexico, Francisco Pizarro sailed from Panama and landed on the western coast of the South American continent to undertake a campaign against the Inca Empire, about which he knew relatively little. His force included about two hundred men armed with guns and swords and equipped with horses, the military power of which the Incas did not understand. In late 1531, Pizarro lured Atahualpa into a conference, where he captured the chief and in the process killed several thousand Indians. The imprisoned Atahualpa then attempted to ransom himself by having a vast horde of gold transported from all over Peru to Pizarro. Needless to say, Pizarro refused to release his captive. After finding he could not use Atahualpa as a puppet ruler, Pizarro had him publicly executed in 1533. Further Indian insurrections took place, with some Inca factions seeking to ally themselves with the Spanish against other factions. The Spanish conquerors also fought among themselves, and effective royal control was not established until the late 1560s.

The conquests of Mexico and Peru stand among the most dramatic and brutal stories in modern western history. One civilization armed with advanced weapons subdued, in a remarkably brief time, two advanced, powerful peoples. But beyond the drama and bloodshed, these conquests, along with lesser ones of smaller groups of Indians, marked a fundamental turning point in the development of western civilization. Never again in the Americas would there be any real possibility that Indian civilizations and their values would produce any significant impact or influence. The Spanish and the Indians did make certain accommodations to each other, but there was never any doubt about which culture held the upper hand. European values, religion, economic goals, and language would dominate, and no group that retained Indian religion, language, or values would be part of the dominant culture or the political power elite. In that sense, the Spanish conquests of the early sixteenth century were the beginning of the process whereby South America (in this context including portions of the southwest United States, Mexico, and Central America) was transformed into Latin America.

The Economy of Exploitation

Almost from the earliest moments of discovery and conquest, the native peoples of America and their lands were drawn into the Atlantic economy and the world of competitive European commercialism. The Spanish set out for America in search of wealth, and they displayed little hesitation in exploiting their unexpected newfound opportunities. For the Indians of Latin America and somewhat later the blacks of Africa, that drive for gain meant various arrangements of forced labor.

There were three major components in the colonial economy of Latin America: mining, agriculture, and shipping. Each of them involved either labor or servitude or a relationship of dependence of the New World economy on that of Spain.

The early *conquistadores* ("conquerors") were primarily interested in gold, but by the middle of the sixteenth century, silver mining provided the chief source of metallic wealth. The great mining centers were Potosí in Peru and somewhat smaller sites in northern Mexico. The Spanish crown was particularly interested in mining because it received one fifth (the *quinto*) of all mining revenues. For this reason, the crown maintained a monopoly over the production and sale of mercury, which was required in the silver-mining process. Silver mining flourished in terms of extracting wealth for the Spanish until the early seventeenth century, when the industry underwent a recession because of lack of new investment and the increasing costs involved in deeper mines. Nonetheless silver never lost predominance during the colonial era, and its production by forced labor for the benefit of Spaniards and the Spanish crown epitomized the wholly extractive economy that stood at the foundation of colonial life.

The major rural and agricultural institution of the Spanish colonies was the *haciendas*. These were large landed estates owned by persons originally born in Spain *(peninsulares)* or persons of Spanish descent born in America *(creoles)*. The establishment of haciendas represented the transfer of the principle of the large unit of privately owned land, which was characteristic of Europe and especially of Spain, to the New World setting. Such estates would become one of the most important features of Latin American life and, in the century after independence, one of the most controversial. Laborers on the hacienda usually stood in some relation of formal servitude to the owner. They were rarely free to move from the services of one landowner to another. There were two major products of the hacienda economy: foodstuffs for mining areas and urban centers and leather goods used in vast quantities on mining machinery. Both farming and ranching thus stood subordinate to the mine economy. However, like mining, the agricultural economy was wholly commercial in nature.

In the West Indies, the basic agricultural unit was the plantation. On Cuba, Hispaniola, Puerto Rico, and other islands, the labor of black slaves from Africa produced sugar to supply what seemed to be the insatiable demand for the product in Europe.

The final major area of economic activity in the Spanish colonies was the variety of service occupations pursued in the cities. These included the governmental bureaucracy, the legal profession, and shipping. These practi-

A Contemporary Describes Forced Indian Labor at Potosí

The Potosí range in Peru was the site of the great silver-mining industry in the Spanish Empire. The vast amount of wealth contained in the region became legendary almost as soon as mining began there in the 1540s. Indians, most of whom were forced laborers working under the *mita* system of conscription, did virtually all of the work underground. This description, written by a Spanish friar in the early seventeenth century, portrays both the large size of the enterprise and the harsh conditions that the Indians endured. At any one time, only one third of the 13,300 conscripted Indians were employed. The labor force was changed every four months.

According to His Majesty's warrant, the mine owners on this massive range have a right to the mita [conscripted labor] of 13,300 Indians in the working and exploitation of the mines, both those which have been discovered, those now discovered, and those which shall be discovered. It is the duty of the Corregidor [municipal governor] of Potosí to have them rounded up and to see that they come in from all the provinces between Cuzco over the whole of El Collao and as far as the frontiers of Tarija and Tomina. . . .

. . . The mita Indians go up every Monday morning to the locality of Guayna Potosí which is at the foot of the range; the Corregidor arrives with all the provincial captains or chiefs who have charge of the Indians assigned them, and he there checks off and reports to each mine and smelter owner the number of Indians assigned him for his mine or smelter; that keeps him busy till 1 P.M., by which time the Indians are already turned over to these mine and smelter owners.

After each has eaten his ration, they climb up the hill, each to his mine, and go in, staying there from that hour until Saturday evening without coming out of the mine; their wives bring them food, but they stay constantly underground, excavating and carrying out the ore from which they get the silver. They all have tallow candles, lighted day and night; that is the light they work with, for as they are underground, they have need of it all the time. . . .

These Indians have different functions in the handling of the silver ore; some break it up with bar or pick, and dig down in, following the vein in the mine; others bring it up; others up above keep separating the good and the poor in piles; others are occupied in taking it down from the range to the mills on herds of llamas; every day they bring up more than 8,000 of these native beasts of burden for this task. These teamsters who carry the metal do not belong to the mita, but are mingados—hired.

Antonio Vázquez de Espinosa, *Compendium and Description of the Indies* (ca. 1620), trans. by Charles Upson Clark (Washington, D.C.: Smithsonian Institution Press, 1968), p. 62, quoted in Helen Delpar (Ed.), *The Borzoi Reader in Latin American History* (New York: Alfred A. Knopf, 1972), pp. 92–93.

tioners were either *peninsulares* or *creoles*, with the former dominating more often than not. The rules they enforced, interpreted, or shipped by were those set by institutions of the Spanish government to realize the goals of a competitive mercantile empire.

All of this extractive and exploitive economic activity required labor, and the Spanish in the New World had decided very early that the Indian population would supply the labor. A series of social devices was used to draw Indians into the economic life imposed by the Spanish.

The first of these was the *encomienda*. This was a formal grant of the right to the labor of a specific number of Indians for a particular period of time. An *encomienda* usually involved a few hundred Indians but might grant the right to the labor of several thousand. *Encomienda* as an institution persisted in some parts of Latin America well into the seventeenth century but generally stood in decline by the middle of the

The great silver mine at Potosí in Peru, as depicted in a drawing of 1584. Potosí was a veritable mountain of silver from which pack trains of llamas carried the ore to the refinery shown in the foreground. [Hispanic Society of America]

sixteenth. The Spanish monarchs feared that the holders of *encomienda* were attempting to become a powerful independent nobility in the New World. The Spanish government was also persuaded by appeals on humanitarian grounds against this particular kind of exploitation of the Indians. The land grants that led to the establishment of haciendas were one means whereby the crown continued to use the resources of the New World for patronage without directly impinging on the Indians.

The passing of the *encomienda* led to a new arrangement of labor servitude, the *repartimiento*. This device required adult male Indians to devote so many days of labor annually to Spanish economic enterprises. In the mines of Peru, the *repartimiento* was known as the *mita,* and in some cases, Indians did not survive their days of labor rotation. The actual limitation of labor time led some Spanish managers to use their workers in an extremely harsh manner, under the assumption that more fresh workers would soon be appearing on the scene.

The eventual shortage of workers and the crown's pressure against extreme versions of forced labor led to the use of free labor. Here again, however, the freedom was more in appearance, and dependence and subservience were the reality. Free Indian laborers were required to purchase goods from the landowner or mine owner. They became indebted and were never able to pay off the debt. This situation was known as *debt peonage* and continued in different forms in Latin America long after the wars of liberation.

Black slavery was the final mode of forced or subservient labor in the New World. Both the Spanish and the Portuguese had used African slaves in Europe. They were used throughout Latin America at one time or another, but the sugar plantations of the West Indies were the major center of slavery.

The conquest and the economy of exploitation and forced labor (and the introduction of European diseases) produced extraordinary demographic consequences for the Indian population. By the early seventeenth century, the Indians were dying off in huge numbers. Estimates of the Pre-Columbian population of America have generated major controversies. Conservative estimates put the Indian population at the time of Columbus's discovery at well over fifty million. In New Spain (Mexico) alone, the decline in population was probably from approximately twenty-five million to less than two million. Whatever the exact figures, there was and is no doubt that the Indian population encountered by the *conquistadores* largely vanished and, with it, the easy supply of labor that they had exploited.

Rise in Prices and the Development of Capitalism

The influx of spices and precious metals into Europe from the Spanish Empire was not an unmixed blessing. It contributed to a steady rise in prices during the sixteenth century that created an inflation rate estimated at 2 per cent a year. The new supply of bullion from the Americas joined with enlarged European production to increase greatly the amount of coinage in circulation, and this increase in turn fed inflation. Fortunately the increase in prices was by and large spread over a long period of time and was not sudden. Prices doubled in Spain by mid-century, quadrupled by 1600. In Luther's Wittenberg the cost of basic food and clothing increased almost 100 per cent between 1519 and 1540. Generally wages and rents remained well behind the rise in prices.

The new wealth enabled governments and private entrepreneurs to sponsor basic research and expansion in the printing, shipping, mining, textile, and weapons industries—the

Jacob Fugger ''the Rich'' (1459–1525) with his chief accountant. As bankers to the Habsburgs, the Fuggers became immensely wealthy. [Robert-Viollet]

growth industries of the Age of Reformation. There is also evidence of mercantilism or large-scale government planning in such ventures as the French silk industry and the Habsburg–Fugger development of mines in Austria and Hungary.

In the thirteenth and fourteenth centuries capitalist institutions and practices had already begun to develop in the rich Italian cities (one may point to the Florentine banking houses of Bardi and Peruzzi). Those who owned the means of production, either privately or corporately, were clearly distinguished from the workers who operated them. Wherever possible, monopolies were created in basic goods. High interest was charged on loans—actual, if not legal, usury. And the "capitalist" virtues of thrift, industry, and orderly planning were everywhere in evidence—all intended to permit the free and efficient accumulation of wealth.

The late fifteenth and the sixteenth centuries saw the maturation of such capitalism together with its peculiar social problems. The new wealth and industrial expansion raised the expectations of the poor and the ambitious and heightened the reactionary tendencies within the established and wealthy classes. This effect, in turn, greatly aggravated the traditional social divisions between the clergy and the laity, the higher and the lower clergy, the urban patriciate and the guilds, masters and journeymen, and the landed nobility and the agrarian peasantry.

Such social divisions may indirectly have prepared the way for the Reformation by making many people critical of traditional institutions and open to new ideas—especially those that seemed to promise a greater degree of freedom and equality.

The far-flung transactions created by the new commerce increased the demand for lawyers and bankers. The Medicis of Florence grew very rich as bankers of the pope, as did the Fuggers of Augsburg as bankers of the Habsburg rulers. The Fuggers lent Charles I of Spain over 500,000 florins to buy his election as Holy Roman Emperor in 1519, and they later boasted that they had created the emperor. But those who paid out their money also took their chances. Both the Fuggers and the Medicis were later bankrupted by popes and kings who defaulted on their heavy debts.

The Northern Renaissance

The scholarly works of northern Humanists created a climate favorable to religious and educational reforms on the eve of the Reformation. Northern Humanism was initially stimulated by the importation of Italian learning through such varied intermediaries as students who had studied in Italy, merchants, and the Brothers of the Common Life (an influential lay religious movement that began in the Netherlands and permitted men and women to live a shared religious life without making formal vows of poverty, chastity, and obedience). The northern Humanists, however, developed their own distinctive culture. They tended to come from more diverse social backgrounds and to

be more devoted to religious reforms than their Italian counterparts. They were also more willing to write for lay audiences as well as for a narrow intelligentsia.

Erasmus

The most famous of the northern Humanists was Desiderius Erasmus (1466–1536), the reputed "prince of the Humanists." Erasmus gained fame as both an educational and a religious reformer. Earning his living by tutoring when patrons were in short supply, Erasmus prepared short Latin dialogues for his students that were intended to teach them how to speak and live well, inculcating good manners and language by encouraging them to imitate what they read. These dialogues were published under the title *Colloquies* and grew in number and length in consecutive editions, coming also

Erasmus of Rotterdam (1466–1536) painted by Hans Holbein the Younger in 1523. Erasmus influenced all of the reform movements of the sixteenth century. He was popularly said to have "laid the egg that Luther hatched." [Kunstmuseum, Basel]

to embrace anticlerical dialogues and satires on popular religious superstition. Erasmus collected ancient and contemporary proverbs, as well, which he published under the title *Adages*, beginning with about eight hundred examples and increasing his collection to over five thousand in the final edition of the work. Among the sayings that the *Adages* popularized are such common modern expressions as "to leave no stone unturned" and "where there is smoke, there is fire."

Erasmus aspired to unite the classical ideals of humanity and civic virtue with the Christian ideals of love and piety. He believed that disciplined study of the classics and the Bible, if begun early enough, was the best way to reform both individuals and society. He summarized his own beliefs with the phrase *philosophia Christi,* a simple, ethical piety in imitation of Christ. He set this ideal in starkest contrast to what he believed to be the dogmatic, ceremonial, and factious religious practice of the later Middle Ages. What most offended him about the Scholastics, both those of the late Middle Ages and, increasingly, the new Lutheran ones, was their letting doctrine and disputation overshadow humble piety and Christian practice.

To promote his own religious beliefs, Erasmus labored to make the ancient Christian sources available in their original versions, for, he believed, only as people drank from the pure, unadulterated sources could moral and religious health result. He edited the works of the Church Fathers and made a Greek edition of the New Testament (1516), which became the basis for his new, more accurate Latin translation (1519).

These various enterprises did not please church authorities, who were unhappy with both Erasmus's "improvements" on the Vulgate, Christendom's Bible for over a thousand years, and his popular anticlerical satires. At one point in the mid-sixteenth century all of Erasmus's works were placed on the *Index of Forbidden Books.* Erasmus also received Luther's unqualified condemnation for his views on the freedom of human will. Still,

---

Erasmus Describes the "Philosophy of Christ"

Although Erasmus called his ideal of how people should live the "philosophy of Christ," he found it taught by classical authors as well. In this selection he comments on its main features, with obvious polemic against the philosophy of the Scholastics.

This kind of philosophy [the philosophy of Christ] is located more truly in the disposition of the mind than in syllogisms. Here life means more than debate, inspiration is preferable to erudition, transformation [of life] a more important matter than intellectual comprehension. Only a very few can be learned, but all can be Christian, all can be devout, and—I shall boldly add—all can be theologians. Indeed, this philosophy easily penetrates into the minds of all; it is an action in special accord with human nature. What else is the philosophy of Christ, which he himself calls a rebirth, than the restoration of human nature . . . ? Although no one has taught this more perfectly . . . than Christ, nevertheless one may find in the books of the pagans very much which does agree with it. There was *never so coarse a school of philosophy that taught that money rendered a man happy. Nor has there ever been one so shameless that fixed the chief good in vulgar honors and pleasures. The Stoics understood that no one was wise unless he was good. . . . According to Plato, Socrates teaches . . . that a wrong must not be repaid with a wrong, and also that since the soul is immortal, those should not be lamented who depart this life for a happier one with the assurance of having led an upright life. . . . And Aristotle has written in the* Politics *that nothing can be a delight to us . . . except virtue alone. . . . If there are things that belong particularly to Christianity in these ancient writers, let us follow them.*

The *Paraclesis* in *Christian Humanism and the Reformation: Desiderius Erasmus,* ed. and trans. by John C. Olin (New York: Harper, 1965), pp. 100–101.

Erasmus's didactic and scholarly works became basic tools of reform in the hands of both Protestant and Catholic reformers.

Humanism in Germany

Peter Luder (d. 1474) and Rudolf Agricola (1443–1485) brought Italian learning to Germany. Agricola, the father of German Humanism, spent ten years in Italy. Like later German Humanists, he aspired to outdo the Italians in classical learning, thereby adding a nationalist motivation to German scholarship. Conrad Celtis (d. 1508), the first German poet laureate, and Ulrich von Hutten (1488–1523), a fiery knight, were exponents of romantic cultural nationalism. The life and work of Von Hutten especially illustrate the union of Humanism, German nationalism, and Luther's religious reform. A poet who admired Erasmus and attacked Scholasticism and bad Latin, von Hutten was also a member of the fading landed nobility who aspired to a revival of ancient German virtue—he died in 1523 in a hopeless knights' revolt against the princes. He was also an advocate of religious reform who attacked indulgences and published an edition of Valla's exposé of the Donation of Constantine.

THE REUCHLIN AFFAIR. The *cause célèbre* that brought von Hutten onto the historical stage and unified many reform-minded German Humanists was the Reuchlin affair. Johann Reuchlin (1455–1522) was Europe's foremost Christian authority on Hebrew and Jewish learning. He had written the first reliable Hebrew grammar by a Christian scholar and was personally attracted to Jewish mysticism. Around 1506 a converted Jew named Pfefferkorn, supported by the Dominican Order in Cologne (the city that was known as "the German Rome"), began a movement to suppress Jewish writings. When Pfefferkorn attacked Reuchlin, many German Humanists, in the name of academic freedom and good scholarship, not for any pro-Jewish sentiment, rushed to Reuchlin's defense. The controversy, which lasted several years, produced one of the great satires of the period, the *Letters of Obscure Men* (1515), a merciless satire on the narrowness and irrelevance of monks and Scholastics, particularly those in Cologne, written by Crotus Rubeanus and Ulrich von Hutten. When Luther came under attack after his famous ninety-five theses against indulgences in 1517, many German Humanists tended to see

in his plight a repetition of the Scholastic attack on Reuchlin; religious reform and academic freedom were again at stake. Although, following Erasmus's lead, many of these same men ceased to support Luther when the revolutionary direction of his theology became clear, German Humanists formed the first identifiable group of Luther's supporters, and many young Humanists became Lutheran pastors.

Humanism in England

Humanists also promoted basic educational and religious reforms in England and France. English scholars and merchants and visiting Italian prelates brought Italian learning to England. The Oxford lectures of William Grocyn (d. 1519) and Thomas Linacre (d. 1524) and the Cambridge lectures of the visiting Erasmus (1510–1513), who worked on his Greek edition of the New Testament while in England, marked the scholarly maturation of English Humanism. John Colet (1467–1519), after 1505 dean of St. Paul's Cathedral, became renowned for his sermons and commentaries on the New Testament and his patronage of Humanist studies for the young. Like the other English Humanists, only more so, he stressed the relevance of Scripture to the problems of religious reform.

The best known of early English Humanists was Thomas More (1478–1535), a close friend of Erasmus. It was while visiting More that Erasmus wrote his most famous work, *The Praise of Folly*, an amusing and profound exposé of human self-deception. More's *Utopia* (1516), a criticism of contemporary society, still rivals the plays of Shakespeare as the most-read sixteenth-century English work. *Utopia* depicted an imaginary society based on reason and tolerance that had overcome social and political injustice by holding all property and goods in common and by requiring all to earn their bread by the sweat of their own brow.

A bureaucrat under Henry VII, More became one of Henry VIII's most trusted diplomats, succeeding Cardinal Wolsey as lord chancellor in 1529. More resigned that position in May 1532 because he could not in good conscience support the king's break with the papacy and his pretension to being head of the English church "so far as the law of Christ allows." More's repudiation of the Act of Supremacy (1534) and his refusal to recognize the king's marriage to Anne Boleyn led to his execution in July 1535.

Thomas More (1478–1535) by Hans Holbein the Younger, painted in 1527. The English statesman and author was beheaded by Henry VIII for his refusal to recognize the king's sovereignty over the English church. [The Frick Collection]

Although More remained staunchly Catholic, Humanism in England, as in Germany, played an important role in preparing the way for the English Reformation. A circle of English Humanists, under the direction of Henry VIII's minister Thomas Cromwell, translated and disseminated, to the king's advantage, such pertinent works as Marsilius of Padua's *Defender of Peace*, a work that exalted the sovereignty of rulers over popes and therefore had been condemned by the church, and writings of Erasmus that urged church reform.

Humanism in France

It was through the French invasions of Italy that Italian learning penetrated France, traffic in books and ideas going hand in hand with the transport of men and matériel to and fro. Guillaume Budé (1468–1540), an accomplished Greek scholar, and Jacques Lefèvre d'Etaples (1454–1536) were the leaders of French Humanism. Lefèvre's two main works—the *Quincuplex Psalterium*, five Latin versions of the psalms arranged in parallel columns, and a translation and commentary on Saint Paul's

Epistle to the Romans—not only exemplified the new critical scholarship but also influenced the theology of Martin Luther. French Humanism had two powerful political patrons: Guillaume Briçonnet (1470–1533), after 1516 the bishop of Meaux, and Marguerite d'Angoulême (1492–1549), sister of Francis I and the future queen of Navarre, who made her own reputation as a writer. The future Protestant reformer John Calvin was a product of this native reform circle. Calvin was the first of three major vernacular writers with Humanist backgrounds who created the modern French language. The others were the physician François Rabelais (1494–1553), an ex-Franciscan and Benedictine monk whose *Gargantua* and *Pantagruel* satirized his age, and the skeptical essayist Michel de Montaigne (1533–1592), who ridiculed the authoritarian Scholastic mind.

Humanism in Spain

Whereas in Germany, England, and France Humanism prepared the way for Protestant reforms, in Spain it entered the service of the Catholic church. Here the key figure was Francisco Jiménez de Cisneros (1437–1517), a confessor to Queen Isabella, and after 1508 Grand Inquisitor—a position from which he was able to enforce the strictest religious orthodoxy. Jiménez was a conduit for Humanist scholarship and learning. He founded the University of Alcalá near Madrid in 1509, printed a Greek edition of the New Testament, and translated many religious tracts that aided clerical reform and control of lay religious life. His greatest achievement, taking fifteen years to complete, was the *Complutensian Polyglot Bible*, a six-volume work that placed the Hebrew, Greek, and Latin versions of the Bible in parallel columns. Such scholarly projects and internal church reforms joined with the repressive measures of Ferdinand and Isabella to keep Spain strictly Catholic throughout the Age of Reformation.

Religious Life

Popular Religious Movements and Criticism of the Church

The Protestant Reformation could not have occurred without the monumental crises of the medieval church during the "exile" in Avignon, the Great Schism, the conciliar period, and the Renaissance papacy. For increasing numbers of people the medieval church had ceased also to provide a viable religious piety. There was a crisis in the traditional teaching and spiritual practice of the church among many of its intellectuals and laity. Between the secular pretensions of the papacy and the dry teaching of Scholastic theologians, laity and clerics alike began to seek a more heartfelt, idealistic, and—often, in the eyes of the pope—increasingly heretical religious piety. The late Middle Ages were marked by independent lay and clerical efforts to reform local religious practice and by widespread experimentation with new religious forms.

A variety of factors contributed to the growth of lay criticism of the church. In the cities the laity were far more knowledgeable about the world and those who controlled their lives. The laity traveled widely—as soldiers, pilgrims, explorers, and traders. New postal systems and the printing press increased the information at their disposal. The new age of books and libraries raised literacy and heightened curiosity. Laypeople were increasingly in a position to take the initiative in shaping the cultural life of their communities.

From the Albigensians, Waldensians, Beguines, and Beghards in the thirteenth century to the Lollards and Hussites in the fifteenth, lay religious movements shared a common goal of religious simplicity in imitation of Jesus. Almost without exception they were inspired by an ideal of apostolic poverty in religion; that is, all wanted a religion of true self-sacrifice like that of Jesus and the first disciples. The laity sought a more egalitarian church, one that gave the members as well as the head of the church a voice, and a more spiritual church, one that lived manifestly according to its New Testament model.

THE MODERN DEVOTION. One of the most constructive lay religious movements in northern Europe on the eve of the Reformation was that of the Brothers of the Common Life, or what came to be known as the *Modern Devotion*. The brothers fostered the religious life outside formal ecclesiastical offices and apart from formal religious vows. Established by Gerard Groote (1340–1384) and centered at Zwolle and Deventer in the Netherlands, the brother and (less numerous) sister houses of the Modern Devotion spread rapidly throughout northern Europe and influenced parts of southern Europe as well. In these houses clerics and laity came together to share a common life, stressing individual piety and practical religion. Lay members were not expected to take special religious vows or to wear special religious dress, nor did they abandon their ordinary secular vocations.

The brothers were also active in education. They worked as copyists, sponsored many religious and a few classical publications, ran hospices for poor students, and conducted schools for the young, especially for boys preparing for the priesthood or a monastic vocation. As youths, Nicholas of Cusa, Johannes Reuchlin, and Desiderius Erasmus were looked after by the brothers. Thomas à Kempis (d. 1471) summarized the philosophy of the brothers in what became the most popular religious book of the period, the *Imitation of Christ,* a semimystical guide to the inner life intended primarily for monks and nuns, but widely appropriated by laity who also wanted to pursue the ascetic life.

The Modern Devotion has been seen as the source of Humanist, Protestant, and Catholic reform movements in the sixteenth century, although some scholars believe that it represented an individualistic approach to religion, indifferent and even harmful to the sacramental piety of the church. It was actually a very conservative movement. The brothers retained the old clerical doctrines and values, while placing them within the new framework of an active common life. They clearly met a need for a more personal piety and a better-informed religious life. Their movement appeared at a time when the laity were demanding good preaching in the vernacular and were even taking the initiative to endow special preacherships to ensure it. The Modern Devotion permitted laity to practice the religious life in the fullest, yet without having to surrender their life in the world.

LAY CONTROL OVER RELIGIOUS LIFE. On the eve of the Reformation, Rome's international network of church offices, which had unified Europe religiously during the Middle Ages, began to fall apart in many areas, hurried along by a growing sense of regional identity—incipient nationalism—and local secular administrative competence. The long-entrenched benefice system of the medieval church, which had permitted important ecclesiastical posts to be sold to the highest bidders and had left residency requirements in parishes unenforced, did not result in a vibrant local religious life.

The substitutes hired by nonresident holders of benefices, who lived elsewhere (mostly in Rome) and milked the revenues of their offices, often performed their chores mechanically and had neither firsthand knowledge of nor much sympathy with local needs and problems. Rare was the late medieval German town that did not have complaints about the maladministration, concubinage, and/or fiscalism of their clergy, especially the higher clergy (i.e., bishops, abbots, and prelates).

Communities loudly protested the financial abuses of the medieval church long before Luther published his famous summary of economic grievances in the *Address to the Christian Nobility of the German Nation.* The sale of indulgences, a practice that was greatly expanded on the eve of the Reformation and seemed now to permit people to buy release from religious punishment in purgatory both for their own and their deceased loved ones' sins, had also been repeatedly attacked before Luther came on the scene. Rulers and magistrates had little objection to and could even encourage the sale of indulgences as long as a generous portion of the income remained within the local coffers. But when an indulgence was offered primarily for the benefit of distant interests, as was the case with the Saint Peter's indulgence protested by Luther, resistance arose for strictly financial reasons, because their sale drained away local revenues.

Indulgences could not pass from the scene until rulers found new ways to profit from religion and a more effective popular remedy for religious anxiety was at hand. The Reformation provided the former by sanctioning the secular dissolution of monasteries and the confiscation of ecclesiastical properties. It held out the latter in its new theology of justification by faith.

City governments also undertook to improve local religious life on the eve of the Reformation by endowing preacherships. These were beneficed positions that provided for well-trained and dedicated pastors and regular preaching and pastoral care, which went beyond the routine performance of the Mass and traditional religious functions. In many instances these preacherships became platforms for Protestant preachers.

Magistrates also carefully restricted the growth of ecclesiastical properties and clerical privileges. During the Middle Ages special clerical rights in both property and person had come to be recognized by canon and civil law.

Because they were holy places, churches and monasteries had been exempted from the taxes and laws that affected others. They were treated as special places of "sacral peace" and asylum. It was considered inappropriate for holy persons (clergy) to be burdened with such "dirty jobs" as military service, compulsory labor, standing watch at city gates, and other obligations of citizenship. Nor was it thought right that the laity, of whatever rank, should sit in judgment on those who were their shepherds and intermediaries with God. The clergy, accordingly, came to enjoy an immunity of place (which exempted ecclesiastical properties from taxes and recognized their right of asylum) and an immunity of person (which exempted the clergy from the jurisdiction of civil courts).

On the eve of the Reformation measures were passed to restrict these privileges and to end their abuses—efforts to regulate ecclesiastical acquisition of new property, to circumvent the right of asylum in churches and monasteries (a practice that posed a threat to the normal administration of justice), and to bring the clergy under the local tax code. Governments had understandably tired of ecclesiastical interference in what seemed to them to be strictly political spheres of competence and authority.

Martin Luther and German Reformation to 1525

Unlike France and England, late medieval Germany lacked the political unity to enforce "national" religious reforms during the late Middle Ages. There were no lasting Statutes of Provisors and *praemunire,* as in England, nor a Pragmatic Sanction of Bourges, as in France, limiting papal jurisdiction and taxation on a national scale. What happened on a unified national level in England and France occurred only locally and piecemeal within German territories and towns. As popular resentment of clerical immunities and ecclesiastical abuses, especially the selling of indulgences, spread among German cities and towns, an unorganized "national" opposition to Rome formed. German Humanists had long given voice to such criticism, and by 1517 it was pervasive enough to provide a solid foundation for Martin Luther's reform.

Luther (1483–1546) was the son of a successful Thüringian miner. He was educated in

Mansfeld; Magdeburg, where the Brothers of the Common Life were his teachers; and Eisenach. Between 1501 and 1505 he attended the University of Erfurt, where the nominalist teachings of William of Ockham and Gabriel Biel (d. 1495) prevailed within the Philosophical Faculty. After receiving his master of arts degree in 1505, Luther registered with the Law Faculty in accordance with his parents' wishes. But he never began the study of law. To the shock and disappointment of his family, he instead entered the Order of the Hermits of Saint Augustine in Erfurt on July 17, 1505. This decision had apparently been building for some time and was resolved during a lightning storm in which a terrified Luther, crying out to Saint Anne for assistance (Saint Anne was the patron saint of travelers in distress), promised to enter a monastery if he escaped death.

Ordained in 1507, Luther pursued a traditional course of study, becoming in 1509 a *baccalaureus biblicus* and *sententiarius,* that is, thoroughly trained in the Bible and the *Sentences* of Peter Lombard. In 1510 he journeyed to Rome on the business of his order, finding there justification for the many criticisms of the church he had heard in Germany. In 1511 he was transferred to the Augustinian monastery in Wittenberg, where he earned his doctorate in theology in 1512, thereafter becoming a leader within the monastery, the new university, and the spiritual life of the city.

Justification by Faith Alone

Reformation theology grew out of a problem common to many of the clergy and the laity at this time: the failure of traditional medieval religion to provide either full personal or intellectual satisfaction. Luther was especially plagued by the disproportion between his own sense of sinfulness and the perfect righteousness that medieval theology taught that God required for salvation. Traditional church teaching and the sacrament of penance proved to be of no consolation. Luther wrote that he came to despise the phrase "righteousness of God," for it seemed to demand of him a perfection he knew neither he nor any other human being could ever achieve. His insight into the meaning of "justification by faith alone" was a gradual process that extended over several years, between 1513 and 1518. The righteousness that God demands, he concluded, was not one that came from many religious works and ceremonies but was present in full measure in

Martin Luther (1483–1546), painted in 1521 by Lucas Cranach the Elder (1472–1553). [Metropolitan Museum of Art, gift of Robert Lehman, 1955]

those who simply believed and trusted in the work of Jesus Christ, who alone was the perfect righteousness satisfying to God. To believe in Christ was to stand before God clothed in Christ's sure righteousness.

The Attack on Indulgences

An indulgence was a remission of the temporal penalty imposed by the priest on penitents as a "work of satisfaction" for their committed mortal sins. According to medieval theology, after the priest had absolved penitents of guilt for their sins, they still remained under an eternal penalty, a punishment God justly imposed on them for their sins. After absolution, however, this eternal penalty was said to be transformed into a temporal penalty, a manageable "work of satisfac-

Martin Luther Discovers Justification by Faith Alone

Many years after the fact, Martin Luther described his discovery that God's righteousness was not an active, punishing righteousness but a passive, transforming righteousness, which made those who believed in Him righteous as God Himself is righteous.

Though I lived as a monk without reproach, I felt that I was a sinner before God with an extremely disturbed conscience. I could not believe that he was placated by my satisfaction. I did not love, yes, I hated the righteous God who punishes sinners, and secretly, if not blasphemously, certainly murmuring greatly, I was angry with God, and said, "As if, indeed, it is not enough, that miserable sinners, eternally lost through original sin, are crushed by every kind of calamity by the law of the decalogue, without having God add pain to pain by the gospel and also by the gospel threatening us with his righteousness and wrath!" Thus I raged with a fierce and troubled conscience. Nevertheless, I beat importunately upon Paul at that place, most ardently desiring to know what St. Paul wanted.

At last, by the mercy of God, meditating day and night, I gave heed to the context of the words, namely, "In it the righteousness of God is revealed, as it is written, 'He who through faith is righteous shall live'" [Romans 1:17].

There I began to understand that the righteousness of God is that by which the righteous lives by a gift of God, namely by faith. And this is the meaning: the righteousness of God is revealed by the gospel, namely, the passive righteousness with which merciful God justifies us by faith, as it is written, "He who through faith is righteous shall live." Here I felt that I was altogether born again and had entered paradise itself through open gates. There a totally other face of the entire Scripture showed itself to me. Thereupon I ran through the Scriptures from memory. I also found in other terms an analogy, as, the work of God, that is, what God does in us, the power of God, with which he makes us strong, the wisdom of God, with which he makes us wise, the strength of God, the salvation of God, the glory of God.

And I extolled my sweetest word with a love as great as the hatred with which I had before hated the word "righteousness of God." Thus that place in Paul was for me truly the gate to paradise.

Preface to the Complete Edition of *Luther's Latin Writings* (1545), in *Luther's Works,* Vol. 34, ed. by Lewis W. Spitz (Philadelphia: Muhlenberg Press, 1960) pp. 336–337.

tion" that the penitent could perform here and now (for example, prayers, fasting, almsgiving, retreats, and pilgrimages). Penitents who defaulted on such prescribed works of satisfaction could expect to suffer for them in purgatory.

At this point indulgences came into play as an aid to a laity made genuinely anxious by a belief in a future suffering in purgatory for neglected penances or unrepented sins. In 1343 Pope Clement VI (1342–1352) had proclaimed the existence of a "treasury of merit," an infinite reservoir of good works in the church's possession that could be dispensed at the pope's discretion. It was on the basis of this declared treasury that the church sold "letters of indulgence," which covered the works of satisfaction owed by penitents. In 1476 Pope Sixtus IV (1471–1484) extended indulgences also to purgatory. Originally indulgences had

been given only for the true self-sacrifice of going on a Crusade to the Holy Land. By Luther's time they were regularly dispensed for small cash payments (very modest sums that were regarded as a good work of almsgiving) and were presented to the laity as remitting not only their own future punishments, but also those of their dead relatives presumed to be suffering in purgatory.

In 1517 a Jubilee indulgence, proclaimed during the pontificate of Pope Julius II (1503–1513) to raise funds for the rebuilding of Saint Peter's in Rome, was revived and preached on the borders of Saxony in the territories of Archbishop Albrecht of Mainz. Albrecht was much in need of revenues because of the large debts he had incurred in order to hold, contrary to church law, three ecclesiastical appointments: the archbishoprics of Mainz and Magdeburg in addition to the bishopric of Halberstadt. The selling of the indulgence was a joint venture by Albrecht, the Augsburg banking-house of Fugger, and Pope Leo X, half the proceeds going to the pope and half to Albrecht and his creditors. The famous indulgence preacher John Tetzel (d. 1519) was enlisted to preach the indulgence in Albrecht's territories because he was a seasoned professional who knew how to stir ordinary people to action. As he exhorted on one occasion:

Don't you hear the voices of your dead parents and other relatives crying out, "Have mercy on us, for we suffer great punishment and pain. From this you could release us with a few alms. . . . We have created you, fed you, cared for you, and left you our temporal goods. Why do you treat us so cruelly and leave us to suffer in the flames, when it takes only a little to save us?"[1]

When on October 31, 1517, Luther posted his ninety-five theses against indulgences, according to tradition, on the door of Castle Church in Wittenberg, he protested especially against the impression created by Tetzel that indulgences actually remitted sins and released the dead from punishment in purgatory—claims Luther believed went far beyond the traditional practice and seemed to make salvation something that could be bought and sold.

Election of Charles V

The ninety-five theses were embraced by Humanists and other proponents of reform. They made Luther famous overnight and prompted official proceedings against him. In April 1518 he was summoned to appear before the general chapter of his order in Heidelberg, and the following October he was called before the papal legate and general of the Dominican Order, Cardinal Cajetan, in Augsburg. As sanctions were being prepared against Luther, Emperor Maximilian I died (January 12, 1519), and this event, fortunate for the Reformation, turned all attention from heresy in Saxony to the contest for a new emperor.

The pope backed the French king, Francis I. However, Charles I of Spain, a youth of nineteen, succeeded his grandfather and became Emperor Charles V. Charles was assisted by both a long tradition of Habsburg imperial rule and a massive Fugger campaign chest, which

A contemporary caricature of John Tetzel, the famous indulgence preacher. The last lines of the jingle read: "As soon as gold in the basin rings, right then the soul to heaven springs." It was Tetzel's preaching that spurred Luther to publish his ninety-five theses. [Staatliche Lutherhalle, Wittenberg]

Pope Leo X (1513–1521), of the Medici family, with two cardinals, as painted about 1517–1518 by Raphael. Leo was pope when the reformation began and condemned Luther for heresy in 1520. [Alinari/SCALA]

[1]*Die Reformation in Augenzeugen berichten,* ed. by Helmar Junghaus (Düsseldorf: Karl Rauch Verlag, 1967), p. 44.

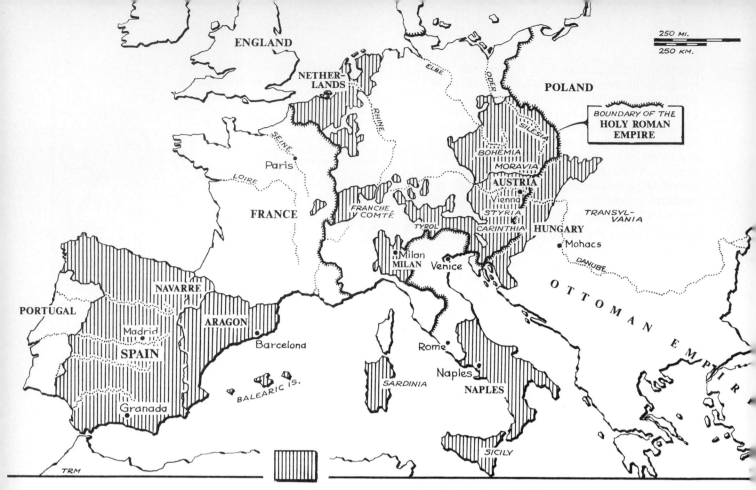

THE EMPIRE OF CHARLES V

MAP 10–2 *Dynastic marriages and simple chance concentrated into Charles's hands rule over the lands shown here, plus Spain's overseas possessions. Crowns and titles rained in on him; election in 1519 as emperor gave him new burdens and responsibilities.*

secured the votes of the seven electors. The electors, who traditionally enhanced their power at every opportunity, wrung new concessions from Charles for their votes. The emperor agreed to a revival of the Imperial Supreme Court and the Council of Regency and promised to consult with a diet of the empire on all major domestic and foreign affairs that affected the empire. These measures also helped the development of the Reformation by preventing unilateral imperial action against the Germans, something Luther could be thankful for in the early years of the Reformation.

Luther's Excommunication and the Diet of Worms

In the same month in which Charles was elected emperor, Luther entered a debate in Leipzig (June 27, 1519) with the Ingolstadt professor John Eck. During this contest Luther challenged the infallibility of the pope and the inerrancy of church councils, appealing, for the first time, to the sovereign authority of Scripture alone. All his bridges to the old church were burned when he further defended certain teachings of John Huss condemned by the Council of Constance. In 1520 Luther signaled his new direction with three famous pamphlets: the *Address to the Christian Nobility of the German Nation*, which urged the German princes to force reforms on the Roman church, especially to curtail its political and economic power in Germany; the *Babylonian Captivity of the Church*, which attacked the traditional seven sacraments, arguing that only two, Baptism and the Eucharist, were proper, and exalted the authority of Scripture, church councils, and secular princes over that of the pope;

and the eloquent *Freedom of a Christian,* which summarized the new teaching of salvation by faith alone. On June 15, 1520, the papal bull *Exsurge Domine* condemned Luther for heresy and gave him sixty days to retract. The final bull of excommunication, *Decet Pontificem Romanum,* was issued on January 3, 1521.

In April 1521 Luther presented his views before a diet of the empire in Worms, over which the newly elected Emperor Charles V presided. Ordered to recant, Luther declared that to do so would be to act against Scripture, reason, and his own conscience. On May 26, 1521, he was placed under the imperial ban and thereafter became an "outlaw" to secular as well as to religious authority. For his own protection friends hid him in Wartburg Castle, where he spent almost a year in seclusion, from April 1521 to March 1522. During his stay, he translated the New Testament into

A Catholic caricature of Martin Luther as a seven-headed monster. This picture served as the title page of a pamphlet by one of Luther's strongest Catholic critics, Johannes Cochlaeus.

Luther Calls on the German Nobility to Reform the Church

In his *Address to the Christian Nobility of the German Nation* (1520), Luther protested against the three "walls" of Rome that had prevented reform in the church by making the pope immune to corrective action on the basis of secular, biblical, and conciliar authority. In the following, Luther urges the nobility to tear down these walls.

The Romanists have with great dexterity built around themselves three walls, which hitherto have protected them against reform; and thereby is Christianity fearfully fallen.

In the first place, when the temporal power has pressed them hard [to reform], they have . . . maintained that the temporal power has no jurisdiction over them, that, on the contrary, the spiritual [power] is above the temporal.

Secondly, when it was proposed to admonish them from the Holy Scriptures they said, "It befits no one but the pope to interpret the Scriptures."

And, thirdly, when they were threatened

with a council, they invented the idea that no one but the pope can call a council.

Thus have they secretly stolen our three rods so that they may go unpunished, and entrenched themselves safely behind these three walls in order to carry on all the knavery and wickedness that we now see. . . .

Now may God help us, and give us one of those trumpets that overthrew the walls of Jericho, so that we may also blow down these walls of straw and paper and . . . regain possession of our Christian rods for the chastisement of sin and expose the craft and deceit of the Devil.

James Harvey Robinson (Ed.), *Readings in European History,* Vol. 2 (Boston: Ginn and Co., 1906), p. 75.

German, using Erasmus's new Greek text, and he attempted by correspondence to oversee the first stages of the Reformation in Wittenberg.

Imperial Distractions: France and the Turks

The Reformation was greatly assisted in these early years by the emperor's war with France and the advance of the Ottoman Turks into eastern Europe. Against both adversaries Charles V, who also remained a Spanish king with dynastic responsibilities outside the empire, needed German troops, and to that end he promoted friendly relations with the German princes. Between 1521 and 1559 Spain (the Habsburg dynasty) and France (the Valois dynasty) fought four major wars over disputed territories in Italy and along their borders. In 1526 the Turks overran Hungary at the Battle of Mohacs, while in western Europe the French-led League of Cognac formed against Charles for the second Habsburg–Valois war.

Thus preoccupied, the emperor agreed through his representatives at the German Diet of Speyer in 1526 that each German territory was free to enforce the Edict of Worms (1521) against Luther ''so as to be able to answer in good conscience to God and the emperor.'' That concession, in effect, gave the German princes territorial sovereignty in religious matters and the Reformation time to put down deep roots. Later (in 1555) such local princely control over religion would be enshrined in imperial law by the Peace of Augsburg.

The Peasants' Revolt

In its first decade the Protestant movement suffered more from internal division than from imperial interference. By 1525 Luther had become as much an object of protest within Germany as was the pope. Original allies, sympathizers, and fellow travelers declared their independence from him.

Peasants plundering a German monastery in 1525. The peasant revolt of 1524–1525 frightened both Protestant and Catholic rulers, who united to suppress the rising. [Bildarchiv Preussischer Kneturbesitz]

German Peasants Protest Rising Feudal Exactions

In the late fifteenth and early sixteenth centuries German feudal lords, both secular and ecclesiastical, tried to increase the earnings from their lands by raising demands on their peasant tenants. As the personal freedoms of peasants were restricted, their properties confiscated, and their traditional laws and customs overridden, massive revolts occurred in southern Germany in 1525. Not a few historians, especially those of Marxist persuasion, see this uprising and the social and economic conditions that gave rise to it, as the major historical force in early modern history. The following, from Memmingen, in modern West Germany, is the most representative and well-known statement of peasant grievances.

1. It is our humble petition and desire . . . that in the future . . . each community should choose and appoint a pastor, and that we should have the right to depose him should he conduct himself improperly. . . .

2. We are ready and willing to pay the fair tithe of grain. . . . The small tithes [of cattle], whether [to] ecclesiastical or lay lords, we will not pay at all, for the Lord God created cattle for the free use of man. . . .

3. We . . . take it for granted that you will release us from serfdom as true Christians, unless it should be shown us from the Gospel that we are serfs.

4. It has been the custom heretofore that no poor man should be allowed to catch venison or wildfowl or fish in flowing water, which seems to us quite unseemly and unbrotherly as well as selfish and not agreeable to the Word of God. . . .

5. We are aggrieved in the matter of woodcutting, for the noblemen have appropriated all the woods to themselves. . . .

6. In regard to the excessive services demanded of us which are increased from day to day, we ask that this matter be properly looked into so that we shall not continue to be oppressed in this way. . . .

7. We will not hereafter allow ourselves to be further oppressed by our lords, but will let them demand only what is just and proper according to the word of the agreement between the lord and the peasant. The lord should no longer try to force more services or other dues from the peasant without payment. . . .

8. We are greatly burdened because our holdings cannot support the rent exacted from them. . . . We ask that the lords may appoint persons of honor to inspect these holdings and fix a rent in accordance with justice. . . .

9. We are burdened with a great evil in the constant making of new laws. . . . In our opinion we should be judged according to the old written law. . . .

10. We are aggrieved by the appropriation . . . of meadows and fields which at one time belonged to a community as a whole. These we will take again into our own hands. . . .

11. We will entirely abolish the due called Todfall *[that is, heriot or death tax, by which the lord received the best horse, cow, or garment of a family upon the death of a serf] and will no longer endure it, nor allow widows and orphans to be thus shamefully robbed against God's will, and in violation of justice and right. . . .*

12. It is our conclusion and final resolution, that if any one or more of the articles here set forth should not be in agreement with the Word of God, as we think they are, such article we will willingly retract.

Translations and Reprints from the Original Sources of European History, Vol. 2 (Philadelphia: Department of History, University of Pennsylvania, 1897).

Like the German Humanists, the German peasantry also had at first believed Luther to be an ally. The peasantry had been organized since the late fifteenth century against efforts by territorial princes to override their traditional laws and customs and to subject them to new regulations and taxes. Peasant leaders, several of whom were convinced Lutherans, saw in Luther's teaching about Christian freedom and his criticism of monastic landowners a point of view close to their own, and they openly solicited Luther's support of their political and economic rights, including their revolutionary request for release from serfdom. Luther and his followers sympathized with the peasants; indeed, for several years Lutheran pamphleteers made *Karsthans*, the burly, honest peasant who earned his bread by the sweat of his brow and sacrificed his own comfort and well-being for others, a symbol of the simple life that God desired all people to live. The Lutherans, however, were not social revolutionaries, and when the peasants revolted against their masters in 1524–1525, Luther, not surprisingly, condemned them in the strongest possible terms as "unchristian" and urged the princes to crush their revolt without mercy. Tens of thousands of peasants (estimates run between 70,000 and 100,000) had died by the time the revolt was put down.

For Luther, the freedom of the Christian was an inner release from guilt and anxiety, not a right to restructure society by violent revolution. Had Luther supported the Peasants' Revolt, he would have contradicted his own teaching and would probably also have ended any chance of the survival of his reform beyond the 1520s. Still, many believe that his decision greatly reduced the social impact of the Reformation.

Zwingli and the Swiss Reformation

Switzerland was a loose confederacy of thirteen autonomous cantons or states and allied areas (see Map 10.3). Some cantons (e.g., Zurich, Bern, Basel, and Schaffhausen) became Protestant, some (especially around the Lucerne heartland) remained Catholic, and a few other cantons and religions managed to effect a compromise. Among the preconditions of the Swiss Reformation were the growth of national sentiment occasioned by opposition to foreign mercenary service (providing mercenaries for Europe's warring nations was a major source of Switzerland's livelihood) and a desire for church reform that had persisted in Switzerland since the councils of Constance (1414–1417) and Basel (1431–1449).

The Reformation in Zurich

Ulrich Zwingli (1484–1531), the leader of the Swiss Reformation, had been humanistically educated in Bern, Vienna, and Basel. He was strongly influenced by Erasmus, whom he credited with having set him on the path to reform. He served as a chaplain with Swiss mercenaries during the disastrous Battle of Marignano in 1515 and thereafter became an eloquent critic of mercenary service. Zwingli believed that this service threatened both the political sovereignty and the moral well-being of the Swiss confederacy. By 1518 Zwingli was also widely known for opposition to the sale of indulgences and to religious superstition. In 1519 he entered the competition for the post of people's priest in the main church of Zurich. His candidacy was contested because of his acknowledged fornication with a barber's daughter, an affair he successfully minimized in a forcefully written self-defense. Actually his conduct was less scandalous to his contemporaries, who sympathized with the plight of the celibate clergy, than it may be to the modern reader. One of Zwingli's first acts as a reformer was to petition for an end to clerical celibacy and for the right of all clergy to marry, a practice that quickly became accepted in all Protestant lands.

From his new position as people's priest in Zurich, Zwingli engineered the Swiss Reformation. In March 1522 he was party to the breaking of the Lenten fast—an act of protest analogous to burning one's national flag today. Zwingli's reform guideline was very simple and very effective: whatever lacked literal support in Scripture was to be neither believed nor practiced. As had also happened with Luther, that test soon raised questions about such honored traditional teachings and practices as fasting, transubstantiation, the worship of saints, pilgrimages, purgatory, clerical celibacy, and certain sacraments. A disputation held on January 29, 1523, concluded with the city government's sanction of Zwingli's Scripture test. Thereafter Zurich became, to all intents and purposes, a Protestant city and the center of the Swiss Reformation. A harsh discipline was imposed by the new Protestant regime, making Zurich one of the first examples of a puritanical Protestant city.

The Marburg Colloquy

Landgrave Philip of Hesse (1504–1567) sought to unite Swiss and German Protestants in a mutual defense pact, a potentially significant political alliance. His efforts were spoiled, however, by theological disagreements between Luther and Zwingli over the nature of Christ's presence in the Eucharist. Zwingli

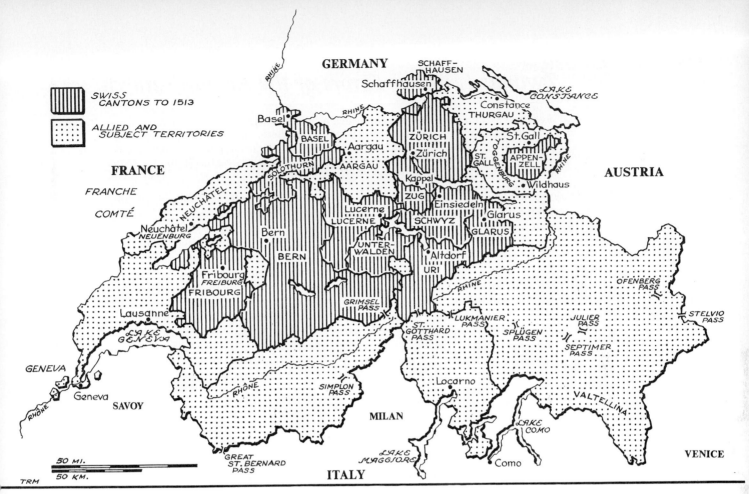

THE SWISS CONFEDERATION

MAP 10-3 *While nominally still a part of the Holy Roman Empire, Switzerland grew from a loose defensive union of the central "forest cantons" in the thirteenth century to a fiercely independent association of regions with different languages, histories, and, finally, religions.*

maintained a symbolic interpretation of Christ's words, "This is my body"; Christ, he argued, was only spiritually, not bodily, present in the bread and wine of the Eucharist. Luther, to the contrary, insisted that Christ's human nature could share the properties of his divine nature; hence, where Christ was spiritually present, he could also be bodily present, for his was a special nature. Luther wanted no part of an abstract, spiritualized Christ. Zwingli, on the other hand, feared that Luther had not broken sufficiently with medieval sacramental theology.

Philip of Hesse brought the two Protestant leaders together in his castle in Marburg in early October 1529, but they were unable to work out their differences on this issue. Luther left thinking Zwingli a dangerous fanatic. Although cooperation between the two sides did not cease, the disagreement splintered the Protestant movement theologically and politically. Separate defense leagues formed, and semi-Zwinglian theological views came to be embodied in the *Confessio Tetrapolitana,* a confession of faith prepared by the Strasbourg reformers Martin Bucer and Caspar Hedio for presentation to the Diet of Augsburg (1530) as an alternative to the Lutheran *Augsburg Confession.*

Swiss Civil Wars

As the Swiss cantons divided between Protestantism and Catholicism, civil wars began.

377

Zwingli Lists the Errors of the Roman Church

Religious argument can become confusing. A clear summary of issues is often helpful—both to the disputants and to interested bystanders. Before the first Zurich Disputation (1523), which effectually introduced the Protestant Reformation in Zurich, the reformer Zwingli prepared such a summary of the new Evangelical truths and the errors of the Roman church, known as the *Sixty-Seven Articles*. Here are some of them.

All who consider other teachings equal to or higher than the Gospel err, and they do not know what the Gospel is.

In the faith rests our salvation, and in unbelief our damnation; for all truth is clear in Christ.

In the Gospel one learns that human doctrines and decrees do not aid in salvation.

That Christ, having sacrificed himself once, is to eternity a certain and valid sacrifice for the sins of all faithful, wherefrom it follows that the Mass is not a sacrifice, but is a remembrance of the sacrifice and assurance of the salvation which Christ has given us.

That God desires to give us all things in his name, whence it follows that outside of this life we need no [intercession of the saints or any] mediator except himself.

That no Christian is bound to do those things which God has not decreed, therefore one may eat at all times all food, wherefrom one learns that the decree about cheese and butter [i.e.,

fasting from such foods at certain times of the year] is a Roman swindle.

That no special person can impose the ban upon [i.e., excommunicate] anyone, but the Church, that is, the congregation of those among whom the one to be banned dwells, together with their watchman, i.e., the pastor.

All that the so-called spiritual [i.e., the papal church] claims to have of power and protection belongs to the lay [i.e., the secular magistracy], if they wish to be Christians.

Greater offense I know not than that one does not allow priests to have wives, but permits them to hire prostitutes.

Christ has borne all our pains and labor. Hence whoever assigns to works of penance what belongs to Christ errs and slanders God.

The true divine Scriptures know naught about purgatory after this life.

The Scriptures know no priests except those who proclaim the word of God.

Ulrich Zwingli (1484–1531): *Selected Works*, ed. by Samuel M. Jackson (Philadelphia: University of Pennsylvania Press, 1972), pp. 111–117.

There were two major battles, both at Kappel, one in June 1529 and a second in October 1531. The first ended in a Protestant victory, which forced the Catholic cantons to break their foreign alliances and to recognize the rights of Swiss Protestants. During the second battle Zwingli was found wounded on the battlefield and was unceremoniously executed, his remains scattered to the four winds so that his followers would have no relics to console and inspire them. The subsequent treaty confirmed the right of each canton to determine its own religion. Heinrich Bullinger (1504–1575), who was Zwingli's protégé and later married his daughter, became the new leader of the Swiss Reformation and guided its development into an established religion.

Anabaptists and Radical Protestants

The moderate pace and seemingly low ethical results of the Lutheran and Zwinglian reformations discontented many people, among them some of the original co-workers of Luther and Zwingli. Many desired a more rapid and thorough implementation of primitive Christianity—that is, a more visible moral transformation—and accused the major reformers of going only halfway. The most important of these radical groups were the Anabaptists, the sixteenth-century ancestors of the modern Mennonites and Amish. The Anabaptists were especially distinguished by their rejection of infant baptism and their insistence on only adult baptism (*unabaptism* derives from the Greek word meaning "to rebaptize"), believing that baptism as a consenting adult conformed to Scripture and was more respectful of human freedom.

Conrad Grebel and the Swiss Brethren

Conrad Grebel (1498–1526), with whom Anabaptism originated, performed the first adult rebaptism in Zurich in January 1525. Initially a coworker with Zwingli and an even greater biblical literalist, Grebel broke openly with Zwingli after a religious disputation in October 1523 in which Zwingli supported the city government's plea for a gradual removal of traditional religious practices. The alternative of the Swiss Brethren, as Grebel's group came to be called, was set forth in the *Schleitheim Confession* of 1527. This document distinguished Anabaptists not only by their practice of adult baptism but also by their refusal to go to war, to swear oaths, and to participate in the offices of secular government. Anabaptists physically separated from society to form a more perfect community in imitation of what they believed to be the example of the first Christians. Because of the close connection between religious and civic life in this period, such separatism was viewed by the political authorities as a threat to basic social bonds.

The Anabaptist Reign in Münster

At first, Anabaptism drew its adherents from all social classes. But as Lutherans and Zwinglians joined with Catholics in opposition to the Anabaptists and persecuted them within the cities, a more rural, agrarian class came to make up the great majority. In 1529, rebaptism became a capital offense throughout the Holy Roman Empire. It has been estimated that between 1525 and 1618 at least one thousand and perhaps as many as five thousand men and women were executed for rebaptising themselves as adults. Brutal measures were universally applied against nonconformists after Anabaptist extremists came to power in the German city of Münster in 1534–1535. Led by two Dutch emigrants, a baker, Jan Matthys of Haarlem, and a tailor, Jan Beukelsz of Leiden, the Anabaptist majority in this city forced Lutherans and Catholics either to convert or to emigrate. As the Lutherans and Catholics left, Münster transformed itself into an Old Testament theocracy, replete with charismatic lead-

The siege of Munster in 1534–1535. A joint Catholic-Protestant army recaptured the city from the Anabaptists led by Jan of Leiden. [*Bilderchiv Foto Marburg*]

ers and the practice of polygamy. The outside world was deeply shocked. Protestant and Catholic armies united to crush the radicals, and the skeletons of their leaders long hung in public view as a warning to all who would so offend traditional Christian sensitivities. After this episode, moderate, pacifistic Anabaptism became the norm among most nonconformists. The moderate Anabaptist leader Menno Simons (1496–1561), the founder of the Mennonites, set the example for the future.

Spiritualists

In addition to the Anabaptists there were radicals known as *Spiritualists*. These were mostly isolated individuals distinguished by their disdain of all traditions and institutions. They believed that the only religious authority was God's spirit, which spoke here and now to every individual. Among them were several former Lutherans: Thomas Müntzer (d. 1525), who had close contacts with Anabaptist leaders in Germany and Switzerland and died as a leader of a peasants' revolt; Sebastian Franck (d. 1541), a free-lance critic of all dogmatic religion who proclaimed the religious autonomy of every individual soul; and Caspar Schwenckfeld (d. 1561), a prolific writer and wanderer after whom the Schwenckfeldian Church is named.

Antitrinitarians

A final group of radical Protestants was the Antitrinitarians, exponents of a commonsense, rational, and ethical religion. Chief among this group were the Spaniard Michael Servetus (1511–1553), executed in 1553 in Geneva for "blasphemies against the Holy Trinity," and the Italians Lelio (d. 1562) and Faustus Sozzini (d. 1604), the founders of Socinianism. These thinkers were the strongest opponents of Calvinism (to be discussed later), especially its belief in original sin and predestination, and have a deserved reputation as defenders of religious toleration.

Political Consolidation of the Lutheran Reformation

The Diet of Augsburg

Charles V, who spent most of his time on politics and military maneuvers outside the empire, especially in Spain and Italy, returned to the empire in 1530 to direct the Diet of Augsburg, a meeting of Protestant and Catholic representatives assembled for the purpose of imposing a settlement of the religious divisions. With its terms dictated by the Catholic emperor, the diet adjourned with a blunt order to all Lutherans to revert to Catholicism. The Reformation was by this time too firmly established for that to occur, and in February 1531 the Lutherans responded with the formation of their own defensive alliance, the Schmalkaldic League. The league took as its banner the *Augsburg Confession*, a moderate statement of Protestant beliefs that had been spurned by the emperor at the Diet of Augsburg. In 1538 Luther drew up a more strongly worded Protestant confession known as the *Schmalkaldic Articles*. Under the leadership of Landgrave Philip of Hesse and Elector John Frederick of Saxony, the league achieved a stalemate with the emperor, who was again distracted by renewed war with France and the ever-resilient Turks.

The Expansion of the Reformation

In the 1530s German Lutherans formed regional consistories, judicial bodies composed of theologians and lawyers, which oversaw and administered the new Protestant churches. These consistories replaced the old Catholic episcopates. Under the leadership of Philip Melanchthon, the "praeceptor of Germany," educational reforms were enacted that provided for compulsory primary education, schools for girls, a Humanist revision of the traditional curriculum, and catechetical instruction of the laity in the new religion.

The Reformation also dug in elsewhere. Introduced into Denmark by Christian II (ruled 1513–1523), Danish Lutheranism throve under Frederick I (1523–1533), who joined the Schmalkaldic League. Under Christian III (1536–1559), Lutheranism became the state religion, and the Wittenberg preacher Johannes Bugenhagen arrived to organize the Danish Lutheran church.

In Sweden, Gustavus Vasa (1523–1560), supported by a Swedish nobility greedy for church lands, confiscated church property and subjected the clergy to royal authority at the Diet of Vesteras (1527).

In politically splintered Poland, Lutherans, Anabaptists, Calvinists, and even Antitrinitarians found room to practice their beliefs, as

The Diet of Augsburg, 1530. Charles V is enthroned beneath the canopy. The principal German princes are seated around him. [Bulloz]

Poland, primarily because of the absence of a central political authority, became a model of religious pluralism and toleration in the second half of the sixteenth century.

REACTION AGAINST PROTESTANTS: THE INTERIM. Charles V made abortive efforts in 1540–1541 to enforce a compromise agreement between Protestants and Catholics. As these and other conciliar efforts failed, he turned to a military solution. In 1547 imperial armies crushed the Protestant Schmalkaldic League. John Frederick of Saxony was defeated in April 1547, and Philip of Hesse was taken captive shortly thereafter.

The emperor established puppet rulers in

Saxony and Hesse and issued as imperial law the *Augsburg Interim,* a new order that Protestants everywhere must readopt old Catholic beliefs and practices. There were a few cosmetic Protestant concessions, for example, clerical marriage (with papal approval of individual cases) and communion in both kinds (that is, bread *and* wine). Although the *Interim* met only surface acceptance within Germany, it forced many Protestant leaders into exile. The Strasbourg reformer Martin Bucer, for example, departed to England, where he played an important role in the drafting of the religious documents of the English Reformation during the reign of Edward VI. In Germany, Magdeburg became a refuge for perse-

381

Charles V (1500–1558), painted by Titian in 1548 after his armies had crushed the Protestant Schmalkaldic League. [The Prado, Madrid]

cuted Protestants and the center of Lutheran resistance.

The Peace of Augsburg

The Reformation was too entrenched by 1547 to be ended even by brute force. Maurice of Saxony, hand-picked by Charles V to rule Saxony, recognized the inevitability of Protestantism and shifted his allegiance to the Protestants. Confronted by fierce Protestant resistance and weary from three decades of war, the emperor was forced to relent. After a defeat by Protestant armies in 1552, Charles reinstated John Frederick and Philip of Hesse and guaranteed Lutheran religious freedoms in the Peace of Passau (August 1552), a declaration that effectively surrendered his lifelong quest for European religious unity.

The division of Christendom was made permanent by the Peace of Augsburg in September 1555. This agreement recognized in law what

had already been well established in practice: *cuius regio, eius religio,* meaning that the ruler of a land would determine the religion of the land. Lutherans were permitted to retain all church lands forcibly seized before 1552. An "ecclesiastical reservation" was added, however, that was intended to prevent high Catholic prelates who converted to Protestantism from retaining their lands, titles, and privileges. Those discontented with the religion of their region were permitted to migrate to another.

Calvinism and Anabaptism were not recognized as legal forms of Christian belief and practice by the Peace of Augsburg. Anabaptists had long adjusted to such exclusion by forming their own separatist communities. Calvinists, however, were not separatists and could not choose this route; they remained determined not only to secure the right to worship publicly as they pleased but also to shape society according to their own religious convictions. While Anabaptists retreated and Lutherans enjoyed the security of an established religion, Calvinists organized to lead national revolutions throughout northern Europe in the second half of the sixteenth century.

The Rise of Russia

Although the Reformation pushed northward into Scandinavia and eastward into Poland, it was not to penetrate into Russia. There another kind of reform, one strictly political in nature, was under way, as the principality of Moscow evolved into a new kind of state under Ivan IV (1533–1584), better known as Ivan the Terrible. His reign displayed a pattern that would be repeated frequently, and often tragically, in later Russian history: early years of reform and solid accomplishment followed by a period of almost inexplicable tyranny.

Ivan came into his political inheritance at the age of three. Consequently, there was a long regency that witnessed numerous clashes among the boyars, or Russian nobles. The first key moment in his personal reign occurred in 1547, when at the age of sixteen he had himself crowned czar (the Russian equivalent of *Caesar* or *Kaiser*) rather than prince of Moscow.

During the opening years of his personal reign, Ivan IV consulted with the great boyars and other able advisers in a relationship of mutual trust. He worked toward formulating a revised law code and a mode of local government that would be responsive to the needs of the areas governed. He reorganized the army, and he established direct economic contact with western Europe. During the 1550s Ivan undertook successful military campaigns against the Ottomans in the south, the Tatars in the south and east, and for a time the Livonians in the northwest. It appeared that his reign would be well regarded at home and abroad.

Beginning in about 1560, however, a profound change took place in his personality. He began to mistrust his most honest advisers and believed that they were plotting against him. When his first wife died in 1560, he thought she had been poisoned by a conspiracy. In the late 1560s he created a set of boyars and officials who were personally loyal to him and an army also loyal to him alone. He loosed these troops, who always dressed in black and who were called the *oprichniki*, against anyone he regarded as an enemy. He imprisoned, tortured, and executed boyars without cause and without trial. In 1581 Ivan killed his own son. He himself died in 1584. While he had pursued this utterly irrational behavior at home, his military forces in Livonia had been defeated by both Sweden and Poland. His reign ended in domestic political turmoil and foreign military defeat.

John Calvin and the Genevan Reformation

In the second half of the sixteenth century Calvinism replaced Lutheranism as the dominant Protestant force in Europe. Calvinism was the religious ideology that inspired or accompanied massive political resistance in France, the Netherlands, and Scotland. It established itself within the Palatinate during the reign of Elector Frederick III (1559–1576). Believing strongly in both divine predestination and the individual's responsibility to reorder society according to God's plan, Calvinists became zealous reformers determined to transform and order society in such a way that men and women would act externally as they believed, or should believe, internally and were destined to live eternally. In a famous study, *The Protestant Ethic and the Spirit of Capitalism* (1904), the German sociologist Max Weber argued that this peculiar combination of confidence and self-disciplined activism produced an ethic that stimulated and reinforced the spirit of emergent capitalism, bringing Calvinism and later

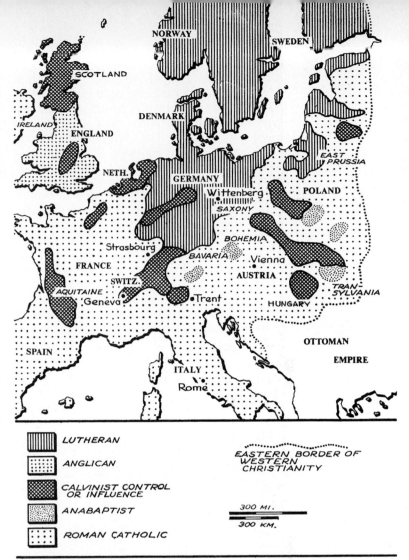

LUTHERAN

ANGLICAN

CALVINIST CONTROL OR INFLUENCE

ANABAPTIST

ROMAN CATHOLIC

EASTERN BORDER OF WESTERN CHRISTIANITY

300 MI.

300 KM.

THE RELIGIOUS SITUATION ABOUT 1560

MAP 10–4 *By 1560 Luther, Zwingli, and Loyola were dead, Calvin near the end of his life, the English break from Rome fully accomplished, and the last session of the Council of Trent about to assemble. Here is the religious geography of Western Europe at this time.*

Puritanism into close association with the development of modern capitalist societies.

The founder of Calvinism, John Calvin (1509–1564), was born into a well-to-do family, the son of the secretary to the bishop of Noyon in Picardy. He received church benefices at age twelve, which financed the best possible education at Parisian colleges and a law degree at Orléans. Calvin associated with members of the indigenous French reform party, a group of Catholic Humanists led by Jacques Lefèvre d'Étaples and Marguerite d'Angoulême, the queen of Navarre after 1527. Although Calvin finally rejected this group as ineffectual, its members contributed to his preparation as a religious reformer. Their sincere but largely hortatory approach to reform was portrayed in Calvin's first published work, a commentary on Seneca's *De Clementia* in 1533.

It was probably in the spring of 1534 that Calvin experienced that conversion to Protestantism by which he said his "long stubborn heart" was "made teachable" by God—a personal model of reform he would later apply to the recalcitrant citizenry of Geneva. His mature theology stressed the sovereignty of God over all creation and the necessity of man's conformity to His will. In May 1534 he dramatically surrendered the benefices he had held for so long and at such profit and joined the Reformation.

The French Reformer and Protestant theologian John Calvin (1509–1564). Between 1540–1564, Calvin made Geneva a Protestant theocracy. [Public and University Library of Geneva]

Political Revolt and Religious Reform in Geneva

Whereas in Saxony religious reform paved the way for a political revolution against the emperor, in Geneva a political revolution against the local prince-bishop laid the foundation for the religious change. Genevans successfully revolted against the House of Savoy and their resident prince-bishop in the late 1520s. Assisted by the Swiss city-states of Fribourg and Bern, the Genevans drove out the prince-bishop in August 1527, and the city councils assumed his legal and political powers. In late 1533 Bern dispatched the Protestant reformers Guillaume Farel (1489–1565) and Antoine Froment (1508–1581) to Geneva. In the summer of 1535, after much internal turmoil, the Protestants triumphed, and the traditional Mass and other religious practices were removed. On May 21, 1536, the city voted officially to adopt the Reformation: "to live according to the Gospel and the Word of God . . . without . . . any more masses, statues, idols, or other papal abuses."

CALVIN AND FAREL. Calvin arrived in Geneva after these events, in July 1536. He might not have come to Geneva at all had the third Habsburg–Valois war not forced him to detour there. Calvin was actually en route to a scholarly refuge in Strasbourg, in flight from Protestant persecution in France, when the war forced him to turn sharply south to Geneva. Farel successfully pleaded with him to stay and assist the Reformation, threatening Calvin with divine vengeance if he turned away from this task.

Before a year had passed, Calvin had drawn up articles for the governance of the new church as well as a catechism to guide and discipline the people, both of which were presented for approval to the city councils in early 1537. Because of the strong measures proposed to govern Geneva's moral life, the reformers were suspected by many of desiring to create a "new papacy." Their orthodoxy was attacked, and Geneva's powerful Protestant ally, Bern, which had adopted a more moderate Protestant reform, pressured Geneva's magistrates to restore the traditional religious ceremonies and holidays abolished by Calvin and Farel. Both within and outside Geneva, Calvin and Farel were perceived as going too far too fast. In February 1538 the four syndics (the chief magistrates of the city) chosen in the annual election turned against Calvin and Farel. Two months later the defiant reformers were exiled from the city.

Calvin went to Strasbourg, a model Protestant city, where he became pastor to the French exiles there. During his long stay in Strasbourg, Calvin wrote biblical commentaries and a second edition of his masterful *Institutes of the Christian Religion*, which many consider the definitive theological statement of the Protestant faith. Calvin also married and participated in the ecumenical discussions urged on Protestants and Catholics by Charles V. Most important, he learned from the Strasbourg reformer Martin Bucer how to implement the Protestant Reformation successfully.

CALVIN'S GENEVA. In 1540 Geneva elected syndics who were both favorable to Calvin and determined to establish full Gene-

van political and religious independence from Bern. They knew Calvin would be a valuable ally in the latter project and invited him to return. This he did in September 1540, never to leave the city again. Within months of his new arrival, new ecclesiastical ordinances were implemented that provided for cooperation between the magistrates and the clergy in matters of internal discipline. Following the Strasbourg model, the Genevan church was organized into four offices: (1) pastors, of whom there were five; (2) teachers or doctors to instruct the populace in and to defend true doctrine; (3) elders, a group of twelve laymen chosen by and from the Genevan councils and empowered to "oversee the life of everybody"; and (4) deacons to dispense church goods and services to the poor and the sick.

Calvin and his followers were motivated above all by a desire to transform society mor-

Theodore Beza Describes John Calvin's Final Days

Calvin's ceaseless labor to make Geneva a bulwark of Protestantism left him an ill and worn-out man at fifty-five. He remained nonetheless a model of discipline to the end. The following description comes from an admiring biography by Calvin's successor, Theodore Beza.

On the 6th of February, 1564, . . . he delivered his last sermon. . . . From this period he taught no more in public, except that he was carried at different times, until the last day of March, to the meeting of the congregation, and addressed them in a few words, His diseases, contracted by incredible labours of mind and body, were various and complicated. . . . He was naturally of a spare and feeble frame, tending to consumption. During sleep he seemed almost awake, and spent a great part of the year in preaching, teaching, and dictating. For at least ten years . . . the only food he [had taken] was at supper, so that it is astonishing how he could so long escape consumption. He frequently suffered from migraine, which he cured only by fasting, so as occasionally to refrain from food for thirty-six hours. But by overstraining his voice and . . . by an immoderate use of aloes, he suffered from hemorrhoids, which degenerated into ulcers, and five years before his death he was occasion-

ally attacked by a spitting of blood. [He also suffered from] gout in the right leg, frequently returning pains of colic, and stone, which he had only felt a few months before his death. . . . The physicians neglected no remedies, and he observed the directions of his medical attendants with a strictness which none could surpass. . . . Though tormented by so many diseases, no one ever heard him utter a word unbecoming a man of bravery, much less a Christian. Only lifting up his eyes to heaven, he used to say, ''How long, O Lord!'' for even in health he often had this sentence on his lips, when he spoke of the calamities of his brethren, with whose sufferings he was both day and night more afflicted than with any of his own. When admonished and entreated by us to forbear, at least in his sickness, from the labour of dictating, or at least of writing, ''What, then,'' he said, ''would you have my Lord find me idle when he cometh?''

Theodore Beza, *The Life of John Calvin*, trans. by Francis Gibson (Philadelphia: Westminster, 1836), pp. 78–79.

ally. Faith, Calvin taught, did not sit idly in the mind but conformed one's every action to God's law. The "elect" should live in a manifestly God-pleasing way, if they were truly God's elect. In the attempted realization of this goal, Calvin spared no effort. The consistory became Calvin's instrument of power. This body was composed of the elders and the pastors and was presided over by one of the four syndics. It enforced the strictest moral discipline, meting out punishments for a broad range of moral and religious transgressions—from missing church services (a fine of 3 sous) to fornication (six days on bread and water and a fine of 60 sous)—and, as time passed, increasingly for criticism of Calvin and the consistory. Calvin ridiculed his opponents as undisciplined "Libertines."

Among the many personal conflicts in Geneva that gave Calvin his reputation as a stern moralist, none proved more damaging than his active role in the capture and execution of the Spanish physician and amateur theologian Michael Servetus in 1553. After 1555, the city's syndics were all devout Calvinists, and Geneva became home to thousands of exiled Protestants who had been driven out of France, England, and Scotland. Refugees (more than

five thousand), most of them utterly loyal to Calvin, came to make up over one third of the population of Geneva. From this time until his death in 1564, Calvin's position in the city was greatly strengthened and the syndics were very cooperative.

Catholic Reform and Counter-Reformation

Sources of Catholic Reform

The Protestant Reformation did not take the medieval church completely by surprise. There were much internal criticism and many efforts at internal reform before there was a Counter-Reformation in reaction to Protestant successes. Before the Reformation ambitious proposals had been set forth to bring about the long-demanded reform of the church in head and members. One of the boldest attempts came on the eve of the Fifth Lateran Council (1513–1517), the last reform council before the Reformation, and was drafted by two Venetian monks, Tommaso Giustiniani and Vincenzo Quirini. Their program went so far as to call for a revision of the *Corpus Juris Canonici*,

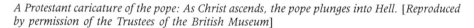

A Protestant caricature of the pope: As Christ ascends, the pope plunges into Hell. [Reproduced by permission of the Trustees of the British Museum]

the massive body of church law that authorized papal practices and ensured papal prerogatives. Sixteenth-century popes, ever mindful of how the councils of Constance and Basel had stripped the pope of his traditional powers, quickly squelched such efforts to bring about basic changes in the laws and institutions of the church. High Renaissance popes preferred the charge given to the Fifth Lateran Council in the keynote address by Giles of Viterbo, the superior general of the Hermits of Saint Augustine: "Men are to be changed by, not to change, religion." The Fifth Lateran Council remained a regional council completely within the pope's control and brought about no significant reforms. The very month after its adjournment Martin Luther posted his ninety-five theses.

As the Fifth Lateran Council suggests, the most important reform initiatives did not always issue from the papal court. Catholic reformers were found within a variety of self-motivated lay and clerical movements. Two important organizations that brought reform-minded clergy and laity together were the Modern Devotion (already discussed) and the Oratory of Divine Love. The latter, founded in Rome in 1517, was an exclusive informal organization of earnest laity and clergy who were both learned and deeply committed to traditional religious devotion. Like that of Erasmus, whose religious writings the members admired, their basic belief was that inner piety and good Christian living, not theological arguments and disputations, were the surest way to reform the church.

Many new religious orders also sprang up in the sixteenth century to lead a broad revival of piety within the church. The first of these was the Theatines, an elitist order, founded in 1524 to groom devout and reform-minded leaders at the higher levels of the church hierarchy. One of the cofounders was Bishop Gian Pietro Carafa, the future Pope Paul IV. Another new order, whose mission pointed in the opposite direction, was the Capuchins. Authorized by the pope in The 1528, they sought to return to the original ascetic and charitable ideals of Saint Francis and became very popular among the ordinary people, to whom they directed their ministry. The Somaschi, who became active in the mid-1520s, and the Barnabites, founded in 1530, endeavored to repair the moral, spiritual, and physical damage done to people in war-torn areas of Italy. The members of the new order of Ursulines, founded in 1535, established convents in Italy and France for the religious education of girls from all social classes and became very influential. Another new religious order, the Oratorians, officially recognized in 1575, was an elite group of secular clerics, who devoted themselves to the promotion of religious literature and church music. Among their members was the great Catholic hymnist and musician Giovanni Palestrina (1526–1594).

In addition to these lay and clerical movements the Spanish mystics Saint Teresa of Avila (1515–1582) and Saint John of the Cross (1542–1591) revived and popularized the mystical piety of medieval monasticism.

Ignatius of Loyola and the Jesuits

Of the various reform groups, none was more instrumental in the success of the Counter-Reformation than the Society of Jesus, the new order of Jesuits, organized by Ignatius of Loyola in the 1530s and officially recognized by the church in 1540. The society grew within the space of a century from its

Ignatius of Loyola (1491–1556), *founder of the Society of Jesus.* [*Bradley Smith*]

Ignatius of Loyola's "Rules for Thinking with the Church"

As leaders of the Counter-Reformation, the Jesuits attempted to live by and instill in others the strictest obedience to church authority. The following are some of the eighteen rules included by Ignatius in his *Spiritual Exercises* to give pious Catholics positive direction. These rules also indicate the Catholic reformers' refusal to compromise with Protestants.

In order to have the proper attitude of mind in the Church Militant we should observe the following rules:

1. Putting aside all private judgment, we should keep our minds prepared and ready to obey promptly and in all things the true spouse of Christ our Lord, our Holy Mother, the hierarchical Church.

2. To praise sacramental confession and the reception of the Most Holy Sacrament once a year, and much better once a month, and better still every week. . . .

3. To praise the frequent hearing of Mass. . . .

4. To praise highly the religious life, virginity, and continence; and also matrimony, but not as highly. . . .

5. To praise the vows of religion, obedience, poverty, chastity, and other works of perfection and supererogation. . . .

6. To praise the relics of the saints . . . [and] the stations, pilgrimages, indulgences, jubilees, Crusade indulgences, and the lighting of candles in the churches.

7. To praise the precepts concerning fasts and abstinences . . . and acts of penance. . . .

8. To praise the adornments and buildings of churches as well as sacred images. . . .

9. To praise all the precepts of the church. . . .

10. To approve and praise the directions and recommendations of our superiors as well as their personal behaviour. . . .

11. To praise both the positive and scholastic theology. . . .

12. We must be on our guard against making comparisons between the living and those who have already gone to their reward, for it is no small error to say, for example: 'This man knows more than St. Augustine'; 'He is another Saint Francis, or even greater.' . . .

13. If we wish to be sure that we are right in all things, we should always be ready to accept this principle: I will believe that the white that I see is black, if the hierarchical Church so defines it. For I believe that between . . . Christ our Lord and . . . His Church, there is but one spirit, which governs and directs us for the salvation of our souls.

The Spiritual Exercises of St. Ignatius, trans. by Anthony Mottola (Garden City, N.Y.: Doubleday, 1964), pp. 139–141.

original ten members to more than fifteen thousand members scattered throughout the world, with thriving missions in India, Japan, and the Americas.

The founder of the Jesuits, Ignatius of Loyola (1491–1556), was a truly heroic figure. A dashing courtier and caballero in his youth, he began his spiritual pilgrimage in 1521 after he had been seriously wounded in the legs during a battle with the French. During a lengthy and painful convalescence, he passed the time by reading Christian classics. So impressed was he with the heroic self-sacrifice of the church's saints and their methods of overcoming mental anguish and pain that he underwent a profound religious conversion; henceforth, he, too, would serve the church as a soldier of Christ.

After recuperating, Ignatius applied the lessons he had learned during his convalescence to a program of religious and moral self-discipline that came to be embodied in the *Spiritual Exercises*. This psychologically perceptive devotional guide contained mental and emotional exercises designed to teach one absolute spiritual self-mastery over one's feelings. It taught that a person could shape his or her own behavior, even create a new religious self, through disciplined study and regular practice.

Whereas in Jesuit eyes Protestants had distinguished themselves by disobedience to church authority and religious innovation, the exercises of Ignatius were intended to teach good Catholics to deny themselves and submit without question to higher church authority and spiritual direction. Perfect discipline and self-control were the essential conditions of such obedience. To these was added the enthusiasm of traditional spirituality and mysticism—a potent combination that helped counter the Reformation and win many Protestants back to the Catholic fold, especially in Austria and Bavaria and along the Rhine.

The Council of Trent (1545–1563)

The broad success of the Reformation and the insistence of the Emperor Charles V forced Pope Paul to call a general council of the church to define religious doctrine. In anticipation Pope Paul appointed a reform commission, chaired by Caspar Contarini (1483–1542). Contarini, a member of the Oratory of Divine Love, was open to many reforms (his critics even described him as "semi-Lutheran"), and his committee consisted of some very liberal Catholic clergy. Their report, presented to the pope in February 1537, bluntly criticized the fiscality and simony of the papal Curia as the primary source of the church's loss of esteem. This report was so critical, in fact, that Pope Paul attempted unsuccessfully to suppress its publication. Protestants reprinted and circulated it as justification of their criticism.

The long-delayed council of the church met in 1545 in the imperial city of Trent in northern Italy. There were three sessions, spread over eighteen years, with long interruptions due to war, plague, and imperial and papal politics. The council met from 1545 to 1547, from 1551 to 1552, and from 1562 to 1563, a period that spanned the careers of four different popes.

Unlike the general councils of the fifteenth century, Trent was strictly under the pope's control, with high Italian prelates very prominent in the proceedings. Initially four of the five attending archbishops and twenty-one of the twenty-three attending bishops were Italians. Even at its final session in 1562, over three quarters of the council fathers were Italians. Voting was limited to high churchmen;

PROGRESS OF PROTESTANT REFORMATION ON THE CONTINENT	
Fifth Lateran Council fails to bring about reform in the church	1513–1517
Luther posts 95 theses against indulgences	1517
Charles I of Spain elected Holy Roman Emperor (as Charles V)	1519
Luther challenges authority of pope and inerrancy of church councils at Leipzig Debate	1519
Papal bull excommunicates Luther for heresy	1521
Diet of Worms condemns Luther	1521
Luther translates the New Testament into German	1521–1522
Peasants' Revolt in Germany	1524–1525
The *Schleitheim Confession* of the Anabaptists	1527
Marburg Colloquy between Luther and Zwingli	1529
Diet of Augsburg fails to settle religious differences	1530
Formation of Protestant Schmalkaldic League	1531
Anabaptists assume political power in city of Münster	1534–1535
Calvin arrives in Geneva	1536
Jesuits, founded by Ignatius of Loyola, recognized as order by pope	1540
Luther dies	1546
Armies of Charles V crush Schmalkaldic League	1547
Augsburg *Interim* outlaws Protestant practices	1548
Peace of Augsburg recognizes rights of Lutherans to worship as they please	1555
Council of Trent institutes reforms and responds to the Reformation	1545–1563

university theologians, the lower clergy, and the laity were not permitted to share in the council's decisions.

The council's most important reforms concerned internal church discipline. Steps were taken to curtail the selling of church offices and other religious goods. Many bishops who resided in Rome rather than within their dioceses were forced to move to their appointed seats of authority. Trent strengthened the authority of local bishops so that they could effectively discipline popular religious practice. The bishops

389

The Council of Trent in session. The Council met in three separate sessions over an eighteen-year period beginning in 1545 and formed the Catholic response to the theological divisions of the later Middle Ages and to the Protestant Reformation. This painting is possibly by the Venetian painter Titian (1477–1576). [Musées du Louvre, Paris. Cliche des Musées Nationaux]

were also subjected to new rules that required them not only to reside in their dioceses, but also to be highly visible by preaching regularly and conducting annual visitations. Trent also sought to give the parish priest a brighter image by requiring him to be neatly dressed, better educated, strictly celibate, and active among his parishioners. To this end Trent also called for the construction of a seminary in every diocese.

Not a single doctrinal concession was made to the Protestants, however. In the face of Protestant criticism the Council of Trent gave a ringing reaffirmation to the traditional Scholastic education of the clergy; the role of good works in salvation; the authority of tradition; the seven sacraments; transubstantiation; the withholding of the Eucharistic cup from the laity; clerical celibacy; the reality of purgatory; the veneration of saints, relics, and sacred images; and the granting of letters of indulgence. The council resolved medieval Scholastic quarrels in favor of the theology of Saint Thomas Aquinas, further enhancing his authority within the church. The strongest resistance was thereafter offered by the church to groups like the Jansenists, who strongly endorsed the medieval Augustinian tradition, a source of alternative Catholic as well as many Protestant doctrines.

Rulers initially resisted Trent's reform decrees, fearing a revival of papal political power within their lands. But with the passage of time and the pope's assurances that religious reforms were his sole intent, the new legislation took hold and parish life revived under the guidance of a devout and better-trained clergy.

The Church in Spanish America

Roman Catholic priests had accompanied the earliest explorers and the conquerors of the Indians. Because of internal reforms within the Spanish church at the turn of the sixteenth century, these first clergy tended to be imbued with many of the social and religious ideals of Christian Humanism. They believed that they could foster Erasmus's concept of the "philosophy of Christ" in the New World. Consequently these missionary priests were filled with zeal not only to convert the Indians to Christianity but also to bring to them learning and civilization of a European kind.

A very real tension existed between the early Spanish conquerors and the mendicant friars who sought to minister to the Indians. Without conquest, the church could not convert the Indians, but the priests often deplored the harsh labor conditions imposed on the native peoples. During the first three quarters of a century of Spanish domination, priests were among the most eloquent and persuasive defenders of the rights of Indians.

By far the most effective and outspoken of these clerics was Bartolomé de Las Casas, a Dominican. He contended that conquest was not necessary for conversion. One result of his campaign was new royal regulation of conquest after 1550. Another result was the emergence of the "Black Legend," which portrayed all Spanish treatment of Indians as unprincipled and inhumane. Advocates of this position drew heavily on Las Casas's writings. Although substantially true, the "Black Legend," nonetheless somewhat exaggerated the case against Spain. Many of the Indian rulers of other Indian tribes had also been exceedingly cruel, as witnessed by the Aztec demands for human sacrifice.

By the end of the sixteenth century, the church in Spanish America had become largely an institution upholding the colonial status quo. On numerous occasions, individual priests did defend the communal rights of Indian tribes, but the colonial church also prospered as the Spanish elite prospered. The church became a great landowner through crown grants and through bequests from Catholics who died in the New World. The monasteries took on an economic as well as a spirit-

Bartolomé de Las Casas (1474–1566). *Las Casas was the most outspoken and effective defender of the Indians of the New World from Spanish exploitation.* [Library of Congress]

ual life of their own. Whatever its concern for the spiritual welfare of the Indians, the church remained one of the indications that Spanish America was a conquered world. And those who spoke for the church did not challenge Spanish domination or any but the most extreme modes of Spanish economic exploitation. By the end of the colonial era in the late eighteenth century, the Roman Catholic church had become one of the most conservative forces in Latin America.

The English Reformation to 1533

The Preconditions of Reform

Late medieval England had a reputation for maintaining the rights of the crown against the pope. Edward I (d. 1307) had rejected efforts by Pope Boniface VIII to prevent secular taxation of the clergy. Parliament passed the first

Statutes of Provisors and *Praemunire* in the mid-fourteenth century curtailing payments and judicial appeals to Rome. The English Franciscan William of Ockham had defended the rights of royalty against Pope John XXII, and John Wycliffe had even sanctioned secular confiscation of clerical property in support of the principle of apostolic poverty. Lollardy, Humanism, and widespread anticlerical sentiment prepared the way religiously and intellectually for Protestant ideas, which began to enter England in the early 1520s.

In the early 1520s future English reformers met at the White Horse Inn in Cambridge to discuss Lutheran writings smuggled into England by merchants and scholars. One of these future reformers was William Tyndale (ca. 1492–1536), who translated the New Testament into English in 1524–1525, while in Germany. Published in Cologne and Worms, Tyndale's New Testament began to circulate in England in 1526, and thereafter the vernacular Bible became the centerpiece of the English Reformation. Cardinal Thomas Wolsey (ca. 1475–1530), the chief minister of King Henry VIII, and Sir Thomas More (1478–1535), Wolsey's successor, guided royal opposition to incipient Protestantism. The king himself defended the seven sacraments against Luther, receiving as a reward the title "Defender of the Faith" from Pope Leo X. Following Luther's intemperate reply to Henry's amateur theological attack, More wrote a lengthy *Response to Luther* in 1523.

THE KING'S AFFAIR. While Lollardy and Humanism may be said to have prepared the soil for the seeds of Protestant reform, it was King Henry's unhappy marriage that furnished the plough that truly broke it. Henry had married Catherine of Aragon (d. 1536), daughter of Ferdinand and Isabella of Spain, and the aunt of Emperor Charles V. By 1527 the union had produced no male heir to the throne and only one surviving child, a daughter, Mary. Henry was justifiably concerned about the political consequences of leaving only a female heir. People in this period believed it unnatural for women to rule over men: at best, a woman ruler meant a contested reign; at worst, turmoil and revolution. Henry even came to believe that his union with Catherine, who had numerous miscarriages and stillbirths, had been cursed by God, because before their marriage Catherine had been the wife of his brother, Arthur. Henry's father, King Henry VII, had

betrothed Catherine to Henry after Arthur's untimely death in order to keep the English alliance with Spain intact. They were officially married in 1509, a few days before Henry VIII received his crown. Marriage to the wife of one's brother was prohibited by both canon and biblical law (see Leviticus 18:16, 20:21), and a special dispensation had been required from Pope Julius II before Henry married Catherine.

By 1527 Henry was thoroughly enamored of Anne Boleyn, one of Catherine's ladies in waiting, and determined to put Catherine aside and take Anne to wife. This he could not do in Catholic England without papal annulment of the marriage to Catherine. And therein lay a special problem. The year 1527 was also the year when soldiers of the Holy Roman Empire mutinied and sacked Rome, and the reigning pope, Clement VII, was at the time a prisoner of Charles V, Catherine's nephew. Even if this had not been the case, it would have been virtually impossible for the pope to grant an annulment of a marriage that had not only survived for eighteen years but had been made possible in the first place by a special papal dispensation, the king's denial of the latter's validity notwithstanding.

Cardinal Wolsey, who aspired to become pope, was placed in charge of securing the royal annulment. Lord Chancellor since 1515 and papal legate-at-large since 1518, Wolsey had long been Henry's "heavy" and the object of much popular resentment. When he failed to secure the annulment, through no fault of his own, he was dismissed in disgrace in 1529. Thomas Cranmer (1489–1556) and Thomas Cromwell (1485–1540), both of whom harbored Lutheran sympathies, thereafter became the king's closest advisers. Finding the way to a papal annulment closed, Henry's new advisers struck a different course: Why not simply declare the king supreme in English spiritual affairs as he was in English temporal affairs? Then the king himself could settle the king's affair.

The Reformation Parliament

In 1529 Parliament convened for what would be a seven-year session that earned it the title the "Reformation Parliament." During this period, it passed a flood of legislation that harassed and finally placed royal reins on the clergy. In January 1531 the clergy in Convocation (a legislative assembly representing the

The Family of Henry VIII, *by Lucas de Heere (1534–1584). This allegorical painting depicts the Tudor succession. To Henry's right stands his Catholic daughter Mary, (1553–1558) and her husband Philip II of Spain. They are accompanied by Mars, the god of war. Henry's son, Edward VI, (1547–1553) is kneeling at the King's left. Elizabeth I (1558–1603) is shown standing in the foreground attended by Peace and Plenty.* [Sudely Castle, The Walter Morrison Collection]

English clergy) publicly recognized Henry as head of the church in England "as far as the law of Christ allows." In 1532 the Act of Supplication of the Commons Against the Ordinaries was passed, a list of grievances against the church ranging from alleged indifference to the needs of the laity to an excessive number of religious holidays. In the same year Parliament passed the Submission of the Clergy, effectively placing canon law under royal control and thereby the clergy under royal jurisdiction. The Act in Conditional Restraint of Annates further gave the English king the power to withhold from Rome these lucrative "first fruits" of new ecclesiastical appointments.

In January 1533 Henry wed the pregnant Anne Boleyn, with Thomas Cranmer officiating. In February 1533 the Act for the Restraint of Appeals made the king the highest court of appeal for all English subjects. In March 1533 Cranmer became archbishop of Canterbury and led the Convocation in invalidating the king's marriage to Catherine. In 1534 Parliament ended all payments by the English clergy and laity to Rome and gave Henry sole jurisdiction over high ecclesiastical appointments. The

Act of Succession in the same year made Anne Boleyn's children legitimate heirs to the throne, and the Act of Supremacy declared Henry "the only supreme head in earth of the church of England." Refusal to recognize these two acts brought the execution of Thomas More and John Fisher, bishop of Rochester—events that made clear the king's determination to have his way regardless of the cost. In 1536 came the first Act for Dissolution of Monasteries, which affected only the smaller ones; three years later a second act dissolved all English monasteries and turned their endowments over to the king.

WIVES OF HENRY VIII. Henry's domestic life proved to lack the consistency of his political life. In 1536 Anne Boleyn was executed for adultery, and her daughter, Elizabeth, was declared illegitimate. Henry had four further marriages. His third wife, Jane Seymour, died in 1537 shortly after giving birth to the future Edward VI. Henry wed Anne of Cleves sight unseen on the advice of Cromwell, the purpose being to create by the marriage an alliance with the Protestant princes. Neither the alliance nor Anne—whom Henry found to have a remarkable resemblance to a horse—proved worth the trouble; the marriage was annulled by Parliament, and Cromwell was dismissed and eventually executed. Catherine Howard, Henry's fifth wife, was beheaded for adultery in 1542. His last wife, Catherine Parr, a patron of Humanists and reformers, for whom Henry was the third husband, survived him to marry still a fourth time—obviously she was a match for the English king.

THE KING'S RELIGIOUS CONSERVATISM. Henry's political and domestic boldness was not carried over to the religious front, although the pope did cease to be the head of the English church and English Bibles were placed in English churches. Despite his political break with Rome, the king remained decidedly conservative in his religious beliefs, and Catholic doctrine remained prominent in a country seething with Protestant sentiment. Despite his many wives and amorous adventures, Henry absolutely forbade the English clergy to marry and threatened any clergy who were twice caught in concubinage with execution. The Ten Articles of 1536 prescribed Catholic doctrine with only mild Protestant concessions. Angered by the growing popularity of Protestant views, even among his chief advisers, Henry struck directly at them in the Six Articles of 1539. These reaffirmed transubstantiation, denied the Eucharistic cup to the laity, declared celibate vows inviolable, provided for private masses, and ordered the continuation of auricular confession. Protestants referred to the articles as the "whip with six stings." Although William Tyndale's English New Testament grew into the Coverdale Bible (1535) and the Great Bible (1539) and the latter was mandated for every English parish during Henry's reign, England had to await Henry's death before it could become a genuinely Protestant country.

The Protestant Reformation Under Edward VI

When Henry died, his son and successor, Edward VI (1547–1553), was only ten years old. Edward reigned under the successive

---

MAIN EVENTS OF THE ENGLISH REFORMATION

Reformation Parliament convenes	1529
Parliament passes the Submission of the Clergy, an act placing Canon law and the English clergy under royal jurisdiction	1532
Henry VIII weds Anne Boleyn; Convocation proclaims marriage to Catherine of Aragon invalid	1533
Act of Succession makes Anne Boleyn's children legitimate heirs to the English throne	1534
Act of Supremacy declares Henry VIII "the only supreme head of the church of England"	1534
Thomas More executed for opposition to Acts of Succession and Supremacy	1535
Publication of Coverdale Bible	1535
Henry VIII imposes the Six Articles, condemning Protestantism and reasserting traditional doctrine	1539
Edward VI succeeds to the throne under protectorships of Somerset and Northumberland	1547
First Act of Uniformity imposes *Book of Common Prayer* on English churches	1549
Mary Tudor restores Catholic doctrine	1553–1558
Elizabeth I fashions an Anglican religious settlement	1558–1603

regencies of Edward Seymour, who became the duke of Somerset (1547–1550), and the earl of Warwick, who became known as the duke of Northumberland (1550–1553), during which time England fully enacted the Protestant Reformation. The new king and Somerset corresponded directly with John Calvin. During Somerset's regency, Henry's Six Articles and laws against heresy were repealed, and clerical marriage and communion with cup were sanctioned.

In 1547 the chantries, places where endowed masses had traditionally been said for the dead, were dissolved. In 1549 the Act of Uniformity imposed Thomas Cranmer's *Book of Common Prayer* on all English churches. Images and altars were removed from the churches in 1550. Still more radical Protestant reforms were carried out by the duke of Northumberland. After Charles V's victory over the German princes in 1547, German Protestant leaders had fled to England for refuge, and several directly assisted the completion of the English Reformation, Martin Bucer prominent among them. The Second Act of Uniformity, passed in 1552, imposed a revised edition of the *Book of Common Prayer* on all English churches. A forty-two-article confession of faith, also written by Thomas Cranmer, was adopted, setting forth a moderate Protestant doctrine. It taught justification by faith and the supremacy of Holy Scripture, denied transubstantiation (although not real presence), and recognized only two sacraments.

All these changes were short-lived, however. In 1553 Catherine of Aragon's daughter, Mary, succeeded Edward (who had died in his teens) to the English throne and proceeded to restore Catholic doctrine and practice with a singlemindedness that rivaled that of her father. It was not until the reign of Anne Boleyn's daughter, Elizabeth (1558–1603), that a lasting religious settlement was worked out in England (to be discussed in Chapter 11).

The Social Significance of the Reformation in Western Europe

It was a common feature of the Lutheran, Zwinglian, and Calvinist reforms to work within the framework of reigning political power. Luther, Zwingli, and Calvin saw themselves and their followers as citizens of the world, subject to definite civic responsibilities and obligations. Their adjustments in this regard have led scholars to characterize them as "magisterial reformers," meaning not only that they were the leaders of the major Protestant movements but also that they succeeded by the force of the magistrate's sword. It was probably not a matter of compromising the principles of the Gospels and choosing the way of brute force, as some have argued. The reformers never contemplated a reform outside or against the societies of which they were members. They wanted a reform that took shape within the laws and institutions of the sixteenth century, and to that end they remained highly sensitive to what was politically and socially possible in their age.

Some scholars believe that these reformers were too conscious of the historically possible, that their reforms went forward with such caution that they not only changed late medieval society very little but actually encouraged acceptance of the sociopolitical status quo.

There was a very conservative side to the Reformation. On the other hand, by the end of the sixteenth century the Reformation had also brought about radical changes in the religious beliefs and practices of many people. As it developed, the Reformation eliminated or put severe restrictions on such traditional practices as mandatory fasting; auricular confession; the veneration of saints, relics, and images; indulgences; pilgrimages and shrines; vigils; weekly, monthly, and annual masses for the dead; the belief in purgatory; Latin worship services; the sacrifice of the Mass; numerous religious ceremonies, festivals, and holidays; the canonical hours; monasteries and mendicant orders; the sacramental status of marriage, extreme unction, confirmation, holy orders, and penance; clerical celibacy; clerical immunity from civil taxation and criminal jurisdiction; nonresident benefices; excommunication and interdict; canon law; episcopal and papal authority; and the traditional Scholastic education of the clergy. Some Protestant lands (Switzerland, for example) enacted more of these reforms, and more radically, than others (England, for example).

It may be argued that by the second half of the sixteenth century Protestant religion had become just as burdensome as medieval religion had ever been. As Protestants won power in cities and towns, they tended to use their new position to erect what critics called "new papacies." In its first decades, however, the

The Injustice of the Law. This woodcut by an unknown artist is entitled the Spider Web. In it the law is compared to a spider web, which easily catches the wealthy and the poor, who are seen hanging on the gallows and the wheel on the left, while permitting the rich and powerful to escape punishment for their crimes. Note the hole in the spider web made by the large bee, while the smaller bugs become hopelessly trapped. [From Max Geisberg, The German Single-Leaf Woodcut, 1500–1550, edited by Walter L. Strauss. Hacker Art Books, 1974. Used by permission of Hacker Art Books.]

Greed. The Power of Money, by Peter Spitzer. The caption reads: "Were my mother a whore (she can be seen in bed with a man in the upper left corner) and my father a thief (he can be seen hanging on the gallows in the upper right corner), still, if I had a lot of money I would have no grief." [From Max Geisberg, The German Single-Leaf Woodcut, 1500–1550, edited by Walter L. Strauss. Hacker Art Books, 1974. Used by permission of Hacker Art Books.]

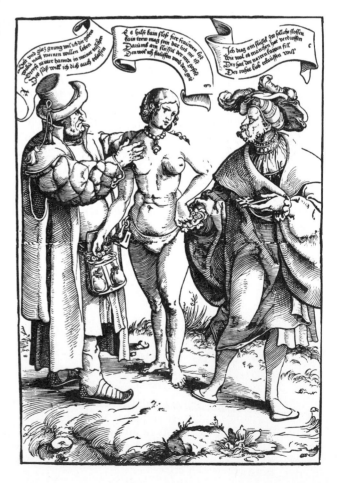

Adultery. The Chasity Belt, by H. Vogtherr gives one view—that of the wronged husband—of this age-old marital problem. Here a husband departing on a business trip has placed his wife, who does not love him, in a chastity belt. She takes his money, which he gladly gives her in exchange for promises of fidelity, to buy a key that will set her free to do as she pleases during his absence. [From Max Geisberg, The German Single-Leaf Woodcut, 1500–1550, edited by Walter L. Strauss. Hacker Art Books, 1974. Used by permission of Hacker Art Books.]

Failed Marriages. The Subservient Husband, by Hans Schaufelein. In the sixteenth century the husband who failed to rule his wife properly was thought to risk creating a shrew who would assume authority in the marriage. Note that in this woodcut the woman has the pocketbook and keys around her waist, for she has become master of the house. Her husband has been forced to do ''woman's work,'' which was considered a sure sign of a house no longer in order. [*From Max Geisberg,* The German Single-Leaf Woodcut, 1500–1550, *edited by Walter L. Strauss. Hacker Art Books, 1974. Used by permission of Hacker Art Books.*]

Tyranny. The Rabbits Catching the Hunters, by Georg Pencz. The rabbits, long brutalized by the hunters and their dogs, organize and then subject the hunters to the treatment the rabbits have long received from them. This woodcut is a warning to all tyrants that tyranny brings rebellion. [*From Max Geisberg,* The German Single-Leaf Woodcut, 1500–1550, *edited by Walter L. Strauss. Hacker Art Books, 1974. Used by permission of Hacker Art Books.*]

Old Age. A Peasant Couple by Christoph Amberger. The man is saying that he is now too old to hunt birds and must therefore depend on an owl to do his hunting. [*From Max Geisberg,* The German Single-Leaf Woodcut, 1500–1550, *edited by Walter L. Strauss. Hacker Art Books, 1974. Used by permission of Hacker Art Books.*]

Drunkenness. The Winebag and His Wheelbarrow, by Hans Weidt. Alcoholism was a very serious problem in the sixteenth century. It was caricatured by artists and railed against by Catholic and Protestant clergymen. [*From Max Geisberg,* The German Single-Leaf Woodcut, 1500–1550, *edited by Walter L. Strauss. Hacker Art Books, 1974. Used by permission of Hacker Art Books.*]

397

Reformation was presented and perceived by those who embraced it as a profound simplification of religious life. It was freeing precisely because it required less rather than more from those who wanted to be pious Christians and because it gave clearer focus to their ethical obligations.

The Reformation and Education

Another important cultural achievement of the Reformation was its implementation of many of the educational reforms of Humanism in the new Protestant schools and universities. Many Protestant reformers in Germany, France, and England were Humanists. Even when their views on church doctrine and humankind separated them from the Humanist movement, the Protestant reformers continued to share with the Humanists a common opposition to Scholasticism and a belief in the unity of wisdom, eloquence, and action. The Humanist program of studies, which provided the language skills to deal authoritatively with original sources, proved to be a more appropriate tool for the elaboration of Protestant doctrine than did Scholastic dialectic.

The connections between Humanism and the Reformation were recognized by the Catholic counterreformers. Ignatius of Loyola observed the way in which the new learning had been embraced by and served the Protestant cause. In his *Spiritual Exercises* he insisted that when the Bible and the Church Fathers were read directly, they be read under the guidance of the authoritative Scholastic theologians: Peter Lombard, Bonaventura, and Thomas Aquinas. The latter, Ignatius argued, being ''of more recent date,'' had the clearer understanding of what Scripture and the Fathers meant and therefore should guide the study of the past.

When in August 1518 Philip Melanchthon (1497–1560), a young Humanist and professor of Greek, arrived at the University of Wittenberg, his first act was to implement curricular reforms on the Humanist model. In his inaugural address, entitled *On Improving the Studies of the Young,* Melanchthon presented himself as a defender of good letters and classical studies against ''barbarians who practice barbarous arts.'' By the latter he meant the Scholastic theologians of the later Middle Ages, whose methods of juxtaposing the views of conflicting authorities and seeking to reconcile them by disputation had, he believed, under-

mined both good letters and sound biblical doctrine. Scholastic dominance in the universities was seen by Melanchthon as having bred contempt for the Greek language and learning and as having encouraged neglect of the study of mathematics, sacred studies, and the art of oratory. Melanchthon urged the careful study of history, poetry, and other Humanist disciplines.

Together Luther and Melanchthon completely restructured the University of Wittenberg's curriculum. Commentaries on Lombard's *Sentences* were dropped, as was canon law, and old Scholastic lectures on Aristotle were replaced by straightforward historical study. Students read primary sources directly, not by way of accepted Scholastic commentators. Candidates for theological degrees defended the new doctrine on the basis of their own exegesis of the Bible. New chairs of Greek and Hebrew were created. Luther and Melanchthon also pressed for universal compulsory education so that both boys and girls could reach vernacular literacy in the Bible.

In Geneva John Calvin and his successor, Theodore Beza, founded the Genevan Academy, which later evolved into the University of Geneva. This institution, created primarily for the purpose of training Calvinist ministers, pursued ideals similar to those set forth by Luther and Melanchthon. Calvinist refugees trained in the academy carried Protestant educational reforms to France, Scotland, England, and the New World. Through such efforts a working knowledge of Greek and Hebrew became commonplace in educated circles in the sixteenth and seventeenth centuries.

Some contemporaries decried what they saw as a narrowing of the original Humanist program as Protestants took it over. Erasmus, for example, came to fear the Reformation as a threat to the liberal arts and good learning, and Sebastian Franck pointed to parallels between Luther's and Zwingli's debates over Christ's presence in the Eucharist and such old Scholastic disputations as that over the Immaculate Conception of the Virgin.

Humanist culture and learning nonetheless remained indebted to the Reformation. The Protestant endorsement of the Humanist program of studies remained as significant for the Humanist movement as the latter had been for the Reformation. Protestant schools and universities consolidated and preserved for the modern world many of the basic pedagogical achievements of Humanism. There the *studia humanitatis,* although often as little more than a handmaiden to theological doctrine, found a permanent home, one that remained hospitable even in the heyday of Protestant Scholasticism.

The Reformation and the Changing Role of Women

The Protestant reformers took a positive stand on clerical marriage and strongly opposed monasticism and the celibate life. From this position they challenged the medieval tendency alternately to degrade women as temptresses (following the model of Eve) and to exalt them as virgins (following the model of Mary). Protestants opposed the popular antiwoman and antimarriage literature of the Middle Ages. They praised woman in her own right, but especially in her biblical vocation as mother and housewife. Although relief of sexual frustration and a remedy of fornication were motives behind Protestant promarriage arguments, and although motherhood and housewifery were considered woman's basic vocation, the reformers also viewed their wives as indispensable companions in their work, and this not solely because they took domestic cares off their husbands' minds. Luther, who married in 1525 at the age of forty-two, wrote of women:

Imagine what it would be like without women. The home, cities, economic life, and government would virtually disappear. Men cannot do without women. Even if it were possible for men to beget and bear children, they still could not do without women.[2]

John Calvin wrote at the death of his wife:

I have been bereaved of the best companion of my life, of one who, had it been so ordered, would not only have been the willing sharer of my indigence, but even of my death. During her life she was the faithful helper of my ministry.[3]

Such tributes were intended in part to overcome Catholic criticism of clerical marriage as a distraction from one's ministry. They were primarily the expression of a new value placed on the estate of marriage and family life. In opposition to the celibate ideal of the Middle Ages, Protestants stressed as no religious movement

before them the sacredness of home and family, and this attitude contributed to a more respectful and sharing relationship between husbands and wives and between parents and children. The ideal of the companionate marriage—that is, of husband and wife as co-workers in a special God-ordained community of the family—led to an important expansion of the grounds for divorce in Protestant cities as early as the 1520s and ensured women an equal right to leave husbands who flagrantly violated the marriage contract. The new stress on companionship in marriage also worked indirectly to make contraception and planned parenthood a respectable choice for married couples, as it made husbands sensitive to the suffering and unhappiness that many pregnancies brought on their wives.

Protestant doctrines were as attractive to women as they were to men. Women who had been maligned as the concubines of priests came to know a new dignity as the "honorable wives" of Protestant ministers. Renegade nuns wrote exposés of the nunnery in the name of Christian freedom and justification by faith. Women in the higher classes, who were enjoying new social and political freedoms during the Renaissance, found in Protestant theology a religious complement to their greater independence in other walks of life.

Because of their desire to have women become pious housewives, Protestants also encouraged the education of girls to vernacular literacy, expecting them thereafter to model their lives on the Bible. Women came in the course of such study, however, to find in the Bible passages that made them the equals to men in the presence of God. Such education further gave them a role in the Reformation as independent authors. These may seem like small advances from a modern perspective, but they were significant, if indirect, steps in the direction of the emancipation of women.

Family Life in Early Modern Europe

LATE MARRIAGES. Between 1500 and 1800 men and women married at later ages than they had done in previous centuries. Men tended to be in their mid- to late twenties rather than in their late teens and early twenties, and women in their early to mid-twenties rather than in their teens. In sixteenth-century Nuremberg, the legal minimum age for marriage without parental permission was set at twenty-five for men and twenty-one for

[2]*Luther's Works,* Vol. 54: *Table Talk,* ed. and trans. by Theodore G. Tappert (Philadelphia: Fortress Press, 1967), p. 161.
[3]*Letters of John Calvin,* Vol. 2, trans. by J. Bonnet (Edinburgh: T. Constable, 1858), p. 216.

A sixteenth-century German family. This was a fairly comfortable household, as witnessed by the many toys and the maidservant. Note that the mother is nursing her youngest child herself.
[*Bildarchiv Preussicher Kulturbesitz*]

women. The canonical or church-sanctioned age for marriage remained fourteen for men and twelve for women, and marriage could still occur at such young ages if the parents agreed. As it had done throughout the high and later Middle Ages, the church also recognized as valid the free, *private* exchange of vows between a man and a woman at these minimal ages. However, after the Reformation, which condemned such "clandestine" unions, the church increasingly required both parental agreement and public vows in church for a fully licit marriage, a procedure it had, in fact, always preferred.

The late marriage pattern, generally observable in western Europe and England, resulted primarily from the difficulty a couple had supporting themselves as an independent family unit. Such support had become difficult because of the large population increase that occurred in the fifteenth and early sixteenth centuries, when western Europe was recovering from the great plague. Larger families meant more heirs and a greater division of resources. In Germanic and Scandinavian countries, the

custom of a fair sharing of inheritance among all male children worked both to delay marriages, as more got less, and to encourage independent family units, as children did not have to hang around the family home indefinitely and live off the charity of the eldest brother after the death of their parents, as more often happened in England where primogeniture (right of the first-born son to inherit all property) remained strong. Still, it took the average couple a longer time to prepare themselves materially for marriage. Many never married. An estimated 20 per cent of all women remained spinsters in the sixteenth century. Combined with the estimated 15 per cent who were unmarried widows, this made up to a sizable unmarried female population.

Marriage tended to be "arranged" in the sense that the male heads of the two families often met and discussed the terms of the marriage before they informed the prospective bride and bridegroom. However, it was rare for the two people involved not to know each other in advance or not to have a prior relationship. Parents did not force total strangers to live together, and children always had a legal right to protest and resist an unwanted marriage. A forced marriage was, by definition, invalid, and no one believed an unwanted marriage would last. The best marriage was one desired by both parties and supported by their families.

Later marriages meant marriages of shorter duration and contributed to more frequent remarriage. Later marriages also worked to slow overall population growth, although not by directly preventing older women from having as many children as younger women. Women who married later in life simply had children in more rapid succession, but with increased risk to health and life and hence with greater maternal mortality. As growing church condemnation confirms, delayed marriage increased fornication. It also raised the number of illegitimate children, as is testified by the rapid growth of orphanages and foundling homes between 1600 and 1800.

FAMILY SIZE. The early modern family was conjugal or nuclear; that is, it consisted of a father and a mother and two to four children who managed to live into adulthood. The average husband and wife had six to eight children, a birth about every two years. Of these, however, an estimated one third died by age five, and one half were gone by age twenty. Rare was the family, at any social level, that did not learn firsthand about infant mortality and child death. The Protestant reformer Martin Luther was typical. He married late in life (at forty-two, here atypical) and fathered six children, two of whom he lost, an infant daughter at eight months and another, more painfully, at thirteen years.

BIRTH CONTROL. Artificial birth control had existed since antiquity. (The ancient Egyptians used acidic alligator dung, and the use of sponges was equally old.) The church's frequent condemnation of *coitus interruptus* (male withdrawal before ejaculation) in the thirteenth and fourteenth centuries suggests that a "contraceptive mentality"—that is, a conscious and regular effort at birth control—may have developed in the later Middle Ages. Birth control was not, however, very effective, and for both historical and moral reasons the church firmly opposed it. During the eleventh century the church suppressed an extreme ascetic sect, the Cathars, that had practiced birth control, when not abstaining from sex alto-gether, on the grounds that to propagate the human species was to encase immortal souls in evil matter. But the church also turned against contraception on moral grounds. According to its most authoritative theologian, Saint Thomas Aquinas, a moral act must always aid and abet, never frustrate, the natural end of a creaturely process. In the eyes of Aquinas and his church, the natural end of sex could be only the production of children and their subsequent rearing to the glory of God within the bounds of holy matrimony and the community of the church.

Despite the church's official opposition on contraception, it is likely that more general Christian moral teaching actually reinforced a contraceptive mentality within the early modern family by encouraging men to be more sensitive husbands and fathers. As men identified emotionally with wives who suffered painful, debilitating, unwanted, life-threatening, serial pregnancies (the chances of dying in childbirth were about one in ten) and with hungry children in overcrowded families, Christian love may also have persuaded a father that *coitus interruptus* was a moral course of action.

WET NURSING. The church allied with the physicians of early modern Europe on another intimate family matter: the condemnation of upper-class women who put their newborn children out to wet nurses for as long as eighteen months. Wet nurses were women who had recently had a baby or were suckling a child of their own, and who, for a fee, agreed also to suckle another child. The practice appears to have greatly increased the risk of infant mortality inasmuch as an infant received a strange and shared milk supply from a woman who was not as healthy as its own mother and who often lived under less sanitary conditions. But nursing a child was a chore some upper-class women, and especially their husbands, found distasteful. Among women, vanity and convenience appear to have been motives for turning to wet nurses. For husbands even more was at stake in the practice. Because the church forbade sexual intercourse while a woman was lactating, and sexual intercourse was believed to spoil a lactating woman's milk (pregnancy, of course, ended her milk supply), a nursing wife often became a reluctant lover. In addition, nursing had a contraceptive effect (about 75 per cent effective). There is good evidence that some women prolonged nursing their children precisely in order to delay a new pregnancy—and loving husbands understood and cooperated in this primitive form of family planning. For other husbands, however, especially wealthy burghers and noblemen who desired an abundance of male heirs, nursing seemed to rob them of sex and offspring and to jeopardize the patrimony. Hence, their strong support of wet nursing.

LOVING FAMILIES? The early modern family had features that seem cold, unloving, even cruel. Not only did parents give infants to wet nurses, but later, when the children were between the ages of eight and thirteen, they sent them out of their houses altogether into apprenticeships or to employment in the homes and businesses of relatives, friends, or even mere acquaintances and strangers. The affective ties between spouses seem to have been as tenuous as those between parents and children. Widowers and widows sometimes remarried within three to six months of their spouse's death, occasionally within weeks, and marriages with extreme disparity in age—especially between old men and young women—also suggest low affection.

Love and affection, however, are as relative to time and culture as other values. A kindness in one historical period can be a cruelty in another; what sends a person to heaven in one culture may damn a person to hell in another culture. "What greater love," an early modern parent would surely have asked a modern critic, "can parents have for their children than to equip them to make their way vocationally in the world?" An apprenticed child was a child with a future. Because of primitive living conditions, contemporaries could also appreciate the purely utilitarian and humane side of marriage and wink at quick remarriages. On the other hand, marriages with extreme disparity in age were no more the norm in early modern Europe than was the practice of wet nursing, and they received just as much criticism and ridicule.

Suggested Readings

ROLAND H. BAINTON, *Erasmus of Christendom* (1960). Charming presentation.

CHARLES BOXER, *Four Centuries of Portuguese Expansion 1415–1825* (1961). Comprehensive survey by a leading authority.

OWEN CHADWICK, *The Reformation* (1964). Among the best short histories and especially strong on theological and ecclesiastical issues.

NORMAN COHN, *The Pursuit of the Millennium* (1957). Traces millennial speculation and activity from the Old Testament to the sixteenth century.

A. G. DICKENS, *The Counter Reformation* (1969). Brief narrative with pictures.

A. G. DICKENS, *The English Reformation* (1974). The best one-volume account.

A. G. DICKENS and JOHN M. TONKIN, *The Reformation in Historical Thought* (1985). The standard critical guide to the main developments of Reformation studies.

G. DONALDSON, *The Scottish Reformation* (1960). Dependable, comprehensive narrative.

H. OUTRAM EVENNETT, *The Spirit of the Counter Reformation* (1968). Essay on the continuity of Catholic reform and its independence from the Protestant Reformation.

JEAN-LOUIS FLANDRIN, *Families in Former Times* (1979). Family life in France.

C. GIBSON, *The Aztecs Under Spanish Rule: A History of the Indians of the Valley of Mexico* (1964). An exceedingly interesting book.

C. GIBSON, *Spain in America* (1966). A splendidly clear and balanced discussion.

HAROLD GRIMM, *The Reformation Era: 1500–1650* (1973). Very good on later Lutheran developments.

WERNER L. GUNDERSHEIMER (Ed.), *French Humanism 1470–1600* (1969). Collection of essays that both summarize and provoke.

L. HANKE, *Bartolomé de Las Casas: An Interpretation of His Life and Writings* (1951). A classic work.

JOYCE L. IRWIN (Ed.), *Womanhood in Radical Protestantism, 1525–1675* (1979). A rich collection of sources.

HUBERT JEDIN, *A History of the Council of Trent*, Vols. 1 and 2 (1957–1961). Comprehensive, detailed, authoritative.

DE LAMAR JENSEN, *Reformation Europe, Age of Reform and Revolution* (1981). Excellent, up-to-date survey.

WILBUR K. JORDAN, *Edward VI: The Young King* (1968). The basic biography.

F. KATZ, *The Ancient American Civilizations* (1972). An excellent introduction.

B. KEEN and M. WASSERMAN, *A Short History of Latin America* (1984). A good survey with very helpful bibliographical guides.

ROBERT M. KINGDON, *Transition and Revolution: Problems and Issues of European Renaissance and Reformation History* (1974). Covers politics, printing, theology, and witchcraft.

ALAN MACFARLANE, *The Family Life of Ralph Josselin: A Seventeenth Century Clergyman* (1970).

JOHN F. MCNEILL, *The History and Character of Calvinism* (1954). The most comprehensive account and very readable.

E. W. MONTER, *Calvin's Geneva* (1967). Dependable sketch derived from authoritative studies.

STEVEN OZMENT, *Mysticism and Dissent* (1973). Treats dissenters from Lutheranism and Calvinism.

STEVEN OZMENT, *The Reformation in the Cities* (1975). An essay on why people thought they wanted to be Protestants.

STEVEN OZMENT, *The Age of Reform 1250–1550: An Intellectual and Religious History of Late Medieval and Reformation Europe* (1980).

STEVEN OZMENT, *When Fathers Ruled: Family Life in Reformation Europe* (1983). Provocative and revisionist.

J. H. PARRY, *The Age of Reconnaissance* (1964). A comprehensive account of explorations from 1450 to 1650.

R. R. POST, *The Modern Devotion* (1968). Currently the authoritative interpretation.

EUGENE F. RICE, JR., *The Foundations of Early Modern Europe 1460–1559* (1970). Broad, succinct narrative.

JASPAR G. RIDLEY, *Thomas Cranmer* (1962). The basic biography.

E. GORDON RUPP, *Patterns of Reformation: Oecolampadius, Karlstadt, Muntzer* (1969). Effort to demonstrate the variety within early Protestantism.

J. J. SCARISBRICK, *Henry VIII* (1968). The best account of Henry's reign.

QUENTIN SKINNER, *The Foundations of Modern Political Thought II: The Age of Reformation* (1978). A comprehensive survey that treats *every* political thinker and tract.

LEWIS SPITZ, *The Religious Renaissance of the German Humanists* (1963). Comprehensive and entertaining.

JAMES STAYER, *Anabaptists and the Sword* (1972).

LAWRENCE STONE, *The Family, Sex and Marriage in England 1500–1800* (1977). Controversial in some respects, but reigning view in most aspects of family history.

GERALD STRAUSS (Ed. and Trans.), *Manifestations of Discontent in Germany on the Eve of the Reformation* (1971). Rich collection of sources for both rural and urban scenes.

R. H. TAWNEY, *Religion and the Rise of Capitalism* (1947). Advances beyond Weber's arguments relating Protestantism and capitalist economic behavior.

ERNST TROELTSCH, *The Social Teaching of the Christian Churches*, Vols. 1 and 2, trans. by Olive Wyon (1960).

MAX WEBER, *The Protestant Ethic and the Spirit of Capitalism*, trans. by Talcott Parsons (1958). First appeared in 1904–1905 and has continued to stimulate debate over the relationship between religion and society.

FRANÇOIS WENDEL, *Calvin: The Origins and Development of His Religious Thought*, trans. by Philip Mairet (1963). The best treatment of Calvin's theology.

GEORGE H. WILLIAMS, *The Radical Reformation* (1962). Broad survey of the varieties of dissent within Protestantism.

The Massacre of the Innocents *by Pieter Brueghel (1520–1569). Brueghel
put his depiction of the Biblical accounting of Herod's massacre of the
children of Bethlehem into a wintry Dutch setting and thereby created
a strong indictment of Spanish atrocities in the Netherlands.
(Kunsthistorisches Museum, Vienna)*

TIIE LATE SIXTEENTH CENTURY and the first half of the seventeenth century are described as an "age of religious wars" because of the bloody opposition of Protestants and Catholics across the length and breadth of Europe. The wars were fueled by both genuine religious conflict and bitter dynastic rivalries. In France, the Netherlands, England, and Scotland in the second half of the sixteenth century, Calvinists fought Catholic rulers for the right to govern their own territories and to practice their chosen religion openly. In the first half of the seventeenth century Lutherans, Calvinists, and Catholics marched against one another in central and northern Europe during the Thirty Years' War. And by the middle of the seventeenth century English Puritans had successfully revolted against the Stuart monarchy and the Anglican church.

In the second half of the sixteenth century the political conflict, which had previously been confined to central Europe and a struggle for Lutheran rights and freedoms, shifted to western Europe—to France, the Netherlands, England, and Scotland—and became a struggle for Calvinist recognition. War-weary German Lutherans and Catholics agreed to live and let live in the Peace of Augsburg (1555): *cuius regio, eius religio,* which means that he who controls the land may determine its religion. Lutheranism thereafter became a legal religion within the Holy Roman Empire. Non-Lutheran Protestants, however, were not recognized by the Peace of Augsburg: both sides scorned Anabaptists and other sectarians as anarchists, and Calvinists were not yet strong enough to demand legal standing.

If German Lutherans had reason to take quiet satisfaction, Protestants elsewhere obviously did not. The struggle for Protestant religious rights had intensified in most countries outside the empire by the mid-sixteenth century. The Council of Trent adjourned in 1563 committed to an international Catholic counteroffensive against Protestants to be led by the Jesuits. At the time of John Calvin's death in 1564, Geneva had become both a refuge for Europe's persecuted Protestants and an international school for Protestant resistance, producing leaders fully equal to the new Catholic challenge.

Genevan Calvinism and Catholicism as revived by the Council of Trent were two equally dogmatic, aggressive, and irreconcilable church systems. Although Calvinists looked like "new papists" to critics when they domi-

11
The Age of Religious Wars

405

Self-portrait by Rembrandt van Rijn (1607–1669). [*The Frick Collection*]

nated cities like Geneva, they were firebrands and revolutionaries when, as minorities, they found their civil and religious rights denied. Calvinism adopted a presbyterian organization that magnified regional and local religious authority; boards of presbyters, or elders, representing the many individual congregations of Calvinists, directly shaped the policy of the church at large. By contrast, the Counter-Reformation sponsored a centralized episcopal church system, hierarchically arranged from pope to parish priest, which stressed absolute obedience to the person at the top. The high clergy—the pope and his bishops—not the synods of local churches, ruled supreme. Calvinism proved attractive to proponents of political decentralization in contest with totalitarian rulers, whereas Catholicism remained congenial to the proponents of absolute monarchy determined to maintain "one king, one church, one law" throughout the land.

The opposition between the two religions can be seen even in the art and architecture that each came to embrace. The Catholic Counter-Reformation found the Baroque style congenial. A successor to Mannerism, Baroque art is a grandiose, three-dimensional display of life and energy. Great Baroque artists like Peter Paul Rubens (1571–1640) and Gianlorenzo Bernini (1598–1680) were Catholics. Protestants by contrast seemed to opt for a simpler, restrained, almost self-effacing art and architecture, as can be seen in the English churches of Christopher Wren (1632–1723) and the gentle, searching portraits of the Dutch Mennonite Rembrandt van Rijn (1606–1669).

As religious wars engulfed Europe, the intellectuals perceived the wisdom of religious pluralism and toleration more quickly than did the politicians. A new skepticism, relativism, and individualism in religion became respectable in the sixteenth and seventeenth centuries. Sebastian Castellio's (1515–1563) pithy censure of John Calvin for his role in the execution of the Antitrinitarian Michael Servetus summarized a sentiment that was to grow in early modern Europe: "To kill a man is not to defend a doctrine, but to kill a man."[1] As a new skepticism greeted the failure of the great reform movements, the French essayist Michel de Montaigne (1533–1592) asked in scorn of the dogmatic mind: "What do I know?" The Lutheran Valentin Weigel (1533–1588), surveying a half century of religious strife in Germany, advised people to look within themselves for religious truth and no longer to churches and creeds.

Such views gained currency in larger political circles only by the most painful experiences. Where religious strife and its attendant civil war were best held in check, rulers tended to subordinate theological doctrine to political unity, urging tolerance, moderation, and compromise—even indifference—in religious matters. Such rulers came to be known as *politiques,* and the most successful among them was Elizabeth I of England. By contrast, rulers like Mary I of England, Philip II of Spain, and Oliver Cromwell, who tended to take their religion with the utmost seriousness and refused every compromise, did not in the long run achieve their political goals.

As we shall see, the wars of religion were both internal national conflicts and truly international wars. While Catholic and Protestant subjects struggled against one another for control of the crown of France, the Netherlands, and England, the Catholic governments of France and Spain conspired and finally sent

406

[1]*Contra libellum Calvini* (N.P., 1562), p. E 2 a.

The Ecstasy of St. Theresa, *by Gianlorenzo Bernini (1598—1680), in the church of Santa
Maria della Vittoria in Rome. This statue of the saint in mystical rapture is part of a richly
decorated altar. Like so much of the art of the Counter-Reformation, the altar was designed to
dazzle and overawe the worshipper.* [Art Resource]

ABOVE: *The splendor of a Baroque church. This is the interior of the eighteenth-century cloister church at Ottobeuren in Bavaria, West Germany. The architect was Johann Michael Fischer. Note how the atmosphere is charged with energy and action.* [Bettmann Archive.]

LEFT: *The interior of St. Paul's Cathedral in London, by Sir Christopher Wren (1632–1723). Although elaborately decorated, the interior is subdued in effect.* [Bettmann Archive.]

armies against Protestant regimes in England and the Netherlands. The outbreak of the Thirty Years' War in 1618 made the international dimension of the religious conflict especially clear; before it ended in 1648, the war drew every major European nation directly or indirectly into its deadly net.

The French Wars of Religion (1562–1598)

Anti-Protestant Measures and the Struggle for Political Power

French Protestants came to be known as *Huguenots,* a term derived from Besançon Hugues, the leader of Geneva's political revolt against the House of Savoy in the 1520s, a prelude to that city's Calvinist Reformation in the 1530s. As early as the 1520s, however, the Sorbonne was vigilant against the Lutheran writings and doctrines that were circulating in Paris.

The capture of the French king Francis I by the forces of Charles V at the Battle of Pavia in 1525 provided a motive for the first wave of Protestant persecution in France. Hoping to pacify their Spanish conqueror, a fierce opponent of German Protestants, and to win their king's swift release, the French government took repressive measures against the native reform movement, led by Jacques Lefèvre d'Étaples and Bishop Briçonnet of Meaux, which had proved a seedbed of Protestant sentiment.

A second major crackdown came a decade later. When Protestants plastered Paris and other cities with anti-Catholic placards on October 18, 1534, mass arrests of suspected Protestants occurred. Government retaliation for this action drove John Calvin and other members of the French reform party into exile. In 1540 the Edict of Fontainebleau subjected French Protestants to the Inquisition. Henry II (1547–1559) established legal procedures against Protestants in the Edict of Chateaubriand in 1551. Save for a few brief interludes, the French monarchy remained a staunch Catholic foe of the Protestants until the ascension to the throne of Henry of Navarre in 1589.

The Habsburg–Valois wars (see Chapter 10) ended with the Treaty of Cateau-Cambrésis in 1559, and Europe experienced a moment of peace. But only a moment. The same year marked the beginning of internal French con-

The Battle of Pavia, 1525. *The French defeat at Pavia and the capture of Francis I by the Habsburg forces under Charles V provided a motive for the first wave of Protestant persecution in France.* [SCALA/Art Resource]

Diane de Poitiers, *by Francois Clouet (1510–1572). The mistress of Henry II of France, Diane (1499–1566) used her influence with the king to further the Catholic cause. After Henry's death in 1559, Diane was forced to retire to her country estates by Queen Catherine de' Medicis.* [*National Gallery of Art*]

flict and the shift of the European balance of power in favor of Spain. It began with an accident. During a tournament held to celebrate the marriage of his thirteen-year-old daughter, Elizabeth, to Philip II, the son of Charles V and heir to the Spanish Habsburg lands, the French king, Henry II, was mortally wounded. (A lance pierced his visor.) This unforeseen event brought to the throne Henry's sickly fifteen-year-old son, Francis II, under the regency of the queen mother, Catherine de Médicis. With the monarchy so weakened by Henry's death, three powerful families saw their chance to control France and began to compete for the young king's ear. They were the Bourbons, whose power lay in the south and west; the Montmorency-Chatillons, who controlled the center of France; and the Guises, who were dominant in eastern France.

The Guises were far the strongest and had little trouble establishing firm control over the young king. Francis, duke of Guise, had been Henry II's general, and his brothers, Charles and Louis, were cardinals of the church. Mary Stuart, Queen of Scots and wife of Francis II, was their niece. Throughout the latter half of the sixteenth century the name of Guise remained interchangeable with militant, reactionary Catholicism. The Bourbon and Montmorency-Chatillon families, in contrast, developed strong Huguenot sympathies, largely for political reasons. The Bourbon Louis I, prince of Condé (d. 1569), and the Montmorency-Chatillon Admiral Gaspard de Coligny (1519–1572) became the political leaders of the French Protestant resistance. They collaborated early in an abortive plot to kidnap Francis II from his Guise advisers in the Conspiracy of Amboise in 1560. This conspiracy was strongly condemned by John Calvin, who considered such tactics a disgrace to the Reformation.

Appeal of Calvinism

Often for quite different reasons ambitious aristocrats and discontented townspeople joined Calvinist churches in opposition to the Guise-dominated French monarchy. In 1561 over two thousand Huguenot congregations existed throughout France, although Huguenots were a majority of the population in only two regions. Dauphiné and Languedoc. Although they made up only about one fifteenth of the population, Huguenots were in important geographic areas and were heavily represented among the more powerful segments of French society. Over two fifths of the French aristocracy became Huguenots. Many apparently hoped to establish within France a principle of territorial sovereignty akin to that secured within the Holy Roman Empire by the Peace of Augsburg (1555). In this way Calvinism indirectly served the forces of political decentralization.

John Calvin and Theodore Beza consciously sought to advance their cause by currying favor with powerful aristocrats. Beza converted Jeanne d'Albert, the mother of the future Henry IV. The Prince of Condé was apparently converted in 1558 under the influence of his Calvinist wife. For many aristocrafts—Condé seems clearly to have been among them—Calvinist religious convictions were attractive primarily as aids to long-sought political goals. The military organization of Condé and

Coligny progressively merged with the religious organization of the French Huguenot churches, creating a potent combination that benefited both political and religious dissidents. Calvinism gave political resistance justification and inspiration, and the forces of political resistance made Calvinism a viable religious alternative in Catholic France. Each side had much to gain from the other. The confluence of secular and religious motives, although beneficial to aristocratic resistance and Calvinist religion alike, tended to cast suspicion on the religious appeal of Calvinism. Clearly religious conviction was neither the only nor always the main reason for becoming a Calvinist in France in the second half of the sixteenth century.

Catherine de Médicis and the Guises

Following Francis II's death in 1560, Catherine de Médicis continued as regent for her minor son, Charles IX (1560–1574). At a colloquy in Poissy she tried unsuccessfully to reconcile the Protestant and Catholic factions. Fearing the power and guile of the Guises, Catherine, whose first concern was always to preserve the monarchy, sought allies among the Protestants. In 1562, after conversations with Beza and Coligny, she issued the January Edict, a measure that granted Protestants freedom to worship publicly outside towns—although only privately within them—and to hold synods. In March this royal toleration came to an abrupt end when the duke of Guise surprised a Protestant congregation at Vassy in Champagne and proceeded to massacre several score—an event that marked the beginning of the French wars of religion (March 1562).

Had Condé and the Huguenot armies rushed immediately to the queen's side after this attack, Protestants might well have secured an alliance with the crown, so great was the queen mother's fear of Guise power at this time. But the hesitation of the Protestant leaders, due primarily to indecision on the part of Condé, placed the young king and the queen mother, against their deepest wishes, in firm Guise control, as cooperation with the Guises became the only alternative to capitulation to the Protestants.

During the first French war of religion, fought between April 1562 and March 1563, the duke of Guise was assassinated. It is a measure of the international character of the struggle in France that troops from Hesse and the Palatinate fought alongside the Huguenots. A brief resumption of hostilities in 1567–1568 was followed by the bloodiest of all the conflicts between September 1568 and August 1570. In this period Condé was killed and Huguenot leadership passed to Coligny—actually a blessing in disguise for the Protestants because Coligny was far the better military strategist. In the Peace of Saint-Germain-en-Laye (1570), which ended the third war, the crown, acknowledging the power of the Protestant nobility, granted the Huguenots religious freedoms within their territories and the right to fortify their cities.

Perpetually caught between fanatical Huguenot and Guise extremes, Queen Catherine had always sought to balance the one side against the other. Like the Guises, she wanted a Catholic France; she did not, however, desire a Guise-dominated monarchy. After the Peace of Saint-Germain-en-Laye the crown tilted manifestly toward the Bourbon faction and the Huguenots, and Coligny became Charles IX's

Catherine de' Medicis (1519–1589). Catherine exercised enormous power in France during the reigns of her three sons Francis II (1559–1560), Charles IX (1560–1574), and Henry III (1574–1589). [Roger-Viollet]

*The Massacre of St. Bartholemew's Day, August 24, 1572, as depicted by the contemporary
Protestant painter Francois Dubois. Three thousand Protestants were slaughtered in Paris, an
estimated 20,000 others died throughout France. The massacre transformed the religious
struggle in France from a conflict for political power to a war for survival between Protestants
and Catholics.* [*Museum of Lausanne*]

most trusted adviser. Unknown to the king,
Catherine began at this time to plot with the
Guises against the ascendant Protestants. As
she had earlier sought Protestant support when
Guise power threatened to subdue the mon-
archy, so she now sought Guise support as
Protestant influence grew.

There was reason for Catherine to fear Coligny's hold on the king. Louis of Nassau, the
leader of Protestant resistance to Philip II in the
Netherlands, had gained Coligny's ear, and
Coligny used his position of influence to win
the king of France over to a planned French
invasion of the Netherlands in support of the
Dutch Protestants. Such a course of action
would have placed France squarely on a collision course with mighty Spain. Catherine recognized far better than her son that France
stood little chance in such a contest. She and
her advisers had been much sobered in this
regard by news of the stunning Spanish victory
over the Turks at Lepanto in October 1571 (to
be discussed later.)

**THE SAINT BARTHOLOMEW'S DAY MAS-
SACRE.** When Catherine lent her support to
the infamous Saint Bartholomew's Day Massacre of Protestants, she did so out of a far less
reasoned judgment. Her decision appears to
have been made in a state of near panic. On
August 22, 1572, four days after the Huguenot
Henry of Navarre had married the king's sister,
Marguerite of Valois—still another sign of
growing Protestant power—Coligny was
struck down, although not killed, by an assassin's bullet. Catherine had apparently been
party to this Guise plot to eliminate Coligny.
After its failure she feared both the king's reaction to her complicity with the Guises and the
Huguenot response under a recovered Coligny.
Summoning all her motherly charm and fury,
Catherine convinced Charles that a Huguenot
coup was afoot, inspired by Coligny, and that
only the swift execution of Protestant leaders
could save the crown from a Protestant attack
on Paris. On Saint Bartholomew's Day, 1572,
Coligny and three thousand fellow Huguenots

Coligny's Death on Saint Bartholomew's Day

The following description of Coligny's murder by henchmen of the duke of Guise was written by an eyewitness to the Saint Bartholomew's Day Massacre, the statesman and historian Jacques-Auguste de Thou.

It was determined to exterminate all the Protestants, and the plan was approved by the queen. . . . The duke of Guise . . . was put in full command of the enterprise. . . . The signal to commence the massacre would be given by the bell of the palace, and the marks by which they [the Catholic Swiss mercenaries and the French soldiers who were to carry it out] should recognize each other in the darkness were a bit of white linen tied around the left arm and a white cross on the hat.

[As the massacre began] Coligny awoke and recognized from the noise that a riot was taking place. . . . When he perceived that the noise increased and that someone had fired an arquebus in the courtyard of his dwelling . . . , conjecturing what it might be, but too late, he arose from his bed and having put on his dressing gown said his prayers. . . . [Then] he said: "I see clearly that which they seek, and I am ready steadfastly to suffer that death which I have never feared. . . ."

Meanwhile the conspirators, having burst through the door of the chamber, entered, and [one named] Besme, sword in hand, demanded of Coligny, who stood near the door, "Are you Coligny?" Coligny replied, "Yes, I am he. . . ." As he spoke, Besme gave him a sword thrust through the body, and having withdrawn his sword, another thrust in the mouth, by which his face was disfigured. So Coligny fell, killed with many thrusts. Others have written that Coligny in dying pronounced . . . these words: "Would that I might at least die at the hands of a soldier and not [at those] of a valet. . . ."

Then the duke of Guise inquired of Besme from the courtyard if the thing were done, and when Besme answered him that it was, the duke replied that the Chevalier d'Angoulême was unable to believe it unless he saw it. . . . [So] they threw the body through the window into the courtyard, disfigured as it was with blood. When the Chevalier d'Angoulême, who could scarcely believe his eyes, had wiped away with a cloth the blood which overran the face and finally recognized him, some say he spurned the body with his foot . . . [and] said: "Cheer up my friends! Let us do thoroughly that which we have begun. The king commands it."

James Harvey Robinson (Ed.), *Readings in European History,* Vol. 2 (Boston: Ginn and Co., 1906), pp. 180–182.

were butchered in Paris. Within three days an estimated twenty thousand Huguenots were executed in coordinated attacks throughout France. It is a date that has ever since lived in infamy for Protestants.

Pope Gregory XIII and Philip II of Spain reportedly greeted the news of the Protestant massacre with special religious celebrations. Philip especially had good reason to rejoice, for the massacre ended for the moment any planned French opposition to his efforts to subdue his rebellious subjects in the Netherlands because France was now thrown into civil war. But the massacre of thousands of Protestants also gave the discerning Catholic world cause for new alarm. The event changed the nature of the struggle between Protestants and Catholics both within and beyond the borders of France. It was thereafter no longer an internal contest between Guise and Bourbon factions for French political influence, nor was it simply a Huguenot campaign to win basic religious freedoms. Henceforth, in Protestant eyes, it became an international struggle to the death for sheer survival against an adversary whose cruelty now justified any means of resistance.

PROTESTANT RESISTANCE THEORY. Only as Protestants faced suppression and sure defeat did they begin to sanction active political resistance. At first, they tried to practice the biblical precept of obedient subjection to worldly authority (Romans 13:1). Luther had only grudgingly approved resistance to the emperor after the Diet of Augsburg in 1530. In 1550 Lutherans in the city of Magdeburg had published a highly influential defense of the right of lower authorities to oppose the emperor's order that all Lutherans return to the Catholic fold.

Calvin, who never faced the specter of total political defeat after his return to Geneva in 1541, had always condemned willful disobedience and rebellion against lawfully constituted governments as unchristian. But he also taught that lower magistrates, as part of the lawfully constituted government, had the right and duty to oppose tyrannical higher authority.

The exiled Scottish reformer John Knox, who had seen his cause crushed by Mary of Guise, the Regent of Scotland, and Mary I of England, had pointed the way for later Calvinists in his famous *Blast of the Trumpet Against the Terrible Regiment of Women* (1558). Knox declared that the removal of a heathen tyrant was not only permissible, but a Christian duty. He had the Catholic queen of England in mind.

After the great massacre of French Protestants on Saint Bartholomew's Day, 1572, Calvinists everywhere came to appreciate the need for an active defense of their religious rights. Classical Huguenot theories of resistance appeared in three major works of the 1570s. The first was the *Franco-Gallia* of François Hotman (1573), a Humanist argument that the representative Estates General of France historically held higher authority than the French king. The second was Theodore Beza's *On the Right of Magistrates over Their Subjects* (1574), which, going beyond Calvin's views, justified the correction and even the overthrow of tyrannical rulers by lower authorities. Finally, there was Philippe du Plessis Mornay's *Defense of Liberty Against Tyrants* (1579), an admonition to

Theodore Beza Defends the Right to Resist Tyranny

One of the oldest problems in political and social theory has been that of knowing when resistance to repression in matters of conscience is justified. Since Luther's day Protestant reformers, although accused by their Catholic critics of fomenting social division and revolution, had urged their followers to strict obedience to established political authority. After the 1572 Massacre of Saint Bartholomew's Day, however, Protestant pamphleteers urged Protestants to resist tyrants and persecutors with armed force. In 1574 Theodore Beza pointed out the obligation of rulers to their subjects and the latter's right to resist rulers who failed to meet the conditions of their office.

It is apparent that there is a mutual obligation between the king and the officers of a kingdom; that the government of the kingdom is not in the hands of the king in its entirety, but only the sovereign degree; that each of the officers has a share in accord with his degree; and that there are definite conditions on either side. If these conditions are not observed by the inferior officers, it is the part of the sovereign to dismiss and punish them. . . . If the king, hereditary or elective, clearly goes back on the conditions without which he would not have been recognized and acknowledged, can there be any doubt that the lesser magistrates of the kingdom, of the cities, and of the provinces, the administration of which they have received from the sovereignty itself, are free of their oath, at least to the extent that they are entitled to resist flagrant oppression of the realm which they swore to defend and protect according to their office and their particular jurisdiction? . . .

We must now speak of the third class of subjects, which though admittedly subject to the sovereign in a certain respect, is, in another respect, and in cases of necessity the protector of the rights of the sovereignty itself, and is established to hold the sovereign to his duty, and even, if need be, to constrain and punish him. . . . The people is prior to all the magistrates, and does not exist for them, but they for it. . . . Whenever law and equity prevailed, nations neither created nor accepted kings except upon definite conditions. From this it follows that when kings flagrantly violate these terms, those who have the power to give them their authority have no less power to deprive them of it.

Constitutionalism and Resistance in the Sixteenth Century: Three Treatises by Hotman, Beza, and Mornay, trans. and ed. by Julian H. Franklin (New York: Pegasus, 1969), pp. 111–114.

princes, nobles, and magistrates beneath the king, as guardians of the rights of the body politic, to take up arms against tyranny in other lands.

The Rise to Power of Henry of Navarre

Henry III (1574–1589), who was Henry II's third son and the last to wear the French crown, found the monarchy wedged between a radical Catholic League, formed in 1576 by Henry of Guise, and vengeful Huguenots. Neither group would have been reluctant to assassinate a ruler whom they considered heretical and a tyrant. Like the queen mother, Henry sought to steer a middle course, and in this effort he received support from a growing body of neutral Catholics and Huguenots, who put the political survival of France above its religious unity. Such *politiques* were prepared to compromise religious creeds as might be required to save the nation.

The Peace of Beaulieu in May 1576 granted the Huguenots almost complete religious and civil freedom. At this time, however, France was not ready for such sweeping toleration. Within seven months of the Peace of Beaulieu, the Catholic League forced Henry to return again to the illusory quest for absolute religious unity in France. In October 1577 the king issued the Edict of Poitiers, which truncated the Peace of Beaulieu, and once again circumscribed areas of permitted Huguenot worship. Thereafter Huguenot and Catholic factions quickly returned to their accustomed anarchical military solutions, the Protestants under the leadership of Henry of Navarre, now heir to the French throne.

In the mid-1580s the Catholic League, supported by the Spanish, became completely dominant in Paris. In what came to be known as the Day of the Barricades, Henry III attempted to rout the league with a surprise attack in 1588. The effort failed badly and the king had to flee Paris. Forced by his weakened position into unkingly guerrilla tactics, and also emboldened by news of the English victory over the Spanish Armada in 1588, Henry successfully plotted the assassination of both the duke and the cardinal of Guise. These assassinations sent France reeling once again. Led by still another Guise brother, Charles, duke of Mayenne, the Catholic League reacted with a fury that matched the earlier Huguenot response to the Massacre of Saint Bartholomew's Day. The king now had only one course

of action: he struck an alliance with the Protestant Henry of Navarre in April 1589.

As the two Henrys prepared to attack the Guise stronghold of Paris, however, a fanatical Jacobin friar stabbed Henry III to death. Thereupon the Bourbon Huguenot Henry of Navarre succeeded the childless Valois king to the French throne as Henry IV (1589–1610). Pope Sixtus V and Philip II stood aghast at the sudden prospect of a Protestant France. They had always wanted France to be religiously Catholic and politically weak, and they now acted to achieve that end. Spain rushed troops to support the besieged Catholic League. Philip II apparently even harbored hopes of placing his eldest daughter, Isabella, the granddaughter of Henry II and Catherine de Médicis, on the French throne.

Direct Spanish intervention in the affairs of France seemed only to strengthen Henry IV's grasp on the crown. The French people viewed his right to hereditary succession more seriously than his espoused Protestant confession. Henry was also widely liked. Notoriously informal in dress and manner—a factor that made him especially popular with the soldiers—Henry also had the wit and charm to neutralize the strongest enemy in a face-to-face confrontation. He came to the throne as a *politique,* long weary with religious strife and fully prepared to place political peace above absolute religious unity. He believed that a royal policy of tolerant Catholicism would be the best way to achieve such peace. On July 25, 1593, he publicly abjured the Protestant faith and embraced the traditional and majority religion of his country. "Paris is worth a mass," he is reported to have said.

It was, in fact, a decision he had made only after a long period of personal agonizing. The Huguenots were understandably horrified by this turnabout and Pope Clement VIII remained skeptical of Henry's sincerity. But the majority of the French church and people, having known internal strife too long, rallied to the king's side. By 1596 the Catholic League was dispersed, its ties with Spain were broken, and the wars of religion in France, to all intents and purposes, had ground to a close.

The Edict of Nantes

On April 13, 1598, a formal religious settlement was proclaimed in Henry IV's famous Edict of Nantes, and the following month, on May 2, 1598, the Treaty of Vervins ended hos-

''Paris is worth a mass'': Henry IV (1589–1610) embraces Catholicism, July 25, 1593, from a contemporary print. [Roger-Viollet]

MAIN EVENTS OF FRENCH WARS OF RELIGION (1562–1598)

Treaty of Cateau-Cambrésis ends Habsburg–Valois wars	1559
Francis II succeeds to French throne under regency of his mother, Catherine de Médicis	1559
Conspiracy of Amboise fails	1560
Protestant worshipers massacred at Vassy in Champagne by the duke of Guise	1562
The Saint Bartholomew's Day Massacre leaves thousands of Protestants dead	1572
Assassination of Henry III brings Huguenot Henry of Navarre to throne as Henry IV	1589
Henry IV embraces Catholicism	1593
Henry IV grants Huguenots religious and civil freedoms in the Edict of Nantes	1598
Henry IV assassinated	1610

tilities between France and Spain. The Edict of Nantes recognized and sanctioned minority religious rights within what was to remain an officially Catholic country. In 1591 Henry IV had already assured the Huguenots of at least qualified religious freedoms. The Edict of Nantes made good that promise. This religious truce—and it was never more than that—granted the Huguenots, who by this time numbered well over one million, freedom of public worship, the right of assembly, admission to public offices and universities, and permission to maintain fortified towns. Most of the new freedoms, however, were to be exercised

The Striding God from Artemisium. This bronze statue dated about 460 B.C. was found in the sea near Artemisium, at the northern tip of the large Greek island of Euboea. Exactly whom the statue represents is not known. Some have thought him to be Poseidon holding a trident; others believe that he is Zeus hurling a thunderbolt. In either case he is a brilliant representative of the early classical period of Greek sculpture and is now located in the Greek National Archaeological Museum in Athens. [Art Resource]

The Athenian Acropolis. The Acropolis in Athens was both a religious and a civic center. In the second half of the fifth century B.C., *Pericles and his successors crowned it with three major temples and a grand entrance building. This picture taken from the northwest shows the reconstructed remains of all the major buildings. The Parthenon, in the upper center, dominates the picture as it does the Acropolis and the city of Athens. In front of it is the entrance building called the Propylaea. At the extreme right is the small temple to Nike (Victory). On the extreme left is the Erechtheum with its famous porch of columns in the shape of young women.* [Art Resource]

OPPOSITE: *The Roman Forum. Originally a market-place, the Roman Forum was the civic center of Rome from its earliest days. It contained many public buildings and temples which were frequently altered and improved or torn down and replaced. Most of the buildings in this picture are from the Imperial period.* [Art Resource]

C-3

Rehearsal of a Satyr Play Depicted in a Roman Mosaic. The satyr play was a Greek art form that originally accompanied a trilogy of tragedies. It was a comic piece in which a chorus confronted the god Dionysus. It became popular among the Romans in its own right, and wealthy Romans often presented a satyr play as part of the entertainment at elaborate banquets. This mosaic from the Villa of Cicero at Pompeii shows actors and musicians preparing for a performance. [Art Resource]

A Street in Herculaneum. Herculaneum was a provincial town just east of Naples. It lay along the lower slopes of Mt. Vesuvius and was destroyed along with Pompeii in the terrible and famous eruption of A.D. *79. Since both towns were well preserved by the covering lava, excavations have given us a good idea of the appearance and daily life of Roman Italy. [Art Resource]*

Ships in the Harbor of Puteoli. This painting of ships moored in the port of Puteoli, a Campanian city on the Bay of Naples, comes from Herculaneum. It now hangs at the National Museum in Naples. [*Art Resource*]

The Colosseum at Rome. The Romans called this building the Flavian Amphitheatre because it was built by three successive emperors of the Flavian family—begun by Vespasian (r. 69–79), dedicated in A.D. 80 by his son Titus (r. 79–81), and finished by his younger son Domitian (r. 81–96). How it acquired its present name is uncertain; it may come from its great size or from its proximity to a colossal statue of the Emperor Nero. Said to have been built by prisoners from the Jewish War (A.D. 66–70), it held 50,000 spectators for the animal hunts, gladiatorial combats, mock sea battles, and other spectacles held in it. [Art Resource]

A reconstruction of imperial Rome. At its peak in the third century A.D., *Rome may well have had more than one million inhabitants, far more than any other city of the ancient world. The large open space in the center beyond the Tiber River is the Circus Maximus, a race course for chariots, which could hold as many as 250,000 spectators. The Coliseum is beyond it. The buildings between the two arenas make up the Roman forum.* [Art Resource]

"Good Government" in Siena. Ambrogio Lorenzetti was an Italian painter who worked in Siena during the fourteenth century. His most famous works are the frescoes of the Hall of Peace (Sala della Pace) of the Public Palace in Siena painted in 1338–1339. They present two allegories, "Good Government" and "Bad Government," and four compositions showing the effects of each on city and country. This section shows the results of good government in both city and country: amid general prosperity, merchants and travelers come and go peacefully, while maidens dance unmolested in the city streets (lower left corner). [Art Resource]

A fourteenth-century depiction of Florence, the center of Renaissance civilization in Italy. The cathedral and major public buildings are shown in the center of the city of the left bank of the Arno River. [Art Resource]

The Baptistry, Dome of the Cathedral, and Bell Tower at Florence. Perhaps the peak of medieval architecture is represented by this complex of buildings that make up the cathedral group at Florence. The Cathedral with its great dome by Filippo Brunelleschi comes chiefly from the fourteenth century; the Bell Tower (Campanile) was built in the mid-fourteenth century by Giotto, and the Baptistry still earlier, in the eleventh century, though some details were added in the fifteenth century. [Art Resource]

The Gates of Paradise, by Ghiberti. These doors, now located on the east side of the Baptistry at Florence, were designed and executed by Lorenzo Ghiberti (1378–1455), one of the early Florentine humanists. In 1401 he won a competition for the commission of a second pair of doors on the Baptistry. After finishing these in 1424 he agreed to make still a third pair, the "Gates of Paradise," ten panels containing some thirty-seven scenes from the Old Testament. The two sets of doors occupied him for about half a century. The two panels shown in close up here depict the stories of Noah (upper) and Esau (lower). [Art Resource]

The Street of the Wool and Silk Merchants in Bologna. This miniature from an illuminated manuscript dated to 1470 shows the street of the wool and silk merchants in Bologna. Like most cities of the Italian Renaissance, Bologna was heavily engaged in the commerce and manufacture of textiles. [Art Resource]

A Visit from the Doctor. These scenes of a physician attending a patient comes from the mid-fifteenth century. It is an illustration on a manuscript of the great Canon of Medicine *by Avicenna (980–1047), a Muslim physician and philosopher. His* Canon, *a summary of Arabic and ancient Greek medical knowledge, was translated into Latin in the twelfth century and became the chief European medical book. The manuscript is in the University Library in Bologna. [Art Resource]*

C-14

A Renaissance Pharmacy. This depiction of a pharmacy comes from the same illustrated manuscript of Avicenna's Canon of Medicine *made in the fifteenth century. Pharmacists, like other professionals in the Middle Ages and Renaissance, belonged to a guild. The assistants shown on the right mixing medicine were apprentices, living as well as working with the master-pharmacist.* [Art Resource]

The main altar of St. Peter's, Rome. The elaborate bronze baldachino or canopy over the altar was designed by Gian Lorenzo Bernini (1598–1680) to be the focal point of the basilica's vast interior space. [Art Resource]

within their own towns and territories. Concession of the right to fortify their towns reveals the continuing distrust between French Protestants and Catholics. As significant as it was, the edict only transformed a long hot war between irreconcilable enemies into a long cold war. To its critics it had only created a state within a state.

A Catholic fanatic assassinated Henry IV in May 1610. Although Henry is remembered most for the religious settlement of the Edict of Nantes, it was he and his finance minister, the duke of Sully, who laid the foundations for the later transformation of France into the absolute state of Cardinal Richelieu and Louis XIV. It would be in pursuit of the political and religious unity that had escaped Henry IV that Louis XIV, calling for "one king, one church, one law," would revoke the Edict of Nantes in 1685 and force France and Europe to learn again by bitter experience the hard lessons of the wars of religion. Rare is the politician who has preferred to learn from the lessons of history rather than repeating its mistakes.

Henry IV Recognizes Huguenot Religious Freedom

By the Edict of Nantes (April 13, 1598) Henry IV recognized Huguenot religious freedoms and the rights of Protestants to participate in French public institutions. Here are some of its provisions.

We have by this perpetual and irrevocable Edict pronounced, declared, and ordained and we pronounce, declare and ordain:

Art. I. Firstly, that the memory of everything done on both sides from the beginning of the month of March, 1585, until our accession to the Crown and during the other previous troubles, and at the outbreak of them, shall remain extinct and suppressed, as if it were something which had never occurred. . . .

Art. II. We forbid all our subjects, of whatever rank and quality they may be, to renew the memory of these matters, to attack, be hostile to, injure or provoke each other in revenge for the past, whatever may be the reason and pretext . . . but let them restrain themselves and live peaceably together as brothers, friends, and fellow-citizens. . . .

Art. III. We ordain that the Catholic, Apostolic, and Roman religion shall be restored and re-established in all places and districts of this our kingdom and the countries under our rule, where its practice has been interrupted. . . .

. . . .

Art. VI. And we permit those of the so-called Reformed religion to live and dwell in all the towns and districts of this our kingdom and the countries under our rule, without being annoyed, disturbed, molested or constrained to do anything against their conscience, or for this cause to be sought out in their houses and districts where they wish to live, provided that they conduct themselves in other respects to the provisions of our present Edict. . . .

. . . .

Art. XXI. Books dealing with the matters of the aforesaid so-called Reformed religion shall not be printed and sold publicly, except in the towns and districts where the public exercise of the said religion is allowed. . . .

Art. XXII. We ordain that there shall be no difference or distinction, because of the aforesaid religion, in the reception of students to be instructed in Universities, Colleges, and schools, or of the sick and poor into hospitals, infirmaries, and public charitable institutions. . . .

. . . .

Art. XXVII. In order to reunite more effectively the wills of our subjects, as is our intention, and to remove all future complaints, we declare that all those who profess or shall profess, the aforesaid so-called Reformed religion are capable of holding and exercising all public positions, honours, offices, and duties whatsoever . . . in the towns of our kingdom . . . notwithstanding all contrary oaths.

Church and State Through the Centuries: A Collection of Historic Documents, trans. and ed. by S. Z. Ehler and John B. Morrall (New York: Biblo and Tannen, 1967), pp. 185–187.

Imperial Spain and the Reign of Philip II (1556–1598)

Pillars of Spanish Power

Until the English defeated his mighty Armada in 1588, no one person stood larger in the second half of the sixteenth century than Philip II of Spain. Philip was heir to the intensely Catholic and militarily supreme western Habsburg kingdom. The eastern Habsburg lands of Austria, Bohemia, and Hungary had been given over by his father, Charles V, to Philip's uncle, the Emperor Ferdinand I, and they remained, together with the imperial title, in the possession of the Austrian branch of the family. Populous and wealthy Castile gave Philip a solid home base. Additional wealth was provided by the regular arrival in Seville of bullion from the Spanish colonies in the New World. In the 1540s great silver mines had been opened in Potosí in present-day Bolivia and in Zacatecas in Mexico. These gave Philip the great sums needed to pay his bankers and mercenaries. He nonetheless never managed to erase the debts left by his father nor to finance his own foreign adventures fully. He later contributed to the bankruptcy of the Fuggers when, at the end of his life, he defaulted on his enormous debts.

The new American wealth brought dramatic social change to the peoples of Europe during the second half of the sixteenth century. As Europe became richer, it was also becoming more populous, especially in the economically and politically active towns of France, England, and the Netherlands, where populations had tripled and quadrupled by the early seventeenth century. Europe's population approached an estimated 100 million by 1600.

The combination of increased wealth and population triggered a serious inflation, a steady 2 per cent a year in much of Europe, with serious cumulative effects by mid-century. As there were more people and greater coinage in circulation, but less food and fewer jobs, wages stagnated while prices doubled and tripled in much of Europe. This was especially the case in Spain. Because the new wealth was concentrated in the hands of a few, the traditional gap between the "haves"—the

Philip II of Spain (1556–1598) by Titian. Philip was the most powerful ruler of his time. [Alinari/Art Resource]

propertied, privileged, and educated classes—and the "have-nots" greatly widened. Nowhere did the unprivileged suffer more than in Spain, where the Castilian peasantry, the backbone of Philip II's great empire, became the most heavily taxed people of Europe. Those who contributed most to making possible Spanish hegemony in Europe in the second half of the sixteenth century prospered least from it.

View of Toledo *by El Greco (1541–1614). Born Domenicos Theotocopoulos in Crete, El Greco (which means "The Greek" in Spanish) did most of his work in Italy and Spain. His depiction of Toledo, the religious capital of Spain, captures the brooding mysticism and intensity of the Spanish Counter Reformation. [Metropolitan Museum of Art. The H.O. Havemeyer Collection]*

A subjugated peasantry and wealth from the New World were not the only pillars of Spanish strength. Philip II shrewdly organized the lesser nobility into a loyal and efficient national bureaucracy. A reclusive man, he managed his kingdom by pen and paper rather than by personal presence. He was also a learned and pious Catholic, although some popes suspected that he used religion as much for political as for devotional purposes. That he was a generous patron of the arts and culture can be seen in his unique retreat outside Madrid, the Escorial, a combination palace, church, tomb, and monastery. Philip also knew personal sorrows. His mad and treacherous son, Don Carlos, died under suspicious circumstances in 1568—some contemporaries suspected that Philip had him quietly executed—only three months before the death of the queen.

During the first half of Philip's reign, atten-tion focused almost exclusively on the Mediterranean and the Turkish threat, a constant European preoccupation. By history, geography, and choice, Spain had traditionally been Catholic Europe's champion against Islam. During the 1560s the Turks advanced deep into Austria, while their fleets dominated the Mediterranean. Between 1568 and 1570 armies under Philip's half-brother, Don John of Austria, the illegitimate son of Charles V, suppressed and dispersed the Moors in Granada. In May 1571 a Holy League of Spain, Venice, and the pope, again under Don John's command, formed to check Turkish belligerence in the Mediterranean. In what became the largest naval battle of the sixteenth century, Don John's fleet engaged the Ottoman navy under Ali Pasha off Lepanto in the Gulf of Corinth on October 7, 1571. Before the engagement ended, thirty thousand Turks had died and

The Escorial, Philip II's massive palace-monastery-mausoleum northwest of Madrid. Built between 1563 and 1584, the Escorial is a monument to the piety of the king. Philip had vowed to build the complex after the Spanish victory at Saint-Quentin over the French in 1577, which was won on St. Lawrence's day. Because the symbol of St. Lawrence is a grill—legend has it that he was martyred by being roasted alive—the Escorial's floor plan was designed to resemble a grill. [Editorial Photocolor Archives.]

The great battle of Lepanto (off the coast of Greece), October 7, 1541. In this, the largest naval engagement of the sixteenth century, the Spanish and their Italian allies under Don John of Austria smashed the Turkish fleet and ended the Ottoman threat to the western Mediterranean. [National Maritime Museum, London]

A sixteenth-century view of Genoa and its war fleet. Unlike its archrival Venice, Genoa tended to support Spanish policy in the Mediterranean. A large Genoese contingent fought under Don Juan at Lepanto. [SCALA/Art Resource]

ABOVE: *The mosque of Ottoman Sultan Suleiman the Magnificent (1520–1566) in Constantinople (modern Istanbul). It was built by Suleiman's architect Sinan at the height of the Ottoman Empire's glory. Like many Ottoman mosques, it was clearly inspired by neighboring Hagia Sophia built by Byzantine Emperor Justinian a thousand years earlier.* [Turkish Government Tourism and Information Office. New York]

LEFT: *St. Peter's in Rome was built in the sixteenth and seventeenth centuries replacing Emperor Constantine's early Christian Basilica of the fourth century on the probable site of the saint's tomb. The great church had many architects, among them Michelangelo, who designed the great dome. The vast piazza in front was designed by Bernini; note how the thrown-open arms extend to embrace pilgrims and draw them into the church. A portion of the pope's residence, the Vatican palace, is at the right center.* [Fotocielo]

over one third of the Turkish fleet had been sunk or captured. The Mediterranean for the moment belonged to Spain, and the Europeans were left to fight each other. Philip's armies also succeeded in putting down resistance in neighboring Portugal, which Spain annexed in 1580. The conquest of Portugal not only added to Spanish seapower but also brought the magnificent Portuguese overseas empire in Africa, India, and the Americas into the Spanish orbit.

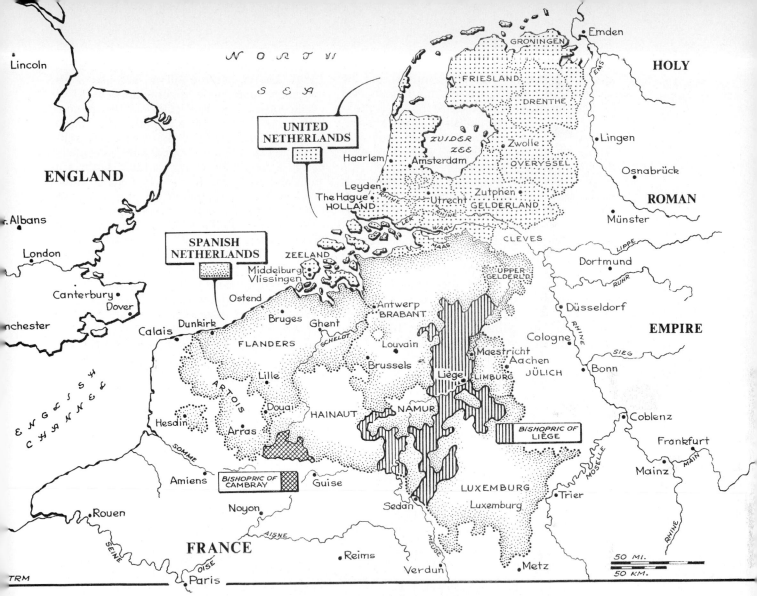

THE NETHERLANDS DURING THE REFORMATION

MAP 11-1 *The northern and southern provinces of the Netherlands. The former, the United Provinces, were mostly Protestant in the second half of the sixteenth century, while the southern, the Spanish Netherlands, made peace with Spain and remained largely Catholic.*

The Revolt in the Netherlands

The spectacular Spanish military success in southern Europe was not repeated in northern Europe. When Philip attempted to impose his will within the Netherlands and on England and France, he learned the lessons of defeat. The resistance of the Netherlands especially proved the undoing of Spanish dreams of world empire.

CARDINAL GRANVELLE. The Netherlands were not only the richest area of Philip's Habsburg kingdom, but of Europe as well. In 1559 Philip had departed the Netherlands for Spain, never again to return. His half-sister, Margaret of Parma, assisted by a special council of state, became regent in his absence. The council was headed by Philip's hand-picked lieutenant, the extremely able Antoine Perrenot (1517–1586), after 1561 Cardinal Gran-

423

velle. Granvelle hoped to check Protestant gains by internal church reforms, and he planned to break down the traditional local autonomy of the seventeen Netherlands provinces by stages and establish in its place a centralized royal government directed from Madrid. A politically docile and religiously uniform country was the objective.

The merchant towns of the Netherlands were, however, Europe's most independent; many, like magnificent Antwerp, were also Calvinist strongholds. By tradition and temperament the people of the Netherlands inclined far more toward variety and toleration than toward obeisant conformity and hierarchical order. Two members of the council of state formed a stubborn opposition to the Spanish overlords, who now sought to reimpose their traditional rule with a vengeance. They were the Count of Egmont (1522–1568) and William of Nassau, the Prince of Orange (1533–1584), known as "the Silent" because of his extremely small circle of confidants.

Like other successful rulers in this period, William of Orange was a *politique* who placed the Netherlands' political autonomy and well-being above religious creeds. He personally passed through successive Catholic, Lutheran, and Calvinist stages. In 1561 he married Anne of Saxony, the daughter of the Lutheran Elector Maurice and the granddaughter of the late Landgrave Philip of Hesse. He maintained his Catholic practices until 1567, at which time he turned Lutheran. After the Saint Bartholomew's Day massacre (1572), Orange became an avowed Calvinist.

In 1561 Cardinal Granvelle proceeded with a planned ecclesiastical reorganization of the Netherlands that was intended to tighten the control of the Catholic hierarchy over the

The Milch Cow, a sixteenth-century satirical painting depicting the Netherlands as a milk cow in whom all the powers are interested. Elizabeth of England is feeding the cow—England had long-standing commercial ties with Flanders; Philip II of Spain is attempting to ride her—Spain was trying to reassert its control over the country; William of Orange is trying to milk the animal—he had placed himself at the head of the anti-Spanish rebellion; and the King of France holds the cow's tail—France sought to profit from the rebellion at Spain's expense. [Rijksmuseum, Amsterdam]

country and to accelerate its consolidation as a Spanish ward. Orange and Egmont, organizing the Dutch nobility in opposition, succeeded in gaining Granvelle's removal from office in 1564, with Regent Margaret's blessing. But aristocratic control of the country after Granvelle's departure proved woefully inefficient, and popular unrest continued to grow, especially among urban artisans, who joined the congregations of radical Calvinist preachers in increasing numbers.

THE COMPROMISE. The year 1564 also saw the first fusion of political and religious opposition to Margaret's government. This opposition resulted from Philip II's unwise insistence that the decrees of the Council of Trent be enforced throughout the Netherlands. William of Orange's younger brother, Louis of Nassau, who had been raised a Lutheran, led the opposition, and it received support from the Calvinist-inclined lesser nobility and townspeople. A national covenant was drawn up called the *Compromise,* a solemn pledge to resist the decrees of Trent and the Inquisition. Grievances were loudly and persistently voiced, and when Margaret's government spurned the protesters as ''beggars'' in 1566, Calvinists rioted through the country. Louis called on French Huguenots and German Lutherans to send aid to the Netherlands, and a full-scale rebellion against the Spanish regency appeared imminent.

THE DUKE OF ALBA. The rebellion failed to materialize, however, because the Netherlands' higher nobility would not support it. Their shock at Calvinist iconoclasm and anarchy was as great as their resentment of Granvelle's more subtle repression. Philip, determined to make an example of the Protestant rebels, dispatched the duke of Alba to suppress the revolt. His army of ten thousand journeyed northward from Milan in 1567 in a show of combined Spanish and papal might. A special tribunal, known to the Spanish as the Council of Troubles and among the Netherlanders as the Council of Blood, reigned over the land. The counts of Egmont and Horn and several thousand suspected heretics were publicly executed before Alba's reign of terror ended.

The Spanish levied new taxes, forcing the Netherlands to pay for the suppression of its own revolt. One of these taxes, the ''tenth penny,'' a 10 per cent sales tax, met such resistance from merchants and artisans that it re-

The Duke of Alba (1507–1582). *His ruthless attempts to stamp out opposition in the Netherlands only inspired greater resistance by the Dutch.* [*Mas*]

mained uncollectable in some areas even after a reduction to 3 per cent. Combined persecution and taxation sent tens of thousands fleeing from the Netherlands during Alba's cruel six-year rule. Alba came to be more hated than Granvelle or the radical Calvinists had ever been.

RESISTANCE AND UNIFICATION. William of Orange was an exile in Germany during these turbulent years. He now emerged as the leader of a broad movement for the Netherlands' independence from Spain. The northern, Calvinist-inclined provinces of Holland, Zeeland, and Utrecht, of which Orange was the *stadholder,* or governor, became his base. As in France, political resistance in the Netherlands gained both organization and inspiration by merging with Calvinism.

The early victories of the resistance attest to the popular character of the revolt. A case in point is the capture of the port city of Brill by the ''Sea Beggars.'' These men were an inter-

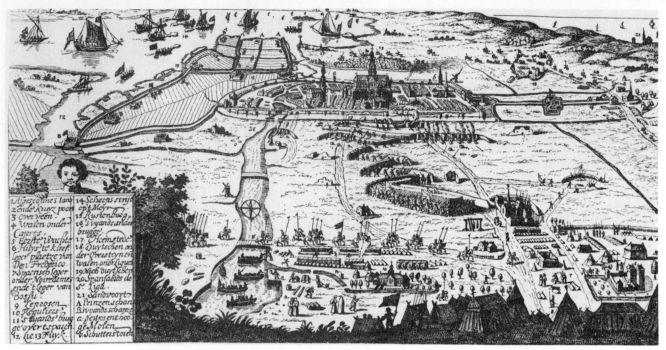

The siege of the Dutch city of Haarlem by Alba's army. The siege was a horrible example of the increasingly bloody struggle in the Netherlands. After resisting heroically for seven months (December 1572–June 1573), the city fell and all of the garrison and about 2000 inhabitants were slaughtered by the Spaniards. [Beschryvinge ende lof der stad Haerlem]

national group of anti-Spanish exiles and criminals, among them many Englishmen. William of Orange did not hesitate to enlist their services. Their brazen piracy, however, had forced Queen Elizabeth to disassociate herself from them and to bar their ships from English ports. In 1572 the Beggars captured Brill and other seaports in Zeeland and Holland. Mixing with the native population, they quickly sparked rebellions against Alba in town after town and spread the resistance southward. In 1574 the people of Leiden heroically resisted a long Spanish siege. The Dutch opened the dikes and flooded their country to repulse the hated Spanish. The faltering Alba had by that time ceded power to Don Luis de Requesens, who replaced him as commander of Spanish forces in the Netherlands in November 1573.

THE PACIFICATION OF GHENT. The greatest atrocity of the war came after Requesens's death in 1576. Spanish mercenaries, leaderless and unpaid, ran amok in Antwerp on November 4, 1576, and they left seven thousand people dead in the streets. The event came to be known as the Spanish Fury.

These atrocities accomplished in four short days what neither religion nor patriotism had previously been able to do. The ten largely Catholic southern provinces (what is roughly modern Belgium) now came together with the seven largely Protestant northern provinces (what is roughly the modern Netherlands) in unified opposition to Spain. This union, known as the Pacification of Ghent, was accomplished on November 8, 1576. It declared internal regional sovereignty in matters of religion, a key clause that permitted political cooperation among the signatories, who were not agreed over religion. It was a Netherlands version of the territorial settlement of religious differences brought about in the Holy Roman Empire in 1555 by the Peace of Augsburg. Four provinces initially held out, but they soon made the resistance unanimous two months later by joining the all-embracing Union of Brussels in January 1577. For the next two years the Spanish faced a unified and determined Netherlands.

Don John, the victor over the Turks at Lepanto in 1571, had taken command of Spanish land forces in November 1576. He now experienced his first defeat. Confronted by unified Netherlands resistance, he signed the Perpetual Edict in February 1577, a humiliating treaty that provided for the removal of all Spanish troops from the Netherlands within twenty days. This withdrawal of troops not only gave the country to William of Orange but also effectively ended for the present whatever plans Philip may have had for using the Netherlands as a staging area for an invasion of England.

THE UNION OF ARRAS AND THE UNION OF UTRECHT. The Spanish, however, were nothing if not persistent. Don Juan and Alessandro Farnese of Parma, the regent Margaret's son, revived Spanish power in the southern provinces, where constant fear of Calvinist extremism had moved the leaders to break the Union of Brussels. In January 1579 the southern provinces formed the Union of Arras, and within five months they made peace with Spain. These provinces later served the cause of the Counter-Reformation. The northern provinces responded with the formation of the Union of Utrecht.

NETHERLANDS INDEPENDENCE. Seizing what now appeared to be a last opportunity to break the back of Netherlands resistance, Philip II declared William of Orange an outlaw and placed a bounty of 25,000 crowns on his head.

Philip II Declares William of Orange an Outlaw (1580)

In the following proclamation the king of Spain accused William of Orange of being the "chief disturber of the public peace" and offered his captors, or assassins, generous rewards.

Philip, by the grace of God king of Castile, etc. to all to whom these presents may come, greeting:

It is well known to all how favorably the late emperor, Charles V, . . . treated William of Nassau. . . . Nevertheless, as everyone knows, we had scarcely turned our back on the Netherlands before the said William . . . (who had become . . . prince of Orange) began . . . by sinister arts, plots, and intrigues . . . to gain [control] over those whom he believed to be malcontents, or haters of justice, or anxious for innovations, and . . . above all, those who were suspected in the matter of religion. . . . With the knowledge, advice, and encouragement of the said Orange, the heretics commenced to destroy the images, altars, and churches. . . . So soon as the said Nassau was received into the government of the provinces, he began, through his agents and satellites, to introduce heretical preaching. . . . Then he introduced liberty of conscience . . . which soon brought it about that the Catholics were openly persecuted and driven out. . . . Moreover he obtained such a hold upon our poor subjects of Holland and Zeeland
. . . that nearly all the towns, one after the other, have been besieged. . . .

Therefore, for all these just reasons, for his evil doings as chief disturber of the public peace . . . we outlaw him forever and forbid our subjects to associate with him . . . in public or in secret. We declare him an enemy of the human race, and in order the sooner to remove our people from his tyranny and oppression, we promise, on the word of a king and as God's servant, that if one of our subjects be found so generous of heart and so desirous of doing us a service and advantaging the public that he shall find the means of executing this decree and of ridding us of the said pest, either by delivering him to us dead or alive, or by depriving him at once of life, we will give him and his heirs landed estates or money, as he will, to the amount of twenty-five thousand gold crowns. If he has committed any crime, of any kind whatsoever, we will pardon him. If he be not noble, we will ennoble him for his valor; and should he require other persons to assist him, we will reward them according to the service rendered, pardon their crimes, and ennoble them too.

James Harvey Robinson (Ed.), *Readings in European History,* Vol. 2 (Boston: Ginn and Co., 1906), pp. 174–177.

The act predictably stiffened the resistance of the northern provinces. In a famous defiant speech to the Estates General of Holland in December 1580, known as the *Apology,* Orange publicly denounced Philip as a heathen tyrant whom the Netherlands need no longer obey. On July 22, 1581, the member provinces of the Union of Utrecht met in The Hague and formally declared Philip no longer their ruler. They turned in his stead to the French duke of Alençon, Catherine de Médicis's youngest and least satisfactory son, a man to whom the southern provinces had also earlier looked as a possible middle way between Spanish and Calvinist overlordship. All the northern provinces save Holland and Zeeland accepted Alençon as their "sovereign" (Holland and Zeeland distrusted him almost as much as they did Philip II), but with the understanding that he would be only a titular ruler. But Alençon, an ambitious failure, saw this as his one chance at greatness. When he rashly attempted to take actual control of the provinces in 1583, he was deposed and returned to France.

Spanish efforts to reconquer the Netherlands continued into the 1580s. William of Orange was assassinated in July 1584, to be succeeded by his seventeen-year-old son, Maurice (1567–1625), who, with the assistance of England and France, continued Dutch resistance. Fortunately for the Netherlands Philip II began at this time to meddle directly in French and English affairs. He signed a secret treaty with the Guises (the Treaty of Joinville in December 1584) and sent armies under Farnese into France in 1590. Hostilities with the English,

---

William of Orange Defends Himself to the Dutch Estates

Branded an outlaw by Philip II of Spain, the Protestant Dutch Prince William of Orange defended himself to his countrymen in an eloquent address known as the *Apology* (1581).

What could be more gratifying in this world, especially to one engaged in the great and excellent task of securing liberty for a good people oppressed by evil men, than to be mortally hated by one's enemies, who are at the same time enemies of the fatherland, and by their mouths to receive a sweet testimony to one's fidelity to his people and to his obstinate opposition to tyrants and disturbers of the peace? Such is the pleasure that the Spaniards and their adherents have prepared for me in their anxiety to disturb me. They have but gratified me by that infamous proscription by which they sought to ruin me. Not only do I owe to them this favor, but also the occasion to make generally known the equity and justice of my enterprises. . . .

My enemies object that I have "established liberty of conscience." I confess that the glow of fires in which so many poor Christians have been tormented is not an agreeable sight to me, although it may rejoice the eyes of the duke of Alba and the Spaniards; and that it has been my opinion that persecutions should cease in the Netherlands. . . .

They denounce me as a hypocrite, which is absurd enough. . . . As their friend, I told them quite frankly that they were twisting a rope to hang themselves when they began the barbarous policy of persecution. . . .

As for me personally . . . it is my head that they are looking for, and that they have vowed my death by offering such a great sum of money. They say that the war can never come to an end so long as I am among you. . . .

If, gentlemen, you believe that my exile, or even my death, may serve you, I am ready to obey your behests. Here is my head, over which no prince or monarch has authority save you. Dispose of it as you will for the safety and preservation of our commonwealth. But if you judge that such little experience and energy as I have acquired through long and assiduous labors, if you judge that the remainder of my possessions and of my life can be of service to you, I dedicate them to you and to the fatherland.

James Harvey Robinson, *Readings in European History,* Vol. 2 (Boston: Ginn and Co., 1906), pp. 177–179.

who had openly aided the Dutch rebels, also increased, gradually building toward the climax of 1588, when Philip's great Armada was defeated in the English Channel. These new Spanish fronts strengthened the Netherlands as Spain became badly overextended. Spanish preoccupation with France and England permitted the northern provinces to drive out all Spanish soldiers by 1593. In 1596 France and England formally recognized the independence of these provinces. Peace was not, however, concluded with Spain until 1609, when the Twelve Years' Truce gave the northern provinces their virtual independence. Full recognition came finally in the Peace of Westphalia in 1648.

England and Spain (1553–1603)

Mary I

Before Edward VI died in 1553, he agreed to a device to make Lady Jane Grey, the teen-age daughter of a powerful Protestant nobleman and, more important, the granddaughter on her mother's side of Henry VIII's younger sister Mary, his successor in place of the Catholic Mary Tudor (1553–1558). But popular support for the principle of hereditary monarchy was too strong to deprive Mary of her rightful rule. Popular uprisings in London and elsewhere led to Jane Grey's removal from the throne within days of her crowning, and she was eventually beheaded.

Once enthroned, Mary proceeded to act even beyond the worst fears of the Protestants. In 1554 she entered a highly unpopular political marriage with Prince Philip (later Philip II) of Spain, a symbol of militant Catholicism to English Protestants, and pursued at his direction a foreign policy that in 1558 cost England its last enclave on the Continent, Calais.

Mary's domestic measures were equally shocking and even more divisive. During her reign Parliament repealed the Protestant statutes of Edward and reverted to the strict Catholic religious practice of her father, Henry VIII. The great Protestant leaders of the Edwardian age—John Hooper, Hugh Latimer, Miles Coverdale, and Thomas Cranmer—were executed for heresy. Hundreds of Protestants either joined them in martyrdom (282 persons were burned at the stake during Mary's reign) or took flight to the Continent. These "Marian

The execution of Thomas Cranmer (1489–1556), Archbishop of Canterbury under Henry VIII and Edward VI. Cranmer was burned by Queen Mary Tudor (1553–1558) for his leading role in the English Reformation. [New York Public library]

exiles," prominent among whom was the future leader of the Reformation in Scotland, John Knox, settled in Germany and Switzerland, forming especially large communities in Frankfurt, Strasbourg, and Geneva. There they worshiped in their own congregations, wrote tracts justifying armed resistance, and waited for the time when a Protestant counteroffensive could be launched in their homelands.

Elizabeth I

Mary's successor was her half-sister, Elizabeth I (1558–1603), the daughter of Henry VIII and Anne Boleyn, and perhaps the most astute politician of the sixteenth century in both domestic and foreign policy. Assisted by a shrewd adviser, Sir William Cecil (1520–1598; Lord Burghley after 1571), Elizabeth built a true kingdom on the ruins of Mary's reign. Between 1559 and 1563 she and Cecil guided a religious settlement through Parliament that prevented England from being torn asunder by religious differences in the sixteenth century, as the Continent was. A *politique* who subordinated religious to political unity, Elizabeth merged a centralized episcopal system, which she firmly controlled, with broadly defined Protestant doctrine and traditional Catholic rit-

429

ual. In the resulting Anglican church inflexible extremes were not permitted in religion.

In 1559 an Act of Supremacy passed Parliament repealing all the anti-Protestant legislation of Mary Tudor and asserting Elizabeth's right as "supreme governor" over both spiritual and temporal affairs. An Act of Uniformity in the same year mandated a revised version of the second *Book of Common Prayer* (1552) for every English parish. The issuance of the Thirty-Nine Articles on Religion in 1563— which were a revision of Thomas Cranmer's original forty-two—made a moderate Protestantism the official religion within the Church of England.

CATHOLIC AND PROTESTANT EXTREMISTS. Elizabeth hoped to avoid both Catholic and Protestant extremism at the official level by pursuing a middle way. Her first archbishop of Canterbury, Matthew Parker (d. 1575), represented this ideal. But Elizabeth could not prevent the emergence of subversive Catholic and Protestant zealots. When she ascended the throne, Catholics were in the majority in England, and the extremists among them, encouraged by the Jesuits, plotted against her. They were also encouraged and later directly assisted by the Spanish, who were piqued both by Elizabeth's Protestant sympathies and by her refusal to follow the example of her half-

---

An Unknown Contemporary Describes Queen Elizabeth

No sixteenth-century ruler governed more effectively than Elizabeth of England (1558–1603), who was both loved and feared by her subjects. An unknown contemporary has left the following description, revealing not only her intelligence and shrewdness but also something of her tremendous vanity.

I will proceed with the description of the queen's disposition and natural gifts of mind and body, wherein she either matched or exceeded all the princes of her time, as being of a great spirit yet tempered with moderation, in adversity never dejected, in prosperity rather joyful than proud; affable to her subjects, but always with due regard to the greatness of her estate, by reason whereof she was both loved and feared.

In her later time, when she showed herself in public, she was always magnificent in apparel; supposing haply thereby that the eyes of her people (being dazzled by the glittering aspect of her outward ornaments) would not so easily discern the marks of age and decay of natural beauty; and she came abroad the more seldom, to make her presence the more grateful and applauded by the multitude, to whom things rarely seen are in manner as new.

She suffered not, at any time, any suitor to depart discontented from her, and though ofttimes he obtained not that he desired, yet he held himself satisfied with her manner of speech, *which gave hope of success in the second attempt. . . .*

Latin, French, and Italian she could speak very elegantly, and she was able in all those languages to answer ambassadors on the sudden. . . . Of the Greek tongue she was also not altogether ignorant. She took pleasure in reading of the best and wisest histories, and some part of Tacitus' Annals *she herself turned into English for her private exercise. She also translated Boethius'* On the Consolation of Philosophy *and a treatise of Plutarch,* On Curiosity, *with divers others. . . .*

It is credibly reported that not long before her death, she had a great apprehension of her own age and declination by seeing her face (then lean and full of wrinkles) truly represented to her in a glass, which she a good while very earnestly beheld; perceiving thereby how often she had been abused by flatterers (whom she held in too great estimation) that had informed her the contrary.

James Harvey Robinson (Ed.), *Readings in European History,* Vol. 2 (Boston: Ginn and Co. 1906), pp. 191–193.

sister Mary and take Philip II's hand in marriage. Elizabeth remained unmarried throughout her reign, using the possibility of a marriage alliance very much to her diplomatic advantage.

Catholic extremists hoped eventually to replace Elizabeth with Mary Stuart, Queen of Scots. Unlike Elizabeth, who had been declared illegitimate during the reign of her father, Mary Stuart had an unblemished claim to the throne by way of her grandmother Margaret, who was the sister of Henry VIII. Elizabeth acted swiftly against Catholic assassination plots and rarely let emotion override her political instincts. Despite proven cases of Catholic treason and even attempted regicide, however, she executed fewer Catholics during her forty-five years on the throne than Mary Tudor had executed Protestants during her brief five-year reign.

Elizabeth dealt cautiously with the Puritans, who were Protestants working within the national church to "purify" it of every vestige of "popery" and to make its Protestant doctrine more precise. The Puritans had two special grievances: (1) the retention of Catholic ceremony and vestments within the Church of England, which made it appear to the casual observer that no Reformation had occurred, and (2) the continuation of the episcopal system of church governance, which conceived of the English church theologically as the true successor to Rome, while placing it politically under the firm hand of the queen and her compliant archbishop.

Sixteenth-century Puritans were not separatists. Enjoying wide popular support and led by widely respected men like Thomas Cartwright (d. 1603), they worked through Parliament to create an alternative national church of semiautonomous congregations governed by representative presbyteries (hence, Presbyterians), following the model of Calvin and Geneva. Elizabeth dealt firmly but subtly with this group, conceding absolutely nothing that lessened the hierarchical unity of the Church of England and her control over it.

The more extreme Puritans wanted every congregation to be autonomous, a law unto itself, with neither higher episcopal nor presbyterian control. They came to be known as *Congregationalists*. Elizabeth and her second archbishop of Canterbury, John Whitgift (d. 1604), refused to tolerate this group, whose views on independence seemed to them to be patently subversive. The Conventicle Act of 1593 gave

Elizabeth I (1558–1603) painted standing on a map of England in 1592. An astute politician in both foreign and domestic policy, Elizabeth was perhaps the most successful ruler of the sixteenth century. [National Portrait Gallery, London]

such separatists the option of either conforming to the practices of the Church of England or facing exile or death.

DETERIORATION OF RELATIONS WITH SPAIN. A series of events led inexorably to war between England and Spain, despite the sincerest desires on the part of both Philip II and Elizabeth to avoid a direct confrontation.

431

In 1567 the Spanish duke of Alba marched his mighty army into the Netherlands, which was, from the English point of view, simply a convenient staging area for a Spanish invasion of England. Pope Pius V (1566–1572), who favored a military conquest of Protestant England, "excommunicated" Elizabeth for heresy in 1570—a mischievous act that only encouraged both internal resistance and international intrigue against the queen. Two years later the piratical Sea Beggars, many of whom were Englishmen, occupied the port city of Brill in the Netherlands and aroused the surrounding countryside against the Spanish.

Following Don John's demonstration of Spain's awesome seapower at the famous naval battle of Lepanto in 1571, England signed a mutual defense pact with France. Also in the 1570s, Elizabeth's famous seamen, John Hawkins (1532–1595) and Sir Francis Drake (1545?–1596), began to prey regularly on Spanish shipping in the Americas. Drake's circumnavigation of the globe between 1577 and 1580 was one in a series of dramatic demonstrations of English ascendancy on the high seas.

After the Saint Bartholomew's Day massacre, Elizabeth's was the only bosom to which Protestants in France and the Netherlands could cleave. In 1585 she signed the Treaty of Nonsuch, which provided English soldiers and cavalry to the Netherlands. Funds that had previously been funneled covertly to support Henry of Navarre's army in France now flowed openly.

MARY, QUEEN OF SCOTS. These events made a tinderbox of English-Spanish relations. The spark that finally touched it off was Elizabeth's reluctant but necessary execution of Mary, Queen of Scots (1542–1587).

Mary was the daughter of King James V of Scotland, and Mary of Guise and had resided in France from the time she was six years old. This thoroughly French and Catholic queen had returned to Scotland after the death of her husband, the French king Francis II, in 1561, there to find a successful, fervent Protestant Reformation that had won legal sanction the year before in the Treaty of Edinburgh (1560). As hereditary heir to the throne of Scotland, Mary remained queen by divine and human right. She was not intimidated by the Protestants who controlled her realm. She established an international French court culture, the gaiety and sophistication of which impressed many Protestant nobles, whose religion tended to make their lives exceedingly dour.

Mary was closely watched by the ever-vigilant eye of the Scottish reformer John Knox, who fumed publicly and always with effect against the queen's private Mass and Catholic practices, which Scottish law made a capital offense for everyone else. Knox won support in his role of watchdog from Elizabeth and Cecil. Elizabeth personally despised Knox and never forgave him for writing the *First Blast of the Trumpet Against the Terrible Regiment of Women*, a work aimed at provoking a revolt against Mary Tudor but published in the year of Elizabeth's ascent to the throne. Elizabeth and Cecil tolerated Knox because he served their foreign policy, never permitting Scotland to succumb to the young Mary and her French and Catholic ways.

In 1568 a public scandal forced Mary's abdication and flight to her cousin Elizabeth in England. Mary's reputed lover, the earl of Bothwell, was, with cause, suspected of having killed her legal husband, Lord Darnley. When a packed court acquitted Bothwell and he subsequently abducted Mary and married her, the outraged reaction from Protestant nobles forced Mary to surrender the throne to her one-year-old son, who became James VI of Scotland (and, later, Elizabeth's successor as King James I of England). Because of Mary's clear claim to the English throne, she remained an international symbol of a possible Catholic England. Her presence in England, where she resided under house arrest for nineteen years, was of constant discomfort to Elizabeth.

In 1583 Elizabeth's vigilant secretary, Sir Francis Walsingham, uncovered a plot against Elizabeth involving the Spanish ambassador Mendoza, a frequent companion of Mary Stuart. After Mendoza's deportation in January 1584, popular antipathy toward Spain and support for Protestant resistance in France and the Netherlands became massive throughout England.

In 1586 Walsingham uncovered still another plot against Elizabeth, the so-called Babington plot, (after Anthony Babington who was caught seeking Spanish support for an attempt on the Queen's life), and this time he had uncontestable proof of Mary's complicity. Elizabeth believed that the execution of a sovereign, even a dethroned sovereign, weakened royalty everywhere. She was also aware of the outcry that Mary's execution would create through-

The execution of Mary, Queen of Scots. [*Scottish National Portrait Gallery*]

out the Catholic world, and Elizabeth sincerely wanted peace with English Catholics. But she really had no choice in the matter and consented to Mary's execution on February 18, 1587. This event dashed all Catholic hopes for a bloodless reconversion of Protestant England. After the execution of the Catholic queen of Scotland, Pope Sixtus V (1585–1590), who feared Spanish domination almost as much as he abhorred English Protestantism, could no longer withhold public support for a Spanish invasion of England. Philip II ordered his Armada to make ready.

THE ARMADA. Spain's war preparations were interrupted in the spring of 1587 by Sir Francis Drake's successful shelling of the port city of Cadiz, an attack that inflicted heavy damage on Spanish ships and stores. After "singeing the beard of Spain's king," Drake raided the coast of Portugal, further incapacitating the Spanish. The success of these strikes forced the Spanish to postpone their planned invasion of England until the spring of 1588. On May 30 of that year, a mighty fleet of 130 ships bearing twenty-five thousand sailors and soldiers under the command of the duke of Medina-Sidonia set sail for England. But the day belonged completely to the English. The invasion barges that were to transport Spanish

soldiers from the galleons onto English shores were prevented from leaving Calais and Dunkirk. The swifter English and Netherlands ships, assisted by what came to be known as an "English wind," dispersed the waiting Spanish fleet, over one third of which never returned to Spain.

The news of the Armada's defeat gave heart to Protestant resistance everywhere. Although Spain continued to win impressive victories in the 1590s, it never fully recovered from this defeat. Spanish soldiers faced unified and inspired French, English, and Dutch armies. By the time of Philip's death on September 13, 1598, his forces had been successfully rebuffed on all fronts. His seventeenth-century successors—Philip III (1598–1621), Philip IV (1621–1665), and Charles II (1665–1700)— were all inferior leaders who never knew responsibilities equal to Philip's. Nor did Spain ever again know such imperial grandeur. The French soon dominated the Continent, while in the New World the Dutch and the English progressively whittled away Spain's once glorious overseas empire.

Elizabeth died on March 23, 1603, knowing comparatively few national wounds and leaving behind her a strong nation, destined to become an empire on which the sun would not set.

The defeat of the Spanish Armada, a defeat from which Spain never fully recovered. [*The Worshipful Society of the Apothecaries of London*]

The Thirty Years' War (1618–1648)

Preconditions for War

FRAGMENTED GERMANY. In the second half of the sixteenth century Germany was an almost ungovernable land of about 360 autonomous political entities. There were independent secular principalities (duchies, landgraviates, and marches); ecclesiastical principalities (archbishoprics, bishoprics, and abbeys); numerous free cities; and castle regions dominated by knights. The Peace of Augsburg (1555) had given each a significant degree of sovereignty within its own borders. Each levied its own tolls and tariffs and coined its own money, practices that made land travel and trade between the various regions difficult, where not impossible. In addition, many of these little "states" were filled with great power pretensions. Political decentralization and fragmentation characterized Germany as the seventeenth century opened; it was not a unified nation like Spain, England, or even strife-filled France.

Germany had always been Europe's highway; during the Thirty Years' War it became its stomping ground. Europe's rulers pressed in on Germany both for reasons of trade and because some of them held lands or legal privileges within certain German principalities. German princes, in their turn, looked to import and export markets beyond German borders. They opposed any efforts to consolidate the Holy Roman Empire, lest their territorial rights, confirmed by the Peace of Augsburg in the principle *cuius regio, eius religio*, be overturned. German princes were not loath to turn to Catholic France or to the kings of Denmark and Sweden for allies against the Habsburg emperor. The latter's dynastic connections with Spain generated policies that were perceived to be against the best interests of the territorial states of the empire. Even the pope found political reasons for supporting Bourbon France against the menacing international Habsburg kingdom.

After the Council of Trent, Protestants in the empire gravely suspected the operation of an imperial and papal conspiracy to re-create the Catholic Europe of pre-Reformation times. The imperial diet, which was controlled by the German princes, demanded that the constitutional rights of Germans, as set forth in electoral agreements with the emperor since the mid-fourteenth century, be strictly observed, and it effectively countered every move by the emperor to impose his will in the empire. In the late sixteenth century the emperor ruled in the empire only to the degree to which he was prepared to use force of arms against his subjects.

RELIGIOUS DIVISION. Religious conflict accentuated the international and internal political divisions (see Map 11.2). During this period the population within the Holy Roman

RELIGIOUS DIVISIONS ABOUT 1600

MAP 11–2 *By 1600 few could seriously expect Christians to return to a uniform religious allegiance. In Spain and southern Italy Catholicism remained relatively unchallenged, but note the existence of large religious minorities, both Catholic and Protestant, elsewhere.*

Empire was about equally divided between Catholics and Protestants, the latter having perhaps a slight numerical edge by 1600. The terms of the Peace of Augsburg (1555) had attempted to freeze the territorial holdings of the Lutherans and the Catholics. In the intervening years, however, the Lutherans had gained political control in some Catholic areas, as had the Catholics in a few previously Lutheran areas. Such territorial reversals, or the threat of them, only increased the suspicion and antipathy between the two sides.

The Lutherans had been far more successful in securing their rights to worship in Catholic lands than the Catholics had been in securing such rights in Lutheran lands, because the Catholic rulers, who were in a weakened position after the Reformation, had no choice but to make concessions to Protestant communities within their territories. Such communities remained a sore point. Also the Catholics wanted a strict enforcement of the "Ecclesiastical Reservation" of the Peace of Augsburg, which Protestants had made little effort to recognize; the Catholics demanded that all ecclesiastical princes, electors, archbishops, bishops,

BOUNDARY OF THE
HOLY ROMAN EMPIRE

⊠ CATHOLIC
GOVERNMENT

▥ LUTHERAN
GOVERNMENT

░ CALVINIST
GOVERNMENT

150 MI.

150 KM.

THE HOLY ROMAN EMPIRE
ABOUT 1618

MAP 11–3 *On the eve of the Thirty Years' War the Empire was politically and religiously fragmented, as revealed by the somewhat simplified map. Lutherans dominated the north and Catholics the south, while Calvinists controlled the United Provinces and the Palatinate and were important in Switzerland and Brandenburg.*

and abbots who had deserted the Catholic for the Protestant side be immediately deprived of their religious offices and positions and that their ecclesiastical principalities be promptly returned to Catholic control. The Lutherans, and especially the Calvinists in the Palatinate, ignored this stipulation at every opportunity.

There was religious strife in the empire not only between Protestants and Catholics but also between liberal and conservative Lutherans and between Lutherans and the growing numbers of Calvinists. The last half of the sixteenth century was a time of warring Protestant factions within German universities. In addition to the heightened religious strife, the anxiety of religious people of all persuasions was increased by the challenge of the new scientific and material culture that was becoming ascendant in important intellectual and political circles. The age of religious wars was also an age of growing preoccupation with magic, mysticism, witchcraft, and the occult, as fears, doubts, and suspicions stampeded religious feeling.

CALVINISM AND THE PALATINATE. As elsewhere in Europe, Calvinism was the political and religious leaven within the Holy Roman Empire on the eve of the Thirty Years' War. Unrecognized as a legal religion by the Peace of Augsburg, Calvinism had established a strong foothold within the empire when Frederick III (1559–1576), a devout convert to Calvinism, had made it the official religion of his land on becoming Elector Palatine (ruler within the Palatinate) in 1559. Heidelberg became a German Geneva in the 1560s: both a great intellectual center of Calvinism and a staging area for Calvinist penetration into the empire. By 1609 Palatine Calvinists headed a Protestant defensive alliance that received outside support from Spain's sixteenth-century

A seventeenth-century Calvinist Church in the Palatinate. Note that all interior decoration has been removed—there is neither altar nor crucifix. [German National Museum, Nuremberg]

enemies: England, France, and the Netherlands. The Lutherans came to fear the Calvinists almost as much as they did the Catholics. Palatine Calvinists seemed to the Lutherans directly to threaten the Peace of Augsburg—and hence the legal foundation of the Lutheran states—by their bold missionary forays into the empire. The more religiously conservative Lutherans were also shocked by outspoken Calvinist criticism of the doctrine of Christ's real presence in the Eucharist. The Elector Palatine once expressed his disbelief in transubstantiation by publicly shredding the host and mocking it as a "fine God." To Lutherans, such religious disrespect and aggressiveness disgraced the Reformation.

MAXIMILIAN OF BAVARIA AND THE CATHOLIC LEAGUE. If the Calvinists were active within the Holy Roman Empire, so also were their Catholic counterparts, the Jesuits. Staunchly Catholic Bavaria, supported by Spain, became militarily and ideologically for the Counter-Reformation what the Palatinate was for Protestantism. From there the Jesuits launched successful missions throughout the empire, winning such major cities as Strasbourg and Osnabrück back to the Catholic fold by 1600. In 1609 Maximilian, duke of Bavaria, organized a Catholic League to counter a new Protestant alliance that had been formed in the same year under the leadership of the Calvinist Elector Palatine, Frederick IV (1583–1610). When the league fielded a great army under the command of Count Johann von Tilly, the stage was set, both internally and internationally, for the worst of the religious wars, the Thirty Years' War.

Four Periods of War

The war went through four distinguishable periods, and during its course it drew in every major western European nation—at least diplomatically and financially if not in terms of direct military involvement. The four periods were the Bohemian (1618–1625); the Danish (1625–1629); the Swedish (1630–1635); and the Swedish-French (1635–1648).

THE BOHEMIAN PERIOD. The war broke out in Bohemia after the ascent to the Bohemian throne in 1618 of the Habsburg Ferdinand, the archduke of Styria, who was also in the line of succession to the imperial throne. Educated by the Jesuits and a fervent Catholic,

Ferdinand was determined to restore the traditional faith throughout Austria, Bohemia, and Poland—the eastern Habsburg lands.

No sooner had Ferdinand become king of Bohemia than he revoked the religious freedoms of Bohemian Protestants. These freedoms had been in force since 1575 and had even been recently broadened by Emperor Rudolf II (1576–1612) in his Letter of Majesty in 1609. The Protestant nobility in Prague responded to Ferdinand's act in May 1618 by literally throwing his regents out the window. The event has ever since been known as the "defenestration of Prague." The three officials feel fifty feet into a dry moat that, fortunately, was padded with manure, which cushioned their fall and spared their lives. When in the following year Ferdinand became Holy Roman Emperor as Ferdinand II, by the unanimous vote of the seven electors, the Bohemians defiantly deposed him in Prague and declared the Calvinist Elector Palatine, Frederick V (1616–1623), their overlord.

What had begun as a revolt of the Protestant nobility against an unpopular king of Bohemia thereafter escalated into an international war. Spain sent troops to Ferdinand, who found more immediate allies in Maximilian of Bavaria and the opportunistic Lutheran Elector John George I of Saxony (1611–1656). John George saw a sure route to territorial gain by joining in an easy victory over the weaker Elector Palatine. This was not the only time politics and greed would overshadow religion during this long conflict, although Lutheran-Calvinist religious animosity also overrode a common Protestantism. We shall find other instances of such conflicts.

Ferdinand's army under Tilly routed Frederick V's troops at the Battle of White Mountain in 1620. By 1622 Ferdinand had managed not only to subdue and re-Catholicize Bohemia but to conquer the Palatinate as well. While he and his allies enjoyed the spoils of these victories, the fighting extended into northwestern Germany as the duke of Bavaria pressed the conflict. Laying claim to land as he went, he continued to pursue Ernst von Mansfeld, one of Frederick's surviving mercenary generals, into the north.

THE DANISH PERIOD. The emperor's subjugation of Bohemia and the Palatinate and Maximilian's forays into northwestern Germany raised new fears that a reconquest and re-Catholicization of the whole empire now loomed. This was in fact precisely Ferdinand II's design. Encouraged by the English, the French, and the Dutch, the Lutheran King Christian IV (1588–1648) of Denmark, who already held territory within the empire as the duke of Holstein and was eager to extend Danish influence over the coastal towns of the North Sea, picked up the Protestant banner of resistance, opening the Danish period of the conflict (1625–1629). Christian's forces were not, however, up to the challenge. Entering Germany with his army in 1626, he was quickly humiliated by Maximilian and forced to retreat back into Denmark.

As military success made Maximilian stronger and more difficult to control, Ferdinand II sought a more pliant tool for his policies by hiring a powerful, complex mercenary,

Albrecht of Wallenstein (1583–1634). Wallenstein was another opportunistic Protestant who had gained a great deal of territory by joining Ferdinand during the conquest of Bohemia. A brilliant and ruthless military strategist, Wallenstein not only completed Maximilian's work by bringing the career of the elusive Ernst von Mansfeld to an end but also penetrated into Denmark with an occupying army. By 1628 Wallenstein commanded a crack army of over 100,000 and became a law unto himself within the empire, completely outside the emperor's control. Pandora's box had now been fully opened.

Wallenstein broke Protestant resistance so successfully that Ferdinand issued the Edict of Restitution in 1629. This proclamation dramatically reasserted the Catholic safeguards of the

This Protestant broadsheet shows two monsters, wearing the papal crown and a cardinal's hat, spewing Catholic priests on the city of Augsburg. Under the Edict of Restitution (1629), Augsburg was returned to Catholic jurisdiction. [British Library]

Peace of Augsburg (1555). It reaffirmed the illegality of Calvinism—a completely unrealistic move in 1629—and it ordered the return of all church lands acquired by the Lutherans since 1552, an equally unrealistic mandate. Compliance with the latter demand would have involved the return of no less than sixteen bishoprics and twenty-eight cities and towns to Catholic allegiance. Although based on legal precedent and certainly within Ferdinand's power to command, the expectations of the edict were not adjusted to the political realities of 1629. It struck panic into the hearts of Protestants and Habsburg opponents everywhere, who now saw clearly the emperor's plan to re-create a Catholic Europe. Resistance quickly reignited.

THE SWEDISH PERIOD. Gustavus Adolphus of Sweden (1611–1632), a deeply pious king of a unified Lutheran nation, became the new leader of Protestant forces within the empire, opening the Swedish period of the war (1630–1635). He was handsomely bankrolled by two very interested bystanders: the French minister Cardinal Richelieu, whose foreign policy was to protect French interests by keeping Habsburg armies tied down in Germany, and the Dutch, who had not forgotten Spanish Habsburg domination in the sixteenth century. The Swedish king found ready allies in the electors of Brandenburg and Saxony and soon won a smashing victory at Breitenfeld in 1630. The Protestant victory at Breitenfeld so dramatically reversed the course of the war that it has been regarded as the most decisive, although far from the final, engagement of the long conflict.

One of the reasons for the overwhelming Swedish victory at Breitenfeld was the military genius of Gustavus Adolphus. The Swedish king brought a new mobility to warfare by having both his infantry and his cavalry master fire and charge tactics. At six deep, his infantry squares were smaller than the traditional ones, and he filled them with equal numbers of musketeers and pikemen. His cavalry also alternated pistol shot with sword charges. His artillery was lighter and more mobile in battle. Each unit of his army—infantry, cavalry, and artillery—had *both* defensive and offensive capability and could quickly change from one to the other.

Gustavus Adolphus died at the hands of Wallenstein's forces during the Battle of Lützen (November 1632)—a very costly engagement

for both sides that created a brief standstill. Ferdinand had long been resentful of Wallenstein's independence, although he was the major factor in imperial success. In 1634 Ferdinand had Wallenstein assassinated. By that time Wallenstein had not only served his purpose for the emperor, but, ever opportunistic, he was even trying openly to strike bargains with the Protestants for his services. The Wallenstein episode is a telling commentary on this war without honor. Despite the deep religious motivations, greed and political gain were the real forces at work in the Thirty Years' War, and even allies that owed one another their success were not above treating each other as mortal enemies.

In the Peace of Prague in 1635 the German Protestant states, led by Saxony, reached a compromise agreement with Ferdinand. The Swedes, however, received continued support from France and the Netherlands. Desiring to maximize their investment in the war, they refused to join the agreement. Their resistance to settlement plunged the war into its fourth and most devastating phase, the Swedish-French period (1635–1648).

THE SWEDISH-FRENCH PERIOD. The French openly entered the war in 1635, sending men and munitions as well as financial subsidies. After their entrance the war dragged on for thirteen years, with French, Swedish, and Spanish soldiers looting the length and breadth of Germany—warring, it seemed, simply for the sake of warfare itself. The Germans, long weary of the devastation, were too disunited to repulse the foreign armies; they simply watched and suffered. By the time peace talks began in the Westphalian cities of Münster and Osnabrück in 1644, an estimated one third of the German population had died as a direct result of the war. It was the worst European catastrophe since the Black Death of the fourteenth century.

The Treaty of Westphalia

The Treaty of Westphalia in 1648 brought all hostilities within the Holy Roman Empire to an end. It rescinded Ferdinand's Edict of Restitution and firmly reasserted the major feature of the religious settlement of the Peace of Augsburg (1555), as the ruler of each land was again permitted to determine the religion of his land. The treaty also gave the Calvinists their long-sought legal recognition. The indepen-

The horror of the Thirty Years' War is captured in this painting by Jan Brueghel (1568–1625) and Sebastien Vranx (1573–1647). During breaks in the actual fighting, marauding armies ravaged the countryside, destroying villages and massacring the rural population. [*Kunsthistorisches Museum, Vienna*]

dence of the Swiss Confederacy and the United Provinces of Holland, long recognized in fact, was now proclaimed in law. And the treaty elevated Bavaria to the rank of an elector state. The provisions of the treaty made the German princes supreme over their principalities. Yet, as guarantors of the treaty, Sweden and France found many occasions to meddle in German affairs until the century's end, France to considerable territorial gain. Brandenburg-Prussia emerged as the most powerful north German state.

France and Spain remained at war outside the empire until 1659, when French victories forced on the Spanish the humiliating Treaty of the Pyrenees. Thereafter France became Europe's dominant power, and the once vast Habsburg kingdom waned.

By confirming the territorial sovereignty of Germany's many political entities, the Treaty of Westphalia perpetuated German division and political weakness into the modern period. Only two German states attained any international significance during the seventeenth century: Austria and Brandenburg-Prussia. The petty regionalism within the empire also reflected on a small scale the drift of larger European politics. In the seventeenth century, distinctive nation-states, each with its own political, cultural, and religious identity, reached maturity and firmly established the competitive nationalism of the modern world.

C. V. Wedgwood described the outcome of the Thirty Years' War:

After the expenditure of so much human life to so little purpose, men might have grasped the essential futility of putting the beliefs of the mind to the judgment of the sword. Instead, they rejected religion as an object to fight for and found others. . . . The war

441

EUROPE IN 1648

SWEDISH
DOMINIONS

BRANDENBURG-
PRUSSIA

SPANISH
MONARCHY

AUSTRIA
HAPSBURGS

CHURCH
LANDS

NORWAY

Bergen

Christiana

FINLAND

S W E D

Reval

ESTON

Stavanger

KINGDOM OF
DENMARK
AND
NORWAY

Stockholm

LIVON

SCOTLAND

Edinburgh

NORTH

DENMARK

Copenhagen

BALTIC SEA

Riga

COURLAND

Memel

SEA

Danzig

EA
PRUS

Belfast

York

SCHLESWIG

P

IRELAND

Dublin

BOUNDARY OF
THE EMPIRE

HOLSTEIN

Posen

BRANDEN-
BURG

Warsaw

ENGLAND

Cork

WALES

UNITED
PROVINCES

SAXONY

Breslau

SILESIA

Cracow

ATLANTIC

London

SPANISH
NETH.

MINOR

Prague

G

Bristol

Brussels

HESSE

GERMAN

BOHEMIA

Plymouth

STATES

MORAVIA

Rouen

Reims

BAVARIA

HUNGARY

Pressburg

Paris

Orleans

AUSTRIA HAPSBURG

Vienna

Budap

OCEAN

Nantes

Tours

FRANCHE
COMTÉ

HUNGA

FRANCE

SWITZ.

SLAVONIA

Lyons

SAVOY

VENICE

CROATIA

SAVA

Belgr

PIED-
MONT

MILAN.

Venice

Venice

BOSNIA

SER

Bordeaux

LANGUEDOC

AVIGNON

PAR.

MOD.

Bologna

(VEN.)

Spalato

MONT
NEGR

Toulouse

Genoa

LUCCA

PAPAL
STATES

(VEN.)

REP.
RAGUSA

Marseilles

TUSCANY

León

NAVARRE

Burgos

Oporto

CASTILE

Saragossa

Salamanca

ARAGON

Madrid

Barcelona

Toledo

SPAIN

PORTUGAL

Lisbon

BALEARIC IS.

Cordova

Seville

Granada

Cadiz

Tangier
(PORT.)

Ceuta (SP.)

FEZ & MOROCCO

Algiers

ALGERIA

CORSICA
(GEN.)

ITALY

Rome

SARDINIA
(SP.)

Capua

Naples

KINGDOM OF THE
TWO SICILIES

MEDITERRANEAN

Cattaro
(VEN.)

ALBA

Bari

SICILY

SEA

Tunis
(OTT.)

SEA

MAP 11–4 *At the end of the Thirty Years' War Spain still had extensive possessions. Austria and Brandenburg-Prussia were prominent, the independence of the United Provinces and Switzerland was recognized, and Sweden held important river mouths in north Germany.*

solved no problem. Its effects, both immediate and indirect, were either negative or disastrous. Morally subversive, economically destructive, socially degrading, confused in its causes, devious in its course, futile in its result, it is the outstanding example in European history of meaningless conflict.[2]

Witchcraft and Witch-hunts in Early Modern Europe

Between 1400 and 1700 courts sentenced an estimated 70,000–100,000 people to death for harmful magic (*malificium*) and diabolical witchcraft. In addition to inflicting harm on their neighbors, these witches were said to attend mass meetings known as *sabbats*, to which they were believed to fly. They were also accused of indulging in sexual orgies with the Devil, who appeared at such gatherings in animal form, most often as a he-goat. Still other charges against them were cannibalism (they were alleged to be especially fond of small Christian children) and a variety of ritual acts and practices designed to insult every Christian belief and value.

Where did such beliefs come from? Their roots were in both popular and elite cultures, especially clerical culture.

In village societies, so-called cunning folk played a positive role in helping people cope with calamity. People turned to them for help when such natural disasters as plague and famine struck or when such physical disabilities as lameness or inability to conceive offspring befell either them or their animals. The cunning folk provided consolation and gave people hope that such natural calamities might be averted or reversed by magical means. In this way they provided an important service and kept village life moving forward.

Possession of magical powers, for good or ill, made one an important person within village society. Not surprisingly, claims to such powers seem most often to have been made by the

[2]In T. K. Rabb, *The Thirty Years' War: Problems of Motive, Extent and Effect* (Boston: D. C. Heath, 1964), pp. 18–19.

Four witches who were burned at the stake at Wittenberg in 1540. The four were accused of commerce with the devil and of directing magic against their neighbors. [*Hacker Art Books*]

their traditional functions within society. Fear of demons and the Devil, which the clergy actively encouraged, allowed them to assert their moral authority over people and to enforce religious discipline and conformity.

In the late thirteenth century the church declared that only its priests possessed legitimate magical power. Inasmuch as such power was not human, theologians reasoned, it had to come either from God or from the Devil. If it came from God, then it was obediently confined to and exercised only on behalf of the church. Those who practiced magic outside the church evidently derived their power from the Devil. From such reasoning grew accusations of "pacts" between non-Christian magicians and Satan. This made the witch-hunts a life-and-death struggle against Christian society's worst heretics and foes, those who had directly sworn allegiance to the Devil himself.

The church based its intolerance of magic outside its walls on sincere belief in and fear of the Devil. But attacking witches was also a way for established Christian society to extend its power and influence into new areas. To accuse, try, and execute witches was also a declaration of moral and political authority over a village or territory. As the "cunning folk" were local spiritual authorities, revered and feared by people, their removal became a major step in the establishment of a Christian beachhead in village society.

A good 80 per cent of the victims of witch-hunts were women, the vast majority between forty-five and sixty years of age and widowed. This fact has suggested to some that misogyny fueled the witch-hunts. Based in male hatred and sexual fear of women, and occurring at a time when women threatened to break out from under male control, witch-hunts, it is argued, were simply woman-hunts. Older women may, however, have been vulnerable for more basic social reasons. As a largely nonproductive and dependent social group, ever in need of public assistance, older and widowed women became natural targets for the peculiar "social engineering" of the witch-hunts.

It may, however, be the case that gender played a purely circumstantial role. Because of their economic straits, more women than men laid claim to the supernatural powers that made them influential in village society. For this reason they found themselves on the front lines in disproportionate numbers when the church declared war against all who practiced magic without its blessing. Also the involve-

people most in need of security and influence, namely, the old and the impoverished, especially single or widowed women. But witch beliefs in village society may also have been a way of defying urban Christian society's attempts to impose its laws and institutions on the countryside. From this perspective, village Satanism became a fanciful substitute for an impossible social revolt, a way of spurning the values of one's new masters. It is also possible, although unlikely, that witch beliefs in rural society had a foundation in local fertility cults, whose semipagan practices, designed to ensure good harvests, acquired the features of diabolical witchcraft under church persecution.

Popular belief in magic was the essential foundation of the great witch-hunts of the sixteenth and seventeenth centuries. Had ordinary people not believed that certain gifted individuals could aid or harm others by magical means, and had they not been willing to make accusations, the hunts could never have occurred. But the contribution of learned society was equally great. The Christian clergy also practiced magic, that of the holy sacraments, and the exorcism of demons had been one of

444

Why More Women Than Men Are Witches

The *Hammer of Witches* (1486), written by two Dominican monks, Heinrich Krämer and Jacob Sprenger, was sanctioned by Pope Innocent VIII as an official guide to the detection and punishment of witches. Here Krämer and Sprenger explain why the great majority of witches are women rather then men.

Why are there more superstitious women than men? The first [reason] is that they are more credulous; and since the chief aim of the devil is to corrupt faith, therefore he rather attacks them. . . . The second reason is that women are naturally more impressionable and ready to receive the influence of a disembodied spirit. . . . The third reason is that they have slippery tongues and are unable to conceal from their fellow-women those things which by evil arts they know; and since they are weak, they find an easy and secret manner of vindicating themselves by witchcraft. . . . [Therefore] since women are feebler both in mind and body, it is not surprising that they should come more under the spell of witchcraft. For as regards intellect, or the understanding of spiritual things, they seem to be of a different nature from men, a fact which is vouched for by the logic of the authorities, backed by various examples from the Scriptures. . . .

But the natural reason [for woman's proclivity to witchcraft] is that she is more carnal than a man, as is clear from her many carnal abominations. And it should be noted that there was a defect in the formation of the first woman, since she was formed from a bent rib, that is, a rib of the breast, which is bent as it were in a contrary direction to a man. And since through this defect she is an imperfect animal, she always deceives. . . .

As to her other mental quality, her natural will, when she hates someone whom she formerly loved, then she seethes with anger and impatience in her whole soul, just as the tides of the sea are always heaving and boiling. . . .

Truly the most powerful cause which contributes to the increase of witches is the woeful rivalry between married folk and unmarried women and men. This [jealousy or rivalry] is so even among holy women, so what must it be among the others . . . ?

Just as through the first defect in their intelligence they are more prone [than men] to abjure the faith, so through their second defect of inordinate affections and passions they search for, brood over, and inflict various vengeances, either by witchcraft or by some other means. Wherefore it is no wonder that so great a number of witches exist in this sex. . . . [Indeed, witchcraft] is better called the heresy of witches than of wizards, since the name is taken from the more powerful party [that is, the greater number, who are women]. Blessed be the Highest who has so far preserved the male sex from so great a crime.

Malleus Maleficarum, trans. by Montague Summers (Bungay, Suffolk: John Rodker, 1928), pp. 41–47.

ment of many of these women in midwifery associated them with the deaths of beloved wives and infants and thus made them targets of local resentment and accusations. Both the church and their neighbors were prepared to think and say the worst about these women. It was a deadly combination.

Why did the witch-hunts come to an end in the seventeenth century? Many factors played a role. The emergence of a new, more scientific worldview made it difficult to believe in the powers of witches. When in the seventeenth century mind and matter came to be viewed as two independent realities, words and thoughts lost the ability to affect things. A witch's curse was merely words. With advances in medicine and the beginning of insurance companies, people learned to rely on themselves when faced with natural calamity and physical affliction and no longer searched for supernatural causes and solutions. Witch-hunts also tended to get out of hand. Accused witches sometimes alleged that important townspeople had attended sabbats; even the judges could be so accused. At this point the trials ceased to serve the purposes of those who were conducting

A Confession of Witchcraft

A confession of witchcraft is here exacted from a burgomaster during a witch panic in seventeenth-century Bamberg in central Germany. The account, an official transcript, accurately describes the process by which an innocent victim was brought, step by step, to confession—from the confrontation with his accusers to the application of increasingly painful tortures. By at last concurring in the accusation (albeit reluctantly and only after torture), the victims were believed by their executioners to be saving the victims' souls as they lost their bodies. Having the victims' own confession may also have helped allay the executioners' consciences.

On Wednesday, June 28, 1628, was examined without torture Johannes Junius, Burgomaster at Bamberg, on the charge of witchcraft: how and in what fashion he had fallen into that vice. Is fifty-five years old, and was born at Nieder-waysich in the Wetterau. Says he is wholly innocent, knows nothing of the crime, has never in his life renounced God; says that he is wronged before God and the world, would like to hear of a single human being who has seen him at such gatherings [as the witch sabbats].

Confrontation of Dr. Georg Adam Haan. Tells him to his face that he will stake his life on it, that he saw him, Junius, a year and a half ago at a witch-gathering in the electoral council-room, where they ate and drank. Accused denies the same wholly.

Confronted with Hopffens Elsse. Tells him likewise that he was on Haupts-moor at a witch-dance; but first the holy wafer was desecrated. Junius denies. Hereupon he was told that his accomplices had confessed against him and he was given time for thought.

On Friday, June 30, 1628, the aforesaid Junius was again without torture exhorted to confess, but again confessed nothing, whereupon, . . . since he would confess nothing, he was put to the torture, and first the

Thumb-screws were applied [both hands bound together, so that the blood ran out at the nails and everywhere]. Says he has never denied God his Saviour nor suffered himself to be otherwise baptized [i.e., initiated into devilish rites]. Will again stake his life on it; feels no pain in the thumb-screws.

Leg-screws. Will confess absolutely nothing; knows nothing about it. He has never renounced God; will never do such a thing; has never been guilty of this vice; feels likewise no pain. Is stripped and examined; on his right side is found a bluish mark, like a clover leaf, is thrice pricked therein, but feels no pain and no blood flows out.

Strappado [the binding of the prisoner's hands behind the back, and pulling them up by a rope attached to a pulley, resulting in the slow dislocation of the shoulders]. Says he never renounced God; God will not forsake him; if he were such a wretch he would not let himself be so tortured; God must show some token of his innocence. He knows nothing about witchcraft. . . .

On July 5, the above named Junius is without torture, but with urgent persuasions, exhorted to confess, and as last he . . . confesses.

Translations and Reprints from the Original Sources of European History, Vol. 3 (Philadelphia: University of Pennsylvania, 1912), pp. 23–24.

them. They not only became dysfunctional but threatened anarchy. Finally, the Reformation may have contributed to an attitude of mind that put the Devil in a more manageable perspective. Protestants ridiculed the sacramental magic of the old church as superstition and directed their faith to a sovereign God absolutely supreme over time and eternity. Even the Devil served God's purposes and acted only with His permission. Ultimately God was the only significant spiritual force in the universe. This belief made the Devil a less fearsome creature. "One little word can slay him," Luther wrote of the Devil in the great hymn of the Reformation, and he often joked outrageously about witches.

Suggested Readings

FERNAND BRAUDEL, *The Mediterranean and the Mediterranean World in the Age of Philip the Second*, Vols. 1 and 2 (1976). Widely acclaimed work of a French master historian.

NATALIE Z. DAVIS, *Society and Culture in Early Modern France* (1975). Essays on popular culture.

RICHARD DUNN, *The Age of Religious Wars 1559–1689* (1979). Excellent brief survey of every major conflict.

J. H. ELLIOTT, *Europe Divided 1559–1598* (1968). Direct, lucid narrative account.

G. R. ELTON, *England Under the Tudors* (1955). Masterly account.

JULIAN H. FRANKLIN, (Ed. and Trans.), *Constitutionalism and Resistance in the Sixteenth Century: Three Treatises by Hotman, Beza, and Mornay* (1969). Three defenders of the right of people to resist tyranny.

PIETER GEYL, *The Revolt of the Netherlands, 1555–1609* (1958). The authoritative survey.

RICHARD KIECKHEFER, *European Witch Trials: Their Foundations in Popular and Learned Culture 1300–1500* (1976).

ALAN KORS AND EDWARD PETERS (Eds.), *European Witchcraft, 1100–1700* (1972).

CHRISTINA LARNER, *Enemies of God: The Witchhunt in Scotland* (1981).

JOHN LYNCH, *Spain Under the Hapsburg I: 1516–1598* (1964). Political narrative.

J. RUSSELL MAJOR, *Representative Institutions in Renaissance France* (1960). An essay in French constitutional history.

GARRETT MATTINGLY, *The Armada* (1959). A masterpiece and novel-like in style.

J. E. NEALE, *The Age of Catherine de Medici* (1962). Short, concise summary.

JOHN NEALE, *Queen Elizabeth I* (1934). Superb biography.

THEODORE K. RABB (Ed.), *The Thirty Years' War* (1972). Excerpts from the scholarly debate over the war's significance.

JASPER G. RIDLEY, *John Knox* (1968). Large, detailed biography.

J. H. M. SALMON (Ed.), *The French Wars of Religion: How Important Were the Religious Factors?* (1967). Scholarly debate over the relation between politics and religion.

J. H. M. SALMON, *Society in Crisis: France in the Sixteenth Century* (1976).

ALFRED SOMAN (Ed.), *The Massacre of St. Bartholomew's Day: Reappraisals and Documents* (1974). Results of an international symposium on the anniversary of the massacre.

KEITH THOMAS, *Religion and the Decline of Magic* (1971).

C. V. WEDGWOOD, *The Thirty Years' War* (1939). The authoritative account.

C. V. WEDGWOOD, *William the Silent* (1944). Excellent political biography.

Louis XIV (1643–1715) was the dominant European monarch in the second half of the seventeenth century. His rule became the prototype of the modern centralized state. [Giraudon]

Constitutional Crisis and Settlement in Stuart England

BETWEEN 1603 AND 1715 England experienced the most tumultuous years of its long history. In this period Puritan resistance to the Elizabethan religious settlement merged with fierce parliamentary opposition to the aspirations to absolute monarchy of the Stuart kings. During these years no fewer than three foreigners occupied the English throne, and between 1649 and 1660 England was without a king altogether. Yet by the end of this century of crisis, England provided a model to Europe of limited monarchy, parliamentary government, and measured religious toleration.

James I

The first of England's foreign monarchs was James VI of Scotland (the son of Mary Stuart, Queen of Scots), who in 1603 succeeded the childless Elizabeth as James I of England. This first Stuart king inherited not only the crown but also a royal debt of almost one-half million pounds, a fiercely divided church, and a Parliament already restive over the extent of his predecessor's claims to royal authority. Under James each of these problems worsened. The new king utterly lacked tact, was ignorant of English institutions, and strongly advocated the divine right of kings, a subject on which he had written a book in 1598 entitled *A Trew Law of Free Monarchies*. He rapidly alienated both Parliament and the politically powerful Puritans.

The breach with Parliament was opened by James's seeming usurpation of the power of the purse. Royal debts, his own extravagance, and an inflation he could not control made it necessary for the king to be constantly in quest of additional revenues. These he sought largely by levying—solely on the authority of ill-defined privileges claimed to be attached to the office of king—new custom duties known as *impositions*. These were a version of the older such duties known as *tonnage* and *poundage*. Parliament resented such independent efforts to raise revenues as an affront to its power, and the result was a long and divisive court struggle between the king and Parliament.

As the distance between king and Parliament widened, the religious problems also worsened. The Puritans, who were prominent among the lesser landed gentry and within

12

England and France in the Seventeenth Century

Parliament, had hoped that James's experience with the Scottish Presbyterian church and his own Protestant upbringing would incline him to favor their efforts to "purify" the Anglican church. Since the days of Elizabeth the Puritans had sought to eliminate elaborate religious ceremonies and to replace the hierarchical episcopal system of church governance with a more representative presbyterian form like that of the Calvinist churches on the Continent. In January 1604 they had their first direct dealing with the new king. James responded in that month to a statement of Puritan grievances, the so-called Millenary Petition, at a special religious conference at Hampton Court. To the dismay of the Puritans the king firmly declared his intention to maintain and even enhance the Anglican episcopacy. "A Scottish presbytery," he snorted, "agreeth as well with monarchy as God and the devil. No bishops, no king." Nonconformists were clearly forewarned.

Both sides departed the conference with their worst suspicions of one another largely confirmed, and as the years passed, the distrust between them only deepened. It was during James's reign in 1620 that Puritan separatists founded Plymouth Colony in Cape Cod Bay in North America, preferring flight from England to Anglican conformity. The Hampton Court conference did, however, sow one fruitful seed. A commission was appointed to render a new translation of the Bible, a mission fulfilled in 1611 when the eloquent Authorized or King James Version of the Bible was published.

Though he inherited major political and religious difficulties, James also created special problems for himself. His court became a center of scandal and corruption. He governed by favorites, the most influential of whom was the duke of Buckingham, whom rumor made the king's homosexual lover. Buckingham controlled royal patronage and openly sold peerages and titles to the highest bidders—a practice that angered the nobility because it cheapened their rank. James's pro-Spanish foreign policy also displeased the English. In 1604 he concluded a much-needed peace with Spain, England's chief adversary during the second half of the sixteenth century. His subjects viewed it as a sign of pro-Catholic sentiment. James further increased suspicions when he attempted unsuccessfully to relax the penal laws against Catholics. The English had not forgotten the brutal reign of Mary Tudor and the acts of treason by Catholics during Elizabeth's reign. In 1618 James hesitated, not unwisely, to rush English troops to the aid of Protestants in Germany at the outbreak of the Thirty Years' War. This hesitation caused his loyalty to the Anglican church to be openly questioned by some. In the king's last years, as his health failed and the reins of government were increasingly given over to his son Charles and Buckingham, parliamentary power and Protestant sentiment combined to undo his pro-Spanish foreign policy, which had also failed to meet the king's own expectations. In 1624 England entered a continental war against Spain.

Charles I

Charles I (1625–1649) flew even more brazenly in the face of Parliament and the Puritans than did his father. Unable to gain adequate funds from Parliament for the Spanish war, Charles, like his father, resorted to extraparliamentary measures. He levied new tariffs and duties, attempted to collect discontinued taxes, and even subjected the English people to a so-called forced loan (a tax theoretically to be repaid), imprisoning those who refused to pay. Troops in transit to war zones were quartered in private English homes.

When Parliament met in 1628, its members were furious. Taxes were being illegally collected for a war that was going badly for England and that now, through royal blundering, involved France as well as Spain. Parliament expressed its displeasure by making the king's request for new funds conditional on his recognition of the Petition of Right. This major document of constitutional freedom declared that henceforth there should be no forced loans or taxation without the consent of Parliament, that no freeman should be imprisoned without due cause, and that troops should not be billeted in private homes. Though Charles agreed to the petition, there was little confidence that he would keep his word.

In August 1628 Charles's chief minister, Buckingham, with whom Parliament had been in open dispute since 1626, was assassinated. His death, while sweet to many, did not resolve the hostility between king and Parliament. In January 1629 Parliament further underscored its resolve to limit royal prerogative. It declared that religious innovations leading to "popery"— Charles's high-church policies were meant— and the levying of taxes without parliamentary consent were acts of treason. Perceiving that

Parliament Attacks Charles I's Royal Abuses of His Subjects

The tension between King Charles I (1625–1649) and Parliament had very few causes that did not go back to earlier reigns. The Petition of Right can, therefore, be seen as a general catalog of reasons for opposing arbitrary royal power. Specifically, angered by Charles and his levying of new taxes and other revenue-gathering devices, his coercion of freemen, and his quartering of troops in transit in private homes, Parliament refused to grant the king any funds until he rescinded such practices by recognizing the Petition of Right (June 7, 1628). Here is the Petition and the king's reply.

[The Lords Spiritual and Temporal, and Commons in Parliament assembled] do humbly pray your Most Excellent Majesty, that no man hereafter be compelled to make or yield any gift, loan, benevolence, tax, or such like charge, without common consent by Act of Parliament; and that none be called to make answer, or take such oath, or to give attendance, or be confined, or otherwise molested or disquieted concerning the same, or for refusal thereof; and that no freeman, in any such manner as is beforementioned, be imprisoned or detained; and that your Majesty will be pleased to remove the said soldiers and mariners [who have been quartered in private homes], and that your people may not be so burdened in time to come; and that the foresaid commissions for proceeding by martial law, may be revoked and annulled; and that hereafter no commissions of like nature may

issue forth to any person or persons whatsoever, to be executed as aforesaid, lest by colour of them any of your Majesty's subjects be destroyed or put to death, contrary to the laws and franchise of the land.

All which they most humbly pray of your Most Excellent Majesty, as their rights and liberties according to the laws and statutes of this realm.

[The King's reply: The King willeth that right be done according to the laws and customs of the realm; and that the statutes be put in due execution, that his subjects may have no cause to complain of any wrong or oppressions, contrary to their just rights and liberties, to the preservation whereof he holds himself as well obliged as of his prerogative.]

Samuel R. Gardiner, Ed. *The Constitutional Documents of the Puritan Revolution* (Oxford, England: Clarendon Press, 1889), pp. 4–5.

things were getting out of hand, Charles promptly dissolved Parliament and did not recall it again until 1640, when war with Scotland forced him to do so.

To conserve his limited resources, Charles made peace with France and Spain in 1629 and 1630, respectively. His chief minister, Thomas Wentworth (after 1640, earl of Stafford), instituted a policy known as *thorough*, that is, strict efficiency and administrative centralization in government. This policy aimed at absolute royal control of England and required for its success the king's ability to operate independently of Parliament. Every legal fundraising device was exploited to the full. Neglected laws suddenly were enforced, and existing taxes were extended into new areas. An example of the latter tactic was the inland col-

lection of "ship money." This tax normally was levied only on coastal areas to pay for naval protection, but after 1634 it was gradually applied to the whole of England, interior and coastal towns alike. A great landowner named John Hampden unsuccessfully challenged its extension in a close legal contest. Although the king prevailed, it was a costly victory, for it deepened the animosity toward him among the powerful landowners, who both elected and sat in Parliament.

Charles had neither the royal bureaucracy nor the standing army to rule as an absolute monarch. This became abundantly clear when he and his religious minister, William Laud (1573–1645; after 1633, the archbishop of Canterbury), provoked a war with Scotland. They tried to impose the English episcopal sys-

Charles I (1625–1649) and his family. Both children in this painting became king. The future Charles II (1660–1685) is clasping his father's knee; the future James II (1685–1688) is in the arms of his mother, Queen Henrietta Marie, the daughter of Henry IV of France. [Metropolitan Museum of Art]

tem and a prayer book almost identical to the Anglican *Book of Common Prayer* on the Scots as they had done throughout England. From his position within the Court of High Commission, Laud had already radicalized the Puritans by denying them the right to publish and preach.

Facing resistance from the Scots, Charles was forced to seek financial assistance from a Parliament that opposed his policies almost as much as it opposed the foreign invaders. Led by John Pym (1584–1643), Parliament refused even to consider funds for war until the king agreed to redress a long list of political and religious grievances. The result was the king's immediate dissolution of Parliament—hence its name, the Short Parliament (April–May 1640). When the Presbyterian Scots invaded England and defeated an English army

at the battle of Newburn in the summer of 1640, Charles found himself forced to reconvene Parliament. This time it was on the latter's terms and for what would be a long and most fateful duration.

THE LONG PARLIAMENT. The landowners and the merchant classes represented by Parliament had resented the king's financial measures and paternalistic rule for some time. To this resentment was added fervent Puritan opposition. Hence the Long Parliament (1640–1660) acted with widespread support and general unanimity when it convened in November 1640. Both the earl of Stafford and Archbishop Laud were impeached by the House of Commons. Disgraced and convicted by a Parliamentary bill of attainder (a judgment of treason entailing loss of civil rights), Stafford was executed in 1641. Laud was imprisoned and later executed (1645). The Court of Star Chamber and the Court of High Commission, royal instruments of political and religious "thorough," respectively, were abolished. The levying of new taxes without consent of Parliament and the inland extension of ship money now became illegal. Finally, it was resolved that no more than three years should elapse between meetings of Parliament and that Parliament could not be dissolved without its own consent.

Marxist historians have seen in these measures a major triumph of the "bourgeoisie" over the aristocracy. But lesser aristocratic groups (the gentry) were actually divided between the parliamentary and royal camps, so more was obviously at issue than simple class warfare. The accomplishment of the Long Parliament was to issue a firm and lasting declaration of the political and religious rights of the many English people represented in Parliament, both high and low, against autocractic royal government.

There remained division within Parliament over the precise direction of religious reform. Both moderate Puritans (the Presbyterians) and extreme Puritans (the Independents) wanted the complete abolition of the episcopal system and the *Book of Common Prayer*. The majority Presbyterians sought to reshape England religiously along Calvinist lines, with local congregations subject to higher representative governing bodies (presbyteries). Independents wanted every congregation to be its own final authority. There was also a considerable number of conservatives in both houses who were determined to preserve the English church in its current form, although their numbers fell dramatically after 1642, when those who sympathized with the present Anglican church departed the House of Commons.

The division within Parliament was further intensified in October 1641, when a rebellion erupted in Ireland requiring an army to suppress it. Pym and his followers, loudly reminding the House of Commons of the king's past misdeeds, argued that Charles could not be trusted with an army and that Parliament should become the commander-in-chief of English armed forces. Parliamentary conservatives, who had winced once at Puritan religious reforms, winced thrice at this bold departure from English practice. On December 1, 1641, Parliament presented Charles with the "Grand Remonstrance," a more-than-200-article summary of popular and parliamentary grievances against the crown.

Charles saw the division within Parliament as a last chance to regain power. In January 1642 he invaded Parliament with his soldiers. He intended to arrest Pym and the other leaders, but they had been forewarned and managed to escape. Shocked by the king's action, a majority of the House of Commons thereafter passed the Militia Ordinance, a measure that gave Parliament control of the army. The die was now cast. For the next four years (1642–1646) civil war engulfed England.

Charles assembled his forces at Nottingham, and in August the civil war began. The main issues were whether England would be ruled by an absolute monarchy or by a parliamentary government and whether English religion would be conformist high Anglican and controlled by the king's bishops or cast into a more decentralized, presbyterian system of church governance. Charles's supporters, known as *Cavaliers*, were located in the northwestern half of England. The parliamentary opposition, known as *Roundheads* because of their close-cropped hair, had its stronghold in the southeastern half of the country. The nobility, identifying the power of their peerage with the preservation of the current form of the monarchy and the church, became prominent supporters of the king, whereas the townspeople supported the Parliamentary army.

Oliver Cromwell and the Puritan Republic

Two factors led finally to Parliament's victory. The first was an alliance with Scotland in 1643 consummated when John Pym persuaded Parliament to accept the terms of the Solemn League and Covenant, an agreement committing Parliament, with the Scots, to a presbyterian system of church government. The second was the reorganization of the parliamentary army under Oliver Cromwell (1599–1658), a middle-aged country squire of iron discipline and strong Independent religious sentiment. Cromwell and his "godly men" favored neither the episcopal system of the king nor the pure presbyterian system of the Solemn League and Covenant. They were willing to tolerate an established majority church, but only if it also permitted Protestant dissenters to worship outside it. The allies won the Battle of Marston Moor in 1644, the largest engagement of the war, and in June 1645 Cromwell's New Model Army, which fought with a disciplined fanaticism, decisively defeated the king at Naseby.

Though defeated militarily, Charles again took advantage of the deep divisions within Parliament, this time seeking to win the Presbyterians and the Scots over to the royalist side. But Cromwell's army firmly imposed its will. In December 1648 Colonel Thomas Pride physically barred the Presbyterians, who made up a majority of Parliament, from taking their seats. After "Pride's Purge," only a "rump" of fewer than fifty members remained. Though small in numbers, this Independent Rump Parliament had supreme military power within England. It did not hesitate to use this power. On January 30, 1649, after trial by a special court, it executed Charles as a public criminal and thereafter abolished the monarchy, the House of Lords, and the Anglican church. The revolution was consummated by events hardly contemplated at its outset.

From 1649 to 1660 England became officially a Puritan republic. During this period Cromwell's army conquered Ireland and Scotland, creating the single political entity of Great Britain. Cromwell, however, was a military man and no politician. He was increasingly frustrated by what seemed to him to be pettiness and dawdling on the part of Parliament. When in 1653 the House of Commons entertained a motion to disband the expensive army of fifty thousand, Cromwell responded by marching in and disbanding Parliament. He ruled thereafter as Lord Protector.

But his military dictatorship proved no more effective than Charles's rule had been and became just as harsh and hated. Cromwell's great

A Portrait of Oliver Cromwell

Statesman and historian Edward Hyde, the earl of Clarendon (1609–1674), was an enemy of Oliver Cromwell. However, his portrait of Cromwell, which follows, mixes criticism with grudging admiration for the Puritan leader.

He was one of those men whom his enemies cannot condemn without at the same time also praising. For he could never have done half that mischief without great parts of courage and industry and judgment. And he must have had a wonderful understanding of the natures and humours of men and a great dexterity in applying them . . . [to] raise himself to such a height. . . .

When he first appeared in the Parliament, he seemed to have a person in no degree gracious, no ornament of discourse, none of those talents which reconcile the affections of the standers-by; yet as he grew into his place and authority, his parts seemed to be renewed, as if he concealed faculties til he had occasion to use them. . . .

After he was confirmed and invested Protector . . . he consulted with very few . . . nor communicated any enterprise he resolved upon with more than those who were to have principal parts in the execution of it; nor to them sooner than was absolutely necessary. What he once resolved . . . he would not be dissuaded from, nor endure any contradiction. . . .

In all other matters which did not concern . . . his jurisdiction, he seemed to have great reverence for the law. . . . And as he proceeded with . . . indignation and haughtiness with those who were refractory and dared to contend with his greatness, so towards those who complied with his good pleasure, and courted his protection, he used a wonderful civility, generosity, and bounty.

To reduce three nations [England, Ireland, and Scotland], which perfectly hated him, to an entire obedience to all his dictates; to awe and govern those nations by an army that was not devoted to him and wished his ruin; this was an instance of a very prodigious address. But his greatness at home was but a shadow of the glory he had abroad. It was hard to discover which feared him most, France, Spain, or the Netherlands. . . . As they did all sacrifice their honour and their interest to his pleasure, so there is nothing he could have demanded that any of them would have denied him.

James Harvey Robinson (Ed.), *Readings in European History,* Vol. 2 (Boston: Ginn and Co., 1906), pp. 248–250.

An Account of the Execution of Charles I

Convicted of "high treason and other high crimes," Charles I was beheaded on January 30, 1649. In his last minutes he conversed calmly with the attending bishop and executioner, anxious only that the executioner not strike before he gave the signal.

To the executioner he said, "I shall say but very short prayers, and when I thrust out my hands—"

Then he called to the bishop for his cap, and having put it on, asked the executioner, "Does my hair trouble you?" and the executioner desired him to put it under his cap, which as he was doing by help of the bishop and the executioner, he turned to the bishop and said, "I have a good cause, and a gracious God on my side."

The bishop said, "There is but one stage more, which, though turbulent and troublesome, yet is a very short one. . . . It will carry you from earth to heaven . . . to a crown of glory. . . ."

Then the king asked the executioner, "Is my hair well?"

And taking off his cloak and George [the Order of the Garter, bearing a figure of Saint George], he delivered his George to the bishop. . . .

Then putting off his doublet and being in his waistcoat, he put on his cloak again, and looking upon the block, said to the executioner, "You must set it fast."

The executioner. "It is fast, sir."
King. "It might have been a little higher."
Executioner. "It can be no higher, sir."
King. "When I put out my hands this way, then—"

Then having said a few words to himself, as he stood with hands and eyes lifted up, immediately stooping down he laid his neck upon the block; and the executioner, again putting his hair under his cap, his Majesty, thinking he had been going to strike, bade him, "Stay for the sign."

Executioner. "Yes, I will, as it please your Majesty."

After a very short pause, his Majesty stretching forth his hands, the executioner at one blow severed his head from his body; which being held up and showed to the people, was with his body put into a coffin covered with black velvet and carried into his lodging.

His blood was taken up by divers persons for different ends; by some as trophies of the villainy; by others as relics of a martyr.

James Harvey Robinson (Ed.), *Readings in European History*, Vol. 2 (Boston: Ginn and Co., 1906), pp. 244–245.

army and foreign adventures inflated his budget to three times that of Charles. Trade and commerce suffered throughout England, as near chaos reigned in many places. Puritan prohibitions of such pastimes as theaters, dancing, and drunkenness were widely resented. Cromwell's treatment of Anglicans came to be just as intolerant as Charles's treatment of Puritans had been. In the name of religious liberty, political liberty had been lost. And Cromwell was unable to get along even with the new Parliaments that were elected under the aus-

pices of his army. By the time of his death in 1658, a majority of the English were ready to end the Puritan experiment and return to the traditional institutions of government.

Charles II and the Restoration of the Monarchy

The Stuart monarchy was restored in 1660 when Charles II (1660–1685), son of Charles I, returned to England amid great rejoicing. A man of considerable charm and political skill, Charles set a refreshing new tone after eleven years of somber Puritanism. His restoration returned England to the status quo of 1642, as once again a hereditary monarch

OPPOSITE: *The execution of Charles I, January 30, 1649. The king's portrait is on the upper left, Cromwell's on the upper right.* [*National Galleries of Scotland*]

Cromwell disbands the House of Commons in 1653. For the next six years, until his death in 1659, Cromwell ruled England as a dictator under the title of Lord Protector. [The Mansell Collection]

sat on the throne and the Anglican church was religiously supreme.

Because of his secret Catholic sympathies the king favored a policy of religious toleration. He wanted to allow all persons outside the Church of England, Catholics as well as Puritans, to worship freely so long as they remained loyal to the throne. But the ultraroyalist Anglicans in Parliament decided otherwise. They did not believe patriotism and religion could be so disjointed. Between 1661 and 1665, through a series of laws known as the Clarendon Code, Parliament excluded Roman Catholics, Presbyterians, and Independents from the religious and political life of the nation. Penalties were imposed for attending non-Anglican worship services, strict adherence to the *Book of Common Prayer* and the Thirty-Nine Articles was required, and all who desired to serve in local government were made to swear oaths of allegiance to the Church of England. This trampling of Puritan sentiments did not go unopposed in Parliament, but the opposition was not strong enough to override the majority.

Under Charles II England stepped up its challenge of the Dutch to become Europe's commercial and business center. Navigation Acts were passed that required all imports into England to be carried either in English ships or in ships registered to the same country as the imports they carried. Because the Dutch were the original suppliers of hardly more than tulips and cheese, these laws struck directly at their lucrative role as Europe's commercial middlemen. A series of naval wars between England and Holland ensued. Charles also undertook at this time to tighten his grasp on the rich English colonies in North America and the Caribbean, many of which had been settled and developed by separatists who desired independence from English rule.

Although Parliament strongly supported the monarchy, Charles, following the habit of his predecessors, required greater revenues than Parliament appropriated. These Charles managed to get in part by increased customs. He also received French aid. In 1670 England and France formally allied against the Dutch in the Treaty of Dover. A secret portion of this treaty pledged Charles to announce his conversion to Catholicism as soon as conditions in England permitted, a declaration for which Louis XIV of

France promised to pay 167,000 pounds. (Such a declaration never came to pass.) Charles also received a French war chest of 250,000 pounds per annum.

In an attempt to unite the English people behind the war with Holland, and as a sign of good faith to Louis XIV, Charles issued a Declaration of Indulgence in 1672 suspending all laws against Roman Catholics and Protestant nonconformists. But again, the conservative Tory Parliament proved less generous than the king and refused to grant money for the war until Charles rescinded the measure. After Charles withdrew the declaration, Parliament passed the Test Act, which required all officials of the crown, civil and military, to swear an oath against the doctrine of transubstantiation—a requirement that no loyal Roman Catholic could honestly meet.

The Test Act was aimed in large measure at the king's brother, James, duke of York, heir to the throne and a recent, devout convert to Catholicism. In 1678 a notorious liar named Titus Oates swore before a magistrate that Charles's Catholic wife, through her physician, was plotting with Jesuits and Irishmen to kill the king so that James could assume the throne. The matter was taken before Parliament, where it was believed. In the ensuing hysteria, known as the *Popish Plot,* several people were tried and executed. In 1680–1681, riding the crest of anti-Catholic sentiment, opposition Whig members of Parliament, led by the earl of Shaftesbury (1621–1683), made an impressive but unsuccessful effort to enact a bill excluding James from succession to the throne.

More suspicious than ever of Parliament, Charles II turned again to increased customs revenue and the assistance of Louis XIV for extra income and was able to rule from 1681 to 1685 without recalling Parliament. In these years Charles suppressed much of his opposition, driving the earl of Shaftesbury into exile, executing several Whig leaders for treason, and bullying local corporations into electing members of Parliament submissive to the royal will. When Charles died in 1685 (after a deathbed conversion to Catholicism), he left James the prospect of a Parliament filled with royal friends.

James II and Renewed Fears of a Catholic England

James II (1685–1688) did not know how to make the most of a good thing. He alienated

Charles II (1660–1685). A man of considerable charm and political skill, Charles was a popular and astute ruler. [Robert Harding Picture Collection]

Parliament by insisting upon the repeal of the Test Act. When Parliament balked, he dissolved it and proceeded openly to appoint known Catholics to high positions in both his court and the army. In 1687 James issued a Declaration of Indulgence, which suspended all religious tests and permitted free worship. Local candidates for Parliament who opposed the declaration were removed from their offices by the king's soldiers and were replaced by Catholics. In June 1688 James went so far as to imprison seven Anglican bishops who had refused to publicize his suspension of laws against Catholics.

Under the guise of a policy of enlightened toleration, James was actually seeking to subject all English institutions to the power of the monarchy. His goal was absolutism, and even conservative, loyalist Tories could not abide this. The English had reason to fear that James planned to imitate the policy of Louis XIV, who in 1685 had revoked the Edict of Nantes (which had protected French Protestants for almost a century) and had returned France to Catholicism, where necessary, with the aid of dragoons. A national consensus very quickly formed against the monarchy of James II.

The direct stimulus for parliamentary action came when on June 20, 1688, James's second wife, a Catholic, gave birth to a son, a male Catholic heir to the English throne. The English had hoped that James would die without a male heir and that the throne would revert to his Protestant eldest daughter, Mary. Mary was the wife of William III of Orange, *stadholder* of the Netherlands, great-grandson of William the Silent, and the leader of European opposition to Louis XIV's imperial designs. Within days of the birth of a Catholic male heir, Whig and Tory members of Parliament formed a coalition and invited Orange to invade England to preserve "traditional liberties," that is, the Anglican church and parliamentary government.

The "Glorious Revolution"

William of Orange arrived with his army in November 1688 and was received without opposition by the English people. In the face of sure defeat James fled to France and the protection of Louis XIV. With James gone, Parliament declared the throne vacant and on its own authority proclaimed William and Mary the new monarchs in 1689, completing a successful bloodless revolution. William and Mary, in turn, recognized a Bill of Rights that limited the powers of the monarchy and guaranteed the civil liberties of the English privileged classes. Henceforth, England's monarchs would rule by the consent of Parliament and would be subject to law. The Bill of Rights also pointedly prohibited Roman Catholics from occupying the English throne. The Toleration Act of 1689 permitted worship by all Protes-

The Bill of Rights being read to William and Mary in 1688. The "Glorious Revolution" established a limited monarchy. Henceforth, while English kings retained real power, they ruled by consent of Parliament and were subject to the law. [Department of the Environment, London]

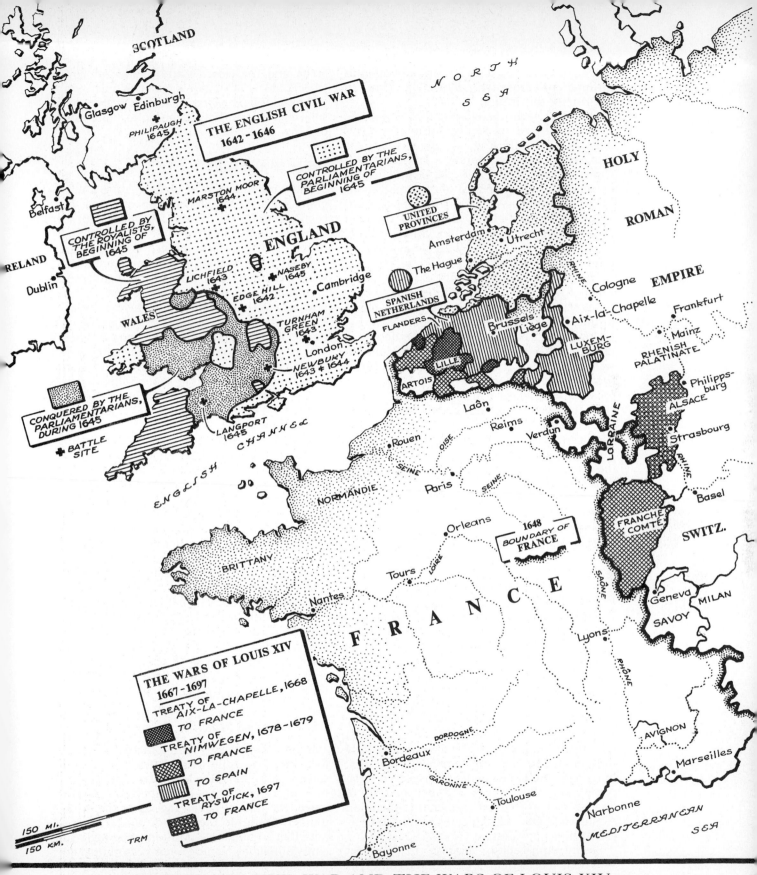

SCOTLAND

Glasgow · Edinburgh
· PHILIPAUGH
1645

THE ENGLISH CIVIL WAR
1642-1646

NORTH
SEA

HOLY
ROMAN
EMPIRE

CONTROLLED BY THE
PARLIAMENTARIANS,
BEGINNING OF
1645

Belfast

· MARSTON MOOR
1644

UNITED
PROVINCES

IRELAND

CONTROLLED BY
THE ROYALISTS,
BEGINNING OF
1645

ENGLAND

Amsterdam · Utrecht

Cologne ·

Frankfurt ·

Dublin

· Cambridge

The Hague

RHINE

Mainz ·

· LICHFIELD
1643
· NASEBY
1645
EDGE HILL
1642

SPANISH
NETHERLANDS

Brussels ·
· Liège
Aix-la-Chapelle ·

RHENISH
PALATINATE

WALES

TURNHAM
GREEN
1643

FLANDERS

LUXEM-
BURG

Philipps-
burg

CONQUERED BY THE
PARLIAMENTARIANS,
DURING 1645

London ·
NEWBURY
1643 ✚ 1644

ARTOIS

LILLE

LORRAINE

ALSACE
Strasbourg ·

✚ BATTLE
SITE

· LANGPORT
1645

ENGLISH
CHANNEL

· Laôn

Reims ·

· Verdun

RHINE

· Basel

· Rouen
SEINE

FRANCHE
COMTÉ

SWITZ.

NORMANDIE

OISE

· Paris

SEINE

1648
BOUNDARY
OF
FRANCE

· Orleans

· Geneva
MILAN ·

BRITTANY

· Tours

F R A N C E

LOIRE

SAÔNE

SAVOY

· Nantes

· Lyons

RHÔNE

THE WARS OF LOUIS XIV
1667-1697
TREATY OF
AIX-LA-CHAPELLE, 1668
TO FRANCE
TREATY OF
NIMWEGEN, 1678-1679
TO FRANCE
TO SPAIN
TREATY OF
RYSWICK, 1697
TO FRANCE

· Bordeaux

DORDOGNE

AVIGNON ·

· Marseilles

GARONNE

· Toulouse

· Narbonne

MEDITERRANEAN
SEA

150 MI.

150 KM.

TRM

· Bayonne

THE ENGLISH CIVIL WAR AND THE WARS OF LOUIS XIV

MAPS 12–1, 12–2 *In the English Civil War, 1645 was a crucial year; here the rapidly deteriorating Royalist position is shown. A bit later in France we see the territorial changes resulting from Louis XIV's first three major wars. The War of the Spanish Succession was yet to come.*

tants and outlawed Roman Catholics and antititrinitarians (those who denied the Christian doctrine of the Trinity).

The final measure closing the century of strife was the Act of Settlement in 1701. This bill provided for the English crown to go to the Protestant House of Hanover in Germany if Queen Anne (1702–1714), the second daughter of James II and the last of the Stuart monarchs, was not survived by her children. Consequently in 1714 the Elector of Hanover became King George I of England, the third foreign monarch to occupy the English throne in just over a century.

The "Glorious Revolution" of 1688 established a framework of government by and for the governed. It received classic philosophical justification in John Locke's *Second Treatise of Government* (1690), in which Locke described the relationship of a king and his people in terms of a bilateral contract. If the king broke that contract, the people, by whom Locke meant the privileged and powerful, had the right to depose him. Although it was, neither in fact nor in theory, a "popular" revolution such as would occur in France and America a hundred years later, the Glorious Revolution did establish in England a permanent check on monarchical power by the classes represented in Parliament.

Rise of Absolutism in France

Regional rights and a degree of religious diversity were recognized within the Holy Roman Empire, England, and the Netherlands during the seventeenth century. The assertion of local autonomy by the numerous member states and cities of the Holy Roman Empire made a strong central government there unthinkable. In England and the Netherlands centuries of parliamentary practice permitted regional freedoms to coexist with a strong central government.

Following the devastation of the Thirty Years' War, the Peace of Westphalia (1648) reaffirmed religious pluralism within the Holy Roman Empire. A degree of religious diversity, long a Netherlands tradition, received final confirmation also in England after decades of dogged Puritan resistance, when the Toleration Act of 1689 granted rights of worship to Protestant nonconformists.

Seventeenth-century France, in contrast, saw both representative government and religious pluralism crushed by the absolute monarchy and the closed Catholic state of Louis XIV (1643–1715). An aggressive ruler who sought glory (*la gloire*) in foreign wars, Louis subjected his subjects at home to "one king, one law, one faith."

Henry IV and Sully

The foundation was well laid for Louis's grand reign by his predecessors and their exceptional ministers. Henry IV (1589–1610; see Chapter 11) began in earnest the curtailment of the privileges of the French nobility necessary for the creation of a strong centralized state. His targets were the provincial governors and the regional *parlements*, especially the powerful Parlement of Paris, where a divisive spirit lived on. Here were to be found the old privileged groups, tax-exempt magnates whose sole preoccupation was to protect their self-interests. During Louis XIV's reign their activities came under the strict supervision of royal civil servants known as *intendants*, who implemented the king's will with remarkable success in the provinces.

Also during Henry IV's reign an economy more amenable to governmental regulation emerged after the long decades of religious and civil war. Henry and his finance minister, the duke of Sully (1560–1641), prepared the way for the mercantilist policies of Louis XIV and his minister Colbert by establishing government monopolies on gunpowder, mines, and salt. A canal system was begun to link the Atlantic and the Mediterranean by joining the Saône, the Loire, the Seine, and the Meuse rivers. An involuntary national labor force emerged with the introduction of a royal *corvée*, and this drafting of workers provided the labor to improve roads and the conditions of internal travel. Sully even dreamed of the political and commercial organization of the whole of Europe in a kind of common market.

Louis XIII and Richelieu

Henry IV was assassinated in 1610, and the following year Sully retired. Because Henry's successor, Louis XIII (1610–1643), was only nine years old when his father was assassinated, the task of governing fell to the queen mother, Marie de Médicis (d. 1642). Finding herself in a vulnerable position, she sought security abroad by signing a ten-year mutual defense pact with arch-rival Spain in the Treaty of Fontainebleau (1611), an alliance that also arranged for the later marriage of Louis XIII to the Spanish infanta as well as for the marriage of the queen's daughter Elizabeth to the heir to the Spanish throne. The queen sought internal security against the French nobility by promoting the career of Cardinal Richelieu (1585–1642) as the king's chief adviser, although Richelieu never became her pawn. Richelieu, loyal and shrewd, aspired to make France a supreme European power and he, more than any one person, was the secret of French success in the first half of the seventeenth century.

An apparently devout Catholic who also believed that the church best served both his own ambition and the welfare of France, Richelieu was strongly anti-Habsburg in politics. On the one hand, he supported the Spanish alliance of the queen and Catholic religious unity within France; on the other, he was determined to contain Spanish power and influence, even when that meant aiding and abetting Protestant Europe. It is an indication both of Richelieu's awkward political situation and of his diplomatic agility that he could, in 1631, pledge funds to the Protestant army of Gustavus Adolphus, while at the same time insisting that Catholic Bavaria be spared from attack and that Catholics in conquered countries be permitted to practice their religion.

At home Richelieu pursued his policies utterly without sentiment. Supported by the king, whose best decision was to let his chief minister make all the decisions of state, Richelieu stepped up the campaign against the separatist provincial governors and *parlements*. He made it clear to all that there was only one law, that of the king, and that none could stand above it. When disobedient noblemen defied his edicts, they were imprisoned and even executed. Louis XIV had Richelieu to thank for the fact that many of the French nobility became docile beggars at his court. Such treatment of the nobility won Richelieu much enmity, even from the queen mother, who was not always prepared to place the larger interests of the state above the pleasure of favorite princes. But the king let no criticism weaken his chief minister, not even that of his mother. The queen mother had largely ignored Louis during his youth—he was educated mostly at the hands of his falconer—and they remained estranged. This was doubtless a factor in the king's firm support of Richelieu when his mother became Richelieu's accuser.

Richelieu inspired the campaign against the Huguenots that would end in 1685 with Louis

Cardinal Richelieu, the mastermind behind French royal power in the seventeenth century. This striking triple portrait is by Philippe de Champaigne (1602–1674). [Courtesy of the Trustees, The National Gallery, London]

XIV's revocation of the Edict of Nantes. Royal armies conquered major Huguenot cities in 1629, and the subsequent Peace of Alais (1629) truncated the Edict of Nantes by denying Protestants the right to maintain garrisoned cities, separate political organizations, and independent law courts. Only Richelieu's foreign policy prevented the earlier implementation of the extreme intolerance of Louis XIV. In the same year that the independent political status of the Huguenots was rescinded, Richelieu also entered negotiations to make Gustavus Adolphus his counterweight to the expansion of Habsburg power within the Holy Roman Empire. By 1635 the Catholic soldiers of France were fighting openly with Swedish Lutherans against the emperor's army in the final phase of the Thirty Years' War.

In the best Machiavellian tradition Richelieu employed the arts and the printing press to defend his actions and to indoctrinate the French in the meaning of *raison d'état* ("reason of state")—again setting a precedent for Louis XIV's elaborate use of royal propaganda and spectacle. It is one measure of Richelieu's success that France made substantial gains in land and political influence when the Treaty of Westphalia (1648) ended hostilities in the Holy Roman Empire and the Treaty of the Pyrenees (1659) sealed peace with Spain.

Young Louis XIV and Mazarin

Richelieu's immediate legacy, however, was strong resentment of the monarchy on the part of the French aristocracy and the privileged bourgeoisie. During the minority of Louis XIV, who was only five years old when Louis XIII died in 1643, the queen mother, Anne of Austria (d. 1666), placed the reins of government in the hands of Cardinal Mazarin (1602–1661), who continued Richelieu's determined policy of centralization. During his regency the long-building backlash occurred. Named after the slingshot used by street boys, the Fronde (1649–1652) was a series of widespread rebellions by segments of the French nobility and townspeople aimed at reversing the drift toward absolute monarchy—a last-ditch effort to preserve their local autonomy. These privileged groups saw their traditional position in French society thoroughly undermined by the crown's steady multiplication of royal offices, the replacement of local by ''state'' agents, and the reduction of their patronage.

The Parlement of Paris initiated the revolt in 1649, and the nobility at large soon followed. The latter were urged on by the influen-

Louis XIV presiding over the council of State. It was a maxim of French law that the king's wish was the law of the land. [Giraudon]

tial wives of princes who had been imprisoned by Mazarin for treason. The many briefly triumphed over the one when Mazarin released the imprisoned princes in February 1651. He and Louis XIV thereafter entered a short exile (Mazarin leaving France, Louis fleeing Paris) and were unable to return to Paris until October 1652, when the inefficiency and near anarchy of government by the nobility made them very welcome. The period of the Fronde convinced a majority of the French that a strong king was preferable to the competing and irreconcilable claims of many regional magnates. After 1652 the French were ready to experiment in earnest with absolute rule.

The World of Louis XIV

Unity at Home

Thanks to the forethought of Mazarin, Louis XIV was well prepared to rule France. The turbulent period of his youth seems also to have made an indelible impression. Louis wrote in his memoirs that the Fronde caused him to loathe ''kings of straw'' and made him determined never to become one. Indoctrinated with a strong sense of the grandeur of his crown, he never missed an opportunity to impress it on the French people. When the dauphin (the heir to the French throne) was born in 1662, for example, Louis appeared for the celebration dressed as a Roman emperor. Although his rule became the prototype of the modern centralized state, its inspiration remained a very narrow ideal of personal glory.

King by Divine Right

Reverence for the king and the personification of government in him had been nurtured in France since Capetian times. It was a maxim of French law and popular opinion that ''the king of France is emperor in his realm,'' that the king's wish is the law of the land.

An important theorist for Louis's even grander concept of royal authority was the devout tutor of the dauphin, Bishop Jacques-Bénigne Bossuet (1627–1704). An ardent champion of the Gallican Liberties—the traditional rights of the French king and church in matters of ecclesiastical appointments and taxation—Bossuet defended what he called the ''divine right of kings.'' He cited the Old Testament example of rulers divinely appointed by and answerable only to God. As medieval popes had insisted that only God could judge a pope, so Bossuet argued that none save God could sit in judgment on the king. Although kings remained duty-bound to reflect God's will in their rule—and in this sense Bossuet considered them always subject to a higher authority—as God's regents on earth they could not be bound to the dictates of mere princes and parliaments. Such were among the assumptions that lay behind Louis XIV's alleged declaration: *"L'état, c'est moi"* ("I am the state").

Jacques-Benigne Bossuet, Bishop of Meaux. Called the "Eagle of Meaux," Bossuet was an eloquent advocate of the "divine right of kings" and a strong defender of the autonomy of the French church against the Pope. This portrait by Hyacinthe Rigaud is in the Louvre. [Giraudon]

Bishop Bossuet Defends the Divine Right of Kings

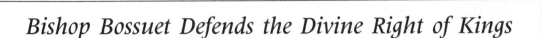

The revolutions of the seventeenth century caused many to fear anarchy far more than tyranny, among them the influential French bishop Jacques-Bénigne Bossuet (1627–1704), the leader of French Catholicism in the second half of the seventeenth century. Louis XIV made him court preacher and tutor to his son, for whom Bossuet wrote a celebrated *Universal History*. In the following excerpt Bossuet defends the divine right and absolute power of kings, whom he depicts as embracing in their person the whole body of the state and the will of the people they govern and, as such, as being immune from judgment by any mere mortal.

The royal power is absolute. . . . The prince need render account of his acts to no one. "I counsel thee to keep the king's commandment, and that in regard of the oath of God. Be not hasty to go out of his sight; stand not on an evil thing for he doeth whatsoever pleaseth him. Where the word of a king is, there is power; and who may say unto him, What doest thou? Whoso keepeth the commandment shall feel no evil thing" [Eccles. 8:2–5]. Without this absolute authority the king could neither do good nor repress evil. It is necessary that his power be such that no one can hope to escape him, and finally, the only protection of individuals against the public authority should be their innocence. This confirms the teaching of St. Paul: "Wilt thou then not be afraid of the power? Do that which is good" [Rom. 13:3].

God is infinite, God is all. The prince, as prince, is not regarded as a private person: he is a public personage, all the state is in him; the will of all the people is included in his. As all perfection and all strength are united in God, so all the power of individuals is united in the person of the prince. What grandeur that a single man should embody so much! . . .

Behold an immense people united in a single person; behold this holy power, paternal and absolute; behold the secret cause which governs the whole body of the state, contained in a single head: you see the image of God in the king, and you have the idea of royal majesty. God is holiness itself, goodness itself, and power itself. In these things lies the majesty of God. In the image of these things lies the majesty of the prince.

From *Politics Drawn from the Very Words of Holy Scripture*, in James Harvey Robinson (Ed.), *Readings in European History*, Vol. 2 (Boston: Ginn and Co., 1906), pp. 275–276.

Versailles

The palace court at Versailles on the outskirts of Paris became Louis's permanent residence after 1682. It was a true temple to royalty, architecturally designed and artistically decorated to proclaim the glory of the Sun King, as Louis was known. A spectacular estate with magnificent fountains and acres of orange groves, it became home to thousands of aristocrats, royal officials, and servants. Although its physical maintenance and new additions, which continued throughout Louis's lifetime, consumed over half his annual revenues—around five million livres a year—Versailles paid political dividends well worth the investment.

Life at court was organized around the king's daily routine. During his rising and dressing, nobles whispered their special requests in Louis's ear.

After the morning mass, which Louis always observed, there followed long hours in council with the chief ministers, assemblies from which the nobility was carefully excluded. Louis's ministers and councilors were hand-picked townsmen, servants who owed everything they had to the king's favor and who served him, for that reason, faithfully and without question. There were three main councils: the Council of State, a small group of four or five who met thrice weekly to rule on all matters of state, but especially on foreign affairs and war policy; the Council of Dispatches, which regularly assessed the reports from the *intendants* in the towns and provinces, a boring business that the king often left to his ministers; and finally, the Council of Finances, which handled matters of taxation and commerce.

Members of the royal court spent the afternoons hunting, riding, or strolling about the lush gardens. Evenings were given over to planned entertainment in the large salons (plays, concerts, gambling, and the like), followed by supper at 10:00 P.M.

Even the king's retirement became a part of day's spectacle. Fortunate nobles held his night candle as they accompanied him to his bed.

Although only five feet four inches in height, the king had presence and was always engaging in conversation. An unabashed ladies' man, he encouraged the belief at court that it was an honor to lie with the king. Married to the Spanish Infanta Marie Thérèse for political reasons in 1660, he kept many mistresses.

After Marie's death in 1683 he settled down in secret marriage with one, Madame de Maintenon, and apparently became much less the philanderer.

All this ritual and play served the political purpose of keeping an impoverished nobility, barred by law from high government positions, busy and dependent so that they had little time to plot revolt. The dress codes and the high-stakes gaming at court contributed to the indebtedness and dependency of the nobility on the king. Court life was a carefully planned and successfully executed domestication of the nobility.

Suppression of the Jansenists

Like Richelieu before him, Louis believed that political unity required religious conformity. To that end he suppressed two groups of religious dissenters: the Catholic Jansenists, who were opponents of the Jesuits, and the Protestant Huguenots.

Although the king and the French church jealously guarded their traditional independence from Rome (the Gallican Liberties), the years following the conversion of Henry IV to Catholicism had seen a great influx of Catholic religious orders into France, prominent among which were the Jesuits. Because of their leadership at the Council of Trent and their close Spanish connections, Catherine de Médicis had earlier banned the Jesuits from France. Henry IV lifted the ban in 1603, with certain conditions: there was to be a limitation on the number of new colleges they could open; special licenses were required for activities outside their own buildings; and each member of the

Cornelis Jansen, Bishop of Ypres (1585–1638), wrote that individuals could do nothing to contribute to their salvation unless they were assisted by divine grace. This teaching, which came to be called Jansenism, was condemned as heretical by the Church because it seemed to deny the doctrine of human free will. [Library of Congress]

order was subjected to an oath of allegiance to the king. The Jesuits were not, however, easily harnessed. They rapidly monopolized the education of the upper classes, and their devout students promoted the religious reforms and doctrine of the Council of Trent throughout France. It is a measure of their success that Jesuits served as confessors to Henry IV, Louis XIII, and Louis XIV.

In the 1630s a group known as *Jansenists* formed an intra-Catholic opposition to both the theology and the political influence of the Jesuits. They were Catholics who adhered to the Augustinian tradition, out of which many Protestant teachings had also come. Serious and uncompromising in their religious doctrine and practice, the Jansenists opposed Jesuit teachings about free will. They believed with Saint Augustine that original sin dominated humankind so completely that individuals could do absolutely nothing good or contribute to their salvation unless they were first specially assisted by the grace of God. The namesake of the Jansenists, Cornelis Jansen

(d. 1638), a Flemish theologian and the bishop of Ypres, was the author of a posthumously published book entitled *Augustinus* (1640), which assailed mainly Jesuit teaching on grace and salvation.

Jean du Vergier de Hauranne (1581–1643), the abbot of Saint-Cyran and Jansen's close friend, was instrumental in bringing into the Jansenist camp a Parisian family, the Arnaulds, who were prominent opponents of the Jesuits. The Arnauld family, like many other French people, believed that the Jesuits had been behind the assassination of Henry IV in 1610. Arnauld support added a strong political element to the Jansenists' theological opposition to the Jesuits. Jansenist communities at Port-Royal and Paris were dominated by the Arnaulds during the 1640s. In 1643 Antoine Arnauld published a work entitled *On Frequent Communion* in which he criticized the Jesuits for confessional practices that permitted the easy redress of almost any sin. The Jesuits, in turn, condemned the Jansenists as "crypto-Calvinists" in their theology.

On May 31, 1653, Pope Innocent X declared heretical five Jansenist theological propositions on grace and salvation. In 1656 the pope banned Jansen's *Augustinus*, and the Sorbonne censured Antoine Arnauld. In this same year Antoine's friend, Blaise Pascal (d. 1662), the most famous of Jansen's followers, published the first of his *Provincial Letters* in defense of Jansenism. A deeply religious man, Pascal tried to reconcile the "reasons of the heart" with growing seventeenth-century reverence for the clear and distinct ideas of the mind. He found Jesuit moral theology to be not only lax and shallow, but also a rationalized approach to religion that did injustice to religious experience.

In 1660 Louis permitted the enforcement of the papal bull *Ad Sacram Sedem* (1656), which banned Jansenism, and he closed down the Port-Royal community. Thereafter Jansenists either capitulated by signing retractions or went underground. At a later date (1710) the French king lent his support to a still more thorough purge of Jansenist sentiment. With the fall of the Jansenists went any hope of a Catholicism broad enough to attract the Huguenots.

Revocation of the Edict of Nantes

Since the Edict of Nantes, a cold war had existed between the great Catholic majority (nine tenths of the French population) and the Protestant minority. Despite their respectable numbers, about 1.75 million by the 1660s, the Huguenots were in decline in the second half of the seventeenth century. Government harassment had forced the more influential members to withdraw their support. Officially the French Catholic church had long denounced Calvinists as heretical and treasonous and had supported their persecution as both a pious and a patriotic act. Following the Peace of Nijmegen in 1678–1679, which halted for the moment Louis's aggression in Europe, Louis launched a methodical government campaign against the French Huguenots in a determined effort to unify France religiously. He hounded the Huguenots out of public life, banned them from government office, and excluded them from such professions as printing and medicine. Subsidies and selective taxation also be-

---

Louis XIV Revokes the Edict of Nantes

Believing that a country could not be under one king and one law unless it was also under one religious system, Louis XIV stunned much of Europe in October 1685 by revoking the Edict of Nantes, which had protected the religious freedoms and civil rights of French Protestants since 1598.

Art. 1. Know that we . . . with our certain knowledge, full power and royal authority, have by this present, perpetual and irrevocable edict, suppressed and revoked the edict of the aforesaid king our grandfather, given at Nantes in the month of April, 1598, in all its extent . . . together with all the concessions made by [this] and other edicts, declarations, and decrees, to the people of the so-called Reformed religion, of whatever nature they be . . . and in consequence we desire . . . that all the temples of the people of the aforesaid so-called Reformed religion situated in our kingdom . . . should be demolished forthwith.

Art. 2. We forbid our subjects of the so-called Reformed religion to assemble any more for public worship of the above-mentioned religion. . . .

Art. 3. We likewise forbid all lords, of whatever rank they may be, to carry out heretical services in houses and fiefs . . . the penalty for . . . the said worship being confiscation of their body and possessions.

Art. 4. We order all ministers of the aforesaid so-called Reformed religion who do not wish to be converted and to embrace the Catholic, Apostolic, and Roman religion, to depart from our kingdom and the lands subject to us within fifteen days from the publication of our present edict . . . on pain of the galleys.

Art. 5. We desire that those among the said

[Reformed] ministers who shall be converted [to the Catholic religion] shall continue to enjoy during their life, and their wives shall enjoy after their death as long as they remain widows, the same exemptions from taxation and billeting of soldiers, which they enjoyed while they fulfilled the function of ministers. . . .

. . . .

Art. 8. With regard to children who shall be born to those of the aforesaid so-called Reformed religion, we desire that they be baptized by their parish priests. We command the fathers and mothers to send them to the churches for that purpose, on penalty of a fine of 500 livres or more if they fail to do so; and afterwards, the children shall be brought up in the Catholic, Apostolic, and Roman religion. . . .

. . . .

Art. 10. All our subjects of the so-called Reformed religion, with their wives and children, are to be strongly and repeatedly prohibited from leaving our aforesaid kingdom . . . or of taking out . . . their possessions and effects. . . .

. . . .

The members of the so-called Reformed religion, while awaiting God's pleasure to enlighten them like the others, can live in the towns and districts of our kingdom . . . and continue their occupation there, and enjoy their possessions . . . on condition . . . that they do not make public profession of [their religion].

Church and State Through the Centuries: A Collection of Historic Documents, trans. and ed. by S. Z. Ehler and John B. Morrall (New York: Biblo and Tannen, 1967), pp. 209–213.

came weapons to encourage their conversion to Catholicism. In 1681 Louis further bullied Huguenots by quartering his troops in their towns. The final stage of the persecution came in October 1685, when Louis revoked the Edict of Nantes. In practical terms the revocation meant the closing of Protestant churches and schools, the exile of Protestant ministers, the placement of nonconverting laity in galleys as slaves, and the ceremonial baptism of Protestant children by Catholic priests.

The revocation of the Edict of Nantes became the major blunder of Louis's reign. Thereafter he was viewed throughout Protestant Europe as a new Philip II, intent on a Catholic reconquest of the whole of Europe, who must be resisted at all costs. Internally the revocation of the Edict of Nantes led to the voluntary emigration of over a quarter million French, who formed new communities and joined the French resistance movement in England, Germany, Holland, and the New World. Thousands of French Huguenots served in the army of Louis's arch foe, William III of the Netherlands, later King William III of England. Those who remained in France became an uncompromising guerrilla force. But despite the many domestic and foreign liabilities created for France by the revocation of the Edict of Nantes, Louis, to his death, considered it his most pious act, one that placed God in his debt.

Louis XIV revoking the Edict of Nantes in 1685. [Bulloz]

War Abroad

War was the normal state of affairs for seventeenth-century rulers and for none more than for Louis XIV, who confessed on his deathbed that he had ''loved war too much.'' Periods of peace became opportunities for the discontented in town and countryside to plot against the king; war served national unity as well as ''glory.'' By the 1660s France was superior to any other nation in administrative bureaucracy, armed forces, and national unity. It had a population of nineteen million, prosperous farms, vigorous trade, and much taxable wealth. By every external measure Louis was in a position to dominate Europe.

LOUVOIS, VAUBAN, AND COLBERT. The great French war machine became the work of three ministers: Louvois, Vauban, and Colbert. The army, which maintained a strength of about a quarter of a million, was the creation of Michel le Tellier and his more famous son, the marquis of Louvois (1641–1691), Louis's war minister from 1677 to 1691 and a superior military tactician.

Before Louvois the French army had been an amalgam of local recruits and mercenaries, uncoordinated groups whose loyalty could not always be counted on. Louvois disciplined the French army and made it a respectable profession. He placed a limit on military commissions and introduced a system of promotion by merit, policies that brought dedicated fighting men into the ranks. Enlistment was for four years and was restricted to single men. The pay was good and regular. *Intendants*, the king's ubiquitous civil servants, carried out regular inspections, monitoring conduct at all levels and reporting to the king.

What Louvois was to military organization, Sebastien Vauban (1633–1707) was to military engineering. He perfected the arts of fortifying and besieging towns. He also devised the system of trench warfare and developed the concept of defensive frontiers that remained basic military tactics through World War I.

War cannot be successful without financing, and here Louis had the guidance of his most brilliant minister, Jean-Baptiste Colbert (1619–1683). Colbert worked to centralize the French economy with the same rigor that Louis had worked to centralize the French government. He put the nation to work under state supervision and carefully regulated the flow of imports and exports through tariffs. He created new

Jean-Baptiste Colbert (1619–1683). His policies transformed France into a major industrial and commercial power. [*Giraudon*]

national industries and organized factories around a tight regimen of work and ideology. Administrative bureaucracy was simplified, unnecessary positions were abolished, and the number of tax-exempt nobles was reduced. Colbert also increased the *taille* on the peasantry, the chief source of royal wealth. Although the French economy continued to be a puppet controlled by many different strings, more of these strings were now in the hand of the king than had been the case in centuries past. This close government control of the economy came to be known as *mercantilism*. Its aim was to maximize foreign exports and the internal reserves of bullion, the gold and silver necessary for making war. Modern scholars argue that Colbert overcontrolled the French economy and cite his "paternalism" as a major reason for French failures in the New World. Be that as it may, Colbert's policies unquestionably transformed France into a major industrial and commercial power, with foreign bases in Africa, India, and the Americas from Canada to the Caribbean.

THE WAR OF DEVOLUTION. Louis's first great foreign adventure was the War of Devolution (1667–1668). It was fought, as still a later and greater war would be, over Louis's claim to a Spanish inheritance through his wife, Marie Thérèse (1638–1683). According to the terms of the Treaty of the Pyrenees (1659), Marie had renounced her claim to the Spanish succession on condition that a

500,000-crown dowry be paid to Louis within eighteen months of the marriage, a condition that was not met. When Philip IV of Spain died in September 1665, he left all his lands to his sickly four-year-old son by a second marriage, Charles II (1665–1700), and explicitly excluded his daughter Marie from any share. Louis had always harbored the hope of turning the marriage to territorial gain and had argued even before Philip's death that Marie was entitled to a portion of the inheritance.

Louis had a legal argument on his side, which gave the war its name. He maintained that because in certain regions of Brabant and Flanders, which were part of the Spanish inheritance, property "devolved" to the children of a first marriage rather than to those of a second, Marie had a higher claim than Charles II to these regions. The argument was not accepted—such regional laws could hardly bind the king of Spain—but Louis was not deterred from sending his armies, under the viscount of Turenne, into Flanders and the Franche-Comté in 1667. In response to this aggression England, Sweden, and the United Provinces of Holland formed the Triple Alliance, a force sufficient to bring Louis to peace terms in the Treaty of Aix-la-Chapelle (1668).

INVASION OF THE NETHERLANDS. In 1670 England and France became allies against the Dutch by signing the Treaty of Dover, a move that set the Stuart monarchy of Charles II on a new international course. With the departure of the English from its membership, the Triple Alliance crumbled. This left Louis in a stronger position to invade the Netherlands for a second time, which he did in 1672. This second invasion was aimed directly at Holland, the organizer of the Triple Alliance in 1667 and the country held accountable by Louis for foiling French designs in Flanders. Louis had been mightily offended by Dutch boasting after the Treaty of Aix-la-Chapelle; cartoons like one depicting the sun (Louis was the "Sun King") eclipsed by a great moon of Dutch cheese cut the French king to the quick. It was also clear that there could be no French acquisition of land in the Spanish Netherlands, nor European hegemony beyond that, until Holland was neutralized.

Louis's successful invasion of the United Provinces in 1672 brought the downfall of Jan and Cornelius De Witt, Dutch statesmen whom the Dutch public blamed for the French success. In their place came the twenty-seven-year-old Prince of Orange, destined after 1689 to become King William III of England. Orange was the great-grandson of William the Silent, who had repulsed Philip II and dashed Spanish hopes of dominating the Netherlands in the sixteenth century.

Orange proved to be Louis's undoing. This unpretentious Calvinist, who was in almost every way Louis's opposite, galvanized the seven provinces into a fierce fighting unit. In 1673 he united the Holy Roman Emperor, Spain, Lorraine, and Brandenburg in an alliance against Louis, "the Christian Turk," a menace to the whole of western Europe, Catholic and Protestant alike. Subsequent battles saw the loss of Louis's ablest generals, Turenne and Condé, in 1675, whereas the defeat of the Dutch fleet by Admiral Duquesne established French control of the Mediterranean in 1676. The Peace of Nimwegen, signed with different parties in successive years (1678, 1679), ended the hostilities of this second war. The settlements were not unfavorable to France—Spain, for example, surrendered the Franche-Comté— but France still fell far short of the European empire to which Louis aspired.

THE LEAGUE OF AUGSBURG. Between the Treaty of Nimwegen and the renewal of full-scale war in 1689, Louis restlessly probed his perimeters. The army was maintained at full strength. In 1681 it conquered the free city of Strasbourg, setting off the formation of new defensive coalitions against Louis. The League of Augsburg, created in 1686 to resist French expansion into Germany, grew by 1689 to include the Emperor Leopold; Spain; Sweden; the United Provinces; the electorates of Bavaria, Saxony, and the Palatinate; and the England of William and Mary. That year saw the beginning of the Nine Years' War (1689–1697) between France and the League of Augsburg. For the third time stalemate and exhaustion forced the combatants into an interim settlement. The Peace of Ryswick in September 1697 became a personal triumph for William of Orange, now William III of England, and the Emperor Leopold, as it secured Holland's borders and thwarted Louis's expansion into Germany. During this same period England and France fought for control of North America in what came to be known as King William's War (1689–1697).

WAR OF THE SPANISH SUCCESSION: TREATIES OF UTRECHT—RASTADT. After Ryswick, Louis, who seemed to thrive on partial success, made still a fourth attempt to realize his grand design of French European domination, this time assisted by an unfore-

An Appraisal of Louis XIV

In his history of the reigns of the first three Bourbon kings, written in 1746, the duc de Saint Simon (1675–1755), an army officer and public official during Louis XIV's reign, left the following highly critical portrait of Louis as a king smitten by vanity.

Louis XIV's vanity was without limit or restraint; it colored everything and convinced him that no one even approached him in military talents, in plans and enterprises, and in government. Hence, those pictures and inscriptions in the gallery at Versailles which disgust every foreigner; those opera prologues that he himself tried to sing; that flood of prose and verse in his praise for which his appetite was insatiable; those dedications of statues copied from pagan sculpture, and the insipid and sickening compliments that were continually offered to him in person and which he swallowed with unfailing relish; hence, his distaste for all merit, intelligence, education, and, most of all, independence of character and sentiment in others; his mistakes of judgment in matters of importance; his familiarity and favor reserved entirely for those to whom he felt himself superior in acquirements and ability; and, above everything else, a jealousy of his own authority which determined and took precedence over every other sort of justice, reason, and consideration whatever.

James Harvey Robinson (Ed.), *Readings in European History*, Vol. 2 (Boston: Ginn and Co., 1906), pp. 286–287.

*The siege of Tournai in 1709 during the War of the
Spanish Succession. Tournai, a fortress city on the border
between France and the Spanish Netherlands, had been
captured by the French in 1667. Here it is beseiged by the
English and Imperial forces under Marlborough and
Prince Eugene. Under the terms of the Treaty of Utrecht
(1713), France ceded Tournai to Austria. This 1709
engraving is by P. Mortier. [BBC Hulton Picture Library]*

seen turn of events. On November 1, 1700,
Charles II of Spain, known as "the Sufferer"
because of his genetic deformities and lingering
illnesses, died. Both Louis and the Austrian
Emperor Leopold had claims to the Spanish
inheritance through their grandsons: Louis by
way of his marriage to Marie Thérèse and Leopold through his marriage to her younger sister, Margaret Thérèse. Although the dauphin
had the higher blood claim, it was assumed
that the inheritance would go to the grandson
of the emperor. The French raised the specter
of a belligerent Habsburg kingdom threatening
the whole of Europe should Spain come under
the imperial crown. Marie Thérèse, however,
had renounced any right to the Spanish inheritance in the Treaty of the Pyrenees (1659).

The nations of Europe feared a union of the
French and Spanish crowns more than they
did a union of the imperial and Spanish
crowns. Indeed, they determined that the
former alliance should not occur. Hence, before Charles's death, negotiations began to partition the inheritance in such a way that the
current balance of power would be maintained.

Charles II upset all plans by leaving the entire Spanish inheritance to Philip of Anjou,
Louis's grandson. At a stroke the Spanish inheritance had fallen to France. Although Louis
had been party to the partition agreements in

THE REIGN OF LOUIS XIV (1643–1715)	
Peace of Westphalia reaffirms religious pluralism in Holy Roman Empire	1648
The Fronde, a revolt of nobility and townsmen against confiscatory policies of the crown	1649–1652
Jansenism declared a heresy by the pope	1653
Treaty of Pyrenees ends hostilities between France and Spain	1659
Louis XIV enforces papal ban on Jansenists	1660
War of Devolution fought over Louis's claims to lands in Brabant and Flanders by virtue of his Spanish inheritance through his wife	1667–1668
The Triple Alliance (England, Sweden, and the United Provinces) repels Louis's army from Flanders and forces the Treaty of Aix-la-Chapelle	1668
Treaty of Dover brings French and English together against the Netherlands	1670
France invades the United Provinces	1672
Peace of Nimwegen ends French wars in United Provinces	1678–1679
Louis XIV revokes Edict of Nantes	1685
Nine Years' War between France and League of Augsburg, a Europe-wide alliance against Louis XIV	1689–1697
Peace of Ryswick ends French expansion into Holland and Germany	1697
England, Holland, and Holy Roman Emperor resist Louis's claim to the Spanish throne in the War of Spanish Succession	1702–1714
Treaty of Utrecht between England and France	1712
Treaty of Rastadt between Spain and France	1714

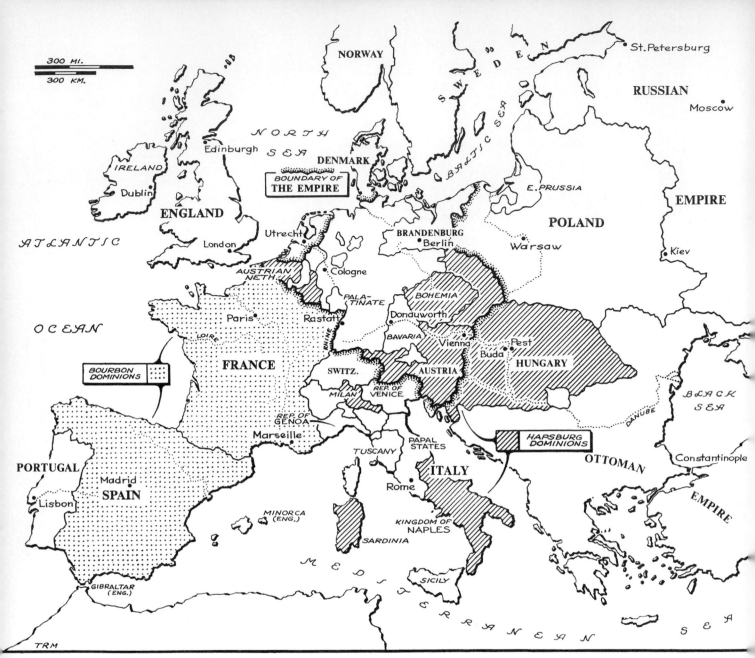

EUROPE IN 1714

MAP 12–3 *The War of the Spanish Succession ended in the year before the death of the aged Louis XIV. By then France and Spain, although not united, were ruled by members of the Bourbon family, and Spain had lost her non-Iberian possessions. Austria had continued to grow.*

advance of Charles's death, he now saw God's hand in Charles's will and chose to enforce its terms fully rather than abide by those of the partition treaty. Philip of Anjou moved to Madrid and became Philip V of Spain, and Louis, in what was interpreted as naked French aggression, sent his troops once again into Flanders, this time to remove Dutch soldiers from Spanish territory in the name of the

new French king of Spain. He also declared Spanish America open to French ships.

In September 1701 the Grand Alliance of England, Holland, and the Holy Roman Emperor formed against Louis. Its intent was to preserve the balance of power by once and for all securing Flanders as a neutral barrier between Holland and France and by gaining for the emperor his fair share of the Spanish inher-

472

itance. After the formation of the alliance Louis increased the stakes of battle by recognizing the son of James II of England as James III, king of England.

Once again total war enveloped western Europe as the twelve-year War of the Spanish Succession (1702–1714) began. France, for the first time, went to war with inadequate finances, a poorly equipped army, and mediocre military leadership. The English had advanced weaponry (flintlock rifles, paper cartridges, and ring bayonets) and superior tactics (thin, maneuverable troop columns rather than the traditional deep ones). John Churchill, the duke of Marlborough, who succeeded William of Orange as military leader of the alliance, bested Louis's soldiers in every major engagement. Marlborough routed French armies at Blenheim in August 1704 and on the plain of Ramillies in 1706—two decisive battles of the war. In 1708–1709 famine, revolts, and uncollectable taxes tore France apart internally. Despair pervaded the French court. Louis wondered aloud how God could forsake one who had done so much for Him.

Though ready to make peace in 1709, Louis could not bring himself to accept the stiff terms of the alliance, which included the demand that he transfer all Spanish possessions to the emperor's grandson Charles and remove Philip V from Madrid. An immediate result of this failure to come to terms was a clash of forces at Malplaquet (September 1709), which left carnage on the battlefield unsurpassed until modern times.

France finally signed an armistice with England at Utrecht in July 1712 and concluded hostilities with Holland and the emperor in the Treaty of Rastadt in March 1714. This agreement confirmed Philip V as king of Spain. It gave England Gibraltar, which made England thereafter a Mediterranean power, and won Louis's recognition of the House of Hanover's right of accession to the English throne.

Politically the eighteenth century would belong to England as the sixteenth had belonged to Spain and the seventeenth to France. Although France remained intact and quite strong, the realization of Louis XIV's ambition had to await the rise of Napoleon Bonaparte. On his deathbed on September 1, 1715, a dying Louis fittingly warned the dauphin not to imitate his love of buildings and his liking for war.

When one looks back on Louis's reign, the grandeur and power of it still remain undimmed by his glory-seeking and military ambitions. One remembers not only a king who loved war too much, but also one who built the palace of Versailles and brought a new majesty to France; a king who managed the French aristocracy and bourgeoisie at court and controlled a French peasantry that had all too many just grievances; a king who raised up skilled and trustworthy ministers, councillors, and *intendants* from the middle classes; and a king who created a new French empire by expanding trade into Asia and colonizing North America.

Suggested Readings

MAURICE ASHLEY, *The Greatness of Oliver Cromwell* (1966). Detailed biography.

TREVOR ASTON (Ed.), *Crisis in Europe 1560–1660* (1965). Essays by major scholars focused on social and economic forces.

PETER BURKE, *Popular Culture in Early Modern Europe* (1978). A journalistic romp.

WILLIAM F. CHURCH (Ed.), *The Greatness of Louis XIV: Myth or Reality?* (1959). Excerpts from the scholarly debate over Louis's reign.

C. H. FIRTH, *Oliver Cromwell and the Rule of the Puritans in England* (1900). Old but still very authoritative work.

WILLIAM HALLER, *The Rise of Puritanism* (1957). Interesting study based largely on Puritan sermons.

CHRISTOPHER HILL, *The Century of Revolution 1603–1714* (1961). Bold, imaginative synthesis by a controversial master.

W. H. LEWIS, *The Splendid Century* (1953). Focuses on society, especially in the age of Louis XIV.

MICHAEL MACDONALD, *Mystical Bedlam: Madness, Anxiety and Healing in Seventeenth Century England* (1981).

DAVID OGG, *Europe in the Seventeenth Century* (1925). Among the most authoritative syntheses.

STUART E. PRALL, *The Puritan Revolution: A Documentary History* (1968). Comprehensive document collection.

LAWRENCE STONE, *The Causes of the English Revolution 1529–1642* (1972). Brief survey stressing social history and ruminating over historians and historical method.

G. R. R. TREASURE, *Seventeenth Century France* (1966). Broad, detailed survey of entire century.

MICHAEL WALZER, *The Revolution of the Saints: A Study in the Origins of Radical Politics* (1965). Effort to relate ideas and politics that depicts Puritans as true revolutionaries.

C. V. WEDGWOOD, *Richelieu and the French Monarchy* (1950). Fine biography.

JOHN B. WOLF, *Louis XIV* (1968). Very detailed political biography.

Galileo Galilei (1564–1642), the Florentine whose observations through a telescope showed the inaccuracy of the Ptolemaic assumption that the earth was the center of the universe and laid the foundations of modern astronomy. [*Library of Congress*]

The Scientific Revolution

New Departures

THE SIXTEENTH AND SEVENTEENTH CENTURIES witnessed a sweeping change in the scientific view of the universe. An earth-centered picture of the universe gave way to one in which the earth was only another planet orbiting about the sun. The sun itself became one of millions of stars. This transformation of humankind's perception of its place in the larger scheme of things led to a vast rethinking of moral and religious matters as well as of scientific theory. At the same time, the new scientific concepts and the methods of their construction became so impressive that subsequent knowledge in the Western world has been deemed correct only as it has approximated knowledge as defined by science. Perhaps no single intellectual development proved to be more significant for the future of European and Western civilization.

The process by which this new view of the universe and of scientific knowledge came to be established is normally termed the *Scientific Revolution*. However, care must be taken in the use of this metaphor. The word *revolution* normally denotes fairly rapid changes in the political world, involving large numbers of people. The Scientific Revolution was not rapid, nor did it involve more than a few hundred human beings. It was a complex movement with many false starts and many brilliant people with wrong as well as useful ideas. It took place in the studies and the crude laboratories of thinkers in Poland, Italy, Bohemia, France, and Great Britain. It stemmed from two major tendencies. The first, as illustrated by Nicolaus Copernicus, was the imposition of important small changes on existing models of thought. The second, as embodied by Francis Bacon, was the desire to pose new kinds of questions and to use new methods of investigation. In both cases, scientific thought changed the current and traditional opinions in other fields.

Nicolaus Copernicus

Copernicus (1473–1543) was a Polish astronomer who enjoyed a very high reputation throughout his life. He had been educated in Italy and corresponded with other astronomers throughout Europe. However, he had not been known for strikingly original or unorthodox thought. In 1543, the year of his death, Coper-

13

New Directions in Science and Thought in the Sixteenth and Seventeenth Centuries

Copernicus Ascribes Movement to the Earth

Copernicus published *De Revolutionibus Orbium Caelestium (On the Revolutions of the Heavenly Spheres)* in 1543. In his preface, which was addressed to Pope Paul III, he explained what had led him to think that the earth moved around the sun and what he thought were some of the scientific consequences of the new theory. The reader should note how important Copernicus considered the opinions of the ancient writers who had also ascribed motion to the earth. This is a good example of the manner in which familiarity with the ancients gave many Renaissance writers the self-confidence to criticize medieval ideas.

I may well presume, most Holy Father, that certain people, as soon as they hear that in this book about the Revolutions of the Spheres of the Universe I ascribe movement to the earthly globe, will cry out that, holding such views, I should at once be hissed off the stage. . . .

So I should like your Holiness to know that I was induced to think of a method of computing the motions of the spheres by nothing else than the knowledge that the Mathematicians [who had previously considered the problem] are inconsistent in these investigations.

For, first, the mathematicians are so unsure of the movements of the Sun and Moon that they cannot even explain or observe the constant length of the seasonal year. Secondly, in determining the motions of these and of the other five planets, they use neither the same principles and hypotheses nor the same demonstrations of the apparent motions and revolutions. . . . Nor have they been able thereby to discern or deduce the principal thing—namely the shape of the Universe and the unchangeable symmetry of its parts. . . .

I pondered long upon this uncertainty of mathematical tradition in establishing the motions of the system of the spheres. At last I began

to chafe that philosophers could by no means agree on any one certain theory of the mechanism of the Universe, wrought for us by a supremely good and orderly Creator. . . . I therefore took pains to read again the works of all the philosophers on whom I could lay hand to seek out whether any of them had ever supposed that the motions of the spheres were other than those demanded by the [Ptolemaic] mathematical schools. I found first in Cicero that Hicetas [of Syracuse, fifth century B.C.] had realized that the Earth moved. Afterwards I found in Plutarch that certain others had held the like opinion. . . .

Thus assuming motions, which in my work I ascribe to the Earth, by long and frequent observations I have at last discovered that, if the motions of the rest of the planets be brought into relation with the circulation of the Earth and be reckoned in proportion to the circles of each planet, not only do their phenomena presently ensue, but the orders and magnitudes of all stars and spheres, nay the heavens themselves, become so bound together that nothing in any part thereof could be moved from its place without producing confusion of all the other parts of the Universe as a whole.

As quoted in Thomas S. Kuhn, *The Copernican Revolution: Planetary Astronomy in the Development of Western Thought* (New York: Vintage Books, 1959), pp. 137–139, 141–142.

---

nicus published *On the Revolutions of the Heavenly Spheres.* Because he died near the time of publication, the fortunes of his work are not the story of one person's crusade for progressive science. Copernicus's book was "a revolution-making rather than a revolutionary text."[1] What Copernicus did was to provide an

intellectual springboard for a complete criticism of the then-dominant view of the position of the earth in the universe.

At the time of Copernicus the standard explanation of the earth and the heavens was that associated with Ptolemy and his work entitled the *Almagest* (A.D. 150). There was not just one Ptolemaic system; rather, several versions had been developed over the centuries by commentators on the original book. Most of these systems assumed that the earth was the

[1]Thomas S. Kuhn, *The Copernican Revolution: Planetary Astronomy in the Development of Western Thought* (New York: Vintage, 1959), p. 135.

center of the universe. Above the earth lay a series of crystalline spheres, one of which contained the moon, another the sun, and still others the planets and the stars. This was the astronomy found in such works as Dante's *Divine Comedy*. At the outer regions of these spheres lay the realm of God and the angels. Aristotelian physics provided the intellectual underpinnings of the Ptolemaic systems. The earth had to be the center because of its heaviness. The stars and the other heavenly bodies had to be enclosed in the crystalline spheres so that they could move. Nothing could move unless something was actually moving it. The state of rest was natural; motion was the condition that required explanation.

Numerous problems were associated with this system, and these had long been recognized. The most important was the observed motions of the planets. Planets could be seen moving in noncircular patterns around the earth. At certain times the planets actually appeared to be going backward. The Ptolemaic systems explained these strange motions primarily through *epicycles*. An epicycle is an orbit upon an orbit, like a spinning jewel on a ring. The planets were said to make a second revolution in an orbit tangent to their primary orbit around the earth. Other intellectual but nonobservational difficulties related to the immense speed at which the spheres had to move around the earth. To say the least, the Ptolemaic systems were cluttered. However, they were effective explanations as long as one assumed Aristotelian physics and the Christian belief that the earth rested at the center of the created universe.

Copernicus's *On the Revolutions of the Heavenly Spheres* challenged this picture in the most conservative manner possible. It suggested that if the earth were assumed to move about the sun in a circle, many of the difficulties with the Ptolemaic systems would disappear or become simpler. Although not wholly eliminated, the number of epicycles would be somewhat fewer. The motive behind this shift away from the earth-centered universe was to find a solu-

Two seventeenth-century armillary spheres, astronomical devices composed of rings that represent the orbits of important celestial bodies. The top one was built on the Copernican model, the bottom sphere reflects the much more complicated Ptolemaic universe. [Museum of the History of Science, Oxford, England]

477

tion to the problems of planetary motion. By allowing the earth to move around the sun, Copernicus was able to construct a more mathematically elegant basis for astronomy. He had been discontented with the traditional system because it was mathematically clumsy and inconsistent. The primary appeal of his new system was its mathematical aesthetics: with the sun at the center of the universe, mathematical astronomy would make more sense. A change in the conception of the position of the earth meant that the planets were actually moving in circular orbits and only seemed to be doing otherwise because of the position of the observers on earth.

Except for the modification in the position of the earth, most of the other parts of Copernicus's book were Ptolemaic. The path of the planets remained circular. Genuine epicycles still existed in the heavens. His system was no more accurate than the existing ones for predicting the location of the planets. He had used no new evidence. The major impact of his work was to provide another way of confronting some of the difficulties inherent in Ptolemaic astronomy. This work did not immediately replace the old astronomy, but it did allow other people who were also discontented with the Ptolemaic systems to think in new directions.

Copernicus's concern about mathematics provided an example of the single most important factor in the developing new science. The key to the future development of the Copernican revolution lay in the fusion of mathematical astronomy with further empirical data and observation, and mathematics became the model to which the new scientific thought would conform. The new empirical evidence helped to persuade the learned public.

Tycho Brahe and Johannes Kepler

The next major step toward the conception of a sun-centered system was taken by Tycho Brahe (1546–1601). He actually spent most of his life opposing Copernicus and advocating a different kind of earth-centered system. He suggested that the moon and the sun revolved around the earth and that the other planets revolved around the sun. However, in attacking Copernicus, he gave the latter's ideas more publicity. More important, this Danish astronomer's major weapon against Copernican astronomy was a series of new naked-eye astronomical observations. Brahe constructed the most accurate tables of observations that had been drawn up for centuries.

When Brahe died, these tables came into the possession of Johannes Kepler (1571–1630), a German astronomer. Kepler was a convinced Copernican, but his reasons for taking that position were not scientific. Kepler was deeply influenced by Renaissance Neoplatonism and its honoring of the sun. These Neoplatonists were also determined to discover mathematical harmonies in those numbers that would support a sun-centered universe. After much work Kepler discovered that to keep the sun at the center of things, he must abandon the Copernican concept of circular orbits. The mathematical relationships that emerged from a consideration of Brahe's observations suggested that the orbits of the planets were elliptical. Kepler published his findings in 1609 in a book entitled *On the Motion of Mars*. He had solved the problem of planetary orbits by using Copernicus's sun-centered universe and Brahe's empirical data.

Kepler had, however, also defined a new problem. None of the available theories could explain why the planetary orbits were elliptical. That solution awaited the work of Sir Isaac Newton.

Galileo Galilei

From Copernicus to Brahe to Kepler there had been little new information about the heavens that might not have been known to Ptolemy. However, in the same year that Kepler published his volume on Mars, an Italian scientist named Galileo Galilei (1564–1642) first turned a telescope on the heavens. Through that recently invented instrument he saw stars where none had been known to exist, mountains on the moon, spots moving across the sun, and moons orbiting Jupiter. The heavens were far more complex than anyone had formerly suspected. None of these discoveries proved that the earth orbited the sun, but they did suggest the complete inadequacy of the Ptolemaic system. It simply could not accommodate itself to all of these new phenomena. Some of Galileo's colleagues at the university of Padua were so unnerved that they refused to look through the telescope. Galileo publicized his findings and arguments for the Copernican system in numerous works, the most famous of which was his *Dialogues on the Two Chief Systems of the World* (1632). This book brought down on him the condemnation of the

479

*New Directions
in Science and
Thought in the
Sixteenth and
Seventeenth
Centuries*

Galileo Discusses the Relationship of Science and the Bible

The religious authorities were often critical of the discoveries and theories of sixteenth- and seventeenth-century science. For many years religious and scientific writers debated the implications of the Copernican theory in the reading of the Bible. For years before his condemnation by the Roman Catholic church in 1633, Galileo had contended that scientific theory and religious piety were compatible. In his *Letter to the Grand Duchess Christiana* (of Tuscany) written in 1615, Galileo argued that God had revealed truth in both the Bible and physical nature and that the truth of physical nature did not contradict the Bible if the latter were properly understood.

*The reason produced for condemning the opinion that the earth moves and the sun stands still is that in many places in the Bible one may read that the sun moves and the earth stands still.
. . .*

With regard to this argument, I think in the first place that it is very pious to say and prudent to affirm that the holy Bible can never speak untruth—whenever its true meaning is understood. But I believe nobody will deny that it is often very abstruse, and may say things which are quite different from what its bare words signify. . . .

This being granted, I think that in discussions of physical problems we ought to begin not from the authority of scriptural passages, but from sense-experiences and necessary demonstrations; for the holy Bible and the phenomena of nature proceed alike from the divine Word, the former as the dictate of the Holy Ghost and the latter as the observant executrix of God's commands. It is necessary for the Bible, in order to be accommodated to the understanding of every man, to speak many things which appear to differ from the absolute truth so far as the bare meaning of the words is concerned. But Nature, on the other hand, is inexorable and immutable; she never transgresses the laws imposed upon her, or cares a whit whether her abstruse reasons and methods of operation are understandable to men. For that reason it appears that nothing physical

which sense-experience sets before our eyes, or which necessary demonstrations prove to us, ought to be called in question (much less condemned) upon the testimony of biblical passages which may have some different meaning beneath their words. For the Bible is not chained in every expression to conditions as strict as those which govern all physical effects; nor is God any less excellently revealed in Nature's actions than in the sacred statements of the Bible. . . .

*From this I do not mean to infer that we need not have an extraordinary esteem for the passages of holy Scripture. On the contrary, having arrived at any certainties in physics, we ought to utilize these as the most appropriate aids in the true exposition of the Bible and in the investigation of those meanings which are necessarily contained therein for these must be concordant with demonstrated truths. I should judge the authority of the Bible was designed to persuade men of those articles and propositions which, surpassing all human reasoning, could not be made credible by science, or by any other means than through the very mouth of the Holy Spirit.
. . .*

But I do not feel obliged to believe that the same God who has endowed us with senses, reason, and intellect has intended to forgo their use and by some other means to give us knowledge which we can attain by them.

Discoveries and Opinions of Galileo, trans. and ed. by Stillman Drake (Garden City, N.Y.: Doubleday Anchor Books, 1957), pp. 181–183.

Roman Catholic church. He was compelled to recant his opinions. However, he is reputed to have muttered after the recantation, *''E pur si muove''* (''It [the earth] still moves'').

Galileo's discoveries and his popularization of the Copernican system were of secondary importance in his life work. His most important achievement was to articulate the concept of a universe totally subject to mathematical laws. More than any other writer of the cen-

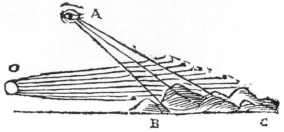

LEFT-*Telescopes built by Galileo. His astronomical observations had revolutionary intellectual and theological implications.* [Science Museum, London]

BELOW-*Galileo's drawing of his method for measuring the heights of lunar mountains* (1611). [Ann Ronan Picture Library and E.P. Goldschmidt and Co., Ltd.]

tury he argued that nature in its most minute details displayed mathematical regularity. He once wrote:

Philosophy is written in that great book which ever lies before our eyes—I mean the universe—but we cannot understand it if we do not first learn the language and grasp the symbols in which it is written. This book is written in the mathematical language, and the symbols are triangles, circles, and other geometrical figures, without whose help it is impossible to comprehend a single word of it; without which one wanders through a dark labyrinth.[2]

The universe was rational; however, its rationality was not that of Scholastic logic but of mathematics. Copernicus had thought that the heavens conformed to mathematical regularity; Galileo saw this regularity throughout all physical nature. He believed that the smallest atom behaved with the same mathematical precision as the largest heavenly sphere.

Galileo's thought meant that a world of quantity was replacing one of qualities. Mathematical quantities and relationships would henceforth increasingly be used to describe nature. Color, beauty, taste, and the like would be reduced to numerical relationships. And eventually social relationships would be envisioned in a mathematical model. Nature was cold, rational, mathematical, and mechanistic. What was real and lasting in the world was what was mathematically measurable. Few intellectual shifts have wrought such momentous changes for Western civilization.

[2]Quoted in E. A. Burtt, *The Metaphysical Foundations of Modern Physical Science* (Garden City, N.Y.: Anchor-Doubleday, 1954), p. 75.

René Descartes

No writer of the seventeenth century more fully adopted the geometric spirit of contemporary mathematics than René Descartes (1596–1650). He was a gifted mathematician who invented analytic geometry, and he was the author of major works on numerous scientific topics. However, his most important contribution was to scientific method. He wanted to proceed by deduction rather than by empirical observation and induction.

In 1637 Descartes published a *Discourse on Method* in which he attempted to provide a basis for all thinking founded on a mathematical model. He published the work in French rather than in Latin because he wanted it to have wide circulation and application. He began by saying that he would doubt everything except those propositions about which he could have clear and distinct ideas. This approach rejected all forms of intellectual authority except the conviction of his own reason. He concluded that he could not doubt his own act of thinking and his own existence. From this base he proceeded to deduce the existence of God. The presence of God was important to Descartes because God was the guarantor of the correctness of clear and distinct ideas. Because God was not a deceiver, the ideas of God-given reason could not be false.

Descartes believed that this powerful human reason could fully comprehend the world. He divided existing things into mind and body. Thinking was the characteristic of the mind, extension of the body. Within the material

René Descartes (1596–1650). Descartes believed that because the material world operated according to mathematical laws it could therefore be understood by the exercise of human reasoning. [Giraudon]

Bacon (1561–1626) was an Englishman of almost universal accomplishment. He was a lawyer, a high royal official, and the author of histories, moral essays, and philosophical discourses. Traditionally he has been regarded as the father of empiricism and of experimentation in science. Much of this reputation is unearned. Bacon was not a scientist except in the most amateur fashion. His accomplishment was setting a tone and helping to create a climate in which other scientists worked. In books such as *The Advancement of Learning* (1605), the *Novum Organum* (1620), and the *New Atlantis* (1627), Bacon attacked the Scholastic belief that most truth had already been discovered and only required explanation, as well as the Scholastic reverence for intellectual authority in general. He believed that Scholastic thinkers paid too much attention to tradition and to knowledge achieved by the ancients. He urged contemporaries to strike out on their own in search of a new understanding of nature. He wanted seventeenth-century

world, mathematical laws reigned supreme. These could be grasped by the human reason. Because the laws were mathematical, they could be deduced from each other and constituted a complete system. The world of extension was the world of the scientist, whereas the mind was related to theology and philosophy. In the material world there was no room for spirits, divinity, or anything nonmaterial. Descartes had separated mind from body in order to banish the former from the realm of scientific speculation. He wanted to resurrect the speculative use of reason, but in a limited manner. It was to be applied only to the mechanical and mathematical realm of matter.

Descartes's emphasis on deduction and rational speculation exercised broad influence. Well into the eighteenth century European thinkers appealed to Descartes's method, which moved from broad intellectual generalizations to specific phenomena. The method then attempted to see how the phenomena could be interpreted so as to mesh with the generalization. However, that method was eventually overcome by the force of scientific induction, whereby the observer or scientist began with observations of empirical data and then attempted to draw generalizations from those observations. The major champion of the inductive method during the early seventeenth century had been Francis Bacon.

Sir Francis Bacon, Viscount St. Albans (1561–1626). By teaching that knowledge should proceed inductively, Bacon became a major champion of the scientific method. [National Portrait Gallery, London]

Europeans to have confidence in themselves and their own abilities rather than in the people and methods of the past. Bacon was one of the first major European writers to champion the desirability of innovation and change.

Bacon believed that human knowledge should produce useful results. In particular, knowledge of nature should be brought to the aid of the human condition. Those goals required the modification or abandonment of Scholastic modes of learning and thinking.

Bacon contended, "The [Scholastic] logic now in use serves more to fix and give stability to the errors which have their foundation in commonly received notions than to help the search after truth."[3] Scholastic philosophers could not escape from their syllogisms to examine the foundations of their thought and intellectual presuppositions. Bacon urged that philoso-

[3]Quoted in Franklin Baumer, *Main Currents of Western Thought*, 4th ed. (New Haven, Conn.: Yale, 1978), p. 281.

Bacon Attacks the Idols that Harm Human Understanding

Francis Bacon wanted the men and women of his era to have the courage to change the way in which they thought about physical nature. In this famous passage from the *Novum Organum* (1620) Bacon attempted to explain why people had such difficulty in asking new questions and seeking new answers. His observations may still be relevant to the manner in which people form and hold their opinions in our own day.

The idols and false notions which are now in possession of the human understanding, and have taken deep root therein, not only so beset men's minds that truth can hardly find entrance, but even after entrance is obtained, they will again in the very instauration of the sciences meet and trouble us, unless men being forewarned of the danger fortify themselves as far as may be against their assaults.

There are four classes of Idols which beset men's minds. To these for distinction's sake I have assigned names,—calling the first class Idols of the Tribe; *the second,* Idols of the Cave; *the third,* Idols of the Marketplace; *the fourth,* Idols of the Theatre.

. . . .

The Idols of the Tribe have their foundation in human nature itself; and in the tribe or race of men. For it is a false assertion that the sense of man is the measure of things. On the contrary, all perceptions as well as the sense as of the mind are according to the measure of the individual and not according to the measure of the universe. And the human understanding is like a false mirror, which, receiving rays irregularly, distorts and discolours the nature of things by mingling its own nature with it.

The Idols of the Cave are the idols of the individual man. For every one (besides the errors common to human nature in general) has a cave or den of his own, which refracts and discolours the light of nature; owing either to his own proper and peculiar nature; or to his education and conversation with others; or to the reading of books, and the authority of those whom he esteems and admires. . . .

There are also Idols formed by the intercourse and association of men with each other, which I call Idols of the Marketplace, on account of the commerce and consort of men there. For it is by discourse that men associate; and words are imposed according to the apprehension of the vulgar. And therefore the ill and unfit choice of words wonderfully obstructs the understanding. . . .

Lastly, there are Idols which have immigrated into men's minds from the various dogmas of philosophies, and also from wrong laws of demonstration. These I call Idols of the Theatre; because in my judgment all the received systems are but so many stage plays, representing worlds of their own creation after an unreal and scenic fashion.

Francis Bacon, *Essays, Advancement of Learning, New Atlantis, and Other Pieces*, ed. by Richard Foster Jones (New York: Odyssey, 1937), pp. 278–280.

The microscope was the telescope's companion as a major optical invention of the seventeenth century. Several people, including Galileo, had a hand in its development, but the greatest progress was made by the Dutchman Anton von Leeuwenhoek (1632–1723) and the Englishman Robert Hooke (1635–1703). Hooke designed this microscope in 1670. [IBM Gallery of Science and Art]

483

*New Directions
in Science and
Thought in the
Sixteenth and
Seventeenth
Centuries*

BELOW-*Another optical aid: spectacles. Spectacles date from at least the fourteenth century and were becoming common during the later 1500s. Here we see a spectacle pedlar selling his wares. Spectacles were selected by trial and error, not made to prescription. [The Mansell Collection]*

phers and investigators of nature examine the evidence of their senses before constructing logical speculations. In a famous passage he divided all philosophers into ''men of experiment and men of dogmas.'' He observed:

The men of experiment are like the ant, they only collect and use; the reasoners resemble spiders, who make cobwebs out of their own substance. But the bee takes a middle course: it gathers its material from the flowers of the garden and of the field, but transforms and digests it by a power of its own. Not unlike this is the true business of philosophy.[4]

By directing scientists toward an examination of empirical evidence, Bacon hoped that they would achieve new knowledge and thus new capabilities for humankind.

Bacon compared himself with Columbus plotting a new route to intellectual discovery. The comparison is significant, because it displays the consciousness of a changing world that appears so often in writers of the late sixteenth and early seventeenth centuries. They were rejecting the past not from simple hatred but rather from a firm understanding that the world was much more complicated than their medieval forebears had thought.

Neither Europe nor European thought could remain self-contained. There were not only new worlds on the globe but also new worlds of the mind. Most of the people in Bacon's day, including the intellectuals, thought that the best era of human history lay in antiquity. Bacon dissented vigorously from that point of view. He looked to a future of material improvement achieved through the empirical examination of nature. His own theory of induction from empirical evidence was quite

[4]Quoted in ibid., p. 288.

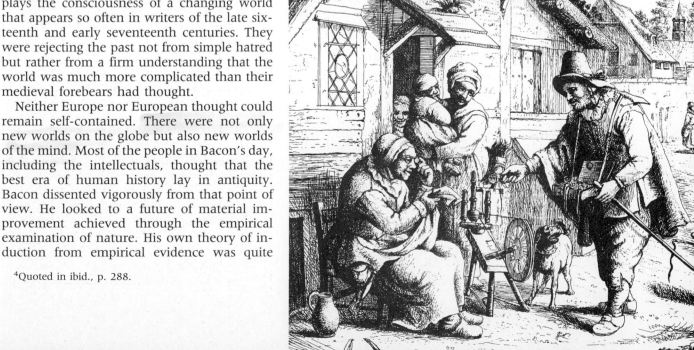

Sir Isaac Newton, discoverer of the mathematical and physical laws governing the force of gravity. Newton believed that religion and science were compatible and mutually supportive. To study nature was to gain a better understanding of the Creator. [New York Public Library Picture Collection]

unsystematic, but his insistence on appeal to experience influenced others whose methods were more productive. His great achievement was persuading increasing numbers of thinkers that scientific thought must conform to empirical experience.

Bacon gave science a progressionist bias. Science was to have a practical purpose and the goal of human improvement. Some scientific investigation does possess this character. Much pure research does not. However, Bacon linked in the public mind the concepts of science and material progress. This was a powerful idea and has continued to influence Western civilization to the present day. It has made science and those who can appeal to the authority of science major forces for change and innovation. Thus, though not making any major scientific contribution himself, Bacon directed investigators of nature to a new method and a new purpose.

Isaac Newton

Isaac Newton (1642–1727) drew on the work of his predecessors and his own brilliance to solve the major remaining problem of planetary motion and to establish a basis for physics that endured more than two centuries. The question that continued to perplex seventeenth-century scientists who accepted the theories of Copernicus, Kepler, and Galileo was how the planets and other heavenly bodies moved in an orderly fashion. The Ptolemaic and Aristotelian answer had been the crystalline spheres and a universe arranged in the order of the heaviness of its parts. Numerous unsatisfactory theories had been set forth to deal with the question.

In 1687 Newton published *The Mathematical*

Principles of Natural Philosophy, better known by its Latin title of *Principia Mathematica.* Much of the research and thinking for this great work had taken place more than fifteen years earlier. Newton was heavily indebted to the work of Galileo and particularly to the latter's view that inertia could exist in either a state of motion or a state of rest. Galileo's mathematical bias permeated Newton's thought. Newton reasoned that the planets and all other physical objects in the universe moved through mutual attraction. Every object in the universe affected every other object through gravity. The attraction of gravity explained why the planets moved in an orderly rather than a chaotic manner. He had found that "the force of gravity towards the whole planet did arise from and was compounded of the forces of gravity towards all its parts, and towards every one part was in the inverse proportion of the squares of the distances from the part."[5] Newton demonstrated this relationship mathematically. He made no attempt to explain the nature of gravity itself.

[5]Quoted in A. Rupert Hall, *From Galileo to Newton, 1630–1720* (London: Fontana, 1970), p. 300.

484

Newton was a great mathematical genius, but he also upheld the importance of empirical data and observation. He believed, in good Baconian fashion, that one must observe phenomena before attempting to explain them. The final test of any theory or hypothesis for him was whether it described what could actually be observed. He was a great opponent of Descartes's rationalism, which he believed included insufficient guards against error. As Newton's own theory of universal gravitation became increasingly accepted, the Baconian bias also became more fully popularized.

With the work of Newton the natural universe became a realm of law and regularity.

Newton Sets Forth Rules of Reasoning in Philosophy

Philosophy was the term that seventeenth-century writers used to describe the new science. In this passage from his *Principia Mathematica* (1687) Isaac Newton laid down what he regarded as the fundamental rules for scientific reasoning. The reader should notice the importance he placed on experimental evidence and his desire to find rules or regularities that exist throughout the natural order.

Rule I. We are to admit no more causes of natural things than such as are both true and sufficient to explain their appearances.

To this purpose the philosophers say that Nature does nothing in vain, and more is in vain when less will serve; for Nature is pleased with simplicity, and affects not the pomp of superfluous causes.

Rule II. Therefore to the same natural effects we must, as far as possible, assign the same causes.

As to respiration in a man and in a beast; the descent of stones in Europe and in America; the light of our culinary fire and of the sun; the reflection of light in the earth, and in the planets.

Rule III. The qualities of bodies, which admit neither intension nor remission of degrees, and which are found to belong to all bodies within the reach of our experiments, are to be esteemed the universal qualities of all bodies whatsoever.

For since the qualities of bodies are only known to us by experiments, we are to hold for universal all such as universally agree with experiments and such as are not liable to diminution can never be quite taken away. We are certainly not to relinquish the evidence of experiments for the sake of dreams and vain fictions of our own devising. . . . We no other way know the extension of bodies than by our senses, nor do these reach it in all bodies; but because we perceive extension in all that are sensible, therefore we ascribe it universally to all others also. That abundance of bodies are hard, we learn by experience; and because the hardness of the whole arises from the hardness of the parts, we therefore justly infer the hardness of the undivided particles not only of the bodies we feel but of all others. That bodies are impenetrable, we gather not from reason, but from sensation. . . .

Lastly, if it universally appears, by experiments and astronomical observations, that all bodies about the earth gravitate towards the earth, and that in proportion to the quantity of matter which they severally contain; . . . we must, in consequence of this rule, universally allow that all bodies whatsoever are endowed with a principle of universal gravitation. . . .

Rule IV. In experimental philosophy we are to look upon propositions collected by general induction from phaenomena as accurately or very nearly true, notwithstanding any contrary hypotheses that may be imagined, till such time as other phaenomena occur, by which they may either be made more accurate, or liable to exceptions.

This rule must follow, that the argument of induction may not be evaded by hypotheses.

Introduction to Contemporary Civilization in the West, 3rd ed., Vol. 1 (New York: Columbia University Press, 1960), pp. 850–852.

Spirits and divinities were no longer necessary to explain its operation. Thus the Scientific Revolution liberated human beings from the fear of a chaotic or haphazard universe. Most of the scientists were very devout people. They saw the new picture of physical nature as suggesting a new picture of God. The Creator of this rational, lawful nature must also be rational. To study nature was to come to a better understanding of that Creator. Science and religious faith were not only compatible but mutually supporting. As Newton wrote, "The main Business of Natural Philosophy is to argue from Phaenomena without feigning Hypothesis, and to deduce Causes from Effects, till we come to the very first Cause, which certainly is not mechanical."[6]

This reconciliation of faith and science allowed the new physics and astronomy to spread rapidly. At the very time when Europeans were finally tiring of the wars of religion, the new science provided the basis for a view of God that might lead away from irrational disputes and wars over religious doctrine. Faith in a rational God encouraged faith in the rationality of human beings and in their capacity to improve their lot once liberated from the traditions of the past. The Scientific Revolution provided the great model for the desirability of change and of criticism of inherited views. Yet at the same time the new science caused some people to feel that the mystery had been driven from the universe and that the rational Creator was less loving and less near to humankind than the God of earlier ages.

Writers and Philosophers

The end of the sixteenth century saw weariness with religious strife and incipient unbelief as many no longer embraced either old Catholic or new Protestant absolutes. Intellectually as well as politically the seventeenth century was a period of transition, one already well prepared for by the thinkers of the Renaissance, who had reacted strongly against medieval intellectual traditions, especially those informed by Aristotle and Scholasticism.

Even as they sought to find a purer culture before the Middle Ages in pagan and Christian antiquity, however, Humanists and Protestants continued to share much of the medieval vision of a unified Christendom. Few wanted to

[6]Quoted in Baumer, p. 323.

embrace the secular values and preoccupations of the growing scientific movement, which found its models in mathematics and the natural sciences, rather than in the example and authority of antiquity. Some strongly condemned the work of Copernicus, Kepler, and Galileo, whose theories seemed to fly in the face of commonsense experience as well as to question hallowed tradition.

The thinkers of the Renaissance and the Reformation nonetheless paved the way for the new science and philosophy, both by their attacks on tradition and by their own failure to implement radical reforms. The Humanist revival of ancient skepticism proved an effective foundation for attacks on traditional views of authority and rationality in both religion and science. Already such thinkers as the Italian Pico della Mirandola (1463–1494), the German Cornelius Agrippa of Nettisheim (1486–1535), and the Frenchman François Rabelais (1494–1553) had questioned the ability of reason to obtain certitude. Sebastian Castellio (1515–1563), Michel de Montaigne (1533–1592), and Pierre Charron (1541–1603) had been as much repelled by the new Calvinist religion as John Calvin had been by medieval religion. It was in the wake of such criticism that René Descartes developed a more modest, yet surer, definition of rationality as the tool of the new scientific philosophy.

The writers and philosophers of the seventeenth century were aware that they lived in a period of transition. Some embraced the new science wholeheartedly (Hobbes and Locke), some tried to straddle the two ages (Cervantes, Shakespeare, and Milton), and still others ignored or opposed the new developments that seemed mortally to threaten traditional values (Pascal and Bunyan). As a group these thinkers helped to make the transition from medieval to modern times by clarifying the intellectual issues involved. In literature, religious thought, and political theory, they established the national landmarks and struck the new directions in Western thought.

Miguel de Cervantes Saavedra (1547–1616)

Spanish literature of the sixteenth and seventeenth centuries reflects the peculiar religious and political history of Spain in this period. Spain was dominated by the Catholic church. Since the joint reign of Ferdinand and Isabella (1479–1504) the church had received the unqualified support of reigning political power. Although there was religious reform in Spain, a Protestant Reformation never occurred, thanks largely to the entrenched power of the church and the Inquisition.

The second influence was the aggressive piety of Spanish rulers. The intertwining of Catholic piety and Spanish political power underlay the third major influence on Spanish literature: preoccupation with medieval chivalric virtues—in particular, questions of honor and loyalty. The novels and plays of the period almost invariably focus on a special decision involving a character's reputation as his honor or loyalty is tested. In this regard Spanish literature may be said to have remained more Catholic and medieval than that of England and France, where major Protestant movements had occurred. Two of the most important Spanish writers in this period became priests (Lope de Vega and Pedro Calderón de la Barca), and the one generally acknowledged to be the greatest Spanish writer of all time, Cervantes, was preoccupied in his work with the strengths and weaknesses of religious idealism.

Cervantes was born in Alcalá, the son of a nomadic physician. Having received only a smattering of formal education, he educated himself by insatiable reading in vernacular literature and immersion in the "school of life." As a young man he worked in Rome for a Spanish cardinal. In 1570 he became a soldier and was decorated for gallantry in the Battle of Lepanto (1571). While he was returning to Spain in 1575, his ship was captured by pirates, and Cervantes spent five years as a slave in Algiers. On his release and return to Spain, he held many odd jobs, among them that of a tax collector. He was several times imprisoned for padding his accounts. He began to write his most famous work, *Don Quixote,* in 1603, while languishing in prison.

The first part of *Don Quixote* appeared in 1605. If, as many argue, the intent of this work was to satirize the chivalric romances so popular in Spain, Cervantes nonetheless failed to conceal his deep affection for the character he created as an object of ridicule, Don Quixote. The work is satire only on the surface and has remained as much an object of study by philosophers and theologians as by students of Spanish literature. Don Quixote, a none-too-stable middle-aged man, was presented by Cervantes as one driven mad by reading too many chivalric romances. He finally comes to believe that he is an aspirant to knighthood and must prove

The author of Don Quixote, *Miguel de Cervantes Saavedra (1547–1616), generally acknowledged to be the greatest Spanish writer.* [*Library of Congress*]

by brave deeds his worthiness of knightly rank. To this end he acquires a rusty suit of armor, mounts an aged steed (named Rozinante), and chooses for his inspiration a quite unworthy peasant girl, Dulcinea, whom he fancies to be a noble lady to whom he can, with honor, dedicate his life.

Don Quixote's foil in the story—Sancho Panza, a clever, worldly-wise peasant who serves as his squire—is an equally fascinating character. Sancho Panza watches with bemused skepticism, but also with genuine sympathy, as his lord does battle with a windmill (which he mistakes for a dragon) and repeatedly makes a fool of himself as he gallops across the countryside. The story ends tragi-

487

cally with Don Quixote's humiliating defeat by a well-meaning friend, who, disguised as a knight, bests Don Quixote in combat and forces him to renounce his quest for knighthood. The humiliated Don Quixote does not, however, come to his senses as a result. He returns sadly to his village to die a shamed and broken-hearted old man.

Throughout *Don Quixote* Cervantes juxtaposed the down-to-earth realism of Sancho Panza with the old-fashioned religious idealism of Don Quixote. The reader perceives that Cervantes admired the one as much as the other and meant to portray both as representing attitudes necessary for a happy life. If they are to be truly happy, men and women need dreams, even impossible ones, just as much as they need a sense of reality.

Don Quixote as imagined by the nineteenth-century French artist Honoré Daumier (1808–1879). Cervantes' novel has delighted readers for four centuries. [Giraudon]

William Shakespeare (1564–1616)

Shakespeare, the greatest playwright in the English language, was born in Stratford-on-Avon, where he lived almost all of his life except for the years when he wrote in London. There is much less factual knowledge about him than one would expect of such an important figure. Shakespeare married in 1582 at the early age of eighteen, and he and his wife, Anne Hathaway, had three children (two were twins) by 1585. He apparently worked as a schoolteacher for a time and in this capacity acquired his broad knowledge of Renaissance learning and literature. The argument of some scholars that he was an untutored natural genius is highly questionable. His own learning and his enthusiasm for the education of his day are manifest in the many learned allusions that appear in his plays.

Shakespeare enjoyed the life of a country gentleman. There is none of the Puritan distress over worldliness in his work. He took the new commercialism and the bawdy pleasures of the Elizabethan Age in stride and with amusement. The few allusions to the Puritans that exist in his works appear to be more critical than complimentary. In matters of politics, as in those of religion, he was very much a man of his time and not inclined to offend his queen.

That Shakespeare was interested in politics is apparent from his history plays and the references to contemporary political events that fill all his plays. He seems to have viewed government simply, however, through the character of the individual ruler, whether Richard III or Elizabeth Tudor, not in terms of ideal systems or social goals. By modern standards he was a political conservative, accepting the social rankings and the power structure of his day and demonstrating unquestioned patriotism.

Shakespeare knew the theater as one who participated in every phase of its life—as a playwright, an actor, and a part owner of a theater. He was a member and principal dramatist of a famous company of actors known as the King's Men. During the tenure of Edmund Tilney, who was Queen Elizabeth's Master of Revels during the greater part of Shakespeare's active period (1590–1610), many of Shakespeare's plays were performed at court. The queen enthusiastically patronized plays and pageants.

Elizabethan drama was already a distinctive form when Shakespeare began writing. Unlike

passion and had a unique talent for psychological penetration.

Shakespeare wrote histories, comedies, and tragedies. *Richard III* (1593), a very early play, stands out among the examples of the first genre, although some historians have criticized as historically inaccurate his patriotic depiction of Richard, the foe of Henry Tudor, as an unprincipled villain. Shakespeare's comedies, although not attaining the heights of his tragedies, surpass in originality his history plays. Save for *The Tempest* (1611), his last play, the

The English dramatist and poet, William Shakespeare. This engraving by Martin Droeshout appears on the title page of the collected edition of his plays published in 1623 and is probably as close as we shall come to knowing what he looked like. [New York Public Library]

This 1596 sketch of the interior of the Swan Theater in London by Johannis de Witt, a Dutch visitor, is the only known contemporary view of an Elizabethan playhouse. In this kind of setting the plays of Marlowe, Shakespeare, Jonson, and their fellows were first seen. [University Library, Utrecht]

French drama of the seventeenth century, which was dominated by the court and classical models, English drama developed in the sixteenth and seventeenth centuries as a blending of many extant forms, ranging from classical comedies and tragedies to the medieval morality play and contemporary Italian short stories. In Shakespeare's own library one could find Holinshed's and other English chronicles; the works of Plutarch, Ovid, and Vergil, among other Latin authors; Arthurian romances and popular songs and fables; the writings of Montaigne and Rabelais; and the major English poets and prose writers.

Two contemporaries, Thomas Kyd and Christopher Marlowe, especially influenced Shakespeare's tragedies. Kyd (1558–1594) was the author of the first dramatic version of *Hamlet* and a master at weaving together motive and plot. The tragedies of Marlowe (1564–1593) set a model for character, poetry, and style that only Shakespeare among the English playwrights of the period surpassed. Shakespeare's work was an original synthesis of the best past and current achievements. He mastered the psychology of human motivation and

comedies most familiar to modern readers were written between 1598 and 1602: *Much Ado About Nothing* (1598–1599), *As You Like It* (1598–1600), and *Twelfth Night* (1602).

The tragedies are considered his unique achievement. Four of these were written within a three-year period: *Hamlet* (1603), *Othello* (1604), *King Lear* (1605), and *Macbeth* (1606). The most original of the tragedies, *Romeo and Juliet* (1597), transformed an old popular story into a moving drama of "star-cross'd lovers." Both Romeo and Juliet, denied a marriage by their factious families, die tragic deaths. Romeo, finding Juliet and thinking her dead after she has taken a sleeping potion, poisons himself. Juliet, awakening to find Romeo dead, stabs herself to death with his dagger.

Throughout his lifetime and ever since, Shakespeare has been immensely popular with both the playgoer and the play reader. As Ben Jonson, a contemporary classical dramatist who created his own school of poets, aptly put it in a tribute affixed to the First Folio edition of Shakespeare's plays (1623): "He was not of an age, but for all time."

The English writer and poet John Milton in an engraving by William Faithorne—one of the few authentic contemporary likenesses of him. [*Library of Congress*]

John Milton (1608–1674)

John Milton was the son of a devout Puritan father. Educated at Saint Paul's School and then at Christ's College of Cambridge University, he became a careful student of Christian and pagan classics. In 1638 he traveled to Italy, where he found in the lingering Renaissance a very congenial intellectual atmosphere. The Phlegraean Fields near Naples, a volcanic region, later became the model for hell in *Paradise Lost*, and it is suspected by some scholars that the Villa d'Este provided the model for paradise in *Paradise Regained*. Milton remained throughout his life a man more at home in the Italian Renaissance, with its high ideals and universal vision, than in the strife-torn England of the seventeenth century.

A man of deep inner conviction and principle, Milton believed that standing a test of character was the most important thing in an individual's life. This belief informed his own personal life and is the subject of much of his literary work. An early poem, *Lycidas*, was a pastoral elegy dealing with one who lived well but not long, Edward King, a close college friend who tragically drowned. In 1639 Milton joined the Puritan struggle against Charles I and Archbishop Laud. Employing his literary talents as a pamphleteer, he defended the pres-

byterian form of church government against the episcopacy and supported other Puritan reforms. After a month-long unsuccessful marriage in 1642 (a marriage later reconciled), he wrote several tracts in defense of the right to divorce. These writings became a factor in Parliament's passage of a censorship law in 1643, against which Milton wrote an eloquent defense of the freedom of the press, *Areopagitica* (1644).

Until the upheavals of the civil war moderated his views, Milton believed that government should have the least possible control over the private lives of individuals. When Parliament divided into Presbyterians and Independents, he took the side of the latter, who wanted to dissolve the national church altogether in favor of the local autonomy of individual congregations. He also defended the execution of Charles I in a tract on the *Tenure of Kings and Magistrates*. After his intense labor on this tract his eyesight failed. Milton was totally blind when he wrote his acclaimed masterpieces.

Paradise Lost, completed in 1665 and published in 1667, is a study of the destructive qualities of pride and the redeeming possibilities of humility. It elaborates in traditional Christian language and concept the revolt of

Satan in heaven and the fall of Adam on earth. The motives of Satan and all who rebel against God intrigued Milton. His proud but tragic Satan, one of the great figures of all literature, represents the absolute corruption of potential greatness.

In *Paradise Lost* Milton aspired to give England a lasting epic like that given Greece in Homer's *Iliad* and ancient Rome in Vergil's *Aeneid*. In choosing biblical subject matter, he revealed the influence of contemporary theology. Milton tended to agree with the Arminians, who, unlike the extreme Calvinists, did not believe that all worldly events, including the Fall of Man, were immutably fixed in the eternal decree of God. Milton shared the Arminian belief that human beings must take responsibility for their fate and that human efforts to improve character could, with God's grace, bring salvation.

Perhaps his own blindness, joined with the hope of making the best of a failed religious revolution, inclined Milton to sympathize with those who urged people to make the most of what they had, even in the face of seemingly sure defeat. That is a manifest concern of his last works, *Samson Agonistes*, which recounts the biblical story of Samson, and *Paradise Regained*, the story of Christ's temptation in the wilderness, both published in 1671.

John Bunyan (1628–1688)

Bunyan was the English author of two classics of sectarian Puritan spirituality: *Grace Abounding* (1666) and *The Pilgrim's Progress* (1678). A Bedford tinker, his works speak especially for the seventeenth-century working people and popular religious culture. Bunyan received only the most basic education before taking up his father's craft. He was drafted into Oliver Cromwell's revolutionary army in 1644 and served for two years, although without seeing actual combat. The visionary fervor of the New Model Army and the imagery of warfare abound in Bunyan's work.

After the restoration of the monarchy in 1660, Bunyan went to prison for his fiery preaching and remained there for twelve years. Had he been willing to agree to give up preaching, he might have been released much sooner. But Puritans considered the compromise of one's beliefs a tragic flaw, and Bunyan steadfastly refused all such suggestions.

During this period of imprisonment Bunyan wrote his famous autobiography, *Grace Abounding*. It is both a very personal statement and a model for the faithful. Like *The Pilgrim's Progress*, Bunyan's later masterpiece, *Grace Abounding* expresses Puritan piety at its most fervent. Puritans believed that individuals could do absolutely nothing to save themselves, and this made them extremely restless and introspective. The individual believer could only trust that God had placed her or him among the elect and try each day to live a life that reflected such a favored status. So long as men and women struggled successfully against the flesh and the world, they had presumptive evidence that they were among God's elect. To falter or to become complacent in the face of temptation was to cast doubt on one's faith and salvation and even to raise the specter of eternal damnation.

This anxious questing for salvation was the subject of *The Pilgrim's Progress*, a work unique in its contribution to Western religious symbolism and imagery. The story of the journey of Christian and his friends Hopeful and Faithful to the Celestial City, it teaches that one must deny spouse, children, and all earthly security and go in search of "Life, life, eternal life." During the long journey, the travelers must resist the temptations of Worldly-Wiseman and Vanity Fair, pass through the Slough of Despond, and endure a long dark night in Doubting Castle, their faith being tested at every turn. Bunyan later wrote a work tracing the progress of Christian's opposite, *The Life and Death of Mr. Badman* (1680), the story of a man so addicted to the bad habits of Restoration society, of which Bunyan strongly disapproved, that he journeyed steadfastly not to heaven but to hell.

MAJOR WORKS OF SEVENTEENTH-CENTURY LITERATURE AND PHILOSOPHY	
King Lear (Shakespeare)	1605
Don Quixote, Part I (Cervantes)	1605
Leviathan (Hobbes)	1651
Provincial Letters (Pascal)	1656–1657
Paradise Lost (Milton)	1667
Ethics (Spinoza)	1677
The Pilgrim's Progress (Bunyan)	1678
Treatises of Government (Locke)	1690
An Essay Concerning Human Understanding (Locke)	1690

The loss of national unity during the Puritan struggle against the Stuart monarchy and the Anglican church took its toll on English literature and drama during the seventeenth century. In 1642 the Puritans had closed the theaters of London. They were reopened after the Restoration of Charles II in 1660, and drama revived following the long Puritan interregnum.

Literary thought thereafter became less experimental and adopted proven classical forms, as a new movement to subject reality to the strict rules of reason began. During the so-called Augustan Age, from John Dryden (1631–1700) to Alexander Pope (1688–1744), writers turned away from the universal ideals and the transcendental concerns of the Elizabethans and the Puritan divines. As in France, where the French comedy writer Molière (1622–1673) is the outstanding example, English writers tried to please the royal court and aristocracy by turning to more earthy and popular topics.

Blaise Pascal (1623–1662)

Pascal, a French mathematician and a physical scientist widely acclaimed by his contemporaries, surrendered all his wealth to pursue an austere, self-disciplined life. Torn between the continuing dogmatism and the new skepticism of the seventeenth century, he aspired to write a work that would refute both the Jesuits, whose casuistry (i.e., arguments designed to

---

Pascal Meditates on Human Beings As Thinking Creatures

Pascal was both a religious and a scientific writer. Unlike other scientific thinkers of the seventeenth century, he was not overly optimistic about the ability of science to improve the human condition. Pascal believed that science and philosophy would instead help human beings to understand their situation better. In these passages from his *Pensées (Thoughts)*, he discussed the uniqueness of human beings as the creatures who alone in all the universe are capable of thinking.

339

I can well conceive a man without hands, feet, head (for it is only experience which teaches us that the head is more necessary than feet). But I cannot conceive man without thought; he would be a stone or a brute.

344

Reason commands us far more imperiously than a master; for in disobeying the one we are unfortunate, and in disobeying the other we are fools.

346

Thought constitutes the greatness of man.

347

Man is but a reed, the most feeble thing in nature; but he is a thinking reed. The entire universe need not arm itself to crush him. A vapour, a drop of water suffices to kill him. But, if the universe were to crush him, man would still be more noble than that which killed him, because he knows that he dies and the advantage which the universe has over him; the universe knows nothing of this.

All our dignity consists, then, in thought. By it we must elevate ourselves, and not by space and time which we cannot fill. Let us endeavour, then, to think well; this is the principle of morality.

348

A thinking reed—It is not from space that I must seek my dignity, but from the government of my thought. I shall have no more if I possess worlds. By space the universe encompasses and swallows me up like an atom; by thought I comprehend the world.

Blaise Pascal, *Pensées and The Provincial Letters* (New York: Modern Library, 1941), pp. 115–116.

493

*New Directions
in Science and
Thought in the
Sixteenth and
Seventeenth
Centuries*

Pascal invented this adding machine, the ancestor of all mechanical calculators, about 1644. It has eight wheels with ten cogs each, corresponding to the numbers 0–9. The wheels move forward for addition, backward for subtraction. [Musee des Techniques, Paris]

minimize and even excuse sinful acts) he considered a distortion of Christian teaching, and the skeptics of his age, who either denied religion altogether (atheists) or accepted it only as it conformed to reason (deists). Such a definitive work was never realized, and his views on these matters exist only in piecemeal form. He wrote against the Jesuits in his *Provincial Letters* (1656–1657), and he left behind a provocative collection of reflections on humankind and religion that was published posthumously under the title *Pensées*.

Pascal allied himself with the Jansenists, seventeenth-century Catholic opponents of the Jesuits. His sister was a member of the Jansenist community of Port-Royal near Paris. The Jansenists shared with the Calvinists Saint Augustine's belief in human beings' total sinfulness, their eternal predestination by God, and their complete dependence on faith and grace for knowledge of God and salvation.

Pascal believed that reason and science, although attesting to human dignity, remained of no avail in matters of religion. Here only the reasons of the heart and a "leap of faith" could prevail. Pascal saw two essential truths in the Christian religion: that a loving God, worthy of

human attainment, exists, and that human beings, because they are corrupted in nature, are utterly unworthy of God. Pascal believed that the atheists and the deists of the age had spurned the lesson of reason. For him rational analysis of the human condition attested humankind's utter mortality and corruption and exposed the weakness of reason itself in resolving the problems of human nature and destiny. Reason should rather drive those who truly heed it to faith and dependence on divine grace.

Pascal made a famous wager with the skeptics. It is a better bet, he argued, to believe that God exists and to stake everything on his promised mercy than not to do so, because if God does exist, everything will be gained by the believer, whereas the loss incurred by having believed in Him should He prove not to exist is by comparison very slight.

Convinced that belief in God improved life psychologically and disciplined it morally, regardless of whether or not God proved in the end to exist, Pascal worked to strengthen traditional religious belief. He urged his contemporaries to seek self-understanding by "learned ignorance" and to discover humankind's

Even before Pascal's day, of course, there was a tradition of elaborate mechanical devices throughout Europe. For example, by 1500, there were public clocks in practically every town. One of the most famous is the astronomical clock of Strasbourg cathedral in France, which presents a parade of allegorical figures every day at noon. [French Government Tourist Office, New York]

The Glockenspiel, or clock performance, occurring hourly at the Munich city hall, is another ingenious time-keeping device. [German Information Center, New York]

greatness by recognizing its misery. Thereby he hoped to counter what he believed to be the false optimism of the new rationalism and science.

Baruch Spinoza (1632–1677)

The most controversial thinker of the seventeenth century was Baruch Spinoza, the son of a Jewish merchant of Amsterdam. Spinoza's philosophy caused his excommunication by his own synagogue in 1656. In 1670 he published his *Treatise on Religious and Political Philosophy,* a work that criticized the dogmatism of Dutch Calvinists and championed freedom of thought. During his lifetime both Jews and Protestants attacked him as an atheist.

Spinoza's most influential writing, the *Ethics,* was published after his death in 1677. Religious leaders universally condemned it for its apparent espousal of pantheism. God and nature were so closely identified by Spinoza that little room seemed left either for divine revelation in Scripture or for the personal immortality of the soul, denials equally repugnant to Jews and to Christians. The *Ethics* was a very complicated work, written in the spirit of the new science as a geometrical system of definitions, axioms, and propositions. Spinoza divided the work into five parts, which dealt with God, the mind, emotions, human bondage, and human freedom.

The most controversial part of the *Ethics* deals with the nature of substance and of God. According to Spinoza, there is but one substance, which is self-caused, free, and infinite, and God is that substance. From this definition it follows that everything that exists is in God and cannot even be conceived of apart from Him. Such a doctrine is not literally pantheistic because God is still seen to be more than the created world that He, as primal substance, embraces. It may perhaps best be described as *panentheism:* the teaching that all that is is within God, yet God remains more than and beyond the natural world. Nonetheless, in Spinoza's view, statements about the natural world are also statements about divine nature. Mind and matter are seen to be extensions of the infinite substance of God; what transpires in the world of humankind and nature is a necessary outpouring of the divine.

Such teaching seemed to portray the world as eternal and human actions as unfree and inevitable. Jews and Christians have traditionally condemned such teachings because they deny the creation of the world by God in time and destroy any voluntary basis for personal reward and punishment.

Spinoza found enthusiastic supporters, however, in the nineteenth-century German philosopher Georg Wilhelm Friedrich Hegel and in romantic writers of the same century, especially Johann Wolfgang von Goethe and Percy Bysshe Shelley. Modern thinkers who are unable to accept traditional religious language and doctrines have continued to find in the teaching of Spinoza a congenial rational religion.

Thomas Hobbes (1588–1679)

Thomas Hobbes was incontestably the most original political philosopher of the seventeenth century. The son of a clergyman, he was educated at Oxford University. Although he never broke with the Church of England, he came to share basic Calvinist beliefs, especially the low view of human nature and the ideal of a commonwealth based on a covenant, both of which found eloquent expression in Hobbes's political philosophy.

An urbane and much-traveled man, Hobbes enthusiastically supported the new scientific movement. He worked as tutor and secretary to three earls of Devonshire over a fifty-year period. During the 1630s he visited Paris, where he came to know Descartes, and after the outbreak of the Puritan Revolution in 1640, he lived as an exile in Paris until 1651. In 1646 Hobbes became the tutor of the Prince of Wales, the future Charles II, and remained on good terms with him after the restoration of the Stuart monarchy. Hobbes also spent time with Galileo in Italy and took a special interest in the works of William Harvey (1578–1657). Harvey was a physiologist famed for the discovery of how blood circulated through the body; his scientific writings influenced Hobbes's own tracts on bodily motions. Hobbes became an expert in geometry and optics. He was also highly trained in classical languages, and his first published work was a translation of Thucydides' *History of the Peloponnesian War*, the first English translation of this work, which is still reprinted today.

The English Civil War made Hobbes a political philosopher. In 1651 his *Leviathan* appeared. Written as the concluding part of a broad philosophical system that analyzed physical bodies and human nature, the work established Hobbes as a major European thinker. Its subject was the political consequences of human passions and its originality lay in (1) its making natural law, rather than common law (i.e., custom or precedent), the basis of all positive law and (2) its defense of a representative theory of absolute authority against the theory of the divine right of kings. Hobbes maintained that statute law found its justification only as an expression of the law of nature and that political authority came to rulers only by way of the consent of the people.

Hobbes viewed humankind and society in a thoroughly materialistic and mechanical way. Human beings are defined as a collection of material particles in motion. All their psychological processes begin with and are derived from bare sensation, and all their motivations are egoistical, intended to increase pleasure and minimize pain. The human power of reasoning, which Hobbes defined unspectacularly as a process of adding and subtracting the consequences of agreed-upon general names of things, develops only after years of concentrated industry. Human will Hobbes defined as simply "the last appetite before choice."

Despite this mechanistic view of human beings, Hobbes believed they could accomplish much by the reasoned use of science. All was contingent, however, on the correct use of that greatest of all human creations, one compounded of the powers of most people: the commonwealth, in which people are united by their consent in one all-powerful person.

The key to Hobbes's political philosophy is a brilliant myth of the original state of humankind. According to this myth, human beings in the natural state are generally inclined to a "perpetual and restless desire of power after power that ceases only in death."[7] As all people desire and, in the state of nature, have a natural right to everything, their equality breeds enmity, competition, diffidence, and desire for glory begets perpetual quarreling— "a war of every man against every man."[8] As Hobbes put it in a famous summary:

In such condition there is no place for industry, because the fruit thereof is uncertain; and consequently no culture of the earth; no navigation nor use of the commodities that may be imported by sea; no commodious building; no instruments of moving and removing such things as require much force; no knowledge of the face of the earth; no account of

[7]*Leviathan Parts I and II*, ed. by H. W. Schneider (Indianapolis: Bobbs-Merrill, 1958), p. 86.
[8]Ibid., p. 106.

Non est potestas Super Terram quæ Comparetur ei Iob. 41. 24.

The famous title-page illustration for Hobbe's Leviathan. *The ruler is pictured as absolute lord of his lands, but note that he incorporates the mass of individuals whose self-interests are best served by their willingness to accept him and cooperate with him.*

time; no arts; no letters; no society; and, which is worst of all, continual fear and danger of violent death; and the life of man solitary, poor, nasty, brutish, and short.[9]

Whereas earlier and later philosophers saw the original human state as a paradise from which humankind had fallen, Hobbes saw it as a corruption from which only society had delivered people. Contrary to the views of Aristotle and Christian thinkers like Thomas Aquinas, in the view of Hobbes human beings are not by nature sociable, political animals; they are self-centered beasts, laws unto themselves, utterly without a master unless one is imposed by force.

According to Hobbes, people escape the impossible state of nature only by entering a social contract that creates a commonwealth tightly ruled by law and order. They are driven to this solution by their fear of death and their desire for "commodious living." The social contract obliges every person, for the sake of peace and self-defense, to agree to set aside personal rights to all things and to be content with as much liberty against others as he or she would allow others against himself or herself. All agree to live according to a secularized version of the golden rule: "Do not that to another which you would not have done to yourself."[10]

Because words and promises are insufficient to guarantee this state, the social contract also establishes the coercive force necessary to com-

[9]Ibid., p. 107.

[10]Ibid., p. 130.

pel compliance with the covenant. Hobbes believed that the dangers of anarchy were always far greater than those of tyranny and conceived of the ruler as absolute and unlimited in power, once established in office. There is no room in Hobbes's political philosophy for political protest in the name of individual conscience, nor for resistance to legitimate authority by private individuals—features of the *Leviathan* criticized by contemporary Catholics and Puritans alike. To his critics, who lamented the loss of their individual liberty in such a government, Hobbes pointed out the alternative:

The greatest that in any form of government can possibly happen to the people in general is scarce sensible in respect of the miseries and horrible calamities that accompany a civil war or that dissolute condition of masterless men, without subjection to laws and a coercive power to tie their hands from rapine and revenge.[11]

It is puzzling why Hobbes believed that absolute rulers would be more benevolent and less egoistic than all other people. He simply placed the highest possible value on a strong, efficient ruler who could save human beings from the chaos attendant on the state of nature. In thc end it mattered little to Hobbes whether this ruler was Charles I, Oliver Cromwell, or Charles II, each of whom received Hobbes's enthusiastic support, once he was established in power.

John Locke (1632–1704)

Locke has proved to be the most influential political thinker of the seventeenth century. His political philosophy found expression in the Glorious Revolution of 1688–1689. Although he was not as original as Hobbes, his political writings became a major source of the later Enlightenment criticism of absolutism, and they gave inspiration to both the American and the French revolutions.

Locke's sympathies lay with the Puritans and the Parliamentary forces that challenged the Stuart monarchy. His father fought with the Parliamentary army during the English Civil War. Locke read deeply in the works of Francis Bacon, René Descartes, and Isaac Newton and was a close friend of the English physicist and chemist Robert Boyle (1627–1691). Some view Locke as the first philosopher to

[11]Ibid., p. 152.

synthesize the rationalism of Descartes and the experimental science of Bacon, Newton, and Boyle.

Locke was for a brief period strongly influenced by the political views of Hobbes. This influence changed, however, after his association with Anthony Ashley Cooper, the earl of Shaftesbury. In 1667 Locke moved into Shaftesbury's London home and served him as physician, secretary, and traveling companion. A zealous Protestant, Shaftesbury was considered by his contemporaries a radical in both religion and politics. He organized an unsuccessful rebellion against Charles II in 1682. Although Locke had no part in the plot, both he and Shaftesbury were forced to flee to Holland after its failure.

Locke's two most famous works are the *Essay Concerning Human Understanding* (1690), completed during his exile in Holland, and the *Two Treatises of Government* (1690). In the *Essay Concerning Human Understanding* Locke stressed the creative function of the human mind. He believed that the mind at birth was a blank tablet. There are no innate ideas; all knowledge is derived from actual sensual experience. Human ideas are either simple (that is, passive receptions from daily experience) or complex (that is, products of sustained mental exercise). What people know is not the external world in itself but the results of the interaction of the mind with the outside world. Locke also denied the existence of innate moral norms. Moral ideals are the product of humankind's subjection of their self-love to their reason—a freely chosen self-disciplining of natural desires so that conflict in conscience may be avoided and happiness attained. Locke also believed that the teachings of Christianity were identical to what uncorrupted reason taught about the good life. A rational person would therefore always live according to simple Christian precepts. Although Locke firmly denied toleration to Catholics and atheists—both were considered subversive in England—he otherwise sanctioned a variety of Protestant religious practice.

Locke wrote *Two Treatises of Government* during the reign of Charles II. They oppose the argument that rulers are absolute in their power. According to the preface of the published edition, which appeared after the Glorious Revolution, the treatises were written "to justify to the world the people of England, whose love of their just and natural rights, with their resolution to preserve them, saved

John Locke Explains the Sources of Human Knowledge

An Essay Concerning Human Understanding (1690) may be the most influential philosophical work ever written in English. Locke's most fundamental idea, which is explicated in the passage below, is that human knowledge is grounded in the experiences of the senses and in the reflection of the mind on those experiences. He rejected any belief in innate ideas. His emphasis on experience led to the wider belief that human beings are creatures of their environment. After Locke, numerous writers argued that human beings could be improved if the environment in which they lived were reformed.

Let us then suppose the mind to be, as we say, white paper void of all characters, without any ideas. *How comes it to be furnished? Whence comes it by that vast store which the busy and boundless fancy of man has painted on it with an almost endless variety? Whence has it all the materials of reason and knowledge? To this I answer, in one word, from* experience; *in that all our knowledge is founded, and from that it ultimately derives itself. Our observation, employed either about* external sensible objects, or about the internal operations of our minds perceived and reflected on by ourselves, is that which supplies our understanding with all the materials of thinking. *These two are the fountains of knowledge, from whence all the ideas we have, or can naturally have, do spring.*

First, our senses, *conversant about particular sensible objects, do* convey into the mind *several distinct* perceptions *of things, according to those various ways wherein those objects do affect them. And thus we come by those* ideas *we have of* yellow, white, heat, cold, soft, hard, bitter, sweet, *and all those which we call sensible qualities. . . . This great source of most of the* ideas *we have, depending wholly upon our senses, and derived by them to the understanding, I call SENSATION.*

Secondly, the other fountain from which experience furnisheth the understanding with ideas *is the* perception of the operations of our own minds *within us, as it is employed about the* ideas *it has got. . . . And such are* perception, thinking, doubting, believing, reasoning, knowing, willing, *and all the different actings of our own minds. . . . I call this* REFLECTION, *the ideas it affords being such only as the mind gets by reflecting on its own operations within itself. . . . These two, I say, viz. external material things as the objects of SENSATION, and the operations of our own minds within as the objects of REFLECTION, are to me the only originals from whence all our* ideas *take their beginnings. . . .*

The understanding seems to me not to have the least glimmering of any ideas *which it doth not receive from one of these two.*

John Locke, *An Essay Concerning Human Understanding*, Vol. 1 (London: Everyman's Library, 1961), pp. 77–78.

the nation when it was on the brink of slavery and ruin.''[12] Locke rejected particularly the views of Sir Robert Filmer and Thomas Hobbes.

Filmer had written a work entitled *Patriarcha, or the Natural Power of Kings* (published in 1680), in which the rights of kings over their subjects were compared with the rights of fathers over their children. Locke devoted his entire first treatise to a refutation of Filmer's argument, maintaining not only that the analogy was inappropriate, but that even the right of a father over his children could not be construed as absolute and was subject to a higher natural law. Both fathers and rulers, Locke argued, remain bound to the law of nature, which is the voice of reason, teaching that ''all mankind [are] equal and independent, [and] no one ought to harm another in his life,

[12]*The Second Treatise of Government*, ed. by T. P. Peardon (Indianapolis: Bobbs-Merrill, 1952), Preface.

health, liberty, or possessions,"[13] inasmuch as all human beings are the images and property of God. According to Locke, people enter into social contracts, empowering legislatures and monarchs to "umpire" their disputes, precisely in order to preserve their natural rights, not to give rulers an absolute power over them. Rulers are rather "entrusted" with the preservation of the law of nature and transgress it at their peril:

Whenever that end [namely, the preservation of life, liberty, and property for which power is given to rulers by a commonwealth] is manifestly neglected or opposed, the trust must necessarily be forfeited and the power devolve into the hands of those that gave it, who may place it anew where they think best for their safety and security.[14]

From Locke's point of view, absolute monarchy is "inconsistent" with civil society and can be "no form of civil government at all."

Locke's main differences with Hobbes stemmed from the latter's well-known views on the state of nature. Locke believed that the natural human state was one of perfect freedom and equality. Here all enjoyed, in unregulated fashion, the natural rights of life, liberty, and property. The only thing lacking in the state of nature was a single authority to give judgment when disputes inevitably arose because of the natural freedom and equality possessed by all. Contrary to the view of Hobbes, human beings in their natural state were creatures not of monomaniacal passion but of extreme goodwill and rationality. And they did not surrender their natural rights unconditionally when they entered the social contract; rather, they established a means whereby these rights could be better preserved. The state of warfare that Hobbes believed characterized the state of nature emerged for Locke only when rulers failed in their responsibility to preserve the freedoms of the state of nature and attempted to enslave people by absolute rule, that is, to remove them from their "natural" condition. Only then did the peace, goodwill, mutual assistance, and preservation in which human beings naturally live and socially ought to live come to an end and a state of war emerge.

[13]Ibid., Ch. 2, sects. 4–6, pp. 4–6.
[14]Ibid., Ch. 13, sect. 149, p. 84.

Suggested Readings

V. M. BRITTAIN, *Valiant Pilgrim: The Story of John Bunyan and Puritan England* (1950). Illustrated historical biography.

K. C. BROWN, *Hobbes Studies* (1965). A collection of important essays.

HERBERT BUTTERFIELD, *The Origins of Modern Science 1300–1800* (1949). An authoritative survey.

JOHN CAIRD, *Spinoza* (1971). Intellectual biography by a philosopher.

NORMAN F. CANTOR (Ed.), *Seventeenth Century Rationalism: Bacon and Descartes* (1969).

CERVANTES, *The Portable Cervantes*, ed. and trans. by Samuel Putnam (1969).

HARDIN CRAIG, *Shakespeare: A Historical and Critical Study with Annotated Texts of Twenty-one Plays* (1958).

MAURICE CRANSTON, *Locke* (1961). Brief biographical sketch.

J. DUNN, *The Political Thought of John Locke; An Historical Account of the "Two Treatises of Government"* (1969). An excellent introduction.

MANUEL DURAN, *Cervantes* (1974). Detailed biography.

GALILEO GALILEI, *Discoveries and Opinions of Galileo*, ed. and trans. by Stillman Drake (1957).

A. R. HALL, *The Scientific Revolution 1500–1800: The Formation of the Modern Scientific Attitude* (1966). Traces undermining of traditional science and rise of new sciences.

THOMAS HOBBES, *Leviathan. Parts I and II*, ed. by H. W. Schneider (1958).

MARGARET JACOB, *The Newtonians and the English Revolution* (1976). A controversial book that attempts to relate science and politics.

T. E. JESSOP, *Thomas Hobbes* (1960). Brief biographical sketch.

H. KEARNEY, *Science and Change 1500–1700* (1971). Broad survey.

ALEXANDER KOYRE, *From the Closed World to the Infinite Universe* (1957). Treated from perspective of the historian of ideas.

THOMAS S. KUHN, *The Copernican Revolution* (1957). A scholarly treatment.

PETER LASLETT, *Locke's Two Treatises of Government*, 2nd ed. (1970). Definitive texts with very important introductions.

JOHN D. NORTH, *Isaac Newton* (1967). Brief biography.

ALAN G. R. SMITH, *Science and Society* (1973). A readable, well-illustrated history of the Scientific Revolution.

E. M. W. TILLYARD, *Milton* (1952). Brief biographical sketch.

RICHARD S. WESTFALL, *Never at Rest: A Biography of Isaac Newton* (1981). A new and very important major study.

Louis XV in coronation robes, painted by Hyacinthe Rigaud in 1730. Although by no means unintelligent, Louis was lazy and pleasure-loving, and his scandalous private life lessened respect for the French monarchy. [Josse/Art Resource]

THE LATE SEVENTEENTH and early eighteenth centuries witnessed significant shifts of power and influence among the states of Europe. Nations that had been strong lost their status as significant military and economic units. Other countries, which had in some cases figured only marginally in international relations, came to the fore. Great Britain, France, Austria, Russia, and Prussia emerged during this period as the powers that would dominate Europe until at least World War I. The establishment of their political and economic dominance occurred at the expense of Spain, the United Netherlands, Poland, Sweden, and the Ottoman Empire. Equally essential to their rise was the weakness of the Holy Roman Empire after the Treaty of Westphalia (1648).

The successful competitors for international power were those states that in differing fashions created strong central political authorities. Farsighted observers in the late seventeenth century already understood that in the future those domains that would become or remain great powers must imitate the political and military organization of Louis XIV. Monarchy alone could impose unity of purpose on the state. The turmoil of seventeenth-century civil wars and aristocratic revolts had impressed people with the value of the monarch as a guarantor of minimum domestic tranquillity. Imitation of French absolutism involved other factors besides belief in a strong monarchy. It usually required building a standing army, organizing an efficient tax structure to support the army, and establishing a bureaucracy to collect the taxes. Moreover the political classes of the country, especially the nobles, had to be converted to a sense of duty and loyalty to the central government that was more intense than their loyalty to other competing political and social institutions.

The waning powers of Europe were those whose leaders failed to achieve such effective organization. They were unable to employ their political, economic, and human resources to resist external aggression or to overcome the forces of domestic dissolution. The internal and external failures were closely related. If a state failed to maintain or establish a central political authority with sufficient power over the nobility, the cities, the guilds, and the church, it could not raise a strong army to defend its borders or its economic interests. More often than not, the key element leading to success or failure was the character, personality, and energy of the monarch.

14

The Waxing and Waning of States (1686–1740)

The Maritime Powers

In western Europe, Britain and France emerged as the dominant powers. This development represented a shift of influence away from Spain and the United Netherlands. Both the latter countries had been quite strong and important during the sixteenth and seventeenth centuries, but they became negligible during the course of the eighteenth century. However, neither disappeared from the map. Both retained considerable economic vitality and influence. The difference was that France and Britain attained so much more power and economic strength.

Spain

Spanish power had depended on the influx of wealth from the Americas and on the capacity of the Spanish monarchs to rule the still largely autonomous provinces of the Iberian peninsula. The economic life of the nation was never healthy. Except for wool Spain had virtually no exports with which to pay for its imports. Instead of promoting domestic industries, the Spanish government financed imports by using the gold and silver mined in its New World empire. This external source of wealth was not certain because the treasure fleets from the New World could be and sometimes were captured by pirates or the navies of other nations. The political life of Spain was also weak. Within Castile, Aragon, Navarre, the Basque provinces, and other districts, the royal government could not operate without the close cooperation of strong local nobles and the church. From the defeat of the Spanish Armada in 1588 to the Treaty of the Pyrenees in 1659, Spain experienced a series of foreign policy reverses that harmed the domestic prestige of the monarchy. Furthermore, between 1665 and 1700 the physically malformed, dull-witted, and sexually impotent Charles II was monarch. Throughout his reign the local provincial estates and the nobility increased their power. On his death the War of the Spanish Succession saw the other powers of Europe contesting the issue of the next ruler of Spain.

The Treaty of Utrecht (1713) gave the Spanish crown to Philip V (1770–1746), who was a Bourbon and the grandson of Louis XIV. The new king should have attempted to consolidate his internal power and to protect Spanish overseas trade. However, his second wife, Elizabeth Farnese, wanted to use Spanish power to carve out interests for her sons on the Italian peninsula. Such machinations diverted government resources and allowed the nobility and the provinces to continue to assert their privileges against the authority of the monarchy. Not until the reign of Charles III (1759–1788) did Spain possess a monarch concerned with efficient administration and internal improvement. By the third quarter of the century the county was better governed, but it could no longer compete effectively in power politics.

The Netherlands

The demise of the United Netherlands occurred wholly within the eighteenth century. After the death of William III of England in 1702, the various local provinces successfully prevented the emergence of another strong *stadtholder*. Unified political leadership therefore vanished. During the earlier long wars of the Netherlands with Louis XIV and England, naval supremacy slowly but steadily had passed to the British. The fishing industry declined, and the Dutch lost their technological superiority in shipbuilding. Countries between which Dutch ships had once carried goods now came to trade directly with each other. For example, the British began to use more and more of their own vessels in the Baltic traffic with Russia. Similar stagnation overtook the Dutch domestic industries, such as textile finishing, paper making, and glass blowing. The disunity of the provinces and the absence of vigorous leadership hastened this economic decline and prevented action that might have slowed or halted it. What saved the United Netherlands from becoming completely insignificant in European matters was their continued dominance of the financial community. Well past the middle of the century their banks continued to provide loans and financing for European trade.

France After Louis XIV

Despite its military losses in the War of the Spanish Succession, France remained a great power. It was less strong in 1715 than in 1680, but it still possessed a large population, an advanced if troubled economy, and the administrative structure bequeathed it by Louis XIV. Moreover, even if France and its resources had been badly drained by the last of Louis's wars, the other major states of Europe emerged from the conflict similarly debilitated. What the country required was a period of economic recovery and consolidation, wiser political leadership, and a less ambitious foreign policy. It did enjoy a period of recovery, but the quality of its leadership was at best indifferent. Louis XIV was succeeded by his five-year-old great-grandson Louis XV (1715–1774). The young boy's uncle, the duke of Orléans, became regent and remained so until 1720. The regency further undermined the already faltering prestige of the monarchy.

The duke of Orléans was a gambler, and for a time he turned over the financial management of the kingdom to John Law (1621–1729), a Scottish mathematician and fellow gambler. Law believed that an increase in the paper money supply would stimulate the postwar economic recovery of the country. With the permission of the regent he established a bank in Paris that issued paper money. Law then organized a monopoly on trading privileges with the French colony of Louisiana in North America.

The Mississippi Company also assumed the management of the French national debt. The company issued shares of its own stock in exchange for government bonds, which had fallen sharply in value. In order to redeem large quantities of bonds, Law encouraged speculation in Mississippi Company stock. In 1719 the price of the stock rose handsomely. However, smart investors took their profits by selling their stock in exchange for money from Law's bank. Then they sought to exchange the currency for gold. To make the second transaction, they went to Law's bank, but that institution lacked sufficient gold to redeem all the money brought to it.

In February 1720 all gold payments were halted in France. Soon thereafter Law himself fled the country. The Mississippi Bubble, as the affair was called, had burst. The fiasco brought disgrace on the government that had made Law its controller general. The Mississippi Company was later reorganized and functioned quite profitably, but fear of paper money and speculation marked French economic life for the rest of the century.

The duke of Orléans made a second departure that also lessened the power of the monarchy. He attempted to draw the French nobility once again into the decision-making

The Amsterdam Exchange. By the mid-seventeenth century, when this picture was painted, Amsterdam had replaced the cities of Italy and south Germany as the leading banking center of Europe. Amsterdam retained this position until the late eighteenth century. [Museum Boymans-van Beuningen, Rotterdam]

Madame de Pompadour (1721–1764), the mistress of Louis XV. A woman of beauty, cultivation, and taste, she was a notable patroness of artists, craftsmen, and writers. This portrait, which captures her grace and elegance, is by Francois Boucher (1703–1770), one of her favorite painters. [National Galleries of Scotland]

the virtues of his great-grandfather. He wanted to hold on to absolute power but was unwilling to work the long hours required. He did not choose many wise advisers after Fleury. He was tossed about by the gossip and intrigues of the court nobles. His personal life was scandalous. His reign became more famous for his mistress, Madame de Pompadour, than for anything else. Louis XV was not an evil person but a mediocre one. And in a monarch, mediocrity was unfortunately often a greater fault than vice.

Despite this political drift France remained a great power. Its army at mid-century was still the largest and strongest military force on the Continent. Its commerce and production expanded. Its colonies produced wealth and spurred domestic industries. Its cities grew and prospered. The wealth of the nation waxed as the absolutism of the monarchy waned. France did not lack sources of power and strength, but it did lack the political leadership that could organize, direct, and inspire its people.

Great Britain: The Age of Walpole

In 1713 Britain had emerged as a victor over Louis XIV, but the nation required a period of recovery. As an institution the British monarchy was not in the degraded state of the

French monarchy, but its stability was not certain. In 1714 the Hanoverian dynasty, designated by the Act of Settlement (1701), came to the throne. Almost immediately George I (1714–1727) confronted a challenge to his new title. The Stuart pretender James Edward (1688–1766), the son of James II, landed in Scotland in December 1715. His forces marched southward but met defeat less than two months later.

Although militarily successful against the pretender, the new dynasty and its supporters saw the need for consolidation. During the seventeenth century England had been one of the most politically restive countries in Europe. The closing years of Queen Anne's reign (1702–1714) had seen sharp clashes between the political factions of Whigs and Tories over the coming Treaty of Utrecht. The Tories had urged a rapid peace settlement and after 1710 had opened negotiations with France. During the same period the Whigs were seeking favor from the Elector of Hanover, who would soon be their monarch. His concern for his domains in Hanover made him unsympathetic to the Tory peace policy. In the final months of Anne's reign, some Tories, fearing loss of power under the waiting Hanoverian dynasty, opened channels of communication with the Stuart pretender; and a few even rallied to his losing cause.

Under these circumstances it was little wonder that George I, on his arrival in Britain, clearly favored the Whigs and proceeded with caution. Previously the differences between the Whigs and the Tories had been vaguely related to principle. The Tories emphasized a strong monarchy, low taxes for landowners, and firm support of the Anglican church. The Whigs supported monarchy but wanted Parliament to retain final sovereignty. They tended to favor urban commercial interests as well as the prosperity of the landowners. They encouraged a policy of religious toleration toward the Protestant nonconformists in England. Socially both groups supported the status quo. Neither was organized like a modern political party. Organizationally, outside of Parliament, each party consisted of political networks based on local political connections and local economic influence. Each group acknowledged a few spokesmen on the national level who articulated positions and principles. However, after the Hanoverian accession and the eventual Whig success in achieving the firm confidence of George I, the chief difference for almost forty years between the Whigs and the Tories was that one group did have access to public office and patronage and the other did not. This early Hanoverian proscription of Tories from public life was one of the most prominent features of the age.

The political situation after 1715 had at first remained in a state of flux, until Robert Walpole (1676–1745) took over the helm of government. This Norfolk squire had been active in the House of Commons since the reign of Queen Anne, and he had served as a cabinet minister. What gave him special prominence under the new dynasty was a British financial scandal similar to the French Mississippi Bubble.

Management of the British national debt had been assigned to the South Sea Company, which exchanged government bonds for company stock. As in the French case, the price of the stock flew high, only to crash in 1720 when prudent investors sold their holdings and took their speculative profits. Parliament intervened and, under Walpole's leadership, adopted measures to honor the national debt. To most contemporaries Walpole had saved the financial integrity of the country and, in so doing, had proved himself a person of immense administrative capacity and political ability.

George I gave Walpole his full confidence. For this reason Walpole has often been regarded as the first prime minister of Great Britain and the originator of the cabinet system of government. However, unlike a modern prime minister, he was not chosen by the majority of the House of Commons. His power largely depended on the goodwill of George I and later of George II (1727–1760). Walpole generally demanded that all of the ministers in the cabinet agree on policy, but he could not prevent frequent public differences on policy. The real source of Walpole's power was the combination of the personal support of the king, his ability to handle the House of Commons, and his iron-fisted control of government patronage. To oppose Walpole on either minor or more substantial matters was to risk the almost certain loss of government patronage for oneself, one's family, or one's friends. Through the skillful use of patronage Walpole bought support for himself and his policies from people who wanted to receive jobs, appointments, favors, and government contracts. Such corruption supplied the glue of political loyalty. Walpole's favorite slogan was "*Quieta non*

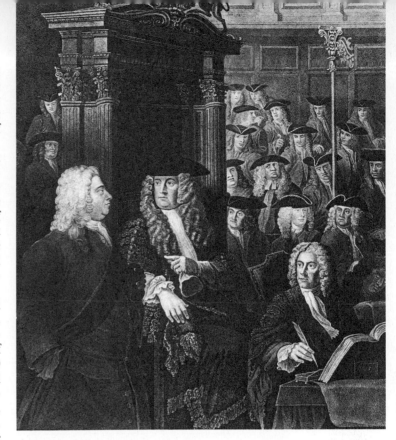

Sir Robert Walpole (1676–1745) left, shown talking to the Speaker of the House of Commons. Walpole, who dominated British political life from 1721 to 1742, is considered the first prime minister of Britain. [The Mansell Collection]

movere" (roughly, "Let sleeping dogs lie"). To that end he pursued a policy of peace abroad and promotion of the status quo at home. In this regard he and Cardinal Fleury were much alike. The structure of the eighteenth-century British House of Commons aided Walpole in his pacific policies. It was neither a democratic nor a representative body. Each of the counties elected two members. But if the more powerful landed families in a county agreed on the candidates, there was no contest. Other members were elected from units called *boroughs*, of which there were a considerable variety. There were many more borough seats than county seats. A few were large enough for elections to be relatively democratic. However, most boroughs had a very small number of electors. For example, a local municipal corporation or council of only a dozen members might have the legal right to elect a member of Parliament. In Old Sarum, one of the most famous corrupt or "rotten" boroughs, the Pitt family for many years simply bought up those pieces of property to which a vote was attached and thus in effect owned a seat in the House of Commons. Through proper electoral management, which involved favors to the electors, the House of Commons could be controlled.

The structure of Parliament and the manner in which it was elected meant that the government of England was dominated by the owners of property and by especially wealthy nobles. They did not pretend to represent people and districts or to be responsive to what would later be called public opinion. They regarded themselves as representing various economic and social interests, such as the West Indian interest, the merchant interest, or the landed interest. These owners of property were suspicious of an administrative bureaucracy controlled by the crown or its ministers. For this reason they or their agents served as local government administrators, judges, militia commanders, and tax collectors. In this sense the British nobility and other substantial landowners actually did govern the nation. And because they regarded the Parliament as the political sovereign, there was no absence of central political authority and direction. Consequently the supremacy of Parliament provided Britain with the kind of unity that elsewhere in Europe was sought through the institutions of absolutism.

British political life was genuinely more free than that on the Continent. There were real limits on the power of Robert Walpole. Parliament could not be wholly unresponsive to popular political pressure. Even with the ex-

---

Lady Mary Wortley Montagu Gives Advice on Election to Parliament

In this letter of 1714 Lady Mary Wortley Montagu discussed with her husband the various paths that he might follow to gain election to the British House of Commons. Note the emphasis she placed on knowing the right people and on having large amounts of money to spend on voters. Eventually her husband was elected to Parliament in a borough that was controlled through government patronage.

You seem not to have received my letters, or not to have understood them: you had been chose undoubtedly at York, if you had declared in time; but there is not any gentleman or tradesman disengaged at this time; they are treating every night. Lord Carlisle and the Thompsons have given their interest to Mr Jenkins. I agree with you of the necessity of your standing this Parliament, which, perhaps, may be more considerable than any that are to follow it; but, as you proceed, 'tis my opinion, you will spend your money and not be chose. I believe there is hardly a borough unengaged. I expect every letter should tell me you are sure of some place; and, as far as I can perceive you are sure of none. As it has been managed, perhaps it will be the best way to deposit a certain sum in some friend's hands, and buy some little Cornish borough: it would, undoubtedly, look better to be chose for a considerable town; but I take it to be now too late. If you have any thoughts of New-

ark, it will be absolutely necessary for you to enquire after Lord Lexington's interest; and your best way to apply yourself to Lord Holdernesse, who is both a Whig and an honest man. He is now in town, and you may enquire of him if Brigadier Sutton stands there; and if not, try to engage him for you. Lord Lexington is so ill at the Bath, that it is a doubt if he will live 'till the elections; and if he dies, one of his heiresses, and the whole interest of his estate, will probably fall on Lord Holdernesse.

'Tis a surprize to me, that you cannot make sure of some borough, when a number of your friends bring in so many Parliament-men without trouble or expense. 'Tis too late to mention it now, but you might have applied to Lady Winchester, as Sir Joseph Jekyl did last year, and by her interest the Duke of Bolton brought him in, for nothing; I am sure she would be more zealous to serve me, than Lady Jekyl.

Lord Wharncliffe (Ed.), *Letters and Works of Lady Mary Wortley Montagu*, 3rd ed., Vol. 1 (London, 1861), p. 211.

tensive use of patronage many members of Parliament maintained independent views. Newspapers and public debate flourished. Free speech could be exercised, as could freedom of association. There was no large standing army. Tories barred from political office and Whig enemies of Walpole could and did voice their opposition to his policies, as would not have been possible on the Continent.

For example, in 1733 Walpole presented to the House of Commons a scheme for an excise tax that would have raised revenue somewhat in the fashion of a modern sales tax. The public outcry in the press, on the public platform, and in the streets was so great that he eventually withdrew the measure. What the English regarded as their traditional political rights raised a real and potent barrier to the power of the government. Again in 1739, the public outcry over the Spanish treatment of British merchants in the Caribbean pushed Britain into the War of Jenkins's Ear, which Walpole opposed and deplored.

Walpole's ascendancy, which lasted until 1742, did little to raise the level of British political morality, but it brought the nation a kind of stability that it had not enjoyed for well over a century. Its foreign trade grew steadily and spread from New England to India. Agriculture improved its productivity. All forms of economic enterprise seemed to prosper. The navy became stronger. As a result of this political stability and economic growth, Great Britain became a European power of the first order and stood at the beginning of its era as a world power. Its government and economy during the next generation became a model for all progressive Europeans.

Central and Eastern Europe

The major factors in the shift of political influence among the maritime nations were naval strength, economic progress, foreign trade, and sound domestic administration. The conflicts among them occurred less in Europe than on the high seas and in their overseas empires. These nations already existed in well-defined geographical areas with established borders. Their populations generally accepted the authority of the central government.

The situation in central and eastern Europe was rather different. Except for the cities on the Baltic, the economy was agrarian. There were fewer cities and many more large estates popu-

FRANCE AND GREAT BRITAIN IN THE EARLY EIGHTEENTH CENTURY	
Treaty of Utrecht ends the War of the Spanish Succession	1713
George I becomes king of Great Britain and thus establishes the Hanoverian dynasty	1714
Louis XV becomes King of France	1715
Regency of the duke of Orléans in France	1715–1720
Mississippi Bubble bursts in France and South Sea Bubble bursts in Great Britain	1720
Robert Walpole dominates British politics	1720–1742
Cardinal Fleury serves as Louis XV's chief minister	1726–1743
George II becomes king of Great Britain	1727
Excise bill crisis in Britain	1733
War of Jenkins's Ear begins between England and Spain	1739

lated by serfs. The states in this region did not possess overseas empires. Changes in the power structure normally involved changes in borders, or at least in the prince who ruled a particular area. Military conflicts took place at home rather than overseas. The political structure of this region, which lay largely east of the Elbe River, was very "soft." The almost constant warfare of the seventeenth century had led to a habit of temporary and shifting political loyalties. The princes and aristocracies of small states and principalities were unwilling to subordinate themselves voluntarily to a central monarchical authority. Consequently the political life of the region and the kind of state that emerged there were different from those of western Europe.

Beginning in the last half of the seventeenth century, eastern and central Europe began to assume the political and social contours that would characterize it for the next two hundred years. After the Peace of Westphalia the Austrian Habsburgs recognized the basic weakness of the position of Holy Roman Emperor and began a new consolidation of their power. At the same time the state of Prussia began to emerge as a factor in north German politics and as a major challenger to Habsburg domination of Germany. Most important, Russia at the opening of the eighteenth century rose to the status of a military power of the first order. These three states (Austria, Prussia, and Russia) achieved their new status largely as a result

509

A series of four Hogarth etchings satirizing an English parliamentary election. In a savage indictment of the notoriously corrupt English electoral system, Hogarth shows the voters going to the polls after having been bribed and intoxicated with free gin. (Note that voting was public. The secret ballot was not introduced in England until 1872.) The fourth etching, Chairing the Member, shows the triumphal procession of the victorious candidate, which is clearly turning into a brawl. [Metropolitan Museum of Art]

of the political decay or military defeat of Sweden, Poland, and the Ottoman Empire.

Sweden: The Ambitions of Charles XII

Under Gustavus Adolphus II (1611–1632), Sweden had played an important role as a Protestant combatant in the Thirty Years' War. During the rest of the seventeenth century Sweden had consolidated its control of the Baltic, preventing Russian possession of a Baltic port and permitting Polish and German access to the sea only on Swedish terms. The Swedes also possessed one of the better armies in Europe. However, Sweden's economy, based primarily on the export of iron, was not strong enough to ensure continued political success.

In 1697 Charles XII (1697–1718) came to the throne. He was headstrong, to say the least, and perhaps insane. In 1700 Russia began a drive to the west against Swedish territory. The Russian goal was a foothold on the Baltic. In the resulting Great Northern War (1700–1721), Charles XII led a vigorous and often brilliant campaign, but one that eventually resulted in the defeat of Sweden. In 1700 he defeated the Russians at the battle of Narva, but then he turned south to invade Poland. The conflict dragged on, and the Russians were able to strengthen their forces. In 1708 the Swedish monarch began a major invasion of Russia but became bogged down in the harsh Russian winter. The next year his army was decisively defeated at the battle of Poltava. Thereafter the Swedes could maintain only a holding action. Charles himself sought refuge with the Ottoman army and then eventually returned to Sweden in 1714. He was shot four years later while fighting the Norwegians.

The Great Northern War came to a close in 1721. Sweden had exhausted its military and economic resources and had lost its monopoly on the Baltic coast. Russia had conquered a large section of the eastern Baltic, and Prussia had gained a portion of Pomerania. Internally, after the death of Charles XII, the Swedish nobles were determined to reassert their power over that of the monarchy. They did so but then fell into quarrels among themselves. Sweden played a very minor role in European affairs thereafter.

The Ottoman Empire

At the southeastern extreme of Europe the Ottoman Empire lay as a barrier to the territorial ambitions of the Austrian Habsburgs and of Poland and Russia. The empire in the late seventeenth century still controlled most of the Balkan peninsula and the entire coastline of the Black Sea. It was an aggressive power that had for two centuries attempted to press its control further westward in Europe. The Ottoman Empire had probably made its greatest military impression on Europe in 1683, when it laid siege to the city of Vienna.

However, the Ottomans had overextended themselves politically, economically, and militarily. The major domestic political groups resisted any substantial strengthening of the central government in Constantinople. Rivalries for power among army leaders and nobles weakened the effectiveness of the government. In the outer provinces, such as Transylvania, Wallachia, and Moldavia (all parts of modern Romania), the empire depended on the goodwill of local rulers, who never submitted themselves fully to the imperial power. The empire's economy was weak, and its exports were primarily raw materials. Moreover the actual conduct of most of its trade had been turned over to representatives of other nations.

By the early eighteenth century the weakness of the Ottoman Empire meant that on the southeastern perimeter of Europe there existed an immense political vacuum. In 1699 the Turks concluded a treaty with their longtime Habsburg enemy and surrendered all pretensions of control over Hungary, Transylvania, Croatia, and Slavonia. From this time onward Russia also attempted to extend its territory and influence at the expense of the empire. For almost two hundred years the decay of the Ottoman Empire constituted a major factor in European international relations. The area always proved tempting to the major powers, but their distrust of each other and their conflicting rivalries, as well as a considerable residual strength on the part of the Turks, prevented the dismemberment of the empire.

Poland

In no other part of Europe was the failure to maintain a competitive political position so complete as in Poland. In 1683 King John III Sobieski (1674–1696) had led a Polish army to rescue Vienna from the Turkish siege. But following that spectacular effort, Poland became little more than a byword for the dangers of aristocratic independence. In Poland as nowhere else on the Continent, the nobility be-

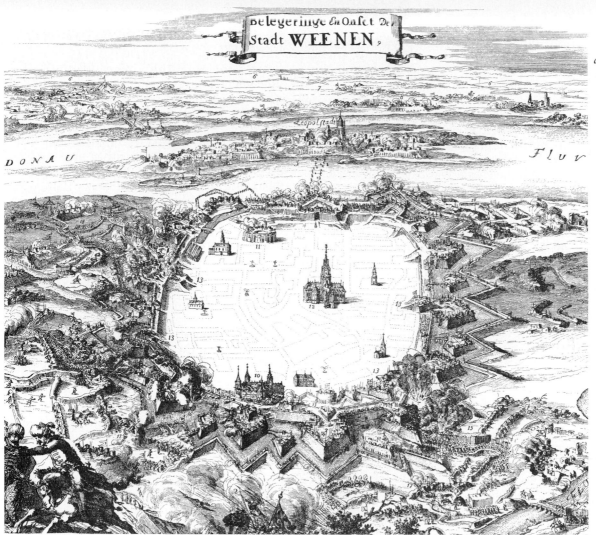

A contemporary Dutch print views the 1683 Turkish siege of Vienna from a remarkably revealing position in the hills west of the city. The scene shows the Turkish forces deciding to give up the summer-long attack; their commanders, the Ottoman Grand Vizier and the Pasha of Adrianople, lower left, and just beginning their flight. Polish and other Christian aid for the beleaguered Habsburg forces had arrived, and the battle was clearly going against the Turks. Never again did the weakened Muslim Ottoman Empire threaten the west. Note the Danube River toward the top, the elaborate zig-zag fortifications outside the walls, and bursts of artillery fire at several points. Most details inside the walled city are omitted, but the central cathedral and the imperial palace, toward the bottom, are shown. One unforeseen lasting social result of the siege was the boost given to coffee drinking by the Viennese discovery of coffee beans in the Turkish camps around the city. [British Museum]

came the single most powerful political factor in the country. Unlike the British nobility and landowners, the Polish nobility would not even submit to a central authority of their own making. There was no effective central authority in the form of either a king or a parliament.

The Polish monarchy was elective, but the deep distrust and divisions among the nobility prevented their electing a king from among their own numbers. Sobieski was a notable exception. Most of the Polish monarchs came from outside the borders of the kingdom and were the tools of foreign powers. The Polish nobles did have a central legislative body called the *Sejm,* or Diet. It included only the nobles and specifically excluded representatives from corporate bodies, such as the towns. In the Diet, however, there existed a practice known as the *liberum veto,* whereby the staunch opposition of any single member could require the body to disband. Such opposition was termed *exploding the Diet.* More often than not, this practice was the work of a group of dissatisfied nobles rather than of one person. Nonetheless, the rule of unanimity posed a major stumbling block to effective government.

Government as it was developing elsewhere in Europe simply was not tolerated in Poland. Localism reminiscent of the Middle Ages continued to hold sway as the nobles used all their energy to maintain their traditional "Polish liberties." There was no way to collect sufficient taxes to build up an army. The price of this noble liberty was eventually the disappearance of Poland from the map of Europe during the last half of the eighteenth century.

John III Sobieski (1624–1696). Elected king of Poland in 1674, Sobieski was a military hero in the wars against the Turks. However, he failed in his attempt to give Poland a strong, national monarchy. [EPA]

The Habsburg Empire and the Pragmatic Sanction

The close of the Thirty Years' War marked a fundamental turning point in the history of the Austrian Habsburgs. Previously, in alliance with the Spanish branch of the family, they had hoped to dominate all of Germany politically and to bring it back to the Catholic fold. They had failed to achieve either goal, and the decline of Spanish power meant that in future diplomatic relations the Austrian Habsburgs were very much on their own. The Treaty of Westphalia permitted Protestantism within the Holy Roman Empire, and the treaty also recognized the political autonomy of more than three hundred corporate German political entities within the empire. These included large units (such as Saxony, Hanover, Bavaria, and Brandenburg) and also scores of small cities, bishoprics, principalities, and territories of independent knights.

After 1648 the Habsburg family retained firm hold on the title of Holy Roman Emperor, but the effectiveness of the title depended less on force of arms than on the cooperation that the emperor could elicit from the various political bodies in the empire. The Diet of the empire sat at Regensburg from 1663 until its dissolution in 1806. The Diet and the emperor generally regulated the daily economic and political life of Germany. The post-Westphalian Holy Roman Empire in many ways resembled Poland in its lack of central authority. However, unlike its Polish neighbor, the Holy Roman Empire was reorganized from within as the Habsburgs attempted to regain their authority and, as will be seen shortly, as Prussia set out on its course toward European power.

While establishing a new kind of position for their Austrian holdings among the German states, the Habsburgs began to consolidate their power and influence within their other hereditary possessions. These included, first, the Crown of Saint Wenceslas encompassing the kingdom of Bohemia (in modern Czechoslovakia) and the Duchies of Moravia and Silesia and, second, the Crown of Saint Stephen, which ruled Hungary, Croatia, and Transylvania. In the middle of the seventeenth century much of Hungary remained occupied by the Turks and was liberated only at the end of the century. In the early eighteenth century the family further extended its domains, receiving the former Spanish (thereafter Austrian) Netherlands, Lombardy in northern Italy, and the

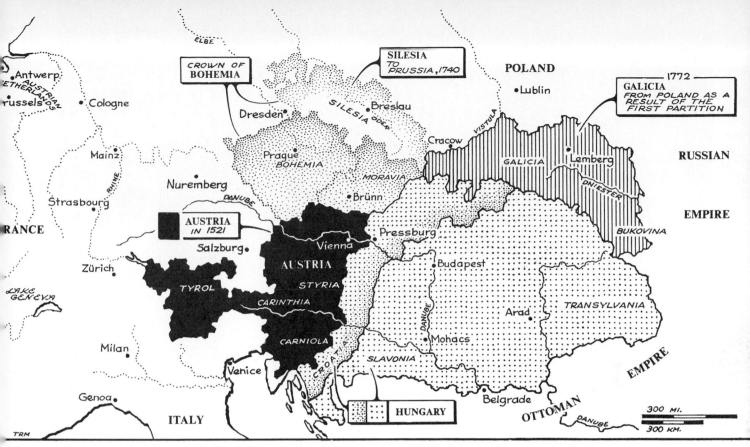

THE AUSTRIAN HAPSBURG EMPIRE, 1521–1772

MAP 14-1 *The Empire had three main units—Austria, Bohemia, Hungary. Expansion was mainly eastward: east Hungary from the Ottomans (17th century) and Galicia from Poland (1772). Meantime, Silesia was lost, but Hapsburgs retained German influence as Holy Roman Emperors.*

Kingdom of Naples in southern Italy through the Treaty of Utrecht in 1713. The Kingdom of Naples was lost relatively quickly and played no considerable role in the Habsburg fortunes. During the eighteenth and nineteenth centuries Habsburgs' power and influence in Europe would be based primarily on their territories located outside Germany.

In the second half of the seventeenth century and later the Habsburg confronted immense problems in these hereditary territories. In each they ruled by virtue of a different title and had to gain the cooperation of the local nobility. The most difficult province was Hungary, where the Magyar nobility seemed ever ready to rebel. There was almost no common basis for political unity among peoples of such diverse languages, customs, and geography. Even the Habsburg zeal for Roman Catholicism no longer proved a bond for unity as they continued to confront the equally zealous Calvinism of the Magyar nobles. Over the years the

Habsburgs established various central councils to chart common policies for their far-flung domains. Virtually all of these bodies dealt with only a portion of the Habsburgs' holdings. Repeatedly they found themselves compelled to bargain with nobles in one part of Europe in order to maintain their position in another.

Despite all these internal difficulties Leopold I (1657–1705) rallied his domains to resist the advances of the Turks and to resist the aggression of Louis XIV. He achieved Ottoman recognition of his sovereignty over Hungary in 1699 and suppressed the long rebellion of his new Magyar subjects between 1703 and 1711. He also extended his territorial holdings over much of what is today Yugoslavia and western Romania. These southeastward extensions allowed the Habsburgs to hope to develop Mediterranean trade through the port of Trieste. The expansion at the cost of the Ottoman Empire also helped the Habsburgs to compensate for their loss of domination over the Holy Roman

Schonnbrunn Palace, outside Vienna. The Habsburg court migrated to this Austrian Versailles each spring, returning to Vienna only in the autumn. [Shostal]

Maria Theresa Discusses One Weakness of Her Throne

Scattered subjects of the multilingual Austrian Empire (Germans, Hungarians, Czechs, Slovaks, Slovenes, Croatians, Poles, and Romanians, for example) made impossible the unifying of the empire into a strong centralized monarchy. Maria Theresa, writing in 1745, explained how previous Habsburg rulers had impoverished themselves by attempting, with little success, to purchase the political and military support of the nobles in different provinces. The more privileges they gave the nobles, the more they were expected to give.

To return once again to my ancestors, these individuals not only gave away most of the crown estates, but absorbed also the debts of those properties confiscated in time of rebellion, and these debts are still in arrears. Emperor Leopold [1658–1705] found little left to give away, but the terrible wars he fought no doubt forced him to mortgage or pawn additional crown estates. His successors did not relieve these burdens, and when I became sovereign, the crown revenues barely reached eighty thousand gulden. Also in the time of my forebears, the ministers received enormous payments from the crown and from the local Estates because they knew not only how to exploit selfishly the good will, grace, and munificence of the Austrian house by convincing each ruler that predecessor had won fame by giving freely but also how to win the ears of the provincial lords and clergy so that these minis-

ters acquired all that they wished. In fact they spread their influence so wide that in the provinces they were more feared and respected than the ruler himself. And when they had finally taken everything from the sovereign, these same ministers turned for additional compensation to their provinces, where their great authority continuously increased. Even though complaints reached the monarch, out of grace and forebearance toward the ministers, he simply allowed the exploitations to continue. . . .

This system gave the ministers such authority that the sovereign himself found it convenient for his own interests to support them because he learned by experience that the more prestige enjoyed by the heads of the provinces, the more of the sovereign's demands these heads could extract from their Estates.

Maria Theresa, *Political Testament*, cited in Karl A. Roider (Ed. and Trans.), *Maria Theresa* (Englewood Cliffs, N.J.: Prentice-Hall, 1973), pp. 32–33.

Empire. Strength in the East gave them greater political leverage in Germany. Leopold was succeeded by Joseph I (1705–1711), who continued his policies.

When Charles VI (1711–1740) succeeded Joseph, he added a new problem to the old chronic one of territorial diversity. He had no male heir, and there was only the weakest of precedents for a female ruler of the Habsburg domains. Charles feared that on his death the Austrian Habsburg lands might fall prey to the surrounding powers, as had those of the Spanish Habsburgs in 1700. He was determined to prevent that disaster and to provide his domains with the semblance of legal unity. To those ends, he devoted most of his reign to seeking the approval of his family, the estates of his realms, and the major foreign powers for a document called the *Pragmatic Sanction*.

This instrument provided the legal basis for a single line of inheritance within the Habsburg dynasty through Charles VI's daughter Maria Theresa (1740–1780). Other members of the Habsburg family recognized her as the rightful heir. The nobles of the various Habsburg domains did likewise after extracting various concessions from Charles. Consequently, when Charles VI died in October 1740, he believed that he had secured legal unity for the Habsburg Empire and a safe succession for his daughter. He had indeed established a permanent line of succession and the basis for future legal bonds within the Habsburg holdings, but he failed to protect his daughter from foreign aggression, either through the Pragmatic Sanction or, more important, by leaving her a strong army and a filled treasury. Less than two months after his death the fragility of the foreign agreements became all too apparent. In December 1740 Frederick II of Prussia invaded the Habsburg province of Silesia. Maria Theresa would now have to fight to defend her inheritance.

Prussia and the Hohenzollerns

The Habsburg achievement had been to draw together into an uncertain legal unity a collection of domains possessed by dint of separate feudal titles. The achievement of the Hohenzollerns of Brandenburg-Prussia was to acquire a similar collection of titular holdings and then to forge them into a centrally administered unit. In spite of the geographical separation of their territories and the paucity of their natural economic resources, they trans-

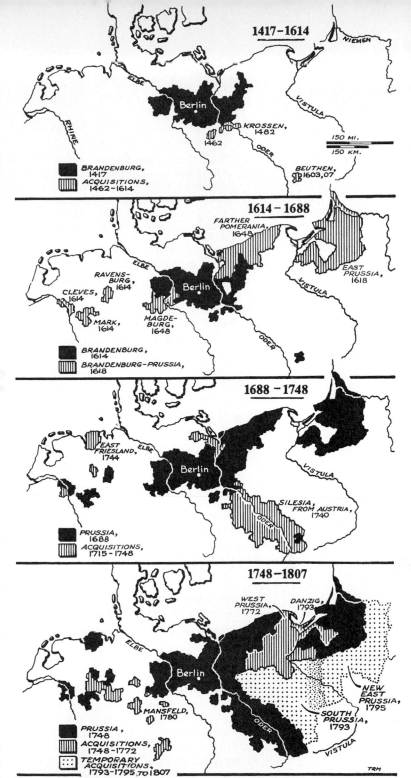

EXPANSION OF BRANDENBURG-PRUSSIA

MAP 14-2 *Seventeenth-century Brandenburg-Prussia expanded mainly by acquiring dynastic titles in geographically separated lands. Eighteenth-century expansion occurred through aggression to the east: Silesia seized in 1740 and various parts of Poland in 1772, 1793, and 1795.*

517

The Great Elector Welcomes Protestant Refugees from France

The Hohenzollern dynasty of Brandenburg-Prussia pursued a policy of religious toleration. The family itself was Calvinist, whereas most of its subjects were Lutherans. When Louis XIV of France revoked the Edict of Nantes in 1685, Frederick William, the Great Elector, seized on the opportunity to invite into his realms French Protestants. As his proclamation indicates, he was quite interested in attracting persons with productive skills who could aid the economic development of his domains.

We, Friedrich Wilhelm, by Grace of God Margrave of Brandenburg. . . .

Do hereby proclaim and make known to all and sundry that since the cruel persecutions and rigorous ill-treatment in which Our co-religionists of the Evangelical-Reformed faith have for some time past been subjected in the Kingdom of France, have caused many families to remove themselves and to betake themselves out of the said Kingdom into other lands, We now . . . have been moved graciously to offer them through this Edict . . . a secure and free refuge in all Our Lands and Provinces. . . .

Since Our Lands are not only well and amply endowed with all things necessary to support life, but also very well-suited to the reestablishment of all kinds of manufactures and trade and traffic by land and water, We permit, indeed, to those settling therein free choice to establish themselves where it is most convenient for their profession and way of living. . . .

The personal property which they bring with them, including merchandise and other wares,

is to be totally exempt from any taxes, customs dues, licenses, or other imposts of any description, and not detained in any way. . . .

As soon as these Our French co-religionists of the Evangelical-Reformed faith have settled in any town or village, they shall be admitted to the domiciliary rights and craft freedoms customary there, gratis and without payment of any fee; and shall be entitled to the benefits, rights, and privileges enjoyed by Our other, native, subjects, residing there. . . .

Not only are those who wish to establish manufacture of cloth, stuffs, hats, or other objects in which they are skilled to enjoy all necessary freedoms, privileges and facilities, but also provision is to be made for them to be assisted and helped as far as possible with money and anything else which they need to realize their intention. . . .

Those who settle in the country and wish to maintain themselves by agriculture are to be given a certain plot of land to bring under cultivation and provided with whatever they need to establish themselves initially. . . .

C. A. Macartney (Ed.), *The Habsburg and Hohenzollern Dynasties in the Seventeenth and Eighteenth Centuries* (New York: Walker, 1970), pp. 270–273.

formed feudal ties and structures into bureaucratic ones. They subordinated every social class and most economic pursuits to the strengthening of the one institution that united their far-flung realms: the army. In so doing they made the term *Prussian* synonymous with administrative rigor and military discipline.

The rise of Prussia occurred within the German power vacuum created by the Peace of Westphalia. It is the story of the extraordinary Hohenzollern family, which had ruled the German territory of Brandenburg since 1417. Through inheritance the family had acquired the duchy of Cleves and the counties of Mark and Ravensburg in 1609, the duchy of East Prussia in 1618, and the duchy of Pomerania in 1637. Except for Pomerania, none of these lands was contiguous with Brandenburg. East Prussia lay inside Poland and outside the authority of the Holy Roman Emperor. All of the territories lacked good natural resources, and many of them were devastated during the Thirty Years' War. At Westphalia the Hohenzollerns lost part of Pomerania to Sweden but were compensated by receiving three more bishoprics and the promise of the archbishopric of Magdeburg when it became vacant, as it did in 1680. By the late seven-

Economically weak, with a small population, Prussia became an important state because it developed a large, well-trained army. The discipline for which Prussian troops were noted was the result of constant drill and harsh punishment. The parade-ground formation shown here was actually meant to be performed on the battlefield. The wooden horse (left) was used for punishment, not exercise. [*Bildarchiv Preussischer Kulturbesitz*]

teenth century the scattered Hohenzollern holdings represented a block of territory within the Holy Roman Empire second in size only to that of the Habsburgs.

Despite its size, the Hohenzollern conglomerate was weak. The areas were geographically separate, and there was no mutual sympathy or common concern among them, In each there existed some form of local noble estates that limited the power of the Hohenzollern prince. The various areas were exposed to foreign aggression.

The person who began to forge these areas and nobles into a modern state was Frederick William (1640–1688), who became known as the Great Elector. He established himself and his successors as the central uniting power by breaking the estates, organizing a royal bureaucracy, and establishing a strong army.

Between 1655 and 1660 Sweden and Poland engaged in a war that endangered the Great Elector's holdings in Pomerania and East Prussia. Frederick William had neither an adequate army nor the tax revenues to confront this foreign threat. In 1655 the Brandenburg estates refused to grant him new taxes; however, he proceeded to collect the required taxes by military force. In 1659 a different grant of taxes, originally made in 1653, elapsed; Frederick William continued to collect them as well as those he had imposed by his own authority. He used the money to build up an army, which allowed him to continue to enforce his will without the approval of the nobility. Similar processes of threats and coercion took place against the nobles in his other territories.

However, there was a political and social trade-off between the elector and his various nobles. These *Junkers,* or German noble landlords, were allowed almost complete control over the serfs on their estates. In exchange for their obedience to the Hohenzollerns, the *Junkers* received the right to demand obedience from their serfs. Frederick William also tended to choose as the local administrators of the tax structure men who would normally have been members of the nobles estates. In this fashion he co-opted potential opponents into his service. The taxes fell most heavily on the backs of the peasants and the urban classes. As the years passed, sons of *Junkers* increasingly dominated the army officer corps, and this practice became even more pronounced during the eighteenth century. All officials and army officers took an oath of loyalty directly to the elector. The army and the elector thus came to embody the otherwise absent unity of the state. The existence of the army made Prussia a valu-

---

Frederick William I of Prussia Demands Truthful Reports from His Royal Officials

On July 20, 1722, Frederick William I issued these orders to his civil servants in charge of Pomerania. He was deeply troubled by inaccuracies in the information being sent to him and to his officials in Berlin. He had no patience with lazy officials. He also intended to discourage officials from hiding bad news from him. Note in particular his concern with the collection of taxes and with all matters relating to the recruitment of troops into the army.

For some time past We have on various occasions remarked with particular displeasure that the reports rendered to Us, especially on matters concerning Our Provinces and towns, often contain statements that are unfounded, or, at least, not based on the necessary conscientious and mature examination of the true circumstances involved, and afterward, after closer scrutiny and examination, show that the event did not occur at all, or at any rate, not in the way in which it was represented, so that in the end We have not known what to believe, and what not. We wish therefore that this improper practice, which is directly contrary to the duty and obligations of Our servants, shall for the future cease absolutely, and no reports be rendered that do not rest on correct and truthful foundations and on mature precedent investigation of all and every attendant circumstance, as their authors have to answer for it before God, Us, and their consciences, under pain of Our extreme disfavor and most severe and active displeasure toward those who do not obey exactly this, Our express command. . . . Our most gracious intention remains, as before, that complete information should be rendered to Us periodically on everything that occurs in the country and the towns, and on the true situation, particularly when there is any deficit in the land tax or the town excise, or any incident in the commercial field; and similarly when, as often occurs in connection with recruiting and billeting, excesses have been committed—real, not hearsay, but actual demonstrable facts which have not been remedied by the commanding officers, to whom the complaints must, by regulation, be first addressed, detailed reports of all such and other similar cases must be sent to Us personally under seal, duplicates to be sent in every case to the General Commissariat of War. We hereby make known to you this, Our considered wish, and command you, not only yourselves to obey in the future, but also to make it known to the magistrates and other persons whom it may concern, in order that each one may safeguard himself against trouble and certain punishment.

C. A. Macartney (Ed.), *The Habsburg and Hohenzollern Dynasties in the Seventeenth and Eighteenth Centuries* (New York: Walker, 1970), pp. 298–299.

able potential ally and a state with which other powers needed to curry favor.

Yet, even with the considerable accomplishments of the Great Elector, the house of Hohenzollern did not possess a crown. The achievement of a royal title was one of the few state-building accomplishments of Frederick I (1688–1713). This son of the Great Elector was the least "Prussian" of his family during these crucial years. He built palaces, founded Halle University (1694), patronized the arts, and lived luxuriously. However, in 1700, at the outbreak of the War of the Spanish Succession, he put his army at the disposal of the Habsburg Holy Roman Emperor. In exchange for this loyal service the emperor permitted Frederick to assume the title of "King in Prussia." Thereafter Frederick became Frederick I, and he passed the much-desired royal title to his son Frederick William I in 1713.

Frederick William I (1713–1740) was both the most eccentric personality to rule the Hohenzollern domains and one of its most effective monarchs. After giving his father a funeral that matched the luxury of his life, Frederick William I immediately imposed policies of strict austerity. In some cases jobs were abolished, and in others salaries were lowered. His political aims seem to have been nothing else than the consolidation of an obedient, compliant bureaucracy and the expansion of the army. He initiated a policy of *Kabinett* government, which meant that lower officials submitted all relevant documents to him in his office, or *Kabinett.* Then he alone examined the papers, made his decision, and issued his orders. Frederick William I thus skirted the influence of ministers and ruled alone.

Frederick William organized the bureaucracy along the lines of military discipline. He united all departments under the *General-Ober-Finanz-Kriegs-und-Domänen-Direktorium*, which is more happily known to us as the *General Directory.* He imposed taxes on the nobility and changed most remaining feudal dues into money payments. He sought to transform feudal and administrative loyalties into a sense of duty to the monarch as a political institution rather than as a person. He once described the perfect royal servant as

an intelligent, assiduous, and alert person who after God values nothing higher than his king's pleasure and serves him out of love and for the sake of honor rather than money and who in his conduct solely seeks and constantly bears in mind his king's service

AUSTRIA AND PRUSSIA IN THE LATE SEVENTEENTH AND EARLY EIGHTEENTH CENTURIES	
Reign of Frederick William, the Great Elector	1640–1688
Leopold I rules Austria and resists the Turkish invasions	1657–1705
Turkish siege of Vienna	1683
Reign of Frederick I of Prussia	1688–1713
Peace treaty between Turks and Habsburgs	1699
Charles VI rules Austria and secures agreement to the Pragmatic Sanction	1711–1740
Frederick William I builds up the military power of Prussia	1713–1740
Maria Theresa succeeds to the Habsburg throne	1740
Frederick II violates the Pragmatic Sanction by invading Silesia	1740

and interests, who, moreover, abhors all intrigues and emotional deterrents.[1]

Service to the state and the monarch was to become impersonal, mechanical, and, in effect, unquestioning.

The discipline that Frederick William applied to the army was little less than fanatical. During his reign the size of the military force grew from about thirty-nine thousand in 1713 to over eighty thousand in 1740. It was the third or fourth largest army in Europe, whereas Prussia ranked thirteenth in size of population. Rather than using recruiters, the king made each canton or local district responsible for supplying a certain number of soldiers.

After 1725 Frederick William always wore an officer's uniform. He built one regiment from the tallest soldiers he could find in Europe. Separate laws applied to the army and to civilians. Laws, customs, and royal attention made the officer corps the highest social class of the state. Military service attracted the sons of *Junkers.* In this fashion the army, the *Junker* nobility, and the monarchy became forged into a single political entity. Military priorities and values dominated Prussian government, society, and daily life as in no other state of Europe. It has often been said that whereas other nations possessed armies, the Prussian army possessed its nation.

[1]Quoted in Hans Rosenberg, *Bureaucracy, Aristocracy, and Autocracy* (Boston: Beacon Press, 1958), p. 93.

Although Frederick William I built the best army in Europe, he followed a policy of avoiding conflict. He wanted to drill his soldiers but not to order them into battle. Although Frederick William terrorized his family and associates and on occasion knocked out teeth with his walking stick, he was not a militarily aggressive monarch. The army was for him a symbol of Prussian power and unity, not an instrument to be used for foreign adventures or aggression. At this death in 1740 he passed to his son Frederick II (1740–1786; Frederick the Great) this superb military machine, but he could not pass to his son the wisdom to refrain from using it. Almost immediately on coming to the throne, Frederick II upset the Pragmatic Sanction and invaded Silesia. He thus crystallized the Austrian-Prussian rivalry for control of Germany that would dominate central European affairs for over a century.

The Entry of Russia into the European Political Arena

Though ripe with consequences for the future, the rise of Prussia and the new consolidation of Austrian Habsburg domains seemed to many at the time only one more shift in the long-troubled German scene. However, the emergence of Russia as an active European power constituted a wholly new factor in European politics. Previously Russia had been considered a part of Europe only by courtesy. Geographically and politically it lay on the periphery of Europe. Hemmed in by Sweden on the Baltic and by the Ottoman Empire on the Black Sea, the country had no warm-water ports. Its chief outlet to the west was Archangel on the White Sea, which was open to ships during only part of the year. There was little trade. What Russia did possess was a vast reserve of largely undeveloped natural and human resources.

The reign of Ivan the Terrible, which had begun so well and closed so frighteningly, was followed by a period of anarchy and civil war known as the *Time of Troubles*. In 1613, hoping to resolve the tension and end the uncertainty, an assembly of nobles elected as czar a seventeen-year-old boy named Michael Romanov (1613–1654). Thus began the dynasty that in spite of palace revolutions, military conspiracies, assassinations, and family strife ruled Russia until 1917.

Michael Romanov and his two successors, Alexis I (1654–1676) and Theodore III (1676–

Ivan the Terrible (1533–1584). He was the first Muscovite ruler to call himself Tsar of Russia. [National Museum Copenhagen]

1682), brought stability and bureaucratic centralization to Russia. However, Russia remained militarily weak and financially impoverished. The bureaucracy after these years of turmoil still remained largely controlled by the boyars. This administrative apparatus was only barely capable of putting down a revolt of peasants and cossacks under Stepan Razin in 1670–1671. Furthermore, the government and the czars faced the danger of mutiny from the *streltsy,* or guards of the Moscow garrison.

Peter the Great

In 1682 another boy—ten years old at the time—ascended the fragile Russian throne as coruler with his half brother. His name was Peter (1682–1725), and Russia would never be the same after him. He and his ill half-brother, Ivan V, had come to power on the shoulders of the *streltsy,* who expected rewards from the persons they favored. Much violence and bloodshed had surrounded the disputed succession. Matters became even more confused when the boys' sister, Sophia, was named regent. Peter's followers overthrew her in 1689. From that date onward Peter ruled personally, although in theory he shared the crown with Ivan, until Ivan died in 1696. The

Peter the Great (1682–1725) studying ship building in Holland. In 1697, the Tsar visited western Europe incognito to study the skills that he considered necessary for Russia to build a strong, modern state. [The Bettmann Archive]

dangers and turmoil of his youth convinced Peter of two things. First, the power of the czar must be made secure from the jealousy of the boyars and the greed of the *streltsy*. Second, the military power of Russia must be increased.

Peter I, who became Peter the Great, was fascinated by western Europe, particularly its military resources. He was an imitator of the first order. The products and workers from the West who had filtered into Russia impressed and intrigued him. In 1697 he made a famous visit in rather weak disguises throughout western Europe. There he dined and talked with the great and the powerful, who considered this almost seven-foot-tall ruler both crude and rude. His happiest moments on the trip were spent inspecting shipyards, docks, and the manufacture of military hardware. He returned to Moscow determined by whatever means necessary to copy what he had seen abroad, for he knew that warfare would be necessary to make Russia a great power. The czar's drive toward westernization, though unsystematic, had four general areas of concern: taming the boyars and the *streltsy*, achieving secular con-

trol of the church, reorganizing the internal administration, and developing the economy. Peter pursued each of these goals with violence and ruthlessness.

He made a sustained attack on the Russian boyars. In 1698, immediately on his return from abroad, he personally shaved the long beards of the court boyars and sheared off the customary long, hand-covering sleeves of their shirts and coats, which had made them the butt of jokes throughout Europe. More important, he demanded that the nobles provide his state with their services.

In 1722 Peter published a Table of Ranks, which henceforth equated a person's social position and privileges with his rank in the bureaucracy or the army rather than with his position in the nobility. However, unlike the case in Prussia, the Russian nobility never became perfectly loyal to the state. They repeatedly sought to reassert their independence and their control of the Russian imperial court.

The *streltsy* fared less well than the boyars. In 1698 they had rebelled while Peter was on his European tour. When he returned and put

---

Bishop Burnet Looks Over a Foreign Visitor

In 1697 and 1698 Peter the Great of Russia toured western Europe to discover how Russia must change its society and economy in order to become a great power. As this description by Bishop Gilbert Burnet in England indicates, the west Europeans found the czar a curious person in his own right.

He came this winter over to England, and stayed some months among us. . . . I had good interpreters, so I had much free discourse with him; he is a man of a very hot temper, soon inflamed, and very brutal in his passion; he raises his natural heat, by drinking much brandy, . . . he is subject to convulsive motions all over his body, and his head seems to be affected with these; he wants not capacity, and has a larger measure of knowledge, than might be expected from his education, which was very indifferent; a want of judgment, with an instability of temper, appear in him too often and too evidently; he is mechanically turned, and seems designed by nature rather to be a ship-carpenter, than a great prince. This was his chief study and exercise, while he stayed here: he wrought much with his own hands, and made all about him work at the models of ships. . . . He was . . . resolved to encourage learning, and to polish his people, by sending some of them to travel in other countries, and to draw strangers to come and live among them. . . . After I had seen him often, and had conversed much with him, I could not but adore the depth of the providence of God, that had raised up such a furious man to so absolute an authority over so great a part of the world.

Bishop Burnet's History of His Own Time, Vol. 4 (Oxford, England: Clarendon Press, 1823), pp. 396–397.

---

down the revolt of these Moscow troops, he directed massive violence and brutality against both leaders and followers. There were private tortures and public executions, in which Peter's own ministers took part. Almost twelve hundred of the rebels were put to death, and their corpses long remained on public display to discourage future disloyalty.

Peter dealt with the potential political independence of the Russian Orthodox Church with similar ruthlessness. Here again, Peter had to confront a problem that had arisen in the turbulent decades that had preceded his reign. The Russian church had long opposed the scientific as well as the theological thought of the West. In the mid-seventeenth century a reformist movement led by Patriarch Nikon arose in the church. In 1667 certain changes had been introduced into the texts and the ritual of the church. These reforms caused great unrest because the Russian church had always claimed to be the protector of the ritual. The Old Believers, a group of Russian Christians who strongly opposed these changes, were condemned by the hierarchy, but they persisted in their opposition. Late in the century thousands of them committed suicide rather than submit to the new rituals. The Old Believers' movement represented a rejection of change and innovation; its presence discouraged the church hierarchy from making any further substantial moves toward modern thought.

In the future Peter wanted to avoid two kinds of difficulties with the Russian church. First, the clergy must not constitute a group within the state that would oppose change and westernization. Second, the hierarchy of the church must not be permitted to reform liturgy, ritual, or doctrine in a way that might again give rise to discontent such as that of the Old Believers. Consequently, in 1721, Peter simply abolished the position of patriarch of the Russian church. In its place he established a synod headed by a layman to rule the church in accordance with secular requirements. So far as transforming a traditional institution was concerned, this action toward the church was the most radical policy of Peter's reign. It produced still further futile opposition from the Old Believers, who saw the czar as leading the church into new heresy.

In his reorganization of domestic administration, Peter looked to institutions then used in Sweden. These were "colleges," or bureaus, composed of several persons rather than departments headed by a single minister. These colleges, which he imposed on Russia, were to look after matters such as the collection of taxes, foreign affairs, war, and economic matters. This new organization was an attempt to breathe life into the generally stagnant and inefficient administration of the country. In 1711 he created a central senate of nine members who were to direct the Moscow government when the czar was away with the army. The purpose of these and other local administrative reforms was to establish a bureaucracy that could collect and spend tax revenues to support an efficient army.

The economic development advocated by Peter the Great was closely related to his military needs. He encouraged the establishment of an iron industry in the Ural Mountains, and by mid-century Russia had become the largest iron producer in Europe. He sent prominent young Russians abroad to acquire technical and organizational skills. He attempted to attract west European craftsmen to live and work in Russia. Except for the striking growth of the iron industry, which later languished, all these efforts had only marginal success.

The goal of these internal reforms and political departures was to support a policy of warfare. Peter was determined to secure warmwater ports that would allow Russia to trade with the West and to have a greater impact of European affairs. This policy led him into wars with the Ottoman Empire and with Sweden. His armies commenced fighting the Turks in 1695 and captured Azov on the Black Sea in 1696. It was a temporary victory, for in 1711 he was compelled to return the port.

Peter had more success against Sweden, where the inconsistency and irrationality of Charles XII were no small aid. In 1700 Russia moved against the Swedish territory on the Baltic. The Swedish king's failure to follow up his victory at Narva in 1700 allowed Peter to regroup his forces and hoard his resources. In 1709, when Charles XII returned to fight Russia again, Peter was ready, and the Battle of Poltava sealed the fate of Sweden. In 1721, at the Peace of Nystad, which ended the Great Northern War, the Russian conquest of Estonia, Livonia, and part of Finland was confirmed. Henceforth Russia possessed warmwater ports and a permanent influence on European affairs.

At one point the domestic and foreign policies of Peter the Great literally intersected. This was at the spot on the Gulf of Finland where Peter founded his new capital city of Saint Petersburg (now Leningrad). There he built government structures and compelled his boyars to construct town houses. In this fashion he imitated those west European monarchs who had copied Louis XIV by constructing smaller versions of Versailles. However, the founding of Saint Petersburg went beyond the construction of a central court. It symbolized a new western orientation of Russia and Peter's determination to hold his position on the Baltic coast. He had begun the construction of the city and had moved the capital there in 1703, even before his victory over Sweden was assured.

Despite his notable success on the Baltic, Peter's reign ended with a great question mark. He had long quarreled with his only son, Alexis. Peter was jealous of the young man and fearful that he might undertake sedition. In 1718 Peter had his son imprisoned, and during

RISE OF RUSSIAN POWER	
Reign of Ivan the Terrible	1533–1584
Time of Troubles	1584–1613
Michael Romanov becomes czar	1613
Peter the Great becomes czar as a boy	1682
Peter assumes personal rule	1689
Russia captures Azov on the Black Sea from the Turks	1696
European tour of Peter the Great	1697
Peter returns to Russia to put down the revolt of the *streltsy*	1698
The Great Northern War opens between Russia and Sweden; Russia defeated at Narva by Swedish Army of Charles XII	1700
Saint Petersburg founded	1703
Russia defeats Sweden at the Battle of Poltava	1709
Charles XII of Sweden dies	1718
Son of Peter the Great dies under mysterious circumstances in prison	1718
Peace of Nystad ends the Great Northern War	1721
Peter establishes a synod for the Russian church	1721
Peter issues the Table of Ranks	1722
Peter dies leaving an uncertain succession	1725

Peter the Great built St. Petersburg (now Leningrad) on the Gulf of Finland to provide Russia with better contact with Western Europe. He moved the capital there from Moscow in 1703. This is an eighteenth-century view of the city. [John R. Freeman]

this imprisonment the presumed successor to the throne died mysteriously. Thereafter Peter claimed for himself the right of naming a successor, but he could never bring himself to designate the person either orally or in writing. Consequently, when he died in 1725, there was no firmer policy on the succession to the throne than when he had acceded to the title. For over thirty years, once again soldiers and nobles would determine who ruled Russia. Peter had laid the foundations of a modern Russia, but he had failed to lay the foundations of a stable state.

Eighteenth-Century European States

By the second quarter of the eighteenth century the major European powers were not yet nation-states in which the citizens felt themselves united by a shared sense of community,

culture, language, and history. They were still monarchies in which the personality of the ruler and the personal relationships of the great noble families exercised considerable influence over public affairs. The monarchs, except in Great Britain, had generally succeeded in making their power greater than the nobility's. However, the power of the aristocracy and its capacity to resist or obstruct the policies of the monarchs were not destroyed. In Britain, of course, the nobility had tamed the monarchy, but even there tension between nobles and monarchs would continue through the rest of the century.

In foreign affairs the new arrangement of military and diplomatic power established during the early years of the century prepared the way for two long-term conflicts. The first was a commercial rivalry for trade and overseas empire between France and Great Britain. During the reign of Louis XIV these two nations had collided over the French bid for dominance in

Europe. During the eighteenth century they dueled for control of commerce on other continents. The second arena of warfare was central Europe, where Austria and Prussia fought for the leadership of the states of Germany.

However, behind these international conflicts and the domestic rivalry of monarchs and nobles, the society of eighteenth-century Europe began to experience momentous change. The character and the structures of the society over which the monarchs ruled were beginning to take on some features associated with the modern age. These economic and social developments would, in the long run, produce transformations in the life of Europe beside which the state building of the early eighteenth-century monarchs paled.

Suggested Readings

M. S. ANDERSON, *Europe in the Eighteenth Century,* 1713–1783 (1961). The best one-volume introduction.

T. M. BARKER, *Army, Aristocracy, Monarchy: Essays in War, Society and Government in Austria,* 1618–1780 (1982). Examines the intricate power relationships among these major institutions.

R. BROWNING, *Political and Constitutional Ideas of the Court Whigs* (1982). An excellent overview of the ideology of Walpole's supporters

F. L. CARSTEN, *The Origins of Prussia* (1954). Discusses the groundwork laid by the Great Elector in the seventeenth century.

A. COBBAN, *A History of Modern France,* 2nd ed., Vol. 1, (1961). A lively and opinionated survey.

L. COLLEY, *In Defiance of Oligarchy: The Tory Party,* 1714–60. (1982) An important study that challenges much conventional opinion about eighteenth-century British politics.

P. DUKES, *The Making of Russian Absolutism:* 1613–1801 (1982). An overview based on recent scholarship.

R. R. ERGANG, *The Potsdam Führer* (1941). The biography of Frederick William I.

R. J. W. EVANS, *The Making of the Habsburg Monarchy,* 1550–1700: *An Interpretation* (1979). Places much emphasis on intellectual factors and the role of religion.

S. B. FAY AND K. EPSTEIN, *The Rise of Brandenburg-Prussia to* 1786 (1937, rev. 1964). A brief outline.

F. FORD, *Robe and Sword: The Regrouping of the French Aristocracy After Louis XIV* (1953). An important book for political, social, and intellectual history.

G. P. GOOCH, *Maria Theresa and Other Studies* (1951). A sound introduction to the problems of the Habsburgs.

G. P. GOOCH, *Louis XV, The Monarchy in Decline* (1956). A discussion of the problems of France after the death of Louis XIV.

J. M. HITTLE, *The Service City: State and Townsmen in Russia,* 1600–1800 (1979). Examines the relationship of cities in Russia to the growing power of the central government.

H. HOLBORN, *A History of Modern Germany,* 1648–1840 (1966). The best and most comprehensive survey in English.

H. C. JOHNSON, *Frederick the Great and His Officials* (1975). An excellent recent examination of the Prussian administration.

R. A. KANN AND Z. V. DAVID, *The Peoples of the Eastern Habsburg Lands,* 1526–1918 (1984). The best overview of the subject.

V. K. KLYUCHEVSKY, *Peter the Great,* tr. by Liliana Archibald (1958). A standard biography.

D. MARSHALL, *Eighteenth-Century England* (1962). Emphasizes social and economic background.

R. K. MASSIE, *Peter the Great: His Life and His World* (1980). A good popular biography.

L. B. NAMIER AND J. BROOKE, *The History of Parliament: The House of Commons,* 1754–1790, 3 vols. (1964). A detailed examination of the unreformed British House of Commons and electoral system.

L. J. OLIVA (Ed.), *Russia and the West from Peter the Great to Khrushchev* (1965). An anthology of articles tracing an important and ambiguous subject.

J. B. OWEN, *The Eighteenth Century* (1974). An excellent introduction to England in the period.

J. H. PLUMB, *Sir Robert Walpole,* 2 vols. (1956, 1961). A masterful biography ranging across the sweep of European politics.

J. H. PLUMB, *The Growth of Political Stability in England,* 1675–1725 (1969). An important interpretive work.

N. V. RIASANOVSKY, *A History of Russia,* 3rd ed. (1977). The best one-volume introduction.

N. V. RIASANOVSKY, *The Image of Peter the Great in Russian History and Thought* (1985). Examines the ongoing legacy of Peter in Russian history.

P. ROBERTS, *The Quest for Security,* 1715–1740 (1947). Very good on the diplomatic problems of the period.

H. ROSENBERG, *Bureaucracy, Aristocracy, and Autocracy: The Prussian Experience,* 1660–1815 (1960). Emphasizes the organization of Prussian administration.

B. H. SUMMER, *Peter the Great and the Emergency of Russia* (1950). A brief, but well-organized discussion.

E. N. WILLIAMS, *The Ancien Régime in Europe* (1972). A state-by-state survey of very high quality.

A. M. WILSON, *French Foreign Policy During the Administration of Cardinal Fleury,* 1726–1743 (1936). The standard account.

J. B. WOLF, *The Emergence of the Great Powers,* 1685–1715 (1951). A comprehensive survey.

Throughout Europe in the eighteenth century, the aristocracy dominated both society and government. This portrait of an English nobleman, Lord Willoughby de Brooke, and his family captures the elegance and luxury of aristocratic life. [Michael Holford]

DURING THE FRENCH REVOLUTION (1789) and the turmoil spawned by that upheaval, it became customary to refer to the patterns of social, political, and economic relationships that had existed in France before 1789 as the *ancien régime*, or the "old regime." The term has come to be applied generally to the life and institutions of prerevolutionary Europe. Politically the term indicated the rule of theoretically absolute monarchies with growing bureaucracies and aristocratically led armies. Economically the old regime was characterized by scarcity of food, the predominance of agriculture, slow transport, a low level of iron production, rather unsophisticated financial institutions, and in some cases competitive commercial overseas empires. Socially, prerevolutionary Europe was based on aristocratic elites possessing a wide variety of inherited legal privileges, established Roman Catholic and Protestant churches intimately related to the state and the aristocracy, an urban labor force usually organized into guilds, and a rural peasantry subject to high taxes and feudal dues. It should be remembered that the men and women living during this period did not know it was the *old* regime. In most cases they earned their livelihoods and went through the various stages of life as their forebears had done for generations before them and as they expected their children to do after them.

Probably the most striking feature of the old regime was the marked contrasts in the lives and experiences of people in different social ranks, different countries, and even different regions of the same country. The bonds created by rapid transport and communication that have today led to similar patterns of life throughout the Western world simply did not yet exist.

Within the major monarchies there was usually no single standard of uniform law, money, or weights and measures. Except in Britain, there were internal tolls that hampered the passage of goods. The nobility of Great Britain lived in the most magnificent luxury the order had ever known. On the Continent some groups of nobles were also very wealthy, but other members of the continental nobility were little better off than the wealthier peasants. So far as the peasantry was concerned, it tended to prosper in western Europe while reaching new depths of social and economic degradation east of the Elbe River.

In Britain, Holland, and parts of France there was a healthy and growing middle class, but

15

Society Under the Old Regime in the Eighteenth Century

such an order hardly existed in the German principalities, the Austrian Empire, or Russia. Finally, there was a stark contrast between the refinement of taste, fashion, and manners of the upper levels of society and the simultaneous presence of public whipping, torture, and executions inflicted on the lower classes. Historians often point to the difficulties of life and the differences in wealth in our industrial society, but these were far more extreme in the society of the old regime.

Eighteenth-century society was traditional. The past weighed more heavily on people's minds than did the future. Few persons outside the government bureaucracies and the movement for reform called the *Enlightenment* considered change or innovation desirable. This was especially true of social relationships. Both nobles and peasants, for very different reasons, repeatedly called for the restoration of traditional or customary rights. The nobles asserted what they considered their ancient rights against the intrusion of the expanding monarchical bureaucracies. The peasants, in petitions and revolts, called for the revival or the maintenance of the customary manorial rights that provided them access to particular lands, courts, or grievance procedures.

With the exception of the early industrial development in Britain, the eighteenth-century economy was also quite traditional. The quality and quantity of the harvest remained the single most important fact of life for the overwhelming majority of the population and the gravest concern of the governments.

Closely related to this traditional social and economic outlook was the hierarchical structure of the society. The medieval sense of rank and degree not only persisted but became more rigid in the course of the century. In several continental cities "sumptuary laws" regulating the dress of the different classes remained on the books. These laws forbade persons in one class or occupation to wear clothes like those worn by people in a socially higher position. The point of such laws, which were largely ineffective in the eighteenth century, was to make the social hierarchy actually visible. Rather than by such legislation, the hierarchy was really enforced through the corporate nature of social relationships. Each state or society was considered a community of numerous smaller communities. People in eighteenth-century Europe did not enjoy what Americans

regard as individual rights. A person enjoyed such rights and privileges as were guaranteed to the particular communities or groups of which she or he was a part. The "community" might include the village, the municipality, the nobility, the church, the guild, or the parish. In turn, each of these bodies enjoyed certain privileges, some of which were great and some small. The privileges might involve exemption from taxation or from some especially humiliating punishment, the right to practice a trade or craft, the right of one's children to pursue a particular occupation, or, in the case of the church, the right to collect the tithe.

Tradition, hierarchy, corporateness, and privilege were the chief social characteristics of the old regime. Yet it was by no means a static society. Factors of change and innovation were fermenting in its midst. There was a strong demand from the colonies in the Americas for European goods and manufactures. Merchants in seaports and other cities were expanding their businesses. By preparing their states for war, the various governments put new demands on the resources and the economic organizations of their nations. The spirit of rationality that had been so important to the Scientific Revolution of the seventeenth century continued to manifest itself in the economic life of the eighteenth century. Perhaps most important, the population of Europe grew rapidly. The old regime itself fostered the changes that eventually transformed it into a very different kind of society.

Family Structures and the Family Economy

In preindustrial Europe the household was the basic unit of production and consumption. That is to say, only the most limited number of productive establishments employed more than a handful of people not belonging to the family of the owner. Those very few establishments employing significant numbers of wage earners who were not members of the owner's family were located in cities. But the overwhelming majority of Europeans lived in rural areas. There, as well as in small towns and cities, the household mode of organization predominated on farms, in artisans' workshops, and in small merchants' shops. With that mode of economic organization there developed what is known as the *family economy*.

Households

What was a household in preindustrial Europe of the old regime? There were two basic models, one characterizing northwestern Europe and the other eastern Europe. In the northwestern part of the continent, the household almost invariably consisted of a married couple, their children through their early teenage years, and their servants. Except for the relatively few very wealthy people, households were quite small, rarely consisting of more than five or six members. Furthermore, in these households, more than two generations of a family rarely lived under the same roof. High mortality and late marriage prevented families of three generations. In other words, grandparents rarely lived in the same household as their grandchildren. In this regard the family structure of northwestern Europe was nuclear rather than extended. That is to say, these families consisted of parents and children rather than of several generations under the same roof. This particular characteristic of the northwestern European household is one of the most major discoveries of recent research

into family history. Previously it had been assumed that before industrialization the European family lived in extended familial settings with several generations inhabiting a household. Recent demographic investigation has sharply reversed this picture. Children lived with their parents only until their early teens. Then they normally left home, usually to enter the work force of young servants who lived and worked in a household other than that of their parents. A child of a skilled artisan might remain with his or her parents in order to acquire the valuable skill, but only rarely would more than one of the children do so because their labor would be more valuable and remunerative elsewhere.

These young men and women who had left home would eventually marry, and they would then begin to form an independent household of their own. This practice of moving away from home is known as *neolocalism*. The age of their marriage would be relatively late. For men it was over twenty-six, and for women over twenty-three. At the time of marriage the couple usually quickly began a family. It was not unusual for the marriage to

A French dairy barn c. 1780. Most eighteenth-century Europeans worked with their families in agriculture. [*Charles Farrell Collection*]

Servant girls making butter and cheese on a family farm. The farmer's wife, at left, is supervising their labor. Being a servant was a way for young people to acquire the skills and savings needed to start a household of their own when they married. [*Bildarchiv Preussischer Kulturbesitz*]

occur at the end of a long courtship when the woman was already pregnant. Family and community pressures seem more often than not to have compelled the man to marry the woman, but in any case premarital sexual relations were not rare, though illegitimate births were not common. The new couple would soon employ a servant, who with their growing children would undertake whatever form of livelihood the household used to support itself.

Servant in this context is a word that may seem confusing. It does not refer to someone looking after the needs of wealthy people. Rather in preindustrial Europe, a servant was a person—either male or female—who was hired, often under a clear contract, to work for the head of the household in exchange for room, board, and wages. The servant was usually young and by no means necessarily of a social position lower than that of his or her employer. Normally the servant was an integral part of the household and took meals with

the family. Young men and women became servants when their labor was no longer needed in their parents' household or when they could earn more money for their family outside the parental household. Being a servant for several years—often as many as eight or ten—was a means of acquiring the productive skills and the monetary savings necessary for young people to begin their own household. This period of working as a servant between leaving home and beginning a new household accounts in a large measure for the late age of marriage in northwestern Europe.

As one moved toward the eastern areas of the continent, the structure of the household and the pattern of marriage changed. There marriage occurred quite early, before the age of twenty for both men and women. Consequently children were born to parents of a much younger age. Quite often, especially among Russian serfs, wives were older than their husbands. Eastern European households tended to be quite large in comparison with those in the West. Often the Russian household in the countryside had more than nine and possibly more than twenty members with three or perhaps even four generations of the same family living together. Early marriage made this situation more likely. In Russia marrying involved not starting a new household but continuing in and expanding one already established.

The landholding pattern in eastern Europe accounts, at least in part, for these patterns of marriage and the family. The lords of the manor who owned land wanted to ensure that it would be cultivated so that they could receive their rents. To that end, for example, in Poland, landlords might forbid marriage between their own serfs and those from another estate. They might also require widows and widowers to remarry so there would be adequate labor for a particular plot of land. Polish landlords also frowned on the hiring of free laborers—the equivalent of servants in the West—to aid land cultivation. The landlords preferred other serfs to be used. This practice inhibited the possible formation of independent households. In Russia, landlords ordered the families of young people in their villages to arrange marriages within a short, set period of time. These lords discouraged single-generation family households because the death or serious illness of a person in such a household might mean that the land assigned to that household would go out of cultivation.

The Family Economy

In both northwestern and eastern Europe, most Europeans worked within the context of the *family economy*. That is to say, the household was the fundamental unit of production and consumption. People thought and worked in terms of sustaining the economic life of the family, and family members saw themselves as working together in an interdependent rather than an independent or individualistic manner. The goal of the family household was to

A family of chimney sweeps. Depending on their ages and skills, everyone in an eighteenth-century family worked to help support the household. [British Museum]

produce or to secure through wages enough food to support its members. In the countryside that effort virtually always involved farming. In cities and towns artisan production or working for another person was the usual pattern. Almost everyone lived within a household of some kind because it was virtually impossible for ordinary people to support themselves independently. Indeed, except for members of religious orders, people living outside a household were viewed with great suspicion. It was assumed that they were potentially criminal or disruptive or, at the very minimum, potentially dependent on the charity of others.

Marriage and the family within this economy meant that all members of the household must work. On a farm much of the effort went directly into raising food or producing other agricultural goods that could be exchanged for food. In the countryside of western Europe, however, very few people had enough land to support their household from farming alone. For this reason one or more family members might work elsewhere and send wages home. For example, the father or older children might work as a harvest picker or might fish or might engage in some other kind of labor, either in the local neighborhood or perhaps many miles from home. If the father was such a migrant worker, the burden of the farm work would fall on his wife and their younger children. This was not an uncommon pattern. Within this family economy all of the goods and income produced went to the benefit of the household rather than to the individual family member. Depending on their ages and skills, everyone in the family worked. The very necessity of survival in the face of poor harvests or economic slumps meant that no one could be idle.

The family economy also dominated the life of skilled urban artisans. The father was usually the chief craftsman. He usually had one or more servants in his employ, but he would expect his children to work in the enterprise also. His eldest child was usually trained in the trade. His wife often contributed to his business by selling the wares, or she might open a small shop of her own. Wives of merchants also often ran their husbands' businesses, especially when the husband traveled to purchase new goods. In any case, everyone in the family was involved. If business was poor, family members would look for employment elsewhere, not to support themselves but to support the survival of the family unit.

In western Europe the death of a father often brought disaster to the economy of the household. The ongoing economic life of the family usually depended on his land or his skills. The widow might take on the farm or the business, or his children might do so. The widow usually sought to remarry quickly in order to have the labor and skills of a male once more in the household and to prevent herself from falling into a state of dependence. The high mortality rate of the time meant that there were many households in which there were stepchildren and reconstituted second family groups. But in some cases, because of the advanced age of the widow or economic hard times, the household simply dissolved. The widow became dependent on charity or relatives, and the children became similarly dependent or moved earlier than they would otherwise have done into the work force of servants. In other cases, the situation could be so desperate that they would resort to crime or to begging. The personal, emotional, and economic vulnerability of the family economy cannot be overemphasized.

In eastern Europe the family economy was also in place, but in the context of serfdom and landlord domination. Peasants clearly thought in terms of their families and of expanding the land available for cultivation. In some measure, the village structure may have mitigated the pressures of the family economy, as did the multigenerational family. There also, dependence on the available land was the chief fact of life, and there were many fewer artisan and merchant households. There was also far less mobility than in western Europe.

Women and the Family Economy

The family economy established many of the chief constraints on the lives and the personal experiences of women in preindustrial society. Most of the historical research that has been undertaken on this subject relates to western Europe. There, a woman's life experience was, in large measure, the function of her capacity to establish and maintain a household. For women, marriage was an institution of economic necessity as well as one that fulfilled sexual and psychological needs. A woman outside a household situation lived in a highly vulnerable and precarious position. Unless she were an aristocrat or a member of a religious order, she probably could not support herself by her own efforts alone. Consequently much of a woman's life was devoted first to aiding the maintenance of her parent's household and then to devising some means of assuring having her own household to live in as an adult. In most cases the bearing and rearing of children were subordinate to these goals.

As a child, certainly by the age of seven, a girl was expected to begin to make contributions to the household work. On a farm this might mean looking after chickens or watering animals or carrying food to adult men and women working the land. In an urban artisan's household, she would do some form of light work, perhaps involving cleaning or carrying and later sewing or weaving. The girl would remain in her parents' home as long as she made a real contribution to the family enterprise or as long as her labor elsewhere was not more valuable and remunerative to the family. An artisan's daughter might not leave home until marriage because she could learn increasingly valuable skills associated with the trade. The situation was quite different for the much larger number of girls growing up on farms. There, the girl's parents and brothers could often do all the necessary farm work, and her labor at home quickly became of little value to the family. She would then leave home, usually between the age of twelve and fourteen. She might take up residence on another farm, but more likely, she would migrate to a nearby town or city. She would rarely travel more than thirty miles from her parents' household. She would then normally become a servant, once again living in a household, but this time in the household of an employer.

Having migrated from home, the young woman's chief goal was to accumulate sufficient capital for a dowry. Her savings would make her eligible for marriage because it would allow her to make the necessary contribution to form a household with her husband. The dowry would thus permit her to become an economic partner in the context of the family economy. It must be emphasized that marriage within the family economy was a joint economic undertaking, and that the wife was expected to make an immediate contribution of capital for the establishment of the household. A young woman might well work for ten years or more to accumulate a dowry. This practice meant that marriage was usually postponed until her mid- to late twenties.

Within the marriage the necessity of earning enough money or producing enough farm goods to ensure an adequate food supply was always the dominant concern. Domestic duties, childbearing, and child rearing were subordi-

Working women in eighteenth-century France: They are crushing clay shards as a first step in making glass. It was common for the wives and daughters of artisans to help with the family trade. [New York Public Library]

nate to the economic situation. Consequently the number of children might very well be limited, usually through the practice of *coitus interruptus* or withdrawal of the male prior to ejaculation. Young children were often placed with wet-nurses so that the mother could continue to make her economic contribution to the household. The wet-nurse, in turn, was making such a contribution to her own household. The child would be fully reintegrated into its family when it was weaned and would be expected to aid the family at a very early age.

The kind of work a married woman did differed markedly between city and country and was in many ways a function of the husband's occupation. If the peasant household possessed enough land to support itself, the wife spent much of her time quite literally carrying things for her husband—water, food, seed, harvested grain, and the like. But there were few such adequate landholdings. If the husband had to do work other than farming, such as fishing or migrant labor, the wife might actually be in charge of the farm and do the ploughing, planting, and harvesting. In the city the wife of an artisan or merchant often acted somewhat in the capacity of a business manager. She might well be in charge of the household finances, and she actively participated in the trade or manufacturing enterprise. When her

535

A Parisian street sweeper. Women of the poorer classes did the same manual work as men. [British Library]

husband died, she might take over the business and perhaps hire an artisan.

Finally, if economic disaster struck the family, more often than not it was the wife who organized what Olwen Hufton has called the "economy of expedients,"[1] within which family members might be sent off to find work elsewhere or even to beg in the streets.

In all phases of life within the family economy, women led active, often decisive roles. Industriousness rather than idleness was their lot in life. Finding a functional place in the household was essential to their well-being, but once that place had been found, their function was essential to the ongoing well-being of the household.

Children and the World of the Family Economy

Under the social and medical conditions of the day, the birth of a child was a time of grave danger to both mother and the infant. Both mother and child were immediately exposed to the possible contraction of contagious diseases. Puerperal fever was frequent, as well as other infections from unsterilized medical instruments. By no means were all midwives skillful practitioners of their profession. Furthermore

[1]Olwen Hufton, "Women and the Family Economy in Eighteenth-Century France," *French Historical Studies*, 9 (1976):19.

the immense poverty and the wretched housing conditions of the vast majority of Europe's population endangered the lives of the newborn child and the mother. For large numbers of women childbirth constituted a time of great fearfulness of personal vulnerability.

Assuming that both mother and child survived, the mother might nurse the infant, but quite often the child would be sent a wet-nurse. Convenience may have led to this practice among the wealthy, but economic necessity dictated it for the poor. The structures and customs of the family economy did not permit a woman the time away from work to devote herself entirely to rearing a child. The wet-nursing industry was quite well organized, and children born in cities might be transported to wet-nurses in the country, where they would remain for months or even years.

However, throughout Europe the birth of a child was not always a welcome event. The child might be illegitimate or it might represent still one more economic burden on an already hard-pressed household. Through at least the end of the seventeenth century and to a lesser degree beyond it, various forms of infanticide were practiced, especially among the poor. The infant might be smothered or left exposed to the elements. These practices were one result of both the ignorance and the prejudice surrounding contraception. Though many married couples seem to have succeeded in limiting their families, young men and women who were unmarried and whose sexual relationships may have been the result of a fleeting acquaintance were less fortunate. Numerous young women, especially among servants, found themselves pregnant and without husbands. This situation and the consequent birth of illegitimate children seem to have become much more frequent over the course of the eighteenth century. The reasons for this development remain uncertain, but it probably arose from the more frequent migration of young people from their homes and the disturbance of traditional village life through enclosures (to be discussed later), the commercialization of agriculture, wars, and the late-century revolutions.

The late seventeenth and the early eighteenth centuries saw a new interest in preserving the lives of abandoned children. Large foundling hospitals were established in all the major nations. Hospitals created to care for abandoned children had existed before, but these years saw an expansion in their size and

Society Under
the Old Regime
in the
Eighteenth
Century

Louis XVI and Marie Antoinette visiting the Paris Orphanage in 1790. [Bulloz]

A Lottery Is Provided for Admission of Children to the London Foundling Hospital

The London Foundling Hospital was established in 1739. The institution soon found that the demand for admission was greater than the facilities available. In 1742 its officers adopted the following policy for admitting children. The goal of the lottery was to ensure fairness. This system continued in use until 1756, when new funds allowed for the expansion of the hospital.

That all the Women who bring any Children be let into the Court Room as they come, and there set on Benches to be placed round the Room. . . . That as many White Balls as there shall be Children to be taken in, and with five red Balls for every Twenty Children who are to be taken in and so in Proportion for any greater or lesser number, and as many black Balls as with the white and red shall be Equal to the number of Women present, shall be put into a Bag or Box and drawn out by the Women who bring the Children. That each Woman who draws a white Ball shall be carried with her Child into the Inspecting Room in order to have the Child examined. That each Woman who draws a red Ball be carried with her Child into another Room there to remain till the Examination of the Children, whose Nurses drew white Balls is ended. That each Woman who draws a black Ball shall be immediately turned out of the Hospital with her Child. If on such Examination any of those Children are rejected but not so many as there be red Balls drawn, there shall be a second Drawing of Lotts by putting into the Bag or Box as many white Balls as there are Children wanting to make up the number ordered to be taken in, And as many black Balls as with the white will be equal to the whole number of red Balls drawn in the first Drawing. And the children whose Nurses draw those white Balls to be taken in if duly qualified, and so on till the whole number be compleated. . . . The Lotts to be drawn in the Court Room in the presence of all the Women to prevent all Suspicion of Fraud or Partiality.

Minutes of the Foundling Hospital's General Committee, as quoted in Ruth K. McClure, *Coram's Children: The London Foundling Hospital in the Eighteenth Century* (New Haven: Yale University Press, 1981), pp. 77–78.

A German elementary school c. 1771. There were two types of students at this school: Upper-class young men and their servant boys. Each was given an education that was considered appropriate to his station. Thus, the young gentlemen are shown in the background being taught riding, fencing, and various sports, while the young servants in the foreground are learning how to garden and sweep. [*Bildarchiv Preussischer Kulturbesitz*]

numbers. These hospitals, two of the most famous of which were the Paris Foundling Hospital (1670) and the London Foundling Hospital (1739), cared for thousands of European children. The demands on their resources vastly increased in the course of the eighteenth century. For example, early in the century, the average number of children admitted to the Paris Foundling Hospital was approximately 1,700 annually. But in the peak year of 1772, that number rose to 7,676 children. Not all of those children came from Paris. Many had been brought to the city from the provinces, where local foundling homes and hospitals were also overburdened. The London Foundling Hospital lacked the income to deal with all of the children brought to it and, in the middle of the eighteenth century, found itself compelled to choose children for admission by a lottery system.

Sadness and tragedy surrounded almost every aspect of abandoned children. The overwhelming majority of them were illegitimate infants drawn from across the social spectrum, but a substantial portion seem to have been left with the foundling hospitals because their parents were encountering difficult economic times. There existed a quite close relationship between rising Paris food prices and increasing numbers of abandoned children. Parents would sometimes leave personal tokens or saints' medals on the abandoned baby in the vain hope that at some future time they might be able to reclaim the child. The number of children so reclaimed was negligible. Leaving a child at a foundling hospital did not guarantee its survival. Again, to cite the situation in Paris, only about 10 per cent of all abandoned children lived to the age of ten years.

Despite all of these perils of early childhood, children did grow up and come of age across Europe. The world of the child may not have received the kind of attention that it does today, but in the course of the eighteenth century the seeds of that modern sensibility were sown. Particularly among the upper classes new interest arose in the education of children. As economic skills became more demanding, literacy became more valuable, and there was a marked improvement in literacy during the century. However, in most areas education remained firmly in the hands of the churches. The overwhelming majority of the European population remained illiterate. It was not until the late nineteenth century that the world of childhood and the process of education became inextricably linked. Then children would be reared to become members of a national citizenry. In the old regime they were reared to make their contribution to the economy of their parents' family and then to set up their own household.

The Land and Its Tillers

Land constituted the economic basis of eighteenth-century life. Well over three fourths of all Europeans lived in the country, and few of these people ever traveled more than a few miles from their birthplace. With the exception of the nobility and the wealthier nonaristocratic landowners, the dwellers on the land were poor, and by any modern standard their lives were difficult. They lived in various modes of economic and social dependency, exploitation, and vulnerability.

Peasants and Serfs

The major forms of rural social dependency related directly to the land. Those who worked the land were subject to immense influence and in some cases direct control by the landowners. This situation prevailed in differing degrees for free peasants, such as English tenants and most French cultivators, and for the serfs of Germany, Austria, and Russia, who were legally bound to a particular plot of land and a particular lord. In all cases the class that owned most of the land also controlled the local government and the courts. For example, in Great Britain all farmers and smaller tenants had the legal rights of English citizens. But the justices of the peace who presided over the county courts and who could call out the local militia were always substantial landowners, as were also the members of Parliament, who made the laws.

William Coxe Describes Serfdom in Eighteenth-Century Russia

William Coxe was an Englishman who traveled widely in eastern Europe. His description of Russian serfdom portrays the brutality of the institution. It also illustrates his amazement at the absence in Russia of civil liberties such as he and more humble citizens enjoyed in England.

Peasants belonging to individuals are the private property of the landholders, as much as implements of agriculture, or herds of cattle; and the value of an estate is estimated, as in Poland, by the number of boors [serfs], and not by the number of acres. . . . If the Polish boor is oppressed, and he escapes to another master, the latter is liable to no pecuniary penalty for harbouring him; but in Russia the person who receives another's vassal is subject to an heavy fine. With respect to his own demands upon his peasants, the lord is restrained by no law, either in the exaction of any sum, or in the mode of employing them. He is absolute master of their time and labour: some he employs in agriculture: a few he makes his menial servants, and perhaps without wages; and from others he exacts an annual payment.

Each vassal, therefore, is rated according to the arbitrary will of his master. Some contribute four or five shillings a year; others, who are engaged in traffic or trade, are assessed in proportion to their supposed profits. . . . With regard to any capital which they may have acquired by their industry, it may be seized, and there can be no redress. . . .

. . . [S]ome of the Russian nobility send their vassals to Moscow or Petersburg for the purpose of learning various handcraft trades: they either employ them on their own estates; let them out for hire; sell them at an advanced price; or receive from them an annual compensation for the permission of exercising trade for their own advantage.

William Coxe, *Travels into Poland, Russia, Sweden, and Denmark*, 4th ed., Vol. 3 (London: T. Cadell 1972, first printed 1784), pp. 174–181.

Eighteenth-century France had some of the best roads in the world, but they were often built with forced labor. French peasants were required to work for part of each year on such projects. This system, called the corvée, *was not abolished until the French Revolution in 1789.* [Giraudon]

The intensity of landlord power increased as one moved from west to east. In France the situation differed somewhat from province to province. Most French peasants owned some land, but there were a few serfs. However, nearly all peasants were subject to certain feudal dues, called *banalités,* that included required use-for-payment of the lord or seigneur's mill to grind grain and his oven to bake bread. The seigneur could also require a certain number of days each year of the peasant's labor. This practice of forced labor was termed the *corvée.* Because even landowning French peasants rarely possessed enough land to support their families, they were also subject to feudal dues attached to the plots of land they rented. In Prussia and Austria, despite attempts by the monarchies late in the century to improve the lot of the serfs, the landlords continued to exercise almost complete control over them. In many of the Habsburg lands law and custom required the serfs to provide service, or *robot,* to the lords. Moreover, throughout continental Europe, in addition to these feudal services, the burden of state taxation fell on the tillers of the soil. Many peasants, serfs, and other agricultural laborers were forced to undertake supplemental work to raise the cash required to pay the tax collector. Through various legal privileges and the ability to demand further concessions from the monarchs, the landlords escaped the payment of numerous taxes. They also presided over the manorial courts.

The condition of the serfs was the worst in Russia. The Russian custom of reckoning one's wealth by the number of "souls" (that is, male serfs) owned rather than by the acreage possessed reveals the contrast. The serfs were, in effect, regarded merely as economic commodities. Russian landlords could demand as many as six days a week of labor, and like Prussian and Austrian landlords they enjoyed the right to punish their serfs. On their own authority alone they could even exile a serf to Siberia. The serfs had no legal recourse against the orders and whims of their lords. There was actually little difference between Russian serfdom and slavery.

The Russian monarchy itself contributed to

541

*Society Under
the Old Regime
in the
Eighteenth
Century*

Catherine the Great Issues a Proclamation Against Pugachev

Against a background of long-standing human degradation, and ever-increasing land-owner authority, the greatest serf rebellion in Russian history was led from 1773 to 1775 by a Don Cossack named Emelyan Pugachev. Empress Catherine the Great's proclamation of 1773 argues that he was alienating the serfs from their natural and proper allegiance to her and their masters.

By the grace of God, we Catherine II . . . make known to our faithful subjects, that we have learnt, with the utmost indignation and extreme affliction, that a certain Cossack, a deserter and fugitive from the Don, named Emelyan Pugachev, after having traversed Poland, has been collecting, for some time past, in the districts that border on the river Irghis, in the government of Orenburg, a troop of vagabonds like himself; that he continues to commit in those parts all kinds of excesses, by inhumanly depriving the inhabitants of their possessions, and even of their lives. . . .

In a word, there is not a man deserving of the Russian name, who does not hold in abomination the odious and insolent lie by which Pugachev fancies himself able to seduce and to deceive persons of a simple and credulous disposition, by promising to free them from the bonds of submission, and obedience to their sovereign, as if the Creation of the universe had established human societies in such a manner as that they can subsist without an intermediate authority between the sovereign and the people.

Nevertheless, as the insolence of this vile refuse of the human race is attended with consequences pernicious to the provinces adjacent to that district; as the report of the flagrant enormities which he has committed, may affright those persons who are accustomed to imagine the misfortunes of others as ready to fall upon them, and as we watch with indefatigable care over the tranquility of our faithful subjects, we inform them . . . that we have taken . . . such measures as are the best adapted to stifle the sedition. . . .

We trust . . . that every true son of the country will unremittingly fulfill his duty, of the contributing to the maintenance of good order and of public tranquility, by preserving himself from the snares of seduction, and by discharging his obedience to his lawful sovereign.

William Tooke, *Life of Catherine II, Empress of Russia,* 4th ed., Vol. 2 (London: T. N. Longman and O. Rees, 1800), pp. 460–461 (spelling modernized).

the degradation of the serfs. Peter the Great gave whole villages to favored nobles. Later in the century Catherine the Great (1762–1796) confirmed the authority of the nobles over their serfs in exchange for the political cooperation of the landowners. The situation in Russia led to considerable unrest. There were well over fifty peasant revolts between 1762 and 1769. These culminated between 1773 and 1775 in Pugachev's rebellion, during which all of southern Russian experienced intense unrest. Emelyan Pugachev (1726–1775) promised the serfs land of their own and freedom from their lords. The rebellion was brutally suppressed. Thereafter any thought of liberalizing or improving the condition of the serfs was set aside for a generation.

Pugachev's was the greatest rebellion in Russian history and the largest peasant uprising of the eighteenth century. Smaller peasant revolts or disturbances occurred outside Russia. Rebellions took place in Bohemia in 1775, in Transylvania in 1784, in Moravia in 1786, and in Austria in 1789. Revolts in western Europe were almost nonexistent, but England experienced numerous local enclosure riots. Rural rebellions were violent, but the peasants and serfs normally directed their wrath against property rather than persons. The rebels usually sought to reassert traditional or customary rights against practices that they perceived as innovations. Their targets were carefully chosen and included unfair pricing, onerous new or increased feudal dues, changes in methods of payment or land use, unjust officials, or extraordinarily brutal overseers and landlords. In this respect the peasant revolts were quite conservative in nature.

The main goal of peasant society was a stability that would ensure the local food supply. In western Europe most rural society was organized into villages, and on about half of the land the owners of individual plots or strips would decide communally what crops would be planted. In eastern Europe, with its great estates of hundreds or thousands of acres, the landlords decided how to use the land. But in either case the tillers resisted changes that might endanger the sure supply of food, which they generally believed to be promised by traditional cultivation. However, throughout the eighteenth century landlords across the Continent began to search for higher profits from their holdings. They embraced innovation in order to increase their own prosperity. They commercialized agriculture and thereby challenged the traditional peasant ways of production. Peasant revolts and disturbances often resulted. The governments of Europe, hungry for new taxes and dependent on the goodwill of the nobility, used their armies and militias to smash the peasants who defended the past. In certain areas, such as the Low Countries and parts of Germany, the peasants themselves began to innovate so that they could more easily raise the cash they needed for tax payments.

The Revolution in Agriculture

Even more basic than the social dependency of peasants and small tenant farmers was their dependency on the productiveness of nature. The quantity and quality of the annual grain harvest was the most fundamental fact in their lives. On the Continent bread was the primary component of the diet of the lower classes. The

Turgot Describes the Results of Poor Harvests in France

Failure of the grain crop and other plantings could bring both hunger and social disruption during the eighteenth century. Anne Robert Jacques Turgot (1727–1781), who later became finance minister of France, emphasized the role of private charity and government policy in relieving the suffering. His description, written in 1769, also provides a brief survey of the diet of the French peasant.

Everyone has heard of the terrible dearth that has just afflicted this generality [a local administrative district]. The harvest of 1769 in every respect proved to be one of the worst in the memory of man. The dearths of 1709 and 1739 were incomparably less cruel. To the loss of the greatest part of the rye was added the total loss of the chestnuts, of the buckwheat, and of the Spanish wheat—cheap food stuffs with which the peasant sustained himself habitually a great part of the year, reserving as much as he could of his corn [grain], in order to sell it to the inhabitants of the towns. . . . The people could exist only by exhausting their resources, by selling at a miserable price their articles of furniture and even their clothes. Many of the inhabitants have been obliged to disperse themselves through other provinces to seek work or to beg, leaving their wives and children to the charity of the parishes. It has been necessary for the public authority to require the proprietors and inhabitants in better circumstances in each parish to assess themselves for the relief of the poor people; nearly a fourth of the population is dependent upon charitable contributions. After these melancholy sufferings which the province has already undergone, and with the reduced condition in which it was left by the dearth of last year, even had the harvest of the present year been a good one, the poverty of the inhabitants would have necessitated the greatest efforts to be made for their relief. But we have now to add the dismal fact of our harvest being again deficient. . . .

W. W. Stephens (Ed.), *The Life and Writings of Turgot* (London: Longmans, Green, 1895), p. 50.

543

*Society Under
the Old Regime
in the
Eighteenth
Century*

*An Austrian nobleman inspecting his flocks. Agriculture became increasingly commercialized
on great estates, as landlords sought more profit from their lands. [Bildarchiv Preussischer
Kulturbesitz]*

food supply was never certain, and the farther east one traveled, the more uncertain it became. Failure of the harvest meant not only hardship but actual death from either outright starvation or protracted debility. Quite often people living in the countryside encountered more difficulty finding food than did city dwellers, whose local government usually stored reserve supplies of grain.

Poor harvest also played havoc with prices. Smaller supplies or larger demand raised grain prices. Even small increases in the cost of food could exert heavy pressure on peasant or artisan families. If prices increased sharply, many of those families fell back on poor relief from their local municipality or county or the church. What made the situation of food supply and prices so difficult was the peasants' sense of helplessness before the whims of nature and the marketplace.

Over the course of the century, historians now believe, there occurred a slow but steady inflation of bread prices, spurred largely by population growth. This inflation put pressure on all of the poor. The prices rose faster than urban wages and brought no appreciable advantage to the very small peasant producer. On the other hand, the rise in grain prices benefited landowners and those wealthier peasants who had surplus grain to sell.

The increasing price of grain presented landlords with an opportunity to improve their incomes and lifestyle. To those ends they began a series of innovations in farm production that are known as the *agricultural revolution*. This movement began during the sixteenth and seventeenth centuries in the Low Countries, where the pressures of the growing population and the shortage of land required changes in cultivation. Dutch landlords and farmers devised better ways to build dykes and to drain land so that they could farm more extensive areas. They also experimented with new crops, such as clover and turnips, that would increase the supply of animal fodder and restore the soil. These improvements became so famous that early in the seventeenth century Cornelius Vermuyden, a Dutch drainage engineer, was hired in England to drain thousands of acres of land around Cambridge.

The methods that the Dutch farmers had pioneered were extensively adopted in England during the early eighteenth century. The major agricultural innovations undertaken by the English included new methods of farming, new crops, and new modes of landholding, all of which eventually led to greater productivity. This advance in food production was necessary for the development of an industrial society. It ensured adequate food for people living in cities and freed agricultural labor for industrial production. The changing modes of agriculture sponsored by the landlords undermined the assumptions of traditional peasant production. Farming now took place not only for the local food supply but also to assure the landlord a handsome profit. The latter goal meant that the landlords began to exert new pressures on their tenants and serfs.

Landlords in Great Britain during the eighteenth century provided the most striking examples of the agricultural improvement. They originated almost no genuinely new methods of farming, but they provided leadership in popularizing ideas developed in the previous century either in the Low Countries or in England. Some of these landlords and agricultural innovators became very famous. For example, Jethro Tull (1674–1741) contributed a willingness to experiment and to finance the experiments of others. Many of his ideas, such as the refusal to use manure as fertilizer, were wrong. Others, however, such as using iron plows to overturn earth more deeply and planting wheat by a drill rather than by casting, were excellent. His methods permitted land to be cultivated for longer periods without having to be left fallow.

Charles "Turnip" Townsend (1674–1738) encouraged even more important innovations. He learned from the Dutch how to cultivate sandy soil with fertilizers. He also instituted crop rotation, using wheat, turnips, barley, and clover. This new system of rotation abolished the fallow field and replaced it with a field sown in a crop that both replaced soil nutrients and supplied animal fodder. The additional fodder meant that more livestock could be raised. The larger number of animals increased the quantity of manure available as fertilizer

for the grain crops. Consequently, in the long run, there was more food for both animals and human beings.

A third British agricultural improver was Robert Bakewell (1725–1795), who pioneered new methods of animal breeding that produced more and better animals and more milk and meat.

These and other innovations received widespread discussion in the works of Arthur Young (1741–1820), who edited the *Annals of Agriculture* and who in 1793 became secretary of the British Board of Agriculture. Young traveled widely across Europe, and his books are among the most important documents of life during the second half of the eighteenth century.

Many of the agriculture innovations, which were adopted only very slowly, were incompatible with the existing organization of land in Britain. Small cultivators who lived in village communities still farmed most of the soil. Each farmer tilled an assortment of unconnected strips. The two- or three-field systems of rotation left large portions of land annually fallow and unproductive. Animals grazed on the common land in the summer and on the stubble of the harvest in the winter. Until at least the middle of the eighteenth century the decisions about what crops would be planted were made communally. The entire system discouraged improvement and favored the poorer farmers, who needed the common land and stubble fields for their animals. The village method provided little possibility of expanding the pasture land to raise more animals that would, in turn, produce more manure, which could be used for fertilizer. Thus, the methods of traditional production aimed at a steady but not a growing supply of food.

In 1700 approximately half the arable land in Britain was farmed by this open-field method. By the second half of the century the rising price of wheat encouraged landlords to consolidate or enclose their lands to increase production. The enclosures were intended to use land more rationally and to achieve greater commercial profits. The process involved the fencing of common lands, the reclamation of previously untilled waste, and the transformation of strips into block fields. These procedures brought turmoil to the economic and social life of the countryside. Riots often ensued. Because many British farmers either owned their strips or rented them in a manner that amounted to ownership, the larger landlords had usually to resort to parliamentary acts to legalize the enclosure of the land, which they owned but rented to the farmers. Because the large landowners controlled Parliament, there was little difficulty in passing such measures. Between 1761 and 1792 almost 500,000 acres were enclosed through parliamentary act, as compared with 75,000 acres between 1727 and 1760. In 1801 a general enclosure act streamlined the process.

The enclosures were at the time and have remained among historians a very controversial topic. They permitted the extension of both farming and innovation. In that regard they increased food production on larger agricultural units. At the same time they disrupted the small traditional communities. They forced off the land some independent farmers, who had needed the common pasturage, and very poor cottagers, who had lived on the reclaimed waste land. However, the enclosures did not depopulate the countryside. In some counties where the enclosures took place, the population increased. New soil had come into production, and services subsidiary to farming also expanded.

The enclosures did not create the labor force for the British Industrial Revolution. What the enclosures most conspicuously displayed was the introduction of the entrepreneurial or capitalistic attitude of the urban merchant into the countryside. This commercialization of agriculture, which spread from Britain very slowly across the Continent during the next century, strained the paternal relationship between the governing and governed classes. Previously the landlords had somewhat looked after the welfare of the lower orders through price controls or alleviation of rents during depressed periods. However, as the landlords became increasingly concerned about profits, they began to leave the peasants to the mercy of the marketplace.

Improving agriculture tended to characterize farm production west of the Elbe. Dutch farming was quite efficient. In France, despite the efforts of the government to improve agriculture, enclosures were restricted. Yet there was much discussion in France about improving agricultural methods. These new procedures benefited the ruling classes because better agriculture increased their incomes and assured a larger food supply, which tended to discourage social unrest.

In Prussia, Austria, Poland, and Russia only very limited agricultural improvement took place. Nothing in the relationship of the serfs to their lords encouraged innovation. In eastern Europe the chief method of increasing production was to extend farming to previously untilled lands. The management of farms was usually under the direction of the landlords or their agents rather than of the villages. By ex-

This view of an English estate in the mid-eighteenth century illustrates many types of agricultural activities: grain and hay growing, cattle, sheep, and pig raising, an orchard, a vegetable garden, and a dairy. Note the landlord's house in the background. [New York Public Library]

tending tillage, the great landlords sought to squeeze more labor from their serfs rather than greater productivity from the soil. As in the West, the goal was increased profits for the landlords. But on the whole, east European landlords were much less ambitious and successful. The only significant nutritional gain

Part of the commercialization of agriculture that occurred in the eighteenth century was the "farming" of forests for saleable timber. This was particularly lucrative in Britain, Scandinavia, and parts of France, where there was a large demand for lumber for ship building. [British Library]

achieved through their efforts was the introduction of maize and the potato. Livestock production did not increase significantly.

Population Expansion

The assault on human dependence on nature through improved farming was both a cause and a result of an immense expansion in the population of Europe. The population explosion with which the entire world must today contend seems to have had its origins in the eighteenth century. Before this time Europe's population had experienced dramatic increases, but plagues, wars, or harvest failures had in time decimated the increase. Beginning in the second quarter of the eighteenth century, the population began to grow without decimation.

Exact figures are lacking, but the best estimates suggest that in 1700 Europe's population, excluding the European provinces of the Ottoman Empire, stood between 100 million and 120 million people. By 1800 the figures had risen to almost 190 million, and by 1850 to 260 million. The population of England and Wales rose from 6 million in 1750 to over 10 million in 1800. France grew from 18 million in 1715 to approximately 26 million in 1789. Russia's population increased from 19 million in 1722 to 29 million in 1766. Such extraordinary, sustained growth put new demands on all resources and considerable pressure on existing social organization.

The population expansion occurred across the Continent in both the country and the cities. Only a limited consensus exists about the causes of this growth. There was a clear decline in the death rate. There were fewer wars and somewhat fewer epidemics in the eighteenth century. Hygiene and sanitation also improved. Better medical knowledge and techniques were once thought to have contributed to the decline in deaths. This factor is now discounted because the more important medical advances came after the initial population explosion or would not have contributed directly to it. Rather, changes in the food supply itself may have provided the chief factor that allowed the population growth to be sustained. The improved and expanding grain production made one contribution. Another and even more important modification was the cultivation of the potato. This tuber was a product of the New World and came into widespread European production during the eighteenth century. On a single acre enough potatoes could be raised to feed one peasant's family for an entire year. With this more certain food supply, more children could be reared, and more could survive.

This impact of the population explosion can hardly be overestimated. It created new demands for food, goods, jobs, and services. It provided a new pool of labor. Traditional modes of production and living had to be revised. More people came to live in the countryside than could find employment there. Migration increased. There were also more people who might become socially and politically discontented. And because the population growth fed on itself, all of these pressures and demands continued to increase. The society and the social practices of the old regime literally outgrew their traditional bounds.

The Industrial Revolution of the Eighteenth Century

The second half of the eighteenth century witnessed the beginning of the industrialization of the European economy. The Industrial Revolution constituted the achievement of sustained economic growth. Previously production had been limited. The economy of a province or a country might grow, but it soon reached a plateau. However, since the late eighteenth century the economy of Europe has managed to expand relatively uninterrupted. Depressions and recessions have been temporary, and even during such economic downturns the western economy has continued to grow.

At considerable social cost, industrialism has made possible more goods and more services than ever before in human history. Industrialism in Europe eventually overcame the economy of scarcity. The new means of production demanded new kinds of skills, new discipline in work, and a large labor force. The goods produced both met immediate consumer demand and created new demands. In the long run, industrialism clearly raised the standard of living and overcame the poverty that had been experienced by the overwhelming majority of Europeans who lived during the eighteenth century and earlier. Industrialization provided human beings greater control over the forces of nature than they had ever known before. The wealth produced by industrialism upset the political structures of the old regime and led to

reforms. The economic elite of the emerging industrial society would eventually challenge the political dominance of the aristocracy.

Industrial Leadership of Great Britain

Great Britain was the home of the Industrial Revolution and, until the middle of the nineteenth century, maintained the industrial leadership of Europe. Several factors contributed to the early start in Britain. The nation constituted the single largest free-trade area in Europe. The British possessed good roads and waterways without internal tolls or other internal trade barriers. The country was endowed with rich deposits of coal and iron ore. The political structure was stable, and property was absolutely secure. Taxation was not especially heavy. In addition to the existing domestic consumer demand, the British economy also benefited from demand from the colonies in North America.

Finally, British society was relatively mobile by the standards of the time. Persons who had money or could earn money could rise socially. The British aristocracy would receive into its midst people who had amassed very large fortunes. No one of these factors preordained the British advance toward industrialism. However, the combination of them plus the progressive state of British agriculture provided the nation with the marginal advantage in the creation of a new mode of economic production.

While this economic development was occurring, people did not call it a *revolution*. That term came to be applied to the British economic phenomena only after the French Revolution. Then continental writers observed that what had taken place in Britain was the economic equivalent of the political events in France; hence the concept of an *industrial* revolution. It was revolutionary less in its speed, which was on the whole rather slow, than in its implications for the future of European society.

New Methods of Textile Production. Although eighteenth-century society was primarily devoted to agriculture, manufacturing permeated the countryside. The same peasants who tilled the land in spring and summer often spun thread or wove textiles in the winter. Under what is termed the *domestic* or *putting-out system*, agents of urban textile

The pithead of an eighteenth-century coal mine in England. The machinery on the left included a steam engine that powered equipment either to bring the mined coal to the surface or to pump water from the mine. Britain's large supply of coal was one of the contributing factors to its early industrialization. [Walker Art Gallery, Liverpool]

Under the domestic or putting-out system, urban textile merchants took unfinished fibers to peasants, who then spun it into thread or wove it into cloth in their homes, as this English family is doing. [Library of Congress]

merchants took wool or other unfinished fibers to the homes of peasants, who spun it into thread. The agent then transported the thread to other peasants, who wove it into the finished product. The merchant sold the wares. In literally thousands of peasant cottages from Ireland to Austria, there stood either a spinning wheel or a handloom. Sometimes the spinners or weavers owned their own equipment, but more often than not, by the middle of the century the merchant capitalist owned the machinery as well as the raw material.

What must be kept constantly in mind is the rather surprising fact that eighteenth-century industrial development took place within a rural setting. The peasant family living in a

549

*Society Under
the Old Regime
in the
Eighteenth
Century*

Manchester's Calico Printers Protest the Use of New Machinery

The introduction of the new machines associated with the Industrial Revolution stirred much protest. Machine labor was replacing human labor; machines were duplicating the skills of laborers. This situation could mean the loss of jobs. It also brought about the loss of status for workers whose chief means of livelihood lay in their possession of those displaced and now mechanized skills. The following letter was sent anonymously to a Manchester manufacturer by English workers. It indicates the outrage of those workers, the modes of intimidation they were willing to use as threats, and their own economic fears.

Mr. Taylor If you dont discharge James Hobson from the House of Correction we will burn your House about your Ears for we have sworn to stand by one another and you must immediately give over any more Mashen Work for we are determined there shall be no more of them made use of in the Trade and it will be madness for you to contend with the Trade as we are combined by Oath to fix Prices we can afford to pay him a Guinea Week and not hurt the fund if you was to keep him there till Dumsday therefore mind you comply with the above or by God we will keep our Words with you we will make some rare Bunfires in this Countey and at your Peril to call any more Meetings mind that we will make the Mosney Pepel shake in their Shoes we are determined to destroy all Sorts of Masheens for Printing in the Kingdom for there is more hands then is work for so no more from the ingerd Gurnemen Rember we are a great number sworn nor you must not advertise the Men that you say run away from you when your il Usage was the Cause of their going we will punish you for that our Meetings are legal for we want nothing but what is honest and to work for selvs and familers and you want to starve us but it is better for you and a few more which we have marked to die then such a Number of Pore Men and their famerles to be starved.

London Gazette, 1786, p. 36, as reprinted in Douglas Hay (Ed.), *Albion's Fatal Tree* (New York: Pantheon Books, 1975), p. 318.

one- or two-room cottage was the basic unit of production rather than the factory. The family economy, rather than the industrial factory economy, characterized the century.

The domestic system of textile production was a basic feature of this family economy. However, by mid-century a series of production bottlenecks had developed within the domestic system. The demand for cotton textiles was growing more rapidly than production. This demand arose particularly in Great Britain, where there existed a large domestic demand for cotton textiles from the growing population. There was a similar foreign demand on British production from its colonies in North America. It was in response to this consumer demand for cotton textiles that the most famous inventions of the Industrial Revolution were devised.

Cotton textile weavers had the technical capacity to produce the quantity of fabric that was in demand. However, the spinners did not possess the equipment to produce as much thread as the weavers needed and could use. This imbalance had been created during the 1730s by James Kay's invention of the flying shuttle, which increased the productivity of the weavers. Thereafter various groups of manufacturers and merchants offered prizes for the invention of a machine to eliminate this bottleneck. About 1765 James Hargreaves (d. 1778) invented the spinning jenny. Initially this machine allowed 16 spindles of thread to be spun, but by the close of the century its capacity had been increased to as many as 120 spindles.

The spinning jenny broke the bottleneck between the productive capacity of the spinners and the weavers, but it was still a piece of machinery that was used in the cottage. The invention that took cotton textile manufacture out of the home and put it into the factory was Richard Arkwright's (1732–1792) water

Richard Arkwright's (1732–1792) cotton mill in Derbyshire, England, in the 1780s. [Art Resource]

frame, patented in 1769. It was a water-powered device designed to permit the production of a purely cotton fabric rather than a cotton fabric containing linen fiber for durability. Eventually Arkwright lost his patent rights, and other manufacturers were able to use his invention freely. As a result, numerous factories sprang up in the countryside near streams that provided the necessary waterpower. From the 1780s onward the cotton industry could meet an ever-expanding demand. In the last two decades of the century cotton output increased by 800 per cent over the production of 1780. By 1815 cotton composed 40 per cent of the value of British domestic exports, and by 1830 just over 50 per cent.

The Industrial Revolution had commenced in earnest by the 1780s, but the full economic and social ramifications of this unleashing of human productive capacity were not really felt until the early nineteenth century. The expansion of industry and the incorporation of new

inventions often occurred rather slowly. For example, Edmund Cartwright (1743–1822) invented the power loom for machine weaving in the late 1780s. Yet not until the 1830s were there more power-loom weavers than hand-loom weavers in Britain. Nor did all of the social ramifications of industrialism appear immediately. The first cotton mills used water-power, were located in the country, and rarely employed more than two dozen workers. Not until the late-century application of the steam engine, perfected by James Watt (1736–1819) in 1769, to the running of textile machinery could factories easily be located in or near existing urban centers. The steam engine not only vastly increased and regularized the available energy but also made possible the combination of urbanization and industrialization.

THE STEAM ENGINE. The new technology in textile manufacture vastly increased cotton production and revolutionized a major con-

James Watt (1736–1819), the Scottish engineer who patented the steam engine in 1769. [Library of Congress]

machines to pump water out of coal and tin mines. By the third quarter of the eighteenth century almost a hundred Newcomen machines were operating in the mining districts of England.

During the 1760s James Watt, a Scottish engineer and machine maker, began to experiment with a model of a Newcomen machine at the University of Glasgow. He gradually understood that if the condenser were separated from the piston and the cylinder, much greater efficiency would result. In 1769 he patented his new invention, but transforming his idea into application presented difficulties. His design required exceedingly precise metalwork. Watt soon found a partner in Matthew Boulton, a toy manufacturer in Birmingham, the city with the most skilled metalworkers in Britain. Watt and Boulton, in turn, consulted with John Wilkinson, a cannon manufacturer, to find ways to drill the precise metal cylinders required by Watt's design. In 1776 the Watt steam engine found its first commercial application pumping water from mines in Cornwall.

The use of the steam engine spread slowly because until 1800 Watt retained the exclusive patent rights. He was also reluctant to make further changes in his invention that would permit the engine to operate more rapidly.

One of Watt's improved steam engines, built in 1784. Pressure in the cylinder on the left forces the beam upwards, while the descending arm sets the large fly wheel in continuous motion. Instead of just pumping, this improved engine could be used to drive every sort of machine. [Science Museum, London]

sumer industry. But the invention that more than any other permitted industrialization to grow on itself and to expand into one area of production after another was the steam engine. This machine provided for the first time in human history a steady and essentially unlimited source of inanimate power. Unlike engines powered by water or the wind, the steam engine, driven by the burning of coal, was a portable source of industrial power that did not fail or falter as the seasons of the year changed. Unlike human power or animal power the steam engine depended on mineral energy that did not tire over the course of a day. Finally, the steam engine could be applied to a very large number of industrial and, eventually, transportation uses.

The first practical engine using steam power had been the invention of Thomas Newcomen in the early eighteenth century. The piston of this device was moved when the steam that had been induced into the cylinder condensed, causing the piston to fall. The Newcomen machine was very large. It was inefficient in its use of energy because both the condenser and the cylinder were heated, and it was practically untransportable. Despite these problems English mine operators employed the Newcomen

Josiah Tucker Praises the New Use of Machinery in England

The extensive use of recently invented machines made the Industrial Revolution possible in England. This passage from a 1757 travel guide illustrates how contemporaries regarded the application of machines to various manufacturing processes as new and exciting.

Few countries are equal, perhaps none excel, the English in the number of contrivances of their Machines to abridge labour. Indeed the Dutch are superior to them in the use and application of Wind Mills for sawing Timber, expressing Oil, making Paper and the like. But in regard to Mines and Metals of all sorts, the English are uncommonly dexterous in their contrivance of the mechanic Powers; some being calculated for landing the Ores out of the Pits, such as Cranes and Horse Engines; others for draining off superfluous Water, such as Water Wheels and Steam Engines; others again for easing the Expense of Carriage such as Machines to run on inclined Planes or Roads downhill with wooden frames, in order to carry many Tons of Material at a Time. And to these must be added the various sorts of Levers used in different processes; also the Brass Battery works, the Slitting Mills, Plate and Flatting Mills, and those for making Wire of different Fineness. Yet all these, curious as they may seem, are little more than Preparations or Introductions for further Operations. Therefore, when we still consider that at Birmingham, Wolverhampton, Sheffield and other manufacturing Places, almost every Master Manufacturer hath a new Invention of his own, and is daily improving on those of others; we may aver with some confidence that those parts of England in which these things are seen exhibit a specimen of practical mechanics scarce to be paralleled in any part of the world.

Josiah Tucker, *Instructions to Travellers* (London: Privately Printed, 1757), p. 20.

Boulton eventually persuaded him to make modifications and improvements. These allowed the engines to be used not only for pumping but also for running cotton mills. By the early nineteenth century the steam engine had become the prime mover for all industry. With its application to ships and then to wagons on iron rails, the steam engine also revolutionized transportation.

MAJOR INVENTIONS IN THE TEXTILE-MANUFACTURING REVOLUTION

James Kay's flying shuttle	1733
James Hargreaves's spinning jenny (patent 1770)	1765
James Watt's steam engine patent	1769
Richard Arkwright's waterframe patent	1769
Edmund Cartwright's power loom	1787

IRON PRODUCTION. The manufacture of high-quality iron has been basic to modern industrial development. It constitutes the chief element of all heavy industry and land or sea transport. Iron has also been the material out of which most productive machinery itself has been manufactured. During the early eighteenth century British ironmakers produced somewhat less than twenty-five thousand tons annually. Three factors held back the production of the metal. Charcoal rather than coke was used to smelt the ore. Charcoal, which is derived from wood, was becoming a scarce commodity, and it did not burn at as high a temperature as coke, which is derived from coal. Until the perfection of the steam engine, insufficient blasts could be achieved in the furnaces. Finally, the demand for iron was limited. The elimination of the first two problems eliminated the third.

In the course of the century British ironmakers began to use coke, and the steam engine provided new power for the blast furnaces. Coke was an abundant fuel because of

Britain's large coal deposits. The existence of the steam engine both improved iron production and increased the demand for iron.

In 1784 Henry Cort (1740–1800) introduced a new puddling process, that is, a new method for melting and stirring the molten ore. Cort's process allowed more slag (the impurities that bubbled to the top of the molten metal) to be removed and a purer iron to be produced. Cort also developed a rolling mill that continuously shaped the still-molten metal into bars, rails, or other forms. Previously the metal had been pounded into these forms.

All of these innovations achieved a better, more versatile product at a lower cost. The demand for iron grew as its price became lower. By the early years of the nineteenth century British iron production amounted to over a million tons annually. The lower cost of iron, in turn, lowered the cost of steam engines and allowed them to be used more widely.

The Aristocracy

Despite the emerging Industrial Revolution, the eighteenth century remained the age of the aristocracy. The nobility of every country was the single wealthiest sector of the population; possessed the widest degree of social, political, and economic power; and set the tone of polite society. Land continued to provide the aristocracy with its largest source of income, but the role of the aristocrat was not limited to the estate. The influence of aristocrats was felt in every area of life. To be an aristocrat was a matter of birth and legal privilege. This much they had in common across the Continent. In almost every other respect they differed markedly from country to country.

The smallest, wealthiest, best-defined, and most socially responsible aristocracy resided in Great Britain. It consisted of about four hundred families, whose eldest male member sat in the House of Lords. Through the corruptions of the electoral system these families also controlled a large number of seats in the House of Commons. The estates of the British nobility ranged from a few thousand to fifty thousand acres, from which they received rents. The nobles owned approximately one fourth of all the arable land in the country. Increasingly the money of the aristocracy was being invested in commerce, canals, urban real estate, mines, and sometimes industrial ventures. Because

only the eldest son inherited the title and the land, younger sons moved into commerce, the army, the professions, and the church. The British landowners in the House of Commons levied taxes in Parliament and also paid taxes. They had almost no significant legal privileges, but their direct or indirect control of local government gave them immense political power and social influence. The aristocracy quite simply dominated the society and the politics of the English counties.

The openness of the English aristocracy and its acceptance of social and political responsibility as well as of power brought a degree of social mobility to English social life that was generally absent from other countries during the old regime. This factor may, in large measure, account for both the economic and the political advancement of Britain during the period.

The situation of the continental nobilities was less clear-cut. In France the nobility was divided between nobles of the sword and those of the robe. The former families enjoyed privileges deriving from military service; the latter had either gained their titles by serving in the bureaucracy or had purchased them. The two groups had frequently quarreled in the past but tended to cooperate during the eighteenth century to defend their common privileges.

The French nobility were also divided between those who held office or favor with the royal court at Versailles and those who did not. The court nobility reaped the immense wealth that could be gained from holding high offices. The noble hold on such offices intensified over the course of the century. By the late 1780s appointments to the church, the army, and the bureaucracy, as well as other profitable positions, tended to go to the nobles already established in court circles. Whereas these well-connected aristocrats were quite rich, other nobles who lived in the provinces were often rather poor. These *hobereaux*, as the poverty-stricken nobles were called, were sometimes little or no better off than wealthy peasants.

Despite differences in rank, origin, and wealth, all French aristocrats enjoyed certain hereditary privileges that set them apart from the rest of society. They were exempt from many taxes. For example, most French nobles did not pay the *taille*, which was the basic tax of the old regime. The nobles were technically liable for payment of the *vingtième*, or the "twentieth," which resembled an income tax. However, by virtue of protests and legal proce-

The court nobility of France were immensely rich and lived in great splendor. This painting depicts a supper concert at the salon of the Princesse de Conti, a member of the royal family. The boy playing the harpsichord on the right is the seven-year-old Wolfgang Amadeus Mozart (1756–1792). [Giraudon/Art Resource]

dures, the nobility rarely felt the entire weight of this tax. The nobles were not liable for the royal *corvées,* or labor donations, which fell on the peasants. In addition to these exemptions, the approximately 400,000 French nobles could collect feudal dues from their tenants and enjoyed hunting and fishing privileges denied their tenants.

East of the Elbe River the character of the nobility became even more complicated and repressive. In Poland there were thousands of nobles, or *szlachta,* who after 1741 were en-

tirely exempt from taxes. Until 1768 these Polish aristocrats possessed the right of life and death over their serfs. Most of the Polish nobility were relatively poor. The political power of the fragile Polish state resided in the few very rich nobles.

In Austria and Hungary the nobility continued to possess broad judicial powers over the peasantry through manorial courts.

In Prussia, after the accession of Frederick the Great in 1740, the position of the *Junker* nobles became much stronger. Frederick's var-

555

*Society Under
the Old Regime
in the
Eighteenth
Century*

ious wars required the support of his nobles. He drew his officers almost wholly from the *Junker* class. The bureaucracy was also increasingly composed of nobles. As in other parts of eastern Europe, the Prussian nobles enjoyed extensive judicial authority over the serfs.

In Russia the eighteenth century saw what amounted to the creation of the nobility. Peter the Great's linking of state service and noble social status through the Table of Ranks (1722) established among Russian nobles a self-conscious class identity that had not previously existed. Thereafter they stood united in their determination to resist compulsory state service. In 1736 Empress Ann reduced such service to a period of twenty-five years. In 1762 Peter III removed the liability for compulsory service entirely from the greatest nobles. In 1785, in the Charter of the Nobility, Catherine the Great granted an explicit legal definition of noble rights and privileges in exchange for assurances of voluntary state service from the nobility. The noble privileges included the right of transmitting noble status to one's wife and children, the judicial protection of noble rights and property, considerable power over the serfs, and exemption from personal taxes.

The Russian Charter of the Nobility constituted one aspect of the broader European-wide development termed the *aristocratic resurgence.* Throughout the century the various nobilities felt their social position and privileges threatened by the expanding power of the monarchies and the growing wealth of merchants, bankers, and other commercial groups. All nobilities attempted to preserve their exclusiveness by making entry into their ranks and institutions more difficult. They also pushed for exclusively noble appointments to the officer corps of the armies, the bureaucracies, the government ministries, and the church. In that manner the nobles hoped to control the power of the monarchies.

On a third level the nobles attempted to use the authority of existing aristocratically controlled institutions against the power of the monarchies. These institutions included the British Parliament and on the Continent the French courts, or *parlements;* the local aristocratic estates; and the provincial diets. Economically the aristocratic resurgence took the form of pressing the peasantry for higher rents or collecting long-forgotten feudal dues. There was a general tendency for the nobility to shore up its position by various appeals to traditional and often ancient privileges that had lapsed over the course of time. To contemporaries this aristocratic challenge to the monarchies and to the rising commercial classes constituted one of the most fundamental political facts of the day.

Aristocratic Protection of Self-Interest in the Countryside: The Case of the English Game Laws

Although the various aristocracies put new pressures on the monarchies during the eighteenth century, the chief area in which they sought to maintain themselves was in the countryside itself. Aristocrats and large landowners who might not hold noble titles but whose social and economic interests were similar to the aristocracies always saw their real power as based on the prestige and power they could command locally. These privileges often accounted for the resentment felt toward the landed classes by both the rural poor and the more prosperous urban classes.

One of the clearest examples of aristocratic domination of the countryside and of aristocratic manipulation of the law to its own advantage was English legislation in regard to the hunting of game. Between 1671 and 1831 English landowners had the exclusive legal right to hunt game animals. These specifically included hares, partridges, pheasants, and moorfowl. Similar legislation covered other animals such as deer, the killing of which became a capital offense in the eighteenth century. By law, only persons owning a particular amount of landed property could hunt these animals. Excluded from the right to hunt were all persons renting land, wealthy city merchants who did not own land, and poor people in cities, villages, and the countryside. The poor were excluded because it was widely believed among the elite classes that allowing them to enjoy the sport of hunting would undermine necessary work habits. The city merchants were excluded in an attempt by the landed gentry in Parliament to give visible and legal demonstration of the superiority of landed wealth over commercial wealth. In other words, the various game laws were intended to uphold the status of the aristocracy and the landed gentry.

The game laws represent a prime example of class legislation because the gentry who benefited from the laws and whose parliamentary representatives had passed them also served as the local justices of the peace who administered the laws and imposed penalties for their violation. The justices of the peace could levy fines and even have poachers impressed into the army. Gentry could also take civil legal action against wealthier poachers, such as rich farmers who did not own land, and thus saddle those persons with immense legal fees. The gentry also took other actions. They employed gamekeepers to protect game from poachers. The gamekeepers were known to kill the dogs belonging to people suspected of poaching. By the middle of the century violent conflicts involving death were not uncommon as gamekeepers confronted poachers. Trapguns were devised to shoot poachers who tripped the hidden levers.

In response to these laws and practices, a small industry arose to circumvent them. Many local poor people living either on the estate or in a nearby village would kill game for food. They believed that the game actually belonged to the community, and this practice increased during economic hard times. In this regard poaching was one way for the poor to find food. But even more important was the black market in game animals sustained by the demand of urban people for this kind of luxury meat. Here there arose the possibility of poaching for profit, and indeed, the technical meaning of *poaching* was the stealing or killing of game for sale. Local people from both the countryside and the villages would steal the game and then sell it to middlemen called *higglers*. Later, coachmen took over this middleman function. The higglers and the coachmen would smuggle the game into the cities, where poulterers would sell it at a premium price. Everyone involved made a bit of money along the way. During the second half of the century English aristocrats began to construct large game preserves, which, in turn, became hunting grounds to organized gangs of poachers. These preserves became the occasion for great resentment among the countryside poor, who had lost their rights to communal land as a result of the enclosures.

A portrait of the English gentry on its estates: Robert Andrews and His Wife *by Thomas Gainsborough (1728–1788). Note the rifle and hunting dog, symbols of Andrews' status as a gentleman and landowner. By law only persons owning a particular amount of land could hunt game animals in England.* [The National Gallery, London]

Over the course of the eighteenth century the game laws became harsher. Penalties against poaching increased in the years after the outbreak of the French Revolution. But during those same years the amount of poaching increased as the economic hardships of the war put a greater burden on poor people and as the demand for food in English cities grew along with their population. By the 1820s there were calls among landowners, as well as from reformers, for a change in the law. In 1831 the game laws were rewritten to make the landowners the possessors of the game but permitting them to allow other people to hunt it. Poaching continued, but the exclusive right of the landed classes to hunt game had ended.

Cities

Patterns of Preindustrial Urbanization

Remarkable changes occurred in the pattern of city growth between 1500 and 1800. In 1500 within Europe (excluding Hungary and Russia), there were approximately 156 cities with a population greater than 10,000. Only 4 of those cities, Paris, Milan, Venice, and Naples, had populations larger than 100,000. By 1800 there existed approximately 363 cities of 10,000 or more inhabitants, and 17 of those had populations larger than 100,000. The percentage of the European population living in urban areas had risen from just over 5 per cent to just over 9 per cent. There had also occurred a major shift in urban concentration from southern, Mediterranean Europe to the north.

These raw figures conceal significant changes that took place in how cities grew and how population distributed itself. A major time of urban development was the sixteenth century. This development was followed by a leveling off and even a decline in the seventeenth. New growth began in the early eighteenth century and became much accelerated in the late eighteenth and the early nineteenth centuries. Between 1500 and 1750 the major urban expansion took place within already-established and generally already-large cities. It was not a period of the emergence and growth of new cities. After 1750 the pattern changed with the birth of new cities and the rapid growth of already-existing smaller cities.

In particular between 1600 and 1750, the urban areas that displayed the most growth and vigor were capitals and ports. This situation reflects the success of monarchical state

The port of Bristol in southwestern England, c. 1735. Bristol was the third busiest port in eighteenth-century Britain after London and Liverpool. [City of Bristol Museum]

building during those years and the consequent burgeoning of bureaucracies, armies, courts, and other groups related to the process of government who lived in the capitals. The growth of port cities, in turn, reflects the expansion of European overseas trade and most especially that of the Atlantic routes. With the exception of Lyons, France, significant growth did not take place in the cases of industrial cities. Furthermore, between 1600 and 1750, cities with populations of less than 40,000 inhabitants declined. These included older landlocked trading centers, medieval industrial cities, and ecclesiastical centers. They contributed less to the new political regimes, and the expansion of the putting-out system transferred much production that had once occurred in medieval cities into the countryside. Rural labor was cheaper than urban labor, and cities with concentrations of labor declined as the site of production was moved from the urban workshop into the country.

In the middle of the eighteenth century a new pattern emerged. The rate of growth of existing large cities declined. New cities began to emerge and existing smaller cities began to grow. Several factors were at work in the process, which Jan De Vries has termed "an urban growth from below."[2] First, there was the general overall population increase. Second, the early stages of the Industrial Revolution, particularly in Britain, occurred in the countryside and tended to aid the growth of smaller towns and cities located nearby the factories. Factory organization itself fostered new concentrations of population. But cities also grew where there was little industrialization. The reason for this growth would seem to have been the new prosperity of European agriculture. Greater agricultural production aided the growth of nearby market towns and other urban centers that served agriculture or allowed more prosperous farmers to have access to the consumer goods and recreation they wanted. This new pattern of urban growth—new cities and the expansion of smaller existing cities—would continue into the nineteenth century.

The Urban Setting

The influence of land and the landed society extended to the cities of the old regime. The cities of the eighteenth century, like those of today, depended on the countryside for their food supply. The specter of famine or food shortages haunted the cities. The governments took great care to ensure adequate supplies of grain by building granaries and by paying careful attention to the fluctuation of bread prices. The nobility were not absent from the cities. They owned homes in the urban centers and often possessed large blocks of city real estate, which they developed as sources of new rents. Frequently nobles controlled the municipal government and sat as judges in the municipal courts.

A two-way migration of people took place between the country and the city. In many cities, especially of central and eastern Europe, rural day laborers lived in the towns and traveled outward to find their work. Other cities witnessed what has become a common modern phenomenon: the migration of people from the countryside into the town to find work, better wages, and possibly a more exciting life. Thousands of men and women born in the country moved to the city to become domestic servants or artisans.

Fernand Braudel rightly described cities as

"so many electric transformers," which "increase tension, accelerate the rhythm of exchange and ceaselessly stir up men's lives."[3] The eighteenth century witnessed a considerable growth of towns. The tumult of the day and the revolutions with which the century closed had a strong relationship to that urban expansion. London grew from about 700,000 inhabitants in 1700 to almost 1 million in 1800. By the time of the French Revolution the population of Paris stood over 500,000. Berlin's population tripled over the course of the century, reaching 170,000 in 1800. Saint Petersburg, founded in 1703, numbered over 250,000 inhabitants a century later. In addition to the growth of these capitals, the number of smaller urban units of 20,000–50,000 people increased considerably. However, this urban growth must be kept in perspective. Even in France and Great Britain probably somewhat less than 20 per cent of the population lived in cities. And the town of 10,000 inhabitants was much more common than the giant urban center.

Nearly all of these urban conglomerates were nonindustrial cities. They grew and expanded for reasons other than being the location of factories or other large manufacturing establishments. Only Manchester in England had experienced such industrial growth, and even its most spectacular expansion occurred after 1800.

Eighteenth-century cities fall into three broad and rather imperfect categories. The first and most common were market centers for the exchange of goods, most of which were produced locally. These relatively small provincial centers might also be the sites of local courts and state administration. The second category consisted of commercial, trading, shipping, and financial centers. These included the major sea and river ports. Finally, there were the great capital cities, which were also frequently commercial centers. In a sense both of the latter kinds of cities were the creation of the expanding bureaucratic states, whose rulers wished to see trade and commerce prosper. The great taxing power of those monarchies meant that vast wealth flowed into the capitals.

With the exception of Saint Petersburg, the cities of the eighteenth century were largely unplanned. A few urban developers might create elegant squares for the wealthy mer-

[2]J. De Vries, "Patterns of Urbanization in Pre-Industrial Europe, 1500–1800," in H. Schnal, ed., *Patterns of European Urbanization Since* 1500 (London: Croom Helm, 1981), p. 103.

[3]Fernand Braudel, *Capitalism and Material Life*, 1400–1800 (New York: Harper Torchbooks, 1973), p. 373.

559

*Society Under
the Old Regime
in the
Eighteenth
Century*

chants of urban-dwelling aristocrats, but most cities simply expanded on the base of their medieval precursors. London had burned in 1666. Its reconstruction benefited from the planning and architecture of Sir Christopher Wren (1632–1723), but expansion was still quite haphazard. On the Continent many cities retained their medieval walls, within which and beyond which growth occurred. There was usually a central square with civic buildings or a cathedral or a fortress nearby. Quite often urban expansion pressed beyond the original city border and onto the territory of nonurban landlords. The authority of the latter would then extend over that part of the city. Consequently some urban areas found themselves governed by manorial courts and other institutions of the countryside.

Visible segregation often existed between the urban rich and the urban poor. The former, including the nobles and the upper middle class, lived in fashionable town-houses, often constructed around newly laid-out green squares. The poorest town dwellers usually congregated along the rivers. Small merchants and craftsmen lived above their shops. Whole families might live in a single room. Sanitary facilities such as now exist were still unknown. There was little pure water. Cattle, pigs, goats, and other animals walked the streets with the people. All reports on the cities of Europe during this period emphasize both the striking grace and beauty of the dwellings of the wealthy and the dirt, filth, and stench that filled the streets.

Despite the more obvious drawbacks, it was still in the cities that men and women from all walks and stations of life found entertainment and excitement. More modes of recreation were available in cities than in the countryside. The cities provided more opportunities for theater, gambling, womanizing, and husband hunting. The season of parties in London drew noble and upper-gentry families from all over England. Here marriages were sought, and friendships were renewed. The French nobility

The city of Tobolesk in western Siberia. It was founded in 1527 at the juncture of two rivers as part of the Russian government's policy of controlling and exploiting the resources of Siberia. By the eighteenth century it was a thriving center for trade in furs and grain. [New York Public Library]

The Place Louis XV (today the Place de la Concorde) in Paris, an example of elegant eighteenth-century urban planning. [*British Museum*]

had learned to enjoy Paris after Louis XIV had initially forced them to come to his court at nearby Versailles. And many Russian nobles came to crave life in Saint Petersburg after having first arrived under the compulsion of Peter the Great. The eighteenth-century town house, as much as the country house, provided the aristocracy with its public stage.

There was, however, another side to urban life. This was the lot of the poor, who often depended on charity in the city. Poverty was not just a city problem; it was usually worse in the countryside. But in the city poverty more visibly manifested itself in terms of crime, prostitution, vagrancy, begging, and alcoholism. Many a young man or woman from the countryside migrated to the nearest city to seek a better life, only to discover poor housing, little food, disease, degradation, and finally death. It did not require the Industrial Revolution and the urban factory to make the cities into hellholes for the poor and the dispossessed. The full darkness of London life during the mid-century "gin age," when consumption of that liquor blinded and killed many poor people, is evident in the engravings of William Hogarth (1697–1764). Also contrasting with the serenity of the aristocratic and upper-commercial-class lifestyle were the public executions that took place all over Europe, the breaking of men and women on the wheel in Paris, and the public floggings in Russia. Bru-

tality condoned and carried out by the ruling classes was quite simply a fact of everyday life.

Urban Classes

Social divisions were as marked in the cities of the eighteenth century as they were in the industrial centers of the nineteenth. At the top of the urban social structure stood a generally small group of nobles, large merchants, bankers, financiers, clergy, and government officials. These men (and they were always men) controlled the political and economic affairs of the town. Normally they constituted a self-appointed and self-electing oligarchy who governed the city through its corporation or city council. These rights of self-government had normally been granted by some form of royal charter that gave the city corporation its authority and the power to select its own members. In a few cities on the Continent, artisan guilds controlled the corporations, but more generally the councils were under the influence of the local nobility and the wealthiest commercial people.

THE MIDDLE CLASS. Another group in the city were the prosperous but not immensely wealthy merchants, tradesmen, bankers, and professional people. These were the most dynamic element of the urban population and constituted the persons traditionally re-

560

garded as the middle class, or *bourgeoisie*. The concept of the middle class was much less clear-cut than that of the nobility. They had less wealth than most nobles but more than urban artisans. The middle-class people lived in the cities and towns, and their sources of income had little or nothing to do with the land. The middle class normally stood on the side of reform, change, and economic growth. The middle-class commercial figures—traders, bankers, manufacturers, and lawyers—often found their pursuit of both profit and prestige blocked by the privileges of the nobility and its social exclusiveness. The bourgeoisie also wanted more rational regulations for trade and commerce, as did some of the more progressive aristocrats.

During the eighteenth century the middle class and the aristocracy were on a collision course. The former often imitated the lifestyle of the latter, and the nobles were increasingly embracing the commercial spirit of the middle class. The bourgeoisie was not rising to challenge the nobility; both were seeking to add new dimensions to their existing power and prestige. However, tradition and political connection gave the advantage to the nobility. Consequently, as the century passed, members of the middle class felt and voiced increasing resentment of the aristocracy. That resentment became more bitter as the wealth and the numbers of the *bourgeoisie* increased and the aristocratic control of political and ecclesiastical power became tighter. The growing influence of the nobility seemed to mean that the middle class would continue to be excluded from the political decisions of the day.

On the other hand, the middle class in the cities tended to fear the lower urban classes as much as they resented the nobility. The lower orders constituted a potentially violent element in the society, a potential threat to property, and, in their poverty, a drain on national resources. However, the lower orders were much more varied than either the city aristocracy or the middle class cared to admit.

ARTISANS. The segment of the urban population that suffered from both the grasping of the middle class and the local nobility was that made up the shopkeepers, the artisans, and the wage earners. These people constituted the single largest group in any city. The lives and experience of this class were very diverse. They included grocers, butchers, fishmongers, carpenters, cabinetmakers, smiths, printers, hand-

By the eighteenth century the drinking of vast quantities of gin, a very cheap liquor, had become a major social problem for the working class in England. This 1750 etching by Hogarth illustrates the social evils that resulted from gin consumption, including debt, child abuse, death, and general disorder. [Metropolitan Museum of Art, Harris Brisbane Dick Fund, 1932]

loom weavers, and tailors, to give but a few examples. They had their own culture, values, and institutions. Like the peasants of the countryside, they were in many respects very conservative. Their economic position was highly vulnerable. If a poor harvest raised the price of food, their own businesses suffered.

The entire life of these artisans and shopkeepers centered on their work. They usually lived near or at their place of employment. Most of them worked in shops with fewer than a half dozen other craftsmen. Their primary institution had historically been the guild, but

561

Several examples of nonagricultural working-class skills can be shown. Printing shops produced the flood of eighteenth-century publications. Type was set and presses operated by hand, and the workmen were among the most highly skilled urban craftsmen. The picture is from Encyclopedia. *[Charles Farrell Collection]*

by the eighteenth century the guilds rarely possessed the influence of their predecessors in medieval or early modern Europe.

Nevertheless the guilds were not to be ignored. They played a conservative role. They played a conservative role. They did not seek economic growth or innovation. They attempted to preserve the jobs and the skills of their members. The guilds still were able in many countries to determine who might and might not pursue a particular craft. They attempted to prevent too many people from learning a particular skill. The guilds also provided a framework for social and economic advancement. A boy might at an early age become an apprentice to learn a craft or trade. After several years he would be made a journeyman. Still later, if successful and sufficiently competent, he might become a master. The ar-

tisan could also receive certain social benefits from the guilds. These might include aid for his family during sickness or the promise of admission for his son. The guilds constituted the chief protection for artisans against the operation of the commercial market. They were particularly strong in central Europe.

The Urban Riot

The artisan class, with its generally conservative outlook, maintained a rather fine sense of social and economic justice. These ideals were based largely on traditional practices. If the collective sense of what was economically "just" was offended, artisans frequently manifested their displeasure through the instrument of the riot. The most sensitive area was the price of bread. If a baker or a grain merchant announced a price that was considered unjustly high, a bread riot might well ensure. Artisan leaders would confiscate the bread or grain and sell it for what the urban crowd considered a "just price." They would then give the money paid for the bread or grain to the baker or merchant. The possibility of bread riots acted as a restraint on the greed of merchants. Such disturbances represented a collective method of imposing the "just price" in place of the price set by the commercial marketplace. In other words, bread and food riots, which occurred throughout Europe, were not irrational acts of screaming hungry people but highly ritualized social phenomena of the old regime and its economy of scarcity.

Other kinds of riots were also a basic characteristic of eighteenth-century society and politics. The riot was a way in which people who were excluded in every other way from the political processes could make their will known. Sometimes urban rioters were incited by religious bigotry. For example, in 1753 London Protestant mobs compelled the government ministry to withdraw an act meant to legalize Jewish naturalization. In 1780 the same rabidly Protestant spirit manifested itself in the Gordon riots, named after Lord George Gordon, who had raised the specter of an imaginary Catholic plot after the government relieved military recruits from having to take specifically anti-Catholic oaths. In these riots and in food riots, violence was normally directed against property rather than against people. The rioters themselves were not "riffraff" but usually small shopkeepers, freeholders, craftsmen, and wage earners. They usually had no other purpose than to restore a traditional right or practice that seemed endangered. Nevertheless considerable turmoil and destruction could result from their actions.

During the last half of the century urban riots increasingly involved political ends. Though often simultaneous with economic disturbances, the political riot always had nonartisan leadership or instigators. In fact, the "crowd" of the eighteenth century was often the tool of the upper classes. In Paris the aristocratic Parlement often urged crowd action in their disputes with the monarchy. In Geneva middle-class citizens supported artisan riots against the local urban oligarchy. In Great Britain in 1792 the government turned out mobs to attack English sympathizers of the French Revolution. All of these and other various outbursts of popular unrest suggest that the crowd

The burning of Newgate Prison, London, in June 1780 during the anti-Catholic Gordon riots which raged for several days. Some three hundred prisoners were released and the unfortunate warden, Mr. Akerman, lost all his furniture in the fire.

or mob first entered the European political and social arena well before the revolution in France.

A Society on the Edge of Modern Times

This chapter opened by describing eighteenth-century society as traditional, hierarchical, corporate, and privileged. These features had characterized Europe for hundreds of years. However, by the close of the eighteenth century each of these facets of European life stood undermined or challenged in a fundamental fashion by developments within the society itself. Europe was on the brink of a new era in which the social, economic, and political relationships of centuries would be destroyed.

Society had remained traditional and corporate largely because of the economy of scarcity. The agricultural and industrial revolutions would eventually overcome most scarcity in Europe and the West generally. The commercial spirit and values of the marketplace clashed with the traditional values and practices of the peasants and the guilds. The desire to make money and accumulate profits was hardly new, but beginning in the eighteenth century, it was permitted fuller play than ever before in European history. The commercial spirit was a major vehicle of social change and, by the early nineteenth century, had led increasingly to a conception of human beings as individuals rather than as members of communities.

The expansion of population provided a further stimulus for change and a challenge to tradition, hierarchy, and corporateness. The traditional economic and social organization had presupposed a stable or declining population. The additional numbers of people meant that new ways had to be devised to solve old problems. More people also meant more labor, more energy, and more minds contributing to the creation and solution of social difficulties. The improvements in health and the longer life span may have given that larger population a new sense of confidence. The social hierarchy had to accommodate itself to more people. Corporate groups, such as the guilds, had to confront the existence of an expanded labor force. Moreover the products and industries arising from the Industrial Revolution made the society and the economy much more complicated. Class structure and social hierarchy remained, but the boundaries became blurred. New wealth meant that birth would eventually become less and less a determining factor in social relationships, except in regard to the social role assigned to the two sexes.

Finally, the conflicting political ambitions of the monarchs, the nobilities, and the middle class generated innovation. The monarchs wanted to make their nations rich enough to wage war. As will be seen, this goal led them to attempt to interfere further with the privileges of the nobles. In the name of ancient rights the nobles attempted to secure and expand their existing social privileges by achieving further political power in the state. By making their privileges so exclusive, they helped to undermine the principle of privilege itself. The middle class, in all of its diversity, was growing wealthier from trade, commerce, and the practice of the professions. Its members wanted social prestige and political influence equal to their wealth. And they wanted the government to function in an efficient and businesslike manner. They resented privileges, frowned at hierarchy, and rejected tradition.

All of these factors meant that the society of the eighteenth century stood at the close of one era in European history and at the opening of another. What began to make contemporaries aware of that fact were the great wars of mid-century, the revolt of the British colonies in North America, and the intellectual currents of the Enlightenment.

Suggested Readings

C. B. A. BEHRENS, *The Ancien Régime* (1967). A brief account of life in France with excellent illustrations.

I. T. BEREND AND G. RANKI, *The European Periphery and Industrialization, 1780–1914* (1982). Examines the experience of eastern and Mediterranean Europe.

J. BLUM, *Lord and Peasant in Russia from the Ninth to the Nineteenth Century* (1961). A thorough and wide-ranging discussion.

J. BLUM, *The End of the Old Order in Rural Europe* (1978). The most comprehensive treatment of life in rural Europe, especially central and eastern, from the early eighteenth through the mid-nineteenth centuries.

F. BRAUDEL, *Capitalism and Material Life, 1400–1800* (1974). An investigation of the physical resources and human organization of preindustrial Europe.

F. BRAUDEL, *The Structures of Everyday Life: The Limits of the Possible,* trans. by M. Kochan (1982). A magisterial survey by the most important social historian of our time.

J. CANNON, *Aristocratic Century: The Peerage of Eighteenth-Century England* (1985). A useful treatment based on the most recent research.

P. DEANE, *The First Industrial Revolution,* 2nd ed. (1979). A well-balanced and systematic treatment.

J. DE VRIES, *The Economy of Europe in an Age of Crisis, 1600–1750* (1976). An excellent overview that sets forth the main issues.

J. DE VRIES, *European Urbanization 1500–1800* (1984). The most important and far-ranging of recent treatments of the subject.

P. EARLE (Ed.), *Essays in European Economic History, 1500–1800* (1974). A useful collection of articles that cover most of the major states of western Europe.

M. W. FLINN, *The European Demographic System, 1500–1820* (1981). A major summary.

F. FORD, *Robe and Sword: The Regrouping of the French Aristocracy After Louis XIV* (1953). An important treatment of the growing social tensions within the French nobility during the eighteenth century.

R. FORSTER, *The Nobility of Toulouse in the Eighteenth Century* (1960). A local study that displays the variety of noble economic activity.

R. FORSTER AND E. FORSTER, *European Society in the Eighteenth Century* (1969). An excellent collection of documents.

R. FORSTER AND O. RANUM, *Deviants and Aban-*

565

*Society Under
the Old Regime
in the
Eighteenth
Century*

doned in *French Society* (1978). This and the following volume contain important essays from the French journal *Annales.*

R. Forster and O. Ranum. *Medicine and Society in France* (1980).

D. V. Glass and D. E. C. Eversley (Eds.), *Population in History: Essays in Historical Demography* (1965). Fundamental for an understanding of the eighteenth-century increase in population.

A. Goodwin (Ed.), *The European Nobility in the Eighteenth Century* (1953). Essays on the nobility in each state.

P. Goubert, *The Ancien Régime: French Society, 1600–1750*, trans. by Steve Cox (1974). A superb account of the peasant social order.

H. J. Habakkuk and M. Postan (Eds.), *The Cambridge Economic History of Europe* (1965). Separate chapters by different authors on major topics.

D. Hay et al., *Albion's Fatal Tree: Crime and Society in Eighteenth-Century England* (1976). Separate essays on a previously little explored subject.

O. H. Hufton, *The Poor of Eighteenth-Century France, 1750–1789* (1975). A brilliant study of poverty and the family economy.

C. Jones, *Charity and Bienfaisance: The Treatment of the Poor in the Montpellier Region, 1740–1815* (1982). An important local French study.

E. L. Jones, *Agriculture and Economic Growth in England, 1650–1815* (1968). A good introduction to an important subject.

H. Kamen, *European Society, 1500–1700* (1985). The best one-volume treatment.

P. Laslett, *The World We Have Lost* (1965). Examination of English life and society before the coming of industrialism.

J. Lough, *An Introduction to Eighteenth-Century France* (1960). A systematic survey with good quotations (in French) from contemporaries.

R. K. McClure, *Coram's Children: The London Foundling Hospital in the Eighteenth Century* (1981). A moving work that deals with the plight of all concerned with the problem.

N. McKendrick (Ed.), *The Birth of a Consumer Society: The Commercialization of Eighteenth Century England* (1982). Deals with several aspects of the impact of commercialization.

P. B. Munsche, *Gentlemen and Poachers: The English Game Laws, 1671–1831* (1981). An excellent analysis of these laws.

S. Pollard, *The Genesis of Modern Management: A Study of the Industrial Revolution in Great Britain* (1965). Treats the issue of industrialization from the standpoint of factory owners.

S. Pollard, *Peaceful Conquest: The Industrialization of Europe, 1760–1970* (1981). A useful survey.

S. Pollard and C. Holmes, *Documents of European Economic History: The Process of Industrialization, 1750–1870* (1968). A very useful collection.

A. Ribeiro, *Dress in Eighteenth Century Europe, 1715–1789* (1985). An interesting examination of the social implication of style in clothing.

G. Rudé, *The Crowd in History 1730–1848* (1964). This and the following work were pioneering studies.

G. Rudé, *Europe in the Eighteenth Century* (1972). A survey with emphasis on social history.

G. Rudé, *Paris and London in the Eighteenth Century* (1973).

H. Schmal (Ed.), *Patterns of European Urbanization Since 1500* (1981). Major revisionist essays.

L. Stone, *The Family, Sex and Marriage in England 1500–1800* (1977). A pioneering study of a subject receiving new interest from historians.

L. Stone, *An Open Elite?* (1985). Raises important questions about the traditional view of open access to social mobility in England.

T. Tackett, *Priest and Parish in Eighteenth-Century France: A Social and Political Study of the Curés in a Diocese of Dauphiné, 1750–1791* (1977). A very important local study that displays the role of the church in the fabric of social life in the old regime.

L. A. Tilly and J. W. Scott, *Women, Work, and Family* (1978). An excellent survey of the issues in western Europe.

R. Wall (Ed.), *Family Forms in Historic Europe* (1983). Essays that cover the entire continent.

C. Wilson, *England's Apprenticeship, 1603–1763* (1965). A broad survey of English economic life on the eve of industrialism.

E. A. Wrigley and R. S. Schofield, *The Population History of England, 1541–1871: A Reconstruction* (1982). One of the most ambitious demographic studies ever undertaken.

William Pitt the Elder, first Earl of Chatham (1708–1778), was the architect of Britain's victory in the Seven Years' War against France and Spain. By the end of the war in 1763, Britain had conquered Canada and had become the dominant European power in India. [*National Portrait Gallery, London*]

THE MIDDLE OF THE EIGHTEENTH CEN-
TURY witnessed a renewal of European warfare on a worldwide scale. The conflict involved two separate but interrelated rivalries.
Austria and Prussia fought for dominance in
central Europe while Great Britain and France
dueled for commercial and colonial supremacy. The wars were long, extensive, and very
costly in both effort and money. They resulted
in a new balance of power on the Continent
and on the high seas. Great Britain gained a
world empire, and Prussia was recognized as a
great power. Moreover the expense of these
wars led every major European government
after the Peace of Paris of 1763 to reconstruct
its policies of taxation and finance. These revised fiscal programs produced internal conditions for the monarchies of Europe that had
most significant results for the rest of the century. These included the American Revolution,
enlightened absolutism on the Continent, a
continuing financial crisis for the French monarchy, and reform of the Spanish Empire in
South America.

16
Empire, War, and Colonial Rebellion

Eighteenth-Century Empires

Periods of European Overseas Empires

Since the Renaissance, European contacts
with the rest of the world have gone through
four distinct stages. The first was that of the
discovery, exploration, and initial conquest
and settlement of the New World. This period
had closed by the end of the seventeenth century. The second era, which is largely the concern of this chapter, was one of colonial trade
rivalry among Spain, France, and Great Britain. The Anglo-French side of the contest has
often been compared to a second Hundred
Years' War. During this second period, which
may be said to have closed during the 1820s,
both the British colonies of the North American seaboard and the Spanish colonies of Central and South America emancipated themselves from European control. The third stage
of European contact with the non-European
world occurred in the nineteenth century,
when new formal empires involving the European administration of indigenous peoples
were carved out in Africa and Asia. Those
nineteenth-century empires also included new
areas of European settlement, such as Australia, New Zealand, and South Africa. The bases
of these empires were trade, national honor,
and military strategy. The last period of European empire came in the present century, with

the decolonization of peoples previously under European colonial rule.

During the four and a half centuries before decolonization, Europeans exerted political dominance over much of the rest of the world. They frequently treated other peoples as social, intellectual, and economic inferiors. They ravaged existing cultures because of greed, religious zeal, or political ambition. These actions are major facts of European history and significant factors in the contemporary relationship of Europe and its former colonies. What allowed the Europeans to exert such influence and domination for so long over so much of the world was not any innate cultural superiority but a technological supremacy closely related to naval power and gunpowder. Ships and guns allowed the Europeans to exercise their will almost wherever they chose.

Mercantile Empires

Navies and merchant shipping were the keystones of the mercantile empires of the eighteenth century. These empires were meant to bring profit to a nation rather than to provide areas for settlement. The Treaty of Utrecht (1713) established the boundaries of empire during the first half of the century. Except for Brazil, which was governed by Portugal, Spain controlled all of mainland South America, and in North America it controlled Florida, Mexico, and California. The Spanish also governed the island of Cuba and half of Hispaniola. The British Empire consisted of the colonies along the North Atlantic seaboard, Nova Scotia, Newfoundland, Jamaica, and Barbados. Britain also possessed a few trading stations on the Indian subcontinent. The French domains covered the Saint Lawrence River valley; the Ohio and Mississippi river valleys; the West Indian islands of Saint Domingue, Guadeloupe, and Martinique; and stations in India. The Dutch controlled Surinam, or Dutch Guiana, in South America; various trading stations in Ceylon and Bengal; and, most important, the trade with Java in what is now Indonesia. All of these powers also possessed numerous smaller islands in the Caribbean. So far as eighteenth-century developments were concerned, the major rivalries existed among the Spanish, the French, and the British.

To the extent that any formal economic theory lay behind the conduct of these empires, it was mercantilism, that practical creed of hardheaded businessmen. Initially, the fundamental point of this outlook was the necessity of acquiring a favorable trade balance of gold and silver bullion. Such bullion was regarded as the measure of a country's wealth, and a nation was truly wealthy only if it amassed more bullion than its rivals. By the late seventeenth century mercantilist thinking, as developed by writers such as Thomas Mun in *England's Treasure of Forraign Trade* (1664), had come to regard general foreign trade and the level of domestic industry as the true indications of a nation's prosperity. But from beginning to end, the economic well-being of the home country was the first concern of mercantilist writers. Colonies were to provide markets and natural resources for the industries of the home country. In turn, the home country was to furnish military security and political administration for the colonies. For decades both sides assumed that the colonies were the inferior partner in the relationship. The mercantilist statesmen and traders regarded the world as an arena of scarce resources and economic limitation. They assumed that one national economy could grow only at the expense of others. The home country and its colonies were to trade only with each other. To that end they attempted to forge trade-tight systems of national commerce through navigation laws, tariffs, bounties to encourage production, and prohibitions against trading with the subjects of other monarchs. National monopoly was the ruling principle.

Mercantilist ideas had always been neater on paper than in practice. By the early eighteenth century mercantilist assumptions were held only in the vaguest manner. They stood too far removed from the economic realities of the colonies and perhaps from human nature. The colonial and home markets simply failed to mesh. Spain could not produce sufficient goods for South America. Economic production in the British North American colonies challenged English manufacturing and led to British attempts to limit certain colonial industries, such as iron and hat making. Colonists of different countries wished to trade with each other. English colonists could buy sugar more cheaply from the French West Indies than from English suppliers. The traders and merchants of one nation always hoped to break the monopoly of another. For all these reasons the eighteenth century became the "golden age of smugglers."[1] The governments could not con-

[1] Walter Dorn, *Competition for Empire, 1740–1763* (New York: Harper, 1940), p. 266.

The Mercantilist Position Stated

One of the earliest discussions of the economic theory of mercantilism appeared in *England's Treasure by Forraign Trade* (1664) by Thomas Mun. In this passage from that work Mun explained why it was necessary to the prosperity of the nation for more goods to be exported than imported. Although later mercantilist theory became somewhat more sophisticated, all writers in the eighteenth century emphasized the necessity of a favorable balance of trade.

The ordinary means therefore to increase our wealth and treasure is by Forraign Trade *wherein wee must ever observe this rule; to sell more to strangers yearly than wee consume of theirs in value. For suppose that when this Kingdom is plentifully served with the Cloth, Lead, Tinn, Iron, Fish and other native commodities, we doe yearly export the overplus to forraign countries to the value of twenty two hundred thousand pounds; by which means we are enabled beyond the Seas to buy and bring in forraign wares for our use and Consumptions, to the value of twenty hundred thousand pounds; By this order duly kept in our trading, we may rest assured that the Kingdom shall be enriched yearly two hundred thousand pounds, which must be brought to us in so much Treasure; because that part of our stock which is not returned to us in wares must necessarily be brought home in treasure [i.e., gold or silver bullion].*

Thomas Mun, *England's Treasure by Forraign Trade,* as quoted in Charles Wilson, *England's Apprenticeship, 1603–1763* (London: Longman, 1965), p. 60

trol the activities of all their subjects. Clashes among colonists could and did bring about conflict between governments.

Neither the French nor the British colonies of North America fit particularly well into the mercantile pattern of empire. Trade with these areas during the early part of the century was smaller than with the West Indies. These mainland colonies were settlements rather than arenas for economic exploitation. The French lands of Canada were quite sparsely populated. Relations with the Indians were troublesome. The economic interests and the development of the colonies were not wholly compatible with those of the home countries. Major flash points existed between France and Britain on the North American continent. Their colonists quarreled endlessly with each other. Both groups of settlers were jealous over rights to the lower Saint Lawrence River valley, upper New England, and later the Ohio River valley. There were other rivalries over fishing rights, fur trade, and relationships with the Indians.

Unlike North America or the West Indies, India was neither the home of migrating Europeans nor an integral part of their imperial schemes. The Indian subcontinent was an area where both France and Britain traded through privileged, chartered companies that enjoyed a legal monopoly. The East India Company was the English institution; the French equivalent was the Compagnie des Indes. The trade of India and Asia figured only marginally in the economics of empire. Some bullion gained by trade or piracy in the West Indies was shipped to India, where it was used to purchase cotton cloth that was shipped to England and then used to purchase slaves in Africa for the West Indies. The commercial problem with the states of India was that the European countries produced little or nothing wanted in the region.

Nevertheless throughout the century trade and involvement on the subcontinent continued. Enterprising Europeans always hoped that in some fashion profitable commerce with India might develop. Others regarded India as a springboard into the even larger potential market of China. The original European footholds in India were trading posts called *factories.* They existed through privileges granted by the various Indian governments. Two circumstances arose during the middle of the eighteenth century to change this situation. First, in several of the Indian states decay occurred in the indigenous administration and government. Second, Joseph Dupleix (1697–1763) for the French and Robert Clive (1725–1774) for the British saw these developments

*The English factory at Surat in India, owned and operated by the East India Company. Here
Indian goods were purchased and stored until British ships arrived to take them to Britain.
[The Mansell Collection]*

as opportunities for expanding the control of
their respective companies (the Compagnie
des Indes and the East India Company). To
maintain their own security and to expand
their privileges, the companies began to fill the
power vacuum and in effect took over the government of some regions. Each group of Europeans hoped to checkmate the other.

The Spanish Colonial System

Spanish control of its American empire involved a system of government and a system of
monopolistic trade regulation. Both were more
rigid in appearance than in practice. Actual
government was often informal, and the trade
monopoly was often breached.

Because Queen Isabella had commissioned
Columbus, the technical legal link between the
New World and Spain was the crown of Castile. Its powers both at home and in America
were subject to few limitations. Government of

America was assigned to the Council of the
Indies, which, in conjunction with the monarch, nominated the persons who served as
viceroys of New Spain and Peru. These viceroys served as the chief executives in the New
World and carried out the laws promulgated by
the Council of the Indies. Within each of the
viceroyalties were established a number of subordinate judicial councils known as *audiencias*.
There were also a variety of local officers, the
most important of which were the *corregidores*,
who presided over municipal councils. All of
these offices provided the monarchy with a
vast array of patronage, usually bestowed on
persons born in Spain. Virtually all political
power flowed from the top of this political
structure downward; in effect, there was little
or no substantial local initiative or self-government.

The colonial political structures existed, in
large measure, to support the commercial goals
of Spain. The Casa de Contratación (House of

Trade) in Seville regulated all trade with the New World. Cádiz was the only port to be used for the American trade. The Casa de Contratación was the single most influential institution of the Spanish Empire, and its members worked closely with the Consulado (Merchant Guild) of Seville and other groups involved with the American commerce in Cádiz.

The key device for maintaining the trade monopoly administered in Seville was a complicated system of trade and bullion fleets. The Seville merchants sought to sell goods in America and to draw back to Spain as much precious metal as possible. They and they alone were to be the link between the New World and Europe. Merchants from other nations were to be excluded from the American routes, and even the Spanish colonists from the various parts of the American empire were prohibited from establishing direct trade with each other and from building their own shipping and commercial industry. Each year, a fleet of commercial vessels (the *flota*), accompanied by protective naval ships, carried merchandise from Spain to a few specified ports in America. These included Portobello, Veracruz, and Cartagena. There were no authorized ports on the Pacific Coast. Areas far to the south, such as Buenos Aires on the Río de la Plata, received shipments only after the shipments had been received at one of the authorized ports. After selling their wares, the ships were loaded with silver and gold bullion, usually wintered in heavily fortified Caribbean ports, and then sailed back to Spain.

The *flota* system always worked imperfectly. First pirates, storms, and hostile navies could ravage the convoy. If, as occurred on more than one occasion over the centuries, the bullion fleet was lost, the Spanish economy went into a depression. Second, Spain alone was not able to produce sufficient consumer goods to meet American demands. The *flota* often carried goods produced in Europe outside Spain, and thus the Casa simply facilitated transactions between the New World and other nations. Third, both non-Spanish European merchants and traders from both the Spanish and the non-Spanish colonies wanted to buy and sell freely in the vast Latin American market. From the mid-seventeenth to the early eighteenth century, the Spanish navy could not effectively enforce its monopoly. The result was an immense amount of smuggling.

A crucial change occurred in the Spanish colonial system during the eighteenth century.

The fortress of El Morro in the harbor of San Juan, Puerto Rico. This massive citadel protected the Spanish treasure fleets that carried gold and silver each year to Spain from the mines of Mexico and Peru. [Commonwealth of Puerto Rico]

The War of the Spanish Succession and the Treaty of Utrecht replaced the Spanish Habsburgs with the Bourbons of France on the Spanish throne. Philip V (1700–1746) and his successors brought with them to Spain the administrative skills and expectations that had been forged by the bureaucrats of Louis XIV. The Bourbon Spanish monarchy was determined to reassert the imperial trade monopoly, which had decayed under the last Spanish Habsburgs, and thus to improve the domestic economy and revive the role of Spain in European affairs.

Under Philip V, attempts were made to suppress smuggling by the use of coastal patrol vessels in American waters. An incident arising from this policy (to be discussed in the next section) eventually led to war with England. In 1739, Philip established the viceroyalty of New Granada in the area that is today made up of Venezuela, Colombia, and Ecuador. The purpose of this new administrative unit was to increase direct royal government in the area. During the reign of Ferdinand VI (1746–1759), the great mid-century wars exposed the vulnerability of the empire to naval attack and economic penetration. As an ally of France,

571

DISPUTED BY
ENGLAND, RUSSIA,
AND SPAIN

VICEROYALTY OF
NEW SPAIN

RIO GRANDE

MISSISSIPPI

ATLANTIC OCEAN

EFFECTIVE FRONTIER OF
SPANISH SETTLEMENT

Mexico City •

Santo Domingo

Caracas

VICEROYALTY OF NEW GRANADA
Separated from
Viceroyalty of Peru,
1717, 1739

Bogotá •

GUIANA

Quito •

AMAZON

VICEROYALTY OF
BRAZIL

Pernambuco •

Lima •

• Bahia

VICEROYALTY OF PERU

PACIFIC OCEAN

São Paulo

Rio de Janeiro

VICEROYALTY OF
LA PLATA
Separated from
Viceroyalty of Peru,
1776

Santiago •

Buenos Aires •

AUDIENCIA OF CHILE
Retained by
Viceroyalty of Peru, 1776

CLAIMED BUT NOT SETTLED BY SPAIN

VICEROYALTIES IN LATIN AMERICA IN 1780
MAP 16–1

Spain emerged as one of the defeated powers in 1763. Government circles were convinced that some changes in the colonial system had to be undertaken.

Charles III (1759–1788) made the most important strides toward imperial reform. What this reform meant was an attempt to reassert Spanish peninsular control of the empire. Like his two Bourbon predecessors, Charles III put more emphasis on royal ministers than on councils. Consequently the role of both the Council of the Indies and the Casa de Contratación diminished. After 1765, Charles abolished the monopolies of Seville and Cádiz and permitted other Spanish commercial centers to trade with America. He also opened more South American and Caribbean ports to trade and authorized some commerce between ports in America. In 1776, he organized a fourth viceroyalty in the region of Rio de la Plata, which included much of present-day Argentina, Uruguay, Paraguay, and Bolivia. While in one sense somewhat freeing trade with and in America, Charles III attempted to increase the efficiency of tax collection and to eliminate bureaucratic corruption. To achieve those ends, he introduced the institution of the *intendent* into the Spanish Empire. These loyal, royal bureaucrats were patterned on the French *intendants* made so famous and effective as agents of the absolutism of Louis XIV.

These late-eighteenth-century Bourbon reforms helped to stimulate the imperial economy. Trade expanded and was somewhat more varied. But first and foremost, these reforms were attempts to bring the empire back under direct Spanish control. *Peninsulares* (persons born in Spain) entered the New World in large numbers to fill new posts. Expanding trade brought more Spanish merchants to Latin America. The export orientation of the economy remained, and economic life was still organized to the benefit of Spain. A major result of these policies was to make the creoles (persons of European descent born in the Spanish colonies) feel that they were second-class subjects. In time, their resentment provided a major source of the discontent leading to the wars of independence in the early nineteenth century. Finally, it should be observed that the new imperial policies of Charles III were the Spanish equivalent of the new colonial directions undertaken by the British government in 1763, which, as will be seen in a later section, led to the American Revolution.

The eighteenth-century City Hall of Buenos Aires. Buenos Aires became the capital of the Viceroyalty of Rio de la Plata in 1776. [Jacques Jangoux, Peter Arnold]

Rivalry and Conflict in the West Indies

The Spanish Empire stood on the defensive throughout the century. It was a sprawling expanse of territory over which the Spanish government wished to maintain a commercial monopoly without possessing the capacity to do so. Spanish colonists looked to illegal imports from French and British traders to supply needed goods. Both France and Britain assumed a very aggressive stance toward the Spanish Empire because they viewed it as a vast potential market and a major source of gold. Their rivalry for intrusion into the mainland Spanish American markets was duplicated by their conflicts in the West Indies.

The heart of the eighteenth-century colonial rivalry was the West Indies. These islands, close to the American continents, constituted the jewels of empire. Here the colonial powers pursued their greedy ambitions in close proximity to each other. The West Indies raised tobacco, cotton, indigo, coffee, and sugar, for which there existed strong markets in Europe. Sugar in particular had become a product of standard consumption rather than a luxury. It was used in coffee, tea, and cocoa; for making candy and preserving fruits; and in the brewing industry. There seemed no limit to its uses. Sugar was also important to the domestic

A sugar mill in the French West Indies. Like all Caribbean plantations, it was worked by slaves from Africa. Europeans had developed an insatiable demand for sugar, and the profits from sugar growing were immense. [*Library of Congress*]

economy of Europe. Sugar refining had become a major industry in France. Sugar and tobacco figured prominently in the reexport industry. For example, large quantities of tobacco were shipped from Scotland to the Continent.

Basic to the economy of the West Indies as well as to that of South America and the British colonies on the south Atlantic seaboard of North America was the institution of slavery. Hundreds of thousands of slaves were imported into the Americas during the eighteenth century. Planters could not attract sufficient quantities of free labor to these areas. They became wholly dependent on slaves. Slavery and the slave trade touched most of the economy of the transatlantic world. Cities such as Newport, Rhode Island; Liverpool, England; and Nantes, France, enjoyed prosperity that rested almost entirely on the slave trade. All of the shippers who handled cotton, tobacco, and sugar depended on slavery, though they might have no direct contact with the institution. There was a general triangle of trade that consisted of carrying goods to Africa to be exchanged for slaves, who were then taken to the West Indies, where they were traded for sugar

and other tropical produce, which were then shipped to Europe. Not all ships necessarily covered all three legs of the triangle. Another major trade pattern existed between New England and the West Indies: New England fish or ship stores were traded for sugar.

Within the rich commerce and agriculture of the West Indies there existed three varieties of colonial rivalry. Producers of different nations were intensely jealous of each other. The quantity of sugar produced had expanded so as to depress the price in Europe. Consequently one group of planters hoped not to conquer the lands of their competitors but rather to destroy the productive capacity of those islands. There was a second form of rivalry among shippers in the Caribbean. Every captain hoped to transport as much sugar as possible to Europe. Finally, the West Indies possessions of France and Britain provided excellent bases for penetration of the trade of the Spanish Empire. Many French and British ship captains in the West Indies were admitted smugglers, and some were little better than pirates.

The close interrelationship of the West Indies and the European economies meant that significant numbers of British, French, and Spanish subjects had an interest in the area. This West India Interest, as it was called in England, consisted of absentee plantation owners, shippers, insurers, merchants, bankers, owners of domestic industries dependent on West Indian products, and all of those involved in the slave trade. In Great Britain it was an articulate and well-organized pressure group. In 1739 the West India Interest, along with the political enemies of Robert Walpole, succeeded in driving Britain into a war with Spain, the War of Jenkins's Ear.

The Treaty of Utrecht (1713) included two special privileges for Great Britain in regard to the Spanish Empire. The British received a thirty-year *asiento*, or contract, to furnish slaves to the Spanish. Britain also gained the right to send one ship each year to the trading fair at Portobello, a major Caribbean seaport on the Panamanian coast. These two privileges al-

---

Visitors Describe the Portobello Fair

The Spanish attempted to restrict all trade within their Latin American empire to a few designated ports. The most famous of these was Portobello on the Isthmus of Panama. In the 1730s, two visitors saw the event and described it. Note the wide variety of goods traded and the vast distances over which products had to be transported. This fair was the chief means of facilitating trade between the western coast of South America and Spain.

The town of Portobello, so thinly inhabited, by reason of its noxious air, the scarcity of provisions, and the soil, becomes, at the time of the [Spanish] galleons one of the most populous places in all South America. . . .

The ships are no sooner moored in the harbour, than the first work is, to erect, in the square, a tent made of the ship's sails, for receiving its cargo; at which the proprietors of the goods are present, in order to find their bales, by the marks which distinguish them. These bales are drawn on sledges, to their respective places by the crew of every ship, and the money given them is proportionally divided.

Whilst the seamen and European traders are thus employed, the land is covered with droves of mules from Panama, each drove consisting of above an hundred, loaded with chests of gold and silver, on account of the merchants of Peru. Some unload them at the exchange, others in the middle of the square; yet, amidst the hurry and confusion of such crowds, no theft, loss, or disturbance, is ever known. He who has seen this place during the tiempo muerto, or dead time, solitary, poor, and a perpetual silence reigning everywhere; the harbour quite empty, and every place wearing a melancholy aspect; must be filled with astonishment at the sudden change, to see the bustling multitudes, every house

crowded, the square and streets encumbered with bales and chests of gold and silver of all kinds; the harbour full of ships and vessels, some bringing by the way of Rio de Chape the goods of Peru, such as cacao, quinquina, or Jesuit's bark, Vicuña wool, and bezoar stones; others coming from Carthagena, loaded with provisions; and thus a spot, at all times detested for its deleterious qualities, becomes the staple of the riches of the old and new world, and the scene of one of the most considerable branches of commerce in the whole earth.

The ships being unloaded, and the merchants of Peru, together with the president of Panama, arrived, the fair comes under deliberation. And for this purpose the deputies of the several parties repair on board the commodore of the galleons, where, in the presence of the commodore, and the president of Panama, . . . the prices of the several kinds of merchandizes are settled. . . . The purchases and sales, as likewise the exchanges of money, are transacted by brokers, both from Spain and Peru. After this, every one begins to dispose of his goods; the Spanish brokers embarking their chests of money, and those of Peru sending away the goods they have purchased, in vessels called chatas and bongos, up the river Chagres. And thus the fair of Porto Bello ends.

George Juan and Antonio de Ulloa, *A Voyage to South America* (London, 1772), Vol. 1 pp. 103–110, quoted in Benjamin Keen (Ed.), *Readings in Latin-American Civilization 1492 to the Present* (New York: Houghton Mifflin, 1955), pp. 107–108.

The war over the Austrian succession and the British-Spanish commercial conflict could have remained separate disputes. They were neither logically nor necessarily politically related. What ultimately united them was the role of France. Cardinal Fleury understood that the long-range interests of France lay in the direction of commercial growth. However, just as British merchant interests had pushed Robert Walpole into war, a group of court aristocrats led by the count of Belle Isle compelled the elderly Fleury to abandon his planned naval attack on British trade and to support the Prussian aggression against Austria. This proved to be one of the most fateful decisions in French history.

Even though the Habsburgs had been the historic enemy of France, a war against Austria was not in the French interest in 1741. In the first place, aid to Prussia had the effect of con-solidating a new and powerful state in Germany. That new power could, and indeed later did, endanger France. Second, the French move against Austria brought Great Britain into the continental war. The British, as usual, wanted to see the Low Countries remain in friendly hands. In the eighteenth century that policy required continued Habsburg control of the Austrian Netherlands. In 1744 the British-French conflict expanded beyond the Continent, as France decided to support Spain against Britain in the New World. As a result, French military and economic resources became badly divided. France could not bring sufficient strength to the colonial struggle. Having chosen to continue a struggle from the past with Austria, France lost the struggle for the future against Great Britain.

By 1748 the war had become a military stalemate for all concerned. Austria had not

The Battle of Fontenoy, 1745, during the War of Austrian Succession. The French under Marechal de Saxe defeated an English army that was defending the territory of Maria Theresa in the Austrian Netherlands. [*Giraudon*]

Prussia and Great Britain Agree to the Convention of Westminster

The Diplomatic Revolution of 1756 saw a reversal of the alliances that had existed during the War of the Austrian Succession. France and Austria became allies against Prussia and Great Britain. The Convention of Westminster was the agreement that created the Prussian-British alliance. That alliance allowed Prussia to receive the financial backing of Britain in case of war and provided Britain with a continental ally that would divert the resources of France from the war for overseas empire. Prussia hoped that the treaty would provide protection from Russia, Austria, and France.

As the differences which have arisen in America between the King of Great Britain and the most Christian King [i.e., the king of France], and the consequences of which become every day more alarming, give room to fear for the public tranquillity of Europe; H.M. the King of Great Britain, etc., and H.M. the King of Prussia, etc., attentive to an object so very interesting, and equally desirous of preserving the peace of Europe in general and that of Germany in particular, have resolved to enter into such measures as may the most effectually contribute to so desirable an end. . . .

I. There shall be, between the said most Serene Kings, a perfect peace and mutual amity, notwithstanding the troubles that may arise in Europe, in consequence of the above-mentioned differences; so that neither of the contracting parties shall attack, or invade, directly or indirectly, the territories of the other; but, on the contrary, shall exert their utmost efforts to prevent their respective allies from undertaking anything against the said territories in any manner whatever.

II. If contrary to all expectation, and in violation of the peace which the high contracting parties propose to maintain by this treaty in Germany, any foreign power should cause troops to enter into the said Germany, under any pretext whatsoever; the two high contracting parties shall unite their forces to punish this infraction of the peace, and maintain the tranquillity of Germany, according to the purport of the present treaty.

H. Butterfield (Ed.), *Select Documents of European History, 1715–1920* (London: Methuen, 1931), pp. 20–21.

been able to regain Silesia, but it had fended off further aggression from other German states. The French army, led by Marshal Maurice de Saxe (1696–1750), won a series of splendid victories over the British and the Austrians in the Netherlands during 1747 and 1748. Britain, for its part, had pursued a very successful colonial campaign. Its forces in America captured the fortress of Louisburg at the mouth of the Saint Lawrence River, and the British more than held their own on the Indian subcontinent. Warfare on French commerce had been highly effective. These victories overseas compensated for the poor showing on the Continent. Consequently the war was brought to a close by the Treaty of Aix-la-Chapelle (1748). In effect the treaty restored the conditions that had existed before the war, with the exception that Prussia retained Silesia. Spain renewed the *asiento* agreement with Great Britain. All observers believed that the treaty constituted a truce rather than a permanent peace.

The "Diplomatic Revolution" of 1756

Before the rivalries again erupted into war, a dramatic shift of alliances took place. In 1756 Prussia and Great Britain signed the Convention of Westminster. It was a defensive alliance aimed at preventing the entry of foreign troops into the Germanies. Frederick II feared invasions by both Russia and France. The convention meant that Great Britain, the ally of Austria since the wars of Louis XIV, had now joined forces with Austria's major eighteenth-century enemy.

Maria Theresa was despondent over this development. However, her foreign minister,

Count Kaunitz (1711–1794). As foreign minister of the Habsburg Monarchy, Kaunitz negotiated the famous reversal of alliances (1756) by which France entered the Seven Years' War allied with Austria against Prussia and Britain. [Bildarchivs der Osterreichischen National-bibliothek, Vienna]

Count Wenzel Anton Kaunitz (1711–1794), was delighted. This brilliant diplomat and servant of the Habsburg dynasty had long hoped for an alliance between Austria and France for the dismemberment of Prussia. The Convention of Westminster made this alliance, unthinkable a few years earlier, possible. France was agreeable because Frederick had not consulted it before coming to his understanding with Britain. Consequently, later in 1756, France and Austria signed a defensive alliance. Kaunitz had succeeded in completely reversing the direction of French foreign policy from Richelieu through Fleury. France would now fight to restore Austrian supremacy in central Europe. But the French monarchy, though having changed its German ally, would remain diverted from its commercial interests on the high seas.

The Seven Years' War (1756–1763)

The Treaty of Aix-la-Chapelle had brought peace in Europe, but the conflict between France and Great Britain continued unofficially on the colonial front. There were continuous clashes between American and French settlers in the Ohio River valley and in upper New England. These were the prelude to what is known in American history as the French and Indian War. These colonial skirmishes would certainly have led in time to a broader conflict. However, once again the factor that opened a general European war that extended into a colonial theater was the action of the king of Prussia.

In August 1756 Frederick II invaded the kingdom of Saxony. He regarded this invasion as a continuation of the defensive strategy of which the Convention of Westminster had been a part. Frederick believed that there existed an international conspiracy on the part of Saxony, Austria, and France to undermine and destroy Prussian power. The attack on Saxony was in Frederick's mind a preemptive strike. The invasion itself created the very destructive alliance that Frederick feared. In the spring of 1757 France and Austria made a new alliance dedicated to the destruction of Prussia. They were eventually joined by Sweden, Russia, and the smaller German states.

Prussia was surrounded by enemies, and Frederick II confronted the gravest crisis of his career. It was after these struggles that he came to be called Frederick the Great. He won several initial battles, the most famous of which was Rossbach on November 5, 1757. Thereafter, however, the Prussians experienced a long series of defeats that might have destroyed the state. Two factors in addition to Frederick's stubborn leadership saved Prussia. The first was major financial aid from Great Britain. The British contributed as much to the Prussian war effort as did the Prussian treasury itself. Second, in 1762 Empress Elizabeth of Russia died. Her successor was Czar Peter III (he also died in the same year), whose admiration for Frederick knew almost no bounds. He immediately made peace with Prussia, thus relieving the country of one enemy and allowing it to hold its own against Austria and France. The treaty of Hubertusburg of 1763 closed the continental conflict with no significant changes in prewar borders. Silesia remained Prussia's province, and Prussia clearly stood in the ranks of the great powers.

The survival of Prussia was less impressive to the rest of Europe than the victories of Great Britain over France in every theater of conflict. The architect of this victory was William Pitt the Elder (1708–1778). He came from a family that had made its fortune from commerce. His grandfather, "Diamond" Pitt, had laid the foundations of the family's wealth by commercial ventures in India. The grandson was no less dedicated to the growth of British trade and economic interests. Pitt was a person of colossal ego and administrative genius. From the time of the War of Jenkins's Ear he had criticized the government as being too timid in its colonial policy. He had been strongly critical of all continental involvement, including the Convention of Westminster. During the 1750s he had gained the favor of the London merchant interest. Once war had begun again, these groups clamored for his appointment to the cabinet. In 1757 he was named the secretary of state in charge of the war. He soon drew into his own hands all the power he could grasp. A person of supreme confidence, he once told his friends, "I am sure that I can save the country, and that no one else can."

Once in office Pitt changed his attitude toward British involvement on the Continent. He came to regard the German conflict as a way to divert French resources and attention from the colonial struggle. He pumped huge financial subsidies to Frederick the Great and later boasted of having won America on the plains of Germany. North America was the center of Pitt's real concern. Put quite simply, he wanted all of North America east of the Mississippi for Great Britain, and that was exactly what he

won. He turned more than forty thousand regular English and colonial troops against the French in Canada. Never had so many soldiers been devoted to a colonial field of warfare. He achieved unprecedented cooperation with the American colonies, whose leaders realized that they might finally defeat their French neighbors. The French government was unwilling and unable to direct similar resources against the English in America. Their military administration was corrupt; the military and political command in Canada was divided; and the food supply to the French army failed. In September 1759, on the Plains of Abraham overlooking the valley of the Saint Lawrence River at Quebec City, the British army under General James Wolfe defeated the French under Lieutenant General Louis Joseph Montcalm. The French empire in Canada was coming to an end.

However, Pitt's colonial vision extended beyond the Saint Lawrence valley and the Great Lakes basin. The major islands of the French West Indies fell to the British fleets. Income from the sale of captured sugar helped finance the British war effort. British slave interests captured the bulk of the French slave trade. Between 1755 and 1760 the value of the French colonial trade fell by over 80 per cent. On the Indian subcontinent the British forces

581

*Empire, War,
and Colonial
Rebellion*

The Battle of the Plains of Abraham, 1759. The British victory at Quebec meant the end of French rule in Canada. [*Courtesy of the Trustees, National Maritime Museum, Greenwich, England*]

France Turns Over French Canada to Great Britain

The Treaty of Paris (1763) concluded the French and English portion of the Seven Years' War. In this particular clause the previously French portion of Canada was turned over to Great Britain.

His Most Christian Majesty [the King of France] renounces all pretensions which he has heretofore formed or might have formed to Nova Scotia or Acadia in all its parts, and guarantees the whole of it, and with all its dependencies, to the King of Great Britain: Moreover, His Most Christian Majesty cedes and guarantees to his said Britannic Majesty, in full right, Canada, with all its dependencies, as well as the island of Cape Breton, and all the other islands and coasts in the gulf and river of St. Laurence, and in general, everything that depends on the said countries, land, islands, and coasts, with the sovereignty, property, possession, and all rights acquired by treaty, or otherwise, which the Most Christian King and the Crown of France have had till now over the said countries, lands, is-lands, places, coasts, and their inhabitants, so that the Most Christian King cedes and makes over the whole to the said King, and to the Crown of Great Britain, and that in the most ample manner and form, without restriction, and without any liberty to depart from the said cession and guarantee under any pretence, or to disturb Great Britain in the possessions above mentioned. His Britannic Majesty, on his side, agrees to grant the liberty of the Catholic Religion, to the inhabitants of Canada: he will, in consequence, give the most precise and effectual orders, that his new Roman Catholic subjects may profess the worship of their religion according to the rights of the Romish Church, as far as the laws of Great Britain permit.

H. Butterfield (Ed.), *Select Documents of European History, 1715–1920* (London: Methuen, 1931), pp. 29–30.

under the command of Robert Clive defeated the French in 1757 at the Battle of Plassey. This victory opened the way for the eventual conquest of Bengal and later of all India by the British East India Company. Never had Great Britain or any other European power experienced such a complete worldwide military victory.

The Treaty of Paris of 1763 reflected somewhat less of a victory than Britain had won on the battlefield. Pitt was no longer in office. George III (1760–1820) had succeeded to the British throne in 1760. He and Pitt had quarreled over policy, and the minister had departed. His replacement was the earl of Bute, a favorite of the new monarch. The new minister was responsible for the peace settlement. Britain received all of Canada, the Ohio River valley, and the eastern half of the Mississippi River valley. Britain partially surrendered the conquest in India by giving France footholds at Pondicherry and Chandernagore. The sugar islands of Guadeloupe and Martinique were restored to the French. Britain could have gained more territory only with further war involving more taxation, against which the country was already complaining.

The Seven Years' War had been a vast conflict. Tens of thousands of soldiers had been killed or wounded. Major battles had been fought around the globe. At great internal sacrifice Prussia had permanently wrested Silesia from Austria and had turned the Holy Roman Empire into an empty shell. Habsburg power now depended largely on the Hungarian domains. France, though still possessing sources of colonial income, was no longer a great colonial power. The Spanish Empire remained largely intact, but the British were still determined to penetrate its markets. On the Indian subcontinent the British East India Company was in a position to continue to press against the decaying indigenous governments and to impose its own authority. The results of that situation would be felt until the middle of the twentieth century. In North America the Brit-

Fort William in Calcutta. This was the base from which Clive was able to conquer Bengal.
[*The British Library*]

ish government faced the task of organizing its new territories. From this time until World War II, Great Britain assumed the status not simply of a European but also of a world power.

The quarter century of warfare also caused a long series of domestic crises among the European powers. The French defeat convinced many people in the nation of the necessity of political and administrative reform. The financial burdens of the wars had astounded all contemporaries. Every power had to begin to find ways to increase revenues to pay its war debt and to finance its preparation for the next combat. Nowhere did this search for revenue lead to more far-ranging consequences than in the British colonies in North America.

CONFLICTS OF THE MID-EIGHTEENTH CENTURY	
Treaty of Utrecht	1713
Outbreak of War of Jenkins's Ear between England and Spain	1739
War of the Austrian Succession commences	1740
Treaty of Aix-la-Chapelle	1748
Convention of Westminster between England and Prussia	1756
Seven Years' War opens	1756
Battle of Plassey	1757
British forces capture Quebec	1759
Treaty of Hubertusburg	1763
Treaty of Paris	1763

The American Revolution and Europe

Events in the British Colonies

The revolt of the British colonies in North America was an event in transatlantic and European history. It erupted from problems of revenue collection common to all the major powers after the Seven Years' War. The War of the American Revolution was a continuation of the conflict between France and Great Britain. The French support of the Americans deepened the existing financial and administrative difficulties of the monarchy.

The political ideals of the Americans had roots in the thought of John Locke and other English political theorists. The colonists raised questions of the most profound nature about

583

MAP 16–2
NORTH AMERICA IN 1763

(diagonal hatching)	13 COLONIES
(vertical hatching)	INDIAN RESERVE
(horizontal hatching)	SPANISH LOUISIANA

It made rational sense that they should henceforth bear part of the cost of their protection and administration. The second problem was the vast expanse of new territory in North America that the British had to organize. This included all the land from the mouth of the Saint Lawrence River to the Mississippi River with its French settlers and, more important, its Indian possessors.

TAXATION AND RESISTANCE IN NORTH AMERICA. As the British ministers pursued solutions to these difficulties, a third and more serious issue arose. The British colonists in North America resisted taxation and were suspicious of the imperial policies toward the western lands. Consequently the British had to search for new ways to exert their authority over the colonies. The Americans became increasingly resistant because their economy had outgrown the framework of mercantilism, because the removal of the French relieved them of dependence on the British army, and because they believed that their liberty was in danger.

The British drive for revenue commenced in 1764 with the passage of the Sugar Act under the ministry of George Grenville (1712–1770). The measure attempted to produce more revenue from imports into the colonies by the rigorous collection of what was actually a lower tax. Smugglers who violated the law were to be tried in admiralty courts without juries. The next year Parliament passed the Stamp Act, which put a tax on legal documents and certain other items such as newspapers. The British considered these taxes legal because they had been passed by Parliament. The taxes seemed just because the money was to be spent in the colonies. The Americans responded that they had the right to tax themselves and that they were not represented in Parliament. The colonists quite simply argued there should be no taxation without representation. Moreover, because the king had granted most of the colonial charters, the Americans claimed that their legal connection to Britain was through the monarch rather than through the Parliament. The expenditure in the colonies of the revenue levied by Parliament did not reassure the colonists. They feared that if colonial government were financed from outside, they would lose control over their government. In October 1765 the Stamp Act Congress met in America and drew up a protest to the crown. There was much dis-

monarchy, political authority, and constitutionalism. These questions had ramifications for all European states. Part of the difficulties from the British side arose because of the characteristic European political friction between the monarch and the aristocracy. Finally, many Europeans saw the Americans as inaugurating a new era in the history of European peoples and indeed of the world.

After the Treaty of Paris of 1763 the British government faced three imperial problems. The first was the sheer cost of empire, which the British felt they could no longer carry alone. The national debt had risen considerably, as had taxation. The American colonies had been the chief beneficiaries of the conflict.

order in the colonies, particularly in Massachusetts. The colonists agreed to refuse to import British goods. In 1766 Parliament repealed the Stamp Act, but through the Declaratory Act it said that Parliament had the power to legislate for the colonies.

The Stamp Act crisis set the pattern for the next ten years. Parliament, under the leadership of a royal minister, would approve a piece of revenue or administrative legislation. The Americans would then resist by reasoned argument, economic pressure, and violence. Then the British would repeal the legislation, and the process would begin again. Each time, tempers on both sides became more frayed and positions more irreconcilable. In 1767 Charles Townshend (1725–1767), as Chancellor of the Exchequer, led Parliament to pass a series of revenue acts relating to colonial imports. The colonists again resisted. The ministry sent over its own customs agents to administer the laws. To protect these new officers, the British sent troops to Boston in 1768. The obvious tensions resulted, and in March 1770 the Boston Massacre, in which British troops killed five citizens, took place. That same year Parliament repealed all of the Townshend duties except for the one on tea.

This view of the "Boston Massacre" of March 5, 1770 by Paul Revere owes more to propaganda than fact. There was no order to fire and the innocent citizens portrayed here were really an angry, violent mob. [Library of Congress]

The "Boston Tea Party," December 16, 1773. This was a serious crime. When Parliament in response determined to teach the Americans a lesson, Britain and the colonies were put on a collision course that would lead to war and independence. [Library of Congress]

In May 1773 Parliament passed a new law relating to the sale of tea by the East India Company. The measure permitted the direct importation of tea into the American colonies. It actually lowered the price of tea while retaining the tax imposed without the colonists' consent. In some cities the colonists refused to permit the unloading of the tea; in Boston a shipload of tea was thrown into the harbor. The British ministry of Lord North (1732–1792) was determined to assert the authority of Parliament over the resistant colonies. During 1774 Parliament passed a series of laws known in American history as the Intolerable Acts. These measures closed the port of Boston, reorganized the government of Massachusetts, allowed troops to be quartered in private homes, and removed the trials of royal customs officials to England. The same year Parliament approved the Quebec Act for the future administration of that province. It extended the boundaries of Quebec to include the Ohio River valley. The Americans regarded the Que-

bec Act as an attempt to prevent the extension of their mode of self-government westward beyond the Appalachian Mountains.

During these years committees of correspondence composed of citizens critical of Britain had been established throughout the colonies. They made the various sections of the eastern seaboard aware of common problems and aided united action. In September 1774 these committees organized the gathering of the First Continental Congress in Philadelphia. This body hoped to persuade Parliament to restore self-government in the colonies and to abandon its attempt at direct supervision of colonial affairs. However, conciliation was not forthcoming. By April 1775 the battles of Lexington and Concord had been fought. In June the colonists suffered defeat at the Battle of Bunker Hill. Despite the defeat, the colonial assemblies soon began to meet under their own authority rather than under that of the king.

The Second Continental Congress gathered in May 1775. It still sought conciliation with

Britain, but the pressure of events led that assembly to begin to conduct the government of the colonies. By August 1775 George III had declared the colonies in rebellion. During the winter Thomas Paine's pamphlet *Common Sense* galvanized public opinion in favor of separation from Great Britain. A colonial army and navy were organized. In April 1776 the Continental Congress opened American ports to the trade of all nations. And on July 4, 1776, the Continental Congress adopted the Declaration of Independence. Thereafter the War of the American Revolution continued until 1781, when the forces of George Washington defeated those of Lord Cornwallis at Yorktown. However, early in 1778 the war had widened

The Second Continental Congress voting independence, July 4, 1776. [Library of Congress]

into a European conflict when Benjamin Franklin persuaded the French government to support the rebellion. In 1779 the Spanish also came to the aid of the colonies. The 1783 Treaty of Paris concluded the conflict, and the thirteen American colonies had established their independence.

This series of events is generally familiar to American readers. The relationship of the American Revolution to European affairs and the European roots of the American revolutionary ideals are less familiar.

NEW IDEOLOGY. The political theory of the American Declaration of Independence derived from the writings of seventeenth-century English Whig theorists, such as John Locke, and eighteenth-century Scottish moral philosophers, such as Francis Hutcheson. Their political ideas had arisen in large measure out of the struggle of seventeenth-century English aristocrats and gentry against the absolutism of

the Stuarts. The American colonists looked to the English Revolution of 1688 as having established many of their own fundamental political liberties as well as those of the English. The colonists claimed that through the measures imposed from 1763 to 1776, George III and the British Parliament had attacked those liberties and dissolved the bonds of moral and political allegiance that had formerly united the two peoples. Consequently the colonists employed a theory that had developed to justify an aristocratic rebellion in order to support their own popular revolution.

These Whig political ideas were only a part of the English ideological heritage that affected the Americans. Throughout the eighteenth century they had become familiar with a series of British political writers called the *Commonwealthmen*. They held republican political ideas and had their intellectual roots in the most radical thought of the Puritan revolution. During the early eighteenth century these writers had relentlessly criticized the government patronage and parliamentary management of Robert Walpole and his successors. They argued that such government was corrupt and that it undermined liberty. They regarded much parliamentary taxation as simply a means of financing political corruption. They also attacked standing armies, which they considered instruments of tyranny. In Great Britain this political tradition had only a marginal impact. The writers were largely ignored because most British subjects regarded themselves as the freest people in the world. However, over three thousand miles away in the colonies, these radical books and pamphlets were read widely and were often accepted at face value. The events in Great Britain following the accession of King George III made many colonists believe that the worst fears of the Commonwealth writers were coming true.

Events in Great Britain

George III (1760–1820) believed that his two immediate royal predecessors had been improperly bullied and controlled by their ministers. Royal power had in effect amounted to little more than the policies carried out by a few powerful Whig families. The new king intended to rule through Parliament, but he was determined to have ministers of his own choice. Moreover George III believed that Parliament should function under royal rather than aristocratic management. When William

George III (1760–1820). Although he never sought to make himself a tyrant as his critics charged, George did try to reassert the political influence of the monarchy which had been eroded under the first two Hanoverian kings, George I and George II. [New York Public Library]

Pitt resigned after a disagreement with George over war policy, the king appointed the earl of Bute as his first minister. In doing so, he ignored the great Whig families that had run the country since 1715. The king sought the aid of politicians whom the Whigs hated. Moreover he attempted to use the same kind of patronage techniques developed by Walpole to achieve royal control of the House of Commons.

Between 1761 and 1770 George tried one minister after another, but each in turn failed to gain sufficient support from the various factions in the House of Commons. Finally, in 1770 he turned to Lord North (1732–1792), who remained the king's first minister until 1782. The Whig families and other political spokesmen claimed that George III was attempting to impose a tyranny. What they meant was that the king was attempting to curb the power of a particular group of the aristocracy. George III certainly was seeking to restore more royal influence to the government of Great Britain, but he was not attempting to make himself a tyrant.

THE CHALLENGE OF JOHN WILKES. Then, in 1763, began the affair of John Wilkes (1725–1797). This London political radical and member of Parliament published a newspaper called *The North Briton*. In issue Number 45 of this paper Wilkes strongly criticized Lord Bute's handling of the peace negotiations with France. Wilkes was arrested under the authority of a general warrant issued by the secretary of state. He pled the privileges of a member of Parliament and was released. The courts also later ruled that the vague kind of general warrant by which he had been arrested was illegal. However, the House of Commons ruled that issue Number 45 of *The North Briton* was a libel and expelled Wilkes from the Commons. He soon fled the country and was outlawed. Throughout these procedures there was very widespread support for Wilkes, and many demonstrations were held in his cause.

In 1768 Wilkes returned to England and again stood for election to Parliament. He won the election, but the House of Commons, under the influence of George III's friends, refused to seat him. He was elected three more times. After the fourth election the House of Commons simply ignored the election results and seated the government-supported candidate. As earlier in the decade, large popular demonstrations of shopkeepers, artisans, and

This satirical portrait of John Wilkes was made by William Hogarth. It suggests the unattractive personal character of Wilkes and also tends to question the sincerity of his calls for liberty. [Charles Farrell Collection]

small property owners supported Wilkes. He also received aid from some aristocratic politicians who wished to humiliate George III. Wilkes himself contended during all of his troubles that his cause was the cause of English liberty. "Wilkes and Liberty" became the slogan of all political radicals and many noble opponents of the monarch. Wilkes was finally seated in 1774, after having become the lord mayor of London.

The American colonists followed all of these developments of the 1760s very closely. The contemporary events in Britain confirmed their fears about a monarchical and parliamentary conspiracy against liberty. The king, as their Whig friends told them, was behaving like a tyrant. The Wilkes affair displayed the arbitrary power of the monarch, the corruption of the House of Commons, and the contempt of both for popular electors. That same monarch and Parliament were attempting to overturn the

589

Major Cartwright Calls for the Reform of Parliament

During the years of the American Revolution there were many demands in England itself for a major reform of Parliament. In this pamphlet of 1777 Major John Cartwright demanded that a much larger number of English citizens be allowed to vote for members of the House of Commons. He also heaped contempt on the opponents of reform.

Suffering as we do, from a deep parliamentary corruption, it is no time to tamper with silly correctives, and trifle away the life of public freedom: but we must go to the bottom of the stinking sore and cleanse it thoroughly: we must once more infuse into the constitution the vivifying spirit of liberty and expel the very last dregs of this poison. Annual parliaments *with an* equal representation of the commons *are the only specifics in this case: and they would effect a radical cure. That a house of commons, formed as ours is, should maintain septennial elections, and laugh at every other idea is no wonder. The wonder is, that the British nation which, but the other day, was the greatest nation on earth, should be so easily laughed out of its liberties. . . .*

Those who now claim the exclusive *right of* sending to parliament the 513 representatives for about six million souls (amongst whom are one million five hundred thousand males, competent as electors) consist of about two hundred and fourteen thousand persons; and 254 of these representatives are elected by 5,723. . . . Their pretended rights are many of them, derived from royal favour; some from antient usage and prescription; and some indeed from act of parliament; but neither the most authentic acts of royalty, nor precedent, nor prescription, nor even parliament can establish any flagrant injustice; much less can they strip one million two hundred and eighty six thousand of an inalienable right, to vest it in a number amounting to only one seventh of that multitude. . . .*

John Cartwright, *Legislative Rights of the Commonality Vindicated,* cited in S. Maccoby, *The English Radical Tradition, 1763–1914* (London: Adam and Charles Black, 1966), pp. 32–33.

traditional relationship of Great Britain to its colonies by imposing parliamentary taxes. The same government had then landed troops in Boston, changed the government of Massachusetts, and undermined the traditional right of jury trial. All of these events fulfilled too exactly the portrait of political tyranny that had developed over the years in the minds of articulate colonists.

MOVEMENT FOR PARLIAMENTARY REFORM IN BRITAIN. The political influences between America and Britain operated both ways. The colonial demand for no taxation without representation and the criticism of the adequacy of the British system of representation struck at the core of the eighteenth-century British political structure. Colonial arguments could be adopted by British subjects at home who were no more directly repre-

sented in the House of Commons than were the Americans. The colonial questioning of the taxing authority of the House of Commons was related to the protest of John Wilkes. Both the Americans and Wilkes were challenging the power of the monarch and the authority of Parliament. Moreover both the colonial leaders and Wilkes appealed over the head of legally constituted political authorities to popular opinion and popular demonstrations. Both were protesting the power of a largely self-selected aristocratic political body. The British ministry was fully aware of these broader implications of the American troubles.

The American colonists also demonstrated to Europe how a politically restive people in the old regime could fight tyranny and protect political liberty. They established revolutionary but orderly political bodies that could function outside the existing political framework. These revolutionary political institutions were the congress and the convention. These began with the Stamp Act Congress of 1765 and culminated in the Constitutional Convention of 1787. The legitimacy of those congresses and conventions lay not in existing law but in the alleged consent of the governed. This approach represented a new way to found a government.

Toward the end of the War of the American Revolution, calls for parliamentary reform were voiced in Britain itself. The method proposed for changing the system was the extralegal Association Movement.

By the close of the 1770s there was much resentment in Britain about the mismanagement of the war, the high taxes, and Lord North's ministry. In northern England in 1778 Christopher Wyvil (1740–1822), a landowner and retired clergyman, organized the Yorkshire Association Movement. Property owners or freeholders of Yorkshire met in a mass meeting to demand rather moderate changes in the corrupt system of parliamentary elections. They organized corresponding societies elsewhere. They intended that the association examine—and suggest reforms for—the entire government. The Association Movement was thus a popular attempt to establish an extralegal institution to reform the government. The movement collapsed during the early 1780s because its supporters, unlike Wilkes and the American rebels, were not willing to appeal for broad popular support. Nonetheless the agitation of the Association Movement provided many people with experience in political protest. Several of its younger figures lived to raise the issue of parliamentary reform after 1815.

Parliament was not insensitive to the demands of the Association Movement. In April 1780 the Commons passed a resolution that called for lessening the power of the crown. In 1782 Parliament adopted a measure for "economical" reform, which abolished some patronage at the disposal of the monarch. However, these actions did not prevent George III from appointing a minister of his own choice. In 1783 shifts in Parliament obliged Lord North to form a ministry with Charles James Fox (1749–1806), a long-time critic of George III. The monarch was most unhappy with the arrangement. In 1783 he approached William Pitt the Younger (1759–1806), son of the victorious war minister, to manage the House of Commons. During the election

EVENTS IN BRITAIN AND AMERICA RELATING TO THE AMERICAN REVOLUTION	
George III ascends the English throne	1760
Treaty of Paris concludes the Seven Years' War	1763
John Wilkes publishes issue Number 45 of *The North Briton*	1763
Sugar Act	1764
Stamp Act	1765
Stamp Act repealed and Declaratory Act passed	1766
Townshend Acts	1767
Parliament refuses to seat John Wilkes after his election	1768
Lord North becomes George III's chief minister	1770
Boston Massacre	1770
Boston Tea Party	1773
Intolerable Acts	1774
First Continental Congress	1774
Second Continental Congress	1775
Declaration of Independence	1776
France enters the war on the side of America	1778
Yorkshire Association Movement founded	1778
British forces surrender at Yorktown	1781
Treaty of Paris concludes War of the American Revolution	1783

of 1784 Pitt received immense patronage support from the crown and constructed a House of Commons favorable to the king. Thereafter Pitt sought to formulate trade policies that would give his ministry broad popularity. He attempted in 1785 one measure of modest parliamentary reform. When it failed, the young prime minister, who had been only twenty-four at the time of his appointment, abandoned the cause of reform.

By the mid-1780s George III had achieved a part of what he had sought beginning in 1761. He had reasserted the influence of the monarchy in political affairs. It proved a temporary victory because his own mental illness, which would finally require a regency, weakened the royal power. The cost of his years of dominance had been very high. On both sides of the Atlantic the issue of popular sovereignty had been raised and widely discussed. The American colonies had been lost. Economically this loss did not prove disastrous. British trade with America after independence actually increased. However, the Americans—through the state constitutions, the Articles of Confederation, and the federal Constitution—had

591

demonstrated to Europe the possibility of government without kings and without aristocracies. They had established the example of a nation in which written documents based on popular consent and popular sovereignty—rather than on divine law, natural law, tradition, or the will of kings—stood as the highest political and legal authority. Writers throughout western Europe sensed that a new kind of political era was dawning. It was to be an age of constituent assemblies, constitutions, and declarations of rights.

Colonies founded to serve the economic requirements of Britain and Europe repaid the debt by serving as laboratories for new political ideals and institutions. The ideas had generally been developed in Europe, but America was the place where most of them were initially put into practice. America for a time served as an experiment station for the advanced political ideas of Europe. Soon the ideas would find their way back to the lands of their origins.

Suggested Readings

B. BAILYN, *The Ideological Origins of the American Revolution* (1967). An important work illustrating the role of English radical thought in the perceptions of the American colonists.

C. BECKER, *The Declaration of Independence: A Study in the History of Political Ideas* (1922). An examination of the political and imperial theory of the Declaration.

J. BREWER, *Party Ideology and Popular Politics at the Accession of George III* (1976). An important series of essays on popular radicalism.

J. BROOKE, *King George III* (1972). The best recent biography.

H. BUTTERFIELD, *George III, Lord North, and the People, 1779–1780* (1949). Explores the domestic unrest in Britain during the American Revolution.

I. R. CHRISTIE, *Stress and Stability in Late Eighteenth-Century Britain: Reflections on the British Avoidance of Revolution* (1985). Thoughtful essays by one of the most important of eighteenth-century British historians.

D. B. DAVIS, *The Problem of Slavery in Western Culture* (1966). A brilliant and far-ranging discussion.

D. B. DAVIS, *The Problem of Slavery in the Age of Revolution, 1770–1823* (1975). A major work for both European and American history.

WALTER DORN, *Competition for Empire, 1740–1763* (1940). Still one of the best accounts of the mid-century struggle.

C. GIBSON, *The Aztecs Under Spanish Rule: A History of the Indians of the Valley of Mexico* (1964). An exceedingly interesting book.

C. GIBSON, *Spain in America* (1966). A splendidly clear and balanced discussion.

L. H. GIPSON, *The British Empire Before the American Revolution*, 13 vols. (1936–1967). A magisterial account of the mid-century wars from an imperial viewpoint.

L. HANKE, *Bartolomé de Las Casas: An Interpretation of His Life and Writings* (1951). A classic work.

F. KATZ, *The Ancient American Civilizations* (1972). An excellent introduction.

B. KEEN AND M. WASSERMAN, *A Short History of Latin America* (1984). A good survey with very helpful bibliographical guides.

J. LOCKHARDT AND S. B. SCHWARTZ, *Early Latin America: A History of Colonial Spanish America and Brazil* (1983). The new standard work.

R. LODGE, *Great Britain and Prussia in the Eighteenth Century* (1923). The standard account.

R. MIDDLETON, *The Bells of Victory: The Pitt-Newcastle Ministry and the Conduct of the Seven Years' War, 1757–1762* (1985). A careful study of the intricacies of eighteenth-century cabinet government that questions the centrality of Pitt's role in the British victory.

E. MORGAN AND H. MORGAN, *The Stamp Act Crisis* (1953). A lively account of the incident from the viewpoint of both the colonies and England.

J. B. OWEN, *The Eighteenth Century* (1974). A recent survey of British politics.

R. PARES, *War and Trade in the West Indies* (1936). Relates the West Indies to Britain's larger commercial and naval concerns.

R. PARES, *King George III and the Politicians* (1953). An important analysis of the constitutional and political structures.

J. H. PARRY, *Trade and Dominion: The European Overseas Empires in the Eighteenth Century* (1971). A comprehensive account with attention to the European impact on the rest of the world.

J. G. A. POCOCK, *The Machiavellian Moment: Florentine Political Thought and the Atlantic Republican Tradition* (1975). An exceedingly important book that traces the origins of Anglo-American radicalism to Renaissance Florence.

J. G. A. POCOCK, *Virtue, Commerce, and History: Essays on Political Thought and History, Chiefly in the Eighteenth Century* (1985). Important articles.

C. D. RICE, *The Rise and Fall of Black Slavery* (1975). An excellent survey of the subject with careful attention to the numerous historiographical controversies.

C. G. ROBERTSON, *Chatham and the British Empire* (1948). A brief study.

G. RUDÉ, *Wilkes and Political Liberty* (1962). A close analysis of popular political behavior.

S. J. AND B. H. STEIN, *The Colonial Heritage of Latin America: Essays on Economic Dependence in Perspective* (1970). An important work emphasizing the long-range impact of the colonial economy.

P. D. G. Thomas, *British Politics and the Stamp Act Crisis: The First Phase of the American Revolution, 1763–1767* (1975). An interesting work from the British point of view.

J. S. Watson, *The Reign of George III; 1760–1815* (1960). Covers the British domestic political scene in a traditional manner.

G. Wills, *Inventing America: Jefferson's Declaration of Independence* (1978). An important study that challenges much of the analysis in the Becker volume noted above.

G. S. Wood, *The Creation of the American Republic, 1776–1787* (1969). A far-ranging work dealing with Anglo-American political thought.

Enlightenment and Revolution in the West

ETWEEN APPROXIMATELY 1750 AND 1850, certain extraordinary changes occurred in Western civilization. Although of immediate significance primarily for the nations of Europe and the Americas, these developments produced in the long run an immense impact throughout the world. No other civilizations eventually escaped the influence of the European intellectual ferment and political turmoil of these years. Most of the intellectual, political, economic, and social characteristics associated with the *modern* world came into being during this era. Europe became the great exporter of ideas and technologies that in time transformed one area after another of the human experience.

Intellectually, the ideals of reform and of challenge to traditional cultural authority captured the imagination of numerous writers. That movement, known as the *Enlightenment,* drew confidence from the scientific worldview that had emerged during the seventeenth century. Its exponents urged the application of the spirit of critical rationalism in one area of social and political life after another. They posed serious historical and moral questions to the Christian faith. They contended that laws of society and economics could be discovered and could then be used to improve the human condition. They embraced the idea of economic growth and development. They called for political reform and more efficient modes of government. They upheld the standard of rationality in order to cast doubt on traditional modes of thought and behavior that seemed to them less than rational. As a result of their labors, in Europe and ultimately throughout the world, the idea of change that has played so important a role in modern life came for the first time to have a generally positive value attached to it.

For many people, however, change seemed to come too rapidly and violently when revolution erupted in France in 1789. Commencing as an aristocratic revolt against the monarchy, the revolution rapidly spread to every corner of French political and social life. The rights of man and citizen displaced those of the monarchy, the aristocracy, and the church. By 1792, the revolution had become a genuinely popular movement and had established a French republic whose armies challenged the other major European monarchies. The reign of terror that saw the execution of the French king unloosed domestic violence unlike anything witnessed in Europe since the age of the religious wars. By the end of the 1790s, to restore order, French political leaders turned themselves over to the leadership of Napoleon. Thereafter, for more than a decade, his armies uprooted institutions of the old regime across the continent. Only in 1815, after the battle of Waterloo, was the power of France and Napoleon finally contained.

The French Revolution in one way or another served as a model for virtually all later popular revolutions. It unleashed new forces and political creeds in one area of the world after another. The French Revolution, with its broad popular base, brought *the people* to the forefront of world political history. In the early revolutionary goals of establishing a legal framework of limited monarchical power, of securing citizen rights, and of making possible relatively free economic activity, the supporters of the revolution spawned the political creed of *liberalism.* The wars of the French Revolution and of Napoleon, stretching from 1792 to 1815, awakened the political force of *nationalism,* which has proved to be the single most powerful ideology of the modern world. Loyalty to the nation defined in terms of a common language, history, and culture replaced loyalty to dynasties. As a political ideology, nationalism could be used both to liberate a people from the domination of another nation and to justify wars of aggression. And nationalism was put to both uses in Europe and throughout the rest of the world in the two centuries following the revolution in France. Nationalism became a kind of secular religion that aroused a degree of loyalty and personal self-sacrifice previously called forth only by the great religious traditions.

Finally, between 1750 and 1850, Europe became not only an exporter of reform and revolution but also of manufactured commodities. The technology and the society associated with industrialism took root throughout the western portion of the continent. Europeans achieved a productive capacity that, in cooperation with their naval power, permitted them to dominate the markets of the world. Thereafter, to be strong, independent, and modern seemed to mean to become industrialized and to imitate the manufacturing techniques of Europe and later of the United States.

But industrialism and its society fostered immense social problems, dislocations, and injustices. The major intellectual and political response was *socialism,* several varieties of which emerged from the European social and economic turmoil of the 1830s and 1840s. History eventually proved the most important of these to be that espoused by Karl Marx, whose *Communist Manifesto* appeared in 1848.

Remarkable ironies are attached to the European achievements of the late eighteenth and the early nineteenth centuries. Enlightenment, revolution, and industrialism contributed to an awakening of European power that permitted the continent to dominate the world for a time at the end of the nineteenth century. Yet those same movements fostered various intellectual critiques, political ideas, and economic skills that twentieth-century non-European peoples would turn against their temporary European masters. It is for that reason that the age of enlightenment and revolution in the West was of such significance not simply in Europe but in the history of the entire modern world.

Denis Diderot (1713–1784), above, *and Jean d'Alembert (1717–1783),* below, *surrounded by the principal contributors to the* Encyclopedia. *Because it contained the most advanced critique of ideas in religion, government, and philosophy, the* Encyclopedia *was bitterly attacked by the Church and condemned by the state.* [Giraudon/Art Resource]

DURING THE EIGHTEENTH CENTURY the conviction began to spread throughout the literate sectors of European society that change and reform were both possible and desirable. This attitude is now commonplace, but it came into its own only after 1700. It represents one of the primary intellectual inheritances from that age. The movement of people and ideas that fostered such thinking is called the *Enlightenment*. Its leading voices combined confidence in the human mind inspired by the Scientific Revolution and faith in the power of rational criticism to challenge the intellectual authority of tradition and the Christian past. These writers stood convinced that human beings could comprehend the operation of physical nature and mold it to the ends of material and moral improvement. The rationality of the physical universe became a standard against which the customs and traditions of society could be measured and criticized. Such criticism penetrated every corner of contemporary society, politics, and religious opinion. As a result the spirit of innovation and improvement came to characterize modern European and Western society.

The *Philosophes*

The writers and critics who forged this new attitude and who championed change and reform were the *philosophes*. They were not usually philosophers in a formal sense; rather, they were people who sought to apply the rules of reason and common sense to nearly all the major institutions and social practices of the day. The most famous of their number included Voltaire, Montesquieu, Diderot, Rousseau, Hume, Gibbon, Smith, Bentham, Lessing, and Kant. A few of them occupied professorships in universities, but most were free agents who might be found in London coffeehouses, Edinburgh drinking spots, the salons of fashionable Parisian ladies, the country houses of reform-minded nobles, or the courts of the most powerful monarchs on the Continent. In eastern Europe persons of this outlook were often to be found in the royal bureaucracies. They were not an organized group; they disagreed on many issues. Their relationship with each other and with lesser figures of the same turn of mind has quite appropriately been compared with that of a fam-

17

The Age of Enlightenment: Eighteenth-Century Thought

ily, in which despite quarrels and tensions a basic unity still remains.[1]

The chief unity of the *philosophes* lay in their desire to reform thought, society, and government for the sake of human liberty. As Peter Gay has suggested, this goal included "freedom from arbitrary power, freedom of speech, freedom of trade, freedom to realize one's talents, freedom of aesthetic response, freedom, in a word, of moral man to make his way in the world."[2] No other single set of ideas has done so much to shape the modern world. The literary vehicles through which the *philosophes* delivered their message included books, pamphlets, plays, novels, philosophical treatises, encyclopedias, newspapers, and magazines. During the Reformation and the religious wars writers had used the printed word to debate the proper mode of faith in God. The *philosophes* of the Enlightenment employed the printed word to proclaim a new faith in the capacity of humankind to improve itself without the aid of God.

Many of the *philosophes* were middle class in their social origins. The bulk of their readership were also drawn from the prosperous commercial and professional people of the eighteenth-century towns and cities. These people discussed the reformers' writings and ideas in local philosophical societies, Freemason lodges, and clubs. They had sufficient income and leisure time to buy and read the *philosophes'* works. Although the writers of the Enlightenment did not consciously champion the goals or causes of the middle class, they did provide an intellectual ferment and a major source of ideas that could be used to undermine existing social practices and political structures. They taught their contemporaries how to pose pointed, critical questions. Moreover the *philosophes* generally supported the economic growth, the expansion of trade, and the improvement of transport that were transforming the society and the economy of the eighteenth century and that were enlarging the middle class.

Formative Influences

The Newtonian world view, the stability and prosperity of Great Britain after 1688, and the

[1] Peter Gay, *The Enlightenment: An Interpretation*, Vol. 1 (New York: Knopf, 1967), p. 4.
[2] Ibid, p. 3.

Edward Jenner (1749–1823), an English physician, discovered that by inoculating human beings with the relatively mild disease of cowpox he could make them immune to the dread disease of smallpox. That discovery eventually led to the complete removal of the danger of smallpox. [Culver Pictures]

degradation that the wars of Louis XIV had brought to France were the chief factors that fostered the discussion of reform throughout Europe.

Isaac Newton (1642–1727) and John Locke (1632–1704) were the major intellectual forerunners of the Enlightenment. Newton's formulation of the laws of universal gravitation exemplified the power of the human mind. His example and his writing encouraged Europeans to approach the study of nature directly and to avoid metaphysics and supernaturalism. Newton had formulated general laws but had always insisted on a foundation of specific empirical evidence for those laws. Empirical experience had provided a constant check on his rational speculation. This emphasis on concrete experience became a keystone for Enlightenment thought. Moreover Newton had discerned a pattern of rationality in natural physical phenomena. During the eighteenth century the ancient idea of following nature became transformed under the Newtonian influence into the idea of following reason. Because nature was rational, society should be organized in a rational manner.

As explained in Chapter 13, Newton's scientific achievement had inspired his fellow countryman John Locke to seek a human psychology based on experience. In *An Essay*

Concerning Human Understanding (1690), Locke argued that each human being enters the world as a *tabula rasa,* or blank page. His or her personality is consequently the product of the sensations that impinge from the external world throughout the course of life. The significant conclusion that followed from this psychology was that human naure is changeable and can be molded by modification of the surrounding physical and social environment. Locke's was a reformer's psychology. It suggested that improvement in the human situation was possible. Locke also, in effect, rejected the Christian view of humankind as creatures permanently flawed by sin. Human beings need not wait for the grace of God or other divine aid to better their lives. They could take charge of their own destiny.

Newton's physics and Locke's psychology provided the theoretical basis for reform. The domestic stability of Great Britain after the Revolution of 1688 furnished a living example of a society in which enlightened reforms functioned for the benefit of all concerned. England permitted religious toleration to all creeds except Unitarianism and Roman Catholicism, whose believers were not actually persecuted. Relative freedom of the press and free speech prevailed. The monarchy was limited in its au-thority, and political sovereignty resided in the Parliament. The courts protected citizens from arbitrary government action. The army was quite small. These liberal policies had produced not disorder and instability but economic prosperity and loyalty to the political system. The continental view of England was somewhat idealized; nevertheless the country was sufficiently freer than any other nation to make the point that the reformers sought.

If the example of Great Britain suggested that change need not be disastrous to a nation and society, France exhibited many of the practices and customs of European politics and society that most demanded reform. Louis XIV had built his power on the bases of absolute monarchy, a large standing army, heavy taxation, and a religious unity requiring persecution. However, the enemies of France had defeated that nation in war. Its people were miserable, and celebrations had marked the death of the great king. His successors had been unable to reform the state. Critics of the monarchy were subject to arbitrary arrest. There was no freedom of worship. Political and religious censors interfered with the press and other literary productions. Offending authors could be imprisoned, although some achieved cooperative relations with the authorities.

A gathering of philosophes *at the salon of Madame Geoffrin in 1755. The Parisian salons presided over by fashionable, intelligent women were the places where the ideas of the Enlightenment were discussed and propagated.* [Musée de Malmaison]

State regulations hampered economic growth. Many aristocrats regarded themselves as a military class and upheld militaristic values. Yet throughout the French social structure there existed people who wanted to see changes brought about. These people read and supported the *philosophes* of their nation and of other countries. Consequently France became the major center for the Enlightenment, for there, more than in any other state, the demand for reform daily confronted writers and political thinkers.

Stages of the Enlightenment

The movement that came to be known as the Enlightenment evolved over the course of the century and involved a number of writers living at different times in various countries. Its early exponents popularized the rationalism and scientific ideas of the seventeenth century. They worked to expose contemporary social and political abuses and argued that reform was necessary and possible. The advancement of their cause and ideas was anything but steady. They confronted the obstacles of vested interests, political oppression, and religious condemnation. Yet by the mid-century they had brought enlightened ideas to the European public in a variety of formats. The *philosophes'* "family" had come into being. They corresponded with each other, wrote for each other as well as for the general public, and defended each other against the political and religious authorities.

By the second half of the century they were sufficiently safe to quarrel among themselves on occasion. They had stopped talking in generalities, and their major advocates were addressing themselves to specific abuses. Their books and articles had become more specialized and more practical. They had become more concerned with politics than with religion. Having convinced Europeans that change was a good idea, they began to suggest exactly what changes were most desirable. They had become honored figures.

Voltaire

One of the earliest and by far the most influential of the *philosophes* was François Marie Arouet, known to posterity as Voltaire (1694–1778). During the 1720s Voltaire had offended the French authorities by certain of his writ-

The young Voltaire (1694–1778). Philosopher, dramatist, poet, historian, scientist—Voltaire was the most famous and influential of the eighteenth-century philosophes. [Bulloz] unfortunately died of yellow fever as pictured here?

ings, and he was arrested and put in prison for a brief time.

Later Voltaire went to England, where he visited in the best literary circles, observed the tolerant intellectual and religious climate, felt free in the atmosphere of moderate politics, and admired the science and the economic prosperity. In 1733 he published *Letters on the English,* which appeared in French the next year. The book praised the virtues of the English and indirectly criticized the abuses of French society. In 1738 he published *Elements of the Philosophy of Newton,* which popularized the thought of the great scientist. Both works were well received and gave Voltaire a reputation as an important writer.

Thereafter Voltaire lived part of the time in France and part near Geneva, just across the French border, where the royal authorities could not bother him. He wrote essays, history, plays, stories, and letters that made him the literary dictator of Europe. He brought the bitter venom of his satire and sarcasm against one evil after another in French and European life. His most famous satire is *Candide* (1759), in which he attacked war, religious persecution, and what he regarded as unwarranted optimism about the human condition. Like most *philosophes,* Voltaire believed that improvement of human society was necessary and possible. But he was never certain that reform, if

601

*The Age of
Enlightenment:
Eighteenth-
Century
Thought*

Voltaire Attacks Religious Fanaticism

The chief complaint of the *philosophes* against Christianity was that it bred a fanaticism that led people to commit crimes in the name of religion. In this passage from his *Philosophical Dictionary* (1764) Voltaire directly reminded his readers of the intolerance of the Reformation era and indirectly referred to examples of contemporary religious excesses. He argued that the philosophical spirit can overcome fanaticism and foster toleration and more humane religious behavior. In a manner that shocked many of his contemporaries, he praised the virtues of Confucianism over those of Christianity.

Fanaticism is to superstition what delirium is to fever and rage to anger. The man visited by ecstasies and visions, who takes dreams for realities and his fancies for prophecies, is an enthusiast; the man who supports his madness with murder is a fanatic. . . .

The most detestable example of fanaticism was that of the burghers of Paris who on St. Bartholomew's Night [1572] went about assassinating and butchering all their fellow citizens who did not go to mass, throwing them out of windows, cutting them in pieces.

Once fanaticism has corrupted a mind, the malady is almost incurable. . . .

The only remedy for this epidemic malady is the philosophical spirit which, spread gradually, at last tames men's habits and prevents the disease from starting; for once the disease has made any progress, one must flee and wait for the air to clear itself. Laws and religion are not strong enough against the spiritual pest; religion, far from being healthy food for infected brains, turns to poison in them. . . .

Even the law is impotent against these attacks of rage; it is like reading a court decree to a raving maniac. These fellows are certain that the holy spirit with which they are filled is above the law, that their enthusiasm is the only law they must obey.

What can we say to a man who tells you that he would rather obey God than men, and that therefore he is sure to go to heaven for butchering you?

Ordinarily fanatics are guided by rascals, who put the dagger into their hands; these latter resemble that Old Man of the Mountain who is supposed to have made imbeciles taste the joys of paradise and who promised them an eternity of the pleasures of which he had given them a foretaste, on condition that they assassinated all those he would name to them. There is only one religion in the world that has never been sullied by fanaticism, that of the Chinese men of letters. The schools of philosophy were not only free from this pest, they were its remedy; for the effect of philosophy is to make the soul tranquil, and fanaticism is incompatible with tranquility. If our holy religion has so often been corrupted by this infernal delirium, it is the madness of men which is at fault.

Voltaire, *Philosophical Dictionary*, trans. by P. Gay (New York: Harcourt, Brace, and World, 1962), pp. 267–269.

achieved, would be permanent. The optimism of the Enlightenment constituted a tempered hopefulness rather than a glib certainty. Pessimism provided an undercurrent to most of the works of the period.

Montesquieu

Among the other pioneers of the early Enlightenment, Charles Louis de Secondat, baron de Montesquieu (1689–1755), was outstanding. He was a lawyer, a noble of the robe, and a member of a provincial *parlement*. He also belonged to the Bordeaux Academy of Science, before which he presented papers on scientific topics. Although living comfortably within the bosom of French society, he saw the need for reform. In 1721 he published *The Persian Letters* to satirize contemporary institutions. The book consisted of letters purportedly written by two Persians visiting Europe. They explained to friends at home how European behavior contrasted with Persian life and customs. Behind the humor lay the cutting edge of criticism and an exposition of the cruelty and irrationality of much contemporary European life. In his most enduring work, *The Spirit of the Laws* (1748), Montesquieu held up the example of the British constitution as the wisest model for regulating the power of government. (We shall examine *The Spirit of the Laws* more closely later in this chapter.)

The Encyclopedia

The mid-century witnessed the publication of one of the greatest monuments of the Enlightenment. Under the heroic leadership of Denis Diderot (1713–1784), and Jean le Rond d'Alembert (1717–1783), the first volume of the *Encyclopedia* appeared in 1751. The project reached completion in 1772, numbering seventeen volumes of text and eleven of plates. The *Encyclopedia* was the product of the collective effort of more than one hundred authors, and its editors had at one time or another solicited articles from all the major French *philosophes*. The project reached fruition only after numerous attempts to censor it and to halt its publication. The *Encyclopedia* set forth the most advanced critical ideas in religion, government, and philosophy. This criticism often had to be hidden in obscure articles or under the cover of irony. The articles represented a collective plea for freedom of expression. However, the large volumes also provided important information on manufacturing, canal building, ship construction, and improved agriculture.

Between fourteen and sixteen thousand copies of various editions of the *Encyclopedia* were sold before 1789. The project had been designed to secularize learning and to undermine the intellectual assumptions remaining from the Middle Ages and the Reformation. The articles on politics, ethics, and society ignored concerns about divine law and concentrated on humanity and its immediate well-being. The encyclopedists looked to antiquity rather than to the Christian centuries for their intellectual and ethical models. The future welfare of humankind lay not in pleasing God or following divine commandments but rather in harnessing the power of the earth and its resources and in living at peace with one's fellow human beings. The good life lay here and now and was to be achieved through the application of reason to human relationships.

With the publication of the *Encyclopedia*, enlightened thought became more fully diffused over the Continent. Enlightened ideas penetrated German and Russian intellectual and political circles. The *philosophes* of the latter part of the century turned from championing the general cause of reform and discussed specific areas of practical application. Gotthold

The Encyclopedia *also contained much practical information. This engraving from the article on plumbing explains how to supply your bath with hot and cold water from taps. [New York Public Library]*

603

*The Age of
Enlightenment:
Eighteenth-
Century
Thought*

Analysis and classification were the hallmarks of Enlightenment science. Thus the French aristocrat Antoine Lavoisier (1743–1794), shown here conducting an experiment in respiration, classified the elements and discovered that human beings need oxygen to breathe. [Ann Ronan Picture Library]

Lessing (1729–1781) wrote plays to plead for religious toleration. Adam Smith (1723–1790) attacked the mercantile system. Cesare Beccaria (1738–1794) and Jeremy Bentham (1748–1832) called for penal and legal reforms. By this time the concepts of reform and the rationalization of existing institutions had become deeply impressed on European thinking and society. The issue then became—and would remain for over a century—how best to implement those reforms.

The Enlightenment and Religion

Throughout the century, in the eyes of the *philosophes* the chief enemy of the improvement of humankind and the enjoyment of happiness was the existence and influence of ecclesiastical institutions. The hatred of the *philosophes* for the church and Christianity was summed up in Voltaire's cry of "Crush the Infamous Thing." Almost all varieties of Christianity, but especially Roman Catholicism, invited the criticism of the *philosophes*.

Intellectually the churches perpetuated a religious rather than a scientific view of humankind and physical nature. The clergy taught that human beings were basically depraved and that they required divine grace to become worthy creatures. The doctrine of original sin in either its Catholic or its Protestant formulation suggested that meaningful improvement in human nature on earth was impossible. Religious concerns turned human interest away from this world to the world to come. In the view of the *philosophes* the concept of predestination suggested that the condition of the human soul after death had little or no relationship to virtuous living during this life. Through disagreements over obscure doctrines the various churches favored the politics of intolerance and bigotry that in the past had caused human suffering, torture, and war.

To attack the Christian churches in this manner was to raise major questions about the life and the society of the old regime. Politically and socially the churches were deeply enmeshed in the power structure. They owned large amounts of land and collected tithes from peasants before any other taxes were collected.

"The Three Imposters," an eighteenth-century attack on religion, inspired by the philosophes, *portrayed Moses, Christ, and Mohammed as imposters who had exploited the gullibility of the human race.* [New York Public Library]

Deism

The *philosophes* believed that religion should be reasonable and should lead to moral behavior. The Newtonian worldview had convinced many writers that nature was rational. Therefore the God who had created nature must also be rational, and the religion through which that God was worshiped should be rational. Moreover Lockean psychology, which limited human knowledge to empirical experience, raised the question whether such a thing as divine revelation to humankind was, after all, possible. These considerations gave rise to a movement for enlightened religion known as *deism.* The title of one of its earliest expositions, *Christianity Not Mysterious* (1696) by John Toland, indicates the general tenor of this religious outlook. Toland and later writers wished to consider religion a natural and rational, rather than a supernatural and mystical, phenomenon. In this respect the deists made a departure from the general piety of Newton and Locke, both of whom regarded themselves as distinctly Christian. Newton had believed that God might interfere with the natural order, whereas the deists regarded God as resembling a divine watchmaker who had set the mechanism of nature to work and had then departed from the scene.

There were two major points in the deists' creed. The first was a belief in the existence of God. They thought that this belief could be empirically deduced from the contemplation of nature. Joseph Addison's poem on the spacious firmament (1712), illustrates this idea:

> The spacious firmament on high,
> With all the blue ethereal sky,
> And spangled heav'n, a shining frame,
> Their great Original proclaim:
> Th' unwearied Sun, from day to day,
> Does his Creator's power display,
> And publishes to every land
> The work of an Almighty hand.

Because nature provided evidence of a rational God, that deity must also favor rational morality. Consequently the second point in the deists' creed was a belief in life after death, when rewards and punishments would be meted out according to the virtue of the life a person led on this earth.

Deism was empirical, tolerant, reasonable, and capable of encouraging virtuous living. It was the major positive religious component of the Enlightenment. Voltaire declared:

Most of the clergy were legally exempt from taxation and made only annual voluntary grants to the government. The upper clergy in most countries were relatives of aristocrats. Churchmen were actively involved in politics, serving in the British House of Lords and advising princes on the Continent. In Protestant countries the local clergyman of a particular parish was usually appointed by the local major landowner. Across the Continent membership in the predominant denomination of the kingdom gave certain subjects political advantages. Nonmembership often excluded other subjects from political participation. Clergymen of all faiths preached the sinfulness of political disobedience, and they provided the intellectual justification for the social and political status quo. They were active where possible in exerting religious and literary censorship. The churches were thus privileged and powerful corporate bodies of the old regime. The *philosophes* chose to attack both their ideas and their power.

The great name of Deist, which is not sufficiently revered, is the only name one ought to take. The only gospel one ought to read is the great book of Nature, written by the hand of God and sealed with his seal. The only religion that ought to be professed is the religion of worshiping God and being a good man.[3]

If such a faith became widely accepted, the fanaticism and rivalry of the various Christian sects might be overcome. Religious conflict and persecutions encouraged by the fulsome zeal would end. There would also be little or no necessity for a priestly class to foment fanaticism, denominational hatred, and bigotry.

The *philosophes* did not rest with the formulation of a rational religious alternative to Christianity. They also attacked the churches and the clergy with great vehemence. Voltaire repeatedly questioned the truthfulness of priests and the morality of the Bible. In his *Philosophical Dictionary* (1764) he humorously pointed out inconsistencies in biblical narratives and immoral acts of the biblical heroes. In the chapter "Of Miracles" published in 1748 as part of his *Inquiry into Human Nature*, the Scottish *philosophe* David Hume (1771–1776) argued that divine miracles, in which the churches put great store, were not grounded in rational belief or empirical evidence. For Hume, the greatest miracle was to believe in

[3] Quoted in J. H. Randall, *The Making of the Modern Mind*, rev. ed. (New York: Houghton Mifflin, 1940), p. 292.

David Hume (1711–1776), the Scottish philosopher, argued against belief in miracles and, implicitly, against belief in Christianity itself. [National Galleries of Scotland]

miracles. In *The Decline and Fall of the Roman Empire* (1776), Edward Gibbon (1737–1794), the English historian, examined the early history of Christianity and explained the rise of that faith in terms of natural causes rather than the influence of miracles and piety. A few *philosophes* went further. Baron d'Holbach (1723–1789) and Julien Offray de La Mettrie (1709–1751) embraced positions very near to atheism and materialism. Theirs was distinctly a minority position, however. Most of the *philosophes* sought not the abolition of religion but its transformation into a humane force that would encourage virtuous living.

Toleration

A primary social condition for such a life was the establishment of religious toleration. Again Voltaire took the lead in championing this cause. In 1762 the Roman Catholic political authorities in Toulouse ordered the execution of a Huguenot named Jean Calas. He stood accused of having murdered his son to prevent him from converting to Roman Catholicism. Calas had been viciously tortured and publicly strangled without ever having confessed his guilt. The confession would not have saved his life, but it would have given the Catholics good propaganda to use against Protestants.

Voltaire learned of the case only after Calas's death. He made the dead man's cause his own. In 1763 he published a *Treatise on Tolerance* and hounded the authorities for a new investigation. Finally, in 1765, the judicial decision against the unfortunate man was reversed. For Voltaire the case illustrated the fruits of religious fanaticism and the need for rational reform of judicial processes. Somewhat later in the century, the German playwright and critic Gotthold Lessing (1729–1781) wrote *Nathan the Wise* (1779) as a plea for toleration not only of different Christian sects but also of religious faiths other than Christianity. All of these calls for toleration stated, in effect, that life on earth and human relationships should not be subordinated to religion. Secular values and considerations were more important than religious ones.

The Enlightenment and Society

Although the *philosophes* wrote much on religion, humanity was the center of their interest.

Beccaria Objects to Capital Punishment as Unenlightened

In the eighteenth century the death penalty was commonly applied throughout Europe for small as well as great crimes. The young north Italian nobleman Cesare Beccaria thought the penalty was unproductive of law and order and was also unenlightened. *On Crimes and Punishments* appeared when he was only twenty-six, and Voltaire, Bentham, and Catherine the Great professed to admire the work. His 1764 comments are a good example of the Enlightenment application of the criteria of reason and utility to social problems.

Is the death penalty really useful and necessary for the security and good order of society? Are torture and torments just, and do they attain the end for which laws are instituted? What is the best way to prevent crimes? Are the same punishments equally effective for all times? What influence have they on customary behavior? These problems deserve to be analyzed with that geometric precision which the mist of sophisms, seductive eloquence, and timorous doubt cannot withstand. . . . If, by defending the rights of man and of unconquerable truth, I should help to save from the spasm and agonies of death some wretched victim of tyranny or of no less fatal ignorance, the thanks and tears of one innocent mortal in his transports of joy would console me for the contempt of all mankind.

. . . .

If one were to cite against me the example of all the ages and of almost all the nations that *have applied the death penalty to certain crimes, my reply would be that the example reduced itself to nothing in the face of truth, against which there is no prescription; that the history of men leaves us with the impression of a vast sea of errors; among which, at great intervals, some rare and hardly intelligible truths appear to float on the surface. Human sacrifices were once common to almost all nations, yet who will dare to defend them? That only a few societies, and for a short time only, have abstained from applying the death penalty, stands in my favor rather than against me, for that conforms with the usual lot of great truths, which are about as long-lasting as a lightning flash in comparison with the long dark night that envelops mankind. The happy time has not yet arrived in which truth shall be the portion of the greatest number, as error has heretofore been.*

Cesare Beccaria, *On Crimes and Punishments*, trans. by Henry M. Paolucci (Indianapolis: Bobbs-Merrill, 1963), pp. 10, 51.

As one writer in the *Encyclopedia* observed, "Man is the unique point to which we must refer everything, if we wish to interest and please amongst considerations the most arid and details the most dry."[4] The *philosophes* believed that the application of human reason to society would reveal laws in human relationships similar to those found in physical nature. Although the term did not appear until later, the idea of social science originated with the Enlightenment. The purpose of discovering social laws was the removal of the inhumanity that existed through ignorance of them. These

[4] Quoted in F. L. Baumer, *Main Currents of Western Thought*, 4th ed. (New Haven, Conn.: Yale University Press, 1978), p. 374.

concerns became especially evident in the work of the *philosophes* on law and prison procedures.

Beccaria

In 1764 Cesare Beccaria (1738–1794), an Italian *philosophe*, published *On Crimes and Punishments*, in which he applied critical analysis to the problem of making punishments both effective and just. He wanted the laws of monarchs and legislatures—that is, positive law—to conform with the rational laws of nature. He rigorously and eloquently attacked both torture and capital punishment. He thought that the criminal justice system should ensure speedy trial, sure punishment, and punishment intended to deter further crime. The purpose of laws was not to impose the will of God or some other ideal of perfection; its purpose was to secure the greatest good or happiness for the greatest number of human beings. This utilitarian philosophy based on happiness in this life permeated most of the Enlightenment writing on practical reforms.

Bentham

Although utilitarianism did not originate with him, it is particularly associated with the English legal reformer Jeremy Bentham (1748–1832). He sought to create codes of scientific law that were founded on the principle of utility, that is, the greatest happiness for the greatest number. In the *Fragment on Government* (1776) and *The Principles of Morals and Legislation* (1789), Bentham explained that the application of the principle of utility would overcome the special interests of privileged groups who prevented rational government. Bentham regarded the existing legal and judicial systems as burdened by traditional practices that harmed the very people whom the law should serve. The application of reason and utility would remove the legal clutter that prevented justice from being realized.

The Physiocrats

Another area of social relationships where the *philosophes* saw existing legislation and administration preventing the operation of natural social laws was the field of economic policy. They believed that mercantilist legislation and the labor regulations established by various governments and guilds actually hampered the expansion of trade, manufacture, and agriculture. In France these economic reformers were called the *physiocrats*. Their leading spokesmen were François Quesnay (1694–1774) and Pierre Dupont de Nemours (1739–1817). They believed that the primary role of government was to protect property and to permit freedom in the use of property. They particularly felt that all economic production was dependent on sound agriculture, and they favored the consolidation of small peasant holdings into larger, more efficient farms. Here as elsewhere there was a close relationship between the rationalism of the Enlightenment and the spirit of improvement at work in eighteenth-century European economic life.

Adam Smith

The most important Enlightenment exposition of economics was Adam Smith's (1723–1790) *Inquiry into the Nature and Causes of the Wealth of Nations* (1776). Smith, who was for a time a professor at Glasgow, urged that the mercantile system of England—including the navigation acts, the bounties, most tariffs, special trading monopolies, and the domestic regulation of labor and manufacture—be abolished. Smith believed that these modes of economic regulation by the state interfered with the natural system of economic liberty. They were intended to preserve the wealth of the nation, to capture wealth from other nations, and to assure a maximum amount of work for the laborers of the country. However, Smith regarded such regulations as preventing the wealth and production of the country from expanding. He wanted to encourage economic growth and a consumer-oriented economy. The means to those ends was the unleashing of individuals to pursue their own selfish economic interest. The free pursuit of economic self-interest would ensure economic expansion as each person sought enrichment by meeting the demands of the marketplace. Consumers would find their wants met as manufacturers and merchants sought their business.

Smith's book challenged the concept of scarce goods and resources that lay behind mercantilism and the policies of the guilds. Smith saw the realm of nature as a boundless expanse of water, air, soil, and minerals. The physical resources of the earth seemed to demand exploitation for the enrichment and comfort of humankind. In effect, Smith was saying that the nations and peoples of Europe need not be poor. The idea of the infinite use of nature's goods for the material benefit of humankind—a concept that has dominated Western life until recent years—stemmed directly from the Enlightenment. When Smith wrote, the population of the world was smaller, its people were poorer, and the quantity of undeveloped resources per capita was much greater. For people of the eighteenth century it was in the uninhibited exploitation of natural resources that the true improvement of the human condition seemed to lie.

Smith is usually regarded as the founder of *laissez-faire* economic thought and policy, which has argued in favor of a very limited role for the government in economic life and regulation. However, *The Wealth of Nations* was a

very complex book. Smith was no simple dogmatist. For example, he was not opposed to all government activity touching on the economy. The state should provide schools, armies, navies, and roads. It should also undertake certain commercial ventures, such as the opening of dangerous new trade routes that were eco-

Adam Smith was one of the most important members of what may be called the Class of 1776—the astonishing outburst of British historical writing that centered on that year. In addition to Smith's Inquiry into the Nature and Causes of the Wealth of Nations, *Gibbon published the first volume of* The Decline and Fall, *Dr. Charles Burney (1726–1814) published the first volume of* A General History of Music *(completed in 1789), and Sir John Hawkins (1719–1789) managed to publish the entire five volumes of his* A General History of the Science and Practice of Music. *Moreover, in 1774, Thomas Warton (1728–1790) published the first volume of* The History of English Poetry *(third volume 1781; never completed), while in 1777 the Scottish historian William Robertson (1721–1793) finished his career with the publication of* History of America. *[Culver Pictures]*

Adam Smith Argues for Individual Industry and Wealth

Adam Smith (1723–1790) wanted to see a general, though not complete, application of individual self-interest to economic activity in place of existing mercantilist policies of state regulation. As he explained in this famous passage from *The Wealth of Nations* (1776), he thought that basically unregulated individual economic actions would produce more goods and services than mercantilist policy.

The annual revenue of every society is always precisely equal to the exchangeable value of the whole annual produce of its industry, or rather is precisely the same thing with that exchangeable value. As every individual, therefore, endeavours as much as he can both to employ his capital in the support of domestic industry, and so to direct that industry that its produce may be of the greatest value; every individual necessarily labours to render the annual revenue of the society as great as he can. He generally, indeed, neither intends to promote the public interest, nor knows how much he is promoting it. By preferring the support of domestic to that of foreign industry, he intends only his own security; and by directing that industry in such a manner as its produce may be of the greatest value, he intends only his own gain, and he is in this, as in many other cases, led by an invisible hand to promote an end which was no part of his intention. Nor is it always the worse for the society that it was no part of it. By pursuing his own interest he frequently promotes that of the society more effectually than when he really intends to promote it. I have never known much good done by those who affected to trade for the public good.

Adam Smith, *The Wealth of Nations* (New York: Modern Library, 1965), p. 423.

nomically desirable but the expense or risk of which discouraged private enterprise. His reasonable tone and recognition of the complexity of social and economic life displayed a very important point about the *philosophes*. Most of them were much less rigid and doctrinaire than any brief summary of their thought may tend to suggest. They recognized the passions of humanity as well as its reason. They adopted reason and nature as tools of criticism through which they might create a climate of opinion that would allow the fully developed human personality to flourish.

Political Thought of the *Philosophes*

Nowhere did the appreciation of the complexity of the problems of contemporary society become more evident than in the *philosophes'* political thought. Nor did any other area of their reformist enterprise so clearly illustrate the tension and conflict within the "family" of the Enlightenment. Most *philosophes* were discontent with certain political features of their countries, but they were especially discontented in France. There the corruptness of the royal court, the blundering of the bureaucracy, the less than glorious mid-century wars, and the power of the church compounded all problems. Consequently it was in France that the most important political thought of the Enlightenment occurred. However, the French *philosophes* stood quite divided as to the proper solution. Their attitudes spanned the whole spectrum from aristocratic reform to democracy to absolute monarchy.

The Spirit of the Laws

Montesquieu's *The Spirit of the Laws* (1748) may well have been the single most influential book of the century. It is a work that exhibits the internal tensions of the Enlightenment. Montesquieu pursued an empirical method, taking illustrative examples from the political experience of both ancient and modern nations. From these he concluded that there could be no single set of political laws that applied to all peoples at all times and in all places. Rather, there existed a large number of political variables, and the good political life depended on the relationship of those variables. Whether a monarchy or a republic was the best form of government was a matter of the size of

the political unit and its population, its social and religious customs, its economic structure, its traditions, and its climate. Only a careful examination and evaluation of these elements could reveal what mode of government would prove most beneficial to a particular people. A century later such speculations would have been classified as sociology.

So far as France was concerned, Montesquieu had some rather definite ideas. He believed in monarchical government, but with a monarchy whose power was tempered and limited by various sets of intermediary institutions. The latter included the aristocracy, the towns, and the other corporate bodies that enjoyed particular liberties that the monarch must respect. These corporate bodies might be said to represent various segments of the general population and thus of public opinion. In France he regarded the aristocratic courts, or *parlements*, as the major example of an intermediary association. Their role was to limit the power of the monarchy and thus to preserve the liberty of the subjects. In championing these aristocratic bodies and the general role of the aristocracy, Montesquieu was a political conservative. However, he adopted that stance in the hope of achieving reform, for in his opinion it was the oppressive and inefficient absolutism of the monarchy that accounted for the degradation of French life.

One of Montesquieu's most influential ideas

Charles de Secondat, Baron de Montesquieu (1689–1744) was the author of The Spirit of the Laws, *which may well have been the most influential work of political thought of the eighteenth century. [Bulloz]*

Montesquieu Defends the Separation of Powers

The Spirit of the Laws (1748) was probably the most influential political work of the Enlightenment. In this passage Montesquieu explained how the division of powers within a government would make that government more moderate and would protect the liberty of its subjects. This idea was adopted by the writers of the United States Constitution when they devised the checks and balances of the three branches of government.

Democratic and aristocratic states are not in their own nature free. Political liberty is to be found only in moderate governments; and even in these it is not always found. It is there only when there is no abuse of power. But constant experience shows us that every man invested with power is apt to abuse it, and to carry his authority as far as it will go. . . .

To prevent this abuse, it is necessary from the very nature of things that power should be a check to power. . . .

In every government there are three sorts of power: the legislative; the executive in respect to things dependent on the law of nations; and the executive in regard to matters that depend on the civil law [the realm of the judiciary]. . . .

The political liberty of the subject is a tranquillity of mind arising from the opinion each person has of his safety. In order to have this liberty, it is requisite that government be so constituted as one man need not be afraid of another.

When the legislative and executive powers are united in the same person, or in the same body of magistrates, there can be no liberty; because apprehensions may arise, lest the same monarch or senate should enact tyrannical laws, to execute them in a tyrannical manner.

Again, there is no liberty, if the judiciary power be not separated from the legislative and executive. Were it joined with the legislative, the life and liberty of the subject would be exposed to arbitrary control; for the judge would be then the legislator. Were it joined to the executive power, the judge might behave with violence and oppression.

There would be an end of everything, were the same man or the same body, whether of the nobles or of the people, to exercise those three powers, that of enacting laws, that of executing the public resolutions, and of trying the causes of individuals.

Baron de Montesquieu, *The Spirit of the Laws,* trans. by Thomas Nugent (New York: Hafner Press, 1949), pp. 150–152.

was that of division of power within any government. For his model of a government with power wisely separated among different branches, he took contemporary Great Britain. There he believed he had found a system in which executive power resided in the king, legislative power in the Parliament, and judicial power in the courts. He thought any two branches could check and balance the power of the other. His perception of the eighteenth-century British constitution was incorrect because he failed to see how patronage and electoral corruption allowed a handful of powerful aristocrats to dominate the government. Moreover he was also unaware of the emerging cabinet system, which meant that the executive power was slowly becoming a creature of the Parliament. Nevertheless the analysis illustrated Montesquieu's strong sense of the need to limit the exercise of power through constitutionalism and the formation of law by legislatures rather than by monarchs. In this manner, although Montesquieu set out to defend the political privileges of the French aristocracy, his ideas had a profound and still-lasting effect on the liberal democracies of the next two centuries.

Rousseau

Jean-Jacques Rousseau (1712–1778) held a view of the exercise and reform of political power quite different from Montesquieu's.

Rousseau was a strange, isolated genius who never felt particularly comfortable with the other *philosophes.* Yet perhaps more than any other writer of the mid-eighteenth century he transcended the thought and values of his own time. Rousseau had a deep antipathy toward the world and the society in which he lived. It seemed impossible for human beings living according to contemporary commercial values to achieve moral, virtuous, or sincere lives. In 1750, in his *Discourse on the Moral Effects of the Arts and Sciences,* he contended that the process of civilization and enlightenment had corrupted human nature. Human beings in the state of nature had been more dignified. In 1755, in a *Discourse on the Origin of Inequality,* Rousseau blamed much of the evil in the world on maldistribution of property.

In both works Rousseau brilliantly and directly challenged the social fabric of the day. He drew into question the concepts of material and intellectual progress and the morality of a society in which commerce and industry were regarded as the most important of human activities. He felt that the real purpose of society was to nurture better people. In this respect Rousseau's vision of reform was much more radical than that of other contemporary writers. The other *philosophes* believed that human life would be improved if people could enjoy more of the fruits of the earth or could produce more goods. Rousseau raised the more fundamental question of what the good life is. This question has haunted European social thought ever since the eighteenth century. Much of the criticism of Europe's post–World War II society is rooted in this Rousseauean approach.

Rousseau carried these same concerns into his political thought. His most extensive discussion of politics appeared in *The Social Contract* (1762). Although the book attracted rather little immediate attention, by the end of the century it was widely read in France. *The Social Contract,* as compared to Montesquieu's *Spirit of the Laws,* is a very abstract book. It does not propose specific reforms but outlines the kind of political structure that Rousseau believed would overcome the evils of contemporary politics and society.

In the tradition of Thomas Hobbes and John Locke, most eighteenth-century political thinkers regarded human beings as individuals and society as a collection of such independent individuals pursuing personal, selfish goals. These writers wished to liberate these individuals from the undue bonds of government. Rousseau picked up the stick from the other end. His book opens with the declaration, "All men are born free, but everywhere

Jean-Jacques Rousseau (1712–1778). His writings raised some of the most profound social and ethical questions of the Enlightenment. [Metropolitan Museum of Art]

they are in chains."[5] The rest of the volume constitutes a *defense* of the chains of a properly organized society over its members. Rousseau suggested that society is more important than its individual members, because they are what they are only because of their relationship to the larger community. Independent human beings living alone can achieve very little. Through their relationship to the larger community, they become moral creatures capable of significant action. The question then becomes what kind of community allows people to behave morally. In his two previous discourses Rousseau had explained that contemporary European society was not such a community. It was merely an aggregate of competing individuals whose chief social goal was to preserve selfish independence in spite of all potential social bonds and obligations.

Rousseau sought to project the vision of a society in which each person could maintain personal freedom while at the same time behaving as a loyal member of the larger community. To that end Rousseau drew on the traditions of Plato and Calvin to define freedom as obedience to law. In his case the law to be

[5] Jean-Jacques Rousseau, *The Social Contract and Discourses,* trans. by G. D. H. Cole (New York: Dutton, 1950), p. 3.

Rousseau Argues That Inequality Is Not Natural

Jean-Jacques Rousseau was one of the first writers to assert the social equality of human beings. He argued, as in this 1755 passage, that inequality had developed through the ages and was not "natural." He directly questioned the sanctity of property based on the assumed natural inequality of human beings.

I have endeavoured to trace the origin and progress of inequality, and the institution and abuse of political societies, as far as these are capable of being deduced from the nature of man merely by the light of reason, and independently of those sacred dogmas which give the sanction of divine right to sovereign authority. It follows from this survey that, as there is hardly any inequality in the state of nature, all the inequality which now prevails owes its strength and growth to the development of our faculties and the advance of the human mind, and becomes at last permanent and legitimate by the establishment of property and laws. Secondly, it follows that moral inequality, authorized by positive right alone, clashes with natural right, whenever it is not proportionate to physical inequality—a distinction which sufficiently determines what we think of that species of inequality which prevails in all civilized countries; since it is plainly contrary to the law of nature, however defined, that children should command old men, fools wise men, and that the privileged few should gorge themselves with superfluities while the starving multitude are in want of the bare necessities of life.

Jean-Jacques Rousseau, *The Social Contract and Discourses,* trans. by G. D. H. Cole (New York: Dutton, 1950), pp. 271–272.

obeyed was that created by the general will. This concept normally indicated the will of the majority of voting citizens who acted with adequate information and under the influence of virtuous customs and morals. Such democratic participation in decision making would bind the individual citizen to the community. Rousseau believed that the general will must always be right and that to obey the general will was to be free. This argument led him to the notorious conclusion that under certain circumstances some people must be forced to be free. Rousseau's politics thus constituted a justification for radical direct democracy and for collective action against individual citizens.

Rousseau had in effect launched an assault on the eighteenth-century cult of the individual and the fruits of selfishness. He stood at odds with the commercial spirit that was transforming the society in which he lived. Rousseau would have disapproved of the main thrust of Adam Smith's *Wealth of Nations,* which he may or may not have read, and would no doubt have preferred a study on the virtue of nations. Smith wanted people to be prosperous; Rousseau wanted them to be good even if being good meant that they might remain economically poor. He saw human beings not as independent individuals but as creatures enmeshed in neccessary social relationships. He believed that loyalty to the community should be encouraged. As one device to that end he suggested a civic religion based on the creed of deism. Such a shared tolerant religious faith would provide unity for the society. Rousseau's chief intellectual inspiration arose from his study of Plato and the ancient Greek *polis.* Especially in Sparta he thought he had discovered human beings dwelling in a moral society inspired by a common purpose. He hoped that modern human beings might also create such a moral commonwealth in which virtuous living would become subordinate to commercial profit.

Rousseau's thought had only a marginal impact on his own time. The other *philosophes* questioned his critique of material improvement. Aristocrats and royal ministers could hardly be expected to welcome his proposal for radical democracy. Too many people were either making or hoping to make money to appreciate his criticism of commercial values. However, he proved to be a figure to whom later generations returned. Many leaders in the French Revolution were familiar with his writing. Thereafter his ideas were important to most writers who felt called on to criticize the general tenor and direction of Western culture. Rousseau hated much about the emerging modern society in Europe, but he contributed much to modernity by exemplifying for later generations the critic who dared to call into question the very foundations of social thought and action. Whatever our opinions of Rousseau, we have not yet escaped him.

Enlightened Absolutism

Most of the *philosophes* favored neither Montesquieu's reformed and revived aristocracy nor Rousseau's democracy as a solution to contemporary political problems. Like other thoughtful people of the day in other stations and occupations, they looked to the existing monarchies. The *philosophes* hoped in particular that the French monarchy might assert really effective power over the aristocracy and the church to bring about significant reform. Voltaire was a very strong monarchist. He and others—such as Diderot, who visited Catherine II of Russia, and physiocrats who were ministers to the French kings—did not wish to limit the power of monarchs but sought to redirect that power toward the rationalization of economic and political structures and the liberation of intellectual life. Most *philosophes* were not opposed to power if they could find a way of using it for their own purposes.

During the last third of the century it seemed to some observers that several European rulers had actually embraced many of the reforms set forth by the *philosophes*. *Enlightened absolutism* is the term used to describe this phenomenon. The phrase indicates monarchical government dedicated to the rational strengthening of the central absolutist administration at the cost of other lesser centers of political power. The monarchs most closely associated with it— Frederick II of Prussia, Joseph II of Austria, and Catherine II of Russia—often found that the political and social realities of their realms caused them to moderate the degree of both enlightenment and absolutism in their policies. Frederick II corresponded with the *philosophes*, for a time provided Voltaire with a place at his court, and even wrote history and political tracts. Catherine II, who was a master of what would later be called public relations, consciously sought to create the image of being enlightened. She read the works of the *philosophes*, became a friend of Diderot and

MAJOR PUBLICATION DATES OF THE ENLIGHTENMENT	
Newton's *Principia Mathematica*	1687
Locke's *Essay Concerning Human Understanding*	1690
Toland's *Christianity Not Mysterious*	1696
Montesquieu's *Persian Letters*	1721
Voltaire's *Letters on the English*	1733
Voltaire's *Elements of the Philosophy of Newton*	1738
Montesquieu's *Spirit of the Laws*	1748
Hume's *Inquiry into Human Nature* with the chapter "Of Miracles"	1748
Rousseau's *Discourse on the Moral Effects of the Arts and Sciences*	1750
First volume of the *Encyclopedia* edited by Diderot	1751
Rousseau's *Discourse on the Origin of Inequality*	1755
Rousseau's *Social Contract*	1762
Voltaire's *Treatise on Toleration*	1763
Voltaire's *Philosophical Dictionary*	1764
Beccaria's *On Crimes and Punishments*	1764
Gibbon's *Decline and Fall of the Roman Empire*	1776
Bentham's *Fragment on Government*	1776
Smith's *Wealth of Nations*	1776
Lessing's *Nathan the Wise*	1779

Voltaire, and made frequent references to their ideas, all in the hope that her nation might seem more modern and Western. Joseph II continued numerous initiatives begun by his mother, Maria Theresa, and imposed a series of religious, legal, and social reforms that contemporaries believed he had derived from suggestions of the *philosophes*.

Despite such appearances, the relationship between these rulers and the writers of the Enlightenment was rather more complicated. They did wish to see their subjects enjoy better health, somewhat more accessible education, the benefits of a more rational political administration, and economic prosperity. In many of these policies they were more advanced than the rulers of western Europe. However, the humanitarian and liberating zeal of the Enlightenment directed only part of their policies. Frederick II, Joseph II, and Catherine II were also determined that their nations would play major diplomatic and military roles in Europe. In no small measure they sought the rational economic and social integration of their realms so they could achieve military strength. All of the states of Europe had emerged from the

*Frederick the Great of Prussia (1740–1786) reviewing his troops in old age. At enormous cost
in blood and treasure, Frederick made Prussia a great power. [The Bettman Archive]*

"The first servant of the State." Frederick the Great inspecting a factory. The king worked continually to strengthen the Prussian economy—it was necessary in order to have a strong state. [Metropolitan Museum of Art]

Seven Years' War understanding that they
would require stronger armed forces in future
conflicts and looking for new sources of taxation to finance their armies. The search for new
revenues and further internal political support
for their rule was an additional factor that led
these central and eastern European monarchs
to make "enlightened" reforms. Consequently,
they and their advisers used rationality to pursue many goals admired by the *philosophes* but
also to further what the *philosophes* considered
irrational militarism.

Frederick the Great of Prussia

After the mid-century wars, during which
Prussia had suffered badly and had almost
been defeated, Frederick II (1740–1786)
hoped to achieve recovery and consolidation.
At grave military and financial cost he had succeeded in retaining Silesia, which he had
seized from Austria in 1740. He worked to
stimulate its potential as a manufacturing district. Like his Hohenzollern forebears he continued to import workers from outside Prussia.
He directed new attention to Prussian agriculture. Under state supervision, swamps were

615

*The Age of
Enlightenment:
Eighteenth-
Century
Thought*

drained, new crops introduced, and peasants encouraged and sometimes compelled to migrate. For the first time in Prussia, potatoes and turnips came into general production. Frederick also established a Land-Mortgage Credit Association to aid landowners in raising money for agricultural improvements.

Throughout this process, the impetus for development came from the state. The monarchy and its bureaucracy were the engine for change. Despite new policies and personal exhortations, the general populace of Prussia did not prosper under Frederick's reign. The burden of taxation still fell disproportionally on peasants and townspeople.

In less material areas Frederick pursued enlightened policies with somewhat more success. He continued the Hohenzollern policy of toleration. He allowed Catholics and Jews to settle in his predominantly Lutheran country, and he protected the Catholics living in Silesia. It should be noted, however, that despite this broad policy of freedom of religious observance, Frederick virtually always appointed Protestants to major positions in the government and army. He ordered a new codification of Prussian law, which was completed after his death. The policy of toleration allowed foreign workers to contribute to the economic growth of the state. The new legal code was to rationalize the existing system, to make it more efficient, to eliminate regional peculiarities, and to eliminate excessive aristocratic influence. The enlightened monarchs were very concerned about legal reforms, primarily as a means of extending and strengthening royal power.

Frederick liked to describe himself as "the first servant of the State." That image represented an important change in the European conception of monarchy. The idea of an impersonal state was beginning to replace the concept of a personal monarchy. Kings might come and go, but the impersonal apparatus of government—the bureaucracy, the armies, the laws, the courts, and the citizens' loyalty arising from fear and from appreciation of state services and protection—remained. The state as an entity separate from the personality of the ruler came into its own after the French Revolution, but it was born in the monarchies of the old regime.

Joseph II of Austria

No eighteenth-century ruler so embodied rational, impersonal force as the emperor Joseph II of Austria. He was the son of Maria Theresa and co-ruler with her from 1765 to 1780. During the next ten years he ruled alone. He has been aptly described as "an imperial puritan and a good deal of a prig."[6] During much of his life he slept on straw and ate little but beef. He prided himself on a narrow, passionless rationality, which he sought to impose by his own will on the various Habsburg domains. Despite his eccentricities and the coldness of his personality, Joseph II genuinely and sincerely wished to improve the lot of his people. He was much less a political opportunist and cynic than either Frederick the Great of Prussia or Catherine the Great of Russia. The ultimate result of his well-intentioned efforts was a series of aristocratic and peasant rebellions extending from Hungary to the Austrian Netherlands.

As explained in Chapter 14, of all the rising states of the eighteenth century, Austria was the most diverse in its people and problems. Robert Palmer likened it to "a vast holding

[6]R. J. White, *Europe in the Eighteenth Century* (New York: St. Martin's, 1965), p. 214.

Two enlightened despots: Joseph II (1780–1790) with his brother and successor the future Leopold II (1790–1792). [Kunsthistorisches Museum]

company."[7] The Habsburgs never succeeded in creating either a unified administrative structure or a strong aristocratic loyalty. The price of the preservation of the monarchy during the War of the Austrian Succession (1740–1748) had been guarantees of considerable aristocratic independence, especially in Hungary. However, during and after the conflict Maria Theresa had taken major steps to strengthen the power of her crown in other of her realms. In Austria and Bohemia, through major administrative reorganization, she imposed a much more efficient system of tax collection that extracted funds even from the clergy and the nobles, and she established several central councils to deal with governmental problems. Her government became, in that regard, more bureaucratic than that of previous Habsburg rulers. She was particularly concerned about bringing all educational institutions into the service of the crown so that she could have a sufficiently large group of educated persons to serve as her officials, and she expanded primary education on the local level. Maria Theresa was also quite concerned about the welfare of the peasants and serfs. The extension of the authority of the royal bureaucracy over that of the local nobilities was of some assistance to the peasants, as were the empress's decrees limiting the amount of labor, or *robot*, that could be demanded from the peasantry by the landowners. This concern was not particularly humanitarian; rather, it arose from her desire to assure a good military recruitment pool in the population. In all these policies and in her general desire to stimulate prosperity and military strength by royal initiative, Maria Theresa anticipated the policies of her son.

However, Joseph II was more determined, and his projected reforms were more wide-ranging than his mother's. He was ambitious to extend the borders of his territories in the direction of Poland, Bavaria, and the Ottoman Empire. But his greatest ambition lay in changing the authority of the Habsburg emperor over his various realms. He sought to overcome the pluralism of the Habsburg holdings by increasing the power of the central monarchy in areas of political and social life where Maria Theresa had wisely chosen not to exert authority. In particular, Joseph sought to lessen the very considerable autonomy enjoyed by Hungary.

[7] Robert R. Palmer, *The Age of the Democratic Revolution*, Vol. 1 (Princeton, N.J.: Princeton University Press, 1959), p. 103.

To that end, he refused to have himself crowned king of Hungary and even had the Crown of Saint Stephen sent to the Imperial Treasury in Vienna. By that means, he avoided having to guarantee existing or new Hungarian privileges at the time of his coronation. He reorganized local government in Hungary so as to increase the authority of his own officials, and he also required the use of the German language in all governmental matters. But eventually, in 1790, Joseph had to rescind most of the imperial centralizing measures he had attempted to impose on Hungary as the Magyar nobility resisted one measure after another.

Another target of Joseph's assertion of royal absolutism was the church. From the reign of Charles V in the sixteenth century to that of Maria Theresa, the Habsburgs had been the single most important dynastic champion of Roman Catholicism. Maria Theresa was quite devout, but she had not allowed the church to limit her authority. Although she had attempted to discourage certain of the more extreme modes of Roman Catholic popular religious piety, such as public flagellation, she stood adamantly opposed to toleration. Joseph II was also a believing Catholic, but from the standpoint of both enlightenment and pragmatic politics, he favored a policy of toleration. In October 1781, Joseph issued a Toleration Patent (decree) that extended freedom of worship to Lutherans, Calvinists, and the Greek Orthodox. They were permitted to have their own places of worship, to sponsor schools, to enter skilled trades, and to hold academic appointments and positions in the public service. From 1781 through 1789 Joseph also issued a series of patents and other enactments that relieved the Jews in his realms of certain taxes and signs of personal degradation. He also extended to them the right of private worship. Although the Jews benefited from these actions, they still did not enjoy general legal rights equal to those of other Habsburg subjects.

Joseph also sought to bring the various institutions of the Roman Catholic church directly under the control of royal authority. He forbade direct communication between the bishops of his realms and the pope. He regarded orders of monks and nuns as generally unproductive. Consequently he dissolved over six hundred monasteries and confiscated their lands, although he excepted certain orders that ran schools or hospitals. He dissolved the tradi-

617

*The Age of
Enlightenment:
Eighteenth-
Century
Thought*

Maria Theresa and Joseph II of Austria Debate the Question of Toleration

In 1765 Joseph, the eldest son of the Empress Maria Theresa, had become coregent with his mother. He began to believe that some measures of religious toleration should be introduced into the Habsburg realms. Maria Theresa, whose opinions on many political issues were quite advanced, adamantly refused to consider adopting a policy of toleration. This exchange of letters between son and mother sets forth their sharply differing positions. It should be noted that the toleration of Protestants in dispute related only to Lutherans and Calvinists. Maria Theresa died in 1780; the next year Joseph, as emperor, issued an edict of toleration.

JOSEPH TO MARIA THERESA, JULY 20, 1777

. . . [I]t is only the word ''toleration'' which has caused the misunderstanding. You have taken it in quite a different meaning [from mine expressed in an earlier letter]. God preserve me from thinking it a matter of indifference whether the citizens turn Protestant or remain Catholic, still less, whether they cleave to, or at least observe, the cult which they have inherited from their fathers! I would give all I possess if all the Protestants of your states would go over to Catholicism.

The word ''toleration,'' as I understand it, means only that I would employ any persons, without distinction of religion, in purely temporal matters, allow them to own property, practice trades, be citizens, if they were qualified and if this would be of advantage to the State and its industry. Those who, unfortunately, adhere to a false faith, are far further from being converted if they remain in their own country than if they migrate into another, in which they can hear and see the convincing truths of the Catholic faith. Similarly, the undisturbed practice of their religion makes them far better subjects and causes them to avoid irreligion, which is a far greater danger to our Catholics than if one lets them see others practice their religion unimpeded. . . .

MARIA THERESA TO JOSEPH, LATE JULY, 1777

Without a dominant religion? Toleration, indifference are precisely the true means of undermining everything, taking away every foundation; we others will then be the greatest losers. . . . He is no friend of humanity, as the popular phrase is, who allows everyone his own thoughts. I am speaking only in the political sense, not as a Christian; nothing is so necessary and salutary as religion. Will you allow everyone to fashion his own religion as he pleases? No fixed cult, no subordination to the Church—what will then become of us? The result will not be quiet and contentment; its outcome will be the rule of the stronger and more unhappy times like those which we have already seen. A manifesto by you to this effect can produce the utmost distress and make you responsible for many thousands of souls. And what are my own sufferings, when I see you entangled in opinions so erroneous? What is at stake is not only the welfare of the State but your own salvation. . . . Turning your eyes and ears everywhere, mingling your spirit of contradiction with the simultaneous desire to create something, you are ruining yourself and dragging the Monarchy down with you into the abyss. . . . I only wish to live so long as I can hope to descend to my ancestors with the consolation that my son will be as great, as religious as his forebears, that he will return from his erroneous views, from those wicked books whose authors parade their cleverness at the expense of all that is most holy and most worthy of respect in the world, who want to introduce an imaginary freedom which can never exist and which degenerates into license and into complete revolution.

C. A. Macarney (Ed.), *The Habsburg and Hohenzollern Dynasties in the Seventeenth and Eighteenth Centuries* (New York: Walker, 1970), pp. 151–153.

tional Roman Catholic seminaries, which he believed taught priests too great a loyalty to the papacy and too little concern for duties to their future parishioners. Having dissolved the existing seminaries, he chose to sponsor eight general seminaries for the training of priests, with an emphasis on parish duties. He also issued decrees that areas needing more priests because of the number of people living there should be supplied with priests. He used funds from the confiscation of the monasteries to pay for these new parishes. In effect, Joseph's policies made Roman Catholic priests the employees of the state and brought the influence of the Roman Catholic church as an independent institution in Habsburg lands to a close. Joseph was willing and even eager to have religious faith and practice flourish, but religious institutions and the people they employed must stand subordinate to the authority of the government. In many respects the ecclesiastical policies of Joseph II, known as *Josephinism,* prefigured those of the French Revolution.

Like Frederick of Prussia, Joseph sought to improve the economic life of his domains. He abolished many internal tariffs and encouraged road building and the improvement of river transport. He went on personal inspection tours of farms and manufacturing districts. Joseph also reconstructed the judicial system to make laws more uniform and rational and to lessen the influence of local landlords. National courts with power over the landlord courts were established. All of these improvements were expected to bring new unity to the state and more taxes into the coffers at Vienna.

In his policies toward serfdom and the land, Joseph II again pursued policies initiated by Maria Theresa to more far-reaching ends. Over the years of his reign Joseph II introduced a series of reforms that touched the very heart of the rural social structure. He did not seek to abolish the authority of landlords over their peasants, but he did seek to make that authority more moderate and subject to the oversight of royal officials. He abolished the legal status of serfdom defined in terms of servitude to another person. He gave peasants a much wider arena of personal freedom. They could marry without approval of the landlord, and they could also engage in skilled work or have their children trained in such skills without permission of the landlord. The procedures of the manorial courts were reformed, and avenues of appeal to royal officials were opened. Joseph also encouraged landlords to change land leases so that it would be easier for peasants to inherit them or to transfer them to another peasant without bringing into doubt the landlord's title of ownership. In all of these actions Joseph believed that the lessening of traditional burdens would make the peasant tillers of the land more productive and industrious.

Near the end of his reign Joseph proposed a new and daring system of land taxation. He decreed in 1789 that all proprietors of the land were to be taxed regardless of social status. No longer were the peasants alone to bear the burden of taxation. He abolished *robot* (the services due a landlord from peasants) and commuted it into a monetary tax, only part of which would in the future go to the landlord while the remainder would revert to the state. The decree was made, but resistence from the nobles led to a delay in its implementation. Then, in 1790, Joseph died, and the decree never went into effect. However, it and others of his measures had stirred up turmoil throughout the Habsburg realms. Peasants revolted over disagreements about the interpretation of their newly granted rights. The nobles of the various realms protested the taxation scheme. The Hungarian Magyars resisted Joseph's centralization measures and compelled him to rescind them.

On Joseph's death, the crown went to his brother Leopold II (1790–1792). Although quite sympathetic to Joseph's goals, Leopold found himself compelled to repeal many of the most controversial decrees, such as that in regard to taxation. In other areas, Leopold thought his brother's policies simply wrong. For example, he returned much political and administrative power to local nobles because he thought it expedient for them to have a voice in government. Still, there was no wholesale repudiation of Joseph's policies, especially in regard to religion and such political centralization as Leopold thought possible to retain. Joseph II had possessed a narrow vision attached to an unbending will. For all his intellectual brilliance and hard work, he had failed to understand that his policies enjoyed few supporters outside the royal bureaucracy. He had ruled without consulting any political constituency. The nobles, the church, the towns with their chartered liberties, and the absence of a strong bureaucracy or army stood as barriers to the realization of his absolutism. His was a mind of classical rationalism in conflict with political and social realities of baroque complexity.

Catherine the Great of Russia

Joseph II never grasped the practical necessity of cultivating political support for his policies. Catherine II (1762–1796), who had been born a German princess but who became empress of Russia, understood only too well the fragility of the Romanov dynasty's base of power.

After the death of Peter the Great in 1725, the court nobles and the army had repeatedly determined the Russian succession. As a result, the crown fell primarily into the hands of people with little talent. Peter's wife, Catherine I, ruled for two years (1725–1727) and was succeeded for three years by Peter's grandson Peter II. In 1730 the crown devolved on Anna, who was a niece of Peter the Great. During 1740 and 1741 a child named Ivan VI, who was less than a year old, was the nominal ruler. Finally, in 1741, Peter the Great's daughter Elizabeth came to the throne. She held the title of empress until 1762, but her reign was not notable for new political departures or sound administration. Her court was a shambles of political and romantic intrigue. Needless to say, much of the power possessed by the czar at the opening of the century had vanished.

Catherine the Great (1762–1796). Catherine sought to introduce Enlightenment reforms into Russia in order to strengthen its position as one of the great powers of Europe. [Novosti]

RUSSIA FROM PETER THE GREAT THROUGH CATHERINE THE GREAT	
Death of Peter the Great	1725
Catherine I	1725–1727
Peter II	1727–1730
Anna	1730–1741
Ivan VI	1740–1741
Elizabeth	1741–1762
Peter III	1762
Catherine II (the Great) becomes empress	1762
Legislative Commission summoned	1767
War with Turkey	1769
Pugachev's Rebellion	1771–1775
First Partition of Poland	1772
Treaty of Kuchuk-Kainardji ends war with Turkey	1774
Reorganization of local government	1775
Russia annexes the Crimea	1783
Catherine issues the Charter of the Nobility	1785
Second Partition of Poland	1793
Third Partition of Poland	1795
Death of Catherine the Great	1796

At her death in 1762 Elizabeth was succeeded by Peter III, one of her nephews. He was a weak ruler whom many contemporaries considered mad. He immediately exempted the nobles from compulsory military service and then made rapid peace with Frederick the Great, for whom he held unbounded admiration. That decision probably saved Prussia from military defeat. The one positive feature of this unbalanced creature's life was his marriage in 1745 to a young German princess born in Pomerania. This was the future Catherine the Great, who for almost twenty years lived in misery and frequent danger at the court of Elizabeth. During that time she befriended important nobles and read widely in the books of the *philosophes.* She was a shrewd person whose experience in a court crawling with rumors, intrigue, and conspiracy had taught her how to survive. She had neither love nor loyalty for her demented husband. After a few months of rule Peter II was deposed and murdered with the approval, if not the aid, of Catherine. On his deposition she was immediately proclaimed empress.

Catherine's familiarity with the Enlightenment and the general culture of western Eu-

619

RUSSIAN EMPIRE, 1689

TERRITORIES ADDED, 1725–1762

TERRITORIES ADDED UNDER PETER THE GREAT, 1689–1725

TERRITORIES ADDED UNDER CATHERINE THE GREAT, 1762–1796

500 MI.

500 KM.

—————EXPANSION OF RUSSIA,—————
1689–1796

MAP 17-1 *The overriding territorial aim of Peter the Great in the first quarter and of Catherine the Great in the last half of the eighteenth century was the securing of northern and southern navigable-water outlets for the vast Russian Empire. Hence Peter's push to the Baltic Sea and Catherine's to the Black Sea. Catherine also managed to acquire large areas of Poland through the partitions of that country.*

rope convinced her that Russia was very backward and that it must make major reforms if it was to remain a great power. She understood that any major reform must have a wide base of political and social support. Such was especially the case because she herself had assumed the throne through a palace coup. Consequently, in 1767, she summoned a Legislative Commission to advise her on revisions in the law and government of Russia. There were over five hundred delegates drawn from all sectors of Russian life. Before the commission convened, Catherine issued a set of *Instructions*, partly written by herself. They contained numerous ideas drawn from the political writings of the *philosophes*. The commission considered the *Instructions* as well as other ideas and complaints raised by its members. The revision of Russian law, however, did not occur for more than a half century. In 1768 Catherine dismissed the commission before several of its key committees had reported. Yet the meeting had not been useless, for a vast amount of information had been gathered about the conditions of local administration and economic life throughout the realm. The inconclusive debates and the absence of programs from the delegates themselves suggested that most Russians saw no alternative to an autocratic monarchy. For her part, it was clear that Catherine had no intention of departing from absolutism.

Catherine proceeded to carry out limited reforms on her own authority. She gave strong support to the rights and local power of the nobility. In 1777 she reorganized local government to solve problems brought to light by the Legislative Commission. She put most local offices into the hands of nobles rather than creating a royal bureaucracy. In 1785 Catherine issued the Charter of the Nobility, which guaranteed many noble rights and privileges. In part the empress had no choice but to favor the nobles. They had the capacity to topple her from the throne. There were too few educated subjects in her realm to establish an independent bureaucracy, and the treasury could not afford an army strictly loyal to the crown. So Catherine wisely made a virtue of necessity. She strengthened the stability of her crown by making convenient friends with her nobles.

Part and parcel of Catherine's program was a continuation of the economic development begun under Peter the Great. She attempted to suppress internal barriers to trade. Exports of grain, flax, furs, and naval stores grew dramatically. She also favored the expansion of the small Russian middle class. Russian trade required such a vital urban class. And through all of these departures Catherine attempted to maintain ties of friendship and correspondence with the *philosophes*. She knew that if she treated them kindly, they would be sufficiently flattered and would give her a progressive reputation throughout Europe.

The limited administrative reforms and the policy of economic growth had a counterpart in the diplomatic sphere. The Russian drive for warm-water ports continued. This goal required warfare with the Turks. In 1769, as a result of a minor Russian incursion, the Ottoman Empire declared war on Russia. The Russians responded in a series of strikingly successful military moves. During 1769 and 1770 the Russian fleet sailed all the way from the Baltic Sea into the eastern Mediterranean. The Russian army won several major victories that by 1771 gave Russia control of Ottoman provinces on the Danube River and the Crimean coast of the Black Sea. The conflict dragged on until 1774, when it was closed by the Treaty of Kuchuk-Kainardji. The treaty gave Russia a direct outlet on the Black Sea, free navigation rights in its waters, and free access through the Bosphorus. Moreover, the province of the Crimea became an independent state, which Catherine painlessly annexed in 1783.

The Partition of Poland

These military successes obviously brought the empress much domestic political support. However, they made the other states of eastern Europe uneasy. These anxieties were overcome by an extraordinary division of Polish territory known as the First Partition of Poland. The Russian victories along the Danube River were most unwelcome to Austria, which also harbored ambitions of territorial expansion in that direction. At the same time, the Ottoman Empire was pressing Prussia for aid against Russia. Frederick the Great made a proposal to Russia and Austria that would give each something it wanted, prevent conflict among the powers, and save appearances. After long, complicated, secret negotiations the three powers agreed that Russia would abandon the conquered Danubian provinces. In compensation Russia received a large portion of Polish territory with almost two million inhabitants. As a reward for remaining neutral, Prussia annexed most of the territory between East Prussia and Prussia proper. This land allowed

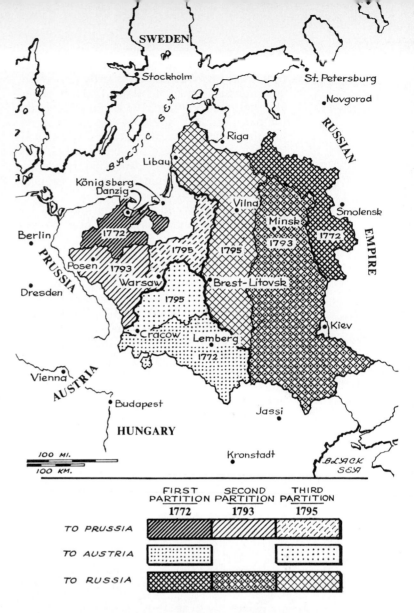

PARTITIONS OF POLAND, 1772–1793–1795

MAP 17-2 *The callous eradication of Poland from the map displayed eighteenth-century power politics at its most extreme. Poland, without strong central governmental institutions, fell victim to those states in central and eastern Europe that had developed such institutions.*

Frederick to unite two previously separate sections of his realm. Finally, Austria took Galicia, with its important salt mines, and other Polish territory with over two and one-half million inhabitants. In September 1772 the helpless Polish aristocracy, paying the price for the maintenance of their internal liberties, ratified this seizure of their territory. The Polish state had lost approximately one third of its territory. That loss was not necessarily fatal to the continued existence of Poland, and a considerable national political revival took place after the partition. Real attempts were made to adjust the Polish political structures to the realities of the time. These proved to be too little and too late. The political and military strength of Poland could not match that of its stronger, more ambitious neighbors.

There were two additional partitions of Poland by Russia and Prussia, and one more by Austria. These occurred in 1793 and 1795 and removed Poland from the map of Europe. Each time the great powers contended that they were saving themselves, and by implication the rest of Europe, from Polish anarchy. The fact of the matter was that the political weakness of Poland made the country and its resources a rich field for plunderous aggression. The last two partitions took place during the French Revolution. The three eastern European absolute monarchies objected to certain reforms undertaken by the Polish nobles for fear that even minor Polish reform might endanger the stability of their own societies.

This French engraving is a satirical comment on the first partition of Poland (1772) by Russia, Austria, and Prussia. The distressed monarch attempting to retain his crown is Stanislaus of Poland. Catherine of Russia, Joseph of Austria, and Frederick of Prussia point out their respective shares of the loot.

The End of the Eighteenth Century in Central and Eastern Europe

During the last two decades of the eighteenth century, all three regimes based on enlightened absolutism became more conservative and politically repressive. In Prussia and Austria the innovations of the rulers stirred resistance among the nobility. In Russia fear of peasant unrest was the chief factor.

Frederick the Great lived much removed from his people during his old age. The aristocracy, looking out for its own self-interest, filled the major Prussian military and administrative posts. There also developed a strong reaction against Enlightenment thought among Prussian Lutheran writers.

As Joseph II confronted growing frustration and political unrest over his plans for restructuring the society and administration of his realms, he made more and more use of censorship and the secret police. Throughout his realms the nobles called for an end to innovation.

Catherine the Great never fully recovered from the fears of social and political upheaval raised by Pugachev's rebellion (1771–1775). Once the French Revolution broke out in 1789, the Russian empress censored books based on Enlightenment thought and sent offensive authors into Siberian exile. By the close of the century fear of and hostility to change permeated the ruling classes throughout the region. Those attitudes had come into existence before 1789, but the events in France froze them for almost half a century. Paradoxically, nowhere did the humanity and liberalism of the Enlightenment encounter more difficulty surviving and entering the mainstream of life and thought than in those states that had been governed by "enlightened" rulers.

Although the enlightened absolute monarchs lacked the humanity of the *philosophes*, they had embraced the Enlightenment spirit of innovation. They wanted to change the political, social, and economic structures of their realms. From the close of the Seven Years' War (1763) until the opening of the French Revolution in 1789, the monarchies of both western and eastern Europe had been the major forces working for significant institutional change. In every case they had stirred up considerable aristocratic and some popular resistance and resentment. George III of Britain fought for years with Parliament and lost the colonies of North America in the process. Frederick II of

Prussia carried out his program of reform only because he accepted new aristocratic influence over the bureaucracy and the army. Catherine II of Russia had to come to terms with her nobility. Joseph II left his domains in turmoil by imposing changes without consulting the nobility.

These monarchs pushed for innovations because of their desires for increased revenue. The same problem existed in France. There the royal drive for adequate fiscal resources also led to aristocratic rebellion. However, in France neither the monarchy nor the aristocracy could control the social and political forces unleashed by their quarrel.

Suggested Readings

R. P. BARTLETT, *Human Capital: The Settlement of Foreigners in Russia, 1762–1804* (1979). Examines Catherine's policy of attracting farmers and skilled workers to Russia.

C. BECKER, *The Heavenly City of the Eighteenth Century Philosophers* (1932). An influential but very controversial discussion.

P. P. BERNARD, *Joseph II* (1968). A brief biography.

T. BESTERMANN, *Voltaire* (1969). A biography by the editor of Voltaire's letters.

D. D. BIEN, *The Calas Affair: Persecution, Toleration, and Heresy in Eighteenth-Century Toulouse* (1960). The standard treatment of the famous case.

E. CASSIRER, *The Philosophy of the Enlightenment* (1951). A brilliant but difficult work by one of the great philosophers of the twentieth century.

H. CHISICK, *The Limits of Reform in the Enlightenment: Attitudes toward the Education of the Lower Classes in Eighteenth-Century France* (1981). An attempt to examine the impact of the Enlightenment on nonelite classes.

G. R. CRAGG, *The Church and the Age of Reason* (1961). A general survey of eighteenth-century religious life.

R. DARNTON, *The Business of Enlightenment: A Publishing History of the Encyclopedia, 1775–1800* (1979). A wide-ranging examination of the printing and dispersion of the *Encyclopedia*.

R. DARNTON, *The Literary Underground of the Old Regime* (1982). Essays on the world of printers, publishers, and booksellers.

P. FUSSELL, *The Rhetorical World of Augustan Humanism* (1969). Examines writers during the Enlightenment.

J. GAGLIARDO, *Enlightened Despotism* (1967). A discussion of the subject in its European context.

P. GAY, *The Enlightenment: An Interpretation*, 2 vols. (1966, 1969). The most important and far-reaching treatment.

P. GAY, *The Enlightenment: A Comprehensive Anthology* (1973). A large, well-edited set of documents.

L. GERSHOY, *From Despotism to Revolution, 1763–1793* (1944). A sound treatment of the political background.

C. C. GILLISPIE, *Science and Polity in France at the End of the Old Regime* (1980). A major survey of the subject.

N. HAMPSON, *A Cultural History of the Enlightenment* (1969). A useful introduction.

P. HAZARD, *The European Mind: The Critical Years, 1680–1715* (1935), and *European Thought in the Eighteenth Century from Montesquieu to Lessing* (1946). The two volumes portray the century as the turning point for the emergence of the modern mind in Europe.

M. C. JACOB, *The Radical Enlightenment: Pantheists, Freemasons, and Republicans* (1981). A treatment of frequently ignored figures in the age of the Enlightenment.

H. C. JOHNSON, *Frederick the Great and His Officials* (1975). An examination of the administrative apparatus of enlightened absolutism.

R. KREISER, *Miracles, Convulsions, and Ecclesiastical Politics in Early Eighteenth-Century Paris* (1978). An important study of the kind of religious life that the *philosophes* opposed.

L. KRIEGER, *Kings and Philosophers, 1689–1789* (1970). A survey that relates the social and political thought of the Enlightenment writers to their immediate political setting.

C. A. MACARTNEY, *The Habsburg Empire, 1790–1918* (1971). Provides useful coverage of major mid-eighteenth-century developments.

I. DE MADARIAGA, *Russia in the Age of Catherine the Great* (1981). The best discussion in English.

F. MANUEL, *The Eighteenth Century Confronts the Gods* (1959). A broad examination of the *philosophes'* treatment of Christian and pagan religion.

R. R. PALMER, *Catholics and Unbelievers in Eighteenth Century France* (1939). A discussion of the opponents of the *philosophes*.

G. RITTER, *Frederick the Great* (trans. 1968). A useful biography.

R. O. ROCKWOOD (ED.), *Carl Becker's Heavenly City Revisited* (1958). Important essays qualifying Becker's thesis.

J. N. SHKLAR, *Men and Citizens, a Study of Rousseau's Social Theory* (1969). A thoughtful and provocative overview of Rousseau's political thought.

R. E. SULLIVAN, *John Toland and the Deist Controversy: A Study in Adaptation* (1982). An important and informative discussion.

A. M. WILSON, *Diderot* (1972). A splendid biography of the person behind the project for the *Encyclopedia* and other major Enlightenment publications.

A poster proclaims the revolutionary program: Liberty, equality, fraternity, and a united, indivisible republic. By 1792, the French monarchy had been swept away, and the Jacobins, whose symbol, the cockade cap, surmounts this poster, were in control of France. [The Mansell Collection]

IN THE SPRING of 1789 the long-festering conflict between the French monarchy and the aristocracy erupted into a new political crisis. This dispute, unlike earlier ones, quickly outgrew the issues of its origins and produced the wider disruption of the French Revolution. The quarrel that began as a struggle between the most exclusive elements of the political nation soon involved all sectors of French society and eventually every major state in Europe. Before the turmoil settled, small-town provincial lawyers and Parisian street orators exercised more influence over the fate of the Continent than did aristocrats, royal ministers, or monarchs. Armies commanded by persons of low birth and filled by conscripted village youths emerged victorious over forces composed of professional soldiers and directed by officers of noble birth. The very existence of the Roman Catholic faith in France was challenged. Politically and socially neither France nor Europe would ever be quite the same after these events.

The Crisis of the French Monarchy

Although the French Revolution constituted one of the central turning points in modern European history, it originated from the basic tensions and problems that characterized practically all late-eighteenth-century states. From the Seven Years' War (1756–1763) onward, the French monarchy was unable to handle its finances on a sound basis. It emerged from the conflict both defeated and in debt. The French support of the American revolt against Great Britain further deepened the financial difficulties of the government. On the eve of the revolution the interest and payments on the royal debt amounted to just over one half of the entire budget. The annual deficit was in the vicinity of 126 million livres. Given the economic vitality of the nation, this debt was neither overly large nor disproportionate to the debts of other European powers. The problem lay with the inability of the royal government to tap the wealth of the French nation through taxes to service and repay the debt. Paradoxically France was a rich nation with an impoverished government.

The debt was symptomatic of the failure of the eighteenth-century French monarchy to come to terms with the resurgent social and political power of the aristocracy. For twenty-

18

The French Revolution

625

five years after the Seven Years' War there was a standoff between them. The monarchy attempted to pursue a program somewhat resembling that associated with enlightened absolutism in eastern Europe. However, both Louis XV (1715–1774) and Louis XVI (1774–1792) lacked the character and the resolution for such a departure. The moral corruption of the former and the indecision of the latter meant that the monarchy could not rally the French public to its side.

In place of a consistent policy to deal with the growing debt, the monarchy gave way to hesitancy, retreat, and even duplicity. In 1763 the monarchy issued a new set of tax decrees that would have extended the collection of certain taxes that were supposed to have been discontinued at the close of the war. There were also new tax assessments. This search for revenue was not unlike the one that led the British government to attempt to tax the American colonies. Several of the provincial *parlements* and finally the Parlement of Paris—all controlled by nobles—declared the taxes illegal. During the ensuing dispute the aristocratic *parlements* set themselves up as the spokesmen of the nation and as the protectors of French liberty against the illegal assertion of monarchical power. This was one of the political functions of the nobility that Montesquieu had outlined in *The Spirit of the Laws* (1748).

In 1770 Louis XV appointed René Maupeou (1714–1792) as chancellor. The new minister was determined to break the *parlements* and impose a greater part of the tax burden on the nobility. He abolished the *parlements* and exiled their members to different parts of the country. He then commenced an ambitious program of reform and efficiency. What ultimately doomed Maupeou's policy was less the resistance of the nobility than the death of Louis XV in 1774. His successor, Louis XVI, in an attempt to regain what he conceived to be popular support, restored all the *parlements* and confirmed their old powers. This action, in conjunction with the later aid to the American colonies, locked the monarchy into a continuing financial bind. Thereafter meaningful fiscal or political reform through existing institutions was probably doomed.

Louis XVI's first minister was the physiocrat Jacques Turgot (1727–1781), who attempted various economic reforms, including the removal of restrictions on the grain trade and the elimination of the guilds. He transformed the *corvée,* or road-working obligation of peasants,

Louis XVI (1774–1792). *Well-meaning but weak and vacillating, Louis stumbled from concession to concession until he finally lost all power to save his throne.* [*Giraudon*]

into money payments. Turgot also intended to restructure the taxation system in order to tap the wealth of the nobility. These and other ideas represented a program of bold new departures for the monarchy. They proved too bold for the tremulous young king, who dismissed Turgot in 1776. By 1781 the debt, as a result of the aid to America, was larger and the sources of revenues were unchanged. However, the new director-general of finances, Jacques Necker (1732–1804), a Swiss banker, produced a public report that suggested that the situation was not so bad as had been feared. He argued that if the expenditures for the American war were removed, the budget was in surplus. However, Necker's report also revealed that a large portion of the royal expenditure went to pensions for aristocrats and other royal court favorites. This information aroused the anger of court aristocratic circles against the banker, who soon left office. His financial sleight of hand, nonetheless, made it more difficult for later government officials to claim a real need to raise new taxes.

The monarchy hobbled along until 1786. By this time Charles Alexandre de Calonne (1734–1802) was the minister of finance. He was probably the most able administrator to serve Louis XVI. More carefully than previous ministers he charted the size of the debt and the deficit. He submitted a program for reform quite similar to that presented by Turgot a decade earlier. Calonne proposed to encourage internal trade; to lower some taxes, such as the *gabelle* on salt; and to transform peasants' services to money payments.

More important, Calonne urged the introduction of a new land tax that would require payments from all landowners regardless of their social status. If this tax could have been imposed, the monarchy would have been able to abandon other indirect taxes. The government would also rarely have had to seek approval for further new taxes from the aristocratically dominated *parlements*. Calonne also intended to establish new local assemblies to approve land taxes; in these assemblies the voting power would depend on the amount of land owned rather than on the social status of the owner. All these proposals would have undermined both the political and the social power of the French aristocracy.

A new clash with the nobility was unavoidable, and the monarchy had very little room for maneuver. The creditors were at the door; the treasury was nearly empty. Consequently, in 1787 Calonne met with an Assembly of Notables drawn from the upper ranks of the aristocracy and the church to seek support and approval for his plan. The assembly adamantly refused any such action; rather, it demanded that the aristocracy be allowed a greater share in the direct government of the kingdom. The notables called for the reappointment of Necker, who they believed had left the country in sound fiscal condition. Finally, they claimed that they had no right to consent to new taxes and that such a right was vested only in the medieval institution of the Estates General of France, which had not met since 1614. The notables believed that the calling of the Estates General, which had been traditionally organized to allow aristocratic and church dominance, would produce a victory for the nobility over the monarchy.

Again Louis XVI backed off. He dismissed Calonne and replaced him with Étienne Charles Loménie de Brienne (1727–1794), who was archbishop of Toulouse and the chief opponent of Calonne at the Assembly of Notables. Once in office, Brienne found, to his astonishment, that the situation was as bad as his predecessor had asserted. Brienne himself now sought to impose the land tax. However, the Parlement of Paris took the new position that it lacked authority to authorize the tax and said that only the Estates General could do so. Shortly thereafter Brienne appealed to the Assembly of the Clergy to approve a large subsidy to allow funding of that part of the debt then coming due for payment. The clergy, like the Parlement dominated by aristocrats, not only refused the subsidy but also reduced their existing contribution, or *don gratuit*, to the government. As these unfruitful negotiations were transpiring at the center of political life, local aristocratic *parlements* and estates in the provinces were demanding a restoration of the privileges they had enjoyed during the early seventeenth century before Richelieu and Louis XIV had crushed their independent power. Consequently, in July 1788 the king, through Brienne, agreed to convoke the Estates General the next year. Brienne resigned and was replaced by Necker. The institutions of the aristocracy—and to a lesser degree, of the church—had brought the French monarchy to its knees. In the country of its origin, royal absolutism had been defeated.

This French cartoon of 1789 shows a peasant carrying a priest and a nobleman on his back. The peasantry could least afford to pay but was most heavily taxed, while the clergy and aristocracy were largely tax exempt. [Giraudon]

Le tems passé

The Revolutions of 1789

The Estates General Becomes the National Assembly

The aristocratic triumph proved to be quite brief. It unloosed social and political forces that neither the nobles nor the monarchy could control. The new difficulties arose from clashes among the groups represented in the Estates General. The body was composed of three divisions: the First Estate of the clergy, the Second Estate of the nobility, and the Third Estate, which represented everyone else in the kingdom. During the widespread public discussions preceding the meeting of the Estates General, it became clear that the Third Estate, which included all the professional, commercial, and middle-class groups of the country, would not permit the monarchy and the aristocracy to decide the future course of the nation. Their spirit was best displayed in a pamphlet published during 1789 in which the Abbé Sieyès (1748–1836) declared, "What is the Third Estate? Everything. What has it been in the political order up to the present? Nothing. What does it ask? To become something."[1]

[1] Quoted in Leo Gershoy, *The French Revolution and Napoleon* (New York: Appleton-Century-Crofts, 1964), p. 102.

The split between the aristocracy and the Third Estate occurred before the Estates General gathered. Debate over the proper organization of the body drew the lines of basic disagreement. Members of the aristocracy demanded an equal number of representatives for each estate. In September 1788 the Parlement of Paris ruled that voting in the Estates General should be conducted by order rather than by head, that is, that each estate, or order, should have one vote, rather than that each member should have one vote. That procedure would ensure that the aristocratic First and Second Estates could always outvote the Third. Both moves on the part of the aristocracy unmasked its alleged concern for French liberty and exposed it as a group determined to maintain its privileges. Spokesmen for the Third Estate denounced the arrogant claims of the aristocracy. The royal council eventually decided that the cause of the monarchy and fiscal reform would best be served by a strengthening of the Third Estate, and in December 1788 the council announced that the Third Estate would elect twice as many representatives as either the nobles or the clergy. This so-called doubling of the Third Estate meant that it could easily dominate the Estates General if voting were allowed by head rather than by order. It was correctly assumed that some liberal nobles

The Estates-General opened at Versailles in 1789 with much pomp and splendour. In this print, Louis XVI is on the throne. The First Estate, the clergy is on the left; the Second Estate, the nobility, sits at the upper right; and the more numerous Third Estate, dressed in black suits and capes, sits at the lower right. [Culver Pictures]

The Third Estate of a French City Petitions the King

The *cahiers de doléances* were the lists of grievances brought to Versailles in 1789 by members of the Estates General. This particular *cahier* originated in Dourdan, a city of central France, and reflects the complaints of the Third Estate. The first two articles refer to the organization of the Estates General. The other articles ask that the king grant various forms of equality before the law and in matters of taxation. These demands for equality appeared in practically all the *cahiers* of the Third Estate.

The order of the third estate of the City . . . of Dourdan . . . supplicates [the king] to accept the grievances, complaints, and remonstrances which it is permitted to bring to the foot of the throne, and to see therein only the expression of its zeal and the homage of its obedience.

It wishes:

1. That his subjects of the third estate, equal by such status to all other citizens, present themselves before the common father without other distinction which might degrade them.

2. That all the orders, already united by duty and a common desire to contribute equally to the needs of the State, also deliberate in common concerning its needs.

3. That no citizen lose his liberty except according to law; that, consequently, no one be arrested by virtue of special orders, or, if imperative circumstances necessitate such orders, that the prisoner be handed over to regular courts of justice within forty-eight hours at the latest.

12. That every tax, direct or indirect, be granted only for a limited time, and that every collection beyond such term be regarded as peculation, and punished as such.

15. That every personal tax be abolished; that thus the capitation *[a poll tax] and the* taille *[tax from which nobility and clergy were exempt] and its accessories be merged with the* vingtièmes *[an income tax] in a tax on land and real or nominal property.*

16. That such tax be borne equally, without distinction, by all classes of citizens and by all kinds of property, even feudal . . . rights.

17. That the tax substituted for the corvée *be borne by all classes of citizens equally and without distinction. That said tax, at present beyond the capacity of those who pay it and the needs to which it is destined, be reduced by at least one-half.*

John Hall Stewart, *A Documentary Survey of the French Revolution* (New York: Macmillan, 1951), pp. 76–77.

and clergy would support the Third Estate. The method of voting was settled by the king only after the Estates General had gathered at Versailles in May 1789.

When the representatives came to the royal palace, they brought with them *cahiers de doléances,* or lists of grievances, registered by the local electors, to be presented to the king. Large numbers of these have survived and provide considerable information about the state of the country on the eve of the revolution. These documents recorded criticisms of government waste, indirect taxes, church taxes and corruption, and the hunting rights of the aristocracy. They included calls for periodic meetings of the Estates General, more equitable taxes, more local control of administration, unified weights and measures, and a free press. The overwhelming demand of the *cahiers* was for equality of rights among the king's subjects.

These complaints and demands could not be discussed until the questions of organization and voting had been decided. From the beginning, the Third Estate, whose members consisted largely of local officials, professional men, and lawyers, refused to sit as a separate order as the king desired. For several weeks there was a standoff. Then on June 1 the Third Estate invited the clergy and the nobles to join them in organizing a new legislative body. A few members of the lower clergy did so. On June 17 that body declared itself the National Assembly.

Three days later, finding themselves accidentally locked out of their usual meeting place, the National Assembly moved to a nearby tennis court, where its members took an oath to continue to sit until they had given France a

The Oath of the Tennis Court, June 20, 1789, *by Jacques Louis David (1748–1825). In the center foreground are members of different Estates joining hands in cooperation as equals. The presiding officer is Jean Sylvain Bailly, soon to become mayor of Paris.* [Art Resource]

The National Assembly Takes the Tennis Court Oath

Throughout the early weeks of the meeting of the Estates General in the late spring of 1789, there was fear that the king would attempt to dissolve the gathering or use troops against it. On June 17 the Estates General had transformed itself into the National Assembly. This was a major act in the unfolding revolutionary situation. Fear of some hostile action on the part of Louis XVI grew stronger. Then, on June 20, the assembly found itself barred from its usual meeting place. Its members then went to a nearby tennis court, where they took an oath to write a new constitution for France.

The National Assembly, considering that it has been summoned to establish the constitution of the kingdom, to effect the regeneration of public order, and to maintain the true principles of monarchy; that nothing can prevent it from continuing its deliberations in whatever place it may be forced to establish itself; and, finally, that wheresoever its members are assembled, there *is the National Assembly.*

Decrees that all members of this Assembly shall immediately take a solemn oath not to separate, and to reassemble wherever circumstances require, until the constitution of the kingdom is established and consolidated upon firm foundations; and that, the said oath taken, all members and each one of them individually shall ratify this steadfast resolution by signature.

John Hall Stewart (Ed.), *A Documentary Survey of the French Revolution* (New York: Macmillan, 1951), p. 88.

constitution. This was the famous Tennis Court Oath. Louis XVI ordered the National Assembly to desist from their actions, but shortly afterward a majority of the clergy and a large group of nobles joined the assembly. On June 27 the king capitulated and formally requested the First and Second Estates to meet with the National Assembly, where voting would occur by head rather than by order. Had nothing further occurred, the government of France would have been transformed. Government by privileged orders had come to an end, for the National Assembly, which renamed itself the National Constituent Assembly, was composed of persons from all three orders, who possessed shared liberal goals for the administrative, constitutional, and economic reform of the country. The revolution in the governing of France had commenced.

Fall of the Bastille

Two new forces soon intruded on the scene. The first was Louis XVI himself, who attempted to regain the initiative by mustering royal troops in the vicinity of Versailles and Paris. It appeared that he might be contemplating disruption of the National Constituent Assembly. Such was the advice of Queen Marie Antoinette, his brothers, and the most conservative nobles, with whom he had begun to consult. On July 11, without consultation with the assembly leaders, Louis abruptly dismissed Necker. These actions marked the beginning of a steady, but consistently poorly executed, royal attempt to undermine the assembly and halt the revolution. Most of the National Constituent Assembly wished to create some form of constitutional monarchy, but from the start Louis's refusal to cooperate thwarted that effort. The king fatally decided to throw his lot in with the aristocracy against the nation.

The second new factor to impose itself on the events at Versailles was the populace of Paris. The mustering of royal troops created anxiety in the city, where throughout the winter and spring of 1789 there had been several bread riots. The Parisians who had elected their rep-

An eye-witness drawing of the fall of the Bastille, July 14, 1789. *The mob was supported by rebel troops and artillery.* [*Mary Evans Picture Library*]

resentatives to the Third Estate had continued to meet after the elections. By June they were organizing a citizen militia and collecting arms. They regarded the dismissal of Necker as the opening of a royal offensive against the National Constituent Assembly and the city. On July 14 somewhat over eight hundred people, most of whom were small shopkeepers, tradespeople, artisans, and wage earners, marched to the Bastille in search of weapons for the militia. This great fortress, with ten-foot-thick walls, had once held political prisoners. Through miscalculations and ineptitude on the part of the governor of the fortress, the troops in the Bastille fired into the crowd, killing ninety-eight people and wounding many others. Thereafter the crowd stormed the fortress and eventually gained entrance. They released the only seven prisoners, none of whom was there for political reasons, and killed several troops and the governor. They found no weapons.

On July 15 the militia of Paris, by then called the National Guard, offered its command to Lafayette. The hero of the American Revolution gave the guard a new insignia in the design of the red and blue stripes of the city of Paris separated by the white stripe of the king. This emblem became the revolutionary cockade worn by the soldiers and eventually the flag of revolutionary France.

The attack on the Bastille marked the first of many crucial *journées,* or days when the populace of Paris would redirect the course of the revolution. The fall of the fortress signaled that the political future of the nation would not be decided solely by the National Constituent Assembly. As the news of the taking of the Bastille spread, similar disturbances took place in the provincial cities. A few days later Louis XVI again bowed to the force of events and personally visited Paris, where he wore the revolutionary cockade and recognized the organized electors as the legitimate government of the city. The king also recognized the National Guard. The citizens of Paris were, for the time being, satisfied.

The Great Fear and the Surrender of Feudal Privileges

Simultaneously with the popular urban disturbances, a movement known as the *Great Fear* swept across much of the French countryside. Rumors had spread that royal troops would be sent into the rural districts. The result was an intensification of the peasant disturbances that had begun during the spring. The Great Fear witnessed the burning of chateaux, the destruction of records and documents, and the refusal to pay feudal dues. The peasants were determined to take possession of food supplies and land that they considered rightfully theirs. They were reclaiming rights and property that they had lost through the aristocratic resurgence of the last quarter century, as well as venting their general anger against the injustices of rural life.

On the night of August 4, 1789, aristocrats in the National Constituent Assembly attempted to halt the spreading disorder in the countryside. By prearrangement a number of liberal nobles and churchmen rose in the assembly and renounced their feudal rights, dues, and tithes. In a scene of great emotion, hunting and fishing rights, judicial authority, and special exemptions were surrendered. In a sense these nobles gave up what they had already lost and what they could not have regained without civil war in the rural areas. Later they would also, in many cases, receive compensation for their losses. Nonetheless, after the night of August 4, all French citizens were subject to the same and equal laws. That dramatic session of the assembly paved the way for the legal and social reconstruction of the nation. Without those renunciations the constructive work of the National Constituent Assembly would have been much more difficult.

Both the attack on the Bastille and the Great Fear displayed varieties of the rural and urban riots that had characterized much of eighteenth-century political and social life. Louis XVI first thought that the turmoil over the Bastille was simply another bread riot. The popular disturbances also were only partly related to the events at Versailles. A deep economic downturn had struck France during 1787 and had continued into 1788. The harvests for both years had been poor, and food prices in 1789 stood higher than at any time since 1703. Wages had not kept up with the rise in prices. Throughout the winter of 1788–1789, an unusually cold one, many people suffered from hunger. Several cities had experienced wage and food riots. These economic difficulties helped the revolution reach such vast proportions. The political, social, and economic grievances of numerous sections of the country became combined. The National Constituent Assembly could look to the popular forces as a source of strength against the king and the

The National Assembly Decrees Civic Equality in France

These famous decrees of August 4, 1789, in effect created civic equality in France. The special privileges previously possessed or controlled by the nobility were removed.

1. The National Assembly completely abolishes the feudal regime. It decrees that, among the rights and dues . . . all those originating in real or personal serfdom, personal servitude, and those which represent them, are abolished without indemnification; all others are declared redeemable, and that the price and mode of redemption shall be fixed by the National Assembly. . . .

2. The exclusive right to maintain pigeon-houses and dove-cotes is abolished. . . .

3. The exclusive right to hunt and to maintain unenclosed warrens is likewise abolished. . . .

4. All manorial courts are suppressed without indemnification.

5. Tithes of every description and the dues which have been substituted for them . . . are abolished, on condition, however, that some

other method be devised to provide for the expenses of divine worship, the support of the officiating clergy, the relief of the poor, repairs and rebuilding of churches and parsonages, and for all establishments, seminaries, schools, academies, asylums, communities, and other institutions, for the maintenance of which they are actually devoted. . . .

. . . .

7. The sale of judicial and municipal offices shall be suppressed forthwith. . . .

8. Pecuniary privileges, personal or real, in the payment of taxes are abolished forever. . . .

. . . .

11. All citizens, without distinction of birth, are eligible to any office or dignity, whether ecclesiastical, civil or military. . . .

Frank Maloy Anderson (Ed. and Trans.), *The Constitutions and Other Select Documents Illustrative of the History of France, 1789–1907,* 2nd ed., rev. and enlarged (Minneapolis: H. W. Wilson, 1908), pp. 11–13.

conservative aristocrats. When the various elements of the assembly later fell into quarrels among themselves, their factions succumbed to the temptation of appealing to the politically sophisticated and well-organized shopkeeping and artisan classes for support. When this turn of events came to pass, the popular classes could demand a price for their cooperation.

The Declaration of the Rights of Man and Citizen

In late August 1789 the National Constituent Assembly decided that before writing a new constitution, it should set forth a statement of broad political principles. On August 27 the assembly issued the Declaration of the Rights of Man and Citizen. This declaration drew together much of the political language of the Enlightenment and was also influenced by the Declaration of Rights adopted by Virginia in America in June 1776. The French declaration

proclaimed that all men were "born and remain free and equal in rights." The natural rights so proclaimed were "liberty, property, security, and resistance to oppression." Governments existed to protect those rights. All political sovereignty resided in the nation and its representatives. All citizens were to be equal before the law and were to be "equally admissible to all public dignities, offices, and employments, according to their capacity, and with no other distinction than that of their virtues and talents." There were to be due process of law and presumption of innocence until proof of guilt. Freedom of religion was affirmed. Taxation was to be apportioned equally according to capacity to pay. Property constituted "an inviolable and sacred right."[2] Although these statements were rather abstract, almost all of them were directed against specific abuses of

[2] Quoted in Georges Lefebvre, *The Coming of the French Revolution,* trans. by R. R. Palmer (Princeton, N.J.: Princeton University Press, 1967), pp. 221–223.

The women of Paris marching to Versailles on October 5, 1789. The following day, the royal family was forced to return to Paris with them. Henceforth, the French government would function under the constant threat of mob violence. [Mary Evans Picture Library]

the old aristocratic and absolutist regime. If any two principles of the future governed the declaration, they were civic equality and protection of property. The Declaration of the Rights of Man and Citizen has often been considered the death certificate of the old regime.

Louis XVI stalled before ratifying both the declaration and the aristocratic renunciation of feudalism. The longer he hesitated, the larger existing suspicions grew that he might again try to resort to the use of troops. Moreover bread continued to be in short supply. On October 5 a large crowd of Parisian women marched to Versailles demanding more bread. They milled about the palace, and many stayed the night. Under this pressure the king agreed to sanction the decrees of the assembly. The next day he and his family appeared on a balcony before the crowd. The Parisians were deeply suspicious of the monarch and believed that he must be kept under the watchful eye of the people. Consequently they demanded that Louis and his family return to Paris. The monarch had no real choice in the matter. On October 6, 1789, his carriage followed the crowd into the city, where he and his family settled in the palace of the Tuileries. The National Constituent Assembly soon followed. Thereafter both Paris and France remained relatively stable and peaceful until the summer of 1792.

The Reconstruction of France

Once established in Paris, the National Constituent Assembly set about reorganizing France. In government it pursued a policy of constitutional monarchy; in administration, rationalism; in economics, unregulated freedom; and in religion, anticlericalism. Throughout its proceedings the assembly was determined to protect property and to limit the impact on national life of the unpropertied elements of the nation and even of possessors of small amounts of property. Although championing civic equality before the law, the assembly spurned social equality and extensive democracy. In all these areas the assembly charted a general course that, to a greater or lesser degree, nineteenth-century liberals across Europe would follow.

Political Reorganization

The Constitution of 1791, which was the product of the National Constituent Assembly's deliberations, established a constitutional monarchy. There was to be a unicameral Legislative Assembly in which all laws would originate and in which the major political authority of the nation would reside. The monarch was allowed a suspensive veto that could

634

ENGLAND

PAS-DE-CALAIS
NORD
SOMME
AISNE
ARDENNES
MEUSE
MOSELLE
MEURTHE
BAS RHIN
SEINE-INFÉRIEURE
OISE
MARNE
VOSGES
HAUT RHIN
EURE
Paris
SEINE-ET-OISE
SEINE-ET-MARNE
AUBE
HAUTE MARNE
HAUTE SAÔNE
CALVADOS
ORNE
EURE-ET-LOIR
LOIRET
YONNE
CÔTE-D'OR
DOUBS
MANCHE
CÔTES-DU-NORD
ILLE-ET-VILAINE
MAYENNE
SARTHE
LOIR-ET-CHER
NIÈVRE
SAÔNE-ET-LOIRE
JURA
FINISTÈRE
MORBIHAN
LOIRE-INFÉRIEURE
MAINE-ET-LOIRE
INDRE-ET-LOIRE
CHER
ALLIER
RHÔNE
AIN
INDRE
LOIRE
ISÈRE
VENDÉE
DEUX-SÈVRES
VIENNE
HAUTE VIENNE
CREUSE
PUY-DE-DÔME
HAUTE LOIRE
ARDÈCHE
DRÔME
HAUTES ALPES
CHARENTE-INFÉRIEURE
CHARENTE
CORRÈZE
CANTAL
LOZÈRE
VAUCLUSE
BASSES ALPES
DORDOGNE
LOT
AVEYRON
GARD
BOUCHES-DU-RHÔNE
VAR
GIRONDE
LOT-ET-GARONNE
TARN-ET-GARONNE
TARN
HÉRAULT
LANDES
GERS
HAUTE GARONNE
AUDE
BASSES PYRÉNÉES
HAUTES PYRÉNÉES
ARIÈGE
PYRÉNÉES ORIENTALES
GOLO
LIAMONE

FRENCH REVOLUTIONARY DEPARTMENTS AFTER 1789

100 MI.
100 KM.

ENGLAND

FLANDERS AND HAINAUT
ARTOIS
PICARDY
METZ AND VERDUN
LORRAINE
ALSACE
ISLE DE FRANCE
Paris
CHAMPAGNE AND BRIE
FRANCHE-COMTÉ
NORMANDIE
MAINE
ORLÉANAIS
NIVERNAIS
BURGUNDY
BRETAGNE
ANJOU
TOURAINE
BERRY
BOURBONNAIS
LYONNAIS
SAUMU-ROIS
POITOU
MARCHE
LIMOUSIN
AUVERGNE
DAUPHINÉ
AUNIS
SAINTONGE AND ANGOUMOIS
PROVENCE
GUIENNE AND GASCONY
LANGUEDOC
ROUSSILLON
BÉARN
FOIX
CORSICA

FRENCH PROVINCES BEFORE 1789

PRUSSIA
BATAVIAN REP.
ENGLAND
Antwerp
Cologne
Amiens
Strasbourg
HELVETIAN REP.
AUSTRIA
Paris
Lunéville
CISALPINE REP.
FRANCE
Marengo
TUSCANY
Lyons
ROMAN REP.
Avignon
Toulon
LIGURIAN REP.
ITALY
PARTHENOPEAN REP.
SPAIN

FIRST FRENCH REPUBLIC 1792–1799

FRENCH REPUBLIC, 1792
ANNEXATIONS IN 1795
INDEPENDENT REPUBLICS, 1799

200 MI.
200 KM.

MAPS 18-1, 18-2, 18-3

delay but not halt legislation. Powers of war and peace were vested in the assembly. The constitution provided for an elaborate system of indirect elections intended to thwart direct popular pressure on the government. The citizens of France were divided into active and passive categories. Only active citizens—that is, men paying annual taxes equal to three days of local labor wages—could vote. They chose electors, who then in turn voted for the members of the legislature. At the levels of electors, or members, still further property qualifications were imposed. Only about fifty thousand citizens of a population of about twenty-five million could qualify as electors or members of the Legislative Assembly.

In reconstructing the local and judicial administration, the National Constituent Assembly applied the rational spirit of the Enlightenment. It abolished the ancient French provinces, such as Burgundy and Brittany, and established in their place eighty-three departments (*départements*) of generally equal size named after rivers, mountains, and other geographical features. The departments in turn were subdivided into districts, cantons, and communes. Most local elections were also indirect. The departmental reconstruction proved to be one of the most permanent achievements of the assembly. The departments exist to the present day. All of the ancient judicial courts, including the seigneurial courts and the *parlements,* were also abolished. In their place were organized uniform courts with elected judges and prosecutors. Procedures were simplified, and the most degrading punishments were removed from the books.

Economic Policy

In economic matters the National Constituent Assembly continued the policies formerly advocated by Louis XVI's reformist ministers. It suppressed the guilds and liberated the grain trade. The assembly established the metric system to provide the nation with uniform weights and measures. These policies of economic freedom and uniformity disappointed both peasants and urban workers caught in the cycle of inflation. By decrees of 1789 the assembly placed the burden of proof on the peasants to rid themselves of the residual feudal dues for which compensation was to be paid. On June 14, 1791, the assembly crushed the attempts of urban workers to protect their wages by enacting the Chapelier Law, which forbade workers' associations. Peasants and workers were henceforth to be left to the freedom and mercy of the marketplace.

While these various reforms were being put into effect, the original financial crisis that had occasioned the calling of the Estates General persisted. The royal debt was not repudiated, because it was owed to the bankers, the merchants, and the commercial traders of the Third Estate. The National Constituent Assembly had suppressed many of the old, hated indirect taxes and had substituted new land taxes, but these proved insufficient. Moreover there were not enough officials to collect them. The continuing financial problem led the assembly to take what may well have been, for the future of French life and society, its most decisive action. The assembly decided to finance the debt by confiscating and then selling the land and property of the Roman Catholic church in France. The results were further inflation, religious schism, and civil war. In effect, the National Constituent Assembly had opened a new chapter in the relations of Church and State in Europe.

Having chosen to plunder the land of the church, in December 1789 the assembly authorized the issuance of *assignats,* or government bonds, the value of which was guaranteed by the revenue to be generated from the sale of church property. Initially a limit was set on the quantity of *assignats* to be issued. However, the bonds proved so acceptable to the public that they began to circulate as currency. The assembly decided to issue an ever larger number of them to liquidate the national debt and to create a large body of new property owners with a direct stake in the revolution. However, within a few months the value of the *assignats* began to fall. Inflation increased and put new stress on the lives of the urban poor.

The Civil Constitution of the Clergy

The confiscation of church lands required an ecclesiastical reconstruction. In July 1790 the National Constituent Assembly issued the Civil Constitution of the Clergy, which transformed the Roman Catholic church in France into a branch of the secular state. This legislation reduced the number of bishoprics from 135 to 83 and brought the borders of the dioceses into conformity with those of the new departments. It also provided for the election of priests and bishops, who henceforth became salaried employees of the state. The assembly consulted neither the pope nor the French clergy about these broad changes. The king approved the measure only with the greatest reluctance.

The Civil Constitution of the Clergy was the major blunder of the National Constituent Assembly. The measure created immense opposition within the French church even from bishops who had long championed Gallican liberties over papal domination. In the face of this resistance the assembly unwisely ruled that all clergy must take an oath to support the Civil Constitution. Only seven bishops and about half the clergy did so. In reprisal the assembly designated the clergy who had not taken the oath as "refractory" and removed them from their clerical functions.

Further reaction was swift. Refractory priests attempted to celebrate Mass. In February 1791 the pope condemned not only the Civil Constitution of the Clergy but also the Declaration of the Rights of Man and Citizen. That condemnation marked the opening of a Roman Catholic offensive against liberalism and the revolution that continued throughout the nineteenth century. Within France itself the pope's action created a crisis of conscience and political loyalty for all sincere Catholics. Religious devotion and revolutionary loyalty became incompatible for many people. French citizens were divided between those who supported the constitutional priests and those who resorted to the refractory clergy. Louis XVI and his family favored the latter clergy.

Counterrevolutionary Activity

The revolution had other enemies besides the pope and the devout Catholics. As it became clear that the old political and social order was undergoing fundamental and probably permanent change, considerable numbers of aristocrats left France. Known as the *émigrés*, they settled in countries near the French border, where they sought to foment counterrevolution. Among the most important of their number was the king's younger brother, the count of Artois (1757–1836). In the summer of 1791 his agents and the queen persuaded Louis XVI to attempt to flee the country. On the night of June 20, 1791, Louis and his immediate family, disguised as servants, left Paris. They traveled as far as Varennes on their way to Metz. At Varennes the king was recognized, and his flight was halted. On June 24 a company of soldiers escorted the royal family back to Paris. The leaders of the National Constitu-

The assignats *were government bonds that were backed by confiscated church lands. They circulated as money. When the government printed too many of them, inflation resulted and their value fell.* [Bettman Archive]

ent Assembly, determined to save the constitutional monarchy, announced that the king had been abducted from the capital. However, such a convenient public fiction could not cloak the reality that the chief counterrevolutionary in France now sat on the throne.

Two months later, on August 27, 1791, under pressure from a group of *émigrés*, Emperor Leopold II of Austria, who was the brother of Marie Antoinette, and Frederick William II, the king of Prussia, issued the Declaration of Pillnitz. The two monarchs promised to intervene in France to protect the royal family and to preserve the monarchy *if* the other major European powers agreed. The latter provision rendered the statement meaningless because at the time Great Britain would not have given its consent. However, the declaration was not so read in France, where the revolutionaries saw the nation surrounded by aristocratic and monarchical foes.

The National Constituent Assembly drew to a close in September 1791. Its task of reconstructing the government and the administration of France had been completed. One of its last acts was the passage of a measure that forbade any of its own members to sit in the Legislative Assembly then being elected. The new body met on October 1 and had to confront the immense problems that had emerged during the earlier part of the year. Within the Legislative Assembly major political divisions also soon developed over the future course of the nation and the revolution.

A Second Revolution

End of the Monarchy

The issues of the Civil Constitution of the Clergy and the trustworthiness of Louis XVI

Marie Antoinette (1755–1793) was beautiful, elegant, and more intelligent than her husband, but her reputation for extravagance and her reactionary political intrigues (she favored war in 1792) were to help destroy the monarchy. [Art Resource]

undermined the unity of the revolution. Much factionalism displayed itself throughout the short life of the Legislative Assembly (1791–1792). Ever since the original gathering of the Estates General, deputies from the Third Estate had organized themselves into clubs composed of politically like-minded persons. The most famous and best organized of these were the Jacobins, whose name derived from the fact that Dominican friars were called *Jacobins,* and the group met in a Dominican monastery in Paris. The Jacobins had also established a network of local clubs throughout the provinces. They had constituted the most advanced political group in the National Constituent Assembly and had pressed for a republic rather than a constitutional monarchy. The events of the summer of 1791 led them to renew those demands.

In the Legislative Assembly a group of Jacobins known as the *Girondists* (because many of them came from the department of the Gironde) assumed leadership.[3] They were determined to oppose the forces of counterrevolution. They passed a measure ordering the *émigrés* to return or suffer loss of property and another requiring the refractory clergy to support the Civil Constitution or lose their state pensions. The king vetoed both acts. On April 20, 1792, the Girondists led the Legislative Assembly to declare war on Austria, by this time governed by Francis II (1768–1835) and allied to Prussia. The Girondists believed that the war would preserve the revolution from domestic enemies and bring the most advanced revolutionaries to power. Paradoxically Louis XVI and other monarchists also favored the war. They thought that the conflict would strengthen the executive power (i.e., the monarchy). The king also entertained the hope that French forces might be defeated and the old regime restored. Both sides were playing dangerously foolish politics.

The war radicalized the revolution and led to what is usually called the *second revolution,* which overthrew the constitutional monarchy and established a republic. Initially the war effort went quite poorly. Both the country and the revolution seemed in danger. In July 1792 the duke of Brunswick, commander of the Prussian forces, issued a manifesto promising the destruction of Paris if harm came to the

---

[3] The Girondists are also frequently called the *Brissotins* after Jacques-Pierre Brissot (1754–1793), who was their chief spokesman in early 1792.

On August 10, 1792, mobs attacked the Tuileries and massacred the royal guards. Louis XVI and his family took refuge with the Legislative Assembly. They can be seen in this print behind the screened reporter's box at the right. [New York Public Library]

French royal family. This statement stiffened support for the war and increased the already significant distrust of the king.

Late in July, under radical working-class pressure, the government of the city of Paris passed from the elected council to a committee, or commune, of representatives from the sections (municipal wards) of Paris. On August 10, 1792, a very large Parisian crowd invaded the Tuileries palace and forced Louis XVI and Marie Antoinette to take refuge in the Legislative Assembly itself. The crowd fought with the royal Swiss guards. When Louis was finally able to call off the troops, several hundred of them and a large number of Parisian citizens lay dead. The monarchy itself was also a casualty of that melee. Thereafter the royal family was imprisoned—in comfortable quarters, but the king was allowed to perform none of his political functions.

The Convention and the Role of the Sans-culottes

Early in September the Parisian crowd again made its will felt. During the first week of the month, in what are known as the *September*

Massacres, the Paris Commune summarily executed or murdered about twelve hundred people who were in the city jails. Many of these people were aristocrats or priests, but the majority were simply common criminals. The crowd had assumed that the prisoners were all counterrevolutionaries. The Paris Commune then compelled the Legislative Assembly to call for the election by universal manhood suffrage of a new assembly to write a democratic constitution. That body, called the *Convention* after its American counterpart of 1787, met on September 21, 1792. The previous day the French army had halted the Prussian advance at the battle of Valmy in eastern France. The victory of democratic forces at home had been conformed by victory on the battlefield.

As its first act, the Convention declared France a republic, that is, a nation governed by an elected assembly without a king. The second revolution had been the work of Jacobins more radical than the Girondists and of the people of Paris known as the *sans-culottes*. The name of the latter means "without breeches" and derived from the long trousers that, as working people, they wore instead of aristocratic knee breeches. The sans-culottes were shopkeepers, artisans, wage earners, and, in a few cases, factory workers. The persistent food shortages and the revolutionary inflation had made their generally difficult lives even more burdensome. The politics of the old regime had ignored them, and the policies of the National Constituent Assembly had left them victims of unregulated economic liberty. However, the nation required their labor and their lives if the war was to succeed. From the summer of 1792 until the summer of 1794 their attitudes, desires, and ideals were the primary factors in the internal development of the revolution.

The sans-culottes generally knew what they wanted. The Parisian tradespeople and artisans sought immediate relief from food shortages and rising prices through the vehicle of price controls. They believed that all people had a right to subsistence and profoundly resented most forms of social inequality. This attitude led them to intense hostility toward the aristocracy and toward the original leaders of the revolution, who they believed simply wanted to take over the social privileges of the aristoc-

racy. Their hatred of inequality did not go so far as to demand the abolition of property. Rather, they advocated a community of relatively small property owners. In politics they were antimonarchical, strongly republican, and suspicious even of representative government. They believed that the people should make the decisions of government to as great an extent as possible. In Paris, where their influence was most important, the sans-culottes' political experience had been gained in meetings of the Paris sections. Those gatherings exemplified direct community democracy and were not unlike a New England town meeting. The economic hardship of their lives made them impatient to see their demands met.

The goals of the sans-culottes were not wholly compatible with those of the Jacobins. The latter were republicans who sought representative government. Jacobin hatred of the aristocracy did not extend to a general suspicion of wealth. Basically the Jacobins favored an unregulated economy. However, from the time of Louis XVI's flight to Varennes onward,

A Pamphleteer Describes a Sans-culotte

This pamphlet is a 1793 description of a sans-culotte written either by one or by a sympathizer. It describes the sans-culotte as a hardworking, useful, patriotic citizen who bravely sacrifices himself to the war effort. It contrasts those virtues to the lazy and unproductive luxury of the noble and the personally self-interested plottings of the politician.

A sans-culotte *you rogues? He is someone who always goes on foot, who has no millions as you would all like to have, no* chateaux, *no valets to serve him, and who lives simply with his wife and children, if he has any, on a fourth or fifth storey.*

He is useful, because he knows how to work in the field, to forge iron, to use a saw, to use a file, to roof a house, to make shoes, and to shed his last drop of blood for the safety of the Republic.

And because he works, you are sure not to meet his person in the Café de Chartres, or in the gaming houses where others conspire and game; nor at the National theatre . . . nor in the literary clubs. . . .

In the evening he goes to his section, not powdered or perfumed, or smartly booted in the hope of catching the eye of the citizenesses in the galleries, but ready to support good proposals with all his might, and to crush those which come from the abominable faction of politicians.

Finally, a sans-culotte *always has his sabre sharp, to cut off the ears of all enemies of the Revolution; sometimes he even goes out with his pike; but at the first sound of the drum he is ready to leave for the Vendée, for the army of the Alps or for the army of the North. . . .*

"Reply to an Impertinent Question: What Is a *Sans-culotte?*" April 1793. Reprinted in Walter Markov and Albert Soboul (Eds.), *Die Sansculotten von Paris,* and republished trans. by Clive Emsley in Merryn Williams (Ed.), *Revolutions: 1775–1830* (Baltimore: Penguin Books, in association with The Open University, 1971), pp. 100–101.

The execution of Louis XVI on January 21, 1793. [New York Public Library]

the more extreme Jacobins began to cooperate with leaders of the Parisian sans-culottes and the Paris Commune for the overthrow of the monarchy. Once the Convention began its deliberations, these advanced Jacobins, known as the *Mountain* because of their seats high in the assembly hall, worked with the sans-culottes to carry the revolution forward and to win the war. This willingness to cooperate with the forces of the popular revolution separated the Mountain from the Girondists, who were also members of the Jacobin Club.

By the spring of 1793 several issues had brought the Mountain and its sans-culottes allies to domination of the Convention and the revolution. In December 1792 Louis XVI was put on trial as mere "Citizen Capet," the family name of extremely distant forebears of the royal family. The Girondists looked for some way to spare his life, but the Mountain defeated the effort. Louis was convicted, by a very narrow majority, of conspiring against the lib-

erty of the people and the security of the state. He was condemned to death and was beheaded on January 21, 1793. The next month the Convention declared war on Great Britain, Holland, and Spain. Soon thereafter the Prussians renewed their offensive and drove the French out of Belgium. To make matters worse, General Dumouriez, the Girondist victor of Valmy, deserted to the enemy. Finally, in March 1793 a royalist revolt led by aristocratic officers and priests erupted in the Vendée in western France and roused much popular support. Consequently the revolution found itself at war with most of Europe and much of the French nation. The Girondists had led the country into the war but had proved themselves incapable either of winning it or of suppressing the enemies of the revolution at home. The Mountain stood ready to take up the task.

Every major European power was now hostile to the revolution.

641

The Revolution and Europe at War

Initially the attitude of the rest of Europe toward the revolutionary events in France had been ambivalent. Those people who favored political reform regarded the revolution as wisely and rationally reorganizing a corrupt and inefficient government. The major foreign governments thought that the revolution meant that France would cease to be an important factor in European affairs for several years. In 1790, however, the Irish-born writer and British statesman Edmund Burke (1729–1799) argued a different position in *Reflections on the Revolution in France*. Burke regarded the reconstruction of French administration as the application of a blind rationalism that ignored the historical realities of political development and the complexities of social relations. He also forecast further turmoil as persons without political experience attempted to govern France. As the revolutionaries proceeded to attack the church, the monarchy, and finally the rest of Europe, Burke's ideas came to have many admirers, and his *Reflections* became the handbook of European conservatives for decades.

By the time of the commencement of the war with Austria in April 1792, the other European monarchies recognized the danger of both the ideas and the aggression of revolutionary France. The ideals of the Rights of Man and Citizen were highly exportable and appli-

---

Burke Condemns the Work of the French National Assembly

Edmund Burke was undoubtedly the most important and articulate foreign critic of the French Revolution. He believed that governments could not be quickly created or organized, as seemed to have occurred in France. He was also deeply opposed to democracy, which he thought would lead to unwise, extreme actions on the part of government. Burke left a legacy of brilliantly argued conservative thought that remained a comfort to many followers, a serious challenge to liberals in nineteenth-century Europe, and an important statement in political theory. This passage is from his 1790 *Reflections on the Revolution in France*.

To make a government requires no great prudence. Settle the seat of power; teach obedience: and the work is done. To give Freedom is still more easy. It is not necessary to guide; it only requires to let go the rein. But to form a free *government; that is, to temper together these opposite elements of liberty and restraint in one consistent work, requires much thought, deep reflection, a sagacious, powerful, and combining mind. This I do not find in those who take the lead in the National Assembly. Perhaps they are not so miserably deficient as they appear. I rather believe it. It would put them below the common level of human understanding. But when the leaders choose to make themselves bidders at an auction of popularity, their talents, in the construction of the state, will be of no service. They will become flatterers instead of legislators;* the instruments, not the guides, of the people. If any of them should happen to propose a scheme of liberty, soberly limited, and defined with proper qualifications, he will be immediately outbid by his competitors, who will produce something more splendidly popular. Suspicions will be raised of his fidelity to his cause. Moderation will be stigmatized as the virtue of cowards; and compromise as the prudence of traitors; until, in hopes of preserving the credit which may enable him to temper, and moderate, on some occasions, the popular leader is obliged to become active in propagating doctrines, and establishing powers, that will afterwards defeat any sober purpose at which he ultimately might have aimed.*

. . . The improvements of the National Assembly are superficial, their errors fundamental.

Edmund Burke, *Reflections on the Revolution in France*, in *The Works of the Right Honourable Edmund Burke*, Vol. 2 (London: Henry G. Bohn, 1864), pp. 515–516.

cable to the rest of Europe. One government after another turned to repressive domestic policies. In Great Britain William Pitt the Younger (1759–1806), the prime minister, who had unsuccessfully supported moderate reform of Parliament during the 1780s, turned against both reform and popular movements. The government suppressed the London Corresponding Society, founded in 1792 as a working-class reform group. In Birmingham the government sponsored mob action to drive Joseph Priestley (1733–1804), a chemist and a radical political thinker, out of the country. In early 1793 Pitt secured parliamentary approval for acts suspending habeas corpus and making it possible to commit treason in writing. With less success Pitt attempted to curb freedom of the press. All political groups who dared to oppose the action of the government were in danger of becoming associated with revolutionary sedition.

In eastern Europe the revolution brought to a close the existence of enlightened absolutism. The aristocratic resistance to the reforms of Joseph II in the Habsburg lands led his brother, Leopold II, to come to terms with the landowners. Leopold's successor, Francis II (1792–1835), became a major leader of the counterrevolution. In Prussia Frederick William II (1786–1797), the nephew of Frederick the Great, looked to the leaders of the Lutheran church and the aristocracy to discourage any potential popular uprisings, such as those of the downtrodden Silesian weavers. In Russia Catherine the Great burned the works of her onetime friend Voltaire and exiled Alexander Radishchev (1749–1802) to Siberia for publishing *Journey from Saint Petersburg to Moscow,* a work critical of Russian social conditions.

In 1793 and 1795 the eastern powers once again combined against Poland. In that unhappy land aristocratic reformers had finally achieved the abolition of the *liberum veto* and had organized a new constitutional monarchy in 1791. Russia and Prussia, which already had designs on Polish territory, saw or pretended to see a threat of revolution in the new Polish constitution. In 1793 they annexed large sections of the country; in 1795 Austria joined the two other powers in a final partition that removed Poland from the map of Europe until after World War I. The governments of eastern Europe had used the widely shared fear of further revolutionary disorder to justify old-fashioned eighteenth-century aggression.

Consequently, in a paradoxical fashion the very success of the revolution in France brought to a rapid close reform movements in the rest of Europe. The French invasion of the Austrian Netherlands and the revolutionary reorganization of that territory roused the rest of Europe to the point of active hostility. In November 1792 the Convention declared that it would aid all peoples who wished to cast off the burdens of aristocratic and monarchical oppression. The Convention had also proclaimed the Scheldt River in the Netherlands open to the commerce of all nations and thus had broken a treaty that Great Britain had made with Austria and Holland. The British were on the point of declaring war on France over this issue when the Convention issued its own declaration of hostilities. By April 1793, when the Mountain began to direct the French government, the nation stood at war with Austria, Prussia, Great Britain, Spain, Sardinia, and Holland. The governments of those nations were attempting to protect their social structures, political systems, and economic interests against the aggression of the revolution.

The Reign of Terror

The Republic Defended

In April 1793 the Convention established a Committee of General Security and a Committee of Public Safety to perform the executive duties of the government. The latter committee became more important and eventually enjoyed almost dictatorial power. The most prominent leaders of the Committee of Public Safety were Jacques Danton (1759–1794), who had provided heroic leadership in September 1792; Maximilien Robespierre (1758–1794), who became for a time the single most powerful member of the committee; and Lazare Carnot (1753–1823), who was in charge of the military. All of these men and the other figures on the committee were strong republicans and had opposed the weak policies of the Girondists. They conceived of their task as saving the revolution from mortal enemies at home and abroad. They generally enjoyed a working political relationship with the sansculottes of Paris, but this was an alliance of expediency on the part of the committee.

The major problem was to wage the war and to secure domestic support for the effort. In early June 1793 the Parisian sans-culottes invaded the Convention and successfully de-

Mary Wollstonecraft Urges the Vindication of the Rights of Woman

Edmund Burke's *Reflections on the Revolution in France* provoked a very large number of replies. Many of these pamphlets defended the principles of the French Declaration of the Rights of Man and Citizen. The terms of the political debate thus brought to prominence the rights of male citizens. In 1790 Mary Wollstonecraft, an English writer, published a tract entitled *A Vindication of the Rights of Men.* Two years later she published her now more famous work *A Vindication of the Rights of Woman* (1792). In that book she explained how the extension to women of the political and social rights enjoyed by most male citizens would raise the condition of all human beings. In particular she argued that existing social and educational arrangements, as well as the absence of political rights, treated women as if they were less than rational creatures and often prescribed for women less than rational roles in life. She argued that women must receive education and social roles like other rational beings and that the consequence would be beneficial to humanity. Note how her language echoes that of the writers of the Enlightenment and the manner in which she extended the call for political liberty into the social realm of relations between the sexes.

It is time to effect a revolution in female manners—time to restore to them their lost dignity—and make them, as a part of the human species, labour by reforming themselves to reform the world. It is time to separate unchangeable morals from local manners. . . .

I wish to sum up what I have said in a few words, for I here threw down my gauntlet, and deny the existence of sexual virtues, not excepting modesty. For man and woman, truth, if I understand the meaning of the word, must be the same; yet the fanciful female character, so prettily drawn by poets and novelists, demanding the sacrifice of truth and sincerity, virtue becomes a relative idea, having no other foundation than utility, and of that utility men pretend arbitrarily to judge, shaping it to their own convenience.

Women, I allow, may have different duties to fulfil; but they are human *duties, and the principles that should regulate the discharge of them, I sturdily maintain, must be the same.*

To become respectable, the exercise of their understanding is necessary, there is no other foundation for independence of character; I mean explicitly to say that they must only bow to the authority of reason, instead of being the modest slaves *of opinion.*

In the superior ranks of life how seldom do we meet with a man of superior abilities, or even common acquirements? The reason appears to me clear, the state they are born in was an unnatural one. The human character has ever been formed by the employments the individual, or class, pursues; and if the faculties are not sharpened by necessity, they must remain obtuse. The argument may fairly be extended to women; for, seldom occupied by serious business, the pursuit of pleasure gives that insignificancy to their character which renders the society of the great *so insipid. The same want of firmness, produced by a similar cause, forces them both to fly from themselves to noisy pleasures, and artificial passions, till vanity takes place of every social affection, and the characteristics of humanity can scarcely be discerned. Such are the blessings of civil governments, as they are at present organized, that wealth and female softness equally tend to debase mankind, and are produced by the same cause; but allowing women to be rational creatures, they should be incited to acquire virtues which they may call their own, for how can a rational being be ennobled by any thing that is not obtained by its own* exertions?

Mary Wollstonecraft, *A Vindication of the Rights of Woman,* ed. by Carol H. Poston (New York: Norton, 1975), pp. 45, 51–52.

manded the expulsion of the Girondist members. That action further radicalized the Convention and gave the Mountain complete control. On June 22 the Convention approved a fully democratic constitution but suspended its operation until the conclusion of the war emergency. On August 23 Carnot began a mobilization for victory by issuing a *levée en masse,* or general military requisition of the population, which conscripted males into the army and directed economic production for military purposes. On September 17 a maximum on prices was established in accord with sans-culotte demands. During these same months the armies of the revolution also successfully crushed many of the counterrevolutionary disturbances in the provinces.

Never before had Europe seen a nation organized in this way nor one defended by a citizen army. Other events within France astounded Europeans even more. The Reign of Terror had begun. Those months of quasi-judicial executions and murders stretching from the autumn of 1793 to the midsummer of 1794 are probably the most famous or infamous period of the

A meeting of the Committee of Public Safety in 1793. The committee had twelve members, but it was said that they never all sat at the same table at the same time, since some were always stationed in the provinces. [Library of Congress]

The French Convention Calls Up the Entire Nation

This proclamation of the *levée en masse,* August 23, 1793, marked the first time in European history that all citizens of a nation were called to contribute to a war effort. The decree set the entire nation on a wartime footing under the centralized direction of the Committee of Public Safety.

1. *From this moment until that in which the enemy shall have been driven from the soil of the Republic, all Frenchmen are in permanent requisition for the service of the armies.*

The young men shall go to battle; the married men shall forge arms and transport provisions; the women shall make tents and clothing and shall serve in the hospitals; the children shall turn old linen into lint; the aged shall betake themselves to the public places in order to arouse the courage of the warriors and preach the hatred of kings and the unity of the Republic.

2. *The national buildings shall be converted into barracks, the public places into workshops for arms, the soil of the cellars shall be washed in order to extract therefrom the saltpetre.*

3. *The arms of the regulation calibre shall be reserved exclusively for those who shall march against the enemy; the service of the interior shall be performed with hunting pieces and side arms.*

4. *The saddle horses are put in requisition to complete the cavalry corps; the draught-horses, other than those employed in agriculture, shall convey the artillery and the provisions.*

5. *The Committee of Public Safety is charged to take all the necessary measures to set up without delay an extraordinary manufacture of arms of every sort which corresponds with the ardor and energy of the French people. . . .*

. . . .

8. *The levy shall be general. . . .*

Frank Maloy Anderson (Ed. and Trans.). *The Constitutions and Other Select Documents Illustrative of the History of France, 1789–1907,* 2nd ed., rev. and enlarged (Minneapolis: H. W. Wilson, 1908), pp. 184–185.

revolution. They can be understood only in the context of the war on the one hand and the revolutionary expectations of the Convention and the sans-culottes on the other.

The Republic of Virtue

The presence of armies closing in on the nation created a situation in which it was relatively easy to dispense with legal due process. However, the people who sat in the Convention and composed the Committee of Public Safety also believed that they had made a new departure in world history. They had established a republic in which civic virtue rather than aristocratic and monarchical corruption might flourish. The republic of virtue manifested itself in the renaming of streets from the egalitarian vocabulary of the revolution, in republican dress copied from that of the sans-culottes or the Roman Republic, in the absence of powdered wigs, in the suppression of plays that were insufficiently republican, and in a general attack against crimes, such as prostitution, that were supposedly characteristic of aristocratic society.

The most dramatic departure of the republic of virtue, and one that illustrates the imposition of political values that would justify the Terror, was an attempt by the Convention to dechristianize France. In October 1793 the Convention proclaimed a new calendar dating from the first day of the French Republic. There were twelve months of thirty days with names associated with the seasons and climate. Every tenth day, rather than every seventh, was a holiday. Many of the most important events of the next few years became known as their dates on the revolutionary calendar.[4] In November 1793 the convention decreed the Cathedral of Notre Dame to be a Temple of Reason. The legislature then sent trusted members, known as *deputies on mission,* into the provinces to enforce dechristianization by closing churches, persecuting clergy and believers, and occasionally forcing priests to marry. Needless to say, this religious policy roused much opposition and deeply separated the French provinces from the revolutionary government in Paris.

During the crucial months of late 1793 and

Maximilien Robespierre (1758–1794). In 1793–1794 he emerged as the most powerful revolutionary figure and dominated the Committee of Public Safety. He considered the Terror essential for the success of the revolution. [Giraudon]

early 1794 the person who emerged as the chief figure on the Committee of Public Safety was Robespierre. He was a complex person who has remained controversial to the present day. He was utterly selfless and from the earliest days of the revolution had favored a republic. The Jacobin Club provided his primary forum and base of power. A shrewd and sensitive politician, he had opposed the war in 1792 as a measure that might aid the monarchy. He largely depended on the support of the sans-culottes of Paris, but he continued to dress as he had before the revolution and opposed dechristianization as a political blunder. For him the republic of virtue meant wholehearted support of republican government and the renunciation of selfish gains from political life. He once told the Convention, "If the mainspring of popular government in peacetime is virtue, amid revolution it is at the same time virtue and *terror:* virtue, without which terror is fatal; terror, without which virtue is impotent. Terror is nothing but prompt, severe, inflexible justice; it is therefore an emanation of virtue."[5] He and those who supported his policies were among the first apostles of secular ideologies who, in the name of humanity, would bring so much suffering to European polities of the left and the right in the next two centuries.

---

[4] From summer to spring the months on the revolutionary calendar were Messidor, Thermidor, Fructidor, Vendémiaire, Brumaire, Frimaire, Nivôse, Pluviôse, Ventôse, Germinal, Floréal, and Prairial.

[5] Quoted in Richard T. Bienvenu, *The Ninth of Thermidor: The Fall of Robespierre* (New York: Oxford University Press, 1968), p. 38.

Progress of the Terror

The Reign of Terror manifested itself through a series of revolutionary tribunals established by the Convention during the summer of 1793. They were to try the enemies of the republic, but the definition of *enemy* remained uncertain and shifted as the months passed. The enemies included those who might aid other European powers, those who endangered republican virtue, and finally good republicans who opposed the policies of the dominant faction of the government. In a very real sense the terror of the revolutionary tribunals systematized and channeled the popular resentment that had manifested itself in the September Massacres of 1792. The first victims were Marie Antoinette, other members of the royal family, and some aristocrats, who were executed in October 1793. They were followed by certain Girondist politicians who had been prominent in the Legislative Assembly.

By the early months of 1794 the Terror had moved to the provinces, where the deputies on mission presided over the summary execution of thousands of people who had allegedly supported internal opposition to the revolution. One of the most infamous incidents occurred in Nantes, where several hundred people were simply tied to rafts and drowned in the river. By early 1794 the victims of the Terror were coming from every social class, including the sans-culottes.

In Paris during the late winter Robespierre began to orchestrate the Terror against republican political figures of the left and right. On March 24 he secured the execution of certain extreme sans-culottes leaders known as the *enragés*. They had wanted further measures regulating prices, securing social equality, and pressing dechristianization. Robespierre then turned against more conservative republicans, including Danton. They were insufficiently militant on the war, had profited monetarily from the revolution, and had rejected any link between politics and moral virtue. Danton was executed during the first week in April. In this fashion Robespierre exterminated the leadership from both groups that might have threatened his position. Finally, on June 10, he secured passage of the Law of 22 Prairial, which permitted the revolutionary tribunal to convict suspects without hearing substantial evidence. The number of executions was growing steadily.

In May 1794, at the height of his power,

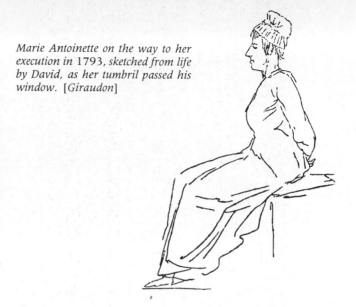

Marie Antoinette on the way to her execution in 1793, sketched from life by David, as her tumbril passed his window. [Giraudon]

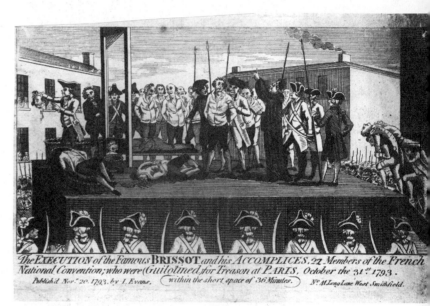

The EXECUTION of the Famous BRISSOT and his ACCOMPLICES, 22 Members of the French National Convention; who were Guillotined for Treason at PARIS, October the 31st 1793.
Publish'd Nov.r 20, 1793, by I. Evans.   within the short space of 36 Minutes.   N.o M Long Lane West Smithfield.

The execution of the Girondists in October 1793 left the Jacobins in full control of the revolution, and marked the victory of Paris over the provinces. [British Library]

Robespierre, considering the worship of Reason too abstract for most citizens, abolished it and established the Cult of the Supreme Being. This deistic cult was in line with Rousseau's idea of a civic religion that would induce morality among citizens. However, Robespierre did not long preside over his new religion. On July 26 he made an ill-tempered speech in the Convention declaring that there existed among other leaders of the government a conspiracy

The Convention Establishes the Worship of the Supreme Being

On May 7, 1794, the Convention passed one of the most extraordinary pieces of revolutionary legislation. It established the worship of the Supreme Being as a state cult. Although the law drew on the religious ideas of deism, the point of the legislation was to provide a religious basis for the new secular French state, which had repeatedly attacked traditional French Catholicism. The reader should pay particular attention to Article 7, which outlines the political and civic values that the Cult of the Supreme Being was supposed to nurture.

1. *The French people recognize the existence of the Supreme Being and the immortality of the soul.*

2. *They recognize that the worship worthy of the Supreme Being is the observance of the duties of man.*

3. *They place in the forefront of such duties detestation of bad faith and tyranny, punishment of tyrants and traitors, succoring of unfortunates, respect of weak persons, defence of the oppressed, doing to others all the good that one can, and being just towards everyone.*

4. *Festivals shall be instituted to remind man of the concept of the Divinity and of the dignity of his being.*

5. *They shall take their names from the glorious events of our Revolution, or from the virtues most dear and most useful to man, or from the greatest benefits of nature.*

. . . .

7. *On the days of* décade *[the name given to a particular day in each month of the revolutionary calendar] it shall celebrate the following festivals:*

To the Supreme Being and to nature; to the human race; to the French people; to the benefactors of humanity; to the martyrs of liberty; to liberty and equality; to the Republic; to the liberty of the world; to the love of the Patrie *[Fatherland]; to the hatred of tyrants and traitors; to truth; to justice; to modesty; to glory and immortality; to friendship; to frugality; to courage; to good faith; to heroism; to disinterestedness; to stoicism; to love; to conjugal love; to paternal love; to maternal tenderness; to filial piety; to infancy; to youth; to manhood; to old age; to misfortune; to agriculture; to industry; to our forefathers; to posterity; to happiness.*

8. *The Committees of Public Safety and Public Instruction are responsible for presenting a plan of organization for said festivals.*

9. *The National Convention summons all talents worthy of serving the cause of humanity to the honor of concurring in their establishment by hymns and civic songs, and by every means which may contribute to their embellishment and utility.*

John Hall Stewart, *A Documentary Survey of the French Revolution* (New York: Macmillan, 1951), pp. 526–527.

OPPOSITE: *The Festival of the Supreme Being that took place in June 1794 inaugurated Robespierre's new civic religion. Its climax occurred when a statue of Atheism was burned and another statue of Wisdom rose from the ashes.* [*Giraudon*]

against himself and the revolution. Such accusations against unnamed persons had usually preceded his earlier attacks. On July 27—the Ninth of Thermidor—by prearrangement, members of the Convention shouted him down when he rose to make another speech. That night Robespierre was arrested, and the next day he was executed. The revolutionary sans-culottes of Paris would not save him because he had deprived them of their chief leaders. The other Jacobins turned against him because after Danton's death they feared becoming the next victims. Robespierre had destroyed rivals for leadership without creating supporters for himself. In that regard he was the selfless creator of his own destruction.

The fall of Robespierre might simply have been one more shift in the turbulent politics of the revolution. Those who brought about his demise were motivated by instincts of self-preservation rather than by major policy differences. They had generally supported the Terror and the executions. Yet within a short time the Reign of Terror, which ultimately claimed over twenty-five thousand victims, did come to a close. The largest number of executions had involved peasants and sans-culottes who had joined rebellions against the revolutionary government. By the late summer of 1794 those provincial uprisings had been crushed, and the war against foreign enemies was also going well. Those factors, combined with the feeling in Paris that the revolution had consumed enough of its own children, brought the Terror to an end.

The fall of Robespierre occurred literally overnight on July 26–27, 1794, when his enemies in the Convention had him and his supporters arrested and executed. In this print he lies on the table a prisoner, clutching a handkerchief to his wounded jaw, where he had been shot when he was arrested. A few hours later he was guillotined. The Terror died with him. [*Library of Congress*]

The closing of the Jacobin Club in November 1794 *was a major event in the* Thermidorean Reaction *that began with the fall of Robespierre.*

The Thermidorian Reaction

The End of the Terror and Establishment of the Directory

A tempering of the revolution called the *Thermidorian Reaction* began in July 1794. It consisted of the destruction of the machinery of terror and the institution of a new constitutional regime. The influence of generally wealthy middle-class and professional people replaced that of the sans-culottes. Within days and weeks of Robespierre's execution the Convention allowed the Girondists who had been in prison or hiding to return to their seats. There was a general amnesty for political prisoners. The Convention restructured the Committee of Public Safety and gave it much less power. The Convention also repealed the notorious Law of 22 Prairial. Some, though by no means all, of the people responsible for the Terror were removed from public life. Leaders of the Paris Commune and certain deputies on mission were executed. The Paris Commune itself was outlawed. The Paris Jacobin Club was closed, and Jacobin clubs in the provinces were forbidden to correspond with each other.

The executions of former terrorists marked the beginning of "the white terror." Throughout the country people who had been involved in the Reign of Terror were attacked and often murdered. Jacobins were executed with little more due process than they had extended to their victims a few months earlier. The Convention itself approved some of these trials. In other cases gangs of youths who had aristocratic connections or who had avoided serving in the army roamed the streets beating known Jacobins. In Lyons, Toulon, and Marseilles these "bands of Jesus" dragged suspected terrorists from prisons and murdered them much as alleged royalists had been murdered during the September Massacres of 1792.

The republic of virtue gave way, if not to one of vice, at least to one of frivolous pleasures. The dress of the sans-culottes and the Roman Republic disappeared among the middle class

650

and the aristocracy. New plays appeared in the theaters, and prostitutes again roamed the streets of Paris. Families of victims of the Reign of Terror gave parties in which they appeared with shaved necks like the victims of the guillotine and red ribbons tied about them. Although the Convention continued to favor the Cult of the Supreme Being, it allowed Catholic services to be held. Many refractory priests returned to the country. One of the unanticipated results of the Thermidorian Reaction was a genuine revival of Catholic worship.

The Thermidorian Reaction also involved still further political reconstruction. The fully democratic constitution of 1793, which had never gone into effect, was abandoned. The Convention issued in its place the Constitution of the Year III, which reflected the Thermidorian determination to reject both constitutional monarchy and democracy. The new document provided for a legislature of two houses. Members of the upper body, or Council of Elders, were to be men over forty years of age who were either husbands or widowers. The lower Council of Five Hundred was to consist of married or single men at least thirty years old. The executive body was to be a five-person Directory chosen by the Elders from a list submitted by the Council of Five Hundred. Property qualifications limited the franchise except for soldiers, who even without property were permitted to vote.

Thermidor became a term associated with political reaction. However, if the French Revolution had originated in political conflicts characteristic of the eighteenth century, it had by 1795 become something very different. A society and a political structure based on rank and birth had given way to one based on civic equality and social status stemming from the ownership or nonownership of property. People who had never been allowed direct, formal access to political power had, to different degrees, been admitted to those activities. Their entrance had given rise to questions of property distribution and economic regulations that could not again be totally ignored. Representation had been established as a principle of practical politics. Henceforth the question before France and eventually before all of Europe would be which new groups would be admitted to representation. In the *levée en masse* the French had demonstrated to Europe the power of the secular ideal of nationhood.

All of these stunning changes in the political and social contours of Europe are not to be for-gotten in a consideration of the post-Thermidorian course of the French Revolution. What triumphed in the Constitution of the Year III was the revolution of the holders of property. For this reason the French Revolution has usually been considered a victory of the bourgeoisie, or middle class. However, the property that won the day was not industrial wealth but the wealth stemming from commerce and the professions. Moreover the largest new propertied class to emerge from the revolutionary turmoil was the peasantry, who as a result of the destruction of aristocratic privileges had achieved personal ownership of the land. Unlike peasants liberated from traditional landholding in other parts of Europe during the next century, French peasants had to pay no monetary compensation.

The most decisively reactionary element in the Thermidorian Reaction and the new constitution was the removal of the sans-culottes from political life. With the war effort succeeding, the Convention severed its ties with the sans-culottes. True to their belief in an unregulated economy, the Thermidorians repealed the ceiling on prices. As a result, the winter of 1794–1795 brought the worst food shortages of the period. There were numerous food riots, which the Convention put down with force to prove that the era of the sans-culottes *journées* had come to a close. Royalist agents, who aimed to restore the monarchy, tried to take advantage of their discontent. On October 5, 1795–13 Vendémiaire—the sections of Paris led by the royalists rose up against the Convention. The government turned the artillery against the royalist rebels. A general named Napoleon Bonaparte (1769–1821) commanded the cannon, and with a "whiff of grapeshot" he dispersed the crowd.

By the Treaty of Basel in March 1795, the Convention concluded peace with Prussia and Spain. However, the legislators feared a resurgence of both radical democrats and royalists in the upcoming elections for the Council of Five Hundred. Consequently the Convention ruled that at least two thirds of the new legislature must have been members of the older body. The Thermidorians did not even trust the property owners as voters. The next year the newly established Directory again faced social unrest. In Paris Gracchus Babeuf (1760–1797) led the Conspiracy of Equals. He and his followers called for more radical democracy and for more equality of property. Babeuf was arrested, tried, and executed. This quite minor plot became famous many decades later when European socialists attempted to find their historical roots in the French Revolution.

The suppression of the sans-culottes, the narrow franchise of the constitution, the rule of the two thirds, and the Catholic royalist revival presented the Directory with problems that it never succeeded in overcoming. It lacked any broad base of meaningful political support. It particularly required active loyalty because France remained at war with Austria and Great Britain. Consequently the Directory came to depend on the power of the army rather than on constitutional processes for gov-

---

THE FRENCH REVOLUTION

1789

The Estates General opens at Versailles	May 5
The Third Estate declares itself the National Assembly	June 17
The National Assembly takes the Tennis Court Oath	June 20
Fall of the Bastille in the city of Paris	July 14
The Great Fear spreads in the countryside	Late July
The nobles surrender their feudal rights in a meeting of the National Constituent Assembly	August 4
Declaration of the Rights of Man and Citizen	August 27
Parisian women march to Versailles and force Louis XVI and his family to return to Paris	October 5–6

1790

Civil Constitution of the Clergy adopted	July 12
A new constitution is accepted by the king	July 14

1791

Louis XVI and his family attempt to flee France and are stopped at Varennes	June 20–24
The Declaration of Pillnitz	August 27
The Legislative Assembly meets	October 1

1792

France declares war on Austria	April 20
The Tuileries palace is stormed, and Louis XVI takes refuge with the Legislative Assembly	August 10
The September Massacres	September 2–7
France wins the battle of Valmy	September 20
The Convention meets, and the monarchy is abolished	September 21

1793

Louis XVI is executed	January 21
France declares war on Great Britain	February 1
Counterrevolution breaks out in the Vendée	March
The Committee of Public Safety is formed	April
The Constitution of 1793 is adopted but not put into operation	June 22
Robespierre enters the Committee of Public Safety	July
Levée en masse proclaimed	August 23
Maximum prices set on foot and other commodities	September 17
Queen Marie Antoinette is executed	October 16
The Cult of Reason is proclaimed; the revolutionary calendar beginning on September 22, 1792, is adopted	November 10

1794

Execution of the Hébertist leaders of the *sans-culottes*	March 24
Execution of Danton	April 6
Cult of the Supreme Being proclaimed	May 7
Robespierre leads the celebration of the Festival of the Supreme Being	June 8
The Law of 22 Prairial is adopted	June 10
The Ninth of Thermidor and the fall of Robespierre	July 27
Robespierre is executed	July 28

1795

The Constitution of the Year III is adopted, establishing the Directory	August 22

erning the country. All of the soldiers could vote. Moreover, within the army, created and sustained by the revolution, stood officers who were eager for power and ambitious for political conquest. The results of the instability of the Directory and the growing role of the army held profound consequences not only for France but for the entire Western world.

Suggested Readings

C. BRINTON, *The Jacobins: An Essay in the New History* (1930). An examination of the social background of these revolutionaries.

C. BRINTON, *A Decade of Revolution, 1789–1799* (1934). A general survey of Europe during the revolutionary years.

R. COBB, *The Police and the People: French Popular Protest, 1789–1820* (1970). An interesting and imaginative treatment of the question of social control during the revolution.

A. COBBAN, *Edmund Burke and the Revolt Against the Eighteenth Century* (1960). Sets Burke's thought in a broader intellectual context.

A. COBBAN, *Aspects of the French Revolution* (1970). Essays on numerous subjects.

C. CONE, *The English Jacobins: Reformers in Late Eighteenth Century England* (1968). The fortunes of English radicals during the repression following the outbreak of war with France.

W. DOYLE, *Origins of the French Revolution* (1980). An outstanding summary of recent historiographical interpretations.

J. EGRET, *The French Pre-Revolution, 1787–88* (1978). A useful survey of the coming crisis for the monarchy.

K. EPSTEIN, *The Genesis of German Conservatism* (1966). A major study of antiliberal forces in Germany before and during the revolution.

A. FORREST, *The French Revolution and the Poor* (1981). A study that expands consideration of the revolution beyond the standard social boundaries.

M. FREEMAN, *Edmund Burke and the Critique of Political Radicalism* (1980). A study of Burke's thought in the general context of modern political theory.

J. GODECHOT, *The Taking of the Bastille, July 14, 1789* (1970). The best modern discussion of the subject and one that places the fall of the Bastille in the context of crowd behavior in the eighteenth century.

J. GODECHOT, *The Counter-Revolution: Doctrine and Action, 1789–1803* (1971). An examination of opposition to the revolution.

A. GOODWIN, *The Friends of Liberty: The English Democratic Movement in the Age of the French Revolution* (1979). A major new work that explores the impact of the French Revolution on English radicalism.

R. GREENLAW (Ed.), *The Social Origins of the French Revolution: The Debate on the Role of the Middle Classes* (1975). A collection of useful articles.

D. M. GREER, *The Incidence of the Terror During the French Revolution: A Statistical Interpretation* (1935). A study of what people in which regions became the victims of the Terror.

N. HAMPSON, *A Social History of the French Revolution* (1963). A clear account with much interesting detail.

D. JOHNSON, (Ed.), *French Society and the Revolution* (1976). A useful collection of important essays on the social history of the revolution.

M. KENNEDY, *The Jacobin Clubs in the French Revolution: The First Years* (1982). A careful scrutiny of the organizations chiefly responsible for the radicalizing of the revolution.

G. LEFEBVRE, *The Coming of the French Revolution* (trans., 1947). An examination of the crisis of the French monarchy and the events of 1789.

G. LEFEBVRE, *The French Revolution*, 2 vols. (1962–1964). A major study by one of the most important modern writers on the subject.

M. LYONS, *France Under the Directory* (1975). A brief survey of the post-Thermidorean governmental experiment.

R. R. PALMER, *Twelve Who Ruled: The Committee of Public Safety During the Terror* (1941). A clear narrative and analysis of the policies and problems of the committee.

R. R. PALMER, *The Age of the Democratic Revolution: A Political History of Europe and America, 1760–1800*, 2 vols. (1959, 1964). An impressive survey of the political turmoil in the transatlantic world.

G. RUDÉ, *The Crowd in the French Revolution* (1959). Examines who composed the revolutionary crowds and why.

S. SCHAMA, *Patriots and Liberators: Revolution in the Netherlands, 1780–1813* (1977). One of the best and most thorough studies of the revolutionary era outside France.

A. SOBOUL, *The Parisian Sans-Culottes and the French Revolution, 1793–94* (1964). The best work on the subject.

A. SOBOUL, *The French Revolution* (trans., 1975). An important work by a Marxist scholar.

J. H. STEWART, *A Documentary Survey of the French Revolution* (1951). Major sources in translation.

B. STONE, *The Parlement of Paris, 1774–1789* (1981). An examination of a key aristocratic institution responsible for precipitating the revolutionary crisis.

T. TACKETT, *Religion, Revolution, and Regional Culture in Eighteenth Century France: The Ecclesiastical Oath of 1791*. (1986). The most important study of this topic.

J. M. THOMPSON, *Robespierre*, 2 vols. (1935). The best biography.

C. TILLY, *The Vendée* (1964). A significant sociological investigation.

M. WALZER (Ed.), *Regicide and Revolution: Speeches at the Trial of Louis XVI* (1974). An important and exceedingly interesting collection of documents with a useful introduction.

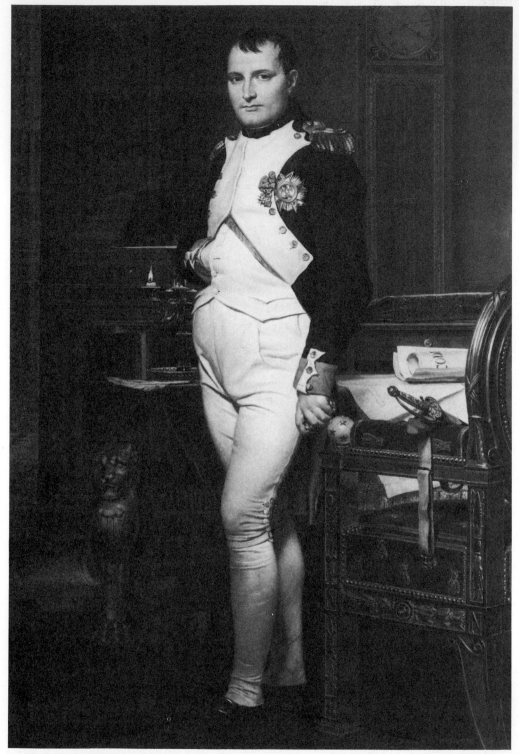

Napoleon in his study. This portrait was painted by Jacques-Louis David (1748–1825) in 1812 at the height of Napoleon's power, when he was about to invade Russia. [*National Gallery of Art*]

THE GOVERNMENT of the Directory represented a new class made up of politicians, merchants, bankers, war speculators, and profiteers sprung from the nonaristocratic order of the old regime, as well as a few undistinguished nobles. Together they formed a society of recently enriched and powerful people whose chief goal was to halt the revolutionary movement without rolling it back. They wanted to perpetuate their own rule. They sought to achieve peace and quiet in order to gain more wealth and to establish a society in which money would become the only requirement for eminence and power. They and their goals confronted a host of enemies.

The Rise of Napoleon Bonaparte

The chief danger to the Directory came from the royalists, who hoped to restore the Bourbon monarchy by legal means. Many of the *émigrés* had drifted back into France. Their plans for a restoration drew support from devout Catholics and from those citizens whom the excesses of the revolution had disgusted. Monarchy seemed to hold the promise of stability. The spring elections of 1797 turned out most of the incumbents and replaced them with a majority of constitutional monarchists and their sympathizers. To prevent an end to the republic and a peaceful restoration of monarchy, the antimonarchist Directory staged a *coup d'état* on 18 Fructidor (September 4, 1797). They put their own supporters into the legislative seats won by their opponents. They then imposed censorship and exiled some of their enemies. Napoleon Bonaparte, the general in charge of the Italian military campaign, had made these political actions possible. At the request of the Directors, he had sent one of his subordinates to Paris to guarantee the success of the *coup*. In 1797, as in 1795, the army and Bonaparte had saved the day for the government installed in the wake of the Thermidorian Reaction.

Napoleon Bonaparte was born in 1769 to a poor family of lesser nobles at Ajaccio, Corsica. Because France had annexed Corsica in the previous year, he went to French schools, pursued a military career, and in 1785 obtained a commission as a French artillery officer. He strongly favored the revolution and was a fiery Jacobin. In 1793 he played a leading role in recovering the port of Toulon from the British.

19

The Age of Napoleon and the Triumph of Romanticism

The siege of Toulon in 1793 was Napoleon's first triumph. Toulon, the principal French naval base in the Mediterranean, had been betrayed by French royalists to the English. As a young artillery officer, Napoleon situated his guns to command the harbor and compelled the British fleet to withdraw. [Mary Evans Picture Library]

In reward for his service the government appointed him a brigadier general. His radical associations threatened his career during the Thermidorian Reaction, but his defense of the new regime on 13 Vendémiaire restored him to favor and won him another promotion and a command in Italy.

By 1795 French arms and diplomacy had shattered the enemy coalition, but France's annexation of Belgium guaranteed continued fighting with Britain and Austria. The attack on Italy was aimed at depriving Austria of the provinces of Lombardy and Venetia. In a series of lightning victories Bonaparte crushed the Austrian and Sardinian armies. On his own initiative, and in many ways contrary to the wishes of the government in Paris, he concluded the Treaty of Campo Formio in October 1797. The treaty took Austria out of the war and crowned Napoleon's campaign and independent policy with success. Before long all of Italy and Switzerland had fallen under French domination.

In November 1797 the triumphant Bonaparte returned to Paris to be hailed as a hero and to confront France's only remaining enemy, Britain. He judged it impossible to cross the channel and invade England at that time. Instead he chose to capture Egypt from the Ottoman Empire. By this strategy he hoped to drive the British fleet from the Mediterranean, cut off British communication with India, damage British trade, and threaten the British Empire. The invasion of Egypt was a failure. Admiral Horatio Nelson (1758–1805) destroyed the French fleet at Abukir on August 1, 1798. The French army could then neither accomplish anything of importance in the Near East nor get home. To make matters worse, the situation in Europe was deteriorating. The French invasion of Egypt had alarmed Russia, which had its own ambitions in the Near East. The Russians, the Austrians, and the Ottomans soon joined Britain to form the Second Coalition. In 1799 the Russian and Austrian armies defeated the French in Italy and Switzerland and threatened to invade France.

Economic troubles and the dangerous international situation eroded the already fragile support of the Directory. One of the Directors, the Abbé Sieyès, proposed a new constitution. The author of the pamphlet *What Is the Third Estate?* (1789) wanted to establish a vigorous executive body independent of the whims of electoral politics, a government based on the principle of "confidence from below, power from above." The change would require another *coup d'état* with military support. News of France's diplomatic misfortunes had reached Napoleon in Egypt. Without orders and leaving his doomed army behind, he returned to France in October 1799. He received much popular acclaim, although some people thought that he deserved a court-martial for desertion. He soon joined Sieyès. On 19 Brumaire (November 10, 1799) his troops drove out the legislators and permitted the success of the *coup*.

Sieyès appears to have thought Napoleon could be used and then dismissed, but if so, he badly misjudged his man. The proposed constitution divided executive authority among three consuls. Bonaparte quickly pushed it aside, as he did Sieyès, and in December 1799 he issued the Constitution of the Year VIII. Behind a screen of universal manhood suffrage that suggested democratic principles, a compli-

cated system of checks and balances that appealed to republican theory, and a Council of State that evoked memories of Louis XIV, the constitution in fact established the rule of one man, the First Consul, Bonaparte. To find a reasonably close historical analogy, one must go back to Caesar and Augustus and the earlier Greek tyrants. The career of Bonaparte, however, pointed forward to the dictators of the twentieth century. He was the first modern political figure to use the rhetoric of revolution and nationalism, to back it with military force, and to combine those elements into a mighty weapon of imperial expansion in the service of his own power and ambition.

The Consulate in France (1799–1804)

The establishment of the Consulate, in effect, closed the revolution in France. The leading elements of the Third Estate—that is, officials, landowners, doctors, lawyers, and financiers—had achieved most of their goals by 1799. They had abolished hereditary privilege, and the careers thus opened to talent allowed them to achieve the wealth and status they sought. The peasants were also satisfied. They had acquired the land they had always wanted and had destroyed oppressive feudal privileges as well. The newly established dominant classes were profoundly conservative. They had little or no desire to share their recently won privileges with the lower social orders. Bonaparte seemed just the person to give them security. When he submitted his constitution to the voters in a plebiscite, they approved it by 3,011,077 votes to 1,567.

Bonaparte quickly justified the public's confidence by setting about achieving peace with France's enemies. Russia had already quarreled with its allies and left the Second Coalition. A campaign in Italy brought another victory over Austria at Marengo in 1800. The Treaty of Lunéville early in 1801 took Austria out of the war and confirmed the earlier settlement of Campo Formio. Britain was now alone and, in 1802, concluded the Treaty of Amiens, which brought peace to Europe. Bonaparte was equally effective in restoring peace and order at home. He employed generosity, flattery, and bribery to win over some of his enemies. He issued a general amnesty and employed in his own service persons from all political factions. He required only that they be

Admiral Viscount Horatio Nelson (1758–1805) *was the greatest naval commander of his age. Between* 1798 *and his death at the battle of Trafalgar in* 1805, *he won a series of brilliant victories that gave Britain mastery of the seas.* [*National Portrait Gallery, London*]

loyal to him. Some of the highest offices were occupied by persons who had been extreme radicals during the Reign of Terror, others by persons who had fled the Terror and favored constitutional monarchy, and still others by former high officials of the old regime.

On the other hand, Bonaparte was ruthless and efficient in suppressing opposition. He established a highly centralized administration in which all departments were managed by prefects directly responsible to the central government in Paris. He employed secret police. He stamped out once and for all the royalist rebellion in the west and made the rule of Paris effective in Brittany and the Vendée for the first time in many years. Nor was he above using or even inventing opportunities to destroy his enemies. When a plot on his life surfaced in 1804, he used the event as an excuse to attack the Jacobins, even though the bombing was the work of royalists. In 1804 his forces invaded the sovereignty of Baden to seize the

---

Napoleon Describes Conditions Leading to the Consulate

In this passage from his memoirs Napoleon described the manner in which the Directory came to an end in 1799 and the Consulate began. In reading of his supposed concern about the army, one should remember that he had abandoned his troops in Egypt to return to Paris to undertake this *coup*.

On my return to Paris I found division among all authorities, and agreement upon only one point, namely, that the Constitution was half destroyed and was unable to save liberty.

All parties came to me, confided to me their designs, disclosed their secrets, and requested my support; I refused to be the man of a party.

The Council of Elders summoned me; I answered its appeal. A plan of general restoration had been devised by men whom the nation has been accustomed to regard as the defenders of liberty, equality, and property; this plan required an examination, calm, free, exempt from all influence and all fear. Accordingly, the Council of Elders resolved upon the removal of the Legislative Body to Saint-Cloud; it gave me the responsibility of disposing the force necessary for its independence. I believed it my duty to my fellow citizens, to the soldiers perishing in our armies, to the national glory acquired at the cost of their blood, to accept the command. . . .

I presented myself at the Council of Five Hundred, alone, unarmed, my head uncovered, just as the Elders had received and applauded me; I came to remind the majority of its wishes, and to assure it of its power.

The stilettos which menaced the deputies were instantly raised against their liberator; twenty assassins threw themselves upon me and aimed at my breast. The grenadiers of the Legislative Body whom I had left at the door of the hall ran forward, placed themselves between the assassins and myself. One of these brave grenadiers had his clothes pierced by a stiletto. They bore me out.

At the same moment cries of ''Outlaw'' were raised against the defender of the law. It was the fierce cry of assassins against the power destined to repress them.

They crowded around the president, uttering threats, arms in their hands; they commanded him to outlaw me; I was informed of this; I ordered him to be rescued from their fury, and six grenadiers of the Legislative Body secured him. Immediately afterwards some grenadiers of the Legislative Body charged into the hall and cleared it.

The factions, intimidated, dispersed and fled. . . .

Frenchmen, you will doubtless recognize in this conduct the zeal of a soldier of liberty, a citizen devoted to the Republic. Conservative, tutelary, and liberal ideas have been restored to their rights through the dispersal of the rebels who oppressed the Councils. . . .

John Hall Stewart, *A Documentary Survey of the French Revolution* (New York: Macmillan, 1951), pp. 763–765.

The Consuls Proclaim the End of the French Revolution

In this proclamation of December 15, 1799, the three new consuls, of whom Napoleon was one, presented the Constitution of the Year VIII to the French people and ceremoniously declared the end of the French Revolution.

Frenchmen!

A Constitution is presented to you.

It terminates the uncertainties which the provisional government introduced into external relations, into the internal and military situation of the Republic.

It places in the institutions which it establishes first magistrates whose devotion has appeared necessary for its success.

The Constitution is founded on the true principles of representative government, on the sacred rights of property, equality, and liberty.

The powers which it institutes will be strong and stable, as they must be in order to guarantee the rights of citizens and the interests of the State.

Citizens, the Revolution is established upon the principles which began it: It is ended.

John Hall Stewart, *A Documentary Survey of the French Revolution* (New York: Macmillan, 1951), p. 780.

Bourbon duke of Enghien. The duke was accused of participation in a royalist plot and put to death, even though Bonaparte knew him to be innocent. The action was a flagrant violation of international law and of due process. Charles Maurice de Talleyrand-Périgord (1754–1838), Bonaparte's foreign minister, later termed the act "worse than a crime—a blunder," because it helped to provoke foreign opposition. On the other hand, it was popular with the former Jacobins, for it seemed to preclude the possibility of a Bourbon restoration. The person who killed a Bourbon was hardly likely to restore the royal family. The execution seems to have put an end to royalist plots.

A major obstacle to internal peace was the steady hostility of French Catholics. Refractory clergy continued to advocate counterrevolution. The religious revival that dated from the Thermidorian Reaction increased discontent with the secular state created by the revolution. Bonaparte regarded religion as a political matter. He approved its role in preserving an orderly society but was suspicious of any such power independent of the state.

In 1801 Napoleon concluded a concordat with Pope Pius VII, to the shock and dismay of his anticlerical supporters. The settlement gave Napoleon what he most wanted. Both the refractory clergy and those who had accepted the revolution were forced to resign. Their replace-

Prince Charles Maurice de Talleyrand was one of the most talented and adaptable diplomats of the age. Born into the highest French aristocracy, he had been a bishop before the Revolution. Later he became foreign minister, first for the Directory, then for Napoleon, and finally for Louis XVIII, whom he represented in 1814–1815 at the Congress of Vienna. [New York Public Library]

ments received their spiritual investiture from the pope, but the state named the bishops and paid their salaries and the salary of one priest in each parish. In return, the church gave up its claims on its confiscated property. The concordat declared that "Catholicism is the religion of the great majority of French citizens." This was merely a statement of fact and fell far short of what the pope had wanted: religious dominance for the Roman Catholic church. The clergy had to swear an oath of loyalty to the state, and the Organic Articles of 1802, which were actually distinct from the concordat, established the supremacy of State over Church. Similar laws were applied to the Protestant and Jewish religious communities as well, reducing

still further the privileged position of the Catholic church.

Peace and efficient administration brought prosperity and security to the French and gratitude and popularity to Bonaparte. In 1802 a plebiscite appointed him consul for life, and he soon produced still another new constitution, which granted him what amounted to full power. The years of the Consulate were employed in reforming and establishing the basic laws and institutions of France. The settlement imposed by Napoleon was an ambiguous combination of liberal principles derived from the Enlightenment and the early years of the revolution and conservative principles and practices going back to the old regime or adapted to

Napoleon Makes Peace with the Papacy

In 1801 Napoleon concluded a concordat with Pope Pius VII. This document was the cornerstone of Napoleonic religious policy. The concordat, which as announced on April 8, 1802, allowed the Roman Catholic church to function freely in France only within the limits of church support for the government as indicated in the oath included in Article 6.

The Government of the French Republic recognizes that the Roman, catholic and apostolic religion is the religion of the great majority of French citizens.

His Holiness likewise recognizes that this same religion has derived and in this moment again expects the greatest benefit and grandeur from the establishment of the catholic worship in France and from the personal profession of it which the consuls of the Republic make.

In consequence, after this mutual recognition, as well for the benefit of religion as for the maintenance of internal tranquility, they have agreed as follows:

1. The catholic, apostolic and Roman religion shall be freely exercised in France: its worship shall be public, and in conformity with the police regulations which the government shall deem necessary for the public tranquility.

. . . .

4. The First Consul of the Republic shall make appointments, within the three months which shall follow the publication of the bull of

His Holiness, to the archbishoprics and bishoprics of the new circumscription. His Holiness shall confer the canonical institution, following the forms established in relation to France before the change of government.

. . . .

6. Before entering upon their functions, the bishops shall take directly, at the hands of the First Consul, the oath of fidelity which was in use before the change of government, expressed in the following terms:

"I swear and promise to God, upon the holy scriptures, to remain in obedience and fidelity to the government established by the constitution of the French Republic. I also promise not to have any intercourse, nor to assist by any counsel, nor to support any league, either within or without, which is inimical to the public tranquility; and if, within my diocese or elsewhere, I learn that anything to the prejudice of the state is being contrived, I will make it known to the government."

F. M. Anderson, *The Constitutions and Other Select Documents Illustrative of the History of France 1789–1907*, 2nd ed. (Minneapolis: H. W. Wilson, 1908), pp. 296–297.

The coronation of Napoleon, December 2, 1804, by David. Having first crowned himself, the emperor is shown about to place the crown on the head of Josephine. Napoleon instructed David to paint Pope Pius VII with his hand raised in blessing. [*Giraudon*]

the conservative spirit that had triumphed at Thermidor.

The abolition of all privileges based on birth, the establishment of equality before the law, the disappearance of all authority except that of the national state and all legal distinctions based on class or locality, and the end of all purchased offices and the substitution of salaried officials chosen for merit represented the application of rationality and the achievement of goals sought by the people who had made the revolution. Most of these were embodied in the general codification of laws carried out under Bonaparte's direction. This was especially true of the Civil Code of 1804, usually called the Napoleonic Code. However, these laws stopped far short of the full equality advocated by liberal rationalists. Fathers were granted extensive control over their children and men over their wives. Labor unions were still forbidden, and the rights of workers were inferior to those of their employers.

In the political arena and in administration Napoleonic institutions ran contrary to the tendencies of the revolution. They aimed at a kind of enlightened absolutism that was similar to but more effective than what had existed

in the old regime. Representative government, local autonomy, and personal freedom were rejected in favor of the centralization of all power and the subordination of personal rights and political freedom to the needs of the state as interpreted by the First Consul. All of this was acceptable to the dominant bourgeoisie and the peasantry. They accepted censorship, the arbitrary and sometimes brutal suppression of dissent, and even the restoration of a new quasi nobility in the Legion of Honor as long as order, prosperity, and security of property were preserved.

In 1804 Bonaparte seized on the bomb attack on his life to make himself emperor. He argued that the establishment of a dynasty would make the new regime secure and make further attempts on his life useless. Another new constitution was promulgated in which Napoleon Bonaparte was called Emperor of the French, instead of First Consul of the Republic. This constitution was also overwhelmingly ratified in a plebiscite.

To conclude the drama, Napoleon invited the pope to Notre Dame to take part in the coronation. But at the last minute the pope agreed that Napoleon should place the crown on his

661

own head. The emperor had no intention of allowing anyone to think that his power and authority depended on the approval of the church. Henceforth he was called Napoleon I. This act was the natural goal of his career. His aims had always been profoundly selfish: power and glory for himself and his family. There was, moreover, a romantic streak in Napoleon. He thought of himself as a rival of Alexander the Great and Caesar, a conqueror as well as a ruler. Had Napoleon wished it, Europe might well have had peace; but his ambition would not permit it.

Napoleon's Empire (1804–1814)

In the decade between his coronation as emperor and his final defeat at Waterloo (1815), Napoleon conquered most of Europe in a series of military campaigns that astonished the world. France's victories changed the map of Europe, put an end to the old regime and its feudal trappings in western Europe, and forced the eastern European states to reorganize themselves to resist Napoleon's armies. Everywhere Napoleon's advance unleashed the powerful force of nationalism. The militarily mobilized French nation, one of the achievements of the revolution, was Napoleon's weapon. He could put as many as 700,000 men under arms at one time, risk as many as 100,000 troops in a single battle, endure heavy losses, and come back to fight again. He could conscript citizen soldiers in unprecedented numbers, thanks to their loyalty to the nation and to their remarkable leader. No single enemy could match such resources, and even coalitions were unsuccessful until Napoleon at last overreached himself and made mistakes that led to his own defeat.

Napoleon deserves his reputation as one of the great commanders of all time. His genius lay not in strategic or tactical invention, in which he had many eighteenth-century French forerunners, but in execution and leadership. His strategy depended on mobility and timing. He liked to divide his forces into units of moderate size, disperse them across the country, and then use their superior speed and his own planning skill to unite them at the critical point at the right time. All of this emphasis on speed of maneuver had a single goal: to bring the hostile armies together for a swift major battle. Napoleon departed from the usual eighteenth-century tactics, which emphasized maneuver and strategic position and the fighting of a battle only as a last resort. His aim was not to control territory nor to gain strong points but to destroy the enemy army. After that, rest for his army might follow. As long as conditions permitted such warfare, Napoleon was unbeatable.

Self-sufficiency was another important Napoleonic military principle that related to his emphasis on swiftness of maneuver. It was this self-sufficiency that allowed him to disperse and reunite his armies so rapidly. The whole army traveled light, with few supplies. By living off the country in which it fought, the army was free of the need to establish and follow a chain of supply depots. This was a great advantage in fertile areas like western and central Europe but proved a problem later against the guerrilla fighters in Spain and in the vast expanse of Russia during the winter. Under those conditions Napoleon's brilliant tactics could not be carried out, and he was eventually defeated. But those events lay many years ahead.

The Peace of Amiens (1802) was doomed to be merely a truce. Napoleon's unlimited ambitions shattered any hope that it might last. He sent an army to restore the rebellious island of Haiti to French rule. This move aroused British fears that he was planning the renewal of a French empire in America, because Spain had restored Louisiana to France in 1800. More serious were his interventions in the Dutch Republic, Italy, and Switzerland and his role in the reorganization of Germany. The Treaty of Campo Formio had required a redistribution of territories along the Rhine River, and the petty princes of the region engaged in a shameful scramble to enlarge their holdings. Among the results were the reduction of Austrian influence in Germany and the emergence of a smaller number of larger German states in the west, all dependent on Napoleon.

The British found all of these developments alarming enough to justify an ultimatum. When Napoleon ignored it, Britain declared war in May 1803. William Pitt the Younger returned to office as prime minister in 1804 and began to construct the Third Coalition. By August 1805 he had persuaded Russia and Austria to move once more against French aggression. A great naval victory soon raised the fortunes of the allies. On October 21, 1805, the British admiral Horatio, Lord Nelson destroyed the combined French and Spanish fleets at the Battle of Trafalgar just off the Spanish coast.

William Pitt, the Younger (1759–1806). As prime minister, Pitt opposed any policy that recognized French domination of Europe. [*New York Public Library*]

Nelson died in the battle, but the British lost no ships. The victory of Trafalgar put an end to all French hope of an invasion of Britain and guaranteed British control of the sea for the rest of the war.

On land the story was very different. Even before Trafalgar Napoleon had marched to the Danube River to attack his continental enemies. In mid-October he forced a large Austrian army to surrender at Ulm and soon occupied Vienna. On December 2, 1805, in perhaps his greatest victory, Napoleon defeated the combined Austrian and Russian forces at Austerlitz. The Treaty of Pressburg, which followed, won major concessions from Austria. The Austrians withdrew from Italy and left Napoleon in control of everything north of Rome. He was recognized as king of Italy.

Extensive changes also came about in Germany. In July 1806 Napoleon organized the Confederation of the Rhine, which included most of the western German princes. The withdrawal of these princes from the Holy Roman Empire led Francis II of Austria to dissolve that ancient political body and hencefore to call himself only emperor of Austria.

Prussia, which had carefully remained neutral up to this point, was now provoked into war against France. The famous Prussian army was quickly crushed at the battles of Jena and Auerstädt on October 14, 1806. Two weeks later Napoleon was in Berlin. There, on November 21, he issued the Berlin Decrees forbidding his allies to import British goods. On June 13, 1807, Napoleon defeated the Russians at Friedland and was able to occupy Königsberg, the capital of East Prussia. The French emperor was master of all Germany.

Napoleon on the field of Austerlitz. Austerlitz is considered Napoleon's most brilliant victory: 73,000 French crushed an Austro-Russian army of 86,000 under the command of the Tsar and the Emperor of Austria. [*Library of Congress*]

THE
CONTINENTAL
SYSTEM
1806 · 1810

NORWAY
SWEDEN
DENMARK
PRUSSIA
POLAND
RUSSIA
RHINE CONF.
FRANCE
AUSTRIA
ENGLAND
PORT.
SPAIN
ITALY

AREAS IN WHICH
BRITISH EXPORTS
WERE PROHIBITED

THE
FRENCH EMPIRE

THE
GRAND EMPIRE

ALLIED WITH
NAPOLEON

300 MI.
300 KM.

BATTLE
SITES

SCOTLAND
Edinburgh
York
UNITED
KINGDOM
London
Dover
Boulogne
WALES
Brest
QUIBERON
Nantes
VENDÉE
FRANCE
Rochefort
Bordeaux
BAY OF
BISCAY
CAPE
FINISTERRE
Corunna
Oporto
ALMEIDA
PORTUGAL
VIMEIRO
CINTRA
Lisbon
ELVAS
BADAJOZ
Cordova
Seville
Cadiz
TRAFALGAR
GIBALTAR
(U.K.)

NORTH
SEA
HELIGO-
LAND
(U.K.)

DENMARK
Christiana
KINGDOM OF
DENMARK
AND
NORWAY
DENMARK

SWEDEN
Stockholm
Gothenburg
GOTHLAND

Copenhagen
BALTIC
SWEDISH
POMERANIA
Lübeck
MECK.
PRUSSIA
THORN
GRAN
BERLIN
Posen
Breslo
BAUTZEN
SAXONY
LEIPZIG
DRESDEN
WEST-
PHALIA
BERG
Cologne
HESSE
Mainz
CONFEDERATION OF THE
RHINE
JENA
Prague
BOHEMIA
AUSTERLITZ
WAGRAM
ASPERN
Vienna
HOLLAND
OLDEN-
BURG
Hamburg
Brussels
WATERLOO
Amiens
Reims
Paris
Versailles
Fontainebleau
Orléans
VALMY
Strasbourg
BADEN
ULM
Munich
HOHENLINDEN
BAVARIA
INNSBRUCK
RATISBON
SWITZ.
ST. GOTTHARD
SAVOY
Lyons
Turin
LOMBARDY
Milan
LODI
MARENGO
Genoa
Avignon
Marseilles
Nice
Leghorn
LUCCA
Toulon
TOULOUSE
VITORIA
Burgos
SALAMANCA
CIUDAD
RODRIGO
TALAVERA
Madrid
SPAIN
OCAÑA
CIUDAD
REAL
BAYLEN
MURCIA
ANDALUCIA
SARAGOSSA
GERONA
Barcelona
TARRAGONA
VALENCIA
VALENCIA
BALEARIC IS.
MEDITERRANEAN
Algiers
CORSICA
K. OF
SARDINIA
Cagliari
ELBA
Rome
ITALY
VENETIA
SACILE
Trieste
ILLYRIAN PROVIN
ADRIA
Urbino
Bari
Naples
K. OF
NAPLES
K. OF
SICILY
Tunis
EMPIR
BO

664

MAPS 19-1, 19-2 *By mid-1812 the areas shown in black were incorporated into France, and most of the rest of Europe was directly controlled by or allied with Napoleon. But Russia had withdrawn from the failing Continental System, and the decline of Napoleon was about to begin.*

CHRONOLOGY

1806 NOV. 21 – NAPOLEON ESTABLISHES THE CONTINENTAL SYSTEM PROHIBITING ALL TRADE WITH ENGLAND.

1807 JULY 7 – THE PEACE CONFERENCE AT TILSIT RESULTS IN RUSSIA JOINING THE CONTINENTAL SYSTEM AND BECOMING AN ALLY OF NAPOLEON.

1809 AND **1810** – NAPOLEON AT THE PEAK OF HIS POWER.

1810 DEC. 31 – RUSSIA WITHDRAWS FROM THE CONTINENTAL SYSTEM AND RESUMES RELATIONS WITH BRITAIN. NAPOLEON PLANS TO CRUSH RUSSIA MILITARILY.

1812 JUNE–DECEMBER – NAPOLEON INVADES RUSSIA. THE RUSSIANS ADOPT A SCORCHED-EARTH POLICY AND BURN MOSCOW. THE THWARTED NAPOLEON DESERTS HIS DWINDLING ARMY AND RUSHES BACK TO PARIS.

Unable to fight another battle and unwilling to retreat into Russia, Czar Alexander I (1801–1825) was ready to make peace. He and Napoleon met on a raft in the middle of the Niemen River while the two armies and the nervous king of Prussia watched from the bank. On July 7, 1807, they signed the Treaty of Tilsit, which confirmed France's gains. Moreover the Prussian state was reduced to half its size and was saved from extinction only by the support of Alexander. Prussia openly and Russia secretly became allies of Napoleon in his war against Britain.

Napoleon organized conquered Europe much like the domain of a great Corsican family. The great French Empire was ruled directly by the head of the clan, Napoleon. On its borders lay a number of satellite states carved out as the portions of the several family members. His stepson ruled Italy for him, and three of his brothers and his brother-in-law were made kings of other conquered states. Napoleon denied a kingdom to his brother Lucien, of whose wife he disapproved. The French emperor expected his relatives to take orders without question. When they failed to do so, he rebuked and even punished them. This establishment of the Napoleonic family as the collective sovereign of Europe was offensive to the growing national feeling in many states and helped to create nationalism in others. The rule of puppet kings was unpopular and provoked

The meeting of Napoleon and Tsar Alexander I (1801–1825) at Tilsit in 1807. [New York Public Library]

leon resisted advice to turn his empire into a free-trade area. Such a policy would have been both popular and helpful. Instead, his tariff policies favored France, increased the resentment of foreign merchants, and made them less willing to enforce the system and more ready to engage in smuggling. It was in part to prevent smuggling that Napoleon invaded Spain in 1808, and the resulting peninsular campaign in Spain and Portugal helped to bring on his ruin.

European Response to the Empire

Napoleon's conquests stimulated the two most powerful political forces in nineteenth-century Europe: liberalism and nationalism. The export of his version of the French Revolution directly and indirectly spread the ideas and values of the Enlightenment and the principles of 1789. Wherever Napoleon ruled, the Napoleonic Code was imposed and class distinction was abolished. Feudal dues disappeared and the peasants were freed from serfdom and manorial dues. In the towns the guilds and the local oligarchies that had been dominant for centuries were dissolved or deprived of their power. New freedom thus came to serfs, artisans, workers, and entrepreneurs outside the privileged circles. The established churches were deprived of their traditional independence and were made subordinate to the state. Church monopoly of religion was replaced by general toleration.

These reforms were not undone by the fall of Napoleon, and along with the demand for representative, constitutional government, they remained the basis of later liberal reforms. However, at the same time it became increasingly clear that Napoleon's policies were intended first and foremost for his own glory and that of France. The Continental System demonstrated that France, rather than Europe generally, was to be enriched by Napoleon's rule. Consequently, before long the conquered states and peoples became restive.

German Nationalism and Prussian Reform

The German response to Napoleon's success was particularly interesting and important. There had never been a unified German state. The great German writers of the Enlightenment, such as Immanuel Kant, the poet and

political opposition that needed only encouragement and assistance to flare up into serious resistance.

After the Treaty of Tilsit such assistance could come only from Britain, and Napoleon knew that he must defeat the British before he could feel safe. Unable to compete with the British navy, he continued the economic warfare begun by the Berlin Decree. His plan was to cut off all British trade with the European continent. In this manner he hoped to cripple the commercial and financial power on which Britain depended to cause domestic unrest and revolution, and thus to drive the British from the war. The Milan Decree of 1807 attempted to stop neutral nations from trading with Britain. For a time it appeared that this Continental System, as it was called, might work. British exports dropped, and riots broke out in England. But in the end the system failed and may even have contributed significantly to Napoleon's defeat.

The British economy survived because of its access to the growing markets of North and South America and of the eastern Mediterranean, all assured by the British control of the seas. At the same time, the Continental System did great harm to the European economies. The system was meant not only to hurt Britain but also to help France economically. Napo-

dramatist Friedrich von Schiller, and Lessing, were neither political nor nationalistic.

At the beginning of the nineteenth century the Romantic movement had begun to take hold. One of its basic features in Germany was the emergence of nationalism. This movement went through two distinct stages. Initially, nationalistic writers emphasized the unique and admirable qualities of German culture, which, they argued, arose from the peculiar history of the German people. Such cultural nationalism prevailed until Napoleon's humiliation of Prussia at Jena in 1806. At that point many German intellectuals began to urge resistance to Napoleon on the basis of German nationalism. The French conquest endangered the independence and achievements of the German people. Many nationalists were also critical of the German princes, who ruled selfishly and inefficiently and who seemed ever ready to lick the boots of Napoleon. No less important in forging a German national sentiment was the example of France, which had attained greatness by enlisting the active support of the entire people in the patriotic cause. Henceforth many Germans sought to solve their internal political problems by establishing a unified German state, reformed to harness the energies of the entire people.

After Tilsit only Prussia could arouse such patriotic feelings. Elsewhere German rulers were either under Napoleon's thumb or actively collaborating with him. Defeated, humiliated, and shrunk in size, Prussia continued to resist, however feebly. To Prussia fled German nationalists from other states, calling for reforms and unification that were, in fact, feared and hated by Frederick William III and the *Junker* nobility. Reforms came about in spite of such opposition because the defeat at Jena had made clear the necessity of new departures for the Prussian state.

The Prussian administrative and social reforms were the work of Baron vom Stein (1757–1831) and Count von Hardenberg (1750–1822). The architects of military reform were General Gerhard von Scharnhorst (1755–1813) and Count von Gneisenau (1760–1831). None of these reformers intended to reduce the autocratic power of the Prussian monarch or to put an end to the dominance of the *Junkers,* who formed the bulwark of the state and of the army officer corps. Rather, they aimed at fighting the revolution and French power with their own version of the French weapons. As Hardenberg declared:

Our objective, our guiding principle, must be a revolution in the better sense, a revolution leading directly to the great goal, the elevation of humanity through the wisdom of those in authority. . . . Democratic rules of conduct in a monarchical administration, such is the formula . . . which will conform most comfortably with the spirit of the age.[1]

Although the reforms came from the top, they brought important changes in Prussian society.

Stein's reforms put an end to the existing system of Prussian landownership. The *Junker* monopoly of landholding was broken. Serfdom was generally abolished. However, the power of the *Junkers* did not permit the total end of the system, as in the western principalities of Germany. Peasants remaining on the land were forced to continue manorial labor, although they were free to leave the land if they chose. They could obtain the ownership of the land they worked only at the price of forfeiting a third of it to the lord. The result was that *Junker* holdings grew larger. Some peasants went to the cities to find work; others became agricultural laborers; and some did actually become small freeholding farmers. Serfdom had come to an end, but new social problems that would fester for another half century had been created as a landless labor force, enlarged by the population explosion, emerged.

The military reforms sought to increase the supply of soldiers and to improve their quality. Jena had shown that an army of free patriots commanded by officers chosen on merit rather than by birth could defeat an army of serfs and mercenaries commanded by incompetent nobles. To remedy the situation, the Prussian reformers abolished inhumane punishments, sought to inspire patriotic feelings in the soldiers, opened the officer corps to commoners, gave promotions on the basis of merit, and organized war colleges that developed new theories of strategy and tactics. These reforms soon put Prussia in a condition to regain its former power. However, because Napoleon had put a strict limit on the size of the Prussian army, universal conscription could not be introduced until 1813. Before that date the Prussians got around the limit of 42,000 men in arms by training one group each year, putting them into the reserves, and then training a new group the same size. In this manner Prussia could boast an army of 270,000 by 1814.

[1]Quoted in Geoffrey Bruun, *Europe and the French Imperium* (New York: Harper & Row, 1938), p. 174.

The French entry into Moscow, September 14, 1812. Despite his expectations, Napoleon found that the fall of their capital did not force the Russians to sue for peace. Within a month, the onset of winter had forced the French to retreat. [Art Resource]

certain. He was able to put down his opponents in Paris and to raise another army of 350,000 men. Neither the Prussians nor the Austrians were eager to risk another bout with Napoleon, and even the Russians hesitated. The Austrian foreign minister, Prince Klemens von Metternich (1773–1859), would have been glad to make a negotiated peace that would leave Napoleon on the throne of a shrunken and chastened France rather than see Europe dominated by Russia. Napoleon might have won a reasonable settlement by negotiation had he been willing to make concessions that would have split his jealous opponents, but he would not consider that solution. As he explained to Metternich, "Your sovereigns born on the throne can let themselves be beaten twenty times and return to their capitals. I cannot do this because I am an upstart soldier. My domination will not survive the day when I cease to be strong, and therefore feared."[2]

In 1813 patriotic pressure and national ambition brought together the last and most powerful coalition against Napoleon. The Russians drove westward and were joined by Prussia and then Austria. All were assisted by vast amounts of British money. From the west Wellington marched his peninsular army into France. Napoleon's new army was inexperienced and poorly equipped. His generals had lost confidence and were tired. The emperor himself was worn out and sick. Still he was able to wage a skillful campaign in central Europe and to defeat the allies at Dresden. In October, however, he met the combined armies of the enemy at Leipzig in what the Germans

[2]Quoted in Felix Markham, *Napoleon and the Awakening of Europe* (New York: Macmillan, 1965), pp. 115–116.

called the Battle of the Nations and was decisively defeated. At the end of March 1814 the allied army marched into Paris, and a few days later Napoleon abdicated and went into exile on the island of Elba off the coast of northern Italy.

The Congress of Vienna and the European Settlement

Fear of Napoleon and hostility to his ambitions had held the victorious coalition together. As soon as he was removed, the allies began to pursue their own separate ambitions. The key person in achieving eventual agreement among the allies was Robert Stewart, Viscount Castlereagh (1769–1822), the British foreign secretary. Even before the victorious armies had entered Paris, he brought about the sign-

ing of the Treaty of Chaumont on March 9, 1814. It provided for the restoration of the Bourbon dynasty to the French throne and the contraction of France to its frontiers of 1792. Even more important was the agreement by Britain, Austria, Russia, and Prussia to form a Quadruple Alliance for twenty years to guarantee the peace terms and to act together to preserve whatever settlement they later agreed on. Remaining problems—and they were many—and final details were left for a conference to be held at Vienna.

The Congress of Vienna assembled in September 1814 but did not conclude its work until November 1815. Although a glittering array of heads of state attended the gathering, the four great powers conducted the important work of the conference. The only full session of the congress met to ratify the arrangements made by the big four. The easiest problem fac-

The leading statesmen of the Congress of Vienna are here portrayed in a single group. Metternich, in white breeches, is standing on the left. Lord Castlereagh is sitting in the center with his legs crossed. Talleyrand is seated on the right with his arm on the table. [By gracious permission of HM the Queen]

EUROPE, 1815 AFTER THE CONGRESS OF VIENNA

NORWAY AND SWEDEN 1814

Bergen

Christiania

Stockholm

FINLAND RUSS., 180

SCOTLAND

Edinburgh

N O R T H

S E A

DENMARK

BALTIC SEA

Belfast

IRELAND

Dublin

Liverpool

Manchester

SCHLESWIG

BOUNDARY OF THE GERMAN CONFEDERATION

HOLSTEIN

PRUSSIA

Danzig

EAST PRUSSIA

(FORMER DUTCH REP.)

HANOVER

UNITED KINGDOM

London

(FORMER AUSTR. NETHS.)

K. OF THE NETHERLANDS

Cologne

Berlin

Breslau

Warsaw

K. OF POLAND (RUSS.)

Brussels

Prague

BOHEMIA

MORAVIA

Cracow

A T L A N T I C

Brest

Rouen

Reims

LORRAINE

Paris

Rennes

Orléans

Strassburg

ALSACE

BAVARIA

Munich

AUSTRIA

Vienna

AUSTRIAN

HUNGARY

Budapest

EMPIRE

O C E A N

Nantes

FRANCE

Berne

SWITZ.

Lyons

SAVOY

TYROL

LOM-BARDY

VENETIA

Trieste

Agram

CROATS

Bordeaux

PIEDMONT

PAR.

MOD.

Bologna

BOSNIA

Belgrade

Montpelier

NICE

LUCCA

Sarajevo

SERBIA

MONTE-NEGRO

Marseilles

ANDORRA

TUSCANY

STATES OF THE CHURCH

ITALY

PORTUGAL

Oviedo

Burgos

KINGDOM OF SARDINIA

CORSICA (FR.)

ELBA

Rome

Lisbon

Madrid

SPAIN

Barcelona

BALEARIC IS. (SP.)

SARDINIA

Naples

Ochr

Jar

Valencia

KINGDOM OF THE TWO SICILIES

Cosenza

Cordova

Seville

M E D I T

E

R

A

N

E

Tangier

GIBRALTAR (U.K.)

Ceuta (SP.)

THE BARBARY STATES

SICILY

Fez

MOROCCO

Algiers

ALGERIA TURK TO 1830

Tunis

TUNISIA (TURK.)

MALTA (U.K.)

A D R I A T I C   S E A

T R MILLER

672

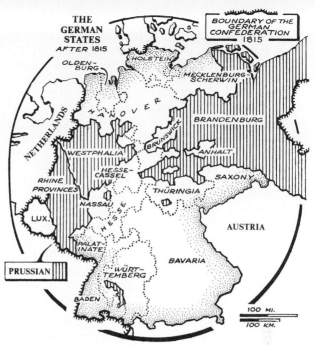

MAPS 19-3, 19-4 *The Congress of Vienna achieved the post-Napoleonic territorial adjustments shown on the map. The most notable arrangements dealt with areas along France's borders (Netherlands, Prussia, Switzerland, and Piedmont) and in Poland and northern Italy.*

ing the great powers was France. All the victors agreed that no single state should be allowed to dominate Europe, and all were determined to see that France should be prevented from doing so again. The restoration of the French Bourbon monarchy, which was again popular, and a nonvindictive boundary settlement kept France calm and satisfied. In addition the powers constructed a series of states to serve as barriers to any new French expansion. They established the kingdom of the Netherlands, including Belgium, in the north and added Genoa to Piedmont in the south. Prussia, whose power was increased by accessions in eastern Europe, was given important new territories in the west along the Rhine River to deter French aggression in that area. Austria was given full control of northern Italy to prevent a repetition of Napoleon's conquests there. As for the rest of Germany, most of Napoleon's arrangements were left untouched. The venerable Holy Roman Empire, which had been dissolved in 1806, was not revived. In all these areas the congress established the rule of

673

legitimate monarchs and rejected any hint of the republican and democratic politics that had flowed from the French Revolution.

On these matters agreement was not difficult, but the settlement of eastern Europe sharply divided the victors. Alexander I of Russia wanted all Poland under his rule. Prussia was willing if it received all of Saxony. But Austria was unwilling to surrender its share of Poland or to see the growth of Prussian power and the penetration of Russia deeper into central Europe. The Polish-Saxon question brought the congress to a standstill and almost brought on a new war among the victors, but defeated France provided a way out. The wily Talleyrand, now representing France at Vienna, suggested that the weight of France added to that of Britain and Austria might bring Alexander to his senses. When news of a

A British cartoon of the battle of Waterloo shows Napoleon fleeing for Paris on a wounded imperial eagle. [British Museum]

secret treaty among the three leaked out, the czar agreed to become ruler of a smaller Poland, and Frederick William III of Prussia agreed to accept only part of Saxony. Thereafter France was included as a fifth great power in all deliberations.

Unity among the victors was further restored by Napoleon's return from Elba on March 1, 1815. The French army was still loyal to the former emperor, and many of the French thought that their fortunes might be safer under his rule than under that of the restored Bourbons. The coalition seemed to be dissolving in Vienna. Napoleon seized the opportunity, escaped to France, and was soon restored to power. He promised a liberal constitution and a peaceful foreign policy. The allies were not convinced. They declared Napoleon an outlaw (a new device under international law) and sent their armies to crush him. Wellington, with the crucial help of the Prussians under Field Marshal von Blücher, defeated Napoleon at Waterloo in Belgium on June 18, 1815. Napoleon again abdicated and was sent into exile on Saint Helena, a tiny Atlantic island off the coast of Africa, where he died in 1821.

The Hundred Days, as the period of Napoleon's return is called, frightened the great powers and made the peace settlement harsher for France. In addition to some minor territorial adjustments, the victors imposed a war indemnity and an army of occupation on France. Alexander proposed a Holy Alliance, whereby the monarchs promised to act in accordance with Christian principles. Austria and Prussia signed; but Castlereagh thought it absurd, and England abstained. The czar, who was then embracing mysticism, believed his proposal a valuable tool for international relations. The Holy Alliance soon became a symbol of extreme political reaction. The Quadruple Alliance between England, Austria, Prussia, and Russia was renewed on November 20, 1815.

The chief aims of the Congress of Vienna were to prevent a recurrence of the Napoleonic nightmare and to arrange an acceptable settlement for Europe that might produce lasting peace. It was remarkably successful in achieving these goals. France accepted the new situation without undue resentment. The victorious powers settled difficult problems in a reasonable way. They established a legalistic balance of power and methods for adjusting to change. The work of the congress has been criticized for failing to recognize and provide for the great forces that would stir the nineteenth century—

nationalism and democracy—but such criticism is inappropriate. The settlement, like all such agreements, was aimed at solving past ills, and in that it succeeded. If the powers failed to anticipate future problems or to yield to forces of which they disapproved, they were more than human to have done so. Perhaps it was unusual enough to produce a settlement that remained essentially intact for almost half a century and that allowed Europe to suffer no general war for a hundred years.

The Romantic Movement

The years of the French Revolution and the conquests of Napoleon saw the emergence of a new and very important intellectual movement thoughout Europe. Romanticism in its various manifestations was a reaction against much of the thought of the Enlightenment. Romantic writers opposed what they considered the excessive scientific narrowness of the eighteenth-century *philosophes*. The latter stood accused of subjecting everything to geometrical and mathematical models and thereby demeaning feelings and imagination. Romantic thinkers refused to conceive of human nature as primarily rational. They wanted to interpret both physical nature and human society in organic rather than in mechanical terms and categories. Where the Enlightenment *philosophes* had often criticized religion and faith, the Romantics saw religion as basic to human nature and faith as a means to knowledge. Expressing this reaction to the rationalism of the previous century, the German Romantic composer Franz Schubert (1797–1828) called the Enlightenment "that ugly skeleton without flesh or blood."

Some historians, most notably Arthur O. Lovejoy, have warned against speaking of a single European-wide Romantic movement. They have pointed out that a variety of such movements—occurring almost simultaneously in Germany, England, and France—arose independently and had their own particular courses of development. Such considerations have not, however, prevented the designation of a specific historical period, dated roughly from 1780 to 1830, as the Age of Romanticism or of the Romantic movement. Despite national differences, a shared reaction to the Enlightenment marked all of these writers and artists. They generally saw the imagination or some such intuitive intellectual faculty supple-

NAPOLEONIC EUROPE	
Napoleon concludes the Treaty of Campo Formio	1797
Nelson defeats the French navy in the harbor of Abukir	1798
Consulate established in France	1799
Concordat between France and the papacy	1801
Treaty of Amiens	1802
War renewed between France and Britain	1803
Execution of Duke of Enghien	1804
Napoleonic Civil Code issued	1804
Napoleon crowned as emperor	1804
Nelson defeats French fleet at Trafalgar (October 21)	1805
Austerlitz (December 2)	1805
Jena	1806
Continental System established by Berlin Decrees	1806
Friedland	1807
Treaty of Tilsit	1807
Beginning of Spanish resistance to Napoleonic domination	1808
Wagram	1809
Napoleon marries Archduchess Marie Louise of Austria	1809
Invasion of Russia and French defeat at Borodino	1812
Leipzig (Battle of the Nations)	1813
Treaty of Chaumont (March) establishes Quadruple Alliance	1814
Congress of Vienna convenes (September)	1814
Napoleon returns from Elba (March 1)	1815
Waterloo (June 18)	1815
Holy Alliance formed at Congress of Vienna (September 26)	1815
Quadruple Alliance renewed at Congress of Vienna (November 20)	1815
Napoleon dies on Saint Helena	1821

menting the reason as a means of perceiving and understanding the world. Many of these writers urged a revival of Christianity such as had permeated Europe during the Middle Ages. And unlike the *philosophes*, the Romantics liked the art, the literature, and the architecture of medieval times. They were also deeply interested in folklore, folk songs, and fairy tales. The Romantics were also fascinated by dreams, hallucinations, sleepwalking, and other phenomena that suggested the existence of a world beyond that of empirical observation, sensory data, and discursive reasoning.

675

Romantic Questioning of the Supremacy of Reason

Several historical streams fed the Romantic movement. These included the individualism of the Renaissance and the Reformation and the pietism of the seventeenth century and the eighteenth-century English Methodist movement, which encouraged a heartfelt, practical religion in place of dogmatism, rationalism, and deism. The sentimental novels of the eighteenth century, such as Samuel Richardson's *Clarissa*, also paved the way for thinkers who would emphasize feeling and emotion. The so-called *Sturm und Drang* ("storm and stress") period of German literature and German idealist philosophy were important to the Romantics. However, two writers who were also closely related to the Enlightenment provided the immediate intellectual foundations for Romanticism. They were Jean-Jacques Rousseau and Immanuel Kant, both of whom raised questions about the sufficiency of the rationalism so dear to the *philosophes*.

It has already been pointed out in Chapter 17 that Jean-Jacques Rousseau, though sharing in some of the reformist spirit of the Enlightenment, opposed many of its other facets. What Romantic writers especially drew from Rousseau was his conviction that society had corrupted human nature. In the two *Discourses* and others of his works, Rousseau had portrayed humankind as created happy and innocent by nature and originally living in a state of equilibrium, able to do what it desired and desiring only what it was able to do. For

The Romantic Movement's glorification of the individual is captured in this drawing entitled Newton *by William Blake (1757–1827). It is not, of course, a portrait of Sir Isaac Newton. Instead, it portrays a God-like scientist solving the mysteries of the universe.* [*The Tate Gallery, London*]

humankind to become happy again, it must remain true to its natural being, while still attempting to realize the new moral possibilities of life in society. In the *Social Contract* (1762) Rousseau had provided his prescription for the reorganization of political life that would achieve that goal.

Rousseau set forth his view on the individual's development toward the good and happy life in a novel entitled *Émile* (1762). Initially this treatise on education was far more influential than the *Social Contract.* In *Émile* Rousseau stressed the difference between children and adults. He distinguished the stages of human maturation and urged that in rearing children, one must give them maximum individual freedom. Each child should be allowed to grow freely, like a plant, and to learn by trial and error what reality is and how best to deal with it. The parent or teacher would help most by providing the basic necessities of life and warding off what was manifestly harmful. Otherwise the adult should stay completely out of the way, like a gardener who waters and weeds a garden but otherwise lets nature take its course.

This was a revolutionary concept of education in an age accustomed to narrow, bookish, and highly regimented vocational education and learning. Rousseau thought that the child's sentiments as well as its reason should be permitted to flourish. To Romantic writers this concept of human development vindicated the rights of nature over those of artificial society, and they thought that such a form of education would eventually lead to a natural society. In its fully developed form, this view of life led the Romantics to place a high value on the uniqueness of each individual person and to explore in great detail the experiences of childhood. Like Rousseau the Romantics saw humankind, nature, and society as organically related to each other.

Immanuel Kant (1724–1804) wrote the two greatest philosophical works of the late eighteenth century: *The Critique of Pure Reason* (1781) and *The Critique of Practical Reason* (1788). He sought to accept the rationalism of the Enlightenment and still to preserve a belief in human freedom, immortality, and the existence of God. Against Locke and other philosophers who saw knowledge rooted in sensory experience alone, Kant argued for the subjective character of human knowledge. For Kant the human mind did not simply reflect the world around it like a passive mirror; rather, it

Immanuel Kant (1724–1804). Romantic writers saw his philosophy as a decisive refutation of the narrow rationality of the Enlightenment. [Bettmann Archive]

actively imposed on the world of sensory experience "forms of sensibility" and "categories of understanding." These categories were generated by the mind itself. In other words, the human mind perceives the world as it does because of its own internal mental categories. What this meant was that human perceptions were as much the product of the mind's own activity as of sensory experience.

Kant found the sphere of reality that was accessible to pure reason to be quite limited. However, he believed that beyond the phenomenal world of sensory experience, over which "pure reason" was master, there existed what he called the "noumenal" world, a sphere of moral and aesthetic reality known by "practical reason" and conscience. Kant thought that all human beings possessed an innate sense of moral duty or an awareness of what he called a *categorical imperative.* This term referred to an inner command to act in every situation as one would have all other people always act in the same situation. Kant regarded the existence of this imperative of conscience as incontrovertible proof of humankind's natural freedom. On the basis of humankind's moral sense Kant went on to postulate the existence of God, eternal life, and future rewards and punishments. He believed that these transcendental truths could not be proved by discursive reasoning. Still, he was convinced that they were realities to which every reasonable person could attest.

To many Romantic writers Kantian philosophy was a decisive refutation of the narrow rationality of the Enlightenment. Whether they called it "practical reason," "fancy," "imagination," "intuition," or simply "feeling," the Romantics believed in the presence of a special power in the human mind that could penetrate beyond the limits of human understanding as set forth by Hobbes, Locke, and Hume. Most of them also believed that poets and artists generally possessed these powers in particular abundance. Other Romantic writers appealed to the limits of human reason in order to set forth new religious ideas or political thought that was often at odds with that of Enlightenment writers.

Romantic Literature

The term *romantic* appeared in English and French literature as early as the seventeenth century. Neoclassical writers then used the word to describe literature that they considered unreal, sentimental, or excessively fanciful. In the eighteenth century the English writer Thomas Warton associated *romantic* with medieval romances. In Germany, a major center of the Romantic literary movement, Johann Gottfried Herder used the terms *romantic* and *Gothic* interchangeably. In both England and Germany the term came to be applied to all literature that failed to observe classical forms and rules and that gave free play to the imagination. English Romantic poets and essayists looked on the period of literature from John Dryden to Alexander Pope, roughly 1670–1750, as a classical "dark age." For both English and German Romantics the French Neoclassicists of the seventeenth century, such as Pierre Corneille and Jean Racine, were slavish imitators of the classics and represented all that literature should not be.

As an alternative to such dependence on the ancients, August Wilhelm von Schlegel (1767–1845) praised the "romantic" literature of Dante, Petrarch, Boccaccio, Shakespeare, the Arthurian legends, Cervantes, and Calderón. According to Schlegel, Romantic literature was to classical literature what the organic and living were to the merely mechanical. He set forth his views in *Lectures on Dramatic Art and Literature* (1809–1811).

The Romantic movement had peaked in Germany and England before it became a major force in France under the leadership of Madame de Staël (1766–1817) and Victor Hugo (1802–1885). So influential was the classical tradition in France that not until 1816

did a French writer openly declare himself a Romantic. That was Henri Beyle (1783–1842), who wrote under the pseudonym Stendhal. He praised Shakespeare and Lord Byron and criticized his own countryman, the seventeenth-century classical dramatist Racine.

The English Romantics believed that poetry was enhanced by freely following the creative impulses of the mind. In this belief they directly opposed Lockean psychology, which regarded the mind as a passive receptor and poetry as a mechanical exercise of "wit" following prescribed rules. For William Blake and Samuel Taylor Coleridge the artist's imagination was God at work in the mind. As Coleridge expressed his views, the imagination was "a repetition in the finite mind of the eternal act of creation in the infinite I AM." Percy Bysshe Shelley believed that "A poet participates in the eternal, the infinite, and the One." So conceived of, poetry could not be considered idle play. It was the highest of human acts, humankind's self-fulfillment in a transcendental world.

William Blake (1757–1827) considered the poet a seer and poetry translated vision. He thought it a great tragedy that so many people understood the world only rationally and could perceive no innocence or beauty in it. In the 1790s he experienced a period of deep personal depression, which seems to have been related to his own inability to perceive the world as he believed it to be. The better one got to know the world, the more the life of the imagination and its spiritual values seemed to recede. Blake saw this problem as evidence of the materialism and injustice of English society. He was deeply impressed by the strong sense of contradiction between a true childlike vision of the world and conceptions of it based on actual experience. Through his own poetry he sought to bring childlike innocence and experience together and to transform experience by imagination. The conflict of which he was so much aware can be seen in *Songs of Innocence* (1789) and *Songs of Experience* (1794). In "The Tyger," published in the latter, he asked:

Tyger, Tyger, burning bright
In the forests of the night.
. . . .
When the stars threw down their spears
And watered heaven with their tears,
Did He smile His work to see?
Did He who made the lamb make thee?

Samuel Taylor Coleridge (1772–1834) was the master of Gothic poems of the supernatural. His three poems "Christabel," "The Ancient Mariner," and "Kubla Khan" are of this character. "The Ancient Mariner" relates the story of a sailor cursed for killing an albatross. The poem treats the subject as a crime against nature and God and raises the issues of guilt, punishment, and the redemptive possibilities of humility and penance. At the end of the poem the mariner discovers the unity and beauty of all things and, having repented, is delivered from his awful curse, which has been symbolized by the dead albatross hung around his neck:

> O happy living things! no tongue
> Their beauty might declare:
> A spring of love gushed from my heart,
> And I blessed them unaware . . .
> The self-same moment I could pray;
> And from my neck so free
> The Albatross fell off, and sank
> Like lead into the sea.

Coleridge also made major contributions to Romantic literary criticism in his lectures on Shakespeare and in *Biographia Literaria* (1817), which presents his theories of poetry.

William Wordsworth (1770–1850) was Coleridge's closest friend. Together they published *Lyrical Ballads* in 1798 as a manifesto of a new poetry that rejected the rules of eighteenth-century criticism. Among Words-

Samuel Taylor Coleridge (1772–1834). A true Romantic, he saw his poetry as similar to the God-like act of creation. [National Portrait Gallery, London]

worth's most important later poems is his "Ode on Intimations of Immortality" (1803), written in part to console Coleridge, who was in the midst of a deep personal crisis. Its subject is the loss of poetic vision, something Wordsworth also keenly felt at this time in himself. Nature, which he had worshiped, no longer spoke freely to him, and he feared that it might never speak to him again:

> There was a time when meadow, grove, and
>   stream,
> The earth, and every common sight,
>   To me did seem
>   Appareled in celestial light,
> The glory and the freshness of a dream.
> It is not now as it hath been of yore—
>   Turn whereso'er I may,
>   By night or day,
> The things which I have seen I now can
>   see no more.

What he had lost was the vision that he believed all human beings lose in the necessary process of maturation: their childlike vision and closeness to spiritual reality. For both Wordsworth and Coleridge childhood was the bright period of creative imagination. Wordsworth held a theory of the soul's preexistence in a celestial state before its creation. The child, being closer in time to its eternal origin and undistracted by much worldly experience, recollects the supernatural world much more easily. Aging and urban living corrupt and deaden the imagination and make one's inner feelings and the beauty of nature less important. Yet Wordsworth took consolation in the occasional moments of later life when he still found in nature "intimations of immortality," a brief glimpse of humankind's eternal origin and destiny:

> O joy! that in our embers
> Is something that doth live,
> That Nature yet remembers
> What was so fugitive!

In his book-length poem *The Prelude* (1850), Wordsworth presented a long autobiographical account of the growth of the poet's mind.

Percy Bysshe Shelley (1792–1822), a very philosophical poet, lived in a Platonic world of ideas more real to him than anything in the sensible world. One of his greatest poetic works, *Prometheus Unbound* (1820), was written in Rome when he was twenty-seven years old. It was stimulated by Aeschylus' *Prometheus Bound*, the story of a defiant Titan who stole fire from the gods and paid for his crime by being eternally bound to a rock and attacked by savage birds. For Shelley, Prometheus was a symbol of all that was good in life, the principle of life itself. He was the friend of humanity, who, like Christ, suffered because he tried to improve humankind. He was the soul's unconquerable desire to create harmony in the world through reasonableness and love. In the poem Prometheus struggles against Jupiter, who represents tyranny and the power of evil in the world. He receives assistance in his struggle from Asia, a symbol of unspoiled nature, and from Mother Earth. In the end Jupiter is overthrown by his own son, Demogorgon, who rewards Prometheus' patience and endurance by setting him free. Demogorgon summarizes the poem's Romantic message:

> To suffer woes which Hope thinks infinite;
> To forgive wrongs darker than death or night;
>   To defy Power, which seems omnipotent;
> To live, and bear; to hope til Hope creates
> From its own wreck the thing it contemplates;
>   Neither to change, nor falter, nor repent;
> This, like thy glory, Titan, is to be
> Good, great and joyous, beautiful and free;
> This alone Life, Joy, Empire, and Victory.

A true rebel among the Romantic poets was Lord Byron (1788–1824). At home, even the other Romantic writers distrusted and generally disliked him. He had little sympathy for their views of the imagination. However, outside England Byron was regarded as the embodiment of the new person of the French Revolution. He rejected the old traditions (he was divorced and famous for his amours) and championed the cause of personal liberty. Byron was outrageously skeptical and mocking, even of his own beliefs. In *Childe Harold's Pilgrimage* (1812) he created the figure of a brooding, melancholy romantic hero. In *Don Juan* (1819) he wrote with ribald humor, acknowledged nature's cruelty as well as its beauty, and even expressed admiration for urban life. Byron tended to be content with the world as he directly knew it. He found his own experience of nature and love, objectively described and reported without embellishment, sufficient for poetic inspiration. He had the rare ability to encompass in his work the whole of his age and to write on subjects that other Romantics considered unworthy of poetry.

The major figures of the early Romantic movement in Germany are August Wilhelm Schlegel and his brother Friedrich (1772–1829); Friedrich von Hardenberg, known under the pseudonym Novalis (1772–1801); Ludwig Tieck (1773–1853), famous for the story *Puss-in-Boots;* and Heinrich Wackenroder (1773–1798). In 1798 this group, under the leadership of the Schlegels, founded the principal organ of German Romanticism, the journal *Athenäum.* Their principles were derived from Shakespeare, Calderón, Johann Wolfgang von Goethe (1749–1832), Friedrich von Schiller (1759–1805), and Friedrich Gottlieb Klopstock (1724–1803). *Athenäum* featured the most definitive Romantic views on art, literature, philosophy, and life, with contributions that were original, provocative, and seminal.

Much Romantic poetry was also written on the Continent, but almost all major German Romantics wrote at least one novel. Romantic novels tended to be highly sentimental and often borrowed material from medieval romances. Novalis's *Heinrich von Ofterdingen* (1802), for example, was the story of a brooding poetical knight in search of a blue flower, symbolic of truth. The characters of Romantic novels were treated as symbols of the larger truth of life. Purely realistic description was avoided. The first German Romantic novel, Ludwig Tieck's *William Lovell* (1793–1795), contrasts the young Lovell, whose life is built on love and imagination, with those who live by cold reason alone and who thus become an easy prey to unbelief, misanthrophy, and egoism. As the novel rambles to its conclusion,

George Gordon, Lord Byron (1788–1824). Brooding, melancholy, aristocratic, dissolute, Byron lived the life of a true Romantic hero, dying in the struggle for Greek independence in 1824. [National Portrait Gallery, London]

Lovell is ruined by a mixture of philosophy, materialism, and skepticism, which are administered to him by two women whom he naively loves.

Friedrich Schlegel wrote a very progressive early Romantic novel, *Lucinde* (1799), which attacked contemporary prejudices against women as capable of being little more than lovers and domestics. Schlegel's novel reveals the ability of the Romantics to become involved in the social issues of their day. He depicted Lucinde as the perfect friend and companion, as well as the unsurpassed lover, of the hero. Like other early Romantic novels the work shocked contemporary morals by frankly discussing sexual activity and by describing Lucinde as equal in all ways to the male hero.

Another important early Romantic novelist, E. T. A. Hoffmann (1776–1822), in *The Devil's Elixir* (1815–1816), traced in psychological detail the moral downfall of a monk aroused by sexuality. In these and other similar works, the Romantics attempted to repudiate many of the more widespread social values of their day. Their writings often reflect the world of dissolving certainties brought about by the continentwide turmoil of the French Revolution and the Napoleonic wars. What began as a movement in rebellion against literary norms became a movement in rebellion against social prejudices.

Towering above all of these German writers stood the figure of Johann Wolfgang von Goethe (1749–1832). Perhaps the greatest German literary figure of modern times, Goethe defies any easy classification. Part of his literary production fits into the Romantic mold, and part of it was a condemnation of Romantic excesses. The book that made his early reputation was *The Sorrows of Young Werther,* published in 1774. This novel, like many of the eighteenth century, is composed of a series of letters. The hero falls in love with Lotte, another man's wife. The letters explore this relationship and display the kind of emotional sentimentalism that was characteristic of the age. Eventually Werther and Lotte part, but in his grief over his abandoned love Werther takes his own life. This novel became very popular throughout Europe. Virtually all later Romantic authors, and especially those in Germany, admired it because of its emphasis on feeling and on living outside the bounds of polite society. Much of Goethe's early poetry was also erotic in nature. However, as he became older, Goethe became much more serious and

Johann Wolfgang von Goethe (1749–1832), the greatest German writer of modern times. He is portrayed here in the garb of a pilgrim against a Romantic background of classical ruins in the fields outside Rome. [Ursula Edelmann]

self-consciously moral. He published numerous other works, including *Wilhelm Meister's Apprenticeship* and *Iphigenia at Tauris,* that explored the manner in which human beings come to live moral lives while still acknowledging the life of the senses.

Goethe's greatest masterpiece was *Faust,* a long dramatic work of poetry in two parts. Part I was published in 1808. It tells the story of Faust, who, weary of life, makes a pact with the Devil: he will exchange his soul for greater knowledge than other human beings. As the story progresses, Faust seduces a young woman named Gretchen. She dies but is received into heaven as the grief-stricken Faust realizes that he must continue to live. In Part II, completed in the year of Goethe's death (1832), Faust is taken through a series of strange adventures involving witches and various mythological characters. This portion of the work has never been admired as much as Part I. However, at the conclusion, Faust dedicates his life, or what remains of it, to the improvement of humankind. In this dedication he feels that he has found a goal that will allow him to overcome the restless striving that first made him make the pact with the Devil. That new knowledge breaks the pact. Faust then dies and is received by angels. In this great work Goethe obviously was criticizing much of his earlier thought and that of contemporary Romantic writers, but he was also attempting

681

to portray the deep spiritual problems that Europeans would encounter as the traditional moral and religious values of Christianity were abandoned. Yet Goethe himself could not reaffirm those values. In that respect both he and his characters symbolized the spiritual struggle of the nineteenth century.

Religion in the Romantic Period

During the Middle Ages the foundation of religion had been the church. The Reformation leaders had appealed to the authority of the Bible. Then, later Enlightenment writers had attempted to derive religion from the rational nature revealed by Newtonian physics. Romantic religious thinkers, on the other hand, appealed to the inner emotions of humankind for the foundation of religion. Their forerunners were the mystics of Western Christianity. One of the first great examples of a religion characterized by Romantic impulses—Methodism—arose in England.

Methodism originated in the middle of the eighteenth century as a revolt against deism and rationalism in the Church of England. The Methodist revival formed an important part of the background of English Romanticism. The leader of the Methodist movement was John Wesley (1703–1791). His education and religious development had been carefully supervised by a remarkable mother, Susannah Wes-

---

Chateaubriand Describes the Appeal of a Gothic Church

Throughout most of the eighteenth century, writers had harshly criticized virtually all aspects of the Middle Ages, which were then considered an unenlightened time. One of the key elements of Romanticism was a new appreciation of all things medieval. In this passage from *The Genius of Christianity* Chateaubriand praised the beauty of the Middle Ages and the strong religious feelings produced by stepping into a Gothic church. The description exemplifies the typically Romantic emphasis on feelings as the chief foundation of religion.

You could not enter a Gothic church without feeling a kind of awe and a vague sentiment of the Divinity. You were all at once carried back to those times when a fraternity of cenobites [a particular order of monks], after having meditated in the woods of their monasteries, met to prostrate themselves before the altar and to chant the praises of the Lord, amid the tranquility and the silence of the night. . . .

Every thing in a Gothic church reminds you of the labyrinths of a wood; every thing excites a feeling of religious awe, of mystery, and of the Divinity.

The two lofty towers erected at the entrance of the edifice overtop the elms and yew trees of the church yard, and produce the most picturesque effect on the azure of heaven. Sometimes their twin heads are illumined by the first rays of dawn; at others they appear crowned with a capital of clouds or magnified in a foggy atmos-

phere. The birds themselves seem to make a mistake in regard to them, and to take them for the trees of the forests; they hover over their summits, and perch upon their pinnacles. But, lo! confused noises suddenly issue from the tops of these towers and scare away the affrighted birds. The Christian architect, not content with building forests, has been desirous to retain their murmurs; and, by means of the organ and of bells, he has attached to the Gothic temple the very winds and thunders that roar in the recesses of the woods. Past ages, conjured up by these religious sounds, raise their venerable voices from the bosom of the stones, and are heard in every corner of the vast cathedral. The sanctuary reechoes like the cavern of the ancient Sibyl; loud-tongued bells swing over your head, while the vaults of death under your feet are profoundly silent.

Vicomte François René de Chateaubriand, *The Genius of Christianity*, trans. by C. I. White (Baltimore: J. Murphy, 1862), as quoted in Howard E. Hugo (Ed.), *The Romantic Reader* (New York: Viking, 1957), pp. 341–342.

ley, who bore eighteen children in addition to John.

While at Oxford, Wesley organized a religious group known as the "Holy Club." He soon left England to give himself to missionary work in Georgia in America, where he arrived in 1735. While crossing the Atlantic, he had been deeply impressed by a group of German Moravians on the ship. These German pietists exhibited unshakable faith and confidence during a violent storm at sea while Wesley despaired of his life. Wesley concluded that they knew far better than he the meaning of justification by faith. When he returned to England in 1738 after an unhappy missionary career, Wesley began to worship with Moravians in London. There, in 1739, he underwent a conversion experience that he described in the words, "My heart felt strangely warmed." From that point on, he felt assured of his own salvation.

Wesley discovered that he could not preach his version of Christian conversion and practical piety in Anglican church pulpits. Therefore, late in 1739, he began to preach in the open fields near the cities and towns of western England. Literally thousands of humble people responded to his message of repentance and good works. Soon he and his brother Charles, who became famous for his hymns, began to organize Methodist societies. By the late eighteenth century the Methodists had become a separate church. They ordained their own clergy and sent missionaries to America, where the Methodists eventually achieved their greatest success and most widespread influence.

The essence of Methodist teaching lay in its stress on inward, heartfelt religion and the possibility of Christian perfection in this life. John Wesley described Christianity as "an inward principle . . . the image of God impressed on a created spirit, a fountain of peace and love springing up into everlasting life." True Christians were those who were "saved in this world from all sin, from all unrighteousness . . . and now in such a sense perfect as not to commit sin and . . . freed from evil thoughts and evil tempers."[3] Many people, weary of the dry rationalism that derived from deism, found Wesley's ideal relevant to their own lives. The Methodist preachers emphasized the role of enthusiastic emotional experience as part of Christian conversion. After Wesley, religious

[3]Quoted in Albert C. Outler (Ed.), *John Wesley: A Representative Collection of His Writings* (New York: Oxford University Press, 1964), p. 220.

John Wesley (1703–1791), *the founder of Methodism, preaching in London. Methodism emphasized the role of enthusiastic emotional experience as part of Christian conversion.* [*New York Public Library*]

revivals became highly emotional in style and content.

Similar religious developments based on feeling appeared on the Continent. After the Thermidorian Reaction, a strong Roman Catholic revival took place in France. Its followers were people who had disapproved of both the religious policy of the revolution and the anticlericalism of the Enlightenment. The most important book to express these sentiments was *The Genius of Christianity* (1802) by Vicomte François René de Chateaubriand (1768–1848). In this work, which became known as the "Bible of Romanticism," Chateaubriand argued that the essence of religion was "passion." The foundation of faith in the church was the emotion that its teachings and sacraments inspired in the heart of the Christian.

Against the Newtonian view of the world and of a rational God, the Romantics found God immanent in nature. No one stated the Romantic religious ideal more eloquently or with greater impact on the modern world than Friedrich Schleiermacher (1768–1834). In 1799 he published *Speeches on Religion to Its Cultured Despisers*. It was a response to Lutheran orthodoxy, on the one hand, and to Enlightenment rationalism, on the other. The advocates of both were the "cultured despisers" of real or heartfelt religion. According to Schleiermacher, religion was neither dogma nor a system of ethics. It was an intuition or feelings of absolute dependence on an infinite reality. Religious institutions, doctrines, and moral activity expressed that primal religious feeling only in a secondary or indirect way.

Although Schleiermacher considered Christianity the "religion of religions," he also believed that every world religion was unique in its expression of the primal intuition of the infinite in the finite. He thus turned against the universal natural religion of the Enlightenment, which he termed "a name applied to loose, unconnected impulses," and defended the meaningfulness of the numerous world religions. Every such religion was seen to be a unique version of the emotional experience of dependence on an infinite being. In so arguing, Schleiermacher interpreted the religions of the world in the same way that other Romantic writers interpreted the variety of unique peoples and cultures.

Romantic Views of Nationalism and History

One of the most distinctive features of Romanticism, especially in Germany, was its glorification of both the individual person and individual cultures. Behind these views lay the philosophy of German idealism, which understood the world as the creation of subjective egos. J. G. Fichte (1762–1814), an important German philosopher and nationalist, identified the individual ego with the Absolute that underlies all existing things. According to him and other similar philosophers, the world is truly the creation of humankind. The world is as it is because especially strong persons conceive of it in a particular way and impose their wills on the world and other people. Napoleon served as the contemporary example of such a great person. This philosophy has ever since served to justify the glorification of great per-

---

Fichte Calls for the Regeneration of Germany

Johann Gottlieb Fichte (1762–1814) began to deliver his famous *Addresses to the German Nation* late in 1807 as a series of Sunday lectures in Berlin. Earlier that year Prussia had been crushed by Napoleon's armies. In this passage from his concluding lecture, presented in early 1808, Fichte challenged the younger generation of Germans to recognize the national duty that historical circumstances had placed on their shoulders. They might either accept their defeat and the consequent slavery or revive the German nation and receive the praise and gratitude of later generations. It is important to note that Fichte saw himself speaking to all Germans as citizens of a single cultural nation rather than as the subjects of various monarchs and princes.

Review in your own minds the various conditions between which you now have to make a choice. If you continue in your dullness and helplessness, all the evils of serfdom are awaiting you; deprivations, humiliations, the scorn and arrogance of the conqueror; you will be driven and harried in every corner, because you are in the wrong and in the way everywhere; until, by the sacrifice of your nationality and your language, you have purchased for yourselves some subordinate and petty place, and until in this way you gradually die out as a people. If, on the other hand, you bestir yourselves and play the man, you will continue in a tolerable and honorable existence, and you will see growing up among and around you a generation that will be the promise for you and for the Germans of most

illustrious renown. You will see in spirit the German name rising by means of this generation to be the most glorious among all peoples; you will see this nation the regenerator and recreator of the world.

It depends on you whether you want to be the end, and to be the last of a generation unworthy of respect and certain to be despised by posterity even beyond its due—a generation of whose history . . . your descendants will read the end with gladness, saying its fate was just; or whether you want to be the beginning and the point of development for a new age glorious beyond all your conceptions, and the generation from whom posterity will reckon the year of their salvation. Reflect that you are the last in whose power this great alteration lies.

Johann Gottlieb Fichte, *Addresses to the German Nation*, ed. by George Armstrong Kelly (New York: Harper Torchbooks, 1968), pp. 215–216.

sons and their actions in overriding all opposition to their will and desires.

In addition to this philosophy the influence of new historical studies lay behind the German glorification of individual cultures. German Romantic writers went in search of their own past in reaction to the copying of French manners in eighteenth-century Germany, the impact of the French Revolution, and the imperialism of Napoleon. An early leader in this effort was Johann Gottfried Herder (1744–1803). Herder had early resented the French cultural preponderance in Germany. In 1778 Herder published an influential essay entitled "On the Knowing and Feelings of the Human Soul." In it he vigorously rejected the mechanical explanation of nature so popular with Enlightenment writers. He saw human beings and societies as developing organically, like plants, over time. Human beings were different at different times and places.

Herder revived German folk culture by urging the collection and preservation of distinctive German songs and sayings. His most important followers in this regard were the

The philosopher J. G. Fichte (1762–1814), shown here in the uniform of a Berlin home guard. Fichte glorified the role of the great individual in history. [Bildarchiv Preussischev Kulturbesitz]

MAJOR PUBLICATION DATES IN THE ROMANTIC MOVEMENT	
Rousseau's *Émile*	1762
Goethe's *Sorrows of Young Werther*	1774
Kant's *Critique of Pure Reason**	1781
Kant's *Critique of Practical Reason**	1788
Blake's *Songs of Innocence*	1789
Blake's *Songs of Experience*	1794
Wordsworth and Coleridge's *Lyrical Ballads*	1798
F. Schlegel's *Lucinde*	1799
Schleiermacher's *Speeches on Religion to Its Cultured Despisers*	1799
Chateaubriand's *Genius of Christianity*	1802
Hegel's *Phenomenology of Mind*	1806
Goethe's *Faust*, Part I	1808
Byron's *Childe Harold's Pilgrimage*	1812
Byron's *Don Juan*	1819
Shelley's *Prometheus Unbound*	1820

*Kant's books were not themselves part of the Romantic movement, but they were fundamental to later Romantic writers.

Grimm brothers, Jakob (1785–1863) and Wilhelm (1786–1859), famous for their collection of fairy tales. Believing that each language and culture was the unique expression of a people, Herder opposed both the concept and the use of a "common" language, such as French, and "universal" institutions, such as those imposed on Europe by Napoleon. These, he believed, were forms of tyranny over the individuality of a people. Herder's writings led to a broad revival of interest in history and philosophy. Although initially directed toward the identification of German origins, such work soon expanded to embrace other world cultures as well. Eventually the ability of the Romantic imagination to be at home in any age or culture spurred the study of non-Western religion, comparative literature, and philology.

Perhaps the most important person to write about history during the Romantic period was the German Georg Wilhelm Friedrich Hegel (1770–1831). He is one of the most difficult philosophers in the history of Western civilization, and he is also one of the most important.

Hegel believed that ideas develop in an evolutionary fashion that involves conflict. At any given time a predominant set of ideas, which he termed the *thesis*, holds sway. They are challenged by other conflicting ideas, which he termed the *antithesis*. As these patterns of thought clash, there emerges a *synthesis*, which

685

eventually becomes the new thesis. Then the process begins all over again. Periods of world history receive their character from the patterns of thought predominating during them. A number of important philosophical conclusions followed from this analysis. One of the most significant was the belief that all periods of history have been of almost equal value because each was, by definition, necessary to the achievements of those that came later. Also all cultures are valuable because each contributes to the necessary clash of values and ideas that allows humankind to develop. Hegel discussed these concepts in *The Phenomenology of Mind* (1806), *Lectures on the Philosophy of History* (1822–1831), and numerous other works, many of which were published only after his death. During his lifetime his ideas became widely known through his university lectures at Berlin.

These various Romantic ideas made a major contribution to the emergence of nationalism, which proved to be one of the strongest motivating forces of the nineteenth and twentieth centuries. The writers of the Enlightenment had generally championed a cosmopolitan outlook on the world. But the emphasis of the Romantic thinkers was on the individuality and worth of each separate people and culture. The factors that helped to define a people or a nation were common language, common history, a homeland that possessed historical associations, and common customs. This cultural nationalism gradually became transformed into a political creed. It came to be widely believed that every people, ethnic group, or nation should constitute a separate political entity, and that only when it so existed could the nation be secure in its own character.

The example of France under the revolution-

Hegel Explains the Role of Great Men in History

Hegel believed that behind the development of human history from one period to the next lay the mind and purpose of what he termed the "World Spirit," a concept somewhat resembling the Christian God. Hegel thought particular heroes from the past (such as Caesar) and in the present (such as Napoleon) were the unconscious instruments of that Spirit. In this passage from his lectures on the philosophy of history Hegel explained how these heroes could change the course of history. All of these concepts are characteristic of the Romantic belief that human beings and human history are always intimately connected with larger, spiritual forces at work in the world.

Such are all great historical men—whose own particular aims involve those large issues which are the will of the World-Spirit. They may be called Heroes, inasmuch as they have derived their purposes and their vocation, not from the calm, regular course of things, sanctioned by the existing order; but from a concealed fount—one which has not attained to phenomenal, present existence—from that inner Spirit, still hidden beneath the surface, which, impinging on the outer world as on a shell, bursts it in pieces, because it is another kernel than that which belonged to the shell in question. They are men, therefore, who appear to draw the impulse of their life from themselves; and whose deeds have produced a condition of things and a complex of historical relations which appear to be only their *interest, and* their *work.*

Such individuals had no consciousness of the general Idea they were unfolding, while prosecuting those aims of theirs; on the contrary, they were practical, political men. But at the same time they were thinking men, who had an insight into the requirements of the time—what was ripe for development. This was the very Truth for their age, for their world; the species next in order, so to speak, and which was already formed in the womb of time. It was theirs to know this nascent principle; the necessary, directly sequent step in progress, which their world was to take; to make this their aim, and to expend their energy in promoting it. World-historical men—the Heroes of an epoch—must, therefore, be recognized as its clear-sighted ones; their deeds, *their* words *are the best of that time.*

G. W. F. Hegel, *The Philosophy of History*, trans. by J. Sibree (New York: Dover, 1956), pp. 30–31.

ary government and then Napoleon had demonstrated the power of nationhood. Other peoples came to desire similar strength and confidence. Napoleon's toppling of ancient political structures, such as the Holy Roman Empire, demonstrated the need for new political organization in Europe. By 1815 these were the aspirations of only a few Europeans, but as time passed, such yearnings came to be shared by scores of peoples from Ireland to the Ukraine. The Congress of Vienna could ignore such feelings, but for the rest of the nineteenth century, statesmen had to confront the growing reality of their power.

Suggested Readings

M. H. ABRAMS, *The Mirror and the Lamp: Romantic Theory and the Critical Tradition* (1958). A standard text on Romantic literary theory that looks at English Romanticism in the context of German Romantic idealism.

M. H. ABRAMS, *Natural Supernaturalism: Tradition and Revolution in Romantic Literature* (1971). A brilliant survey of Romanticism across West European literature.

J. S. ALLEN, *Popular French Romanticism: Authors, Readers, and Books in the Nineteenth Century* (1981). Relates Romanticism to popular culture.

L. BERGERON, *France Under Napoleon* (1981). An in-depth examination of Napoleonic administration.

J. F. BERNARD, *Talleyrand: A Biography* (1973). A useful account.

H. BLOOM, *The Visionary Company*, rev. ed. (1971). A standard reading of the major English Romantic poetic texts.

G. BRUUN, *Europe and the French Imperium, 1799–1814* (New York, 1938). A good survey.

E. CASSIRER, *Kant's Life and Thought* (1981). A brilliant work by one of the major philosophers of this century.

D. G. CHANDLER, *The Campaigns of Napoleon* (New York, 1966). A good military study.

K. CLARK, *The Romantic Rebellion* (1973). A useful discussion that combines both art and literature.

O. CONNELLY, *Napoleon's Satellite Kingdoms* (1965). The rule of Napoleon and his family in Europe.

H. C. DEUTSCH, *The Genesis of Napoleon's Imperialism, 1801–1805* (1938). Basic for foreign policy.

Dictionary of the History of Ideas, Vol. 4 (1973), pp. 198–208. Contributions by René Wellek, "Romanticism in Literature"; Franklin L. Baumer, "Romanticism (ca. 1780–ca. 1830)"; and Jacques Droz, "Political Romanticism in Germany." Excellent and succinct.

J. ENGELL, *The Creative Imagination: Enlightenment to Romanticism* (1981). An important book on the role of the imagination in Romantic literary theory.

P. GEYL, *Napoleon: For and Against* (1949). A fine survey of the historical debate.

M. GLOVER, *The Peninsular War, 1807–1814: A Concise Military History* (1974). An interesting account of the military campaign that so drained Napoleon's resources in western Europe.

E. HECKSCHER, *The Continental System: An Economic Interpretation* (1922). Napoleon's commercial policy.

J. C. HEROLD, *The Age of Napoleon* (1968). A lively, readable account.

R. HOLTMAN, *The Napoleonic Revolution* (1950). Good on domestic policy.

H. KISSINGER, *A World Restored: Metternich, Castlereagh and the Problems of Peace, 1812–1822* (1957). A provocative study by an author who became an American Secretary of State.

S. KÖRNER, *Kant* (1955). A very clear introduction to a difficult thinker.

M. LeBRIS, *Romantics and Romanticism* (1981). A recent work, lavishly illustrated, that relates politics and Romantic art.

G. LEFEBVRE, *Napoleon*, 2 vols., trans. by H. Stockhold, (1969). The fullest and finest biography.

A. O. LOVEJOY, "The Meaning of Romanticism for the Historian of Ideas," in Franklin L. Baumer, (Ed.), *Intellectual Movements in Modern European History* (1965). A very influential summary of the basic characteristics of Romanticism.

F. MARKHAM, *Napoleon and the Awakening of Europe* (1954). Emphasizes the growth of nationalism.

F. MARKHAM, *Napoleon* (1963). A good biography strong on military questions.

H. NICOLSON, *The Congress of Vienna* (1946). A good, readable account.

R. PLANT, *Hegel: An Introduction* (1983). Emphasis on his political thought.

Z. A. PELCZYNSKI, *The State and Civil Society: Studies in Hegel's Political Philosophy* (1984). An important series of essays.

S. PRAWER (Ed.), *The Romantic Period in Germany* (1970). Contributions covering all facets of the movement.

J. L. TALMON, *Romanticism and Revolt: Europe. 1815–1848* (1967). An effort to sketch the Romantic movements and relate them to one another and to the larger political history of the period.

C. TAYLOR, *Hegel* (1975). The best one-volume introduction.

J. M. THOMPSON, *Napoleon Bonaparte: His Rise and Fall* (1952). A sound biography.

J. E. TOEWS, *Hegelianism: The Path Toward Dialectical Humanism, 1805–1841* (1980). A brilliant treatment of German philosophy after Hegel.

A. WALICKI, *Philosophy and Romantic Nationalism: The Case of Poland* (1982). Examines the manner in which philosophy influenced the character of Polish nationalism.

Prince Clemens von Metternich (1773–1859), the statesman who epitomized nineteenth-century conservatism. [By gracious permission of HM the Queen]

THE DEFEAT of Napoleon and the diplomatic settlement of the Congress of Vienna restored a conservative political and social order in Europe. Legitimate monarchies, landed aristocracies, and established churches constituted the major pillars of conservatism. The institutions themselves were ancient, but the self-conscious alliance of throne, land, and altar was new. Throughout the eighteenth century these groups had been in frequent conflict. Only the upheavals of the French Revolution and the Napoleonic era transformed them into natural, if sometimes reluctant, allies. They retained their former arrogance but neither their former privileges nor their old confidence. They knew they could be toppled by the political groups that hated them. They understood that revolution in one country could spill over into another. The conservatives regarded themselves as surrounded by enemies and as standing permanently on the defensive against the forces of liberalism, nationalism, and popular sovereignty. These potential sources of unrest had to be confronted both at home and abroad.

Conservative Governments on the Domestic Scene

The course of nineteenth-century history is frequently associated with the emergence of the liberal, national state and industrial society. But the staying power of the restored conservative institutions, especially in Great Britain and eastern Europe, is an equally and perhaps even more striking feature of the century. Actually not until World War I did their power and pervasive influence come to an end. One need not admire these institutions or the policies and personalities associated with them, yet one must admit that their persistence constituted one of the most important features of nineteenth-century political and social life. To ignore or to disparage their relatively successful attempts at self-preservation is to underestimate the grave obstacles that confronted liberals and nationalists.

The more theoretical political and religious ideas of the conservative classes were associated with Romantic thinkers, such as Burke and Hegel. Conservatives shared other, less formal attitudes forged by the revolutionary experience. The fate of Louis XVI convinced most monarchs that they could trust only aristocratic governments or governments of aristo-

20
Restoration, Reaction, and Reform (1815–1832)

Czar Alexander I (1802–1825). A mild reformer when he succeeded to the throne, Alexander became increasingly reactionary after 1815. [By gracious permission of HM the Queen]

crats in alliance with the very wealthiest middle-class and professional people. The European aristocracies believed that their property and influence would rarely be safe under any form of genuinely representative government. All conservatives spurned the idea of a written constitution unless they were permitted to promulgate the document themselves. Even then, some could not be reconciled to the concept.

The churches were equally apprehensive of popular movements except their own revivals. The ecclesiastical leaders throughout the Continent regarded themselves as entrusted with the educational task of supporting the social and political status quo. They also feared and hated most of the ideas associated with the Enlightenment because those rational concepts and reformist writings enshrined the critical spirit and undermined revealed religion. Conservative Europeans came to regard as *liberal* any idea or institution that they opposed. However, as will be seen, that word actually had rather different meanings in different countries.

Russia and Alexander I

The pursuit of Napoleon's army across Europe after the burning of Moscow created a new image of vast Russian power. The image remained until the Russian defeat in the Crimean War (1854–1856). In Vienna Czar Alexander I had played a more important personal role than any other participating monarch. Both in those negotiations and in his governance of Russia, Alexander was and has remained a puzzling figure. He was torn between an intellectual attraction to the doctrines of the Enlightenment and reform and a very pragmatic adherence to traditional autocracy. His own development as a person and as a ruler reflected the turn of eastern European states from enlightened absolutism to rigid conservatism and defense of the status quo.

Alexander I came to the Russian throne in 1801 after the murder of his father, Czar Paul. The son had condoned the palace revolution. Paul had been an unstable person who ruled in an arbitrary and unpredictable manner. Paul had attempted to reverse the policies of his mother, Catherine the Great, whom he loathed. He attacked the privileges of the nobility. The result was a *coup d'état* led by court nobles and the army. Alexander I intended to return to the policies of his grandmother and to consider at least the possibility of political and administrative change in Russia. He confirmed the privileges of the nobles and abolished the security police. He was well educated in the ideas of the Enlightenment. In 1801 he appointed a government reform committee composed of liberal friends. Little came from the reformist plans submitted by this group, and by 1803 Alexander had declared that no group had a right to challenge the legality of the decrees of the czar.

Once Alexander had led Russia into war against Napoleon, even the mild reformist tendencies began to wane. In 1807 the security police were, in effect, reestablished. Yet the military reverses of the campaign and his personal admiration of Napoleon's administrative genius convinced the czar that a reconstruction of the Russian government was necessary. In 1808 he turned to Michael Speransky (1772–1839) to guide his thinking on matters of administrative reform. This enlightened minister, who held a series of government appointments, drew up a plan for constitutional government that included an elected legislative body. He even dared talk about an eventual, gradual abolition of serfdom. The czar could not support such bold departures. Speransky had to be satisfied with a restructuring of the ministries and the bureaucracy. In 1812 he introduced new, progressive taxes on landed income. Each of these policies alienated the nobility. In March 1812 Alexander, fearing the discontent among the nobles, dismissed his once-trusted minister. Again reform came to a close almost without having begun.

Thereafter Alexander, though occasionally using liberal rhetoric, became an increasingly hardened conservative. For the renewed struggle against Napoleon, he needed the support of his nobility and the army. Also, during this post-Speransky period, he was deeply drawn to those mystical religious feelings that lay behind his project for forming the Holy Alliance in 1815. The czar came to regard the Enlightenment, the French Revolution, and Napoleon as one vast attack on Christianity. His new chief adviser was Alexis Arakcheiev (1769–1834), a general and a political opponent of Speransky. This reactionary military figure became the most powerful person in the country except for Alexander himself. Together they pursued a consistently conservative policy. Censorship and religiously dominated education became the order of the day. They also established "military farms." These institutions transformed whole districts of the country into military establishments where the army farmed and supported itself when not fighting. There was little or no toleration of political opposition or criticism of the regime. By the early 1820s, the czar, whose early years had seemed

to hold out the promise of possible reform, had become a leading symbol of conservative reaction.

Austria and the Germanies

The early nineteenth-century statesman who more than any other epitomized conservatism was the Austrian Prince Metternich, whom we have already met at the Congress of Vienna. This devoted servant of the Habsburg emperor had been, along with Castlereagh, the chief architect of the Vienna settlement. It was he who seemed to exercise chief control over the forces of the European reaction. The conservative foreign and domestic policy that he forged for Austria stemmed from the pragmatic needs of that peculiar state rather than from ideology. The Austrian government could make no serious compromises with the new political forces in Europe. To no other country were the programs of liberalism and nationalism potentially more dangerous. The Habsburg domains were peopled with Germans and Hungarians, as well as Poles and other nationalities or ethnic groups. Through puppet governments Austria also dominated the Italian peninsula. Pursuit of dynastic integrity required Austrian domination of the newly formed German Confederation to prevent the formation of a German national state that might absorb the heart of the empire and exclude the other realms governed by the Habsburgs. So far as Metternich and other officials were concerned, the recognition of the political rights and aspirations of any of the various national groups would mean the probable dissolution of the empire. If Austria permitted representative government, Metternich feared that the national groups would fight their battles internally at the probable cost of Austrian international influence.

During the immediate postwar years Metternich's primary concern lay with Germany. The Congress of Vienna had created the German Confederation to replace the defunct Holy Roman Empire. It consisted of thirty-nine states under Austrian leadership. Each state remained more or less autonomous, but Austria was determined to prevent any movement toward constitutionalism in as many of them as possible.

The majority victory for this holding policy came in Prussia. In 1815 Frederick William III (1797–1840), during the exhilaration after the War of Liberation, as Germans termed the last

Metternich Criticizes the Political Activity of the Middle Class

In 1820 the emperor of Austria asked Prince Klemens von Metternich to compose a political "confession of faith" to be sent to Alexander I of Russia. In the course of that document Metternich described what he regarded as the political evil of middle-class liberals. He argued that liberals sought to undermine the natural loyalty of subjects to monarchs. This action stemmed from the intellectual pride or presumption of these liberals, who had adopted many of the ideas of the Enlightenment. Metternich also pointed to the role of a free press in causing political unrest. Metternich himself did much to foster extensive press censorship in eastern Europe.

The evil exists and it is enormous. We do not think we can better define it and its cause at all times and in all places than we have already done by the word ''presumption,'' that inseparable companion of the half-educated, that spring of an unmeasured ambition, and yet easy to satisfy in times of trouble and confusion.

It is principally the middle classes of society which this moral gangrene has affected, and it is only among them that the heads of the party [working for liberal reform] are found. . . .

Europe thus presents itself to the impartial observer under an aspect at the same time deplorable and peculiar. We find everywhere the people praying for the maintenance of peace and tranquility, faithful to God and their Princes, remaining proof against the efforts and seductions of the factious who call themselves friends of the people and wish to lead them to an agitation which the people themselves do not desire!

The Governments, having lost their balance, are frightened, intimidated, and thrown into confusion by the cries of the intermediary class of society, which placed between Kings and their subjects, breaks the sceptre of the monarch, and usurps the cry of the people. . . .

We see this intermediary class abandon itself with a blind fury and animosity which proves much more its own fears than any confidence in the success of its enterprises, to all the means which seem proper to assuage its thirst for power, applying itself to the task of persuading Kings that their rights are confined to sitting upon a throne, while those of the people are to govern, and to attack all that centuries have bequeathed as holy and worthy of man's respect— denying, in fact, the value of the past, and declaring themselves the masters of the future. . . . It takes possession of the press, and employs it to promote impiety, disobedience to the laws of religion and the State, and goes so far as to preach murder as a duty for those who desire what is good. . . .

If the same elements of destruction which are now throwing society into convulsion have existed in all ages . . . yet ours, by the single fact of the liberty of the press, possesses more than any preceding age the means of contact, seduction, and attraction whereby to act on these different classes of men.

Prince Richard Metternich (Ed.), *Memoirs of Prince Metternich, 1815–1829,* Vol. 5 (New York: Charles Scribner's, 1881), pp. 465–466, 468, 472–473.

part of their conflict with Napoleon, had promised some mode of constitutional government. However, he immediately stalled on keeping his pledge. In 1817 he formally reneged and created a new Council of State, which did bring about more efficient administration but which was not a constitutional mode of government. In 1819 the king moved further away from thoughts of reform. After a major disagreement over the organization of the army,

his chief reform-minded ministers resigned. The monarch replaced them with hardened conservatives. On their advice in 1823 Frederick William III established eight provincial estates, or diets, which were dominated by the *Junkers* and which exercised only an advisory function. The old alliance between the Prussian monarchy, the army, and the landholders stood reestablished. This conservative alliance opposed German nationalist aspirations that seemed to threaten the social and political order.

Three south German states—Baden, Bavaria, and Württemberg—had received constitutions after 1815 as their monarchs attempted to secure wider political support. Each of these constitutions was a very limited document that refused to recognize popular sovereignty and that defined political rights as the gift of the monarch. But the nationalist and liberal aspirations raised by the collective national experience of defeating the French armies remained alive in the hearts and minds of many young Germans. The most important of these groups was the university students. They had grown up during the days of the reforms of Stein and Hardenburg and the initial circulation of the writings of Fichte and other German nationalists. Many of them had fought Napoleon. When they went to the universities, they continued to dream their dream of a united Germany. They formed *Burschenschaften*, or student associations. Like student groups today, these clubs served numerous social functions, but one of them was severing old provincial loyalties and replacing them with loyalty to the concept of a united German state.

In 1817 in Jena one such student club organized a large celebration of the fourth anniversary of the battle of Leipzig and of the tercentenary of Luther's Ninety-five Theses. There were bonfires, songs, and processions as more than five hundred people gathered for the festivities. The event made German rulers uneasy, for it was known that some republicans were involved with the student clubs. Two years later, in March 1819, a young man named Karl Sand, who was a *Burschenschaft* member, assassinated the conservative dramatist August von Kotzebue. Sand, who was tried, condemned, and publicly executed, became a martyr in the eyes of some nationalists. Although the assassin had acted alone, Metternich decided to use the incident to suppress the student clubs and other potential institutions of liberalism.

In July 1819 Metternich persuaded representatives of the major German states to issue the Carlsbad Decrees, which dissolved the *Burschenschaften*. The decrees also provided for university inspectors and press censors. The next year the German Confederation promulgated the Final Act, which limited the subjects that might be discussed in the constitutional chambers of Bavaria, Württemberg, and Baden. The measure also asserted the right of the monarchs to resist demands of the constitutionalists. Thereafter, for many years the secret police of the various German states harassed potential dissidents. In the opinion of the princes these included almost anyone who sought even moderate social or political change.

Great Britain

The years 1819 and 1820 marked a high tide for conservative influence and repression in western as well as eastern Europe. After 1815 Great Britain experienced two years of poor harvests. There was also considerable industrial unemployment, to which discharged sailors and soldiers added their numbers.

A caricature of George IV (1820–1830) as a self-indulgent voluptuary. Although a discerning patron of the arts, George was extremely unpopular both as Prince of Wales and as king. His extravagant, dissolute way of life cast the monarchy itself into disrepute. [*The Mansell Collection*]

The Tory ministry of Lord Liverpool (1770–1828) was unprepared to deal with these problems of postwar dislocation. Instead, it sought to protect the interests of the landed and other wealthy classes. In 1815 Parliament passed a Corn Law to maintain high prices for domestically produced grain through import duties on foreign grain. The next year Parliament abolished the income tax paid by the wealthy and replaced it with excise or sales taxes on consumer goods paid by both the wealthy and the poor. These laws represented a continuation of previous legislation through which the British ruling class had abandoned much of its traditional role of paternalistic protector of the poor. In 1799 Parliament had passed the Combination Acts forbidding workers' organizations or unions. During the war, wage protection had been removed. The taxpaying classes grumbled about supporting the poor law that provided public relief for those destitute or without work; many people called for its abolition.

In light of these policies and the postwar economic downturn, it is hardly surprising that the lower social orders began to doubt the wisdom of their rulers and to call for a reform of the political system. Mass meetings calling for

the reform of Parliament were held. Reform clubs were organized. Radical newspapers, such as William Cobbett's *Political Registrar,* demanded political change. In the hungry, restive agricultural and industrial workers the government could see only images of continental sans-culotte crowds ready to hang aristocrats from the nearest lamppost. Government ministers regarded radical leaders, such as Cobbett (1763–1835), Major John Cartwright (1740–1824), and Henry "Orator" Hunt (1773–1835), as demagogues who were seducing the people away from allegiance to their natural leaders. The answer of the government to the discontent was repression. In December 1816 a very unruly mass meeting took place at Spa Fields near London. This disturbance provided an excuse to pass the Coercion Act of March 1817. These measures temporarily suspended habeas corpus and extending existing laws against seditious gatherings.

This initial repression, accompanied by improved harvests, brought calm for a time to the political landscape. However, by 1819 the people were restive again. Throughout the industrial north a large number of well-organized mass meetings were held to demand the re-

Shelley Deplores the Condition of England in 1819

Percy Bysshe Shelley, one of the greatest of the Romantic poets, was a political radical. In 1819 he was living in Italy. On hearing the news of the Peterloo Massacre, he wrote the most famous of his political poems, "Sonnet: England in 1819." In it he attacked George III, who had long been mentally unstable; the Church of England, which was insensitive the plight of the common people; and Parliament, which had passed repressive laws after Peterloo.

An old, mad, blind, despised, and dying
  king,—
Princes, the dregs of their dull race, who flow
Through public scorn,—mud from a muddy
  spring,—
Rulers who neither see, nor feel, nor know,
But leech-like to their fainting country cling,
Till they drop, blind in blood, without a
  blow,—
A people starved and stabled in the untilled
  field,—

An army, which liberticide and prey
Makes as a two-edged sword to all who
  wield,—
Golden and sanguine laws which tempt and
  slay;
Religion Christless, Godless—a book sealed;
A Senate,—Time's worst statute
  unrepealed,—
Are graves, from which a glorious Phantom
  may
Burst, to illumine our tempestuous day.

The Complete Poetical Works of Percy Bysshe Shelley, ed. by Thomas Hutchinson (London: Oxford University Press, 1929), p. 570.

form of Parliament. Major radical leaders gave speeches to thousands of people. The radical reform campaign culminated on August 16, 1819, with a meeting in Manchester at Saint Peter's Fields. Royal troops and the local militia were on hand to ensure order. Just as the speeches were about to begin, a local magistrate ordered the militia to move into the audience. The result was panic and death. At least eleven people in the crowd were killed; scores were injured. The event became known as the "Peterloo" Massacre through a contemptuous comparison with the victory at Waterloo.

Peterloo had been the act of the local Manchester officials. However, the Liverpool ministry felt that those officials must be supported. The Cabinet also decided to act once and for all to end these troubles. Most of the radical leaders were arrested and thus taken out of circulation. In December 1819, a few months after the German Carlsbad Decrees, Parliament passed a series of laws called the Six Acts. These forbade large meetings, raised the fines for seditious libel, speeded up the trials of political agitators, increased newspaper taxes, prohibited the training of armed groups, and allowed local officials to search homes in certain disturbed counties. In effect, the Six Acts attempted to remove the instruments of agitation from the hands of radical leaders and to provide the authorities with new powers.

Two months after the passage of the Six Acts, the Cato Street Conspiracy was unearthed. Under the guidance of a possibly demented figure named Thistlewood, a group of extreme radicals had plotted to blow up the entire British Cabinet. The plot was foiled. The leaders were arrested and tried, and four of them were executed. The conspiracy had been little more than a half-baked plot, but it provided new support for repression by the government. More important, the conspiracy helped further to discredit the movement for parliamentary reform.

The arrest of the Cato Street conspirators in 1820. This half-baked plot was used by the government as a pretext for further repression. [The Mansell Collection]

Bourbon Restoration in France

The abdication of Napoleon in 1814 opened the way for a restoration of Bourbon rule in the homeland of the great revolution. The new king was the former count of Provence and a brother of Louis XVI. The son of the executed monarch had died in prison. Royalists had regarded the dead boy as Louis XVII, and so his uncle became Louis XVIII (1814–1824). This fat, awkward man had become a political realist during his more than twenty years of exile. He understood that he could not govern if he attempted to turn back the clock. France had undergone too many irreversible changes. Consequently Louis XVIII agreed to become a constitutional monarch, but under a constitution of his own making.

The constitution of the French restoration was the Charter. It provided for a hereditary

Louis XVIII (1814–1824). Unlike his more reactionary supporters, who were said to be ''more royalist than the king,'' Louis was a political realist and agreed to reign as a constitutional monarch. [Library of Congress]

monarchy and a bicameral legislature. The monarch appointed the upper house; the lower house, the Chamber of Deputies, was elected according to a very narrow franchise that upheld a high property qualification. The Charter guaranteed most of the rights enumerated by the Declaration of the Rights of Man and Citizen. There was to be religious toleration, but Roman Catholicism was designated as the official religion of the nation. Most important for thousands of the French at various stations of life who had profited from the revolution, the Charter promised not to disturb the property changes brought about by the confiscation and sale of aristocratic and church land. In this manner Louis XVIII attempted to reconcile to his restored regime those classes that had benefited from the revolution.

This moderate spirit did not penetrate deeply into the ranks of royalist supporters. Their families had suffered much at the hands of the revolution. They now demanded their revenge. The king's brother, the count of Artois (1757–1836), served as a rallying point for those people who were more royalist than the monarch. In the months after Napoleon's final defeat at Waterloo, royalists in the south and west carried out a White Terror against former revolutionaries and supporters of the deposed emperor. The king could do little or nothing to halt this bloodbath of royalist revenge. Similar extreme royalist sentiment existed in the Chamber of Deputies. The ultraroyalist majority elected in 1816 proved so dangerously reactionary that the king soon dissolved the chamber. The majority returned by the second election were more moderate. Under the ministry of the duke of Richelieu the country paid off the war indemnity to the allies, and the occupation troops withdrew in 1818. Yet royalist discontent remained. Louis XVIII attempted to pursue a policy of mild accommodation with liberals through his minister Decazes, who took office in 1818, but the king's younger brother, the count of Artois, pushed for reactionary departures.

This give and take might have continued for some time. However, in February 1820 the duke of Berri, son of Artois and heir to the throne after his father, was murdered by a lone assassin. The ultraroyalists persuaded Louis XVIII that the murder was the result of Decazes's cooperation with liberal politicians. The duke of Richelieu was recalled. The electoral laws were revised to give wealthy electors two votes. Press censorship was imposed. Persons suspected of dangerous political activity could be easily arrested. By 1821 the direction of secondary education in France had been put under the control of the Roman Catholic bishops. All of these actions revealed the basic contradiction of the French restoration. There had been no intention of creating a genuinely parliamentary system. The king rather than the Chamber of Deputies chose the ministers. The government constantly tinkered with the electoral apparatus to disqualify opponents from voting. By the early 1820s the veneer of constitutionalism had worn away. Liberals were being driven out of legal political life and into near-illegal activity.

The Conservative International Order

The Congress System

At the Congress of Vienna, the major powers—Russia, Austria, Prussia, and Great Britain—had agreed to consult with each other from time to time on matters affecting Europe as a whole. The vehicle for this consultation was a series of postwar congresses. Later, as differences arose among the powers, the consultations became more informal. This mode of working out issues of foreign policy was known as the *Concert of Europe*. It meant that no one nation could take a major action in international affairs without the assent of the others. The major goal of the Concert of Europe was to maintain the balance of power against new French aggression and against the military might of Russia. The Concert of Europe continued to function on large and small issues until the third quarter of the century.

The years that witnessed the domestic conservative consolidation of power also saw a generally successful functioning of the congress system. The first congress occurred in 1818 at Aix-la-Chapelle. As a result of this congress the four major powers removed their troops from France, which had paid its war reparations, and readmitted that nation to good standing among European nations. Despite unanimity on these decisions, problems did arise during the conference. Czar Alexander I, displaying his full reactionary colors, suggested that the Quadruple Alliance agree to uphold the borders and the existing governments of all European countries. Castlereagh, representing Britain, flatly rejected the pro-

posal. He contended that the Quadruple Alliance was intended only to prevent future French aggression.

THE SPANISH REVOLUTION OF 1820. These disagreements appeared somewhat academic in 1818. But two years later a series of revolutions began in southern Europe. The Spanish rebelled against Ferdinand VII (1814–1833). When placed on his throne at the time of Napoleon's downfall, this Bourbon monarch had promised to govern according to a written constitution. Once securely in power, Ferdinand simply ignored that pledge. He dissolved the parliament (the Cortes) and ruled alone. In 1820 a group of army officers about to be sent to suppress revolution in Spain's Latin American colonies rebelled. In March Ferdinand once again announced that he would abide by the provisions of the constitution. For the time being, the revolution had succeeded. Almost at the same time, in July 1820, the revolutionary spirit erupted in Naples, where the king of the Two Sicilies very quickly accepted a constitution. There were other, lesser revolts in Italy, but none of them succeeded.

These events frightened the ever-nervous Metternich. Italian disturbances were especially troubling to him. Austria hoped to dominate the peninsula to provide a buffer against the spread of revolution on its own southern flank. The other powers were divided on the best course of action. Britain opposed joint intervention in either Italy or Spain. Metternich turned to Prussia and Russia for support. The three eastern powers, along with unofficial delegations from Britain and France, met at the Congress of Troppau in late October 1820. The members of the Holy Alliance, led by Alexander of Russia, issued the Protocol of Troppau. This declaration asserted that stable governments might intervene to restore order in countries experiencing revolution. Yet even Russia hesitated to authorize Austrian intervention in Italian affairs. That decision was finally reached in January 1821 at the Congress of Laibach. Shortly thereafter Austrian troops marched into Naples and restored the king of the Two Sicilies to unconstitutional government.

The final postwar congress took place in October 1822 at Verona. Its primary purpose was to resolve the situation in Spain. Once again Britain balked at joint action. Shortly before the meeting Castlereagh had committed suicide. George Canning (1770–1827), the new foreign minister, was much less sympathetic to Metternich's goals. At Verona, Britain, in effect, withdrew from continental affairs. Austria, Prussia, and Russia agreed to support French intervention in Spain. In April 1823 the French army crossed the Pyrenees and within a few months suppressed the Spanish revolu-

Greece Dying on the Ruins of Missolonghi, *by Eugene Delacroix (1799–1863), illustrates how small nationalities were sentimentalized by Romantic artists in Western Europe. Greece is personified as a beautiful, defenceless woman appealing for help against the triumphant Turk pictured in the background. The painting was inspired by the fall of the fortress of Missolonghi in southern Greece to the Turks. Lord Byron died of typhus during the siege.* [Giraudon]

tion. Liberals and revolutionaries were tortured, executed, and driven from the country. The intervention in Spain in 1823 was one of the most bloody examples of reactionary politics during the entire century.

There was a second diplomatic result of the Congress of Verona and the Spanish intervention. George Canning was much more interested in the fate of British commerce and trade than Castlereagh had been. Consequently Canning sought to prevent the politics of European reaction from being extended to the Spanish colonies then revolting in Latin America (to be discussed later). He intended to use those South American revolutions as the occasion for British penetration of the old Spanish trading monopoly in that area. To that end the British foreign minister supported the American Monroe Doctrine in 1823, prohibiting further colonization and intervention by European powers in the Americas. Britain soon recognized the Spanish colonies as independent states. Through the rest of the century British commercial interests dominated Latin America. In this fashion Canning may be said to have brought to a successful conclusion the War of Jenkins's Ear (1739).

The Greek Revolution of 1821

While the powers were plotting the new restorations in Italy and Spain, a third Mediterranean revolt had erupted in Greece. The Greek revolution became one of the most famous of the century because it attracted the support and participation of many illustrious literary figures. Liberals throughout Europe, who were seeing their own hopes crushed at home, imagined that the ancient Greek democracy was being reborn. "The world's great age begins anew," wrote Shelley. Lord Byron went to fight and in 1824 died in the cause of Greek liberty. Philhellenic societies were founded in nearly every major country.

The Greeks were rebelling against the Ottoman Empire. The weakness of that empire troubled Europe for the entire century and raised what was known as the *eastern question.* The residue of the problem remains alive today in the tensions between Greece and Turkey and in the instability in the Middle East. Most of the major powers were interested in what happened to the Ottoman holdings for reasons less idealistic than the poets'. Russia and Austria coveted land in the Balkans. France and Britain were concerned with the empire's com-

The battle of Navarino, October 20, 1827 in which a combined British-French-Russian fleet that was supporting the Greek revolt destroyed the Turkish navy. [*Bildarchiv Preussischev Kulturbesitz*]

merce and with control of key naval positions in the eastern Mediterranean. There was also the issue of protection of Christian access to the shrines in the Holy Land.

These conflicting interests, as well as mutual distrust, prevented any direct intervention in Greek affairs for several years. In 1827 a joint British, French, and Russian fleet supported the Greek revolt. The fleet was enforcing the Treaty of London of 1827, in which those powers demanded Turkish recognition of Greek independence. They had decided that their domestic security would not be endangered by an independent Greek state and that their several foreign-policy concerns in the area would prosper from such a new nation. In 1828 Russia sent troops against the Ottoman holdings in what is today Romania. By the treaty of Adrianople of 1829, Russia gained effective control of that territory. The treaty further stipulated that the Turks would allow Britain, France, and Russia to decide the future of Greece.

In 1830 Greece was declared an independent kingdom by a second Treaty of London.

Two years later Otto I (1832–1862), the son of the king of Bavaria, was chosen as the first king of the new Greek royal dynasty. The Greek revolt was the only successful national revolution of the first quarter of the century. Elsewhere the conservative powers had defeated the attempts at revolution.

The Wars of Independence in Latin America

The wars of the French Revolution, and more particularly those of Napoleon, sparked movements for independence from European domination throughout Latin America. In less than two decades, between 1804 and 1824, France was driven from Haiti, Portugal lost control of Brazil, and Spain lost control of all but Cuba and Puerto Rico. Three centuries of Iberian colonial government over the South American continent came to an end.

Haiti achieved independence in 1804 following a slave revolt that began in 1794, led by Toussaint L'Ouverture and Jean-Jacques Dessalines. Such a revolution, involving the popu-

699

Toussaint L'Ouverture (1743–1803) began the revolt that led to Haitian independence in 1804. [Culver Pictures]

lar uprising of a repressed social group, was the great exception in the Latin American drive for liberty from European masters. Generally speaking, on the South American continent, the creole elite, composed of Spanish merchants, landowners, and professional persons born in America, led the movements against Spain and Portugal. Very few Indians, blacks, people of mixed race, or slaves became involved or benefited from the end of Iberian rule. Indeed, the example of the Haitian slave revolt haunted the creoles, and they were determined that any drive for political independence from Spain and Portugal should not cause social disruption or the loss of their existing social and economic privileges. In this respect, the creole revolutionaries were not unlike American revolutionaries in the southern colonies who wanted to reject British rule but to keep their slaves, or French revolutionaries who wanted to depose the king but not to extend liberty to the French working class.

There were several sources of creole discontent with Spanish colonial government. (The Brazilian situation will be discussed separately.) Some of the creole complaints against Spain resembled those of the American colonists against Great Britain. Latin American merchants wanted to trade more freely within the region and throughout the North American and European markets. They wanted commercial regulations that would benefit them rather than Spain. The late-eighteenth-century Bourbon imperial reforms, though liberating trade, had hurt Latin American exports. Creoles also feared that Spanish imperial regulations might attempt to make changes in landholding, access to army officer commissions, local government, and the treatment of slaves and Indians. The creoles deeply resented the favors granted to persons born in Spain and the clear discrimination against themselves in matters of appointments and patronage in the colonial government, church, and army.

Creole leaders had read the Enlightenment *philosophes* and regarded their reforms as potentially beneficial to the region. They were also well aware of the events and the political philosophy of the American Revolution. But something more than reform programs and revolutionary example was required to transform creole discontent into revolt against the Spanish government. That transforming event occurred in Europe when Napoleon toppled the Portuguese monarchy in 1807 and the Spanish government in 1808 and placed his own brother on those thrones. The Portuguese royal family fled to Brazil and established its government there. But the Bourbon monarchy of Spain stood, for the time being, wholly vanquished. That situation created an imperial political vacuum throughout Spanish Latin America and provided both the opportunity and the necessity for action by creole leaders.

The creole elite feared that a liberal Napoleonic monarchy in Spain would attempt to impose reforms in Latin America that would harm their economic and social interests. They also feared that a Spanish monarchy controlled by France would attempt to drain the region of the wealth and resources needed for Napoleon's wars. To protect their interests and to seize the opportunity to take over direction of their own political destiny, between 1808 and 1810 various creole juntas, or political committees, claimed the right to govern different regions of Latin America. Many of them quite insincerely declared that they were ruling in the name of the deposed Spanish monarch Ferdinand VII. After the establishment of these local juntas, the Spanish would not again directly govern the continent; after ten years of politically and economically exhausting warfare, they were required to make Latin American independence permanent.

The vast size of Latin America, its geographical barriers, and its distinct regional differences meant that there would be several different paths to independence. The first region to assert itself was the Río de la Plata, or modern Argentina. The center of revolt was Buenos Aires, whose citizens, as early as 1806, had fought off a British invasion against the Spanish commercial monopoly and thus had learned that they could look to themselves rather than Spain for effective political and military action. In 1810, the junta in Buenos Aires not only thrust off Spanish authority but also sent forces against both Paraguay and Uruguay in the cause of liberation from Spain and control by their own region. The armies were defeated, but Spanish control was lost in the two areas. Paraguay asserted its own independence. Uruguay was eventually absorbed by Brazil.

The Buenos Aires government was not discouraged by these early defeats and remained determined to liberate Peru, the greatest stronghold of royalist power. By 1814, José de San Martín had become the leading general of the Río de la Plata forces. He organized a disciplined army and led his forces in a daring march over the Andes Mountains. By early 1817, he had occupied Santiago in Chile, where the Chilean independence leader Bernardo O'Higgins was established as supreme dictator. From Santiago, San Martín oversaw the construction and organization of a naval force that, in 1820, he used to carry his army by sea to an assault on Peru. The next year, San Martín drove royalist forces from the city of Lima and took for himself the title of Protector of Peru.

While the army of San Martín had been liberating the southern portion of the continent, Simón Bolívar had been pursuing a similar task in the north. Bolívar had been involved in the organization of a liberating junta in Caracas, Venezuela, in 1810. He was a firm advocate of both independence and republican modes of government. Between 1811 and 1814, civil war took place throughout Venezuela as both royalists, on the one hand, and slaves and *llaneros* (Venezuelan cowboys), on the other, challenged the authority of the republican government. Bolívar had to go into exile first in Colombia and then in Jamaica. In 1816, with help from Haiti, he launched a new

Simón Bolívar (1783–1830), the Liberator of South America. [Collection of Alfredo Boulton, Caracas]

invasion against Venezuela. He first captured Bogotá, capital of New Granada (including modern Colombia, Bolivia, and Ecuador), to secure a base for the attack on Venezuela. The tactic worked. By the summer of 1821, Bolívar's forces had captured Caracas, and he had been named president.

A year later, in July 1822, the armies of Bolívar and San Martín joined as they moved to liberate Quito. At a famous meeting of the two liberators in Guayaquil, a sharp disagreement occurred about the future political structure of Latin America. San Martín believed that monarchies were required; Bolívar maintained his republicanism. Not long after the meeting, San Martín quietly retired from public life and went into exile in Europe. Meanwhile Bolívar purposely allowed the political situation in Peru to fall into confusion, and in 1823 he sent in troops to establish his control. On December 9, 1824, at the battle of Ayacucho, the Spanish royalist forces suffered a major defeat at the hands of the liberating army. The battle marked the conclusion of the Spanish effort to retain their American empire. That final Spanish retreat left Latin Americans to confront directly the kind of political questions that had so profoundly divided San Martín and Bolívar.

The drive for independence in New Spain (present-day Mexico) illustrates better than that of any other region the socially conservative outcome of the Latin American colonial revolutions. As elsewhere, a local governing junta was organized. But before it had undertaken any significant measures, a creole priest, Miguel Hidalgo y Costilla, issued a call for rebellion to the Indians in his parish. They and other repressed groups of black and mestizo urban and rural workers responded. Father Hidalgo set forth a program of social change, including hints of changes in landholding. Soon he stood at the head of a rather unorganized group of eighty thousand followers who captured several major cities and then marched on Mexico City. Hidalgo's forces and the royalist army that opposed them committed numerous atrocities. In July 1811 the revolutionary priest was captured and executed. Leadership then fell to José María Morelos y Pavón, a mestizo priest. Far more radical than Hidalgo, he called for an end to forced labor and substan-

Father Miguel Hidalgo y Costilla (d. 1811) led an unsuccessful peasant revolt in 1810–1811 that marked the beginning of the struggle for Mexican independence. [Organization of American States]

tial land reforms before his execution in 1815. These five years of popular uprising that ended with Morelos's death had resulted in thousands of other fatalities.

The popular uprising and demand for fundamental social reform united all conservative political groups in Mexico whether they were creole or Spanish. They were unwilling to undertake any kind of reform that might cause loss of their privileges. In 1820 they found their recently achieved security challenged from an unexpected source. As already explained, the revolution in Spain had forced Ferdinand VII to accept a liberal constitution. Conservative Mexicans feared that the new liberal monarchy would attempt to impose liberal reforms in Mexico. Therefore, for the most conservative of reasons, they rallied to a former royalist general, Agustín de Iturbide, who in 1821 declared Mexico independent of Spain. Shortly thereafter Iturbide was declared emperor. His own regime did not last long, but an independent Mexico governed by persons determined to resist any significant social reform had been created.

Brazilian independence, in contrast to that of Spanish Latin America, came relatively simply and peacefully. As already noted, the Portuguese royal family took refuge in Brazil in 1807. The prince regent João addressed many of the local complaints, equivalent to those of the Spanish creoles, by measures such as the expansion of trade. In 1815, he made Brazil a kingdom, which meant that it was no longer to be regarded merely as a colony of Portugal. Then, in 1820, a revolution occurred in Portugal, and its leaders demanded João's return to Lisbon. They also demanded the return of Brazil to colonial status. João left his son Dom Pedro as regent in Brazil and encouraged him to be sympathetic to the political aspirations of the Brazilians. In September 1822 Dom Pedro embraced the cause of Brazilian independence against the recolonializing efforts of Portugal. By the end of the year, he had become emperor of an independent Brazil, which maintained that form of government until 1889.

The era of the wars of independence left Latin America liberated from direct colonial control but economically exhausted. The new republics felt themselves to be very weak and vulnerable and looked to Britain for protection and for markets and capital investment.

The most disadvantaged citizens received only the most marginal improvement as a result of independence. Caste distinctions and

Map labels: RIO GRANDE, San Antonio, ATLANTIC OCEAN, MEXICO 1821, GULF OF MEXICO, Mexico City, Veracruz, CUBA, HAITI 1804, BR. HONDURAS, PUERTO RICO, Guatemala, CARIBBEAN SEA, TRINIDAD, UNITED PROVINCES OF CENTRAL AMERICA 1823-1839, Panama, Caracas, BR. GUIANA, DUTCH GUIANA, FR. GUIANA, Bogotá, GRAN COLOMBIA 1819-1830, GALAPAGOS IS., Quito, AMAZON, PERU 1821, INDEFINITE BOUNDARY, EMPIRE OF BRAZIL 1822, PACIFIC OCEAN, Lima, Bahia, BOLIVIA 1825, Sucre, PARAGUAY 1813, Rio de Janeiro, CHILE 1817, Asunción, Santiago, URUGUAY 1828, Buenos Aires, Montevideo, UNITED PROVINCES OF LA PLATA 1816

MAP 20–1

LATIN AMERICA IN 1830

most racial distinctions were removed from the law, but the societies themselves remained very conscious of class and racial divisions. The Indian populations were not incorporated into political life. Landowners replaced urban colonial officials as the major governing section in the nations. Very considerable portions of the population of each republic felt little or no loyalty to the new regimes, which more often than not functioned almost entirely in the interests of the creole elites that had brought them into being.

Liberalism in the Early Nineteenth Century

The nineteenth century is frequently considered the great age of *isms*. Throughout the Western world, secular ideologies began to take hold of the popular and learned imagination in opposition to the political and social status quo. These included liberalism, nationalism, socialism, republicanism, and communism. One noted historian has called all such words "trouble-breeding and usually thought-obscuring terms."[1] They are just that if one uses them as an excuse to avoid thinking or if one fails to see the variety of opinions concealed beneath each word.

It was just such intellectual laziness that characterized European conservatives as they faced their political opposition after the Napoleonic wars. They tended to call "liberal" almost anything or anyone who drew into questions their own political, social, or religious values. Moreover, the word *liberal* for twentieth-century Americans carries with it meanings and connotations that have little or nothing to do with its significance to nineteenth-century Europeans. European conservatives of the last century saw liberals as more radical than they actually were; present-day Americans think of them as being more conservative than they were.

Liberal Goals and Their Circumstances

POLITICS. Liberals derived their political ideas from the writers of the Enlightenment, the example of English liberties, and the so-called principles of 1789 as embodied in the French Declaration of the Rights of Man and Citizen. Liberal political figures sought to establish a framework of legal equality, religious toleration, and freedom of the press. Their general goal was a political structure that would limit the arbitrary power of the government against the persons and property of individual citizens. They generally believed that the legitimacy of government emanated from the freely given consent of the governed. The popular basis of such government was to be expressed through elected, representative or parliamentary bodies. Most important, free government required that state or crown ministers must be responsible to the representatives rather than to the monarch.

These goals may seem very limited, and they were. However, such responsible government existed in none of the major European countries in 1815. Even in Great Britain the Cabinet ministers were at least as responsible to the monarch as to the House of Commons. The kinds of people who espoused these changes in government tended to be those who were excluded from the existing political processes but whose wealth and education made them feel that such exclusion was unjustified. Liberals were often academics, members of the learned professions, and people involved in the rapidly expanding commercial and manufacturing segments of the economy. They believed in and were products of the career open to talent. The existing monarchical and aristocratic regimes often failed to recognize sufficiently their new status and to provide for their economic and professional interests.

Although the liberals wanted broader political participation, they were *not* advocates of democracy. Second only to their hostility to the privileged aristocracies was their general contempt for the lower, unpropertied classes. Liberals transformed the eighteenth-century concept of aristocratic liberty into a new concept of privilege based on wealth and property rather than on birth. As the French liberal theorist Benjamin Constant (1767–1830) wrote in 1814:

Those whom poverty keeps in eternal dependence are no more enlightened on public affairs than children, nor are they more interested than foreigners in national prosperity, of which they do not understand the basis and of which they enjoy the advantages only indirectly. Property alone, by giving sufficient leisure, renders a man capable of exercising his political rights.[2]

By the middle of the century this widely shared attitude meant that throughout Europe liberals had separated themselves from both the rural and the urban working class.

ECONOMICS. The economic goals of the liberals also furthered that important future split in European politics and society. Here the Enlightenment and the economic thought deriving from Adam Smith set the pattern. The manufacturers of Great Britain, the landed and manufacturing middle class of France, and the

[1]Arthur O. Lovejoy, *The Great Chain of Being: A Study in the History of an Idea* (New York: Harper Torchbook, 1936), p. 6

[2]Quoted in Frederick B. Artz, *Reaction and Revolution, 1814–1832* (New York: Harper, 1934), p. 94.

The abolition of the Paris tolls, May 1, 1791. Most European countries had a system of internal tolls by which goods entering a city or region were taxed as if they were foreign imports. Nineteenth-century liberals considered these a barrier to trade and worked for their removal. [Mary Evans Picture Library]

commercial interests of Germany and Italy sought the removal of the economic restraints associated with mercantilism. They wanted to be able to manufacture and sell goods freely. To that end they favored the general removal of internal barriers to trade and of international tariffs. Economic liberals opposed the old paternalistic legislation that established wages and labor practices by government regulation or by guild privileges. Labor was simply one more commodity to be bought and sold freely. Liberals sought an economic structure in which people were at liberty to use whatever talents and property they possessed to enrich themselves. By this means, the liberals contended, there would be more goods and more

services for everyone at lower prices. Such a system of economic liberty was to provide the basis for material progress.

NATIONALISM. Another major ingredient of liberalism, as it developed in Germany, Italy, and the Austrian Empire, was nationalism. The idea of nationhood was not necessarily or logically linked to liberalism. There were conservative nationalists. However, liberalism and nationalism were often complementary. Behind the concept of a people joined naturally together by the bonds of common language, customs, culture, and history lurked the idea of popular sovereignty. The idea of the career open to talent could be applied to suppressed

705

national groups who were not permitted to realize their cultural or political potential. The efficient government and administration required by commerce and industry would mean the replacement of the petty dynasties of the small German and Italian states with larger political units. Moreover nationalist groups in one country could gain the sympathy of liberals in other nations by espousing the cause of representative government and political liberty.

Because the social and political circumstances of various countries differed, the specific programs of their liberals also differed. Great Britain already possessed institutions, such as Parliament, that could be reformed to provide more nearly representative government. The monarchy was already limited, and most individual liberties had been secured. Links between land, commerce, and industry existed. French liberals possessed a code of modern law in the Napoleonic Code. They could appeal to the widely accepted "principles of 1789." As in England, representatives of the different economic interests had worked together. Their problem was to protect the civil liberties by law, to define the respective powers of the monarch and the elected representative body, and to expand the electorate moderately while avoiding democracy.

The situation in Germany was quite different and very complex. Distinct social divisions existed between the aristocratic landowning classes, which filled the bureaucracies and officer corps, and the small middle-class commercial and industrial interests. There was little or no precedent for the latter groups' participating in the government or the army. There was no strong tradition of civil or individual liberty. From the time of Martin Luther through Kant and Hegel, freedom in Germany had meant conformity to a higher moral law rather than participation in politics. Consequently the mainstream of German liberalism differed from its British and French counterparts. There was much greater opposition from both the monarchs and the aristocracies. German liberals had little direct access to political influence. Most of them favored a united Germany that was to be created through the instrument of either the Austrian or the Prussian monarchy. This policy meant that they tended to stress the power of the state and the monarchy rather more than did other liberals. Once unification had been achieved, a freer social and political order might be established. The great difficulty

for German liberals was the refusal of the Austrian or the Prussian monarchy to cooperate. Thus, in Germany, liberals were generally frustrated and had to remain satisfied with the lowering of internal trade barriers.

Between 1819 and 1822 the institutions of the restored conservative order had held back the forces of liberalism. In the Germanies, Austria, and Italy, the liberal challenge was smothered for at least another twenty-five years. However, during the 1820s, the conservative governments of Russia, France, and Great Britain faced new stirrings of political discontent. In Russia, the result was suppression; in France, revolution; and in Britain, accommodation.

Russia: The Decembrist Revolt of 1825 and the Autocracy of Nicholas I

During the mid-1820s Russia took the lead in suppressing both liberal and nationalistic tendencies within its domains. In the process of driving Napoleon's army across Europe and then of occupying defeated France, many officers in the Russian army were introduced to the ideas of the French Revolution and the Enlightenment. They realized how economically backward and politically stifled their own nation remained. The domestic repression in Russia hardened as Alexander I became more conservative. Under these conditions groups within the army officer corps formed secret societies. One such reformist coterie was the Southern Society. Led by an officer named Pestel, these men sought a representative government and the abolition of serfdom. Pestel himself favored democracy and a moderately independent Poland. The Northern Society was a second, more moderate group. It favored constitutional monarchy and the abolition of serfdom but protection for the interests of the aristocracy. Both societies were very small; there was much friction between them. They agreed only that there must be a change in the government of Russia. Sometime during 1825 they seem to have decided to carry out a *coup d'état* in 1826.

Other events intervened. In late November 1825 Czar Alexander I suddenly and unexpectedly died. His death created two crises. The first was a dynastic one. Alexander had no direct heir. His brother Constantine stood next in line to the throne. However, Constantine, who was then the commander of Russian forces in occupied Poland, had married a woman who was not of royal blood. He had thus excluded himself from the throne and was more than willing to renounce any claim. Through a series of secret instructions made public only after his death, Alexander had named his younger brother, Nicholas (1825–1855), as the new czar. Once Alexander was dead, the legality of these instructions became uncertain. Constantine acknowledged Nicholas as czar, and Nicholas acknowledged Constantine. This family muddle continued for about three weeks, during which Russia actually had no ruler, to the astonishment of all Europe. Then, during the early days of December, the army command reported to Nicholas the existence of a conspiracy among certain officers. Able to wait no longer for the working out of legal niceties, Nicholas had himself declared czar, much to the delight of the by-now-exasperated Constantine.

The second crisis now proceeded to unfold. There was a plot devised by a number of junior officers intent on rallying the troops under their command to the cause of reform. On December 26, 1825, the army was to take the oath of allegiance to Nicholas, who was less popular than Constantine and was regarded as more conservative. Nearly all of the regiments did so. But the Moscow regiment, whose chief officers, surprisingly, were not secret society members, marched into the Senate Square in Saint Petersburg and refused to swear allegiance. Rather, they called for Constantine and a constitution. Attempts to settle the situation peacefully failed. Late in the afternoon Nicholas ordered the cavalry and the artillery to attack the insurgents. Over sixty people were killed. Early in 1826 Nicholas himself presided over the commission that investigated the Decembrist Revolt and the secret army socie-

The Decemberist coup, December 26, 1825. Troops loyal to Nicholas I are in the foreground, facing insurgent forces massed before the Winter Palace in St. Petersburg. [Bildarchiv Preussichev Kulturbesitz]

ties. Five of the plotters were executed and over one hundred other officers were exiled to Siberia.

Although the Decembrist Revolt completely failed, it was the first rebellion in modern Russian history whose instigators had had specific political goals. They wanted constitutional government and the abolition of serfdom. As the century passed, the Decembrists, in their political martyrdom, came to symbolize the yearnings of all Russian liberals, whose numbers were always quite small. The more immediate result of the revolt was the crushing of liberalism as even a moderate political influence in Russia. Nicholas I was determined that never again would his power come under question. He eventually epitomized the most extreme form of nineteenth-century autocracy.

Nicholas was neither an ignorant nor a bigoted reactionary. He was quite simply afraid of change. He knew that Russia required reforms for economic growth and social improvement. In 1842 he told his State Council, "There is no doubt that serfdom, in its present form, is a flagrant evil which everyone realizes, yet to attempt to remedy it now would be, of course, an evil more disastrous."[3] To remove serfdom would necessarily, in his view, have undermined the nobles' support of the czar. Consequently Nicholas turned his back on this and practically all other reforms. Literary and political censorship and a widespread system of secret police flourished throughout his reign. There was little attempt to forge even an efficient and honest administration. The only significant reform of his rule was a codification of Russian law published in 1833.

In place of reform Nicholas and his closest

[3]Quoted in Michael T. Florinsky, *Russia: A History and an Interpretation,* Vol. 2 (New York: Macmillan, 1953), p. 755.

Uvarov Praises the Policy of Official Nationality

Uvarov was the Russian minister of education under Nicholas I. In that capacity he was largely responsible for the policy of Official Nationality and its program of orthodoxy, autocracy, and nationality. In 1843 he explained that this ideology was to prevent Russia from experiencing the political turmoil that had occurred in western Europe.

In the midst of rapid collapse in Europe of religious and civil institutions, at the time of a general spread of destructive ideas, at the sight of grievous phenomena surrounding us on all sides, it was necessary to establish our fatherland on firm foundations upon which is based the well-being, strength, and life of a people; it was necessary to find the principles which form the distinctive character of Russia, and which belong only to Russia; it was necessary to gather into one whole the sacred remnants of Russian nationality and to fasten to them the anchor of our salvation. Fortunately, Russia had retained a warm faith in the sacred principles without which she cannot prosper, gain in strength, live. Sincerely and deeply attached to the church of his fathers, the Russian has of old considered it the guarantee of social and family happiness. Without a love for the faith of its ancestors a

people, as well as an individual must perish. A Russian devoted to his fatherland, will agree as little to the loss of a single dogma of our Orthodoxy as to the theft of a single pearl from the tsar's crown. Autocracy constitutes the main condition of the political existence of Russia. The Russian giant stands on it as on the cornerstone of his greatness. An innumerable majority of the subjects of Your Majesty feel this truth; they feel it in full measure although they are placed on different rungs of civil life and although they vary in education and in their relations to the government. The saving conviction that Russia lives and is protected by the spirit of a strong, humane, and enlightened autocracy must permeate popular education and must develop with it. Together with these two national principles there is a third, no less important, no less powerful: nationality.

Cited in Nicholas Riasanovsky, *Nicholas I and Official Nationality in Russia, 1825–1855* (Berkeley: University of California Press, 1959), pp. 74–75.

advisers embraced a program called *Official Nationality*. Its slogan, published repeatedly in government documents, newspapers, journals, and schoolbooks, was "Orthodoxy, Autocracy, and Nationalism." The Russian Orthodox faith was to provide the basis for morality, education, and intellectual life. The church, which since the days of Peter the Great had been an arm of the secular government, controlled the schools and universities. Young Russians were taught to accept their place in life and to spurn rising in the social structure. The program of autocracy championed the unrestrained power of the czar as the only authority that could hold the vast expanse of Russia and its peoples together in an orderly fashion. Political writers stressed that only under the autocracy of Peter the Great, Catherine the Great, and Alexander I had Russia prospered and exerted a major influence on world affairs. Through the glorification of Russian nationality, the country was urged to see its religion, language, and customs as a source of perennial wisdom that separated the nation from the moral corruption and political turmoil of the West. The person who presided over the program of Official Nationality was Count S. S. Uvarov, minister of education from 1833 to 1849. The result of his efforts and those of the czar was the profound alienation of serious Russian intellectual life from the czarist government.

Nicholas I also manifested extreme conservatism in foreign affairs. After the Congress of Vienna, Poland had been given a constitutional government, but within the limits of the Russian domination that dated back to the eighteenth-century partitions of Poland. Grand Duke Constantine, the brother of Alexander I and Nicholas I, was in charge of the Polish government by authority delegated by the czars. Although both czars frequently infringed on the constitutional arrangement and quarreled with the Polish Diet, the constitution itself remained. Nevertheless Polish nationalists continued to agitate for change.

In late November 1830, after the news of the French and Belgian revolutions of that summer had penetrated Poland, a small military insurrection broke out in Warsaw. Disturbances soon spread throughout the rest of the country. On December 18 the Polish Diet declared the revolution to be a nationalist movement. In early January 1831 the Diet voted to depose Nicholas as ruler of Poland. The czar reacted by sending troops into the country. After several months the revolt was thoroughly suppressed.

Czar Nicholas I (1825–1855) resisted all attempts to reform Russia and offered the use of Russian troops to other rulers threatened by revolution. [Culver Pictures]

In February 1832 Nicholas issued the Organic Statute, which declared Poland to be an integral part of the Russian empire. The statute guaranteed certain Polish liberties, but they were systematically ignored. The Polish uprising had confirmed all the czar's worst fears. Henceforth Russia and Nicholas became the gendarme of Europe, ever ready to provide troops to suppress liberal and nationalist movements.

Revolution in France (1830)

The Polish revolt was the most distant of several disturbances that flowed from the overthrow of the Bourbon dynasty in France during July 1830. In 1824 Louis XVIII had died. He was succeeded by his brother, the count of Artois, who became Charles X (1824–1830). The new king, who had been the chief leader of the ultraroyalists at the time of the restoration, considered himself a monarch by divine right. He was crowned with elaborate cere-

Benjamin Constant Discusses the Character of Modern Liberty

In 1819 the French liberal political theorist Benjamin Constant delivered lectures on the character of ancient and modern liberty. In the passage below, he emphasized the close relationship of modern liberty to freedom of action in economic activity and to general freedom in the private lives of human beings. He then tied that desire for a free private life to the need for representative government. Modern life did not leave people enough time to make the kind of political commitment that had been required by the ancient *polis*. Consequently, modern citizens turned over much of their political concern and activity to representatives. In this discussion Constant clearly set forth the desire of nineteenth-century liberals to maximize private freedom of action and to minimize areas of life in which government might interfere.

[Modern liberty] is, for each individual, the right not to be subjected to anything but the law, not to be arrested, or detained, or put to death, or mistreated in any manner, as a result of the arbitrary will of one or several individuals. It is each man's right to express his opinions, to choose and exercise his profession, to dispose of his property and even abuse it, to come and go without obtaining permission and without having to give an account of either his motives or his itinerary. It is the right to associate with other individuals, either to confer about mutual interests or to profess the cult that he and his associates prefer or simply to fill his days and hours in the manner most conforming to his inclinations and fantasies. Finally, it is each man's right to exert influence on the administration of government, either through the election of some or all of its public functionaries, or through remonstrances, petitions, and demands which authorities are more or less obliged to take into account. . . .

Just as the liberty we now require is distinct from that of the ancients, so this new liberty itself requires an organization different from that suitable for ancient liberty. For the latter, the more time and energy a man consecrated to the exercise of his political rights, the more free he believed himself to be. Given the type of liberty to which we are now susceptible, the more the exercise of our political rights leaves us time for our private interests, the more precious we find liberty to be. From this . . . stems the necessity of the representative system. The representative system is nothing else than an organization through which a nation unloads on several individuals what it cannot and will not do for itself. Poor men handle their own affairs; rich men hire managers. This is the story of ancient and modern nations. The representative system is the power of attorney given to certain men by the mass of the people who want their interests defended but who nevertheless do not always have the time to defend these interests themselves.

Benjamin Constant, *Ancient and Modern Liberty,* as translated and quoted in Stephen Holmes, *Benjamin Constant and the Making of Modern Liberalism* (New Haven, Conn.: Yale University Press, 1984), pp. 66, 74.

mony and ritual at the Cathedral of Reims. At long last in power, he intended to roll back as much of the revolution as possible and to repay the loyalty of the French royalists.

His first action was to have the Chamber of Deputies in 1824 and 1825 provide for the indemnification of aristocrats who had lost their lands in the revolution. The existing land settlement was confirmed. However, by lowering the interest rates on government bonds, the Chamber created a fund from which the survivors of the *émigrés* who had forfeited land would be paid an annual sum of money. The middle-class bondholders, who lost income, naturally resented this measure. Another measure restored the rule of primogeniture, whereby only the eldest son of an aristocrat inherited the family domains. Charles X supported the Roman Catholic church by a law punishing sacrilege with sentences of imprisonment or death. Liberals disapproved of all of these measures.

The results of the elections of 1827 compelled Charles X to appease the liberals, who in conjunction with more moderate royalists could muster a majority in the Chamber of Deputies. He appointed a less conservative ministry. Laws directed against the press and those allowing the government to dominate education were eased. Yet the liberals, who wanted a genuinely constitutional regime, remained unsatisfied. In 1829 the king decided that his policy of accommodation had failed. He dismissed his ministers and in their place appointed an ultraroyalist ministry headed by the Prince de Polignac (1780–1847). The opposition was now forced to the desperate action of opening negotiations with the liberal Orléanist branch of the royal family.

In 1830 Charles X called for new elections, in which the liberals scored a stunning victory. He might have relented and tried to accommodate the new Chamber of Deputies. Instead the king and his ministers decided to attempt a royalist seizure of power. In June and July 1830 Polignac had sent a naval expedition against Algeria. On July 9 reports of its victory reached Paris. The foundation of a French empire in North Africa had been laid. On July 25, 1830, under the euphoria of this foreign diversion, Charles X issued the Four Ordinances, which amounted to a royal *coup d'état*. The ordinances restricted freedom of the press, dissolved the recently elected Chamber of Deputies, restricted the franchise to the wealthiest people in the country, and called for new elections under the new royalist franchise.

The Four Ordinances provoked swift and decisive popular political reactions. Liberal newspapers called on the nation to reject the monarch's actions. The laboring populace of Paris, burdened since 1827 by an economic downturn, took to the streets and erected barricades. The king called out troops, and over eighteen hundred people died during the ensuing battles in the city. On August 2 Charles X abdicated and left France for exile in England. The liberals in the Chamber of Deputies named a new ministry composed of constitutional monarchists. They proclaimed Louis Philippe (1830–1848), the duke of Orléans, the new monarch. The July Days had brought to a final close the rule of the Bourbon dynasty in France.

In the Revolution of 1830 the liberals of the Chamber of Deputies had filled a power vacuum created by the popular Paris uprising and the failure of effective royal action. Had

Liberty Leading the People, *Delacroix's famous depiction of the Revolution of* 1830. [*Giraudon*]

Guizot Fits the July Monarchy into the Context of French History

François Guizot (1787–1874) was a liberal French historian who became the most important minister of Louis Philippe during the July Monarchy. In this speech of 1831 to the French Chamber of Deputies, Guizot defined the goal of the new government as establishing both liberty and order. He argued that previous regimes had attained only one or the other. As the years passed, both Guizot and Louis Philippe would become more concerned about order than about liberty.

Each epoch has its special task. The Revolution of 1789 was under obligation to destroy the an-cien régime; it accomplished this with principles and powers which were adequate for the job, but when it tried to establish its own government with these principles and these powers which had just destroyed the ancien régime, it was able to give us nothing but tyranny mixed with anarchy. We had this combination in two forms, powerful under the Convention, weak under the Directory. . . .

The Empire [of Napoleon] arose to re-establish order, order of an exterior, material sort which was the basis of the civil society as the Revolution had founded it. The Empire spread this idea throughout all of Europe; this was its mission and it succeeded at it. It was incapable, however, of establishing a lasting political government; the necessary conditions were lacking.

The Empire fell in its turn, to be succeeded by the Restoration.

What did the Restoration promise? It promised to resolve the problem, to reconcile order with liberty. . . . It was unable to solve the problem. It died in the process, overwhelmed by the burden.

It is on us, on the Revolution of July, that this job has been imposed; it is our duty and responsibility to establish definitively, not order alone, not liberty alone, but order and liberty at the same time. There is no way of escaping this double duty. Yes, gentlemen, our duty is twofold. We are commissioned to establish at the same moment the principle and the institutions of order, the principle and the institutions of liberty: there is the promise of the Revolution of July.

Cited in Thomas C. Mendenhall, Basil D. Henning, and Archibald S. Foord, *The Quest for a Principle of Authority in Europe, 1715–Present* (New York: Henry Holt, 1948), p. 144.

Charles X provided himself with sufficient troops in Paris, the outcome could have been quite different. Moreover, had the liberals, who favored constitutional monarchy, not acted quickly, the workers and shopkeepers of Paris might have formed a republic. By seizing the moment, the middle class, the bureaucrats, and the moderate aristocratic liberals over-threw the restoration monarchy and still avoided a republic. These liberals feared a new popular revolution such as had swept France in 1792 on the overthrow of the old monarchy. They had no desire for another sans-culotte republic. Consequently a fundamental political and social tension marked the new monarchy as the hard-pressed laborers and the prosper-ous middle-class people whose temporary alliance had achieved the revolution realized that their basic goals had been quite different.

Politically the July Monarchy, as it was called, was more liberal than the restoration government. Louis Philippe was called the king of the French rather than of France. The tri-color flag of the revolution replaced the white flag of the Bourbons. The new constitution was regarded as a right of the people rather than a concession of the monarch. Catholicism be-came the religion of the majority of the people rather than the official religion. Censorship was abolished. The franchise became some-what wider but remained on the whole re-stricted. The king had to cooperate with the Chamber of Deputies; he could not dispense with laws on his own authority.

Socially, however, the Revolution of 1830 proved quite conservative. The hereditary peerage was abolished in 1831, but the every-day economic, political, and social influence of

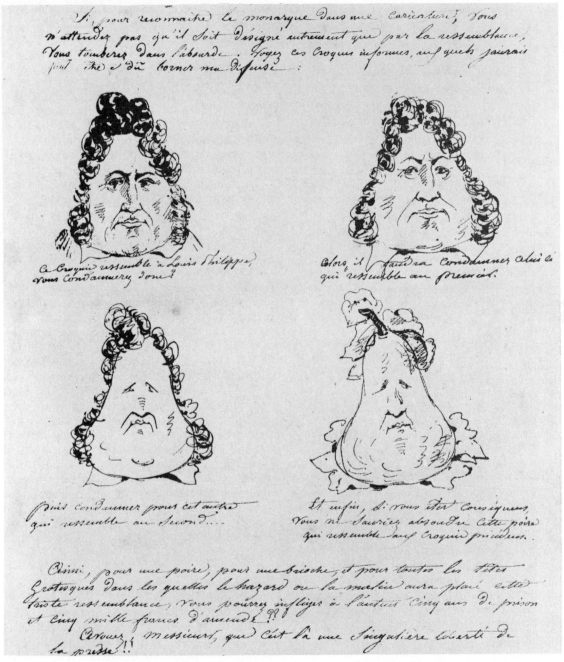

Despite laws forbidding disrespect to the government, political cartoonists had a field day with Louis Philippe. Here, the artist emphasizes the king's resemblance to a pear and in the process attacks restraints on freedom of the press. [Library of Congress]

the landed oligarchy continued. Money was the path to power and influence in the government. There was much corruption. Most important, the liberal monarchy displayed little or no sympathy for the lower and working classes. The Paris workers in 1830 had called

for the protection of jobs, better wages, and the preservation of the traditional crafts rather than for the usual goals of political liberalism. The government of Louis Philippe ignored their demands and their plight. The laboring classes of Paris and the provincial cities seemed

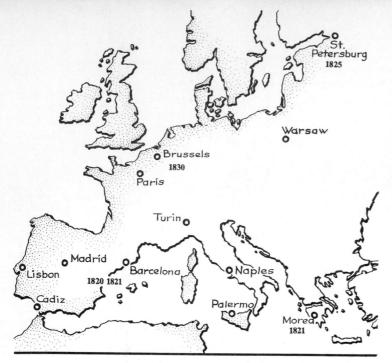

CENTERS OF REVOLUTION, 1820–1830

MAP 20–2 *Conservative governments and cooperation among repressive great powers in post-Napoleonic Europe were challenged by uprisings and revolutions, beginning in 1820–1821 in Spain, Naples, and Greece and appearing in Russia, France, and Belgium later in the decade.*

just one more possible source of disorder. In late 1831 troops suppressed a workers' revolt in the city of Lyons. In July 1832 an uprising occurred in Paris during the funeral of a popular Napoleonic general. Again the government called out troops and over eight hundred people were killed or wounded. In 1834 a very large strike of silkworkers in Lyons was crushed. Such discontent might be smothered for a time, but without attention to the social and economic conditions creating that tension, new turmoil would eventually erupt.

Belgium Becomes Independent (1830)

The July Days in Paris sent sparks to other political tinder on the Continent. The revolutionary fires first lighted in neighboring Belgium. The former Austrian Netherlands had in 1815 been merged with the kingdom of Holland. The upper classes of Belgium had never reconciled themselves to rule by a country with a different language, religion, and economic life. On August 25, 1830, disturbances broke

out in Brussels following the performance of an opera that portrayed a rebellion of Naples against Spanish rule. To put an end to the rioting, the municipal authorities and persons from the propertied classes formed a provisional national government. When compromise between the Belgians and the Dutch failed, William of Holland sent troops and ships against Belgium. By November 10, 1830, the Dutch had been defeated. A national congress then wrote a liberal Belgian constitution, which was promulgated in 1831.

The major powers saw the revolution in Belgium as upsetting the boundaries established by the Congress of Vienna. Russia could not intervene because of the Polish revolt. Prussia and the other German states were suppressing small risings in their own domains. The Austrians were busy putting down disturbances in Italy. France under Louis Philippe favored an independent Belgium and hoped to dominate it. Britain felt that it could tolerate a liberal Belgium as long as it was free of foreign domination. In December 1830 Lord Palmerston (1784–1865), the British foreign minister, gathered representatives of the powers in London. Through skillful negotiations he persuaded them to recognize Belgium as an independent and neutral state. In July 1831 Leopold of Saxe-Coburg (1831–1865) became king of the Belgians. By the Convention of 1839 the great powers guaranteed the neutrality of Belgium. For almost a century Belgian neutrality remained one of the articles of faith in European international relations. In 1914 it was German violation of the neutrality convention that technically brought Great Britain into World War I.

The Great Reform Bill in Britain (1832)

The revolutionary year of 1830 saw in Great Britain the election of a House of Commons that debated the first major bill to reform Parliament. The death of George IV (1820–1830) and the accession of William IV (1830–1837) required the calling of an election. It was once believed that the July revolution in France had influenced the British elections in the summer of 1830. This theory has been shown to be incorrect through a close analysis of the time and character of the individual county and borough elections. The passage of the Great Reform Bill, which became law in 1832, was the result of a series of events very different from those that occurred on the Continent. In Britain the forces of conservatism and reform made accommodations with each other.

Several factors made this situation possible and meant that Great Britain would become "the chief laboratory of liberal thought during the century."[4] First, there was a larger commercial and industrial class in Britain than in other countries. No matter what group might control the government, British prosperity required attention to those economic interests. Second, there existed in Britain the long tradition of liberal Whig aristocrats, who regarded themselves as the protectors of constitutional

liberty. They saw their role as that of making moderate political changes that would render revolutionary changes unnecessary. Their early sympathy for the French Revolution had lessened their influence. However, after 1815 they reentered the political arena and waited to be recalled to power. Finally, there also existed in British law, tradition, and public opinion a strong respect for civil liberties.

In 1820, the year after the passage of the notorious Six Acts, Lord Liverpool shrewdly moved to change his Cabinet. New faces began to appear. They included George Canning, Sir Robert Peel (1788–1850), and William Huskisson (1770–1830). These men, sometimes called liberal Tories, favored conservative politics but also knew that the nation and the gov-

[4]George L. Mosse, *The Culture of Western Europe: The Nineteenth and Twentieth Centuries* (New York: Rand McNally, 1965), p. 97.

Thomas Babington Macaulay Defends the Great Reform Bill

Macaulay (1800–1859) was a member of the House of Commons that passed the Great Reform Bill in 1831, only to have it rejected by the House of Lords before another measure was successfully enacted in 1832. His speeches in support of the bill derived from his views on the need for Parliament to give balanced representation to major elements in the population. Specifically, he supported the Great Reform Bill because, without creating a democratic government, it allowed the middle class to obtain political influence. He saw the reform of Parliament as a way to prevent political revolution in England. His argument had wide appeal.

[The principle of the ministers] is plain, rational, and consistent. It is this,—to admit the middle class to a large and direct share in the Representation, without any violent shock to the institutions of our country. . . . I hold it to be clearly expedient, that in a country like this, the right of suffrage should depend on a pecuniary qualification. Every argument . . . which would induce me to oppose Universal Suffrage, induces me to support the measure which is now before us. I oppose Universal Suffrage, because I think that it would produce a destructive revolution. I support this measure, because I am sure that it is our best security against a revolution. . . . I . . . do entertain great apprehension for the fate of my country. I do in my conscience believe, that unless this measure, or some similar measure, be speedily adopted, great and terrible calamities will befall us. Entertaining

this opinion, I think myself bound to state it, not as a threat, but as a reason. I support this measure as a measure of Reform: but I support it still more as a measure of conservation. That we may exclude those whom it is necessary to exclude, we must admit those whom it may be safe to admit. . . . All history is full of revolutions, produced by causes similar to those which are now operating in England. A portion of the community which had been of no account, expands and becomes strong. It demands a place in the system, suited, not to its former weakness, but to its present power. If this is granted, all is well. If this is refused, then comes the struggle between the young energy of one class, and the ancient privileges of another. . . . Such . . . is the struggle which the middle classes in England are maintaining against an aristocracy of mere locality. . . .

Hansard's Parliamentary Debates, 3rd series, Vol. 2, pp. 1191–1197.

Alexander I of Russia dismisses Speransky	1812
Louis XVIII restored in France under the Charter	1814
Holy Alliance formed among Russia, Austria, and Prussia	1815
Quadruple Alliance renewed among Russia, Austria, Prussia, and Britain	1815
Wartburg Festival at Jena	1817
Congress of Aix-la-Chapelle	1818
(March 23) Assassination of Kotzebue	1819
(July) Carlsbad Decrees	1819
(August 16) Peterloo Massacre	1819
(December) Six Acts passed in Great Britain	1819
(January) Spanish revolution	1820
(February 13) Assassination of the Duke of Berri	1820
(October) Congress of Troppau	1820
(January) Congress of Laibach	1821
(February) Greek revolution	1821
Congress of Verona	1822
France intervenes to crush the Spanish revolution	1823
Charles X becomes king of France	1824
Decembrist Revolt in Russia	1825
Catholic Emancipation Act in Great Britain	1829
(July 9) News of French victory in Algeria reaches Paris	1830
(July 25) Charles X issues the Four Ordinances	1830
(August 2) Charles X abdicates; Louis Philippe proclaimed king	1830
(August 25) Belgian revolution	1830
(November 29) Polish revolution	1830
Great Reform Bill passed in Great Britain	1832

tionalists might again rebel as they had in 1798 and perhaps turn Ireland into a base for a French invasion, William Pitt the Younger had persuaded Parliament to enact the Act of Union between England and Ireland. Ireland now sent one hundred members to the House of Commons. However, because of the religious scruples of King George III, Pitt was unable to secure the passage of a law to permit Roman Catholics to sit in the House of Commons. Consequently only Protestant Irishmen, who usually had close ties to England, could be elected to represent overwhelmingly Catholic Ireland.

During the 1820s, under the leadership of Daniel O'Connell (1775–1847), Irish nationalists organized the Catholic Association to agitate for Catholic emancipation. In 1828 O'Connell secured his own election to Parliament, where he could not legally take his seat. The British ministry of the duke of Wellington realized that henceforth an entirely Catholic delegation might be elected from Ireland. If they were not seated, civil war might erupt

Daniel O'Connell was the most dynamic and effective Irish nationalist leader in the first half of the nineteenth century. This portrait was made in 1834 when O'Connell was fifty-nine.

ernment must accommodate themselves to the new economic and political forces of the day. Canning introduced the more liberal foreign policy that led to the recognition of the Latin American republics. Peel set about reforming the criminal law and reducing the number of capital offenses. Huskisson was an economic liberal who began a slow process of lowering tariffs for the benefit of the commercial classes. In 1824 the Combination Acts were repealed, and labor organization became possible.

Economic considerations had generally led to these moderate reforms. English determination to maintain the union with Ireland brought about another key reform. England's relationship to Ireland was not unlike that of Russia's to Poland or Austria's to its several national groups. In 1800, fearful that Irish na-

across the Irish Sea. Consequently, in 1829 Wellington and Robert Peel steered the Catholic Emancipation Act through Parliament. Roman Catholics could now become Members of Parliament. This measure, together with the repeal in 1828 of restrictions against Protestant nonconformists, meant that the Anglican monopoly on British political life was over.

Catholic emancipation was a liberal measure that was passed for the conservative purpose of preserving order in Ireland. It included a provision raising the franchise in Ireland so that only the wealthier Irish could vote. Nonetheless this measure alienated many of Wellington's Anglican Tory supporters in the House of Commons. In the election of 1830 a large number of supporters of parliamentary reform were returned to Parliament. Even some Tories believed that parliamentary reform was necessary because they had concluded that Catholic emancipation could have been passed only by a corrupt House of Commons. The Wellington

ministry soon fell. The Tories were badly divided. Consequently King William IV turned to the Whigs under the leadership of Earl Grey (1764–1845) to form a government.

The Whig ministry soon presented the House of Commons with a major reform bill that had two broad goals. The first was to abolish "rotten" boroughs, which had small numbers of voters, and to replace them with representatives for the previously unrepresented manufacturing districts and cities. Second, the number of voters in England and Wales was increased by about 50 per cent through a series of new franchises. In 1831 the House of Commons narrowly defeated the bill. Grey called for a new election, in which a majority in favor of the bill was returned. The House of Commons passed the reform bill, but the House of Lords rejected it. Mass meetings were held throughout the country. Riots broke out in several cities. Finally, William IV agreed to create enough new peers to give a third reform

The first meeting of the reformed House of Commons in 1833. Most seats were still filled by the gentry and the wealthy. But the elimination of rotten boroughs and the election of members from the new urban centers began to transform the House of Commons into a representative national body. [National Portraiot Gallery, London]

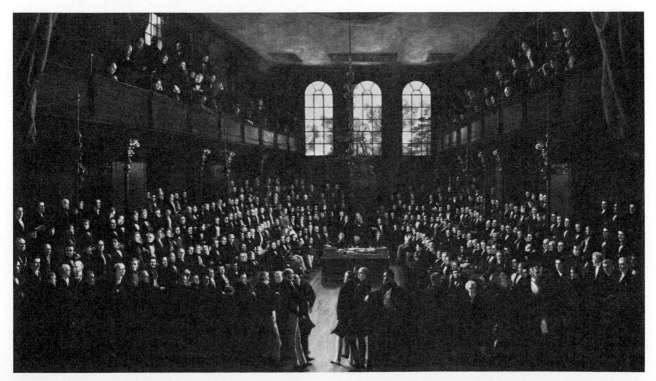

bill a majority in the House of Lords. Under this pressure the House of Lords yielded, and in 1832 the measure became law.

The Great Reform Bill expanded the size of the English electorate, but it was not a democratic measure. The number of voters was increased by over 200,000 persons, or by almost 50 per cent. However, the basis of voting remained a property qualification. (Gender was also a qualification. No thought was given to enfranchising women.) Some working-class voters actually were disenfranchised because of the abolition of certain old franchise rights. New urban boroughs were created to allow the growing cities to have a voice in the House of Commons. Yet the passage of the reform act did not, as it was once thought, constitute the triumph of the middle-class interest in England. For every new urban electoral district, a new rural district was also drawn. It was expected that the aristocracy would dominate the rural elections.

The success of the reform bill was its reconciliation of previously unrepresented property owners and economic interests to the existing political institutions of the country. The act created a political situation in which further reforms of the church, the municipal government, and commercial policy could be achieved in an orderly fashion. Revolution in Britain was unnecessary because the people who sought change had been admitted to the political forum that could legislate those changes. In this manner the historic institutions of Great Britain were maintained while the persons and groups who influenced them became more diverse.

Suggested Readings

D. BEALES, *From Castlereagh to Gladstone,* 1815–1885 (1969). A survey to be read in conjunction with Briggs (below).

R. J. BEZUCHA, *The Lyon Uprising of 1834: Social and Political Conflict in the Early July Monarchy* (1974). An excellent discussion of the tensions in France after the Revolution of 1830.

A. BRIGGS, *The Making of Modern England* (1959). The best survey of English history during the first half of the nineteenth century.

M. BROCK, *The Great Reform Act* (1974). The standard work.

G. A. CRAIG, *The Politics of the Prussian Army,* 1640–1945 (1955). A splendid study of the conservative political influence of the army on Prussian development.

D. DAKIN, *The Struggle for Greek Independence* (1973). An excellent explanation of the intricacies of the Greek independence question.

G. DE BERTIER DE SAUVIGNY, *The Bourbon Restoration* (trans., 1966), and *Metternich and His Times* (1962). Sympathetic, but not uncritical, studies of the forces of political conservatism.

G. DE RUGGIERO, *The History of European Liberalism* (1927). The major treatment of the subject.

J. DROZ, *Europe Between Revolutions,* 1815–1848 (1967). An examination of Europe as created by the Vienna settlement.

E. HALÉVY, *England in* 1815 (1913). One of the most important and influential books written on nineteenth-century Britain.

C. J. HAYES, *Essays on Nationalism* (1926). Pioneering, but still useful studies.

E. J. HOBSBAWM, *The Age of Revolution,* 1789–1848 (1962). A very comprehensive survey emphasizing the social ramifications of the liberal democratic and industrial revolutions.

S. HOLMES, *Benjamin Constant and the Making of Modern Liberalism* (1984). An outstanding study of a major liberal theorist.

A. JARDIN AND A. J. TUDESQ, *Restoration and Reaction,* 1815–1848 (1984). Surveys this period in France.

W. B. KAUFMANN, *British Policy and the Independence of Latin America,* 1802–1828 (1951). A standard discussion of an important relationship.

H. KOHN, *The Idea of Nationalism: A Study in Its Origin and Background* (1944). An examination of the roots of nationalism in Western culture.

L. KRIEGER, *The German Idea of Freedom* (1957). A far-ranging examination of the problems and ideology of German liberalism.

W. B. LINCOLN, *Nicholas I: Emperor and Autocrat of All the Russians* (1978). A serious scholarly treatment.

J. LYNCH, *The Spanish American Revolutions,* 1808–1826 (1973). An excellent one-volume treatment.

C. A. MACARTNEY, *The Habsburg Empire,* 1790–1918 (1971). An outstanding survey.

P. MANSEL, *Louis XVIII* (1981). A recent biography that captures much of the tone of life among *émigrés* and royalists.

J. MERRIMAN (Ed.), *1830 in France* (1976). A collection of important essays on the Revolution of 1830.

A. PALMER, *Alexander I: Tsar of War and Peace* (1974). An interesting biography that captures much of the rather mysterious personality of this ruler.

D. H. PINKNEY, *The French Revolution of* 1830 (1972). The best account in English.

M. RAEFF, *The Decembrist Movement* (1966). An examination of the unsuccessful uprising, with documents.

N. V. RIASANOVSKY, *Nicholas I and Official Nationality in Russia,* 1825–1855 (1959). A lucid discussion of the conservative ideology that made Russia the major opponent of liberalism.

C. A. RUUD, *Fighting Words: Imperial Censorship and the Russian Press, 1804–1906* (1982). Examines the government attempt to shape and control public opinion.

D. THOMSON, *Europe Since Napoleon* (1962). A survey of political developments during the past century and a half.

A. B. ULAM, *Russia's Failed Revolutionaries* (1981). Contains a useful discussion of the Decembrists as a background for other nineteenth-century Russian revolutionary activity.

M. WALKER, *Metternich's Europe* (1968). A useful collection of documents.

P. S. WANDYCZ, *The Lands of Partitioned Poland, 1795–1918* (1974). The best study of Poland during the nineteenth century.

Behind the barricade: Paris 1848. The street barricade was a hallmark of the revolutionary outbreaks that erupted across Europe in the 1830s and 1840s. Constructed of paving stones, carts, barrels, and whatever else was handy, these barricades across narrow, twisting streets could present formidable obstacles to troops. [Library of Congress]

BY 1830 Europe was headed toward an industrial society. Only Great Britain had already attained that status, but the pounding of new machinery and the grinding of railway engines soon began to echo across the entire continent. Further urbanization, the disintegration of traditional social bonds and work habits, and eventually class conflict accompanied the economic development. However, what characterized the second quarter of the century was not the triumph of industrialism but the final gasps of those economic groups who opposed it. Intellectually the period saw the formulation of the major creeds supporting and criticizing the new society. These were years of uncertainty for almost everyone. Even the most confident entrepreneurs knew that the trade cycle might bankrupt them in a matter of weeks. For the industrial workers and the artisans unemployment became a haunting and recurring problem. For the peasants the question was sufficiency of food. It was a period of self-conscious transition that culminated in 1848 with a continentwide outbreak of revolution. People knew that one mode of life was passing, but they were uncertain what would replace it.

21

Economic Advance and Social Unrest (1830–1850)

Toward an Industrial Society

Population and Migration

The Industrial Revolution had begun in eighteenth-century Great Britain with the advances in textile production described in Chapter 15. Natural resources, adequate capital, native technological skills, a growing food supply, a social structure that allowed considerable mobility, and strong foreign and domestic demands for goods had given Britain an edge in achieving a vast new capacity for production in manufacturing. Its factories and recently invented machines allowed British producers to furnish customers with more products and better products at lower prices than any competitors. The wars of the French Revolution and of Napoleon brought about the final collapse of the French Atlantic trade. The same conflicts had destroyed capital, led to inflated currencies, and killed off much of the labor supply in the continental countries. Consequently Britain's initial lead became further extended, so that in 1850 the nation still remained a generation ahead of its future continental competitors.

Despite the economic lag the continental

nations were beginning to make material progress. By the 1830s, in Belgium, France, and Germany the number of steam engines in use was growing steadily. Exploitation of the coalfields of the Ruhr and the Saar basins had begun. Coke was replacing charcoal in iron and steel production.

Industrial areas were generally less concentrated than in Britain, and large manufacturing districts, such as the British Midlands, did not yet exist across the English Channel. There were major pockets of production in western Europe, such as the cities of Lyons, Rouen, Liège, and Lille, but most continental manufacturing still took place in the countryside. New machines were integrated into the existing domestic system. The extreme slowness of continental imitation of the British example meant that at mid-century, peasants and urban artisans remained more important politically than industrial factory workers.

While the process of industrialization spread, the population of Europe continued to grow on the base of the eighteenth-century population explosion. The number of people in France rose from 32.5 million in 1831 to 35.8 million in 1851. The population of Germany rose from 26.5 million to 33.5 million during approximately the same period. That of Britain grew from 16.3 million to 20.8 million. More and more of the people of Europe lived in cities. By mid-century one half of the population of England and Wales had become town dwellers; the proportion for France and Germany was about one quarter. The sheer numbers of human beings put considerable pressure on the physical resources of the cities. Migration from the countryside meant that existing housing, water, sewers, food supplies, and lighting were completely inadequate. Slums with indescribable filth grew, and disease, especially cholera, ravaged the population. Crime in-

Stockport, an English industrial center, about 1840. Note the railway viaduct running through the city. [Mary Evans Picture Library]

Parliament Hears About German Imitation of English Machinery

In 1841 a committee of the British Parliament heard evidence on the exportation of English machinery. In the passage below, a Mr. Charles Noyes informed the committee of the activities supported by the Prussian government to imitate English textile machines. His testimony reveals the contemporary recognition of English technological superiority and the attempts of other European nations to compete with England. Despite efforts such as those described, Britain continued to maintain its domination in textile production even as manufacturers on the Continent began to adopt English methods.

I found at Berlin the most enterprising and systematic exertions made on the part of the Government to obtain a command of the manufacture of machinery; I found no expense spared for that purpose; and the exertions quite astonished me. There is one very important [training] institution at Berlin, called the "Gerwerbe Institut" [Trade Institute], which is a large establishment for practical education, combining design with almost every branch of manufactures into which science and mechanics enter. . . . In going through the rooms of this institution with the professor, Mr. Wedding, I saw suites of apartments completely filled with models of English machines: the professor informed me that they had in it models of every machine in use in Great Britain for the manufacture of cotton, flax, silk, and wool, and likewise a number from America and [elsewhere in] Germany; that by these means they were not only enabled to have our recent improvements, but, what was a matter of importance which we cannot command, that they were enabled frequently to combine in the same machine two distinct patents. The system he told me was, that this machinery, as soon as produced in England, was immediately imported at the expense of the [Prussian] Government, and set up at the Gerwerbe Institut; that it was proved [tested]; that a working model was immediately made from it, to be deposited in the institution, and that the original was presented as an honorary prize by the Government to some manufacturer in Prussia, who had distinguished himself in the peculiar branch to which it was applicable. In the Institut, likewise, the pupils were taught to make the machinery themselves; they were supplied with the tools, and they were permitted to carry away the machines which they themselves had constructed; I cannot but look upon the whole of this system as the most surprising effort made on the part of the [Prussian] Government to obtain a command of the manufacture of machinery, which is at the present moment so important a feature in English manufactures.

From "Minutes of Evidence taken before the Select Committee . . . [on] The Exportation of Machinery" (1841), as cited in S. Pollard and C. Holmes (Eds.), *Documents of European Economic History*, Vol. 1 (London: Edward Arnold, 1968), p. 429.

creased and became a way of life for those who could make a living in no other manner. Human misery and degradation in numerous early nineteenth-century cities seemed to have no bounds.

The situation in the countryside was little or no better. During the first half of the century the productive use of the land still remained the overwhelming fact of life for the majority of Europeans. The enclosures of the late eighteenth century, the land redistribution of the French Revolution, and the emancipation of serfs in Prussia and later in Austria (1848) and Russia (1861) commercialized landholding. Liberal reformers had hoped that the legal revolution in ownership would transform peasants into progressive, industrious farmers. Most of them had instead become very conservative landholders who possessed too little soil to innovate or, in many cases, even to support themselves. The specter of poor harvests still haunted Europe. The worst such experience of the century was the Irish famine of 1845–1847. Perhaps as many as half a million

Starving Irish peasants begging for relief in 1847. The failure of the Irish potato crop in 1845–1847 led to the worst famine of nineteenth-century Europe. About 500,000 people starved and more than one million emigrated. [*Mary Evans Picture Library*]

Irish peasants with no land or small plots simply starved when disease blighted the potato crop. Hundreds of thousands emigrated. By mid-century the revolution in landholding had led not only to greater agricultural production but also to a vast uprooting of people from the countryside into cities and from Europe into the rest of the world.

Railways

Industrial advance itself had also contributed to this migration. The decades of the 1830s and 1840s were the great age of railway building. The Stockton and Darlington Line opened in England in 1825. By 1830 another major line had been built between Manchester and Liverpool and had several hundred daily passengers. Belgium had undertaken railway construction by 1835. The first French line opened in 1832, but serious construction came only in the 1840s. Germany entered the railway age in 1835. At mid-century Britain had 9,797 kilometers of railway; France, 2,915; and Germany, 5,856. The railroads, plus canals and improved regular roads, meant that people could leave the place of their birth more easily than ever before. The improvement in transportation also allowed cheaper and more rapid passage of raw materials and finished products.

Railways epitomized the character of the industrial economy during the second quarter of the century. They represented investment in capital goods rather than in consumer goods. There was consequently somewhat of a shortage of consumer goods at cheap prices. This favoring of capital over consumer production was one reason that the working class often found itself able to purchase so little for its wages. The railways in and of themselves also brought about still more industrialization. They created a sharply increased demand for iron and steel and then for a more skilled labor force. The new iron and steel capacity soon permitted the construction of ironclad ships and iron rather than wooden machinery. These great capital industries led to the formation of vast industrial fortunes that would be invested in still newer enterprises. Industrialism had begun to grow on itself.

An 1837 view of one of the first French railways, the line between Paris and the suburb of St. Germain. The line was built by Baron James de Rothschild, of the famous Jewish banking family. [Mary Evans Picture Library]

The Middle Classes

It was the age of the career open to talent. The middle class of entrepreneurs, traders, shippers, factory owners, doctors, lawyers, shopkeepers, and schoolteachers benefited most from the economic and material progress. Their incomes, unlike those of laborers, allowed them to buy consumer goods. Their skills and education permitted them to rise socially. They often had sufficient savings to make either large or small investments in the railroads and other heavy industries. Many of them were able to rise well above the social status of their birth.

The middle *classes*—for the group was very diverse—believed that merit and competition should replace good birth and patronage as avenues to social position and political influence. In place of the former aristocratic value of leisure, they raised the values of thrift and hard work. They tended to measure success and respectability in terms of money. This attitude made them very unsympathetic toward the plight of the poor. They believed that the poor experienced poverty from either lack of ability or laziness. The middle classes were the people whom the English novelist Charles Dickens (1812—1870) pilloried in *Hard Times* and other novels and whose amoral existence the French novelist Honoré de Balzac (1799—1850) dissected in his fiction. But the confidence of the middle classes was a reflection of the new economic order that their members had created. They were also arrogant because they had learned from the aristocracy that pride and self-confidence were the marks of socially superior people.

Yet for all their economic success and apparent self-confidence, in several countries, the middle classes at mid-century still generally lacked effective political power. They were best off in Britain, where aristocratic leaders did listen to them and where they were being absorbed into the political process, as the careers of prime ministers Robert Peel and William Gladstone demonstrated.

In France, by contrast, a very small group of extremely wealthy persons affected politics. During the July Monarchy only about 250,000

Charles Dickens (1812–1870). Like other novelists of his age, Dickens' novels portrayed the harsh effects of the industrial revolution on the poor. [New York Public Library]

males had the right to vote. In the states of Germany, the Habsburg Empire, and Russia the small middle classes were relatively powerless. Throughout Europe these people were coming increasingly to resent a lack of political influence equal to their wealth and ability. Their enemies were the aristocracy and inefficient royal administrations. Through philosophical and scientific societies, chambers of commerce, and where possible newspapers, they were by the late 1840s voicing their complaints and ambitions.

Some writers from the early nineteenth-century middle class, however, were critical of the social conditions arising from industrialism. During the second quarter of the century numerous physicians who had to enter working-class districts to treat disease wrote books describing the suffering of the poor. Novelists, such as Elizabeth Gaskell (1810–1865), in *Mary Barton,* Frances Trollope (1780–1863) in *Michael Armstrong,* and Benjamin Disraeli (1804–1881; a notable political figure and later a prime minister) in *Sybil,* featured the plight of the British working class. Social commentators, such as Thomas Carlyle (1795–

1881) in *Past and Present,* denounced the sacrifice of social welfare to the naked profit motive. Henry Mayhew (1812–1887), a reporter for the London *Morning Chronicle,* wrote a long series of articles in 1849–1850 about the life of the laboring poor in the city. He revealed a world of which middle-class readers had neither knowledge nor experience. Edwin Chadwick (1800–1890), a pioneer of sanitary reform, presented government reports on the degradation of urban and industrial life in Britain. Various parliamentary commissions also published papers describing the harsh realities of the conditions of the working class. All of these materials provided Karl Marx (1818–1883) with some of the most important sources for his denunciation of capitalism.

The Labor Force

The composition and experience of the early nineteenth-century labor force was quite varied. No single description could include all of the factory workers, urban artisans, domestic system craftsmen, household servants, countryside peddlers, farm workers, or railroad navvies. The work force was composed of some persons who were reasonably well off, enjoying steady employment and decent wages. It also numbered the "laboring poor," who held jobs but whose wages allowed them little more than the subsistence. The condition of any particular working-class family depended on the skills of its members, the nature of the local labor market, and the trade cycle. But all of these working people faced possible unemployment, with little or no provision for their security. They confronted over the course of their lives the dissolution of many of the traditional social ties of custom and community. Most of the economic relationships in their lives became those of the marketplace or, as Thomas Carlyle said, of the "cash nexus."

Within the life of this immensely various European work force historians of the nineteenth century have traditionally emphasized the role and experience of industrial factory workers. In many respects this emphasis has been correct because factory labor and factory discipline did constitute the wave of the economic future. In the long run the industrial system affected almost every aspect of economic and social life. However, during the first half of the century only the textile-manufacturing industry became thoroughly mechanized and moved into the factory setting. A vastly larger number of the nonrural, nonagricultural work force consisted of skilled urban artisans who were attempting to maintain the value of their skills and control over their trades in the face of changing features of production.

Proletarianization of Factory Workers and Urban Artisans

During the century both artisans and factory workers underwent a process of *proletarianization*. This term is used to indicate the entry of workers into a wage economy and their gradual loss of significant ownership of the means of production, such as tools and equipment, and of control over the conduct of their own trades. The process occurred rapidly wherever the factory system arose. The factory owner provided the financial capital to construct the factory, to purchase the machinery, and to secure the raw materials. The factory workers contributed their labor for a wage. Those workers also submitted to various kinds of factory discipline. This discipline meant that in large measure, work conditions became determined by the demands for smooth operation of the machines. Closing of factory gates to late workers, fines for such lateness, dismissal for drunkenness, and public scolding of faulty laborers constituted attempts to create human discipline that would match the regularity of the cables, wheels, and pistons. The factory worker also had no direct say in regard to the quality of the product or its price. It should be noted that for all the difficulties of factory conditions the situation was often better than for the textile workers who resisted the factory mode of production. In particular English hand-loom weavers, who continued to work in their homes, experienced decades of declining trade and growing poverty in their unsuccessful competition with power looms.

Urban artisans in the nineteenth century experienced proletarianization more slowly than factory workers, and machinery had little to do with the process. The emergence of factories in and of itself did not harm urban artisans. Many even prospered from the development. For example, the construction and maintenance of the new machines generated major demand for metalworkers, who consequently prospered. The actual erection of factories and the expansion of cities benefited all craftsmen in the building trades, such as car-

penters, roofers, joiners, and masons. The lower prices for machine-made textiles aided artisans involved in the making of clothing, such as tailors and hatters, by reducing the costs of their raw materials. Where the urban artisans encountered difficulty and where they found their skills and livelihood threatened was in the organization of production.

In the eighteenth century a European town or city workplace had usually consisted of a few artisans laboring for a master, first in the capacity of apprentices and then as journeymen, according to established guild regulations and practices. The master owned the workshop and the larger equipment, and the apprentices and journeymen owned their tools. The journeyman could well expect to become a master. This guild system had allowed very considerable worker control over labor recruitment and training, pace of production, quality of product, and price.

British metal workers in the ship-building industry, c. 1840. Skilled laborers such as these often prospered with increasing industrialization. [Michael Holford]

In the nineteenth century the situation of the urban artisan underwent very considerable change. It became increasingly difficult for artisans to continue to exercise corporate or guild direction and control over their trades. The legislation of the French Revolution had outlawed such organizations in France. Across Europe political and economic liberals disapproved of labor and guild organizations and attempted to make them illegal.

Other destructive forces were also at work. The masters often found themselves under increased competitive pressure from larger, more heavily capitalized establishments or from the possibility of the introduction of machine production into a previously craft-dominated industry. In many workshops masters began to follow a practice, known in France as *confection*, whereby goods such as shoes, clothing, and furniture were produced in standard sizes and styles rather than by special orders for individual customers. The result of this practice was to increase the division of labor in the workshop. Each artisan produced a smaller part of the more-or-less uniform final product. Consequently less skill was required of each artisan, and the particular skills possessed by a worker became less valuable. Masters also attempted to increase production and reduce their costs by lowering the wages paid for piecework. Those attempts often led to work stoppages or strikes. Migrants from the countryside or small towns into the cities created, in some cases, a surplus of relatively unskilled workers who were willing to work for lower wages or under less favorable and protected conditions than traditional artisans. The dilution of skills and possible lower wages, caused not by machinery but by changes in the organization of artisan production, made it much more difficult for urban journeymen ever to hope to become masters with their own workshops, in which they would be in charge. Increasingly these artisans became lifetime wage laborers whose skills were simply bought and sold in the marketplace.

Working-class Political Action

By the middle of the century, such artisans, proud of their skills and frustrated in their social expectations, became the most radical political element in the European working class. From at least the 1830s onward, these artisans took the lead in one country after another in attempting to formulate new ways of protecting their social and economic interests. Within the workplace they bargained and sometimes carried out strikes, as did the shoemakers of Marseilles in 1845. Other attempts to improve their situation included the formation of mutual aid societies, to which workers contributed to look after their needs in time of poor health or to ensure that they would have a proper funeral. Other artisans became involved in the various early socialist ideologies and the early trade-union movements. But repeatedly, artisans turned to collective action of a political nature. The most important of these in the first half of the century was British Chartism.

CHARTISM IN GREAT BRITAIN. By the late 1830s the British working class had turned to direct political activity. They linked the solution of their economic plight to a program of political reform known as *Chartism*. In 1836 William Lovett (1800–1877) and other London radical artisans formed the London Working Men's Association. In 1838 the group issued the Charter, demanding six specific reforms. The Six Points of the Charter included universal manhood suffrage, annual election of the House of Commons, the secret ballot, equal electoral districts, abolition of property qualifications for Members of Parliament, and payment of members. For over ten years the Chartists, who were never tightly organized, agitated for their reforms. On three occasions the Charter was presented to Parliament, which refused to pass it. Mass petitions were presented to the House of Commons with millions of signatures. Strikes were called. A Chartist newspaper called *The Northern Star* was published. Feargus O'Connor (1794–1855), the most important Chartist leader, made speeches up and down the island. Despite this vast activity Chartism as a national movement failed. Its ranks were split between those who favored violence and those who wanted to use peaceful tactics. However, locally the Chartists scored several successes and controlled the city councils in Leeds and Sheffield.

The economic foundation of Chartism had been the depression of the late 1830s and early 1840s. As prosperity returned, many working people abandoned the movement. Chartism came to a close in March 1848. A mass march on Parliament planned for that month fizzled. The reviving economy took care of the rest of the problem. Nevertheless the Chartist movement constituted the first large-scale working-

A Chartist procession in London. Chartism constituted the first large-scale working-class political movement. [The Mansell Collection]

class political movement. It had specific goals and largely working-class leadership. Eventually several of the Six Points were enacted into law. Continental working-class observers saw in Chartism the kind of mass movement that workers must eventually adopt if they were to improve their situation.

Family Structures and the Industrial Revolution

It is more difficult to write in generalities about the European family structure in the age of early industrialism than under the old regime. The reason is that industrialism developed at very different rates across the continent and because the impact of industrialism cannot be separated from that of migration and urbanization. Furthermore, industrialism did not touch all families directly. In that regard, the structures and customs of many peasant families changed relatively little in the early and even in the later nineteenth century. Yet the process of factory expansion, proletarianization, and the growth of commercial and service sectors related to industrialism did change the structures of much family life and the character of gender roles within families. Much more is known about the relationships of the new in-

dustry to the family in Great Britain than elsewhere. It would seem that many of the British developments foreshadowed those in other countries as the factory system spread.

Contrary to the opinion once held, the adoption of new machinery and factory production in and of itself did not destroy the working-class family. Before the late-eighteenth-century revolution in textile production in England, the individual family involved in textiles was the chief unit of production. The earliest textile inventions, such as the spinning jenny, did not change that situation. The new machine was simply brought into the home. It was the mechanization of weaving that led to the major change. The father who became a machine weaver was employed in a factory. His work was thus separated from his home. However, the structure of early English factories allowed him to preserve many of his traditional family roles as they had existed before the factory system. In the domestic system of the family economy the father and mother had worked with their children in textile production as a family unit. They had trained and disciplined the children within the home setting. Their home life and their economic life were largely the same. In the early factories the father was permitted to employ his wife and children as his assistants. The tasks of education and discipline were not removed from the work place nor from the institution of the family. Parental training and discipline were thus transferred from the home into the early factory. In some cases, in both Britain and France, whole families would move near a new factory so that the family as a unit could work there.

A major shift in this family and factory structure began in the mid-1820s in England and had been more or less completed by the mid-1830s. As spinning and weaving were put under one roof, the size of factories and of the machinery became larger. These newer machines required fewer skilled operators but many relatively unskilled attendants. The ma-

Child laborers. Concern about the plight of child labor in England only became acute in the 1830s when whole families ceased to work in the mills together, and children had to toil without their parents being present. [The Mansell Collection]

chine tending became the work of unmarried women and children, whom factory owners found would accept lower wages and were less likely than adult men to attempt any form of worker or union organization. However, factory wages for skilled adult males became sufficiently high to allow some fathers to remove their children from the factory and to send them to school. The children who were now working in the factories as assistants were often the children of the economically depressed handloom weavers. The wives of the skilled operatives also tended no longer to be working in the factories. Consequently the original links of the family in the British textile factory that had existed for well over a quarter century largely disappeared.

It was at this point in the 1830s that much concern about the plight of child labor came to dominate workers' attention. They were concerned about the treatment of factory children because discipline was no longer being exercised by parents over their own children in the factories. The English Factory Act of 1833, passed to protect children by limiting their workday to eight hours and requiring two hours of education paid for by the factory owner, further divided work and home life. The workday for adult males remained twelve hours. Children often worked in relays of four or six hours. Consequently the parental link was thoroughly broken. The education requirement began the process of removing nurturing and training from the home and family and setting them into a school, where a teacher rather than the parents was in charge of education. After this act was passed, many of the working-class demands for shorter workdays for adults related to the desire to reunite, in some manner, the workday of adults with that of their children, or at least to allow adults to spend more hours with their children. In 1847 Parliament mandated a ten-hour day. By present standards this was very long, but at that time it allowed parents and children more hours together as a domestic unit because their relationship as a work or production unit had ceased wherever the factory system prevailed. By the middle of the 1840s, in the lives of industrial workers the role of men as breadwinners and men as fathers and husbands had become distinct in the British textile industry.

What occurred in Britain presents a general pattern for what would happen elsewhere with the spread of industrial capitalism and of public education. The European family was in the process of passing from the chief unit of both production and consumption to becoming the chief unit of consumption alone. This development did not mean the end of the family as an economic unit. However, parents and children now came to depend on sharing of wages often derived from several sources rather than on sharing of work in the home or in the factory. And ultimately the wage economy meant that families were somewhat less closely bound together than in the past. Because wages could be sent over long distances to parents, children might now move farther away from home. Once they moved far away, the economic link was, in time, often broken. On the other hand, when a family settled in an industrial city, the wage economy might, in that or the next generation, actually discourage children from leaving home as early as they had in the past. Children could find wage employment in the same city and then live at home until they had accumulated enough savings to marry and begin their own household. That situation meant that children often remained with their parents to a later age than in the past.

Women in the Early Industrial Revolution

The industrial economy ultimately produced an immense impact on the home and the family life of women. First, it took virtually all productive work out of the home and put it elsewhere and allowed many families to live from the wages of the male spouse. That transformation prepared the way for a new concept of gender-determined roles in the home and in domestic life generally. Women came to be associated with domestic duties such as housekeeping, food preparation, child rearing and nurturing, and household management. The man came to be associated almost exclusively with breadwinning. Children were reared to match these expected gender patterns. Previously this domestic division of labor had prevailed among the relatively small middle class and gentry class. During the nineteenth century it came to characterize the working class as well. Second, industrialization created for many young women new modes of employment that allowed them to earn enough money to marry or, if necessary, to support themselves independently. Third, industrialism, though fostering more employment for women, lowered the skills required of employed women.

Because the early Industrial Revolution had

begun in textile production, women and their labor were deeply involved from the very start. While both spinning and weaving were still domestic industries, women usually worked in all stages of production. Hand spinning was virtually always a woman's task. When spinning was moved into factories and involved large machines, women tended to be displaced by men. The higher wages commanded by male cotton-factory workers allowed many women to stop work or to work only to supplement their husband's wages.

With the next generation of machines in the 1820s, unmarried women rapidly became employed in the factories. However, in the factories their jobs tended to be less skilled than those they had previously exercised in the home production of textiles. They were also less skilled than most work done by men. Tending a machine required less skill than actually spinning or weaving or acting as foreman. There was thus a certain paradox in the impact of the factory on women. Many new jobs were opened to women, but the level of skills was lowered. Moreover, almost always, the women in the factories were young single women or widows. On marriage or perhaps the birth of the first child, they usually found that their husband earned enough money for them to leave the factory. Or they found themselves unwanted by the factory owners, who disliked employing married women because of the likelihood of pregnancy, the influence of their husbands, and the duties of child rearing.

In Britain and elsewhere by mid-century, industrial factory work accounted for less than half of all employment for women. The largest group of employed women in France continued to work on the land. In England they were domestic servants. Domestic industries such as lacemaking, glove making, garment making, and other kinds of needlework employed a vast number of women. In almost all such cases their conditions of labor were harsh, whether they worked in their homes or in sweated workshops. Generally it cannot be overemphasized that all work by women commanded low wages and involved low skills. They had virtually no effective modes of protecting themselves from exploitation. The charwoman, in that regard, was a common sight across the continent and symbolized the plight of working women.

One of the most serious problems facing women in the work force was the uncertainty of employment. Because they virtually always

Women Industrial Workers Explain Their Economic Situation

In 1832 there was much discussion in the British press about factory legislation. Most of that discussion was concerned with the employment of children, but the *Examiner* newspaper made the suggestion that any factory laws should not only address the problem of child labor but also in time eliminate women from employment in factories. That article provoked the following remarkable letter in response. This letter to the editor, composed by or on behalf of women factory workers, eloquently stated the very real necessity of such employment for women and the very unattractive alternatives. Their emphasis on not having a male to support them is an indication that the overwhelming majority of women in factories were either unmarried or widowed. No legislation excluding women from factories was passed, though later legislation, in effect, sharply reduced female employment in the mines.

Sir,

Living as we do, in the densely populated manufacturing districts of Lancashire, and most of us belonging to that class of females who earn their bread either directly or indirectly by manufactories, we have looked with no little anxiety for your opinion on the Factory Bill. . . . You are for doing away with our services in manufactories altogether. So much the better, if you had pointed out any other more eligible and practical employment for the surplus female labour, that will want other channels for a subsistence. If our competition were withdrawn, and short hours substituted, we have no doubt but the effects would be as you have stated, "not to lower wages, as the male branch of the family would be enabled to earn as much as the whole had done," but for the thousands of females who are employed in manufactories, who have no legitimate claim on any male relative for employment or support, and who have, through a variety of circumstance, been early thrown on their own resources for a livelihood, what is to become of them?

In this neighbourhood, hand-loom has been almost totally superseded by power-loom weaving, and no inconsiderable number of females, who must depend on their own exertions, or their parishes for support, have been forced, of necessity into the manufactories, from their total inability to earn a livelihood at home.

It is a lamentable fact, that, in these parts of the country, there is scarcely any other mode of employment for female industry, if we except servitude and dressmaking. Of the former of these, there is no chance of employment for one-twentieth of the candidates that would rush into the field, to say nothing of lowering the wages of our sisters of the same craft; and of the latter, galling as some of the hardships of manufactories are (of which the indelicacy of mixing with the men is not the least), yet there are few women who have been so employed, that would change conditions with the ill-used genteel little slaves, who have to lose sleep and health, in catering to the whims and frivolities of the butter-flies of fashion.

We see no way of escape from starvation, but to accept the very tempting offers of the newspapers, held out as baits to us, fairly to ship ourselves off to Van Dieman's Land [Tasmania] on the very delicate errand of husband hunting, and having safely arrived at the "Land of Goshen," jump ashore, with a "Who wants me?" Now, then, as we are a class of society who will be materially affected by any alteration of the present laws, we put it seriously to you, whether, as you have deprived us of our means of earning bread, you are not bound to point out a more eligible and suitable employment for us?

Waiting with all humility, for your answer to our request, we have the honour to subscribe ourselves, the constant readers of the Examiner,
*THE FEMALE OPERATIVES
OF TODMORDEN*

The Examiner, February 26, 1832, as quoted in Ivy Pinchbeck, *Women Workers and the Industrial Revolution, 1750–1850* (New York: Augustus M. Kelley, 1969), pp. 199–200.

Machinery in early textile mills was often tended by unmarried women or widows. There were many such jobs, but the women were paid less than men because it was unskilled labor. [Bettmann Archive]

found themselves in the least skilled jobs and trades, security of employment was never certain. Much of their work was seasonal. This was one reason that so many working-class women feared that at one time or another in their lives they might be compelled to turn to prostitution. On the other hand, cities and the more complex economy did allow a greater variety of jobs. Movement to cities and entrance into the wage economy also gave women wider opportunities for marriages. Cohabitation before marriage seems not to have been uncommon. Parents had less to do with arranging marriages than in the past. Marriage also now generally meant that a woman would leave the work force to live on her husband's earnings. If all went well, that arrangement might improve the woman's situation, but if the husband became ill or died, or if the husband deserted his wife, she would find herself again required to enter the market for unskilled labor at a much advanced age.

Despite all of these changes, many of the traditional practices associated with the family economy survived into the industrial era. As a young woman came of age, both family needs and her desire to marry still directed what she would do with her life. The most likely early occupation for a young woman was domestic service. A girl born in the country normally migrated to a nearby town or city for such employment, often living initially with a relative. As in the past, she would attempt to earn enough in wages to give her a dowry, so that she might marry and establish her own household. If she became a factory worker, she would probably live in a supervised dormitory. Such dormitories were one of the ways that factory owners attracted young women into their employ by convincing parents that they would be safe. The life of young women in the cities seems to have been more precarious than earlier. There seem to have been fewer family and community ties. There were also perhaps more available young men. These men, who worked for wages rather than in the older apprenticeship structures, were more mobile, so that relationships between men and women seem to have been more fleeting. In any case, illegitimate births increased. That is to say,

733

fewer women who became pregnant before marriage found the father willing to marry them.

Marriage in the wage industrial economy was also different in certain respects from earlier marriages. Marriage still involved the starting of a separate household, but the structure of gender relationships within the household was different. Marriage was less an economic partnership. The husband's wages might well be able to support the entire family. The wage economy and the industrialization separating workplace and home made it very difficult for women to combine domestic duties with work. When married women worked, it was usually in the nonindustrial sector of the economy. More often than not, children were sent to work rather than the wife. This may provide one explanation for the increase of fertility within marriages, as children in the wage economy tended to be an economic asset. Married women worked outside the home only when family needs or illness or the death of a spouse really required them to do so. As Louise

---

A French Physician Describes a Working-class Slum in Lille

The work of medical doctors frequently carried them into working-class areas of industrial cities rarely visited by other members of the middle class. Louis Villermé was such a French physician. He wrote extensive descriptions of the slums and the general living conditions of industrial workers. The passage quoted below describes a particularly notorious section of Lille, a major cotton-manufacturing town in northern France.

The poorest live in the cellars and attics. These cellars . . . open onto the streets or courtyards, and one enters them by a stairway which is very often at once the door and the window. . . . Commonly the height of the ceiling is six or six and a half feet at the highest point, and they are only ten to fourteen or fifteen feet wide.

It is in these somber and sad dwellings that a large number of workers eat, sleep, and even work. The light of day comes an hour later for them than for others, and the night an hour earlier.

Their furnishings normally consist, along with the tools of their profession, of a sort of cupboard or a plank on which to deposit food, a stove . . . a few pots, a little table, two or three poor chairs, and a dirty pallet of which the only pieces are a straw mattress and scraps of a blanket. . . .

In their obscure cellars, in their rooms, which one would take for cellars, the air is never renewed, it is infected; the walls are plastered with garbage. . . . If a bed exists, it is a few dirty,

greasy planks; it is damp and putrescent straw; it is a coarse cloth whose color and fabric are hidden by a layer of grime; it is a blanket that resembles a sieve. . . . The furniture is dislocated, worm-eaten, covered with filth. Utensils are thrown in disorder all over the dwelling. The windows, always closed, are covered by paper and glass, but so black, so smoke-encrusted, that the light is unable to penetrate . . . everywhere are piles of garbage, of ashes, of debris from vegetables picked up from the streets, of rotten straw; of animal nests of all sorts; thus, the air is unbreathable. One is exhausted, in these hovels, by a stale, nauseating, somewhat piquante odor, odor of filth, odor of garbage. . . .

And the poor themselves, what are they like in the middle of such a slum? Their clothing is in shreds, without substance, consumed, covered, no less than their hair, which knows no comb, with dust from the workshops. And their skin? . . . It is painted, it is hidden, if you wish, by indistinguishable deposits of diverse exudations.

Louis Réné Villermé, *Tableau de l'état physique et moral des employés dans les manufactures de coton, de laine et de soie* (Paris, 1840), as quoted and trans. in William H. Sewell, Jr., *Work and Revolution in France: The Language of Labor from the Old Regime to 1848* (Cambridge: Cambridge University Press, 1980), p. 224.

Tilly and Joan Scott wrote, "Most women resolved the conflict between home and work by withdrawing from permanent employment, becoming temporary workers when their family need for their wages outweighed the advantages of their remaining at home and fulfilling economically important, but unpaid, domestic responsibilities."[1]

In the home, working-class women were by no means idle. Their domestic duties were an essential factor in the family wage economy. If work took place elsewhere, someone had to be directly in charge of maintaining the home front. Homemaking came to the fore when a life at home had to be organized that was separate from the place of work. Wives were primarily concerned with food and cooking, but they often also were in charge of the family's finances. The role of the mother expanded when the children still living at home became wage earners. She was now providing home support for her entire wage-earning family. She created the environment to which the family members returned after work. The longer period of home life of working children may also have increased and strengthened familial bonds of affection between those children and their hardworking, homebound mothers.

Problems of Crime and Order

Throughout the nineteenth century the political and economic elite in Europe were profoundly concerned about social order. The revolutions of the late eighteenth and early nineteenth centuries made them fearful of future disorder and threats to life and property. The process of industrialization and urbanization also contributed to this problem of order. Thousands of Europeans migrated from the countryside to the towns and cities. There they often encountered poverty or unemployment and general social frustration and disappointment. Cities became places associated with criminal activity and especially crimes against property, such as theft and arson. Throughout the first sixty years of the nineteenth century, there appears to have occurred a relatively

[1]Louise A. Tilly and Joan W. Scott, *Women, Work, and Family* (New York: Holt, Rinehart and Winston, 1978), p. 136.

slow but steady increase in crime, which then more or less plateaued.

Historians and social scientists are divided about the reasons for this rise in the crime rate. So little is known about crime in rural settings that comparisons are difficult. There are also many problems with crime statistics in the nineteenth century. No two nations kept them in the same manner. Different legal codes and systems of judicial administration were in effect in different areas of the continent, thus giving somewhat different legal definitions of criminal activity. The result has been confusion, very difficult research, and tentative conclusions. Scholars have long believed that much nineteenth-century crime was the result of social deprivation. That is to say, many people living in cities were desperately poor and consequently turned to crime simply to allow their families to survive. This explanation may hold through the 1840s, when there did seem to be a straightforward relationship between theft and subsistence. The 1840s saw a great deal of economic hardship across the continent, but after that decade Europe, except in wartime, did not experience real food shortages, which had previously accounted for much theft. An alternative explanation is that nineteenth-century crime against property was less the result of actual deprivation than of the rising social and economic expectations fueled after mid-century by an expanding economy. Some people who found their own social and economic expectations unfulfilled turned to crime. Another theory prevalent both at the time and since simply assumed the existence of a criminal class. None of these explanations is wholly satisfactory, and far more research is needed on the subject.

New Police Forces

From the propertied elite classes there emerged, during the century, two major views about containing crime and criminals. These were prison reform and better systems of police. The result of these efforts was the triumph in Europe of the concept of a policed society. This concept means the presence in a nation of a paid, professionally trained group of law-enforcement officers charged with keeping order, protecting property and lives, investigating crime, and apprehending offenders. These officers are distinct from the army and are charged specifically with domestic security. It is to them that the civilian population normally

London policemen in 1850. Professional police forces did not exist before the early nineteenth century. The London police force was created by Parliament in 1828. [The Mansell Collection]

turns for law enforcement. One of the key features of the theory of a policed society is that crime may be prevented by the visible presence of law-enforcement officers. These police forces, at least in theory, did not perform a political role, though in many countries that distinction was often ignored. Such professional police forces did not really exist until the early nineteenth century. They differed in the various countries in terms of both authority and organization, but their creation proved to be one of the main keys to the emergence of an orderly European society. Although police were viewed and have continued to be viewed with a certain suspicion at various times, the remarkable fact is that by the end of the century most Europeans held friendly views toward police and regarded them as their protectors. Persons from the upper and middle classes felt their property to be more secure. Persons from the working class also frequently turned to the police to protect their lives and property and aid them in other ways in emergencies. It is, of course, important to add that such was not the attitude toward political or secret po-

lice, who were hated and dreaded wherever governments created them.

In the late eighteenth century France was regarded as the best-policed state in Europe. Paris was regarded as the safest city on the Continent. Louis XIV had originally created the Paris police force. During the French Revolution the various revolutionary governments devised several different police organizations. There were important experiments that gave local municipalities responsibility for police enforcement. There was always fear that the police would be used by one political group against another. Under Napoleon the *police général* was a force used for political surveillance. There were further attempts to reorganize the police forces under the restored Bourbon government, but politics again came to the fore. From the revolution onward, the French governments depended on the *gendarmerie*, or military police, to patrol the provincial highways and, when necessary, to put down public disturbances. In 1828 a new departure was taken. A new concept of policing was announced by the prefect of Paris: "Safety by day and night, free traffic movement, clean streets, the supervision of and precaution against accidents, the maintenance of order in public places, the seeking out of offences and their perpetrators. . . . The municipal police is a parental police.''[2] The next year *sergents* in blue uniforms appeared on the streets of Paris. The uniform was important because it meant that the police officers could not disappear like a secret agent. They were very lightly armed to distinguish them from soldiers. There were never very many police in Paris or in other French cities during the nineteenth century. Paris had fewer than 500 at mid-century, and in the second half of the century only about 4,000. In 1900 Marseilles had fewer than 300 police. The rapidly changing French governments tended to tolerate a rather confused and decentralized system of police. Those governments also continued to depend on the *gendarmerie* to put down major public and political disturbances.

The situation in Prussia was not unlike that in France. There was always a combination of small local police forces and troops to ensure order. The militarized character of Prussian society meant that many subjects lived in cities or towns where there were regularly stationed military garrisons. After the revolution of 1848, a new police force called the *Schutzmannschaft* was organized in Berlin. Originally a civilian force, it became over the years much more military in character. The police president of Berlin established a network of information with police presidents in other Prussian cities to increase criminal and political surveillance. Yet, at the same time, these Prussian police improved the delivery of municipal services and the general administration of their cities. This latter activity would appear to be one reason why many people, especially those of the middle classes, accepted the political activity of the police as well.

The most famous example of the creation of a domestic police force that came to command immense public confidence occurred in Great Britain. The British had always resisted the introduction of a professional police force. They feared that any such force would resemble the secret police of the major continental powers. However, in the early nineteenth century the British confronted two major problems. Local authorities using amateur constables and troops had not been able to maintain order. The Peterloo Massacre of 1819 had made that problem all too clear. Second, despite the fact that scores of capital offenses were on the law books, the threat of capital punishment was not deterring crimes against property. Gradually but dramatically, Britain lowered the number of capital offenses from more than two hundred in 1800 to eleven in 1841. After that date, only murder even actually led to execution except during wartime. The reduction in penalties was tied to an effort to see that juries would actually convict and that criminals would actually be apprehended. In 1828 Parliament passed the Metropolitan Police Act, creating a new police force for London. The minister who sponsored this legislation was Sir Robert Peel, after whom the members of the force came to be known as *bobbies*. By 1830 there were almost three thousand police serving in London. In 1839 Parliament extended permissive legislation to the countryside by permitting counties to organize police forces, and in 1856 it mandated the establishment of those county forces. The English police during the nineteenth century tended to enjoy much popular support from all classes in the society. Members of the working class no less than members of the middle class turned to the police to ensure order and to apprehend persons who had disturbed their lives.

Prison Reform

The motives for establishing and reorganizing police forces were straightforward desires for order. Prison reform involved the impulse for both order and humanitarian improvement of the situation of prisoners. Before the nineteenth century European prisons tended to be local jails, quite large in the case of cities, or state prisons, such as the Bastille, or prison ships called *hulks*. Some nations sentenced prisoners to naval galleys, where, chained to their benches, they rowed until they died or were eventually released. Prisoners in prisons lived under the most wretched of conditions. Men and women were housed together. Children might be housed with adults. Persons guilty of minor offenses were left in the same room with persons guilty of the most serious offenses.

The late eighteenth century saw several developments that eventually fostered reform. The philosophy of the Enlightenment, as noted in Chapter 17, had raised questions about the

---

[2]Quoted in Clive Emsley, *Policing and Its Context, 1750–1870* (London: Macmillan, 1983), p. 58.

treatment of criminals. Then, reformers such as John Howard in England made visits to prisons and widely publicized the terrible conditions. In 1813 Elizabeth Frey took up the cause of prison reform. In France Charles Lucas demanded change. All of these efforts made very slow progress. There was a host of local authorities to convince, and the building of new and better prisons was very expensive.

The British government had for sometime used the penalty of *transportation* for persons convicted of the most serious offenses. Begin-

LEFT: *British convicts in Australia, around 1820. Transporting prisoners to Australia was regarded as an alternative to hanging and was practiced until the mid-nineteenth century.* [*Mary Evans Picture Library*]

BELOW: *Prisoners working on the treadmill at the Brixton prison in Britain, around 1830. The treadmill in prisons was advocated by social reformers as a way of improving discipline.* [*Library of Congress*]

ning in the late eighteenth century these people were shipped to the colony of New South Wales in Australia. Transportation was regarded as an alternative to capital punishment. It was used by the British until the middle of the nineteenth century, when the colonies began to object. Thereafter the British government established public works prisons in Britain to house long-term prisoners. The point of this mode of imprisonment was punishment and removing offenders from society. These had been the general purposes of imprisonment for decades in Europe.

However, in the 1840s both the French and the English undertook several bold efforts in prison reform. New prisons were designed according to what were regarded as scientific modes of understanding criminals and criminal reform. These prisons were intended to rehabilitate the criminal and to transform him or her during the period of incarceration. The original models for these prisons had been established in the United States. All of these experiments depended on various ways of separating prisoners from each other. One was known as the Auburn system after the Auburn Prison in New York State. According to it, prisoners were separated during the night but could associate in worktime during the day. The other was the Philadelphia system, in which prisoners were kept rigorously separated at all times. Europeans used various versions of these systems, but the keys to all of these systems were an individual cell for each prisoner and long periods of separation and silence between prisoners. The most famous example of this kind of prison in Europe was the Pentonville Prison near London. There, each prisoner was placed in a separate cell. The prisoners were never allowed to speak to each other while working or to see each other. They wore masks when in the prison yard, and in the chapel, they had separate stalls. The point of the system was to turn the prisoner's mind in on itself to a mode of contemplation that would reform the criminal. As time passed, the system was allowed to become more relaxed because the intense isolation led to mental collapse.

In France imprisonment became more repressive as the century passed. French prisons similar to Pentonville were constructed in the 1840s. One of the strongest advocates of the Philadelphia system in France was Alexis de Tocqueville, the author of *Democracy in America* (1833). Inspection of American prisons had been the occasion of his famous journey through the United States. The growing rigor of French prisons and the general treatment of crimes seems to have been closely related to fears of social and political disorder. In 1851 the French government adopted transportation to the colonies at about the time the English gave up that system. In 1875 the French also adopted a firm general policy of isolation of prisoners in prison. This policy led to the construction of sixty prisons based on that principle by 1908. Prisoners were supposed to be trained in some kind of trade or skill while in prison so that they could reemerge as reformed citizens. It was the vast increase in repeat offenses that led the French government in 1885 to declare transportation the penalty for repeated offenses of serious crimes. The idea of this transportation to places, such as the infamous Devil's Island off the coast of South America, was literally to purge the nation of its worst criminals and to ensure that they would never return.

All of these attempts to create a police force and to reform prisons illustrate the new post–French Revolution concern about order and stability on the part of the European political and social elites. They also reflect attempts to impose some kind of new order on a European social order put under immense pressures by a growing and migrating population, the emergence of industrial modes of production, urbanization, and political and economic discontent. New disturbances of a serious nature would occur, such as the revolutions of 1848 to be discussed later in this chapter. But on the whole, by the end of the century an orderly society had been established and the new police and prisons had no small role in that development.

Intellectual Responses to Industrial Society

Classical Economics

Economists whose thought largely derived from Adam Smith's *Wealth of Nations* (1776) dominated private and public discussions of industrial and commercial policy. Their ideas are generally associated with the phrase *laissez-faire*. Although they thought that the government should perform many important functions, the classical economists favored economic growth through competitive free enterprise. The economists conceived of society as consisting of atomistic individuals from whose competitive efforts the demands of the consumers in the marketplace were met. Most economic decisions should be made through the mechanism of the marketplace. They distrusted government action, believing it to be mischievous and corrupt. The government should maintain a sound currency, enforce contracts, protect property, impose low tariffs and taxes, and leave the remainder of economic life to private initiative. The economists naturally assumed that the state would maintain sufficient armed forces and naval power to protect the economic structure and the foreign trade of the nation.

The classical economists suggested complicated and very pessimistic ideas about the working class. Thomas Malthus (1766–1834) and David Ricardo (1772–1823), probably the most influential of all these writers, suggested, in effect, that the condition of the working class could not be improved. In 1798 Malthus published the first edition of his *Essay on the Principle of Population*. His ideas have haunted the world ever since. He contended that population must eventually outstrip the food supply. Although the human population grows geometrically, the food supply can expand only arithmetically. There was little hope of averting the disaster, in Malthus's opinion, except through late marriage, chastity, and contraception, the last of which he considered a vice. It took three quarters of a century for contraception to become a socially acceptable method of containing the population explosion.

Malthus contended that the immediate plight of the working class could only become worse. If wages were raised, the workers would simply produce more children, who would, in turn, consume both the extra wages and more food. Later in his life Malthus suggested, in a more optimistic vein, that if the working class could be persuaded to adopt a higher standard of living, their increased wages might be spent on consumer goods rather than on more children.

In the *Principles of Political Economy* (1817), David Ricardo transformed the concepts of Malthus into the Iron Law of Wages. If wages were raised, more children would be produced. They, in turn, would enter the labor market, thus expanding the number of workers and lowering wages. As wages fell, working people would produce fewer children. Wages would then rise, and the process would start all over again. Consequently, in the long run, wages would always tend toward a minimum level. These arguments simply confirmed employers in their natural hesitancy to raise wages. These concepts also provided strong theoretical support for opposition to labor unions. The ideas of the economists were spread to the public during the 1830s through journals, newspapers, and even short stories, such as Harriet Martineau's series of *Illustrations of Political Economy*.

The working class of France and Great Britain, needless to say, resented these attitudes, but the governments embraced them. Louis Philippe and his minister François Guizot told the French to go forth and enrich themselves. People who simply displayed sufficient energy need not be poor. A goodly number of the French middle class did just that. The July Monarchy saw the construction of major social overhead capital, such as roads, canals, and railways. Little was done about the poverty in the cities and the countryside.

In Germany the middle classes made less headway. However, the Prussian reformers after the Napoleonic wars had seen the desirability of abolishing internal tariffs that impeded economic growth. In 1834 all the major German states, with the exception of Austria, formed the *Zollverein,* or free trading union.

Harriet Martineau (1802–1876) was one of the most important popularizers of the ideas of the British classical economists. She illustrated their principles through moral tales.

Classical economics had somewhat less influence in Germany because of the tradition dating from enlightened absolutism of state direction of economic development. The German economist Friedrich List (1789–1846) argued for this approach to economic growth during the second quarter of the century.

Britain was the home of the major classical economists, and their policies were widely accepted. In 1834 the reformed House of Commons passed a new Poor Law. This measure established a Poor Law Commission, which set out to make poverty the most undesirable of all social situations. Government poor relief was to be disbursed only in workhouses. Life in the workhouse was consciously designed to be more unpleasant than life outside. Husbands and wives were separated; the food was bad; and the work assigned in the house was distasteful. The social stigma of the workhouse was even worse. The law and its administration presupposed that people would not work because they were lazy. The laboring class, not unjustly, regarded the workhouses as new "bastilles."

The second British monument to applied classical economics was the repeal of the Corn Laws in 1846. The Anti-Corn Law League, organized by manufacturers, had sought this goal for over six years. The league wanted the tariffs protecting the domestic price of grain to be abolished. That change would lead to lower food prices, which would then allow lower wages at no real cost to the workers. In turn, the prices on British manufactured goods could be lowered to allow a stronger competitive position in the world market. The actual reason for Robert Peel's repeal of the Corn Laws in 1846 was the Irish famine. Peel had to open British ports to foreign grain to feed the starving Irish. He realized that the Corn Laws could not be reimposed. Peel accompanied the abolition measure with a program for government aid to modernize British agriculture and to make it more efficient. The repeal of the Corn Laws was the culmination of the lowering of British tariffs that had begun during the 1820s. The repeal marked the opening of an era of free trade that continued until late in the century.

UTILITARIANISM. Closely related to the classical economists were the British utilitarians. Their major figures included Jeremy Bentham (1748–1832), James Mill (1773–1836), John Stuart Mill (1806–1873), and Sir Edwin Chadwick (1800–1890). They were a set of

John Stuart Mill (1806–1873), the most distinguished spokesman for utilitarianism. [National Portrait Gallery, London]

radical political reformers who urged that the principle of utility—the greatest good for the greatest number—should constitute the guiding principle of public policy. They lacked all reverence for tradition. They felt that political, economic, and social problems should be addressed rationally and without reference to special interests or privileged groups. They have frequently been considered spokesmen for the middle class, but it would be more correct to see them as forerunners of an efficient bureaucracy. The utilitarians and their disciples were often civil servants, and they frequently worked on governmental commissions. They were the actual authors of much reform legislation, such as the Factory Act of 1833, the Poor Law of 1834, and the Sanitation Act of 1848.

The utilitarians have achieved a bad reputation for lacking emotion and an understanding of humanity. Some of this reputation is deserved. However, their most distinguished spokesman, John Stuart Mill, was anything but doctrinaire. As a young man he revolted against the rigid Benthamite education imposed on him by his father, James Mill. In his *Principles of Political Economy* (1848), John Stuart Mill advocated the education of the working class as a means of raising their standard of living. He believed workers capable of as high a moral existence as any other social group. He urged the formation of labor cooperatives. In 1859 Mill published *On Liberty* to plead for freedom of thought and expression and for the protection of the individual against the intrusion of the state. In 1869 he took up the cause of women's rights in a pioneering essay on *The Subjection of Women*. If utilitarianism had been narrow in its origins, by the close of Mill's life in 1873 the creed had proved itself capable of considerable moderation.

Socialism

Today the socialist movement, in the form of either communist or social democratic political parties, constitutes one of the major political forces in Europe. Less than 150 years ago the advocates of socialism lacked any meaningful political following. Their doctrines were blurred and often seemed silly to their contemporaries. The confusion in early socialist thought reflected its pioneering nature. The social and economic conditions being analyzed were new, and the exact problems to be solved still had to be defined. The early socialists generally applauded the new productive capacity of industrialism, but they denied that the free market could adequately produce and distribute goods in the fashion claimed by the classical economists. The socialists saw primarily mismanagement, low wages, maldistribution of goods, and suffering arising from the unregulated industrial system. Moreover the socialists thought that human society should be organized as a community rather than merely as a conglomerate of atomistic, selfish individuals.

UTOPIAN SOCIALISM. Among the earliest people to define the social question were a group of writers called the *utopian socialists* by their later critics. They were considered utopian because their ideas were often visionary and because they frequently advocated the creation of ideal communities. They were called *socialists* because they questioned the structures and values of the existing capitalistic framework. In some cases they actually deserved neither description.

Count Claude Henri de Saint-Simon (1760–1825), was the earliest of the socialist pioneers. As a young liberal French aristocrat he had fought in the American Revolution. Later he welcomed the French Revolution, during which he made and lost a fortune. By the time of Napoleon's ascendancy he had turned to a career of writing and social criticism. Saint-Simon believed that history oscillated between organic and critical periods. During organic periods, such as the Middle Ages, order, harmony, and shared values prevailed. During critical periods, such as the Reformation, the structures, values, and customs of a society underwent severe criticism and disintegration. He saw the late eighteenth and early nineteenth centuries as a critical age. He hoped to set forth a body of ideas and to organize a group of disciples that could project a social blueprint for the inevitable new organic period.

Above all else Saint-Simon believed that modern society would require rational management. Private wealth, property, and enterprise should be subject to an administration other than that of its owners. His ideal government would have consisted of a large board of directors organizing and coordinating the activity of individuals and groups to achieve social harmony. In a sense he was the ideological father of technocracy. Not the redistribution of wealth but its management by experts would alleviate the poverty and social dislocation of the age. His faith in experts was similar to the Enlightenment *philosophes'* advocacy of political absolutism. Like his eighteenth-century forebears Saint-Simon had little sympathy with democracy. The order and harmony of the new organic age was to come from the genius of great thinkers such as himself. When Saint-Simon died in 1825, he had persuaded only a handful of people that his ideas were correct. Interestingly enough, several of those disciples later became leaders in the French railway industry during the 1850s.

The major British contributor to the early socialist tradition was Robert Owen (1771–1858), a self-made cotton manufacturer. In his early twenties Owen became a partner in one of the largest cotton factories in Britain at New Lanark, Scotland. Owen was a firm believer in the environmentalist psychology of the Enlightenment. If human beings were placed in the correct surroundings, they and their character could be improved. Moreover Owen saw no incompatibility between creating a humane industrial environment and making a good profit. At New Lanark he put his ideas into practice. Workers were provided with good quarters. Recreational possibilities abounded,

A dance recital by the students in the factory school in New Lanark. Robert Owen's industrial community there included free schooling for the children of his workers. [The Mansell Collection]

and the children received an education. There were several churches, although Owen himself was a notorious freethinker on matters of religion and sex. In the factory itself various rewards were given for good work. His plant made a fine profit. Visitors flocked from all over Europe to see what Owen had accomplished through enlightened management.

In numerous articles and pamphlets, as well as in letters to influential people, Owen pleaded for a reorganization of industry based on his own successful model. He envisioned a series of communities shaped like parallelograms in which factory and farm workers might live together and produce their goods in cooperation. During the 1820s Owen sold his New Lanark factory and then went to the United States, where he established the community of New Harmony, Indiana. When quarrels among the members led to the community's failure, he refused to give up his reformist causes. He returned to Britain, where he became the moving force behind the organization of the Grand National Union. This was an attempt to draw all British trade unions into a single body. It collapsed with other labor organizations during the early 1830s. Owen possessed an exaggerated sense of his own impor-

tance and was a difficult person. His version of socialism amounted to little more than old-fashioned paternalism transported to the industrial setting. However, he contributed to the socialist tradition a strong belief in the practicality of cooperative production and proof that industrial production and humane working conditions were compatible.

Charles Fourier (1772–1837) was the French intellectual counterpart of Owen. He was a commercial salesman who never succeeded in attracting the same kind of public attention as Owen. He wrote his books and articles and waited at home each day at noon, hoping to meet a patron who would undertake his program. No one ever arrived to meet him. Fourier believed that the industrial order ignored the passionate side of human nature. Social discipline ignored all the pleasures that human beings naturally seek. Fourier advocated the construction of communities, called *phalanxes*, in which liberated living would replace the boredom and dullness of industrial existence. Agrarian rather than industrial production would predominate in these communities. Sexual activity would be relatively free, and marriage was to be reserved only for later life. Fourier also urged that no person be re-

Friedrich Engels Describes the Plight of English Workers

As the most industrially advanced country, England offered a vast object lesson for study by social critics like Karl Marx and Friedrich Engels. Engels had visited England, where his father owned a factory. At age twenty-five he already believed that the major difficulty confronting industrial workers was the almost total lack of security in their lives. They seemed to be the victims of chance and of the economic interests of the middle class.

Insecurity is even more demoralising than poverty. English wage-earners live from hand to mouth, and this is the distinguishing mark of their proletarian status. The lower ranks of the German peasantry are largely filled with men who are also poor, and often suffer want, but they are less subject to that sort of distress which is due solely to chance. They do at least enjoy some measure of security. But the proletarian is in quite a different position. He possesses nothing but his two hands and he consumes to-day what he earned yesterday. His future is at the mercy of chance. He has not the slightest guarantee that his skill will in the future enable him to earn even the bare necessities of life. Every commercial crisis, every whim of his master, can throw him out of work. He is placed in the most revolting and inhuman position imaginable. A slave is at least assured of his daily bread by the self-interest of his master. . . . . Slaves and serfs are both guaranteed a basic minimum existence.

The proletarian on the other hand is thrown wholly upon his own resources, and yet at the same time is placed in such a position that he cannot be sure that he can always use those resources to gain a livelihood for himself and his family. Everything that the factory worker can do to try and improve his position vanishes like a drop in the bucket in face of the flood of chance occurrences to which he is exposed and over which he has not the slightest control. He is the passive sufferer from every possible combination of mishaps, and can regard himself as fortunate if he keeps his head above water even for a short time. . . . He may fight for survival in this whirlpool; he may try to maintain his dignity as a human being. This he can do only by fighting the middle classes, who exploit him so ruthlessly and then condemn him to a fate which drives him to live in a way unworthy of a human being.

Friedrich Engels, *The Condition of the Working Class in England*, trans. by W. O. Henderson and W. H. Chaloner (Stanford, Calif.: Stanford University Press, 1970), p. 131.

larger and larger, smaller middle-class units would be squeezed out by the competitive pressures. Competition among the few remaining giant concerns would lead to more intense suffering on the part of the proletariat. As the workers suffered increasingly from the competition among the ever-enlarging firms, they would eventually begin to foment revolution and finally overthrow the few remaining owners of the means of production. For a time the workers would organize the means of production through a dictatorship of the proletariat, which would eventually give way to a propertyless and classless communist society.

This proletarian revolution was inevitable, according to Marx and Engels. The structure of capitalism required competition and consolidation of enterprise. Although the class conflict involved in the contemporary process resembled that of the past, it differed in one major respect. The struggle between the capitalistic bourgeoisie and the industrial proletariat would culminate in a wholly new society that would be free of class conflict. The victorious proletariat, by its very nature, could not be a new oppressor class: "The proletarian movement is the self-conscious, independent movement of the immense majority, in the interest of the immense majority."[4] The result of the

[4]Robert C. Tucker (Ed.), *The Marx–Engels Reader* (New York: W. W. Norton, 1972), p. 353.

proletarian victory would be "an association, in which the free development of each is the condition for the free development of all."[5] The victory of the proletariat over the bourgeoisie would represent the culmination of human history. For the first time in human history one group of people would not be oppressing another.

Marx's analysis was conditioned by his own economic environment. The 1840s had been a period of much unemployment and deprivation. However, capitalism did not collapse as he had predicted, nor did the middle class during the rest of the century become proletarianized. Rather, more and more people came to benefit from the industrial system. Nonetheless, within a generation Marxism had captured the imagination of many socialists and large segments of the working class. The doctrines were based on the empirical evidence of hard economic fact. This scientific aspect of Marxism helped the ideology as science became more influential during the second half of the century. Marx had made the ultimate victory of socialism seem certain. His writings had also portrayed, for the first time, the actual magnitude of the revolutionary transformation. His works also suggested that the path to socialism lay with revolution rather than with reform. The days of the utopians were over.

1848: Year of Revolutions

In 1848 a series of liberal and nationalistic revolutions spread across the Continent. No single factor caused this general revolutionary ground swell; rather, a number of similar conditions existed in several countries. Severe food shortages had prevailed since 1846. The harvests of grain and potatoes had been very poor. The famine in Ireland was simply the worst example of a more widespread situation. The commercial and industrial economy was also in a period of downturn. Unemployment was very widespread. All systems of poor relief were overburdened. These difficulties, added to the wretched living conditions in the cities, heightened the sense of frustration and discontent of the urban artisan and laboring classes.

However, the dynamic force for change in 1848 originated not with the working classes but with the political liberals, who were generally drawn from the middle classes. Through-

[5]Ibid.

out the Continent liberals were pushing for their program of more representative government, civil liberty, and unregulated economic life. The repeal of the English Corn Laws and the example of peaceful agitation by the Anti-Corn Law League encouraged them. The liberals on the Continent wanted to pursue similar peaceful tactics. However, to put additional pressure on their governments, they began to appeal for the support of the urban working classes. The goals of the latter were improved working and economic conditions rather than a liberal framework of government. Moreover the tactics of the working classes were frequently violent rather than peaceful. The temporary alliance of liberals and workers in several states overthrew or severely shook the old order; then the allies commenced to fight each other.

Finally, outside France nationalism was an important common factor in the uprisings. Germans, Hungarians, Italians, and smaller national groups in eastern Europe sought to create national states that would reorganize or replace existing political entities. The Austrian Empire, as usual, was the state most profoundly endangered by nationalism. The nationalists were also frequently liberal and sometimes benefited from lower- and working-class economic discontent in the major cities.

The immediate results of the 1848 revolutions were quite stunning. The French monarchy fell, and many of the others were badly shaken. Never in a single year had Europe known so many major uprisings. Yet the revolutions proved a false spring for progressive Europeans. Without exception they failed to establish genuinely liberal or national states. The conservative order proved stronger and more resilient than anyone had expected. Moreover the liberal middle-class political malcontents in each country discovered that they could no longer push for political reform without at the same time raising the social question. The liberals refused to follow political revolution with social reform and thus isolated themselves from the working classes. Once separated from potential mass support, the liberal revolutions became an easy prey to the armies of the reactionary classes.

France: The Second Republic and Louis Napoleon

As twice before, the revolutionary tinder first blazed in Paris. The liberal political opponents of the corrupt regime of Louis Philippe and his minister Guizot had organized a series of political banquets. These occasions were used to criticize the government and to demand further middle-class admission to the political process. The poor harvests of 1846 and 1847 and the resulting high food prices and unemployment brought working-class support to the liberal campaign. On February 21, 1848, the government forbade further banquets. A very large one had been scheduled for the next day. On February 22 disgruntled Parisian workers paraded through the streets demanding reform and Guizot's ouster. The next morning the crowds grew, and by afternoon Guizot had resigned. The crowds had erected barricades, and numerous clashes had occurred between the citizenry and the municipal guard. On February 24, 1848, Louis Philippe abdicated and fled to England.

The liberal opposition, led by the poet Alphonse de Lamartine (1790–1869), organized a provisional government. They intended to call an election for an assembly that would write a republican constitution. The various working-class groups in Paris had other ideas; they wanted a social as well as a political revolution. Led by Louis Blanc, they demanded

---

Paris Workers Complain About the Actions of Their Government

In the late spring of 1848 the government of the recently formed French Republic abolished the national workshops that it had created a few weeks earlier to provide aid for the unemployed. The first selection below illustrates the anger caused by the abolition of the workshops and the sense of betrayal felt by the workers. The second document describes the experience of a cabinetmaker who had for a time enrolled in one of the workshops.

TO THE FINANCE MINISTER OF THE REPUBLIC

Are you really the man who was the first finance minister of the Republic, of the Republic won at the cost of blood thanks to the workers' courage, of this Republic whose first vow was to provide bread every day for all its children by proclaiming the universal right to work? Work, who will give it to us if not the state at a time when industry has everywhere closed its workshops, shops and factories? Yesterday martyrs for the Republic out on the barricades, today its defenders in the ranks of the national guard, the workers might consider it owed them something. . . .

Why do the national workshops so rouse your reprobation . . . ? You are not asking for their reform, but for their total abolition. But what is to be done with this mass of 110,000 workers who are waiting each day for their modest pay, for the means of existence for themselves and their families? Are they to be left a prey to the evil influences of hunger and of the excesses that follow in the wake of despair?

A LETTER TO A NEWSPAPER EDITOR

I live in the fauborg [working class neighborhood]; by trade I am a cabinet-maker and I am enrolled in the national workshops, waiting for trade to pick up again.

I went into the workshops when I could no longer find bread elsewhere. Since then people have said we were given charity there. But when I went in I did not think that I was becoming a beggar. I believed that my brothers who were rich were giving me a little of what they had to spare simply because I was their brother.

I admit that I have not worked very hard in the national workshops, but then I have done what I could. I am too old now to change my trade easily—that is one explanation. But there is another: the fact is that, in the national workshops, there is absolutely nothing to do.

Roger Price (Ed. and Trans.), *1848 in France* (Ithaca, N.Y.: Cornell University Press, 1975), pp. 103–104.

representation in the Cabinet. Blanc and two other radical leaders were made ministers. Under their pressure the provisional government organized national workshops to provide work and relief for thousands of unemployed workers.

On Sunday, April 23, an election based on universal manhood suffrage chose the new National Assembly. The result was a legislature dominated by moderates and conservatives. In the French provinces there had been much resentment against the Paris radicals. The church and the local notables still exercised considerable influence. Small landowning peasants feared possible confiscation of their holdings by Parisian socialists. The new conservative National Assembly had little sympathy for the very expensive national workshops, which they incorrectly perceived to be socialistic. Throughout May government troops and the Parisian crowd of unemployed workers and artisans clashed. As a result, the assembly closed the workshops to new entrants and

planned the removal of many enrolled workers. By the latter part of June barricades again appeared in Paris. On June 24, under orders from the government, General Cavaignac, with troops drawn largely from the conservative countryside, moved to destroy the barricades and to quell potential disturbances. During the next two days over four hundred people were killed. Thereafter troops hunted down another three thousand persons in street-to-street fighting. The drive for social revolution had come to an end.

The so-called June Days confirmed the political predominance of conservative property holders in French life. They wanted a republic, but a republic safe for small property. This search for social order received further confirmation late in 1848. The victor in the presidential election was Louis Napoleon Bonaparte (1808–1873), a nephew of the great emperor. For most of his life he had been an adventurer living outside France. Twice he had unsuccessfully attempted to lead a *coup* against the July

Government troops capture the National Assembly building from the insurgents during the June Days in Paris in 1848. [New York Public Library]

De Tocqueville Analyzes the June Revolution in Paris

Alexis de Tocqueville (1805–1859) was a French liberal politician, historian, and political scientist and also a keen social observer. By the time of the 1848 uprising in Paris, he had lived two years in the United States in the 1830s; *Democracy in America* is still an important analysis of our early institutions. In this passage from his memoirs he described the manner in which the conflict of the June Days of 1848 in Paris differed from earlier political upheavals in France. He understood that what had occurred was a mode of class warfare and that it might characterize European political life for many decades to come.

I come at last to the insurrection of June. . . .

What distinguished it also, among all the events of this kind which have succeeded one another in France for sixty years, is that it did not aim at changing the form of government, but at altering the order of society. . . . It was not, strictly speaking, a political struggle, in the sense which until then we have given to the word, but a combat of class against class, a sort of Servile War. It represented the facts of the Revolution of February in the same manner as the theories of Socialism represented its ideas; or rather it issued naturally from these ideas, as a son does from his mother. We beheld in it nothing more than a blind and rude, but powerful, effort on the part of the workmen to escape from the necessities of their condition, which had been depicted to them as one of unlawful oppression, and to open up by main force a road towards

that imaginary comfort with which they had been deluded. It was this mixture of greed and false theory which first gave birth to the insurrection and then made it so formidable. These poor people had been told that the wealth of the rich was in some way the product of a theft practised upon themselves. They had been assured that the inequality of fortunes was as opposed to morality and the welfare of society as it was to nature. Prompted by their needs and their passions, many had believed this obscure and erroneous notion of right, which, mingled with brute force, imparted to the latter an energy, a tenacity and a power which it would never have possessed unaided.

It must be observed that this formidable insurrection was not the enterprise of a certain number of conspirators, but the revolt of one whole section of the population against another.

Alexis de Tocqueville, *Recollections*, trans. by A. T. de Mattos (New York: Macmillan, 1896), pp. 187–188.

Monarchy. The disorder of 1848 provided him a new opportunity to enter the French political scene. After the corruption of Louis Philippe and the turmoil of the early months of the Second Republic, the voters turned to the name of Bonaparte as a source of stability and greatness.

The election of the "Little Napoleon" doomed the Second Republic. Louis Napoleon was dedicated to his own fame rather than to republican institutions. He was the first of the modern dictators who, by playing on unstable politics and social insecurity, have so changed European life. He constantly quarreled with the National Assembly and claimed that he rather than they represented the will of the nation. In 1851 the assembly refused to amend the constitution to allow the president to succeed himself. Consequently, on December 2, 1851, the anniversary of the great Napoleon's victory at Austerlitz, Louis Napoleon seized personal power. Troops dispersed the assembly, and the president called for new elections. Over 200 people died resisting the *coup*, and over 26,000 persons were arrested throughout the country. Almost 10,000 persons who opposed the *coup* were transported to Algeria. Yet, in the plebiscite of December 21, 1851, over 7.5 million voters supported the actions of Louis Napoleon and approved a new constitution that consolidated his power. Only about 600,000 citizens dared to vote against him. A year later, in December 1852, an Empire was proclaimed, and Louis Napoleon became Emperor Napoleon III. Again a plebiscite approved the action. For the second time in just over fifty years France had turned from republicanism to caesarism.

The Habsburg Empire: Nationalism Resisted

The events of February 1848 in Paris immediately reverberated throughout the Habsburg domains. The empire was susceptible to revolutionary challenge on every score. Its government rejected liberal institutions. Its geographical borders disregarded the principle of nationalism. Its society perpetuated serfdom. During the 1840s even Metternich had urged reform, but none was forthcoming. In 1848 the regime confronted major rebellions in Vienna, Prague, Hungary, and Italy. It was also intimately involved in the disturbances that broke out in Germany.

The Habsburg troubles began on March 3, 1848, when Louis Kossuth (1802–1894), a Magyar nationalist, attacked Austrian domination of Hungary. He called for the independence of Hungary and a responsible ministry under the crown of Habsburg. Ten days later, inspired by Kossuth's demands, students led a series of major disturbances in Vienna. The army failed to restore order. Metternich resigned and fled the country. The feeble-minded Emperor Ferdinand (1835–1848) promised a moderately liberal constitution. Unsatisfied, the radical students then formed democratic clubs to press the revolution further. On May 17 the emperor and the imperial court fled to Innsbruck. The government of Vienna at this point lay in the hands of a committee of over two hundred persons primarily concerned with alleviating the economic plight of Viennese workers.

What the Habsburg government most feared was not the urban rebellions but a potential uprising of the serfs. Already there had been isolated instances of serfs invading manor houses and burning records. Almost immediately after the Vienna uprising, the imperial government had emancipated the serfs in large areas of Austria. The Hungarian Diet also abolished serfdom in March 1848. These actions smothered the most serious potential threat to order in the empire. The emancipated serfs now had little reason to support the revolutionary movement in the cities.

The Vienna revolt had further encouraged the Hungarians. The leaders of the Hungarian March revolution were primarily liberal Magyars supported by Magyar nobles who wanted their aristocratic liberties guaranteed against

A caricature in the flight of Metternich in March 1848. Although he had advocated limited reform of the Austrian government during the 1840s, Metternich in the eyes of the people was the symbol of reaction. His fall evoked great popular rejoicing. [Culver Pictures]

the central government in Vienna. The Hungarian Diet passed a series of March Laws that ensured equality of religion, jury trials, the election of a lower chamber, a relatively free press, and payment of taxes by the nobility. Emperor Ferdinand approved these measures because in the spring of 1848 he was in a position to do little else.

The Magyars also hoped to establish a separate Hungarian state within the Habsburg domains. They would retain considerable local autonomy while Ferdinand remained their emperor. As part of this scheme for a partially independent state, the Hungarians attempted to annex Transylvania, Croatia, and other territories on the eastern border of the Habsburg empire. That policy of annexation would bring

751

of a strong, unified state on their southern border. Moreover protection of the pope was good domestic politics for the French Republic and its president, Louis Napoleon. In early June 1849 ten thousand French soldiers laid siege to the Eternal City. By the end of the month the Roman Republic had dissolved. Garibaldi attempted to lead an army north against Austria but was defeated. On July 3 Rome fell to the French forces, which continued to occupy it as protection for the pope until 1870. Pius IX returned, having renounced his previous liberalism. He became one of the archconservatives of the next quarter century. Leadership toward Italian unification would have to come from another direction.

Germany: Liberalism Frustrated

The revolutionary contagion had also spread rapidly through numerous states of Germany. Württemberg, Saxony, Hanover, and Bavaria all experienced insurrections calling for liberal government and greater German unity. The major revolution, however, occurred in Prussia. By March 15, 1848, large popular disturbances had erupted in Berlin. Frederick William IV (1840–1861), believing that the trouble stemmed from foreign conspirators, refused to turn his troops on the Berliners. He even announced certain limited reforms. Nevertheless, on March 18, several citizens were killed when troops cleared a square near the palace. The monarch was still hesitant to use his troops forcefully, and there was much confusion in the government. The king also called for a Prussian constituent assembly to write a constitution. The next day, as angry Berliners crowded around the palace, Frederick William IV appeared on the balcony to salute the corpses of his slain subjects. He made further concessions and implied that henceforth Prussia would aid the movement toward German unification. For all practical purposes the Prussian monarchy had capitulated.

Frederick William IV appointed a cabinet headed by David Hansemann (1790–1864), a widely respected moderate liberal. However, the Prussian constituent assembly proved to be radical and democratic. As time passed, the king and his conservative supporters decided that they would ignore the assembly. The liberal ministry resigned and was replaced by a conservative one. In April 1849 the assembly was dissolved, and the monarch proclaimed his own constitution. One of its key elements was a system of three-class voting. All adult males were allowed to vote. However, they voted according to three classes arranged by ability to pay taxes. Thus the largest taxpayers, who constituted only about 5 per cent of the population, elected one third of the Prussian Parliament. This system prevailed in Prussia until 1918. In the finally revised Prussian constitution of 1850, the ministry was responsible to the king alone. Moreover, the Prussian army and officer corps swore loyalty directly to the monarch.

While Prussia was moving from revolution to reaction, other events were unfolding in Germany as a whole. On May 18, 1848, representatives from all the German states gathered in Saint Paul's Church in Frankfurt to revise the organization of the German Confederation. The Frankfurt Parliament intended to write a moderately liberal constitution for a united Germany. The liberal character of the Frankfurt Parliament alienated both German conservatives and the German working class. The offense to the conservatives was simply the challenge to the existing political order. The Frankfurt Parliament lost the support of the industrial workers and artisans by refusing to restore the protection once afforded by the guilds. The liberals were too much attached to the concept of a free labor market to offer meaningful legislation to workers. This failure marked the beginning of a profound split between German liberals and the German working class. For the rest of the century Germany conservatives would be able to play on that division.

As if to demonstrate its disaffection from workers, in September 1848 the Frankfurt Parliament called in troops of the German Confederation to suppress a radical insurrection in the city. The liberals in the parliament wanted nothing to do with workers who erected barricades and threatened the safety of property.

The Frankfurt Parliament floundered on the issue of unification as well as on the social question. Members differed over the inclusion of Austria in the projected united Germany. The large German (*grossdeutsch*) solution favored inclusion, whereas the small German (*kleindeutsch*) solution advocated exclusion. The latter formula prevailed because Austria rejected the whole notion of German unification. It raised too many other nationality problems within the Habsburg domains. Consequently the Frankfurt Parliament looked to Prussian leadership. On March 27, 1849, the

The Frankfurt Parliament met in a church in that city in September 1848. Its deputies wanted to create a liberal, united Germany. However, as their debate dragged out, the forces of reaction regained strength and the parliament failed. [Bettmann Archive]

parliament produced its constitution. Shortly thereafter its delegates offered the crown of a united Germany to Federick William IV of Prussia. He rejected the offer, asserting that kings ruled by the grace of God rather than by the wisdom of man-made constitutions. On his refusal the Frankfurt Parliament began to dissolve. Not long afterwards troops drove off the remaining members.

German liberals never fully recovered from this defeat. The Frankfurt Parliament had alienated the artisans and the working class without gaining any compensating support from the conservatives. The liberals had proved themselves to be awkward, hesitant, unrealistic, and ultimately dependent on the armies of the monarchies. They had failed to unite Ger-

many or to confront effectively the realities of political power in the German states. What was achieved through the various revolutions was an extension of the franchise in some of the German states and the establishment of conservative constitutions. The gains were not negligible, but they were a far cry from the hopes of March 1848.

The events of 1848 and 1849 had one important footnote for Frederick William IV. He gave much more thought to possible German unification under Prussia. In 1850 he attempted to create a German federation, which would have been a union of princes headed by the king of Prussia and excluding Austria. The Austrian Empire firmly rejected the proposal, which would have diminished Habsburg influ-

THE REVOLUTIONARY CRISIS OF 1848–1851

1848

Revolution in Paris forces the abdication of Louis Philippe	February 22–24
National workshops established in Paris	February 26
Kossuth attacks the Habsburg domination of Hungary	March 3
Revolution in Vienna	March 13
The Habsburg emperor accepts the Hungarian March Laws	March 15
Revolution in Berlin	
Frederick William IV of Prussia promises a constitution	March 18
Revolution in Milan	
Frederick William IV is forced to salute the corpses of slain revolutionaries in Berlin	March 19
Piedmont declares war on Austria	March 22
Election of the French National Assembly	April 23
Worker protests in Paris lead the National Assembly to close the national workshops	May 15
Habsburg Emperor Ferdinand flees from Vienna to Innsbruck	May 17
The Frankfurt Assembly gathers to prepare a German constitution	May 18
A Czech revolution in Prague is suppressed	June 17
A workers' insurrection in Paris is suppressed by the troops of the National Assembly	June 23–26
Austria defeats Piedmont	July 24
General Jellachich invades Hungary	September 17
Vienna falls to the bombardment of General Windisch-Graetz	October 31
Papal minister Rossi is assassinated in Rome	November 15

Revolution in Rome	November 16
Pope Pius IX flees Rome	November 25
Habsburg Emperor Ferdinand abdicates and Francis Joseph becomes emperor	December 2
Louis Napoleon is elected president of the Second French Republic	December 10

1849

General Windisch-Graetz occupies Budapest	January 5
The Roman Republic is proclaimed	February 2
War is resumed between Piedmont and Austria	March 12
Piedmont is defeated, and Charles Albert abdicates the crown of Piedmont in favor of Victor Emmanuel II	March 23
The Frankfurt Parliament completes a constitution for Germany	March 27
The Frankfurt Parliament elects Frederick William IV of Prussia to be emperor of Germany	March 28
Frederick William IV of Prussia rejects the crown offered by the Frankfurt Parliament	April 21
The remaining members of the Frankfurt Parliament are dispersed by troops	June 18
Collapse of the Roman Republic after invasion by French troops	July 3
The Hungarian forces are defeated by Austria aided by the troops of Russia	August 9–13

1850

The Punctation of Olmütz	November 29

1851

Coup d'état of Louis Napoleon	December 2

The King of Prussia Declines the Crown Offered by the Frankfurt Parliament

In the spring of 1849 the Frankfurt Parliament completed the writing of a constitution for a united Germany that would exclude Austria. The Parliament offered the crown of a constitutional German monarchy to Frederick William IV of Prussia. He declined the offer. In this letter of May 15, 1849, addressed to the people of Prussia, the monarch explained his reasons and attacked the liberal political thought of the Parliament and the revolutionary events that had allowed it to be called in the first place.

Taking as a pretense the interests of Germany, the enemies of the fatherland have raised the standard of revolt, first in neighboring Saxony, then in several districts of south Germany. To my deep chagrin, even in parts of our own land some have permitted themselves to be seduced into following this standard and attempting, in open rebellion against the legal government, to overturn the order of things established by both divine and human sanction. In so serious and dangerous a crisis I am moved publicly to address a word to my people.

I was not able to return a favorable reply to the offer of a crown on the part of the German National Assembly [the Frankfurt Parliament], because the Assembly has not the right, without the consent of the German governments, to bestow the crown which they tendered me, and moreover, because they offered the crown upon condition that I would accept a constitution which could not be reconciled with the rights and safety of the German states.

I have exhausted every means to reach an understanding with the German National Assembly. . . . Now the Assembly has broken with Prussia. The majority of its members are no longer those men upon whom Germany looked with pride and confidence. The greater part of the deputies voluntarily left the Assembly when they saw that it was on the road to ruin, and yesterday I ordered all the Prussian deputies who had not already withdrawn to be recalled. The other governments [of the several German states] will do the same.

A party now dominates the Assembly which is in league with the terrorists. While they urge the unity of Germany as a pretense, they are really fighting the battle of godlessness, perjury, and robbery, and kindling a war against monarchy; but if monarchy were overthrown, it would carry with it the blessings of law, liberty, and property. . . .

James Harvey Robinson (Ed.), *Readings in European History* (Boston: Ginn and Co., 1906), pp. 571–572.

ence in Germany. In November 1850, in what is known as the Punctation of Olmütz, the Prussian monarch renounced his scheme at the demand of Austria. Prussian historians later called this event the Humiliation of Olmütz.

The turmoil of 1848 through 1850 brought to a close the era of liberal revolution that had begun in 1789. Liberals and nationalists had discovered that rational argument and small insurrections would not achieve their goals. The political initiative passed for a time to the conservative political groups. Nationalists henceforth were less romantic and more hardheaded. Railways, commerce, guns, soldiers, and devious diplomacy rather than language and cultural heritage became the weapons of national unification. The working class also adopted new tactics and organization. The era of the riot and urban insurrection was coming to a close. In the future, workers would turn to trade unions and political parties to achieve their political and social goals. Perhaps most important after 1848 the European middle class ceased to be revolutionary. It became increasingly concerned about the protection of its property against radical political and social movements. The middle class remained politically liberal only as long as liberalism seemed to promise economic stability and social security for its own style of life.

Suggested Readings

S. A v i n e r i, *The Social and Political Thought of Karl Marx* (1969). An advanced treatment.

I. B e r l i n, *Karl Marx: His Life and Environment* (1948). An excellent introduction.

A. B r i g g s (Ed.), *Chartist Studies* (1959). An anthology of significant essays.

S. G. C h e c k l a n d, *The Rise of Industrial Society in England, 1815–1885* (1964). Strong on economic institutions.

G. D. H. C o l e, *A History of Socialist Thought*, 5 vols. (1953–1960). An essential work that spans the entire nineteenth century.

W. C o l e m a n, *Death Is a Social Disease: Public Health and Political Economy in Early Industrial France* (1982). One of the first works in English to study this problem.

I. D e a k, *The Lawful Revolution: Louis Kossuth and the Hungarians, 1848–1849* (1979). The most significant study of the topic in English.

G. D u v e a u, *The Making of a Revolution* (trans., 1968). A lively book that explores the attitudes of the various French social classes.

E. H a l é v y, *The Growth of Philosophic Radicalism* (1928). The basic discussion of utilitarianism.

T. H a m e r o w, *Restoration, Revolution, and Reaction: Economics and Politics in Germany, 1815–1871* (1958). Traces the forces that worked toward the failure of revolution in Germany.

J. F. C. H a r r i s o n, *Quest for the New Moral World: Robert Owen and the Owenites in Britain and America* (1969). Now the standard work.

R. H e i l b r o n e r, *The Worldly Philosophers*, rev. ed. (1972). A useful, elementary introduction to nineteenth-century economic thought.

W. O. H e n d e r s o n, *The Industrialization of Europe, 1780–1914* (1969). Emphasizes the Continent.

G. H i m m e l f a r b, *The Idea of Poverty: England in the Early Industrial Age* (1984). A major work covering the subject from the time of Adam Smith through 1850.

M. I g n a t i e f f, *A Just Measure of Pain: The Penitentiary in the Industrial Revolution, 1750–1850* (1978). An important treatment of early English penal thought and practice.

K. K o l a k o w s k i, *Main Currents of Marxism: Its Rise, Growth, and Dissolution*, 3 vols. (1978). A very important and comprehensive survey.

D. L a n d e s, *The Unbound Prometheus: Technological Change and Industrial Development in Western Europe from 1750 to the Present* (1969). The best one-volume treatment of technological development in a broad social and economic context.

W. L. L a n g e r, *Political and Social Upheaval, 1832–1852* (1969). A remarkably thorough survey strong in both social and intellectual history as well as political narrative.

F. M a n u e l, *The Prophets of Paris* (1962). A stimulating treatment of French utopian socialism and social reform.

T. W. M a r g a d a n t, *French Peasants in Revolt: The Insurrection of 1851* (1979). A study of the rural resistance to Louis Napoleon.

J. M. M e r r i m a n, *The Agony of the Republic: The Repression of the Left in Revolutionary France, 1848–1851* (1978). A major study of the manner in which the Second French Republic and popular support for it were suppressed.

J. M. M e r r i m a n (Ed.), *Consciousness and Class Experience in Nineteenth-Century Europe* (1979). A collection of important revisionist essays in social and intellectual history covering topics across the Continent.

P. O'B r i e n, *The Promise of Punishment: Prisons in Nineteenth-Century France* (1982). An excellent treatment of the problems of life within the prison.

H. P e r k i n, *The Origins of Modern English Society, 1780–1880* (1969). A provocative attempt to look at the society as a whole.

D. P h i l i p s, *Crime and Authority in Victorian England: The Black Country 1835–1860* (1977). One of the few works to examine the problem in an industrial setting.

I. P i n c h b e c k, *Women Workers and the Industrial Revolution, 1750–1850* (1930, reprinted 1969). A pioneering study that remains of great value.

D. R o b e r t s, *Paternalism in Early Victorian England* (1979). An interesting study of the paternalistic response to early ninteenth-century social problems.

P. R o b e r t s o n, *Revolutions of 1848: A Social History* (1952). Covers the developments of each nation.

P. R o b e r t s o n, *An Experience of Women: Pattern and Change in Nineteenth-Century Europe* (1982). A useful survey.

W. H. S e w e l l, J r., *Work and Revolution in France: The Language of Labor from the Old Regime to 1848* (1980). A very fine analysis of French artisans.

N. S m e l z e r, *Social Change in the Industrial Revolution: An Application of Theory to the British Cotton Industry* (1959). Important sections on the working-class family.

P. S t e a r n s, *Eighteen Forty-Eight: the Tide of Revolution in Europe* (1974). A good discussion of the social background.

G. D. S u s s m a n, *Selling Mother's Milk: The Wetnursing Business in France, 1715–1914* (1982). An examination of an important subject in the history of the family and of women.

A. J. T a y l o r (Ed.), *The Standard of Living in Britain in the Industrial Revolution* (1975). A collection of major articles on the impact of industrialism.

D. T h o m p s o n, *The Chartists: Popular Politics in the Industrial Revolution* (1984). An important new study.

E. P. T h o m p s o n, *The Making of the English Working Class* (1964). An important, influential, and controversial work.

L. A. T i l l y and J. W. S c o t t, *Women, Work, and Family* (1978). A useful and sensitive survey.

A. S. W o h l, *Endangered Lives: Public Health in Victorian Britain (1983). An important and wide-ranging examination of the health problems created by urbanization and industrialization.

C. WOODHAM-SMITH, The Great Hunger: Ireland, 1845–1849 (1962). A moving account of one of the great social tragedies of the nineteenth century.

G. WRIGHT, Between the Guillotine and Liberty: Two Centuries of the Crime Problem in France (1983). A useful overview.

H. ZEHR, Crime and the Development of Modern Society: Patterns of Criminality in Nineteenth-Century Germany and France (1976). An examination of crimes against property in urban society.

Toward the Modern World

he century between approximately 1850 and 1945 may quite properly be regarded as the European era of world history. The nations of Europe achieved and exercised an unprecedented measure of political, economic, and military power across the globe. No less impressive than the vastness of this influence was its brevity. By 1945, much of Europe, from Britain to the Soviet Union, literally lay in ruins. Within a few years, the United States and the Soviet Union would emerge as superpowers with whom no European state could compete. Furthermore, nations throughout Asia, Africa, and Latin America that had once experienced direct or indirect European rule would thrust off their colonial status. Both the rise and the decline of European world dominance fostered violence, warfare, and human exploitation all over the globe.

The half century after 1850 witnessed political consolidation and economic expansion that paved the way for the momentary dominance of Europe. The skillful diplomats and armies of the conservative monarchies of Piedmont and Prussia united Italy and Germany by military force. As a major new political and economic power in central Europe, Germany loomed as a potential rival to Great Britain, France, and Russia. For a time, shrewd diplomacy and a series of complex alliances contained that rivalry. At the same time, while sorting out the new power relationships on the continent, the nations of Europe exported potential conflicts overseas. The result of this externalized rivalry was a period of imperialistic ventures. By the turn of the century these had resulted in the outright partition of Africa into areas directly governed by Europeans and in the penetration of China by European merchants, administrators, and missionaries.

What permitted this unprecedented situation to arise was the economic and technological base of late-nineteenth-century European civilization. Europeans possessed the productive capacity to dominate world markets. Their banks controlled or influenced vast amounts of capital throughout the world economy. Their engineers constructed and later often managed railways on all the continents. Their military technology, especially their navies, allowed Europeans to back up economic power with armed force.

Simultaneously with the expansion of industrial power new political ideologies came to the fore in Europe. Across the continent socialists challenged the ideology of liberalism and spawned internal disputes that have influenced European political life to the present day. Nationalism was the other dominant political ideology whose supporters challenged the legitimacy of any political arrangement that failed to recognize a politics based on ethnicity. Nowhere was nationalism a more troubling force than in the multinational Habsburg Empire.

In 1914 the more general situation of European dominance came to an abrupt end when war growing out of imperialistic and nationalistic rivalry erupted among the major states of Europe. That conflict may be regarded as the central event of the twentieth century. Its effects continue to influence the world today. The Austro-Hungarian monarchy collapsed. Germany became a republic. The revolutionary socialist government of the Bolsheviks replaced the imperial government of the Russian czars.

Social turmoil and economic dislocation accompanied the political revolutions. The victorious nations of Britain, France, and Italy had been bled white of young men, and much of their wealth had been exhausted by wartime expenditures. The military and financial participation of the United States blocked the establishment of independent economic policy by the European powers. Ongoing nationalistic resentments fostered by the Paris Peace Settlement of 1919, in combination with the political and economic pressures of the 1920s and 1930s, created conditions from which arose the authoritarian movements of Italian Fascism and German Nazism. By 1939 the aggression of Germany and the hesitant response of the other major powers led again to the outbreak of war in Europe. From that conflict, Europe failed to reemerge as the dominant political or economic force in the world.

Two other developments also contributed to the end of the European era of world history. First, the principle of national self-determination applied to Europeans in the 1919 settlement was adopted by colonial peoples seeking to assert their own right to national independence. Second, the demand for self-determination soon became linked to criticism of the foreign capitalistic domination of colonial economic life. The latter development flowed directly from the spread of communist ideas throughout the colonial world after the Russian Revolution. In this respect, the ideologies of nationalism and revolutionary socialism developed by Europeans in the nineteenth century to solve certain problems in their own political and economic life were turned against them as peoples in Asia, Africa, and Latin America sought to solve their own political problems in the mid-twentieth century.

Napoleon III (1852–1870) was the most influential European ruler of the mid-nineteenth century. Although his regime ended in military defeat, its economic policies led to a rapid expansion of French industry and trade. (Lauros-Giraudon)

THE REVOLUTIONS of 1848 collapsed in defeat for both liberalism and nationalism. Throughout the early 1850s authoritarian regimes entrenched themselves across the Continent. Yet only a quarter century later many of the major goals of early-nineteenth-century liberals and nationalists stood accomplished. Italy and Germany were each at long last united under constitutional monarchies. The Habsburg emperor had accepted constitutional government; the Hungarian Magyars had attained recognition of their liberties. In Russia the serfs had been emancipated. France was again a republic. Liberalism and even democracy flourished in Great Britain.

Paradoxically most of these developments occurred under the direction and leadership of conservative leaders. Events within European international affairs compelled some of them to pursue new policies at home as well as abroad. They had to find novel methods of maintaining the loyalty of their subjects. In some cases conservative leaders preferred to carry out a popular policy on their own terms so that they, rather than the liberals, would receive credit. Finally, some political leaders moved as they did because they had no choice.

The Crimean War (1854–1856)

As has so often been true in modern European history, the impetus for change originated in war. The Crimean War (1854–1856) was rooted in the long-standing rivalry between Russia and the Ottoman Empire. There were two disputes that led to the conflict. First, the Ottoman Empire had recently granted Catholic France rather than Orthodox Russia the oversight of the Christian shrines in the Holy Land. Second, Russia wanted to extend its control over the Ottoman provinces of Moldavia and Walachia (now in Romania). The czar's duty to protect Orthodox Christians in the Ottoman Empire furnished the pretext for the Russian aggression. Russia occupied the two provinces in the summer of 1853. The Ottoman Empire declared war on Russia in the autumn of that year. The other great powers soon became involved, and a war among major European states resulted. Both France and Great Britain opposed Russian expansion in the eastern Mediterranean, where they had extensive naval and commercial interests. Napoleon III also thought that an activist foreign policy would shore up domestic support for his re-

22

The Age of Nation-States

OPPOSITE: *The Crimean War (1854–1856) was the first major military conflict recorded by photography. The British photographer Roger Fenton, who accompanied the expeditionary force to the siege of Sevastopol, took these pictures of a cavalry camp (above) and of the supply depot at Balaklava (below).*

gime. On March 28, 1854, France and Britain declared war on Russia. Much to the disappointment of Czar Nicholas I, Austria and Prussia remained neutral. The Austrians had their own ambitions in the Balkans, and after the humiliation of Olmütz Prussia followed Austrian leadership for some time.

The war was ineptly waged on both sides. The ill-equipped and poorly commanded armies became bogged down along the Crimean coast of the Black Sea. In September 1855, after a long siege, the Russian fortress of Sevastopol finally fell. In March 1856 a conference in Paris concluded the Treaty of Paris, which was highly unfavorable to Russia. It was required to surrender territory near the mouth of the Danube River, to recognize the neutrality of the Black Sea, and to renounce claims of protection over Christians in the Ottoman Empire. Even before the conference Austria had forced Russia to withdraw from Moldavia and Walachia. The image of an invincible Russia that had prevailed across Europe since the close of the Napoleonic wars was totally shattered.

Also shattered was the Concert of Europe (see Chapter 20) as a means of dealing with international relations on the Continent. There was much less fear of revolution than in the early part of the century and consequently much less reverence for the Vienna settlement. As Gordon Craig commented, "After 1856 there were more powers willing to fight to overthrow the existing order than there were to take up arms to defend it."[1] Napoleon III had little respect for the Congress of Vienna and favored redrawing the map along lines of nationality. The Austrians hoped to compensate for the poor figure they had cut in remaining neutral during the conflict by asserting more influence within the German Confederation. Prussia became increasingly discontented with a role in Germany subordinate to Austria's. Russia, which had been among the chief defenders of the Vienna settlement, now sought to overcome the disgrace of the 1856

Treaty of Paris. The mediocre display of British military prowess led that nation to hesitate about future continental involvement.

Consequently, for about twenty-five years after the Crimean War, instability prevailed in European affairs, allowing a largely unchecked adventurism in foreign policy. Without the restraining influence of the Concert of Europe, each nation believed that only the limits of its military power and its diplomatic influence should act as constraints on its international ambitions. Moreover foreign policy increasingly became an instrument of domestic policy. The two most significant achievements to result from this new international situation were the unifications of Italy and of Germany. Those events, in turn, generated further pressures on neighboring countries.

Italian Unification

Nationalists had long wanted the small, absolutist principalities of the Italian peninsula united into a single state. However, during the first half of the century there had existed broad differences of opinion about the manner and goals of unification.

One approach to the issue had been that of romantic republicans. After the Congress of Vienna numerous secret republican societies were founded, the most famous of which was the *Carbonari* ("charcoal burners"). They were singularly ineffective.

Following the failure of nationalist uprisings in 1831, the leadership of romantic republican nationalism passed to Giuseppe Mazzini (1805–1872). He became the most important nationalist leader in all Europe and brought to the cause of nationalism new emotional fervor. He once declared, "Nationality is the role assigned by God to a people in the work of humanity. It is its mission, its task on earth, to the end that God's thought may be realized in the world."[2] In 1831 he founded the Young Italy Society for the purposes of driving Austria from the peninsula and establishing an Italian republic. During the 1830s and 1840s Mazzini and fellow republican Giuseppe Garibaldi (1807–1882) led insurrections. Both were deeply involved in the ill-fated Roman Republic of 1849. Throughout the next decade they continued to conduct what amounted to guer-

[1]*The New Cambridge Modern History,* Vol. 10 (Cambridge: Cambridge University Press, 1967), p. 273.

[2]Quoted in William L. Langer, *Political and Social Upheaval,* 1832–1852 (New York: Harper Torchbook, 1969), p. 115.

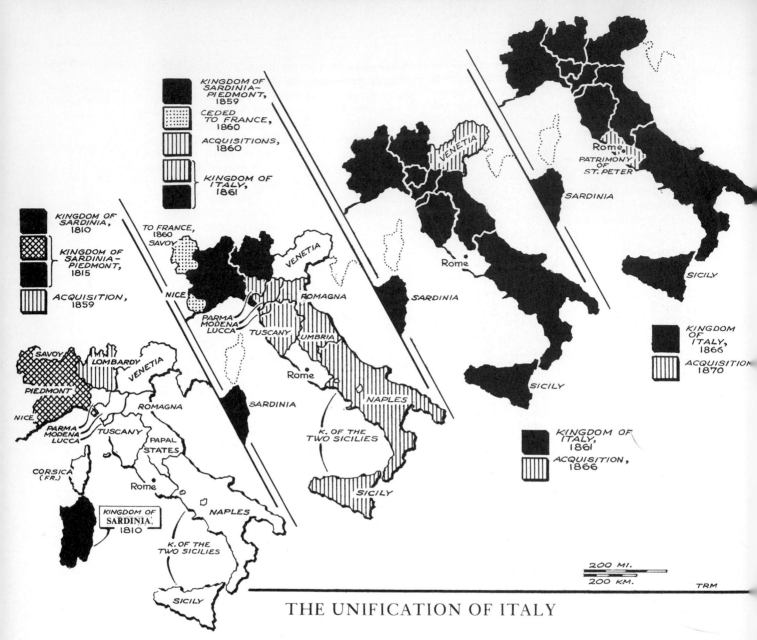

KINGDOM OF SARDINIA-PIEDMONT, 1859

CEDED TO FRANCE, 1860

ACQUISITIONS, 1860

KINGDOM OF ITALY, 1861

KINGDOM OF SARDINIA, 1810

KINGDOM OF SARDINIA-PIEDMONT, 1815

ACQUISITION, 1859

KINGDOM OF ITALY, 1866

ACQUISITION 1870

KINGDOM OF ITALY, 1861

ACQUISITION, 1866

TO FRANCE, 1860
SAVOY

NICE

VENETIA

ROMAGNA

PARMA MODENA LUCCA

TUSCANY

UMBRIA

Rome

SARDINIA

NAPLES

K. OF THE TWO SICILIES

SICILY

SAVOY

LOMBARDY

VENETIA

PIEDMONT

NICE

PARMA MODENA LUCCA

TUSCANY

ROMAGNA

PAPAL STATES

Rome

SARDINIA

CORSICA (FR.)

KINGDOM OF SARDINIA 1810

NAPLES

K. OF THE TWO SICILIES

SICILY

VENETIA

Rome

SARDINIA

SICILY

Rome
PATRIMONY OF ST. PETER

SARDINIA

SICILY

200 MI.

200 KM.

TRM

THE UNIFICATION OF ITALY

MAP 22–1 *Beginning with the association of Sardinia and Piedmont by the Congress of Vienna in 1800, unification was achieved through the expansion of Piedmont between 1859 and 1870. Both Cavour's statesmanship and the campaigns of ardent nationalists played large roles.*

rilla warfare. Because both men spent much time in exile, they became well known across the Continent and in the United States.

Republican nationalism frightened the more moderate Italians, who wanted to rid themselves of Austrian domination but not at the cost of establishing a republic. For a time these people had looked to the pope as a possible vehicle for unification. That solution became impossible after the experience of Pius IX with the Roman Republic in 1849. Consequently, at mid-century "Italy" remained a geographical expression rather than a political entity. However, between 1852 and 1860 the area was transformed into a national state. The process was carried out not by romantic republican nationalists but by Count Camillo Cavour (1810–1861), the moderately liberal prime

tates, and editing a newspaper. He was deeply imbued with the ideas of the Enlightenment, classical economics, and utilitarianism. Cavour was a nationalist of a new breed who had no respect for Mazzini's ideals. A strong monarchist, Cavour rejected republicanism. It was economic and material progress rather than romantic ideals that required a large, unified state on the Italian peninsula.

Cavour believed that if Italians proved themselves to be efficient and economically progressive, the great powers might decide that Italy could govern itself. He joined the Piedmontese Cabinet in 1850 and became premier two years later. He worked for free trade, railway construction, credit expansion, and agricultural improvement. He felt that such material and economic bonds, rather than fuzzy Romantic yearnings, must unite the Italians. However, Cavour also recognized the need to capture the loyalties of the Italians who possessed other varieties of nationalistic feelings. To that end he

Giuseppi Mazzini (1805–1872). His fervent republican nationalism excited emotional support for Italian unity, but also frightened moderate Italians. [Ullstein Bilderdienst]

Cavour was the moderately liberal prime minister of the Kingdom of Piedmont. He was determined to make the idea of a united Italy respectable and acceptable to the rest of Europe. [Culver Pictures]

minister of Piedmont. The method of unification was that of force of arms tied to secret diplomacy. The spirit of Machiavelli must have smiled over the enterprise.

Cavour's Policy

Piedmont (officially styled the Kingdom of Sardinia), in northwestern Italy, was the most independent state on the peninsula. The Congress of Vienna had restored the kingdom as a buffer between French and Austrian ambitions in the area. As we have seen, during 1848 and 1849 King Charles Albert of Piedmont, after having promulgated a conservative constitution, twice unsuccessfully fought Austria. Following the second defeat, he abdicated in favor of his son, Victor Emmanuel II. In 1852 the new monarch chose as his prime minister Count Camillo Cavour. This cunning statesman had begun political life as a strong conservative but had gradually moved toward a moderately liberal position. He had made a personal fortune by investing in railroads, reforming agricultural methods on his own es-

Cavour Explains Why Piedmont Should Enter the Crimean War

As prime minister of Piedmont, Cavour attempted to prove that the Italians were capable of progressive government. In 1855, addressing the Parliament of Piedmont, he urged entry into the Crimean War so that the other Europeans would consider Piedmont a military power. Earlier politics in Italy had been characterized by petty absolute princes and Romantic nationalist conspiracies, both of which Cavour scorned. He understood that in the nineteenth century a nation must possess good government, economic prosperity, and a strong army.

The experience of recent years and previous centuries has proved (at least in my opinion) how little Italy has benefited by conspiracies, revolutions and disorderly uprisings. Far from helping her, they have been a tremendous calamity for this beautiful part of Europe. And not only, gentlemen, because individual people so often suffered from them, not only because revolutions became the cause or pretext for repression, but above all because continual conspiracies, repeated revolutions and disorderly uprisings damaged the esteem and, up to a certain point, the sympathy that other European peoples cherished for Italy.

Now, gentlemen, I believe that the principal condition for the improvement of Italy's fate, the condition that stands out above all others, is to lift up her reputation once more, so to act that all the peoples of the world, those governing and those governed, may do justice to her qualities. And for this two things are necessary: first, to

prove to Europe that Italy has sufficient civic sense to govern herself freely and according to law, and that she is in a condition to adopt the very best forms of government; second, to prove that her military valor is as great as that of her ancestors.

You have done Italy one service by your conduct over the last seven years. You have shown Europe in the most luminous way that Italians are capable of governing themselves with wisdom, prudence, and trustworthiness. But it still remains for you to do Italy an equal, if not a greater, service; it is our country's task to prove that Italy's sons can fight valiantly on battlefields where glory is to be won. And I am sure, gentlemen, that the laurels that our soldiers will win in Eastern Europe will help the future state of Italy more than all that has been done by those people who hoped to regenerate her by rhetorical speeches and writings.

Denis Mack Smith (Ed. and Trans.), *The Making of Italy, 1796–1870* (New York: Walker and Company, 1968), pp. 199–200.

fostered the Nationalist Society, which established chapters in other Italian states to press for unification under the leadership of Piedmont. Finally, the prime minister believed that Italy could be unified only with the aid of France. The recent accession of Napoleon III in France seemed to open the way for such aid at some time in the future.

Cavour used the outbreak of the Crimean War to enter the larger European picture. In 1855 Piedmont joined the conflict on the side of France and Britain and sent ten thousand troops to the front. This small but significant participation in the war allowed Cavour to raise the Italian question at the Paris conference. He left Paris with no diplomatic reward,

but he had impressed everyone with his intelligence and political capacity. Cavour also gained the sympathy of Napoleon III. During the rest of the decade Cavour achieved further international respectability for Piedmont by opposing various plots of Mazzini, who was still attempting to lead nationalist uprisings. By the close of the decade Cavour represented a moderate liberal alternative to both republicanism and reactionary absolutism in Italy.

The Piedmontese prime minister continued to bide his time. Then, in January 1858, an Italian named Orsini attempted to assassinate Napoleon III. The incident made the French emperor, who had once belonged to a nationalist group, newly aware of the Italian issue. He began to fancy himself as continuing his more famous uncle's liberation of the peninsula. He also saw Piedmont as a potential ally against Austria. In July 1858 Cavour and Napoleon III met at Plombières. Riding alone in a carriage, with the emperor at the reins, the two men plotted to provoke a war in Italy that would permit their two nations to intervene against Austria. A formal treaty in December 1858 confirmed the agreement. France was to receive Nice and Savoy for its aid.

During the winter and spring of 1859 tension grew between Austria and Piedmont as the latter country mobilized its army. On April 22 Austria presented Piedmont with an ultimatum ordering a halt to mobilization. That demand provided sufficient grounds to claim that Austria was provoking a war. France intervened to aid its ally. On June 4 the Austrians were defeated at Magenta and on June 24 at Solferino. In the meantime revolutions had broken out in Tuscany, Modena, Parma, and Romagna. With the Austrians in retreat and the new revolutionary states calling for union with Piedmont, Napoleon III feared too extensive a Piedmontese victory. On July 11 he independently concluded a peace with Austria at Villafranca. Piedmont received Lombardy, but Venetia remained under Austrian control. Cavour felt betrayed by France, but nonetheless the war had driven Austria from most of northern Italy. Later that summer, Parma, Modena, Tuscany, and Romagna voted to unify with Piedmont.

At this point the forces of romantic republican nationalism entered the picture and compelled Cavour to pursue the complete unification of northern and southern Italy. In May 1860 Garibaldi landed in Sicily with more than a thousand troops, who had been outfitted in the north. He captured Palermo and prepared to attack the mainland. By September the city and kingdom of Naples, probably the most corrupt example of Italian absolutism, lay under Garibaldi's control. The popular leader had for over two decades hoped to form a republican Italy, but Cavour moved to forestall that possibility. He rushed Piedmontese troops south to confront Garibaldi. On the way they conquered the Papal States except for the area around Rome, which remained under the direct control of the pope. Garibaldi's nationalism won out over his republicanism, and he unhappily accepted the Piedmontese domination. In late 1860 the southern Italian states joined the northern union forged by Piedmont.

The New Italian State

In March 1861 Victor Emmanuel II was proclaimed king of Italy. Three months later Cavour died. The new state more than ever needed his skills because Italy had, in effect, been more nearly conquered than united by Piedmont. The republicans resented the treatment of Garibaldi. The clericals resented the conquest of the Papal States. In the south armed resistance continued until 1866 against the intrusion of Piedmontese administration. The economies of the two areas were incompatible. The south was rural, poor, and backward. In the north industrialism was under way. The social structures reflected those differences, with landholding groups being dominant in the south and an urban working class emerging in the north.

The political framework of the united Italy did little to help overcome the problems. The constitution, which was that promulgated for Piedmont in 1848, provided for a rather conservative constitutional monarchy. The Senate was appointed, and the Chamber of Deputies was elected on a very narrow franchise. Ministers were responsible to the monarch. These arrangements did not foster a vigorous parliamentary life. The major problems of the nation were often simply avoided by the political leaders. In place of efficient, progressive government such as Cavour had brought to Piedmont, a system of *transformismo* developed. This process meant the transformation of political opponents into government supporters through bribery and favors or inclusion in cabinet coalitions. Italian politics became a byword for corruption.

There also remained territories that many Italians believed should be added to their nation. The most important of these were Venetia and Rome. The former was gained in 1866 as one result of the Austro-Prussian War. Rome and the papacy continued to be guarded by French troops, first sent there in 1849, until the Franco-Prussian War of 1870 forced the withdrawal of the garrison. The Italian state then annexed Rome and transferred the capital there from Florence. The papacy remained confined to the Vatican, and its relations with the Italian state remained hostile until the Lateran Accord of 1929. By 1870 only the small territories of Trent and Trieste remained outside the state. In and of themselves these areas were not important, but they served to fuel the continued hostility of Italian patriots toward

Austria. The desire to bring *Italia Irredenta* or "Unredeemed Italy" into the nation was one reason for the Italian support of the Allies against Austria and Germany in 1915.

German Unification

The construction of a united German nation was the single most important political development in Europe between 1848 and 1914. It transformed the balance of economic, military, and international power. Moreover the character of the united German state was largely determined by the method of its creation. Germany was united by the conservative army, monarchy, and prime minister of Prussia, among whose chief motives was the outflanking of Prussian liberals. The goal of a unified Germany, sought for two generations by German liberals, was actually achieved for the most illiberal of reasons.

During the 1850s German unification still seemed very far away. The major states continued to trade with each other through the *Zollverein*, and railways linked the various economic regions. However, Frederick William IV of Prussia had given up his short-lived thoughts of unification under Prussian leadership. Austria continued to oppose any mode of closer union that might lessen its influence.

Prince Otto von Bismarck (1815–1898). Through shrewd diplomacy and successful wars he made Germany a united nation. [German Information Center]

Liberal nationalists had not recovered from the humiliating experiences of 1848 and 1849. What modified this situation rather quickly was a series of domestic political changes and problems within Prussia.

In 1858 Frederick William IV was adjudged insane, and his brother William assumed the regency. William I (1861–1888), who became king in his own right in 1861, was less of an idealist than his brother and rather more of a Prussian patriot. In the usual tradition of the Hohenzollern dynasty, his first concern was for the strength of the Prussian army. In 1860 his war minister and chief of staff proposed to enlarge the army, to increase the number of officers, and to extend the period of conscription from two to three years. The Prussian Parliament, created by the Constitution of 1850, refused to approve the taxes necessary for the military expansion. The liberals, who dominated the body, did not wish to place so much additional power in the hands of the monarchy. A deadlock continued for two years between the monarch and the Parliament.

Bismarck

In September 1862 William I turned for help to the person who, more than any other single individual, shaped the next thirty years of European history: Otto von Bismarck (1815–1898). Bismarck came from *Junker* stock. He attended the university, joined a *Burschenschaft,* and for a time displayed an interest in German unification. Then he retired to his father's estate. During the 1840s he was elected to the local provincial diet. At the time of the revolutions of 1848 his stand was so reactionary as to disturb even the king and the leading state ministers. Yet he had made his mark. From 1851 to 1859 Bismarck was the Prussian minister to the Frankfurt Diet of the German Confederation. Later he served as Prussian ambassador to Saint Petersburg. Just before William I called him to become prime minister of Prussia, Bismarck had been transferred to the post of ambassador to Paris.

Although Bismarck had entered public life as a reactionary, he had mellowed into a conservative. He opposed parliamentary government but not a constitutionalism that provided a strong monarch. His origins were those of a *Junker,* but he understood that Prussia—and later, Germany—must have a strong industrial base. He was a fervent Prussian patriot. His years in Frankfurt arguing with his Austrian

THE UNIFICATION OF GERMANY

MAP 22–2 *Under Bismarck's leadership, and with the strong support of its royal house, Prussia used most of the available diplomatic and military means, on both the German and international stages, to force the unification of German states into a strong national entity.*

counterpart had only hardened that patriotism. In politics he was a pragmatist who put more trust in power and action than in ideas. As he declared in his first speech as prime minister, "Germany is not looking to Prussia's liberalism but to her power. . . . The great questions of the day will not be decided by speeches and majority decisions—that was the mistake of 1848–1849—but by iron and blood."[3] Yet this

same minister, after having led Prussia into three wars, spent the next nineteen years seeking to ensure peace.

After being appointed prime minister in 1862, Bismarck immediately moved against the liberal Parliament. He contended that in the absence of new levies, the Prussian constitution permitted the government to carry out its functions on the basis of previously granted taxes. Therefore taxes could be collected and spent despite the parliamentary refusal to vote them. The army and most of the bureaucracy

[3]Quoted in Otto Pflanze, *Bismarck and the Development of Germany: The Period of Unification: 1815–1871* (Princeton, N.J.: Princeton University Press 1963), p. 177.

771

supported this interpretation of the constitution. However, in 1863 new elections sustained the liberal majority in the Parliament. Bismarck had to find some way to attract popular support away from the liberals and toward the monarchy and the army. To that end Bismarck set about uniting Germany through the conservative institutions of Prussia. The tactic amounted to diverting public attention from domestic matters to foreign affairs.

THE DANISH WAR (1864). Bismarck pursued a *kleindeutsch,* or small German, solution to the question of unification. Austria was to be ultimately excluded from German affairs when an opportunity presented itself. This maneuver required highly complex diplomacy. The Schleswig-Holstein problem provided the handle for Bismarck's policy. These two duchies had long been administered by Denmark without being incorporated into that kingdom. Their populations were a mixture of Germans and Danes. Holstein, where Germans predominated, belonged to the German Confederation. In 1863 the Danes moved to annex both duchies. The smaller states of the German Confederation proposed an all-German war to halt the annexation. Bismarck wanted Prussia to act alone or only in cooperation with Austria. Together the two large states defeated Denmark in a short war in 1864. They took over the joint administration of the two provinces in question.

The Danish defeat gave Bismarck new personal prestige. The joint holding of the duchies allowed him to prod Austria into war with Prussia. In August 1865 the two powers negotiated the Convention of Gastein, which put Austria in charge of Holstein and Prussia in charge of Schleswig. Bismarck then moved to mend other diplomatic fences. He had gained Russian sympathy by supporting the 1863 suppression of the Polish revolt. Conversations with Napoleon III achieved promises of neutrality in case of an Austro-Prussian conflict. In April 1866 Bismarck concluded a treaty with Italy that stated that Italy would annex Venetia in exchange for support of Prussia should war break out with Austria. Now the issue became the provocation of hostilities.

THE AUSTRO-PRUSSIAN WAR (1866). There had been constant Austro-Prussian tension over the administration of Schleswig and Holstein. Bismarck ordered the Prussian forces to do whatever was necessary to be obnoxious to the Austrians. On June 1, 1866, Austria appealed to the German Confederation to intervene in the dispute. Bismarck claimed that the request violated the terms of the 1864 alliance and the Convention of Gastein. The Seven Weeks' War of the summer of 1866 led to the decisive defeat of Austria at Königgrätz. However, the Treaty of Prague, which ended the conflict on August 23, was quite lenient toward Austria. It lost no territory except Venetia, which was ceded to Napoleon III, who in turn ceded it to Italy. The exchange could not be direct because Austria had actually defeated Italy when the latter honored its commitment to Prussia. The Prussian defeat of Austria and the treaty permanently excluded the Habsburgs from German affairs. Prussia had become the only major power among the German states.

THE NORTH GERMAN CONFEDERATION. In 1867 the states of Hanover, Hesse, and Nassau, and the city of Frankfurt, which had supported Austria during the war, were incorporated into Prussia, and their ruling dynasties were deposed. Prussia and these newly incorporated territories, plus Schleswig and Holstein and the rest of the German states north of the Main River, constituted the North German Confederation. The constitution of this body provided for a federation under Prussian leadership. Each state retained its own local government, but the military forces were under federal control. The president of the federation was the king of Prussia, represented by his chancellor. There was a federal council, or *Bundesrat,* composed of nominated members. The lower house, or *Reichstag,* was chosen by universal manhood suffrage. Bismarck had little fear of this broad franchise because he sensed that the peasants would tend to vote conservatively. Moreover the *Reichstag* had little real power because the ministers were responsible only to the monarch. Even legislation did not originate in the *Reichstag.* The legislature did have the right to approve military budgets, but these were usually submitted to cover several years at a time. The constitution of the confederation, which after 1871 became the governing document of the German Empire, possessed some of the appearances but none of the substance of liberalism. Germany was in effect a military monarchy.

The spectacular success of Bismarck's policy overwhelmed the liberal opposition in the Prussian Parliament. The liberals were split between those who prized liberalism and those who supported unification. In the end nationalism proved more attractive than liberalism. In 1866 the Prussian Parliament passed an indemnity measure that retroactively approved the earlier military budget. Bismarck had crushed the Prussian liberals by making the monarchy and the army the most popular institutions in the country. The drive toward unification had achieved Bismarck's domestic political goal.

The Franco-Prussian War and the German Empire (1870–1871)

Bismarck now awaited an opportunity to complete unification by bringing the states of southern Germany into the confederation. Events in Spain provided the excuse. In 1868 a revolution led by conservatives deposed the corrupt Bourbon queen of Spain. In searching for a new monarch, the Spaniards chose Prince Leopold of Hohenzollern-Sigmaringen,

---

Bismarck Edits the Ems Dispatch

On July 13, 1870, William I of Prussia sent Bismarck a telegram reporting his meeting with Benedetti, the French Ambassador, at Ems, a watering place in northwest Germany. The telegram also included a comment by the king's private secretary on later events of the day. Before releasing the dispatch to the press, Bismarck edited it so that the telegram appeared to report that the king of Prussia had treated the French ambassador in a brusque and insulting fashion. Bismarck thus hoped to goad France into a declaration of war. In the text of both telegrams "His Majesty" is William I, and "the Prince" is Charles Anthony, the father of Prince Leopold, the candidate for the Spanish throne. Throughout the negotiations Charles Anthony had spoken on behalf of his son.

THE ORIGINAL MESSAGE SENT BY WILLIAM I TO BISMARCK

"M. Benedetti intercepted me on the Promenade in order to demand of me most insistently that I should authorize him to telegraph immediately to Paris that I shall obligate myself for all future time never again to give my approval to the candidacy of the Hohenzollerns should it be renewed. I refused to agree to this, the last time somewhat severely, informing him that one dare not and cannot assume such obligations à tout jamais [forever]. Naturally, I informed him that I had received no news as yet, and since he had been informed earlier than I by way of Paris and Madrid, he could easily understand why my government was once again out of the matter."

Since then His Majesty has received a dispatch from the Prince. As His Majesty has informed Count Benedetti that he was expecting news from the Prince, His Majesty himself, in view of the above-mentioned demand and in consonance with the advice of Count Eulenburg and myself, decided not to receive the French envoy again but to inform him through an adjutant that His Majesty had now received from the Prince con-firmation of the news which Benedetti had already received from Paris, and that he had nothing further to say to the Ambassador. His Majesty leaves it to the judgement of Your Excellency whether or not to communicate at once the new demand by Benedetti and its rejection to our ambassadors and to the press.

BISMARCK'S EDITED VERSION RELEASED TO THE PRESS

After the reports of the renunciation by the Hereditary Prince of Hohenzollern had been officially transmitted by the Royal Government of Spain to the Imperial Government of France, the French Ambassador presented to His Majesty the King at Ems the demand to authorize him to telegraph to Paris that His Majesty the King would obligate himself for all future time never again to give his approval to the candidacy of the Hohenzollerns should it be renewed.

His Majesty the King thereupon refused to receive the French envoy again and informed him through an adjutant that His Majesty had nothing further to say to the Ambassador.

Louis L. Snyder (Ed. and Trans.), *Documents of German History* (New Brunswick, N.J.: Rutgers University Press, 1958), pp. 215–216.

The proclamation of the German Empire in the Hall of Mirrors at Versailles, January 18, 1871. Kaiser Wilhelm I is standing at the top of the steps under the flags. Bismarck is in the center in a white uniform. [German Information Center]

a cousin of William I of Prussia. On June 19, 1870, Leopold accepted the Spanish crown with Prussian blessings. Bismarck knew that France would react strongly against the idea of a second bordering state ruled by a Hohenzollern. On July 2 the Spanish publicized Leopold's acceptance, and the French reacted as expected. France sent Count Vincent Benedetti (1817–1900) to consult with William I, who was vacationing at Bad Ems. They discussed the matter at several meetings. On July 12 Leopold's father renounced his son's candidacy for the Spanish throne, fearing that the issue would cause war between Prussia and France. William I seems to have been relieved

that conflict had been avoided and that he had not been required to order Leopold to renounce his claim to the Spanish title.

There the matter might have rested had it not been for the impetuosity of the French and the guile of Bismarck. On July 13 the French government instructed Benedetti to ask William I for assurances that he would tolerate no future Spanish candidacy for Leopold. The king refused but said that he might take the question under further consideration. Later that day he sent Bismarck, who was in Berlin, a telegram reporting the substance of the meeting. The chancellor, who desperately wanted a war with France to complete unification, had been disappointed by the peaceful resolution of the Spanish candidacy question. The telegram provided a new opportunity. Bismarck released an edited version of the dispatch. The revised Ems telegram made it appear that William I had insulted the French ambassador. The idea was to goad France into a declaration of war.

The French government of Napoleon III quickly fell for Bismarck's bait, and on July 19 the French declared war. The French emperor had been almost as eager for war as Bismarck because he believed that victory over the North German Confederation would give his regime a new and stronger popular base of support. Once the conflict erupted, the south German states honored treaties signed with Prussia in 1866 and eagerly joined the northern cause against France, whose defeat was not long in coming. On September 1, at the Battle of Sedan, the Germans not only beat the French army but also captured the French emperor. By late September Paris stood besieged; it finally capitulated on January 28, 1871. Ten days earlier, in the Hall of Mirrors at the Palace of Versailles, the German Empire had been declared. During the war the states of south Germany had joined the North German Confederation, and their princes had requested William I to accept the imperial title. The princes of the southern states retained their positions as heads of their respective states within the new federation. From the peace settlement with France, Germany received the additional territory of Alsace and part of Lorraine.

Both the fact and the manner of German unification produced long-range effects in Europe. A powerful new state had been created in north central Europe. It was rich in natural resources and talented citizens. Militarily and economically the German Empire would be stronger than Prussia had been alone. The unification of Germany was also a blow to European liberalism because the new state was a conservative creation. Conservative politics was now backed not by a weak Austria or an economically retrograde Russia but by the strongest state on the Continent. The two nations most immediately affected by German and also Italian unification were France and Austria. The emergence of the two new unified states revealed the weakness of both France and the Habsburg Empire. Change had to come in each: France returned to republican government, and the Habsburgs organized a dual monarchy.

GERMAN AND ITALIAN UNIFICATION

Crimean War opens	1854
Cavour leads Piedmont into the war on the side of France and England	1855
Treaty of Paris concludes the Crimean War	1856
(January 14) Attempt to assassinate Napoleon III	1858
(July 20) Secret conference between Napoleon III and Cavour at Plombières	1858
War of Piedmont and France against Austria	1859
Garibaldi lands his forces in Sicily and invades southern Italy	1860
(March 17) Proclamation of the Kingdom of Italy	1861
(June 6) Death of Cavour	1861
Bismarck becomes prime minister of Prussia	1862
Danish-Prussian War	1864
Convention of Gastein	1865
Austro-Prussian War	1866
Venetia ceded to Italy	1866
North German Confederation formed	1867
(June 19–July 12) Crisis over Hohenzollern candidacy for the Spanish throne	1870
(July 13) Bismarck publishes the Ems dispatch	1870
(July 19) France declares war on Prussia	1870
(September 1) France defeated at Sedan and Napoleon III captured	1870
(September 4) French Republic proclaimed	1870
(October 2) Italian state annexes Rome	1870
(January 18) Proclamation of the German Empire at Versailles	1871
(March 18–May 28) Paris Commune	1871
(May 1) Treaty of Frankfurt between France and Prussia	1871

France: From Liberal Empire to the Third Republic

The reign of Emperor Napoleon III (1851–1870) is traditionally divided into the years of the authoritarian empire and those of the liberal empire. The point of division is 1860. Initially, after the *coup* in December 1851, Napoleon III had kept a close rein on the legislature, had strictly controlled the press, and had made life difficult for political dissidents. His support came from property owners, the French Catholic church, and businessmen. They approved the security he brought to property, his protection of the pope, and his aid to commerce and railroad construction. The French victory in the Crimean War had further confirmed the emperor's popularity.

From the late 1850s onward, Napoleon III began to modify his policy. In 1860 he concluded a free trade treaty with Britain and permitted the legislature to discuss matters of state more freely. By the late 1860s he had relaxed the press laws and had permitted labor unions. In 1870 he allowed the leaders of the moderates in the legislature to form a ministry. That same year Napoleon III agreed to a liberal constitution that made the ministers responsible to the legislature. All of these liberal moves were closely related to problems in foreign policy. He had lost control of the diplomacy of Italian unification. Between 1861 and 1867 he had supported a military expedition against Mexico

From September 1870 to January 1871, Paris was besieged by the Germans and cut off from the rest of France. This photo shows the escape from the city of Leon Gambetta (1838–1882), the Minister of War in the Government of National Defense. Gambetta left Paris to organize French resistance to the Germans. [Bildarchiv Preussicher Kulturbesitz]

led by Archduke Maximilian of Austria. The venture ended in defeat and the execution of the archduke. In 1866 Napoleon III and France rather sat on the sidelines while Bismarck and Prussia reorganized German affairs. The liberal concessions on domestic matters were attempts to compensate for an increasingly unsuccessful foreign policy. The war of 1870 against Germany was simply Napoleon III's last and most disastrous attempt to shore up French foreign policy and to secure domestic popularity.

Whether Napoleon III would have succeeded in sustaining liberal government or his own position became a moot point. The Second Empire, but not the war, came to an inglorious end with the Battle of Sedan in September 1870. The emperor was captured, imprisoned, and then allowed to go to England, where he died in 1873. Shortly after news of the Sedan disaster reached Paris, a republic was proclaimed and a Government of National Defense was established. Paris itself was soon under Prussian siege. During the siege of Paris, the French government was transferred to Bordeaux. Paris finally surrendered in January 1871, but the rest of France had been ready to sue for peace long before the capital surrendered.

The Paris Commune

The division between the provinces and Paris became even more decided after the fighting stopped. Monarchists dominated the new National Assembly elected in February. For the time being, executive power was turned over to Adolphe Thiers (1797–1877), who had been active in French politics since 1830. He negotiated a settlement with Prussia (the Treaty of Frankfurt) whereby France was charged with a large indemnity, remained occupied by Prussian troops until the indemnity had been paid, and surrendered territories in Alsace and Lorraine. The city of Paris, which had suffered much during the siege, resented what it regarded as a betrayal by the monarchist National Assembly sitting at Versailles. Thiers, familiar with a half-century of Parisian political turmoil, ordered the disarmament of the Paris National Guard on March 17. The attempt on the next day to seize the guard's cannon was bungled. Paris then regarded the National Assembly as its new enemy.

On March 26, 1871, the Parisians elected a new municipal government, called the *Paris Commune.* It was formally proclaimed on

March 28. Its goal was to administer the city separately from the rest of the country. Political radicals and socialists of all stripes participated in the Paris Commune at one time or another. The National Assembly moved rapidly against the commune. By early April, Paris was again a besieged city, but this time it stood surrounded by a French army. On May 8 the Army bombarded Paris. On May 21, the day on which the formal treaty with Prussia was signed, the National Assembly forces broke through the city's defenses. During the next seven days the troops restored order to Paris and in the process killed about twenty thousand inhabitants. The communards claimed their own victims as well.

The short-lived Paris Commune very quickly became a legend throughout France and Europe. Marxists regarded it as a genuine proletarian government which the troops of the French bourgeoisie had suppressed. This interpretation is largely mistaken. The commune, though of shifting composition, was dominated by petty bourgeois members. The socialism that was a part of the commune had its roots in Blanqui and Proudhon rather than in

The Paris Commune is Proclaimed

In September 1870 the French Republic was proclaimed, and shortly thereafter a National Assembly was elected. The city of Paris, which had held out against Prussia longer than any other part of France, was hostile to the National Assembly. On March 18, 1871, a revolt against the assembly occurred in Paris. The National Guard of Paris sought to organize the city as a separate part of France. Below is an excerpt of the proclamation of March 28 of the separation of Paris into an autonomous commune. The rebellious Parisians wanted all of France to be organized into a federation of politically autonomous communes. This communal concept was directly opposed to that of the large national state. Two months after this proclamation the troops of the assembly crushed the commune.

By its revolution of the 18th March, and the spontaneous and courageous efforts of the National Guard, Paris has regained its autonomy. . . . On the eve of the sanguinary and disastrous defeat suffered by France as the punishment it has to undergo for the seventy years of the Empire, and the monarchical, clerical, parliamentary, legal and conciliatory reaction, our country again rises, revives, begins a new life, and retakes the tradition of the Communes of old and of the French Revolution. This tradition, which gave victory to France, and earned the respect and sympathy of past generations, will bring independence, wealth, peaceful glory and brotherly love among nations in the future.

Never was there so solemn an hour. The Revolution which our fathers commenced and we are finishing . . . is going on without bloodshed, by the might of the popular will. . . . To secure the triumph of the Communal idea . . . it is necessary to determine its general principles, and to draw up . . . the programme to be realized. . . .

The Commune is the foundation of all political states, exactly as the family is the embryo of human society. It must have autonomy; that is to say, self-administration and self-government, agreeing with its particular genius, traditions, and wants; preserving, in its political, moral, national, and special groups its entire liberty, its own character, and its complete sovereignty, like a citizen of a free town.

To secure the greatest economic development, the national and territorial independence, and security, association is indispensable; that is to say, a federation of all communes, constituting a united nation.

The autonomy of the Commune guarantees liberty to its citizens; and the federation of all the communes increases, by the reciprocity, power, wealth, markets, and resources of each member, the profit of all.

It was the Communal idea . . . which triumphed on the 18th of March, 1871. It implies, as a political form, the Republic, which is alone compatible with liberty and popular sovereignty.

G. A. Kertesz (Ed.), *Documents in the Political History of the European Continent, 1815–1939* (Oxford: Clarendon Press, 1968), pp. 312–313.

*Mass graves were dug for the thousands of Parisians killed or executed during the fighting that
marked the suppression of the Paris Commune in 1871. [Snark International]*

Marx. The goal of the commune was not a
workers' republic but a nation composed of
relatively independent, radically democratic
enclaves. The suppression of the commune
consequently represented not only the protection of property but also the triumph of the
centralized nation-state over an alternative
mode of political organization. Just as the armies of Piedmont and Prussia had united the
small states of Italy and Germany, the army of
the French National Assembly destroyed the
particularistic political tendencies of Paris and,
by implication, those of any other French community.

The Third Republic

The National Assembly put down the commune directly, but it backed into a republican
form of government indirectly and much
against its will. The monarchists, who constituted its majority, were divided in loyalty between the House of Bourbon and the House of

Orléans. They could have surmounted this
problem because the Bourbon claimant had no
children. He could have become king on the
condition that the Orléanist heir would follow
him to the throne. However, the Bourbon
count of Chambord refused to become king if
the nation retained the revolutionary tricolor
flag. Even the conservative monarchists would
not return to the white flag of the Bourbons,
which symbolized extreme political reaction.

While the monarchists quarreled over the
proper heir, and the heir over the proper flag,
time passed and events marched on. By September 1873 the indemnity had been paid and
the Prussian occupation troops had withdrawn. Thiers was ousted from office because
he had displayed clear republican sentiments.
The monarchists wanted a person more sympathetic with their goals to be executive. They
elected as president Marshal MacMahon
(1808–1893), who was conservative and who
was expected to prepare for an eventual monarchist restoration. In 1875 the National As-

sembly, still monarchist in sentiment but unable to find a candidate for the throne, decided to regularize the political system. It adopted a law that provided for a Chamber of Deputies elected by universal manhood suffrage, a Senate chosen indirectly, and a president elected by the two legislative houses. This relatively simple republican system had resulted from the bickering and frustration of the monarchists.

MacMahon remained as president. He would have liked to transform that office into a much stronger position. After numerous quarrels with the Chamber of Deputies, he resigned in 1879. His departure meant that people dedicated to a republic generally controlled the national government. But France remained an uncertain and unconfident republic. A considerable body of public opinion within the army, the church, and the wealthy families still favored government by a single strong figure. During the late 1880s they looked to General Georges Boulanger (1837–1891) as such a leader. In 1886 and 1887 he had been a popular minister of war who initiated a number of military reforms. When a financial scandal touched several major political figures, Boulanger became all the more appealing for his honesty and integrity. He was elected to the Chamber of Deputies from numerous districts, though afterward he sat for only one. In 1889 there was much talk and expectation of his carrying out a *coup d'état*. Nothing came of these speculations. The good general had talked with too many different political groups to be trusted by any. He also lacked real drive and political ambition. In the end he left France for life with his Belgian mistress and in 1891 committed suicide on her grave in Brussels.

The political structure of the Third Republic proved much stronger than many citizens suspected at the time. It was able to survive a series of major scandals. In the late 1880s the son of the president was discovered to be selling positions in the Legion of Honor. Early in the next decade a number of ministers and deputies were implicated in the Panama affair. Ferdinand de Lesseps, who had constructed the Suez Canal, organized a company to build a canal in Panama. Various people in authority in France accepted bribes for their public support of the venture. These two *causes célèbres* made the republic look rather sleazy in the eyes of its conservative enemies. But the institutions of the republic allowed new ministers to replace those whose corruption was exposed.

THE DREYFUS AFFAIR. The greatest trauma of the republic occurred over the Dreyfus affair. On December 22, 1894, a French military court found Captain Alfred Dreyfus (1859–1935) guilty of passing secret information to the German army. The evidence supporting his guilt was at best flimsy and was later revealed to have been forged. Someone in the officer corps had been passing documents to the Germans, and it suited the army investigators to accuse Dreyfus, who was Jewish. However, after Dreyfus had been sent to Devil's Island, secrets continued to flow to the German army. In 1896 a new head of French counterintelligence reexamined the Dreyfus file and found evidence of forgery. A different officer was implicated, but a military court quickly acquitted him of all charges. The officer who had discovered the forgeries was transferred to a distant post.

By then the matter had become one of widespread and sometimes near-hysterical public debate. The army, the French Catholic church, political conservatives, and vehemently anti-Semitic newspapers repeatedly contended that

Captain Alfred Dreyfus (1859–1935) leaving the courtroom after his second trial in 1898. Dreyfus was not fully vindicated until 1906. [Snark International]

Dreyfus was guilty. Such anti-Dreyfus opinion was quite powerful at the beginning of the affair. In 1898, however, the novelist Émile Zola published a newspaper article entitled *"J'accuse"* ("I Accuse") in which he contended that the army had consciously denied due process to Dreyfus and had plotted to suppress evidence and to forge other evidence. Zola was convicted of libel and received a one-year prison sentence, which he avoided only by leaving France for exile in England.

Zola was only one of numerous liberals, radicals, and socialists who had begun to demand a new trial for Dreyfus. Although these forces of the political left had come to Dreyfus's support rather slowly, they soon realized that his cause could aid their own public image. They portrayed the conservative institutions of the nation as having denied Dreyfus the rights belonging to any citizen of the republic. They also claimed, and quite properly so, that Dreyfus had been singled out so that the guilty persons, who were still in the army, could be protected. In August 1898 further evidence of forged material came to light. The officer responsible for those forgeries committed suicide in jail. A new military trial took place, but Dreyfus was again found guilty by officers who refused to admit the original mistake. The president of France immediately pardoned the captain, and eventually, in 1906, a civilian court set aside the results of both previous military trials.

The Dreyfus case divided France as no issue had done since the Paris Commune. By its conclusion the conservative political forces of the nation stood on the defensive. They had for a number of years allowed themselves to persecute an innocent person and to manufacture false evidence against him to protect themselves from disclosure. They had also embraced a strongly anti-Semitic posture. On the political left, radicals, republicans, and socialists developed an informal alliance that outlived the fight over the Dreyfus case itself. These groups realized that republican institutions must be preserved in a conscious fashion if the political left were to achieve any of its goals. Outside political circles, ever larger numbers of French citizens understood that their rights and liberties were safer under a republic than under some alternative mode of conservative government. The divisions, suspicions, and hopes growing out of the Dreyfus affair would continue to mark and to divide the Third French Republic until its defeat by Germany in 1940.

The Habsburg Empire: Formation of the Dual Monarchy

After 1848 the Habsburg Empire remained a problem both to itself and to the rest of Europe. An ungenerous critic remarked that the empire was supported by a standing army of soldiers, a kneeling army of priests, and a crawling army of informers. In the age of national states, liberal institutions, and industrialism, the Habsburg domains remained primarily dynastic, absolutist, and agrarian. The response to the revolts at the end of the 1840s has been the reassertion of absolutism. Francis Joseph, who became emperor in 1848 and ruled until 1916, was honest, hardworking, and unimaginative. He reacted to events but rarely commanded them.

During the 1850s his ministers attempted to impose a centralized administration on the empire. The system amounted to a military and bureaucratic government dominated by German-speaking Austrians. The Vienna government abolished all internal tariffs in the empire. It divided Hungary, which had been so revolutionary in 1848, into military districts. The Roman Catholic church received control of education. Although these actions stirred much domestic resentment and opposition, this system of neoabsolutism actually floundered because of a series of major setbacks in Habsburg foreign policy. Austrian refusal to support Russia during the Crimean War meant that the new czar would not in the future help to preserve Habsburg rule in Hungary as Nicholas I had done in 1849. An important external support of Habsburg power for the past half century thus disappeared. The Austrian defeat in 1859 at the hands of France and Piedmont and the subsequent loss of territory in Italy confirmed the necessity for new structures of domestic government. For seven years the emperor, the civil servants, the aristocrats, and the politicians attempted to construct a viable system of government.

In 1860 Francis Joseph issued the October Diploma, which created a federation among the states and provinces of the empire. There were to be local diets dominated by the landed classes and a single imperial parliament. The Magyar nobility of Hungary rejected the plan. Consequently, in 1861 the emperor promulgated the February Patent. Technically it interpreted the Diploma, but in point of fact it

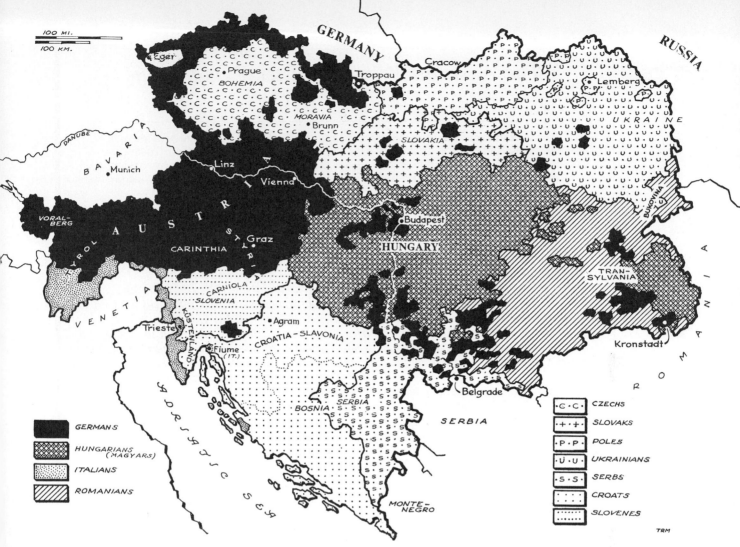

NATIONALITIES WITHIN THE HABSBURG EMPIRE

MAP 22–3 *The patchwork appearance reflects the unusual problem of the numerous ethnic groups that the Habsburgs could not, of course, meld into a modern national state. Only the Magyars were recognized in 1867, leaving nationalist Czechs, Slovaks, and the others chronically dissatisfied.*

constituted an entirely different form of government. It established a bicameral imperial parliament, or *Reichsrat*, with an appointed upper chamber and an indirectly elected lower chamber. Again the Magyars refused to cooperate in a system designed to permit German-speaking Austrian domination of the empire. The Hungarians sent no delegates to the legislature. Nevertheless, for six years, the February Patent governed the empire, and it prevailed in Austria proper until World War I. There was no ministerial responsibility to the *Reichsrat*. Few genuine guarantees existed for civil liberties. Armies could be levied and taxes raised without parliamentary consent. When the *Reichsrat* was not in session, the emperor could simply promulgate laws on his own authority.

Meanwhile negotiations continued between the emperor and the Magyars. These produced no concrete result until the defeat of Austria by Prussia in the summer of 1866 and the consequent exclusion of Austria from German affairs. The military disaster compelled Francis Joseph to come to terms with the Magyars. The

781

The Austrian Prime Minister Explains the Dual Monarchy

The multinational character of the Austrian Empire had long been a source of internal weakness and political discontent. After the defeat of Austria by Prussia in 1866, the Austrian government attempted to regain the loyalty of the Hungarians by making Hungary a separate kingdom within a dual monarchy known thereafter as Austria-Hungary.

The dangers which Austria has to face are of a twofold nature. The first is presented by the tendency of her liberal-minded German population to gravitate toward that larger portion of the German-speaking people . . . the second is the diversity of language and race in the empire. Of Austria's large Slav population, the Poles have a natural craving for independence after having enjoyed and heroically fought for it for centuries; while the other nationalities are likely at a moment of dangerous crisis to develop pro-Russian tendencies.

Now my object is to carry out a bloodless revolution—to show the various elements of this great empire that it is to the benefit of each of them to act in harmony with its neighbor. . . . But to this I have made one exception. Hungary is an ancient monarchy, more ancient as such than Austria proper. . . . I have endeavoured to give Hungary not a new position with regard to the Austrian empire, but to secure her in the one which she has occupied. The Emperor of Austria is King of Hungary; my idea was that he should revive in his person the Constitution of which he and his ancestors have been the heads. The leading principles of my plan are . . . the resuscitation of an old monarchy and an old Constitution; not the separation of one part of the empire from the other, but the drawing together of the two component parts by the recognition of their joint positions, the maintenance of their mutual obligations, their community in questions affecting the entire empire, and their proportional pecuniary responsibility for the liabilities of the whole State. It is no plan of separation that I have carried out: on the contrary, it is one of close union, not by the creation of a new power, but by the recognition of an old one. . . .

Memoirs of Friedrich Ferdinand Count von Beust, Vol. 1, ed. by Baron Henry de Worms (London: Remington, 1887), pp. xx–xxvi.

subsequent *Ausgleich,* or Compromise, of 1867 transformed the Habsburg Empire into a dual monarchy. Francis Joseph was separately crowned king of Hungary in Budapest. Except for the common monarch, Austria and Hungary became almost wholly separate states. They shared ministers of foreign affairs, defense, and finance, but the other ministers were different for each state. There were also separate parliaments. Each year sixty parliamentary delegates from each state were to meet to discuss matters of mutual interest. Every ten years Austria and Hungary were to renegotiate their trade relationship. By this cumbersome machinery, unique in all European history, the Hungarian Magyars were reconciled to Habsburg rule. They had achieved the free hand they had long wanted in local Hungarian matters.

Many of the other national groups within the empire—including the Czechs, the Ruthenians, the Romanians, and the Serbo-Croatians—opposed the Compromise of 1867. The dual monarchy, in effect, permitted the German-speaking Austrians and the Hungarian Magyars to dominate all other nationalities in their respective states. The most vocal critics were the Czechs of Bohemia. They favored a policy of trialism or triple monarchy. In 1871 Francis Joseph was willing to accept this concept. However, the Hungarian Magyars vetoed the proposal for fear that they might have to make similar concessions to their own subject nationalities.

For over twenty years the Czechs were conciliated by an extension of generous Austrian patronage and admission to the Austrian bureaucracy. By the 1890s Czech nationalism

The coronation of Francis Joseph as King of Hungary in 1867, The so-called Ausgleich, or Compromise, of 1867 transformed the Habsburg Empire into a dual monarchy in which Austria and Hungary became almost separate states except for defense and foreign affairs. [Bildarchiv der Osterreichischen Nationalbibliothek, Vienna]

had again become more vocal. In 1897, through a series of ordinances, Francis Joseph gave the Czechs and the Germans equality of language in various localities. The Germans in the Austrian *Reichsrat* set out on a course of parliamentary disruption to oppose these measures. The Czechs replied in kind. By the turn of the century this obstructionist activity, which included the playing of musical instruments in the parliament chamber, had paralyzcd parliamentary life. The emperor ruled by imperial decree with the support of the bureaucracy. In 1907 universal manhood suffrage was introduced in Austria, but it did not change the situation in the *Reichsrat*. In effect, by 1914 constitutionalism was a dead letter in Austria. It flourished in Hungary, but only because the Magyars relentlessly exercised politi-

cal supremacy over all other competing national groups.

Russia: Emancipation and Revolutionary Stirrings

Reforms of Alexander II

The defeat in the Crimean War and the humiliation of the Treaty of Paris compelled the Russian government to reconsider its domestic situation. Nicholas I had died in 1855 during the conflict. Because of extensive travel in Russia and an early introduction to government procedures, Nicholas's son Alexander II (1855–1881) was quite familiar with the chief difficulties facing the nation. The debacle of the war had created a situation in which reform was both necessary and possible. Alexander II took advantage of this turn of events to institute the most extensive restructuring of Russian society and administration since Peter the Great. Like Peter, Alexander imposed his reforms from the top.

In every area of economic and public life a profound cultural gap existed between Russia and the rest of Europe. Nowhere was this fact more true than in the matter of serfdom. Everywhere else on the Continent it had been abandoned. In Russia the institution had changed very little since the eighteenth century. Landowners had a very free hand with their serfs, and the serfs had little recourse against the lords. In March 1856, at the conclusion of the Crimean War, Alexander II announced his intention to abolish serfdom. He had decided that only abolition of the institution would permit Russia to organize its human and natural resources so as to maintain its status as a great power. Serfdom had become economically inefficient: the threat of large or small revolts of serfs was always present; the serfs recruited into the army had performed poorly in the Crimean conflict; and the moral opinion of the day had come increasingly to condemn serfdom. Only Russia, Brazil, and certain portions of the United States among the Western nations still retained such forms of involuntary servitude. For over five years government commissions wrestled over the way to implement the czar's desire. Finally, in February 1861, against much opposition from the nobility and the landlords, Alexander II promulgated the long statute ending serfdom in Russia.

The technicalities of the emancipation statute meant that freedom was often more theoretical than practical. The procedures were so complicated and the results so limited that many serfs believed that real emancipation was still to come. Serfs immediately received the personal rights to marry without their landlord's permission as well as to purchase and sell property freely, to engage in court actions, and to pursue trades. What they did not receive immediately was free title to their land. They were required to pay the landlords for frequently insufficient allotments of land over a period of forty-nine years. They were also charged interest during this period. The serfs made the payments to the government, which had already reimbursed the landlords for their losses. The serfs did not receive title to the land until the debt was paid. The redemption payments led to almost unending difficulty. Poor harvests caused the debts to fall into arrears, and the situation was not remedied until 1906. With widespread revolutionary unrest following the Japanese defeat of Russia in 1905, the government grudgingly completed the process of emancipation by canceling the remaining debts.

The abolition of serfdom required the reor-

Alexander II Decides to Emancipate the Serfs

Shortly after becoming czar, Alexander II reached the decision that the Russian serfs should eventually be emancipated. On March 30, 1856, he announced his decision to a group of Moscow nobles. He told them that the serfs would be freed and then asked them to help him to devise the best way to carry out the emancipation, which did not occur for another five years. Note the czar's emphasis on the wisdom of freeing the serfs by a deliberate decision rather than being forced to that action by a revolt.

I have learned, gentlemen, that rumors have spread among you of my intention to abolish serfdom. To refute any groundless gossip on so important a subject I consider it necessary to inform you that I have no intention of doing so immediately. But, of course, and you yourselves realize it, the existing system of serf owning cannot remain unchanged. It is better to begin abolishing serfdom from above than to wait for it to begin to abolish itself from below. I ask you, gentlemen, to think of ways of doing this. Pass on my words to the nobles for consideration.

George Vernadsky (Ed.), *A Source Book for Russian History from Earliest Times to* 1917, Vol. 3 (New Haven, Conn.: Yale University Press, 1972), p. 589.

ganization of local government and the judicial system. The authority of village communes replaced that of the landlord over the peasant. The village elders settled family quarrels, imposed fines, issued internal passports, and collected taxes. In many cases also, the emancipated serfs owned land communally rather than individually. The nobility were permitted a larger role in local administration through a system of provincial and county *zemstvos*, or councils, organized in 1864. These councils were to oversee local matters such as bridge and road repair, education, and agricultural improvement. However, because the councils received inadequate funds, local government never became vigorous.

The flagrant inequities and abuses of the preemancipation judicial system could not continue. In 1864 Alexander II promulgated a new statute on the judiciary. For the first time principles of western European legal systems were introduced into Russia. These included equality before the law, impartial hearings, uniform procedures, judicial independence, and trial by jury. The new system was far from perfect. The judges were not genuinely independent, and the czar could increase as well as reduce sentences. For certain offenses, such as those involving the press, jury trials were not held. Nonetheless the system was an improvement both in its efficiency and in its relative lack of the old corruption.

Reforms were also instituted in the army. Russia possessed the largest military establishment on the Continent, but it had floundered badly in the Crimean War. The usual period of recruitment was twenty-five years. Villages had to provide quotas of serfs. Often the recruiters had come to the villages and simply seized serfs from their families. Once in the army, the recruits rarely saw their homes again. Life in the army was exceedingly harsh, even by the usually brutal standards of most mid-century armies. In the 1860s the army lowered the period of recruitment to fifteen years and slightly relaxed disciplinary procedures. In 1874 the enlistment period was lowered to six years of active duty, followed by nine years in the reserves. All males were subject to military service after the age of twenty.

Alexander's reformist departures became more measured shortly after the Polish Rebellion of 1863. As in 1830, Polish nationalists attempted to overthrow Russian dominance. Once again the Russian army suppressed the rebellion. Alexander II then moved to "rus-

Even after emancipation, the life of Russian peasants was difficult. They attempted to secure a livelihood partly from farming and partly from small handcraft industries, such as those seen in this picture of a Russian village in the late nineteenth century. [Culver Pictures]

sify" Poland. In 1864 he emancipated the Polish serfs as a move against the politically restive Polish nobility. Russian law, language, and administration were imposed on all areas of Polish life. Henceforth, until the close of World War I, Poland was treated merely as one other Russian province.

As revealed by the Polish suppression, Alexander II was a reformer only within the limits of his own autocracy. His changes in Russian life failed to create new loyalty or gratitude among his subjects. The serfs felt that their emancipation had been inadequate. The nobles and the wealthier educated segments of Russian society resented the czar's persistent refusal to allow them a meaningful role in government and policymaking. Consequently, although Alexander II became known as the Czar Liberator, he was never a popular ruler. He could be very indecisive and was rarely open to new ideas. These characteristics became more pronounced after 1866, when an attempt was made on his life. Thereafter Russia increasingly became a police state. This new repression fueled the activity of radical groups within Russia. Their actions, in turn, made the autocracy more reactionary.

Revolutionaries

The czarist regime had long had its critics. One of the most prominent was Alexander Herzen (1812–1870), who lived in exile. From

London he published a newspaper called *The Bell* in which he set forth reformist positions. The initial reforms of Alexander II had raised great hopes among Russian students and intellectuals, but they soon became discontented with the limited character of the restructuring. Drawing on the ideas of Herzen and other radicals, these students formed a revolutionary movement known as *Populism*. They sought a social revolution based on the communal life of the Russian peasants. The chief radical society was called *Land and Freedom*. In the early 1870s hundreds of young Russians, including both men and women, took their revolutionary message into the countryside. They intended to live with the peasants, to gain their trust, and to teach them about the peasant role in the coming revolution. The bewildered and distrustful peasants turned most of the youths over to the police. In the winter of 1877–1878 almost two hundred students were tried. Most were acquitted or given very light sentences, because they had been held for months in preventive detention and because the court believed that a display of mercy might lessen public sympathy for the young revolutionaries. The court even suggested that the czar might wish to pardon those students given heavier

The assassination of Czar Alexander II (1855–1881) on March 1, 1881. Two bombs were thrown. The first wounded several Imperial guards. The Czar stopped his carriage to see to the wounded. The assassins then threw another bomb which killed Alexander. [*Bildarchiv Preussicher Kulturbesitz*]

sentences. The czar refused and let it become known that he favored heavy penalties for all persons involved in revolutionary activity.

Thereafter the revolutionaries decided that the czarist regime must be attacked directly. They adopted a policy of terrorism. In January 1878 Vera Zasulich attempted to assassinate the military governor of Saint Petersburg. At her trial the jury acquitted her because the governor she had shot had a special reputation for brutality and because some people at the time believed that Zasulich had a personal rather than a political grievance against her victim. Nonetheless the verdict further encouraged the terrorists.

In 1879 Land and Freedom split into two groups. One held to the idea of educating the peasants, and it soon dissolved. The other, known as *People's Will*, was dedicated to the overthrow of the autocracy. Its members decided to assassinate the czar himself. Several assassination attempts failed, but on March 1, 1881, a bomb hurled by a member of People's Will killed Czar Alexander II. Four men and two women were sentenced to death for the deed. All of them had been willing to die for their cause. The emergence of such dedicated revolutionary opposition constituted as much a part of the reign of Alexander II as did his reforms, for the limited character of those reforms convinced many people from various walk of life that the autocracy could never truly redirect Russian society.

Alexander III, whose reign (1881–1894) further underscored that pessimistic conviction, possessed all the autocratic and repressive characteristics of his grandfather Nicholas I and none of the better qualities of his father. Some slight attention was directed toward the improvement of life in the Russian factories, but primarily Alexander III sought to roll back the reforms of the third quarter of the century. He favored centralized bureaucracy over the new limited modes of self-government. He strengthened the secret police and increased press censorship. In effect, he confirmed all the evils that the revolutionaries saw inherent in autocratic government. His son, Nicholas II, who became czar in 1894, would discover that autocracy could not survive the pressures of the twentieth century.

OPPOSITE: *The American engineer George Kennan took this photo of Siberian exiles in 1889. In Czarist Russia exile was the most extreme punishment short of death.* [*Library of Congress*]

George Kennan Describes Siberian Exile in Alexander III's Russia

Under Alexander III the police-state character of the Russian monarchy intensified. Exile was the most extreme form of punishment short of death. In effect, it robbed the person exiled not only of legal rights but almost of his or her identity, as pointed out in this account by a noted American observer who spent long periods in Siberia in the 1860s and 1880s. It should be noted that he was not the person of the same name who has been an important spokesman in mid-twentieth-century American foreign policy.

Exile by administrative process means the banishment of an obnoxious person from one part of the empire to another without the observance of any of the legal formalities that, in most civilized countries, precede the deprivation of rights and the restriction of personal liberty. The obnoxious person may not be guilty of any crime, and may not have rendered himself unamenable in any way to the laws of the state, but if, in the opinion of the local authorities, his presence in a particular place is "prejudicial to public order," or "incompatible with public tranquillity," he may be arrested without a warrant, may be held from two weeks to two years in prison, and may then be removed by force to any other place within the limits of the empire and there be put under police surveillance for a period of from one year to ten years. He may or may not be informed of the reasons for this summary proceeding, but in either case he is perfectly helpless. He cannot examine the witness upon whose testimony his presence is declared to be "prejudicial to public order." He cannot summon friends to prove his loyalty and good character, without great risk of bringing upon them the same calamity that has befallen him. He has no right to demand a trial, or even a hearing. He cannot sue out a writ of habeas corpus. He cannot appeal to his fellow-citizens through the press. His communications with the world are so suddenly severed that sometimes even his own relatives do not know what has happened to him. He is literally and absolutely without any means whatever of self-defense.

George Kennan, *Siberia and the Exile System,* Vol. 1 (London: Century Co., 1891), pp. 242–243.

Great Britain:
Toward Democracy

While the continental nations became unified and struggled toward internal political restructuring, Great Britain continued to symbolize the confident liberal state. Britain was not without its difficulties and domestic conflicts, but it seemed able to deal with these through existing political institutions. The general prosperity of the third quarter of the century took the edge off the class hostility of the 1840s. A large body of shared ideas emphasizing competition and individualism was accepted by the members of all classes. Even the leaders of trade unions during these years asked for little more than to receive a portion of the fruits of prosperity and to prove their own social respectability. Parliament itself continued to provide an institution that permitted the absorption of new groups and interests into the existing political processes. In short, the British did not have to create new liberal institutions and then learn how to live within them.

The major political figure of mid-century was Henry John Temple, Lord Palmerston (1784–1865). He became prime minister early in 1855 as the nation became weary of blunders in the conduct of the Crimean War. Except for a seventeen-month interlude in 1858 and 1859, he governed until late 1865. Palmerston was a liberal Whig whose chief interest was foreign policy. He generally championed free trade and the right of European nationalities to determine their own political destinies. His bombastic patriotism made him very popular with voters; he rarely hesitated to parade British naval power before the world. Yet Palmerston was a person of the past. He had little sympathy with those political and working-class figures who wanted to extend the franchise beyond the limits of the Great Reform Act of 1832. By the time of his death Palmerston had become the chief obstacle to further political and social reform.

The Second Reform Act (1867)

By the early 1860s it had become clear to most observers that in one way or another the franchise would again have to be expanded. The prosperity and the social respectability of the working class convinced many politicians that the workers truly deserved the vote. Organizations such as the Reform League, led by John Bright (1811–1889), were agitating for parliamentary action. In 1866 Lord John Russell's Liberal ministry introduced a reform bill that was defeated by a coalition of traditional Conservatives and antidemocratic liberals. Russell resigned, and the Tory Lord Derby replaced him. What then occurred surprised everyone.

The Conservative ministry, led in the House of Commons by Benjamin Disraeli (1804–1881, introduced its own reform bill in 1867. As the debate proceeded, Disraeli accepted one amendment after another and expanded the electorate well beyond the limits earlier proposed by the Liberals. When the final measure was passed, the number of voters had been increased from approximately 1,430,000 to 2,470,000. Britain had taken a major step toward democracy. Large numbers of male working-class voters had been admitted to the electorate. Disraeli hoped that by sponsoring the measure, the Conservatives would receive the gratitude of the new voters. Because reform was bound to come, it was best for the Conservatives to enjoy the credit. Disraeli thought that eventually significant portions of the working class would support Conservative candidates who proved themselves responsive to social issues. He also thought that the growing suburban middle class would become more conservative. In the long run, his intuition proved correct, for in the past century the Conservative Party has dominated British politics.

The immediate election of 1868, however, dashed Disraeli's hopes. William Gladstone (1809–1898) became the new prime minister. Gladstone had begun political life in 1833 as a strong Tory, but over the next thirty-five years he moved steadily toward liberalism. He had supported Robert Peel, free trade, repeal of the Corn Laws, and efficient administration. As chancellor of the exchequer during the 1850s and early 1860s he had lowered taxes and government expenditure. He had also championed Italian nationalism. For many years he continued to oppose a new reform bill. Yet by the early 1860s he had also modified his position on that issue. In 1866 he had been Russell's spokesman in the House of Commons for the unsuccessful liberal reform bill.

Gladstone's Great Ministry (1868–1874)

Gladstone's ministry of 1868–1874 witnessed the culmination of classical British liberalism. Those institutions that still remained the preserve of the aristocracy and the Anglican church were opened to people from other classes and religious denominations. By an Order in Council of 1870, competitive examinations replaced patronage as a means of entering the civil service. In 1871 the purchase of officers' commissions in the army was abolished. The same year saw the removal of Anglican religious requirements for the faculties of Oxford and Cambridge universities. The Ballot Act of 1872 introduced voting by secret ballot. The most momentous measure of Gladstone's first ministry was the Education Act of 1870. For the first time in British history, the government assumed the responsibility for establishing and running elementary schools. Previously British education had been a task relegated to the religious denominations, which received small amounts of state support for the purpose.

All of these reforms were typically liberal. They sought to remove long-standing abuses without destroying existing institutions and to permit all able citizens to compete on the grounds of ability and merit. They attempted to avoid the potential danger to a democratic state of an illiterate citizenry. These reforms also constituted a mode of state building because they created new bonds of loyalty to the nation by abolishing many sources of present and future discontent.

Disraeli in Office (1874–1880)

The liberal policy of creating popular support for the nation through the extension of political liberty and the reform of abuses had its conservative counterpart in concern about social reform. Disraeli succeeded Gladstone as prime minister in 1874, when the election produced sharp divisions among Liberal Party voters over matters of liquor regulation, religion, and education. The two men had stood on different sides of most issues for over a quarter century. Whereas Gladstone looked to individualism, free trade, and competition to solve social problems, Disraeli had believed that the ruling classes of the country must confront those matters through paternalistic legislation. Disraeli

---

Gladstone Praises the Education Act of 1870

The British Education Act of 1870 marked the creation of the first national system of schools in Britain. Prime Minister Gladstone and others admired the measure because it still permitted private religious schools, because it was relatively inexpensive, and because it depended largely on the initiative of local government. In other words, it permitted the liberty and the low taxes that liberals prized.

The great object of all was to make education universal and effective. This was to be done, and doing it we sought, and I think reason and common sense required us to seek, to turn to account for that purpose the vast machinery of education already existing in the country, which had been devised and mainly provided by the Christian philanthropy and the voluntary action of the people. That was the second condition under which the Act was framed. The third was, and I think it was not less wise than the two former, that we should endeavour to separate the action of the State in the matter of education, and the application of State funds, in which I include funds raised by rate [taxes], from all subjects on which, unhappily, religious differences prevail.

Those, I may say, were three of the principles of the measure; and the fourth principle, not less important than the others, was this: that we should trust for the attainment of these great objects, as little as possible to the central Government, and as much as possible to the local authorities and the self-governing power of the people. And let me say in passing, that in my opinion if there be one portion of our institutions more precious in my view than another, it is that portion in which the people are locally organized for the purposes of acquiring the habits and instincts of political action, and applying their own free consciences and free understandings to dealing with the affairs of the community.

A. T. Bassett (Ed.), *Gladstone's Speeches* (London: Methuen, 1916), pp. 412–413.

A House of Commons debate: Gladstone, standing on the right, is attacking Disraeli, who is sitting with legs crossed and arms folded. [Mary Evans Picture Library]

believed in state action to protect weak groups of citizens. In his view such paternalistic legislation would alleviate class antagonism.

Disraeli personally talked a better line than he produced. He had very few specific programs or ideas. The significant social legislation of his ministry stemmed primarily from the efforts of his Home Secretary, Richard Cross. The Public Health Act of 1875 consolidated previous sanitary legislation and reaffirmed the duty of the state to interfere with private property on matters of health and physical well-being. Through the Artisans Dwelling Act of 1875, the government became actively involved in providing housing for the working class. The same year, in an important symbolic gesture, the Conservative majority in Parliament passed a law that gave new protection to British trade unions and allowed them to raise picket lines. The Gladstone ministry, although recognizing the legality of unions, had refused such extensive protection.

The Irish Question

In 1880 a second Gladstone ministry took office as an agricultural depression and unpopular foreign policy undermined Disraeli's popularity. In 1884, with Conservative cooperation, a third reform act was passed extending the vote to most male farm workers. However, the major issue of the decade was Ireland. From the late 1860s onward Irish nationalists had sought to achieve home rule for Ireland, by which they meant more Irish control of local government. During his first ministry Gladstone had addressed the Irish question through two major pieces of legislation. In 1869 he carried a measure to disestablish the Church of Ireland, which was the Irish branch of the Anglican church. Henceforth Irish Roman Catholics would not pay taxes to support the hated Protestant church, to which only a small fraction of the population belonged. Second, in 1870 the Liberal ministry sponsored a land act that provided compensation to evicted Irish tenants and loans for tenants who wished to purchase their land.

Throughout the 1870s the Irish question continued to fester. Land remained the center of the agitation. Today the matter of Irish economic development seems more complicated and who owned the land seems less important that the methods of management and cultivation. Nevertheless the organization of the Irish Land League in the late 1870s brought a period of intense agitation and intimidation against the landlords, who were often English. The leader of the Irish movement for a just land settlement and for home rule was Charles Stewart Parnell (1846–1891). In 1881 the second Gladstone ministry passed another Irish land act, which provided further guarantees of tenant rights. This measure only partly satisfied Irish opinion because it was accompanied by a Coercion Act intended to restore law and order to Ireland.

By 1885 Parnell had organized eighty-five Irish members of the House of Commons into a tightly disciplined party that often voted as a bloc. They pursued disruptive tactics to gain attention for the cause of home rule. They bargained with the two English political parties. In the election of 1885 the Irish Party emerged with the balance of power between the English Liberals and Conservatives. The Irish could decide which party would take office. In December 1885 Gladstone announced support of home rule for Ireland. Parnell gave his votes to the formation of a Liberal ministry. However, the issue split the Liberal Party. In 1886 a group of Liberals known as the Liberal Unionists joined with the Conservatives to defeat Gladstone's Home Rule Bill. Gladstone called for a new election, in which Liberals were defeated. They remained a permanently divided party.

The new Conservative ministry of Lord Salisbury (1830–1903) attempted to reconcile the Irish to English government through public works and administrative reform. The policy, which was tied to further coercion, had only marginal success. In 1892 Gladstone returned to power. A second Home Rule Bill passed the House of Commons but was defeated in the House of Lords. There the Irish question stood until after the turn of the century. The Conservatives sponsored a land act in 1903 that carried out the final transfer of land to tenant ownership. Ireland became a country of small farms. In 1912 a Liberal ministry passed the third Home Rule Bill. Under the provisions of the House of Lords Act of 1911, which curbed the power of that body, the bill had to pass the Commons three times over a Lords veto to become law. The third passage occurred in the summer of 1914, and the implementation of the home rule provisions of the bill was suspended for the duration of World War I.

The Irish question affected British politics in a manner not unlike that of the Austrian nationalities problem. Normal British domestic issues could not be adequately addressed because of the political divisions created by Ireland. The split of the Liberal Party proved especially harmful to the cause of further social and political reform. The people who could agree on matters of reform could not agree on Ireland, and the latter problem seemed more important. As the two traditional parties failed to deal with the social questions, by the turn of the century a newly organized Labour Party began to fill the vacuum.

Charles Stewart Parnell (1846–1891) led the fight for Irish home rule, until his political career ended in scandal when his affair with a married woman became public knowledge. [Library of Congress]

The European Political Scene: 1850–1875

Between 1850 and 1875 the major contours of the political systems that would dominate Europe until World War I had been drawn. Those systems and political arrangements solved, so far as such matters can be solved, many of the political questions and problems that had troubled the Europeans during the first half of the nineteenth century. The concept of the nation-state had on the whole triumphed. Support for governments no longer stemmed from loyalty to dynasties but from various degrees of citizen participation. Moreover the unity of nations was no longer based on dynastic links but on ethnic, cultural, linguistic, and historical bonds. The parliamentary governments of western Europe and the autocracies of eastern Europe were quite different, but both political systems had been compelled to recognize the force of nationalism and the larger role of citizens in political affairs. Only Russia failed to make such concessions, but the emancipation of serfs had constituted a concession to a mode of popular opinion. The major sources of future discontent would arise from the demands of labor to enter the political processes and the still unsatisfied aspirations of subject nationalities. Those two areas of unrest would trouble Europe for the next forty years and would eventually undermine the political structures created during the third quarter of the nineteenth century.

Suggested Readings

M. BENTLEY, *Politics Without Democracy, 1815–1914* (1984). A well-informed survey of British development.

G. F. A. BEST, *Mid-Victorian Britain* (1972). A good book on the social structure.

R. BLAKE, *Disraeli* (1967). The best recent biography.

J. BLUM, *Lord and Peasant in Russia from the Ninth to the Nineteenth Century* (1961). A clear discussion of emancipation in the later chapters.

W. L. BURN, *The Age of Equipoise* (1964). A thoughtful and convincing discussion of Victorian social stability.

M. BURNS, *Rural Society and French Politics: Boulangism and the Dreyfus Affair, 1886–1900* (1984). An examination of the subject from the rural perspective.

G. CHAPMAN, *The Dreyfus Affair: A Reassessment* (1955). A detached treatment of a subject that still provokes strong feelings.

G. CRAIG, *Germany, 1866–1945* (1978). An excellent new survey.

S. EDWARDS, *The Paris Commune of 1871* (1971). A useful examination of a complex subject.

I. V. HULL, *The Entourage of Kaiser Wilhelm II, 1888–1918* (1982). An important discussion of the scandals of the German court.

R. A. KANN, *The Multinational Empire*, 2 vols. (1950). The basic treatment of the nationality problem of Austria-Hungary.

G. KITSON CLARK, *The Making of Victorian England* (1962). The best introduction.

R. R. LOCKE, *French Legitimists and the Politics of Moral Order in the Early Third Republic* (1974). An excellent study of the social and intellectual roots of monarchist support.

P. MAGNUS, *Gladstone: A Biography* (1955). A readable biography.

A. J. MAY, *The Habsburg Monarchy, 1867–1914* (1951). Narrates in considerable detail and with much sympathy the fate of the dual monarchy.

W. N. MEDLICOTT, *Bismarck and Modern Germany* (1965). An excellent brief biography.

W. E. MOSSE, *Alexander II and the Modernization of Russia* (1958). A brief biography.

N. M. NAIMARK, *Terrorists and Social Democrats: The Russian Revolutionary Movement Under Alexander III* (1983). Based on the most recent research.

C. C. O'BRIEN, *Parnell and His Party* (1957). An excellent treatment of the Irish question.

O. PFLANZE, *Bismarck and the Development of Germany* (1963). Carries the story through the achievement of unification.

A. PLESSIS, *The Rise and Fall of the Second Empire, 1852–1871* (1985). A useful survey of France under Napoleon III.

N. RICH, *The Age of Nationalism and Reform*, rev. ed. (1976). A sound volume based on recent research.

R. SHANNON, *Gladstone: 1809–1865* (1982). Best coverage of his early career.

D. M. SMITH, *Cavour* (1984). An excellent biography.

D. M. SMITH, *Cavour and Garibaldi in 1860: A Study in Political Conflict* (1954). Explores the two key personalities in Italian unification.

D. M. SMITH, *The Making of Italy, 1796–1870* (1968). A narrative that incorporates the major documents.

A. J. P. TAYLOR, *The Habsburg Monarchy, 1809–1918* (1941). An opinionated but highly readable work.

D. THOMPSON, *Democracy in France Since 1870*, rev. ed. (1969). A clear guide to a complex problem.

J. M. THOMSON, *Louis Napoleon and the Second Empire* (1954). A straightforward account.

R. TOMBS, *The War Against Paris, 1871* (1981). Examines the role of the army in suppressing the Commune.

A. B. ULAM, *Russia's Failed Revolutionaries* (1981). A recent study of revolutionary societies and activities prior to the Revolution of 1917.

F. VENTURI, *The Roots of Revolution* (trans., 1960). A major treatment of late nineteenth-century revolutionary movement.

H. S. Watson, *The Russian Empire, 1801–1917* (1967). A far-ranging narrative.

H. U. Wehler, *The German Empire, 1871–1918* (1985). An important, controversial work.

A. J. Whyte, *The Evolution of Modern Italy* (1965). An interesting survey of the Italian problem in nineteenth-century diplomacy.

R. Williams, *The World of Napoleon III*, rev. ed. (1965). Examines the cultural setting.

C. B. Woodham-Smith, *The Reason Why* (1953). A lively account of the Crimean War and the charge of the Light Brigade.

T. Zeldin, *The Political System of Napoleon III* (1958). An examination of the local sources of political support for Louis Napoleon.

T. Zeldin, *France: 1848–1945*, 2 vols. (1973, 1977). Emphasizes the social developments.

R. E. Zelnick, *Labor and Society in Tsarist Russia: The Factory Workers of St. Petersburg, 1855–1870* (1971). An important volume that considers the early stages of the Russian industrial labor force in the era of serf emancipation.

The Eiffel Tower under construction, March 1889. Built entirely of iron by the French engineer Gustave Eiffel (steel was still too expensive), the tower was a symbol not only of Paris, but of the new industrial age. It was the centerpiece of the great Exhibition of 1889 that was held in Paris to celebrate the one hundredth anniversary of the French Revolution. [Library of Congress]

BETWEEN 1860 and 1914 European political, economic, and social life assumed many of the features characteristic of our world today. Nation-states with large electorates, political parties, centralized bureaucracies, and universal military service emerged. Business adopted large-scale corporate structures, and the labor force organized itself into trade unions. Large numbers of white-collar workers appeared. Urban life came to predominate throughout western Europe. Socialism became a major ingredient in the political life of all nations. The foundations of the welfare state and of vast military establishments were laid. Taxation increased accordingly.

During this half-century the extensive spread of industrialism created an unparalleled productive capacity in Europe. The age of the automobile, the airplane, the bicycle, the refrigerated ship, the telephone, the radio, the typewriter, and the electric light bulb dawned. The world's economies, based on the gold standard, became increasingly interdependent. European goods flowed into markets all over the globe. In turn, foreign products, raw materials, and foodstuffs were imported. Europe had also quietly become dependent on the resources and markets of the rest of the world. Changes in the weather conditions in Kansas, Argentina, or New Zealand might now affect the European economy. However, before World War I the dependence was concealed by Europe's industrial, military, and financial supremacy. At the time people rather assumed that such supremacy was a natural situation, but the twentieth century would reveal it to have been quite temporary. Nevertheless, while that condition prevailed, Europeans were able to dominate most of the other peoples of the earth and to display the most extreme self-confidence.

23

The Building of European Supremacy: Society and Politics to World War I

Population Trends and Migration

There seem to have been more Europeans proportionally about 1900 than ever before or since. Europe then contained just under one quarter of the estimated world population. The demographic expansion to which so much attention has already been paid continued through the second half of the century. The number of Europeans rose from approximately 266 million in 1850 to 401 million in 1900 and 447 million in 1910. However, the rate of European growth began to slow, whereas the population expansion elsewhere did not recede. Depending on the country in Europe, the birth rate either fell or remained stationary. The death rate did likewise. In the long run that ratio meant a more slowly growing population. This situation also meant that the grave demographic differential between the developed and the undeveloped world—which is so much a part of the present food and resource crisis—had been established.

Europe's peoples were on the move in the last half of the century as never before. Legal movement and migration became easier as the role of the landlords lessened. Railways, steamships, and better roads allowed greater physical mobility. The development of the European economy and the economies of North America, Latin America, and Australia meant better wages and cheap land, which enticed people to move.

Europeans migrated away from their continent in record numbers. Between 1846 and 1932 over fifty million Europeans left their homelands. The major areas to benefit from this movement were the United States, Canada, Australia, South Africa, Brazil, and Argentina. At mid-century most of the emigrants were from Great Britain (and especially Ireland), Germany, and Scandinavia. After 1885 the migration drew its numbers from southern and eastern Europe. This exodus helped to relieve the social and population pressures on the Continent. The outward movement of peoples in conjunction with Europe's economic and technological superiority contributed heavily to the Europeanization of the world. Not since the sixteenth century had European civilization produced such an impact on other cultures.

The Middle Classes in Ascendancy

The sixty years before World War I were definitively the age of the middle classes. The Great Exhibition of 1851 held in the Crystal Palace in

European immigrants on their way to the United States, 1906. Between 1846 and 1932, over 50 million Europeans immigrated to the United States, Canada, South America, Australia, and South Africa. [Library of Congress]

London had displayed the products and the new material life they had forged. Thereafter the middle classes became the arbiter of much consumer taste and the defender of the status quo. After the revolutions of 1848 the middle classes ceased to be a revolutionary group. Most of their political goals had been attained, even if imperfectly. Once the question of social equality had been raised, large and small property owners across the Continent moved to protect what they possessed. In the late-century drive toward protective tariffs, new business organization, militarism, and empire, the upper levels of the middle class often joined political forces with the aristocracy and other groups, such as the church and landowners, from traditionally conservative social and political backgrounds.

The middle classes, which had never been perfectly homogeneous, now became even more diverse. Their most prosperous members were the owners and managers of great businesses and banks. They lived in a splendor that rivaled and sometimes excelled that of the aristocracy. Some, such as W. H. Smith, the owner of railway newsstands in England, were made members of the House of Lords. The Krupp family of Germany were pillars of the state and received visits from the German emperor and his court. Only a few hundred families acquired such wealth. Beneath them were the comfortable small entrepreneurs and professional people, whose incomes permitted private homes, large quantities of furniture, pianos, pictures, books, journals, education for their children, and vacations. There were also the shopkeepers, the schoolteachers, the librarians, and others who had either a bit of property or a skill derived from education that provided respectable, nonmanual employment. Finally there was a wholly new element, namely the white-collar workers. These included secretaries, retail clerks, and lower-level bureaucrats in business and government. The white-collar labor force was often working class in its origins and might even belong to unions, but its aspirations for lifestyle were middle class. This lower-middle-class or petty-bourgeois element in society consciously sought to set itself off from the lifestyle of the working class. People from the lower middle class actively pursued educational opportunities and chances for even the slightest career advancement for themselves and their children. They also tended to spend a considerable portion of their disposable income on con-

The elegance of Bon Marché, one of the great Parisian department stores, is depicted in this print from the 1890s. Bon Marché was one of the first department stores in Paris and still exists. Built of wrought iron and marble, illuminated by huge glass domes, equipped with the newly invented electric lighting, it was a place for the middle classes to promenade as well as to shop. One nineteenth-century writer called these stores ''cathedrals of commerce.'' [Mary Evans Picture Library]

sumer goods, such as stylish clothing and furniture, that were distinctively middle-class in appearance.

Significant tensions began to exist among the various strata of middle-class society during the latter part of the century. The small businessmen and shopkeepers, whose numbers rose steadily until shortly after 1900, often resented the power of the great capitalists. The little people of the middle class feared being

797

Paris Department Stores Expand Their Business

The department store in Europe and the United States became a major institution of retailing in the last half of the nineteenth century. It was one of the reasons for the expansion in late-century consumer demand. This description, written by the Frenchman E. Levasseur in 1907, follows the growth of such stores in Paris and explains why they exerted such considerable economic power. The reader will notice how many of their techniques of retailing are still used today.

It was in the reign of Louis-Philippe [1830–1848] that department stores for fashion goods and dresses . . . began to be distinguished. The type was already one of the notable developments of the Second Empire; it became one of the most important ones of the Third Republic. These stores have increased in number and several of them have become extremely large. Combining in their different departments all articles of clothing, toilet articles, furniture and many other ranges of goods, it is their special object so to combine all commodities as to attract and satisfy customers who will find conveniently together an assortment of a mass of articles corresponding to all their various needs. They attract customers by permanent display, by free entry into the shops, by periodic exhibitions, by special sales, by fixed prices, and by their ability to deliver the goods purchased to customers' homes, in Paris and to the provinces. Turning themselves into direct intermediaries between the producer and the consumer, even producing sometimes some of their articles in their own workshops, buying at lowest prices because of their large orders and because they are in a position to profit from bargains, working with large sums, and selling to most of their customers for cash only, they can transmit these benefits in lowered selling prices. They can even decide to sell at a loss, as an advertisement or to get rid of out-of-date fashions. . . .

The success of these department stores is only possible thanks to the volume of their business, and this volume needs considerable capital and a very large turnover. Now capital, having become abundant, is freely combined nowadays in large enterprises. . . . [T]he large urban agglomerations, the ease with which goods can be transported by the railways, the diffusion of some comforts to strata below the middle classes, have all favoured these developments. . . .

According to the tax records of 1891, these stores in Paris, numbering 12, employed 1,708 persons and rated their site values at 2,159,000 francs; the largest had then 542 employees. These same stores had, in 1901, 9,784 employees; one of them over 2,000 and another over 1,600; their site value was doubled.

Sidney Pollard and Colin Holmes, *Documents of European Economic History,* Vol. 3 (London: Edwin Arnold, 1972), pp. 95–96.

edged out of the marketplace by large companies, with whom they could not hope to compete. The shopkeeping class always had to work very hard simply to maintain their lifestyle and were often dependent on banks for commercial credit. Department stores and mail-order catalogs endangered their livelihood. There is also good reason to believe that the learned professions were becoming overcrowded. To be a professional person no longer ensured a sound income. The new white-collar work force had just attained respectability and a non-working-class status. They profoundly feared slipping back to their social origins.

Before World War I these social groups were reasonably secure but remained quite apprehensive: they feared that the business cycle might turn against them; that their small supplementary incomes from stocks, bonds, or interest from savings might disappear; that somehow the socialists might confiscate their property. After World War I many of those fears were realized. The profound insecurity that the middle classes then experienced became one of the most significant factors of twentieth-century political life.

Middle-class people lived in every community in western Europe. But nowhere did they exert their influence and set the social and economic tenor of the day as they did in the cities.

Late-Nineteenth-Century Urban Life

Europe became more urbanized than ever in the sixty years before World War I. Migration within the Continent and Great Britain continued to move toward the cities. In France the percentage of the urban population within the whole population rose between 1850 and 1911 from approximately 25 per cent to 44 per cent, and in Germany the shift was from 30 per cent to 60 per cent. In other countries of western Europe by 1900, similar proportions of national populations lived in urban areas. The rural migrants to the cities were largely uprooted from traditional social ties. They often confronted poor housing, social anonymity, and potential unemployment because they rarely possessed skills that would make them easily employable. The difficulties that peoples from different ethnic backgrounds had in mixing socially and the competition for too few jobs generated new varieties of urban political and social discontent, such as were experienced by the thousands of Russian Jews who

GROWTH OF MAJOR EUROPEAN CITIES (FIGURES IN THOUSANDS)			
	1850	*1880*	*1910*
Berlin	419	1,122	2,071
Birmingham	233	437	840
Frankfurt	65	137	415
London	2,685	4,470	7,256
Madrid	281	398	600
Paris	1,053	2,269	2,888
Vienna	444	1,104	2,031

migrated to western Europe. Much of the political anti-Semitism of the latter part of the century had its social roots in these problems of urban migration.

The Redesign of Cities

The inward urban migration placed new social and economic demands on already-strained city resources and gradually produced

The hustle and bustle of a European capital in the late nineteenth century is captured in this photograph of the center of Berlin, taken in 1898. Horses still dominated transportation, but one of the first motor cars, small and fragile-looking, can be seen in the center of the picture. [Ullstein Bilderdienst]

significant transformations in the patterns of urban living. The central portions of many major European cities were redesigned during the second half of the century. Previously the central areas of cities had been places where large numbers of people from all social classes both lived and worked. From the middle of the century onward, they became transformed into districts where relatively few people resided and where businesses, government offices, large retail stores, and theaters were located. Commerce, trade, government, and leisure activities now dominated central cities.

The commercial development of the central portion of cities, the clearing of slums, and the building of railways into cities displaced large numbers of people who had previously lived in city centers. These developments also raised the price of centrally located urban land and of the rents charged on buildings located in the center of cities. Consequently, both the middle classes and the working class began to seek housing elsewhere. The middle classes looked for neighborhoods removed from urban congestion. The working class were in search of affordable housing. Consequently, outside the urban center proper, there arose in virtually all countries suburbs that housed the families whose breadwinner worked in the central city or in factories located within the city limits. The expansion of railways with cheap workday fares and the introduction of mechanical and later electric tramways allowed tens of thousands of workers from all classes to move daily between the city and the outlying suburbs. For hundreds of thousands of Europeans, home and work became physically separated as never before.

This remarkable social change and the values it reflected became embodied in the new designs of many European cities. The most famous and extensive transformation of a major city occurred in Paris. Like so many other European cities, Paris had expanded from the Middle Ages onward with little or no design or planning. Great public buildings and squalid hovels stood near each other. The Seine River was little more than an open sewer. The streets were narrow, crooked, and crowded. It was impossible to cross easily from one part of Paris to another either on foot or by carriage. In 1850 there did not even exist a fully correct map of the city. Of more concern to the government of Napoleon III, those streets had for sixty years provided the battleground for urban insurrections that had, on numerous occasions, most recently in 1848, toppled French governments.

Napoleon III personally determined that Paris must be redesigned. He wished the city to be beautiful and to reflect the achievements of his regime and of modern technology. The person whom he put in charge of the rebuilding program was Georges Haussmann. As prefect of the Seine from 1853 to 1870, Haussmann oversaw a vast urban reconstruction program. Whole districts were destroyed to open the way for the broad boulevards and streets that became the hallmark of modern Paris. Much, though by no means all, of the purpose of this street planning was political. The wide vistas were not only beautiful but also allowed for the quick deployment of troops to put down riots. The eradication of the many small streets and alleys removed areas where barricades could be and had been erected. The project was also political in another sense. In addition to the new boulevards, there were also constructed or completed parks, such as the Bois de Boulogne, and major public buildings, such as the Paris Opera. These projects, along with the demolition and street building, created a vast number of public jobs for thousands of people. Many other laborers found employment in the private construction that paralleled the public action.

The Franco-Prussian War ended the Second Empire, and the Paris Commune brought destruction to parts of the city. Further rebuilding and redesign took place under the Third Republic. There was much private construction of department stores, office complexes, and largely middle-class apartment buildings. By the late 1870s mechanical trams were operating in Paris. After long debate a subway system (the "Métro") was begun in 1895, long after that of London (1863). New railway stations were also erected near the close of the century. This transport linked the refurbished central city to the suburbs. In 1889 the Eiffel Tower was built, originally as a temporary structure for the international trade exposition of that year. Not all the new structures of Paris bespoke the impact of middle-class commerce and the reign of iron and steel. Between 1873 and 1914 the French Roman Catholic church oversaw the construction of the Basilica of the Sacred Heart high atop Montmartre as an act of national penance for the sins that had led to French defeat in the Franco-Prussian War. Those two landmarks—the Eiffel Tower and the Basilica of the Sacred Heart—visibly sym-

One of the new Parisian boulevards around 1900. Between 1852 and 1870, Napoleon III and his prefect Baron Haussmann transformed Paris from a medieval warren of narrow, crooked streets into a planned city of wide, elegant boulevards and sweeping vistas. [*Library of Congress*]

bolized the social and political divisions between liberals and conservatives in the Third Republic.

There were other important urban transformations in Europe during the second half of the century. They also involved battles over social and political symbols. For example, in Manchester, the English city most associated with the harshness of the Industrial Revolution in textiles, the city fathers built a great town hall according to a neo-Gothic medieval design. They wanted to remind citizens of the power and pride of the medieval city merchants, whom they regarded as their cultural and economic forebears. The situation was somewhat reversed in Vienna, from which the politically conservative Habsburg court governed its troubled multinational empire. But political liberals gained control of the Vienna city council in the early part of the second half of the century. They employed Camillo Sitte

and Otto Wagner to redesign the central area of the city. The old medieval fortifications were removed, and in their place were constructed the great boulevards of the Ringstrasse. These new streets allowed the emperor and the army to exercise control over potential political disturbances. Yet those same boulevards allowed magnificent views of the parliament building, the university, and the city hall, which stood as symbols in the heart of Habsburg Vienna of the aspirations and values of the middle classes. As Carl Schorske observed, the Ringstrasse "embodied in stone and space a cluster of social values."[1] And beyond those civic buildings rose new structures devoted to shopping, commerce, and the leisured occupations of the middle classes. Such was the case in one city after another across Europe as the values of

[1]Carl E. Schorske, *Fin-de-Siecle Vienna: Politics and Culture* (New York: Knopf, 1980), p. 62.

801

business, commerce, and material progress captured the urban civic imagination.

Urban Sanitation and Housing

The efforts of governments and of the increasingly conservative middle classes to maintain public order after 1848 led to a growing concern with the problems of public health and housing for the poor. There arose a widespread feeling that only when the health and housing of the working class were improved would the health of the middle classes also be secure and the political order stable.

These concerns first manifested themselves as a result of the great cholera epidemics of the 1830s and 1840s, during which thousands of Europeans, especially those in cities, had died from this disease of Asian origin, previously unknown in Europe. Cholera, unlike many

The Basilica of the Sacred Heart in Paris is a monument to the late nineteenth-century Roman Catholic revival in France. Its construction was begun in 1876 as part of an effort to atone for national sins that were considered by many to be the cause of French defeat in the Franco-Prussian War. [French Government Tourist Office, New York]

other common deadly diseases of the day that touched only the poor, struck persons from all classes and thus generated much middle-class demand for a solution. Before the development of the bacterial theory of disease, which was achieved only late in the century, physicians and sanitary reformers believed that cholera and other diseases were spread through infection from miasmas in the air. The miasmas, the presence of which was noted by their foul odors, were believed to arise from filth. The way to get rid of the dangerous, foul-smelling air was to clean up the cities.

During the 1840s numerous medical doctors and some government officials had begun to publicize the dangers posed by the unsanitary conditions associated with overcrowding in cities and with businesses such as basement slaughterhouses. In 1840 Louis René Villermé published his *Tableau de l'état physique et moral des ouvriers (Catalog of the Physical and Moral State of Workers)*. In 1842 Edwin Chadwick's *Report on the Sanitary Condition of the Labouring Population* shocked the English public. In Germany, Rudolf Virchow published similar findings. These and various other private and public commission reports closely linked the issues of wretched living conditions and public health. They also demonstrated that these dangers were removable and that the threat to health was preventable through sanitary reform. These reports have become some of the most important sources of information about working-class living conditions in the middle of the century.

The proposed solution to the health hazard was cleanliness, to be achieved through new water and sewer systems. The construction of these new facilities proceeded very slowly. They were usually first begun in capital cities and then much later in provincial cities. Some major urban areas did not have good water systems until after the turn of the century. Nonetheless the building of these systems constituted one of the major health and engineering achievements of the second half of the nineteenth century. The sewer system of Paris became one of the most famous parts of Haussmann's rebuilding program. In London the construction of the Albert Embankment along the Thames involved not only large sewers discharging into the river but gas mains and water pipes as well, encased in thick walls of granite and concrete, the latter being one of the new building materials of the day. Wherever these sanitary reforms were undertaken, con-

Building the sewers in the Albert Embankment along the Thames in London. New water and sewer systems did much to lower the mortality rate in nineteenth-century cities. [Mary Evans Picture Library]

siderable decreases in the mortality rate resulted.

This concern with public health led to a considerable expansion of governmental power on various levels. In Britain the Public Health Act of 1848, in France the Melun Act of 1851, and various laws in the still-disunited German states, as well as later legislation, introduced new restraints on private life and enterprise. This legislation allowed medical officers and building inspectors to enter homes and other structures in the name of public health. Private property could be condemned for posing health hazards. Private land could be excavated for the construction of the sewers and water mains required to protect the public. New building regulations put restraints on the activities of private contractors. And when the bacterial theory of disease had become fully accepted at the close of the century, the necessity of cleanliness assumed an ever greater role in public life. The discoveries of Louis Pasteur in France, Robert Koch in Germany, and Joseph Lister in Britain paved the way for the slow acceptance of the use of antiseptics in the practice of medicine and in public health policy. Thereafter, throughout Europe, issues related to the maintenance of public health and the physical well-being of national populations repeatedly opened the way for new modes of government intervention in the lives of citizens and expanded to vast new dimensions the social role of medical and scientific experts and governmental bureaucracies.

The information about working-class living conditions brought to light by the sanitary reformers also led to heated debates over the housing problem. The wretched dwellings of the poor were themselves a cause of poor sanitation and thus became one of the newly perceived health hazards. Furthermore, middle-

Working-class housing in the slums of Glasgow around 1870. Nineteenth-century Glasgow was the booming industrial center of Scotland, but slums such as this, filthy, vermin-infested, disease-ridden, had not changed for centuries. [Library of Congress]

class reformers and bureaucrats found themselves shocked by the domestic arrangements of the poor, whose large families might live in a single room lacking all forms of personal privacy. A single toilet facility might be furnished for a whole block of tenements. After the revolutions of 1848, the overcrowding in housing and the social discontent that it generated also appeared as a political danger that demanded remedy.

Middle-class reformers thus turned to housing reform as a solution to the medical, moral, and political dangers posed by slums. They praised the home, as it was understood by the middle class, as a remedy for these dangers. Proper, decent housing would foster a good home life, which would, in turn, lead to a healthy, moral, and politically stable population. As A. V. Huber, one of the early German housing reformers, declared, "Certainly it would not be too much to say that the home is the communal embodiment of family life. Thus the purity of the dwelling is almost as important for the family as is the cleanliness of the body for the individual. Good or bad housing is a question of life and death if ever there was one."[2] Later advocates of housing reform, such as Jules Simon in France, saw good housing as leading to good family life and then to strong national patriotism on the part of the well-housed family. It was widely believed that if the poor and the working class could enjoy adequate, respectable, cheap housing, much social and political discontent would be overcome. It was also believed that the personal saving and investment required for owning a home would lead the working class to adopt the thrifty habits of the middle classes.

The first attacks on the housing problem came from private philanthropy. Companies that operated on a very low margin of profit or that loaned money for housing construction at low interest rates encouraged the building of housing for the poor. Some major industrial companies undertook similar housing programs. They tended to favor the construction of small individual houses or cottages that would ensure for the working class the kind of detached dwellings associated with the middle classes. Model housing projects and industrial communities were constructed by industrial firms, such as the German Krupp armament

[2]Quoted in Nicholas Bullock and James Read, *The Movement for Housing Reform in Germany and France, 1840–1914* (Cambridge: Cambridge University Press, 1985), p. 42.

concern, in all the major European nations. All of them were seeking to ensure a contented, healthy, and stable work force. These early private efforts to address the housing problem reflected the usual liberal tendency to favor private rather than governmental enterprise.

By the mid-1880s, as a result of record-breaking migration into the cities of Europe, the housing issue had come to the fore as a political question. Some form of governmental action seemed inescapable. The actual policies differed markedly in each country, but all were quite hesitant. In England the first steps toward public housing came in the form of an act of 1885 that lowered interest rates for the construction of cheap housing. A few years later, local town councils, especially that of London, began to construct public housing. In Germany action came somewhat later in the century, primarily through the initiative of local municipalities. In 1894 France passed legislation making credit available on an easier basis for the housing of the poor, and the terms of this legislation were somewhat expanded after the turn of the century. No government had undertaken really large-scale housing experiments before World War I. Most legislation, though not all, was permissive in nature and facilitated the construction of cheap housing by the private sector.

By 1914 the housing problem stood fully recognized if not adequately addressed. What had been recognized was the necessity for planning and action. The middle-class housing reformers had, moreover, defined the terms or the debate and of future planning. The values and the character of the middle-class family house and home had become the ideal. The goal of housing reform across western Europe came to be that of a dwelling, whether in the form of a detached house or some kind of affordable city apartment with several rooms, a private entrance, and separate toilet facilities that would allow the working class to enjoy a family life more or less along the lines of the middle classes.

Furthermore, the desire for light and clean air led to greater consideration for gardens and other kinds of urban green spaces. Many urban planners embraced the concept of garden cities in which houses and apartment buildings would be constructed in green spaces far removed from city centers or factories. Their inhabitants would return to them from work each evening to enjoy parks, fresh air, and a sense of community that would, in turn, foster close-knit family life. This kind of urban vision, like so many aspects of turn-of-the-century European social life and culture, was made possible by the technological advance of the Second Industrial Revolution.

The Second Industrial Revolution

As David Landes suggested, "The period from 1850 to 1873 was the Continental industry's coming-of-age."[3] The gap that had existed for half a century between British and continental economic development was closed. The basic heavy industries of Belgium, France, and Germany underwent major expansion. French development was relatively slow, but steady. The rate of growth became more rapid after the Franco-Prussian War. The expansion of German industry was stunning. Coal mining, iron and steel production, and the chemical industry made rapid progress. German steel production surpassed that of Britain in 1893 and had almost doubled the British effort by the outbreak of World War I. This emergence of an industrial Germany was the major fact of European economic and political life at the turn of the century.

The systematic spread of railways continued to make a key contribution to economic development during the third quarter of the century. Railways cheapened transport costs and made wider regional and continental marketing possible. Railway building by Europeans in other parts of the globe created new overseas markets. The money spent on railways created demand elsewhere in the economy. Rail transportation, besides fostering capital industry and investment, put new pressure on European agriculture. Trains running into the great plains of the United States and steamships crossing the oceans sharply lowered the cost of grain and other foodstuffs imported into Europe. Continental farmers facing this foreign competition received lower prices for their produce.

Factors other than continued railway construction also accounted for the prosperity that followed hard on the heels of the economic troubles of the 1840s. From the 1850s to the

[3]David S. Landes, *The Unbound Prometheus: Technological Change and Industrial Development in Western Europe from 1750 to the Present* (Cambridge: Cambridge University Press, 1969), p. 193.

early 1870s numerous countries negotiated treaties lowering tariffs, so that goods could flow more easily and cheaply from one nation to another. New laws permitting the formation of joint stock companies and easier business incorporation allowed the garnering of vast capital funds for investment. Such legal reforms favoring capital expansion were enacted in Britain in 1856, in France in 1863, and in Prussia in 1870. The gold standard, whereby any major currency could be exchanged for gold, brought new confidence to international trade. Throughout Europe the various national currencies became more uniform. Currency rationalization was a major achievement of German unification. Finally, large banks, such as the French Crédit Mobilier and the German Darmstädter Bank, channeled funds into capital investment rather than commerce. Finance capitalism had the power to determine to a large extent what enterprises would and would not be undertaken. Banks rather than individual entrepreneurs now seemed to guide the economy.

New Industries

Initially the economic expansion of the third quarter of the century involved the spread of industries similar to those pioneered earlier in Great Britain. Thereafter, however, wholly new industries emerged. It is this latter development that is usually termed the *Second Industrial Revolution*. The first Industrial Revolution was associated with textiles, steam, and iron; the second with steel, chemicals, electricity, and oil. Steel began to replace iron in manufacture and construction. It was stronger, more flexible, and more adaptable. Its uses seemed infinite. In the 1850s Henry Bessemer (1830–

The Second Industrial Revolution was a period of innovation and experimentation. These early experimental engines were used at Owens Colle Engineering in Manchester, England, around 1900. [Bettmann Archive]

1898), an English engineer, discovered a new process, named after him, for manufacturing steel cheaply in large quantities. Bessemer had air injected directly into molten iron. The subsequent process of rapid oxidation allowed steel to be produced from the iron in larger quantities over the same period of time. In 1860 Great Britain, Belgium, France, and Germany had produced 125,000 tons of steel. By 1913 the figure had risen to 32,020,000 tons. Tied to the increased production were new processes for rolling and forming the molten metal for use in shipbuilding, machinery, and automobiles.

The chemical industry also came of age during this period. The Solway process of alkali production replaced the older Leblanc process. The new process allowed more chemical by-products to be recovered. More sulfuric acid could be produced and so could more laundry soap. New dyestuffs and plastics were also developed. The chemical industry, which has been so fundamental to the quality of life in the twentieth century, represented the earliest example of a combination of scientific and industrial development. Formal scientific research had played only the most minimal role in early industrial development. Trial-and-error amateurism was then the order of the day. By late in the second half of the century, chemists and physicists were increasingly called on to solve the problems of industry. This alliance of science, technology, and industry proved to be fundamental to economic development from the 1890s onward. As in so many other fields of the Second Industrial Revolution, Germany led the way in fostering scientific research and education.

The most significant change for industry and eventually for everyday life was the application of electrical energy to production. Electricity was the most versatile and transportable source of power ever discovered. It could be used to run either large or small machines and to make factory construction more efficient. Electricity was a mode of energy that could be taken to the machinery. The first major public power plant was constructed in Great Britain in 1881. Soon electric poles, lines, and generating stations dotted the European landscape. Electric lights were beginning to be used in homes. Streetcar and subway systems were electrified. The industries powered by electricity, in turn, produced more and more products that were run by electricity, so that the electrical industry grew rapidly on itself. Probably no

The invention of electricity revolutionized European life, not least in public transport. Before the 1890s, streetcars in European cities were pulled by horses, which severely limited their size and speed. The electric trolley was bigger, faster, cleaner, and cheaper. This photograph was taken in Berlin in 1901 when electric streetcars were rapidly replacing horsedrawn buses. [Ullstein Bilderdienst]

single late-nineteenth-century development has so influenced the material lifestyle of this century.

The turn of the century also saw the emergence of the first large European demand for petroleum. The internal combustion engine was invented in 1876. When the German engineer Gottlieb Daimler (1834–1900) put it on four wheels and obtained a French patent in 1885, the automobile was born. France initially took the lead in auto manufacture, but for many years the car remained a novelty item that only the wealthy could afford. It was the American Henry Ford (1863–1947) who later made the automobile accessible to large numbers of people. The automobile and the new industrial and chemical uses for oil greatly expanded the demand for petroleum. Before the 1890s petroleum had been used primarily for lighting; soon it became the basis for transportation and much of the new chemical industry. Europe, then as now, was almost wholly dependent on imported oil. The major supplying

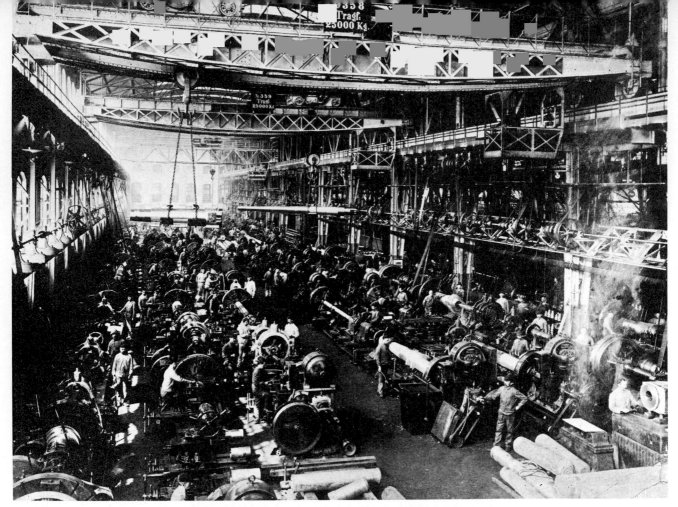

The Krupp armaments works at Essen, Germany. In the late nineteenth century, Krupp was one of the largest industrial firms in Europe, employing some 30,000 workers. In the Second Industrial Revolution, Germany not Britain, led the way. [Culver Pictures]

companies were Standard Oil of the United States, British Shell Oil, and Royal Dutch.

The Second Industrial Revolution witnessed a shift in the European economic balance of power. In almost all areas of the new industrial expansion, Great Britain, which had pioneered the first Industrial Revolution, fell behind the Continent and especially Germany. Britain ceased to be a leader and became simply one more competitor. There was no lack of invention on the part of individual British citizens, but the early industrial lead meant that the nation's industries were often locked into existing production processes and could not easily incorporate new techniques. The British did too little to encourage scientific and technical education. Managers put too much faith in the inventive amateur, who had so brilliantly fostered the early Industrial Revolution. British investors put too little capital into new industry. Management was immensely complacent. There was too much dependence on old mar-

keting techniques. Attempts to improve the situation came only after the lead had been lost. All of these factors meant that by 1900, while still a great industrial power, Britain was falling behind German competition. This situation greatly affected the international political rivalry of the two powers.

Wider Economic Trends

Business Difficulties

The second half of the century was not a period of uninterrupted or smooth economic growth. The years from 1850 to 1873 saw a general boom in both industry and agriculture. The last quarter of the century witnessed economic advance but of a much slower nature. Bad weather and foreign competition put grave pressures on European agriculture. Grain producers suffered the most. In Britain thousands of acres of land went out of tillage. In eastern Europe the landlords demanded new protective tariffs. There were moves to specialize farming. Denmark, for example, at this time changed to dairy production. Other countries adopted more scientific and mechanized modes of agriculture. Farmers used fertilizers more frequently and took steam-driven tractors into the fields to aid in plowing. These techniques made farming more costly, and farms became larger. From the consumers' standpoint these developments meant lower food prices. Nevertheless the difficulties of the agricultural sector put a drag on the economy.

During 1873 a number of major banks failed, and the rate of capital investment slowed. The major railway systems had been built. During the next two decades stagnation occurred in several industries. Prices and profits fell. Wages also became lower, but the simultaneous fall in prices meant that real wages generally held firm and, in some countries, even improved. There were pockets of unemployment. (In fact the word *unemployment* was coined during this period.) Despite the stagnation, the general standard of living in the industrialized nations improved, although many workers still lived and labored in abysmal conditions. What made this depression less cruel and disruptive than the turmoil of the 1840s was the greater availability of consumer goods and the assurance of a food supply. By the turn of the century the demand for consumer goods and the development of new employing industries made possible by the Second Industrial Revolution had lifted Europe from its economic doldrums.

What brought the economy out of this period of stagnation, which contemporaries regarded as a depression, was a new expansion of consumer demand. The lower food prices eventually allowed all classes to spend a marginally larger amount of their income on consumer goods. Urbanization in and of itself created a larger market. People living in cities simply saw more things they wanted to buy than they would have seen in the countryside. The new industries of the late century were largely directed toward consumer goods. Retailing techniques changed. Department stores, retail chains, new packaging, mail-order catalogs, and advertising were developed. Marketing itself was creating new demand. The foundations of a consumer economy were being laid. Furthermore the overseas imperialism of this period also opened new markets for European consumer goods.

The Drift Away from Competition and Free Trade

The economic pressures of the last quarter of the century brought about a shift from economic competition to business consolidation. Big business firms and corporations were organized. They had no desire to compete because they had far too much to lose. Cartels and trade associations, which were the European version of the American trusts, were organized. They attempted to divide markets and to fix prices so as not to drive each other out of business. The great examples were the German General Electric Company, the German Siemens Electric Company, and the British Glass Manufacturers' Association. Other industries, such as the Krupp armaments company, organized vertically in order to control the sources of raw materials and product marketing as well as manufacturing. These new forms of business organization tended to stabilize industries, to make jobs more secure, and to increase consumer demand by creating more steady wages. They did not, however, necessarily produce the lowest consumer prices.

The mid-century ideal of free trade also came under increasing attack as both farming and manufacturing interests sought to ensure a monopoly in their national markets. Governments across the Continent raised new protective tariff barriers. Austria and Russia turned to this device in 1874 and in 1877, respectively. In 1879 Bismarck imposed a tariff to protect German industry and the *Junker* landlords. Italy moved to protection in 1887, and the Third French Republic passed the Méline Tariff in 1892. Each of these measures was passed to bring new domestic political support to the various governments. Great Britain remained true to free trade. Yet even there, after the turn of the century Joseph Chamberlain (1836–1914) led a campaign for tariff reform. The drive for tariffs meant that business was seeking the kind of government aid that it had largely spurned half a century earlier.

Europeans also looked outside their continent for markets. The late-century age of imperialism was closely related to internal economic problems. European bankers invested large amounts of money in the rest of the world, with the largest portion going to the development of the United States. But traders and investors also hoped to reap profits from Latin America, Asia, and Africa. The early British textile industry had depended to a great extent on foreign markets. Britain's emulators in the latter part of the century also believed that they must penetrate those areas. They needed both raw materials and new outlets for finished goods.

It was once argued that the Europeans carved out their colonies in order to create those needed markets. The process is now considered more complicated. In establishing sources for raw materials and in creating markets for finished goods, the Europeans undermined the existing governments and the traditional societies in the underdeveloped portions of the globe. The result was political instability in those areas. It was after such turmoil had been created that the European governments moved in to protect the already-existing commercial presence of their nations. The foreign markets never proved to be as profitable as their promoters had hoped. Right up to World War I, Europe itself remained the single largest market for its own goods.

At the close of the nineteenth century Europe clearly predominated in the world economy. It had the most capital, and its industries provided it with the military might to control other areas. However, within Europe two distinct economic zones had come into existence. One consisted of the advanced industrial states, including Britain, Belgium, France, Germany, northern Italy, and the western part of Austria. These areas enjoyed a relatively high standard of living, good transport systems, and healthy, educated populations. The second area consisted of Ireland, the Iberian Peninsula, southern Italy, the Balkans, most of Austria-Hungary, and Russia. There agricultural production dominated, and education was backward. These areas exported grain and foodstuffs to the industrialized sector. This European economic division, which came into being in the late nineteenth century, was not overcome until after World War II, and even then only partially.

Varieties of Late-Nineteenth-Century Women's Experience

The complexities of general European society reflected themselves in the variety of social experiences encountered by women. The lives of women in the various social ranks partook of the general lifestyle of those particular classes. Yet, within each of those social ranks, the experience of women was distinct from that of men. Women remained, generally speaking, in positions of economic dependence and legal inferiority, whatever their social class.

The pattern of gender-defined social roles that had begun to develop in the early nineteenth century in the industrialized sections of western Europe spread during the later part of the century wherever industrialism and urbanization came to dominate, and especially wherever middle-class values predominated. Men worked as the chief family wage earner. Young women in the working class and the lower middle class still spent part of their youth working to support themselves and to accumulate enough money to marry. After these women married, they tended to work at home. Such was the expected social pattern for late-nineteenth-century women. The problem arose as the lives of many women did not or could not conform to this pattern. There was little or no provision for women who did not marry or who had to support themselves independently, and they became very much the victims of the general social expectations of the lives of women.

New Employment Patterns for Women

During the decades of the Second Industrial Revolution, two major developments affected the economic lives of women. The first was an explosion in the variety of available jobs. The second was a significant withdrawal of married women from the work force. These two seemingly contradictory situations require some explanation.

The expansion of governmental bureaucracies, the emergence of corporations and other large-scale businesses, the new and growing demand for schoolteachers resulting from compulsory education laws, and the vast expansion of retail stores of all kinds opened many new employment opportunities for women. Technological inventions and innovations such as the typewriter and eventually the telephone exchange fostered female employment. Women by the thousands became secretaries and clerks for governments and for private businesses. Still more thousands became shop assistants. These new jobs did mean new and often somewhat better employment opportunities for women, but these new jobs still required relatively low levels of skill and involved minimal training. They were occupied

The first telephone exchange in Berlin exhibits the role of both communication and electricity in the Second Industrial Revolution. In this picture men are attending the switchboard; soon, however, women took over these jobs. Telephone companies eventually opened a large area of employment for women. [Bettmann Archive]

primarily by unmarried women or widows. Schoolteaching also became rapidly identified as a female occupation, but women very rarely entered the university world or the learned professions. They were even more rarely to be found in major positions of private or public management. Furthermore, employers continued to pay women low wages because they assumed, quite often knowing better, that a woman did not need to support herself independently but could expect additional financial support from her father or from her husband. Consequently a woman who did need to support herself independently was almost always unable to find a job paying an adequate income or a position that paid as well as one held by a man, who was supporting himself independently.

Most of the women in this new service work force were young and unmarried. At the time of marriage, or certainly after the birth of her first child, a woman normally withdrew from the labor force. She either did not work or she worked at some occupation that could be pursued in the home. Such withdrawal in and of itself was not new by the latter part of the century, but the extent of it was much more significant. The kinds of industrial occupations that women had filled in the middle of the nineteenth century, especially textile and garment making, were shrinking. There were consequently fewer opportunities for employment in those industries for either married or unmarried women. Employers in offices and retail stores seem to have preferred young, unmarried women whose family responsibilities would not interfere with their work. The shrinkage in the number of children being born meant that fewer married women were needed to look after other women's children. The real wages paid to male workers increased during this period, so that there was a somewhat reduced need for the supplementary wages of their wives. Also, men tended to live longer as a result of improving health conditions, and their wives had to enter the work force less frequently in emergencies. The smaller size of families also lowered the need for supplementary wages. Working children stayed longer at home and continued to contribute to the family's wage pool. Finally, the cultural dominance of the middle class, with its generally idle wives, established a pattern of social expectations according to which the more prosperous a working-class family became, the less involved in employment its women were supposed to be. Indeed, the less income-producing work a wife did, the more prosperous and stable the family was considered.

Women working in the Cadbury candy factory in England. In the late nineteenth century, although most working women continued to be domestic servants, for the first time large numbers of women began to work in factories and retail stores. [Cadbury Limited, Bournville, England.]

Yet behind these generalities stands a vast variety of different social and economic experiences encountered by women. As might be expected, the chief determinant of those individual experiences was social class.

Working-class Women

Although the textile industry and garment making were much less dominant than earlier in the century, they continued to employ large numbers of women. The situation of women in the German clothing-making trades illustrates the kind of vulnerable economic situation that they could encounter as a result of their limited skills and the organization of the trade. The system of manufacturing mass-made clothes of uniform sizes in Germany was quite complex. It was designed to require minimal capital investment on the part of the manufacturers and to protect them from significant risk. A major manufacturer would arrange for the production of clothing through a putting-out system. He would purchase the material and then put it out for tailoring. The clothing was produced not in a factory but usually in numerous, independently owned, small sweatshops or by workers in their homes. In Berlin in 1896 there were over eighty thousand garment workers, mostly women, who were so employed. When business was good and the demand strong, there was much employment for these women. But as the seasons shifted or business became poor, these workers became unemployed as less and less work was put out for production. In effect, the workers who actually sewed the clothing carried much of the risk of the enterprise. Some women did work in factories, but they, too, were subject to loss of work. Furthermore, women in the clothing trade were nearly always in positions less skilled than those of the male tailors or the male middlemen who owned the workshops.

In a very real sense the expectation of separate social and economic spheres for men and women and the definition of the chief work of women as pertaining to the home contributed mightily to the exploitation of women workers outside the home. Because their wages were regarded merely as supplementing their husbands', they became particularly vulnerable to economic exploitation. The entire German putting-out system for clothing production and similar systems of clothing production elsewhere depended on this situation. What was regarded as an adequate wage for a woman was always seen in terms of a wage supplementary to the husband's. Consequently, women were nearly always treated as casual workers everywhere in Europe.

Prostitution

One of the major but little recognized social facts of most large and small nineteenth-century cities was the presence of a very considerable surplus of women workers whose social situation did not allow them to conform to those normal expectations of working only for wages supplementary to a father's or a husband's. There were almost always many more women seeking employment than there were jobs. The economic vulnerability of women and the consequent poverty encountered by many of them was one of the chief causes of prostitution. In any major late-nineteenth-century European city, there were thousands of prostitutes. The presence of prostitution was, of course, not new. It had always been one way for very poor women to find some income, but in the late nineteenth century it seems to have been quite closely related to the difficulty encountered by very poor women who were attempting to make their way in an overcrowded female labor force. On the Continent, prostitution was generally legalized and was subject to governmental and municipal regulations. Those regulations were, it should be noted, passed and enforced by male legislatures and councils and were enforced by male police and physicians. In Great Britain, prostitution received only minimal regulation.

Numerous myths and much misunderstanding have surrounded the subject of prostitution. The most recent studies of the subject in England emphasize that most prostitutes were active on the streets for a very few years, generally from their late teens to about age twenty-five. They tended to be very poor women who had recently migrated from nearby rural areas. Others were born in the towns where they became prostitutes. Certain cities, such as towns with large army garrisons or naval port cities or cities with large transient populations, such as London, fostered the presence of considerable numbers of prostitutes. There seem to have been many fewer prostitutes in manufacturing towns, where there were more opportunities for steady employment and where community life was more stable.

Women who became prostitutes tended to

An unflattering view of French prostitutes in 1894, by Henri de Toulouse-Lautrec (1864–1901). In France and in most Continental countries, female prostitution was legal but subject to government regulation. [Metropolitan Museum of Art]

have minimal skills and education and to have come from families of unskilled workers. Many had been servants. They also tended to be from broken homes or to be orphaned. Contrary to many sensational late-century newspaper accounts, there seem to have been very few child prostitutes. Furthermore, rarely were these women seduced into their occupations by middle-class employers or middle-class clients. The customers of poor working-class prostitutes seem to have been primarily working-class men. Women remained prostitutes for relatively few years. Thereafter they seem to have moved back into the regular work force or to have married.

Poverty was not the only problem confronting English prostitutes. Venereal disease was another. Special institutions known as *lock hospitals* received women suffering from these diseases. It was nearly always assumed that a woman suffering from a venereal disease was a prostitute, and that she should be isolated from other patients. Because many people regarded venereal disease as the wages of vice, these hospitals were badly underfinanced. Within the hospitals women were submitted to rigor-

813

ous moral and religious instruction. In contrast, men who suffered from venereal disease were not subjected to medical isolation or moral instruction.

Between 1864 and 1886 English prostitutes became subject to the Contagious Diseases Acts, which provided for the medical examination of prostitutes in certain naval and military cities. Any woman whom the police identified as or suspected of being a prostitute could be required to undergo immediate internal medical examination for venereal disease. Those found to have the disease could be confined to a lock hospital for a number of months. These measures, in effect, enacted the double standard of sexual morality into law. No action of any kind was taken against the male customers of these women.

By 1869 opposition had arisen to the Acts from a number of quarters. The most important of these opposition organizations was the Ladies' National Association for the Repeal of the Contagious Diseases Acts. This was a distinctly middle-class organization led by Josephine Butler. It achieved the suspension of the Acts in 1883 and their repeal in 1886. The advocates of repeal based their arguments on English liberty and on public repugnance at women being dragged from the streets on vague charges and then being forced to submit to physical examination. Further, middle-class women were angered that the laws in no manner affected or penalized men. They also believed that the causes of prostitution lay primarily in the work conditions and the poverty imposed on so many working-class women. They also saw poor women being made victims of the same kind of discrimination that prevented middle-class women from entering the universities and professions. Middle-class women were attempting to prove that they were just as human and rational as men and thus properly subject to equal treatment. The Contagious Diseases Acts were designed to prove that women were otherwise and to treat them as less than human and less than rational creatures. The laws literally took women's bodies from their own control and put them under the control of male customers, medical men, and the police. The movement to repeal the Contagious Diseases Acts provided the first experience of many British middle-class women in the political arena. It also provided an example of one of the rare instances of active cooperation between women of markedly different social classes. Another result of the

movement and of the repeal were purity crusades and calls for chastity to end the social evil of prostitution and venereal disease, and thus to make such repressive legislation unnecessary.

Women of the Middle Class

It is difficult to communicate the vast social gap that lay between the experience of poor working-class women whose economic situation led them into prostitution or into the sweated textile trades and those of their middle-class counterparts. Middle-class women participated as their fathers' and husbands' incomes permitted in the vast expansion of consumerism and domestic comfort

The cover of this French fashion magazine from March 1910 conveys an idealized portrait of middle-class femininity—modest, serene, elegant. Such a woman was expected to have no other role in life than that of dutiful daughter, wife, and mother. [Art Resource]

The Virtues of a French Middle-class Lady Praised

One of the chief social roles assigned to middle-class French women was that of charitable activity. This obituary of Mme. Émile Delesalle from a Roman Catholic church paper of the late nineteenth century describes the work of this woman among the poor. It is a very revealing document because it clearly shows the class divisions that existed in the giving of charity. It also is a document that instructed its women readers through the kind of virtues praised. Note the emphasis on home life, spirituality, and instruction of children in charitable acts.

The poor were the object of her affectionate interest, especially the shameful poor, the fallen people. She sought them out and helped them with perfect discretion which doubled the value of her benevolent interest. To those whom she could approach without fear of bruising their dignity, she brought, along with alms to assure their existence, consolation of the most serious sort—she raised their courage and their hopes. To others, each Sunday, she opened all the doors of her home, above all when her children were still young. In making them distribute these alms with her, she hoped to initiate them early into practices of charity.

In the last years of her life the St. Gabriel Orphanage gained her interest. Not only did she accomplish a great deal with her generosity, but she also took on the task of maintaining the clothes of her dear orphans in good order and in good repair. When she appeared in the courtyard of the establishment at recreation time, all her protégés surrounded her and lavished her with manifestations of their profound respect and affectionate gratitude.

Annales de l'archiconfrérie des mères chrétiennes, as quoted and trans. in Bonnie G. Smith, *Ladies of the Leisure Class: The Bourgeoises of Northern France in the Nineteenth Century* (Princeton, N.J.: Princeton University Press, 1981), pp. 147–148.

that marked the end of the nineteenth century and the early twentieth century. Their homes were filled with manufactured items, including clothing, china, furniture, carpets, drapery, wallpaper, and prints. They enjoyed all the improvements of sanitation and electricity. They could command the services of numerous domestic servants. They moved into the fashionable new houses being constructed in the rapidly expanding suburbs.

For the middle classes the gender distinction between work and family had become complete and constituted the model for all other social groups. Middle-class women, if at all possible, did not work. More than any other group of women, they became limited to the role of wife and mother. That situation allowed them to enjoy much domestic luxury and comfort, but it also no less markedly circumscribed what they might do with their lives, their talents, their ambitions, and their intelligence. Middle-class women became, in large measure, the product of a particular understanding of social life. The home and its occupants were to have lives very different from the life of busi-

ness and the marketplace. The home was not only to be distinct from the world of work and business, it was also to be a private refuge from that life. This view was set forth in scores of women's journals across Europe.

As studies of the lives of middle-class women in northern France have suggested, this image of the middle-class home and of the role of women in the home is quite different from the one that had existed earlier in the nineteenth century. During the first half of the century the spouse of a middle-class husband might very well contribute directly to the business, handling accounts or correspondence. These women also frequently had little to do with rearing their children, leaving that task first to nurses and later to governesses. This situation was very different later in the century. The reasons for the change are not certain, but it would appear that men began to insist on doing business with other men. Magazines and books directed toward women began to praise motherhood, domesticity, religion, and charity as the proper work of women.

For these middle-class French women, as

well as for middle-class women elsewhere, the home came to be praised as the center of virtue, of children, and of the proper life for women. Marriages were usually arranged for some kind of family economic benefit. Romantic marriage was presented as a danger to social stability. Most middle-class women in northern France married by the age of twenty-one. Children were expected to follow very soon after marriage. Quite often a child was born within the first year, and the rearing and nurturing of that child and of later children was the chief task in life for the woman. Such a woman would have had no experience of or training for any role other than that of a dutiful daughter, wife, and mother.

Within the home a middle-class woman performed major roles. She was largely in charge of the household. She oversaw virtually all domestic management and child care. She was in a very real sense in charge of the home as a major unit of consumption. It was for this reason that so much advertising was directed toward women. But all of this domestic activity occurred within the limits of the approved middle-class lifestyle and set relatively strict limits on a woman's initiative. She and her conspicuous idleness served to symbolize first her father's and then her husband's worldly success. This cult of domesticity in France and elsewhere assigned to women very firm religious duties. The Roman Catholic church strongly supported these domestic and religious roles for French women. Frequent attendance at mass and religious instruction of their children were part of this role. Women were charged with observing meatless Fridays and with participating in religious observances. Prayer was a major part of their lives and daily rituals. Those portions of the Christian religion that stressed meekness and passivity became a major part of the mind set of these middle-class French women. In other countries as well, religion and religious activities became part of the expected work of women. For this reason women were regarded by political liberals as especially susceptible to the influence of priests. This close association between religion and a strict domestic life for women was one of the reasons that as time passed, there often arose tension between feminism and religious authorities.

Another important role for these middle-class women was the administration of charity. Women were judged especially prepared to carry out charitable roles because of their supposed innate spirituality and their capacity to instill domestic and personal discipline. Middle-class women were often in charge of clubs for poor youth, societies to protect poor young women, schools for infants, and societies for visiting the poor. Women were supposed to be particularly interested in the problems of poor women, their families, and their children. Quite often charity from middle-class women required the poor recipient to indicate in some manner the possession of a good character. By the end of the century middle-class women who were attempting to expand their spheres of activity became social workers either for the church, for private charities, or for the government. It was a vocation that was a natural extension of the roles socially assigned to them.

The world of the middle-class wife and her family is now understood to have been much more complicated than was once thought. Not all such women or their families conformed to the stereotypes. First, recent studies have suggested that the middle classes of the nineteenth century enjoyed sexual relations within marriage far more fully than was once thought. Diaries, letters, and even early medical and sociological sex surveys indicate that sexual enjoyment rather than sexual repression was fundamental to middle-class marriages. Much of the inhibition about sexuality stemmed from the actual dangers of childbirth rather than from any dislike or disapproval of sexuality. Second, one of the major changes in this regard during the second half of the century was the acceptance of small family size among the middle classes. The fertility rate in France dropped throughout the nineteenth century. It began to fall in England steadily from the 1870s onward. Middle-class married couples seem to have begun to make conscious decisions to limit the size of their families. During the last decades of the century, various new contraceptive devices became available and were used by middle-class families. One of the chief reasons for this change was the apparently conscious decision made by couples to maintain a relatively high level of material consumption by rearing fewer children. Children had become much more expensive to rear, and at the same time, more material comforts had become available. The presence of fewer children in the middle-class household probably meant that more attention was focused on the child and that mothers and their children became emotionally closer.

As can be seen from the previous discussion, liberal society and its values neither automatically nor inevitably improved the lot of women. Divorce was difficult everywhere. Most property laws until well into the second half of the century favored husbands or gave them virtually complete control over their wives' property. In France, for example, the major political legislation of the revolution and the Napoleonic Code excluded women from voting and made them subject to their husbands. There was a general apprehension among male political liberals that granting the vote to women would benefit political conservatives because it was widely assumed that women were unduly controlled by Roman Catholic priests. There was a similar apprehension about the alleged influence of the Anglican clergy over women in England. Consequently anticlerical liberals had difficulty working with feminists.

Those few women who pioneered female entry into the professions, activity on government commissions and school boards, or dispersal of birth control information faced grave social obstacles, personal humiliation, and often outright bigotry. These women and their male supporters were challenging that clear separation of life into male and female spheres that had emerged in middle-class European

J. S. Mill Analyzes the Causes of the Subjection of Women

John Stuart Mill (1806–1873) was one of the key nineteenth-century advocates of women's rights. In this 1869 essay he was concerned that society benefit from the various talents and capacities that women could bring to the social, political, and intellectual problems of the day. He attempted to explain how custom, public opinion, and traditional education not only denied women their rightful place in society but also cunningly convinced them in numerous subtle ways that they could not achieve such a place.

Men do not want solely the obedience of women, they want their sentiments. . . . They have therefore put everything in practice to enslave their minds. . . . The masters of women wanted more than simple obedience, and they turned the whole force of education to effect their purpose. All women are brought up from the very earliest years in the belief that their ideal of character is the very opposite to that of men; not self-will, and government by self-control, but submission, and yielding to the control of others. All the moralities tell them that it is the duty of women, and all the current sentimentalities that it is their nature, to live for others; to make complete abnegation of themselves, and to have no life but in their affections. And by their affections are meant the only ones they are allowed to have—those to the men with whom they are connected, or to the children who constitute an additional and indefeasible tie between them and a man.

When we put together three things—first, the natural attraction between opposite sexes; secondly, the wife's entire dependence on the husband, every privilege or pleasure she has being either his gift, or depending on his will; and lastly, that the principal object of human pursuit, consideration, and all objects of social ambition, can in general be sought or obtained by her only through him—it would be a miracle if the object of being attractive to men had not become the polar star of feminine education and formation of character. And, this great means of influence over the minds of women having been acquired, an instinct of selfishness made men avail themselves of it to the utmost as a means of holding women in subjection, by representing to them meekness, submissiveness, and resignation of all individual will into the hands of a man, as an essential part of sexual attractiveness.

John Stuart Mill, *On Liberty, Representative Government, and the Subjection of Women* (London: Oxford University Press, 1960), pp. 443–444.

social life during the nineteenth century. Women themselves were often hesitant to support feminist causes because they had been so thoroughly acculturated into the recently stereotyped roles. Many women as well as men saw a real conflict between family responsibilities and feminism.

But there was another important reason for the frequent absence of support for feminist causes by women. Issues of gender constituted only one of several priorities in the minds and social concerns of women. Some women were very sensitive to their class and economic interests. Others subordinated feminist issues to national unity and nationalistic patriotism. Still others would not support particular feminist organizations because of differences over tactics. The various social and tactical differences among women led quite often to sharp divisions within the feminists' own ranks. Except in England, it was often difficult for working-class and middle-class women to cooperate. Roman Catholic feminists were uncomfortable with radical secularist feminists. There were other disagreements about which goals for improvement in women's legal and social conditions were most important.

Liberal society and law had set up many obstacles to women's developing their lives fully, and the necessity of working within the political structures of liberal states raised many of the issues that divided women. However, the intellectual and political tools for feminists' social and political criticisms were also present in the ideology of liberal society. The rationalism and the penchant for self-criticism that have characterized modern Western society manifested themselves in the movement to emancipate women. As early as 1792 in Britain, Mary Wollstonecraft (1759–1797), in *The Vindication of the Rights of Woman* (see document in Chapter 18), had applied the revolutionary doctrines of the rights of man to the predicament of the members of her own sex. John Stuart Mill (1806–1873), in conjunction with his wife Harriet Taylor, had applied the logic of liberal freedom to the position of women in *The Subjection of Women* (1869). The arguments for utility and efficiency so dear to middle-class liberals could be used to expose the human and social waste implicit in the inferior role assigned to women. Furthermore, the socialist criticism of capitalist society often, though by no means always, included a harsh indictment of the social and economic position to which women had been relegated. Yet the

Mary Wollstonecraft (1759–1797) was one of the first writers to call for equal rights for women. Shortly before her early death she was married to William Godwin, the English political writer and novelist. Their child was the future Mary Shelley, author of Frankenstein *and wife of the Romantic poet. [National Portrait Gallery, London]*

very fact that the earliest statements of feminism arose from critics of the existing order and were often associated with people who had unorthodox opinions about sexuality, family life, and property hardened resistance to the feminist message. This seems to have been especially true on the Continent, where feminists were never able to stir up massive public support or demonstrations as they were in Great Britain and the United States.

Much of the discussion of the social position of women remained merely theory and talk. Some women did gain meaningful employment in the professions, but their numbers were quite small. Women did not rise rapidly through the work force. However, to some extent, theory was transformed into practice, or at least into protest, as far as political life was concerned. The political tactics used by men to expand the electoral franchise and to influence the governing process earlier in the century could be and were used by women later in the century to pursue the same goal. The claims to political participation set forth by the respectable, prosperous, and educated working class applied equally well to respectable, prosperous, and educated women. Nonetheless, virtually everywhere, the feminist cause was badly divided.

The most advanced women's movement in Europe was that in Great Britain. There Millicent Fawcett (1847–1929) led the moderate National Union of Women's Suffrage Societies. Her view was that Parliament would grant women the vote only when convinced that women would be respectable and responsible in their political activity. In 1908 this organization could rally almost half a million women in London. Fawcett was the wife of a former liberal party Cabinet minister and economist. Her tactics were those of English liberals. Emmeline Pankhurst (1858–1928) led a different and much more radical branch of British feminists. Pankhurst's husband, who had died near the close of the century, had been active in labor and Irish nationalist politics. Irish nationalists had developed numerous disruptive political tactics. Early labor politicians had also sometimes had confrontations with police over the right to hold meetings. In 1903 Pankhurst and her daughters, Christabel and Sylvia, founded the Women's Social and Political Union. For several years they and their followers, known derisively as *suffragettes*, lobbied publicly and privately for the extension of the

---

An English Feminist Defends the Cause of the Female Franchise

Frances Power Cobbe wrote widely on numerous religious and social issues of the second half of the century. She had been a feminist since early adulthood. In this letter to an English women's feminist magazine in 1884, she explained why women should seek the vote. More important, she attempted to refute the argument that possession of the franchise would in some manner make women less womanly.

If I may presume to offer an old woman's counsel to the younger workers in our cause, it would be that they should adopt the point of view—that it is before all things our duty *to obtain the franchise. If we undertake the work in this spirit, and with the object of using the power it confers, whenever we gain it, for the promotion of justice and mercy and the kingdom of God upon earth, we shall carry on all our agitation in a corresponding manner, firmly and bravely, and also calmly and with generous good temper. And when our opponents come to understand that this is the motive underlying our efforts, they, on their part, will cease to feel bitterly and scornfully toward us, even when they think we are altogether mistaken. . . .*

The idea that the possession of political rights will destroy ''womanliness,'' absurd as it may seem to us, is very deeply rooted in the minds of men; and when they oppose our demands, it is *only just to give them credit for doing so on grounds which we should recognize as valid, if their premises were true. It is not so much that our opponents (at least the better part of them) despise women, as that they really prize what women now are in the home and in society so highly that they cannot bear to risk losing it by any serious change in their condition. These fears are futile and faithless, but there is nothing in them to affront us. To remove them, we must not use violent words, for every such violent word confirms their fears; but, on the contrary, show the world that while the revolutions wrought by men have been full of bitterness and rancor and stormy passions, if not of bloodshed, we women will at least strive to accomplish our great emancipation calmly and by persuasion and reason.*

Letter to the *Woman's Tribune*, May 1, 1884, quoted in Frances Power Cobbe, *Life of Frances Power Cobbe by Herself* (Boston: Houghton, Mifflin, 1894).

Mrs. Emmeline Pankhurst (1858–1928) led a long struggle for female suffrage in Britain. British women were finally given the vote in 1918. [Mary Evans Picture Library]

vote to women. By 1910, having failed to move the government, they turned to the violent tactics of arson, window breaking, and sabotage of postal boxes. They marched en masse on Parliament. The Liberal government of Henry Asquith imprisoned many of the women and force-fed those who went on hunger strikes in jail. The government refused to extend the franchise. Only in 1918 did some British women receive the vote as a result of their contribution to the war effort.

How advanced the British women's movement was can be seen by the contrast in France and Germany. In France, Hubertine Auclert (1848–1914) had begun campaigning for the vote in the 1880s. She stood virtually alone. During the 1890s the National Council of French Women (CNFF) was organized among upper-middle-class women, but it did not support the idea of the vote for women until after the turn of the century. French Roman Catho-

lic feminists such as Marie Mauguet (1844–1928) supported the franchise also. But almost all French feminists rejected any form of violence. They also were never able to organize mass rallies. The leaders of French feminism believed that the vote could be achieved through careful legalism. In 1919 the French Chamber of Deputies passed a bill granting the vote to women, but in 1922 the French Senate defeated the bill. It was not until after World War II that French women received the right to vote.

In Germany the situation of feminist awareness and action was even more underdeveloped. German law actually forbade German women from political activity. Because no group in the German Empire enjoyed extensive political rights, women were not certain that they would benefit from demanding them. Any such demand would be regarded as subversive not only of the political state but also of the society. In 1894 the Union of German Women's Organizations (BDFK) was founded. By 1902 it was supporting a call for the right to vote. But it was largely concerned with improvement of women's social conditions, access to education, and other protections. The group also worked to see that women might be admitted to political or civic activity on the municipal level. This work usually included education, child welfare, charity, and public health. The German Social Democratic Party supported women's suffrage, but this position made the demand all the more suspect in the eyes of the German authorities and especially in the view of German Roman Catholics. Women received the vote in Germany only in 1918, when the constitution of the Weimar Republic was promulgated after German defeat in war and revolution at home.

Throughout Europe in the years before World War I, the demands for women's rights were raised widely and vocally. But the extent of their success and their tactics tended in very large measure to reflect the political and class structures of the individual nations. Before World War I, only in Norway (1907) could women vote on national issues.

Labor, Socialism, and Politics to World War I

The late-century industrial expansion wrought further changes in the life of the labor force. In all industrializing continental countries the numbers of the urban proletariat rose. Proportionally there were many fewer artisans and highly skilled workers. For the first time factory wage-earners came to predominate. The increasingly mechanized factories often required less highly technical skills from its operatives. There also occurred considerable growth in the very unskilled work associated with shipping, transportation, and building. Work assumed a more impersonal character. Factories were located in cities, and almost all links between factory or day-labor employment and home life dissolved. Large corporate enterprise meant less personal contact between employers and their workers.

On the whole, the standard of living improved throughout the second half of the century. However, that improvement was often more statistical than real. There still existed widespread poverty, poor housing, sweatshop working conditions, and the haunting fears of accident, disability, unemployment, and old age. Between 1900 and World War I, industrial labor discontent was distinctly on the rise as wages failed to keep up with rising prices. During the latter years of the nineteenth century a few big businesses attempted to provide some security for their employees through company housing and pension plans. Although these efforts were, in a few cases, pioneering, they could not prove adequate for the mass of the labor force.

Trade Unionism

Workers still had to look to themselves for the improvement of their situation. However, after 1848 European workers ceased taking to the streets to voice their grievances in the form of riots. They also stopped trying to revive the paternal guilds and similar institutions of the past. After mid-century the labor force accepted the fact of modern industrial production and its general downgrading of skills and attempted to receive more benefits from that system. Workers turned to new institutions and ideologies. Chief among these were trade unions, democratic political parties, and socialism.

Trade unionism came of age as legal protections were extended to unions throughout the second half of the century. Unions became

French glass workers strike at Carmaux in 1896. The right to strike was fiercely opposed by European industrialists and strikes were often long and bitter. This strike at Carmaux, for instance, lasted eighteen months. [Musee Jaures, Castres, France]

fully legal in Great Britain in 1871 and were allowed to picket in 1875. In France Napoleon III had first used troops against strikes, but as his political power waned, he allowed weak labor associations in 1868. The Third French Republic fully legalized unions in 1884. After 1890 they could function in Germany with little disturbance. Initially most trade unions entered the political process in a rather marginal fashion. As long as the representatives of the traditional governing classes looked after labor interests, members of the working class rarely sought office themselves.

The mid-century organizational efforts of the unions were directed toward skilled workers. The goal was the immediate improvement of wages and working conditions. By the close of the century, industrial unions for unskilled workers were being organized. They were very large and included thousands of workers. They confronted extensive opposition from employers, and long strikes were frequently required to bring about employer acceptance. In the prewar decade there were an exceedingly large number of strikes throughout Europe as the unions attempted to raise wages to keep up with inflation. However, despite the advances of unions and the growth of their memberships in 1910 to approximately 3 million in Britain, 2 million in Germany, and 977,000 in France, they never included a majority of the industrial labor force. What the unions did represent was a new collective fashion in which workers could associate to confront the economic difficulties of their lives and to attain better security.

Democracy and Political Parties

The democratic franchise provided workers with direct political influence, which meant that they could no longer be ignored. With the exception of Russia all the major European states adopted broad-based, if not perfectly democratic, electoral systems. Great Britain passed its second voting-reform act in 1867 and its third in 1884. Bismarck brought universal manhood suffrage to the German Empire in 1871. The French Chamber of Deputies was democratically elected. Universal manhood suffrage was adopted in Switzerland in 1879, in Spain in 1890, in Belgium in 1893, in the Netherlands in 1896, and in Norway in 1898. Italy finally fell into line in 1912. Democracy brought new modes of popular pressure to bear on all governments. It meant that

discontented groups could now voice their grievances and advocate their programs within the institutions of government rather than from the outside.

The advent of democracy witnessed the formation for the first time in Europe of organized mass political parties, which had existed throughout the nineteenth century in the United States. In the liberal European states with narrow electoral bases, most voters had been people of property who knew what they had at stake in politics. Organization had been minimal. The new expansion of the electorate brought into the political processes many people whose level of political consciousness, awareness, and interest was quite low. This electorate had to be organized and taught the nature of power and influence in the liberal democratic state. The organized political party—with its workers, newspapers, offices, social life, and discipline—was the vehicle that mobilized the new voters. The largest single group in these mass electorates was the working class. The democratization of politics presented the socialists with opportunities and required the traditional ruling classes to vie with the socialists for the support of the new voters.

Along with new opportunities, the trade unions and the democratic electorates created ideological and practical problems for European socialists. Both the economic dislocation of early industrialization and the exclusion of the workers from politics had conditioned early socialist doctrines. Socialists of various kinds had called for major social changes, often involving violent revolution. However, unions, democracy, and rising standards of living meant that the ends of socialism might be attained within the existing political framework and without violent revolution. Moreover, as the labor force began to receive direct benefits from the expanding economy, they were less likely to desire its destruction. It was while working out these ideological and tactical problems that the European socialists entered the mainstream of European politics. The internal socialist conflicts of these years have continued to influence the movement in Europe and elsewhere to the present day.

Marx and the First International

Karl Marx himself made considerable accommodation to the new practical realities that developed during the third quarter of the cen-

The delegates to the Second Congress of the German Social Democratic Party in 1871. The German socialists were the most important Marxist party in Europe before World War I. [Bildarchiv Preussicher Kulturbesitz]

tury. He did not abandon the revolutionary doctrines of *The Communist Manifesto,* and in *Capital* (Vol. 1, 1867) he continued to predict the disintegration of capitalism. His private thoughts, as revealed in his letters, also remained quite revolutionary, but his practical, public political activity reflected a somewhat different approach.

In 1864 a group of British and French trade unionists founded the International Working Men's Association. Known as the First International, it encompassed in its membership a vast array of radical political types, including socialists, anarchists, and Polish nationalists. The First International allowed Marx, who was by then quite active in the London radical community, to write its inaugural address. In it he urged radical social change and the economic emancipation of the working class, but he also supported and approved efforts by workers and trade unions to reform the conditions of labor within the existing political and economic processes. He urged revolution but tempered the means. Privately he often criticized such reformist activity, but those writings were not

made public until near the end of the century, and after his death.

During the late 1860s the First International gathered statistics, kept labor groups informed of mutual problems, provided a forum for the debate of socialist doctrine, and extravagantly proclaimed its own size and influence. From these debates and activities Marxism emerged as the single most important strand of socialism. In 1872 Marx and his supporters drove the anarchists out of the First International. Marx was determined to preserve the role of the state against the anarchist attack on authority and large political organizations. Through the meetings and discussions of the First International, German socialists became deeply impressed by Marx's thought. Because, as will be seen, they became the most important socialist party in Europe, they became the chief channel for the preservation and development of Marxist thought.

The First International proved to be a very fragile structure. The events surrounding the Paris Commune presented the final blow to its existence. Few socialists and only one real

823

Marxist were involved in the commune. However, Marx, in a major pamphlet, glorified the commune as a genuine proletarian uprising. British trade unionists, who in 1871 were finally receiving new legal protection, wanted no connection with the crimes of the Parisians. The French authorities used the uprising to suppress socialist activity. Throughout Europe the events in Paris cast a pall over socialism. The First International held its last European congress in 1873. Its offices were then transferred to the United States, where it was dissolved in 1876. Thereafter the fate of socialism and the labor movement depended largely on the economic and political conditions of the individual European countries.

Great Britain: Fabianism and Early Welfare Programs

Neither Marxism nor any other form of socialism made significant progress in Great Britain, the most advanced industrial society of the day. There trade unions grew steadily and the members normally supported Liberal Party candidates. The "new unionism" of the late 1880s and the 1890s organized the dock workers, the gas workers, and similar unskilled groups. Employer resistance to unions heightened class antagonism. In 1892 Keir Hardie became the first independent working man to be elected to Parliament. The next year the small, socialist Independent Labour Party was founded, but it remained ineffective.

Until 1901 general political activity on the part of labor remained quite limited. The Taff Vale decision in that year by the House of Lords, however, removed the legal protection previously accorded union funds. The Trades Union Congress responded by launching the Labour Party. In the election of 1906 the fledgling party sent twenty-nine members to Parliament. Their goals as trade unionists did not yet encompass socialism. Along with this new political departure, the British labor movement became more militant. There were scores of strikes before the war, as workers fought for wages to meet the rising cost of living. The government took a larger role than ever before in mediating these strikes, which in 1911 and 1912 involved the railways, the docks, and the mines.

British socialism itself remained primarily the preserve of intellectuals. H. M. Hyndman (1842–1921), a wealthy graduate of Eton, and William Morris (1834–1896), the poet and

George Bernard Shaw (1856–1950), the most important modern British playwright, was an active Fabian socialist. [Mary Evans Picture Gallery]

designer, read Marx's works avidly, but their Social Democratic Federation, founded in 1881, never had more than a handful of members. The socialists who exerted the most influence were the Fabian Society, founded in 1884. The society took its name from Q. Fabius Maximus, the Roman general whose tactics against Hannibal was that of avoiding direct conflict that might lead to defeat. Through its name the society intended to indicate a gradual approach to major social reform. Its leading members were Sidney (1859–1947) and Beatrice (1858–1943) Webb, H. G. Wells (1866–1946), Graham Wallas (1858–1932), and George Bernard Shaw (1856–1950). Many of the Fabians were civil servants who believed that the problems of industry, the expansion of ownership, and the state direction of production could be achieved gradually, peacefully, and democratically. They sought to educate the country to the rational wisdom of socialism. They were particularly interested in modes of collective ownership on the municipal level, the so-called gas-and-water socialism.

Sidney Webb Relates Socialism to Democracy

Members of the Fabian Society represented a major force in British socialism. They believed that through democracy the great social questions of the day could be addressed. They hoped to replace individualism by state action. In their view the goals of socialism could be achieved without revolution. Sidney Webb, whose views follow, and his wife, Beatrice, were frequent voices for the Fabians.

The main stream which has borne European society towards Socialism during the past 100 years is the irresistible progress of Democracy. . . .

In the present Socialist movement these two streams are united: advocates of social reconstruction have learnt the lesson of Democracy, and know that it is through the slow and gradual turning of the popular mind to new principles that social reorganization bit by bit comes. All students of society who are abreast of their time, Socialists as well as Individualists, realize that important organic changes can only be (1) democratic, and thus acceptable to a majority of the people, and prepared for in the minds of all; (2) gradual, and thus causing no dislocation, however rapid may be the rate of progress; (3) not regarded as immoral by the mass of the people, and thus not subjectively demoralizing to them; and (4) in this country at any rate, constitutional and peaceful. Socialists may therefore be quite one with Radicals in their political methods. Radicals, on the other hand, are perforce realizing that mere political levelling is insufficient to save a State from anarchy and despair. Both sections have been driven to recognize that the root of the difficulty is economic; and there is every day a wider consensus that the inevitable outcome of Democracy is the control by the people themselves, not only of their own political organization, but, through that, also of the main instruments of wealth production; the gradual substitution of organized cooperation for the anarchy of the competitive struggle. . . . The economic side of the democratic ideal is, in fact, Socialism itself.*

Sidney Webb, *Fabian Essays in Socialism* (Gloucester, Mass.: Peter Smith, 1967, originally published 1889), pp. 50–52.

The British government and the major political parties responded slowly to these various pressures. In 1903 Joseph Chamberlain launched his unsuccessful tariff-reform campaign to match foreign tariffs and to finance social reform through higher import duties. The campaign badly split the Conservative Party. After 1906 the Liberal Party, led by Sir Henry Campbell-Bannerman (1836–1908) and after 1908 by Herbert Asquith (1852–1928), pursued a two-pronged policy. Fearful of losing seats in Parliament to the new Labour Party, they restored the former protection of the unions. Then, after 1909, with Chancellor

Beatrice and Sidney Webb, in a photograph from the late 1920s. These most influential British Fabian socialists wrote many books on governmental and economic matters, served on special parliamentary commissions, and agitated for the enactment of socialist policies. [Radio Times Hulton Picture Library]

of the Exchequer David Lloyd George (1863–1945) as the guiding light, the Liberal ministry undertook a broad program of social legislation. This included the establishment of labor exchanges; the regulation of the sweated labor trades, such as tailoring and lacemaking; and the National Insurance Act of 1911, which provided unemployment benefits and health care. The financing of these programs brought the House of Commons into conflict with the Conservative-dominated House of Lords. The result was the Parliament Act of 1911, which allowed the Commons to override the legislative veto of the upper chamber. The new taxes and social programs meant that in Britain, the home of nineteenth-century liberalism, the state was taking on an expanded role in the life of its citizens. The early welfare legislation was only marginally satisfactory to labor, many of whose members still thought they could gain more from the direct action of strikes.

France: "Opportunism" Rejected

French socialism gradually revived after the suppression of the Paris Commune. The institutions of the Third Republic provided a framework for legal activity. The major problem for French socialists was their own internal division rather than government opposition. There were no fewer than five separate parties, plus other independent socialists. They managed to elect approximately forty members to the Chamber of Deputies by the early 1890s. Despite the lack of a common policy, the socialist presence aided the passage of measures to relieve workers from carrying identity cards and to provide for factory safety inspection, health care, and limited working hours. In 1910 the republic inaugurated a scheme for voluntary pensions. However, the most important developments of French labor and socialism were not legislative.

At the turn of the century the two major factions of French socialism were led by Jean Jaurès (1859–1914) and Jules Guesde (1845–1922). Jaurès believed that socialists should cooperate with radical middle-class ministries to ensure the enactment of needed social legislation. Guesde opposed this policy, arguing that socialists could not, with integrity, support a bourgeois cabinet that they were theoretically dedicated to overthrow. The quarrel came to a head as a by-product of the Dreyfus affair. In 1899, as a means of uniting all supporters of Dreyfus, Prime Minister René Waldeck-Rous-

seau (1846–1904) appointed the socialist Alexander Millerand to the Cabinet. By 1904 the issue of "opportunism," as such Cabinet participation by socialists was termed, came to be debated at the Amsterdam Congress of the Second International. This organization had been founded in 1889 in a new effort to unify the various national socialist parties and trade unions. The Amsterdam Congress condemned "opportunism" in France and ordered the French socialists to form a single party. Jaurès, believing socialist unity the most important issue in France, accepted the decision. French socialists began to work together, and by 1914 the recently united Socialist Party was the second largest group in the Chamber of Deputies. Socialist Party members would not again serve in a French Cabinet until the Popular Front Government of 1936.

The French labor movement, with deep roots in the Proudhonian doctrines of anarchism, was uninterested in both politics and socialism. French workers tended to vote socialist, but the unions avoided active political participation. The Confédération Générale du Travail was founded in 1895 and regarded itself as a rival to the socialist parties. Its leaders sought to improve the workers' conditions through direct action. They embraced the doctrines of syndicalism, which were most persuasively expounded by Georges Sorel (1847–1922) in *Reflections on Violence* (1908). This book enshrined the idea of the general strike as a means of generating worker unity and power. The strike tactic was quite different from the socialist idea of aiding the situation of labor through the action of the state. Strike action on the part of unions flourished between 1905 and 1914, and the Radical ministry on more than one occasion used troops against the strikers. Consequently, in France the forces of labor were suppressed by the liberal state, and the Socialist Party was locked into a doctrine of nonparticipation in the Cabinet, which effectively undermined its potential political influence.

Germany: Social Democrats and Revisionism

The judgment rendered by the Second International against French socialist participation in bourgeois ministries reflected a policy of permanent hostility to nonsocialist governments previously adopted by the German Social Democratic Party, or SPD. The organizational success of this party, more than any other single factor, kept Marxist socialism alive into the latter part of the century. The party was founded in 1875. Its origins lay in the labor agitation of Ferdinand Lasalle (1825–1864), who wanted worker participation in German politics. His followers were joined by Wilhelm Liebknecht (1826–1900) and August Bebel (1840–1913), who were Marxists. Consequently the party was divided from its founding between those who wanted reformist political activity and those who advocated revolution.

The forging experience of the SPD was twelve years of persecution by Bismarck. The so-called Iron Chancellor believed that socialism would undermine German politics and society. Shortly after its founding, he moved against the young SPD. In 1878 there was an attempt to assassinate William I. Although the socialists were not involved, Bismarck used the opportunity to steer a number of antisocialist laws through the Reichstag. The measures suppressed the organization, meetings, newspapers, and other public activities of the SPD. To

The German Empire Legislates Against the Socialists

Through these 1878 laws Bismarck hoped to destroy the young Social Democratic Party. The measures were intended to make it difficult for the SPD to hold meetings, publish newspapers and pamphlets, and collect money to support its activities. The antisocialist laws remained in effect until 1891.

1. *Associations which aim, by Social Democratic, Socialistic, or Communistic endeavours, at the destruction of the existing order in State or society, are to be forbidden. . . .*

9. *Meetings in which Social Democratic, Socialistic, or Communistic tendencies, directed to the destruction of the existing order in State or society, make their appearance, are to be dissolved.*

Meetings, of which facts justify the assumption that they are destined to further such tendencies, are to be forbidden.

Public festivities and processions are placed under the same restrictions.

11. *Printed matter, in which Social Democratic, Socialistic, or Communistic tendencies, directed to the destruction of the existing order in State and society in a manner dangerous to the peace, and, in particular, to the harmony between different classes of the population, make their appearance, is to be forbidden.*

In the case of periodical literature, the prohibition can be extended to any further issue, as soon as a single number has been forbidden under this law.

16. *The collection of contributions for the furthering of Social Democratic, Socialistic, or Communistic endeavours, directed toward the destruction of the existing order in State or society, as also the public instigation to the furnishing of such contributions, are [sic] to be forbidden by the police.*

28. *For districts or localities which are threatened, by the above-mentioned endeavours, with danger to the public safety, the following provisions can be made, for the space of a year at most, by the central police of the state in question, and subject to the permission of the Bundesrath [the upper chamber of the Parliament].*

(1) That meetings may only take place with the previous permission of the police; this prohibition does not extend to meetings for an election to the Reichstag or the Diet.

(2) That the distribution of printed matter may not take place in public roads, streets, or places, or other public localities.

(3) That residence in such districts or localities can be forbidden to all persons from whom danger to the public safety or order is to be feared.

(4) That the possession, import, or sale of weapons is forbidden, limited, or confined by certain conditions.

Bertrand Russell, *German Social Democracy* (London: Longmans, Green, 1896), pp. 100–102.

The parliamentary leadership of the German Social Democratic Party in 1889. August Bebel is seated in the center. Wilhelm Liebknecht is standing directly behind him. [*Bildarchiv Preussicher Kulturbesitz*]

remain a socialist meant to remove oneself from the mainstream of respectable German life and possibly to lose one's job. The antisocialist legislation proved politically counterproductive. From the early 1880s onward, the SPD steadily polled more and more votes in elections to the Reichstag.

As simple repression failed to separate German workers from socialist loyalties, Bismarck undertook a program of social welfare legislation. In 1883 the German Empire adopted a health insurance measure. The next year saw the enactment of accident insurance legislation. Finally, in 1889, Bismarck sponsored a plan for old age and disability pensions. These programs, to which both workers and employers contributed, represented a paternalistic, conservative alternative to socialism. The state itself would organize a system of social security that did not require any change in the system of property holding or politics. Germany became the first major industrial nation to enjoy this kind of welfare program.

In 1890, after forcing Bismarck's resignation, Emperor William II (1888–1918) allowed the antisocialist legislation to expire the next year in hopes of thus building new support for the monarchy among the working class. Even under the repressive laws, members

of the SPD could sit in the Reichstag. Now, however, the question became what attitude the recently legalized party should assume toward the German Empire. The answer came in the Erfurt Program of 1891, formulated under the political guidance of Bebel and the ideological tutelage of Karl Kautsky (1854–1938). In good Marxist fashion the program declared the imminent doom of capitalism and the necessity of socialist ownership of the means of production. However, these goals were to be achieved by legal political participation rather than by revolutionary activity. Because by its very nature capitalism must fall, the immediate task of socialists was to work for the improvement of workers' lives rather than for the revolution, which was inevitable. In theory the SPD was vehemently hostile to the German Empire, but in practice the party functioned within its institutions. The SPD members of the Reichstag maintained clear consciences by refusing to enter the Cabinet, to which they were not invited anyway, and by refraining for many years from voting for the military budget.

The situation of the SPD, however, generated the most important internal socialist challenge to the orthodox Marxist analysis of capitalism and the socialist revolution. Eduard Bernstein (1850–1932) was the author of this socialist heresy. He had spent over a decade of his life in Great Britain and was quite familiar with the Fabians. Bernstein questioned whether Marx and his later orthodox followers, such as Kautsky, had been correct in their pessimistic appraisal of capitalism and the necessity of revolution. In *Evolutionary Socialism* (1899) Bernstein pointed to the rising standard of living in Europe. Ownership of capitalist industry was becoming more widespread through stockholding. The middle class was not falling into the ranks of the proletariat and was not identifying its problems with those of the workers. The inner contradictions of capitalism as expounded by Marx had simply not developed. Moreover the opening of the franchise to the working class meant that revolutionary change might be achieved through parliamentary methods. What was required to realize a humane socialist society was not revolution but more democracy and social reform.

Bernstein's doctrines, known as *revisionism*, were widely debated among German socialists and were finally condemned as theory. His critics argued that evolution toward social democracy might be possible in liberal, parliamentary Britain, but not in authoritarian, militaristic Germany, with its basically powerless Reichstag. The critics were probably correct about the German political scene. Nonetheless, while still calling for revolution, the SPD pursued a course of action similar to that advocated by Bernstein. Its trade union members, prospering within the German economy, did not want revolution. Its grass-roots members wanted to consider themselves patriotic Germans as well as good socialists. Its leaders feared any actions that might renew the persecution that they had experienced under Bismarck. Consequently the party worked at elections, membership expansion, and short-term political and social reform. It prospered and became one of the most important institutions of imperial Germany. Even some middle-class Germans voted for it as a means of opposing the illiberal institutions of the empire. And in August 1914, after long debate among themselves, the SPD members of the Reichstag abandoned their former stance and unanimously voted for the war credits that would finance World War I.

Russia: Industrial Development and the Birth of Bolshevism

During the last decade of the nineteenth century Russia entered the industrial age and confronted many of the problems that the more advanced nations of the Continent had experienced fifty or seventy-five years earlier. Unlike those other countries, Russia had to deal with major political discontent and economic development simultaneously. Russian socialism reflected that peculiar situation.

WITTE'S PROGRAM FOR INDUSTRIAL GROWTH. The emancipation of the serfs in 1861 had brought little agricultural progress. The peasants remained burdened with redemption payments, local taxes, excessive national taxes, and falling grain prices. There were few attempts to educate the peasantry in the more advanced techniques of farming. Most of the land held by free peasants was owned communally through the *mir*, or village. This system of ownership was extremely inefficient and employed strip farming and the farming of small plots. Between 1860 and 1914 the population of European Russia rose from approximately 50 million to approximately 103 million people. Land hunger spread among the peasants. There was intense

agrarian discontent. Peasants with too little land still had to work on larger noble estates or for more prosperous peasant farmers known as *kulaks*. Uprisings in the countryside were a frequent problem. The agricultural sector benefited little from the late-century industrialism.

Alexander III and, after him, Nicholas II were determined that Russia should become an industrial power. Only by this means could the country maintain its military position and its diplomatic role in Europe. The person who led Russia into the industrial age was Sergei Witte (1849–1915). After a career in railways and other private business, he was appointed finance minister in 1892. Witte epitomized the nineteenth-century modernizer who pursued a policy of planned economic development, protective tariffs, high taxes, the gold standard, and efficiency. He established a strong financial link with the French money market, which led to later diplomatic cooperation between Russia and France.

Witte favored heavy industries. Between 1890 and 1904 the Russian railway system grew from 30,596 kilometers to 59,616 kilometers. The 5,000-mile Trans-Siberian Railroad was almost completed. Coal output more than tripled during the same period. There was

Count Sergei Witte (1849–1915) sought to modernize Russia with a program of industrial development, protective tariffs, high taxes, and an adherence to the gold standard.

a vast increase in pig-iron production, from 928,000 tons in 1890 to 4,641,000 tons in 1913. During the same period steel production rose from 378,000 tons to 4,918,000 tons. Textile manufacturing continued to expand and still constituted the single largest industry. The factory system began to be used more extensively throughout the country.

A Russian Social Investigator Describes the Condition of Children in the Moscow Tailoring Trade

E. A. Oliunina was a young Russian woman who had been active among union organizers during the Revolution of 1905. Later, as a student at the Higher Women's Courses in Moscow, a school for women's post-secondary education, she began to investigate and to write about garment workers. In the passage below, she discusses the plight of children who were apprentices in the tailoring trade in Moscow. Between seven and eight thousand children worked in the Moscow garment trade. Their apprenticeships lasted three to five years, during which time they worked for little or even no wages. As often as not, these children were not taught real skills but were simply exploited. The conditions under which they labored indicate both indifference to their welfare and the rather purposeless existence confronted by adult workers in these small tailoring establishments.

Children begin their apprenticeship between the ages of twelve and thirteen, although one can find some ten- and eleven-year-olds working in the shops. . . .

Apprenticeship is generally very hard on children. At the beginning, they suffer enormously, particularly from the physical strain of having to do work well beyond the capacity of their years. They have to live in an environment where the level of morality is very low. Scenes of drunkenness and debauchery induce the boys to smoke and drink at an early age.

For example, in one subcontracting shop that made men's clothes, a fourteen-year-old boy worked together with twelve adults. When I visited there at four o'clock one Tuesday afternoon, the workers were half-drunk. Some were lying under the benches, others in the hallway. The boy was as drunk as the rest of them and lay there with a daredevil look on his face, dressed only in a pair of longjohns and a dirty, tattered shirt. He had been taught to drink at the age of twelve and could now keep up with the adults.

"Blue Monday" is a custom in most subcontracting shops that manufacture men's clothes. The whole workshop gets drunk, and work comes to a standstill. The apprentices do nothing but hang around. Many of the workers live in the workshop, so the boys are constantly exposed to all sorts of conversations and scenes. In one shop employing five workers and three boys, "Blue Monday" was a regular ritual. Even the owner himself is prone to alcoholic binges. In these kinds of situations, young girls are in danger of being abused by the owner or his sons.

Conditions such as these make a deep impression on children. Especially in subcontracting shops, the environment fosters coarse manners and cynicism. . . .

In Russia, there have been no measures taken to improve the working conditions of apprentices. As I have tried to show, the situation in workshops in no way provides apprentices with adequate training in their trade. The young workers are there only to be exploited. Merely limiting the number of apprentices would not better their position, nor would it eradicate the influx of cheap labor. An incomparably more effective solution would be to replace apprenticeship with a professional educational system and well-established safeguards for child workers. However, the only real solution to the exploitation of unpaid child labor is to introduce a minimum wage for minors.

From E. A. Oliunina. *The Tailoring Trade in Moscow and the Villages of Moscow and Riazan Provinces: Material on the History of the Domestic Industry in Russia* (1914), as reprinted in Victoria E. Bonnell, *The Russian Worker: Life and Labor Under the Tsarist Regime* (Berkeley: University of California Press, 1983), pp. 177, 180–181, 182–183.

Industrialism brought considerable social discontent to Russia, as it had elsewhere. Landowners felt that foreign capitalists were earning too much of the profit. The peasants saw their grain exports and tax payments finance development that did not measurably improve their lives. A small but significant industrial proletariat arose. At the turn of the century there were approximately three million factory workers in Russia. Their working and living conditions were very bad by any standard. They enjoyed little state protection, and trade unions were illegal. In 1897 Witte did enact a measure providing for an 11½-hour workday. But needless to say, discontent and strikes continued.

New political departures accompanied the economic development. In 1901 the Social Revolutionary Party was founded. Its members and intellectual roots went back to the Populists of the 1870s. The party opposed industrialism and looked to the communal life of rural Russia as a model for the economic future. In 1903 the Constitutional Democratic Party, or Cadets, was formed. They were liberal in outlook and were drawn from people who partici-

Alexander III (1881–1894) attempted to reimpose arbitrary rule after the reforms of Alexander II. The future Czar Nicholas II (1894–1917) is standing directly behind his father.

pated in the local *zemstvos.* They wanted a parliamentary regime with responsible ministries, civil liberties, and economic progress. The Cadets hoped to model themselves on the liberal parties of western Europe.

LENIN'S EARLY THOUGHT AND CAREER. The situation for Russian socialists differed radically from that in other major European countries. Russia had no representative institutions and only a small working class. The compromises and accommodations that had been achieved elsewhere were meaningless in Russia, where socialism in both theory and practice had to be revolutionary. The Russian Social Democratic Party had been established in 1898, but the repressive policies of the czarist regime meant that the party had to function in exile. It was Marxist, and its members greatly admired the German Social Democratic Party.

The leading late-nineteenth-century Russian Marxist was Gregory Plekhanov (1857–1918), who wrote from his exile in Switzerland. At the turn of the century his chief disciple was Vladimir Illich Ulyanov (1870–1924), who later took the name of Lenin. The future leader of the Communist Revolution had been born in 1870 as the son of a high bureaucrat. His older brother, while a student in Saint Petersburg, had become involved in radical politics. He was arrested for participating in a plot against Alexander III and was executed in 1887. In 1893 Lenin moved to Saint Petersburg, where he studied to become a lawyer. Soon he, too, was drawn to the revolutionary groups among the factory workers. He was arrested in 1895 and exiled to Siberia. In 1900, after his release, Lenin left Russia for the West. He spent most of the next seventeen years in Switzerland.

Once in Switzerland Lenin became deeply involved in the organizational and policy disputes of the exiled Russian Social Democrats. They all considered themselves Marxists, but they held differing positions on the proper nature of a Marxist revolution in primarily rural Russia and on the structure of their own party. Unlike the backward-looking Social Revolutionaries, the Social Democrats were modernizers who favored further industrial development. The majority believed that Russia must develop a large proletariat before the revolution could come. This same majority hoped to mold a mass political party like the German SPD.

Lenin dissented from both positions. In *What*

Is to Be Done? (1902) he condemned any accommodations, such as those practiced by the German SPD. He also criticized a trade unionism that settled for short-term gains rather than true revolutionary change for the working class. Lenin further rejected the concept of a mass party composed of workers. Revolutionary consciousness would not arise spontaneously from the working class. It must be carried to them by "people who make revolutionary activity their profession."[4] Only a small elite party would possess the proper dedication to revolution and would be able to resist penetration by police spies. The guiding principle of that party should be "the strictest secrecy, the strictest selection of members, and the training of professional revolutionaries."[5]

[4]Quoted in Albert Fried and Ronald Sanders (Eds.); *Socialist Thought: A Documentary History* (Garden City, N.Y.: Anchor Doubleday, 1964), p. 459.
[5]Ibid., p. 468.

In 1903, at the London Congress of the Russian Social Democratic Pary, Lenin forced a split in the party ranks. During much of the congress Lenin and his followers lost votes on various questions put before the body. But near the close Lenin's group mustered a very slim majority. Thereafter Lenin's faction assumed the name *Bolsheviks,* meaning "majority," and the other, more moderate, democratic revolutionary faction became known as the *Mensheviks,* or "minority." There was, of course, a considerable public relations advantage to the name *Bolshevik.* (In 1912 the Bolsheviks organized separately.) in 1905 Lenin complemented his organizational theory with a program for revolution in Russia. *Two Tactics of Social Democracy in the Bourgeois-Democratic Revolution* urged that the socialist revolution unite the proletariat and the peasants. Lenin grasped better than any other revolutionary the profound discontent in the Russian coun-

---

Lenin Argues for the Necessity of a Secret and Elite Party of Professional Revolutionaries

Social democratic parties in Western Europe had mass memberships and generally democratic structures of organization. In this passage from *What Is to Be Done?* (1902), Lenin explained why the autocratic political conditions of Russia demanded a different kind of organization for the Russian Social Democratic Party. Lenin's ideas became the guiding principles of Bolshevik organization.

I assert that it is far more difficult [for government police] to unearth a dozen wise men than a hundred fools. This position I will defend, no matter how much you instigate the masses against me for my "anti-democratic" views, etc. As I have stated repeatedly, by "wise men," in connection with organisation, I mean professional revolutionaries, *irrespective of whether they have developed from among students or working men. I assert:* (1) *that no revolutionary movement can endure without a stable organisation of leaders maintaining continuity;* (2) *that the broader the popular mass drawn spontaneously into the struggle, which forms the basis of the movement and participates in it, the more urgent the need for such an organisation, and the more solid this organisation must be . . . ;*

(3) *that such an organisation must consist chiefly of people professionally engaged in revolutionary activity;* (4) *that in an autocratic state [such as Russia], the more we* confine *the membership of such an organisation to people who are professionally engaged in revolutionary activity and who have been professionally trained in the art of combating the political police, the more difficult will it be to unearth the organisation; and* (5) *the* greater *will be the number of people from the working class and from other social classes who will be able to join the movement and perform active work in it. . . .*

The only serious organisation principle for the active workers of our movement should be the strictest secrecy, the strictest selection of members, and the training of professional revolutionaries.

Albert Fried and Ronald Sanders (Eds.), *Socialist Thought: A Documentary History* (Garden City, N.Y.: Anchor Doubleday, 1964), pp. 460, 468.

London Coffee House, c. 1688. *During the seventeenth and eighteenth centuries coffee houses were centers for political activity and business agreements as well as leisure.* [Michael Holford]

Two pictures from the Rake's Progress. *London was viewed in the eighteenth century as a place of moral danger. William Hogarth (1697–1764) was one of the great moralists among British painters. These two scenes from his series on the Rake's Progress depict the arrest of the rake and his later imprisonment. Hogarth in these works captured the harsh and bitter side of urban life where so many people seeking to enrich themselves led to personal depravity. [Art Resource/Sir John Sloane's Museum, London]*

St. Paul's Cathedral in London painted by Antonio Canaletto (1697–1768) in 1754. Canaletto was a Venetian whose views of Venice were immensely popular with wealthy Britons making the Grand Tour of Europe. In 1746 his English patrons induced him to move to London, where his paintings of London and of various English country houses were equally successful with the British upper classes. St. Paul's was designed by Sir Christopher Wren (1632–1723) after the Great Fire of London had destroyed its medieval predecessor in 1666. [Yale Center for British Art, Paul Millon collection]

C-21

Canaletto painted this view of Westminster Abbey in 1749. In the foreground is a procession of the Knights of the Bath, an order of chivalry founded in 1725 by the first Hanoverian king, George I (1714–1727).

View of Paris, 1834. In the early part of the nineteenth century, Paris was largely an unplanned city. The Seine River remained an important commercial route. Many of the chief buildings were from the seventeenth century or earlier. [Giraudon/Art Resource]

The Taking of the Pantheon. *The Revolution of 1848 saw troops attacking revolutionary forces throughout the city. In this painting troops have broken through a barricade erected in front of the Pantheon, a church built in the eighteenth century, where revolutionary heroes including Voltaire and Rousseau and Napoleonic generals had been buried. [Giraudon/Art Resource]*

OPPOSITE: *Two views of the boulevards of Paris:* The Boulevard de Sebastopol *by A. Decaen in 1870 (top),* and The Boulevard Montmartre *by Camille Pissaro (1830–1903) in 1897. Under Napoleon III the city of Paris underwent extensive reconstruction. Broad new boulevards replaced the narrow streets. These boulevards made possible the rapid movement of troops against potential revolutionaries and also allowed easy passage of carriages and horse cabs. The department store in the foreground of the picture at the top was one of many shops that catered to the rapidly growing middle class of late-nineteenth-century Paris and the pleasure boats on the Seine. [EPA/Art Resource]*

The Bar at the Folies Bergère (1882) by Edouard Manet (1832–1883). The Folies Bergère, which is still in business, was among the most famous Parisian pleasure palaces of the late nineteenth century. Its elaborate musical revues featuring scantily clad young dancers titillated audiences from all over the world. The Folies appealed to all social classes—from wealthy bourgeois to shop assistants on a once-a-year spree. Manet's barmaid seems completely withdrawn and remote from the festive crowd reflected in the mirror behind her. She was there only to serve. [Courtald Institute, London]

In the late nineteenth century Paris had become synonymous with leisure and pleasure. Its nightlife was famous throughout the Western World. The sights of food, dance, and sensuality caught the attention of many of the leading artists of the day. In the Moulin de la Galette, *Auguste Renoir (1841–1919) caught the mood of gaity in one of the many open-air gardens where the middle classes went to eat, dance, and flirt.* [Art Resource]

A different, darker view of sensuality was expressed in this view of two dancers at the famous Moulin Rouge by Henri de Toulouse-Lautrec (1864–1901) in 1892. The son of a count, Toulouse-Lautrec was a leading member of Paris' rakish night life where dandies and society figures mixed with artists and prostitutes. [Library of Congress]

Late nineteenth-century Paris was also a city of restaurants and cafes, such as this one at the Place Clichy, painted by Pierre Bonnard (1867–1947). In an age before radio and television, Parisians went to cafes as much for entertainment as for refreshment. [Art Resource]

The Exposition of 1889. The Eiffel Tower was erected for the great exposition of 1889. Such fairs and expositions were common in the late nineteenth century. They allowed manufacturers from around the world to display their wares and provided leisure activity for thousands of visitors. [Art Resource]

C-30

OPPOSITE: *Paris was not all light and laughter. It was also a working-class city, and many of its inhabitants were desperately poor. No one captured the harsh realities of daily life for these people better than Honoré Daumier (1808–1879), as in this sympathetic portrayal of a weary washerwoman and her daughter.* [*Louvre*]

In The Third-Class Carriage *Daumier depicted the poor doing something that they had never been able to do so easily or so cheaply in the past—travelling. The invention of the railway for the first time gave mobility to millions whose horizon had always been restricted to their native village or province.* [*Metropolitan Museum of Art*]

The St. Lazare Railroad Station (1877) *by Claude Monet (1840–1926), one of the masters of French Impressionism. This was one of seven stations that were built in the heart of Paris. From these terminals railway lines spread like a web across France linking the whole country to the capital and the rest of Europe.*

tryside. He knew that an alliance of workers and peasants in rebellion probably could not be suppressed. Lenin's two principles of an elite party and a dual social revolution allowed the Bolsheviks, in late 1917, to capture leadership of the Russian Revolution and to transform the political face of the modern world.

THE REVOLUTION OF 1905 AND ITS AFTERMATH. The quarrels among the Russian socialists and Lenin's doctrines had no immediate influence on events in their country itself. Industrialization proceeded and continued to stir resentment in many sectors. In 1903 Nicholas II dismissed Witte, hoping to quell the criticism. The next year Russia went to war with Japan, partly in expectation that public opinion would rally to the czar. However, the result was Russian defeat and political crisis. The Japanese captured Port Arthur early in 1905. A few days later, on January 22, a priest named Father Gapon led several hundred workers to present a petition to the czar for the improvement of industrial life. As the petitioners approached the Winter Palace in Saint Petersburg, the czar's troops opened fire. About one hundred people were shot down in cold blood, and many more were wounded. Never again after this event, known as Bloody Sunday, would the Russian people see the czar as their protector and "little father."

During the next ten months revolutionary

Russian Workers Attempt to Present a Petition to the Czar

Growing unrest in Russia led to, among other things, the organization in 1903 of the Assembly of Russian Factory and Mill Workers of Saint Petersburg under a priest, Father Gapon. On January 22, 1905, the assembly was able to muster a large crowd of workers to converge on Czar Nicholas II's Winter Palace in the hope of peacefully presenting a petition detailing urban grievances and outlining a program of widespread industrial, political, and economic reform. Rather than allow access to the czar, security forces, commanded by the czar's uncle, fired on the crowd. This is the petition's preamble.

We, working men and inhabitants of St. Petersburg of various classes, our wives and our children and our helpless old parents, come to Thee, Sire, to seek for truth and defence. We have become beggars; we have been oppressed; we are burdened by toil beyond our powers; we are scoffed at; we are not recognized as human beings; we are treated as slaves who must suffer their bitter fate and who must keep silence. We suffered, but we are pushed farther into the den of beggary, lawlessness, and ignorance. We are choked by despotism and irresponsibility, and we are breathless. . . . The first request which we made was that our masters should discuss our needs with us; but this they refused, on the ground that no right to make this request is recognized by law. They also declared to be illegal our requests to diminish the working hours to eight hours daily, to agree with us about the prices for our work, to consider our misunder-

standings with the inferior administration of the mills, to increase the wages for the labour of women and of general labourers, so that the minimum daily wage should be one ruble per day, to abolish overtime work, to give us medical attention without insulting us, to arrange the workshops so that it might be possible to work there, and not find in them death from awful draughts and from rain and snow. All these requests appeared to be, in the opinion of our masters and of the factory and mill administrations, illegal. Everyone of our requests was a crime, and the desire to improve our condition was regarded by them as impertinence, and as offensive to them.

. . . In reality in us, as in all Russian people, there is not recognized any human right, not even the right of speaking, thinking, meeting, discussing our needs, taking measures for the improvement of our condition.

James Mavor, *An Economic History of Russia* (London: J. M. Dent, 1914), pp. 469–470.

On "Bloody Sunday," January 22, 1905 troops of Czar Nicholas II fired on a peaceful procession of workers who sought to present a petition at the Winter Palace in St. Petersburg. After this day there was little chance that the Russian working class could be reconciled with the existing government. [Soviet Life from Sovfoto.]

disturbances spread throughout Russia: sailors mutinied; peasant revolts erupted; and property was attacked. The uncle of Nicholas II was assassinated. Liberal Constitutional Democrat leaders from the *zemstvos* demanded political reform. Student strikes occurred in the universities. Social Revolutionaries and Social Democrats were active among urban working groups. In early October 1905 strikes broke out in Saint Petersburg, and for all practical purposes worker groups, called *soviets*, controlled the city. Nicholas II recalled Witte and issued the October Manifesto, which promised Russia constitutional government.

Early in 1906 Nicholas II announced the election of a representative body, the Duma,

with two chambers. However, he reserved to himself ministerial appointments, financial policy, military matters, and foreign affairs. The April elections returned a very radical group of representatives. The czar dismissed Witte and replaced him with P. A. Stolypin (1862–1911), who had little sympathy for parliamentary government. Within four months Stolypin persuaded Nicholas to dissolve the Duma. A second assembly was elected in February 1907. Again cooperation proved impossible, and dissolution of that Duma came in June of that year. The czar then changed the franchise to ensure a conservative Duma. The third Duma, elected on the new basis in late 1907, proved sufficiently pliable for the czar and his minister. Thus, within two years of the 1905 Revolution, Nicholas II had recaptured much of the ground he had conceded.

Stolypin set about repressing rebellion, removing some causes of the revolt, and rallying property owners behind the czarist regime. Early in 1907 special field courts-martial tried rebellious peasants, and almost seven hundred executions resulted. Before turning to this repression, the minister had canceled any redemptive payments that the peasants still owed to the government from the emancipation of the serfs in 1861. This step, undertaken in November 1906, was part of a more general policy to eradicate communal land ownership. The peasants were encouraged to assume individual proprietorship of their land holdings and to abandon the communal system associated with the *mirs*. Stolypin believed that farmers working for themselves would be more productive. Agriculture did improve through this policy and through instruction of the peasants in better farming methods. The very small peasant proprietors who sold their land increased the size of the industrial labor force.

Russian moderate liberals who sat in the Duma approved of the new land measures. They liked the idea of competition and individual property ownership. The Constitutional Democrats wanted a more genuinely parliamentary mode of government, but they compromised out of fear of new revolutionary disturbances. There still existed widespread hatred of Stolypin among the older conservative groups in the country. The industrial workers were antagonistic to the czar. In 1911 Stolypin was shot by a Social Revolutionary, who may have been a police agent in the pay of conservatives. Nicholas II found no worthy successor. His government simply continued to muddle along. At court the monk Grigory Efimovich Rasputin (1871?–1916) came into ascendancy because of his alleged power to heal the czar's hemophilic son, the heir to the throne. The undue influence of this strange and uncouth man, the continued social discontent, and the conservative resistance to any further liberal reforms rendered the position and the policy of the czar uncertain after 1911. Once again, as in 1904, he and his ministers thought that some bold move on the diplomatic front might bring the regime the broad popular support that it so desperately needed.

The domestic political situation in Russia was only the most extreme version of a pattern that appeared in several of the major European

MAJOR DATES IN THE DEVELOPMENT OF SOCIALISM	
International Working Men's Association (The First International) founded.	1864
German Social Democratic Party founded	1875
First International dissolved	1876
German antisocialist laws passed	1878
British Fabian Society founded	1884
Second International founded	1889
German antisocialist laws permitted to expire	1891
German Social Democratic Party's Erfurt Program	1891
French Confédération Générale du Travail founded	1895
Eduard Bernstein's *Evolutionary Socialism*	1899
Formation of the British Labour Party	1902
Lenin's *What Is to Be Done?*	1902
Bolshevik–Menshevik split	1903
"Opportunism" debated at the Amsterdam Congress of the Second International	1904

Prince Peter Stolypin (1862–1911), the last great statesman of Imperial Russia, sought to counter the rising tide of discontent with a program that combined repression of rebellion with land reform. [*Ullstein Bilderdienst*]

states. Potential or actual political and social unrest existed in Great Britain, France, Germany, Austria, and Russia. It was not at all certain that moderate political concessions could quiet the unrest of the working classes. Conservative governments were looking for some means whereby they might overcome social divisions and avoid further social change and revolution. From the French Revolution onward, war had been the one vehicle that had overcome the social and political cleavages in nations. It would be incorrect to say that this desire for national unity led the European governments to adopt war policies in 1914, but those anxieties may have made them less eager to turn back from the wider conflict. In other words, the domestic social problems experienced by the major governments of Europe were closely related to their diplomatic policy.

Suggested Readings

J. ALBISETTI, *Secondary School Reform in Imperial Germany* (1983). Examines the relationship between politics and education.

A. ASHWORTH, *A Short History of the International Economy Since* 1850, rev. ed. (1967). An introductory survey.

J. A BANKS, *Prosperity and Parenthood: A Study of Family Planning among the Victorian Middle Classes* (1954). Probably the most sensitive and sensible study of the subject.

J. H. BATES, *St. Petersburg: Industrialization and Change* (1976). Impact of industrialization on the major city of imperial Russia.

G. BEHLMER, *Child Abuse and Moral Reform in England*, 1870–1908 (1982). An important study of changes in the treatment of children.

L. R. BERLANSTEIN, *The Working People of Paris*, 1871–1914 (1985). Interesting and comprehensive.

D. BLACKBOURN AND G. ELEY, *The Peculiarities of German History: Bourgeois Society and Politics in Nineteenth-Century Germany* (1985). An important and probing study.

P. BRANCA, *Silent Sisterhood: Middle Class Women in the Victorian Home* (1975). A well researched work.

N. BULLOCK AND J. READ, *The Movement for Housing Reform in Germany and France*, 1840–1914 (1985). An important and wide-ranging study of the housing problem.

R. E. CAMERON, *France and the Industrial Development of Europe*, 1800–1914, rev. ed. (1968). The best treatment of the subject.

C. M. CIPOLLA, *The Economic History of World Population* (1962). A basic introduction.

R. J. EVANS AND W. R. LEE, *The German Family: Essays on the Social History of the Family in Nineteenth and Twentieth-Century Germany* (1981). Very useful.

W. H. FRASER, *The Coming of the Mass Market*, 1850–1914 (1981). Exploration of the expansion of consumer society.

P. GAY, *The Dilemma of Democratic Socialism: Eduard Bernstein's Challenge to Marx* (1952). A clear presentation of the problems raised by Bernstein's revisionism.

P. GAY, *The Bourgeois Experience: Victoria to Freud*, Vol. 1, *Education of the Senses* (1984). Vol. 2, *The Tender Passion* (1986). A major study of middle-class sexuality.

H. GOLDBERG, *A Life of Jean Jaurès* (1962). A splendid biography that explains the problems of the French socialists.

D. F. GOOD, *The Economic Rise of the Hapsburg Empire*, 1750–1914 (1985). The best available study.

O. J. HALE, *The Great Illusion*, 1901–1914 (1971). An excellent treatment.

S. HARCAVE, *First Blood: The Russian Revolution of 1905* (1964). A useful introduction.

S. C. HAUSE, *Women's Suffrage and Social Politics in the French Third Republic* (1984). A wide-ranging examination of the question.

C. J. H. HAYES, *A Generation of Materialism*, 1871–1900 (1941). A classic account of the close of the century.

W. HENDERSON, *The Rise of German Industrial Power* (1976). A straightforward account.

E. J. HOBSBAWM, *The Age of Capital* (1975). Explores the consolidation of middle-class life after 1850.

L. HOLCOMBE, *Wives and Property: Reform of the Married Women's Property Law in Nineteenth-Century England* (1983). The standard work on the subject.

K. H. JARAUSCH, *Students, Society, and Politics in Imperial Germany: The Rise of Academic Illiberalism* (1982). The reaction of the academic community to the threat of socialism.

L. JENKS, *The Migration of British Capital to 1875* (1927). The basic discussion of a key topic in European economic history.

J. JOLL, *The Second International* (1954). A straightforward treatment of the divisions among socialists before World War I.

P. JOYCE, *Work, Society, and Politics: The Culture of the Factory in Later Victorian England* (1980). Explores what actually happened in factories.

S. KERN, *The Culture of Time and Space*, 1880–1918 (1983). A lively discussion of the impact of the new technology.

D. I. KERTZER, *Family Life in Central Italy*, 1880–1910: *Sharecropping, Wage Labor, and Coresidence* (1984). One of the few studies of rural family life.

K. KOLAKOWSKI, *Main Currents of Marxism: Its Rise, Growth, and Dissolution*, 3 vols. (1978). The relevant sections on the last years of the nineteenth century and the early years of the twentieth are especially good.

D. LANDES, *The Unbound Prometheus: Technological Change and Industrial Development in Western Europe from 1750 to the Present* (1969). Includes excellent discussions of late-century development.

G. LICHTHEIM, *Marxism: An Historical and Critical Study* (1961). Perhaps the clearest one-volume discussion of the development of Marxist thought.

A. J. MAYER, *The Persistence of the Old Regime in Europe to the Great War* (1981). An interesting and very controversial book that argues that less political and social change occurred in the nineteenth century than has usually been thought.

A. H. McBRIAR, *Fabian Socialism and English Politics, 1884–1918* (1962). The standard discussion.

T. McBRIDE, *The Domestic Revolution: The Modernization of Household Service in England and France, 1820–1920* (1976). Important for understanding the character of gender roles in the family.

A. MacLAREN, *Sexuality and Social Order: The Debate over the Fertility of Women and Workers in France, 1770–1920* (1983). Examines the debate over birth control in France.

H. MOLLER (Ed.), *Population Movements in Modern European History* (1964). A collection of helpful and important articles.

S. MUTHESIUS, *The English Terraced House* (1982). A well-illustrated examination of English housing.

R. A. NYE, *Crime, Madness, and Politics in Modern France: The Medical Concept of National Decline* (1984). Relevant to issues of family and women.

D. OWEN, *The Government of Victorian London, 1855–1889* (1982). A study of how one city met the problems of urban development.

H. PELLING, *The Origins of the Labour Party, 1880–1900* (1965). Examines the sources of the party in the activities of British socialists and trade unionists.

D. H. PINKNEY, *Napoleon III and the Rebuilding of Paris* (1958). A classic study.

F. K. PROCHASKA, *Women and Philanthropy in Nineteenth-Century England* (1980). Studies the role of women in charity.

J. RENDALL, *The Origins of Modern Feminism: Women in Britain, France and the United States, 1780–1860* (1985). An exceedingly well-informed introduction.

H. ROGGER, *Russia in the Age of Modernization and Revolution, 1881–1917* (1983). The best synthesis of the period.

D. L. RUSSEL (Ed.), *The Family in Imperial Russia* (1978). A collection of essays on a little investigated subject.

C. E. SCHORSKE, *German Social Democracy, 1905–1917* (1955.) A brilliant study of the difficulties of the Social Democrats under the empire.

J. SCOTT, *The Glassworkers of Carmaux: French Craftsmen and Political Action in a Nineteenth-Century City* (1974). A classic analysis of the manner in which highly skilled craftsmen confronted and were eventually defeated by the mechanization of their industry.

M. SEGALEN, *Love and Power in the Peasant Family: Rural France in the Nineteenth Century* (1983). A pioneering work.

A. L. SHAPIRO, *Housing the Poor of Paris, 1850–1902* (1985). Examines what happened to working-class housing at the time of the remodeling of Paris.

B. G. SMITH, *Ladies of the Leisure Class: The Bourgeoises of Northern France in the Nineteenth Century* (1981). Emphasizes the importance of the reproductive role of women.

R. A. SOLOWAY, *Birth Control and the Population Question in England, 1877–1930* (1982). An important book that should be read with MacLaren (listed above).

N. STONE, *Europe Transformed* (1984). A sweeping survey that emphasizes the difficulties of late nineteenth-century liberalism.

F. M. L. THOMPSON (Ed.), *The Rise of Suburbia* (1982). Important for understanding middle-class lifestyles.

C., R., AND L. TILLY, *The Rebellious Century, 1830–1930* (1975). A pioneering study of the nature of collective violence in European society.

A. B. ULAM, *The Bolsheviks: The Intellectual and Political History of the Triumph of Communism in Russia* (1965). Early chapters discuss prewar developments and the formation of Lenin's doctrines.

M. VICINUS, *Suffer and Be Still: Women in the Victorian Age* (1972). A series of excellent essays on Victorian women.

M. VICINUS (Ed.), *A Widening Sphere: Changing Roles of Victorian Women* (1980). Examines late-century developments.

T. H. VON LAUE, *Sergei Witte and the Industrialization of Russia* (1963). A useful account of the last great minister of czarist Russia.

J. R. WALKOWITZ, *Prostitution and Victorian Society: Women, Class, and the State* (1980). A work of great insight and sensitivity.

E. WEBER, *Peasants into Frenchmen: The Modernization of Rural France, 1870–1914* (1976). An important and fascinating work on the transformation of French peasants into self-conscious citizens of the nation state.

M. J. WIENER, *English Culture and the Decline of the Industrial Spirit, 1850–1980* (1981). The best study of the problem.

Charles Darwin (1809–1882). In two works of seminal importance, The Origin of Species (1859) *and* The Descent of Man (1871), *Darwin enunciated the theory of evolution by natural selection and applied that theory to human beings. The result was a storm of controversy that affected not only biology, but also religion, philosophy, sociology, and even politics.* [National Portrait Gallery, London]

DURING the same period that the modern nation-state developed and the Second Industrial Revolution laid the foundations for the modern material lifestyle, the ideas and concepts that have marked European thought for much of the present century took shape. Like previous intellectual changes, these arose from earlier patterns of thought. The Enlightenment provided late-nineteenth-century Europeans with a heritage of rationalism, toleration, cosmopolitanism, and appreciation of science. Romanticism led them to value feelings, imagination, national identity, and the autonomy of the artistic experience. By 1900 these strands of thought had become woven into a new fabric. Many of the traditional intellectual signposts were disappearing. The death of God had been proclaimed. Christianity had undergone the most severe attack in its history. The picture of the physical world that had dominated since Newton had undergone major modification. The work of Darwin and Freud had challenged the special place that Western thinkers had assigned to humankind. The value long ascribed to rationality was being questioned. The political and humanitarian ideals of liberalism and socialism gave way for a time to new, aggressive nationalism. At the turn of the century European intellectuals were more daring than ever before, but they were also probably less certain and less optimistic.

The New Reading Public

The social context of intellectual life changed in the last half of the nineteenth century. For the first time in Europe, a mass reading public came into existence. In 1850 approximately half the population of western Europe and a much higher proportion of Russians were illiterate. Even those people who might technically be capable of reading and writing did so very poorly. The literacy of the continent improved steadily, as from the 1860s onward one government after another undertook state-financed education. Hungary provided elementary education in 1868; Britain, in 1870; Switzerland, in 1874; Italy, in 1877; and France, between 1878 and 1881. The already advanced education system of Prussia was extended in various ways throughout the German Empire after 1871. The attack on illiteracy proved most successful in Britain, France, Belgium, the Netherlands, Germany, and Scandinavia, where by 1900 approximately 85 per

24

The Birth of Contemporary European Thought

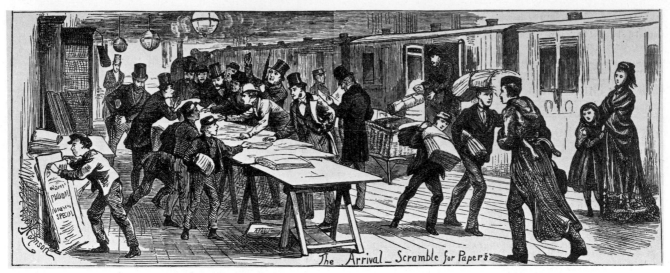

Travelers at an English railway station rushing to buy newspapers in 1875. The late nineteenth century was the heyday of the cheap, mass-circulation newspaper. The enormous new reading public had an insatiable appetite for news. [New York Public Library Picture Collection]

cent or more of the people could read. Italy, Spain, Russia, Austria-Hungary, and the Balkans lagged well behind, with illiteracy rates of between 30 and 60 per cent.

The new primary education in the basic skills of reading and writing and elementary arithmetic reflected and generated social change. Both liberals and conservatives regarded such minimal training as necessary for orderly political behavior on the part of the newly enfranchised voters. There was also hope that literacy might help the poor to help themselves and might create a better, more productive labor force. This side of the educational crusade embodied the rationalist faith that right knowledge will lead to right action. However, literacy and its extension soon became forces in their own right. The schoolteaching profession grew rapidly in numbers and prestige. Those people who learned to read the little they were taught could continue to read much more on their own. They soon discovered that the education that led to better jobs and political influence was still open only to those who could afford it. Having created systems of primary education, the major nations had to give further attention to secondary education by the time of World War I. In yet another generation the question would become one of democratic university instruction.

The expanding literate population created a vast market for new reading material. There was nothing less than an explosion of printed matter. Advances in printing and paper technology lowered production costs. The number of newspapers, books, and libraries grew rapidly. Cheap mass-circulation newspapers, such as *Le Petit Journal* of Paris and the *Daily Mail* and *Daily Express* of London, enjoyed their first heyday. Newspapers with very specialized political or religious viewpoints were also published. The number of monthly and quarterly journals for families, women, and free-thinking intellectuals increased. Probably more people with more different kinds of ideas could get into print in the late nineteenth century than ever before in European history. And more people could read their ideas than ever before.

The quantity of readers and reading material did not ensure quality. The cheap newspapers prospered on stories of sensational crimes and political scandal and on pages of advertising. Religious journals depended on denominational rivalry. A brisk market existed for pornography. There was much cutthroat journalism, as portrayed in George Gissing's (1857–1903) novel *New Grub Street* (1892). Newspapers became major factors in the emerging mass politics. The news could be managed, but in central Europe more often by the government censor than by the publisher. Editorials appeared on the front page.

The mass audience and the new literary world created problems for the literary artist. Much of the contempt for democracy and for the "people" found in late-nineteenth-century literature arose in reaction to the recently established conditions for publication. The new sense of distance between the artist and the public was in part a result of the changed character of the literate public. As publishers sought to make profits, they often feared offending the sensibilities of their potential readership. Some writers accepted this situation and happily wrote harmless verbiage that supported current moral and political opinion. Others, such as Matthew Arnold (1822–1888), worked to raise the level of popular taste. Still others, such as the French novelist Émile Zola (1840–1902), deliberately offended the complaisant bourgeois values of their readers. These anxieties and tensions were closely

Matthew Arnold Contemplates the Loss of Intellectual Certainties

In this poem, written in 1867, Matthew Arnold (1822–1888) portrayed a man and a woman looking across the waters of the English Channel on a moonlit night. The speaker in the poem notes that Sophocles, the ancient Greek dramatist, had drawn lessons about the misery of life from the ebb and flow of the Aegean Sea. The speaker then compares the movement of the sea to the withdrawal of the Christian faith from the lives of nineteenth-century men and women. Finally, he says that the world that seems so beautiful is really a place where there can be no certainty, love, light, or peace. This pessimism reflects the state of mind of many writers who were no longer sure of the truth of the Christian faith.

DOVER BEACH

*The sea is calm to-night.
The tide is full, the moon lies fair
Upon the Straits;—on the French coast the
    light
Gleams and is gone; the cliffs of England
    stand,
Glimmering and vast, out in the tranquil
    bay.*

*Come to the window, sweet is the night air!
Only, from the long line of spray
Where the sea meets the moon-blanch'd land,
Listen! you hear the grating roar
Of pebbles which the waves draw back, and
    fling,
At their return, up the high strand,
Begin, and cease, and then again begin,
With tremulous cadence slow, and bring
The eternal note of sadness in.*

* Sophocles long ago
Heard it on the Aegean, and it brought
Into his mind the turbid ebb and flow*

*Of human misery; we
Find also in the sound a thought,
Hearing it by this distant northern sea.*

*The Sea of Faith
Was once, too, at the full, and round earth's
    shore
Lay like the folds of a bright girdle furl'd.
But now I only hear
Its melancholy, long, withdrawing roar,
Retreating, to the breath
Of the night-wind, down the vast edges drear
And naked shingles of the world.*

*Ah, love, let us be true
To one another! for the world, which seems
To lie before us like a land of dreams,
So various, so beautiful, so new,
Hath really neither joy, nor love, nor light,
Nor certitude, nor peace, nor help for pain;
And we are here as on a darkling plain
Swept with confused alarms of struggle and
    flight,
Where ignorant armies clash by night!*

In Donald J. Gray and G. B. Tennyson, *Victorian Literature: Poetry* (New York: Macmillan, 1976), pp. 479–480.

related to some writers' criticism of democracy. Artists and their middle-class audience became the subjects of novels, such as James Joyce's (1882–1941) *Portrait of the Artist As a Young Man* (1914).

Because many of the new readers were only marginally literate and still quite ignorant on many scores, the books and journals catering to them seemed and often were thoroughly mediocre. Social and artistic critics were correct in pointing out this low level of public taste. Nevertheless the new education, the new readers, and the hundreds of new books and journals permitted a monumental popularization of knowledge that has become a hallmark of the contemporary world. The new literacy was the intellectual equivalent of the railroad and the steamship. People could leave their original intellectual surroundings.

Literacy is not an end in itself. It leads to other skills and the acquisition of other knowledge. People who can read may not necessarily change their world for the better, but they have a better chance to do so than those who remain illiterate.

Science at Mid-Century

In about 1850 Voltaire would still have felt at home in a general discussion of scientific concepts. The basic Newtonian picture of physical nature that he had popularized still prevailed. Scientists continued to believe that nature operated as a vast machine according to mechanical principles. During the first half of the century scientists had extended mechanistic explanation into several important areas. John Dalton (1766–1844) had formulated the modern theory of chemical composition. However, at mid-century and long thereafter atoms and molecules were thought to resemble billiard balls. During the 1840s several independent researchers had arrived at the concept of the conservation of energy, according to which energy is never lost in the universe but is simply transformed from one form to another. The principles of mechanism had been extended to geology through the work of Charles Lyell (1797–1875), whose *Principles of Geology* (1830) postulated that various changes in geological formation were the result of the mechanistic operation of natural causes over great spans of time.

At mid-century the physical world was thus regarded as rational, mechanical, and depend-able. Its laws could be ascertained objectively through experiment and observation. Scientific theory purportedly described physical nature as it really existed. Moreover almost all scientists also believed, like Newton and the deists of the eighteenth century, that their knowledge of nature demonstrated the existence of a God or a Supreme Being.

Darwin

In 1859 Charles Darwin (1809–1882) published *The Origin of Species,* which carried the mechanical interpretation of physical nature into the world of living things. The book proved to be one of the seminal works of Western thought and earned Darwin the honor of being regarded as the Newton of biology. Both Darwin and his book have been much misunderstood. He did not originate the concept of evolution, which had been discussed widely before he wrote. What he and Alfred Russel Wallace (1823–1913) did, working independently, was to formulate the principle of natural selection, which explained how species had changed or evolved over time. Earlier writers had believed that evolution might occur; Darwin and Wallace explained how it could occur.

Drawing on Malthus, the two scientists contended that more seeds and living organisms

Alfred Russel Wallace (1823–1913), here photographed in his later years, also came upon the principle of evolution by natural selection independently of Darwin.

come into existence than can survive in their environment. Those organisms possessing some marginal advantage in the struggle for existence live long enough to propagate their kind. This principle of survival of the fittest Darwin called *natural selection*. The principle was naturalistic and mechanistic. Its operation required no guiding mind behind the development and change in organic nature. What neither Darwin nor anyone else in his day could explain was the origin of those chance variations that provided some living things with the marginal chance for survival. Only when the work on heredity of the Austrian monk Gregor Mendel (1822–1884) received public attention after 1900, several years following his death,

did the mystery of those variations begin to be unraveled.

Darwin's and Wallace's theory represented the triumph of naturalistic explanation, which removed the idea of purpose from organic nature. Eyes were not made for seeing according to the rational wisdom and purpose of God but had developed mechanistically over the course of time. In this manner the theory of evolution through natural selection not only contradicted the biblical narrative of the Creation but also undermined the deistic argument for the existence of God from the design of the universe. Moreover Darwin's work undermined the whole concept of fixity in nature or the universe at large. The world was a realm of flux

Darwin Defends a Mechanistic View of Nature

In the closing paragraphs of *The Origin of Species* (1859), Charles Darwin contrasted the view of nature he championed with that of his opponents. He argued that interpreting the development of organic nature through mechanistic laws actually suggested a nobler concept of nature than interpreting its development in terms of some form of divine creation. Darwin, however, added the term *Creator* to these paragraphs in the second edition of the *Origin*.

Authors of the highest eminence seem to be fully satisfied with the view that each species has been independently created. To my mind it accords better with what we know of the laws impressed on matter by the Creator, that the production and extinction of the past and present inhabitants of the world should have been due to secondary causes, like those determining the birth and death of the individual. When I view all beings not as special creations, but as the lineal descendants of some few beings which lived long before the first bed of the Cambrian [geological] system was deposited, they seem to me to become ennobled. . . .

It is interesting to contemplate a tangled bank, clothed with many plants of many kinds, with birds singing on the bushes, with various insects flitting about, and with worms crawling through the damp earth, and to reflect that these elaborately constructed forms, so different from each other, and dependent upon each other in so

complex a manner, have all been produced by laws acting around us. These laws, taken in the largest sense, being Growth with Reproduction; Inheritance which is almost implied by reproduction; Variability from the indirect and direct action of the conditions of life, and from use and disuse: a Ratio of Increase so high as to lead to a Struggle for Life, and as a consequence to Natural Selection, entailing Divergence of Character and the Extinction of less-improved forms. Thus, from the war of nature, from famine and death, the most exalted object which we are capable of conceiving, namely the production of the higher animals, directly follows. There is grandeur in this view of life, with its several powers, having been originally breathed by the Creator into a few forms or into one; and that, whilst this planet has gone cycling on according to the fixed law of gravity, from so simple a beginning endless forms most beautiful and most wonderful have been, and are being evolved.

Charles Darwin, *The Origin of Species and the Descent of Man* (New York: Modern Library, n.d.), pp. 373–374.

and change. The fact that physical and organic nature might be constantly changing allowed people in the late nineteenth century to believe that society, values, customs, and beliefs should also change.

In 1871 Darwin carried his work a step further. In *The Descent of Man* he applied the principle of evolution by natural selection to human beings. Darwin was hardly the first person to treat human beings as animals, but his arguments brought greater plausibility to that point of view. He contended that humankind's moral nature and religious sentiments, as well as its physical frame, had developed naturalistically in response largely to the requirements of survival. Neither the origin nor the character of humankind on earth, in Darwin's view, required the existence of a God for their explanation. Not since Copernicus had removed the earth from the center of the universe had the pride of Western human beings received so sharp a blow.

Darwin's theory of evolution by natural selection was very controversial from the moment of the publication of the *Origin of Species*. It encountered criticism from both the religious and the scientific communities. By the end of the century the concept of evolution was widely accepted by scientists, but not yet Darwin's mechanism of natural selection. The acceptance of the latter within the scientific community really dates from the 1920s and 1930s, when Darwin's theory became combined with the insights of modern genetics.

The Prestige of Science

Darwin's ideas remained highly controversial. They were widely debated in popular and scientific journals. He changed some of them in the course of his writings. However, at issue was not only the correctness of the theory and the place of humankind in nature but also the role of science and scientists in society. The prestige of Darwin's achievement, progress in medicine, and the links of science to the technology of the Second Industrial Revolution made the general European public aware of science as never before. The British Fabian Socialist Beatrice Webb recalled this situation from her youth:

Who will deny that the men of science were the leading British intellectuals of that period; that it was they who stood out as men of genius with international reputations; that it was they who were the self-confident militants of the period; that it was they who were routing the theologians, confounding the mystics, imposing their theories on philosophers, their inventions on capitalists, and their discoveries on medical men; whilst they were at the same time snubbing the artists, ignoring the poets, and even casting doubts on the capacity of the politicians?[1]

Contemporaries spoke of a religion of science that would explain all without resort to supernaturalism. Popularizers, such as Thomas Henry Huxley (1825–1895) and John Tyndall (1820–1893) in Britain and Ernst Haeckel (1834–1919) in Germany, wrote and lectured widely on scientific topics. They argued that science held the answer to the major questions of life. They worked for government support of scientific research and for inclusion of science in the schools and universities.

Scientific knowledge and theories became models for thought in other fields even before the impact of Darwinian ideas. The French philosopher Auguste Comte (1798–1857), a late child of the Enlightenment and a onetime follower of Saint-Simon, developed a philosophy of human intellectual development that culminated in science. In *The Positive Philosophy* (1830–1842), Comte argued that human thought had gone through three stages of development. In the theological stage, physical nature was explained in terms of the action of divinities or spirits. In the second or metaphysical stage, abstract principles became regarded as the operative agencies of nature. In the final or positive stage, explanations of nature became matters of exact description of phenomena, without recourse to an unobservable operative principle. Physical science had, in Comte's view, entered the positive stage, and similar thinking should penetrate other areas of analysis. In particular Comte thought that positive laws of social behavior could be discovered in the same fashion as laws of physical nature. For this reason he is generally regarded as the father of sociology. Works like Comte's helped to convince learned Europeans that genuine knowledge in any area must resemble scientific knowledge. This belief had its roots in the Enlightenment and continues to permeate Western thought to the present day.

Theories of ethics were modeled on science during the last half of the century. The concept of the struggle for survival was widely applied

[1]Beatrice Webb, *My Apprenticeship* (London: Longmans, Green, 1926), pp. 130–131.

Auguste Comte (1798–1857), the founder of Positivism. Comte argued that all natural phenomena, including the workings of human society, could be explained by empirical scientific evidence—natural laws that human beings could describe and understand. [French Cultural Services, New York]

demonstrate how human beings should not behave.

Scientific thought even affected the way in which authors wrote novels. The movement to literary realism, which is considered more fully later in this chapter, was a product of the influence of science. Certain writers wanted to portray the world as they observed it. In France, Gustave Flaubert's (1821–1880) *Madame Bovary* (1857); in England, George Eliot's (1819–1880) *Adam Bede* (1859); and in Russia, Ivan Turgenev's (1818–1883) *A Sportsman's Sketches* (1852) paid new attention to minute physical and natural details. Émile Zola (1840–1902) found artistic inspiration in Claude Bernard's (1813–1878) *An Introduction to the Study of Experimental Medicine* (1865). Zola, a French novelist, believed that he could write an experimental novel in which the characters and their actions would be observed and reported as the scientist might relate events within a laboratory experiment. Zola and others believed that absolute physical (and psychological) determinism ruled human events, just as in the physical world determinism prevailed.

Scientists and their admirers enjoyed a supreme confidence during the last half of the century. They genuinely believed that they had, for all intents and purposes, discovered all that might be discovered. The issues for science in the future would be the extension of acknowledged principles and the refinement of measurement. However, the turn of the century held a much more brilliant future for science. That confident, self-satisfied world of late-nineteenth-century science and scientism vanished. A much more complicated picture of nature developed. Before examining those new departures, we must see how the cult of science affected religious thought and practice.

to human social relationships. The phrase "survival of the fittest" predated Darwin and reflected the competitive outlook of classical economics. Darwin's use of the phrase gave it the prestige associated with advanced science.

The most famous advocate of evolutionary ethics was Herbert Spencer (1820–1903), the British philosopher. Spencer, a strong individualist, believed that human society progressed through competition. If the weak received too much protection, the rest of humankind was the loser. In Spencer's work, struggle against one's fellow human beings became a kind of ethical imperative. The concept could be applied to justify the avoidance of aiding the poor and the working class or to justify the domination of colonial peoples or to urge aggressively competitive relationships among nations. Evolutionary ethics and similar concepts, all of which are usually termed *social Darwinsim*, often came very close to saying that might makes right.

Interestingly enough, one of the chief opponents of such thinking was Thomas Henry Huxley, the great defender of Darwin. In 1893 Huxley declared that the physical cosmic process of evolution was at odds with the process of human ethical development. The struggle in nature held no ethical implications except to

Christianity and the Church Under Siege

The nineteenth century was one of the most difficult periods in the history of the organized Christian churches. Many European intellectuals left the faith. The secular, liberal nation-states attacked the political and social influence of the church. The expansion of population and the growth of cities challenged its organizational capacity to meet the modern age. Yet during all of this turmoil the Protestant and

Catholic churches still made considerable headway at the popular level.

The intellectual attack on Christianity arose on the grounds of its historical credibility, its scientific accuracy, and its pronounced morality. The *philosophes* of the Enlightenment had delighted in pointing out contradictions in the Bible. The historical scholarship of the nineteenth century brought new issues to the fore.

In 1835 David Friederich Strauss (1808–1874) published a *Life of Jesus* in which he questioned whether the Bible provided any genuine historical evidence about Jesus. Strauss contended that the story of Jesus was a myth that had arisen from the particular social and intellectual conditions of first-century Palestine. Jesus' character and life represented the aspirations of the people of that time and place rather than events that had occurred. Other skeptical lives of Jesus were written and published elsewhere.

During the second half of the century scholars such as Julius Wellhausen (1844–1918) in Germany, Ernst Renan (1823–1892) in France, and William Robertson Smith (1847–1894) in Great Britain contended that the books of the Bible had been written and revised with the problems of Jewish society and politics in the minds of human authors. They were not inspired books but had, like the Homeric epics, been written by normal human beings in a primitive society. This questioning of the historical validity of the Bible caused more literate men and women to lose faith in Christianity than any other single cause.

The march of science also undermined Christianity. This blow was particularly cruel because many eighteenth-century writers had led Christians to believe that the scientific examination of nature provided a strong buttress for their faith. William Paley's (1743–1805) *Natural Theology* (1802) and books by numerous scientists had enshrined this belief. The geology of Charles Lyell (1797–1875) suggested that the earth was much older than the biblical records contended. By appealing to natural causes to explain floods, mountains, and valleys, Lyell removed the miraculous hand of God from the physical development of the earth. Darwin's theory cast doubt on the doctrine of the Creation. His ideas and those of other writers suggested that the moral nature of humankind could be explained without appeal to the role of God. Finally, anthropologists, psychologists, and sociologists suggested that religion itself and religious sentiments were just one more set of natural phenomena.

Other intellectuals questioned the morality of Christianity. The old issue of immoral biblical stories was again raised. Much more important, the moral character of the Old Testament God came under fire. His cruelty and unpredictability did not fit well with the progressive, tolerant, rational values of liberals. They also wondered about the morality of the New Testament God, who would sacrifice for His own satisfaction the only perfect being ever to walk the earth. Many of the clergy began to ask themselves if they could honestly preach doctrines they felt to be immoral.

During the last quarter of the century this moral attack on Christianity came from another direction. Writers like Friedrich Nietzsche (1844–1900) in Germany portrayed Christianity as a religion of sheep that glorified weakness rather than the strength that life required. Christianity demanded a useless and debilitating sacrifice of the flesh and spirit rather than full-blooded heroic living and daring. Nietzsche once observed, "War and courage have accomplished more great things than love of neighbor."[2]

These widespread skeptical intellectual currents seem to have directly influenced only the upper levels of educated society. Yet they created a climate in which Christianity lost much of its intellectual respectability. Fewer educated people joined the clergy. More and more people found that they could lead their lives with little or no reference to Christianity. The secularism of everyday life proved as harmful to the faith as the direct attacks. This situation especially prevailed in the cities, which were growing faster than the capacity of the churches to meet the challenge. There was not even enough room in urban churches for the potential worshipers to sit. Whole generations of the urban poor grew up with little or no experience of the church as an institution or of Christianity as a religious faith.

Conflict of Church and State

The secular state of the nineteenth century clashed with both the Protestant and the Roman Catholic churches. Liberals generally disliked the dogma and the political privileges of the established churches. National states

---

[2]Walter Kaufmann (Ed. and Trans.), *The Portable Nietzsche* (New York: Viking, 1967), p. 159.

were often suspicious of the supranational character of the Roman Catholic church. However, the primary area of conflict between the state and the churches was the expanding systems of education. The churches feared that future generations would emerge from the schools without the rudiments of religious teaching. The advocates of secular education feared the production of future generations more loyal to religion or the church than to the nation. From 1870 through the turn of the century, the issue of religious education was heatedly debated in every major country.

GREAT BRITAIN. In Great Britain the Education Act of 1870 provided for the construction of state-supported school-board schools, whereas earlier the government had given small grants to religious schools. The new schools were to be built in areas where the religious denominations failed to provide satisfactory education. There was rivalry not only between the Anglican church and the state but also between the Anglican church and the Nonconformist denominations, that is, those Christian denominations that were not part of the Church of England. There was intense local hostility among all these groups. The churches of all denominations had to oppose improvements in education because these increased the costs of their own schools. In the Education Act of 1902 the government decided to provide state support for both religious and nonreligious schools but imposed the same educational standards on each.

FRANCE. The British conflict was relatively calm compared with that in France, where there existed a dual system of Catholic and public schools. Under the Falloux Law of 1850 the local priest provided religious education in the public schools. The very conservative French Catholic church and the Third French Republic were mutually hostile to each other. Between 1878 and 1886 the government passed a series of educational laws sponsored by Jules Ferry (1832–1893). The Ferry Laws replaced religious instruction in the public schools with civic training. Members of religious orders were no longer permitted to teach in the public schools, the number of which was to be expanded. After the Dreyfus affair the French Catholic church again paid a price for its reactionary politics. The Radical government of Waldeck-Rousseau, drawn from pro-Dreyfus groups, suppressed the religious or-

The shrine at Lourdes, in southwestern France, where, it is believed, the Virgin Mary appeared to a young girl, Bernadette Soubirous, in 1858. Millions of pilgrims visit the shrine each year seeking miraculous cures. [Ullstein Bilderdienst]

ders. In 1905 the Napoleonic Concordat was terminated, and Church and State were totally separated.

GERMANY AND THE KULTURKAMPF. The most extreme example of Church–State conflict occurred in Germany during the 1870s. At the time of unification the German Catholic hierarchy had wanted freedom for the churches guaranteed in the constitution. Bismarck left the matter to the discretion of each federal state, but he soon felt the activity of the Roman Catholic church and the Catholic Center Party to be a threat to the political unity of the new state. Through administrative orders

847

in 1870 and 1871 Bismarck removed both Catholic and Protestant clergy from overseeing local education and set education under state direction. The secularization of education was merely the beginning of a concerted attack on the independence of the Catholic church in Germany.

The "May Laws" of 1873, which applied to Prussia and not the entire German Empire, required priests to be educated in German schools and universities and to pass state-administered examinations. The state could veto the appointments of priests. The disciplinary power of the pope and the church over the clergy was abolished and transferred to the state. When the bishops and many of the clergy refused to obey these laws, Bismarck used the police against them. In 1876 he had either arrested or driven from Prussia all the Catholic bishops. In the end, Bismarck's *Kulturkampf* ("cultural struggle") against the Catholic church failed. Not for the first time, Christian martyrs aided resistance to persecution. By the close of the decade the chancellor had abandoned his attack. He had gained state control of education and civil laws governing marriage only at the price of lingering Catholic resent-

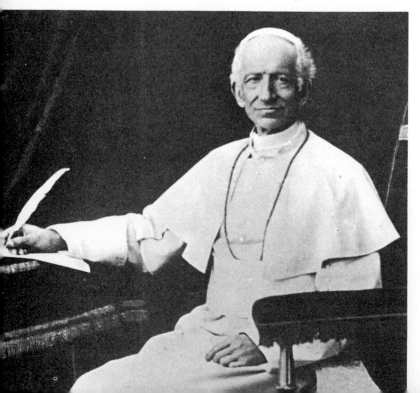

Pope Leo XIII (1878–1903) led the Roman Catholic Church toward a recognition of the problems of industrial democracy. His encyclical Rerum Novarum (1891) *was the Church's major statement on social justice. [Bildarchiv Preussicher Kulturbesitz]*

ment against the German state. The *Kulturkampf* was probably the greatest blunder of Bismarck's career.

Areas of Religious Revival

The successful German Catholic resistance to the intrusions of the secular state illustrates the continuing vitality of Christianity during this period of intellectual and political hardship. In Great Britain both the Anglican church and the Nonconformist denominations experienced considerable growth in membership. Vast sums of money were raised for new churches and schools. In Ireland the 1870s saw a widespread Catholic devotional revival. Priests in France after the defeat by Prussia organized special pilgrimages by train for thousands of penitents who believed that France had been defeated because of their sins. The cult of the miracle of Lourdes originated during these years. There were efforts by churches of all denominations to give more attention to the urban poor.

In effect, the last half of the nineteenth century witnessed the final great effort to Christianize Europe. It was well organized, well led, and well financed. It failed not from want of effort but because the population had simply outstripped the resources of the churches. This persistent liveliness of the church accounts in part for the intense hostility of its enemies.

The Roman Catholic Church and the Modern World

Perhaps the most striking feature of this religious revival amidst turmoil and persecution was the resilience of the papacy. The brief hope for a liberal pontificate from Pope Pius IX (1846–1878) vanished on the night in 1848 when he fled the turmoil in Rome. In the 1860s Pius IX, embittered by the mode of Italian unification, launched a counteroffensive against liberalism in thought and deed. In 1864 he issued the *Syllabus of Errors,* which condemned all the major tenets of political liberalism and modern thought. He set the Roman Catholic church squarely against the worlds of contemporary science, philosophy, and politics. In 1869 the pope called into session the First Vatican Council. The next year, through the political manipulations of the pontiff and against much opposition from numerous members, the council promulgated the dogma of the infallibility of the pope when speaking officially on matters of faith and morals. No earlier pope had gone so far. The First Vatican Council came to a close in 1870, when Italian troops invaded Rome at the outbreak of the Franco-Prussian War.

Pius IX died in 1878 and was succeeded by Leo XIII (1878–1903). The new pope, who was sixty-eight years old at the time of his election, sought to make accommodation with the modern age and to address the great social questions. He looked to the philosophical tradition of Thomas Aquinas to reconcile the claims of faith and reason. His encyclicals of 1885 and 1890 permitted Catholics to participate in the politics of liberal states.

Leo XIII's most important pronouncement on public issues was the encyclical *Rerum Novarum* (1891). In that document Leo XIII defended private property, religious education, and religious control of the marriage laws, and he condemned socialism and Marxism. However, he also declared that employers should treat their employees justly, pay them proper wages, and permit them to organize labor unions. He supported laws and regulations to protect the conditions of labor. The pope urged that modern society be organized according to corporate groups, including people from various classes, which might cooperate according to Christian principles. The corporate society, derivative of medieval social organization, was

---

Leo XIII Considers the Social Question in European Politics

In his 1891 encyclical *Rerum Novarum,* Pope Leo XIII addressed the social question in European politics. It was the answer of the Catholic church to secular calls for social reforms. The pope denied the socialist claim that class conflict was the natural state of affairs. He urged employers to seek just and peaceful relations with workers.

The great mistake that is made in the matter now under consideration is to possess oneself of the idea that class is naturally hostile to class; that rich and poor are intended by Nature to live at war with one another. So irrational and so false is this view that the exact contrary is the truth. . . . Each requires the other; capital cannot do without labour, nor labour without capital. Mutual agreement results in pleasantness and good order; perpetual conflict necessarily produces confusion and outrage. Now, in preventing such strife as this, and in making it impossible, the efficacy of Christianity is marvellous and manifold. . . . Religion teaches the labouring man and the workman to carry out honestly and well all equitable agreements freely made; never to injure capital, or to outrage the person of an employer; never to employ violence in representing his own cause, or to engage in riot or disorder; and to have nothing to do with men of evil principles, who work upon the people with artful promises and raise foolish hopes which usually end in disaster and in repentance when too late. Religion teaches the rich man and the employer that their work people are not their slaves; that they must respect in every man his dignity as a man and as a Christian; that labour is nothing to be ashamed of, if we listen to right reason and to Christian philosophy, but is an honourable employment, enabling a man to sustain his life in an upright and creditable way; and that it is shameful and inhuman to treat men like chattels to make money by, or to look upon them merely as so much muscle or physical power. Thus, again, Religion teaches that, as among the workman's concerns are Religion herself and things spiritual and mental, the employer is bound to see that he has time for the duties of piety; that he be not exposed to corrupting influences and dangerous occasions; and that he be not led away to neglect his home and family or to squander his wages. Then, again, the employer must never tax his work people beyond their strength, nor employ them in work unsuited to their sex or age. His great and principal obligation is to give every one that which is just.

F. S. Nitti, *Catholic Socialism,* trans. by Mary Mackintosh (London: S. Sonnenschein, 1895), p. 409.

to be an alternative to both socialism and competitive capitalism. On the basis of Leo XIII's pronouncements democratic Catholic parties and Catholic trade unions were founded throughout Europe.

The emphasis of Pius X, who reigned from 1903 to 1914 and who has been proclaimed a saint, was intellectually reactionary. He hoped to restore traditional devotional life. Between 1903 and 1907 he condemned Catholic Modernism, a movement of modern biblical criticism within the church, and in 1910 he required an anti-Modernist oath from all priests. By these actions Pius X set the church squarely against the intellectual currents of the day, and the struggle between Catholicism and modern thought continued. Although Pius X did not strongly support the social policy of Leo XIII, the Catholic church continued to permit its members active participation in social and political movements.

Toward a Twentieth-Century Frame of Mind

World War I is often regarded as the point of departure into the contemporary world. Although this view is possibly true of political and social developments, it is an incorrect assessment of intellectual history. The last quarter of the nineteenth century and the first decade of the twentieth century constituted the crucible of contemporary Western and European thought. During this period the kind of fundamental reassessment that Darwin's work had previously made necessary in biology and in understanding the place of human beings in nature became writ large in other areas of thinking. Philosophers, scientists, psychologists, and artists began to portray physical reality, human nature, and human society in ways quite different from those of the past. Their new concepts challenged the major presuppositions of mid-nineteenth-century science, rationalism, liberalism, and bourgeois morality.

Science: The Revolution in Physics

The modifications in the scientific world view originated within the scientific community itself. By the late 1870s considerable discontent existed over the excessive realism of mid-century science. It was thought that many scientists believed that their mechanistic models, solid atoms, and absolute time and space actually described the real universe. In 1883 Ernst Mach (1838–1916) published *The Science of Mechanics*, in which he urged that the concepts of science be considered descriptive not of the physical world but of the sensations experienced by the scientific observer. Science could describe only the sensations, not the physical world that underlay the sensations. In line with Mach, the French scientist and mathematician Henri Poincaré (1854–1912) urged that the concepts and theories of scientists be regarded as hypothetical constructs of the human mind rather than as descriptions of the true state of nature. In 1911 Hans Vaihinger (1852–1933) suggested that the concepts of science be considered "as if" descriptions of the physical world. By World War I few scientists believed any longer that they could portray the "truth" about physical reality. Rather, they saw themselves as recording the observations of instruments and as setting forth useful hypothetical or symbolic models of nature.

New discoveries in the laboratory paralleled the philosophical challenge to nineteenth-century science. With those discoveries the comfortable world of supposedly "complete" nineteenth-century physics vanished forever. In December 1895 Wilhelm Roentgen (1845–1923) published a paper on his discovery of X rays, a form of energy that penetrated various opaque materials. The publication of his paper was followed within a matter of months by major steps in the exploration of radioactivity. In 1896 Henri Becquerel (1852–1908), through a series of experiments following on Roentgen's work, found that uranium emitted a similar form of energy. The next year J. J. Thomson (1856–1940), working in the Cavendish Laboratory of Cambridge University, formulated the theory of the electron. The interior world of the atom had become a new area for human exploration. In 1902 Ernest Rutherford (1871–1937), who had been Thomson's assistant, explained the cause of radiation through the disintegration of the atoms of radioactive materials. Shortly thereafter he speculated on the immense store of energy present in the atom.

The discovery of radioactivity and discontent with the existing mechanical models led to revolutionary theories in physics. In 1900 Max Planck (1858–1947) pioneered the articulation of the quantum theory of energy, according to which energy is a series of discrete quantities or packets rather than a continuous stream. In 1905 Albert Einstein (1879–1955) published his first epoch-making papers on relativity. He contended that time and space exist not separately but rather as a combined continuum. Moreover the measurement of space and time depend on the observer as well as on the entities being measured. In 1927 Werner Heisenberg (1901–1976) set forth the uncertainty

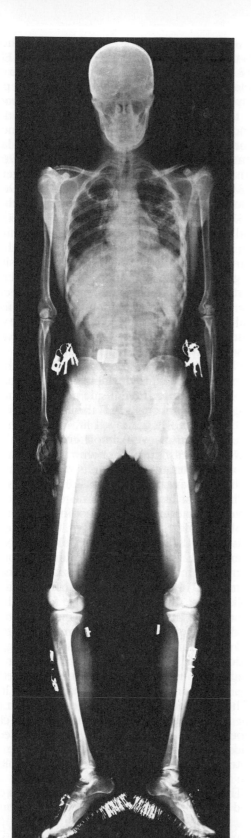

LEFT: *In an early demonstration Roentgen took an X ray of the entire body of a man. Note the buckle of his belt, his keys, and the tacks in the soles and heels of his shoes.* [Deutsches Museum, Munich]

BELOW: *Marie (1869–1934) and Pierre Curie (1859–1906), two of the most important figures in the advance of physics and chemistry. Marie was born in Poland but worked in France for most of her life. She is credited with the discovery of radium, for which she was awarded the Nobel Prize in Chemistry in 1911.* [Ullstein Bilderdienst]

readers unable to sustain old values and uncertain about the sources of new ones.

Philosophy: Revolt Against Reason

Within philosophical circles the adequacy of rational thinking to address the human situation was being questioned. No late-nineteenth-century writer better exemplified this new attitude than the German philosopher Friedrich Nietzsche (1844–1900), who had been educated as a classical philologist rather than as an academic philosopher. His books remained unpopular until late in his life, when his brilliance had deteriorated into an almost totally silent insanity. He was a person wholly at odds with the predominant values of the age. At one time or another he attacked Christianity, democracy, nationalism, rationality, science, and progress. He sought less to change values than to probe the very sources of values in the human mind and character. He wanted not only to tear away the masks of respectable life but also to explore the ways in which human beings made such masks.

His first important work was *The Birth of Tragedy* (1872), in which he urged that the nonrational aspects of human nature were as important and noble as the rational characteristics. Here and elsewhere he insisted on the positive function of instinct and ecstasy in human life. To limit human activity to strictly rational behavior was to impoverish human life and experience. In this work Nietzsche regarded Socrates as one of the major contributors to Western decadence because of the Greek philosopher's appeal for rationality in human affairs. In Nietzsche's view the strength for the heroic life and the highest artistic achievement arose from sources beyond rationality.

In later works, such as the prose poem *Thus Spake Zarathustra* (1883), Nietzsche criticized democracy and Christianity. Both would lead only to the mediocrity of sheepish masses. He announced the death of God and proclaimed the coming of the Overman (*Übermensch*), who would embody heroism and greatness. This latter term was frequently interpreted as some mode of superman or super race, but such was not Nietzsche's intention. He was highly critical of contemporary racism and anti-Semitism. What he sought was a return to the heroism that he associated with Greek life in the Homeric age. He thought that the values of Christianity and of bourgeois morality prevented

Friedrich Nietzsche (1844–1900), the most influential German philosopher of the late nineteenth century. His books challenged existing morality and values. He has exerted a vast influence on twentieth-century literature and philosophy. [New York Public Library Picture Collection]

humankind from achieving life on a heroic level. Those moralities forbade too much of human nature from fulfilling and expressing itself.

Two of Nietzsche's most profound works are *Beyond Good and Evil* (1886) and *The Genealogy of Morals* (1887). Both are difficult books. Much of the former is written in brief, ambiguous aphorisms. Nietzsche sought to discover not what is good and what is evil but the social and psychological sources of the judgment of good and evil. He declared, "There are no moral phenomena at all, but only a moral interpretation of phenomena."[4] He dared to raise the question of whether morality itself was valuable: "We need a critique of moral values; the value of these values themselves must first be called in question."[5] In Nietzsche's view morality was a human convention that had no independent existence apart from humankind.

[4]Walter Kaufmann (Ed. and Trans.), *The Basic Writings of Nietzsche* (New York: The Modern Library, 1968), p. 275.
[5]Ibid., p. 456.

For Nietzsche this discovery did not condemn morality but liberated human beings to create life-affirming instead of life-denying values. Christianity, utilitarianism, and middle-class respectability could, in good conscience, be abandoned, and human beings could, if they so willed, create a new moral order for themselves that would glorify pride, assertiveness, and strength rather than meekness, humility, and weakness.

What Nietzsche said about morality was indicative of what other philosophers were saying about similar subjects. There was a growing tendency to see all conceptual categories as useful creations rather than exact descriptions.

The American philosopher William James (1842–1910) was one of the most influential figures to question the adequacy of nineteenth-century rationalism and science. He and his philosophy of pragmatism were very influential in Europe. James suggested that the truth of an idea or a description depended primarily on how well it worked. Knowledge was less an instrument for knowing than for acting.

The most important European philosopher to pursue such lines of thought was the Frenchman Henri Bergson (1859–1941). His most significant works were *Time and Free Will* (1889), *Creative Evolution* (1907), and *Two Sources of Morality and Religion* (1932). Bergson glorified instinct, will, and subjectivism. He regarded human beings as living in a world of becoming, where the only certain thing was their sense of themselves. The world was permeated with a great vital force in which all things participated to a greater or lesser degree. The evolutionary nature of the universe meant that both the knower and the object of knowledge were constantly changing. What Bergson did was to set down much of the thought of earlier mystics in the language of evolutionary science.

In their appeal to the feelings and the emotions and in their questioning of the adequacy of rationalism, these writers drew on the Romantic tradition. The kind of creative impulse that earlier Romantics had considered the gift of artists, these later writers saw as the burden of all humans beings. The character of the human situation that these philosophers urged on their contemporaries was that of an ever-changing flux in which little or nothing but change itself was permanent. Human beings had to forge from their own inner will and determination the truth and values that were to exist in the world. In their impact on twen-

The Thinker *by Auguste Rodin (1840–1917). Perhaps the most famous sculpture since the Renaissance, it can be seen as symbolic of the new view of the human condition that emerged in the nineteenth century: Human beings had to forge truth and values from their own inner will and determination. Rationality alone was no longer adequate. [Roger-Viollet]*

tieth-century developments these philosophies threw into doubt not only the rigid domestic and religious morality of the nineteenth century but also the values of toleration, cosmopolitanism, and benevolence that had been championed during the Enlightenment.

The Birth of Psychoanalysis

A determination to probe beneath surface or public appearances united the major figures of late-nineteenth-century science, art, and philosophy. They sought to discern the various undercurrents, tensions, and complexities that

855

lay beneath the smooth, calm surfaces of hard atoms, respectable families, rationality, and social relationships. Their theories and discoveries meant that articulate, educated Europeans could never again view the surface of life with smugness or complacency or even much confidence. No single intellectual development more clearly and stunningly exemplified this trend than the emergence of psychoanalysis through the work of Sigmund Freud.

Freud was born in 1856 into an Austrian Jewish family that shortly thereafter settled in Vienna. He originally planned to become a lawyer but soon moved to the study of physiol-

Sigmund Freud (1856–1939), photographed in his Vienna office in 1914. Freud revolutionized the concept of human nature in Western thought. After Freud it was no longer possible to see reason as the sole determinant of behavior. [Ullstein Bilderdienst]

ogy and then to medicine. In 1886 he opened his medical practice in Vienna, where he continued to live until driven out by the Nazis in 1938, a year before his death. All of Freud's research and writing was done from the base of his medical practice. His earliest medical interests had been psychic disorders, to which he sought to apply the critical method of science. In late 1885 he had studied for a few months in Paris with Jean-Martin Charcot, who used hypnosis to treat cases of hysteria. In Vienna he collaborated with another physician, Josef Breuer (1842–1925), and in 1895 they published *Studies in Hysteria.*

In the mid-1890s Freud changed the technique of his investigations. He abandoned hypnosis and allowed his patients to talk freely and spontaneously about themselves. Repeatedly he found that they associated their particular neurotic symptoms with experiences related to earlier experiences, going back to childhood. He also noticed that sexual matters were significant in his patients' problems. For a time he thought that perhaps some sexual incident during childhood accounted for the illness of his patients. However, by 1897 he had privately rejected this theory. In its place he formulated a theory of infantile sexuality, according to which sexual drives and energy exist in infants and do not simply emerge at puberty. In Freud's view human beings are creatures of sexuality from birth through adulthood. He thus questioned in the most radical manner the concept of childhood innocence. He also portrayed the little-discussed or little-acknowledged matter of sex as one of the bases of mental order and disorder.

During the same decade Freud was also examining the psychic phenomena of dreams. Romantic writers had taken dreams very seriously, but most psychologists had not examined dreams scientifically. As a good rationalist Freud believed that there must exist a reasonable, scientific explanation for the irrational contents of dreams. That examination led him to a reconsideration of the general nature of the human mind. He came to the conclusion that during dreams, unconscious wishes, desires, and drives that had been excluded from everyday conscious life and experience enjoyed relatively free play in the mind. He argued, "The dream is the (disguised) fulfillment of a (suppressed, repressed) wish."[6] During the

[6]*The Basic Writings of Sigmund Freud,* trans. by A. A. Brill (New York: The Modern Library, 1938), p. 235.

Freud Explains an Obstacle to the Acceptance of Psychoanalysis

In addition to spawning numerous divergent views, the radical nature of Freud's theories caused them to be heard with misunderstanding, scorn, and opposition. In this 1915 passage, Freud was at pains to give a rational explanation for the nonrational popular reaction to his work. He contended that civilization had been built largely through channeling sexual energies into nonsexual activity. For him, psychoanalysis revealed this important role of the sexual impulses. By so revealing them, psychoanalysis tended to make people uncomfortable. Consequently public opinion played down the discoveries of psychoanalysis by claiming it was either dangerous or immoral.

We believe that civilization has been built up, under the pressure of the struggle for existence, by sacrifices in gratification of the primitive impulses, and that it is to a great extent for ever being recreated, as each individual, successively joining the community, repeats the sacrifice of his instinctive pleasures for the common good. The sexual are among the most important of the instinctive forces thus utilized: they are in this way sublimated, that is to say, their energy is turned aside from its sexual goal and diverted towards other ends, no longer sexual and socially more valuable. But the structure thus built up is insecure, for the sexual impulses are with difficulty controlled; in each individual who takes up his part in the work of civilization there is a danger that a rebellion of the sexual impulses may occur, against this diversion of their energy. *Society can conceive of no more powerful menace to its culture than would arise from the liberation of the sexual impulses and a return of them to their original goal. Therefore society dislikes this sensitive place in its development being touched upon; that the power of the sexual instinct should be recognized, and the significance of the individual's sexual life revealed, is very far from its interests; with a view to discipline it has rather taken the course of diverting attention away from this whole field. For this reason, the revelations of psychoanalysis are not tolerated by it, and it would greatly prefer to brand them as aesthetically offensive, morally reprehensible, or dangerous. . . . It is characteristic of human nature to be inclined to regard anything which is disagreeable as untrue, and then without much difficulty to find arguments against it.*

Sigmund Freud, *A General Introduction to Psychoanalysis*, trans. by J. Riviere (Garden City, N.Y.: Garden City Publishing Company, 1943), pp. 23–24.

waking hours the mind repressed or censored those wishes, which were as important to one's psychological makeup as conscious thought. In fact, those unconscious drives and desires contributed to conscious behavior. Freud developed these concepts and related them to his idea of infantile sexuality in *The Interpretation of Dreams*, published in 1900. It was his most important book.

In later books and essays Freud continued to urge the significance of the role played by the human unconscious. He portrayed a new internal organization of the mind. That inner realm was the arena for struggle and conflict among entities that he termed the *id*, the *ego*, and the *superego*. The first of these consisted of amoral, irrational, driving instincts for sexual gratification, aggression, and general physical and sensual pleasure. The superego constituted the external moral imperatives and expectations imposed on the personality by its society and culture. The ego stood as the mediator between the impulses of the id and the asceticism of the superego. The ego allowed the personality to cope with the inner and outer demands of its existence. Consequently, everyday behavior displayed the activity of the personality as its inner drives were partially repressed through the ego's coping with the external moral expectations as interpreted by the superego. It has been a grave misreading of Freud to see him as urging humankind to thrust off all repression. He believed that excessive repression could lead to mental disorder but that a certain degree of repression of sexuality and aggression was necessary for civilized living and the survival of humankind.

Freud's work led to nothing less than a revolution in the understanding of human nature. As his views gained adherents just before and after World War I, new dimensions of human life became widely recognized. Human beings were seen as attaining rationality rather than merely exercising it. Civilization itself came to be regarded as a product of repressed or sublimated aggressions and sexual drive.

In Freud's appreciation of the role of instinct, will, dreams, and sexuality, his thought pertained to the Romantic tradition of the nineteenth century. However, Freud must stand as a son of the Enlightenment. Like the *philosophes* he was a realist who wanted human beings to live free of fear and illusions by rationally understanding themselves and their world. He saw the personalities of human beings as being determined by finite physical and mental forces in a finite world. He was hostile to religion and spoke of it as an illusion. Freud, like the writers of the eighteenth century, wished to see civilization and humane behavior prevail. However, more fully than those predecessors, he understood the immense sacrifice of instinctual drives required for civilized behavior. He understood how many previously unsuspected obstacles lay in the way of rationality. Freud believed that the sacrifice and struggle were worthwhile, but he was pessimistic about the future of civilization in the West.

Freud's work marked the beginning of the psychoanalytic movement. By 1910 he had gathered around him a small but highly able group of disciples. Several of his early followers soon moved toward theories of which the master disapproved. The most important of these dissenters was Carl Jung (1875–1961). He was a Swiss whom for many years Freud regarded as his most distinguished and promising student. Before World War I the two men had, however, come to a parting of the ways. Jung had begun to question the primacy of sexual drives in forming human personality and in contributing to mental disorder. He also put much less faith in the guiding light of reason. Jung believed that the human subconscious contained inherited memories from previous generations of human beings. These collective memories, as well as the personal experience of an individual, constituted his or her soul. Jung regarded human beings in the twentieth century as alienated from these useful collective memories. One of his more famous books is entitled *Modern Man in Search of a Soul* (1933). Here and elsewhere Jung's thought tended toward mysticism and toward ascribing positive values to religion. Freud was highly critical of most of Jung's work. If Freud's thought derived primarily from the Enlightenment, Jung's was more dependent on Romanticism.

By the 1920s psychoanalysis had become even more fragmented as a movement. Nonetheless, in its several varieties, the movement touched not only psychology but also sociology, anthropology, religious studies, and literary theory. It has been one of the most important set of ideas whereby intellectuals in the twentieth century have come to understand themselves and their civilization.

Retreat from Rationalism in Politics

Both nineteenth-century liberals and nineteenth-century socialists agreed that society and politics could be guided according to rational principles. Rational analysis could discern the problems of society and prepare solutions. They generally felt that once given the vote, individuals would behave in their rational political self-interest. Improvement of society and the human condition was possible through education. By the close of the century these views were under attack in both theory and practice. Political scientists and sociologists painted politics as frequently irrational. Racial theorists questioned whether rationality and education could affect human society at all.

During this period, however, one major social theorist stood profoundly impressed by the role of reason in human society. The German sociologist Max Weber (1864–1920) regarded the emergence of rationalization throughout society as the major development of human history. Such rationalization displayed itself in both the development of scientific knowledge and the rise of bureaucratic organization. Weber saw bureaucratization as the most fundamental feature of modern social life. He used this view to oppose Marx's concept of the development of capitalism as the driving force in modern society. Bureaucratization involved the extreme division of labor as each individual person began to fit himself or herself into a particular small role in much larger organizations. Furthermore Weber believed that in modern society people derived their own self-images

*Max Weber (1864–1920) considered bureaucratization
as the most fundamental feature of modern social life. In
contrast to Marx and Freud, Weber stressed the role of the
individual and of rationality in human affairs. [German
Information Center]*

and sense of personal worth from their position in these organizations. Weber also contended—again, in contrast to Marx—that noneconomic factors might account for major developments in human history. For example, in his most famous essay, *The Protestant Ethic and the Spirit of Capitalism* (1905), Weber traced much of the rational character of capitalist enterprise to the ascetic religious doctrines of Puritanism. The Puritans, in his opinion, had accumulated wealth and worked for worldly success less for its own sake than to furnish themselves the assurance that they stood among the elect of God.

In his emphasis on the individual and on the dominant role of rationality, Weber differed from many contemporary social scientists, such as Gustave LeBon, Émile Durkheim, and Georges Sorel in France; Vilfredo Pareto in Italy; and Graham Wallas in England. LeBon (1841–1931) was a psychologist who explored the activity of crowds and mobs. He believed that in crowd situations rational behavior was abandoned. Sorel (1847–1922) argued in *Reflections on Violence* (1908) that people did not pursue rationally perceived goals but were led to action by collectively shared ideals. Durkheim (1858–1917) and Wallas (1858–1932) became deeply interested in the necessity of shared values and activities in a society. These elements, rather than a logical analysis of the social situation, bound human beings together. Instinct, habit, and affections instead of reason

directed human social behavior. Besides playing down the function of reason in society, all of these theorists emphasized the role of collective groups in politics rather than that of the individual formerly championed by liberals.

RACISM. The same tendencies to question or even to deny the constructive activity of reason in human affairs and to sacrifice the individual to the group manifested themselves in theories of race. Racial thinking had long existed in Europe. Renaissance explorers had displayed considerable prejudice against nonwhite peoples. Since the least the eighteenth century, biologists and anthropologists had classified human beings according to the color of their skin, their language, and their stage of civilization. Late-eighteenth-century linguistic scholars had observed similarities between many of the European languages and Sanskrit. They then postulated the existence of an ancient race called the *Aryans*, who had spoken the original language from which the rest derived. During the Romantic period writers had called the different cultures of Europe *races*. The debates over slavery in the European colonies and the United States had given further opportunity for the development of racial theory. However, in the late nineteenth century the concept of race emerged as a single dominant explanation of the history and the character of large groups of people.

Arthur de Gobineau (1816–1882), a reactionary French diplomat, enunciated the first important theory of race as the major determinant of human history. In his four-volume *Essay on the Inequality of the Human Races* (1853–1854), Gobineau portrayed the troubles of Western civilization as being the result of the long degeneration of the original white Aryan race. It had unwisely intermarried with the inferior yellow and black races, thus diluting the qualities of greatness and ability that originally existed in its blood. Gobineau was deeply pessimistic because he saw no way to reverse the degeneration that had taken place.

Gobineau's essay remained relatively obscure for many years. In the meantime a growing literature by anthropologists and explorers helped to spread racial thinking. In the wake of Darwin's theory, the concept of survival of the fittest was applied to races and nations. The recognition of the animal nature of humankind made the racial idea all the more persuasive. At the close of the century Houston Stewart Chamberlain (1855–1927), an Englishman

H. S. Chamberlain Exalts the Role of Race

Houston Stewart Chamberlain's *Foundations of the Nineteenth Century* (1899) was one of the most influential works of the day to argue for the primary role of race in history. Chamberlain believed that most people in the world were racially mixed and that this mixture weakened those human characteristics most needed for physical and moral strength. However, as demonstrated in the passage below, he also believed that those persons who were assured of their racial purity could act with the most extreme self-confidence and arrogance. Chamberlain's views had a major influence on the Nazi Party in Germany and on others who wished to prove their alleged racial superiority for political purposes.

Nothing is so convincing as the consciousness of the possession of Race. The man who belongs to a distinct, pure race, never loses the sense of it. The guardian angel of his lineage is ever at his side, supporting him where he loses his foothold, warning him like the Socratic Daemon where he is in danger of going astray, compelling obedience, and forcing him to undertakings which, deeming them impossible, he would never have dared to attempt. Weak and erring like all that is human, a man of this stamp recognises himself, as others recognise him, by the sureness of his character, and by the fact that his actions are marked by a certain simple and peculiar greatness, which finds its explanation in his distinctly typical and super-personal qualities. Race lifts a man above himself; it endows him with extraordinary—I might almost say supernatural—powers, so entirely does it distinguish him from the individual who springs from the chaotic jumble of peoples drawn from all parts of the world: and should this man of pure origin be perchance gifted above his fellows, then the fact of Race strengthens and elevates him on every hand, and he becomes a genius towering over the rest of mankind, not because he has been thrown upon the earth like a flaming meteor by a freak of nature, but because he soars heavenward like some strong and stately tree, nourished by thousands and thousands of roots—no solitary individual, but the living sum of untold souls striving for the same goal.

Houston Stewart Chamberlain, *Foundations of the Nineteenth Century*, Vol. 1, trans, by John Lees (London: John Lane, 1912), p. 269.

who settled in Germany, drew together these strands of racial thought into the two volumes of his *Foundations of the Nineteenth Century* (1899). He championed the concept of biological determinism through race, but he was somewhat more optimistic than Gobineau. Chamberlain believed that through genetics the human race could be improved and even that a superior race could be developed. Chamberlian added another element. He pointed to the Jews as the major enemy of European racial regeneration. Chamberlain's book and the lesser works on which it drew aided the spread of anti-Semitism in European political life. Also in Germany the writings of Paul de Lagarde and Julius Langbehn emphasized the supposed racial and cultural dangers posed by the Jews to traditional German national life.

ANTI-SEMITISM. Political and racial anti-Semitism, which have cast such dark shadows across the twentieth century, emerged in part from this atmosphere of racial thought and the retreat from rationality in politics. Religious anti-Semitism dated from at least the Middle Ages. Since the French Revolution, west European Jews had gradually gained entry into the civil life of Britain, France, and Germany. Popular anti-Semitism continued to exist as the Jewish community was identified with money and banking interests. During the last third of the century, as finance capitalism changed the economic structure of Europe, people pressured by the changes became hostile toward the Jewish community. This was especially true of the socially and economically insecure middle class. In Vienna Mayor Karl Lueger (1844–1910) used such anti-Semitism as a major attraction to his successful Christian Socialist Party. In Germany the ultraconservative Lutheran chaplain Adolf Stoecker (1835–1909) revived anti-Semitism. The Dreyfus af-

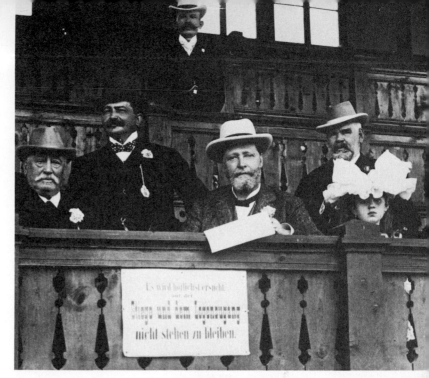

Karle Lueger (1844–1910), in the center wearing a white hat, anti-Semitic mayor of Vienna. That Lueger was able to attract votes because of his party's anti-Semitism was an evil omen for the future. [Ullstein Bilderdienst]

fair in France allowed a new flowering of hatred toward the Jews.

To this already ugly atmosphere, racial thought contributed the belief that no matter to what extent Jews assimilated themselves and their families into the culture of their country, their Jewishness—and thus their alleged danger to the society—would remain. The problem of race was not in the character but in the blood of the Jew. An important Jewish response to this new, rabid outbreak of anti-Semitism was the launching in 1896 of the Zionist movement to found a separate Jewish state. Its founder was the Austro-Hungarian Theodor Herzl (1860–1904). The conviction in 1894 of Captain Dreyfus in France and the election of Karl Lueger in 1895 as mayor of Vienna, as well as his personal experience of discrimination, convinced Herzl that liberal politics and the institutions of the liberal state could not protect the Jews in Europe or ensure that they would be treated justly. In 1896 Herzl published *The Jewish State,* in which he called for the organization of a separate state in which the Jews of the world might be assured of those rights and liberties that they should be enjoying in the liberal states of Europe. Furthermore Herzl followed the tactics of late-century mass democratic politics by particularly directing his appeal to the economically poor Jews who lived in the ghettos of eastern Europe and the slums of western Europe. The original call to Zionism thus combined a rejection of the anti-Semitism of Europe and a desire to establish some of the ideals of both liberalism and socialism in a state outside Europe.

Racial thinking and revived anti-Semitism were part of a wider late-century movement toward more aggressive nationalism. Previously nationalism had been a movement among European literary figures and liberals. The former had sought to develop what they

Theodor Herzl (1860–1904), on a visit to Palestine in 1898. Herzl's vision of a Jewish state would eventually lead to the creation of Israel in 1948. [Bildarchiv Preussicher Kulturbesitz]

of this aggressive racist variety would prove to be the most powerful ideology of the early twentieth century.

Suggested Readings

J. L. ALTHOLZ, *The Churches in the Nineteenth Century* (1967). A useful overview.

R. ARON, *Main Currents in Sociological Thought,* 2 vols. (1965, 1967). An introduction to the founders of the science.

S. AVINERI, *The Making of Modern Zionism: The Intellectual Origins of the Jewish State* (1981). An excellent introduction to the development of Zionist thought.

S. BARROWS, *Distorting Mirrors: Visions of the Crowd in Late Nineteenth-Century France* (1981). An important and imaginative examination of crowd psychology as it related to social tension in France.

F. L. BAUMER, *Religion and the Rise of Scepticism* (1960). Traces the development of religious doubt from the seventeenth to the twentieth centuries.

F. L. BAUMER, *Modern European Thought: Continuity and Change in Ideas, 1600–1950* (1977). The best work on the subject for this period.

M. D. BIDDIS, *Father of Racist Ideology: The Social and Political Thought of Count Gobineau* (1970). Sets the subject in the more general context of nineteenth-century thought.

P. BOWLER, *The Eclipse of Darwinism: Anti-Darwinian Evolution Theories in the Decades Around* 1900 (1983). A major study of the fate of Darwinian theory in the nineteenth-century scientific community.

P. BOWLER, *Evolution: The History of an Idea* (1984). An outstanding survey of the subject.

J. W. BURROW, *Evolution and Society: A Study in Victorian Social Theory* (1966). An important study of evolutionary sociology.

O. CHADWICK, *The Secularization of the European Mind in the Nineteenth Century* (1975). The best treatment available.

D. G. CHARLTON, *Positivist Thought in France During the Second Empire, 1852–1870* (1959), and *Secular Religions in France, 1815–1870* (1963). Two clear introductions to important subjects.

C. M. CIPOLLA, *Literacy and Development in the West* (1969). Traces the explosion of literacy in the past two centuries.

A. DANTO, *Nietzsche as Philosopher* (1965). A very helpful and well-organized introduction.

A. J. ENGEL, *From Clergyman to Don: The Rise of the Academic Profession in Nineteenth-Century Oxford* (1983). An interesting survey of a changing profession.

P. GAY, *Freud, Jews, and Other Germans: Masters and Victims in Modernist Culture* (1978). A collection of wide-ranging essays on German intellectual and cultural life.

regarded as the historically distinct qualities of particular national or ethnic literatures. The liberal nationalists had hoped to redraw the map of Europe to reflect ethnic boundaries. The drive for the unification of Italy and Germany had been major causes, as had been the liberation of Poland from foreign domination. The various national goups of the Habsburg Empire had also sought emancipation from Austrian domination. From the 1870s onward, however, nationalism became a movement with mass support, well-financed organizations, and political parties. Nationalists tended to redefine nationality in terms of race and blood. The new nationalism opposed the internationalism of both liberalism and socialism. The ideal of nationality was used to overcome the pluralism of class, religion, and geography. The nation and its duties replaced religion in the lives of many secularized peoplc. It sometimes became a secular religion in the hands of state schoolteachers, who were replacing the clergy as the instructors of youth. Nationalism

C. C. GILLISPIE, *Genesis and Geology* (1951). An excellent discussion of the impact of modern geological theory during the early nineteenth century.

C. C. GILLISPIE, *The Edge of Objectivity* (1960). One of the best one-volume treatments of modern scientific ideas.

J. C. GREENE, *The Death of Adam: Evolution and Its Impact on Western Thought* (1959). Emphasizes pre-Darwinian thought.

H. S. HUGHES, *Consciousness and Society: The Reorientation of European Social Thought, 1890–1930* (1958). A wide-ranging discussion of the revolt against positivism.

W. IRVINE, *Apes, Angels, and Victorians* (1955). A lively and sound account of Darwin and Huxley.

W. A. KAUFMANN, *Nietzsche: Philosopher, Psychologist, Antichrist,* rev. ed. (1968). An exposition of Nietzsche's thought and its sources.

T. A. KSELMAN, *Miracles and Prophesies in Nineteenth-Century France* (1983). A study of popular religion.

E. MAYR, *The Growth of Biological Thought: Diversity, Evolution, and Inheritance* (1982). A major survey by a scientist of note.

J. MCMANNERS, *Church and State in France, 1870–1914* (1972). The standard treatment.

J. T. MERZ, *A History of European Thought in the Nineteenth Century,* 4 vols. (1897–1914). Still a useful mine of information.

J. MOORE, *The Post-Darwinian Controversies: A Study of the Protestant Struggle to Come to Terms with Darwin in Great Britain and America, 1870–1900* (1979). A major examination of the impact of Darwinian thought on both science and religion.

J. MORRELL AND A. THACKRAY, *Gentlemen of Science: Early Years of the British Association for the Advancement of Science* (1981). An important study that examines the role of science in early and mid-nineteenth-century Britain.

G. L. MOSSE, *Toward the Final Solution: A History of European Racism* (1978). A sound introduction.

R. PASCAL, *From Naturalism to Expressionism: German Literature and Society, 1880–1918* (1973). A helpful survey.

L. POLIAKOV, *The Aryan Myth: A History of Racist and Nationalist Ideas in Europe* (1971). The best introduction to the problem.

P. G. J. PULZER, *The Rise of Political Anti-Semitism in Germany and Austria* (1964). A sound discussion of anti-Semitism in the world of central European politics.

P. RIEF, *Freud: The Mind of the Moralist* (1959). Probably the best one-volume treatment.

C. E. SCHORSKE, *Fin de Siècle Vienna: Politics and Culture* (1980). Major essays on the explosively creative intellectual climate of Vienna.

J. SPERBER, *Popular Catholicism in Nineteenth-Century Germany* (1984). A significant new study.

F. STERN, *The Politics of Cultural Despair: A Study in the Rise of the German Ideology* (1965). An important examination of antimodern and anti-Semitic thought in imperial Germany.

F. M. TURNER, *The Greek Heritage in Victorian Britain* (1981). An examination of the role of Greek antiquity in Victorian thought.

A. VIDLER, *The Church in an Age of Revolution* (1961). A sound account of the problems of Church and State in the nineteenth century.

J. P. VON ARX. *Progress and Pessimism: Religion, Politics, and History in Late Nineteenth Century Britain* (1985). A major study that casts much new light on the nineteenth-century view of progress.

R. WILLIAMS, *The Long Revolution* (1961). Explores the impact of literacy and popular publishing on English culture.

R. WOLLHEIM, *Sigmund Freud* (1971). An excellent introduction to Freud's intellectual development and his major concepts.

Kaiser William II (1888–1918), at left, and his six sons on parade in Berlin in January 1913. William was intelligent but unstable. His penchant for military swagger and tough talk convinced many in Europe that he was an irresponsible militarist. [Bildarchiv Preussicher Kulturarchiv]

Expansion of European Power and the "New Imperialism"

DURING the second half of the nineteenth century, and especially after 1870, European influence and control over the rest of the world grew to an unprecedented degree. North and South America, as well as Australia and New Zealand, became almost integral parts of the European world as the great streams of European immigrants populated them. Until the nineteenth century Asia (with the significant exception of India) and most of Africa had gone their own ways, having little contact with Europe. But the latter part of that century brought the partition of Africa among a number of European nations and the establishment of European economic and political power from the eastern to the western borders of Asia. By the next century this growth of European dominance had brought every part of the globe into a single world economy and had made events in any corner of the world significant thousands of miles away.

The explosive developments in nineteenth-century science, technology, industry, agriculture, transportation, communication, and military weapons provided the chief sources of European power. They made it possible for a small number of Europeans (or Americans) to impose their will on other peoples many times their number by force or by the threat of force. Institutional as well as material advantages allowed Westerners to have their way. The growth of national states that commanded the loyalty, service, and resources of their inhabitants to a degree previously unknown was a Western phenomenon, and it permitted the European nations to deploy their resources in the most effective way. The Europeans also possessed another, less tangible weapon: a sense of superiority of their civilization and way of life. This gave them a confidence that often took the form of an unpleasant arrogance and that fostered the expansionist mood.

The expansion of European influence was not anything new. Spain, Portugal, France, and Britain had controlled territories overseas for centuries, but by the mid-nineteenth century only Great Britain retained extensive holdings. The first half of the century was generally a period of hostility to colonial expansion. Even the British had been sobered by their loss of the American colonies. The French acquired Algeria and part of Indochina, and

25
Imperialism, Alliances, and War

the British made some additional gains in territories adjacent to their holdings in Canada, India, Australia, and New Zealand. For the most part, however, the doctrine of free trade was dominant, and it opposed the idea of political interference in other lands.

Because Britain ruled the waves and had great commercial advantages as a result of being first in the Industrial Revolution, the British were usually content to let commerce go forward without annexations. Yet they were quite prepared to interfere forcefully if some "backward" country placed barriers in the way of their trade. Still, at mid-century, in Britain as elsewhere, opinion stood predominantly against further political or military involvement overseas.

In the last third of the century, however, the European states swiftly spread their control over perhaps 10 million square miles and 150 million people, about a fifth of the world's land area and a tenth of its population. The movement has been called the *New Imperialism*.

The New Imperialism

Imperialism is a word that has come to be used so loosely as almost to be deprived of meaning. It may be useful to offer a definition that might be widely accepted: "The policy of extending a nation's authority by territorial acquisition or by the establishment of economic and political hegemony over other nations."[1] That definition seems to apply equally well to human actions as far back as ancient Egypt and Mesopotamia and to the performance of European nations in the late nineteenth century. But there were some new elements in the latter case. Previous imperialisms had taken the form either of seizing land and settling it with the conqueror's people or of establishing trading centers to exploit the resources of the dominated area. The New Imperialism did not completely abandon these devices, but it introduced new ones.

The usual pattern of the New Imperialism was for the European nation to invest capital in the "backward" country, to build productive enterprises and improved means of transportation, to employ great numbers of natives in the process, and thereby to transform the entire economy and culture of the dominated area. To guarantee their investments, the European

states would make favorable arrangements with the local government either by enriching the rulers or by threatening them. If these arrangements proved inadequate, the dominant power established different degrees of political control, ranging from full annexation as a colony to protectorate status (whereby the local ruler was controlled by the dominant European state and maintained by its military power), to "spheres-of-influence" status (whereby the European state received special commercial and legal privileges without direct political involvement). Other novelties included the great speed with which European expansion went forward and the way in which participation in this expansion came to be regarded as necessary to retaining status as a great power.

Motives for the New Imperialism: The Economic Interpretation

There has been considerable debate about the motives for the New Imperialism, and after more than a century there is still no agreement. The most widespread interpretation has been economic, most typically in the form given by the English radical economist J. A. Hobson and later adapted by Lenin. As Lenin put it. "Imperialism is the monopoly stage of capitalism,"[2] the last stage of a dying capitalist system. According to this interpretation, competition inevitably leads to the elimination of inefficient capitalists and, therefore, to monopoly. Powerful industrial and financial capitalists soon run out of profitable areas of investment in their own countries and persuade their governments to gain colonies in "backward" countries, where they can find higher profits from their investments, new markets for their products, and safe sources of the needed raw materials.

The facts of the matter do not support this viewpoint. The European powers did export considerable amounts of capital in the form of investments abroad, but not in such a manner as to fit the model of Hobson and Lenin. Britain, for example, made heavier investments abroad before 1875 than during the next two decades. Only a very small percentage of British and European investments overseas, moreover, went to the new colonial areas. Most went into Europe itself or into older, well-established areas like the United States, Can-

---

[1] *American Heritage Dictionary of the English Language* (New York: Houghton Mifflin, 1969), p. 660.

[2] V. I. Lenin, *Imperialism, the Highest Stage of Capitalism* (New York: International Publishers, 1939), p. 88.

ada, Australia, and New Zealand. Even when investments were made in the new areas, they were not necessarily put into colonies held by the investing country.

The facts are equally discouraging for those who emphasize the need for markets and raw materials. Colonies were not usually important markets for the great imperial nations, and all were forced to rely on areas that they did not control as sources of vital raw materials. It is not even clear that control of the new colonies was particularly profitable. Britain, to be sure, benefited greatly from its rule of India. It is also true that some European businessmen and politicians hoped to find a cure for the great depression of 1873–1896 in colonial expansion. Nevertheless, as one of the leading students of the subject has said, "No one can determine whether the accounts of empire ultimately closed with a favorable cash balance."[3] That is true of the European imperial nations collectively, but it is certain that for some of them, like Italy and Germany, empire was a losing proposition. Some individuals and companies, of course, were able to make great profits from particular colonial ventures, but such people were able to influence national policy only occasionally. Economic motives certainly played a part, but a full understanding of the New Imperialism requires a search for further motives as well.

Cultural, Religious, and Social Interpretations

Advocates of imperialism put forth various justifications. Some argued that it was the responsibility of the advanced European nations to bring the benefits of their higher culture and superior civilization to the people of "backward" lands, but few people were influenced by such arrogant arguments, though many shared the intellectual assumptions. Religious groups argued for the responsibility of Western nations to bring the benefits of Christianity to the heathen with more extensive efforts and aid from their governments. Some politicians and diplomats argued for imperialism as a tool of social policy. In Germany, for instance, some people suggested that imperial expansion might serve to deflect public interest away from domestic politics and social reform. But Germany acquired only a few colonies, and

[3]D. K. Fieldhouse, *The Colonial Empires* (New York: Delacorte, 1966), p. 393.

Queen Victoria (1837–1901) at work on state papers in 1893. Note the Indian attendant. The Queen was also Empress of India. India was by far the most important possession in the British Empire. [National Portrait Gallery, London]

such considerations played little if any role.

In Britain such arguments were made, as was their opposite. The statesman Joseph Chamberlain argued for the empire as a source of profit and economic security that would finance a great program of domestic reform and welfare. To the extent that they had any influence, these arguments were not important as motives for imperialism because they were made well after the British had acquired most of their empire. Another common and apparently plausible justification was that colonies would provide a good place to settle surplus population. In fact, most European emigrants went to areas not controlled by their countries, chiefly to North and South America and Australia.

The Scramble for Africa: Strategic and Political Interpretations

Strategic and political considerations seem to have been more important in bringing on the New Imperialism. The scramble for Africa in

IMPERIAL EXPANSION IN AFRICA TO 1880

MAP 25–1

A contemporary French view of the fall of Algiers in 1830. The French conquest of Algeria took some seventeen years (1830–1847). [New York Public Library]

the 1880s is one example. Britain was the only great power with extensive overseas holdings on the eve of the scramble. The completion of the Suez Canal in 1869 made Egypt an area of vital interest to the British because it sat astride the shortest rout to India. Under Disraeli, Britain purchased a major, but not a controlling, interest in the canal in 1875. When Egypt's stability was threatened by internal troubles in the 1880s, the British moved in and established a protectorate. Then, to protect Egypt, they advanced into the Sudan.

France became involved in Africa in 1830 by sending a naval expedition to Algeria to attack the pirates based there. Before long, French settlers arrived and established a colony. By 1882 France was in full control of Algeria, and at about the same time, to prevent Tunisia from falling into Italy's hands, France took over that area of North Africa also. Soon lesser states like Belgium, Portugal, Spain, and Italy were scrambling for African colonies. By the 1890s their intervention had compelled Britain to expand northward from the Cape of Good Hope into what is now Zimbabwe. Britain may have had significant strategic reasons for protecting the Suez and Cape routes to India, but France and the smaller European nations did not have such reasons. Their motives were political as well as economic, for they equated status as a great power (Britain stood as the chief model) with the possession of colonies. They therefore sought colonies as evidence of their own importance.

Bismarck appears to have pursued an imperial policy, however brief, from coldly political motives. In 1884 and 1885 Germany declared protectorates over Southwest Africa, Togoland, the Cameroons, and East Africa. None of these places was particularly valuable or of intrinsic strategic importance. Bismarck himself had no interest in overseas colonies and once compared them to fine furs worn by impoverished Polish nobles who had no shirts underneath. His concern lay in Germany's exposed position in Europe. On one occasion he said, "My map of Africa lies in Europe. Here is Russia, and there is France, and here in the middle are we. That is my map of Africa."[4] He acquired colonies chiefly to improve Germany's diplomatic position in Europe. He tried to turn France from hostility against Germany by diverting the French toward colonial interests. At the

[4]Quoted by J. Remak in *The Origins of World War I, 1871–1914* (New York: Holt, Rinehart & Winston, 1967), p. 5.

Cecil Rhodes (1835–1902) resting on the African plain. Rhodes's dream, never realized, was for a railway from Capetown to Cairo running throughout on British-controlled territory. [Bettmann Archive]

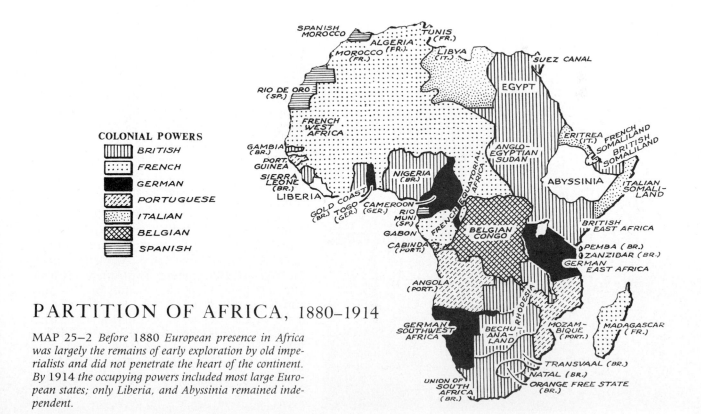

COLONIAL POWERS

|||||||	*BRITISH*
⋮⋮⋮⋮	*FRENCH*
▓▓	*GERMAN*
⋰⋰	*PORTUGUESE*
⋱⋱	*ITALIAN*
⊠⊠	*BELGIAN*
≡≡≡	*SPANISH*

PARTITION OF AFRICA, 1880–1914

MAP 25–2 *Before 1880 European presence in Africa was largely the remains of early exploration by old imperialists and did not penetrate the heart of the continent. By 1914 the occupying powers included most large European states; only Liberia, and Abyssinia remained independent.*

same time German colonies in Africa could be used as a subtle weapon with which to persuade the British to be reasonable.

The Irrational Element

Germany's annexations started a wild scramble by the other European powers to establish claims on what was left of Africa. By 1890 almost all of the continent was parceled out. Great powers and small expanded into areas neither profitable nor strategic for reasons less calculating and rational than Bismarck's. "Empire in the modern period," D. K. Fieldhouse observed, "was the product of European power: its reward was power or the sense of power."[5]

Such motives were not new. They had been well understood by the Athenian spokesman at

[5]Fieldhouse, p. 393.

United States sailors in action off the coast of Cuba in 1898 during the Spanish-American War. Victory in the war made the United States an imperial power in the Caribbean and the Pacific. [*National Archives*]

Melos in 416 B.C., whose words were reported by Thucydides: "Of the gods we believe and of men we know clearly that by a necessity of their nature where they have the power they rule."[6]

In Asia the emergence of Japan as a great power in touch with the rest of the world frightened the other powers interested in China. The Russians were building a railroad across Siberia to Vladivostok and were afraid of any power that might threaten Manchuria. Together with France and Germany they applied diplomatic pressure that forced Japan out of the Liaotung Peninsula and its harbor, Port Arthur, and all pressed feverishly for concessions in China. Fearing that China, its markets, and its investment opportunities would soon be closed to its citizens, the United States in 1899 proposed the "Open Door Policy," which opposed foreign annexations in China and allowed entrepreneurs of all nations to trade there on equal terms. The support of Britain helped win acceptance of the policy by all the powers except Russia.

The United States had only recently emerged as a force in international affairs. After freeing itself of British rule and consolidating its independence during the Napoleonic Wars, the Americans had busied themselves with westward expansion on the North American continent until the end of the nineteenth century. The Monroe Doctrine of 1823 had, in effect, made the entire Western Hemisphere an American protectorate. Cuba's attempt to gain independence from Spain was the spark for the new United States involvement in international affairs. Sympathy for the Cuban cause, American investments on the island, the desire for Cuban sugar, and concern over the island's strategic importance in the Caribbean all helped win the Americans over to the idea of a war with Spain.

Victory in the Spanish-American War of 1898 brought the United States an informal protectorate over Cuba and the annexation of Puerto Rico and drove Spain completely out of the Western Hemisphere. The Americans also purchased the Philippine Islands and Guam, and Germany acquired the other Spanish islands in the Pacific. The Americans and the Germans also divided Samoa between them. What was left of the Pacific islands was soon taken by France and England. Hawaii had been under American influence for some time and

[6]Thucydides, *The Peloponnesian War*, 5.105.2.

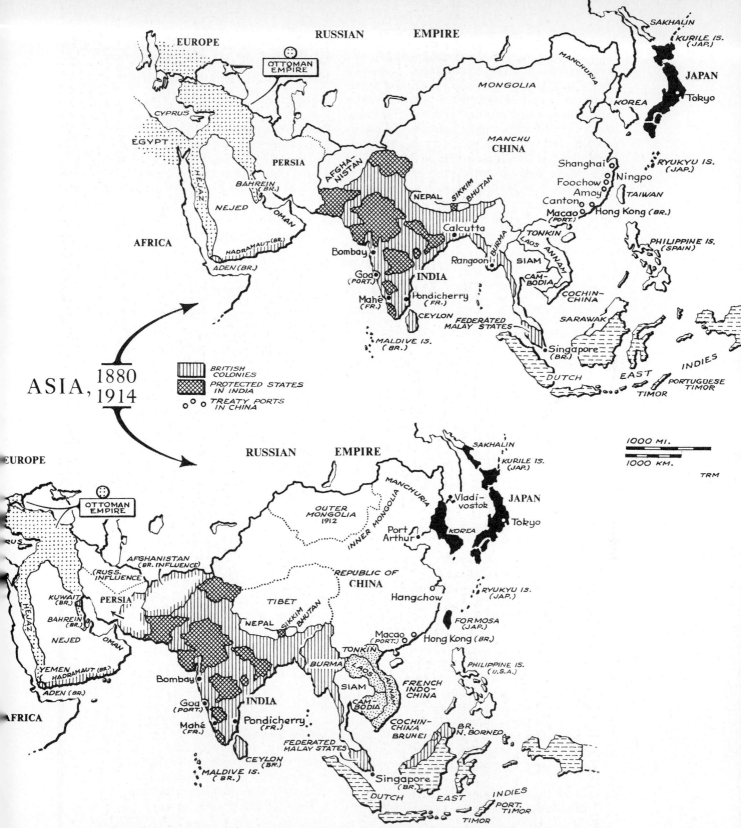

ASIA, 1880 1914

BRITISH COLONIES

PROTECTED STATES IN INDIA

TREATY PORTS IN CHINA

1000 MI.

1000 KM.

TRM

MAPS 25–3, 25–4 *As in Africa, the decades before World War I saw imperialism spread widely and rapidly in Asia. Two new powers, Japan and the United States joined the British, French, and Dutch in extending control both to islands and to mainland and in exploiting an enfeebled China.*

had been asking for annexation, which was accomplished in 1898. This outburst of activity after the Spanish war made the United States an imperial and Pacific power. Soon after the turn of the century most of the world had come under the control of the industrialized Western nations. The one remaining area of great vulnerability was the Ottoman Empire, but its fate was closely tied up with European developments and must be treated in that context.

Emergence of the German Empire and the Alliance Systems (1873–1890)

Prussia's victories over Austria and France and its creation of a large, powerful German Empire in 1871 revolutionized European diplomacy. The sudden appearance of a vast new political unit that brought together the major-

---

Kipling Advises the Americans: The Responsibility for Empire

THE WHITE MAN'S BURDEN
1899
(*The United States and the Philippine
Islands*)

Take up the White Man's burden—
  Send forth the best ye breed—
Go bind your sons to exile
  To serve your captives' need;
To wait in heavy harness
  On fluttered folk and wild—
Your new-caught, sullen peoples,
  Half devil and half child.

Take up the White Man's burden—
  The savage wars of peace—
Fill full the mouth of Famine
  And bid the sickness cease;
And when your goal is nearest
  The end for others sought,
Watch Sloth and heathen Folly
  Bring all your hope to nought.

Take up the White Man's burden—
  And reap his old reward:
The blame of those ye better,
  The hate of those ye guard—
The cry of hosts ye humour
  (Ah, slowly!) toward the light:—
"Why brought ye us from bondage,
  "Our loved Egyptian night?"

Take up the White Man's burden—
  In patience to abide,

To veil the threat of terror
  And check the show of pride;
By open speech and simple,
  An hundred times made plain,
To seek another's profit,
  And work another's gain.

Take up the White Man's burden—
  No tawdry rule of kings,
But toil of serf and sweeper—
  The tale of common things.
The ports ye shall not enter,
  The roads ye shall not tread,
Go make them with your living,
  And mark them with your dead!

Take up the White Man's burden—
  Ye dare not stoop to less—
Nor call too loud on Freedom
  To cloak your weariness;
By all ye cry or whisper,
  By all ye leave or do,
The silent, sullen peoples
  Shall weigh your Gods and you.

Take up the White Man's burden—
  Have done with childish days—
The lightly proffered laurel,
  The easy, ungrudged praise.
Comes now, to search your manhood
  Through all the thankless years,
Cold-edged with dear-bought wisdom,
  The judgment of your peers!

"The White Man's Burden (1899)," from *Rudyard Kipling's Verse: Definitive Edition* (New York: Doubleday, 1940) pp. 321–323.

ity of the German people to form a nation of great and growing population, wealth, industrial capacity, and military power posed new problems. The balance of power created at the Congress of Vienna was altered radically. Britain retained its position and so did Russia, even though somewhat weakened by the Crimean War. Austria, however, had fallen quite a distance, and its position was destined to deteriorate further as the forces of nationalism threatened to disintegrate the Austro-Hungarian Empire. French power and prestige were badly damaged by the Franco-Prussian War and the German annexation of Alsace-Lorraine. The weakened French were both afraid of their powerful new neighbor and at the same time resentful of the defeat, the loss of territory and population, and the loss of their traditional position of dominance in western Europe.

Until 1890 Bismarck continued to guide German policy. He insisted after 1871 that Germany was a satisfied power and wanted no further territorial gains, and he meant it. He only wanted to consolidate the new international situation by avoiding a new war that might undo his achievement. Aware of French resentment, he tried to assuage it by friendly relations and by supporting French colonial aspirations in order to turn French attention away from European discontents. At the same time he prepared for the worst. If France could not be conciliated, it must be isolated. The kernel of Bismarck's policy was to prevent an alliance between France and any other European power—especially Austria or Russia—that would threaten Germany with a war on two fronts.

WAR IN THE BALKANS. His first move was to establish the Three Emperors' League in 1873. It brought together the three great conservative empires of Germany, Austria, and Russia. The league soon collapsed as a result of the Russo-Turkish War, which broke out in 1875 because of an uprising in the Ottoman Balkan provinces of Bosnia and Herzegovina. The tottering Ottoman Empire was held together chiefly by the competing aims of those powers who awaited its demise. The weakness of the Ottoman Empire encouraged Serbia and Montenegro to come to the aid of their fellow Slavs. Soon the rebellion spread to Bulgaria. Then Russia entered the fray and turned it into a major international crisis. The Russians hoped to pursue their traditional policy of expansion at Ottoman expense and especially hoped to achieve their most cherished goal: control of Constantinople and the Dardanelles. The Russian intervention also reflected the influence of the Pan-Slavic movement, which sought to bring together all the Slavic peoples, even those under Austrian or Ottoman rule, under the protection of Holy Mother Russia.

The Ottoman Empire was weak, and before long it was forced to ask for peace. The Treaty of San Stefano of March 1878 was a Russian triumph. The Slavic states in the Balkans were freed of Ottoman rule, and Russia itself obtained territorial gains and a heavy monetary indemnity. But the Russian victory was not lasting. The other great powers were alarmed by the terms of the settlement. Austria feared that the great Slavic victory and the powerful increase in Russian influence in the Balkans would cause dangerous shock waves in its own Balkan provinces. The British were alarmed by the damage the Russian victory would do to the European balance of power and especially by the thought of possible Russian control of the Dardanelles. Disraeli was determined to resist, and British public opinion supported him. A music-hall song that became popular gave the language a new word for superpatriotism: *jingoism.*

> We don't want to fight,
> But by jingo if we do,
> We've got the men,
> We've got the ships,
> We've got the money too!

THE CONGRESS OF BERLIN. Even before the Treaty of San Stefano, Disraeli sent a fleet to Constantinople. After the magnitude of Russia's appetite was known, Britain and Austria forced Russia to agree to an international conference at which the provisions of the treaty would be reviewed by the other great powers. The resulting Congress of Berlin met in June and July of 1878 under the presidency of Bismarck. The choice of site and presiding officer was a clear recognition of Germany's new importance and of its chancellor's claim that this policy called for no further territorial gains and aimed at preserving the peace. Bismarck referred to himself as an "honest broker," and the title seems justified. He agreed to the congress simply because he wanted to avoid a war between Russian and Austria into which he feared Germany would be drawn with nothing to gain and much to lose. From the collapsing Ottoman Empire he wanted nothing. "The

Eastern Question," he said, "is not worth the healthy bones of a single Pomeranian musketeer."[7]

The decisions of the congress were a blow to Russian ambitions. Bulgaria was reduced in size by two thirds and was deprived of access to the Aegean Sea. Austria-Hungary was given Bosnia and Herzegovina to "occupy and administer," although those provinces remained formally under Ottoman rule. Britain received Cyprus, and France gained permission to expand into Tunisia. These privileges were compensation for the gains that Russia was permitted to keep. Germany asked for nothing but got little credit from Russia for its restraint. The Russians believed that they had saved Prussia in 1807 from complete dismemberment by Napoleon and had expected a show of German gratitude. They were bitterly disappointed, and the Three Emperors' League was dead.

All of the Balkan states were also annoyed by the Berlin settlement. Romania wanted Bessarabia; Bulgaria wanted a return to the bor-

ders of the Treaty of San Stefano; and Greece wanted a part of the Ottoman spoils. The major trouble spot, however, was in the south Slavic states of Serbia and Montenegro. They deeply resented the Austrian occupation of Bosnia and Herzegovina, as did many of the natives of those provinces. The south Slavic question, no less than the estrangement between Russia and Germany, was a threat to the peace of Europe.

GERMAN ALLIANCES WITH RUSSIA AND AUSTRIA. For the moment Bismarck could ignore the Balkans, but he could not ignore the breach in his eastern alliance system. With Russia alienated, he turned to Austria and concluded a secret treaty in 1879. The resulting Dual Alliance provided that if either Germany or Austria were attacked by Russia the ally would help the attacked party. If the signatory countries were attacked by someone else, each promised at least to maintain neutrality. The treaty was for five years and was renewed regularly until 1918. As the central point in German policy, it was criticized at the time, and some have judged it mistaken in retrospect. It appeared to tie the German fortunes to those of

[7]Quoted by Hajo Holborn, *A History of Modern Germany, 1840–1945* (New York: Knopf, 1969), p. 239.

The Congress of Berlin, 1878. Bismarck is in the center greeting the Russian Ambassador. Disraeli is standing on the left with his hand on his hip. [Bildarchiv Preussicher Kulturbesitz]

the troubled Austro-Hungarian Empire and in that way to borrow trouble. At the same time, by isolating the Russians, it pushed them in the direction of seeking alliances in the West.

Bismarck was fully aware of these dangers but discounted them with good reason. At no time did he allow his Austrian alliance to drag Germany into Austria's Balkan quarrels. As he put it himself, in any alliance there is a horse and a rider, and in this one Bismarck meant Germany to be the rider. He made it clear to the Austrians that the alliance was purely defensive and that Germany would never be a party to an attack on Russia. "For us," he said, "Balkan questions can never be a motive for war."[8]

Bismarck believed that monarchical, reactionary Russia would not seek an alliance either with republican, revolutionary France or with increasingly democratic Britain. In fact, he expected the news of the Austro-German negotiations to frighten Russia into seeking closer relations with Germany, and he was right. Russian diplomats soon approached him, and by 1881 he had concluded a renewal of the Three Emperors' League on a firmer basis. The three powers promised to maintain friendly neutrality in case either of the others was attacked by a fourth power. Other clauses included the right of Austria to annex Bosnia-Herzegovina whenever it wished and closed the Dardanelles to all nations in case of war. The agreement allayed German fears of a Russian-French alliance and Russian fears of a combination of Austria and Britain against it, of Britain's fleet sailing into the Black Sea, and of a hostile combination of Germany and Austria. Most importantly, the agreement aimed at a resolution of the conflicts in the Balkans between Austria and Russia. Though it did not put an end to such conflicts, it was a significant step toward peace.

THE TRIPLE ALLIANCE. In 1882 Italy, ambitious for colonial expansion and annoyed by the French preemption of Tunisia, asked to join the Dual Alliance. The provisions of its entry were defensive and were directed against France. At this point Bismarck's policy was a complete success. He was allied with three of the great powers and friendly with the other, Great Britain, which held aloof from all alliances. France was isolated and no threat. Bismarck's diplomacy was a great achievement,

but an even greater challenge was to maintain this complicated system of secret alliances in the face of the continuing rivalries among Germany's allies. In spite of another Balkan war that broke out in 1885 and again estranged Austria and Russia, he succeeded. Although the Three Emperors' League lapsed, the Triple Alliance (Germany, Austria, and Italy) was renewed for another five years. To restore German relations with Russia, he negotiated the Reinsurance Treaty of 1887, in which both powers promised to remain neutral if either was attacked. All seemed smooth, but a change in the German monarchy soon overturned everything.

In 1888 William II (1888–1918) came to the German throne. He was twenty-nine years old, ambitious and impetuous. He was imperious by temperament and believed in monarchy by divine right. He had suffered an injury at birth that left him with a withered arm, and he compensated for this disability by means of vigorous exercise, by a military bearing and outlook, and sometimes by an embarrassingly loud and bombastic rhetoric.

Like many Germans of his generation, William II was filled with a sense of Germany's destiny as the leading power of Europe. He wanted to achieve recognition at least of equality from Britain, the land of his mother and of his grandmother, Queen Victoria. To achieve a "place in the sun," he and his contemporaries wanted a navy and colonies like Britain's. These aims, of course, ran counter to Bismarck's limited continental policy. When William argued for a navy as a defense against a British landing in north Germany, Bismarck replied, "If the British should land on our soil, I should have them arrested." This was only one example of the great distance between the young emperor, or Kaiser, and his chancellor. In 1890 William used a disagreement over domestic policy to dismiss Bismarck.

As long as Bismarck held power, Germany was secure, and there was peace among the great European powers. Although he made mistakes and was not always successful, there was much to admire in his understanding and management of international relations in the hard world of reality. He had a clear and limited idea of his nation's goals. He resisted pressures for further expansion with few and insignificant exceptions. He understood and used the full range of diplomatic weapons: appeasement and deterrence, threats and promises, secrecy and openness. He understood the

[8]Quoted by J. Remak, p. 14.

Bismarck and the young Kaiser William II in 1888. The two disagreed over many issues, and in 1890 William dismissed the aged chancellor. [German Information Center]

needs and hopes of other countries and, where possible, tried to help to accomplish them or used them to his own advantage. His system of alliances created a stalemate in the Balkans at the same time that it ensured German security.

During Bismarck's time Germany was a force for European peace and was increasingly understood to be so. This position would not, of course, have been possible without its great military power, but it also required the leadership of a statesman who was willing and able to exercise restraint and who could make a realistic estimate of what his country needed and what was possible.

Forging of the Triple Entente (1890–1907)

FRANCO-RUSSIAN ALLIANCE. Almost immediately after Bismarck's retirement his system of alliances collapsed. His successor was General Leo von Caprivi (1831–1899), who had once asked, "What kind of jackass will dare to be Bismarck's successor?" Caprivi refused the Russian request to renew the Reinsurance Treaty, in part because he felt incom-

petent to continue Bismarck's complicated policy and in part because he wished to draw Germany closer to Britain. The results were unfortunate, as Britain remained aloof and Russian was alienated. Even Bismarck had assumed that ideological differences were too great to permit a Franco-Russian alliance, but political isolation and the need for foreign capital unexpectedly drove the Russians toward France. The French, who were even more isolated, were glad to encourage their investors to pour capital into Russia if it would help produce an alliance and security against Germany. In 1894 the Franco-Russian alliance against Germany was signed.

BRITAIN AND GERMANY. Britain now became the key to the international situation. Colonial rivalries pitted the British against the Russians in Central Asia and against the French in Africa. Traditionally Britain had also opposed Russian control of Constantinople and the Dardanelles and French control of the Low Countries. There was no reason to think that Britain would soon become friendly to its traditional rivals or abandon its accustomed friendliness toward the Germans. Yet, within a decade of William II's accession, Germany had become the enemy in the minds of the British. Before the turn of the century popular British thrillers about imaginary wars portrayed the French as the invader; after the turn of the century the enemy was always German. This remarkable transformation has often been attributed to the economic rivalry of Germany and Britain, in which Germany made vast strides to challenge and even overtake British production in various materials and markets. There can be no doubt that Germany made such gains and that many Britons resented them, but the problem was not a serious cause of hostility and waned as the first decade of the century wore on. The real problem lay in the foreign and naval policies of the German emperor and his ministers.

William II's attitude toward Britain was respectful and admiring, especially with regard to its colonial empire and its mighty fleet. At first, Germany tried to win the British over to the Triple Alliance, but when Britain clung to its policy of "splendid isolation," German policy took a different tack. The idea was to demonstrate Germany's worthiness as an ally by withdrawing support and even making trouble for Britain. This odd manner of gaining an ally reflected the Kaiser's confused feelings toward

German battleships in the North Sea, 1914. The British were antagonized by the threat posed by the powerful German navy. [Ullstein Bilderdienst]

Britain, which consisted of dislike and jealousy mixed with admiration. These feelings reflected those of many Germans, especially in the intellectual community, who like William were eager for Germany to pursue a "world policy" rather than Bismarck's limited one that confined German interests to Europe. They, too, saw England as the barrier to German ambitions, and their influence in the schools, the universities, and the press guaranteed popular approval of actions and statements hostile to Britain.

The Germans began to exert pressure against Britain in Africa by barring British attempts to build a railroad from Capetown to Cairo. They also openly sympathized with the Boers of South Africa in their resistance to British expansion. In 1896 William insulted the British by sending a congratulatory telegram to Paul Kruger (1825–1904), president of the Transvaal, for repulsing a British raid "without having to appeal to friendly powers for assistance."

In 1898 William's dream of a German navy began to achieve reality with the passage of a naval law providing for nineteen battleships. In 1900 a second law doubled that figure. The architect of the new navy was Admiral Alfred von Tirpitz (1849–1930), who openly proclaimed that Germany's naval policy was aimed at Britain. His "risk" theory argued that Germany could build a fleet strong enough, not to defeat the British, but to do sufficient damage to make the British navy inferior to that of other powers like France or the United States. The theory was, in fact, absurd because as Germany's fleet became menacing, the British would certainly build ships to maintain their advantage, and British financial resources were greater than Germany's. The naval policy, therefore, was doomed to failure. Over time its main achievements were to waste German resources and to begin a great naval race with Britain. It is not too much to say, moreover, that the threat posed by the German navy did more to antagonize British opinion than

877

anything else. As the German navy grew and German policies seemed to become more threatening, the British were alarmed enough to abandon their traditional attitudes and policies.

At first, however, Britain was not unduly concerned. The British were embarrassed by the general hostility of world opinion during the Boer War (1899–1902) and were suddenly alarmed that their isolation no longer seemed so splendid. The Germans had acted with restraint during the war. Between 1898 and 1901 Joseph Chamberlain, the colonial secretary, made several attempts to conclude an alliance with Germany. The Germans, confident that a British alliance with France or Russia was impossible, refused and expected the British to make greater concessions in the future.

THE ENTENTE CORDIALE. The first breach in Britain's isolation came in 1902, when an alliance was concluded with Japan to relieve the pressure of defending British interests in the Far East against Russia. Next Britain abandoned its traditional antagonism toward France and in 1904 concluded a series of agreements with the French, collectively called the *Entente Cordiale*. It was not a formal treaty and had no military provisions, but it settled all outstanding colonial differences between the two nations. The Entente Cordiale was a long step toward aligning the British with Germany's great potential enemy.

Britain's new relationship with France was surprising, but in 1904 hardly anyone believed that the British whale and the Russian bear would ever come together. The Russo-Japanese war of 1904–1905 made such a development seem even less likely because Britain was allied with Russia's enemy. But Britain had behaved with restraint, and the Russians were chastened by their unexpected and humiliating defeat. The defeat had also led to the the Russian Revolution of 1905. Although the revolution was put down, it left Russia weak and reduced British apprehensions in that direction. At the same time the British were concerned that Russia might again drift into the German orbit.

THE FIRST MOROCCAN CRISIS. At this point Germany decided to test the new understanding between Britain and France and to press for colonial gains. In March 1905 Emperor William II landed at Tangier, challenged the French protectorate there in a speech in favor of Moroccan independence, and by implication asserted Germany's right to participate in Morocco's destiny. Germany's chancellor, Prince Bernhard von Bülow (1849–1929), intended to show France how weak it was and how little it could expect from Britain and at the same time to gain significant colonial concessions.

The Germans might well have achieved their aims and driven a wedge between France and Britain, but they pushed too far and demanded an international conference to show their power more dramatically. The conference met in 1906 at Algeciras in Spain. Austria sided with its German ally, but Spain, Italy, and the United States voted with Britain and France. The Germans had overplayed their hand, receiving trivial concessions, and the French were confirmed in their position in Morocco. German bullying had, moreover, driven Britain and France closer together. In the face of the threat of a German attack on France, Sir Edward Grey, the British foreign secretary, without making a firm commitment, authorized conversations between the British and the French general staffs. Their agreements became morally binding as the years passed. By 1914 French and British military and naval plans were so mutually dependent that they were effectively, if not formally, allies.

BRITISH AGREEMENT WITH RUSSIA. Britain's fear of Germany's growing naval power, its concern over German ambitions in the Near East as represented by the German-sponsored plan to build a railroad from Berlin to Baghdad, and its closer relations with France made it desirable for Britain to become more friendly with France's ally, Russia, With French support the British made overtures to the Russians and in 1907 concluded an agreement with them much like the Entente Cordiale with France. It settled Russo-British quarrels in Central Asia and opened the door for wider cooperation. The Triple Entente, an informal, but powerful association of Britain, France, and Russia, was now ranged against the Triple Alliance. Because Italy was unreliable, Germany and Austria-Hungary stood surrounded by two great land powers and Great Britain.

William II and his ministers had turned Bismarck's nightmare of the prospect of a two-front war with France and Russia into a reality and had made it more horrible by adding Britain to the hostile coalition. The equilibrium that Bismarck had worked so hard to achieve was destroyed. Britain could no longer support Austria in restraining Russian ambitions in the Balkans. Germany, increasingly terrified by a sense of encirclement, was less willing to restrain the Austrians for fear of alienating them. In the Dual Alliance of Germany and Austria it had become less clear who was the horse and who was the rider. Bismarck's alliance system had been intended to maintain peace, but the new one increased the risk of war and made the Balkans a likely spot for it to break out. Bismarck's diplomacy had left France isolated and impotent; the new arrangement found France associated with the two greatest powers in Europe apart from Germany. The Germans could rely only on Austria, and such was the condition of that troubled empire that it was less likely to provide aid than to need it.

The Road to War

Growing Tensions (1908–1914)

The situation in the Balkans in the first decade of this century was exceedingly complicated. The weak Ottoman Empire controlled the central strip running west from Constantinople to the Adriatic. North and south of it were the independent states of Romania, Serbia, and Greece, as well as Bulgaria, technically still part of the empire but legally autonomous and practically independent. The Austro-Hungarian Empire included Croatia and Slovenia and since 1878 had "occupied and administered" Bosnia and Herzegovina.

With the exception of the Greeks and the Romanians, most of the inhabitants of the Balkans spoke variants of the same Slavic language and felt a cultural and historical kinship with one another. For centuries they had been ruled by Austrians, Hungarians, or Turks, and the growing nationalism that characterized late-nineteenth-century Europe made many of them eager for liberty. The more radical among them longed for a union of the south Slavic, or Yugoslav, peoples in a single nation. They looked to independent Serbia as the center of the new nation and hoped to detach all the Slavic provinces (especially Bosnia, which bordered on Serbia) from Austria. In this regard Serbia was to unite the Slavs at the expense of Austria, as Piedmont had united the Italians and Prussia the Germans.

In 1908 a group of modernizing reformers called the *Young Turks* brought about a revolution in the Ottoman Empire. Their actions threatened to revive the life of the empire and to interfere with the plans of the European jackals preparing to pounce on the Ottoman corpse. These events brought on the first of a series of Balkan crises that would eventually lead to war.

THE BOSNIAN CRISIS. In 1908 the Austrian and Russian governments decided to act quickly before Turkey became strong enough to resist. They struck a bargain in which it was agreed that they would call an international conference where each of them would support the other's demands. Russia would agree to the Austrian annexation of Bosnia and Herzegovina, and Austria would support Russia's request to open the Dardanelles to Russian warships.

Austria, however, declared the annexation before any conference was called. The British, ever concerned about their own position in the Mediterranean, refused to agree to the Russian demand. The Russians felt betrayed by the British, humiliated, and furious. Their "little brothers," the Serbs, were frustrated and angered by the loss of Bosnia, which they had hoped one day to include in an independent south Slavic nation led by Serbia. The Russians were too weak to do anything but accept the new situation. The Germans had not been warned in advance of Austria's plans and were unhappy because the action threatened their relations with Russia. But Germany felt so dependent on the Dual Alliance that it assured Austria of its support. Austria had been given a free hand, and to an extent German policy was being made in Vienna. It was a dangerous precedent. At the same time, the failure of Britain and France to support Russia strained the Triple Entente and made it harder for them to oppose Russian interests again in the future if they were to retain Russian friendship.

THE SECOND MOROCCAN CRISIS. The second Moroccan crisis, in 1911, emphasized the French and British need for mutual support. When France sent in an army to put down a rebellion, Germany took the opportunity to "protect German interests" in Morocco as a means of extorting colonial concessions in the French Congo. To add force to their demands, the Germans sent the gunboat *Panther* to the port of Agadir, allegedly to protect German citizens there. Once again, as in 1905, the

"The Mailed Fist of the Kaiser Strikes Agadir." This cartoon refers to the landing of the German gunboat Panther *at Agadir in Morocco in 1911. William II's purpose was to press the French to make colonial concessions to Germany in Africa and, perhaps, to break up the Entente between the French and the British. The result, instead, was the second Moroccan crisis, which drew the Entente closer together and helped bring on World War I.*

Germans went too far. The *Panther's* visit to Agadir provoked a strong reaction in Britain. For some time Anglo-German relations had been growing worse, chiefly because of the intensification of the naval race. In 1907 Germany had built its first new battleship of the dreadnought class, which Britain had developed in 1906. In 1908 Germany had passed still another naval law, which accelerated the schedule of production to challenge British naval supremacy. These actions frightened and angered the British because of the clear threat to the security of the island kingdom and its empire. The German actions also forced Britain to increase taxes to pay for new armaments just when the Liberal government was launching its expensive program of social legislation. Negotiations failed to persuade William II and Tirpitz to slow down naval construction.

In this atmosphere the British heard of the *Panther's* arrival in Morocco. They wrongly believed that the Germans meant to turn Agadir into a naval base on the Atlantic. The crisis passed when France yielded some insignificant bits of the Congo and Germany withdrew from Morocco. The main result was to increase British fear and hostility and to draw the Britons closer to France. Specific military plans were formulated for a British expeditionary force to defend France in case of German attack, and the British and French navies agreed to cooperate. Without any formal treaty the German naval construction and the Agadir crisis had turned the Entente Cordiale into an alliance that could not have been more binding. If France were attacked by Germany, Britain must defend the French, for its own security was inextricably tied up with that of France.

WAR IN THE BALKANS. The second Moroccan crisis also provoked another crisis in the Balkans. Italy sought to gain colonies and to take its place among the great powers. It wanted Libya, which though worth little at the time was at least available. Italy feared that the recognition of the French protectorate in Morocco would encourage France to move into Libya. Consequently, in 1911, Italy attacked the Ottoman Empire to anticipate the French, defeated the faltering Turks, and obtained Libya and the Dodecanese Islands. The Italian victory encouraged the Balkan states to try their luck. In 1912 Bulgaria, Greece, Montenegro, and Serbia joined an attack on the Ottoman Empire and won easily. After this First Balkan War, the victors fell out among themselves. The Serbs and the Bulgarians quarreled about the division of Macedonia, and in 1913 a Second Balkan War erupted. This time Turkey and Romania joined the other states against Bulgaria and stripped away much of what the Bulgarians had gained since 1878.

After the First Balkan War, the alarmed Austrians were determined to limit Serbian gains and especially to prevent the Serbs from gaining a port on the Adriatic. This policy meant keeping Serbia out of Albania, but the Russians backed the Serbs, and tensions mounted. An

OPPOSITE: MAPS 25–5, 25–6 *Two maps show the Balkans before and after the two Balkan wars; note the Ottoman retreat. In the center we see the geographical relationship of the Central Powers and their Bulgarian and Turkish allies. Tables give relative strength of World War I combatants.*

	GREAT BRITAIN	FRANCE	ITALY	RUSSIA	BELGIUM	ROMANIA	GRFECE
POPULATION (TOTAL)	OVERSEAS EMP. 390 MILLION — 45 000 000	OVERSEAS EMP. 58 MILLION — 40 000 000	OVERSEAS EMP. 2 MILLION — 35 000 000	164 000 000	7 500 000	7 500 000	5 000 000
SOLDIERS POTENTIALLY AVAILABLE	711 000	1 250 000	750 000	1 200 000	180 000	420 000	120 000
MILITARY EXPENDITURES 1913–1914 (MILLIONS OF $)	250 000 000	185 000 000	50 000 000	335 000 000	13 750 000	15 000 000	3 750 000
BATTLESHIPS IN SERVICE OR BEING BUILT	64	28	14	16			
CRUISERS	121	34	22	14			
SUBMARINES	64	73	12	29			
MERCHANT SHIPS MILLIONS OF TONS	20 000 000	2 000 000	1 750 000	750 000			

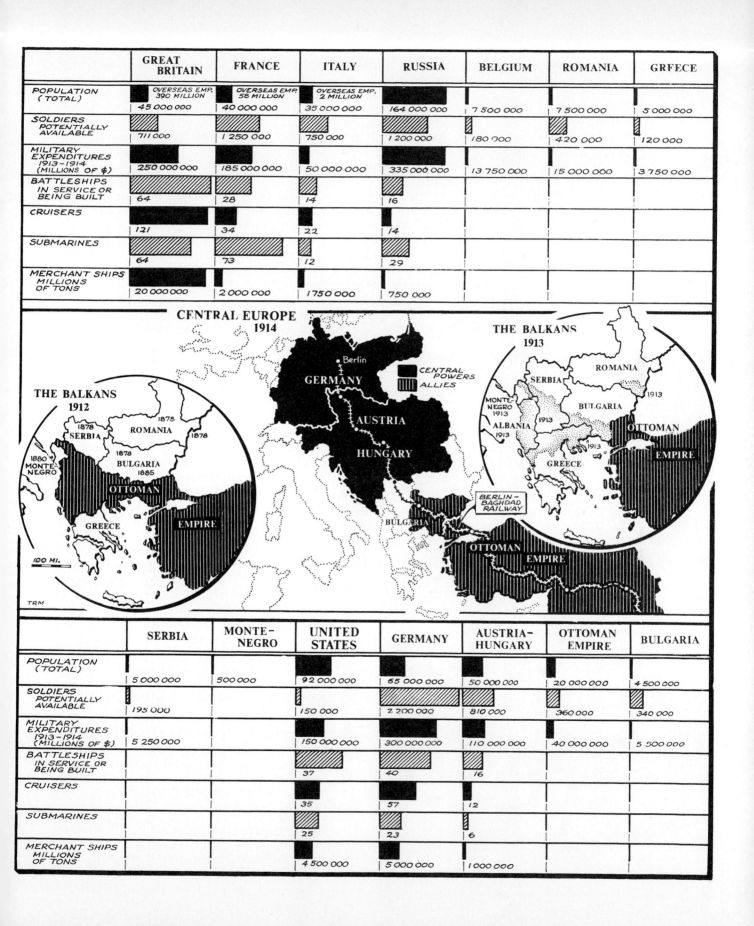

THE BALKANS 1912

1878 ROMANIA
1878 SERBIA 1878
1878 BULGARIA 1885
1880 MONTE-NEGRO
OTTOMAN EMPIRE
GREECE
100 MI.
TRM

CENTRAL EUROPE 1914

Berlin
GERMANY
AUSTRIA HUNGARY
CENTRAL POWERS
ALLIES
BULGARIA
BERLIN–BAGHDAD RAILWAY
OTTOMAN EMPIRE

THE BALKANS 1913

ROMANIA
SERBIA
MONTE-NEGRO 1913
BULGARIA 1913
ALBANIA 1913
1913
GREECE 1913
OTTOMAN EMPIRE

	SERBIA	MONTE-NEGRO	UNITED STATES	GERMANY	AUSTRIA-HUNGARY	OTTOMAN EMPIRE	BULGARIA
POPULATION (TOTAL)	5 000 000	500 000	92 000 000	65 000 000	50 000 000	20 000 000	4 500 000
SOLDIERS POTENTIALLY AVAILABLE	195 000		150 000	2 200 000	810 000	360 000	340 000
MILITARY EXPENDITURES 1913–1914 (MILLIONS OF $)	5 250 000		150 000 000	300 000 000	110 000 000	40 000 000	5 500 000
BATTLESHIPS IN SERVICE OR BEING BUILT			37	40	16		
CRUISERS			35	57	12		
SUBMARINES			25	23	6		
MERCHANT SHIPS MILLIONS OF TONS			4 500 000	5 000 000	1 000 000		

international conference sponsored by Britain in early 1913 resolved the matter in Austria's favor and called for an independent kingdom of Albania. But Austria felt humiliated by the public airing of Serbian demands. Then, for some time, the Serbs defied the powers and continued to occupy parts of Albania. Under Austrian pressure they withdrew, but in September 1913, after the Second Balkan War, the Serbs reoccupied sections of Albania. In mid-October Austria unilaterally issued an ultimatum to Serbia, and the latter country again withdrew its forces from Albania. During this crisis many people in Austria had wanted an all-out attack on Serbia to remove its threat once and for all from the empire. Those demands had been resisted by Emperor Francis Joseph and the heir to the throne, Archduke Francis Ferdinand. At the same time Pan-Slavic sentiment in Russia pressed Czar Nicholas II to take a firm stand, but Russia once again let Austria have its way in its confrontation with Serbia. Throughout the crisis Britain, France, and Germany restrained their respective allies, although each worried about seeming too reluctant to help its friends.

The lessons learned from this crisis of 1913 profoundly influenced behavior in the final crisis, the crisis of 1914. The Russians had once again, as in 1908, been embarrassed by their passivity, and their allies were more reluctant to restrain them again. The Austrians were embarrassed by what had resulted from accepting an international conference and were determined not to repeat the experience. They had seen that better results might be obtained from a threat of direct force; they and their German allies did not miss the lesson.

Sarajevo and the Outbreak of War (June–August 1914)

THE ASSASSINATION. On June 28, 1914, a young Bosnian nationalist shot and killed the Austrian Archduke Francis Ferdinand, heir to the throne, and his wife as they drove in an open car through the Bosnian capital of Sarajevo. The assassin was a member of a conspiracy hatched by a political terrorist society called *Union or Death,* better known as the *Black Hand.* A major participant in the planning and preparation of the crime was the chief of intelligence of the Serbian army's general staff. Even though his role was not actually known at the time, it was generally believed that Serbian officials were involved. The glee of the Serbian press lent support to that belief. The archduke was not a popular person in his own land, and his funeral evoked few signs of grief. He had been known to favor a form of federal government that would have given a higher status to the Slavs in the empire. This position alienated the conservatives and the

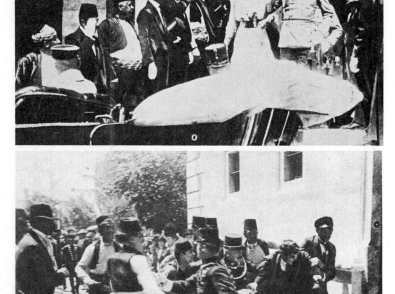

ABOVE: *The Austrian Archduke Franz Ferdinand and his wife at Sarajevo, June 28, 1914. Later in the day the royal couple were assassinated by young revolutionaries trained and supplied in Serbia. The murders set off the crisis that led to World War I.*

BELOW: *Moments after the assassination of Archduke Ferdinand and his wife the Austrian police captured one of the assassins in Sarajevo.* [*Brown Brothers*]

Hungarians. It also alarmed radical Yugoslav nationalists, who feared that reform might end their dream of an independent south Slav state.

GERMANY AND AUSTRIA'S RESPONSE. News of the assassination produced outrage and condemnation everywhere. To those Austrians who had long favored an attack on Serbia as a solution to the empire's Slavic problem, the opportunity seemed irresistible. But it was never easy for the Dual Monarchy to make a decision. Conrad von Hötzendorf, chief of the Austrian general staff, urged an attack as he had often done before. Count Stefan Tisza, speaking for Hungary, resisted. Leopold Berchtold, the Austro-Hungarian foreign minister, felt the need for strong action, but he knew that German support would be required in the likely event that Russia should decide to intervene to protect Serbia. He also knew that nothing could be done without Tisza's approval and that only German support could persuade the Hungarians to accept the policy of war. The question of peace or war, therefore, had to be answered in Berlin.

William II and Chancellor Theobald von Bethmann-Hollweg (1856–1921) readily promised German support for an attack on Serbia. It has often been said that they gave the Austrians a "blank check," but their message was firmer than that. They urged the Austrians to move swiftly while the other powers were still angry at Serbia, and they made the Austrians feel that a failure to act would be taken as evidence of Austria-Hungary's weakness and uselessness as an ally. Therefore the Austrians never wavered in their determination to make war on Serbia. They hoped, with the protection of Germany, to fight a limited war that would not bring on a general European conflict, but they were prepared to risk even the latter. The Germans also knew that they risked a general war, but they hoped to "localize" the fight between Austria and Serbia.

Some scholars believe that Germany had long been plotting war, and some even think that a specific plan for war in 1914 was set in motion as early as 1912. The vast body of evidence on the crisis of 1914 gives little support to such notions. The German leaders plainly

The Austrian Ambassador Gets a "Blank Check" from the Kaiser

It was at a meeting at Potsdam on July 5, 1914, that the Austrian ambassador received from the Kaiser assurance that Germany would support Austria in the Balkans, even at the risk of war.

After lunch, when I [the Austro-Hungarian Ambassador] again called attention to the seriousness of the situation, the Kaiser authorised me to inform our gracious Majesty that we might in this case, as in all others, rely upon Germany's full support. He must, as he said before, first hear what the Imperial Chancellor has to say, but he did not doubt in the least that Herr von Bethmann-Hollweg would agree with him. Especially as far as our action against Serbia was concerned. But it was his (Kaiser Wilhelm's) opinion that this action must not be delayed. Russia's attitude will no doubt be hostile, but for this he had been for years prepared, and should a war between Austria-Hungary and

Russia be unavoidable, we might be convinced that Germany, our old faithful ally, would stand at our side. Russia at the present time was in no way prepared for war, and would think twice before it appealed to arms. But it will certainly set other powers on the Triple Alliance and add fuel to the fire in the Balkans. He understands perfectly well that His Apostolic Majesty [Francis Joseph] in his well-known love of peace would be reluctant to march into Serbia; but if we had really recognised the necessity of warlike action against Serbia, he (Kaiser Wilhelm) would regret if we did not make use of the present moment, which is all in our favour.

Outbreak of the World War: German Documents Collected by Karl Kautsky, ed. by Max Montgelas and Walther Schücking (New York: Carnegie Endowment for International Peace, 1924), p. 76.

reacted to a crisis that they had not foreseen and just as plainly made decisions in response to events. The fundamental decision to support Austria, which made it very difficult if not impossible to avoid war, was made by the emperor and chancellor without significant consultation with either their military or their diplomatic advisers.

William II appears to have reacted violently to the assassination. He was moved by his friendship for the archduke and by outrage at an attack on royalty. It is doubtful that a different provocation would have moved him so much. Bethmann-Hollweg was less emotional but under severe pressure. To resist the decision would have meant flatly to oppose the emperor. The chancellor, moreover, was suspected of being "soft" in the powerful military circles favored by his master. A conciliatory position would have been difficult. Beyond these considerations, Bethmann-Hollweg, like

many other Germans, viewed the future with apprehension. Russia was recovering its strength and would reach a military peak in 1917. The Triple Entente was growing more powerful, and Germany's only reliable ally was Austria. The chancellor recognized the danger of support for Austria, but he believed it to be even more dangerous to withhold that support. If Austria did not crush Serbia, the empire would soon collapse before the onslaught of Slavic nationalism defended by Russia. If Germany did not defend its ally, the Austrians might look elsewhere for help. His policy was one of "calculated risk."

The calculations proved to be incorrect. Bethmann-Hollweg hoped that the Austrians would strike swiftly and present the powers with a *fait accompli* while the outrage of the assassination was still fresh, and that German support would deter Russian involvement. Failing that, he was prepared for a continental war that would bring rapid victory over France and allow a full-scale attack on the Russians, who were always slow to bring their strength into action. All of this policy depended on British neutrality, and the German chancellor convinced himself that the British could be persuaded to stand aloof.

However, the Austrians were slow to act, as always, and did not even deliver their deliberately unacceptable ultimatum to Serbia until July 24, when the general hostility toward Serbia had begun to subside. Serbia further embarrassed the Austrians by returning so soft and conciliatory an answer that the mercurial German emperor thought it removed all reason for war. But the Austrians were determined not to turn back, and on July 28 the Austrians declared war on Serbia, even though they could not put an army into the field until mid-August.

THE TRIPLE ENTENTE'S RESPONSE. The Russians, previously so often forced to back off, angrily responded to the Austrian demands on Serbia. The most conservative elements of the Russian government opposed war, fearing that it would bring on revolution as it had in 1905. But nationalists, Pan-Slavs, and most of the politically conscious classes in general demanded action. The government responded by ordering partial mobilization, against Austria only. This policy was militarily impossible, but its intention was the diplomatic one of putting pressure on Austria to hold back its attack on Serbia. Mobilization of any kind, however,

The aged Emperor Francis Joseph (1830–1916) in 1913. After the assassination of his nephew and heir at Sarajevo, the Emperor was convinced by his advisors that a war against Serbia was necessary for the survival of the Habsburg Empire. [Ullstein Bilderdienst]

was a dangerous political weapon because it was generally understood to be equivalent to an act of war. It was especially alarming to General Helmuth von Moltke (1848–1916), head of the German general staff. The possibility that the Russians might start mobilization before the Germans could move would upset the delicate timing of Germany's only battle plan, the Schlieffen Plan, which required an attack on France first, and would put Germany in great danger. From this point on, Moltke pressed for German mobilization and war, and the pressure of military necessity mounted until it became irresistible.

The western European powers were not eager for war. France's president and prime minister were on their way back from a visit to Russia when the crisis flared up again on July 24. The Austrians had, in fact, timed their ultimatum precisely so that these two men would be at sea at the crucial moment. Had they been at their desks, they might have attempted to restrain the Russians, but the French ambassador to Russia gave the Russians the same assurances that Germany had given its ally. The British worked hard to avoid trouble by traditional means: a conference of the powers. Austria, still smarting from its humiliation after the London Conference of 1913, would not hear of it. The Germans privately supported the Austrians but publicly took on a conciliatory tone in the hope of keeping the British neutral. Soon, however, Bethmann-Hollweg came to realize what he should have known from the first: if Germany attacked France, Britain must fight. Until July 30 his public appeals to Austria for restraint were a sham. Thereafter he sincerely tried to persuade the Austrians to negotiate and to avoid a general war, but it was too late. While Bethmann-Hollweg was urging restraint on the Austrians, Moltke was pressing them to act. The Austrians wondered who was in charge in Berlin, but they could not turn back without losing their own self-respect and the respect of the Germans.

On July 30 Austria ordered mobilization against Russia. Bethmann-Hollweg resisted the enormous pressure to mobilize, not because he had any further hope of avoiding war but because he wanted Russia to mobilize against Germany first and appear to be the aggressor. Only in that way could he win the support of the German nation for war, especially the pacifistic Social Democrats. His luck was good for a change. The news of Russian general mobilization came only minutes before Germany

THE COMING OF WORLD WAR I	
The end of the Franco-Prussian War; creation of the German Empire; German annexation of Alsace-Lorraine	1871
The Three Emperors' League (Germany, Russia, and Austria-Hungary)	1873
The Russo-Turkish War	1875
The Congress of Berlin	1878
The Dual Alliance between Germany and Austria	1879
The Three Emperors' League is renewed	1881
Italy joins Germany and Austria in the Triple Alliance	1882
William II becomes the German emperor	1888
Bismarck is dismissed	1890
The Franco-Russian alliance	1894
Germany begins to build a battleship navy	1898
The British alliance with Japan	1902
The Entente Cordiale between Britain and France	1904
The Russo-Japanese War	1904–1905
The first Moroccan crisis	1905
The British agreement with Russia	1907
The Bosnian crisis	1908–1909
The second Moroccan crisis	1911
Italy attacks Turkey	1911
The First and Second Balkan Wars	1912–1913
Outbreak of World War I	1914

would have mobilized in any case. The Schlieffen Plan went into effect. The Germans invaded Luxembourg on August 1 and Belgium on August 3. The latter invasion violated the treaty of 1839 in which the British had guaranteed Belgian neutrality. This factor undermined the considerable sentiment in Britain for neutrality and united the nation against Germany. Germany then invaded France, and on August 4 Britain declared war on Germany. The Great War had begun. As Sir Edward Grey, the British foreign secretary, put it, the lights were going out all over Europe. They would come on again, but Europe would never be the same.

World War I (1914–1918)

Throughout Europe jubilation greeted the outbreak of war. No general war had been fought since Napoleon, and the horrors of modern

The Kaiser's Comments on the Outbreak of the World War

On July 30, 1914, the German Foreign Office received the news that Russian mobilization had been started and would not be stopped. German strategy, based on the Schlieffen Plan, required an immediate mobilization and a swift attack on France before the weight of the Russian armies in the east could take full effect. The telegram from the German ambassador in Saint Petersburg, therefore, meant that war had come. The Kaiser, as usual, filled the margins of the document with his comments. On this occasion he concluded with a long note that reveals his own understanding of the situation.

If mobilization can no longer be retracted—WHICH IS NOT TRUE—*why, then, did the Czar appeal for my mediation three days afterward without mention of the issuance of the mobilization order? That shows plainly that the mobilization appeared to him to have been precipitate, and that after it he made this move* pro forma *in our direction for the sake of quieting his uneasy conscience, although he knew that it would no longer be of any use, as he did not feel himself to be strong enough to* STOP *the mobilization. Frivolity and weakness are to plunge the world into the most frightful war, which eventually aims at the destruction of Germany. For I have no doubt left about it: England, Russia and France have* AGREED *among themselves— after laying the foundation of the* casus foederis *for us through Austria—to take the Austro-Serbian conflict for an* EXCUSE *for waging a* WAR OF EXTERMINATION *against us. Hence Grey's [Sir Edward Grey, The British Foreign Secretary] cynical observation to Lichnowsky [The German Ambassador to Britain] "as long as the war is* CONFINED *to Russia and Austria, England would sit quiet, only when we and France* MIXED INTO IT *would he be compelled to make an active move against us ("); i.e., either we are shamefully to betray our allies,* SACRIFICE *them to Russia—thereby breaking up the Triple Alliance, or we are to be attacked in common by the Triple Entente for our* FIDELITY TO OUR ALLIES *and punished, whereby they will satisfy their jealousy by joining in totally* RUINING *us. That is the real naked situation* in nuce, *which, slowly and cleverly set going, certainly by Edward VII, has been carried on, and systematically built up by disowned conferences between England and Paris and Petersburg; finally brought to a conclusion by George V and set to work. And thereby the stupidity and ineptitude of our ally is turned into a snare for us. So the famous "*CIRCUMSCRIPTION*" of Germany has finally become a complete fact, despite every effort of our politicians and diplomats to prevent it. The net has been suddenly thrown over our head, and England sneeringly reaps the most brilliant success of her persistently prosecuted purely* ANTI-GERMAN WORLD-POLICY, *against which we have proved ourselves helpless, while she twists the noose of our political and economic destruction out of our fidelity to Austria, as we squirm* ISOLATED *in the net. A great achievement, which arouses the admiration even of him who is to be destroyed as its result! Edward VII is stronger after his death than am I who am still alive! And there have been people who believed that England could be won over or pacified, by this or that puny measure!!! Unremittingly, relentlessly she has pursued her object, with notes, holiday proposals, scares, Haldane, etc., until this point was reached. And we walked into the net and even went into the one-ship-program in construction with the ardent hope of thus pacifying England!!! All my warnings, all my pleas were voiced for nothing. Now comes England's so-called gratitude for it! From the dilemma raised by our fidelity to the venerable old Emperor of Austria we are brought into a situation which offers England the desired pretext for annihilating us under the hypocritical cloak of justice, namely, of helping France on account of the reputed "balance of power" in Europe, i.e., playing the card of all the European nations in England's favor against us! This whole business must now be ruthlessly uncovered and the mask of Christian peaceableness publicly and brusquely torn from its face in public, and the pharisaical hypocrisy exposed on the pillory!! And our consuls in Turkey and India, agents, etc., must fire the whole Mohammedan world to fierce rebellion against this hated, lying, conscienceless nation of shop-keepers; for if we are to be bled to death, England shall at least lose India.*

Max Montgelas and Walther Schücking (Eds.), *Outbreak of the World War: German Documents Collected by Karl Kautsky*, No. 401 (1924), pp. 348–350, trans. by Carnegie Endowment for International Peace. Reprinted by permission of Carnegie Endowment for International Peace.

warfare were not yet understood. The dominant memory was of Bismarck's swift and decisive campaigns, in which costs and casualties were light and the rewards great. After the repeated crises of recent years and the fears and resentments they had created, war came as a release of tension. The popular press had increased public awareness of and interest in foreign affairs and had fanned the flames of patriotism. The prospect of war moved even a rational man of science like Sigmund Freud to say, "My whole libido goes out to Austria-Hungary."[9]

Strategies and Stalemate: 1914–1917

Both sides expected to take the offensive, force a battle on favorable ground, and win a quick victory. The Triple Entente powers—or the Allies, as they came to be called—held superiority in numbers and financial resources as well as command of the sea. Germany and Austria, the Central Powers, had the advantages of internal lines of communication and of having launched their attack first.

After 1905 Germany's only war plan was the one developed by Count Alfred von Schlieffen (1833–1913), chief of the German general staff from 1891 to 1906. It aimed at going around the French defenses by sweeping through Bel-

[9]Quoted in J. Remak, p. 134.

THE SCHLIEFFEN PLAN OF 1905

MAP 25–7 *Germany's grand strategy for quickly winning the war against France in 1914 is shown by the wheeling arrows on the map. The crushing blows at France were, in the original plan, to be followed by the release of troops for use against Russia on Germany's Eastern front. But the plan was not adequately implemented, and the war on the Western front became a long contest in place.*

The outbreak of World War I was greeted with jubilation throughout Europe. In Berlin, women put flowers in the guns of soldiers leaving for the front. [EPA]

887

gium to the Channel, then wheeling to the south and east to envelop the French and to crush them against the German fortresses in Lorraine. The secret of success lay in making the right wing of the advancing German army immensely strong and deliberately weakening the left opposite the French frontier. The weakness of the left was meant to draw the French into the wrong place while the war was decided on the German right. As one keen military analyst has explained, "It would be like a revolving door—if a man pressed heavily on one side, the other side would spring round and strike him in the back. Here lay the real subtlety of the plan, not in the mere geograph-

In 1914 few Europeans could imagine the carnage of modern war. These French cavalrymen with their brass breastplates, swords, and lances had no idea in August 1914 they were riding to a war of machine guns, poison gas, and trench warfare. [Bildarchiv Preussicher Kulturbesitz]

ical detour."[10] In the east the Germans planned to stand on the defensive against Russia until France had been crushed, a task they thought would take only six weeks.

The apparent risk, besides the violation of Belgian neutrality and the consequent alienation of Britain, lay in weakening the German defenses against a direct attack across the frontier. The strength of German fortresses and the superior firepower of German howitzers made that risk more apparent than real. The true danger was that the German striking force on the right through Belgium would not be powerful enough to make the swift progress vital to success. Schlieffen is said to have uttered the dying words, "It must come to a fight. Only make the right wing strong." The execution of his plan, however, was left to Helmuth von Moltke, the nephew of Bismarck's most effective general. The younger Moltke was a gloomy and nervous man who lacked the talent of his illustrious uncle and the theoretical daring of Schlieffen. He added divisions to the left wing and even weakened the Russian front for the same purpose. The consequence of this hesitant strategy was the failure of the Schlieffen Plan by a narrow margin.

THE WAR IN THE WEST. The French had also put their faith in the offensive, but with less reason than the Germans. They badly underestimated the numbers and the effectiveness of the German reserves and set too much store by the importance of the courage and spirit of their troops. These proved insufficient against modern weapons, especially the machine gun. The French offensive on Germany's western frontier failed totally. In a sense this defeat was better than a partial success because it released troops for use against the main German army. As a result the French and the British were able to stop the Germans at the Battle of the Marne in September 1914.

Thereafter the nature of the war in the west changed completely and became one of position instead of movement. Both sides dug in behind a wall of trenches protected by barbed wire that stretched from the North Sea to Switzerland. Strategically placed machine-gun nests made assaults difficult and dangerous. Both sides, nonetheless, attempted massive attacks prepared for by artillery barrages of unprecedented and horrible force and duration.

[10]B. H. Liddell Hart, *The Real War*, 1914–1918 (Boston: Little, Brown, 1964; first published in 1930), p. 47.

Still the defense was always able to recover and to bring up reserves fast enough to prevent a breakthrough. Sometimes assaults that cost hundreds of thousands of lives produced advances that could be measured in hundreds of yards. The introduction of poison gas as a solution to the problem proved ineffective. In 1916 the British introduced the tank, which proved to be the answer to the machine gun, but throughout the war defense was supreme. For three years after its establishment, the western front moved only a few miles in either direction.

THE WAR IN THE EAST. In the east the war began auspiciously for the Allies. The Russians advanced into Austrian territory and in-

RIGHT: *Trench warfare on the western front. The trenches were defended by barbed wire and machine guns, which gave the defense the advantage. The masks worn by the French soldiers in this picture were the response to the German attempts to break the deadlock by using poison gas.* [*Collection Violet*]

BELOW: *A British tank in action on the Western Front in 1917. The tank was impervious to machine gun fire. Had tanks been used in great numbers before 1918, they could have broken the stalemate in the West.* [*National Archives*]

WORLD WAR I IN EUROPE

T R MILLER

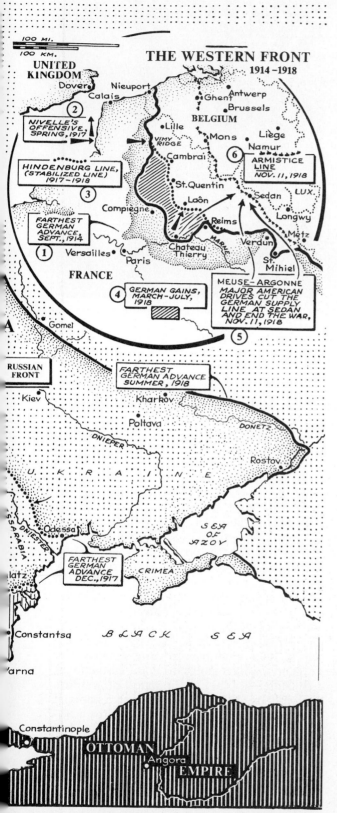

THE WESTERN FRONT
1914-1918

100 MI.
100 KM.

UNITED KINGDOM

Dover
Calais
Nieuport
Ghent
Antwerp
Brussels
BELGIUM
(2) NIVELLE'S OFFENSIVE, SPRING, 1917
Lille
Mons
Liège
Namur
VIMY RIDGE
Cambrai
(6) ARMISTICE LINE NOV. 11, 1918
(3) HINDENBURG LINE, (STABILIZED LINE) 1917-1918
St.Quentin
Laôn
Sedan
LUX.
Compiegne
(1) FARTHEST GERMAN ADVANCE, SEPT., 1914
Reims
Longwy
Metz
Versailles
Paris
Chateau Thierry
MARNE
Verdun
St. Mihiel
FRANCE
(4) GERMAN GAINS, MARCH-JULY, 1918
MEUSE-ARGONNE MAJOR AMERICAN DRIVES CUT THE GERMAN SUPPLY LINE AT SEDAN AND END THE WAR, NOV. 11, 1918

A
Gomel
RUSSIAN FRONT
Kiev
FARTHEST GERMAN ADVANCE SUMMER, 1918
Kharkov
Poltava
DONETZ
DNIEPER
Rostov
U K R A I N E
Odessa
DNIESTER
SARABIA
SEA OF AZOV
FARTHEST GERMAN ADVANCE DEC., 1917
CRIMEA
Jatz
Constantsa
B L A C K   S E A
Varna
Constantinople
OTTOMAN
Angora
EMPIRE

MAPS 25–8, 25–9 *Despite the importance of military action in the Far East, in the Arab world, and at sea, the main theaters of activity in World War I were in the European areas shown here. The crucial Western front is seen in somewhat greater detail in the inset map.*

flicted heavy casualties, but Russian incompetence and German energy soon reversed the situation. A junior German officer, Erich Ludendorff (1865–1937), under the command of the elderly General Paul von Hindenburg (1847–1934), destroyed or captured an entire army at the Battle of Tannenberg and defeated the Russians at the Masurian Lakes. In 1915 the Central Powers pressed their advantage in the east and drove into the Baltic states and western Russia, inflicting over two million casualties in a single year. Russian confidence was badly shaken, but the Russian army stayed in the field.

As the battle lines hardened, both sides sought new allies. Turkey (because of its hostility to Russia) and Bulgaria (the enemy of Serbia) joined the Central Powers.

Italy seemed an especially valuable prize, and both sides bid for Italian support with promises of a division of the spoils of victory. Because what the Italians wanted most was held by Austria, the Allies were able to make the more attractive promises. In a secret treaty of 1915 the Allies agreed to deliver to Italy most of *Italia Irredenta* (i.e., the Trentino, the South Tyrol, Trieste, and some of the Dalmatian Islands) after victory. By the spring of 1915 Italy was engaging Austrian armies. Although the Italian campaign drained the strength of the Central Powers to a degree, the alliance with Italy generally proved a disappointment to the Allies and never produced significant results.

Romania joined the Allies in 1916 but was quickly defeated and driven from the war.

In the Far East, Japan honored its alliance with Britain and entered the war. The Japanese quickly overran the German colonies in China and the Pacific and used the opportunity to improve their own position against China.

Both sides also tried the tactic of subversion by appealing to nationalist sentiment in areas held by the enemy. The Germans supported nationalist movements among the Irish, the Flemings in Belgium, and the Poles and the Ukrainians under Russian rule, They even tried to persuade the Turks to lead a Muslim upris-

Austrian troops relaxing on the Italian front in 1916. Despite repeated assaults, the Austrian armies managed to hold the Italians at bay until Austria-Hungary disintegrated in 1918. [*National Archives*]

ing against the British and the French in North Africa.

The Allies also used the device of subversion, with greater success. They sponsored movements of national autonomy for the Czechs, the Slovaks, the south Slavs, and the Poles that were under Austrian rule. They also favored a movement of Arab independence from Turkey. Guided by Colonel T. E. Lawrence (1888–1935), this last scheme proved especially successful in the later years of the war.

In 1915 the Allies undertook to break the deadlock in the fighting by going around it. The idea came chiefly from Winston Churchill (1874–1965), First Lord of the British Admiralty. He proposed an attack on the Dardanelles and the swift capture of Constantinople. This policy would knock Turkey from the war, bring help to the Balkan front, and ease communication with Russia. The plan was daring but promising and, in its original form, presented little risk. British naval superiority and the element of surprise would allow the forcing of the straits and the capture of Constantinople by purely naval action. Even if the scheme failed, the fleet could escape with little loss. Success depended on timing, speed, and daring leadership, but all of these were lacking. The execution of the attack was inept and overly

cautious. Troops were landed, and as resistance continued, the Allied commitment increased. Before the campaign was abandoned, the Allies lost almost 150,000 men and diverted three times that number from more useful occupation.

RETURN TO THE WEST. Both sides turned back to the west in 1916. General Erich von Falkenhayn (1861–1922), who had succeeded Moltke in September 1914, sought success by an attack on the French stronghold of Verdun. His plan was not to take the fortress or to break through the line but to inflict enormously heavy casualties on the French, who must defend it against superior firepower coming from several directions. He, too, underestimated the superiority of the defense, and the French were able to hold Verdun with comparatively few men and to inflict almost as many casualties as they suffered. The commander of Verdun, Henri Pétain (1856–1951), became a national hero, and "They shall not pass" became a slogan of national defiance. The Allies tried to end the impasse by launching a major offensive along the River Somme in July. Aided by a Russian attack in the east that drew off some German strength and by an enormous artillery barrage, they hoped at last to break through.

Verdun, 1916. The battle at Verdun was the longest battle in history. For ten months millions of shells rained down on the city and the surrounding battlefield, as the French and the Germans stayed locked in the most terrible endurance test of the war. [United Press International Photo].

Once again, the superiority of the defense was demonstrated. Enormous casualties on both sides brought no result. On all fronts the losses were great and the results meager. The war on land dragged on with no end in sight.

THE WAR AT SEA. As the war continued, control of the sea became more important. The British ignored the distinction between war supplies (which were contraband according to international law) and food or other peaceful cargo, which was not subject to seizure. They imposed a strict blockade meant to starve out the enemy, regardless of international law. The Germans responded with submarine warfare meant to destroy British shipping and to starve the British. They declared the waters around the British Isles a war zone, where even neutral ships would not be safe. Both policies were unwelcome to neutrals, and especially to the United States, which conducted extensive trade in the Atlantic, but the sinking of neutral ships by German submarines was both more dramatic and more offensive. In 1915 the British liner *Lusitania* was torpedoed by a German submarine. Among the 1,200 drowned were 118 Americans. President Woodrow Wilson (1856–1924) warned Germany that a repetition would not be accepted, and the Germans desisted for the time being rather than further anger the United States. This development gave the Allies a considerable advantage. The German fleet that had cost so much money and had caused so much trouble played no significant part in the war. The only battle it fought was at Jutland in the spring of 1916. The battle resulted in a standoff and confirmed British domination of the surface of the sea.

AMERICA ENTERS THE WAR. In December 1916 President Woodrow Wilson of the

The British liner Lusitania, *docked in New York. The sinking of this ship in May 1915 with the loss of 1200 lives, many of them Americans, produced a wave of revulsion against Germany in the United States. [Culver Pictures]*

United States intervened in an attempt to bring about a negotiated peace, but neither side was willing to renounce war aims that its opponent found unacceptable. The war seemed likely to continue until one or both sides reached exhaustion. Two events early in 1917 changed the situation radically. On February 1 the Germans announced the resumption of unrestricted submarine warfare, which led the United States to break off diplomatic relations. On April 6 the United States declared war on the Central Powers. One of the deterrents to an earlier American intervention had been the presence of autocratic czarist Russia among the Allies. Wilson could conceive of the war only as an idealistic crusade "to make the world safe for democracy." That problem was resolved in March of 1917 by a revolution in Russia that overthrew the czarist government.

The Russian Revolution

The March Revolution in Russia was neither planned nor led by any political faction. It was the result of the collapse of the monarchy's ability to govern. Although public opinion had strongly supported Russian entry into the war, the conflict put far too great demands on the resources of the country and the efficiency of the czarist government. Nicholas II was weak and incompetent and was suspected of being under the domination of his German wife and the insidious monk Rasputin, who was assassinated by a group of Russian noblemen in 1916. Military and domestic failures produced massive casualties, widespread hunger, strikes by workers, and disorganization in the army. The peasant discontent that had plagued the countryside before 1914 did not subside during the conflict. In 1916 the czar adjourned the Duma and proceeded to rule alone. All political factions were in one way or another discontented.

In early March 1917 strikes and worker demonstrations erupted in Petrograd, as Saint Petersburg had been renamed. The ill-disciplined troops in the city refused to fire on the demonstrators, and the czar abdicated on March 15. The government of Russia fell into the hands of members of the reconvened Duma, who soon constructed a provisional government composed chiefly of Constitutional Democrats with Western sympathies. At the same time the various socialists, including both Social Revolutionaries and Social Democrats of the Menshevik wing, began to organize

Grigori Rasputin was the sinister Russian holy man who claimed the power to heal the ill son of Czar Nicholas II and acquired great influence at court. His presence scandalized many politically important persons. Rasputin was finally assassinated in 1916 by a group of Russian nobles.

the workers into soviets. Initially they allowed the provisional government to function without actually supporting it. As relatively orthodox Marxists, the Mensheviks believed that a bourgeois stage of development must come to Russia before the revolution of the proletariat could be achieved. They were willing to work temporarily with the Constitutional Democrats (Cadets) in a liberal regime, but they became estranged as the Cadets failed to control the army or to purge "reactionaries" from the government.

In this climate the provisional government made the important decision to remain loyal to the existing Russian alliances and to continue the war against Germany. In this regard the provisional government was accepting the czarist foreign policy and was associating itself with the source of much domestic suffering and discontent. The fate of the provisional government was sealed by the collapse of the new offensive in the summer of 1917. Disillusionment with the war, shortages of food and other necessities at home, and the growing demand by the peasants for land reform undermined the government, even after its leadership had been taken over by the moderate socialist Al-

The Outbreak of the Russian Revolution

The great Russian revolution of 1917 started with a series of ill-organized demonstrations in Petrograd early in the month of March. The nature of these actions and the incompetence of the government's response are described in the *memoirs* of Maurice Paléologue, the French ambassador.

Monday, March 12, 1917

At half-past eight this morning, just as I finished dressing, I heard a strange and prolonged din which seemed to come from the Alexander Bridge. I looked out: there was no one on the bridge, which usually presents such a busy scene. But, almost immediately, a disorderly mob carrying red flags appeared at the end which is on the right bank of the Neva, and a regiment came towards it from the opposite side. It looked as if there would be a violent collision, but on the contrary the two bodies coalesced. The army was fraternizing with revolt.

Shortly afterwards, someone came to tell me that the Volhynian regiment of the Guard had mutinied during the night, killed its officers and was parading the city, calling on the people to take part in the revolution and trying to win over the troops who still remain loyal.

At ten o'clock there was a sharp burst of firing and flames could be seen rising somewhere on the Liteïny Prospekt which is quite close to the embassy. Then silence.

Accompanied by my military attaché, Lieutenant-Colonel Lavergne, I went out to see what was happening. Frightened inhabitants were scattering through the streets. There was indescribable confusion at the corner of the Liteïny. Soldiers were helping civilians to erect a barricade. Flames mounted from the Law Courts. The gates of the arsenal burst open with a crash. Suddenly the crack of machine-gun fire split the air: it was the regulars who had just taken up position near the Nevsky Prospekt. The revolutionaries replied. I had seen enough to have no doubt as to what was coming. Under a hail of bullets I returned to the embassy with Lavergne who had walked calmly and slowly to the hottest corner out of sheer bravado.

About half-past eleven I went to the Ministry for Foreign Affairs, picking up Buchanan [the British ambassador to Russia] on the way.

I told Pokrovski [the Russian foreign minister] everything I had just witnessed.

''So it's even more serious than I thought,'' he said.

But he preserved unruffled composure, flavoured with a touch of scepticism, when he told me of the steps on which the ministers had decided during the night:

''The sitting of the Duma has been prorogued to April and we have sent a telegram to the Emperor, begging him to return at once. With the exception of M. Protopopov [the Minister of the Interior, in charge of the police], my colleagues and I all thought that a dictatorship should be established without delay; it would be conferred upon some general whose prestige with the army is pretty high, General Russky for example.''

I argued that, judging by what I saw this morning, the loyalty of the army was already too heavily shaken for our hopes of salvation to be based on the use of the ''strong hand,'' and that the immediate appointment of a ministry inspiring confidence in the Duma seemed to me more essential than ever, as there is not a moment to lose. I reminded Pokrovski that in 1789, 1830, and 1848, three French dynasties were overthrown because they were too late in realizing the significance and strength of the movement against them. I added that in such a grave crisis the representative of allied France had a right to give the Imperial Government advice on a matter of internal politics.

Buchanan endorsed my opinion.

Pokrovski replied that he personally shared our views, but that the presence of Protopopov in the Council of Ministers paralyzed action of any kind.

I asked him:

''Is there no one who can open the Emperor's eyes to the real situation?'

He heaved a despairing sigh.

''The Emperor is blind!''

Deep grief was writ large on the face of the honest man and good citizen whose uprightness, patriotism and disinterestedness I can never sufficiently extol.

Maurice Paléologue, *An Ambassador's Memoirs* (London: Doubleday & Company, Inc., Hutchinson Publishing Group Ltd., 1924), pp. 221–225, Reprinted by permission.

Russian troops demonstrating for peace, May 1917. By the summer of 1917, discipline in the Russian armies had virtually collapsed. Thousands of soldiers deserted, while those who stayed at the front often refused to fight or obey orders. [*National Archives*]

exander Kerensky (1881–1970). Moreover discipline in the army had badly disintegrated.

Ever since April the Bolshevik wing of the Social Democratic Party had been working against the provisional government. The Germans, in their most successful attempt at subversion, had rushed the brilliant Bolshevik leader V. I. Lenin in a sealed train from his exile in Switzerland across Germany to Petrograd in the hope that he would cause trouble for the revolutionary government.

Lenin saw the opportunity to achieve the political alliance of workers and peasants that he had discussed theoretically before the war. In speech after speech he hammered away on the theme of peace, bread, and land. The Bolsheviks soon gained control of the soviets, or councils of workers and soldiers. They demanded that all political power go to the soviets. The failure of the summer offensive encouraged them to attempt a *coup*, but the effort

was premature and a failure. Lenin fled to Finland, and his chief collaborator, Leon Trotsky (1877–1940), was imprisoned.

The failure of a right-wing counter *coup* gave the Bolsheviks another chance. Trotsky, released from prison, led the powerful Petrograd Soviet. Lenin returned in October, insisted to his doubting colleagues that the time was ripe to take power, and by the extraordinary force of his personality persuaded them to act. Trotsky organized the *coup* that took place on November 6 and that concluded with an armed assault on the provisional government. The Bolsheviks, almost as much to their own astonishment as to that of the rest of the world, had come to rule Russia.

The victors moved to fulfill their promises and to assure their own security. The provisional government had decreed an election for late November to select a Constituent Assembly. The Social Revolutionaries won a large majority over the Bolsheviks. When the assembly gathered in January, it met for only a day before the Red Army, controlled by the Bolsheviks, dispersed it. All other political parties also ceased to function in any meaningful fashion. In November and January the Bolshevik government promulgated decrees that nationalized the land and turned it over to its peasant proprietors. Factory workers were put in charge of their plants. Banks were taken from their owners and seized for the state, and the debt of the czarist government was repudiated. Property of the church reverted to the state.

The Bolshevik government also took Russia out of the war, which they believed benefited only capitalism. They signed an armistice with Germany in December 1917. On March 3, 1918, they accepted the Treaty of Brest-Litovsk, by which Russia yielded Poland, the Baltic states, and the Ukraine. Some territory in the Transcaucasus region went to Turkey. In addition the Bolsheviks agreed to pay a heavy war indemnity. These terms were a terribly high price to pay for peace, but Lenin had no choice. Russia was incapable of renewing the war effort, and the Bolsheviks needed time to impose their rule on a devastated and chaotic

Lenin Establishes His Dictatorship

After the Bolshevik *coup* in October, elections for the Constituent Assembly were held in November. The results gave a majority to the Social Revolutionary Party and embarrassed the Bolsheviks. Using his control of the Red Army, Lenin closed the Constituent Assembly in January 1918, after it had met for only one day, and established the rule of a revolutionary elite and his own dictatorship. Here is the crucial Bolshevik decree.

. . . The Constituent Assembly, elected on the basis of lists drawn up prior to the October Revolution, was an expression of the old relation of political forces which existed when power was held by the compromisers and the Cadets. When the people at that time voted for the candidates for the Socialist-Revolutionary Party, they were not in a position to choose between the Right Socialist-Revolutionaries, the supporters of the bourgeoisie, and the Left Socialist-Revolutionaries, the supporters of Socialism. Thus the Constituent Assembly, which was to have been the crown of the bourgeois parliamentary republic, could not but become an obstacle in the path of the October Revolution and the Soviet power.

The October Revolution, by giving the power to the Soviets, and through the Soviets to the toiling and exploited classes, aroused the desperate resistance of the exploiters, and in the crushing of this resistance it fully revealed itself as the beginning of the socialist revolution . . . the majority in the Constituent Assembly which met on January 5 was secured by the party of the Right Socialist-Revolutionaries, the party of Kerensky, Avksentyev and Chernov. Naturally, this party refused to discuss the absolutely clear, precise and unambiguous proposal of the supreme organ of Soviet power, the Central Executive Committee of the Soviets, to recognize the program of the Soviet power, to recognize the ''Declaration of Rights of the Toiling and Exploited People,'' to recognize the October Revolution and the Soviet power. . . .

The Right Socialist-Revolutionary and Menshevik parties are in fact waging outside the walls of the Constituent Assembly a most desperate struggle against the Soviet power. . . .

Accordingly, the Central Executive Committee resolves: The Constituent Assembly is hereby dissolved.

R. V. Daniels (Ed.), *A Documentary History of Communism*, Vol. 1 (New York: Random House, 1960), pp. 133–135.

Russia. Moreover Lenin believed that communist revolutions might soon sweep across other nations in Europe as a result of the war and the Russian example.

Until 1921 the New Bolshevik government confronted major domestic resistance. A civil war erupted between the "Red" Russians supporting the revolution and the "White" Russians, who opposed the Bolshevik triumph. In the summer of 1918 the czar and his family were murdered. Loyal army officers continued to fight the revolution and eventually received aid from the Allied armies. However, under the leadership of Trotsky the Red Army eventually overcame the domestic opposition. By 1921 Lenin and his supporters were in firm control.

The End of World War I

The internal collapse of Russia and the later Treaty of Brest-Litovsk brought Germany to the peak of its success. The Germans controlled eastern Europe and its resources, especially food, and by 1918 they were free to concentrate their forces on the western front. This turn of events would probably have been decisive had it not been balanced by American intervention. Still American troops would not arrive in significant numbers for about a year, and both sides tried to win the war in 1917. An Allied attempt to break through in the west failed disastrously, bringing heavy losses to the British and the French and causing a mutiny in the French army. The Austrians, supported by the Germans, defeated the Italians at Caporetto

and threatened to overrun Italy, but they were checked with the aid of Allied troops. The deadlock continued, but time was running out for the Central Powers.

In 1918 the Germans—persuaded chiefly by Ludendorff, by then Quartermaster-General, second in command to Hindenburg, but the real leader of the army—decided to gamble everything on one last offensive. The German army pushed forward and even reached the Marne again but got no farther. They had no more reserves, and the entire nation was exhausted. The Allies, on the other hand, were bolstered by the arrival of American troops in ever-increasing numbers. They were able to launch a counteroffensive that proved to be irresistible. As the Austrian fronts in the Balkans and Italy collapsed, the German high command knew that the end was imminent.

Ludendorff was determined that peace should be made before the German army could be thoroughly defeated in the field and that the responsibility should fall on civilians. For some time he had been the effective ruler of Germany under the aegis of the emperor. He now allowed a new government to be established on democratic principles and to seek peace immediately. The new government, under Prince Max of Baden, asked for peace on the basis of the Fourteen Points that President Wilson had declared as the American war aims. These were idealistic principles, including self-determination for nationalities, open diplomacy, freedom of the seas, disarmament, and establishment of a league of nations to keep the

American troops moving toward the trenches on the Western Front. The arrival of increasing numbers of fresh American troops in France in 1918 tipped the balance decisively in the Allies' favor. [*National Archives*]

peace. Wilson insisted that he would deal only with a democratic German government because he wanted to be sure that he was dealing with the German people and not merely their rulers.

The disintegration of the German army forced William II to abdicate on November 9, 1918. The majority branch of the Social Democratic Party proclaimed a republic to prevent the establishment of a soviet government under the control of their radical, Leninist wing, which had earlier broken away as the Independent Socialist Party. Two days later this republican, socialist-led government signed the armistice that ended the war by accepting German defeat. At the time of the armistice the German people were, in general, unaware that their army had been defeated in the field and was crumbling. No foreign soldier stood on German soil. It appeared to many Germans that they could expect a negotiated and mild settlement. The real peace was quite different and embittered the German people, many of whom came to believe that Germany had not been defeated but had been tricked by the enemy and betrayed—even stabbed in the back—by republicans and socialists at home.

The victors rejoiced, but they also had much to mourn. The casualties on all sides came to about ten million dead and twice as many wounded. The economic and financial resources of the European states were badly strained. The victorious Allies, formerly creditors to the world, became debtors to the new American colossus, itself barely touched by the calamities of war.

The old international order, moreover, was dead. Russia was ruled by a Bolshevik dictatorship that preached world revolution and the overthrow of capitalism everywhere. Germany was in chaos, and Austria-Hungary had disintegrated into a swarm of small national states competing for the remains of the ancient empire. These kinds of change stirred the colonial territories ruled by the European powers, and overseas empires would never again be as secure as they had seemed before the war. Europe was no longer the center of the world, free to interfere when it wished or to ignore the outer regions if it chose. Its easy confidence in material and moral progress was shattered by the brutal reality of four years of horrible war. The memory of that war lived on to shake the nerve of the victorious Western powers as they confronted the new conditions of the postwar world.

The Settlement at Paris

The representatives of the victorious states gathered at Versailles and other Parisian suburbs in the first half of 1919. Wilson speaking for the United States, David Lloyd George (1863–1945) for Britain, Georges Clemenceau (1841–1929) for France, and Vittorio Emanuele Orlando (1860–1952) for Italy made up the Big Four. Japan, now recognized for the first time as a great power, also had an important part in the discussions. The diplomats who met in Paris had a far more difficult task than the one facing those who had sat at Vienna a century earlier. Both groups attempted to restore order to the world after long and costly wars, but Metternich and his associates could confine their thoughts to Europe. France had acknowledged defeat and was willing to take part in and uphold the Vienna settlement. The diplomats at Vienna were not much affected by public opinion, and they could draw the new map of Europe along practical lines determined by the realities of power and softened by compromise.

The Peacemakers

The negotiators at Paris in 1919 were not so fortunate. They represented constitutional, generally democratic governments, and public opinion had become a mighty force. Though there were secret sessions, the conference often worked in the full glare of publicity. Nationalism had become almost a secular religion, and Europe's many ethnic groups could not be relied on to remain quiet while they were distributed on the map at the whim of the great powers. World War I, moreover, had been transformed by propaganda and especially by the intervention of Woodrow Wilson into a moral crusade to achieve a peace that would be just as well as secure. The Fourteen Points set forth the right of nationalities to self-determination as an absolute value, in spite of the fact that there was no way to draw the map of Europe to match ethnic groups perfectly with their homelands. All these elements made compromise difficult.

Wilson's idealism, moreover, came into conflict with the more practical war aims of the victorious powers and with many of the secret treaties that had been made before and during the war. The British and French people had been told that Germany would be made to pay for the war. Russia had been promised control

WORLD WAR I PEACE SETTLEMENT IN EUROPE AND THE MIDDLE EAST

OPPOSITE: MAP 25–10 *The map of central and Eastern Europe, as well as that of the Middle East, underwent drastic revision after World War I. The enormous geographical losses suffered by Germany, Austria-Hungary, the Ottoman Empire, Bulgaria, and Russia were the other side of the coin represented by gains for France, Italy, Greece, and Romania and the appearance, or reappearance, of at least eight new independent states from Finland in the north to Yugoslavia in the south. The mandate system for former Ottoman territories outside Turkey proper laid foundations for several new, mostly Arab, states in the Middle East.*

Woodrow Wilson (1856–1924) arriving in Britain in 1919. King George V (1865–1936) is on the President's right. Wilson saw the war as a moral crusade. His triumphal tour of Europe in 1919 convinced him that he had the support of peoples everywhere for an equally moral peace. [*National Archives*]

of Constantinople in return for recognition of the French claim to Alsace-Lorraine and British control of Egypt. Romania had been promised Transylvania at the expense of Hungary. Some of the agreements contradicted others: Italy and Serbia had competing claims to the islands and shore of the Adriatic. During the war the British had encouraged Arab hopes of an independent Arab state carved out of the Ottoman Empire, but those plans conflicted with the Balfour Declaration (1917), in which the British seemed to accept Zionist ideology and to promise the Jews a national home in Palestine. Both of these plans stood in conflict with an Anglo-French agreement to divide the Near East between the two Western powers.

The continuing national goals of the victors presented further obstacles to an idealistic "peace without victors." France, keenly conscious of its numerical inferiority to Germany and of the low birth rate that would keep it inferior, was naturally eager to achieve a settlement that would permanently weaken Germany and preserve French superiority. Italy continued to seek the acquisition of *Italia Irredenta*; Britain continued to look to its imperial interests; Japan pursued its own advantage in Asia; and the United States insisted on freedom of the seas, which favored American commerce, and on its right to maintain the Monroe Doctrine.

Finally, the peacemakers of 1919 faced a world still in turmoil. The greatest immediate threat appeared to be posed by the spread of Bolshevism. While Lenin and his colleagues were distracted by civil war, the Allies landed small armies at several places in Russia in the hope of overthrowing the Bolshevik regime. The revolution seemed likely to spread as communist governments were established in Bavaria and Hungary, and Berlin experienced a dangerous communist uprising led by the "Spartacus group." The Allies were sufficiently worried by these developments to allow and to support suppression of these communist movements by right-wing military forces, and they even allowed an army of German volunteers to operate against the Bolsheviks in the Baltic states. The fear of the spread of communism played a part in the thinking of the diplomats at Versailles, but it was far from dominant. The Germans kept playing on such fears as a way of getting better terms, but the Allies, and especially the French, would not hear of it. Fear of Germany remained the chief concern for France, whereas attention to interests that were more traditional and more immediate governed the policies of the other Allies.

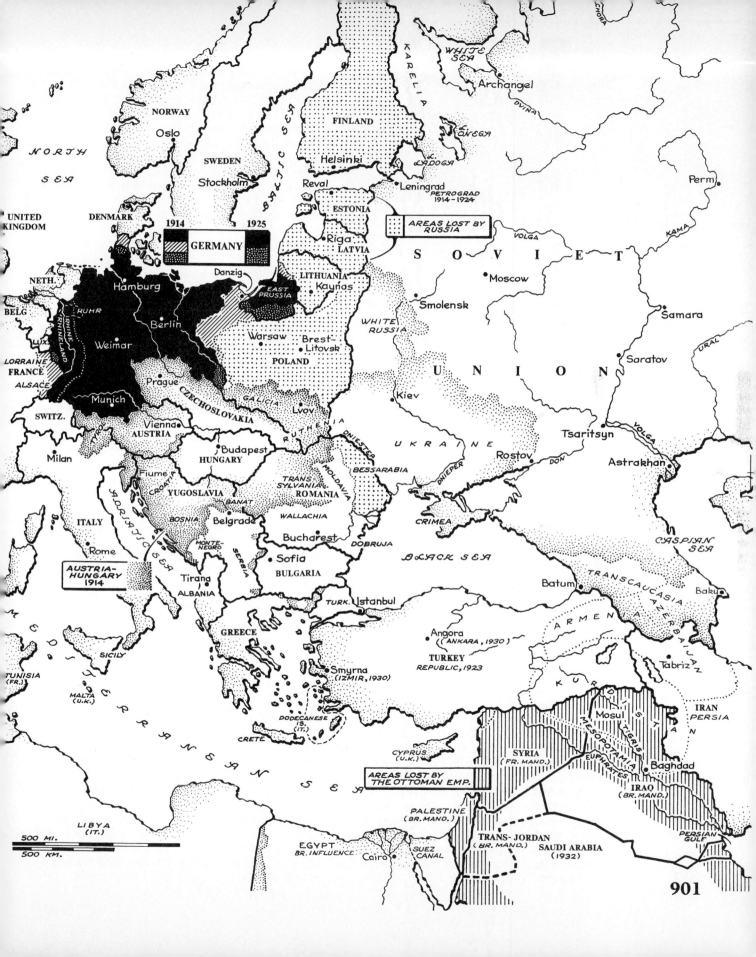

NORTH SEA

NORWAY
Oslo

SWEDEN
Stockholm

BALTIC SEA

KARELIA

WHITE SEA

Archangel

DVINA

FINLAND

Helsinki

L. ONEGA

L. LADOGA

Leningrad
PETROGRAD
1914-1924

Perm

KAMA

UNITED KINGDOM

DENMARK

1914 1925
GERMANY

Danzig

ESTONIA
Reval

Riga
LATVIA

LITHUANIA
Kaunas

EAST PRUSSIA

AREAS LOST BY RUSSIA

VOLGA

S O V I E T

Moscow

Smolensk

Samara

NETH.

Hamburg

BELG

RUHR

RHINE
RHINELAND

Berlin

Weimar

LUX.

Warsaw

Brest-Litovsk

POLAND

WHITE RUSSIA

U N I O N

Saratov

URAL

LORRAINE
FRANCE
ALSACE

Munich

Prague

CZECHOSLOVAKIA

GALICIA

Lvov

RUTHENIA

Kiev

Rostov

DON

Tsaritsyn

VOLGA

Astrakhan

SWITZ.

TYROL

Vienna
AUSTRIA

Budapest
HUNGARY

DNIESTER

U K R A I N E

DNIEPER

Milan

ADRIATIC SEA

Fiume

CROATIA

YUGOSLAVIA

BANAT

Belgrade

TRANS-SYLVANIA

MOLDAVIA

ROMANIA

BESSARABIA

ITALY

Rome

BOSNIA

MONTE-NEGRO

SERBIA

WALLACHIA

Bucharest

DOBRUJA

CRIMEA

C A S P I A N   S E A

TRANSCAUCASIA

AUSTRIA-HUNGARY
1914

Tirana
ALBANIA

Sofia
BULGARIA

B L A C K   S E A

Batum

AZERBAIJAN

Baku

TUNISIA (FR.)

MEDITERRANEAN SEA

SICILY

MALTA (U.K.)

GREECE

TURK. Istanbul

Smyrna
(IZMIR, 1930)

DODECANESE IS. (IT.)

CRETE

Angora
(ANKARA, 1930)

TURKEY
REPUBLIC, 1923

ARMENIA

KURDISTAN

Tabriz

IRAN
PERSIA

CYPRUS (U.K.)

Mosul

TIGRIS

EUPHRATES

Baghdad

AREAS LOST BY THE OTTOMAN EMP.

SYRIA
(FR. MAND.)

MESOPOTAMIA

IRAQ
(BR. MAND.)

PERSIAN GULF

500 MI.

500 KM.

LIBYA (IT.)

EGYPT
BR. INFLUENCE

Cairo

SUEZ CANAL

PALESTINE
(BR. MAND.)

TRANS-JORDAN
(BR. MAND.)

SAUDI ARABIA
(1932)

901

The Big Four at Versailles: Lloyd George of Britain, Orlando of Italy, Clemenceau of France, and Wilson of the United States. [*National Archives*]

The Peace

The Paris settlement consisted of five separate treaties between the victors and the defeated powers. Formal sessions began on January 18, 1919, and the last treaty was signed on August 10, 1920. Wilson arrived in Europe to unprecedented acclaim. Liberals and idealists expected a new kind of international order achieved in a new and better way, but they were soon disillusioned. "Open covenants openly arrived at" soon gave way to closed sessions in which Wilson, Clemenceau, and Lloyd George made arrangements that seemed cynical to outsiders. The notion of "a peace without victors" became a mockery when the Soviet Union (as Russia was now called) and Germany were excluded from the peace conference. The Germans were simply presented with a treaty and compelled to accept it in a manner that fully justified their complaint that the treaty had not been negotiated but dictated. The principle of national self-determination was violated many times, as was unavoidable, but the diplomats of the small nations were angered by their exclusion from decisions. The undeserved adulation accorded Wilson on his arrival gradually turned into equally undeserved scorn. He had not abandoned his ideals lightly but had merely given way to the irresistible force of reality.

THE LEAGUE OF NATIONS. Wilson was able to make unpalatable concessions without abandoning his ideals because he put great faith in a new instrument for peace and justice, the League of Nations. Its convenant was an essential part of the peace treaty. The league was not intended as an international government but as a body of sovereign states who agreed to pursue some common practices and to consult in the common interest, especially when war threatened. In that case the members promised to submit the matter to arbitration or to an international court or to the League Council. Refusal to abide by this agreement would justify league intervention in the form of economic and even military sanctions. But the league was unlikely to be effective because it had no armed forces at its disposal, and any action required the unanimous consent of its council, consisting of Britain, France, Italy, the United States, and Japan, as well as four other states that had temporary seats. The Covenant of the League bound its members to "respect and preserve" the territorial integrity of all its members, and this was generally seen as a device to ensure the security of the victorious powers. The exclusion from the League Assembly of Germany and the Soviet Union further undermined the league's claim to evenhandedness.

COLONIES. Another provision of the covenant dealt with colonial areas. These were to be placed under the "tutelage" of one of the great powers under league supervision and encouraged to advance toward independence. Because there were no teeth in this provision, very little advance was made. Provisions for disarmament were doomed to be equally ineffective. Members of the league remained fully sovereign and continued to pursue their own national interests. Only Wilson seems to have put much faith in its future ability to produce peace and justice, and this belief allowed him to approve territorial settlements that violated his own principles.

GERMANY. In the west the main territorial issue was the fate of Germany. Although a united Germany was less than fifty years old, no one seems to have thought of undoing Bismarck's work and dividing it into its component parts. The French would have liked to detach the Rhineland and set it up as a separate buffer state, but Lloyd George and Wilson would not permit that. Still, they could not ignore France's need for protection against a resurgent Germany. France received Alsace-Lorraine and the right to work the coal mines of the Saar for fifteen years. Germany west of the Rhine and fifty kilometers east of it was to be a demilitarized zone, and Allied troops on the west bank could stay there for fifteen years. In addition to this physical barrier to a new German attack, the treaty provided that Britain and the United States would guarantee to aid France if it were attacked by Germany. Such an attack was made more unlikely by the permanent disarmament of Germany. Its army was limited to 100,000 men on long-term service; its fleet was all but eliminated; and it was forbidden to have war planes, submarines, tanks, heavy artillery, or poison gas. As long as these provisions were observed, France would be safe.

THE EAST. The settlement in the east ratified the collapse of the great defeated empires that had ruled it for centuries. Germany's frontier was moved far to the west, excluding much of Silesia and most of Prussia. What was left of East Prussia was cut off from the rest of Germany by a corridor carved out to give the revived state of Poland access to the sea. The Austro-Hungarian Empire disappeared entirely, giving way to many smaller successor states. Most of its German-speaking people were gathered in the small Republic of Austria, cut off from the Germans of Bohemia and forbidden to unite themselves with Germany. The Magyars occupied the much-reduced kingdom of Hungary. The Czechs of Bohemia and Moravia joined with the Slovaks and Ruthenians to the east to form Czechoslovakia, and this new state included several million unhappy Germans. The southern Slavs were united in the kingdom of Serbs, Croats, and Slovenes, or Yugoslavia. Italy gained the Trentino and Trieste. Romania was enlarged by receiving Transylvania from Hungary and Bessarabia from Russia. Bulgaria was diminished by the loss of territory to Greece and Yugoslavia. Russia lost vast territories in the west. Finland, Estonia, Latvia, and Lithuania became independent states, and a good part of Poland was carved out of formerly Russian soil. The old Ottoman Empire disappeared. The new republic of Turkey was limited to little more than Constantinople and Asia Minor, and the former Ottoman territories of Palestine and Iraq came under British control and Syria and Lebanon under French control as mandates of the League of Nations. Germany's former colonies in Africa were divided among Britain, France, and South Africa, and the German Pacific possessions went to Australia, New Zealand, and Japan.

In theory the mandate system was meant to have the "advanced nations" govern the former colonies in the interests of the native peoples until they became ready to govern themselves. For this purpose they were divided into three categories, A, B, and C, in descending order of their readiness for independence. In practice most mandated territories were treated as colonies by the powers under whose "tutelage" they came. Not even one Class A mandate had achieved full independence twenty years after the signing of the treaty. The legacy of colonialism was to remain a problem even after World War II.

REPARATIONS. Perhaps the most debated part of the peace settlement dealt with reparations for the damage done by Germany during the war. Before the armistice the Germans promised to pay compensation "for all damages done to the civilian population of the Allies and their property." The Americans judged that the amount would be between $15 billion and $25 billion and that Germany would be able to pay that amount. However, France and Britain, worried about repaying their war debts to the United States, were eager to have Germany pay the full cost of the war, including pensions to survivors and dependents. There was general agreement that Germany could not afford to pay such a sum, whatever it might be, and no sum was fixed at the conference. In the meantime Germany was to pay $5 billion annually until 1921. At that time a final figure would be set, which Germany would have to pay in thirty years. The French did not regret the outcome. Either Germany would pay and be bled into impotence, or Germany would refuse to pay and justify French intervention.

To justify these huge reparations payments, the Allies inserted the notorious Clause 231 into the treaty:

The Allied and Associated Governments affirm, and Germany accepts, the responsibility of Germany and her allies for causing all the loss and damage to which the Allied and Associated Governments and their nationals have been subjected as a consequence of the war imposed upon them by aggression of Germany and her allies.

The Germans, of course, did not believe that

they were solely responsible for the war and bitterly resented the charge. They had suffered the loss of vast territories containing millions of Germans and great quantities of badly needed natural resources; they were presented with an astronomical and apparently unlimited reparations bill. To add insult to injury, they were required to admit to a war guilt that they did not feel. Finally, to heap insult on insult, they were required to accept the entire treaty as it was written by the victors, without any opportunity for negotiation. German's Prime Minister Philipp Scheidemann (1865–1939) spoke of the treaty as the imprisonment of the German people and asked, "What hand would not wither that binds itself and us in these fetters?" But there was no choice. The Social Democrats and the Catholic Center Party formed a new government, and their representatives signed the treaty. These were the parties that formed the backbone of the Weimar government that ruled Germany until 1933, and they never overcame the stigma of accepting the Treaty of Versailles.

Evaluation of the Peace

Few peace settlements have undergone more severe attacks than the one negotiated in Paris in 1919. It is natural that the defeated powers should object to it, but the peace soon came under bitter criticism in the victorious countries as well. Many of the French thought that it failed to provide adequate security for France, because it tied that security to promises of aid from the unreliable Anglo-Saxon countries. In England and the United States a wave of bitter criticism arose in liberal quarters because the treaty seemed to violate the idealistic and liberal aims and principles that the Western leaders had professed. It was not a peace without victors, did not put an end to imperialism, attempted to promote the national interests of the winning nations, and violated the principles of national self-determination by leaving significant pockets of minorities outside the borders of their national homelands.

The most influential critic was John Maynard Keynes (1883–1946), a brilliant British economist who took part in the peace conference. He resigned in disgust when he saw the direction it was taking and wrote a book called *The Economic Consequences of the Peace* (1920). It was a scathing attack, especially on reparations and the other economic aspects of the peace. It was also a skillful assault on the negotiators

and particularly on Wilson, who was depicted as a fool and a hypocrite. Keynes argued that the Treaty of Versailles was both immoral and unworkable. He called it a Carthaginian peace, referring to the utter destruction of Carthage by Rome after the Third Punic War. He argued that such a peace would bring economic ruin and war to Europe unless it were repudiated. Keynes had a great effect on the British, who were already suspicious of France and glad of an excuse to withdraw from continental affairs. The decent and respectable position came to be one that aimed at revision of the treaty in favor of Germany. Even more important was the book's influence in the United States. It fed the traditional tendency toward isolationism and gave powerful weapons to Wilson's enemies. Wilson's own political mistakes helped prevent American ratification of the treaty. Consequently America was out of the League of Nations and not bound to defend France. Britain, therefore, was also free from its obligation to France. France was left to protect itself without adequate means to do so for long.

Many of the attacks on the Treaty of Versailles are unjustified. It was not a Carthaginian peace. Germany was neither dismembered nor ruined. Reparations could be and were scaled down, and until the great world depression of the 1930s, the Germans recovered a high level of prosperity. Complaints against the peace should also be measured against the peace that the victorious Germans had imposed on Russia at Brest-Litovsk and the plans they had made for a European settlement in case of victory. Both were far more severe than anything enacted at Versailles. The attempt at achieving self-determination for nationalities was less than perfect, but it was the best solution Europe had ever accomplished in that direction.

The peace, nevertheless, was unsatisfactory in important ways. The elimination of the Austro-Hungarian Empire, however inevitable that might seem, created a number of serious problems. Economically it was disastrous, for it separated raw materials from manufacturing areas and producers from their markets by new boundaries and tariff walls. In hard times this separation created friction and hostility that aggravated other quarrels also created by the peace treaties. Poland contained unhappy German minorities, and Czechoslovakia was a collection of nationalities that did not find it easy to live together as a nation. Disputes over territories in eastern Europe promoted further tension. The peace was inadequate on another level, as well. It rested on a victory that Germany did not admit. The Germans believed that they had been cheated rather than defeated. At the same time the high moral principles proclaimed by the Allies undercut the validity of the peace, for it plainly fell far short of those principles.

Finally, the great weakness of the peace was its failure to accept reality. Germany and Russia must inevitably play an important part in European affairs, yet they were excluded from the settlement and from the League of Nations. Given the many discontented parties, the peace was not self-enforcing; yet no satisfactory machinery for enforcing it was established. The league was never a serious force for this purpose. It was left to France, with no guarantee of support from Britain and no hope of help from the United States, to defend the new arrangements. Finland, the Baltic states, Poland, Romania, Czechoslovakia, and Yugoslavia were created as a barrier to the expansion westward of Russian Communism and as a threat in the rear to deter German revival. Most of these states, however, would have to rely on France in case of danger, and France was simply not strong enough for the task if Germany should rearm. The tragedy of the Treaty of Versailles was that it was neither conciliatory enough to remove the desire for change, even at the cost of war, nor harsh enough to make another war impossible. The only hope for a lasting peace required the enforcement of the disarmament of Germany while the more obnoxious clauses of the peace treaty were revised. Such a policy required continued attention to the problem, unity among the victors, and far-sighted leadership; but none of these was present in adequate supply during the next two decades.

Suggested Readings

L. ALBERTINI, *The Origins of the War of* 1914, 3 vols. (1952, 1957). Discursive but invaluable.

M. BALFOUR, *The Kaiser and His Times* (1972). A fine biography of William II.

V. R. BERGHAHN, *Germany and the Approach of War in* 1914 (1973). A work similar in spirit to Fischer's [see below] but stressing the importance of Germany's naval program.

R. BOSWORTH, *Italy and the Approach of the First World War* (1983). A fine analysis of Italian policy.

S. B. FAY, *The Origins of the World War*, 2 vols. (1928). The best and most influential of the revisionist accounts.

D. K. FIELDHOUSE, *The Colonial Experience: A Comparative Study from the Eighteenth Century* (1966). An excellent recent study.

F. FISCHER, *Germany's Aims in the First World War* (1967). An influential interpretation that stirred a great controversy in Germany and around the world by emphasizing Germany's role in bringing on the war.

F. FISCHER, *War of Illusions* (1975). A long and diffuse book that tries to connect German responsibility for the war with internal social, economic, and political developments.

I. GEISS, *July* 1914 (1967). A valuable collection of documents by a student of Fritz Fischer's. The emphasis is on German documents and responsibility.

O. J. HALE, *The Great Illusion* 1900–1914 (1971). A fine survey of the period, especially good on public opinion.

P. KENNEDY, *The Rise of the Anglo-German Antagonism* 1860–1914 (1980). An unusual and thorough analysis of the political, economic and cultural roots of important diplomatic developments.

J. M. KEYNES, *The Economic Consequences of the Peace* (1920). The famous and influential attack on the Versailles Treaty.

L. LAFORE, *The Long Fuse* (1965). A readable account of the origins of World War I that focuses on the problem of Austria-Hungary.

W. L. LANGER, *The Diplomacy of Imperialism* (1935). A continuation of the previous study for the years 1890–1902.

W. L. LANGER, *European Alliances and Alignments*, 2nd ed. (1966). A splendid diplomatic history of the years 1871–1890.

B. H. LIDDELL HART, *The Real War* 1914–1918 (1964). A fine short account by an outstanding military historian.

D. C. B. LIEVEN, *Russia and the Origins of the First World War* (1983). A good account of the forces that shaped Russian policy.

E. MANTOUX, *The Carthaginian Peace* (1952). A vigorous attack on Keynes's view [see Keynes, above].

J. STEINBERG, *Yesterday's Deterrent* (1965). An excellent study of Germany's naval policy and its consequences.

Z. STEINER, *Britain and the Origins of the First World War* (1977). A perceptive and informed account of the way British foreign policy was made in the years before the war.

A. J. P. TAYLOR, *The Struggle for Mastery in Europe*, 1848–1918 (1954). Clever but controversial.

L. C. F. TURNER, *Origins of the First World War* (1970). Especially good on the significance of Russia and its military plans.

Benito Mussolini (1883–1945), addressing the nation from the balcony of his headquarters in Rome in 1935. In the 1920s Mussolini was widely admired. Many Europeans believed that Fascism had given Italy a strong, modern, stable government. Yet, in reality, Fascist rule was corrupt, inefficient, and completely opportunistic. [Bildarchiv Preussicher Kulturbestiz]

PURSUIT of experimentation in politics and of normality in economic life marked the decade following the conclusion of the Paris settlement. Many of the experiments failed, and the normality proved quite elusive. By the close of the decade the political path had been paved for the nightmares of brutally authoritarian governments and international aggression. Yet many of the people who had survived the Great War had hoped and worked for a better outcome. Authoritarianism and aggression were not the inescapable destiny of Europe. Their emergence was the result of failures in securing alternative modes of political life and international relations.

Political and Economic Factors After the Paris Settlement

New Governments

In 1919 experimental political regimes studded the map of Europe. From Ireland to Russia new governments were seeking to gain the active support of their citizens and to solve the grievous economic problems caused by the war. In the Soviet Union the Bolsheviks regarded themselves as forging nothing less than a new kind of civilization. They gave little significant consideration to anything but an authoritarian rule.

It was otherwise elsewhere on the Continent. Democratically elected parliamentary governments appeared where the autocratic, military empires of Germany and Austria-Hungary had previously held sway. Their goals were substantially more modest than those of the Bolsheviks. Yet to pursue parliamentary politics where it had never been meaningfully practiced proved no simple task. The Wilsonian vision of democratic, self-determined nations floundered on the harsh realities of economics, aggressive nationalism, and revived political conservatism. Too often the will for democratic, parliamentary government, as well as experience in its exercise, was absent from the nations on which it had been bestowed. Moreover, in many of the new democracies important sectors of the citizenry believed that parliamentary politics was by its very nature corrupt or unequal to great nationalistic enterprise.

26

Political Experiments of the 1920s

Demands for Revision of Versailles

Several other Europe-wide problems haunted the early interwar period and directly affected the decisions and actions of individual nations. The Paris settlement fostered both resentment and discontent in numerous countries. Germany had been humiliated. The arrangements for reparations led to seemingly endless haggling over payments. Various national groups in the successor states of eastern Europe felt that injustice had been done in their particular case of self-determination. There were demands for further border adjustments. On the other side the victorious powers, and especially France, often believed that the provisions of the treaty were being inadequately enforced. Consequently, throughout the 1920s, calls either to revise or to enforce the Paris treaties contributed to domestic political turmoil across the Continent. All too many political figures were willing to fish in these troubled international waters for a large catch of domestic votes.

Postwar Economic Problems

Simultaneous with the move toward political experiment and demands for revision of the recently established international order was a widespread desire to return to the economic prosperity of the prewar years. However, after 1918 it was impossible to restore what American President Warren Harding would shortly term "normalcy." During the conflict Europeans had turned against themselves and their civilization the vast physical power that they had created in the previous century. More than 750,000 British soldiers had perished. The combat deaths for France and Germany were 1,385,000 and 1,808,000, respectively. Russia had lost no fewer than 1,700,000 troops. Scores of thousands more from other belligerent nations had also been killed. Still more millions had been wounded. These casualties meant not only the waste of human life and talent but also the loss of producers and consumers. There had also been widespread destruction of transport facilities, mines, and industry.

Another casualty of the conflict was the financial dominance and independence of Europe. At the opening of hostilities, Europe had been the financial and credit center of the world. At the close of the fighting, Europeans stood deeply in debt to each other and to the United States. The Bolsheviks had repudiated the debt of the czarist government, much of which was owed to French creditors. Other nations could not pursue this revolutionary course. The Paris settlement had imposed heavy financial obligations on Germany and its allies. The United States refused to ask reparations from Germany but firmly demanded repayment of war debts from its own allies. On the one hand, the reparation and debt structure meant that no nation was fully in control of its own economic life. On the other hand, the absence of international economic cooperation meant that more than ever, individual nations felt compelled to pursue or to attempt to pursue selfish, nationalistic economic aims. It was perhaps the worst of all possible international economic worlds.

The market and trade conditions that had prevailed before 1914 had also changed radically. Russia, in large measure, withdrew from the European economic order. The political reconstruction of eastern and central Europe into the multitude of small successor states broke up the trade region formerly encompassed by Germany and Austria-Hungary. Most of those new states had weak economies hardly capable of competing in modern economic life. The new boundaries separated raw materials from the factories using them. Railway systems on which finished and unfinished products traveled might now lie under the control of two or more nations. Political and economic nationalism went together. New customs barriers were raised.

International trade also followed new patterns. The United States became less dependent on European production and assumed the status of a major competitor. During the war the belligerents had been forced to sell many of their holdings on other continents to finance the conflict. As a consequence Europeans exercised less dominance over the world economy. Postwar economic growth within colonies or former colonies lowered the demand for European goods. The United States and Japan began to penetrate markets in Latin America and Asia previously dominated by European producers and traders.

New Roles for Government and Labor

The war effort in all countries occasioned new dimensions of state interference and direction in the economy. Large government bureaucracies had been organized to plan the

One of the last British soldiers killed on the Western Front in November 1918. The millions killed or maimed in the war were one of the main causes for European weakness and instability in the 1920s and 1930s. [Library of Congress]

course of production and the distribution of goods. Prices had been controlled, raw materials stockpiled, consumer goods rationed, and economic priorities set by government technocrats. The mechanism of the freely operating market so dear to nineteenth-century liberals had been rejected as a vehicle for economic decision-making. The economic planning skills learned during the war could be transferred to peacetime operations. Moreover governments had learned about the immense productive and employment power of an economy placed under state control.

Labor had achieved new prominence within the wartime economic setting. The unions had actively supported the war effort of their nations. They had ensured labor peace for production. In turn, their members had received better wages, and their leaders had been admitted to high political councils. This wartime cooperation of unions and labor leaders with the various national governments destroyed the internationalism of the prewar labor movement, but it also meant that henceforth the demands of labor could not be ignored by governments. Although in peacetime wages might

be lowered, they could very rarely be reduced to prewar levels. European workers intended to receive their just share of the fruits of their labor. Collective bargaining and union recognition brought on by the war also could not be abandoned. This improvement in both the status and the effective influence of labor was one of the most significant social and political changes to flow from World War I.

The social condition of the work force seemed to be improving while that of the middle class seemed to be stagnating or declining. Throughout the 1920s people from the various segments of the middle class remained very suspicious of the new role of labor and of socialist political parties. This suspicion and fear of potential loss of property on the part of the middle classes led them to seek to perpetuate the status quo and to fend off further social and economic advances of the working classes. In this regard, the European middle classes, once the vanguard of the liberal revolution, had become a thoroughly conservative political force.

The war and the peace settlement wrought one other major change that affected the course of political and economic life. The turn to liberal democracy and the extension of the franchise to women and previously disenfranchised males meant that for the first time in European history the governments handling economic matters were responsible to mass electorates. Economics and politics had become more intimately connected than ever before. The economic and social anxieties of the electorate could and eventually did overcome its political scruples. Whereas previously economic discontent had been articulated through riots and later through unions, it could now be voiced through the ballot box.

Joyless Victors

France and Great Britain, with the aid of the United States, had won the war. France became the strongest military power on the Continent. Britain had escaped with almost no physical damage. Both nations, however, had lost vast numbers of young men in the conflict. Their economies were weak, and their overseas wealth and power stood much diminished. Compared with contemporary events in Germany, Italy, and Russia, the interwar political development of the two major democracies seems rather tame. Neither experienced a revolution or a shift to authoritarian government. Yet this surface calm was largely illusory. Both were troubled democracies. To neither did victory in war bring the good life in peace.

France: The Search for Security

At the close of World War I, as after Waterloo, the revolution of 1848, and the defeat of 1871, the French voters elected a doggedly conservative Chamber of Deputies. The preponderance of military officers among its members led to the nickname of the "Horizon Blue Chamber." The overwhelmingly conservative character of the chamber was registered in 1920 by its defeat of Georges Clemenceau's bid for the presidency. The crucial factor had been, of all things, the alleged leniency of the Paris treaties and the failure to establish a separate Rhineland state. The deputies wanted to achieve future security against Germany and Russian Communism. They intended to make as few concessions to domestic social reform as possible. The 1920s were marked by fluctuations in ministries and a drift in domestic policy. The political turnstile remained ever active. Between the end of the war and January 1933,

France was governed by no fewer than twenty-seven different cabinets.

NEW ALLIANCES. During the first five years after the Treaty of Versailles, France accepted its role as the leading European power. The French plan was to enforce strictly the clauses of the treaty that were meant to keep Germany weak and, at the same time, to build a system of eastern alliances to replace the lost prewar alliance with Russia. In 1920 and 1921 three eastern states that had much to lose from revision of the treaty—Czechoslovakia, Romania, and Yugoslavia—formed the Little Entente. Before long France made military alliances with these states as well as with Poland. A dispute with Czechoslovakia over the control of Teschen prevented the Poles from joining the Little Entente, but the independent existence of Poland depended on the maintenance of the Versailles settlement. This new system of eastern alliances was the best France could do, but it was far weaker than the old Franco-Russian alliance. The new states combined were no match for the former power of imperial Russia, and they were neither united nor reliable. Poland and Romania were more concerned about Russia than about Germany, and the main target of the Little Entente was Hungary. If one of the eastern states were threatened by a resurgent Germany, there was considerable doubt that the others would be eager to come to its aid.

The formation of this new alliance system heightened the sense of danger and isolation felt by the two excluded powers, Germany and the Soviet Union. In 1922, while the European states were holding an economic conference at Genoa, the Russians and the Germans met at Rapallo nearby and signed a treaty of their own. It established diplomatic and economic relations that proved useful to both sides. Although the treaty contained no secret political or military clauses, such arrangements were suspected to exist. And it is now known that the Germans helped train the Russian army and gave their own army valuable experience in the use of tanks and planes in the Soviet Union. The news of Rapallo confirmed the French in their growing belief that Germany was unwilling to live up to the terms of the Versailles Treaty and helped move them to strong action.

QUEST FOR REPARATIONS. In early 1923 the Allies, and France in particular, declared

Raymond Poincaré (1860–1934). As prime minister of France in the 1920s, Poincaré used force to compel Germany to pay reparations. [Bildarchiv Preussicher Kulturbesitz]

Germany to be in technical default of its reparations payments. Raymond Poincaré (1860–1934), France's powerfully nationalistic prime minister, took the opportunity to teach the Germans a lesson and force them to comply. On January 11, to ensure receipt of the hardwon reparations, the French government ordered its troops to occupy the Ruhr mining and manufacturing district. The response of the Weimar Republic was to order passive resistance. This policy amounted to calling a general strike in the largest industrial region of the nation. Confronted with this tactic, Poincaré sent French civilians to run the German mines and railroads. France got its way. The Germans paid, but France confronted a great price for its victory. The English were alienated by the French heavy-handedness and took no part in the occupation. They became more suspicious of France and more sympathetic to Germany. The cost of the Ruhr occupation, moreover, vastly increased French as well as German inflation and damaged the French economy. As one scholar explained, the French "threatened to choke Germany to death; the Germans threatened to die. Neither side dared carry its threat to extremity."[1] From the French viewpoint, consequently, victory in the war and the achievement of considerable military power

[1]A. J. P. Taylor, *The Origins of the Second World War* (New York: Fawcett, 1961), p. 33.

seemed to have brought the nation little of the prestige and effective influence it sought.

In 1924 the conservative ministry gave way to a coalition of leftist parties, the so-called *Cartel des Gauches*, led by Edouard Herriot (1872–1957). The chief policy changes of the new Cabinet were recognition of the Soviet Union and a more conciliatory policy toward Germany. Leadership on this score came from Aristide Briand (1862–1932), who was foreign minister for the remainder of the decade. He championed the League of Nations and attempted to persuade his own nation that its military power did not give it unlimited influence on the foreign affairs of Europe. Under the leftist coalition a mild inflation also occurred. It had begun under the conservatives but picked up intensity in 1925. When the value of the franc fell sharply on the international money market in 1926, Poincaré returned to office as head of a national government composed of several parties. The value of the franc recovered somewhat, and inflation cooled. For the rest of the 1920s the conservatives remained in power. The country enjoyed a general prosperity that lasted until 1931, longer than in any other nation.

Great Britain

World War I profoundly changed British politics if not the political system. In 1918 Parliament expanded the electorate to include all men aged twenty-one and women aged thirty. (In 1928 the age for women voters was also lowered to twenty-one.) The prewar structure of parties and leadership also shifted. A coalition Cabinet composed of Liberal, Conservative, and Labour ministers had directed the war effort. The wartime ministerial participation of the Labour Party did much to dispel its radical image. For the Liberal Party, however, the conflict brought unexpected division. Until 1916 Liberal Prime Minister Herbert Asquith had presided over the Cabinet. As disagreements over war management developed, he was ousted by fellow Liberal David Lloyd George. The party then became sharply split between followers of the two men. In 1918, against the wishes of both the Labour Party and the Asquith Liberals, Lloyd George decided to maintain the coalition through the tasks of the peace conference and the domestic reconstruction. The wartime coalition, now minus its Labour members, won a stunning victory at the polls. However, Lloyd George could thereafter remain prime minister only as long as his dominant Conservative partners wished to keep him.

During the 1918 election campaign there had been much talk about creating "a land fit for heroes to live in." It did not happen. Except for the three years immediately after the war, the British economy was depressed throughout the 1920s. Genuine postwar recovery simply did not get under way. Unemployment never dipped below 10 per cent and often hovered near 11 per cent. There were never fewer than a million workers unemployed. Government insurance programs to cover unemployed workers, widows, and orphans were expanded. But there was no similar meaningful expansion in the number of jobs available. From 1922 onward, accepting the "dole" with little expectation of future employment became a wretched and degrading way of life for scores of thousands of poor British families.

THE FIRST LABOUR GOVERNMENT.

In October 1922 the Conservatives dropped Lloyd George and replaced him with Bonar Law (1858–1923), one of their own. A Liberal would never again be prime minister. Stanley Baldwin (1867–1947) soon replaced Law, who fell victim to throat cancer. Baldwin decided to attempt to cure Britain's economic plight by abandoning free trade and imposing protective tariffs. The voters rejected the proposed policy in 1923. At the election the Conservative Party lost its majority in the House of Commons, but only votes from both Liberal and Labour party members could provide an alternative majority. Labour had elected the second largest group of members to the Commons. Consequently, in December 1923, King George V (1910–1936) asked Ramsay MacDonald (1866–1937) to form the first Labour ministry in British history. The Liberal Party did not serve in the Cabinet but provided the necessary votes in the House of Commons to give the Labour ministry a working majority.

The Labour Party was socialistic in its platform, but not revolutionary. The party had expanded beyond its early trade-union base. MacDonald himself had opposed World War I and for a time had also broken with the party. His own version of socialism owed little, if anything, to Marx. His program consisted of plans for extensive social reform rather than for the nationalization or public seizure of industry. A sensitive politician, if not a great leader, Mac-Donald understood that the most important task facing the ministry was proving to the nation that the Labour Party was both respectable and responsible. His nine months in office achieved just that goal if little else of major importance. The establishment of Labour as a viable governing party signaled the permanent demise of the Liberal Party. It has continued to exist, but the bulk of its voters have drifted into either the Conservative or the Labour ranks.

THE GENERAL STRIKE OF 1926.

The Labour government fell in the autumn of 1924 over charges of inadequate prosecution of a communist writer. Stanley Baldwin returned to office, where he remained until 1929. The problem of the stagnant economy remained uppermost in the public mind. Business and political leaders continued to believe that all

Stanley Baldwin was the Conservative Party Prime Minister during the general strike of 1926. His solid, calm appearance suggested to many voters the qualities most needed in their government. [Bettmann Archive]

Stanley Baldwin Reflects on the British General Strike

After halting much economic activity for more than a week in 1926, the British general strike came to a peaceful conclusion. Baldwin, who was the Conservative prime minister at the time, thought the outcome spoke well for British character and British freedom. In examining the impact of the strike, he was particularly concerned to present British institutions in a favorable light, as contrasted with the new social order then emerging in the Soviet Union. He hoped that communist doctrines would not come to influence the British labor movement.

It may have been a magnificent demonstration of the solidarity of labour, but it was at the same time a most pathetic evidence of the failure of all of us to live and work together for the good of all. . . . But if that strike showed solidarity, sympathy with the miners—whatever you like— it showed something else far greater. It proved the stability of the whole fabric of our own country, and to the amazement of the world not a shot was fired. We were saved by common sense and the good temper of our own people. We have been called a stupid people; but the moment the public grasped that what was at stake was not the solidarity of labour nor the fate of the miners, but the life of the State, then there was a response to the country's need deep and irresistible. And mark this: in my view there was that feeling in the country because the leaders of the strike and the men who were on strike felt it in their innermost hearts, too. They felt a conflict of loyalties. They knew that same conflict was raging in the breasts of thousands of men who had fought for their country ten years ago. Many of the strikers were uneasy in their minds and their consciences, because the British workman, as I know him, does not like breaking contracts, as so many of them did. I do not think many of them

like stopping food supplies and shutting down the Press. I sometimes amuse myself with wondering what their language would have been like if these things had been done by the Government. And, after all, when all has been said about England, about the mistakes we make, and about our stupidity, and about how much better they do things in Russia, yet how many of those men or any of us, would prefer to have been born and brought up in any country in the world but this, or to send our children to be brought up there. In these postwar years, in spite of all the depression, in spite of all our troubles, never before has the wealth of this country, through the taxes and the rates, been so distributed to those less fortunate and for the provision of those thrown out of work. . . .

I want to see our British Labour movement free from alien and foreign heresy. I want to see it pursued and developed on English lines, led by English men. The temptations that beset the growth of these vast organizations [the labor unions], in many respects as they are today outside the law, controlling multitudes of men and large sums of money—the temptation to set such a machine in motion and make people follow it is great indeed.

Stanley Baldwin, *Our Inheritance* (London: Hodder and Stoughton, 1928), pp. 222–224.

would be well if they could restore the prewar conditions of trade. A major element in these conditions had been the gold standard as the basis for international trade. In 1925 the Conservative government returned to the gold standard, abandoned during the war, in hopes of re-creating the former monetary stability. However, the government set the conversion rate for the pound against other currencies too high and thus, in effect, raised the price of British goods to foreign customers.

In order to make their products competitive on the world market, British management attempted to lower prices by cutting wages. The coal industry was the sector most directly affected by the wage cuts. It was inefficient and poorly managed and had been in trouble ever since the end of the war.

Labor relations in the coal industry had been unruly for some time. In 1926, after cuts in wages and a breakdown in negotiations, the coal miners went out on strike. Soon thereaf-

The British general strike of May 1926 produced much tension but little violence. Armored cars were used to protect food convoys in London and other big cities against attacks by strikers which never occurred. [Mary Evans Picture Library]

ter, in May 1926, sympathetic workers in other industries engaged in a general strike lasting nine days. There was much tension but little violence. In the end the miners and the other unions capitulated. With such high levels of unemployment organized labor was in a relatively weak position. After the general strike the Baldwin government attempted to reconcile labor primarily through an expansion of housing and reforms in the poor laws. Despite the economic difficulties of these years the actual standard of living of most British workers, including those receiving government insurance payments, actually improved somewhat.

EMPIRE. World War I also modified Britain's imperial position. The aid given by the dominions, such as Canada and Australia, demonstrated a new independence on their part. Empire was a two-way proposition. The idea of self-determination as applied to Europe could not be prevented from filtering into imperial relationships. In India the Congress Party, led by Mohandas Gandhi (1869–1948), was beginning to attract widespread support. The British started to talk more about eventual self-government for the nation. Moreover,

during the 1920s the Indian government achieved the right to impose tariffs for the protection of its own industry rather than for the advantage of British manufacturers. The British textile producers no longer had totally free access to the vast Indian market.

IRELAND. A new chapter was written in the unhappy relations between Britain and Ireland during and after the war. In 1914 the Irish Home Rule Bill had passed Parliament, but its implementation was postponed for the duration of the conflict. As the war dragged on, Irish nationalists became determined to wait no longer. On Easter Monday, 1916, a nationalist uprising occurred in Dublin. It was the only rebellion of a national group to occur against any government engaged in the war. The British suppressed it in less than a week but then made a grave tactical blunder. They executed the Irish nationalist leaders who had been responsible for the uprising. Overnight those rebels became national martyrs. Leadership of the nationalist cause quickly shifted from the Irish Party in Parliament to the extremist Sinn Fein ("Ourselves Alone") movement.

In the election of 1918 the Sinn Fein Party won all but four of the Irish parliamentary seats outside Ulster. They refused to go to the Parliament at Westminster. Instead they constituted themselves into a Dail Eireann, or Irish Parliament. On January 21, 1919, they declared Irish independence. The military wing of Sinn Fein became the Irish Republican Army (IRA). The first president was Eamon De Valera (1882–1975), who had been born in the United States. Very quickly what amounted to a guerrilla war broke out between the IRA and the British army supported by auxiliaries known as the Black and Tans. There was unusually intense bitterness and hatred on both sides.

In late 1921 secret negotiations began between the two governments. In the treaty concluded in December 1921 the Irish Free State took its place beside the earlier dominions in the British Commonwealth: Canada, Australia, New Zealand, and South Africa. The six counties of Ulster, or Northern Ireland, were permitted to remain part of what was now called the United Kingdom of Great Britain and Northern Ireland, with provisions for home rule. No sooner had the treaty been signed than a new Irish civil war broke out between Irish moderates and diehards. The moderates supported the treaty; the diehards wanted the oath to the British monarch abolished and a totally independent republic established. The second civil war continued until 1923. De Valera, who supported the diehards, resigned the presidency and organized resistance to the treaty. In 1932 he was again elected president. The next year the Dail Eireann abolished the oath of allegiance to the monarch.

During World War II Ireland remained neutral. In 1949 it declared itself the wholly independent republic of Eire.

Trials of the New Democracies

Both France and Great Britain had prewar experience in liberal democratic government. Their primary challenges lay in responding to economic pressures and allowing new groups, such as the Labour Party, to share political power. In Germany, Poland, Austria, Czechoslovakia, and the other successor states, the issue for the 1920s was to make new parliamentary governments function in a satisfactory and stable manner. Before the war both Germany and Austria-Hungary had possessed elected parliaments, but those bodies had not exercised genuine political power. The question after the war became whether those groups that had previously sat powerless in parliaments could assume both power and responsibility. Another question was how long conservative institutions, such as the armies and the conservative political groups, would tolerate or cooperate with the liberal experiments. At the same time all of these newly organized states confronted immense postwar economic difficulties.

Successor States in Eastern Europe

Only the barest outline can be given of the dreary political story of the successor states. It had been an article of faith among nineteenth-century liberals that only good could flow from the demise of Austria-Hungary. The new states in eastern Europe were to symbolize the principle of national self-determination and to provide a buffer against the westward spread of Bolshevism. However, they were in trouble from the beginning. They were poor and overwhelmingly rural nations in an industrialized world. Nationality problems continued to exist. The major social and political groups were generally unwilling to make compromises. With the exception of Czechoslovakia, all of these states succumbed to some form of authoritarian government.

In Hungary during 1919 the Bolsheviks had erected a socialist government led by Béla Kun (1885–1937). The Allies quickly authorized an invasion by Romanian troops to remove the Communist danger. They then established Admiral Miklós Horthy (1858–1957) as regent, a position he held until 1944. During the 1920s the effective ruler of Hungary was Count Stephen Bethlen (1874–1947). He presided over a government that was parliamentary in form but aristocratic in character. In 1932 he was succeeded by General Julius Gömbös (1886–1936), who pursued policies of anti-Semitism and rigged elections. No matter how the popular vote turned out, the Gömbös party controlled the Parliament. There was also deep resentment in Hungary over the territory it had lost to other nations through the Paris settlement.

The situation in Austria was little better. The new Austria consisted of a capital city surrounded by some other territory. A quarter of the eight million Austrians lived in Vienna. Viable economic life was almost impossible, and union with Germany was forbidden by the Paris settlement. Throughout the 1920s the leftist Social Democrats and the conservative Christian Socialists contended for power. Unwilling to use only normal political methods, both groups employed small armies to terrorize their opponents and to impress their followers. In 1933 the Christian Socialist Engelbert Dollfuss (1892–1934) became chancellor. He tried to steer a course between the Austrian Social Democrats and the German Nazis, who had begun to penetrate Austria. In 1934 he outlawed all political parties except the Christian Socialists, the agrarians, and the paramilitary groups, which composed his own Fatherland Front. He used government troops against the Social Democrats. During an unsuccessful Nazi *coup* in 1934, Dollfuss was shot. His successor, Kurt von Schuschnigg (1897–1977) presided over Austria until Hitler annexed it in 1938.

In southeastern Europe revision of the Versailles Treaty arrangements was somewhat less of an issue. Parliamentary government floun-

In 1934 Engelbert Dollfuss (1892–1934), the conservative chancellor of Austria, used troops and heavy artillery to suppress the Social Democratic party. The heaviest fighting occurred in working-class districts where apartment buildings, such as this, were taken by direct assault. [Ullstein Bilderdienst]

dered nevertheless. In Yugoslavia (known as the kingdom of the Serbs, Croats, and Slovenes until 1929), the clash of nationalities eventually led to the imposition of royal dictatorship in 1929 under King Alexander I (1921–1934), himself a Serb. His dictatorship saw the outlawing of political parties and the jailing of popular politicians. Alexander I was assassinated in 1934, but the authoritarian government continued under the regency for his son. Other royal dictatorships were imposed: in Romania by King Carol II (1930–1940) and in Bulgaria by King Boris III (1918–1943). They regarded their own illiberal regimes as countering even more extreme antiparliamentary movements and as quieting the discontent of the varied nationalities within their borders. In Greece the parliamentary monarchy floundered amidst military *coups* and calls for a republic. In 1936 General John Metaxas (1871–1941) instituted a dictatorship that for the time being ended parliamentary life in Greece.

The nation whose postwar fortunes probably most disappointed liberal Europeans was Poland. For over a hundred years the country had been erased from the map. Restoration of an independent Poland had been one of Woodrow Wilson's Fourteen Points. When the country was finally reconstructed in 1919, nationalism proved an insufficient bond to overcome political disagreements stemming from class, diverse economic interests, and regionalism. The new Parliament was plagued with a vast number of small political parties. The constitution assigned too little power to the executive. In 1926 General Josef Pilsudski (1857–1935) carried out a military *coup*. He ruled personally until the close of the decade, when the government passed into the hands of a group of military leaders.

Only one central European successor state escaped the fate of self-imposed authoritarian government. Czechoslovakia possessed a strong industrial base, a substantial middle class, and a tradition of liberal values. During the war Czechs and Slovaks had cooperated to aid the Allies. They had learned to work together and to trust each other. After the war the new government had carried out agrarian reform and had broken up large estates in favor of small peasant holdings. In the person of Thomas Masaryk (1850–1937), the nation possessed a gifted leader of immense integrity and fairness. The country had a real chance of constructing a viable modern nation-state. However, it was plagued with discontent among its smaller national groups, including the German population of the Sudetenland assigned to Czechoslovakia by the Paris settlement. The parliamentary regime might very well have been able to deal with this problem, but extreme German nationalists looked to Hitler for aid. For his part, the German dictator wished to expand into eastern Europe. In 1938, at Munich, the great powers divided liberal Czechoslovakia to appease the aggressive instincts of Hitler.

The fate of the successor states proved most disappointing to those who had hoped for political liberty to result from the dissolution of the Habsburg Empire and other border adjustments in eastern Europe. By the early 1930s, in most of those states, the authoritarianism of the Habsburgs had been replaced by that of other rulers. However, the most momentous democratic experiment between the wars was conducted in Germany. There, after a century of frustration and disappointment, a liberal state had been constructed. It was in Germany that parliamentary democracy and its future in Western civilization faced its major trial.

The Weimar Republic

The German Weimar Republic was born from the defeat of the imperial army, the revolution of 1918 against the Hohenzollerns, and the hopes of German Liberals and Social Democrats. Its name derived from the city in which its constitution was written and promulgated in August 1919. While the constitution was being debated, the republic, headed by the Social Democrats, accepted the humiliating terms of the Versailles Treaty. Although its officials had signed only under the threat of an Allied invasion, the republic was nevertheless permanently associated with the national disgrace and the economic burdens of the treaty. Throughout the 1920s the government of the republic was required to fulfill the economic and military provisions imposed by the Paris settlement. It became all too easy for nationalists and military figures whose policies had brought on the tragedy and defeat of the war to blame the young republic and the socialists for the results of the conflict. In Germany, more than in other countries, the desire to revise the treaty was closely related to a desire to change the mode of domestic government.

The Weimar Constitution was a highly enlightened document. It guaranteed civil liberties and provided for direct election, by universal suffrage, of the Reichstag and the president. However, it also contained certain crucial structural flaws that allowed the eventual overthrow of its institutions. Within the Reichstag a complicated system of proportional representation was adopted. This system made it relatively easy for very small political parties to gain seats in the Reichstag and resulted in shifting party combinations that led to considerable instability. Ministers were technically responsible to the Reichstag, but the president appointed and removed the chancellor. Perhaps most importantly, Article 48 allowed the president, in times of emergency, to rule by decree. In this manner the constitution permitted the possibility of presidential dictatorship.

Beyond the burden of the Versailles Treaty and the potential constitutional pitfalls, the Weimar Republic suffered from a lack of sympathy and a lack of loyalty on the part of many Germans. A social revolution had not accompanied the changes in political structure. Many important political figures actually favored a constitutional monarchy. The schoolteachers, civil servants, and judicial officials of the republic were generally the same people who had previously served the Kaiser and the empire. Before the war they had distrusted or even hated the Social Democratic Party, which figured so prominently in the establishment and the politics of the republic. The officer corps was deeply suspicious of the government and profoundly resentful of the military provisions of the peace settlement. They and other nationalistic Germans perpetuated the myth that the German army had surrendered on foreign soil only because it had been stabbed in the back by civilians at home. In other words, large numbers of Germans in significant social and political positions wanted both to revise the peace treaty and to modify the system of government. The early years of the republic only solidified those sentiments.

A number of major and minor humiliations as well as considerable economic instability impinged on the new government. In March 1920 the right-wing Kapp *Putsch*, or armed insurrection, erupted in Berlin. Led by a conservative civil servant and supported by army officers, the attempted *coup* failed. But the collapse occurred only after government officials had fled the city and German workers had carried out a general strike. In the same month a series of strikes took place in the Ruhr mining district. The government sent in troops. Such extremism from both the left and the right would haunt the republic for all its days. In May 1921 the Allies presented a reparations bill for 132 billion gold marks. The German republican government accepted this preposterous demand only after new Allied threats of occupation. Throughout the early 1920s there were numerous assassinations or attempted assassinations of important republican leaders. Violence was the hallmark of the first five years of the republic.

INVASION OF THE RUHR AND INFLATION. Inflation brought the major crisis of this period. The financing of the war and the continued postwar deficit spending generated an immense rise in prices. Consequently the value of German currency fell. By early 1921 the German mark traded against the American dollar at a ratio of 64 to 1, compared with a ratio of 4.2 to 1 in 1914. The German financial community contended that the value of the currency could not be stabilized until the reparations issue had been solved. In the meantime the printing presses kept pouring forth paper money, which was used to redeem government bonds as they fell due.

The French invasion of the Ruhr in January 1923 and the German response of economic passive resistance produced cataclysmic

During the hyper-inflation that followed the French occupation of the Rhineland, Germans found it cheaper to burn money than to spend it on fuel. [Library of Congress]

The French occupy the Rhineland, January 1923. [Bilderdienst Suddeutscher Verlag]

inflation. The Weimar government paid subsidies to the Ruhr labor force, who had laid down their tools. Unemployment soon spread from the Ruhr to other parts of the country, creating a new drain on the treasury and also reducing tax revenues. The printing presses by this point had difficulty providing enough paper currency to keep up with the daily rise in prices. In November 1923 an American dollar was worth more than 800 million German marks. Money was literally not worth the paper it was printed on. Stores were unwilling to exchange goods for the worthless currency, and farmers withheld produce from the market. The moral and social values of thrift and prudence were thoroughly undermined. The security of middle-class savings, pensions, and insurance policies was wiped out, as were investments in government bonds. Simultaneously debts and mortgages could be paid off. Speculators in land, real estate, and industry

Lilo Linke Recalls the Mad Days of the German Inflation

In 1923 the presses that were printing paper currency in Germany could hardly keep up with the rising prices. This memoir recounts the difficulties of those days and the resentments that arose as money became worth less than the paper on which it was printed.

The whole population had suddenly turned into maniacs. Everyone was buying, selling, speculating, bargaining, and dollar, dollar, dollar was the magic word which dominated every conversation, every newspaper, every poster in Germany. Nobody understood what was happening. There seemed to be no sense, no rules in the mad game, but one had to take part in it if one did not want to be trampled underfoot at once. Only a few people were able to carry through to the end and gain by the inflation. The majority lost everything and broke down, impoverished and bewildered.

The middle class was hurt more than any other, the savings of a lifetime and their small fortunes melted into a few coppers. They had to sell their most precious belongings for ten milliard inflated marks to buy a bit of food or an absolutely necessary coat, and their pride and dignity were bleeding out of many wounds. Bitterness remained for ever in their hearts. Full of hatred, they accused the international financiers, the Jews and Socialists—their old enemies—of having exploited their distress. They never forgot and never forgave and were the first to lend a willing ear to Hitler's fervent preaching.

In the shop, notices announced that we should receive our salaries in weekly parts, after a while we queued up at the cashier's desk every evening, and before long we were paid twice daily and ran out during the lunch hour to buy a few things, because as soon as the new rate of exchange became known in the early afternoon our money had again lost half its value.

Lilo Linke, *Restless Days* (New York: Knopf, 1935), pp. 131–132.

made great fortunes. Union contracts generally allowed workers to keep up with rising prices. Inflation thus was not a disaster to everyone. However, to the middle class and the lower middle class the inflation was still one more traumatic experience coming hard on the heels of the military defeat and the peace treaty. Only when the social and economic upheaval of these months is grasped can the later German desire for order and security at almost any cost be comprehended.

HITLER'S EARLY CAREER. Late in 1923 Adolf Hitler (1889–1945) made his first major appearance on the German political scene. In 1889 he had been born the son of a minor Austrian customs official. By 1907 he had gone to Vienna, where his hopes of becoming an artist were soon dashed. He lived off money sent by his widowed mother and later off his Austrian orphan's allowance. He also painted postcards for further income and later found work as a day laborer. In Vienna he became acquainted with Mayor Karl Lueger's Christian Social Party, which prospered on an ideology of anti-Semitism and from the social anxieties of the lower middle class. Hitler's own relatively precarious situation and his own social observations taught him how desperately the lower middle class feared slipping into a working-class condition. He also absorbed the rabid German nationalism and extreme anti-Semitism that flourished in Vienna. He came to hate Marxism, which he associated with Jews. During World War I Hitler fought in the German army, was wounded, was promoted to the rank of corporal, and was awarded the Iron Cross for bravery. The war gave him his first sense of purpose.

After the conflict Hitler settled in Munich. In the new surroundings he became associated with a small nationalistic, anti-Semitic political party that in 1920 adopted the name of National Socialist German Workers' Party, better

The National Socialist German Workers' Party Issues a Platform

These statements from the Nazi Party's Twenty-five Points of 1920 illustrate the calls for nationalism, territorial expansion, anti-Semitic public policy, and aid for the poor and the lower middle class that in time attracted broad support throughout Germany.

1. We demand the union of all Germans to form a Great Germany on the basis of self-determination enjoyed by nations.

2. We demand equality of rights for the German people in its dealings with other nations, and abolition of the peace treaties of Versailles and Saint-Germain.

3. We demand land and territory (colonies) for the nourishment of our people and for settling our excess population.

4. None but members of the nation may be citizens of the state. None but those of German blood, whatever their creed, may be members of the nation. No Jew, therefore, may be a member of the nation.

5. Anyone who is not a citizen of the state may live in Germany only as a guest and must be regarded as being subject to foreign laws.

. . . .

7. We demand that the state shall make it its first duty to promote the industry and livelihood of citizens of the state. If it is not possible to nourish the entire population of the state, foreign

nationals (non-citizens of the state) must be excluded from the Reich.

. . . .

10. It must be the first duty of each citizen of the state to work with his mind or with his body. The activities of the individual may not clash with the interests of the whole, but must proceed within the frame of the community and be for the general good.

. . . .

15. We demand extensive development of provision for old age.

16. We demand creation and maintenance of a healthy middle class, immediate communalization of wholesale business premises, and their lease at a cheap rate to small traders, and that extreme considerations shall be shown to all small purveyors to the state, district authorities, and smaller localities.

. . . .

22. We demand abolition of a paid army and formation of a national army.

. . . .

Raymond E. Murphy (Ed.), *National Socialism,* U.S. Department of State, Publication 1864 (Washington, 1943), pp. 222–224.

known simply as the Nazis. The same year, the group began to parade under a red banner with a black swastika. It issued a platform, or program, of Twenty-five Points. Among other things these called for the repudiation of the Versailles Treaty, the unification of Austria and Germany, the exclusion of Jews from German citizenship, agrarian reform, the prohibition of land speculation, the confiscation of war profits, state administration of the giant cartels, and the replacement of department stores with small retail shops. Originally the Nazis had called for a broad program of nationalization of industry in an attempt to compete directly with the Marxist political parties for the vote of the workers. As the tactic failed, the Nazis redefined the meaning of the word *socialist* in the

party name so that it suggested a *nationalistic* outlook. In 1922 Hitler said:

Whoever is prepared to make the national cause his own to such an extent that he knows no higher ideal than the welfare of his nation; whoever has understood our great national anthem, *Deutschland, Deutschland, über Alles* ["Germany, Germany, over All"], to mean that nothing in the wide world surpasses in his eyes this Germany, people and land, land and people—that man is a Socialist.[2]

This definition, of course, had nothing to do with traditional German socialism. The "socialism" that Hitler and the Nazis had in mind

[2]Alan Bullock, *Hitler: A Study in Tyranny,* rev. ed. (New York: Harper & Row, 1962), p. 76.

was not state ownership of the means of production but the subordination of all economic enterprise to the welfare of the nation. It often implied protection for very small economic enterprise. Increasingly over the years the Nazis discovered that their social appeal was to the lower middle class, which found itself squeezed between well-organized big business and socialist labor unions or political parties. The Nazis tailored their message to this very troubled economic group.

Soon after the promulgation of the Twenty-five Points, the storm troopers or SA (Sturmabteilung), were organized under the leadership of Captain Ernst Roehm. It was a paramilitary organization that initially provided its members with food and uniforms and later in the decade with wages. In the mid-1920s the SA adopted its famous brown-shirted uniform. The storm troopers were the chief Nazi instrument for terror and intimidation before the party came into control of the government. They were a law unto themselves. The organization constituted a means of preserving military discipline and values outside the small army permitted by the Paris settlement. The existence of such a private party army was a sign of the potential for violence in the Weimar Republic and the widespread contempt for the law and the institutions of the republic.

The social and economic turmoil following the French occupation of the Ruhr and the German inflation provided the fledgling party with an opportunity for direct action against the Weimar Republic, which at that point seemed incapable of providing military or economic security to the nation. By this time, because of his immense oratorical skills and organizational abilities, Hitler personally dominated the Nazi Party. On November 9, 1923, Hitler and a band of followers, accompanied by General Ludendorff, attempted an unsuccessful *Putsch* at a beer hall in Munich. When the local authorities crushed the rising, sixteen Nazis were killed. Hitler and Ludendorff were arrested and tried for treason. The general was acquitted. Hitler employed the trial to make himself into a national figure. In his defense he condemned the republic, the Versailles Treaty, the Jews, and the weakened condition of his adopted country. He was convicted and sentenced to five years in prison. He actually spent only a few months in jail before being paroled. During this time he wrote *Mein Kampf* ("My Struggle"). Another result of the brief imprisonment was a decision on Hitler's part that in

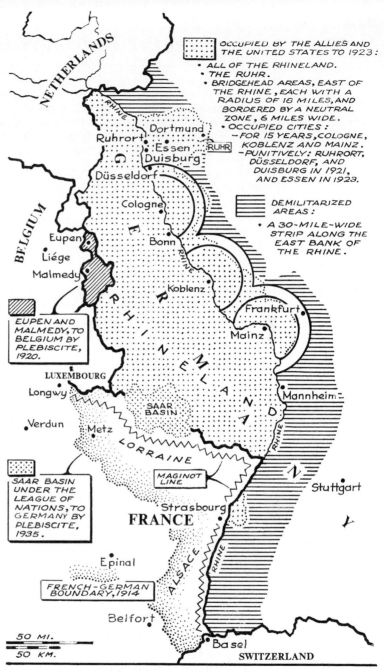

GERMANY'S
WESTERN FRONTIER

MAP 26–1 *The sensitive French-Belgian-German border area between the two world wars. In spite of efforts to restrain tension in the twenty-year period, there were persistent difficulties related to the Ruhr, Rhineland, Saar, and Eupen-Malmédy regions that necessitated strong defenses.*

Hitler Denounces the Versailles Treaty

One of the chief complaints of the National Socialist movement was the unfairness of the Versailles Treaty of 1919. Virtually all German public figures, including leaders of the Weimar Republic, hoped to see an eventual revision of that settlement, but Hitler and his followers made denunciation of the treaty their single most uncompromising demand. In this speech of April 17, 1923, Hitler explained how the treaty had undermined the German nation.

With the armistice begins the humiliation of Germany. If the Republic on the day of its foundation had appealed to the country: "Germans, stand together! Up and resist the foe! The Fatherland, the Republic expects of you that you fight to your last breath," then millions who are now the enemies of the Republic would be fanatical Republicans. To-day they are the foes of the Republic not because it is a Republic but because this Republic was founded at the moment when Germany was humiliated, because it so discredited the new flag that men's eyes must turn regretfully towards the old flag.

It was no Treaty of Peace which was signed, but a betrayal of Peace.

The Treaty was signed which demanded from Germany that she should perform what was for ever impossible of performance. But that was not the worst; after all that was only a question of material values. This was not the end: Commissions of Control were formed! For the first time in the history of the modern world there were planted on a State agents of foreign Powers to act as Hangmen, and German soldiers were set to serve the foreigner. And if one of these Commissions was "insulted," a company of the German army had to defile before the French flag. We no

longer feel the humiliation of such an act; but the outside world says, "What a people of curs!"

So long as this Treaty stands there can be no resurrection of the German people: no social reform of any kind is possible! The Treaty was made in order to bring 20 million Germans to their deaths and to ruin the German nation. But those who made the Treaty cannot set it aside. At its foundation our Movement formulated three demands:

1. Setting aside of the Peace Treaty.
2. Unification of all Germans.
3. Land and soil to feed our nation.

Our Movement could formulate these demands, since it was not our Movement which caused the War, it has not made the Republic, it did not sign the Peace Treaty.

There is thus one thing which is the first task of this Movement: it desires to make the German once more National, that his Fatherland shall stand for him above everything else. It desires to teach our people to understand afresh the truth of the old saying: He who will not be a hammer must be an anvil. An anvil are we today, and that anvil will be beaten until out of the anvil we fashion once more a hammer, a German sword!

Norman H. Baynes (Ed.), *The Speeches of Adolph Hitler, April 1922–1939* (Oxford: Oxford University Press, 1942).

the future he and his party must seek to seize political power by legal methods.

THE STRESEMANN YEARS. Elsewhere the officials of the republic were attempting to repair the damage from the inflation. Gustav Stresemann (1878–1929) was primarily responsible for the reconstruction of the republic and for its achievement of a sense of self-confidence. He served as chancellor only from August to November 1923, but he provided the nation with a new basis for stability. Strese-

mann abandoned the policy of passive resistance in the Ruhr. The country simply could not afford it. Then, with the aid of banker Hjalmar Schacht, he introduced a new German currency. The rate of exchange was one trillion of the old German marks for one new *Rentenmark*. Stresemann also moved against challenges from both the left and the right. He supported the crushing of both Hitler's abortive *Putsch* and smaller communist disturbances. In late November 1923 he resigned as chancellor and assumed the position of foreign minister, a

This picture of Adolf Hitler was taken in May 1927. He was not yet a major political figure, and the Nazi movement was relatively small. [*United Press International Photo*]

post that he held until his death in 1929. In that office he exercised considerable influence over the affairs of the republic.

In 1924 the Weimar Republic and the Allies agreed to a new systematization of the reparation payments. The Dawes Plan, submitted by the American banker Charles Dawes, lowered the annual payments and allowed them to fluctuate according to the fortunes of the German economy. The French were to evacuate the Ruhr, and the last French troops left that region in 1925. The same year Friedrich Ebert (1871–1925), the Social Democratic president of the republic, died. Field Marshal Paul von Hindenburg, a military hero and a conservative monarchist, was elected as his successor. He governed in strict accordance with the constitution, but his election suggested that a new conservative tenor had come to German politics. It looked as if conservative Germans had become reconciled to the republic. This conservatism was in line with the prosperity of the latter part of the decade. The new political and economic stability meant that foreign capital flowed into Germany, and employment, which had been poor throughout most of the postwar

years, improved smartly. Giant industrial combines spread. The prosperity helped to establish broader acceptance and appreciation of the republic.

In foreign affairs Stresemann pursued a conciliatory course. He was committed to a policy of fulfilling the provisions of the Versailles Treaty, even as he attempted to revise it by diplomacy. He was willing to accept the settlement in the west but was a determined, if sometimes secret, revisionist in the east. He aimed to recover German territories lost to Poland and Czechoslovakia and possibly to unite with Austria, chiefly by diplomatic means. The first step, however, was to achieve respectability and economic recovery. That goal required a policy of accommodation and "Fulfillment," for the moment at least.

LOCARNO. These developments gave rise to the Locarno Agreements of October 1925. The spirit of conciliation led politicians Austen Chamberlain for Britain and Aristide Briand for France to accept Stresemann's proposal for a fresh start. France and Germany both accepted the western frontier established at Ver-

923

The signing of the Locarno Agreements in October of 1925, which brought a new, if temporary, spirit of conciliation and hope to Europe. [*United Press International Photo*]

sailles as legitimate. Britain and Italy agreed to intervene against the aggressor if either side violated the frontier or if Germany sent troops into the demilitarized Rhineland. Significantly, no such agreement was made about Germany's eastern frontier, but the Germans made treaties of arbitration with Poland and Czechoslovakia, and France strengthened its ties with the Little Entente. France supported German membership in the League of Nations and agreed to withdraw its occupation troops from the Rhineland in 1930, five years earlier than specified at Versailles.

Germany was pleased to have achieved respectability and a guarantee against another Ruhr occupation, as well as the possibility of revision in the east. Britain was pleased to be allowed to play a more evenhanded role. Italy was glad to be recognized as a great power. The French were happy, too, because the Germans voluntarily accepted the permanence of their western frontier, which was also guaranteed by Britain and Italy, while France maintained

its allies in the east. As A. J. P. Taylor put it, "Any French statesman of 1914 could have been bewildered with delight by such an achievement."[3]

The Locarno Agreements brought a new spirit of hope to Europe. Germany's entry into the League of Nations was greeted with enthusiasm. Chamberlain, Briand, and Stresemann jointly received the Nobel Peace Prize in 1926. The spirit of Locarno was carried even further when the leading European states, Japan, and the United States signed the Kellogg–Briand Pact in 1928, renouncing "war as an instrument of national policy." The joy and optimism were not justified. France had merely recognized its inability to coerce Germany without help. Britain had shown its unwillingness to uphold the settlement in the east. Austen Chamberlain declared that no British government ever would "risk the bones of a British grenadier" for the Polish corridor. Ger-

[3]Taylor, p. 58.

many was by no means reconciled to the eastern settlement. It continued its clandestine military connections with the Soviet Union, which had begun with the Treaty of Rapallo, and planned to continue to press for revision.

In both France and Germany, moreover, the conciliatory politicians represented only a part of the nation. In Germany, especially, most people continued to reject Versailles and regarded Locarno as only an extension of it. When the Dawes Plan ran out in 1929, it was replaced by the Young Plan, named after the American businessman Owen D. Young, which lowered the reparation payments, put a term on how long they must be made, and removed Germany entirely from outside supervision and control. The intensity of the outcry in Germany against the continuation of any reparations showed how far the Germans were from accepting their situation. In spite of these problems, major war was by no means inevitable. Europe, aided by American loans, was returning to prosperity. German leaders like Stresemann would certainly have continued to press for change, but there is little reason to think that they would have resorted to force, much less to a general war. Continued prosperity and diplomatic success might have won the loyalty of the German people for the Weimar Republic and moderate revisionism, but the Great Depression of the 1930s brought new forces to power.

The Fascist Experiment in Italy

While its wartime allies continued to pursue parliamentary politics and its former enemies set out on the troubled path of democracy, Italy moved toward a new form of authoritarian government. From the Italian Fascist movement of Benito Mussolini (1883–1945) was derived the general term of *fascist*, which has frequently been used to describe the various right-wing dictatorships that arose between the wars.

The exact meaning of *fascism* as a political term remains much disputed among both historians and political scientists. However, a certain consensus does exist. The governments regarded as fascist were antidemocratic, anti-Marxist, antiparliamentary, and frequently anti-Semitic. They hoped to hold back the spread of Bolshevism, which seemed at the time a very real threat. They sought a world

safe for the middle class, small businesses, owners of moderate amounts of property, and small farmers. The fascist regimes rejected the political inheritance of the French Revolution and of nineteenth-century liberalism. Their adherents believed that normal parliamentary politics and parties sacrificed national honor and greatness to petty party disputes. They wanted to overcome the class conflict of Marxism and the party conflict of liberalism by consolidating the various groups and classes within the nation for great national purposes. As Mussolini declared in 1931, "The fascist conception of the state is all-embracing, and outside of the state no human or spiritual values can exist, let alone be desirable."[4] The fascist governments were usually single-party dictatorships characterized by terrorism and

[4]Quoted in Denis Mack Smith, *Italy: A Modern History* (Ann Arbor: University of Michigan Press, 1959), p. 412.

Mussolini was a powerful orator. His gestures, which often appear comic today, were part of a carefully cultivated image designed to make him appear the leader at all times. Here, for example, he poses bare-chested to speak to farmers after having helped harvest a field of grain. [*Ullstein Bilderdienst*]

police surveillance. These dictatorships were rooted in the base of mass political parties.

The Rise of Mussolini

The Italian *Fasci di Combattimento* ("Band of Combat") was founded in 1919 in Milan. Its members came largely from Italian war veterans who felt that the sacrifices of the conflict had been in vain. They resented the failure of Italy to gain the city of Fiume, toward the northern end of the Adriatic Sea, at the Paris conference. They feared socialism and inflation.

Their leader, Benito Mussolini, had been born the son of a blacksmith. For a time he had been a schoolteacher, then a day laborer. He became active in Italian socialist politics and by 1912 had become editor of the socialist newspaper *Avanti*. In 1914 Mussolini broke with the socialists and supported Italian entry into the war on the side of the Allies. His interventionist position lost him the editorship of *Avanti*. He then established his own paper, *Il Popolo d'Italia*. Later he served in the army and was wounded. In 1919, although of some prewar political stature, Mussolini was simply one of many Italian politicians. His *Fasci* organization was, for its part, simply one of numerous small political groups in a country characterized by such entities. As a politician Mussolini was an opportunist par excellence. He proved capable of changing his ideas and principles to suit every new occasion. Action for him was always more important than thought or rational justification. His one real rule was that of political survival.

Postwar Italian politics was a muddle. During the conflict the Italian Parliament had for all intents and purposes ceased to function. It had been quite willing to allow ministers to rule by decree. However, the parliamentary system as it then existed had begun to prove quite unsatisfactory to large sectors of the citizenry. Many Italians besides those in Mussolini's band of followers felt that Italy had emerged from the war as less than a victorious nation, had not been treated as a great power at the peace conference, and had not received the territories it deserved. The main spokesman for this discontent was the extreme nationalist poet and novelist Gabriele D'Annunzio (1863–1938). In 1919 he successfully led a force of patriotic Italians in an assault on Fiume. Troops of the Italian parliamentary government eventually drove him out. D'Annunzio

had provided the example of the political use of a nongovernmental military force. The action of the government in removing him from Fiume gave the parliamentary ministry a somewhat-less-than-patriotic appearance.

Between 1919 and 1921 Italy also experienced considerable internal social turmoil. Numerous industrial strikes occurred, and workers occupied factories. Peasants seized uncultivated land from large estates. Parliamentary and constitutional government seemed incapable of dealing with this unrest. The Socialist Party had captured a plurality of seats in the Chamber of Deputies during the 1919 election. A new Catholic Popular Party had also done quite well. Both appealed to the working and agrarian classes. However, neither party would cooperate with the other, and parliamentary deadlock resulted. Under these conditions many Italians honestly and still others conveniently believed that there existed the danger of a communist revolution.

Initially Mussolini was uncertain of the direction of the political winds. He first supported the factory occupations and land seizures. However, never one to be concerned with consistency, he soon reversed himself. He had discovered that large numbers of both upper-class and middle-class Italians who were pressured by inflation and who feared property loss had no sympathy for the workers or the peasants. They wanted order rather than some vague social justice that might harm their own interests. Consequently Mussolini and his Fascists took direct action in the face of the government inaction. They formed local squads of terrorists who disrupted Socialist Party meetings, mugged Socialist leaders, and terrorized Socialist supporters. They attacked strikers and farm workers and protected strikebreakers. Conservative land and factory owners were grateful. The officers and institutions of the law simply ignored the crimes of the Fascist squads. By early 1922 the Fascists had turned their intimidation through arson, beatings, and murder against local officials in cities such as Ferrara, Ravenna, and Milan. They controlled the local government in many parts of northern Italy.

In the election of 1921 Mussolini and thirty-four of his followers were sent to the Chamber of Deputies. Their importance grew as the local Fascists gained more direct power. The movement now had hundreds of thousands of supporters. In October 1922 the Fascists, dressed in their characteristic black shirts, began a

Scenes from the Fascist march on Rome in October 1922. When it was clear the king would not authorize force against them, the marchers, in their characteristic black shirts, posed for the friendly photographer. [United Press International Photo]

march on Rome. King Victor Emmanuel III (1900–1946), because of both personal and political fear, refused to sign a decree that would have authorized the use of the army against the marchers. Probably no other single decision so ensured a Fascist seizure of power. The Cabinet resigned in protest. On October 29 the monarch telegraphed Mussolini in Milan and asked him to become prime minister. The next day Mussolini arrived in Rome by sleeping car and greeted his followers as head of the government when they entered the city.

Technically Mussolini had come into office by legal means. The monarch did possess the power to appoint the prime minister. However, Mussolini had no majority or even near majority in the Chamber of Deputies. Behind the legal facade of his assumption of power lay the months of terrorist disruption and intimidation and the threat of the Fascist march itself. The non-Fascist politicians, whose ineptitude had prepared the way for Mussolini, believed that his regime, like others of previous months, would be temporary. They failed to comprehend that he was not a traditional Italian politician.

The Fascists in Power

Mussolini had not really expected to be appointed prime minister. He moved cautiously to shore up his support and to consolidate his power. His success was the result of the impotence of his rivals, his own effective use of his office, his power over the masses, and his sheer ruthlessness. On November 23, 1922, the king and Parliament granted Mussolini dictatorial authority for one year to bring order to the lower levels of the government. Wherever possible Mussolini appointed Fascists to office. Late in 1924, under Mussolini's guidance, the Parliament changed the election law. Previously parties had been represented in the Chamber of Deputies in proportion to the popular vote cast for them. According to the new election law, the party that gained the largest popular vote (with a minimum of at least 25 per cent) received two thirds of the seats in the chamber. Coalition government, with all its compromises and hesitant policies, would no longer be necessary. In the election of 1924 the Fascists won a great victory and complete control of the Chamber of Deputies. They used

927

Mussolini Heaps Contempt on Political Liberalism

The political tactics of the Italian Fascists wholly disregarded the liberal belief in the rule of law and the consent of the governed. In 1923 Mussolini explained why the Fascists so hated and repudiated these liberal principles. The reader should note his emphasis on the idea of the twentieth century as a new historical epoch requiring a new kind of politics and his undisguised praise of force in politics.

Liberalism is not the last word, nor does it represent the definitive formula on the subject of the art of government. . . . Liberalism is the product and the technique of the 19th century. . . . It does not follow that the Liberal scheme of government, good for the 19th century, for a century, that is, dominated by two such phenomena as the growth of capitalism and the strengthening of the sentiment of nationalism, should be adapted to the 20th century, which announces itself already with characteristics sufficiently different from those that marked the preceding century. . . .

I challenge Liberal gentlemen to tell if ever in history there has been a government that was based solely on popular consent and that renounced all use of force whatsoever. A government so constructed there has never been and never will be. Consent is an ever-changing thing like the shifting sand on the sea coast. It can never be permanent: It can never be complete. . . . If it be accepted as an axiom that any system of government whatever creates malcontents, how are you going to prevent this discontent from overflowing and constituting a menace to the stability of the State? You will prevent it by force. By the assembling of the greatest force possible. By the inexorable use of this force whenever it is necessary. Take away from any government whatsoever force—and by force is meant physical, armed force—and leave it only its immortal principles, and that government will be at the mercy of the first organized group that decides to overthrow it. Fascism now throws these lifeless theories out to rot. . . . The truth evident now to all who are not warped by [liberal] dogmatism is that men have tired of liberty. They have made an orgy of it. Liberty is today no longer the chaste and austere virgin for whom the generations of the first half of the last century fought and died. For the gallant, restless and bitter youth who face the dawn of a new history there are other words that exercise a far greater fascination, and those words are: order, hierarchy, discipline. . . .

Know then, once and for all, that Fascism knows no idols and worships no fetishes. It has already stepped over, and if it be necessary it will turn tranquilly and step again over, the more or less putrescent corpse of the Goddess of Liberty.

Benito Mussolini, "Force and Consent" (1923), as cited and trans. in Jonathan F. Scott and Alexander Baltzly, *Readings in European History Since 1814* (New York: F. S. Crofts, 1931), pp. 680–682.

that majority to end legitimate parliamentary life. A series of laws passed in 1925 and 1926 permitted Mussolini, in effect, to rule by decree. In 1926 all other political parties were dissolved. By the close of that year Italy had been transformed into a single-party dictatorial state.

Their growing dominance over the government had not, however, diverted the Fascists from their course of violence and terror. They were put in charge of the police force, and the terrorist squads became institutionalized into government militia. In late 1924 their thugs murdered Giacomo Matteotti (1885–1924), a major non-Communist socialist leader. He had persistently criticized Mussolini and had exposed the criminality of the Fascist movement. In protest against the murder, a number of opposition deputies withdrew from the Chamber of Deputies. That tactic gave the prime minister an even freer hand. The deputies were refused readmission.

The parallel organization of the party and the government sustained support for the regime. For every government institution there existed a corresponding party organization. In this manner the Fascist Party dominated the political structure at every level. When all other political parties were outlawed, the citizens had to look to the Fascists in their community for political favors. They also knew the high price of opposition. By the late 1920s the Grand Council of the party had become an organ of the state. It drew up and presented the list of persons who would stand for election to the Chamber of Deputies. Major policies to be approved by the chamber first passed the Grand Council. And Mussolini himself controlled the council.

The party used propaganda quite effectively. A cult of personality surrounded Mussolini. His skills in oratory and his general intelligence allowed him to hold his own with both large crowds and the leaders of the more respectable portions of the community. The latter tolerated and often admired him in the belief that he had saved them from Bolshevism. The persons who did have the courage to oppose Mussolini were usually driven into exile, and some were murdered.

The Italian dictator made one important domestic departure that brought him significant political dividends. Through the Lateran Accord of February 1929, the Roman Catholic church and the Italian state made peace with each other. Ever since the armies of Italian unification had seized papal lands in the 1860s, the church had been hostile to the state. The popes had remained virtual prisoners in the Vatican after 1870. The agreement of 1929 recognized the pope as the temporal ruler of Vatican City. The Italian government agreed to pay an indemnity to the papacy for confiscated land. The state also recognized Catholicism as the religion of the nation, exempted church property from taxes, and allowed church law to govern the institution of marriage. The Lateran Accord brought further respectability to Mussolini's authoritarian regime.

The Beginning of the Soviet Experiment

The political right had no monopoly on authoritarianism between the wars. The consolidation of the Bolshevik Revolution in Russia established the most extensive and durable of all twentieth-century authoritarian governments. However, the dictatorships of the left

The signing of the Lateran treaty, February 11, 1929. Cardinal Gasparri, the Vatican's Secretary of State is seated at the center; Mussolini is sitting on his left. [Bildarchiv Preussicher Kulturbesitz]

The Third International Issues Conditions of Membership

After the Russian Revolution, the Russian Communist Party organized the Third Communist International. Any communist party outside the Soviet Union was required to accept these Twenty-one Conditions, adopted in 1919, in order to join the International. In effect, this program demanded that all such parties adopt a distinctly revolutionary program and cease operating as legal parties within their various countries. By this means, the Soviet Union sought to achieve leadership of the socialist movement throughout Europe. As non-Russian socialist parties debated whether to join the Third International, they quickly split into social democratic parties that remained independent of Moscow and communist parties that adopted the policy imposed by the Russian Communist Party.

1. *The daily propaganda and agitation must bear a truly communist character and correspond to the program and all the decisions of the Third International. All the organs of the press that are in the hands of the party must be edited by reliable communists who have proved their loyalty to the cause of the proletarian revolution. . . .*

    .   .   .   .

3. *The class struggle in almost all of the countries of Europe and America is entering the phase of civil war. Under such conditions the communists can have no confidence in bourgeois law. They must* everywhere *create a parallel illegal apparatus, which at the decisive moment could assist the party in performing its duty of revolution. . . .*

4. *The obligation to spread communist ideas includes the particular necessity of persistent, systematic propaganda in the army. . . .*

5. *It is necessary to carry on systematic and steady agitation in the rural districts. . . .*

    .   .   .   .

7. *The parties desiring to belong to the Communist International must recognize the necessity of a complete and absolute rupture with reformism . . . , and they must carry on propaganda in favor of this rupture among the broadest circles of the party membership. . . .*

8. *. . . . Every party desirous of belonging to the Third International must ruthlessly denounce the methods of ''their own'' imperialists*

in the colonies, supporting, not in words, but in deeds, every independence movement in the colonies. . . .

    .   .   .   .

14. *Every party that desires to belong to the Communist International must give every possible support to the Soviet Republics in their struggle against all counterrevolutionary forces. . . .*

    .   .   .   .

16. *All decisions of the congresses of the Communist International . . . are binding on all parties affiliated to the Communist International. . . .*

17. *In connection with all this, all parties desiring to join the Communist International must change their names. Every party that wishes to join the Communist International must bear the name:* Communist party *of such-and-such country. This question as to name is not merely a formal one, but a political one of great importance. The Communist International has declared a decisive war against the entire bourgeois world and all the yellow social democratic parties. Every rank-and-file worker must clearly understand the difference between the communist parties and the old official ''social democratic'' or ''socialist'' parties which have betrayed the cause of the working class.*

18. *Members of the party who reject the conditions and thesis of the Communist International, on principle, must be expelled from the party.*

International Communism in the Era of Lenin: A Documentary History, ed. by Helmut Gruber (Garden City, N.Y.: Doubleday, 1972), pp. 241–246.

and the right did differ from each other. Unlike the Italian Fascists or the German National Socialists, the Bolsheviks had seized power illegally through revolution. For several years they confronted effective opposition, and their leaders long felt insecure about their hold on the country. The Communist Party was not a mass party nor a nationalistic one. Its early membership rarely exceeded 1 per cent of the Russian population. The Bolsheviks confronted a much less industrialized economy than existed in Italy or Germany. They believed in and practiced the collectivization of economic life attacked by the right-wing dictatorships. The Marxist-Leninist ideology was far more all-encompassing than the nationalism of the Fascists and the racism of the Nazis. Communism was an exportable commodity. The Communists regarded their government and their revolution not as local events in a national history but as epoch-making events in the history of the world and the development of humanity.

The Third International

The policies of the early Russian Communist Revolution directly and importantly affected the rise of the Fascists and the Nazis in western Europe. The success of the revolution in Russia had the paradoxical effect of dividing socialist parties and socialist movements in the rest of Europe. In 1919 the Soviet Communists founded the Third International of the European socialist movement. It became better known as the Comintern. A year after its inception the Comintern imposed its Twenty-one Conditions on any other socialist party that wished to become a member. The conditions included acknowledgment of leadership from Moscow, rejection of reformist or revisionist socialism, and repudiation of previous socialist leaders. The Comintern wished to make the Russian model of socialism, as developed by Lenin, the rule for all socialist parties outside the Soviet Union.

The decision whether to join or not to join the Comintern under these conditions split every major socialist party on the Continent. As a result, separate communist parties and social democratic parties emerged. The former modeled themselves after the Soviet party and pursued policies dictated by Moscow. The social democratic parties attempted to pursue both social reform and liberal parliamentary politics. Throughout the 1920s and early 1930s the communists and the social democrats

Lenin addressing a May Day demonstration in Moscow in 1918. [Culver Pictures]

tended to fight each other more intensely than they fought either capitalism or conservative political parties. This division of the European political left meant that right-wing political movements rarely had to confront a united opposition on the political left.

War Communism

Within the Soviet Union the Red Army under the organizational genius of Leon Trotsky (1879–1940) had suppressed internal and foreign military opposition to the new government. Within months of the revolution a new secret police, known as *Cheka*, appeared. Throughout the civil war Lenin had declared that the Bolshevik Party, as the vanguard of the revolution, was imposing the dictatorship of the proletariat. Political and economic administration became highly centralized. All major decisions flowed from the top in a nondemocratic manner. Under the economic policy of "War Communism" the revolutionary government confiscated and then operated the banks, the transport facilities, and heavy industry. The state also forcibly requisitioned grain produced

931

Lenin and Trotsky (saluting) in Red Square in Moscow in 1919, from a documentary film made by Herman Axelbank. Trotsky's organizational skill was largely responsible for the Red Army's victory in the Russian Civil War of 1918–1920. [*United Press International Photo*]

by the peasants and shipped it from the countryside to feed the army and the workers in the cities. The fact of the civil war permitted suppression of possible resistance to this economic policy.

"War Communism" aided the victory of the Red Army over its opponents. The revolution had survived and triumphed. However, the policy generated domestic opposition to the Bolsheviks, who in 1920 numbered only about 600,000 members. The alliance of workers and peasants forged by the slogan of "Peace, Bread, and Land" had begun to come apart at the seams. Many Russians were no longer willing to make the sacrifices demanded by the central party bureaucrats. In 1920 and 1921 major strikes occurred in numerous factories. Peasants were discontented and resisted the requisition of grain. In March 1921 the navy mutinied at Kronstadt. The Red Army crushed the rebellion with grave loss of life. Each of these incidents suggested that the proletariat itself was opposing the dictatorship of the proletariat. Also, by late 1920 it had become clear that further revolution would not sweep across the rest of Europe. For the time being, the Soviet Union would constitute a vast island of revolutionary socialism in the larger sea of worldwide capitalism.

The New Economic Policy

Under these difficult conditions Lenin made a crucial strategic retreat. In March 1921, following the Kronstadt mutiny, he outlined the New Economic Policy, normally referred to as *NEP*. Apart from what he termed "the commanding heights" of banking, heavy industry, transportation, and international commerce, there was to be considerable private economic enterprise. In particular, peasants were to be permitted to farm for a profit. They would pay taxes like other citizens, but they could sell their surplus grain on the open market. The NEP was in line with Lenin's earlier conviction that the Russian peasantry held the key to the success of revolution in the nation. After 1921 the countryside did become more stable, and a secure food supply seemed assured for the cities. Similar free enterprise flourished within light industry and domestic retail trade. By 1927 industrial production had reached its 1913 level. The revolution seemed to have transformed Russia into a land of small family farms and small, privately owned shops and businesses.

Stalin Versus Trotsky

The New Economic Policy had caused sharp disputes within the Politburo, the highest governing committee of the Communist Party. The partial return to capitalism seemed to some members nothing less than a betrayal of sound Marxist principles. These frictions increased as Lenin's firm hand disappeared. In 1922 he suffered a stroke that broke his health. He returned to work but never again dominated party affairs. In 1924 Lenin died. As the power vacuum developed, an intense struggle for future leadership of the party began. Two factions emerged. One was led by Trotsky; the other by Joseph Stalin (1879–1953), who had become general secretary of the party in 1922. Shortly before his death Lenin had criticized both men. He was especially harsh toward Stalin. However, the general secretary's base of power lay with the party membership and with the daily management of party affairs. Consequently he was able to withstand the posthumous strictures of Lenin.

The issue between the two factions was power within the party, but the struggle was fought out over the question of Russia's path toward industrialization and the future of the communist revolutionary movement. Trotsky, speaking for what became known as the left wing, urged rapid industrialization financed through the expropriation of farm production. Agriculture should be collectivized, and the peasants should be made to pay for industrialization. Trotsky further argued that the revolution in Russia could succeed only if new revolutions took place elsewhere in the world. Russia needed the skills and wealth of other nations to build its own economy. As Trotsky's influence within the party began to wane, he also demanded that party members be permitted to criticize the policies of the government and the party. However, Trotsky was very much a latecomer to the advocacy of open discussion. When in control of the Red Army, he had been known as an unflinching disciplinarian.

A right-wing faction opposed Trotsky. Its chief ideological voice was that of Nikolai Buk-

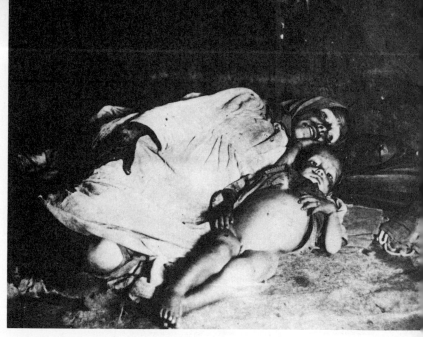

Victims of the Russian famine, 1921. Between 1918 and 1921 an estimated seven million Russians died from hunger or sickness. The famine was particularly severe during the winter of 1920–1921, when only massive relief from the United States prevented even more people from starving. Lenin's New Economic Policy, which sought to stimulate food production, was a reaction to these conditions. [Library of Congress]

MAJOR POLITICAL EVENTS OF THE 1920s	
(August) Constitution of the Weimar Republic promulgated	1919
Kapp *Putsch* in Berlin	1920
(March) Kronstadt mutiny leads Lenin to initiate his New Economic Policy	1921
(December) Treaty between Great Britain and the Irish Free State	1921
(April) Treaty of Rapallo between Germany and the Soviet Union	1922
(October) Fascist March on Rome leads to Mussolini's assumption of power	1922
(January) France invades the Ruhr	1923
(November) Hitler's Beer Hall *Putsch*	1923
(December) First Labour Party government in Britain	1923
Death of Lenin	1924
Locarno Agreements	1925
General strike in Britain	1926
Kellogg–Briand Pact	1928
(January) Trotsky expelled from the Soviet Union	1929
(February) Lateran Accord between the Vatican and the Italian state	1929

harin (1888–1938), the editor of *Pravda*, the official party paper. Stalin was the major political manipulator. In the mid-1920s this group pressed for the continuation of Lenin's NEP and a policy of relatively slow industrialization. Stalin emerged as the victor in these intraparty rivalries.

Stalin had been born in 1879 into a very poor family. Unlike the other early Bolshevik leaders, he had not spent a long period of exile in western Europe. He was much less an intellectual and internationalist. He was also much more brutal. His handling of various recalcitrant national groups within Russia after the revolution had shocked even Lenin. Stalin's power lay in his command of bureaucratic and administrative methods. He was neither a brilliant writer nor an effective public speaker; however, he mastered the crucial, if dull, details of party structure, including admission and promotion. That mastery meant that he could draw on the support of the lower levels of the party apparatus when he came into conflict with other leaders.

In the middle of the decade Stalin supported Bukharin's position on economic develop-

Lenin and Stalin in the summer of 1922, after Stalin's appointment as General Secretary of the Communist Party. The following December Lenin suffered a paralytic stroke and was unable to check Stalin's increasing dominance of party affairs. Lenin died in January 1924.

ment. In 1924 he also enunciated, in opposition to Trotsky, the doctrine of "socialism in one country." He urged that socialism could be achieved in Russia alone. Russian success did not depend on the fate of the revolution elsewhere. In this manner Stalin nationalized the previously international scope of the Marxist revolution. Stalin cunningly used the apparatus of the party and his control over the Central Committee of the Communist Party to edge out Trotsky and his supporters. By 1927 Trotsky had been removed from all his offices, expelled from the party, and exiled to Siberia. In 1929 he was sent out of Russia and eventually took up residence in Mexico, where he was murdered in 1940, presumably by one of Stalin's agents. With the removal of Trotsky from all positions of influence, Stalin was firmly in control of the Soviet state. It remained to be seen where he would direct its course and what "socialism in one country" would mean in practice.

Results of the Decade of Experiment

At the close of the 1920s it appeared that Europe had finally emerged from the difficulties of the World War I era. The initial resentments over the peace settlement seemed to have abated. The major powers were cooperating. Democracy was still functioning in Germany. The Labour Party was about to form its second ministry in Britain. France had settled into a less assertive international role. Mussolini's Fascism seemed to have little relevance to the rest of the Continent. The successor states had not fulfilled the democratic hopes of the Paris conference, but their troubles seemed their own. The Soviet Union, though still harboring a communist menace, stood largely withdrawn into its own internal development and power struggles.

The European economy seemed finally to be on an even keel. The frightening inflation was over, and unemployment had eased. American capital was flowing into the Continent. The reparations payments had been systematized by the Young Plan. Yet both this economic and this political stability proved illusory and temporary. What brought them to an end was the deepest economic depression in the modern history of the West. As the governments and electorates responded to the economic collapse, the search for liberty gave way in more than one instance to a search for security. The political experiments of the 1920s gave way to the political tragedies of the 1930s.

Suggested Readings

D. H. ALDCROFT, *From Versailles to Wall Street: The International Economy in the* 1920s (1976). A useful introduction.

R. BESSEL, *Political Violence and the Rise of Nazism: The Storm Troopers in Eastern Germany,* 1925–1934 (1984). A study of the uses of violence by the Nazis.

K. D. BRACHER, *The German Dictatorship* (1970). A comprehensive treatment of both the origins and the functioning of the Nazi movement and government.

A. BULLOCK, *Hitler: A Study in Tyranny,* rev. ed. (1964). The best biography.

E. H. CARR, *A History of Soviet Russia,* 9 vols. (1950–19—). An extensive and important study.

S. F. COHEN, *Bukharin and the Bolshevik Revolution: A Political Biography,* 1888–1938 (1973). An interesting examination of Stalin's chief opponent on the Communist right.

R. DAHRENDORF, *Society and Democracy in Germany* (1967). An important commentary by a leading sociologist.

I. DEUTSCHER, *The Prophet Armed* (1954), *The Prophet Unarmed* (1959), and *The Prophet Outcast* (1963). A major biography of Trotsky.

E. EYCK, *A History of the Weimar Republic,* 2 vols. (trans. 1963). The story as narrated by a liberal.

L. FISCHER, *The Life of Lenin* (1964). A sound biography by an American journalist.

P. FUSSELL, *The Great War and Modern Memory* (1975). A brilliant account of the literature arising from World War I during the 1920s.

P. GAY, *Weimar Culture; The Outsider as Insider* (1968). A sensitive analysis of the intellectual life of Weimar.

H. J. GORDON, *Hitler and the Beer Hall Putsch* (1972). An excellent account of the event and the political situation in the early Weimar Republic.

N. GREENE, *From Versailles to Vichy: The Third Republic,* 1919–1940 (1970). A useful introduction to a difficult subject.

H. GRUBER, *International Communism in the Era of Lenin: A Documentary History* (1967). An excellent collection of otherwise difficult-to-find documents.

C. A. MACARTNEY AND A. W. PALMER, *Independent Eastern Europe: A History* (1962). The best one-volume survey.

C. S. MAIER, *Recasting Bourgeois Europe: Stabilization in France, Germany, and Italy in the Decade after World War I* (1975). An important interpretation written from a comparative standpoint.

A. MARWICK, *The Deluge: British Society and the First World War* (1965). Full of insights into both major and more subtle minor social changes.

E. NOLTE, *Three Faces of Fascism* (1963). An important, influential, and difficult work on France, Italy, and Germany.

R. PIPES, *The Formation of the Soviet Union,* 2nd ed. (1964). A study of internal policy with emphasis on Soviet minorities.

H. ROGGER AND E. WEBER (Eds.), *The European Right: A Historical Profile* (1965). An anthology of articles on right-wing political movements in various European countries.

S. A. SCHUKER, *The End of French Predominance in Europe: The Financial Crisis of 1924 and the Adoption of the Dawes Plan* (1976). An excellent study of a very complicated issue.

C. SETON-WATSON, *Italy from Liberalism to Fascism,* 1870–1925 (1967). A useful survey.

H. SETON-WATSON, *Eastern Europe Between the Wars,* 1918–1941 (1946). Somewhat dated but still a useful work.

D. P. SILVERMAN, *Reconstructing Europe after the Great War* (1982). Examines the difficulties confronted by the major powers.

D. MACK SMITH, *Italy: A Modern History,* rev. ed. (1969). Very good chapters on the Fascists and Mussolini.

R. J. SONTAG, *A Broken World,* 1919–1939 (1971). An exceptionally thoughtful and well-organized survey.

M. STEINBERG, *Sabers and Brownshirts: The German Students' Path to National Socialism,* 1918–1935 (1977). An interesting study of the recruitment of young Germans.

A. J. P. TAYLOR, *English History,* 1914–1945 (1965). Lively and opinionated.

M. TRACTENBERG, *Reparations in World Politics: France and European Economic Diplomacy,* 1916–1923 (1980). Points to the special role of reparations in French calculations.

R. TUCKER, *Stalin as Revolutionary,* 1879–1929: *A Study in History and Personality* (1973). A useful and readable account of Stalin's rise to power.

N. TUMARKIN, *Lenin Lives: The Lenin Cult in Soviet Russia* (1983). An interesting work on the uses of Lenin's reputation after his death.

H. A. TURNER, JR. (Ed.), *Reappraisals of Fascism* (1975). A collection of very important articles on Fascist movements.

T. WILSON, *The Downfall of the Liberal Party,* 1914–1935 (1966). A close examination of the surprising demise of a political party in Britain.

E. WISKEMANN, *Fascism in Italy: Its Development and Influence* (1969). A comprehensive treatment.

R. WOHL, *The Generation of 1914* (1979). An important work that explores the effect of the war on political and social thought.

For works on diplomatic developments, see end of Chapter 29.

Adolf Hitler (1889–1945) at a Nazi party rally in Nuremburg in 1934. [*National Archives*]

IN EUROPE, unlike in the United States, the 1920s had not been "roaring." Economically they had been a decade of much insecurity, of a search for elusive stability, of a short-lived upswing, and then of collapse in finance and production. The Depression that began in 1929 was the most severe downturn ever experienced by the capitalist economies. The unemployment, low production levels, financial instability, and contracted trade arrived and would not depart. Marxists thought that the final downfall of capitalism was at hand. Capitalist businessmen and political leaders despaired over the failure of the market mechanism to save them. Voters looked for new ways out of the doldrums and politicians sought escapes from the pressures that the Depression had brought on them. One result of the fight for economic security was the establishment of the Nazi dictatorship in Germany. Another was the piecemeal construction of what has since become known as the *mixed economy*; that is, governments became directly involved in economic decisions. In both cases most of the political and economic guidelines of nineteenth-century liberalism were abandoned for good. Two other casualties of these years were decency and civility in political life.

27

Europe and the Depression of the 1930s

Toward the Great Depression

Three factors combined to bring about the intense severity and the extended length of the Depression. There was a financial crisis that stemmed directly from the war and the peace settlement. To this was added a crisis in the production and distribution of goods in the world market. These two problems became intertwined in 1929, and as far as Europe was concerned, they reached the breaking point in 1931. Finally, both of these difficulties became worse than might have been necessary because of the absence of strong economic leadership and responsibility on the part of any major west European country or the United States. Without cooperation or leadership in the Atlantic economic community, the economic collapse in finance and production simply lingered and deepened.

The Financial Tailspin

Most European nations emerged from World War I with inflated currencies. Immediately after the armistice the unleashed demand for

Crowds gathered on Wall Street in New York on October 29, 1929, the day the Stock Market crashed. The Depression in the United States meant that no American capital was available to loan to Europe. [Brown Brothers]

consumer and industrial goods continued to drive up prices. The price and wage increases generally subsided after 1921, but the problem of maintaining the value of their currencies still haunted political leaders—and even more after the German financial disaster of 1923. This frightening experience accounted in part for the refusal of most governments to run budget deficits when the Depression struck. They feared inflation as a political danger in the same manner that European governments since World War II have feared unemployment.

The problems of reparation payments and international war-debt settlement further complicated the picture. France and the United States provided the stumbling blocks in these matters. France had paid reparations as a defeated nation after 1815 and 1871. As a victor it now intended to receive reparations and to finance its postwar recovery through them.

The 1923 invasion of the Ruhr demonstrated French determination on this question.

The United States was no less determined to receive repayments of the wartime loans extended to its allies. There were also various debts that the European Allies owed to each other. It soon became apparent that German reparations were to provide the means of repaying the American and other Allied debts. Most of the money that the Allies collected from each other also went to the United States.

In 1922 Great Britain announced that it would collect payment on its own debts only to the extent that the United States required payments from Britain. However, the American government would not relent. The reparations and the war debts made normal business, capital investment, and international trade very difficult and expensive for the European nations. Various modes of government controls were exercised over credit, trade, and currency.

Speculation in currency drew funds away from capital investment in productive enterprise. The monetary problems served to reinforce the general tendency toward high tariff policies. If a nation imported too many goods from abroad, it might have difficulty meeting those costs and the expenses of debt or reparations payments. The financial and money muddle thus discouraged trade and production and, in turn, harmed employment.

In 1924 the Dawes Plan brought more system to the administration and transfer of reparations. Those procedures, in turn, smoothed the debt repayments to the United States. Thereafter large amounts of private American capital flowed into Europe and especially into Germany. Much of this money, which provided the basis for Europe's brief prosperity after 1925, was in the form of short-term loans. In 1928 this lending began to contract as American money became diverted from European investments into the booming New York stock market. The crash of Wall Street in October 1929—the result of virtually unregulated financial speculation—saw the loss of large amounts of money. United States banks had made very large loans to customers who then invested the money in the stock market. When stock prices fell, the customers could not repay the banks. Consequently, within the United States there occurred a major contraction of all kinds of credit, and numerous banks failed. Thereafter little American capital was available for investment in Europe. Furthermore loans already made to Europeans were not renewed, as American banks used their available funds to cover domestic shortages.

As the credit to Europe began to run out, a major financial crisis struck the continent. In May 1931 the Kreditanstalt, a major bank in Vienna, collapsed. It was a primary lending institution for much of central and eastern Europe. The German banking system came under severe pressure and was saved only through government guarantees. However, it became clear that under this crisis situation Germany would be unable to make its next reparation payment as stipulated in the 1929 Young Plan. As the German difficulties reached such large proportions, American President Herbert Hoover announced in June 1931 a one-year moratorium on all payments of international debts. The Hoover moratorium was a prelude to the end of reparations. Hoover's action was a sharp blow to the French economy, for which reparations had continued to be important. The French agreed to the moratorium most reluctantly but really had little alternative because the German economy was in a state of virtual collapse. The Lausanne Conference of the summer of 1932 in effect brought the era of reparations to a close. The next year the debts owed to the United States were settled either through small token payments or simply through default. Nevertheless the financial politics of the 1920s had done its damage.

Problems in Agricultural Commodities

In addition to the dramatic financial turmoil and collapse there was also a less dramatic, but equally fundamental, downturn in production and trade. The 1920s witnessed a contraction in the market demand for European goods relative to the continent's productive capacity. Part of this problem originated within Europe and part outside. In both instances the difficulty arose from agriculture. Better methods of farming, improved strains of wheat, expanded tillage, and more extensive transport facilities all over the globe vastly increased the quantity of grain produced. World wheat prices fell to record lows. This development was, of course, initially good for consumers. However, it meant lower incomes for European farmers and especially for those of central and eastern Europe. At the same time higher industrial wages raised the cost of the industrial goods used by the farmer or peasant. The farmers could not purchase those products. Moreover farmers began to have difficulty paying off their mortgages and normal annual operation debts. They borrowed money to plant their fields, expecting to pay the debt when the crops were sold. The fall in commodity prices raised problems of repayment.

The difficulties of agricultural finance became especially pressing in eastern Europe. Immediately after the war numerous land-reform programs had been undertaken in this region. The democratic franchise in the successor states had opened the way for considerable redistribution of tillable soil. In Romania and Czechoslovakia large amounts of land changed hands. This occurred to a lesser extent in Hungary and Poland. However, the new relatively small farmers proved to be inefficient and were unable to earn sufficient incomes. Protective tariffs often prevented the export of grain among European countries. The credit and cost squeeze on east European farmers and on their counterparts in Germany played a major role

The League of Nations Reports the Collapse of European Agriculture

A crisis in agriculture was as much a cause of the Depression as was the turmoil in the financial community. The League of Nations reported in 1931 how, in part, the desperate situation in agriculture had developed.

It is the lowness of prices that constitutes the agricultural crisis. It is becoming difficult to sell products, and in many cases prices have reached a level at which they are scarcely, if at all, sufficient to cover the cost of production.

The reason for the crisis and for its continuance is to be found in the fact that agricultural prices are low in comparison with the expenditure which the farmer must meet. . . . Agricultural products cost a lot to produce and then fetch very little in the market. In spite of the great technical progress achieved, operating costs remain implacably higher than selling prices, farmers obtain no longer a fair return on their labour or on their capital. Frequently the returns of agricultural undertakings are not enough to cover the necessary outlay for the purchase of the material or products necessary for continued operation or for the payment of wages and taxes and so forth.

This disproportion between the income and expenditure of agricultural undertakings . . . appears to constitute the dominant and decisive element of the prevailing agricultural depression.

Until 1929, prices were low as compared with prices of industrial products, but were above prewar prices. The predominating tendency to a fall which was observed was not altogether general nor was it abnormally rapid. The general character of the price movement completely changed in 1930. A fall, sometimes catastrophic, spread with extreme violence to almost all agricultural produce. It was so rapid that at the end of the year, whilst some products reached the pre-war level of prices, others fell as low as one-quarter or one-half below the 1913 level. . . . Farmers throughout the world have suffered from it.

League of Nations, Economic Committee, *The Agricultural Crisis*, Vol. 1 (1931), pp. 7–8, reprinted in S. B. Clough, T. Moodie, and C. G. Moodie, *Economic History of Europe: The Twentieth Century* (New York: Harper & Row, 1968), pp. 216–217.

in their disillusionment with liberal politics. For example, in Germany farmers provided the Nazis with a major source of political support.

Outside Europe similar problems affected other producers of agricultural commodities. The prices that they received for their products plummeted. Government-held reserves accumulated to record levels. This glut of major world commodities involved the supplies of wheat, sugar, coffee, rubber, wool, and lard. The people who produced these goods in underdeveloped nations could no longer make enough money to buy finished goods from industrial Europe. As world credit collapsed, the economic position of these commodity producers became all the worse. Commodity production had simply outstripped world demand.

The result of the collapse in the agricultural sector of the world economy and the financial turmoil was stagnation and depression for European industry. Coal, iron, and textiles had depended largely on international markets. Unemployment spread from these industries to those producing finished consumer goods. The persistent unemployment of Great Britain and to a lesser extent of Germany during the 1920s had already meant "soft" domestic markets. The policies of reduced government spending with which the governments confronted the Depression further weakened domestic demand. By the early 1930s the Depression was growing on itself.

Areas of Growth Within the Depressed Economies

Despite the Depression, some economic growth did take place between the wars. Depression did not mean economic regression. The economic growth was spotty, unsteady, and concentrated in special areas. Three of these industries deserve brief mention. They were radios, automobiles, and synthetic goods. The technological basis for each of them had been developed before World War I, but their major impact on the economy occurred afterward.

RADIO. Radio and radio technology came of age in the 1920s and 1930s. The wartime requirements for communication had speeded up the development and the production of the wireless. In 1922 broadcasting facilities had been established in Britain. The nationalized British Broadcasting Corporation was organized in 1926. Other radio broadcasting facilities spread across the Continent during the same years. The radio was a consumer gadget of the first order. The expanding electrical systems made its use possible. The radio itself was sold and then required other businesses to supply service parts. The radio industry, in turn, expanded the scope and transformed the na-

ture of advertising. By the end of the 1920s millions of radios were in European homes. It was a product bought not by the wealthy, who had various other modes of leisure, but by the relatively poor and middle-class groups of the population. It was the first product of sophisticated electrical technology to capture the mass market. Radio—like its successor, television—transformed European life and tended to produce a more nearly uniform culture. Radio also helped to make the propaganda programs of the authoritarian states possible.

AUTOMOBILES. Automobiles were a second interwar growth industry. Only during those years did the motor car become a product of widespread consumption. In France Louis Renault and André Citroën built cars that the middle class wanted and could afford to buy. The automobile revolutionized European life rather less than it did American life. But the auto did bring new mobility and also possessed obvious military uses. Its production called forth new demand for steel, glass, rubber, petroleum, and highways. The automobile, like

---

George Orwell Observes a Woman in the Slums

Although Great Britain was beginning to emerge from the Great Depression by the late 1930s, much poverty and human degradation remained. This scene, described in 1937 by the social critic and novelist George Orwell (1903–1950), captures a glimpse of the sadness and hopelessness that many British citizens experienced every day of their lives.

The train bore me away, through the monstrous scenery of slag-heaps, chimneys, piled scrap-iron, foul canals, paths of cindery mud crisscrossed by the prints of clogs. . . . As we moved slowly through the outskirts of the town we passed row after row of little grey slum houses running at right angles to the embankment. At the back of one of the houses a young woman was kneeling on the stones, poking a stick up the leaden waste-pipe which ran from the sink inside, and which I suppose was blocked. I had time to see everything about her—her sacking apron, her clumsy clogs, her arms reddened by the cold. . . . She had a round pale face, the usual exhausted face of the slum girl who is *twenty-five and looks forty, thanks to miscarriages and drudgery; and it wore, for the second in which I saw it, the most desolate, hopeless expression I have ever seen. It struck me then that we are mistaken when we say that "It isn't the same for them as it would be for us," and that people bred in the slums can imagine nothing but the slums. For what I saw in her face was not the ignorant suffering of an animal. She knew well enough what was happening to her—understood as well as I did how dreadful a destiny it was to be kneeling there in the bitter cold, on the slimy stones of a slum backyard, poking a stick up a foul drain-pipe.*

George Orwell, *The Road to Wigan Pier* (New York: Berkley Medallion Books, 1967; originally printed in 1937), p. 29.

Motor Cars Become More Popular in France

The Depression came to France later than to other countries. During the late 1920s and early 1930s the motor-car industry grew. More French citizens drove cars, and the manufacture of cars became more standardized. This passage from a report on the French economy describes this development and emphasizes the desire of French consumers to have real choices in regard to motor-car styles.

Nearly twelve times as many passenger cars are in use today in France as there were in 1913, the number of registered or tax-paying passenger cars having grown from 107,857 in that year to 1,279,142 at the end of 1932; since 1928, when the number was 757,668, the increase has been over half a million. . . .

In the French motor-car industry noteworthy progress has been made in standardization during the last seven years. The industry is one in which there was particular scope for the introduction of some form of standardization, for owing to the multiplicity of small manufacturers (50 or more of whom produced between them only about 10 per cent of the total output of the country, each seeking to strike a note of individuality), there was an inevitable tendency towards an unduly large variety of designs and dimensions, even of the most ordinary parts. A normalization bureau was set up in 1926 by the association of accessory and spare parts manufacturers, and by 1928 standards had been established for 29 parts, resulting in price reductions, in some cases, of 86 to 95 per cent. For instance, the number of different types of caps for radiators and petrol tanks has been reduced from 88 to five. . . .

Government departments and public utility concerns, such as the Ministry of War and the motor transport concession holders working in collaboration with the railways, are lending useful support to the normalization movement by inserting a clause in their specifications requiring suppliers of vehicles to employ only parts conforming to the accepted standards. . . .

The tendency towards standardization was further manifested about 1929, by a fairly general decision of leading French motor-car manufacturers, whereby each firm concentrated its energies on two or three types of cars, instead of trying to cater for the whole range of motor-car users, private and industrial; the Citroën and Peugeot firms, in particular, being prominent protagonists of the new policy. The individualistic French temperament, however, proved itself too strong for this policy to be followed for long; and at the motor shows of 1931–1933 a reversion to the former practice of putting on the markets as many different types of cars as each producer thought he had a chance of selling, was clearly apparent.

J. R. Cahill, *Economic Conditions in France* (London: 1934), pp. 253, 257–258, as cited in Sidney Pollard and Colin Holmes, *Documents of European Economic History*, Vol. 3 (London; Edward Arnold, 1973), pp. 587–588.

the radio, required a sales and service—as well as a production—industry.

SYNTHETICS. During these years the production of synthetic goods began to assume major economic significance. Rayon, invented before World War I, led the way in this area. Its production and consumption for hose and underwear grew rapidly. The product itself was soon much improved through the acetate process. Rayon began to replace cotton as the cheap textile for everyday use. The production of this synthetic fabric proved especially attractive to governments, such as those of Germany and Italy, that sought economic self-sufficiency. The prospect of war in the late 1930s led various governments to encourage the chemical industries to search for other synthetic substances that might replace natural products if foreign sources for the latter were shut off.

Depression and Government Policy

It is important to remember these areas of industrial expansion between the wars. The

A Citroen automobile of the late 1920s with Michelin tires. In the interwar period, France had more private automobiles than any other country except the United States. [Bilderdienst Suddeutscher Verlag]

Depression did not mean absolute economic decline. Nor did it mean that everyone was out of a job. The numbers of employed always well exceeded those without work. What the economic downturn did mean was the spread of actual or potential insecurity. People in nearly all walks of life feared that their own economic security and lifestyle might be the next to go. The Depression also brought on a frustration of social and economic expectations. People with jobs frequently improved their standard of living or received promotion much more slowly than they might have under sound economic conditions. Although they were employed, they seemed in their own eyes to be going nowhere. Their anxieties created a major source of social discontent.

The governments of the late 1920s and the early 1930s were not particularly well fitted in either structure or ideology to confront these problems. The demand from the electorates was to do something. What the government did depended in large measure on the severity of the Depression in a particular country and the self-confidence of the nation's political system. The Keynesian theory of governments' spending the economy out of Depression was not yet available. John Maynard Keynes's *General Theory of Employment, Interest, and Money* was not published until 1936. The orthodox economic policy of the day called for cuts in government spending so as to prevent inflation. It was then expected that eventually the market mechanism would bring the economy back to prosperity. However, the length and severity of the Depression, plus the possibility of direct democratic political pressure, led governments across Europe to interfere with the economy as never before.

Government participation in economic life was not new. One need only recall the policies of mercantilism and the government encouragement of railway building. But from the early 1930s onward, government involvement increased rapidly. Private economic enterprise became subject to new trade, labor, and currency regulations. The political goals of the restoration of employment and the provision for defense established new state-related economic priorities. Generally speaking, as in the past, the extent of state intervention increased as one moved from west to east across the continent. These new economic policies, in most cases, also involved further political experimentation.

Confronting the Depression in the Democracies

The Depression brought to an end the business-as-usual attitude that had marked the political life of Great Britain and France during the late 1920s. In Britain the emergency led to a new coalition government and the abandonment of economic policies considered almost untouchable for a century. The economic stagnation in France proved to be the occasion for a bold political and economic program sponsored by the parties of the left. The relative success of the British venture gave the nation new confidence in the democratic processes; the new departures in France created social and political hostilities that undermined faith in republican institutions.

Great Britain: The National Government

In 1929 a second minority Labour government, headed by Ramsay MacDonald, assumed office. As the number of British unemployed rose to more than 2.5 million workers in 1931, the ministry became divided over the remedy for the problem. MacDonald believed that the budget should be slashed, government salaries reduced, and the benefits to people on government unemployment insurance lowered. This was a bleak program for a Labour government. MacDonald's strong desire to make the Labour Party respectable led him away from more radical programs. Many of the Cabinet ministers rejected MacDonald's proposals. They would not consent to taking income away from the poor and the unemployed. The prime minister requested the resignations of his Cabinet and arranged for a meeting with King George V.

Everyone assumed that the entire Labour ministry was about to leave office. However, to the surprise of his party and the nation, MacDonald did not resign. At the urging of the king and probably of his own ambition, MacDonald

formed a coalition ministry called the *National Government* composed of Labour, Conservative, and Liberal ministers. The bulk of the Labour Party believed that their leader had sold out. In the election of 1931 the National Government received a very comfortable majority. After the election, however, MacDonald, who remained prime minister until 1935, was little more than a tool of the Conservatives. They held a majority in their own right in the House of Commons, but the appearance of a coalition was useful for imposing unpleasant programs.

The National Government took three decisive steps to attack the Depression. To balance the budget, it raised taxes, cut insurance benefits to the unemployed and the elderly, and lowered government salaries. Its leaders argued that the fall in prices that had taken place meant that lowering those benefits and salaries did not appreciably cut real income. In September 1931 the National Government went off the gold standard. The value of the British pound on the international money market fell by about 30 per cent. Exports were somewhat stimulated by this move. In 1932 Parliament passed the Import Duties Bill, which placed a 10 per cent *ad valorem* tariff on all imports except those from the empire. In the context of previous British policy, all of these steps were nothing less than extraordinary. Gold and free trade, the hallmarks of almost a century of British commercial policy, stood abandoned.

The policies of the National Government produced significant results. Great Britain avoided the banking crisis that hit other countries. By 1934 industrial production had expanded somewhat beyond the level for 1929. Britain was the first nation to achieve restoration of that level of production. Of course, the mediocre British industrial performance of the 1920s made the British task easier. The government also encouraged lower interest rates. These, in turn, led to the largest private housing boom in British history. Industries related to housing and the furnishing of homes prospered. Those people who were employed generally experienced an improvement in their standard of living. Nonetheless the hard core of unemployment remained. In 1937 the number of jobless had fallen to just below 1.5 million. That same year, when George Orwell described the laboring districts of the nation in *The Road to Wigan Pier*, the poverty and the workless days of the people whom he met dominated his picture.

Britain had entered the Depression with a

stagnant economy and left the era with a stagnant economy. Yet the political system itself was not fundamentally challenged. There were demonstrations of the unemployed, but social insurance, though hardly generous, did support them. To the employed citizens of the country the National Government seemed to pursue a policy that avoided the extreme wings of both the Labour and the Conservative parties. When MacDonald retired in 1935, Stanley Baldwin again took office. He was succeeded in 1937 by Neville Chamberlain (1869–1940). The new prime minister is today known for the disaster of the Munich agreement. When he took office, he was known as one of the more progressive thinkers on social issues in the Conservative Party.

Britain did see one movement that flirted with the extreme right-wing politics of the Continent. In 1932 Sir Oswald Mosley (1896–1980) founded the British Union of Fascists. He had held a minor position in the second Labour government and was disappointed in its feeble attack on unemployment. Mosley urged a program of direct action through a new corporate structure for the economy. His group wore black shirts and attempted to hold mass meetings. He gained only a few thousand adherents. Mosley's popularity reached its height in 1934. Thereafter his anti-Semitism began to alienate supporters, and by the close of the decade he had become little more than a political oddity.

France: The Popular Front

The timing of the Depression in France was the reverse of that in Britain. It came later and lasted much longer. Only in 1931 did the economic slide begin to affect the French economy. Even then unemployment did not become the major problem that it did elsewhere. Rarely were more than half a million workers without jobs. However, in one industry after another, wages were lowered. Tariffs were raised to protect French goods and especially French agriculture. Ever since that time French farmers have enjoyed unusual protection from the government. These measures helped to maintain the home market but did little to overcome industrial stagnation. Relations between labor and management were tense.

The first political fallout of the Depression was the election of another Radical coalition government in 1932. Fearful of contributing to inflation as it had after 1924, the Radical gov-

The cabinet of the National Government that was formed in Britain in January 1931. Ramsay MacDonald is seated in the center with Stanley Baldwin on his right. Neville Chamberlain, who would become prime minister in 1937, is standing second from the right. [AP]

ernment pursued a generally deflationary policy. In the same year that the new ministry took office, reparation payments had stopped. As the economic crisis tightened, normal parliamentary and political life became difficult and confused.

Outside the Chamber of Deputies politics assumed a very ugly face. The old divisions between left and right hardened. Various right-wing groups with authoritarian tendencies became active. These leagues included the Action Française, founded before World War I in the wake of the Dreyfus affair, and the Croix de Feu ("Cross of Fire"), composed of army veterans. The memberships of these and other similar groups numbered somewhat more than two million persons. Some wanted a monarchy; others favored what would have amounted to military rule. They were hostile to the idea of parliamentary government, socialism, and communism. They wanted what they regarded as the greater good and glory of the nation to be set above the petty machinations of political parties. In this regard they resembled the Fascists and the Nazis. Their activities and propaganda aided the dissolution of loyalty to republican government and injected bitterness and vindictiveness into French political life. These leagues also created one moment of extraordinary havoc that produced important long-range political consequences.

945

The incident grew out of the Stavisky affair, the last of those curious *causes célèbres* that punctuated the political fortunes of the Third Republic. Serge Stavisky was a small-time gangster who appears to have had good connections within the government. In 1933 he became involved in a fraudulent bond scheme. When finally tracked down by the police, he committed suicide in January 1934. The official handling of the matter suggested a political cover-up. It was alleged that people in high places wished to halt the investigation. To the right wing in France the Stavisky incident symbolized all the seaminess, immorality, and corruption of republican politics. On February 6, 1934, a very large demonstration of the right-wing leagues took place in Paris. The exact purpose and circumstances of the rally remain uncertain, but the crowd did attempt to march on the Chamber of Deputies. Violence erupted between right and left political groups and between them and the police. Fourteen demonstrators were killed; scores of others were in-

jured. It was the largest disturbance in Paris since the Commune of 1871.

In the wake of the night of February 6, the Radical ministry of Edouard Daladier (1884–1970) resigned and was replaced by a national coalition government composed of all living former premiers. The Chamber of Deputies permitted the ministry to deal with economic matters by decree. However, the major result of the right-wing demonstrations was a political self-reassessment by the parties of the left. Radicals, Socialists, and Communists began to realize that a right-wing *coup* might be possible in France. Consequently, between 1934 and 1936, the French left began to make peace within its own ranks. This was no easy task. French Socialists, led by Léon Blum (1872–1950), had been the major target of the French Communists since the split over joining the Comintern in 1920. Only Stalin's fear of Hitler as a danger to the Soviet Union made this new cooperation possible. In spite of deep suspicions on all sides, the Popular Front had been

Right-wing crowds attempted to storm the French Parliament on February 6, 1934 in the wake of the Stavisky scandal. [Ullstein Bilderdienst]

The Right Wing Attacks the Third French Republic

The Stavisky affair provided new opportunity for various French right-wing political groups to criticize the liberal institutions of the Third Republic. In this proclamation of January 7, 1934, one such organization, the *Camelots du Roi*, accused one minister, and by implication all French politicians, of having aided Stavisky in a fraudulent bond scheme. The minister did later resign, but he was not directly implicated in the theft. Also, the reader should note how this proclamation invites the people of Paris to demonstrate against the Chamber of Deputies and to take the law into their own hands. The violence of the night of February 6, 1934, resulted from such invitations to right-wing demonstration.

To the People of Paris.

At a time when the Government and the Parliament of the Republic declare themselves incapable of balancing our budget, and continue to defend the topsy-turvy foundations of their regime; while they refuse to reduce the burden of taxation and are actually inflicting more taxes on the French people a scandal breaks out. This scandal shows that, far from protecting the savings of the people, the Republican Authorities have given free course to the colossal rackets of an alien crook. A Minister, M. Dalimier, by his letters of 25 June and 23 September 1932, deliberately provided an instrument which enabled the thief Stavisky to rob the insurance companies and the Social Insurance Fund of over half a milliard francs. He has been urged to resign; but he has refused to do so. He should be in prison together with his pals Stavisky and Dubarry [another person implicated in the plot]; instead of which, he continues to be a member of the
Government whose duty it is to inquire into this affair. Dalimier is not alone; we can see behind him a crowd of other ministers and influential members of Parliament, all of whom have, in one way or another, favoured the adventurer's rackets, especially by instructing the police to leave him alone, and by suspending during many years the legal proceedings that should have been taken against him. There is no law and no justice in a country where magistrates and the police are the accomplices of criminals. The honest people of France who want to protect their own interests, and who care for the cleanliness of public life, are forced to take the law into their own hands.

At the beginning of this week, Parliament will reassemble and we urge the people of Paris to come in large numbers before the Chamber of Deputies, to cry "Down with the Thieves" and to clamour for honesty and justice.

Sidney Pollard and Colin Holmes, *Documents of European Economic History*, Vol. 3 (London: Edward Arnold, 1973), p. 369.

established by Bastille Day in 1935. Its purpose was to preserve the republic and to press for social reform.

The election of 1936 gave the Popular Front a majority in the Chamber of Deputies. The Socialists were the largest single party for the first time in French history. Consequently they organized the Cabinet as they had long promised they would do when they constituted the majority party of a coalition. Léon Blum assumed the premiership on June 5, 1936. From the early 1920s this Jewish intellectual and humanitarian had opposed the communist version of socialism. Cast as the successor to Jean Jaures, who had been assassinated in 1914, Blum wanted socialism in the context of democratic, parliamentary government. He hoped to bring France a program akin to the New Deal that President Franklin Roosevelt had carried out in the United States.

During May 1936, before the Popular Front came to power, strikes had begun to spread throughout French industry. Immediately after assuming office on June 6, the Blum government faced further spontaneous work stoppages involving over half a million workers who had occupied factories in sit-down strikes. These were the most extensive labor disturbances in the history of the Third Republic. They aroused new fears in the conservative business community, which had already been frightened by the election of the Popular Front.

A display of unity by leaders of the French Popular front at a Bastille Day rally in Paris, July 14, 1935. Léon Blum of the Socialist Party is on the left with Mme. Blum; Maurice Thorez (1900–1964), the Secretary of the French Communist Party, stands beside him on the right. [Photo Trends]

Blum acted swiftly to bring together representatives of labor and management. On June 8 he announced the conclusion of the Matignon Accord, which reorganized labor–management relations in France. Wages were immediately raised from 7 to 15 per cent, depending on the job involved. Employers were required to recognize unions and to bargain collectively with them. Annual, paid two-week vacations for workers were adopted. The forty-hour week was established throughout French industry. Blum hoped to overcome labor hostility to French society, to establish a foundation for justice in labor–management relations, and to increase the domestic consumer demand of the nation.

Blum followed his labor policy with other bold departures. He raised the salaries of civil servants and instituted a program of public works. Government loans were extended to small industry. Spending on armaments was increased, and some armament industries were nationalized. To aid agriculture, he set up a National Wheat Board to manage the produc-

tion and sale of grain. Initially he had promised to resist devaluation of the franc. However, by the autumn of 1936 international monetary pressure forced him to devalue. He did so again in the spring of 1937. The devaluations brought little aid to French exports because they came too late. All of these moves enraged the conservative banking and business community. In March 1937 they brought sufficient influence to bear on the ministry to cause Blum to halt the program of reform. It was not taken up again. Blum's Popular Front colleagues considered the pause in reform an unnecessary compromise. In June 1937 Blum resigned. The Popular Front ministry itself held on until April 1938, when it was replaced by a Radical ministry under Daladier.

The Popular Front had brought much hope to labor and to socialists, but it did not lead France out of the Depression. Some of its programs actually harmed production. The business community, because of its apprehensions and hostility, became even less venturesome after the Popular Front reforms. Not until 1939

948

did French industrial production reach the level of 1929. In a sense the Popular Front had come too late to give either the economy or French political life new vitality. Internal divisions and conservative opposition meant that the Popular Front had enjoyed less than a free hand. By the close of the 1930s citizens from all walks of life had begun to wonder if the republic was worth preserving. The left continued to remain divided. Business people found the republic inefficient and, in their opinion, too much subject to socialist pressures. The right wing hated the republic in principle. When the time came in 1940 to defend the republic, there were too many citizens who were less than sure that it was worth defending.

Germany: The Nazi Seizure of Power

Depression and Political Deadlock

The outflow of foreign, and especially American, capital from Germany beginning in 1928 undermined the economic prosperity of the Weimar Republic. The resulting economic crisis brought parliamentary government to an end. In 1928 a coalition of center parties and the Social Democrats governed. All went reasonably well until the Depression struck. Then the coalition partners differed sharply on economic policy. The Social Democrats wanted no reduction in social and unemployment insurance. The more conservative parties, remem-

French Management and Labor Reach an Agreement

When the Popular Front government came to power in France in 1936, it immediately confronted widespread strikes. Premier Léon Blum called together the representatives of labor and management. The result of these negotiations was the Matignon Accord, which gave the unions more secure rights, raised wages, and brought the strikes to an end.

The delegates of the General Confederation of French Production (CGPF) and the General Confederation of Labour (CGT) have met under the chairmanship of the Premier (Léon Blum) and have concluded the following agreement, after arbitration by the Premier:

1. The employer delegation agrees to the immediate conclusion of collective agreements.

2. These agreements must include, in particular, articles 3. . . .

3. All citizens being required to abide by law, the employers recognize the freedom of opinion of workers and their right to freely join and belong to trade unions.

In their decisions on hiring, organization or assignment of work, disciplinary measures or dismissals, employers agree not to take into consideration the fact of membership or nonmembership in a union. . . .

The exercise of trade union rights must not give rise to acts contrary to law.

4. The wages actually paid to all workers as of 25 May 1936 will be raised, as of the resumption of work, by a decreasing percentage ranging from 15 per cent for the lowest rates down to 7 per cent for the highest rates. In no case must the total increase in any establishment exceed 12 per cent. . . .

The negotiations, which are to be launched at once, for the determination by collective agreement of minimum wages by regions and by occupations must take up, in particular, the necessary revision of abnormally low wages. . . .

6. The employer delegation promises that there will be no sanctions for strike activities.

7. The CGT delegation will ask the workers on strike to return to work as soon as the managements of establishments have accepted this general agreement and as soon as negotiations for its application have begun between the managements and the personnel of the establishments.

V. R. Lorwin, *The French Labour Movement* (Cambridge: Harvard University Press, 1954), pp. 313–315.

Nazi storm troopers on the streets of Berlin in 1932. [Ullstein Bilderdienst]

bering the inflation of 1923, insisted on a balanced budget. The coalition dissolved in March 1930. To resolve the parliamentary deadlock in the Reichstag, President von Hindenburg appointed Heinrich Brüning (1885–1970) as chancellor. Lacking a majority in the Reichstag, the new chancellor governed through emergency presidential decrees as authorized by Article 48 of the constitution. The party divisions in the Reichstag prevented the overriding of the decrees. In this manner the Weimar Republic was transformed into a presidential dictatorship.

German unemployment rose from 2,258,000 in March 1930 to over 6,000,000 in March 1932. There had been persistent unemployment during the 1920s, but nothing of such magnitude or duration. The economic downturn and the parliamentary deadlock worked to the advantage of the more extreme political parties. In the election of 1928 the Nazis had won only 12 seats in the Reichstag, and the Communists had won 54 seats. Two years later, after the election of 1930, the Nazis held 107 seats and the Communists 77.

The power of the Nazis in the streets was also on the rise. The unemployment fed thousands of men into the storm troopers, which had 100,000 members in 1930 and almost 1 million in 1933. The SA freely and viciously attacked Communists and Social Democrats. For the Nazis, politics meant the capture of power through the instruments of terror and intimidation as well as by legal elections. Anything resembling decency and civility in political life vanished. The Nazis held rallies that resembled secular religious revivals. They paraded through the streets and the countryside. They gained powerful supporters and sympathizers in the business, military, and newspaper communities. Some intellectuals were also sympathetic. The Nazis were able to transform this discipline and enthusiasm born of economic despair and nationalistic frustration into impressive electoral results.

Hitler Comes to Power

For two years Brüning continued to govern through the confidence of Hindenburg. The economy did not improve, and the political situation deteriorated. In 1932 the eighty-three-year-old president stood for reelection. Hitler ran against him and forced a runoff. In the first election the Nazi leader garnered 30.1 per cent of the vote, and he later gained 36.8 per cent in the second. Although Hindenburg was returned to office, the results of the poll convinced him that Brüning no longer commanded sufficient confidence from conservative German voters. On May 30, 1932, he dismissed Brüning, and on the next day he appointed Franz von Papen (1878–1969) in his place. The new chancellor was one of a small group of extremely conservative advisers on whom the aged Hindenburg had become increasingly dependent. Others included the president's son and several military figures. With the continued paralysis in the Reichstag, their influence over the president virtually amounted to control of the government. Consequently the crucial decisions of the next several months were made by only a handful of people.

Papen and the circle around the president wanted to find some way to draw the Nazis into cooperation with them without giving any effective power to Hitler. The government needed the mass popular support that only the Nazis seemed able to generate. The Hindenburg circle decided to convince Hitler that the Nazis could not come to power on their own.

Papen removed the ban on Nazi meetings that Brüning had imposed and then called a Reichstag election for July 1932. The Nazis won 230 seats and polled 37.2 per cent of the vote. As the price for his entry into the Cabinet, Hitler demanded appointment as chancellor. Hindenburg refused. Another election was called in November, partly as a means of wearing down the Nazis' financial resources. It was successful in that regard. The number of Nazi seats fell to 196, and their percentage of the popular vote dipped to 33.1 per cent. The advisers around Hindenburg still refused to appoint Hitler to office.

In early December 1932 Papen resigned, and Kurt von Schleicher (1882–1934) became chancellor. There now existed much fear of civil war between groups on the left and the right. Schleicher decided to attempt the construction of a broad-based coalition of conservative groups and trade unionists. The prospect of such a coalition, including groups from the political left, frightened the Hindenburg circle even more than the prospect of Hitler. They did not trust Schleicher's motives, which have never been very clear. Consequently, they persuaded Hindenburg to appoint Hitler as chancellor. To control him and to see that he did

President von Hindenburg (1847–1934) *with Chancellor Hitler in* 1930 *at the anniversary of the battle of Tannenberg. To Hitler's left are two prominent Nazis: Herman Goering* (1893–1946) *and Ernst Roehm* (1887–1934), *the commander of the SA, who was murdered by Hitler the following year.* [*Library of Congress*]

The Nazis Pass Their Racial Legislation

Anti-Semitism had been a fundamental tenet of the Nazi Party and became a major policy of the Nazi government. This comprehensive legislation of September 15, 1935, carried anti-Semitism into all areas of public life and into some of the most personal areas of private life as well. It was characteristically titled the Law for the Protection of German Blood and Honor. Hardly any aspect of Nazi thought and action was as shocking to the non-German world as was this policy toward the Jews.

Imbued with the knowledge that the purity of German blood is the necessary prerequisite for the existence of the German nation, and inspired by an inflexible will to maintain the existence of the German nation for all future times, the Reichstag has unanimously adopted the following law, which is now enacted:

Article I: (1) Any marriages between Jews and citizens of German or kindred blood are herewith forbidden. Marriages entered into despite this law are invalid, even if they are arranged abroad as a means of circumventing this law.

(2) Annulment proceedings for marriages may be initiated only by the Public Prosecutor.

Article II: Extramarital relations between Jews and citizens of German or kindred blood are herewith forbidden.

Article III: Jews are forbidden to employ as servants to their households female subjects of German or kindred blood who are under the age of forty-five years.

Article IV: (1) Jews are prohibited from displaying the Reich and national flag and from showing the national colors.

(2) However, they may display the Jewish colors. The exercise of this right is under state protection.

Article V: (1) Anyone who acts contrary to the prohibition noted in Article I renders himself liable to penal servitude.

(2) The man who acts contrary to the prohibition of Article II will be punished by sentence to either a jail or penitentiary.

(3) Anyone who acts contrary to the provisions of Articles III and IV will be punished with a jail sentence up to a year and with a fine, or with one of these penalties.

Article VI: The Reich Minister of Interior, in conjunction with the Deputy to the Führer and the Reich Minister of Justice, will issue the required legal and administrative decrees for the implementation and amplification of this law.

Article VII: This law shall go into effect on the day following its promulgation, with the exception of Article III, which shall go into effect on January 1, 1936.

Louis L. Snyder (Ed. and Trans.), *Documents of German History* (New Brunswick, N.J.: Rutgers University Press, 1958), pp. 427–428.

support. In 1935 a series of measures known as the *Nuremberg Laws* robbed German Jews of their citizenship. All persons with at least three Jewish grandparents were defined as Jews. The professions and the major occupations were closed to Jews. Marriage and sexual intercourse between Jews and non-Jews were prohibited. Legal exclusion and humiliation of the Jews became the order of the day.

The persecution of the Jews increased again in 1938. Business careers were forbidden. In November 1938, under orders from the Nazi Party, thousands of Jewish stores and synagogues were burned or otherwise destroyed.

The Jewish community itself was required to pay for the damage because the government confiscated the insurance money. In all manner of other ways, large and petty, the German Jews were harassed. This persecution allowed the Nazis to inculcate the rest of the population with the concept of a master race of pure German "Aryans" and also to display their own contempt for civil liberties. After the war broke out, Hitler decided in 1942 to destroy the Jews in Europe. It is thought that over six million Jews, mostly from east European nations, died as a result of that staggering decision, unprecedented in its scope and implementation.

An anti-Jewish rally in Berlin, 1935. The banners read: ''The Jews are our ruin.'' ''The Jews are our disaster.'' [AP]

Nazi Economic Policy

Besides consolidating power and persecuting allegedly inferior races, Hitler still had to confront the reality of the Depression. German unemployment had been a major factor in his rise to power. The Nazis attacked this problem and achieved a degree of success that astonished and frightened the rest of Europe. By 1936, while the rest of the European economy continued to stagnate, the specter of unemployment and other difficulties associated with the Depression for all intents and purposes no longer haunted Germany. As far as the economic crisis was concerned, Hitler had become the most effective political leader in Europe. This fact was a most important element in accounting for the internal strength and support of his tyrannical regime. The Nazi success against the Depression provided the regime with considerable contemporary credibility. As might be expected, the cost in terms of liberty and human dignity had been very high.

Hitler reversed the deflationary policy of the cabinets that had preceded him. He instituted what amounted to a massive program of public works and spending. Many of these projects related directly or indirectly to rearmament. Canals were built, and land was reclaimed. Construction of a large system of highways with clear military uses was begun. Some unemployed workers were sent back to farms if they had originally come from there. Other laborers were frozen in their jobs and were not permitted to change employment. In 1935 renunciation of the military provisions of the Versailles Treaty led to open rearmament and

During the night of November 9, 1938, all across Germany the windows of stores owned by Jews were smashed and synagogues burned. The Nazis then confiscated the insurance money and refused to allow the Jewish businesses to be compensated for their losses. [AP]

May 1, 1938: Hitler introduces the first volkswagen *("people's car"). The volkswagens were supposed to provide cheap transportation for German workers. The coming of war, however, meant that few volkswagens were ever built. [Ullstein Bilderdienst]*

expansion of the army with little opposition, as will be explained in Chapter 28. These measures essentially restored full employment. In 1936 Hitler instructed Hermann Göring (1893–1946), who had headed the air force since 1933, to undertake a Four-Year Plan to prepare the army and the economy for war. The state determined that Germany must be economically self-sufficient. Armaments received top priority. This economic program satisfied both the yearning for social and economic security and the desire for national fulfillment.

Nazi economic policies maintained private property and private capitalism. However, all significant economic enterprise and decisions became subordinated to the goals of the state. Prices were controlled and investments restricted. Currency regulation interfered with

trade. Production that related to the military buildup received top priority and even redirected some industries. For example, in the late 1930s, the German chemical producers diverted a large proportion of their resources toward the manufacture of various synthetics.

With the crushing of the trade unions in 1933, strikes became illegal. There was no genuine collective bargaining. The government handled labor disputes through compulsory arbitration. Both workers and employers were required to participate in the Labor Front, the existence of which was intended to prove that class conflict had ended. It sponsored a "Strength Through Joy" program that provided vacations and other forms of recreation for the labor force.

However, behind the direction of both business and labor stood the Nazi terror and police. The Nazi economic experiment proved that with the sacrifice of all political and civil liberty, of a free trade-union movement, of private exercise of capital, and of consumer satisfaction, full employment for the purposes of war and aggression could be achieved.

Herman Goring (1892–1946) talking with Dr. Josef Goebbels (1897–1945). Goring was Hitler's second in command, head of the air force, and director of Germany's plan for rearmament. Goebbels was the Nazi Minister of Propaganda, in control of the press, radio, and cinema. [Library of Congress]

As part of the Nazi program of public works, a network of superhighways (Autobahnen) *was built across Germany. Here Hitler inaugurates a highway in eastern Germany.* [*Bilderdienst Suddeutscher Verlag*]

Fascist Economics In Italy

The Fascists had promised to bring order to the instability of Italian social and economic life. Discipline was a substitute for economic policy and creativity. During the 1920s Mussolini undertook programs of public works, such as draining the Pontine Marshes for settlement. The shipping industry was subsidized, and protective tariffs were introduced. Mussolini desperately sought to make Italy self-sufficient. He embarked on the "battle of wheat" to prevent foreign grain from appearing in products on Italian tables. There was an extraordinary expansion of wheat farming in Italy. However, these policies did not keep the Depression from affecting Italy. Production, exports, and wages fell. Even the increased wheat production backfired. So much poor marginal land that was expensive to cultivate came into production that the domestic price of wheat, and thus of much food, actually rose.

Both before and during the Depression the Fascists sought to steer an economic course between socialism and a liberal *laissez-faire* system. Their policy was known as *Corporatism*. It constituted a planned economy linked to the private ownership of capital and to government arbitration of labor disputes. Major industries were first organized into syndicates representing labor and management. The two groups negotiated labor settlements within this framework and submitted differences to compulsory government arbitration. The Fascists contended that class conflict would be avoided if both labor and management looked to the greater goal of productivity for the nation. It is a matter of considerable dispute whether this arrangement favored workers or managers. What is certain is that from the mid-1920s Italian labor unions lost the right to strike and to pursue their own independent economic goals. In that respect management clearly profited.

After 1930 these industrial syndicates were further organized into entities called *corporations*. These bodies included all industries relating to a major area of production, such as agriculture or metallurgy, from raw materials through finished product and distribution. A total of twenty-two such corporations was established to encompass the whole economy. In 1938 Mussolini abolished the Italian Chamber of Deputies and replaced it with a Chamber of Corporations. This vast organizational framework did not increase production; instead, it led to excessive bureaucracy and corruption. The corporate state allowed the government to direct much of the nation's economic life without a formal change in ownership. Consumers and owners simply no longer could determine what was to be produced. The Fascist government gained further direct economic power through the Institute for Industrial Reconstruction, which extended loans to businesses in financial difficulty. The loans, in effect, established partial state ownership.

How corporatism might have affected the Italian economy in the long run cannot really be calculated. In 1935 Italy invaded Ethiopia. Economic life was put on a formal wartime footing. The League of Nations imposed economic sanctions, urging member nations to refrain from purchasing Italian goods. The sanctions had little effect. Thereafter taxes rose. During 1935 the government imposed a forced loan on the citizenry by requiring property owners to purchase bonds. Wages continued to be depressed. As the international tensions increased during the late 1930s, the Italian state assumed more and more direction over the economy. The order of Fascism in Italy had not proved to be an order of prosperity. It had brought economic dislocation and a falling standard of living.

Stalin's Five-Year Plans and Purges

While the capitalist economies of western Europe floundered in the doldrums of the Depression, the Soviet Union entered on a period of tremendous industrial advance. Like similar eras of past Russian economic progress, the direction and impetus came from the top. Stalin far exceeded his czarist predecessors in the intensity of state coercion and terror he brought to the task. Russia achieved its stunning economic growth during the 1930s only at the cost of literally millions of human lives and the degradation of still other millions. Stalin's economic policy clearly proved that his earlier rivalry with Trotsky had been a matter of political power rather than one of substantial ideological difference.

The Decision for Rapid Industrialization

Through 1928 Lenin's New Economic Policy (NEP), as championed by Bukharin with Stalin's support, had charted the course of Soviet economic development. Private ownership and enterprise were permitted to flourish in the countryside as a means of ensuring an adequate food supply for the workers in the cities. A few farmers, the *kulaks*, had become quite

prosperous. They probably numbered less than 5 per cent of the rural population. During 1928 and 1929 these and other farmers withheld grain from the market because of dissatisfaction with prices. Food shortages occurred in the cities and provided a cause of potential unrest against the regime. The goals of the NEP were no longer being fulfilled. Sometime during these troubled months Stalin came to a momentous decision. Russia must industrialize rapidly in order to match the economic and military power of the West. Agriculture must be collectivized to produce sufficient grain for food and export and to free peasant labor for the factories. This program, which basically embraced Trotsky's earlier economic position, unleashed nothing less than a second Russian revolution. The costs and character of "Socialism in One Country" now became clear.

AGRICULTURAL POLICY. In 1929 Stalin ordered party agents into the countryside to confiscate any hoarded wheat. The *kulaks* bore the blame for the grain shortages. As part of the general plan to erase the private ownership of land and to collectivize farming, the government undertook a program to eliminate the *kulaks* as a class. However, the definition of a *kulak* soon embraced anyone who opposed Stalin's policy. In the countryside there was extensive resistance from peasants and farmers at all levels of wealth. The stubborn peasants were determined to keep their land. They wreaked their own vengeance on the policy of collectivization by slaughtering more than 100 million horses and cattle between 1929 and 1933. The situation in the countryside amounted to nothing less than open warfare. The peasant resistance caused Stalin to call a brief halt to the process in March 1930. He justified the slowdown on the grounds of "dizziness from success."

Soon thereafter the drive to collectivize the farms was renewed with vehemence, and the costs remained very high. As many as ten million peasants were killed, and millions of others were sent forcibly to collective farms or labor camps. Initially, because of the turmoil on the land, agricultural production fell. There was famine in 1932 and 1933. Milk and meat remained in short supply because of the livestock slaughter. Yet Stalin persevered. The uprooted peasants were moved to thousand-acre collective farms. The machinery for these units was provided by the state through machine-tractor stations. In this fashion the state retained control over major farm machines. That monopoly was a powerful weapon.

The upheaval of collectivization did change Russian farming in a very dramatic way. In 1928 approximately 98 per cent of Russian farmland consisted of small peasant holdings. Ten years later, despite all the opposition, over 90 per cent of the land had been collectivized, and the quantity of farm produce directly handled by the government had risen by 40 per cent. Those shifts in control meant that the government now had primary direction over the food supply. The farmers and peasants could no longer determine whether there would be stability or unrest in the cities. Stalin and the Communist Party had won the battle of the wheat fields, but they had not solved the problem of producing sufficient quantities of grain. That difficulty has continued to plague the Soviet Union to the present day.

THE FIVE-YEAR PLANS. The revolution in agriculture had been undertaken for the sake of industrialization. The increased grain supply was to feed the labor force and provide exports to finance the imports required for industrial development. The scope of the industrial achievement of the Soviet Union between 1928 and World War II stands as one of the most striking accomplishments of the twentieth century. Russia made a more rapid advance toward economic growth than any other nation in the Western world has ever achieved during any similar period of time. By even the conservative estimates of Western observers, Soviet industrial production rose approximately 400 per cent between 1928 and 1940. Emphasis was placed on the production of iron, steel, coal, electrical power, tractors, combines, railway cars, and other heavy machinery. Few consumer goods were produced. The labor for this development was supplied internally. Capital was raised from the export of grain even at the cost of internal shortage. The technology was generally borrowed from already-industrialized nations.

The organizational vehicle for industrialization was a series of Five-Year Plans first begun in 1928. The State Planning Commission, or Gosplan, oversaw the program. It set goals of production and organized the economy to meet them. The task of coordinating all facets of production was immensely difficult and complicated. Deliveries of materials from mines or factories had to be assured before the next unit could carry out its part of the plan.

Russian collective farmers on their way to work in 1931. Stalin's forced collectivization of Russian agriculture gave the Soviet government control of the food supply, but it also led to the Soviet Union's chronic inability to produce enough grain to feed its citizens. [Wide World Photos]

There was many a slip between the cup and the lip. The troubles in the countryside were harmful. A vast program of propaganda was undertaken to sell the Five-Year Plans to the Russian people and to elicit cooperation. However, the industrial labor force soon became subject to regimentation similar to that being imposed on the peasants. By the close of the 1930s the accomplishment of the three Five-Year Plans was truly impressive and probably allowed the Soviet Union to survive the German invasion. Industries that had never existed in Russia now challenged and in some cases, such as tractor production, surpassed their counterparts in the rest of the world. Large, new industrial cities had been built and populated by hundreds of thousands of people.

Many non-Russian contemporaries looked at the Soviet economic experiment quite uncritically. While the capitalist world lay in the throes of the Depression, the Soviet economy had grown at a pace never realized in the West. The American writer Lincoln Steffens reported after a trip to Russia, "I have seen the future and it works." Beatrice and Sidney Webb, the British Fabian Socialists, spoke of "a new civilization" in the Soviet Union. These and other similar writers ignored the shortages in consumer goods and the poor housing. More important, they seem to have had little idea of the social cost of the Soviet achievement. Millions of human beings had been killed and millions more uprooted. The total picture of suffering and human loss during those years will probably never be known; however, the deprivation and sacrifice of Soviet citizens far exceeded anything described by Marx and Engels in relation to nineteenth-century industrialization in western Europe.

The internal difficulties caused by collectivization and industrialization led Stalin to make an important shift in foreign policy. In 1934 he began to fear that the nation might be left isolated against future aggression by Nazi Ger-

---

Stalin Praises the Results of the First Five-Year Plan

The first Five-Year Plan was carried out between 1928 and 1932. The goal was to transform Soviet industry and agriculture so that the nation could compete with the capitalist world. The plan involved immense disruption of Russian society, and most especially of agriculture, in the pursuit of industrialism. In this passage of 1933 Stalin explained what the purpose of the plan had been and boasted of its successes with only the barest indication of the resistance that the Communist Party had encountered in the countryside. These disturbances were so considerable that Stalin had had to pull back from the full implementation of the plan, but that fact was never openly admitted.

The fundamental task of the Five-Year Plan was to transfer our country, with its backward, and in part medieval, technique, to the lines of new, modern technique.

The fundamental task of the Five-Year Plan was to convert the U.S.S.R. from an agrarian and weak country, dependent upon the caprices of the capitalist countries, into an industrial and powerful country, fully self-reliant and independent of the caprices of world capitalism.

The fundamental task of the Five-Year Plan was, in converting the U.S.S.R. into an industrial country, fully to eliminate the capitalist elements, to widen the front of socialist forms of economy, and to create the economic base for the abolition of classes in the U.S.S.R., for the construction of socialist society.

The fundamental task of the Five-Year Plan was to create such an industry in our country as would be able to re-equip and reorganize, not only the whole of industry, but also transport and agriculture—on the basis of socialism.

The fundamental task of the Five-Year Plan was to transfer small and scattered agriculture to the lines of large-scale collective farming, so as to ensure the economic base for socialism in the rural districts and thus to eliminate the possibility of the restoration of capitalism in the U.S.S.R.

Finally, the task of the Five-Year Plan was to create in the country all the necessary technical and economic prerequisites for increasing to the utmost the defensive capacity of the country, to enable it to organize the determined resistance to any and every attempt at military intervention from outside, to any and every attempt at military attack from without.

. . . The object of the Five-Year Plan in the sphere of agriculture was to unite the scattered and small individual peasant farms, which lacked the opportunity of utilizing tractors and modern agricultural machinery, into large collective farms, equipped with all the modern implements of highly developed agriculture, and to cover unoccupied land with model state farms. . . .

The party has succeeded in routing the kulaks as a class, although they have not yet been dealt the final blow; the laboring peasants have been emancipated from kulak bondage and exploitation and a firm economic basis for the Soviet government, the basis of collective farming, has been established in the countryside.

The party has succeeded in converting the U.S.S.R. from a land of small peasant farming into a land where agriculture is run on the largest scale in the world.

Joseph Stalin, *Selected Writings* (New York: International Publishers, 1942), pp. 242, 253–254.

many. The Soviet Union was not yet strong enough to withstand such an attack. Consequently that year he ordered the Comintern to permit Communist parties in other countries to cooperate with non-Communist political parties against Nazism and Fascism. This marked a reversal of the Comintern policy established by Lenin as part of the Twenty-one Conditions in 1919. The new Stalinist policy originating from Moscow allowed the formation of the Popular Front government in France. After more than a decade of vicious rivalry between Communists and Democratic Socialists, for a few years the two groups would attempt to cooperate against the common right-wing foe.

The Purges

Stalin's decisions to industrialize rapidly, to move against the peasants, and to reverse the Comintern policy did arouse internal political opposition. They were all departures from the policies of Lenin. In 1929 Stalin forced Bukharin, the fervent supporter of the NEP and his own former ally, off the Politburo. Little detailed information is known about further opposition, but it does seem to have existed among lower-level party followers of Bukharin and other previous opponents of rapid industrialization. Sometime in 1933 Stalin began to fear loss of control over the party apparatus and the emergence of possibly effective rivals. These fears were probably produced as much by his own paranoia as by real plots. Nevertheless they resulted in the Great Purges, one of the most mysterious and horrendous political events of this century. The purges were not understood at the time and have not been fully comprehended either inside or outside the Soviet Union to the present day.

By the late 1930s the cult of Stalin was an ever-present fact of Soviet life. Even at beach resorts his picture was always near. In this 1950 photograph swimmers in the Black Sea carry large pictures of him on small rafts. Note the war ships in the background. [Sovfoto]

On December 1, 1934, Sergei Kirov (1888–1934), the popular party chief of Leningrad (formerly Saint Petersburg and Petrograd) and a member of the Politburo, was assassinated. In the wake of the shooting thousands of people were arrested, and still larger numbers were expelled from the party and sent to labor camps. At the time it was believed that Kirov had been murdered by opponents of the regime. Direct or indirect complicity in the crime became the normal accusation against the persons whom Stalin attacked. It now seems almost certain that Stalin himself authorized Kirov's assassination in fear of eventual rivalry with the Leningrad leader.

The purges after Kirov's death were just the beginning of a larger process. Between 1936 and 1938 a series of spectacular show trials were held in Moscow. Previous high Soviet leaders, including former members of the Politburo, publicly confessed all manner of political crimes. They were convicted and executed. It is still not certain why they made their palpably false confessions. Still other leaders and lower-level party members were tried in private and shot. Thousands of people received no trial at all. The purges touched persons in all areas of party life. There was apparently little rhyme or reason to why some were executed, others sent to labor camps, and still others left unmolested. After the civilian party members had been purged, the prosecutors turned against the army. Important officers, including heroes of the civil war, were sent to their deaths. Within the party itself hundreds of thousands of members were expelled, and applicants for membership were removed from the rolls. The exact numbers of executions, imprisonments, and expulsions are unknown but certainly ran into the millions.

The trials and purges astonished Western observers. Nothing quite like this phenomenon had been seen before. Political murders and executions were not new, but the absurd confessions were novel. The scale of the political turmoil was also unprecedented. The Russians themselves did not believe or comprehend what was occurring. There existed no national emergency or crisis. There were only accusations of sympathy for Trotsky or of complicity in Kirov's murder or of other nameless crimes. If a rational explanation is to be sought, it probably must be found in Stalin's concern over his own power. In effect, the purges created a new party structure absolutely loyal to him. The "old Bolsheviks" of the October Revolution were among his earliest targets. They and others active in the first years of the revolution knew how far Stalin had moved from Lenin's policies. New, younger members appeared to replace all of the party members executed or expelled. The newcomers had little knowledge of old Russia or of the ideals of the original Bolsheviks. They had not been loyal to Lenin, to Trotsky, or to any Soviet leader except Stalin himself.

POLITICAL DEVELOPMENTS OF THE LATE 1920s and the 1930s

First Five-Year Plan launched in the Soviet Union	1928
(June) Second Labor Party government in Britain	1929
(October) New York stock market crash	
(November) Bukharin expelled from his offices in the Soviet Union; Stalin's central position thus affirmed	
(March) Brüning government begins in Germany; Stalin calls for moderation in his policy of agricultural collectivization because of "dizziness from success"	1930
(September) Nazis capture 107 seats in German Reichstag	
(August) National Government formed in Britain	1931
(March 13) Hindenburg defeats Hitler for German presidency	1932
(May 31) Franz von Papen forms German Cabinet	
(July 31) German Reichstag election	
(November 6) German Reichstag election	
(December 2) Kurt von Schleicher forms German Cabinet	
(January 30) Hitler is made German chancellor	1933
(February 27) Reichstag Fire	
(March 5) Reichstag election	
(March 23) Enabling Act consolidates Nazi power	
(February 6) Stavisky affair riots in Paris	1934
(June 30) Blood purge of the Nazi Party	
(August 2) Death of Hindenburg	
(December 1) Assassination of Kirov leads to the beginning of Stalin's purges	
(May) Popular Front government in France	1936
(July–August) Most famous of public purge trials in Russia	

Scope of the Dictatorships

By the middle of the 1930s dictators of the right and the left had established themselves across much of Europe. Political tyranny was hardly new to Europe, but several factors combined to give these rules unique characteristics. They drew their immediate support from well-organized political parties. Except for the Bolsheviks, these were mass parties. The roots of support for the dictators lay in nationalism, the social and economic frustration of the Depression, and political ideologies that promised to transform the social and political order. As long as the new rulers seemed successful, they were not lacking in support. They had in the eyes of many citizens brought an end to the pettiness of everyday politics.

After coming to power, these dictators possessed a practical monopoly over mass communications. Through armies, police forces, and party discipline, they also held a monopoly on terror and coercive power. They could propagandize large populations and compel large groups of people to obey them and their followers. Finally, as a result of the Second Industrial Revolution, they commanded a vast amount of technology and a capacity for immense destruction. Earlier rulers in Europe may have shared the ruthless ambitions of Hitler, Mussolini, and Stalin, but they had not found at their disposal the ready implements of physical force to impose their wills. Mass political support, monopoly of police and military power, and technological capacity meant that the dictators of the 1930s held more extensive sway over their nations than any other group of rulers who had ever governed on the continent. Soon the issue would become whether they would be able to maintain peace among themselves and with their democratic neighbors.

Suggested Readings

W. S. ALLEN, *The Nazi Seizure of Power: The Experience of a Single German Town, 1930–1935* (1965). A classic treatment of Nazism in a microcosmic setting.

K. E. BAILES, *Technology and Society Under Lenin and Stalin: Origins of the Soviet Technical Intelligentsia, 1917–1941* (1978). An important study of the people who actually put the programs of modernization into place.

N. BRANSON AND M. HEINEMANN, *Britain in the Nineteen Thirties* (1971). Primarily considers the social and economic problems of the day.

T. CHILDERS, *The Nazi Voter: The Social Foundations of Fascism in Germany, 1919–1933* (1983). An attempt to examine who in the German voting population voted for the Nazis.

J. COLTON, *Léon Blum: Humanist in Politics* (1966). One of the best biographies of any twentieth-century political figure.

R. CONQUEST, *The Great Terror: Stalin's Purges of the Thirties* (1968). The best treatment of the subject to this date.

G. CRAIG, *Germany, 1866–1945* (1978). An important new survey.

I. DEUTSCHER, *Stalin: A Political Biography,* 2nd ed. (1967). The best biography in English.

M. DOBB, *Soviet Economic Development Since 1917,* 6th ed. (1966). A basic introduction.

R. F. HAMILTON, *Who Voted for Hitler?* (1982). An examination of voting patterns.

E. C. HELMREICH, *The German Churches Under Hitler: Background, Struggle, and Epilogue* (1979). A useful study.

H. HOLBORN, *A History of Modern Germany: 1840–1945* (1969). A very comprehensive treatment.

C. KINDLEBERGER, *The World in Depression, 1929–1939* (1973). An account by a leading economist whose analysis is comprehensible to the layperson.

C. KINDLEBERGER, *A Financial History of Western Europe* (1984). A major study.

D. LANDES, *The Unbound Prometheus: Technological Change and Industrial Development in Western Europe from 1750 to the Present* (1969). Includes an excellent analysis of both the Great Depression and the few areas of economic growth.

W. LAQUEUR AND G. L. MOSSE (Eds.), *The Great Depression* (1970). A useful collection of articles.

V. R. LORWIN, *The French Labor Movement* (1954). A good introduction.

D. SCHOENBAUM, *Hitler's Social Revolution: Class and Status in Nazi Germany* (1966). A fascinating analysis of Hitler's appeal to various social classes.

D. MACK SMITH, *Mussolini's Roman Empire* (1976). A general description of the Fascist regime in Italy.

A. SOLZHENITSYN, *The Gulag Archipelago,* 3 vols. (1974–1979). A major examination of the labor camps under Stalin by one of the most important of contemporary Russian writers.

J. STEPHENSON, *The Nazi Organization of Women* (1981). Examines the attitude and policies of the Nazis toward women.

H. A. TURNER, JR., *German Big Business and the Rise of Hitler* (1985). An important major study of the subject.

Reference should also be made to the works cited in Chapter 26.

Global Conflict and Detente

The people of Europe and the United States saw the great conflict of 1914–1918 as a world war, but by far the largest part of the fighting and suffering was confined to the European continent. The consequences of that war, however, affected the whole world. Though Germany and Russia lost their colonies, these and the other colonial areas remained under the control of one or another of the victorious European powers, Japan, or the United States, under the guise of mandates from the new League of Nations. Advances in transportation and communication and the rapid growth of an interrelated world economy meant that both economic and political problems would not long remain isolated in a single country, or even on one continent. The failure of the League of Nations to bring international stability, widespread dissatisfaction with the peace settlement, a terrible worldwide economic depression, and the rise of fiercely nationalistic and militaristic regimes in Europe and Japan brought an end to an uneasy peace that lasted only two decades.

The second great upheaval of the twentieth century, the war of 1939–1945, was truly global in scope and even more devastating than the first in effect. Heavy fighting took place in Africa, Asia, and Europe, and the people of every inhabited continent were involved. Battle casualties were many, and the assault on civilians was unprecedented. Massive aerial bombardment of cities began with the German attack on Britain in 1940 and concluded with the use of the new and terrifying atomic weapons against Japan in 1945. Hitler in Germany and Stalin in the Soviet Union made war on designated populations within their own countries, and the Japanese treated civilians under their control with great brutality. The cost of World War II in life and property was even greater than that of World War I.

After World War II the hopes of many for peace and stability in the future rested with a new international organization, the United Nations. Unlike the League of Nations, which the United States had never joined, the new organization included all the victorious powers and came to include almost all the nations of the world. Its success, however, required the cooperation of the great powers, but the coalition of the victors was always tenuous because of differences between the political and economic systems of the western nations and those of the Soviet Union and because of the mutual suspicion between them. The western powers' insistence on free, democratic elections in the liberated states of eastern Europe was incompatible with the Soviet Union's desire to establish secure control over the areas on its western border. Disputes over Poland, the Balkan states, and Germany led to a division of Germany and of all of Europe into east and west and began a period of competition and sometimes open hostility called the *Cold War*. The division hardened with the formation of the North Atlantic Treaty Organization in 1949 and the Warsaw Pact in 1955. Since that time the former Allies have faced each other across what Winston Churchill called an "Iron Curtain" with ever-increasing collections of deadly weapons and with continuing tension, occasionally relaxed by hopes for cooperation.

The Cold War quickly spread to Asia, where the Communist Party under Mao Tse-tung gained control of China and allied itself with the Soviet Union, supporting the Communist regime of North Korea against South Korea, which was supported by the United States and its allies. Later, the same alignment appeared in Vietnam, but by the 1960s a split between the Chinese and the Russians became apparent and international relations became more complex. By the 1980s China and the United States had established reasonably friendly relations, and a new Chinese regime had even begun to introduce elements of a free-market economy. This action followed similar steps in such Communist nations as Yugoslavia, Hungary, and Romania, all of them undoubtedly influenced by the remarkable success of free-market economies in the defeated nations of West Germany and Japan. Both of these countries had swiftly recovered from a condition of devastation and poverty to achieve unprecedented prosperity in what was widely seen as an economic miracle. Similar advances took place in the other western countries and in such Asian lands as South Korea and Taiwan. In contrast, the socialist economies of eastern Europe and the Soviet Union were in serious trouble by the 1980s, and Mao's desperate attempts to produce economic progress through state control had been badly disappointed.

World War II had destroyed the capacity of the European nations to maintain their colonial empires and had led to the establishment of new, independent nations in former colonial territories in Africa, Asia, and the islands of the Pacific. The withdrawal of foreign control was joyously welcomed, but independence brought new problems. Rapid growth of population; ethnic, religious, and tribal rivalries; inadequate educational systems and political experience; and a shortage of technological expertise and investment capital—all of these often led to civil wars and to political and economic crisis. A wave of Islamic fundamentalism with serious political implications swept through the Arab world, dividing it and threatening the stability of more moderate Arab states. This instability in the so-called Third World created further tensions between the two great power blocs.

The defeat of the Axis powers in World War II had saved the world from a terrible threat to freedom and civility, but it had not, of course, produced universal peace, prosperity, and democracy. Advances in science and technology made it easier than ever for tyrants to abuse their subjects and totalitarian regimes to stamp out freedom. The new and varied means of destruction that these advances provided also threatened the very existence of the human race. Yet, for four decades, the presence of such dangerous weapons seems to have contributed to the avoidance of such general and terrible conflicts as the two world wars. The wonders of science and technology have also brought longer spans of life, better health, and unprecedented prosperity to people in the advanced nations and have offered the promise of the same to the developing countries. Both the dangers and the opportunities present challenges to humanity's capacity for wisdom, restraint, and patience.

Nuremburg, 1945: By the end of the war, most of Germany's cities had been reduced to rubble. Nuremburg, where the Nazis had held their annual rally, was soon to witness the trial of the leading Nazis as war criminals. [National Archives]

Again the Road to War (1933–1939)

World War I and the Versailles Treaty in and of themselves had only a marginal relationship to the world depression of the 1930s. But in Germany, where the reparations settlement had contributed to the vast inflation of 1923, economic and social discontent focused on the Versailles settlement as the cause of all ills. Throughout the late 1920s Adolf Hitler and the Nazi Party had never ceased denouncing Versailles as the source of all Germany's trouble, and the economic woes of the early 1930s seemed to bear them out. Nationalism and attention to the social question, along with party discipline, had been the sources of Nazi success. They continued to influence Hitler's foreign policy after he became chancellor in early 1933. Moreover the Nazi destruction of the Weimar Constitution and of political opposition meant that to an extraordinary degree German foreign policy lay in Hitler's own hands. Consequently it is important to know what his goals were and what plans he had for achieving them.

Hitler's Goals

For almost twenty years after the outbreak of World War II there was general agreement that the war was the outcome of Hitler's expansionist ambitions, which might have been unlimited and which certainly included vast conquests in eastern Europe and dominance of the European continent. A more recent view is that Hitler was not very much different from any other German statesman, wanting only a revision of Germany's eastern boundaries, elimination of the restrictions of the Versailles Treaty, "and then to make Germany the greatest power in Europe by her natural weight."[1] The same view asserts that Hitler did not have a consistent plan in foreign policy but was an opportunist who went the way that events and opportunity took him, emphasizing his own statement: "I go the way that Providence dictates with the assurance of a sleepwalker."[2]

The truth appears to be a combination of these apparently contradictory views. From the

---

28

World War II and the Cold War

---

[1]A. J. P. Taylor, *The Origins of the Second World War* (New York: Atheneum, 1968), p. 70.

[2]Quoted by Alan Bullock in "Hitler and the Origins of the Second World War," in E. M. Robertson (Ed.), *The Origins of the Second World War* (London: Macmillan, 1971), p. 192.

first expression of his goals in *Mein Kampf* to his last days in the bunker where he died, Hitler's racial theories and goals held the central place in his thought. He meant to go far beyond Germany's 1914 boundaries, which were the limit of the vision of his predecessors. He meant to bring the entire German people *(Volk)*, understood as a racial group, together into a single nation. The new Germany would include all the Germanic parts of the old Habsburg Empire, including Austria. This virile and growing nation would need more space to live *(Lebensraum)*, which would be taken from the Slavs, a lesser race, fit only for servitude. The new Germany would be purified by the removal of the Jews, another inferior race in Nazi theory. The plan always required the conquest of Poland

and the Ukraine as the primary areas for the settlement of Germans and for the provision of badly needed food. Neither *Mein Kampf* nor later statements of policy were blueprints for action. Hitler was a brilliant improviser who sought after and made good use of opportunities as they arose, but he never lost sight of his goal, which would almost certainly require a major war.

THE DESTRUCTION OF VERSAILLES. When Hitler came to power, Germany was far too weak to permit the direct approach. The first problem was to shake off the fetters of Versailles and to make Germany a formidable military power. In October of 1933 Germany withdrew from an international disarmament

---

Hitler Describes His Goals in Foreign Policy

From his early career, Hitler had certain long-term general views and goals. They were set forth in his *Mein Kampf*, which appeared in 1925, and included consolidation of the German *Volk* (People), provision of more land for the Germans, and contempt for such "races" as Slavs and Jews. Here are some of Hitler's views on land.

The National Socialist movement must strive to eliminate the disproportion between our population and our area—viewing this latter as a source of food as well as a basis for power politics—between our historical past and the hopelessness of our present impotence. . . .

.   .   .   .

The demand for restoration of the frontiers of 1914 is a political absurdity of such proportions and consequences as to make it seem a crime. Quite aside from the fact that the Reich's frontiers in 1914 were anything but logical. For in reality they were neither complete in the sense of embracing the people of German nationality, nor sensible with regard to geomilitary expediency. . . .

As opposed to this, we National Socialists must hold unflinchingly to our aim in foreign policy, namely, to secure for the German people the land and soil to which they are entitled on this earth. . . .

. . . The soil on which some day German generations of peasants can beget powerful sons will sanction the investment of the sons of today,

and will some day acquit the responsible statesmen of blood-guilt and sacrifice of the people, even if they are persecuted by their contemporaries. . . .

Much as all of us today recognize the necessity of a reckoning with France, it would remain ineffectual in the long run if it represented the whole of our aim in foreign policy. It can and will achieve meaning only if it offers the rear cover for an enlargement of our people's living space in Europe. . . .

If we speak of soil in Europe today, we can primarily have in mind only Russia and her vassal border states. . . .

. . . See to it that the strength of our nation is founded, not on colonies, but on the soil of our European homeland. Never regard the Reich as secure unless for centuries to come it can give every scion of our people his own parcel of soil. Never forget that the most sacred right on this earth is a man's right to have earth to till with his own hands, and the most sacred sacrifice the blood that a man sheds for this earth.

Adolf Hitler, *Mein Kampf*, trans. by Ralph Manheim (Boston: Houghton, Mifflin, 1943), pp. 646, 649, 652, 653, 656.

conference and also from the League of Nations. Hitler argued that because the other powers had not disarmed as they had promised, it was wrong to keep Germany helpless. These acts alarmed the French but were merely symbolic. In January of 1934 Germany made a nonaggression pact with Poland that was of greater concern, for it put into question France's chief means of containing the Germans. At last, in March 1935, Hitler formally renounced the disarmament provisions of the Versailles Treaty with the formation of a German air force, and soon he reinstated conscription, which aimed at an army of half a million men.

His path was made easier by growing evidence that the League of Nations was ineffective as a device for keeping the peace and that collective security was a myth. In September 1931 Japan occupied Manchuria, provoking an appeal to the League of Nations by China. The league responded by sending out a commission under the Earl of Lytton. The Lytton Report condemned the Japanese for resorting to force, but the powers were unwilling to impose sanctions. Japan withdrew from the league and kept control of Manchuria.

When Hitler announced his decision to rearm Germany, the league formally condemned that action, but it took no steps to prevent Germany's rearming. The response of France and Britain was hostile, but they felt unable to object because they had not carried out their own promises to disarm. Instead, they met with Mussolini in June 1935 to form the so-called Stresa Front, making an agreement to use force to maintain the status quo in Europe. But Britain, desperate to maintain superiority at sea, even contrary to the Stresa accords and at the expense of French security needs, soon made a separate naval agreement with Hitler, allowing him to rebuild the German fleet to 35 per cent of the British navy, and Italy's expansionist ambitions in Africa soon brought it into conflict with the Western powers. Hitler had taken a major step toward his goal without provoking serious opposition.

Italy Attacks Ethiopia

The Italian attack on Ethiopia made the impotence of the League of Nations and the timidity of the Allies even clearer. Using a border incident as an excuse, Mussolini attacked Ethiopia in October 1935 to avenge a humiliating defeat that the Italians had suffered in 1896, to begin the restoration of Roman imperial glory,

Emperor Haile Selassie of Ethiopia (1892–1975) appealing in Geneva to the League of Nations in June 1936 for help against the Italian invasion of his country. The League condemned Italian aggression but took no practical steps to counter it. [Bilderdienst Suddeutscher Verlag]

and, perhaps, to turn the thoughts of Italians away from the corruption of the Fascist regime and their economic misery. France and Britain were eager to appease Mussolini in order to offset the growing power of Germany. They were prepared to allow him the substance of conquest if he would only maintain Ethiopia's formal independence, but for Mussolini the form was more important than the substance. His attack outraged opinion in the West, and the French and British governments were forced at least to appear to resist. The League of Nations condemned Italian aggression and, for the first time, voted economic sanctions. It imposed an arms embargo that limited loans and credits to and imports from Italy. But Britain and France were afraid of alienating Mussolini, so they refused to place an embargo on oil, the one economic sanction that could have prevented Italian victory. Even more impor-

969

tant, the British fleet did not prevent the movement of Italian troops and munitions through the Suez Canal. The results of this wavering policy were disastrous. The League of Nations and collective security were totally discredited, and Mussolini was alienated as well. He now turned to Germany, and by November 1, 1936, he could speak publicly of a Rome–Berlin "Axis."

Remilitarization of the Rhineland

No less important a result of the Ethiopian affair was its effect on Hitler's evaluation of the strength and determination of the western powers. On March 7, 1936, he took his greatest risk yet, sending a small armed force into the demilitarized Rhineland. This was a breach not only of the Versailles Treaty but of the Locarno Agreements of 1925 as well, agreements that Germany had made voluntarily. It also removed one of the most important elements of French security. France and Britain had every right to resist, and the French especially had a claim to retain the only element of security left after the failure of the Allies to guarantee her defense, yet neither did anything but make a feeble protest with the League of Nations. British opinion would not permit any support for France. The French themselves were paralyzed by internal division and by military ideas that concentrated on defense and feared taking the offensive. Both countries were further weakened by a growing pacifism.

In retrospect it appears that the Allies lost a great opportunity to stop Hitler before he became a serious menace. The failure of his gamble, taken against the advice of his generals, might have led to his overthrow; at the least it would have made German expansion to the east dangerous if not impossible. Nor is there much reason to doubt that the French army could easily have routed the tiny German force in the Rhineland. As the German General Alfred Jodl said some years later, "The French covering army would have blown us to bits."[3]

A Germany that was rapidly rearming and had a defensible western frontier presented a completely new problem to the western powers. Their response was the policy of "appeasement." It was based on the assumption that Germany had real grievances, that Hitler's goals were limited and ultimately acceptable,

[3]Quoted by W. L. Shirer in *The Collapse of the Third Republic* (New York: Simon & Schuster, 1969), p. 281.

and that the correct policy was to bring about revision by negotiation and concession before a crisis could arise and lead to war. Behind this approach was the general horror at the thought of another war. Memories of the losses in the last war were still fresh, and the advent of aerial bombardment made the thought of a new war terrifying. A firmer policy, moreover, would have required rapid rearmament, but British leaders especially were reluctant to pursue this path because of the expense and because of the widespread belief that the arms race had been a major cause of the last war. As Germany armed, the French huddled behind their newly constructed defensive wall, the Maginot Line, and the British hoped things would go well.

The Spanish Civil War

The new European alignment that found the Western democracies on one side and the fascist states on the other was made clearer by the Spanish Civil War, which broke out in July 1936. In 1931 the Spaniards had driven out their king and established a democratic republic. The new government followed a program of moderate reform that antagonized landowners, the Catholic church, nationalists, and conservatives without satisfying the demands of peasants, workers, Catalan separatists, or radicals. Elections in February 1936 brought to power a Spanish Popular Front government ranging from republicans of the left to communists and anarchists. The defeated groups, especially the Falangists, the Spanish version of fascists, would not accept defeat at the polls. In July, General Francisco Franco (1892–1975) led an army from Spanish Morocco in rebellion against the republic.

Thus began a civil war that lasted almost three years, cost hundreds of thousands of lives, and provided a training ground for World War II. Germany and Italy aided Franco with troops, airplanes, and supplies. The Soviet Union sent airplanes, equipment, and advisers to the republicans. Liberals and leftists from Europe and America volunteered to fight in the republican ranks against fascism.

The civil war, fought on blatantly ideological lines, had a profound effect on world politics. It brought Germany and Italy closer together, leading to the Rome–Berlin Axis Pact. The Axis powers were joined in the same year by Japan in the Anti-Comintern Pact, ostensibly against communism but really a new and pow-

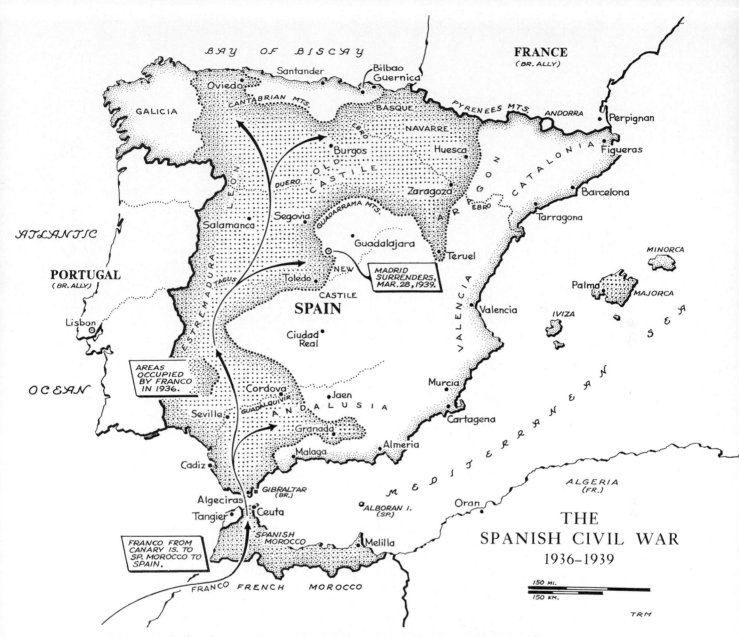

MAP 28–1 *The dotted area on the map shows the large portion of Spain quickly overrun by Franco's insurgent armies during the first year of the war. In the following two years, progress came more slowly for the fascists as the war became a kind of international rehearsal for the coming World War II. Madrid's fall to Franco in the spring of 1939 had been preceded by that of Barcelona a few weeks earlier*

erful diplomatic alliance. Western Europe, especially France, had a great interest in preventing Spain from falling into the hands of a fascist regime closely allied with Germany and Italy, but the appeasement mentality reigned. Although international law permitted the sale of weapons and munitions to the legitimate republican government, France and Britain forbade the export of war materials to either side, and the United States passed new neutrality

Loyalist troops in action during the Spanish Civil War (September 1936–March 1939).
[*Magnum*]

legislation to the same end. When the city of Barcelona fell to Franco early in 1939, the fascists had won effective control of Spain.

Austria and Czechoslovakia

Hitler made good use of his new friendship with Mussolini. He had always planned to make his native Austria a part of the new Germany. In 1934 the Nazi Party in Austria assassinated the prime minister and tried to seize power. Mussolini, not yet allied with Hitler, and suspicious of German intentions, moved an army to the Brenner Pass in the Alps between Austria and Italy, preventing German intervention and causing the *coup* to fail. In 1938 the new diplomatic situation encouraged Hitler to try again. He seems to have hoped to achieve his goal by propaganda, bullying, and threats, but the Austrian Premier Kurt Schuschnigg refused to collapse. On March 9 the premier announced a plebiscite on the fol-

lowing Sunday, March 13, in which the Austrian people could decide the question of union with Germany for themselves. Hitler dared not let the plebiscite take place and sent his army into Austria on March 12. To his great relief Mussolini made no objection and Hitler could march into Vienna to the cheers of his Austrian sympathizers. This peaceful outcome was fortunate for the Germans. Their army was far from ready for combat, and a high percentage of German tanks and trucks broke down along the roads of Austria.

The *Anschluss*, or union of Germany and Austria, was another clear violation of Versailles, but the treaty was now a dead letter; the latest violation produced no reaction from the West. It had great strategic significance, however, especially for the position of Czechoslovakia, one of the bulwarks of French security. The union with Austria left the Czechs surrounded by Germany on three sides.

The very existence of Czechoslovakia was an

affront to Hitler. It was democratic and pro-Western; it had been created as a check on Germany and was allied both to France and to the Soviet Union. It also contained about 3.5 million Germans who lived in the Sudetenland near the German border. These Germans had been the dominant class in the old Austro-Hungarian Empire and resented their new minority position. Supported by Hitler and led by Konrad Henlein, the chief Nazi in Czechoslovakia, they made ever-increasing demands for privileges and autonomy within the Czech state. The Czechs made many concessions, but Hitler did not want to improve the lot of the Sudeten Germans. He wanted to destroy Czechoslovakia. He told Henlein, "We must always demand so much that we can never be satisfied."[4]

As pressure mounted, the Czechs grew nervous. In May 1938 they received false rumors of an imminent attack by Germany and mobilized their army. The French, British, and Russians all issued warnings that they would support the Czechs. Hitler, who had not planned an attack at that time, was forced to make a public denial of any designs on Czechoslovakia. The public humiliation infuriated him, and from that moment he planned a military attack on the Czechs. The affair stiffened Czech resistance, but it appears to have frightened the French and British. The French, as had become their custom, deferred to British leadership. The British prime minister was Neville Chamberlain, a man thoroughly committed to the policy of appeasement. He was determined not to allow Britain to come close to war again. He put pressure on the Czechs to make further concessions to Germany, but no concession was enough.

On September 12, 1938, Hitler made a provocative speech at the Nuremberg Nazi Party rally. His assertions led to rioting in the Sudetenland and the declaration of martial law by the Czech government. German intervention seemed imminent. Chamberlain, aged sixty-nine, had never flown before, but between September 15 and September 29 he made three flights to Germany in an attempt to appease Hitler at Czech expense and thus to avoid war. At Hitler's mountain retreat, Berchtesgaden, on September 15 Chamberlain accepted the separation of the Sudetenland from Czechoslovakia. And he and the French pre-mier, Daladier, forced the Czechs to agree by threatening to desert them if they did not. A week later Chamberlain flew yet again to Germany only to find that Hitler had raised his demands: he wanted cession of the Sudetenland in three days and immediate occupation by the German army.

Munich

Chamberlain returned to England thinking that he had failed, and France and Britain prepared for war. Almost at the last moment Mussolini proposed a conference of Germany, Italy, France, and Britain. It met on September 29 at Munich. Hitler received almost everything he had demanded. The Sudetenland, the key to Czech security, became part of Germany, thus depriving the Czechs of any chance of self-defense. In return the powers agreed to spare the rest of Czechoslovakia. Hitler promised, "I have no more territorial demands to make in Europe." Chamberlain returned to England with the Munich agreement and told a cheering crowd that he had brought "peace with honour. I believe it is peace for our time."

Even in the short run the appeasement of Hitler at Munich was a failure. Soon Poland and Hungary tore bits of territory from Czechoslovakia, and the Slovaks demanded autonomy. Finally, on March 15, 1939, Hitler broke his promise and occupied Prague, putting an end to Czechoslovakia and to illusions that his only goal was to restore Germans to the Reich. Defenders of the appeasers have argued that their policy was justified because it bought valuable time in which the West could prepare for war. But that argument was not made by the appeasers themselves, who thought that they were achieving peace, nor does the evidence appear to support it.

If the French and the British had been willing to attack Germany from the west while the Czechs fought in their own defense, there is reason to think that their efforts might have been successful. High officers in the German army were opposed to Hitler's risky policies and might have overthrown him. Even failing such developments, a war begun in October 1938 would have forced Hitler to fight without the friendly neutrality and material assistance of the Soviet Union and without the resources of eastern Europe that became available to him as a result of appeasement. If, moreover, the West ever had a chance of alliance with the Soviet Union against Hitler, the exclusion of

[4]Quoted by Alan Bullock in *Hitler, A Study in Tyranny* (New York: Harper & Row, 1962), p. 443.

the Russians from Munich and the appeasement policy helped destroy it. Munich remains an example of short-sighted policy that helped bring on a war in disadvantageous circumstances because of the very fear of war and the failure to prepare for it.

Hitler's occupation of Prague discredited appeasement in the eyes of the British people. In the summer of 1939 a Gallup Poll showed that three quarters of the British public believed it worth a war to stop Hitler. Though Chamberlain himself had not lost all faith in his policy, he felt the need to respond to public opinion, and he responded to excess. It was apparent that Poland was the next target of German expansion. In the spring of 1939 the Germans put pressure on Poland to restore the formerly German city of Danzig and to allow a railroad and a highway through the Polish Corridor to connect East Prussia with the rest of Germany. When the Poles would not yield, the usual propaganda campaign began, and the pressure mounted. On March 31 Chamberlain announced a Franco-British guarantee of Polish independence. Hitler appears to have expected to fight a war with Poland but not with the western allies, for he did not take their guarantee seriously. He had come to hold their

The Munich Conference, October 1938. The figures in front are, from left to right, Chamberlain of Great Britain, Daladier of France, Hitler of Germany, and Mussolini of Italy. [Imperial War Museum, London]

Winston Churchill Warns of the Effects of the Munich Agreement

Churchill delivered his speech on the Munich agreement before the House of Commons on October 5, 1938. Following are excerpts from it.

The Chancellor of the Exchequer [Sir John Simon] said it was the first time Herr Hitler had been made to retract—I think that was the word—in any degree. We really must not waste time after all this long Debate upon the difference between the positions reached at Berchtesgaden, at Godesberg and at Munich. They can be very simply epitomized, if the House will permit me to vary the metaphor. One pound was demanded at the pistol's point. When it was given, £2 were demanded at the pistol's point. Finally, the dictator consented to take £1 17s. 6d. and the rest in promises of good will for the future. . . .

. . . .

I do not grudge our loyal, brave people, who were ready to do their duty no matter what the cost, who never flinched under the strain of last week—I do not grudge them the natural, spontaneous outbursts of joy and relief when they *learned that the hard ordeal would no longer be required of them at the moment; but they should know the truth. They should know that there has been gross neglect and deficiency in our defenses; they should know that we have sustained a defeat without a war, the consequences of which will travel far with us along our road; they should know that we have passed an awful milestone in our history, when the whole equilibrium of Europe has been deranged, and that the terrible words have for the time being been pronounced against the Western democracies: "Thou art weighed in the balance and found wanting." And do not suppose that this is the end. This is only the beginning of the reckoning. This is only the first sip, the first foretaste of a bitter cup which will be proffered to us year by year unless, by a supreme recovery of moral health and martial vigor, we arise again and take our stand for freedom as in the olden time.*

Winston S. Churchill, *Blood, Sweat, and Tears* (New York: G. P. Putnam's Sons, 1941), pp. 56, 66.

leaders in contempt. He knew that both countries were unprepared for war and that large segments of their populations were opposed to fighting a war to save Poland.

Belief in the Polish guarantee was further undermined by the inability of France and Britain to get effective help to the Poles. An attack on Germany's western front was out of the question for the French, still dominated by the defensive mentality of the Maginot Line. The only way to defend Poland was to bring Russia into the alliance against Hitler, but a Russian alliance posed many problems. Each side was profoundly suspicious of the other. The French and the British were hostile to Russia's Communist ideology, and since Stalin's purge of the officer corps of the Red Army, they stood unconvinced of the military value of an alliance with Russia. Besides, the Russians could not help Poland without the right of transit through Romania and the right of entry into Poland. Both nations, suspicious of Rus-

sian intentions, and with good reason, refused to grant these rights. As a result Western negotiations with Russia moved forward slowly and cautiously.

The Nazi–Soviet Pact

The Russians had at least equally good reason to hesitate. They resented being left out of the Munich agreement. They were annoyed by the low priority that the West seemed to give to negotiations with Russia compared with the urgency with which they dealt with Hitler. They feared, quite rightly, that the western powers meant them to bear the burden of the war against Germany. As a result they opened negotiations with Hitler, and on August 23, 1939, the world was shocked to learn of a Nazi–Soviet nonaggression pact. Its secret provisions, which were easily guessed and soon carried out, divided Poland between the two powers and allowed Russia to take over the

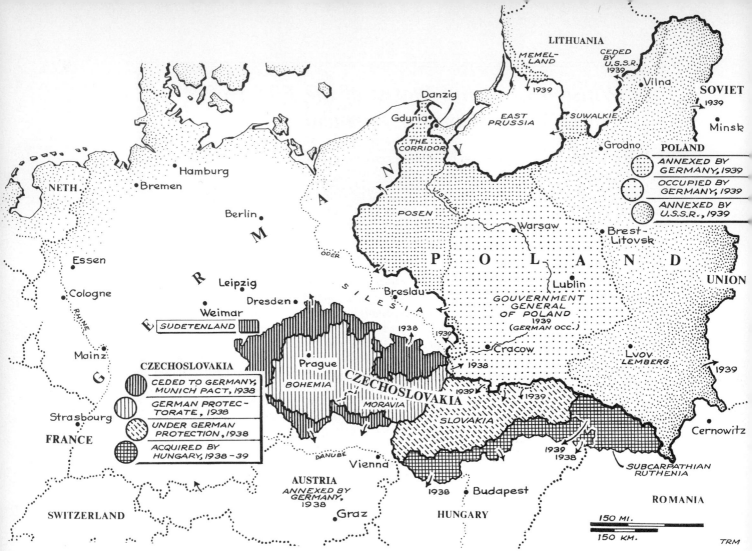

PARTITIONS OF CZECHOSLOVAKIA AND POLAND, 1938–1939

MAP 28–2 *The immediate background of World War II is found in the complex international drama unfolding on Germany's eastern frontier in 1938 and 1939. Germany's expansion inevitably meant the victimization of Austria, Czechoslovakia, and Poland. With the failure of the Western powers' appeasement policy and the signing of a German-Soviet pact, the stage for the war was set.*

Baltic states and to take Bessarabia from Romania. The most bitter ideological enemies had become allies. Communist parties in the West changed their line overnight from the ardent advocacy of resistance to Hitler to a policy of peace and quiet. Ideology gave way to political and military reality. The West offered the Russians danger without much prospect of gain. Hitler offered Stalin gain without immediate danger. There could be little doubt about the decision.

The Nazi–Soviet Pact sealed the fate of Poland, and the Franco-British commitment guaranteed a general war. On September 1, 1939, the Germans invaded Poland. Two days later Britain and France declared war on Germany. World War II had begun.

World War II (1939–1945)

World War II has a better claim to its name than its predecessor, for it was truly global. Fighting took place in Europe and Asia, the Atlantic and the Pacific oceans, the Northern and Southern Hemispheres. The demand for

*The Nazi-Soviet Pact of August, 1939, which shocked the
world, sealed the fate of Poland and made the imminent
outbreak of World War II inevitable. This photo shows
Soviet foreign minister Molotov (1890–1986) signing
the treaty, while Nazi foreign minister von Ribbentrap
(1893–1946) and Stalin (1879–1953) look on. [Li-
brary of Congress]*

the fullest exploitation of material and human
resources for increased production, the use of
blockades, and the intensive bombing of civilian targets made the war of 1939 even more
"total,"—that is, comprehensive and intense—
than that of 1914.

The German Conquest of Europe

The German attack on Poland produced
swift success. The new style of "lightning warfare," or *Blitzkrieg*, employed fast-moving,
massed armored columns supported by air
power. The Poles were inferior in tanks and
planes, and their defense soon collapsed. The
speed of the German victory astonished everyone, not least the Russians, who hastened to
collect their share of the booty before Hitler
could deprive them of it. On September 17
they invaded Poland from the east, dividing the
country with the Germans. They then forced

THE COMING OF WORLD WAR II	
(June) The Versailles Treaty	1919
(January) France occupies the Ruhr	1923
(October) The Locarno Agreements	1925
(Spring) Onset of the Great Depression in Europe	1931
(January) Hitler comes to power	1933
(October) Germany withdraws from the League of Nations	
(March) Hitler renounces disarmament, starts an air force, and begins conscription	1935
(October) Mussolini attacks Ethiopia	
(March) Germany reoccupies and remilitarizes the Rhineland	1936
(July) Outbreak of the Spanish Civil War	
(October) Formation of the Rome–Berlin Axis	
(March) *Anschluss* with Austria	1938
(September) The Munich Conference and partition of Czechoslovakia	
(March) Hitler occupies Prague; France and Great Britain guarantee Polish independence	1939
(August) The Nazi–Soviet pact	
(September 1) Germany invades Poland	
(September 3) Britain and France declare war on Germany	

the encircled Baltic countries to sign treaties with them. By 1940 Estonia, Latvia, and Lithuania were absorbed as constituent republics into the USSR (Union of Soviet Socialist Republics, or the Soviet Union). In November 1940 the Russians invaded Finland, but the Finns put up a surprisingly effective resistance. Although they were finally worn down and compelled to yield territory and bases to Russia, they retained their independence. Russian difficulties in Finland may well have encouraged Hitler to invade the Soviet Union in June 1941, just twenty-two months after the 1939 treaty.

Through the fall of 1939 and the winter of 1939–1940, the western front was quiet. The French remained quiet behind the Maginot Line while Hitler and Stalin swallowed Poland and the Baltic states. Britain hastily rearmed and reorganized the traditional naval blockade. Cynics in the West called it the phony war, or

German troops stage a victory parade past the Arc de Triomphe in Paris in June, 1940. [Ullstein Bilderdienst]

''*Sitzkrieg*,'' but Hitler shattered the stillness in the spring of 1940. In April, without warning and with swift success, the Germans invaded Denmark and Norway. Hitler's northern front was secure, and he now had both air and naval bases closer to Britain. A month later a combined land and air attack struck Belgium, the Netherlands, and Luxembourg. German airpower and armored divisions were irresistible. The Dutch surrendered in a few days, and the Belgians, though aided by the French and the British, surrendered less than two weeks later. The British and French armies in Belgium were forced to flee to the English Channel to seek escape from the beaches of Dunkerque. By the heroic effort of hundreds of Britons manning small boats, over 200,000 British and 100,000 French soldiers were saved, but casualties were high and much valuable equipment was abandoned.

The Maginot Line ran from Switzerland to the Belgian frontier. Until 1936 the French had expected the Belgians to continue the fortifications along their German border. After Hitler remilitarized the Rhineland without opposition, the Belgians lost faith in their French alliance and returned to neutrality, leaving the Maginot Line exposed on the left flank. Hitler's swift advance through Belgium therefore circumvented France's main line of defense. The French army, poorly and hesitantly led by superannuated generals who lacked a proper understanding of the use of tanks and planes, quickly collapsed. Mussolini, eager to claim the spoils of victory when it was clearly safe to do so, sent an army across the French border on June 10, less than a week before the new French government, under the ancient hero of Verdun, Henri Philippe Pétain, asked for an armistice. In two months Hitler had accomplished what Germany had failed to achieve in four years of bitter fighting in the previous war.

The terms of the armistice, signed June 22, 1940, allowed the Germans to occupy more than half of France, including the Atlantic and English Channel coasts. In order to prevent many of the French from fleeing to North Africa to continue the fight, and even more to prevent the French from turning their fleet over to Britain, Hitler left southern France unoccupied. Pétain set up a dictatorial regime at the resort city of Vichy and followed a policy of collaboration with the Germans in order to preserve as much autonomy as possible. Most of the French were too stunned to resist. Many thought that Hitler's victory was certain and saw no alternative to collaboration. A few, most notably General Charles de Gaulle (1890–1969), fled to Britain, where they organized the French National Committee of Liberation, or "Free French." The Vichy government controlled most of French North Africa and the navy, but the Free French began operating in central Africa and from London beamed messages of hope and defiance to their compatriots in France. As the passage of time dispelled expectations of a quick German victory, a French underground movement arose that organized many forms of resistance.

The Battle of Britain

The fall of France left Britain isolated, and Hitler expected the British to come to terms. He was prepared to allow Britain to retain its empire in return for a free hand for Germany on the Continent. The British had never been willing to accept such an arrangement and had fought the long and difficult war against Napoleon to prevent the domination of the Continent by a single power. If there was any chance that the British would consider such terms, that chance disappeared when Winston Churchill (1874–1965) replaced Chamberlain as prime minister in May of 1940.

Churchill had been an early and forceful critic of Hitler, the Nazis, and the policy of appeasement. A descendant and biographer of the duke of Marlborough (1650–1722), who had fought to prevent the domination of Europe by Louis XIV in the seventeenth century, Churchill's sense of history, his feeling for British greatness, and his hatred of tyranny and love of freedom made him reject any thought of compromise. His skill as a speaker and a writer allowed him to infuse the British people with his own courage and determination and to undertake what seemed almost a hopeless fight. Hitler and his allies, including the Soviet Union, controlled all of Europe. Japan was having its way in Asia. The United States was neutral, dominated by isolationist sentiment, and determined to avoid involvement outside the Western Hemisphere.

One of Churchill's greatest achievements was establishing a close relationship with the American President Franklin D. Roosevelt, who found ways to help the British in spite of strong political opposition. In 1940 and 1941, before the United States was at war, America sent military supplies, traded badly needed warships for leases on British naval bases, and

Prime Minister Winston Churchill (1874–1965) standing amid the ruins of the House of Commons, which was badly damaged during the German bombing of London. Churchill's eloquence and resolution helped preserve British morale during the darkest days of the war. [UPI/ Bettmann Newsphotos]

even convoyed ships across the Atlantic to help the British survive.

As weeks passed and Britain remained defiant, Hitler was forced to contemplate an invasion, and that required control of the air. The first strikes by the German air force (*Luftwaffe*), directed against the airfields and fighter planes in southeastern England, began in August 1940. There is reason to think that if these attacks had continued, Germany might soon have gained control of the air and, with it, the chance of a successful invasion. In early September, however, seeking revenge for some British bombing raids on German cities, the *Luftwaffe* made London its major target. For two months London was bombed every night. Much of the city was destroyed and about fif-

979

Londoners returning home after a raid. Despite many casualties and wide-spread devastation, the German bombing of London did not break British morale or prevent the city from functioning. [*UPI/Bettmann Newsphotos*]

teen thousand people were killed, but the theories of victory through air power alone proved vain. Casualties were many times fewer than expected and morale was not shattered. In fact, the bombings brought the British people together and made them more resolute. At the same time the Royal Air Force (RAF) inflicted heavy losses on the *Luftwaffe*. Aided by the newly developed radar and an excellent system of communications, the Spitfire and Hurricane fighter planes destroyed more than twice as many enemy planes as were lost by the RAF. Hitler had lost the Battle of Britain in the air and was forced to abandon his plans for invasion.

980

The German Attack on Russia

From the first, the defeat of Russia and the conquest of the Ukraine to provide *Lebensraum* ("living room") for the German people had been a major goal for Hitler. Even before the assault on Britain he had informed his staff of his intention to attack Russia as soon as conditions were favorable. In December of 1940, even while the bombing of England continued, he ordered his generals to prepare for an invasion of Russia by May 15, 1941. He appears to have thought that a *Blitzkrieg* victory in the east would destroy all hope and bring the British to their senses.

Operation Barbarossa, the code name for the invasion of Russia, was aimed at knocking Russia out of the war before winter could set in. Success depended in part on an early start, but here Hitler's Italian alliance proved costly. Mussolini was jealous of Hitler's success and annoyed by the treatment he had received from the German dictator. Unable to make progress against the French army even while Hitler was crushing the part of it that was on his own frontier, Mussolini was not allowed any gain at the expense of France or even of French Africa. Instead he launched an attack against the British in Egypt and drove them back some sixty miles. Encouraged by this success, he invaded Greece from his base in Albania (which he had seized in 1939). His purpose was revealed by his remark to his son-in-law, Count Ciano: "Hitler always faces me with a *fait accompli*. This time I am going to pay him back in his own coin. He will find out in the newspapers that I have occupied Greece."[5] But in North Africa the British counterattacked and drove the Italians back into Libya, and the Greeks themselves pushed into Albania. In March 1941 the British sent help to the Greeks, and Hitler was forced to divert his attention to the Balkans and to Africa. General Erwin Rommel (1891–1944), later to earn the title "The Desert Fox," went to Africa and soon got the British out of Libya and back into Egypt. In the Balkans the German army swiftly occupied Yugoslavia and crushed Greek resistance, but the price was a delay of six weeks. The diversion caused by Mussolini's vanity proved to be costly the following winter in the Russian campaign.

Operation Barbarossa was launched against Russia on June 22, 1941, and it came very

[5]Quoted in Gordon Wright, *The Ordeal of Total War, 1939–1945* (New York: Harper & Row, 1968), pp. 35–36.

With Goring in the podium, Hitler announces the invasion of Russia to the Reichstag on June 22, 1941. "The world," he said, "will hold its breath." [Reuters/Bettmann Newsphotos]

close to success. In spite of their deep suspicion of Germany and the excuse later offered by apologists for the Soviet Union that the Nazi–Soviet Pact was meant to give Russia time to prepare, the Russians were taken quite by surprise. Stalin appears to have panicked. He had not fortified his frontier, not had he issued orders for his troops to withdraw when attacked. In the first two days some two thousand planes were destroyed on the ground. By November Hitler had gone further into Russia than Napoleon: the German army stood at the gates of Leningrad, on the outskirts of Moscow, and on the Don River. Of the 4.5 million troops with which the Russians had begun the fighting, they had lost 2.5 million; of their 15,000 tanks only 700 were left. Moscow was in panic, and a German victory seemed imminent.

But the Germans could not deliver the final blow. In August there was a delay in their advance to decide on a course of action. One plan was to drive directly for Moscow and take it before winter. There is some reason to think that such a plan might have worked and brought victory, for unlike the situation in Napoleon's time, Moscow was the hub of the

German tanks rolling across the plains of the Ukraine in June, 1941. Despite many signs that war was imminent, the German invasion took the Soviets by surprise. German armies were able to penetrate to the edge of Moscow before stiffening Russian resistance—and the onset of winter—halted them. [Library of Congress]

Russian system of transportation. Hitler, however, imposed his own view on his generals and diverted a significant part of his forces to the south. By the time he was ready to return to the offensive near Moscow, it was too late. Winter struck the German army, which was neither dressed nor equipped to face it. Given precious time, Stalin was able to restore order and to build defenses for the city. Even more important, there was time for troops to come from Siberia, where they had been placed to check a possible Japanese attack. In November and December the Russians were able to counterattack. The *Blitzkrieg* had turned into a war of attrition, and the Germans began to have visions of Napoleon's retreat.

Hitler's Europe

Hitler often spoke of the "new order" that he meant to impose after he had established his Third Reich throughout Europe. The first two German empires (*Reich*) were those of Charlemagne in the ninth century and William II in the nineteenth, and Hitler predicted that his own would last for a thousand years. If his organization of Germany before the war is a proper index, he had no single plan of government but relied frequently on intuition and pragmatism. His organization of conquered Europe had the same characteristics of spontaneity and patchwork. Some conquered territory was annexed to Germany; some was administered directly by German officials; some lands were nominally autonomous but were ruled by puppet governments.

The demands and distractions of war and the fact that Hitler's defeat prevented him from fully carrying out his plans make it hard to be sure what his intentions were, but the measures he took before his death provide indications. They give evidence of a regime probably unmatched in history for carefully planned terror and inhumanity. To accomplish his plan of giving *Lebensraum* to the Germans at the expense of people he deemed inferior, Hitler established colonies of Germans in parts of Poland, driving the local people from their land and employing them as cheap labor. He had similar plans on an even higher scale for Russia. The Russians would be driven eastward to central Asia and Siberia; they would be kept in check by frontier colonies of German war veterans, and the more desirable lands of European Russia would be settled by Germans.

Hitler's long-range plans included Germanization as well as colonization. In lands inhabited by people racially akin to the Germans, like the Scandinavian countries, the Netherlands, and Switzerland, the natives would be absorbed into the German nation. Such peoples would be reeducated and purged of dissenting elements, but there would be little or no colonization. He even had plans, only slightly realized, of adopting selected people from the lesser races into the master race. One of these plans involved bringing half a million Ukrainian girls into Germany as servants and finding German husbands for them; about fifteen thousand actually did reach Germany.

In the economic sphere Hitler regarded the conquered lands merely as a source of plunder. From eastern Europe he removed everything useful, including entire industries. In Russia and Poland the Germans simply confiscated the land. In the west the conquered countries were forced to support the occupying army at a rate several times the real cost. The Germans used the profits to buy up everything useful and desirable, stripping the conquered peoples of most necessities. The Nazis were frank about their policies. One of Hitler's high officials said, "Whether nations live in prosperity or starve to death interests me only insofar as we need them as slaves for our culture.[6]

Racism and the Holocaust

The most horrible aspect of the Nazi rule in Europe arose not from military or economic necessity but from the inhumanity and brutality inherent in Hitler's racial doctrines. He considered the Slavs *Untermenschen*, subhuman creatures like beasts who need not be thought of or treated as people. In parts of Poland the upper and professional classes were entirely removed—either jailed, deported, or killed. Schools and churches were closed; marriage was controlled by the Nazis to keep down the Polish birth rate; and harsh living conditions were imposed. In Russia things were even worse. Hitler spoke of his Russian campaign as a war of extermination. Heinrich Himmler, head of Hitler's elite SS guard, planned the elimination of thirty million Slavs to make room for the Germans, and he formed extermination squads for the purpose. The number of Russian prisoners of war and deported civilian

[6]Quoted by Gordon Wright, *The Ordeal of Total War, 1939–1945* (New York: Harper & Row, 1968), p. 117

AXIS EUROPE, 1941

MAP 28–3 *On the eve of the German invasion of the Soviet Union the Germany-Italy Axis bestrode most of Western Europe by annexation, occupation, or alliance—from Norway and Finland in the north to Greece in the south and from Poland to France. Britain, the Soviets, a number of insurgent groups, and, finally, America had before them the long struggle of conquering this Axis "fortress Europe."*

workers who died under Nazi rule may have reached six million.

Hitler had special plans for the Jews. He meant to make all Europe *Judenrein* ("free of Jews"). For a time he thought of sending them to the island of Madagascar, but later he arrived at the "final solution of the Jewish prob-lem": extermination. The Nazis built extermi-nation camps in Germany and Poland and used the latest technology to achieve the most efficient means of killing millions of men, women, and children for no other reason than their birth into the designated group. Before the war was over, perhaps six million Jews had

983

RIGHT: *A Jewish couple in Berlin in October 1941 wearing yellow stars of David marked* Jude *(Jew). The wearing of the stars was required of all German Jews by a law passed the previous month. The final step in the Nazi's anti-Jewish campaign, the deportation of Jews to death camps in Eastern Europe, began in early 1942. [Wide World Photos]*

BELOW: *The dead at the Nordhausen concentration camp, which was liberated by the American army in April 1945. The Nazis set up their first concentration camps in Germany 1933 to hold opponents of their regime. After the conquest of Poland, new camps were established there as part of the ''final solution,'' the extermination of the Jews. About six million Jews were murdered in these camps. Even in those camps not dedicated to extermination, in which political prisoners and ''undesirables,'' such as gypsies, homosexuals, and Jehovah's Witnesses, were held, conditions were brutal in the extreme, and tens of thousands died. The crimes of the Nazi regime have no precedent in human history. [National Archives]*

died in what has come to be called the *Holocaust*. Only about a million remained alive, those mostly in pitiable condition.

World War II was unmatched in modern times in cruelty. When Stalin's armies conquered Poland and entered Germany, they

---

An Observer Describes the Mass Murder of Jews in the Ukraine

After World War II some German officers and officials were put on trial at Nuremberg by the victorious powers for crimes they were charged with having committed in the course of the war. The following selections from the testimony of a German construction engineer who witnessed the mass murder of Jews at Dubno in the Ukraine on October 5, 1942, reveal the brutality with which Hitler's attempt at a "final solution of the Jewish problem" was carried out.

On October 5, 1942, when I visited the building office at Dubno, my foreman told me that in the vicinity of the site, Jews from Dubno had been shot in three large pits, each about 30 metres long and 3 metres deep. About 1,500 persons had been killed daily. All the 5,000 Jews who had still been living in Dubno before the pogrom were to be liquidated. As the shooting had taken place in his presence, he was still much upset.

Thereupon, I drove to the site accompanied by my foreman and saw near it great mounds of earth, about 30 metres long and 2 metres high. Several trucks stood in front of the mounds. Armed Ukrainian militia drove the people off the trucks under the supervision of an S.S. man. The militiamen acted as guards on the trucks and drove them to and from the pit. All these people had the regulation yellow patches on the front and back of their clothes, and thus could be recognized as Jews.

My foreman and I went directly to the pits. Nobody bothered us. Now I heard rifle shots in quick succession from behind one of the earth mounds. The people who had got off the trucks— men, women and children of all ages—had to undress upon the orders of an S.S. man, who carried a riding or dog whip. They had to put down their clothes in fixed places, sorted according to shoes, top clothing and underclothing. I saw a heap of shoes of about 800 to 1,000 pairs, great piles of underlinen and clothing.

Without screaming or weeping, these people undressed, stood around in family groups, kissed each other, said farewells, and waited for

a sign from another S.S. man, who stood near the pit, also with a whip in his hand. During the fifteen minutes that I stood near I heard no complaint or plea for mercy. I watched a family of about eight persons, a man and a woman both about fifty with their children of about one, eight and ten, and two grown-up daughters of about twenty to twenty-nine. An old woman with snow-white hair was holding the one-year-old child in her arms and singing to it and tickling it. The child was cooing with delight. The couple were looking on with tears in their eyes. The father was holding the hand of a boy about ten years old and speaking to him softly; the boy was fighting his tears. The father pointed to the sky, stroked his head, and seemed to explain something to him.

At that moment the S.S. man at the pit shouted something to his comrade. The latter counted off about twenty persons and instructed them to go behind the earth mound. Among them was the family which I have mentioned. I well remember a girl, slim and with black hair, who, as she passed close to me pointed to herself and said "23." I walked around the mound and found myself confronted by a tremendous grave. People were closely wedged together and lying on top of each other so that only their heads were visible. Nearly all had blood running over their shoulders from their heads. Some of the people shot were still moving. Some were lifting their arms and turning their heads to show that they were still alive. The pit was already two-thirds full. I estimated that it already contained about 1,000 people.

From the *Nuremberg Proceedings*, as quoted in Louis L. Snyder. *Documents of German History*, (New Brunswick: Rutgers University Press, 1958), pp. 462–464.

raped, pillaged, and deported millions to the east. The British and American bombing of Germany killed thousands of civilians, and the dropping of atomic bombs on Japan inflicted terrible harm on civilian populations. The bombings, however, were thought of as acts of war that would help defeat the enemy. Stalin's atrocities were not widely known in the West at the time and are not even today. The victorious Western Allies, therefore, were shocked by what they saw when they came on the Nazi extermination camps and their pitiful survivors; little wonder that they were convinced that the effort of resistance to the Nazis and all the pain it had cost were well worth it.

Japan and America's Entry into the War

The sympathies of the American government were very much on the British side, and the various forms of assistance that Roosevelt gave Britain would have justified a German declaration of war. Hitler, however, held back, and it is not clear that the United States government would have overcome isolationist sentiment and entered the war in the Atlantic if war had not been thrust on America in the Pacific. Since the Japanese conquest of Manchuria in 1931, American policy toward Japan had been suspicious and unfriendly. The outbreak of the war in Europe emboldened the Japanese to move forward more quickly in their drive to dominate Asia. They allied themselves with Germany and Italy, made a treaty of neutrality with the Soviet Union, and penetrated into Indochina at the expense of defeated France. At the same time they continued their war in China and made plans to gain control of Malaya and the East Indies at the expense of beleaguered Britain and the conquered Netherlands. The only barrier to Japanese expansion was the United States.

The Americans had temporized, unwilling to cut off vital supplies of oil and other materials for fear of provoking a Japanese attack on Southeast Asia and Indonesia. The Japanese seizure of Indochina in July 1941 changed that policy, which had already begun to stiffen. The United States froze Japanese assets and cut off oil supplies; the British and Dutch did the same. Japanese plans for expansion could not continue without the conquest of the Indonesian oil fields and Malayan rubber and tin. In October a war faction led by General Hideki Tojo (1885–1948) took power in Japan and decided to risk a war rather than yield. On Sunday morning, December 7, 1941, even while Japanese representatives were discussing a settlement in Washington, Japan launched an air attack on Pearl Harbor, Hawaii, the chief American naval base in the Pacific. The technique was similar to the one Japan had used against the Russian fleet at Port Arthur in 1904, and it caught the Americans equally by surprise. A large part of the American fleet and many airplanes were destroyed, and the American capacity to wage war in the Pacific was destroyed for the time being. The next day the United States and Britain declared war on Japan, and three days later Germany and Italy declared war on the United States.

The Tide Turns

The potential power of the United States was enormous, but right after Pearl Harbor, America was ill prepared for war. Though conscription had been introduced in 1940, the army was tiny, inexperienced, and ill supplied. American industry was not ready for war. The Japanese swiftly captured Guam, Wake Island, and the Philippine Islands. At the same time they attacked Hong Kong, Malaya, Burma, and Indonesia. By the spring of 1942 they controlled these places and the southwest Pacific as far as New Guinea. They were poised for an attack on Australia, and it seemed that nothing could stop them.

In the same year the Germans advanced deeper into Russia and almost reached the Caspian Sea in their drive for Russia's oil fields. In Africa, too, Axis fortunes were high. Rommel drove the British back into Egypt toward the Suez Canal and finally was stopped at El Alamein, only seventy miles from Alexandria. Relations between the democracies and their Soviet ally were still far from close; German submarine warfare was threatening British supplies; the Allies were being thrown back on every front; and the future looked bleak.

The first good news for the Allied cause in the Pacific came in the spring of 1942. A naval battle in the Coral Sea sent many Japanese ships to the bottom and gave security to Australia. A month later the United States defeated the Japanese in a fierce air and naval battle off Midway Island, blunting the chance of another assault on Hawaii and doing enough damage to halt the Japanese advance. Soon American Marines landed on Guadalcanal in the Solomon Islands and began in a small way to reverse the momentum of the war. The war in

Pearl Harbor, December 7, 1941. The successful Japanese attack on the American base at Pearl Harbor in Hawaii, together with simultaneous attacks on other Pacific bases, brought the United States into war against the Axis powers. This picture shows the effects of the Japanese bombing upon the battleships Arizona, Tennessee, *and* West Virginia. [*Official United State Navy Photograph*]

the Pacific was far from over, but Japan was checked sufficiently to allow the Allies to concentrate their efforts first in Europe.

The nations opposed to the Axis powers numbered more than twenty and were located all over the world, but the main combatants were Great Britain, the Soviet Union, and the United States. The two Western democracies cooperated in everything to an unprecedented degree, but suspicion between them and their Soviet ally continued. Although the Russians accepted all the aid they could get, they did not trust their allies, complained of inadequate help, and demanded that the democracies open a "second front" on the mainland of Europe. In 1942 American preparation and production were inadequate for an invasion of

Europe, and control of the Atlantic by German submarines was such as to prevent safe crossing by the required number of troops. Not until 1944 were conditions right for the invasion, but in the meantime other developments forecast the doom of the Axis.

ALLIED LANDINGS IN AFRICA, SICILY, AND ITALY. In November 1942 an Allied force landed in French North Africa. Even before that landing, the British Field Marshal Bernard Montgomery (1887–1976), after stopping Rommel at El Alamein, had begun a drive to the west, and the American General Dwight D. Eisenhower (1890–1969) had pushed eastward through Morocco and Algeria. The two armies caught the German army

987

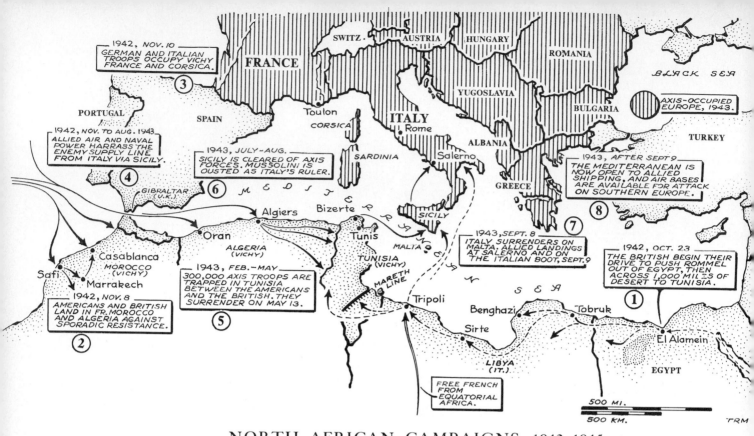

NORTH AFRICAN CAMPAIGNS, 1942–1945

MAP 28–4 *Control of North Africa was important to the Allies in order to have access to Europe from the south. The map diagrams this theater of the war from Morocco to Egypt and the Suez Canal.*

between them in Tunisia and crushed it. The Suez Canal and the Mediterranean were now under Allied control, and southern Europe was exposed. In July and August 1943 the Allies took Sicily. Mussolini was driven from power, and the new government tried to make peace, but the Germans moved into Italy. The Allies landed in Italy, and Marshal Pietro Badoglio (1871–1956), the leader of the new Italian government, went over to their side, declaring war on Germany. Churchill had spoken of Italy as the "soft underbelly" of the Axis, but German resistance was tough and determined. Still the need to defend Italy put a strain on the Germans' energy and resources and left them vulnerable on other fronts.

BATTLE OF STALINGRAD. The Russian campaign became especially demanding. In the summer of 1942 the Germans resumed the offensive on all fronts but were unable to get very far except in the south. The goal was the oil fields near the Caspian Sea, and they got as far as Stalingrad on the Volga, a key point for the protection of the flank of the German army in

the south. Hitler was determined to take the city and Stalin to hold it. The Battle of Stalingrad raged for months with unexampled ferocity. The Russians lost more men than the Americans lost in combat during the entire war, but their heroic defense prevailed. Because Hitler again overruled his generals and would not allow a retreat, an entire German army was lost. Stalingrad marked the turning point of the Russian campaign. Thereafter material help from America and, even more, increased production from their own industry, which had been moved to or built up in the safety of the central and eastern regions of the U.S.S.R., allowed the Russians to gain and keep the offensive. As the German military and material resources dwindled, the Russians advanced westward inexorably.

STRATEGIC BOMBING. In 1943 the Allies began to gain ground in production and logistics as well. The industrial might of the United States began to come into full force, and at the same time new technology and tactics made great strides in eliminating the submarine menace. In the same year the American and British air forces began a series of massive bombardments of Germany by night and day. The Americans were more committed to the theory of the "precision bombing" of military and industrial targets vital to the enemy war effort, so they flew the day missions. The British regarded precision bombing as impossible and therefore useless. They preferred indiscriminate "area bombing" aimed at destroying the morale of the German people, and this kind of mission could be done at night. It does not appear that either kind of bombing had much effect on the war until 1944. Then the Americans introduced long-range fighters that could protect the bombers and allow accurate missions by day. By 1945 the Allies had cleared the skies of German planes and could bomb at will. Concentrated attacks on industrial targets, especially communications centers and oil refineries, did very real damage and helped to shorten the war. Terror bombing continued, too, but seems not to have had any useful result. The bombardment of Dresden in February 1945 was especially savage and destructive. It was much debated within the British government and has raised moral questions since, but the aerial war over Germany took a heavy toll of the German air force and diverted vital resources away from other military purposes.

The Defeat of Nazi Germany

On June 6, 1944 ("D-Day"), American, British, and Canadian troops landed in force on the coast of Normandy. The "second front" was opened. General Dwight D. Eisenhower, the commander of the Allied armies, faced a difficult problem. The European coast was heavily fortified. Amphibious assaults, moreover, are especially vulnerable to changes of wind and weather. Success depended on meticulous planning, advance preparation by heavy bombing, and successful feints to mask the point of attack. The German defense was strong, but the Allies were able to establish a beachhead and then to break out of it. In mid-August the Allies landed in southern France to put more pressure on the enemy. By the beginning of September, France had been liberated.

All went smoothly until December, when the Germans launched a counterattack on the Belgian front through the Forest of Ardennes. Because the Germans were able to push forward into the Allied line, this was called the Battle of the Bulge, and it brought heavy losses

Stalingrad after the battle, February 1943. The German defeat at Stalingrad marked the turning point of the Russian campaign. Thereafter, the Russians advanced inexorably westward. [*Sovfoto*]

Allied forces land on the Normandy beaches on D-Day, June 6, 1944. [*U.S. Air Force Photo*]

500 MI.
500 KM.

Trondheim

NORWAY
Oslo
Stavanger

FINLAND
Viborg
Leningrad
Helsinki
Reval
L. LADOGA

SWEDEN
Stockholm

NORTH SEA

N. IRELAND
EIRE

UNITED KINGDOM
Liverpool
Hull
Coventry
London

DENMARK
Copenhagen
NETH.
Rotterdam

BALTIC SEA

ESTONIA
Novgorod
Riga
LATVIA
LITHUANIA
Memel
Vitebsk
Smolensk
Kaunas
BYELO-
Vilna
RUSSIA
KATYN FOREST
Brya

GERMAN SURRENDER IN REIMS, MAY 7, 1945 BERLIN, MAY 8, 1945

Danzig
EAST PRUSSIA

Hamburg
Bremen
Berlin
GREATER GERMANY
Essen
Torgau
POSEN
Cologne
Dresden
Warsaw
Remagen
Breslau
POLAND
Kiev

NORMANDY INV. JUNE 6, 1944

BELG.
Dunkirk

BATTLE OF THE BULGE DEC. 1944

Gomel

RHINE CROSSING, MAR. 7, 1945

Cracow

Reims
Paris
Nürnberg
St. Nazaire
Orléans
Strassburg
BOHEMIA
MORAVIA
Lemberg

RUSSIAN FRONT JUNE 23, 1944

Tours
Munich
SLOVAKIA
DNIESTER
Kir

FRANCE
Vichy
SWITZ.
TYROL
Vienna
AUSTRIA
HUNGARY
BESSARABIA

Lyons
Budapest
Jassi
Odessa

Bordeaux

Milan
ROMANIA

Bologna
CROATIA
Bucharest

AXIS TROOPS OCCUPY VICHY FRANCE, NOV. 10 AND 11, 1942

Florence
Belgrade
YUGOSLAVIA
SERBIA

PROVENCE
ADRIATIC SEA

ALLIES LAND IN PROVENCE, AUG. 15, 1944

Marseilles
Toulon

SPAIN
Barcelona

CORSICA (VICHY)

ITALY
Rome

MONTE-NEGRO
BULGARIA
Varna

Tirana
Sofia
Skoplje

Istanbul

Valencia

Anzio
Cassino
ALBANIA
(TURK.)

BALEARIC IS.
SARDINIA (IT.)
Naples
Salerno
Salonika

MEDITERRANEAN
CALABRIA
GREECE
AEGEAN SEA
Izmir

Algiers
Bizerte

ALLIES INVADE SICILY & ITALY, JULY–SEPT. 1943

Athens

RHODE

AXIS TROOPS EVACUATED, MAY 1943

Tunis
SICILY

ITALIAN SURRENDER, SEPT. 8, 1943

SEA
Candia

ALGERIA (VICHY)
TUNISIA (VICHY)
MALTA (U.K.)
CRETE

990

DEFEAT OF THE AXIS
IN EUROPE,
1942–1945

MAP 28–5 *This is the sequel to the map on page 901. Here we see some major steps in the progress toward allied victory against Axis Europe. From the south through Italy, from the west through France, and from the east through Russia the Allies gradually conquered the continent to bring the war in Europe to a close.*

and considerable alarm to the Allies. That effort, however, was the last gasp for the Germans. The Allies recovered the momentum and pushed eastward. They crossed the Rhine in March of 1945, and German resistance crumbled. This time there could be no doubt that the Germans had lost the war on the battlefield.

In the east the Russians swept forward no less swiftly. By March 1945 they were within reach of Berlin. Because the Allies insisted on unconditional surrender, the Germans fought on until May. Hitler and his intimates committed suicide in an underground hideaway in Berlin on May 1, 1945. The Russians occupied Berlin by agreement with their Western allies. The Third Reich had lasted a dozen years instead of the millennium predicted by Hitler.

Fall of the Japanese Empire

The war in Europe ended on May 8, 1945, and by then victory over Japan was in sight. The original Japanese attack on the United States had been a calculated risk against the odds. The longer the war lasted, the greater was the advantage to the American superiority in industrial production and human resources. Beginning in 1943 the American forces, still relatively small in number, began a campaign of "island hopping." They did not try to recapture every Pacific island held by the Japanese but selected major bases and places strategically located along the enemy supply line. Starting from the Solomons, they moved northeast toward the Japanese homeland. By June of 1944 they had reached the Mariana Islands, which they could use as bases for bombing the Japanese in the Philippines, in China, and in Japan itself. In October of the same year the Americans recaptured most of the Philippines and drove the Japanese fleet back into its home waters. In 1945 Iwo Jima and Okinawa fell, in spite of a determined Japanese resistance that included "kamikaze" attacks, suicide missions in which specially trained pilots deliberately flew their explosive-

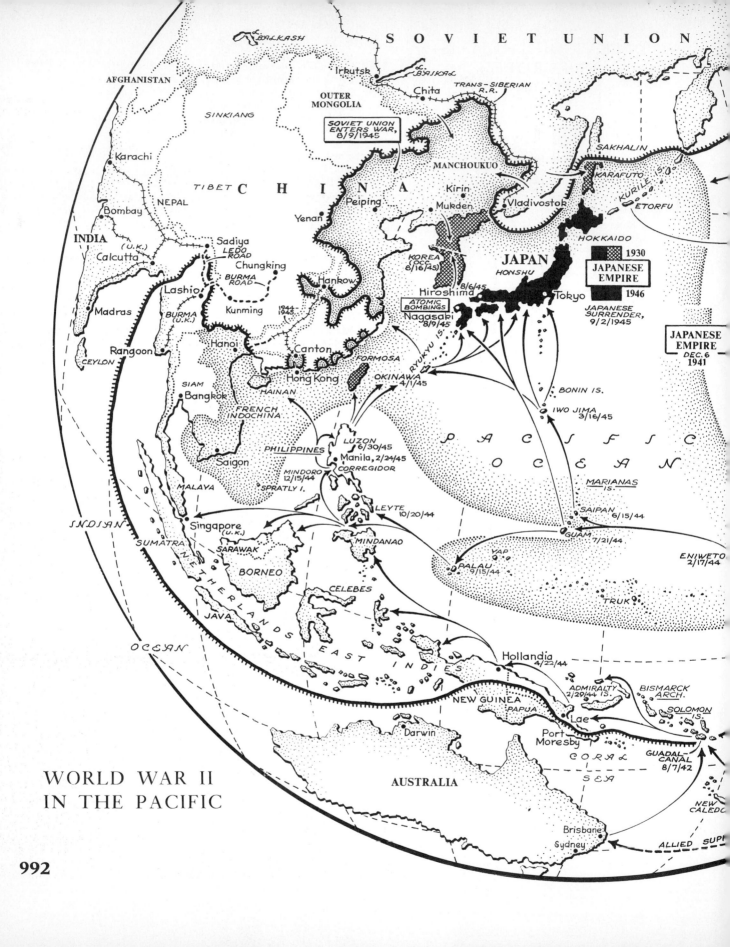

WORLD WAR II
IN THE PACIFIC

992

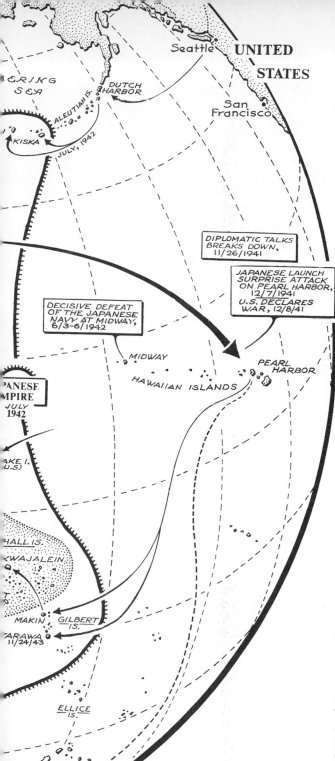

MAP 28–6 *As in Europe, the Pacific war was a problem in Allied recapture of areas that had been quickly taken earlier by the enemy. The enormous area represented by the map shows the initial expansion of Japanese holdings to cover half the Pacific and its islands, as well as huge sections of eastern Asia, and the long struggle to push the Japanese back to their homeland and defeat them by the summer of 1945.*

filled planes into American warships. From these new bases, closer to Japan, the American bombers launched a terrible wave of bombings that destroyed Japanese industry and disabled the Japanese navy, but still the Japanese government, dominated by a military clique, refused to surrender.

Confronted with Japan's determination, the Americans made plans for a frontal assault on the Japanese homeland, which, they calculated, might cost a million American casualties and even greater losses for the Japanese. At this point science and technology presented the Americans with another choice. Since early in the war a secret program had been in progress. Its staff, made up in significant part of exiles from Hitler's Europe, was working to use atomic energy for military purposes. On August 6, 1945, an American plane dropped an atomic bomb on the city of Hiroshima. The city was destroyed, and more than 70,000 of its 200,000 residents were killed. Two days later the Soviet Union declared war on Japan and invaded Manchuria. The next day a second atomic bomb fell, this time on Nagasaki. Even then the Japanese did not yield. The Japanese Cabinet was prepared to resist further, to face an invasion rather than give up. It was only the unprecedented intervention of Emperor Hirohito that convinced the government to surrender on August 14. Even then they made the condition that Japan could keep its emperor. Although the Allies had continued to insist on unconditional surrender, President Harry S Truman (1884–1972), who had come to office on April 12, 1945, on the death of Franklin D. Roosevelt, accepted the condition, and peace was formally signed aboard the U.S.S. *Missouri* in Tokyo Bay on September 2, 1945.

Revulsion and horror at the only use of atomic bombs as well as hindsight arising from the Cold War have surrounded with debate the decision to use the bomb against Japanese cities. Some have suggested that the bombings were unnecessary to win the war and that their main purpose was to frighten the Russians into

Hiroshima after the bomb, August, 1945. The atomic blast destroyed the city and killed 70,000 of its 200,000 inhabitants. [U.S. Air Force Photo]

a more cooperative attitude after the war. Others have emphasized the bureaucratic, almost automatic nature of the decision, once it had been decided to develop the bomb. To the decision makers and their contemporaries, however, matters were simpler. The bomb was a way to end the war swiftly without the need of invasion or an extended period of bombardment, and it would save American lives. The

decision to use it was conscious, not automatic, and required no ulterior motive.

The Cost of War

World War II was the most terrible war in history. Military deaths are estimated at some fifteen million, and at least as many civilians were killed. If deaths linked indirectly to the war are included, the figure of victims might reach as high as forty million. Most of Europe and significant parts of Asia were devastated. Yet the end of so terrible a war brought little opportunity for relaxation. The dawn of the Atomic Age and the dramatic end it brought to the war made people conscious that another major war might bring an end to humanity. Everything depended on the conclusion of a stable peace, but even as the fighting came to an end, conflicts among the victors made the prospects of a lasting peace doubtful.

Preparations for Peace and the Onset of the Cold War

The split between the Soviet Union and its wartime allies should cause no surprise. As the self-proclaimed center of world communism, the Soviet Union was openly dedicated to the overthrow of the capitalist nations, though this message was muted when the occasion demanded. On the other side, the western allies were no less open about their hostility to communism and its chief purveyor, the Soviet Union. Though they had been friendly to the early stages of the Russian Revolution, they had sent troops in hopes of overthrowing the Bolshevik regime. The United States did not grant formal recognition to the Union of Soviet Socialist Republics until 1933. The Western powers' exclusion of the Soviets from the Munich conference and Stalin's pact with Hitler did nothing to improve relations.

Though cooperation against a common enemy and strenuous propaganda efforts in the West helped improve Western feeling toward the Soviet ally, Stalin remained suspicious and critical of the Western war effort, and Churchill never ceased planning to contain the Soviet advance into Europe. For some time Roosevelt seems to have been hopeful that the Allies could continue to work together after the war, but even he was losing faith as the war and his life drew to a close. Differences in historical development and ideology, as well as traditional conflicts over political power and influence, soon dashed whatever hopes there were of a mutually satisfactory peace settlement and continued cooperation to uphold it.

The Atlantic Charter

In August 1941, even before the Americans were at war, Roosevelt and Churchill had met on a ship off Newfoundland and agreed to the Atlantic Charter, a broad set of principles in the spirit of Wilson's Fourteen Points, which provided a theoretical basis for the peace they sought. When Russia and the United States joined Britain in the war, the three powers entered a purely military alliance in January 1942, leaving all political questions aside. The first political conference was the meeting of foreign ministers in Moscow in October 1943. The ministers reaffirmed earlier agreements to fight on until the enemy surrendered without condition and to continue cooperating after the war in a united-nations organization.

Tehran

The first meeting of the three leaders of state took place at Tehran, the capital of Iran, in 1943. Western promises to open a second front in France the next summer (1944) and Stalin's agreement to join in the war against Japan when Germany was defeated created an atmosphere of goodwill in which to discuss a postwar settlement. Stalin wanted to retain what he had gained in his pact with Hitler and to dismember Germany. Roosevelt and Churchill were conciliatory, but they made no firm commitments. The most important decision was the one that chose Europe's west coast as the point of attack instead of southern Europe, by the way of the Mediterranean. That meant, in retrospect, that Soviet forces would occupy eastern Europe and control its destiny. At Tehran in 1943 the western allies did not foresee this clearly, for the Russians were still fighting deep within their own frontiers, and military considerations were paramount everywhere.

By 1944, the situation was different. In August, Soviet armies were in sight of Warsaw, which had risen in expectation of liberation. But the Russians halted, allowing the Polish rebels to be annihilated while they turned south into the Balkans. They gained control of Romania and Hungary, advances of which centuries of expansionist czars had only dreamed. Alarmed by these developments, Churchill went to Moscow and met with Stalin in October. They agreed to share power in the Balkans on the basis of Soviet predominance in Romania and Bulgaria, Western predominance in Greece, and equality of influence in Yugoslavia and Hungary. These agreements were not enforceable without American approval, and the Americans were known to be hostile to such un-Wilsonian devices as "spheres of influence."

Agreement on European questions was more difficult. On Germany the three powers easily agreed on its disarmament and denazification and on its division into four zones of occupation by France and the Big Three (the USSR, Britain, and the United States). Churchill, however, began to balk at Stalin's plan to dismember Germany and objected to his demand for reparations in the amount of $20 billion as well as forced labor from all the zones, with Russia to get half of everything. These matters were left undecided to fester and to cause dissension in the future.

The settlement of eastern Europe was no less a problem. Everyone agreed that the Soviet Union deserved neighboring governments that were friendly, but the West insisted that they also be independent, autonomous, and democratic. The western leaders, and especially Churchill, were not eager to see eastern Europe fall under Russian domination; they were also, especially Roosevelt, truly committed to democracy and self-determination. But Stalin knew that independent, freely elected governments in Poland and Romania would not be safely friendly to Russia. He had already established a subservient government in Poland at Lublin in competition with the Polish government-in-exile in London. Under pressure from the western leaders, however, he agreed to reorganize the government and to include some Poles friendly to the West. He also signed a Declaration on Liberated Europe promising self-determination and free democratic elections. Stalin may have been eager to avoid conflict before the war with Germany was over—he never was free of the fear that the Allies might still make an arrangement with Germany and betray him—and he probably thought it worth endorsing some meaningless principles as the price of continued harmony. In any case, he wasted little time in violating these agreements.

Yalta

The next meeting of the Big Three was at Yalta in the Crimea in February 1945. The western armies had not yet crossed the Rhine, and the Soviet army was within a hundred miles of Berlin. The war with Japan continued, and no atomic explosion had yet taken place. Roosevelt, faced with an invasion of Japan and prospective heavy losses, was eager to bring

the Russians into the Pacific war as soon as possible. As a true Wilsonian he also suspected Churchill's determination to maintain the British Empire and Britain's colonial advantages. The Americans thought that Churchill's plan to set up British spheres of influence in Europe would encourage the Russians to do the same and lead to friction and war. To encourage Russian participation in the war against Japan, Roosevelt and Churchill made extensive concessions to Russia in Sakhalin and the Kurile Islands, in Korea, and in Manchuria. Again in the tradition of Wilson, Roosevelt laid great stress on a united-nations organization: "Through the United Nations, he hoped to achieve a self-enforcing peace settlement that would not require American troops, as well as an open world without spheres of influence in which American enterprise could work freely."[7] Soviet agreement on these points seemed well worth concessions elsewhere.

Potsdam

The Big Three met for the last time in the Berlin suburb of Potsdam in July 1945. Much had changed since the last conference. Germany was defeated, and news of the successful experimental explosion of an atomic weapon reached the American president during the meetings. The cast of characters was also different: President Truman replaced Roosevelt, and Clement Attlee (1883–1967), leader of the Labour Party that had defeated Churchill's Conservatives in a general election, replaced Churchill as Britain's spokesman during the conference. Previous agreements were reaffirmed, but progress on undecided questions was slow.

Russia's western frontier was moved far into what had been Poland and included part of German East Prussia. In compensation Poland was allowed "temporary administration" over the rest of East Prussia and Germany east of the Oder–Neisse river line, a condition that became permanent. In effect, Poland was moved about a hundred miles west, at the expense of Germany, to accommodate the Soviet Union. The Allies agreed that Germany would be divided into occupation zones until the final peace treaty was signed. As no such treaty has ever been made, Germany remains divided to this day.

[7]Robert O. Paxton, *Europe in the Twentieth Century* (New York: Harcourt Brace Jovanovich, 1975), p. 487.

A Council of Foreign Ministers was established to draft peace treaties for Germany's allies. Growing disagreements made the job difficult, and it was not until February 1947 that Italy, Romania, Hungary, Bulgaria, and Finland signed treaties. The Russians were dissatisfied with the treaty that the United States made with Japan in 1951 and signed their own agreements with the Japanese in 1956. These disagreements were foreshadowed at Potsdam.

Causes of the Cold War

Some scholars attribute the hardening of the atmosphere to the advent of Truman in place of the more sympathetic Roosevelt and to the American possession of an effective atomic bomb. The fact is that Truman was trying to carry Roosevelt's policies forward, and there is

MAP 28–7 *"The Big Three", Roosevelt, Churchill, Stalin, met at Yalta in the Crimea in February of 1945. At the meeting concessions were made to Stalin concerning the settlement of Eastern Europe, as Roosevelt was eager to bring the Russians into the Pacific war as soon as possible. This map shows the positions held at the time of the surrender.*

The "Big Three" at Yalta, February 1945. [*Library of Congress*]

YALTA TO THE SURRENDER

The first meeting of the United Nations in San Francisco in April, 1945. Initial hopes that the U.N. would be able to resolve international conflicts soon foundered on the realities of great power conflict in the post-war world. [AP/Wide World Photos]

evidence that Roosevelt himself had become distressed by Soviet actions in eastern Europe. Nor did Truman use the successful test of the atomic bomb to try to keep Russia out of the Pacific. On the contrary, he worked hard to ensure Russian intervention against Japan. In part, the new coldness among the Allies arose from the mutual feeling that each had violated previous agreements. The Russians were plainly asserting permanent control of Poland and Romania under puppet Communist governments. The United States, on the other hand, was taking a harder line on the extent of German reparations to the Soviet Union.

In retrospect, however, it appears unlikely that friendlier styles on either side could have avoided a split that rested on basic differences of ideology and interest. The Soviet Union's attempt to extend its control westward into central Europe and the Balkans and southward into the Middle East was a continuation of the policy of czarist Russia. It had been Britain's traditional role to try to restrain Russian expansion into these areas, and it was not sur-

TERRITORIAL CHANGES AFTER WORLD WAR II

MAP 28–8 *The map pictures the shifts in territory following the defeat of the Axis. No treaty of peace has formally ended the war with Germany.*

prising that the United States should inherit that task as Britain's power waned. The alternative was to permit a major change in the balance of power in the world in favor of a huge nation, traditionally hostile, dedicated in its official ideology to overthrow nations like the United States, and governed by an absolute dictator who had already demonstrated many times his capacity for the most amazing deceptions and the most horrible cruelties. Few nations would be likely to take such risks.

Nevertheless the Americans made no attempt to roll back Soviet power where it existed, though American military forces were the greatest in their history, their industrial power was unmatched in the world, and atomic weapons were an American monopoly. In less than a year from the war's end, American forces in Europe were reduced from 3.5 million to half a million. The speed of the withdrawal was the result of pressure to "get the boys home" but was fully in accord with American plans and peacetime goals. These were the traditional ones of support for self-determination, autonomy, and democracy in the political area, free trade, freedom of the seas, no barriers to investment, and the Open Door in the economic sphere. These goals agreed with American principles, and they served American interests well. As the strongest, richest nation in the world, the one with the greatest industrial plant and the strongest currency, the United States would benefit handsomely if such an international order were established.

American hostility to colonial empires created tension with France and Britain, but these were minor. The main conflict came with the Soviet Union. From the Soviet perspective the extension of its frontiers and the domination of formerly independent states in eastern Europe were necessary for the security of the USSR and a proper compensation for the fearful losses that the Russians had suffered in the war. American resistance to the new state of things could be seen as a threat to the Soviets' security and legitimate aims. American objections over Poland and other states could be seen as attempts to undermine regimes friendly to Russia and to encircle the Soviet Union with hostile neighbors. Such behavior might be seen to justify Russian attempts to overthrow regimes friendly to the United States in western Europe and elsewhere.

The growth in France and Italy of large Communist parties plainly taking orders from Moscow led the Americans to believe that Stalin was engaged in a great worldwide plot to destroy capitalism and democracy by subversion. In the absence of reliable evidence about Stalin's intentions, certainty is not possible, but most people in the West thought the suspicions plausible. Rivalry between the Soviet Union and the United States dominated international relations for the next three decades, and in the flawed world of reality it is hard to see how things could have been otherwise. The important question was whether the conflict would take a diplomatic or a military form.

The Cold War

Evidence of the new mood of hostility among the former allies was not long in coming. In February 1946 both Stalin and his foreign minister, Vyacheslav Molotov, gave public speeches in which they spoke of the western democracies as enemies. A month later Churchill gave a speech in Fulton, Missouri, in

Churchill Invents the Iron Curtain; Cold War Declared

In 1946 Winston Churchill chose an American audience (at Westminster College in Fulton, Missouri) for the speech that contributed *iron curtain* to the language and, more important, defined the existence of what came to be known as the *Cold War* between the Communist and the democratic camps.

A shadow has fallen upon the scenes so lately lighted by the Allied victory. Nobody knows what Soviet Russia and its Communist international organization intends to do in the immediate future, or what are the limits, if any, to their expansive and proselytizing tendencies. . . .

From Stettin in the Baltic to Trieste in the Adriatic, an iron curtain has descended across the Continent. Behind that line lie all the capitals of the ancient states of central and eastern Europe. Warsaw, Berlin, Prague, Vienna, Budapest, Belgrade, Bucharest and Sofia; all these famous cities and the populations around them lie in the Soviet sphere and all are subject in one form or another, not only to Soviet influence but to a very high and increasing measure of control from Moscow. Athens alone, with its immortal glories, is free to decide its future at an election under British, American, and French observation. The Russian-dominated Polish government has been encouraged to make enormous and wrongful inroads upon Germany, and mass

expulsions of millions of Germans on a scale grievous and undreamed of are now taking place. The Communist parties, which were very small in all these eastern states of Europe, have been raised to preeminence and power far beyond their numbers and are seeking everywhere to obtain totalitarian control. Police governments are prevailing in nearly every case, and so far, except in Czechoslovakia, there is no true democracy. . . .

. . . I do not believe that Soviet Russia desires war. What they desire is the fruits of war and the indefinite expansion of their power and doctrines. . . .

. . . If the western democracies stand together in strict adherence to the principles of the United Nations Charter, their influence for furthering these principles will be immense and no one is likely to molest them. If, however, they become divided or falter in their duty, and if these all-important years are allowed to slip away, then indeed catastrophe may overwhelm us all.

"Winston Churchill's Speech at Fulton," in *Vital Speeches of the Day*, Vol. 12 (New York: City News Publishing), March 15, 1946, pp. 331–332.

which he viewed Russian actions in eastern Europe with alarm. He spoke of an Iron Curtain that had descended on Europe, dividing a free and democratic West from an East under totalitarian rule. He warned against Communist subversion and urged western unity and strength as a response to the new menace. In this atmosphere difficulties grew.

The attempt to deal with the problem of atomic energy was an early victim of the Cold War. The Americans put forward a plan to place the manufacture and control of atomic weapons under international control, but the Russians balked at the proposed requirements for on-site inspection and for limits on the veto power in the United Nations. The plan fell through. The United States continued to develop its own atomic weapons in secrecy, and the Russians did the same. By 1949, with the help of information obtained by Soviet spies in Britain and the United States, the Soviet Union exploded its own atomic bomb, and the race for nuclear weapons was on.

Any hopes that the new United Nations organization, with its headquarters in New York as a symbol of firm American adherence to international responsibility, would resolve the world's conflicts were soon disappointed. Like the League of Nations, it is dependent on voluntary contributions of money and troops. The UN Charter, moreover, forbids interference in the internal affairs of nations, and many of the problems of the 1940s were internal in nature. Finally, the Security Council, which is responsible for maintaining world peace, gives a veto to each of the permanent members. Because the Soviet Union was generally in the minority, it used the veto repeatedly, making it clear that the United Nations was not adequate to resolve existing problems.

Western resistance to what the West increasingly perceived as Soviet intransigence and Communist plans for subversion and expansion took clearer form in 1947. Since 1944 civil war had been raging in Greece between the royalist government restored by Britain and insurgents supported by the Communist countries, chiefly Yugoslavia. In 1947 Britain informed the United States that it was financially no longer able to support the Greeks. On March 12 President Truman asked Congress for legislation to support Greece and also Turkey, which was under Soviet pressure to yield control of the Dardanelles. Congress voted funds to aid Greece and Turkey, but the Truman Doctrine, as enunciated in a speech of March 12,

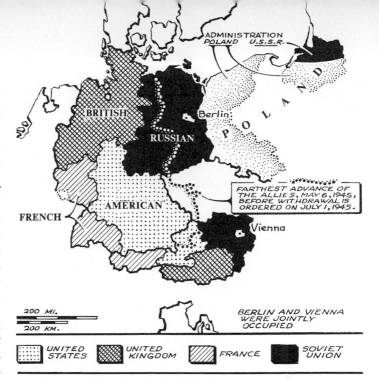

OCCUPIED GERMANY AND AUSTRIA

MAP 28–9 *At the war's end, defeated Germany, including Austria, was occupied by the victorious Allies in the several zones shown here. Austria, by prompt agreement, was reerected into an independent, neutral state and no longer occupied. But the German zones have hardened into an ''East'' Germany (the former Soviet zone) and a ''West'' Germany (the former British, French, and American zones). The city of Berlin, within the Soviet zone, was similarly divided.*

had a broader significance. The president advocated a policy of supporting "free people who are resisting attempted subjugation by armed minorities or by outside pressures," by implication anywhere in the world.

American aid to Greece and Turkey took the form of military equipment and advisers, but the threat in Western Europe was the growth of Communist parties fed by postwar poverty and hunger. To deal with this menace, the Americans devised the European Recovery Program, named the Marshall Plan after George C. Marshall, the secretary of state who introduced it. This was a plan for broad economic aid to European states on condition only that they work together for their mutual benefit. The invitation included the Soviet Union and its satellites. Finland and Czechoslovakia were willing to participate, and Poland and Hungary showed interest. The Soviets, fearing that American economic aid would attract many satellites out of their orbits, forbade them to take part. The Marshall Plan was a great success in restoring prosperity to West-

---

The Truman Doctrine

In 1947 the British informed the United States that they could no longer support the Greeks in their fight against a Communist insurrection supported from the outside. On March 12 of that year, President Truman asked Congress for legislation in support of both Greece and Turkey, which was also in danger. The spirit behind that request, which became known as the *Truman Doctrine,* appears in the following selections from Truman's speech to the Congress.

I am fully aware of the broad implications involved if the United States extends assistance to Greece and Turkey, and I shall discuss these implications with you at this time.

One of the primary objectives of the foreign policy of the United States is the creation of conditions in which we and other nations will be able to work out a way of life free from coercion. This was a fundamental issue in the war with Germany and Japan. Our victory was won over countries which sought to impose their will, and their way of life, upon other nations.

To insure the peaceful development of nations, free from coercion, the United States has taken a leading part in establishing the United Nations. The United Nations is designed to make possible lasting freedom and independence for all its members. We shall not realize our objectives, however, unless we are willing to help free peoples to maintain their free institutions and their national integrity against aggressive movements that seek to impose upon them totalitarian regimes. This is no more than a frank recognition that totalitarian regimes imposed upon free peoples, by direct or indirect aggression, undermine the foundations of international peace and hence the security of the United States.

The peoples of a number of countries of the world have recently had totalitarian regimes forced upon them against their will. The Government of the United States has made frequent protests against coercion and intimidation, in violation of the Yalta agreement, in Poland, Rumania, and Bulgaria. I must also state that in a number of other countries there have been similar developments.

At the present moment in world history nearly every nation must choose between alternative ways of life. The choice is too often not a free one.

One way of life is based upon the will of the majority, and is distinguished by free institutions, representative government, free elections, guaranties of individual liberty, freedom of speech and religion, and freedom from political oppression.

The second way of life is based upon the will of a minority forcibly imposed upon the majority. It relies upon terror and oppression, a controlled press and radio, fixed elections, and the suppression of personal freedoms.

I believe that it must be the policy of the United States to support free peoples who are resisting attempted subjugation by armed minorities or by outside pressures.

I believe that we must assist free peoples to work out their own destinies in their own way.

I believe that our help should be primarily through economic and financial aid, which is essential to economic stability and orderly political processes.

The world is not static, and the status quo *is not sacred. But we cannot allow changes in the* status quo *in violation of the Charter of the United Nations by such methods as coercion, or by such subterfuges as political infiltration. In helping free and independent nations to maintain their freedom, the United States will be giving effect to the principles of the Charter of the United Nations.*

Senate Committee on Foreign Relations, *A Decade of American Foreign Policy: Basic Documents 1941–1949* (1950), pp. 1235–1237.

ern Europe and in setting the stage for Europe's unprecedented postwar economic growth. It also led to the waning of Communist strength in the West and to the establishment of solid democratic regimes.

From the Western viewpoint this policy of "containment" was a new and successful response to the Soviet and Communist challenge. To Stalin it may have seemed a renewal of the old Western attempt to isolate and encircle the USSR. His answer was to put an end to all multiparty governments behind the Iron Curtain and to replace them with thoroughly Communist regimes completely under his control. He also called a meeting of all Communist parties around the world at Warsaw in the autumn of 1947. There they organized the Communist Information Bureau (Cominform), a revival of the old Comintern, dedicated to spreading revolutionary communism throughout the world. The era of the popular front was officially over. Communist leaders in the West who favored friendship, collaboration, and reform were replaced by hard-liners who attempted to sabotage the new structures.

In February 1948 a more dramatic and brutal display of Stalin's new policy took place in Prague. The Communists expelled the democratic members of what had been a coalition government and murdered Jan Masaryk, the foreign minister and son of the founder of Czechoslovakia, Thomas Masaryk. President Eduard Beneš (1884–1948) was also forced to resign, and Czechoslovakia was brought fully under Soviet rule.

These Soviet actions, especially those in Czechoslovakia, increased American determination to go ahead with its own arrangements in Germany. The wartime Allies had never agreed on the details of a German settlement and kept putting off decisions. At first they all agreed on the dismemberment of Germany but not on the form it should take. By the time of Yalta, Churchill had come to fear Russian control of Eastern and Central Europe and began to oppose dismemberment. There were differences in economic policy, too. The Russians proceeded swiftly to dismantle German industry in the eastern zone, but the Americans acted differently. They concluded that such a policy would require the United States to support Germany for the foreseeable future. It would also cause political chaos and open the way for communism. They preferred, therefore, to try to make Germany self-sufficient, and this meant restoring rather than destroying

The American airlift in action during the Berlin blockade. Every day for almost a year a stream of planes supplied the city until Stalin lifted the blockade in May, 1949. [Bildarchiv Preussicher Kulturbesitz]

its industrial capacity. To the Soviets the restoration of a powerful industrial Germany, even in the western zones only, was frightening and unacceptable. The same difference of approach hampered agreement on reparations because the Soviets claimed the right to the industrial equipment in all the zones, and the Americans resisted their demands.

Disagreement over Germany produced the most heated of postwar debates. When the Western powers agreed to go forward with a separate constitution for the western sectors of Germany in February 1948, the Soviets walked out of the joint Allied Control Commission. In the summer of that year the Western powers issued a new currency in their zone. Berlin, though well within the Soviet zone, was governed by all four powers. The Soviets feared the new currency that was circulating in Berlin at better rates than their own and chose to seal the city off by closing all railroads and highways to West Germany. Their purpose was to drive the Western powers out of Berlin. The Western allies responded to the Berlin Blockade with an airlift of supplies to the city that

1003

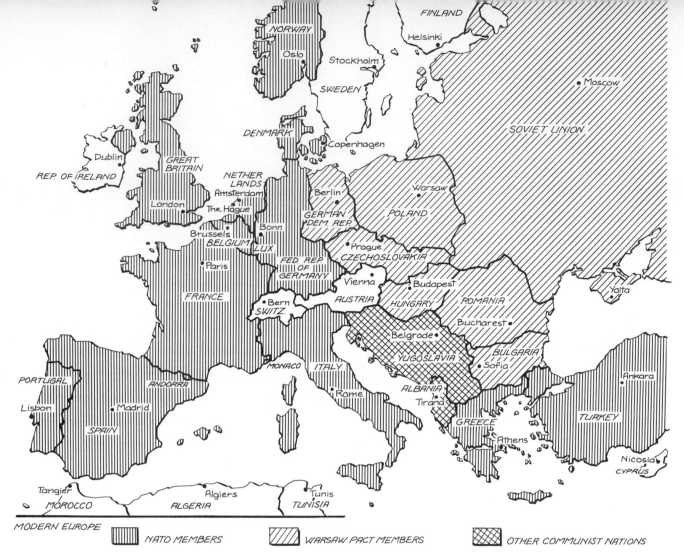

MAJOR EUROPEAN ALLIANCE SYSTEMS

MAP 28–10 *The North Atlantic Treaty Organization, which includes both Canada and the United States, stretches as far east as Turkey. By contrast, the Warsaw Pact nations are contiguous communist states of eastern Europe, with the Soviet Union, of course, as the dominant member.*

lasted almost a year. In May 1949 the Russians were forced to back down and to open access to Berlin, but the incident was decisive. It greatly increased tensions and suspicions between the opponents, and it hastened the lasting separation of Germany into two states. West Germany formally became the German Federated Republic in September 1949, and the eastern region became the German Democratic Republic a month later. Ironically Germany had been dismembered in a way no one had planned or expected.

NATO AND THE WARSAW PACT. Meanwhile the nations of Western Europe had been coming closer together. The Marshall Plan encouraged international cooperation, and in March 1948 Belgium, the Netherlands, Luxembourg, France, and Britain signed the Treaty of Brussels, providing for cooperation in economic and military matters. In April 1949 these nations joined with Italy, Denmark, Norway, Portugal, and Iceland to sign a treaty with Canada and the United States that formed the North Atlantic Treaty Organization (NATO).

NATO committed its members to mutual assistance in case any of them was attacked. For the first time in history the United States was committed to defend allies outside the Western Hemisphere. The NATO treaty formed the West into a bloc. A few years later West Germany, Greece, and Turkey joined the alliance.

Soviet relations with the states of Eastern Europe were governed by a series of bilateral treaties providing for close ties and mutual assistance in case of attack. In 1949 the Council of Mutual Assistance (COMECON) was formed to integrate the economies of these states. Unlike the NATO states, the Eastern alliance system was under direct Soviet domination through local Communist parties controlled from Moscow and overawed by the presence of the Red Army. The Warsaw Pact of May 1955, which included Albania, Bulgaria, Czechoslovakia, East Germany, Hungary, Poland, Romania, and the Soviet Union, merely gave formal recognition to a system that already existed. Europe was divided into two unfriendly blocs. The Cold War had taken firm shape in Europe.

Suggested Readings

A. ADAMTHWAITE, *France and the Coming of the Second World War, 1936–1939* (1977). A careful account making good use of the newly opened French archives.

A. BULLOCK, *Hitler: A Study in Tyranny,* rev. ed. (1964). A brilliant biography.

W. S. CHURCHILL, *The Second World War,* 6 vols. (1948–1954). The memoirs of the great British leader.

H. FEIS, *From Trust to Terror: The Onset of the Cold War, 1945–1950* (1970). The best general account.

H. W. GATZKE, *Stresemann and the Rearmament of Germany* (1954). An important monograph.

M. GILBERT AND R. GOTT, *The Appeasers,* rev. ed. (1963). A revealing study of British policy in the 1930s.

B. H. LIDDELL HART, *History of the Second World War,* 2 vols. (1971). A good military history.

K. HILDEBRAND, *The Foreign Policy of the Third Reich* (1970).

M. KNOX, *Mussolini Unleashed* (1982). An outstanding study of Fascist Italy's policy and strategy in World War II.

G. KOLKO, *The Politics of War* (1968). An interesting example of the new revisionist school that finds the causes of the Cold War in economic considerations and emphasizes American responsibility.

W. L. LANGER AND S. E. GLEASON, *The Challenge of Isolation* (1952). American foreign policy in the 1930s.

S. MARKS, *The Illusion of Peace* (1976). A good discussion of European international relations in the 1920s and early 1930s.

W. MURRAY, *The Change in the European Balance of Power 1938–1939* (1984). A brilliant study of the relationship between strategy, foreign policy, economics, and domestic politics in the years before the war.

N. RICH, *Hitler's War Aims,* 2 vols. (1973–1974).

M. SHERWIN, *A World Destroyed: The Atomic Bomb and the Grand Alliance* (1975). An analysis of the role of the atomic bomb in the years surrounding the end of World War II.

R. J. SONTAG, *A Broken World 1919–1939* (1971). An excellent survey.

A. J. P. TAYLOR, *The Origins of the Second World War* (1966). A lively, controversial, even perverse study.

C. THORNE, *The Approach of War 1938–1939* (1967). A careful analysis of diplomacy.

G. WRIGHT, *The Ordeal of Total War 1939–1945* (1968). An excellent survey.

President Reagan meets with Soviet leader Mikhail Gorbachev in Geneva in November 1985. Since 1945 Europe has been dominated by the rivalry of two superpowers, the United States and the Soviet Union. Summit meetings between leaders of the two states have achieved little beyond short-lived periods of detente. [Sygma]

OVER FORTY YEARS have passed since the conclusion of World War II and the onset of the Cold War. In this period of considerably more than a human generation, Europe has remained divided between Communist and non-Communist states and between allies of the United States and those of the Soviet Union. Such division is hardly a new feature of European history. For centuries the continent was separated into Roman and barbarian areas; later into Christian and Islamic spheres; then into Protestant, Catholic, and Orthodox camps; and finally into liberal and conservative states. Each of these divisions left an imprint on the culture of Europe. This seems no less true of the Cold War separation, although the latter may prove less long-lived than the previous divisions.

The four decades of the Cold War and its aftermath have witnessed extraordinary changes in European political and economic life. These, in turn, have produced significant results for the rest of the world once dominated by Europeans. Leadership in the western part of the continent has shifted to the United States and in the eastern part to the Soviet Union. The successor states of the Austro-Hungarian Empire previously coveted by Hitler fell under Soviet domination. Britain, France, Belgium, the Netherlands, and Portugal have conducted what is no doubt a permanent retreat from world empire. They have thus concluded an era of European world dominance that began during the Renaissance.

Many of those same nations have begun to cooperate economically and politically with each other as at no time in previous European experience. Peaceful economic integration and possible political unity have become facts of everyday life. During these same years much of the continent has experienced the most extensive material prosperity in its history.

Europe and the Soviet– American Rivalry

From approximately 1848 to 1948 the nation-state characterized European political life and rivalry. Generally these countries sought to expand their political influence and economic power at each other's expense. During the same century Europe's economic and technological supremacy allowed certain of its states to rule or administer a vast area of the globe inhabited by non-European peoples. These

29

Europe in the Era of the Superpowers

Repairing the Suez Canal, 1957. The Egyptians had sunk ships to block the canal during the Anglo-French-Israeli invasion in 1956. [United Nations]

nation-states have obviously continued to exist, but the economic and political collapse occasioned by World War II led them to become more interrelated and interdependent. The loss of economic and military superiority coincided with and in some cases aided the rise of nationalism throughout the colonial world. The United States and the Soviet Union—with their extensive economic resources, military forces, and nuclear capacities—have filled the power vacuum created by the European collapse.

The first round of Cold War confrontation culminated in the formation of NATO (1949) and the intervention of United States and United Nations forces in Korea (1950). In 1953 Stalin died, and later that year an armistice was concluded in Korea. Both events produced hope that international tensions might lessen. In early 1955 Austria agreed to become a neutral state, and Soviet occupation forces left. Later that year the leaders of France, Great Britain, the Soviet Union, and the United States held a summit conference at Geneva. Nuclear weapons and the future of divided Germany were the chief items on the agenda. Although there was much public display of

friendliness among the participants, there were few substantial agreements on major problems. Nonetheless the fact that world leaders were discussing problems and issues produced the so-called spirit of Geneva. This atmosphere proved to be short-lived, and the rivalry of power and polemics soon resumed.

The Crises of 1956

S UEZ. The year 1956 was one of considerable significance for both the Cold War and the recognition of the realities of European power in the postwar era. In July President Gamal Abdel Nasser (1918–1970) of Egypt nationalized the Suez Canal. Great Britain and France feared that this action would close the canal to their supplies of oil in the Persian Gulf. In October 1956 war broke out between Egypt and the eight-year-old state of Israel (for a discussion of the formation of Israel, see the section later in this chapter titled "The Arab–Israeli Dispute"). The British and the French seized the opportunity of this conflict to intervene. Publicly they spoke of acting to separate the combatants, but their real motive was to recapture the canal. The Anglo-French military operation was a fiasco of the first order and resulted in a humiliating diplomatic defeat. The United States refused to support the Anglo-French action. The Soviet Union protested in the most severe terms. The Anglo-French forces had to be withdrawn, and control of the canal remained with Egypt. The Suez intervention proved that without the support of the United States the nations of Western Europe could no longer undertake meaningful military operations. They could no longer impose their will on the rest of the world. At the same time it appeared that the United States and the Soviet Union had acted to restrain their allies from undertaking actions that might result in a wider conflict. The fact that neither of the superpowers wanted war put limitations on the actions of both Egypt and the Anglo-French forces.

POLAND. The autumn of 1956 also saw important developments in Eastern Europe. These demonstrated in a similar fashion the limitations on independent action among the Soviet bloc nations. When the prime minister of Poland died, the Polish Communist Party leaders refused to choose as his successor the person selected by Moscow. Considerable tension developed. The Soviet leaders even visited Warsaw to make their opinions known. In the end Wladyslaw Gomulka (1905–1982) emerged as the new Communist leader of Poland. He was the choice of the Poles, and he proved acceptable to the Soviets because he promised continued economic and military cooperation and most particularly continued Polish membership in the Warsaw Pact. Within those limits he moved to halt the collectivization of Polish agriculture and to improve the relationship between the Communist government and the Polish Roman Catholic church.

UPRISING IN HUNGARY. Hungary provided the second trouble spot for the Soviet Union. In late October, as the Polish problem was approaching a solution, demonstrations of sympathy for the Poles occurred in Budapest. The Communist government moved to stop

Budapest, October 1956. Street battles raged for several days until Soviet tanks finally put down the Hungarian revolt. [Raymond Darolle. Sygma]

the demonstrations, and street fighting erupted. A new ministry headed by former premier Imre Nagy (1896–1958) was installed by the Hungarian Communist Party. Nagy was a Communist who sought a more independent position for Hungary. He went much further in his demands than had Gomulka in Poland, and Nagy made direct appeals for political support from non-Communist groups in Hungary. Nagy called for the removal of Soviet troops and the ultimate neutralization of Hungary. He even went so far as to call for Hungarian withdrawal from the Warsaw Pact. These demands were wholly unacceptable to the Soviet Union. In early November Soviet troops invaded the country; deposed Nagy, who was later executed; and imposed Janos Kadar (b. 1912) as premier. The Suez intervention had provided an international diversion that helped to permit free action by the Soviet Union. The Polish and Hungarian disturbances had several results. They demonstrated the limitations of independence within the Soviet bloc, but they did not bring an end to independent action. They also demonstrated that the example of Austrian neutrality would not be imitated elsewhere in Eastern Europe. Finally, the failure of the United States to take any action in the Hungarian uprising proved the hollowness of American political rhetoric about liberating the captive nations of Eastern Europe.

The Cold War Intensified

The events of 1956 brought to a close the era of fully autonomous action by the European nation-states. In very different ways and to differing degrees the two superpowers had demonstrated the new political realities. After 1956 the Soviet Union began to talk about "peaceful coexistence" with the United States. In 1958 negotiations began between the two countries for limitations on the testing of nuclear weapons. However, that same year the Soviet Union announced that the status of West Berlin must be changed and the Allied occupation forces must be withdrawn. The demand was refused. In 1959 tensions relaxed sufficiently for several Western leaders to visit Moscow and for Soviet Premier Nikita Khrushchev (1894–1971) to tour the United States. A summit meeting was scheduled for May 1960, and American President Dwight D. Eisenhower (1890–1969) was to go to Moscow.

The Paris Summit Conference of 1960 proved anything but a repetition of the friendly days of 1955. Just before the gathering, the Soviet Union shot down an American U-2 aircraft that was flying reconnaissance over Soviet territory. Khrushchev demanded an apology from President Eisenhower for this air surveillance. Eisenhower accepted full responsibility for the policy but refused to issue any apology. Khrushchev then refused to take part in the summit conference just as the participants arrived in the French capital. The conference was thus aborted, and Eisenhower's proposed trip to the Soviet Union never took place.

The Soviet actions to destroy the possibility of the summit conference on the eve of its opening were not simply the result of the American spy flights. The Soviets had long been aware of the American flights but chose to protest at this time for two reasons. Khrushchev had hoped that the leaders of Britain, France, and the United States would be sufficiently divided over the future of Germany so that a united Allied front would be impossible. The divisions did not come about as he had hoped. Consequently the conference would have been of little use to him. Second, by 1960 the Communist world itself had become split between the Soviets and the Chinese. The latter were portraying the Russians as lacking sufficient revolutionary zeal. Khrushchev's action was, in part, a response to those charges and proof of the hard-line attitude of the Soviet Union toward the capitalist world.

The abortive Paris conference opened the most difficult period of the Cold War. In 1961 the new U.S. president, John F. Kennedy (1917–1963), and Premier Khrushchev met in Vienna. The conference was inconclusive, but the American president left wondering if the two nations could avoid war. Throughout 1961 thousands of refugees from East Germany were crossing the border into West Berlin. This outflow was a political embarrassment to East Germany and a detriment to its economic life. In August 1961 the East Germans erected a concrete wall along the border between East and West Berlin. Henceforth it was possible to cross only at designated checkpoints and with proper papers. The United States protested and sent Vice President Lyndon Johnson (1908–1973) to Berlin to reassure its citizens, but the Berlin Wall remained—and does so to the present day. The refugee stream was halted, and the United States' commitment to West Germany was brought into doubt.

A year later the most dangerous days of the

Cold War occurred during the Cuban missile crisis. The Soviet Union attempted to place missiles in Cuba, which was a nation friendly to Soviet aims lying less than a hundred miles from the United States. The United States blockaded Cuba, halted the shipment of new missiles, and demanded the removal of existing installations. After a very tense week, with numerous threats and messages between Moscow and Washington, the crisis ended and the Soviets backed down.

The Cuban missile crisis was the last major Cold War confrontation that would have involved Europe directly because there had existed the possibility of the launching of missiles over Europe or from European bases. Thereafter the American-Soviet rivalry shifted to the war in Vietnam and the Arab–Israeli conflict in the Near East. A "hotline" communications system was installed between Moscow and Washington for more rapid and direct exchange of diplomatic messages in times of crisis.

Detente and After

In 1963 the two powers concluded a Nuclear Test Ban Treaty. This agreement marked the beginning of a lessening in the tensions between the United States and the Soviet Union. The German problem somewhat subsided in the late 1960s as West Germany, under Premier Willy Brandt (b. 1913), moved to improve its relations with the Soviet Union and Eastern Europe. In 1968 the Soviet Union in-

President John F. Kennedy (1917–1963) and Premier Nikita Krushchev (1894–1971) in Vienna in June, 1961. Secretary of State Dean Rusk (b. 1909) is on the left. The meeting between the two leaders was not a success. Kennedy considered Krushchev a war-monger. Krushchev felt that Kennedy was weak. [AP/Wide World Photos]

President Kennedy Defines the Cold War Arena

This passage is from President John F. Kennedy's speech at the time of the Berlin Wall crisis of 1961. He called for a democratic challenge to communism throughout the world. The commitment to Southeast Asia would later lead to the major war in Vietnam.

The immediate threat to free men is in West Berlin. But that isolated outpost is not an isolated problem. The threat is worldwide. Our effort must be equally wide and strong, and not be obsessed by any single manufactured crisis. We face a challenge in Berlin, but there is also a challenge in Southeast Asia, where the borders are less guarded, the enemy harder to find, and the dangers of Communism less apparent to those who have so little. We face a challenge in our own hemisphere, and indeed wherever else the freedom of human beings is at stake.

Public Papers of the Presidents of the United States, John F. Kennedy, January 20 to December 31, 1961, ed. by Wayne C. Gover (Washington: U.S. Government Printing Office, 1962), p. 533.

vaded Czechoslovakia to prevent its emergence into further independence. Although deplored by the United States, this action led to no renewal of tensions. During the presidency of Richard Nixon (1969–1974), the United States embarked on a policy of detente or reduction of tension with the Soviet Union. This policy involved trade agreements and mutual reduction of strategic armaments.

In 1975 President Gerald Ford attended a conference in Helsinki, Finland, that in effect recognized the Soviet sphere of influence in Eastern Europe. The Helsinki Accords also committed its signatory powers, including the Soviet Union, to recognize and protect the human rights of their citizens.

The foreign policy of President Jimmy Carter (b. 1924) placed much stress on the observance of these human rights clauses. However, the Soviet invasion of Afghanistan in 1979, though not directly affecting Europe, hardened relations between Washington and Moscow. The United States refused to participate in the 1980 Olympic Games held in Moscow and placed an embargo on American grain being shipped to the Soviet Union. Furthermore, in 1979 President Carter signed a second Strategic Arms Limitation Treaty with the Soviet Union. The U.S. Senate refused to ratify it.

The administration of President Ronald Reagan (b. 1911) adopted a much tougher policy and rhetoric toward the Soviet Union though it relaxed the trade embargo and placed less emphasis on human rights. Under the Reagan administration, the United States sharply slowed arms limitation negotiations and successfully deployed a major new missile system in Europe. The United States also launched a new arms proposal known as the Strategic Arms Defense initiative. It would involve a system of highly developed technology designed to provide defense against nuclear attack. The proposal has been very controversial and has played a major role in recent arms negotiations between the United States and the Soviet Union. President Reagan and Mikhail S. Gorbachev held a friendly summit meeting in 1985. It was the first East–West Summit in six years. However, in early 1986 the Reagan administration announced that it would no longer abide by the 1979 Strategic Arms Limitation Treaty the terms of which the United States had observed even though the treaty had not been ratified. This also proved to be a highly controversial step. Throughout the next few years ongoing negotiations over arms limi-

tation will no doubt be the chief issue between the two superpowers.

A new factor that may to some extent influence those superpower discussions is the emergence in Europe of various popular peace and anti-nuclear movements. These are relatively small but have aimed at establishing a Europe free of nuclear weapons. They have primarily directed their attention to the United States missile and air force bases in Western Europe. The Soviet Union has seen these peace movements as presenting the possibility of creating a desire for a politically neutral Europe within West European public opinion. At the same time the very limited information made available by the Soviet Union in regard to the Chernobyl nuclear plant disaster of 1986 seems to have raised doubts about intentions and good faith. Nevertheless, American military policy initiatives in Western Europe now require much more careful negotiation with the allies and more attention to public opinion than in the past.

Decolonization and the Cold War

Retreat from Empire

At the onset of World War II many of the nations of Europe were still imperial powers. Great Britain, France, the Netherlands, Belgium, Italy, and Portugal governed millions of non-European peoples. One of the most striking and significant postwar developments has been the decolonization of these imperial holdings and the consequent emergence of the so-called Third World political bloc. The process of retreat from empire involved the colonial powers in three major stages of difficulties. The first was the turmoil created by nationalist movements and revolts in the colonies. The second was the injection of Cold War diplomacy and rivalries into the power vacuums formed by the European withdrawals. Finally, in recent years the control of important natural resources and particularly of oil by the new nations of the Third World has put considerable economic pressure on both Western Europe and the United States. This last condition may well prove one of the most important factors in world politics for the remainder of this century.

The decolonization that has occurred since 1945 has been a direct result of both the war itself and the rise of indigenous nationalist

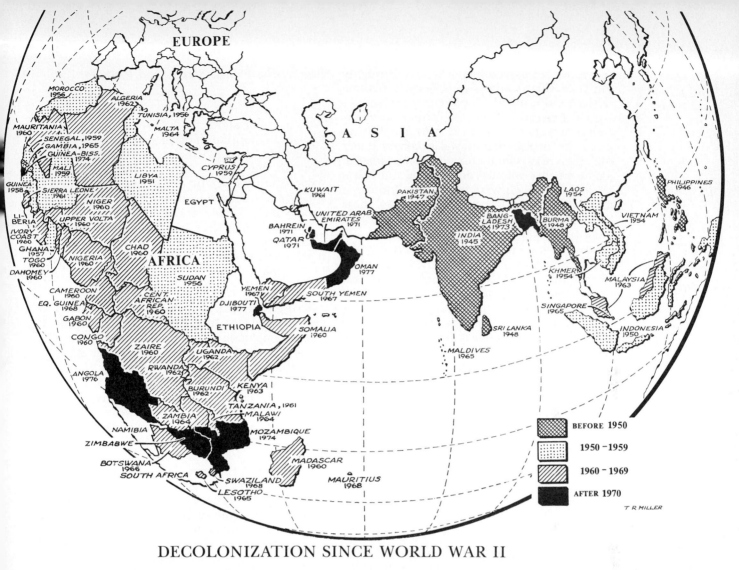

DECOLONIZATION SINCE WORLD WAR II

MAP 29–1 *The extent of the rapid retreat from imperialism on the part of the Western powers after World War II is graphically shown on this outline map covering half the globe— from West Africa, to the Southwest Pacific.*

movements within the European colonial world. World War II drew the military forces of the colonial powers back to Europe. The Japanese conquests of Asia helped to turn out the European powers from that area. After the military and political dislocations of the war came the postwar economic collapse, which meant that the colonial powers could no longer afford to maintain their positions abroad.

Finally, the war aims of the Allies undermined colonialism. It was difficult to fight against tyranny in Europe while maintaining colonial dominance abroad. Moreover the postwar policy of the United States generally opposed the continuation of European empires. Within the colonies there had also arisen nationalist movements of varying strength.

These were often led by gifted persons who had been educated in Europe. The values and the political ideologies that they had learned in Europe itself helped them to present effective critiques of the colonial situation. Such leadership, as well as the frequently blatant injustice imposed on colonial peoples, paved the way for effective nationalist movements.

There was a wide variety in decolonization. Some cases were relatively systematic; in others the European powers simply beat a hasty retreat. In 1947 Britain left India. The result of internal disputes, including religious differences, was the creation of two states, India and Pakistan. In 1948 Burma and Sri Lanka (formerly Ceylon) became independent. During the 1950s the British attempted to prepare col-

1013

onies for self-government. Ghana (formerly the Gold Coast) and Nigeria—which became self-governing in 1957 and 1960, respectively—were the major examples of planned decolonization. In other areas, such as Malta and Cyprus, the British withdrawal occurred under the pressure of militant nationalist movements.

The smaller colonial powers had much less choice. The Dutch were forced from Indonesia in 1950. In 1960 the Belgian Congo, now Zaire, became independent in the midst of great turmoil. For a considerable time, as will be seen, France attempted to maintain its position in Southeast Asia but met defeat in 1954. It was similarly driven from North Africa. President Charles de Gaulle carried out a policy of referendums on independence within the remaining French colonial possessions. By the late 1960s only Portugal remained a traditional colonial power. In 1975 it finally abandoned its African colony of Angola.

Kwame Nkrumah of Ghana (1900–1966) and the Duchess of Kent, representing Queen Elizabeth II, at the ball held to celebrate Ghana's independence on March 6, 1957. Ghana was the first colony of Black Africa to gain its independence. [AP/Wide World Photos]

France, the United States, and Vietnam

As far as the general history of the West is concerned, the decolonization policies of France produced the major postwar upheavals. French decolonization became an integral part of the Cold War and led directly to the involvement of the United States in the Southeast Asian country of Vietnam. The problem of decolonization helped to transfer the Cold War rivalry that had developed in Europe to other continents. Nowhere did those rivalries become more intense than in Asia. Moreover, there was a close relationship between events in Asia and in Europe.

KOREA. To elucidate how the United States became so deeply involved in the French attempt to maintain its position in Vietnam, brief attention must first be given to the policy of the United States in regard to the Korean War.

Between 1910 and 1945, Japan, as an Asian colonial power in its own right, occupied and exploited Korea. By the close of World War II the Japanese had been driven out of the Korean peninsula. At home, under the direction of the United States, the Japanese nation was politically reconstructed into a democracy. The influence of the army and of large business combines was reduced. Women were allowed to vote, and representative institutions were imposed. General Douglas MacArthur (1880–1964) was the representative of the United States during this crucial period. Maintenance of a democratic Japan was to be a cornerstone of postwar United States policy.

The Japanese empire still had to be dealt with. Consequently the United States and the Soviet Union presided over the division of Korea into two parts with the thirty-eighth parallel as the line of separation. It was anticipated that the country would eventually be reunited. However, by 1948 two separate states had been organized: the Democratic People's Republic of Korea under Kim Il Sung in the north and the Republic of Korea under Syngman Rhee in the south. The former was supported by the Soviet Union and the latter by the United States.

Numerous border clashes occurred between the two states. In late June 1950 forces from North Korea invaded across the thirty-eighth parallel. The United States intervened and was soon supported by a mandate of the United Nations. Great Britain, Turkey, and Australia sent token forces. The troops were commanded by General MacArthur. The Korean police action was technically a United Nations venture to halt aggression. (It had been made possible by a boycott by the Soviet ambassador to the United Nations at the time of the key vote.) From the standpoint of the United States the point of the Korean conflict was to contain the spread and to halt the aggression of communism. The United States policymakers tended to conceive of the Communist world as a single unit directed from Moscow. The movement of forces into South Korea was, in their view, simply another example of Communist pressure against a non-Communist state similar to that previously confronted in Europe.

General MacArthur's forces had initially repelled the North Koreans. He then pushed them almost to Manchuria. Late in 1950, however, the Chinese, responding to the pressure against their border, sent troops to support North Korea. The American forces had to retreat. The United States policymakers believed that the Chinese, who since 1949 had been under the Communist government of Mao Tsetung (1893–1976), were simply the puppets of Moscow. For over two years the war bogged down. Eventually a border near the thirty-eighth parallel was restored. The war lasted until June 16, 1953, when an armistice was signed. In Korea limited military action had halted and contained the military advance of a Communist nation. The lessons of the Cold War learned in Europe appeared to have been successfully applied to Asia. The American government was confirmed in its faith in a policy of containment.

VIETNAM. During the years of the Korean conflict another war was being fought in Asia between France and the Viet Minh nationalist movement in Indochina. France, in its push for empire, had occupied this territory (which contained Laos, Cambodia, and Vietnam) between 1857 and 1883. It had administered the area and had invested heavily in it, but the economy of Indochina remained overwhelmingly agrarian. During World War I tens of thousands of Indochinese troops supported France. The French also educated many people from the colony. However, neither the aid during the war nor the achievement of Western education allowed the Vietnamese to escape discrimination from their French colonial rulers.

By 1930 a movement against French colonial rule had been organized by Ho Chi Minh

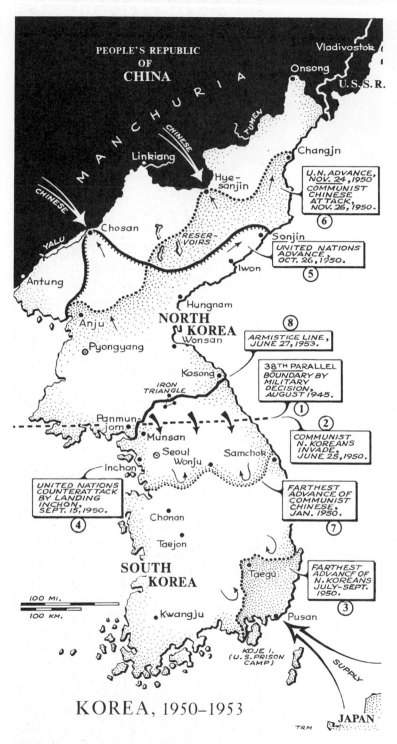

KOREA, 1950–1953

MAP 29–2 *The North Korean invasion of South Korea in 1950 and the bitter three-year war to repulse the invasion and stabilize a firm boundary near the thirty-eighth parallel are outlined here. The war was a dramatic application of the American policy of "containment" of communism.*

PEOPLE'S REPUBLIC OF CHINA

VIETNAM AND ITS NEIGHBORS

MAP 29–3 *The Southeast Asia scene of the long and complex struggle centered in Vietnam is shown by the map.*

(1892–1969) into the Indochinese Communist Party. Ho had traveled throughout the world and had held jobs in several places in Europe before World War I. He and other Indochinese had lobbied at the Versailles Conference in 1919 to have the principle of self-determination applied to their country. In 1920 he was part of the wing of the French Socialist Party that formed the French Communist Party. In 1923 he was sent to Moscow. By 1925 he had formed the Vietnam Revolutionary Youth. After organizing the Indochinese Communist Party, he traveled in Asia and spent considerable time in the Soviet Union. Throughout the 1930s, however, the French succeeded in suppressing most activities by the Communist Party in their colony.

World War II provided new opportunities for Ho Chi Minh and other nationalists. When Japan invaded, it found the pro-Vichy French colonial administration ready to collaborate. Consequently action against the Japanese thereafter meshed quite neatly with action against the French. It was during these wartime circumstances that Ho Chi Minh established his position as a major nationalist leader. He was a Communist to be sure, but he was first and foremost a nationalist. Most important, he had achieved his position in Vietnam during the war independent of the support of the Chinese Communist movement.

In September 1945 Ho Chi Minh declared the independence of Vietnam under the Viet Minh. There was considerable internal Vietnamese resistance to this claim of political control. The opposition arose from religious groups and non-Communist nationalists. After the war the French immediately took advantage of these divisions to establish a government favorable to their own interests. The United States, in line with its wartime anticolonialist position, urged the French to make some kind of accommodation with Ho Chi Minh. In 1946 France and the Viet Minh reached an armistice. It proved to be quite temporary, and in 1947 full-fledged war broke out. The next year the French established a friendly Vietnamese government under Bao Dai. It was to be independent within a loose union with France. This arrangement would have meant very limited independence and was clearly unacceptable to both the Viet Minh and most other nationalists.

Until 1949 the United States had displayed only the most minimal concern about the Indochina War. However, the defeat in China of Chiang Kai-shek (1887–1975) in 1949 and the establishment of the Communist People's Republic of China changed that situation dramatically. This turn of events led the United States to regard the French colonial war against Ho Chi Minh as an integral part of the Cold War conflict. The French government, hoping for United States support, worked to maintain that point of view. Early in 1950 the United States recognized the Bao Dai government. At approximately the same time the Soviet Union and the People's Republic of China recognized the government of Ho Chi Minh. Indochina was thus transformed from a colonial battleground into an area of Cold War confrontation.

In May 1950 the United States announced that it would supply financial aid to the French war effort. Between that time and 1954 more than $4 billion flowed from the United States to France. However, the war itself deteriorated for the French. In the spring of 1954 their army was overrun by the Viet Minh forces at the battle of Dien Bien Phu. Psychologically and militarily the French could not muster new energy for the war. Pierre Mendès-France (b. 1907) was elected premier in Paris on the promise of concluding the conflict. At this point the United States government was badly divided, but it decided against military intervention.

During the late spring and the early summer of 1954 a conference was held at Geneva to

Ho Chi Minh (1892–1969), center, and advisors during the war against the French in 1954. [Black Star]

French troops under bombardment at Dien Bien Phu. The fall of this fortress in May 1954 to the Viet Minh broke the French will to resist. [Magnum]

1017

settle the Indochina conflict. All in all it proved a most unsatisfactory gathering. To one degree or another, all of the major powers were involved in the proceedings, but they did not sign the agreements. Technically the agreements existed between the armed forces of France and those of the Viet Minh. The precedents for such arrangements were the surrender of the German army in 1945 and the Korean armistice of 1953. The Geneva conference provided for the division of Vietnam at the seventeenth parallel. This was to be a temporary border. By 1956 elections were to be held to reunify the country. North of the parallel, centered on the city of Hanoi, the Viet Minh were in charge; below it, the French were in charge, and Saigon was the major city. The prospect of elections meant that theoretically both groups could function politically in the territory of the other. In effect, the conference attempted to transform a military conflict into a political one.

The United States was less than happy about the results of the Geneva discussions. Its first major response came in September 1954, with the formation of the Southeast Asia Treaty Organization (SEATO). It was a collective security agreement that in some respects paralleled the European NATO alliance. However, it did not involve the integration of forces achieved in NATO, nor did it include all the major states of the region. Its membership consisted of the United States, Great Britain, France, Australia, New Zealand, Thailand, Pakistan, and the Philippines.

By 1955 American policymakers had begun to think about the Indochina region, and more especially Vietnam, largely in terms of the Korean example. The United States government assumed that the government being established in North Vietnam was, like the government of North Korea, basically a Communist puppet state. The same year French troops began to withdraw from the south. As they left, the various Vietnamese political groups began to fight for power. Into the turmoil of the power vacuum stepped the United States with military and economic aid. Among the Vietnamese politicians, it chose to support Ngo Dinh Diem. He was a strong non-Communist nationalist who had not collaborated with the French. The Americans hoped that he would become a leader around whom a non-Communist Vietnamese nationalist movement might rally. However, because the United States had publicly been deeply committed to the French, any government it supported

would be, and was, viewed with suspicion by Vietnamese nationalists. In October 1955 Diem established a Republic of Vietnam in the territory for which the Geneva conference had made France responsible. By 1956 the United States was training troops and government officials, paying salaries, and providing military equipment.

In the meantime Diem announced that he and his newly established government were not bound by the Geneva agreements and that elections would not be held in 1956. The American government, which had not signed the Geneva documents, supported his position. Diem undertook an anti-Communist campaign, attacking many citizens who had earlier resisted the French. This was the beginning of a program of political repression that characterized his regime and those that followed. There was a long series of ordinances that gave the government extraordinary power over its citizens. Diem alienated the peasants by restoring rents to landlords and generally strengthening large landowners. He abolished elected village councils and replaced them with his own officials, who had often come from the north. In fact, Diem's major base of political support lay with the more than one million Vietnamese who had migrated to the south after 1954.

By 1960 Diem's policy had created considerable internal resistance in South Vietnam. In that year the National Liberation Front was founded, with the goals of overthrowing Diem, unifying the country, reforming the economy, and ousting the Americans. It was anticolonial, nationalist, and Communist. Its military arm was called the Viet Cong. Sometime in the very late 1950s the government of North Vietnam began to aid the insurgent forces of the south. The Viet Cong and their supporters carried out a program of widespread terrorism and political disruption. They imposed an informal government through much of the countryside. Many peasants voluntarily supported them; others supported them from fear of reprisals. In addition to the Communist opposition, Diem confronted mounting criticism from non-Communist citizens. The Buddhists agitated against the Roman Catholic president. The army was less than satisfied with him. Diem's response to all of these pressures was further repression and dependence on an ever smaller group of advisers.

The Eisenhower and early Kennedy administrations in America continued to support Diem while demanding reforms. The American

United States marines in Vietnam, May 1968. At the war's peak, more than 500,000 American troops were stationed in South Vietnam. For a decade, this effort seriously weakened the U.S. commitment to Western Europe. [Griffiths/Magnum]

military presence grew from somewhat more than six hundred persons in early 1961 to over sixteen thousand troops in late 1963. The political situation in Vietnam became increasingly unstable. On November 1, 1963, Diem was overthrown and murdered in an army *coup*. The United States was deeply involved in this plot. Its officials hoped that if the Diem regime were eliminated, the path would be opened for the establishment of a new government in South Vietnam capable of generating popular support. Thereafter the political goal of the United States was to find a leader who could fill this need. It finally settled on Nguyen Van Thieu, who governed South Vietnam from 1966 to 1975.

President Kennedy was assassinated on November 22, 1963. His successor, Lyndon Johnson, continued and vastly expanded the commitment to South Vietnam. In August 1964, after an attack on an American ship in the Gulf of Tonkin, the first bombing of North Vietnam was authorized. In February 1965 major bombing attacks began that continued, with only brief pauses, until the early weeks of 1973. The land war grew in extent, with over

500,000 Americans stationed in South Vietnam. In 1969 President Richard Nixon commenced a policy of gradual withdrawal of troops. The program was called *Vietnamization*. From the spring of 1968 onward, long-drawn-out peace negotiations were conducted in Paris. In January 1973 a cease-fire was finally arranged. The troops of the United States were pulled back, and prisoners of war held in North Vietnam were returned. Thereafter violations of the cease-fire occurred on both sides. In early 1975 an evacuation of South Vietnamese troops from the northern part of their country turned into a complete rout as they were attacked by the troops of North Vietnam. On April 30, 1975, the city of Saigon fell to the troops of the Viet Cong and North Vietnam. The Second Indochina War had come to an end.

The Second Indochina War, which was, in effect, a continuation of the first war, which the French had lost, was an event of immense controversy and complexity. It was widely debated throughout the world at the time and will continue to be debated for many years. The United States saw the conflict as part of the

Cold War and as a repetition of Korea. Aggression from the north had to be halted. There was also hope that the military power of the United States might buy time so that a strong nationalist, non-Communist regime could be established in South Vietnam. However, the United States misread the situation in Vietnam and especially its superficial resemblance to what had taken place in Korea. The United States ignored the basic colonial character of the Vietnamese political scene. It also overlooked the larger size of Vietnam, the different topography, the weakness of the South Vietnamese army, and the corruption of the government of South Vietnam.

The war grew out of a power vacuum left by decolonization. It produced a major impact on all the Western world. For a decade after the Cuban missile crisis the attention of the United States was largely diverted from Europe. American prestige suffered, and the American commitment to Western Europe came into question. Moreover the blundering of American policy in Southeast Asia made many Europeans wonder about the basic wisdom of the American government. Many young Europeans—and not a few Americans—born after World War II came to regard the United States not as a protector of liberty but as an ambitious, aggressive, and cruel power trying to keep colonialism alive after the end of the colonial era. The American involvement in Vietnam probably proved fundamental to the emergence of a new commitment to unity and economic integration in Europe. That involvement allowed Europeans still living in the shadow of American power and influence to reassert their own independence and to strike out in new directions.

Toward Western European Unification

Post-War Cooperation

Since 1945 the nations of Western Europe have taken unprecedented steps toward cooperation and potential unity. The moves toward unification have related primarily to economic integration. These actions have arisen from American encouragement in response to the Soviet domination of Eastern Europe, and from a sense of lack of effective political power on the part of the states of Western Europe. The process of economic integration has not been steady, nor is it near completion; but it has provided a major new factor in the domestic politics of the states involved.

The movement toward unity could have occurred in at least three ways: politically, militarily, or economically. The economic path was taken largely because the other paths were blocked. In 1949 ten European states organized the Council of Europe, which meets in Strasbourg, France. Its organization involved foreign ministers and a Consultative Assembly elected by the parliaments of the participants. The Council of Europe was and continues to be only an advisory body. It had been hoped by some persons that the council might become a parliament of Europe, but during the early 1950s none of the major states was willing to surrender any of its sovereignty to the newly organized body. The initial failure of the council to bring about significant political cooperation meant that for the time being unity would not come about by political or parliamentary routes.

Between 1950 and 1954 there was some interest in a more thorough integration of the military forces of NATO. When the Korean War broke out, the United States began to urge the rearmament of Germany. The German forces would provide Western Europe with further protection against possible Soviet aggression while the United States was involved in Korea. France continued to fear a German army. In 1951 the French government suggested the creation of a European Defense Community that would constitute a supranational military organization. It would require a permanent British commitment of forces to the Continent to help France, in effect, counter any future German threat. The proposal continued to be considered for some time, but in 1954 the French Parliament itself vetoed the program. In 1955 Germany was permitted to rearm and to enter NATO. Supranational military organization had not been achieved.

Rather than in politics or the military, the major moves toward European cooperation and potential unity came in the economic sphere. Unlike the other two possible paths of cooperation, economic activity involved little or no immediate loss of political sovereignty. Moreover the material benefits of combined economic activity brought new popular support to all of the governments involved.

The Marshall Plan of the United States created the Organization for European Economic Cooperation (OEEC). It was a vehicle set up to require common planning and cooperation among the participating countries and to discourage a return to the prewar economic nationalism. The OEEC and later NATO gave the countries involved new experience in working with each other and demonstrated the productivity, the efficiency, and the simple possibility of cooperative action.[1] Although neither organization provided a means of political or economic integration, the experience was most important.

Among European leaders and civil servants there existed a large body of opinion that only through the abandonment of economic nationalism could the newly organized democratic states avoid the economic turmoil that had proved such fertile ground for dictatorship. Economic cooperation carried the possibility of greater efficiency, prosperity, and employment. The leading figures holding these opinions were Robert Schuman (1886–1963), the foreign minister of France; Konrad Adenauer (1876–1967), the chancellor of the Federal Republic of Germany; Alcide De Gasperi

1021

*Europe in the
Era of the
Superpowers*

[1]The OEEC continued in existence until 1961, when it was reorganized as the Organization for Economic Cooperation and Development (OECD). Both organizations included nations not involved in the more formal moves toward unity. The OECD also included Japan and has been interested in Third World economic development.

The signing of the Treaty of Rome in 1957. This pact created the European Economic Community, or Common Market. The original members were France, West Germany, Italy, Belgium, Netherlands, and Luxembourg. Subsequently, Greece, Ireland, Denmark, and Britain also joined, while Spain and Portugal are negotiating for membership. [AP/Wide World Photos]

(1881–1954), the prime minister of Italy; and Paul-Henri Spaak (1899–1972), the prime minister of Belgium. Among major civil servants and bureaucrats, Jean Monnet (1885–1981) of France was the leading spokesman.

In 1950 Schuman proposed that the coal and steel production of Western Europe be undertaken on an integrated, cooperative basis. The next year France, West Germany, Italy, and the "Benelux" countries (Belgium, the Netherlands, and Luxembourg) organized the European Coal and Steel Community. Its activity was limited to a single part of the economy, but that was a sector that affected almost all other industrial production. An agency called the *High Authority* administered the plan. The authority was genuinely supranational, and its members could not be removed during their appointed terms. The Coal and Steel Community prospered. By 1955 coal production had grown by 23 per cent. Iron and steel production was up by almost 150 per cent. The community both benefited from and contributed to the immense growth of material production in Western Europe during this period. Its success reduced the suspicions of government and business groups about the concept of coordination and economic integration.

The European Economic Community

It took more than the prosperity of the European Coal and Steel Community to draw European leaders toward further unity. The unsuccessful Suez intervention and the resulting diplomatic isolation of France and Britain persuaded many Europeans that only through unified action could they exert any significant influence on the two superpowers or control their own destinies. Consequently, in 1957, through the Treaty of Rome, the six members of the Coal and Steel Community agreed to form a new organization: the European Economic Community. The *Common Market*, as the EEC soon came to be called, envisioned more than a free-trade union. Its members sought to achieve the eventual elimination of tariffs, a free flow of capital and labor, and similar wage and social benefits in all the participating countries. Its chief institutions were a Council of Foreign Ministers and a High Commission composed of technocrats. The former came to be the dominant body.

The Common Market achieved a stunning degree of success during its early years. By 1968 all tariffs among the six members had been abolished well ahead of the planned schedule. Trade and labor migration among the members grew steadily. Moreover nonmember states began to copy the community and later to seek membership. In 1959 Britain, Denmark, Norway, Sweden, Switzerland, Austria, and Portugal formed the European Free Trade Area. However, by 1961 Great Britain had decided to seek Common Market membership. Twice, in 1963 and 1967, British membership was vetoed by President de Gaulle of France. The French president felt that Britain was too closely related to the United States and its policies to support the European Economic Community wholeheartedly.

The French veto of British membership demonstrated the major difficulty confronting the Common Market during the 1960s. The Council of Ministers, representing the individual national interests of member states, came to have more influence than the High Commission. Political as well as economic factors increasingly entered into decision making. France particularly was unwilling to compromise on any matter that it regarded as pertaining to its sovereignty. On more than one occasion President de Gaulle demanded his own policies and refused French participation under any other conditions. This attitude caused major problems over agricultural policy.

Despite the French actions the Common Market survived and continued to prosper. In 1973 Great Britain, Ireland, and Denmark became members. Discussions continued on further steps toward integration, including a common currency. Throughout the late 1970s, however, and into the 1980s, there seemed to be a loss of momentum. Norway and Sweden, with relatively strong economies, declined to join. Although in 1982 Spain, Portugal, and Greece applied for membership and were admitted, there continued to be sharp disagreements and a sense of stagnation within the Community. The Community will no doubt survive, but a decade of major internal controversy seems to lie ahead.

Internal Political Developments in Western Europe

After the war, with the exceptions of Portugal and Spain, which remained dictatorships until the mid-1970s, the nations of Western Europe

The European Economic Community Is Established

The 1957 Treaty of Rome identified the major goals of the European Economic Community (Common Market) for the original six members.

Article 2: It shall be the aim of the Community, by establishing a Common Market and progressively approximating the economic policies of Member States, to promote throughout the Community a harmonious development of economic activities, a continuous and balanced expansion, an increased stability, an accelerated raising of the standard of living and closer relations between its Member States.

Article 3: For the purposes set out in the preceding Article, the activities of the Community shall include, under the conditions and with the timing provided for in this Treaty:

(a) the elimination, as between Member States, of customs duties and of quantitative restrictions in regard to the importation and exportation of goods, as well as of all other measures with equivalent effect;

(b) the establishment of a common customs tariff and a common commercial policy towards third countries;

(c) the abolition, as between Member States, of the obstacles to the free movement of persons, services and capital;

(d) the inauguration of a common agricultural policy;

(e) the inauguration of a common transport policy;

(f) the establishment of a system ensuring that competition shall not be distorted in the Common Market;

(g) the application of procedures which shall make it possible to co-ordinate the economic policies of Member States and to remedy disequilibria in their balances of payments;

(h) the approximation of their respective municipal law to the extent necessary for the functioning of the Common Market;

(i) the creation of a European Social Fund in order to improve the possibilities of employment for workers and to contribute to the raising of their standard of living;

(j) the establishment of a European Investment Bank intended to facilitate the economic expansion of the Community through the creation of new resources; and

(k) the association of overseas countries and territories with the Community with a view to increasing trade and to pursuing jointly their effort towards economic and social development.

Treaty Establishing the European Economic Community (Brussels: Secretariat of the Interim Committee for the Common Market and Euratom, 1957), pp. 17–18.

continued to pursue the path of liberal democracy. But their leaders realized that the prewar democratic political structures alone had been insufficient to ensure peace, stability, material prosperity, and domestic liberty for their peoples. It had become clear that democracy required a social and economic base as well as a political structure. Economic prosperity and social security in the eyes of most Europeans became a duty of government as a way of staving off the kind of turmoil that had brought on tyranny and war. They also regarded such programs as a means of avoiding communism.

Except for the British Labour Party, the vehicles of the new postwar politics were not, as might have been expected, the democratic socialist parties. On the whole those parties did not prosper after the onset of the Cold War. They stood opposed by both Communists and groups more conservative than themselves. Rather, the new departures were led by various Christian Democratic parties, usually leading coalition governments. These Christian Democratic political parties were a major new feature of postwar politics. They were largely Roman Catholic in leadership and membership. Catholic parties had previously existed in Europe. But from the late nineteenth century through the 1930s they had been very conservative and had tended to protect the social, political, and educational interests of the church. They had traditionally opposed communism but had few positive programs of their own. The postwar Christian Democratic parties of Germany, France, and Italy were progressive. They accepted democracy and advocated social reform. They welcomed non-Catholics to membership. Democracy, social reform, economic growth, and anticommunism were their hallmarks. Not until the late 1960s were those goals seriously challenged or questioned.

The events of the war years in large measure determined the political leadership of the postwar decade. On the Continent those groups and parties that had been active in the resistance against Nazism and Fascism held an initial advantage. Until 1947 those groups frequently included the Communist Party. Thereafter Communists were quite systematically excluded from all Western European governments. This policy was quite naturally favored and encouraged by the United States. The immediate domestic problems after the war included not only those created by the physical damage of the conflict but often those that had existed in 1939. The war in most cases had not solved those prewar difficulties, but it had often opened new opportunities or possibilities for solution.

Great Britain: Power in Decline

In July 1945 the British electorate overwhelmingly voted for a Labour Party government. For the first time the Labour Party commanded in its own right a majority of the House of Commons. Clement Attlee (1883–1967) replaced Winston Churchill as prime

The British Labour Party Issues a Cautious Platform

The Labour Party in 1945 was committed to a program of socialism. However, its platform of that year made clear that the party would move cautiously in carrying out its policy. Both the commitment to social change and the promise of caution proved attractive to the electorate, with the result that Labour came to power.

By the test of war some industries have shown themselves capable of rising to new heights of efficiency and expansion. Others, including some of our older industries fundamental to our economic structure, have wholly or partly failed. . . .

Each industry must have applied to it the test of national service. If it serves the nation, well and good; if it is inefficient and falls down on its job, the nation must see that things are put right.

These propositions seem indisputable, but for years before the war anti-Labour Governments set them aside, so that British industry over a large field fell into a state of depression, muddle, and decay. Millions of working and middle-class people went through the horrors of unemployment and insecurity. It is not enough to sympathise with these victims: we must develop an acute feeling of national shame—and act.

The Labour Party is a Socialist Party, and proud of it. Its ultimate purpose at home is the establishment of the Socialist Commonwealth of Great Britain—free, democratic, efficient, progressive, public-spirited, its material resources organised in the service of the British people.

But Socialism cannot come overnight, as the product of a week-end revolution. The members of the Labour Party, like the British people, are practical-minded men and women.

There are basic industries ripe and over-ripe for public ownership and management in direct service of the nation. There are many smaller businesses rendering good service which can be left to go on with their useful work.

There are big industries not yet ripe for public ownership which must nevertheless be required by constructive supervision to further the nation's needs and not to prejudice national interests by restrictive anti-social monopoly or cartel agreements—caring for their own capital structures and profits at the cost of a lower standard of living for all.

Let Us Face the Future, cited in J. F. C Harrison, *Society and Politics in England, 1790–1960* (New York: Harper & Row, 1965), pp. 450–451.

minister. The British had not so much rejected the great wartime leader as they had renounced the Conservative Party, which had, in effect, governed since 1931. In the public mind the Conservatives were associated with the economic problems of the 1930s. For purposes of postwar reconstruction and redirection, the Labour Party seemed to have a better program.

Atlee's ministry was socialist but clearly non-Marxist. It made a number of bold departures in both economic and social policy. The government assumed ownership of certain major industries, including the Bank of England, the airlines, public transport, coal, electricity, and steel. The ministry also undertook a major housing program. Probably its most popular accomplishment was the establishment of a major program of welfare legislation. This involved further unemployment assistance, old-age pensions, school lunches, and, most important, free medical service to all citizens. All of these departures were expensive, and immediate postwar economic recovery was slow. By the close of 1948 the drive toward further social reform had come to a halt. During the next several years the Labour Party itself became badly divided between one wing that advocated more socialism and government services and another that contended that the nation could, for the time being, afford few or no new programs.

The forward domestic policy of the Labour government was matched by a policy of gradual retreat on the world scene. In 1947 the enunciation of the Truman Doctrine in regard to Greece and Turkey marked Britain's admission that it could not afford to oversee the security of those areas. In the same year Britain recognized the independence of Pakistan and India. In the postwar era Britain would be repeatedly confronted by nationalist movements within the empire and would gradually, and usually gracefully, retreat from those outposts.

In 1951 the Conservative Party under Churchill returned to office, and the party remained there until 1964. This was the longest period of continuous government by any party in modern British history. Internal Labour Party divisions contributed to this development, but so did the policies of the Conservatives. Under Churchill and then under his successors, Anthony Eden in 1955–1957, Harold Macmillan in 1957–1963, and Alec Douglas-Home in 1963–1964, the Conservatives attempted to draw a picture of major differences between themselves and the Labour Party. In

reality the differences were of degree rather than of kind. The Conservative government did return the steel industry to private ownership, but it did not return to a free economy. The program of national welfare and health services continued, and the Conservatives actually undertook a building program larger than that of the Labour Party.

The problem of the decline of power and prestige continued. From the mid-1950s onward, one part of the empire after another became independent. The Suez intervention of 1956 brought an end to independent British military intervention. Increasingly, British policy was made subservient to that of the United States. However, the economy constituted the most persistent difficulty. Throughout the decade the slogan "Export or die" was heard. Exports did grow rapidly, yet more slowly than imports. Productivity remained discouragingly low. There was a low rate of capital investment in both privately and nationally owned industries. The trade unions were often more interested in carving up existing wealth than in creating new wealth to be distributed. The government too often favored economic programs that were not aimed at long-term growth.

In 1964 the Labour Party returned to office under Harold Wilson. It promised to right the economic situation, but the economy only worsened. Wilson renewed the attempt to join the Common Market, which Macmillan had begun in 1963. Labour, like the Conservatives, confronted the veto of France. In 1970 the electorate again turned to the Conservative Party, then led by Edward Heath. His major accomplishment was to take Britain into the Common Market in 1973. However, domestically Heath floundered badly in his dealings with the trade unions. The country suffered a crippling coal strike in the winter of 1973–1974.

In 1974 Wilson returned to office, primarily on the grounds that the Labour Party might have better relations with the unions. The Labour government was able to reach some agreements on limitations for pay raises. Still inflation raged. The same year Wilson voluntarily resigned and was replaced by James Callaghan. The new prime minister took virtually no new departures, and the problem of a stagnant economy linked to inflation continued. In March of 1979, after a defeat in the House of Commons, Callaghan called for new elections. Labour lost decisively to the Conservative

Prime Minister Margaret Thatcher at the annual conference of the British Conservative Party in 1979. Thatcher has been the most right-wing prime minister of post-war Britain. [*Magnum*]

Party, which since 1975 has been led by Margaret Thatcher, the first woman to be the British prime minister.

Within the context of the British Conservative Party, Thatcher stood much farther to the right than had Heath. Her Cabinet pursued a policy of very high interest rates, sharp tax cuts, and somewhat reduced government spending. Generally Thatcher also took a very hard line with the trade unions. The results of these policies, popularly known as Thatcherism, have been quite mixed. Inflation did come under limited control, but the rate of unemployment in the early 1980s reached the levels of the Great Depression years.

The summer of 1981, however, saw an important new problem arise for British society and political leadership. Riots broke out in several of the major cities, including Liverpool and London. The riots were violent and involved extensive property damage and loss of life. Two factors seemed to account for these disturbances. First, thousands of British youth were without jobs, and they saw Thatcher's policies as being responsible for that situation. Second, during the past two decades tens of thousands of nonwhite immigrants had come to settle in Britain from the nation's former colonies. The clash of cultures and the competition for scarce employment led to widespread racism of a very public character. Some of the riots of 1981, and later ones, involved racial clashes; others involved both white and nonwhite youths jointly attacking the police, who had come to be viewed in some urban areas as symbols of political repression. The Thatcher government took only the most minimal action to address the economic conditions that fostered the riots. Some government funds were appropriated to create new jobs. But in the years ahead both the economic stagnation and the racial animosity promise the possibility of further instability.

The fragmentation in British society and economic life was matched by new factionalism in politics. Thatcher's emergence represented the victory of the right wing of the British Conservative Party over its more moderate center. Throughout the Callaghan ministry and after, the Labour Party experienced even more disunity. The left wing of the Labour Party, led by Anthony Benn, challenged the leadership of Callaghan, who was replaced by Michael Foot in 1980. Thereafter several members of the Labour Party who were former government ministers, including David Owen, Roy Jenkins, and Shirley Williams, resigned from the Labour Party. They joined with a few lesser-known Conservatives to form a new political party in 1980 known as the Social Democratic Party. This new party saw itself as carving out a broad middle position between the Conservative and Labour parties in alliance with the Liberal Party. Public opinion polls have showed considerable support for the new alliance, but has not been able to translate this support into a large number of seats in Parliament.

In the spring of 1982, after years of fruitless negotiations over the question of legal ownership, the government of Argentina ordered the invasion of the Falkland Islands (Malvinus), which are located in the South Atlantic off the shore of South America and which have been governed by Great Britain for over a century and a half. The Argentines claimed that the dispute involved the recapture of territory held by a colonial power. The British contended that

1027

*Europe in the
Era of the
Superpowers*

the Argentines had committed an act of international aggression, an opinion in which the government of the United States concurred. The invasion occurred on April 3. Shortly thereafter the British dispatched a very large fleet to the South Atlantic. During the following weeks the largest naval engagements since World War II took place between the British and Argentine navies. Both forces sustained major losses before the British emerged the victors.

The election of 1983 held in the wake of the Falklands military success proved a great victory for Mrs. Thatcher. Her party retained firm control of Parliament. Throughout 1984 the government confronted a long miners' strike the eventual conclusion of which worked to the benefit of the government's policies of closing inefficient mines. Shortly after the election leadership of the Labour Party fell to Neil Kinnock. His party has remained badly divided over matters of policy and ideology, but its popularity has grown in the public opinion polls. Thatcher's popularity has waned, but it would be premature to write off her dominance of both the Conservative Party and British politics. Until the Labour Party overcomes

its divisions and moderates its more extreme left wing, so as clearly to re-establish itself as a viable alternative, the Conservatives will retain an edge.

In addition to the war in the South Atlantic and the gravest economic situation in the Western world, Britain has also had to confront in recent years a major internal disturbance in Northern Ireland. By the treaty of 1921 the Ulster counties remained a part of the United Kingdom while retaining a large measure of self-government. The Protestant majority used its power to discriminate systematically against the Roman Catholic minority in the province. In 1968 a Catholic civil rights movement was launched. Demonstrations and counterdemonstrations resulted. Units of the Provisional Wing of the Irish Republican Army became active in seeking to unite Ulster with the Irish Republic. In turn, militant Protestant organizations became mobilized. The British government sent in units of the army to restore order. Soon the army units became the target of both groups of militant Irish. In 1972 the British suspended the Northern Irish Parliament and began to govern the province di-

*British troops landing on the Falklands June 1982. The Falklands war generated immense
support for the Thatcher government in Britain.* [*Sygma*]

Children in Belfast stoning British armored cars. An entire generation of Northern Irish children has grown up in an atmosphere of continuous violence. [Sygma]

rectly. Thus far, the troops remain, and well over thirteen hundred people have been killed in terrorist activity. During 1981 certain Irish Republican Army prisoners held in government prisons took part in hunger strikes to protest the conditions of their imprisonment. No less than ten prisoners starved themselves to death. Riots followed each death, but the British government steadfastly refused to grant the status of political prisoner to persons who it believed had been properly convicted for acts of terrorism. No peaceful solution has yet proved forthcoming in the Irish situation, despite ongoing consultation between the governments of Great Britain and Ireland and a historic agreement in 1985 giving the Irish Republic an advisory role in the government of Northern Ireland.

West Germany: The Economic Miracle

No country in Europe since the war has so contrasted with Britain as the Federal Republic of Germany. The nation was organized in 1949 from the three Western Allied occupation sectors. Its amazing material progress from the ruins of the conflict became known as the economic miracle of postwar Europe. Between 1948 and 1964 West German industrial production grew by 600 per cent. Unemployment became almost unknown. All of this time the country remained the center of Cold War disputes and was occupied by thousands of foreign troops. In the midst of Cold War tensions the Germans prospered.

The economic growth of the nation stemmed from a number of favorable factors. The Marshall Plan provided a strong impetus to recovery. The government of the republic throughout the 1950s and 1960s pursued a policy of giving private industry a relatively free hand while providing sufficient planning to avoid economic crisis. The goods produced by Germany proved attractive to the customers of other nations. *Volkswagen* became a household word throughout the world. Moreover domestic demand was vigorous, and skilled labor and energetic management were available. Finally, Germany had very few foreign commitments or responsibilities. A relatively small portion of its national income had to be spent on defense. This situation aided capital formation.

In a very real sense postwar West Germany indulged in economic expansion rather than in politics or active international policy. Unlike the Weimar Constitution, the constitution of the Federal Republic did not permit the proliferation of splinter parties. Nor did the president possess extraordinary power. The Federal Republic returned to the arena of nations very slowly. In 1949 it participated in the Marshall Plan and two years later in the European Coal and Steel Community. In 1955 the nation joined NATO, and in 1957 it was one of the charter members of the European Economic Community. The Federal Republic has been perhaps the major champion of European cooperation.

Throughout this period political initiative lay with the Christian Democrats led by Konrad Adenauer. His domestic policies were relatively simple and consistent: West Germany must become genuinely democratic and economically stable and prosperous. His foreign policy was profoundly anti-Communist. Under what was known as the Hallstein Doctrine, the Federal Republic refused to have diplomatic ties with any nation, except the Soviet Union, that extended diplomatic recognition to East Germany. Adenauer's position on East Germany contributed to the Cold War climate, and it may have led the United States to overestimate the threat of Communist aggression in Europe. The Hallstein Doctrine separated the Federal Republic from all the nations of Eastern Europe.

Adenauer remained in office until 1963, when he retired at the age of eighty-seven. The Christian Democrats remained in power, led first by Ludwig Erhard and later by Kurt Kiesinger. In 1966, however, they were compelled to form a coalition with the Social Democratic Party (SDP). After the war this party had revived but had been unable to capture a parliamentary majority. By the early 1960s the SDP had expanded its base beyond the working class and had become more a party of social and economic reform than a party of socialism. This shift reflected the growing prosperity of the German working class. The major leader of

Few sights better illustrate the astounding economic recovery of Europe after 1945 than the contrast between these two views of Berlin. The ghostly picture shows the heavy destruction caused by the intense wartime bombing of the city. The contrasting photograph shows the rebuilt center of West Berlin that emerged in the 1950s and 1960s. Only the ruins of the Emperor William I Memorial church were left as a reminder of war's destruction. [UPI/Bettmann Newsphotos; German Information Center, New York]

A Former West German Chancellor Looks Toward the Close of This Century

In January 1982, Helmut Schmidt, then chancellor of West Germany, gave an interview that provided his thoughts on the major issues confronting Europe during the closing years of this century. His remarks remain relevant.

I would like to stress that I do not believe in prophecies by politicians. Having said this, . . .

There will not be a world war or another great war between now and the end of the century. But the year 2000 is about the span of my lifetime; I will be 82 in the year 2000, and I think I can look as far as that.

There will be no world war, because the responsibility of governments and the awareness of the danger of war are much greater nowadays than they have ever been in the first three-quarters of the 20th century. And they will get, in the long last, they will have arms reductions and arms control.

Secondly, as in the past also in the future there will be ups and downs in the economic well-being of their governments. After Keynes and after Lord Beveridge, two great Englishmen [who were the economists whose thought was largely responsible for government management of Western economies], they seemed to have learned how to manage their economies only to learn in the last decade that this doesn't hold

true under any possible circumstances. But I think we will again learn to overcome our economic, our structural economic deficiencies.

This leads me to the third aspect, which might in the end be the prevailing one.

When this century started, we had quite a few less than two billion people on the earth. At the end of the century, the number will have more than tripled to more than six billion people.

It is not industry that has to be blamed for the overexhaustion of natural resources. Of course industry is to be blamed for many things, but generally speaking if you want not only to feed but to give a fair standard of living to four billion people today, try to do this for six billion people within the next 18 years or so. It will necessarily mean additional overexhaustion of natural resources, the so-called natural environment and so on. And what mankind will have to learn during the last 20 years of this century is not only to set the goal for stabilization of global population but also to find the means to achieve that goal.

The New York Times, January 3, 1982, p. 15.

the SDP in the 1960s was Willy Brandt, the mayor of West Berlin. In 1966 he became vice-chancellor in the coalition government. In 1969 Brandt and the SDP carried the election in their own right.

The most significant departure of the SDP occurred in the area of foreign policy. While continuing to urge further Western unity through the Common Market, Brandt moved carefully but swiftly to establish better relations with Eastern Europe (a policy called *Ostpolitik*). In 1970 he met with the leadership of East Germany. Later that year he went to Moscow to sign a treaty of cooperation. By November 1970 Brandt had completed a reconciliation treaty with Poland that recognized the Oder–Neisse river line as the Polish western border. A treaty with Czechoslovakia soon followed.

In 1973 both the Federal Republic of Germany and the German Democratic Republic were admitted to the United Nations. Brandt's policy of *Ostpolitik*, to a large extent, regularized the German situation, but that regularity will probably remain only as long as the two superpowers desire it. Brandt's moves were in part a subdevelopment of the policy of detente on the part of the United States and the Soviet Union. In 1974 Brandt resigned. He was succeeded by Helmut Schmidt, who continued a policy of conversations with the Communist bloc nations and Moscow. Schmidt also took a lead in asserting the necessity of close United States consultation with its West European allies on both economic and military matters.

In 1982 Helmut Kohl, a conservative Christian Democrat, became the West German chancellor. His first years in office were marked by a number of political and financial scandals. He also pursued a controversial policy of allowing Germany to begin to acknowledge more openly its Nazi epoch in an effort to bring about full reconciliation with Germany's allies. He visited World War I battlefields with President Mitterand of France. In 1985 he persuaded President Reagan to visit the German military cemetary at Bitburg among whose graves were those of SS officers. Kohl and his party have also generally maintained the strength of the German economy.

France: Search for Stability and Glory

France experienced the most troubled postwar domestic political scene of any major European nation. The Third Republic had been in very deep difficulty in 1940. It had come to satisfy neither the left nor the right of the political world. More important, the republic had been incapable of staving off military defeat. To these inherited problems was added, after the war, the fact of wide-scale collaboration with the Nazi conquerors. A few trials, executions, and prison sentences superficially handled the problem of the Vichy collaborators, but much bitterness remained.

After the defeat of 1940 a little-known general named Charles de Gaulle (1890–1970) had organized a Free French government in London. In 1944 De Gaulle presided over the provisional government in liberated France. He was an immensely proud, patriotic person who seemed to regard himself as personally embodying the spirit of France. He had a low regard for traditional liberal democratic politics and hated the machinations of political parties, which he thought unnecessarily divided the nation. In 1946 De Gaulle suddenly resigned from the government, believing that the newly organized Fourth Republic, like the Third, gave far too little power to the executive. The Fourth French Republic thus lost the single strong leader it had possessed. After De Gaulle's departure the republic returned to the rapid turnover of ministries that had characterized the Third Republic during the 1920s and 1930s. Between 1948 and 1958 there were no less than nineteen ministries. The faces of the ministers changed, but the problems remained.

A major source of domestic discontent related to colonial problems in North Africa and Indochina. Between 1947 and 1954 France fought the long, bitter war to retain some mea-

sure of control over Indochina. That conflict has been examined more closely earlier in this chapter. By 1954, however, Premier Mendès-France's government admitted defeat and began to preside over a withdrawal from the region. It marked a major defeat for a Western nation by a former colony. The Mendès-France government also granted independence to Tunisia. Morocco was soon moving toward independence. The Suez fiasco of 1956 marked another conspicuous loss of power and prestige for France.

Indochina, Tunisia, and Morocco were regarded as colonial problems by the French. However, in their eyes Algeria, conquered in 1830 and now possessing over a million French citizens, was not a colony but an integral part of France. In 1954 a revolt broke out in Algeria, led by the Algerian Liberation Movement (the FLN). The revolt deeply divided France. The army and right-wing political groups were determined to hold Algeria. Nevertheless the war, which was intensely bitter and brutal, became increasingly unpopular. There were demands for a negotiated settlement. When the civilian government began to make moves in that direction in 1958, an army mutiny occurred in Algeria and unrest soon spread to Corsica. France seemed on the brink of civil war.

At this point the politicians in Paris turned to General de Gaulle, whom the army trusted would uphold their cause. The general accepted office only on the condition that he be given a free hand to govern and to submit a new constitution to the nation. De Gaulle created the Fifth French Republic, in which the president possesses extraordinary power. He can appoint and dismiss the premier and dissolve the Chamber of Deputies. De Gaulle submitted the constitution to a popular referendum, in which it was overwhelmingly approved. Having secured his own power, De Gaulle moved to attack the Algerian problem. He believed that France could not win militarily in Algeria and that a continued struggle might bring even more political disruption in France itself. French public opinion had also shifted in favor of making some kind of accommodation that would end the bloodshed. De Gaulle made large concessions to the FLN, and by 1962 Algeria was independent. There was much domestic opposition to De Gaulle's policy. Hundreds of thousands of French citizens in Algeria returned to France, putting new pressures on its economy and resources. However, the president of the republic held the nation behind him. He had become a symbol of stability and nationalism. There always existed the fear in the late 1950s and early 1960s that De Gaulle might again resign and leave the nation subject to possible disruptive forces.

De Gaulle combined the methods of Louis Napoleon with the patriotism of Clemenceau. Throughout the 1960s he pursued a policy of making France the leading nation in a united Europe. Often De Gaulle pursued strictly nationalist goals that frustrated those who favored united action. His nationalism was probably necessary as a means of healing the internal wounds to French pride and prestige brought about by the colonial and Algerian defeats. He pursued systematically good relations with Germany but was never friendly with Great Britain. He deeply resented the influence of the United States in Western Europe.

De Gaulle wanted Europe to become a third force in the world between the superpowers. For that reason he pushed for the development of a French nuclear capacity and refused to become a party to the 1963 Nuclear Test Ban Treaty. He took French military forces out of NATO in 1967 and caused its headquarters to be moved from Paris to Brussels, but he did not take France out of the alliance itself. He was highly critical of the American involvement in Vietnam. That American adventure served to convince him even further that Europe under French leadership must prepare to fend for itself.

It is not certain that the rest of the world ever understood De Gaulle or he them. He imposed a kind of presidential dictatorship on France but permitted civil liberties to be observed and parliamentary politics to function. Yet what was important was what the president and his ministers decided. For ten years he succeeded. Then in 1968 he confronted a domestic unrest

---

President de Gaulle Insists on Maintaining French Autonomy

De Gaulle was determined to maintain the national independence of France both in Europe and in the Atlantic community. In this 1966 speech he criticized those who would compromise that independence by having France subordinate itself to various international organizations, such as NATO and the United Nations. He particularly resented the influence of the United States in European affairs.

It is true that, among our contemporaries, there are many minds—and often some of the best—who have envisaged that our country renounce its independence under the cover of one or another international grouping. Having thus handed over to foreign bodies the responsibility for our destiny, our leaders would—according to the expression sanctioned by that school of thought—have nothing more to do than ''plead France's case.''

. . . Thus some—exulting in the dream of the international—wanted to see our country itself, as they placed themselves, under the obedience of Moscow. Thus others—invoking either the supranational myth, or the danger from the East, or the advantage that the Atlantic West could derive from unifying its economy, or even *the imposing utility of world arbitration—maintained that France should allow her policy to be dissolved in a tailor-made Europe, her defense in NATO, her monetary concepts in the Washington Fund, her personality in the United Nations, et cetera.*

Certainly, it is a good thing that such institutions exist, and it is only in our interest to belong to them; but if we had listened to their extreme apostles, these organs in which, as everyone knows, the political protection, military protection, economic power and multiform aid of the United States predominate—these organs would have been for us only a cover for our submission to American hegemony. Thus, France would disappear swept away by illusion.

Cited in Ronald C. Monticone, *Charles de Gaulle* (Boston: Twayne Publishers, 1975), pp. 67–68.

President Charles de Gaulle (1890–1969), *the most important and successful French political leader since World War II.* [Magnum]

in France that was even more widespread than that confronted by Léon Blum in the spring of 1936. The troubles began among student groups in Paris, and then they spread to other major sectors of French life. Hundreds of thousands of workers went on strike. Having assured himself of the support of the army, De Gaulle made a brief television speech to rally his followers. Soon they, too, came into the streets to demonstrate for De Gaulle and stability. The strikes ended. Police often moved against the student groups. The government itself quickly moved to improve the wages and benefits to workers. May 1968 had revealed the fragile strength of the Fifth Republic. It had also revealed that the economic progress of France since the war had created a large body of citizens with sufficient stake in the status quo to fear and prevent its disruption.

In 1969 President de Gaulle resigned after some relatively minor constitutional changes were rejected in a referendum. Georges Pompidou (1911–1974), who succeeded to the presidency, was reelected in the next election. He was a strong supporter of De Gaulle and his policies. He and his own successor, Valéry Giscard d'Estaing (b. 1926), set about to improve the economic conditions that had fostered discontent among factory workers in 1968. They also continued to favor a strong policy favoring European unity. In 1973, three years after De Gaulle's death in political retirement, France permitted Great Britain to join the Common Market.

The center-right government of Valéry Giscard d'Estaing was elected in 1974 on a platform of social reform. The new president also spoke of an "opening" to the political left. It seemed that he might be willing to accept the support of the French Socialist Party for his programs. Giscard d'Estaing was essentially a technocrat who wanted to see the traditionally harsh ideological split in France healed. He and others of his persuasion saw such splits as preventing the serious handling of major economic problems. Yet his interest in some mode of alliance with the left remained a matter of rhetoric. Indeed, during the parliamentary elections of 1978 he made major election-eve speeches deploring the possibility of a political victory for the left.

Such a victory had for a time seemed possible, on the one hand, because of disillusionment with Giscard d'Estaing's timid policies and, on the other, because of new cooperation between the French Socialist Party and the French Communist Party. Beginning in the late 1960s, François Mitterand had led an impressive drive to reorganize the Socialist Party. Its membership increased, as did its performance at the polls. In 1972 the Socialist Party and the Communist Party led by Georges Marchais formed a Common Front and agreed on a social and economic program that would be enacted if they were elected. The Socialists accepted the alliance because it seemed the only way that a left-wing majority could be achieved. The motives of the Communists were less clear, but it would seem that they thought such an alliance would give them considerable political leverage within left-wing politics. They hoped to become the tail that wagged the dog.

However, after 1972 the strength of the Socialist Party continued to grow and that of the Communist Party did not. It became clear by 1977 that if the proposed coalition won the election, the Communists would be able to exert relatively little pressure within the Cabinet. Consequently, in the middle of 1977, the Communist Party resumed its traditional stance of harshly criticizing the Socialists. In September 1977 the Common Front, in effect, came to an end. During the parliamentary elections of 1978 the two left-wing parties failed to cooperate. Communists refused to vote for Socialists, and Socialists refused to vote for Communists. The result of the election was a victory for the right and the center.

The presidential election of 1980 witnessed a

*Francois Mitterand, a socialist, was elected president in
1980, ending twenty-two years of right-wing domination
of French politics. However, the right recaptured control
of parliament in 1986. [UPI/Bettmann Newsphotos]*

sharp turnaround in French politics. Mitter-
and, the Socialist Party candidate, decisively
defeated Giscard d'Estaing. A few weeks later
the Socialists also captured control of the
French Parliament. Both Socialist victories
were achieved without formal alliance with or
support from the Communists.

Mitterand became president of France for
several reasons. Giscard d'Estaing had become
personally unpopular and was regarded as increasingly aloof from the French people. The
electorate had also become tired of techno-
cratic politics that tended to impose economic
and social solutions from above. Giscard d'Estaing's traditional supporters were divided because groups further to the right of him failed
to give support. These factors, however, should
not detract from the very remarkable accomplishment of political rebuilding of the left carried out by Mitterand over the past decade.
During those years he slowly but steadily
wooed traditional Communist voters away
from support of that party and toward support
of the Socialists. When a Socialist victory
rather than a Communist victory appeared the
likely result of turning out the Gaullists, the
French voters decided to try the Socialists. For
the first time in twenty-three years a genuinely
new administration had come to power in
France.

The Mitterand government initially pursued
a policy of active socialism in rhetoric and
rather moderate policies in action. Govern-

ment ownership of several large industries increased. There was an unsuccessful attempt to
reform the educational system to the detriment
of Roman Catholic influence. In the realm of
foreign policy Mitterand pursued a strong anti-
Soviet line and a moderately strong pro-
American position. This stance differed from
the traditional Gaullist position, which put
France on a course of independent mediation
between the two superpowers. Mitterand,
however, strongly supported the continuation
of the independent French nuclear capability.
Numerous tests were carried out in the South
Pacific. In 1985 that policy led to considerable
embarrassment when French agents were
caught and tried for the sinking of a peace-
movement ship, the *Rainbow Warrior*, in the
harbor of Auckland, New Zealand.

The French parliamentary elections of 1986
resulted in two new situations for the Fifth
Republic. First, the election saw the emergence
on the national scene of the National Front, an
extreme right wing group led by Jean-Marie
LePen, which gained approximately 10 per
cent of the popular vote. Its support seemed to
come from certain working-class and lower-
middle-class constituencies that had in the past
often voted with the political left. The appeal of
LePen's group seems to have been rooted in
racial and ethnic tensions that have arisen especially in southern France as groups of workers have immigrated from North Africa and
entered the local French job market. Second
and of more immediate importance, a coalition
of traditional French conservative parties won
control of the National Assembly. This victory
meant that a Socialist president had to do business with a hostile Assembly. The French Constitution which had been tailored by and for De
Gaulle had not envisioned a situation in which
the Presidency would be held by one party and
the Assembly controlled by another. Mitterand
appointed Jacques Chirac, a former Gaullist
minister and mayor of Paris, as prime minister.
Through an arrangement, known popularly as
cohabitation, the two opposing party leaders
have handled matters of state. Needless to say,
this arrangement has often proved cumbersome and has sharply reduced the area for political manoeuvre on the part of all concerned.

Instability in the Mediterranean World

For a quarter century after World War II
the major Mediterranean states were stable,
though for very different reasons. Spain and

Portugal remained governed by General Francisco Franco (1892–1975) and Antonio Salazar (1889–1970), respectively. They had established themselves during the turmoil between the wars and continued to preside over illiberal regimes. Italy had attained a course of reasonably steady progress under the leadership of the Christian Democrats. Greece had become stabilized during the 1950s, primarily thanks to American military and economic aid. By the middle of the 1960s each of these nations had begun to experience internal tensions that have since led to considerable turmoil throughout the region. Moreover, at the far southeastern end of the Mediterranean the Arab–Israeli conflict has proved a continuing source of instability.

PORTUGAL. Salazar ruled Portugal with an iron hand until 1968, when a stroke removed him from the political scene. His successor, Marcelo Caetano, continued to pursue authoritarian policies. The government remained determined to hold its possessions in Africa long after other European states had abandoned traditional colonial policies. Both at home and abroad major opposition to the government developed within the army officer corps. In 1974 General Antonio de Spinola led a successful army revolt against Caetano.

Since that time Portugal has indulged itself in the kind of political activity that had been forbidden for almost half a century. There have been large numbers of popular demonstrations, intense political party activity, and broad discussion of economic, social, and political problems. The Portuguese Communist Party proved to be exceedingly well organized. It was able to contribute to the overthrow of the Spinola government. However, in the elections of 1975 the Communists did not do well. The government came under the control of the Socialists, led by Mario Soares. In 1976 a democratic constitution was promulgated. Thereafter considerable political shifting and instability took place. Nonetheless, for the moment democracy in Portugal seems secure.

SPAIN. Spain has also entered on a period of considerable uncertainty. As long as he lived, Franco tolerated virtually no political life outside that of his own supporters. The Spanish police were active against any political opposition. Many political activists remained either in exile or in jail. However, opposition continued to grow. A large number of illegal

political parties had been organized. Franco died in 1975. As he had provided, his successor was Juan Carlos, from the old Bourbon royal family of Spain, who became king. The new monarch, though trained by Franco, made it clear that he wished Spain to be liberalized both politically and culturally. In December 1976 the Spanish voters approved a more liberal constitution. The question now became whether Juan Carlos could obtain the cooperation and trust of the recently legalized political parties. One event of 1981 would seem to have solidified their working relationship and mutual respect. In February 1981 a small group of military officers attempted a right-wing coup against the legislative assembly. Juan Carlos very quickly made himself the symbol of the ongoing democracy and called for the continuation of the democratic experiment, which has maintained itself with considerable success.

1035

*Europe in the
Era of the
Superpowers*

Francisco Franco (1892–1975) at a rally of the Falange Party in 1971. Behind Franco is Prince Juan Carlos of Bourbon, who became king of Spain when Franco died in 1975. To the surprise of many, under Juan Carlos Spain has become a liberal, democratic state. [AP/Wide World Photos]

GREECE. At the other end of the Mediterranean, Greece has also experienced a decade of upheaval. In 1965 King Constantine II (b. 1940) came into conflict with the political left. During the next several months leftist and liberal Greek politicians hoped to exert new influence on the monarch. In the spring of 1967 conservative army officers, claiming to be saving Greece from a Communist takeover, staged a *coup.* A few months later Constantine failed in his attempt at a counter-*coup,* and he fled the country. The strongly authoritarian army junta imposed tight control over the population and imprisoned political opponents. In the summer of 1974, however, confrontation between Greece and Turkey over the future of Cyprus led to the collapse of the Greek military government. Turkey had invaded Cyprus under the pretext of protecting the Turkish part of the population. The Greek junta was incapable of dealing with the crisis, and a civilian government, headed by former premier Constantine Karamanlis (b. 1907), took over. In 1975 a referendum by the Greek people decided against restoration of the monarchy. The problem of the future of Cyprus remained a source of friction between Greece and Turkey. In October 1981, the Greek Socialist Party, led by Andreas Papandreou, won the elections and has governed ever since.

ITALY. Instability has threatened Italy from different sources. The transformation from a fascist to a nonfascist government commenced during the war. In 1943 the Grand Fascist Council had ousted Mussolini. He was later summarily executed by Italian partisans. A government friendly to the Allies was installed in southern Italy, and it expanded its control as the Allied armies moved northward. At the close of the conflict the profascist political parties quickly reemerged. In 1946 the nation voted to abolish the monarchy.

The Christian Democrats governed under the leadership of Alcide de Gasperi. Until 1947 the Italian Communist Party served in the coalition, but it was excluded in that year. Thereafter Italy remained a nation with a single major large political party, the Christian Democrats, who formed coalitions with other smaller parties. Government by bargained coalition became the order of the day. Under this system, which resembled the system of *transformismo* that had prevailed before Mussolini, the Italian economy experienced a period of growth not unlike that of West Germany. Italy became a genuinely modern nation. It manufactured autos, refrigerators, and office equipment. The nation was very active in the drive for European unity.

However, by the late 1960s and early 1970s discontent was stirring against the Christian Democrats. Their methods of government had led to corruption, inefficiency, and political paralysis. Inflation became intense as economic growth stagnated. As a result, the Italian Communist Party, the largest and best organized in Western Europe, began to make significant inroads into political life. It won a considerable number of municipal elections. During 1976 the Communists won over 35 per cent of the popular vote for the Chamber of Deputies. They were refused admission to the Cabinet but were granted several important posts within the Chamber of Deputies.

The architect of the Communist advance within Italian politics was Enrico Berlinguer (1922–1984). He set forth a policy known as the *historic compromise.* The policy represented a major break not only with the previous stand of the Italian Communist Party but also with a Moscow-dominated Communist movement. By the "historic compromise" Berlinguer announced the willingness of the Italian Communist Party to enter a coalition government with the Christian Democrats and other non-Communist parties. In other words, the Italian Communists have, for the time being, renounced revolution as the path to political power. They have also agreed to participate in a government that they would not dominate or control. The Italian Communist Party has also promised that as a partner in a coalition or as the governing party, should it be elected, it will govern constitutionally and will respect individuals' civil liberties. It has also urged continued Italian participation in NATO and criticized the recent authoritarian policies of the Polish Communist government. To date these promises have not been put to the test. The compromises, however, represent an important example of the strains emerging among Communist parties in Europe.

The Italian Communist success, stemming from its announced willingness to cooperate with middle-class and Christian political parties, has led to a further radicalization of the political left in Italy. The "historic compromise" has made the Italian Communist Party seem quite conservative to the unknown numbers of people who wish to see radical, but so far unclearly defined, political and social change in the nation. These groups have resorted to terrorism to make their power felt and to illustrate that the Communists have now become a pillar of the existing establishment. The best known of the terrorist organizations is the Red Brigades. In the spring of 1978, while several members of the Red Brigades were on trial for earlier violence, other members kidnapped Aldo Moro, a former premier of Italy and a major leader of the Christian Democratic Party. The government refused to negotiate for his release. After several weeks of captivity Moro was assassinated, and his body was left in a car on a street in Rome. During the crisis both the Christian Democratic Party and the Italian Communist Party condemned terrorism. Since the Moro assassination Italian politics has resumed its familiar pattern. The Christian Democrats rule and have experienced some electoral gains. The Communists govern several major cities but cannot win a national election or gain seats in the Cabinet. Terrorism still continues to be a factor in public life.

In 1983 Bettino Craxi came to the prime ministership. He is a Socialist leading a coalition government supported by the Christian Democrats. The Craxi ministry remained in office longer than any other of the post-war era. It has confronted a number of crises during which it was virtually out of office, but it then returned each time after a few days when no satisfactory alternative ministry could be organized.

THE ARAB—ISRAELI DISPUTE. A final source of instability in the Mediterranean world is the Arab—Israeli conflict. This dispute involves Europe because many of the citizens of Israel are immigrants from Europe and because Europe, like the United States, is highly dependent on oil from Arab countries. Moreover the Middle East also remains an arena for potential problems between the United States and the Soviet Union.

The modern state of Israel was the achievement of the world Zionist movement founded in 1897 by Theodore Herzl and later led by Chaim Weizmann. The British Balfour Declaration of 1917 had favored the establishment of a national home for the Jewish people in Palestine. Between the wars thousands of Jews, mainly from Europe, immigrated into the area, which was then governed by Great Britain under a mandate of the League of Nations. During the interwar period the Yishuv or

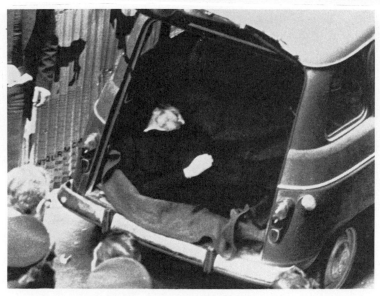

On May 9, 1978, *the body of former Italian Premier Aldo Moro was found in the rear of an automobile on a street in Rome. He had been kidnapped on March 16 by an Italian terrorist organization known as the Red Brigades and was murdered when the Italian government refused to negotiate for his release.* [*United Press International Photo*]

Jewish community in Palestine developed its own political parties, press, labor unions, and educational system. There were numerous conflicts with the Arabs already living in Palestine, for they considered the Jewish settlers intruders. The British rather unsuccessfully attempted to mediate those clashes.

This situation might have prevailed longer in Palestine except for the outbreak of World War II and the attempt by Hitler to exterminate the Jewish population of Europe. The Nazi persecution united Jews throughout the world behind the Zionist ideal of a Jewish state in Palestine. At the same time the knowledge of Nazi atrocities mobilized the conscience of the United States and the other Western powers. It seemed morally right that something be done for Jewish refugees from Nazi concentration camps. In 1947 the British turned over to the United Nations the whole problem of the relationship of Arabs and Jews in Palestine. That same year the United Nations passed a resolution calling for a division of the territory into a Jewish state and an Arab state.

The Arabs in Palestine and the surrounding area resisted the United Nations resolution. Not unnaturally, they resented the influx of

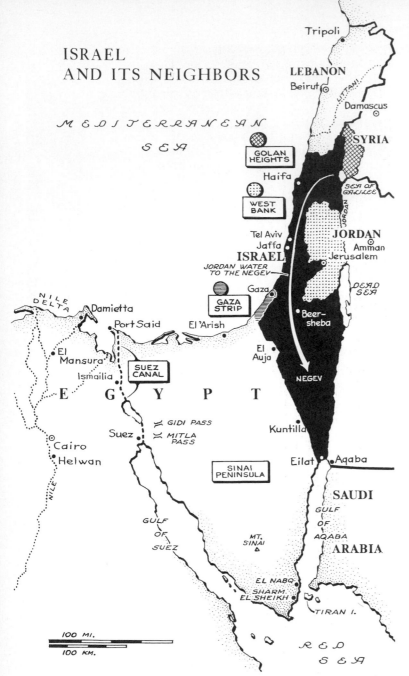

ISRAEL
AND ITS NEIGHBORS

MEDITERRANEAN
SEA

LEBANON
Tripoli
Beirut
Damascus
SYRIA
GOLAN HEIGHTS
Haifa
SEA OF GALILEE
WEST BANK
Tel Aviv
Jaffa
ISRAEL
JORDAN
Amman
Jerusalem
JORDAN WATER TO THE NEGEV
Gaza
GAZA STRIP
DEAD SEA
Beer-sheba
NILE DELTA
Damietta
Port Said
El 'Arish
El Auja
El Mansura
Ismailia
SUEZ CANAL
NEGEV
E G Y P T
Kuntilla
Cairo
Helwan
Suez
GIDI PASS
MITLA PASS
Eilat
Aqaba
SINAI PENINSULA
SAUDI
GULF OF SUEZ
MT. SINAI
GULF OF AQABA
ARABIA
EL NABQ
SHARM EL SHEIKH
TIRAN I.
RED SEA

100 MI.
100 KM.

MAP 29–4 *The map shows the geography of the difficult problem of Israel and its surrounding Arab neighbors. Syria, Jordan, and Egypt are the states with lands
now occupied by Israel. The future of those lands and of
earlier Palestinian refugees makes up the major set of
problems still unresolved in the area.*

new settlers. Large numbers of Palestinian
Arabs were displaced and themselves became
refugees. In May 1948 the Yishuv declared the
independence of a new Jewish state called Israel. The United States, through President Truman, almost immediately recognized the new
nation, whose first prime minister was David
Ben-Gurion (1886–1973). During 1948 and
1949 Israel fought its war of independence
against the Arabs. In that war Israel expanded
its borders beyond the limits originally set forth
by the United Nations. By 1949 Israel had,
through force of arms, secured its existence
and peace, but it had not secured diplomatic
recognition by its Arab neighbors—Egypt, Jordan, Syria, and Saudi Arabia, to name those
closest. The peace amounted to little more than
an armed truce.

Then in 1952 a group of Egyptian army officers seized power in Egypt. Their leader was
Gamal Abdel Nasser. He established himself as
a dictator and, more important, as a spokesman for militant Arab nationalism. His policy
was marked by a clear hatred of all the old
imperial powers. In 1956 Nasser nationalized
the Suez Canal. That same year, as noted previously, Great Britain and France responded to
Nasser's action by attacking the canal. Israel
joined with France and Britain. This alliance
helped Israel fend off certain Arab guerilla attacks but associated Israel with the former imperial powers. After 1956 a United Nations
peacekeeping force separated the armies of Israel and Egypt. The bases of the UN force were
located in Egypt. Still there was no official
Arab recognition of the existence of Israel.

An uneasy peace continued until 1967.
Meanwhile, the Soviet Union increased its influence in Egypt, and the United States increased its influence in Israel. Both great powers supplied weapons to their friends in the
area. In 1967 President Nasser made the calculation, which proved to be quite wrong, that
the Arab nations could defeat Israel, which by
then was nearly two decades old. He began to
mass troops in the Sinai Peninsula, and he attempted to close the Gulf of Aqaba to Israeli
shipping. He also demanded the withdrawal of
the UN peacekeeping force. Diplomatic activity
failed to stem the crisis and the Arab attempt to
isolate Israel. On June 5, 1967, the armed
forces of Israel, under the direction of Defense
Minister Moshe Dayan (1915–1981), attacked
Egyptian airfields rather than endure additional provocation by Egypt. Almost immediately Syria and Jordan entered the war on the
side of Egypt. Yet, by June 11, the Six Days'
War was over, and Israel had won a stunning
victory. The military forces of Egypt lay in
shambles. Moreover Israel occupied the entire
Egyptian Sinai Peninsula, as well as the West
Bank region along the Jordan River that had

previously been part of the state of Jordan. This victory marked the height of Israeli power and prestige.

In 1970 President Nasser died. He was succeeded by Anwar el-Sadat (1918–1981). Sadat had first to shore up his support at home. The existing tensions between Israel and the defeated Egypt, of course, continued, and the Soviet Union still poured weapons into Egypt. However, Sadat deeply distrusted the Russians and in 1972 ordered them to leave the country. He and his advisers also felt that only another war with Israel could return to Egypt the lands lost in 1967. In October 1973, on the Jewish holy day of Yom Kippur, the military forces of Egypt and Syria launched an attack across the Suez Canal into Israeli-held territory. The invasion came as a complete surprise to the Israelis. Initially the Egyptian forces made considerable headway. Then the Israeli army thrust back the invasion. In November 1973 a truce was signed between the forces in the Sinai. Although Israel had been successful in repelling the Egyptians, the cost in troops and prestige was very high.

The Yom Kippur War added a major new element to the Middle East problem. In the fall of 1973, when the war broke out, the major Arab oil-producing states shut off the flow of oil to the United States and Europe. This dramatic move was an attempt to force the Western powers to use their influence to moderate the policy of Israel. The threat of the loss of oil was particularly frightening to Europeans, who possess almost no major sources of oil, on which their industry depends. In the future this Arab oil can be expected to play an even more influential part in Middle East developments.

In November 1977, President Sadat of Egypt, in a dramatic personal gesture, flew to Israel, addressed the Israeli Parliament, and held discussions with Prime Minister Menachem Begin (b. 1913), although the two states were still technically at war. In effect, for the first time the head of a major Arab state recognized the existence of Israel. Previously all contacts had taken place through either the United Nations or other third parties. The Sadat initiative, roundly condemned in many Arab quarters, resulted in direct conversations, the most important of which occurred at Camp David in the United States with President Carter as moderator. The Camp David Accords of September 1978 have provided one framework through which negotiations on Middle East questions have taken place. Since 1978 nu-

Israeli troops occupy the Golan Heights in Syria during the Six Days' War of 1967. Israel annexed the Golan in 1981. [Black Star]

Announcement of the historic Camp David Accords in 1978. Left to right, President Sadat of Egypt, President Carter, and Prime Minister Begin of Israel. [UPI]

United States stationed marines in Lebanon. After a terrorist bombing killed more than three hundred troops, they were withdrawn. In 1985 Israeli troops withdrew. However, at present and into the foreseeable future, Lebanon remains a center of crisis and a base from which terrorists may operate against all sides.

In 1983 Prime Minister Begin, who was in ill health, resigned. He was succeeded by a coalition government in which the major party leaders are to take turns in the prime ministership. In 1986 Premier Shimon Peres met with King Hassan II of Morocco. This was the first public meeting between an Israeli leader and an Arab head of state since the Sadat initiative that led to the Camp David Accords. It remains unclear what developments will result from these new initiatives.

The Israeli–Arab conflict has in recent years seen increased activity in the region on the part of the United States. The temporary stationing of troops in Lebanon was one indication of this action. But in 1986 as a result of numerous incidents of terrorism directed against American citizens by Libya, the United States carried out an air raid on Tripoli. The policy of the United States in the region so far as terrorism is concerned would now seem to be one of direct response.

The Soviet Union and Eastern Europe

The Soviet Union Since the Death of Stalin (1953)

Many Russians had hoped that the end of the war would signal a lessening of Stalinism. No other nation had suffered greater losses or more deprivation than the Soviet Union. Its people anticipated some immediate reward for their sacrifice and heroism. They desired a reduction in the scope of the police state and a redirection of the economy away from heavy industry to consumer products. They were disappointed. Stalin did little or nothing to modify the character of the regime he had created. The police remained ever-present. The cult of personality expanded, and the central bureaucracy continued to grow. Heavy industry was still favored over production for consumers. Agriculture continued to be troubled. Stalin's personal authority over the party and the nation remained unchallenged. In foreign policy Stalin moved to solidify Soviet control over

merous meetings have occurred between Egyptian and Israeli officials. Until 1986 no other Arab states have joined these talks. The major stumbling block to future agreements is the Palestine refugee problem. The Palestine Liberation Organization (PLO) remains the major spokesman for the refugees. The PLO continues to demand a separate Palestinian state. The government of Israel has steadily refused to recognize the PLO. Israel also believes that virtually any independent Palestinian state would be a threat to its own independence and ultimate survival.

In early 1981 Prime Minister Begin's coalition was reelected, but in October of that year President Sadat was assassinated by Muslim extremists. The death of the Egyptian president cast doubt on the long-range stability of the Camp David process. Further strains appeared in late December 1981, when the Israeli Parliament suddenly annexed the Golan Heights while the attention of most of the Western world was on the crisis in Poland.

In 1982 Israeli troops invaded Lebanon in an effort to destroy PLO bases and to disperse the PLO leadership. They were largely successful in that effort. However, at the same time the fragile Lebanese state, long racked by civil war, virtually collapsed. For a few months in 1983 the

1041

*Europe in the
Era of the
Superpowers*

Eastern Europe for the purposes of both Communist expansion and Soviet national security. He attempted to impose the Soviet model on those nations. The Cold War stance of the United States simply served to confirm Stalin in his ways.

By late 1952 and early 1953 it appeared that Stalin might be ready to unloose a new series of purges. In January 1953 a group of Jewish physicians was arrested and charged with plotting the deaths of important leaders. Charges of extensive conspiracy appeared in the press. All of these developments were similar to the events that had preceded the purges of the 1930s. Then, quite suddenly, in the midst of this new furor, on March 6, 1953, Stalin died.

For a time no single leader replaced Stalin. Rather the Presidium (the renamed Politburo) pursued a policy of collective leadership. A considerable amount of reshuffling occurred among the top party leaders. Lavrenty Beria (1899–1953), the dreaded director of the secret police, was removed from his post and eventually executed. Georgy Malenkov (b. 1902) became premier, a position he held for about two years. Gradually, however, power and influence began to devolve on Nikita Khrushchev (1894–1971), who in 1953 had been named party secretary. By 1955 he had edged out Malenkov and had successfully urged the appointment of Nikolai Bulganin (1895–1975) in his place. Three years later Khrushchev himself became premier. His rise constituted the end of collective leadership, but at no time did he enjoy the extraordinary powers of Stalin.

THE KHRUSHCHEV YEARS. The Khrushchev era, which lasted until the autumn of 1964, witnessed a marked retreat from Stalinism, though not from extreme authoritarianism. Indeed, the political repression of Stalin had been so extensive that there was considerable room for relaxation of surveillance within the limits of tyranny. Politically the demise of Stalinism meant shifts in leadership and party structure by means other than purges. In 1956, at the Twentieth Congress of the Communist Party, Khrushchev made a secret speech (later published outside the Soviet Union) in which he denounced Stalin and his crimes against socialist justice during the purges of the 1930s. The speech caused shock and consternation in party circles and opened the way for limited, but genuine, internal criticism of the Soviet government. Gradually the strongest support-

ers of Stalinist policies were removed from the Presidium. By 1958 all of Stalin's former supporters were gone, but none had been executed.

Under Khrushchev, intellectuals were somewhat more free to express their opinions. This so-called thaw in the cultural life of the country was closely related to the premier's interest in the opinions of experts on problems of industry and agriculture. He often went outside the usual bureaucratic channels in search of information and new ideas. Novels such as Aleksandr Solzhenitsyn's (b. 1918) *One Day in the Life of Ivan Denisovich* (1963) could be published. However, Boris Pasternak (1890–1960), the author of *Dr. Zhivago,* was not permitted to accept the Nobel Prize for literature in 1958. The intellectual liberalization of Soviet life during this period should not be overestimated. It looked favorable only in comparison with what had preceded it and has continued to seem so because of the decline of such freedom of expression since Khrushchev's fall.

The economic policy also somewhat departed from the strict Stalinist mode. By 1953 the economy had recovered from the strains and destruction of the war, but consumer goods and housing still remained in very short supply. The problem of an adequate food supply also continued. Malenkov had favored improvements in meeting the demand for consumer goods; Khrushchev also favored such a departure. Khrushchev also moved in a moderate fashion to decentralize economic planning and execution. During the late 1950s he often boasted that Soviet production of consumer goods would overtake that of the West. Steel, oil, and electric-power production continued to grow, but the consumer sector improved only marginally. The ever-growing defense budget and the space program that successfully launched the first human-engineered satellite of the earth, *Sputnik,* in 1957 made major demands on the nation's productive resources. Economically Khrushchev was attempting to move the country in too many directions at once.

Khrushchev strongly redirected Stalin's agricultural policy. He recognized that in spite of the collectivization of the 1930s the Soviet Union had not produced an agricultural system capable of feeding its own people. Administratively Khrushchev removed many of the most restrictive regulations on private cultivation. The machine tractor stations were abandoned. Existing collective farms were further amalga-

Khrushchev Denounces the Crimes of Stalin: The Secret Speech

In 1956 Khrushchev denounced Stalin in a secret speech to the Party Congress. *The New York Times* published a text of that speech smuggled from Russia.

Stalin acted not through persuasion, explanation, and patient cooperation with people, but by imposing his concepts and demanding absolute submission to his opinion. Whoever opposed this concept or tried to prove his viewpoint and the correctness of his position was doomed to removal from the leading collective [group] and to subsequent moral and physical annihilation. . . .

Stalin originated the concept of "enemy of the people." This term automatically rendered it unnecessary that the ideological errors of a man or men engaged in a controversy be proved; this term made possible the usage of the most cruel repression violating all norms of revolutionary legality, against anyone who in any way disagreed with Stalin, against those who were only suspected of hostile intent, against those who had bad reputations.

This concept "enemy of the people" actually eliminated the possibility of any kind of ideological fight or the making of one's views known on this or that issue, even those of a practical character. In the main, and in actuality, the only proof of guilt used, against all norms of current legal science, was the "confession" of the accused himself; and, as a subsequent probing proved, "confessions" were acquired through physical pressures against the accused. . . .

Lenin used severe methods only in the most necessary cases, when the exploiting classes were still in existence and were vigorously opposing the revolution, when the struggle for survival was decidedly assuming the sharpest forms, even including civil war.

Stalin, on the other hand, used extreme methods and mass repressions at a time when the revolution was already victorious, when the Soviet State was strengthened, when the exploiting classes were already liquidated and Socialist relations were rooted solidly in all phases of national economy, when our party was politically consolidated and had strengthened itself both numerically and ideologically. It is clear that here Stalin showed in a whole series of cases his intolerance, his brutality and his abuse of power. Instead of proving his political correctness and mobilizing the masses, he often chose the path of repression and physical annihilation, not only against actual enemies, but also against individuals who had not committed any crimes against the party and the Soviet Government. . . .

The New York Times, June 5, 1956, pp. 13–16.

mated. The government undertook an extensive "virgin lands" program to extend wheat cultivation by hundreds of thousands of acres. This policy initially increased grain production to new records. However, in a very few years the new lands became subject to erosion. The farming techniques applied had been inappropriate for the soil. The agricultural problem has simply continued to grow. Currently the Soviet Union imports vast quantities of grain from the United States and other countries. United States grain imports have constituted a major facet of the policy of detente.

Adventuresomeness also characterized Khrushchev's foreign policy. In 1956 the Soviet Union adopted the phrase "peaceful coexistence" in regard to its relationship with the United States. The policy implied no less competition with the capitalist world but suggested that war might not be the best way to pursue Communist expansion. The previous year Khrushchev had participated in the Geneva summit meeting alongside Bulganin. Thereafter followed visits around the world, culminating with one to the United States in 1959. By the early 1960s it had become clear that Khrushchev had made few inroads on Western policy. He was under increasing domestic pressure and also pressure from the Chinese. The militancy of the denunciation of the U-2 flight, the aborting of the Paris summit meeting, the Berlin Wall, and the Cuban missile crisis were all responses to those pressures. The last of these adventures brought a clear Soviet retreat.

By 1964 numerous high Russian leaders and many people lower in the party had concluded that Khrushchev had tried to do too much too soon and had done it too poorly. On October 16, 1964, after defeat in the Central Committee of the Communist Party, Khrushchev resigned. He was replaced by Alexei Kosygin

RIGHT: *Krushchev visiting one of the new wheat-growing collectives on the "virgin lands" of southeastern Russia. Soviet agriculture has been weak since the 1930s. The "virgin lands" program initially increased grain yields, but was ultimately a costly failure.* [*Sovfoto*]

BELOW: *Krushchev was the most popular Soviet leader outside the U.S.S.R. since Stalin. Part of his appeal lay in his earthy, unpretentious style. His emotional approach is captured by this series of photos taken during his speech denouncing the U-2 flights in Paris in 1959. The man seated to his left is Marshal Rodion Malinovsky, the Soviet Defense Minister.* [*AP/Wide World Photos*]

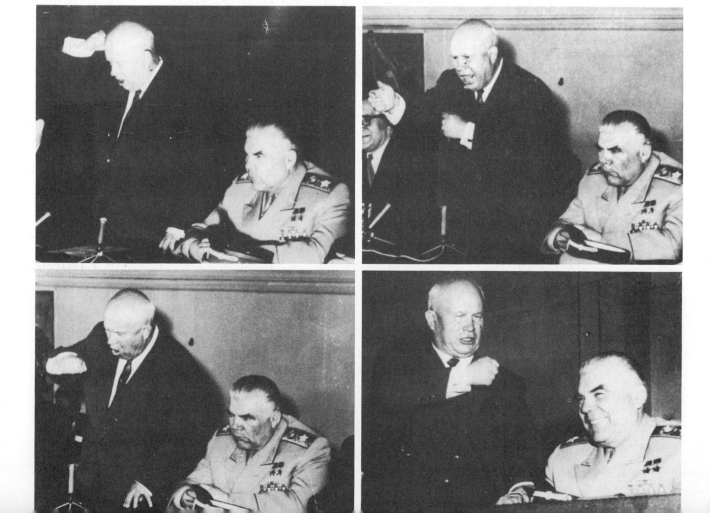

(1904–1980) as premier and Leonid Brezhnev (1906–1982) as party secretary. The latter eventually emerged as the dominant figure. In 1977 the constitution of the Soviet Union was changed to combine the offices of president and party secretary. Brezhnev became president, and thus head of the state as well as of the party. He held more personal power than any Soviet leader since Stalin.

BREZHNEV AND AFTER. Domestically the Soviet government has become markedly more repressive since 1964. All intellectuals have enjoyed less and less freedom and little direct access to the government leadership. In 1974 the government expelled Solzhenitsyn. Perhaps most important among recent developments, Jewish citizens of the Soviet Union have become subject to harassment. Major bureaucratic obstacles have been placed in the way of the emigration of Soviet Jews to Israel. These policies suggest a return to the limitations of the Stalinist period.

The internal repression has given rise to a dissident movement. Certain Soviet citizens have dared to criticize the regime in public and to carry out small demonstrations against the government. They have accused the Soviet government of violating the human rights provisions of the 1975 Helsinki Accords. The dissidents have included a number of prominent citizens, such as the Nobel Prize physicist Andrei Sakharov. The response of the Soviet government to the dissident movement has been further repression. Prominent dissidents, such as Anatoly Shcharansky (since released), Aleksandr Ginzburg, and Vladimir Slepak, have been arrested, tried on clearly trumped-up charges, and sentenced to long periods of imprisonment or internal exile in Siberia. The Soviet government obviously feels it cannot tolerate the dissident movement. The questions that now arise and cannot be answered have to do with how much internal opposition to the government exists in the Soviet Union and what, if any, possibility the opposition has of making its thought and will known.

In foreign policy the Brezhnev years witnessed attempts to reach accommodation with the United States while continuing to press for expanded Soviet influence and further attempts to maintain Soviet leadership of the Communist movement. During the Vietnam war the Soviet Union pursued a policy of restrained support for North Vietnam. Under President Richard Nixon the United States pursued a policy of detente based on arms limitation and trade agreements. Nonetheless Soviet spending on defense, and particularly on naval expansion, continued to grow. During the Ford and Carter administrations in the United States, Soviet involvement in African affairs was troubling.

More important in leading to a cooling of relations between the superpowers was the Soviet invasion of Afghanistan in December 1979. A Soviet presence had already existed in that country, but for reasons that still remain unclear the Soviet government felt that it was required to send in troops to ensure its influence in central Asia. As noted earlier, the invasion brought a grain embargo and a boycott on participation in the Moscow Olympic Games from the United States government. The invasion also dashed any hope for U.S. Senate ratification of the arms limitation treaty signed by President Carter and President Brezhnev in 1979. The Reagan administration has continued a similar policy but has stiffened it by postponing arms negotiations. It has, however, relaxed the grain embargo. The Afghanistan invasion also seems to have tied the hands of the Soviet government in its own sphere of influence in Eastern Europe. There seems little doubt that the Soviet hesitation to react more strongly to events in Poland, which are discussed in the next section, stemmed in part from having military resources committed to Afghanistan and from having encountered broad condemnation for the invasion from some West European Communist parties and from the governments of nations not aligned with the West.

Brezhnev died in 1982. Both of his immediate successors, Yuri Andropov and Constantine Chernenko, died after holding office for very short periods. Neither put any particular new mark on Soviet policy. In 1984 Mikhail S. Gorbachev came to power. He immediately made numerous important changes in personnel. Several new persons about whom relatively little is known in the West now hold major positions in the Soviet Union. He also began an effective and vigorous public-relations campaign to command the attention of the western press.

In the spring of 1986 a major malfunction and fire occurred at a Soviet nuclear reactor at Chernobyl near Kiev in the Ukraine. For several days the Soviet government released very little information about the disaster while large amounts of nuclear fallout were deposited

1045

*Europe in the
Era of the
Superpowers*

*Anti-Soviet freedom fighters in Afghanistan. Since 1979 the Soviet army has been bogged
down there in a bloody and expensive guerilla war in an effort to prop up a puppet communist
regime.* [Raymond Deparon—Magnum]

across Western Europe. The long-range environmental impact of this event cannot yet be determined, though it is likely to be considerable. The political impact was immediate. Throughout Western Europe new suspicions arose about the good intentions of the Soviet Union and particularly about its recent assertions of openness. The internal problem of assessing blame and devising better future controls has presented Gorbachev with major and unexpected problems. His Soviet peers will judge him according to his response to these difficulties. One almost inevitable result will be a slowing of the various initiatives he had intended to undertake in terms of domestic policy, party reorganization, and bureaucratic reform.

In addition to these problems there is growing evidence that the Soviets feel bogged down in Afghanistan and would like to extricate themselves. This situation will also prove a major challenge to Gorbachev's new leadership.

Polycentrism in the Communist World

Throughout the Cold War observers in the West have concentrated their attention on the tensions between the Soviet Union and the United States. But beyond its continuing confrontation of and rivalry with America, the Soviet government has also had to deal with growing tension and division within the world Communist movement. During most of the Stalin era the Soviet Union was the center of world communism. Stalin hoped to impose his model on other parties. Immediately after the war the Soviets attempted to construct governments in the peoples' democracies of Eastern Europe in the Stalinist mold. Since the late 1940s the unity of world communism, which was always more frail than Cold War rhetoric suggested, became strained and finally shattered. As early as 1948 Yugoslavia began to construct its own model for socialism independent of Moscow. From 1956 onward, the governments of Eastern Europe began to seek a freer hand in internal affairs. By the late 1950s the monumental split between the Soviet Union and the People's Republic of China had developed. The Communist world has come to have many centers—thus the descriptive term *polycentrism*— and the Soviet Union has had to compete for leadership.

There have been three stages in postwar relations between the Soviet Union and Eastern Europe. They were the years of Stalinism, then of revolt, and finally of socialist polycentrism. These stages closely paralleled internal developments in the Soviet Union itself.

Before the death of Stalin in 1953 the so-called peoples' democracies were brought steadily into line with Soviet policy. By 1948 single-party Communist governments had been established in Bulgaria, Romania, Hungary, Yugoslavia, Albania, Czechoslovakia, Poland, and East Germany. Yugoslavia, headed by Marshal Tito (1892–1980), pursued an independent course of action and was bitterly denounced by Stalin. Elsewhere, however, Soviet troops and Stalinist party leaders prevailed. The economies of those states were made to conform to the requirements of Soviet economic recovery and growth. The Soviet Union paid low prices for its imports from Eastern Europe and demanded high prices for its exports. In this fashion and through outright reparations, it drained the resources of the region for its own uses. The Soviet Union prevented the Eastern European nations from participating in the Marshall Plan and responded with its own Council for Economic Mutual Assistance in 1949. In 1955 it organized the Warsaw Pact to confront NATO.

The Stalinist system of control was bound to generate discontent. This first manifested itself shortly after Stalin's death in 1953, when a brief revolt occurred in East Berlin. It was immediately crushed. Talk in the early Eisenhower administration in America about the "liberation" of Eastern Europe may have contributed to this disturbance by raising hopes of some form of United States support. Khrushchev's speech of 1956 in which he denounced Stalin sent reverberations throughout Eastern Europe as well as the Soviet Union. It was no accident that following the speech came the Polish October Revolution and the Hungarian Revolution of 1956. In the short run the bids for independence had the most limited kind of success; however, in retrospect they can be seen as marking the close of the Stalinist period and as paving the way for the emergence of polycentrism.

During the early years of the Cold War it was common in the West to regard the Communist movement as a single monolithic structure. There was a failure to take into account the role of nationalism in Eastern Europe and the potential for division between the Soviet Union and China. The events of 1956 delineated the limits of acceptable independence for the Soviet-dominated successor states. Those nations of Eastern Europe must remain members of the Warsaw Pact, and their leaders had to be willing to consult and cooperate with the Soviet Union. They might trade with Western Europe and the United States and even establish cultural contacts, but their chief political and economic orientation must remain with the Soviet Union.

Since 1956, within these limits considerable diversity has appeared within the communist bloc in Eastern Europe. In Hungary the Janos Kadar government, which was installed by Soviet troops, pursued a program of economic growth and consumer satisfaction. Hungary is now probably the most prosperous and stable country in the region. East Germany and Bulgaria retained the closest relationships with the Soviet Union. After the Berlin Wall crisis of 1961 and the subsequent halt in the outflow of refugees, East Germany experienced very substantial economic growth. Romania has witnessed a resurgence of limited nationalism. Under the leadership of President Nicolae Ceauşescu (b. 1918), it has maintained ties with both the Soviet Union and China. Moreover, it has also cultivated friendly relations with the United States, as witnessed by President Nixon's visit in 1969 and President Ceauşescu's visit to America in 1977. However, in all of these countries the independence achieved is extremely limited and exists within the limits of one-party government, authoritarianism, and absence of the traditional civil liberties.

THE CZECHOSLOVAKIAN CRISIS. In 1968 the Soviet Union moved to crush an experiment in developing a socialist model independent of Soviet domination. In that year the nations of the Warsaw Pact invaded Czechoslovakia to halt the political experimentation of the Alexander Dubcek government. It was quite clear that the Soviet Union felt that it could not tolerate so liberal a Communist regime on its own borders. Dubcek was permitting in Czechoslovakia the very kind of intellectual freedom and discussion that was simultaneously being suppressed within Russia itself. At the time of the invasion Soviet Party Chairman Brezhnev declared the right of the Soviet Union to interfere in the domestic politics of other Communist countries. Such direct interference has nevertheless not occurred since 1968. Moreover, at a conference of Communist parties held in East Berlin in 1976, the Soviet Union accepted a declaration stating that there could be several paths to socialism. The main proponents of this policy were the Communist parties of Western Europe. As the

1047

*Europe in the
Era of the
Superpowers*

Soviet tanks in Prague, August, 1968. Unlike the Hungarians in 1956, the Czechs did not resist the Soviets. The invasion demonstrated that the nations of eastern Europe would be compelled to remain politically and economically tied to the Soviet Union. [Ullstein Bilderdienst]

Communist Party of Italy in particular, as well as that of France, has seen election to full or shared power as a genuine possibility, it has attempted to put a distance between itself and the Soviet Union. However, to date none of these declarations and acknowledgments of socialist independence from Soviet domination has been put to a meaningful test.

THE POLISH CRISIS. Such a test seems to have occurred in Poland since the summer of 1980. The Soviet Union has a deep strategic interest in that nation because it was across Poland that the armies of both Napoleon and Hitler invaded Russia. After 1956 the Polish Communist Party, led by Wladyslaw Gomulka (1905–1982) made peace with the Roman Catholic church, halted land collectivization, established trade with the West, and participated in cultural exchange programs with non-Communist nations. However, Poland experienced chronic economic mismanagement and persistent shortages in food and consumer goods. In 1970 food shortages led to a series of strikes, the most famous of which occurred in the shipyards at Gdansk. In December 1970 the Polish authorities broke the strike at the

cost of a number of workers' lives. These events led to the departure of Gomulka. His successor was Edward Gierek (b. 1913).

In the decade after 1970 the Polish economy made very little progress. Food and other consumer goods remained in very short supply. The government tried to work its way out of these difficulties through very large loans from banks in the United States and Western Europe. In early July 1980 the Polish government raised meat prices. The result was hundreds of protest strikes across the country. The strikes were directed against the economic situation and against what was regarded as the mismanagement of the nation's affairs by the current leaders of the Polish Communist Party. On August 14 workers occupied the Lenin shipyard at Gdansk. They demanded the reinstatement of certain workers who had led the 1970 strike, the building of a memorial to the workers killed in 1970, a guarantee of no reprisals against the strikers of 1980, family subsidies, and raises in wages. The strike soon spread to other shipyards, transport facilities, and factories connected with the shipbuilding industry. The most important leader to emerge from among the strikers was Lech Walesa (b. 1944).

Lech Walesa (b. 1944) and the members of the Solidarity Committee in Gdansk in August 1980. At Soviet urging, Solidarity was suppressed after the Polish military took power in December 1981. Walesa was not imprisoned, but his activities are closely monitored. [*Jean Gaumy—Magnum*]

He and the other strike leaders refused to negotiate with the government through any of the traditionally government-controlled unions. The Gdansk strike ended on August 31 with the workers having been promised the right to organize an independent union and the right of access to television and the press on the part of the union (by then called *Solidarity*) and the Polish Roman Catholic church. Less than a week later, on September 6, Edward Gierek was dismissed as the head of the Polish Communist Party by the Polish Politburo and was replaced by Stanislaw Kania. Later in September the Polish courts recognized Solidarity as an independent union, and the state-controlled radio, for the first time in thirty years, broadcast a Roman Catholic mass.

The Soviet Union watched these events with growing unease and displeasure. It feared that other Eastern European states might attempt to copy Poland. Throughout 1980 and 1981 Soviet leaders sent warning messages to the Poles, and troop maneuvers were carried out on the Polish borders. Despite these pressures the early months of 1981 witnessed still further changes in Poland. Solidarity carried out new strikes demanding a five-day work week. The small independent farmers in the countryside soon organized a rural union known as *Rural Solidarity*, and it too was recognized by the courts. In the midst of this external and internal pressure the Polish Communist government still had to attempt to redirect economic policy toward greater production and the payment of its massive foreign debts. Food shortages led to rationing. In order to set out on a new course and to give itself a further appearance of legitimacy, the Polish Communist Party called a special party congress for July of 1981. The calling of the congress was in itself extraordinary, but the manner in which it was carried out was even more surprising. For the first time in any European Communist state, there were secret elections, and real choices were permitted among the candidates. When the congress met and elected new members for the Polish Politburo, those congress elections were also secret and allowed real choice. By making these concessions, admitting past mistakes, and erecting a memorial to the 1970 strikers, the Polish Communist Party had clearly sought to make itself more acceptable to the political grass roots of the nation. Poland remained a nation governed by a single party, but for the time being, real debate was permitted within that party. These political changes, which were

The Premier of Poland Announces the Imposition of Martial Law

On December 13, 1981, General Wojciech Jaruzelski, the premier of Poland and head of the Polish Communist Party, announced the imposition of martial law. The action was taken after months of liberal reform in Poland led by the independent trade union Solidarity. The government turned to military rule out of fear that the political activity of Solidarity would endanger the rule of the Communist Party in Poland. The announced reason for the imposition of martial law was to prevent disorder.

Our country is on the edge of the abyss. Achievements of many generations, raised from the ashes, are collapsing into ruin. State structures no longer function. New blows are struck each day at our flickering economy. Living conditions are burdening people more and more.

Through each place of work, in many Polish people's homes, there is a line of painful division. The atmosphere of unending conflict, misunderstanding and hatred sows mental devastation and damages the tradition of tolerance.

Strikes, strike alerts, protest actions have become standard. Even students are dragged into it. . . .

With our aims, it cannot be said that we [the Communist Party government] did not show good will, moderation, patience, and sometimes there was probably too much of it. It cannot be said the Government did not honor the social agreements [made with Solidarity in 1980 at Gdansk]. We even went further. The initiative of the great national understanding was backed by the millions of Poles. It created a chance, an opportunity to deepen the system of democracy of

people ruling the country, widening reforms. Those hopes failed.

Around the negotiating table there was no leadership from Solidarity. Words said in Radom and in Gdansk [strike calls and political demands from Solidarity] showed the real aims of its leadership. These aims are confirmed by everyday practice, growing aggressiveness of the extremists, clearly aiming to take apart the Polish state system.

How long can one wait for a sobering up? How long can a hand reached for accord meet a fist? I say this with a broken heart, with bitterness. It could have been different in our country. It should have been different. But if the current state had lasted longer, it would have led to a catastrophe, to absolute chaos, to poverty and starvation. . . .

I declare that today the army Council of National Salvation has been constituted, and the Council of State obeying the Polish Constitution declared a state of emergency at midnight on the territory of Poland. . . .

The New York Times, December 14, 1981, p. 16.

very considerable, did not lead to the solving of the underlying economic problem. Strikes continued, as did the duel between Solidarity and the government.

In October 1981 Kania was dismissed by the Politburo and was replaced as head of the party by General Wojciech Jaruzelski (b. 1923). This move brought the army to the center of Polish events. Early in December 1981 General Jaruzelski, in a surprise move, declared martial law in Poland. The army suspended civil liberties and moved against Solidarity. Many of the chief leaders of Solidarity were placed under arrest, and many other Poles were also impris-

oned. In an attempt to make the action appear evenhanded, the military also arrested a number of former Communist Party leaders suspected of corruption. The imposition of martial law met some resistance from Polish workers, and several miners were killed. The United States reacted to these events by blaming the Soviet Union and placing economic sanctions against the Soviet Union and against Poland. The West European allies of the United States gave little support to the action because they feared disrupting their own economic ties to the Soviet Union. The Polish military leaders succeeded in repressing the Poles, but they were not successful in addressing the major economic problems of the country.

By the mid-1980s the military and the Polish Communist Party had succeeded in suppressing the activity of Solidarity as both a political and a trade union force. The events in Poland made clear that the Soviet Union stands willing to tolerate virtually no independent institutions within those nations in its Eastern European sphere of influence.

Suggested Readings

K. L. BAKER, R. J. DALTON, AND K. HILDEBRANDT, *Germany Transformed: Political Culture and the New Politics* (1981). Useful essays on the functioning of German democracy.

S. BEER, *Modern British Politics: Parties and Pressure Groups in the Collectivist Age* (1982). The best introduction to the subject.

C. D. BLACK AND G. DUFFY, eds., *International Arms Control Issues and Agreements* (1985). Useful essays.

E. BOTTOME, *The Balance of Terror: Nuclear Weapons and the Illusion of Security, 1945–1985* (1986). A pessimistic evaluation.

Z. BRZEZINSKI, *The Soviet Block: Unity and Conflict* (1967). A somewhat dated discussion of Eastern Europe.

C. BURDICK, H–A. JACOBSEN, AND W. KUDSZUR, eds., *Contemporary Germany: Politics and Culture* (1984). A collection of wideranging essays.

L. T. CALDWELL AND W. DIEBOLD, JR., *Soviet American Relations in the 1980's: Superpower Politics and East-West Trade* (1980). An attempt to delineate the major problems in Soviet-American relations during the present decade.

A. W. DE PORTE, *Europe Between the Superpowers: The Enduring Balance* (1979). A very important study.

R. EMERSON, *From Empire to Nation: The Rise to Self-assertion of Asian and African Peoples* (1960). An important discussion of the origins of decolonization.

B. B. FALL, *The Two Vietnams: A Political and Military Analysis,* rev. ed. (1967). A discussion by a journalist who spent many years on the scene.

M. FRANKLIN, *The Decline of Class Voting in Britain* (1986). The argument is stated in the title.

J. R. FREARS, *France in the Giscard Presidency* (1981) A survey.

D. GILMOUR, *The Transformation of Spain from Franco to the Constitutional Monarchy* (1985). A useful overview.

R. HISCOCKS, *The Adenauer Era* (1966). A treatment of postwar German political development.

D. HOLLOWAY, *The Soviet Union and the Arms Race* (1985). Excellent treatment of internal Soviet decisionmaking.

S. HOFFMAN (Ed.), *In Search of France* (1963). A useful collection of essays on the problems of postwar France.

R. W. HULL, *The Irish Triangle: Conflict in Northern Ireland* (1976). A thoughtful and generally dispassionate treatment of a difficult problem.

J. JOSEPHS, *Inside the Alliance: An Inside Account of the Development and Prospects of the Liberal-SDP Alliance* (1983). A discussion of the founding of a new political party in Britain.

N. R. KEDDIE, *Roots of Revolution: An Interpretative History of Modern Iran* (1981). A useful treatment of an important, controversial, and ongoing event.

W. W. KULSKI, *De Gaulle and the World: The Foreign Policy of the Fifth French Republic* (1968). A straightforward treatment of De Gaulle's drive toward French and European autonomy.

W. LEONHARD, *Three Faces of Communism* (1974). An analysis of the ideological divisions within the communist world.

R. F. LESLIE, *The History of Poland Since 1863* (1981). An excellent collection of essays that provide the background for current tensions in Poland.

L. MARTIN (Ed.), *Strategic Thought in the Nuclear Age* (1979). A collection of useful essays on an issue that lies at the core of the American relationship to Western Europe.

R. MAYNE, *The Recovery of Europe, 1945–1973* (1973). A sound treatment emphasizing the movement toward economic integration.

M. MCCAULEY, *The German Democratic Republic since 1945* (1983). Useful survey of East Germany.

Z. A. MEDVEDEV, *Gorbachev* (1986). The best available biography.

G. MYRDAL, *Asian Drama: An Inquiry into the Poverty of Nations,* 3 vols. (1968). A significant discussion of the economic and social problems of the postcolonial world by a thoughtful economist.

M. M. POSTAN, *An Economic History of Western Europe, 1945–1964* (1967). A basic survey.

D. ROBERTSON, *Class and the British Electorate* (1986). Emphasizes the decline of class voting.

R. ROSE, *Governing Without Consensus: An Irish Perspective* (1971). An excellent exploration of the origins and development of the Irish problem.

G. ROSS, *Workers and Communists in France: From Popular Front to Eurocommunism* (1982) An important issue in recent French politics.

J. RUSCOE, *The Italian Communist Party, 1976–81: On the Threshold of Government* (1982). Examines the party at the height of its influence.

A. SAMPSON, *The Changing Anatomy of Britain* (1982). An exploration of the social and political elites.

L. SCHAPIRO, *The Communist Party of the Soviet Union* (1960). A classic analysis of the most important institution of Soviet Russia.

R. SHAPLEN, *The Lost Revolution: The U.S. in Vietnam* (1965). A clear analysis of the problems that confronted the United States.

H. SIMONIAN, *The Privileged Partnership: Franco-German Relations in the European Community, (1969–1984)* (1985). An important examination of the dominant role of France and Germany in the E.E.D.

J. STEELE, *Soviet Power: The Kremlin's Foreign Policy— Brezhnev to Andropov* (1983) A broad survey.

C. TUGENHAT, *Making Sense of Europe* (1986). Evaluation of Common Market by one of its commissioners.

A. ULAM, *Expansion and Coexistence: The History of Soviet Foreign Policy, 1917–1967* (1968). The best one-volume treatment.

D. M. WILLIAMS, *French Politicians and Elections, 1951–1969* (1970). Excellent coverage of the establishment and early years of the Fifth Republic.

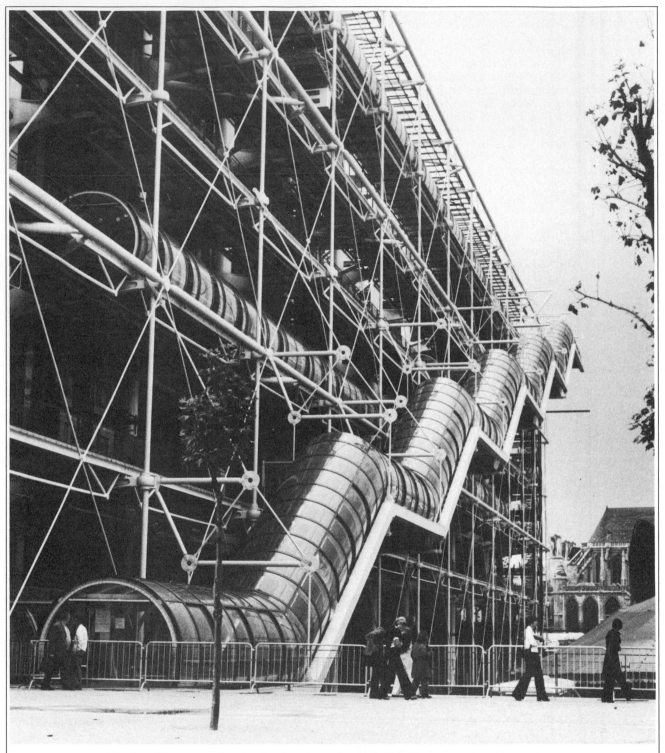

The Pompidou Center of Art and Culture in Paris was built in the 1970s. The architects have made the building appear to be almost all skeleton by placing its engineering and functional elements on the outside, so that it seems permanently encased in scaffolding. [EPA/Art Resource]

THE PLURAL form of the word *state* in the title of this chapter is quite intentional. No single characteristic has so marked the thought of the twentieth-century West as the absence of unity and shared values. As discussed in Chapter 24, many of the traditional religious and intellectual certainties dissolved during the fifty years before 1914. Already philosophers, theologians, writers, and social thinkers had found themselves compelled to look for new paths of thought and new intellectual signposts. The crises that flowed from the two world wars, the Great Depression, the conflict of political ideologies, and the shadow of nuclear warfare have, in turn, created problems more rapidly, perhaps, than solutions can be formulated. The pressure of events, as well as the absence of intellectual certainty, has caused major thinkers to go in more different directions than ever before in the Western experience. Anxiety, fear, and even desperation have been the chief features of that search for new values.

The intellectual life of this century has taken place amidst the most extreme social and political conditions. The world wars confirmed the power of human beings not simply to do great harm to each other but actually to destroy the species. From the opening months of World War I onward, Westerners have known that they could kill scores of thousands of each other between a single rising and setting of the sun. Since 1945 the entire world has been aware of the devastating potential of nuclear weapons. Within individual nation-states, people have experienced the most extreme forms of political repression in the history of the West, and that repression has occurred under both right-wing and left-wing governments. In sheer magnitude the racial atrocities of the Nazis and the peasant slaughters under Stalin's agricultural policy were unprecedented. The economic unrest of the 1920s and 1930s brought uncertainty and in many cases extreme suffering to millions of people. Throughout the colonial world the onetime subject nations began to rebel and to condemn the major values of western civilization. The attempts by western nations to maintain colonial dominance and influence gave rise to widespread internal criticism. During all of these developments the technology that had brought Europe and the West to its pinnacle of world domination seemed to be turning against its creators, first in the destructiveness of war and then as a danger to the environment.

30

Twentieth-Century States of Mind

Such a time of turmoil was not entirely new to the western experience. The third and fourth centuries had seen a variety of differing attempts to come to grips with the social and political disintegration of the Roman Empire. The problems of the late empire brought about major political reorganization and the conversion to Christianity. Many twentieth-century intellectuals have regarded themselves as living in no less a tumultuous period.

Extreme social and political conditions have encouraged extreme intellectual solutions. Between the wars distinguished writers and philosophers in considerable numbers supported either fascism or communism. Other writers began to identify with the aspirations of the restive colonial peoples. These intellectuals condemned both colonialism and the civilization that fostered it. A major segment of the intellectual community rejected rationalism, reason, and science as the primary guides to a better and more humane life. Equally significantly, most of the intellectual movements addressing themselves to modern problems have been very short-lived. Whereas one can see the Enlightenment as extending over most of the eighteenth century, the chief intellectual developments of this century have often sustained themselves for only a decade.

Although writers and thinkers have been testing new solutions for the new problems of this century, there has also been considerable continuity with the past. New departures have not meant total separation. For example, although rationalism and the prestige of science have been challenged, science, medicine, and rational business and government practices have touched the realities of everyday life as never before. Through World War II the most extreme modes of nationalism flourished in Europe, but since 1945 the kind of international cooperation that the *philosophes* of the eighteenth century desired has made unprecedented progress. This century has been one of ever-growing secularism, but Christian theologians and religious institutions have demonstrated considerable vitality. Finally, in its very self-criticism the civilization of twentieth-century Europe has displayed its links with the past. For it has been the capacity of the West to nurture internal criticism that has permitted it to adapt itself to new problems and conditions.

Chariot, *by the Italian sculptor Alberto Giacometti* (1901–1966), *was completed in* 1950 *and displays the questioning spirit of the years immediately after World War II. It brings humanity and the machine together but suggests the idea of the diminution of humankind by forces larger than itself in the twentieth century.* [*The Museum of Modern Art, New York*]

The Diffusion of Knowledge and Culture

The twentieth century has witnessed unparalleled changes in the pursuit and diffusion of knowledge. The invention and institutionalization of radio, television, and computers have created an informational revolution. The communications revolution has made the world smaller and has led to a wider uniformity of culture. The daily events of politics are reported instantaneously. Different nations can share the same programming, and the same products can be advertised. Through computer science more information of all kinds can be gathered and stored. There has also been a

Recumbent Figure, *by the English sculptor Henry Moore (1898–1986), uses basic shapes and materials in a traditional manner, but it exemplifies the twentieth-century search for new perspectives on human and physical nature. Although the statue is clearly modern, its "eroded" form suggests less separation from past culture than do many contemporary works.* [*The Tate Gallery, London*]

continuation of the vast explosion of printed matter that began about the middle of the nineteenth century. In the face of radio and television, Europeans have not ceased to read and write books. This century has seen more books of every kind printed than ever before; storage is now a problem for libraries. However, the printed word has become only one mode of public communication. The sheer quantity of information now available on nearly every subject has in itself contributed to the fragmentation of public opinion and intellectual endeavor.

The increase in the quantity of information has been accompanied by a growing number of Europeans' receiving some form of university education. At the turn of the century in every major European country only a few thousand people were enrolled in the universities. By the 1970s that figure had risen to hundreds of thousands. More people from more different kinds of social and economic backgrounds were receiving higher education. Equally important, for the first time large numbers of women were receiving such training. This expansion in the student and educated populations has been closely related to the intense self-criticism of Europeans. Millions of citizens

1055

have become equipped with those critical intellectual skills that in previous centuries were usually the possession of very small literate elites.

The "student experience"—that is, leaving home and settling for several years in a community composed primarily of late adolescents—has come to be widely shared. Previously only a relatively few privileged persons had known this experience. Since World War II it has become one of the major features of European and Western society. One of its most striking results was the student rebellion of the 1960s. Student uprisings began in the early 1960s in the United States and then spread into Europe and other parts of the world. Students at the Sorbonne in Paris were the leading instigators of the events in France that in May 1968 shook the foundations of the Gaullist government. About the same time German students forced the entire restructuring of the university system. Students were also in the forefront of the socialist experiment in Czechoslovakia, which was suppressed by the Soviet invasion in 1968. Student disturbances occurred in several of the British universities, and Italian students have been no less active. The growth in the number of students and their political activities has accounted in part for the disunity of intellectual life. As more different kinds of people come to participate in university and intellectual life, there is bound to be less unity.

The expansion in the number of students has

The University of Bochum in West Germany. Since World War II many new universities have been built in western Europe, and the number of university students has vastly increased. [German Information Center]

also meant a general increase in the numbers of university teachers. As a result, there have been more scientists, historians, economists, literary critics, and other professional intellectuals during the last seventy-five years than in all previous human history. Moreover, not since the early years of the Reformation have university intellectuals exerted such widespread influence. The major intellectual developments of the seventeenth, eighteenth, and nineteenth centuries took place primarily, though not entirely, outside the university. In the twentieth century the university has become the most likely home for the intellectual. And the symbol of success for a writer in almost any field has been the inclusion of his or her work in the university curriculum.

All of these factors, in addition to the difficult political and social events of the century, have meant that the former unity of Western thought has become shattered. Some observers have regarded this development as opening the possibility for new creativity.

New Patterns in the Work and Expectations of Women

The decades since World War II have witnessed notable changes in the work patterns and the social expectations of women. In all social ranks women have begun to assert larger economic and wider political roles. Women have entered the learned professions and have achieved more major managerial roles than ever before in European history.

One of the patterns that was firmly established at the turn of the century has reversed itself. The number of married women in the work force has sharply risen. Both middle-class and working-class married women have sought to find jobs outside the home. The largest sector of employment became positions in service industries. The postwar population growth increased the demand for such services as were associated with the rearing of children. The larger number of children, in turn, spurred the growth of consumer industries that employed women. Because there had been relatively few women born in the 1930s, there were, in turn, relatively few young single women to be employed in the years just after the war. Married women entered the job market to replace them. Some factories changed the nature of the hours and their workshifts in order to accommodate the needs of the mar-

In the decades since World War II, women have achieved more managerial roles than ever before in European history. [German Information Center]

ried women in their employment. It was also easier for married women to enter the work force because improvements in health care and in consumer conveniences meant that child rearing demanded somewhat less time than in the past.

In the twentieth century, children were no longer expected to make substantial contributions to family income. They spent large amounts of their time in compulsory schools. If the family needed further income to supplement that of the father, the mother would now enter the work force. There is also considerable evidence to suggest that married women began to work in order to escape the boredom of housework and to find company among other female workers.

The work pattern of a European woman's life displayed much more continuity than it had in the nineteenth century. After schooling, the young single woman went to work. But she also continued to work after marriage. She might withdraw from the work force during her children's earliest years, and then return to it when her children began to go to school. A number of factors have created this new pattern, but one of the most important is the much longer life span of women.

1057

At the time when women died relatively young, child rearing necessarily filled a large proportion of their short lives. The extension of the life span has meant that child rearing fills a much smaller proportion of women's lives. Consequently, women throughout the Western world have come to have new concerns about how they will spend those years when they are not involved in rearing children.

Many women have begun to choose to limit sharply the number of children they bear or to forego childbearing and child rearing altogether. Marriage remains a standard expectation of both men and women, but the new kinds of careers open to women and the possibility of greater consumption on the part of married couples without children have led to a decline in the birth rate in some countries and to a sharp stabilization in others.

These changing patterns have spurred sharp social debates in Europe, as in the United States. Feminist groups in Europe have emphasized the need to assert the rights of women as equal citizens.

The liberalization of divorce laws has been one of the chief results of these demands. In turn, however, there has arisen much criticism of the new social expectations of women. The Roman Catholic church has often taken the lead in this matter. Generally speaking, the European women's movement is less well organized and has been somewhat less successful than its counterpart in the United States.

The French novelist and existential writer Albert Camus (1913–1960). Camus won the Nobel Prize for literature in 1957. His two most famous novels, The Stranger *(1942) and* The Plague *(1947) reflect his belief in the meaningless absurdity of the universe and of the need for human beings to revolt against this absurdity. [Bresson-Magnum]*

Existentialism

The single intellectual movement that perhaps best characterizes the predicament and mood of twentieth-century European culture is existentialism. It is symptomatic that most of the philosophers associated with this movement disagree with each other on major issues. Like the modern Western mind in general, existentialism, which has been termed the philosophy of Europe in the twentieth century, has been badly divided. The movement represents in part a continuation of the revolt against reason that began in the nineteenth century.

Friedrich Nietzsche, whose thought was considered in Chapter 24, was one of the major forerunners of existentialism. Another was the Danish writer Sören Kierkegaard (1813–1855), who wrote during the second quarter of the nineteenth century but received little attention until after World War I. He was a rebel against Hegelian philosophy and Christianity as he found them in Denmark. In works such as *Fear and Trembling* (1843), *Either/Or* (1843), and *Concluding Unscientific Postscript* (1846), he urged that the truth of Christianity could not be contained in creeds, doctrines, and church organizations. It could be grasped only in the living experience of those who faced extreme human situations. This emphasis on lived experience as the true test of the validity of philosophy and religion has characterized most twentieth-century existential writers. Kierkegaard also criticized Hegelian philosophy and, by implication, all modes of academic rational philosophy. Its failure, he felt, was the attempt to contain all of life and human experience within abstract categories. Kierkegaard spurned this faith in the power of mere reason. "The conclusions of passion," he once declared, "are the only reliable ones."[1]

The intellectual and ethical crisis of World

---

[1]Quoted in Walter Kaufmann (Ed.), *Existentialism from Dostoevsky to Sartre* (Cleveland: The World Publishing Company, 1962), p. 18.

War I brought Kierkegaard's thought to the fore and also created new interest in Nietzsche's critique of reason. The human sacrifice and the destruction of property made many people doubt whether human beings were actually in control of their own destiny. The conflict stood as an affront to the concept of human improvement and the view of human beings as creatures of rationality. The war itself had been fought with the instruments developed through rational technology. The pride in rational human achievement that had characterized much nineteenth-century European civilization lay in ruins. The sunny faith in rational human development and advancement had not been able to withstand the extreme experiences of war.

Existential thought came to thrive in this climate and received further encouragement from the trauma of World War II. The major existential writers included the Germans Martin Heidegger (1889–1976) and Karl Jaspers (1883–1969) and the French Jean-Paul Sartre (1905–1980) and Albert Camus (1913–1960). Their books are often very difficult and in some cases simply obscure, and the writers frequently disagreed with each other. Yet all of them in one way or another questioned the primacy of reason and scientific understanding as ways of coming to grips with the human situation. Heidegger went so far as to argue, "Thinking only begins at the point where we have come to know that Reason, glorified for centuries, is the most obstinate adversary of thinking."[2] The tradition of the Enlightenment suggested that analysis or the separation of human experience into its component parts was the proper path to understanding. Existential writers rejected this approach. They argued that the human condition was greater than the sum of its parts and must be grasped as a whole.

The Romantic writers of the early nineteenth century had also questioned the primacy of reason, but they did so in a much less radical manner than the existentialists. The Romantics emphasized the imagination and intuition, but the existentialists tended to dwell primarily on the extremes of human experience. Death, dread, fear, and anxiety provided their themes. The titles of their works illustrate their sense of foreboding and alienation: *Being and Time* (1962) by Heidegger; *Nausea* (1938) and *Being*

and Nothingness (1943) by Sartre; *The Plague* (1947) and *The Stranger* (1942) by Camus. The touchstone of philosophic truth became the experience of individual human beings under such extreme situations. The existentialists saw human beings as compelled to formulate their own ethical values rather than being able to find ethical guidance from traditional religion, rational philosophy, intuition, or social customs. This opportunity and necessity to lay down values for oneself became the dreadful freedom of existentialist philosophy.

In large measure the existentialists were protesting against a world in which reason, technology, and the political policies of war and genocide had produced unreasonable results. Their thought reflected the uncertainty of social institutions and ethical values that existed during the era of the two world wars. However, since the 1950s their thought has become the subject of study in universities throughout the world. They will probably continue to be subjects of philosophy and literature classes, but it seems unlikely that they will again achieve their former popularity. In that respect their somewhat lessening influence reflects the relative prosperity and material comfort achieved by a growing majority of Europeans during the last quarter century. The new generation of Europeans born after World War II has not known the experiences that gave rise to existential philosophy. Existentialism was the philosophy of the political and social crisis of Europe in the first half of the twentieth century. As the perceived crisis has passed, so also has the immediate influence of existentialism.

Intellectuals and Politics

After World War I, writers, philosophers, critics, and artists throughout Europe believed that a new course had to be set for their culture. Many of them thought that the political values and institutions of liberal democracy had failed. Liberalism had neither prevented the war nor achieved a minimum standard of decent living for the general population. Conservative intellectuals saw liberalism as fostering social and political unrest and undermining national greatness. Consequently considerable numbers of intellectuals during the 1920s and the 1930s felt that they must align themselves with either fascism or communism. Political ideology had become the order of the day. Art, literature, and philosophy were subordinated to political ends.

---

[2]Quoted in William Barrett, *Irrational Man* (Garden City, N.Y.: Doubleday, 1962), p. 20.

Sartre Discusses the Character of His Existentialism

Jean-Paul Sartre, dramatist, novelist, and philosopher, was the most important French contemporary existentialist. He is widely read in European and American universities. In the first paragraph of this 1946 statement Sartre asserted that all human beings must experience a sense of anguish or the most extreme anxiety when undertaking a major commitment. That anguish arises because consciously or unconsciously they are deciding whether all human beings should make the same decision. In the second paragraph Sartre argued that the existence or nonexistence of God would make no difference in human affairs. What humankind must do is to discover the character of its own situation by itself.

The existentialist frankly states that man is in anguish. His meaning is as follows—When a man commits himself to anything, fully realizing that he is not only choosing what he will be, but is thereby at the same time a legislator deciding for the whole of mankind—in such a moment a man cannot escape from the sense of complete and profound responsibility. There are many, indeed, who show no such anxiety. But we affirm that they are merely disguising their anguish or are in flight from it. Certainly, many people think that in what they are doing they commit no one but themselves to anything: and if you ask them, ''What would happen if everyone did so?'' they shrug their shoulders and reply, ''Everyone does not do so.'' But in truth, one ought always to ask oneself what would happen if everyone did as one is doing; nor can one escape from that disturbing thought except by a kind of self-deception. The man who lies in self-excuse, by saying ''Everyone will not do it'' must be ill at ease in his conscience, for the act of lying implies the universal value which it denies.

By its very disguise his anguish reveals itself.

. . . .

Existentialism is nothing else but an attempt to draw the full conclusions from a consistently atheistic position. Its intention is not in the least that of plunging men into despair. And if by despair one means—as the Christians do—any attitude of unbelief, the despair of the existentialist is something different. Existentialism is not atheist in the sense that it would exhaust itself in demonstration of the nonexistence of God. It declares, rather, that even if God existed that would make no difference from its point of view. Not that we believe God does exist, but we think that the real problem is not that of His existence; what man needs is to find himself again and to understand that nothing can save him from himself, not even a valid proof of the existence of God. In this sense existentialism is optimistic. It is a doctrine of action, and it is only by self-deception, by confusing their own despair with ours that Christians can describe us as without hope.

Jean-Paul Sartre, *Existentialism and Humanism,* trans. by Philip Mairet (London: Methuen, 1960), in Walter Kaufman (Ed.), *Existentialism from Dostoevsky to Sartre* (New York: Meridian Books, 1956), pp. 292, 310–311.

Hitler and Mussolini attracted numerous intellectuals and university teachers to support their policies. Some of these writers were little more than paid literary hacks, but others were persons of considerable standing in the academic community. However, the most important political movement to attract the allegiance of twentieth-century European intellectuals was communism. It seemed to provide a very direct manner of dealing with the social question and a vehicle for opposing the spread of fascism.

As the liberal democracies floundered in the Depression and as right-wing regimes spread across the continent, communism seemed to many people at the time a way to protect humane values. Throughout Europe students in the universities affiliated with the Communist Party. They and older intellectuals visited the Soviet Union and praised Stalin's achievements. Some of these writers did not know of Stalin's terror; others simply closed their eyes to it, somehow believing that humane ends might come from inhumane methods. During the late 1920s and the 1930s communism became little less than a substitute religion. One group of former Communists, writing after World War II, described their attraction and later disillusionment with communism in a book entitled *The God That Failed* (1949).

The Russian Revolution and its later developments led both to the attraction of intellectuals to communism and eventually to their later rejection of the ideology. In Russia the revolution had seemed to construct a new social order in the name of and on the behalf of the proletariat. Under Lenin there had occurred a brief period of literary and artistic experimentation. Later the Soviet Union had also taken a lead in opposing fascism. However, the revolution had also split the ranks of socialists between Communists and "democratic" socialists. Many writers and philosophers of left-wing orientation had chosen communism because of its discipline and because of its supposedly proved success in Russia. But as the brutal nature of Stalinism became known, numerous intellectuals attempted to set a distance between themselves and the Soviet experiment.

Four events proved crucial to the disillusionment of the intellectuals. These were the great public purge trials of 1936 and, later, the Spanish Civil War (1936–1939), the Nazi–Soviet Pact of 1939, and the Soviet invasion of Hungary in 1956. Arthur Koestler's play *Darkness at Noon* (1940) recorded a former Communist's view of the purges. George Orwell, who had never been a Communist but who had sympathized, presented the disappointment with Stalin's policy in Spain in *Homage to Catalonia* (1938). The Nazi–Soviet Pact removed the image of Stalin as an opponent of fascism. Jean-Paul Sartre long put faith in the Soviet Union, but the Hungarian invasion cooled his ardor.

Yet disillusionment with the Soviet Union or with Stalin did not in all cases mean disillusionment with Marxism or with a radical socialist criticism of European society. Some writers and social critics looked to the establishment of alternative Communist governments based on non-Soviet modes. During the decade after World War II, Yugoslavia provided such a different model. Since the late 1950s radical students and intellectuals have looked for inspiration to the Chinese Revolution. Still other groups have hoped for the development of a European Marxist system. Among the more important contributors to this non-Soviet tradition was the Italian Communist Antonio Gramsci (1891–1937) and his work *Letters*

Jean-Paul Sartre (1905–1980) and Simone de Beauvoir (1908–1986), two leading French intellectuals of the mid-century. His was a major voice of the existentialist movement, and she wrote extensively on the social position, experience, and psychology of women. [*United Press International Photo*]

George Orwell (1903–1950). In his essays and novels, the most popular of which were Animal Farm *(1945) and* 1984 *(1949), Orwell attacked the totalitarian tendencies that threaten human values in the twentieth century.* [*Ullstein Bilderdienst*]

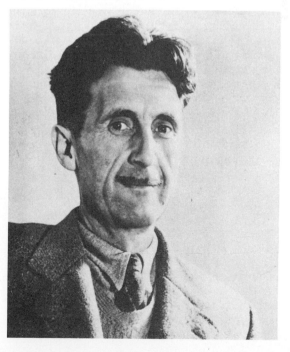

from Prison (published posthumously in 1947). The thought of such non-Soviet Communists has become very important to West European Communist parties, such as that of Italy, which hope to gain office democratically.

Another mode of Marxist accommodation within mid-twentieth-century European thought has been a redefinition of the basic message of Marx himself. During the 1930s a considerable body of previously unprinted essays by Marx was published. These books and articles are quite abstract and philosophical and were written by Marx before *The Communist Manifesto* of 1848. They make the "young Marx" appear to belong more nearly to the humanist than to the revolutionary tradition of European thought. Since World War II these works, including *Philosophic Manuscripts of 1844* and *German Ideology*, have been widely read. Today many people are more familiar with them than with the *Manifesto* or *Capital*. The writings of the young Marx have allowed many people to consider themselves sympathetic to Marxism without also seeing themselves as revolutionaries or supporters of the Soviet Union.

In effect, by the last quarter of this century Marxism and even communism had become fragmented. Politically their supporters stand divided in loyalty to the differing models of the Soviet Union, China, Yugoslavia, and others in the non-European world. Ideologically there are divisions among Soviet ideologues, Maoists, and the more independent thinkers of Western Europe. Yet in its various forms Marxism still remains probably the single most influential tradition of political thought in Europe today. Even for people who may not wish a Communist state, Marxism has come to provide a vehicle for the criticism of contemporary European society. Moreover the impact of various modes of Marxist thought in the non-European world may now constitute the most important Western influence in the postcolonial age.

The Christian Heritage

In most ways Christianity has continued to be hard-pressed during the twentieth century. Material prosperity and political ideologies have replaced religious faith as the dominant factors in many people's lives. However, despite their loss of much popular support and former legal privileges, the Christian churches still exercise considerable social and political influence. In Germany the churches were one of the few major institutions not wholly conquered by the Nazis. Lutheran clergymen, such as Martin Neimöller and Dietrich Bonhoeffer, were leaders of the opposition to Hitler. After the war, in Poland and elsewhere in Eastern Europe, the Roman Catholic church actively opposed the influence of communism. In western Europe religious affiliation provided much of the initial basis for the Christian Democratic parties. Across the continent the churches have raised critical questions about colonialism, nuclear weapons, human rights, and other moral issues. Consequently, in the most secular of all ages, the church has affected numerous issues of state.

A theological revival took place during the first half of the century. Nineteenth-century theologians had frequently softened the concept of sin and had tended to portray human nature as not very far removed from the divine. The horror of World War I destroyed that optimistic faith. Many Europeans felt that evil had stalked the continent.

The most important Christian response to this experience was the theology of Karl Barth (1886–1968). In 1919 this Swiss pastor published *A Commentary on the Epistle to the Romans*, which reemphasized the transcendence of God and the dependence of humankind on the divine. Barth portrayed God as wholly other than, and different from, humankind. In a sense Barth was returning to the Reformation theology of Luther, but the work of Kierkegaard had profoundly influenced his reading of the reformer. Barth, like the Danish writer, regarded the lived experience of men and women as the best testimony to the truth of his theology. Those extreme moments of life described by Kierkegaard provided the basis for a real knowledge of humankind's need for God. This view totally challenged much nineteenth-century writing about human nature. Barth's theology, which became known as *neo-orthodoxy*, proved to be very influential throughout the West in the wake of new political disasters and human suffering.

Liberal theology, however, was not swept away by neo-orthodoxy. The German-American Paul Tillich (1886–1965) was the most important liberal theologian. He looked to a theology of culture and tended to regard religion as a human rather than a divine phenomenon. Whereas Barth saw God as dwelling outside humankind, Tillich believed that evidence of the divine had to be sought from within human nature and human culture. Other liberal theologians, such as Rudolf Bultmann (1884–1976), continued to work out the problems of naturalism and supernaturalism that had plagued earlier writers. Bultmann's major writing took place before World War II but was popularized thereafter in Anglican Bishop John Robinson's *Honest To God* (1963). Another liberal Christian writer from Britain, C. S. Lewis (1878–1963), attracted millions of readers during and after World War II. He was a layman and his books were often in the form of letters or short stories. His most famous work is *The Screwtape Letters* (1942).

Perhaps the most significant postwar religious departures occurred within the Roman Catholic church. Pope John XXIII (1958–1963) undertook the most extensive changes to occur in Catholicism for over a century—and some would say, since the Council of Trent in the sixteenth century. In 1959 Pope John summoned the twenty-first ecumenical council of the church to be called since the series started under the emperor Constantine in the fourth century. It was known as *Vatican II*. He died before it had completed its work; but his successor, Pope Paul VI, continued the council, which met between 1962 and 1965. Among the numerous changes in liturgy, the Mass became celebrated in the vernacular. Free relations were established with other Christian

Pope John XXIII (1958–1963) at the opening of the Vatican Council in October 1962. The council, known as Vatican II, effected the most extensive changes in the Catholic Church since the Council of Trent in the sixteenth century. [AP/World Wide Photos]

denominations. More power was shared with bishops. Pope Paul also appointed a number of cardinals from nations of the former colonial world. However, after having taken these very liberal moves, the pope firmly upheld the celibacy of priests and maintained the church's prohibition on contraception. The former position caused many men and women to leave the priesthood and religious orders, and many of the laity deeply resented the policy on family planning.

Paul VI died in 1978, as did John Paul I, his immediate successor, whose reign lasted only thirty-four days. The second new pope of 1978 was Karol Wojtyla of Poland, the former archbishop of Cracow. John Paul II was the youngest pope to be elected in over a century. The college of cardinals clearly anticipated a long reign in which the changes made in the church during the past quarter of a century might be consolidated. John Paul II, who survived an assassination attempt in 1981, has pursued a three-pronged policy. He has reasserted a traditional policy in regard to the priesthood and the nature of family life. He has stressed the authority of the papacy in doctrinal matters and has attempted to limit doctrinal and liturgical experiment on the part of those Catholics regarded as either exceedingly liberal or exceedingly conservative. Finally, he has encouraged the expansion of the church in the non-Western world. In this last effort he has stressed the need for social justice while at the same time limiting the political activity of

---

Pope John Paul II Discusses the Role of Women and Work

In the encyclical "On Human Work," issued in 1981, Pope John Paul II examined the character of work and proper labor relations as understood by the Roman Catholic church. In the context of a plea for the dignity of labor and the necessity for social justice, the pope set forth his views on the issue of women in the workplace. Although recognizing the necessity for many women to work, the pope emphasized the view of the church that women should first and foremost fulfill their roles in the life of the home and family.

Experience confirms that there must be a social reevaluation of the mother's role, of the toil connected with it and of the need that children have for care, love and affection in order that they may develop into responsible, morally and religiously mature and psychologically stable persons. It will redound to the credit of society to make it possible for a mother—without inhibiting her freedom, without psychological or practical discrimination and without penalizing her as compared with other women—to devote herself to taking care of her children and educating them in accordance with their needs, which vary with age.

Having to abandon these tasks in order to take up paid work outside the home is wrong from the point of view of the good of society and of the family when it contradicts or hinders these primary goals of the mission of a mother.

In this context it should be emphasized that, *on a more general level, the whole labor process must be organized and adapted in such a way as to respect the requirements of the person and his or her forms of life, above all life in the home, taking into account the individual's age and sex. It is a fact that in many societies women work in nearly every sector of life.*

But it is fitting that they should be able to fulfill their tasks in accordance with their own nature, without being discriminated against and without being excluded from jobs for which they are capable, but also without lack of respect for their family aspirations and for their specific role in contributing, together with men, to the good of society. The true advancement of women requires that labor should be structured in such a way that women do not have to pay for that advancement by abandoning what is specific to them and at the expense of the family, in which women as mothers have an irreplaceable role.

The New York Times, September 16, 1981, p. D26.

priests. All of these policies have provoked controversy within the church and between the church and the rest of the world. These policies have also commanded broad support in the church, largely because of the attractive and charismatic personal qualities of John Paul II.

Toward the Twenty-first Century

A century ago a book like this one might have concluded with a statement of the superiority of Western over all other cultures. In that hundred years the position of Europe in power politics has changed. The century has seen vast destruction and inhumanity. Consequently this volume must conclude with an affirmation of the continuity of Western culture with its past, its potential for new creativity, and its capacity for new interaction with other cultures.

Europeans have not outgrown their history. Many of the formative influences traced in this book continue to hold sway. For some observers technology may appear to be an enemy and a threat to the environment, but science touches in a positive manner the lives of more people than might have been imagined even fifty years ago. And it will be from scientific understanding that the problems of the environment and of resource shortages will be solved. Although many intellectuals have praised the irrational, rationalism in the processes of everyday life has never been more present, and the use of reason still promises the best hope to humankind. Since World War II the problems of constitutional order and human rights have continued to be major concerns of political life and discussion. Within both Communist and non-Communist Europe, the spirit of criticism still thrives, though in very different ways.

These persistent features of European life have not ensured that its civilization, as well as the results flowing from it, will be morally good, but they have meant that it has possessed in itself the possibility of correcting itself and of raising questions about what are the good life and the good society. The possibility of asking those questions is necessary before the desired improvement and reform can be attained. Perhaps the chief carriers of Western culture today are those within its midst who most criticize it and demand that it justify itself.

Pope John Paul II (1978), the first non-Italian to be elected pope since 1522, has reasserted traditional Catholic practices and values while also emphasizing the Church's commitment to social justice. [*Ullstein Bilderdienst*]

Suggested Readings

W. M. ABBOTT (Ed.), *The Documents of Vatican II* (1966). A useful way of looking at the changes in contemporary Catholicism.

P. ANDERSON, *Considerations on Western Marxism* (1976). A discussion of developments in this century.

R. ARON, *The Opium of the Intellectuals* (1957). A critical discussion of communism and the intellectual community.

B. BARBER, *Science and the Social Order* (1952). A good introduction to the institutional impact of science in this century.

W. BARRETT, *Irrational Man* (1958). A sound treatment of existentialism in its broader intellectual context.

1065

F. L. BAUMER, *Modern European Thought: Continuity and Change in Ideas,* 1600–1950 (1977). Excellent chapters on this century.

R. CROSSMAN (Ed.), *The God That Failed* (1949). Essays from former Communist intellectuals.

W. P. DIZARD, *Television: A World Review* (1966). A useful discussion of an important topic.

J. DUNN, *Western Political Theory in the Face of the Future* (1979). A thoughtful work that relates traditional political theory to new modes of thinking.

D. FLEMING AND B. BAILYN (Eds.), *The Intellectual Migration: Europe and America,* 1930–1960 (1969). An important collection of essays on the migration of European intellectuals to the United States largely due to the political situation in twentieth-century Europe.

E. FROMM (Ed.), *Socialist Humanism: An International Symposium* (1965). Essays dealing with humanistic approaches to Marxism.

H. S. HUGHES, *The Obstructed Path: French Social Thought in the Years of Desperation,* 1930–1960 (1968). A book that well illustrates the fragmentation of twentieth-century thought.

G. G. IGGERS, *New Directions in European Historiography* (1975). Still a useful work.

M. JAY, *The Dialectical Imagination* (1973). An important work on the development of Marxist thought among German intellectuals.

W. KAUFMANN (Ed.), *Existentialism from Dostoevsky to Sartre* (1956). An excellent introduction to this movement of thought.

D. LaCapra AND S. L. KAPLAN, (Eds.), *Modern European Intellectual History: Reappraisals and New Perspectives* (1982). An important collection of essays.

G. MONTEFIORE, *Philosophy in France Today* (1983). A good introduction to one of the centers of contemporary thought.

J. PASSMORE, *A Hundred Years of Philosophy* (1968). An exceptionally fine one-volume history.

M. POSTER, *Existential Marxism in Postwar France* (1975). An excellent and clear work.

S. P. SCHILLING, *Contemporary Continental Theologians* (1966). A basic survey of modern theology.

Q. SKINNER, *The Return to Grand Theory in the Human Sciences* (1985). Individual essays on major contemporary thinkers.

R. N. STROMBERG, *After Everything: Western Intellectual History Since* 1945 (1975). A lively and thoughtful account of a very difficult subject.

W. WAGAR (Ed.), *European Intellectual History Since Darwin and Marx* (1966). A collection of high-quality essays.

W. WAGAR (Ed.), *Science, Faith, and Man: European Thought Since* 1914 (1968). A collection of documents with good introductions.

J. D. WILKINSON, *The Intellectual Resistance in Europe* (1981). An important treatment of intellectuals who resisted the Nazis.

R. WOHL, *The Generation of* 1914 (1979). A major work that considers the impact of World War I on European intellectual life.

Index

Atom, 850
Atomic bomb
  Cold War and, 997, 998
  on Japan, 993, 994
  Soviet Union and, 1001
  United States and, 1001
  see also Nuclear weapons
Atomists, 85
Aton, 19, 20, 21
Attalus, King, 132
Attalus I, 103
Attila the Hun, 202
Attlee, Clement, 996, 1024–1025
Atzcapotzalco, 358
Auburn system, 739
Auckland, 1034
Audiencias, 570
Auerstädt, battle of, 663
Augsburg
  Diet of (1530), 377, 380, 381, 413
  League of, 374, 382
  Peace of, 374, 382, 405, 410, 434, 435,
    437, 438, 439, 440
Augsburg Confession, 377, 380
Augsburg Interim, 381
Augustine of Hippo, Saint, 195–196, 214,
    256, 466, 493
Augustinus (Jansen), 466
Augustus, 3, 146, 147, 151–154, 155,
    156–158, 160, 163
  see also Octavian; Octavianus; C. Julius
    Caesar; Octavius, Gaius
Aurelian, 182
Ausculta Fili, 320
Ausgleich [Compromise] of 1867, 782, 783
Austerlitz, battle of, 663
Australia, 738, 739, 903, 914, 915
Austrasia, 218
Austria, 362, 418, 441–443, 509, 512,
    541, 674, 781, 920
  foreign relations, *see also* war and war-
    fare, *below*
    Concert of Europe, 697
    Congress of Berlin, 873–874
    Congress of Vienna, 673, 674
    France and, 580, 776
    Germany and, 691–693, 875, 879,
      923, 972, 976
    Italy and, 697, 752, 765, 767, 769–
      770
    late nineteenth century, 873
    Middle East, 698–699
    neutrality, 1008
    Quadruple Alliance, 671, 674
    Spain, 698
    Three Emperors' League, 873
    Triple Alliance, 875
  French Revolution and, 643
  German unification and, 754
  Habsburgs of, 514–517, 576, 577, 582,
    691, 751–752
  Hungary and, 576–577, 751–752, 780–
    782, 783
  Joseph II of, 613, 615–618, 623
  late nineteenth-century economy, 810
  Metternich, 670, 691–693
  middle classes in, 726
  nationalism in, 705–706
  nobility in, 554
  Poland and, 621–622
  political parties, 916

Nazi Party, 972
religion, 616–618
Republic of, 903
serfs in, 723, 751
war and warfare
  Austro–Prussian War, 769, 772
  Crimean War, 765
  France, 638, 643, 656, 657, 662, 663,
    668, 670
  Seven Weeks' War, 772
  War of the Austrian Succession, 576–
    579, 616
  see also under World War I
Austria-Hungary, 782, 783, 810, 840, 883,
    892, 899
  Bosnia and, 874, 875, 879
  Herzegovina and, 874, 875, 879
  see also Austro-Hungarian Empire
Austrian Succession, War of the, 576–579,
    616
Austro-Hungarian Empire, 873, 875, 879
  World War I and, 903, 904
  see also Austria-Hungary
Austro–Prussian War, 769, 772
Autobahnen, 957
Automobiles
  interwar growth industry, 941–942, 943
  invention of, 807
Avanti, 926
Avars, 220
Averroës, 258
Avignon, 338
  pope in, 318, 321–325, 326
Axelbank, Herman, 932
Ayacucho, battle of, 701
Azov, 525
Aztecs, 357–358

Babeuf, Gracchus, 651
Babington plot, 432
Babylon, 10, 23, 97, 99, 102
Babylonia, 10, 27, 28, 59
Babylonian captivity, 27, 325–326
  see also Avignon, papacy at
Babylonian Captivity of the Church (Luther),
    372–373
Bacchus. *See* Dionysus
Bacon, Francis, 481–484
Bactrians, 99
Baden, 658, 693
Badoglio, Pietro, 988
Baghdad, 209
Bailiffs, 329
Baillis, 302
Bailly, Jean Sylvain, 630
Bakewell, Robert, 544
Baldwin of Bouillon, 247
Baldwin, Stanley, 912–914, 945
Balearic Islands, 120
Balfour Declaration, 900, 1037
Balkans, 205, 810, 840
  Congress of Berlin and, 873–874
  First Balkan War, 880
  Middle East and, 698–699
  Russo–Turkish War, 873, 874
  Second Balkan War, 880, 882
  World War I and, 879, 880, 881–884
  World War II and, 995
Ball, John, 311–312

Ballot Act of 1872, 789
Baltic Sea, 180, 355, 512, 621
Baltic States, World War I and, 896, 905
Balzac, Honoré de, 725, 852
Bamberg, 446
Banalités, 270, 540
Banks and banking
  Bardis, 336, 362
  Fuggers, 356, 362, 363, 371, 418
  in late nineteenth century, 806, 809
  Peruzzis, 335, 362
  Rothschilds, 725
  Welsers, 356
Bao Dai, 1016, 1017
Baptism, 179
Barbados, 568
Barbarian invasions, in ancient Rome, 153,
    180–181, 182, 186, 189, 202–204
Barcelona, 972
Bardi, banking house of, 336, 362
Barnabites, 387
Baroque, 406, 408
Basel, Council of, 325, 327–328, 328, 376,
    387, 651
Basil the Great, 212
Basilica of the Sacred Heart, 800, 802
Basque, 502
Bastille, 737
  fall of, 631–632
Baths, of ancient Rome, 169, 171, 184
Battles. *See under name of specific battle, e.g.,*
    Normandy, battle of
Battle of the Seven Arts, The, 257
Bavaria, 218, 228, 238, 438, 441, 461,
    514, 616, 693, 754
Bay of Sluys, battle of, 310
Beauharnais, Josephine de, 668
Beaulieu, Peace of, 415
Bebel, August, 827, 828
Beccaria, Cesare, 606–607
Beccaria, Jeremy, 603
Becket, Thomas à, 285
Becquerel, Henri, 850
Bedford, duke of, 312
Beghards, 295
Begin, Menachem, 1039, 1040
Beguinages, 267
Beguines, 295, 296
Being and Nothingness (Sartre), 1059
Being and Time (Heidegger), 1059
Belfast, 1028
Belgian Congo, 1014
Belgium, 673
  African colonies, 868, 869
    Congo, 1014
  democracy in, 822
  Flemings and, 891
  France and, 656
  independence, 714
  industrialism in, 722, 805, 807
  late nineteenth-century economy, 810
  World War I and, 885, 887
  World War II and, 978, 989
Bell, The, 786
Belle Isle, comte de, 578
Ben-Gurion, David, 1038
Benedetti, Vincent, Count, 773, 774
Benedict XI, Pope, 321
Benedict XII, Pope, 324
Benedict XIII, Pope, 327
Benedict of Nursia, 211, 212

I-3

Bulganin, Nikolai, 1041
Bulgaria, 879, 880, 903
    Congress of Vienna and, 874
    Russo–Turkish War and, 873
    Soviet Union and, 1046
    World War I aftermath and, 916
    World War II treaties and, 997
Bulge, Battle of the, 989, 991
Bullinger, Heinrich, 378
Bülow, Bernhard von, 878
Bultmann, Rudolf, 1063
Bundesrat, 772
Bunker Hill, Battle of, 586
Bunyan, John, 491–492
Burghley, Lord, 429
Burgundians, 202, 217
Burgundy, 218, 297, 311, 312, 314, 330, 636
Burke, Edmund, 642, 644
Burma, 1013
    Japan and, 986
Burnet, Gilbert, 524
Burney, Charles, 608
Burschenschaften, 693
Business, in late nineteenth century, 808–810
    see also Industrialism
Bute, earl of, 589
Butler, Josephine, 814
Buttresses, in Gothic architecture, 287–291
Byron, Lord, 680, 698
Byzantine Empire, 188–189, 204–216, 301
    Christianity in, 206–207, 211–216
    Islam in, 207–211
Byzantium, 95, 184, 200

Cadets. *See* Constitutional Democratic Party
Cadiz, 433, 571, 573
Caesar, Augustus. *See* Augustus; Octavian
Caesar, Gaius Julius, 3, 140, 141–144, 146–147, 151, 154, 155–156
Caetano, Marcelo, 1035
Cahiers de doléances, 629
Cajetan, Cardinal, 371
Calabria, 216
Calais, 310, 311, 314, 429, 433
Calas, Jean, 605
Calculi, 130
Calcutta, 356
Calderón de la Barca, Pedro, 487, 680
Calendar
    French revolutionary, 646
    Roman, 144
    Sumerian, 11
California, 568
Caligula. *See* Gaius
Caliphs, 209
Calixtines, 328
Calixtus II, Pope, 243, 245
Callaghan, James, 1025, 1026
Calonne, Charles Alexandre de, 626–627
Calvin, John, 383–386, 395, 398, 399, 405, 406, 409, 410, 414, 431
Calvinism
    in Austria, 616, 617
    in France, 410–411, 413–415
    in the Netherlands, 424, 425, 427

Thirty Years' War and, 434–443
Cambridge, University of, 255, 256
Cambyses, 60
Cameades, 101
Camelots du Roi, 947
Cameroons, Bismarck and, 868
Camp David Accords, 1039–1040
Campania, 110
Campbell-Bannerman, Henry, 825
Campo Formio, 656
    Treaty of, 657, 662
Campus Martius, 116, 158
Camus, Albert, 1058, 1059
Canaanites, in Palestine, 23–24
Canada, 569, 914, 915, 1004
    France and England in, 581
Candide (Voltaire), 600
Cannae, battle of, 123
Canning, George, 697–698, 715, 716
Canon law, 254, 266
Canons Regular, 267
Canossa, Henry IV's Penance at, 243
Canterbury Tales (Chaucer), 285
Canute, the Dane, 282–283
Cape Cod Bay, 450
Cape of Good Hope, 356
Capet, Citizen, 641
Capetian dynasty, 239, 292, 302, 308
Capital (Marx), 745, 823, 1062
Capitalism
    development of, 362–363
    Marxism and, 745–746
Capitoline hill, 111, 166, 167
Caporetto, battle at, 898
Caprivi, Leo von, 876
Capuchins, 387
Caracas, 701
Carafa, Gian Pietro, Bishop, 387
    see also Paul IV, Pope
Carbonari, 765
Cardinals, College of, 240, 241, 319
Carlos, Don, 420
Carlsbad Decrees, 693, 695
Carlyle, Thomas, 726
Carmaux, 821
Carnot, Lazare, 643, 645
Carol II of Romania, 916
Carolingian minuscule, 225
Carolingians, 218, 219, 224–225, 228–230, 233, 234, 279, 338
Carrhae, 143
Cartagena, 571
Cartel des Gauches, 911
Cartels, in late nineteenth century, 809
Carter, Jimmy, 1012, 1039, 1044
Carthage, 24, 102, 110, 120–124, 125, 126
Carthusians, 267
Cartwright, Edmund, 550
Cartwright, John, Major, 590, 694
Cartwright, Thomas, 431
Casa de Contratación, 570–571, 573
Caspian Sea, 98, 986, 988
Cassiodorus, 256
Cassius, 147
Castellio, Sebastian, 406, 486
Castiglione, Baldassare, 339
Castile, 329, 330, 331, 418, 419, 502
Castlereagh, Robert Stewart, Viscount, 671, 674, 697
Catacombs, of the Jordani, 179
Catalan, 970

Cateau-Cambrésis, Treaty of, 409
Categories (Aristotle), 256
Cathars, 318
    Crusade against, 293
Cathedral of Amiens, 288
Cathedral of Reims, 288
Cathedral schools, 255, 256, 338
Catherine I of Russia, 619
Catherine II (the Great) of Russia, 541, 555, 613, 619–621, 622–623, 643, 690
Catherine of Aragon, 331, 392, 393, 395
Catholic Association, 716
Catholic Center Party, 847
Catholic Emancipation, 717
Catholic League, 415, 438
Catholic Modernism, 850
Catholicism, 180, 195, 239, 294, 406, 847
    in Austria, 616, 618
    Carolingian kings and, 219
    Christian Democratic political parties and, 1023–1024
    Cluny reform movement, 239–240
    communism and, 1062
    emergence of, 179
    in England, 429, 430–431, 432–433, 450, 456–457, 458, 460
    Enlightenment and, 603–604, 605
    in France, 349, 410, 411–413, 415–417, 461, 464, 466–468, 636–637, 646, 647, 651, 655, 659–660, 696, 697, 710, 712, 800, 802, 816, 817, 848
    in Germany, 847–848
    investiture struggle and, 241–245
    in Ireland, 716–717, 790, 848, 1027–1028
    in Italy, 929; *see also* Christianity
    Jesuits, 387–389, 405, 430, 438, 464, 466
    in Latin America, 391
    in Netherlands, 423–429
    in nineteenth century, 845–850
    in Poland, 1009, 1048
    popes and papacy, *see* Christianity
    Protestant Reformation and, 377–378, 381–382
    in Prussia, 615
    reform and Counter-Reformation, 386–391, 406, 438
    in Spain, 331, 356, 366, 415, 420, 487
    in Switzerland, 377–378
    see also Religious wars
Catiline, 140–141, 155
Cato, Marcus Porcius, 125, 126, 127, 128
Cato the Elder, 128
Cato Major (Plutarch), 128
Cato Street Conspiracy, 695
Catullus, 156
Cavaignac, General, 749
Cavaliers, 453
Cavour, Camillo, Count, 766–769
Ceauşescu, Nicolae, 1046
Cecil, William, 429, 432
Celestine V, Pope, 320, 329
Celtic, 21
Celtis, Conrad, 365
Celts, 109, 110
Cenicula, 159–160
Central Powers, 887
Centuriate assembly, 115–116
Cerularius, Michael, 215
Cervantes Saavedra, Miguel de, 486–488

Great Depression and, 940, 941, 949–950, 955–956
Habsburgs, 509
Hanseatic League, 252
Hitler, 917, 919–922, 923, 936, 946, 950–956, 967–969, 972, 973, 974, 975, 978–979, 982, 986, 991, 1060
Hohenstaufens in, 296–301
Humanism in, 365
industrialism in, 722, 724
    Second Industrial Revolution in, 805, 806, 807–808, 811
inflation and, 918–919, 921
Krupp family, 797, 804–805, 808, 809
late nineteenth-century
    business and, 809
    cities and, 799
    economy and, 810, 812
middle classes in, 726
nationalism in, 666–667, 705–706
New Imperialism, 867
    African colonies, 868, 869, 870
    Pacific Islands, 870
Ottonians in, 230, 238–239, 292
peasants' revolt in, 374–376
political parties
    Catholic Center Party, 847, 904
    Communist Party, 950, 952
    Independent Socialist Party, 899
    Liberal Party, 917
    Nazi Party, 950–956; see also Hitler, above
    Social Democratic Party, 820, 822, 823, 826–829, 885, 904, 917, 923, 949–950, 952
public housing in, 805
rearmament of, 1020
Reichstag, 332, 772, 827, 828, 829, 917, 950, 951, 952, 981
religion
    anti-Semitism, 860, 919, 920, 921, 953–954, 955, 968, 982–986
    Catholicism, 847–848
    Lutheranism, 405
    Protestant Reformation in, 368–376
Romantic movement in, 678, 680–682, 684–687
Stresemann, 922–923
trade unionism, 822
unification, 754–755, 757, 770–775, 806
war and warfare
    France, 662, 663, 670–671, 691–692
    Thirty Years' War, 441, 443
    World War I reparations, 903–904, 939
    see also World War I; World War II
Weimar Republic, 820, 904, 911, 917–925, 950, 952
William II, 828, 864, 875–877, 878, 880, 883, 884, 886, 899
women's movement in, 820
see also East Germany; Holy Roman Empire; Prussia; West Germany
Gerson, Jean, 326
Ghana, 1014
Ghent, 251, 310
    Pacification of, 426–427
Ghibellines, 334
Ghosts (Ibsen), 853
Giacometti, Alberto, 1054
Gibbon, Edward, 605

Gibraltar, 473
Gierek, Edward, 1047, 1048
Giles of Viterbo, 387
Gilgamesh, 11, 16
Ginsburg, Aleksandr, 1044
Giotto, 335, 342
Girondist Legislative Assembly, 647
Girondists, 638, 641, 643, 650
Giscard d'Estaing, Valéry, 1033, 1034
Gissing, George, 840
Giustiniani, Tommaso, 386
Gladiators, of ancient Rome, 172, 173
Gladstone, William, 725, 788–789, 790, 791
Glass Manufacturers' Association, 809
Glockenspiel, 494
Glorious Revolution, 458, 460, 497
Glossa Ordinaria (Anselm), 256
Gneisenau, count von, 667
Goa, 356
Gobineau, Arthur de, 859
Godfrey of Bouillon, 247, 248
Godwin, William, 818
Godwinsson, Harold, 282
Goebbels, Josef, 956
Goethe, Johann Wolfgang von, 495, 680, 681
Golan Heights, 1039
Gold Coast, 1014
Golden Bull, 332
Golden Horde, 301
Gömbös, Julius, General, 915
Gomorrah, 29
Gomulka, Wladyslaw, 1009, 1047
Gorbachev, Mikhail S., 1006, 1012, 1044, 1045
Gordon, George, Lord, 563
Gordon riots, 563
Göring, Hermann, 951, 956, 981
Gorky, Maxim, 852
Gospels, 174, 176, 180, 214, 395
Gosplan, 959
Gothic architecture, 287–289, 291, 292
Goths, 180, 186, 191, 196, 202, 203, 204, 217
Government, 1
Government of National Defense, 776
Goya, Francisco, 668
Gracchus, Gaius, 133–134
Gracchus, Tiberius, 132–133
Grace Abounding (Bunyan), 491
Grain Embargo, 1012
Grammaticus, 128, 130
Gramsci, Antonio, 1061–1062
Granada, 331, 420
Grand Alliance, of England, Holland, and the Holy Roman Emperor, 472–473
Grand National Union, 743
Grand Remonstrance, 453
Grandi, 251–252, 335
Granicus River, battle of, 97
Granvelle, Cardinal, 423–425
Gratian, 254, 256
Great Bible, 394
Great Britain
    Chartism in, 728–729
    classical economics in, 741
    conservatism in, 693–696
    democracy in, 510, 822
    Disraeli, 788, 789–790
    empire, 867
        Africa, 867, 868, 869, 877, 878, 1014

    Burma, 1013
    China, 870
    Cyprus, 874, 1014
    Egypt, 868
    in eighteenth century, 568, 569–570, 575–576, 581–582
    India, 581–582, 867, 868, 914, 1013
    Pacific Islands, 870
    Palestine, 1037–1038; see also Israel
    Sri Lanka, 1013
    Sudan, 868
    World War I and, 914
European Economic Community, 1022, 1025, 1033
Fabianism in, 824–826
foreign relations, see also war and warfare, below
    Belgium, 714
    Congress of Berlin, 873–874
    Entente Cordiale, 878
    France, 666, 878
    Germany, 868, 870, 875, 876–878, 923, 924, 969, 970, 973
    Greece, 1001
    Iraq, 903
    Ireland, 716–717, 790–791, 914–915, 1028
    Israel, 903, 1038
    Italy, 969–970
    Japan, 878
    Latin America, 698, 716
    Palestine, 903
    Prussia, 579
    Quadruple Alliance, 671, 674
    Russia, 878
    Soviet Union, 975, 998–999
    Spain, 697–698
    Suez crisis (1956), 1008–1009
    World War II aftermath and, 995–997
French Revolution and, 643
Gladstone, 788–789, 790, 791
Great Depression and, 940, 941, 944–945
Great Reform Bill, 714–718, 788
Hanoverian dynasty, 506, 507
industrialism in
    family and, 729–735
    Industrial Revolution, 545, 547–553, 721–722, 723
    in late nineteenth century, 805, 806, 807–808
    railways, 724
    women and, 731, 732
landholding in, 539
in late nineteenth century
    cities, 799
    economy, 810
    literacy, 839
middle classes in, 725
National Government, 944–945
nobility in, 553, 555–557
Parliament, 507–509, 539, 545, 555, 576, 584, 585, 586, 588, 589, 590–592, 599, 643, 694, 695, 706, 714, 716, 717, 723, 728, 730, 737, 819, 820, 824, 825, 911, 914, 915, 944, 1026, 1027
    House of Commons, 507–508, 509, 553, 589, 590, 714, 716, 718, 741, 788, 791, 826, 912, 975, 1024, 1025

Henry VI of Germany, 248, 298
Henry VII of England, 329, 365, 392
Henry VII of Spain, 331
Henry VIII of England, 331, 365, 366, 392, 393–394, 429
Henry the Fowler, 238
Henry of Guise, 415
Henry of Langenstein, 326
Henry the Lion, 248, 297, 298
Henry of Navarre, 409, 412, 415
Henry the Navigator, 355
Henry Tudor. *See* Henry VII of England
Hephaestus, 57
Hera, 57
Heracles, 93
Heraclidae, 36
Heraclides of Pontus, 104
Heraclitus, 85
Heraclius, 207, 208
Herder, Johann Gottfried, 678, 685
Hermandad, 331
Hermann (Arminius), 153
Hermes, 57
Hermes (Praxiteles), 90
Hermit monasticism, 211–212
Hermits of Saint Augustine, 387
Herodes Atticus, 166
Herodotus, 14, 45, 88
Herriot, Edouard, 911
Herzegovina, 873, 874, 875, 879
Herzen, Alexander, 785–786
Herzl, Theodore, 861, 1037
Hesiod, 46–47, 156
Hesse, 381, 772
Hestia, 57
Hidalgo y Costilla, Miguel, 702
Hiero, 120
Hieroglyphics, 16
Higglers, 556
Himmler, Heinrich, 953, 982
Hindenburg, Paul von, 891, 898, 923, 950, 951
Hipparchus, 55
Hipparchus of Nicaea, 105
Hippias, 54, 55, 60, 61
Hippias, or the Bath (Lucian), 171
Hippocrates of Cos, 30, 88, 281
Hippodamus of Miletus, 103
Hirohito, emperor, 993
Hiroshima, atomic bomb on, 993, 994
Hispaniola, 359, 568
Historic compromise, 1036
Histories (Polybius), 115
History, 5, 7
    Romantic movement and, 684–685
History (Herodotus), 88
History of America (Robertson), 608
History of English Poetry, The (Warton), 608
History of the Peloponnesian War (Thucydides), 495
History of Rome (Livy), 119, 158, 194
Hither Spain, ancient Rome and, 127
Hitler, Adolf, 917, 919–922, 923, 936, 946, 950–056, 967–969, 972, 973, 974, 975, 978–979, 983, 986, 991, 1060
    see also Nazi Party
Hittites, 10, 17, 21–22, 36
Ho Chi Minh, 1015–1016, 1017
Hobbes, Thomas, 6, 495–497, 498, 499, 678
Hobereaux, 553

Hoffmann, E. T. A., 681
Hogarth, William, 510–511, 560, 561, 589
Hohenstaufen empire, 296–301, 319, 517–522
Hohenzollern dynasty, 773–774, 917
Holbein, Hans, the Younger, 363, 366
Holland, 425, 426, 428, 714
    eighteenth century and agriculture, 544–545
    empire, 568
    England and, 456–457
    France and, 643, 669
    United Provinces of, 441
    War of the Spanish Succession, 470–473
    see also Netherlands
Holstein, 772
Holy Alliance, 691, 697
"Holy Club," 683
Holy League, 349, 420
Holy Roman Empire, 221, 296–301, 320, 330, 332–333, 377, 379, 392, 410, 434–435, 436, 437, 438, 509, 514, 518, 519, 582, 663, 687, 691
    Congress of Vienna and, 673
    Lutheranism in, 405
    Thirty Years' War, 434–443
    War of the Spanish Succession, 470–473
Holy war, in Islam, 208
Homage to Catalonia (Orwell), 1061
Homer, 36, 38–40, 157
Honest to God (Robinson), 1063
Honestiores, 182
Hong Kong, Japan and, 986
Hooper, John, 429
Hoover, Herbert, 939
Hoplites, 41, 53, 71
Horace, 3, 145, 157
Horemhab, 21
Horizon Blue Chamber, 910
Horn, count of, 425
Horthy, Miklós, 915
Hotman, François, 414
Hötzendorf, Conrad von, 883
House of Commons, 452, 453, 507–508, 509, 553, 589, 590, 714, 716, 717, 718, 728, 741, 788, 791, 826, 912, 975, 1024, 1025
House of Lords, 453, 553, 604, 717, 718, 791, 797, 824, 826
House of Lords Act of 1911, 791
Housing, in cities of late nineteenth century, 804–805
Howard, Catherine, 394
Howard, John, 738
Huber, A. V., 804
Hubertusburg, Treaty of, 580
Hubris, 57
Hugo, Victor, 678
Huguenots, 409–410, 411–417, 461, 464, 466–468, 518
Hugues, Besançon, 409
Hulks, 737
Humanism, 322, 333, 392, 398
    civic, 341
    in England, 365–366
    in France, 366
    in Germany, 365
    in Italy, 336–341
    northern, 363–366
    Reformation and, 398–399
    rhetoricians and, 257
    scholasticism and, 256–257

in Spain, 366
Humanitas, 128, 337
Humbert, Cardinal, 241
Hume, David, 605, 678
Humiliation of Olmütz, 757
Humiliores, 182
Hundred Days, 674
Hundred Years' War, 266, 273, 284, 302, 308–314, 318, 320, 324, 329, 330, 332
Hungarians. *See* Magyars
Hungary, 362, 418, 512, 514
    agriculture in 1920s, 939
    Austria and, 616, 751–752
    Czechoslovakia and, 973
    Habsburg Empire and, 780–782
    literacy in late nineteenth century, 839
    Little Entente and, 910
    Magyars, 230, 231, 238, 515, 577, 751–752, 780, 781, 903
    nobility in, 554
    Soviet Union and, 995, 1009–1010, 1046
    Turks and, 374
    World War I and, 903, 915
    World War II treaties and, 997
Huns, 186, 189, 202, 220
Hunt, Henry "Orator," 694
Hunting, in Middle Ages, 265
Hurricane plane, 980
Huskisson, William, 715, 716
Huss, John, 325, 372
Hussites, 324, 327–328
Hutcheson, Francis, 588
Huxley, Thomas Henry, 844, 845
Hyde, Edward, 454
Hyksos, 17, 19, 24
Hyndman, H. M., 824

Iberian Peninsula, 810
    see also Portugal; Spain
Ibsen, Henrik, 824, 852–853
Iceland, 1004
Iconoclasm, 207
Id, 857
Ignatius of Loyola, 387–389, 398
Île-de-France, 292
Iliad (Homer), 36, 38–40
Illustrations of Political Economy (Martineau), 740
Illyria, 182
Illyricum, 141
Immigration
    industrialism and, 722–724
    in late nineteenth century, 796
Imperator, 151, 160
Imperial Supreme Court, 372
Imperialism, 809–810
    new, 865–872
    see also Colonialism
Imperium, 111, 112, 114, 115, 116, 122, 123, 139
Imperium maius, 152
Import Duties Bill, 944
Imposition, 449
Improving the Studies of the Young (Melanchthon), 398
Incas, 357, 358–359
Independent Labor Party, in Great Britain, 824

United States, 924
war and warfare
  Russo–Japanese War, 833, 878
  World War II, 986–987, 991–994
Jaruzelski, Wojciech, 1049
Jaspers, Karl, 1059
Jaurès, Jean, 826, 947
Jena, 692
  battle of, 663, 667
Jenkins, Robert, 576
Jenkins, Roy, 1026
Jenkins's Ear, War of, 509, 575, 576, 581, 698
Jenner, Edward, 598
Jerome, Saint, 195, 212
Jerome of Prague, 325
Jerusalem, 24, 25, 168, 175, 179, 247
Jesuits, 387–389, 405, 430, 438, 464, 466
Jesus of Nazareth, 174–176, 177, 178, 179, 194, 203, 207, 208, 211–212, 214, 216, 369
Jewish State, The (Herzl), 861
Jews and Judaism, 2, 24
  anti-Semitism
    ancient Rome and, 164, 168
    Hitler and Nazis and, 860, 919, 920, 921, 953–954, 955, 968, 982–986
    late nineteenth century and, 799, 860–861
    in Middle Ages, 316
    Mussolini and, 925
    Palestine and, 1037
    Soviet Union and, 1041, 1044
    Spanish Inquisition and, 331
  Arabs and, 208
  in Austria, 616
  basis of, 26, 27, 28–29
  in Byzantine Empire, 207
  Christianity and, 176
    Pharisees, 176
  in Prussia, 615
  Reuchlin affair and, 365
  see also Israel
Jiménez de Cisneros, Francisco, 266, 331
Jingoism, 873
Joan of Arc, 309, 310, 312–313, 330
Joanna the Mad, 331
João of Brazil, 702
John, Gospel of, 174
John I of England, 252, 284, 285, 286, 292, 310
John II, the Good, 310
John III Sobieski, 512, 513, 514
John VIII, Pope, 230
John XII, Pope, 238–239
John XXII, Pope, 323, 324, 392
John XXIII, Pope, 326, 327, 1063
John of Austria, Don, 420, 421, 426–427, 432
John Cassian, 212
John of the Cross, Saint, 387
John the Fearless, 312
John Frederick of Saxony, 380, 381, 382
John of Gaunt, 311
John George I of Saxony, 438
John the Good, 311
John of Paris, 320
John of Salisbury, 256
John Paul I, Pope, 1064
John Paul II, Pope, 1064–1065
Johnson, Lyndon, 1010, 1019
Joinville, Treaty of, 428

Jonson, Ben, 490
Jordan, Israel and, 1038
Jordan River, 1038–1039
Joseph I of Austria, 517
Joseph II of Austria, 613, 615–618, 623, 643
Josephinism, 618
Journées, 632, 651
Journey from Saint Petersburg to Moscow (Radishchev), 643
Joyce, James, 842
Juan Carlos of Spain, 1035
Judaea, 173, 175
Judah, 2, 24, 25
Judaism. *See* Jews and Judaism
Judith of Bavaria, 228–229
Jugurtha, 134, 135
Jugurtha (Sallust), 135
Jugurthine War, 134, 155
Julia, daughter of Augustus, 154
Julia, daughter of Caesar, 143
Julian "the Apostate," 186, 192, 193
Julius II, Pope, 345, 346, 349, 370, 392
Julius Excluded from Heaven (Erasmus), 349
July Monarchy, 711–712, 725, 740
June Days, 749
Jung, Carl, 858
Junkers, 520, 521, 554–555, 692, 770, 809
Juntas, in Latin America, 700, 701
Jus gentium, 156
Jus naturale, 156
Justices of the peace, 329
Justinian, 91, 205, 206, 207, 254
Justinian Code, 207
Juvenal, 129, 159, 160

*K*abinett, 521
Kadar, Janos, 1010, 1046
Kamikaze attacks, 991
Kania, Stanislaw, 1048, 1049
Kant, Immanuel, 666, 677–678
Kapp *Putsch*, 917
Kappel, battle at, 378
Karamanlis, Constantine, 1036
Karsthans, 376
Kassites, 10, 17, 21
Kaunitz, Wenzel Anton, 580
Kautsky, Karl, 828
Kay, James, 549
Kellogg-Briand Pact, 924
Kennan, George, 787
Kennedy, John F., 1010, 1011, 1018, 1019
Kent, Duchess of, 1014
Kepler, Johannes, 478
Kerensky, Alexander, 895–896
Keynes, John Maynard, 904, 943
Khan, Genghis, 301
Khrushchev, Nikita, 1010, 1041–1044, 1046
Khufu, 14
Khyber Pass, 99
Kierkegaard, Sören, 1058, 1059, 1062
Kiev, 301
King, Edward, 490
King James Version, of Bible, 450
King Lear (Shakespeare), 490
King William's War, 470
King's men, 488
Kinnock, Neil, 1027
Kipling, Rudyard, 872

Kirov, Sergei, 962
Klopstock, Friedrich Gottlieb, 680
Knights, of Middle Ages, 264, 265, 277
Knights Hospitalers, 247
Knights of the Round Table, 284
Knights Templars, 247, 321
Knox, John, 414, 429, 432
Koch, Robert, 803
Koestler, Arthur, 1061
Kohl, Helmut, 1030–1031
Koinē, 106
Königgrätz, battle of, 772
Königsberg, 663
Koran, 208
Korean War, 1008, 1014–1015
Kossuth, Louis, 751, 752
Kosygin, Alexei, 1043–1044
Kottabos, 48
Kotzebue, August von, 693
Krämer, Heinrich, 445
Kreditanstalt, 939
Kruger, Paul, 877
Krupp family, 797, 804–805, 808, 809
Kuchuk-Kainardji, Treaty of, 621
Kulaks, 829, 958
Kulturkampf, 848
Kun, Béla, 915
Kurile Islands, 996
Kutuzov, Mikhail, 669
Kyd, Thomas, 489

*L*a Mettrie, Julien Offray de, 605
Labor
  Great Britain and, 912–914
  industrialism and, 726–729
  late nineteenth century and, 820–821
  World War I aftermath and, 904–905
  see also Socialism; Trade unionism
Labour Party, of Great Britain, 824, 911, 912, 944–945, 1023, 1024–1026, 1027
Laconia, 52
Lade, 61
Ladies' National Association for the Repeal of the Contagious Diseases Acts, 814
Lafayette, 632
Lagarde, Paul de, 860
Lagash, 9
Laibach, Congress of, 697
Laissez-faire, 607, 739
Lamartine, Alphonse de, 748
Lancaster, House of, 332
Lancelot, Sir, 284
Land and Freedom, 786
Land-Mortgage Credit Association, 615
Lanfranc, 258
Langbehn, Julius, 860
Languedoc, 293, 410
Las Casas, Bartolomé de, 391
Lasalle, Ferdinand, 827
L'Assommoir (Zola), 852
Last Judgment, The (Michelangelo), 346
Late Middle Ages. *See* Middle Ages
Lateran Accord, 929
Latifundia, 132
Latimer, Hugh, 429
Latin, as language, 21, 163, 186, 204, 225, 256
  Humanism and, 337–338

I-17

Loyola, Ignatius of, 383
Lublin, 996
Luca, 142
Lucania, 119
Lucas, Charles, 738
Lucinde (Schlegel), 681
Lucretius, 156
Lucullus, Lucius Licinius, 140
Ludendorff, Erich, 891, 898, 921
Luder, Peter, 365
Ludovico il Moro, 336, 343, 347, 348, 349
Lueger, Karl, 860, 861, 919
Luftwaffe, 979, 980
Lunéville, Treaty of, 657
Lusitania, 893
Luther, Martin, 341, 362, 364, 365, 368–376, 377, 395, 398, 399, 401, 413, 693
Lutheranism, 365, 373, 376, 382, 405
    in Austria, 616
    in Prussia, 615
    Thirty Years' War, 434–443
Luxembourg
    World War I and, 885
    World War II and, 978
Lyceum, of Aristotle, 91, 92, 101
Lycidas (Milton), 490
Lydia, 59, 61
Lyell, Charles, 842, 846
Lyons, 330, 557, 714, 722
    Council of, 318
Lyrical Ballads (Wordsworth and Coleridge), 679
Lysander, 79, 81
Lysippus, 90
Lytton, earl of, 969
Lytton Report, 969

M

MacArthur, Douglas, 1014, 1015
Macbeth (Shakespeare), 490
MacDonald, Ramsay, 912, 944–945
Macedon, 91, 125
Macedonia, 2, 42, 69, 78, 880
    ancient Rome and, 127
Macedonian dynasty, 82, 209
Macedonian Wars, 125, 126
Mach, Ernst, 850
Machiavelli, Niccolò, 329, 336, 341, 349–351
Machine guns, World War I and, 888, 889
Machu Picchu, 358
MacMahon, Marshal, 778, 779
Madagascar, 983
Madame Bovary (Flaubert), 845, 852
Madonna and Child (Giotto), 341
Madrid, 366, 799
Maecenas, 145, 157
Magdeburg, 369, 381–382, 413
Magellan, Ferdinand, 356
Magenta, battle of, 769
Magic, witchcraft as, 443–446
Maginot Line, 970, 975, 978
Magna Carta, 248, 285–286, 292, 299, 310
Magna Graecia, 42
Magnesia, battle of, 125
Magyars, 230, 231, 238, 515, 577, 751–752, 780, 781, 903
Main River, 772

Maintenon, Madame de, 464
Mainz, 354
Malabar Coast, 356
Malaya, Japan and, 986
Maleficium, 443
Malenkov, Georgy, 1041
Manifesto, 1062
Malleus maleficarum (Krämer and Sprenger), 445
Mallus, 222
Malplaquet, battle of, 473
Malta, 120, 1014
Malthus, Thomas, 740
Mamertines, 120
Man and Superman (Shaw), 853
Manchester, 558, 695, 724
    in late nineteenth century, 801
Manchuria, 1015
    Japan and, 969, 986
    Soviet Union and, 993
Mandate system, 903
Mani, 190
Manichaeism, 190–191
Mannerism, 346
Manorialism, in Middle Ages, 211, 226–227, 268–273, 275
Mansfeld, Ernst von, 369, 438, 439
Mansi, 233–234
Mantinea, battle of, 82
Mao Tse-tung, 1015
Marathon, battle of, 61–62, 69, 88
Marburg Colloquy, 376–377
Marcel, Étienne, 310
March Laws, 751
Marchais, George, 1033
Marcus Aurelius, 3, 150, 161, 163, 168, 173, 180
Mardonius, 65
Marduk, 27
Marengo, battle of, 657
Margaret, sister of Henry VIII, 431
Margaret of Parma, 423, 425
Margaret Thérèse, 471
Marguerite of Valois, 412
Maria Theresa of Austria, 516, 517, 576–577, 579, 613, 615, 616, 617, 618
Mariana Islands, 991
Marie, countess of Champagne, 284
Marie, daughter of Philip II of Spain, 469
Marie Antoinette of France, 631, 638, 639, 647
Marie Louise, Austrian archduchess, 668, 669
Marie Thérèse, 464, 469, 471
Marignano, battle of, 349, 376
Marius, 134–136, 137, 140
Mark, county of, 518
Mark, Gospel of, 174
Marlborough, duke of, 979
Marlowe, Christopher, 489
Marne, 898
    battle of the, 888
Marriages, in early modern Europe, 399–401
Mars, 120
Mars the Avenger, temple of, 158
Marseilles, 728
Marshall, George C., 1001
Marshall Plan, 1001–1003, 1004, 1020, 1028, 1029, 1046
Marsilius of Padua, 323–324, 329, 366

Marston Moor, battle of, 453
Martin V, Pope, 326–327, 328
Martin of Tours, Saint, 212, 224
Martineau, Harriet, 740
Martinique, 582
Marx, Karl, 726, 822–824, 828, 858, 1062
Marxism, 744–749, 822–824, 973
    Germany and, 919
    Hitler and, 920
    mid-twentieth century and, 1061–1062
    Paris Commune and, 777
    see also Socialism
Mary I of England, 392, 393, 395, 406, 429, 430, 431, 432–433, 450, 458
Mary Barton (Gaskell), 726
Mary of Guise, 414, 432
Mary Stuart, Queen of Scots, 410, 431, 449
Masaccio, 342
Masaryk, Jan, 1003
Masaryk, Thomas, 916
Massachusetts, 585, 586
Master Builder, The (Ibsen), 853
Masurian Lakes, battle of, 891
Matignon accord, 948, 949
Matteotti, Giacomo, 928
Matthew, 180, 216
    Gospel of, 180, 214
Matthew of Paris, 300
Matthys, Jan, 379
Mauguet, Marie, 820
Maupeou, René, 626
Maurice of Nassau, 424, 428
Maurice of Saxony, 382
Max of Baden, Prince, 898
Maximian, 183
Maximilian I, emperor, 330, 331, 332, 333, 348, 349, 371
Maximilian of Austria, archduke, 776
Maximilian of Bavaria, 438–439
Maximum Prices, Edict of, 186
Maximus, Fabius, 824
"May Laws," 848
Mayan civilization, 357
Mayhew, Henry, 726
Mayor of the palace, 218
Mazarin, Cardinal, 462
Mazzini, Giuseppe, 753, 765, 767, 768
Meaux, Bishop Briçonnet of, 366, 409
Mecca, 208
Medes, 59
Medians, 23
Medici, 351, 363, 371
    Cosimo de', 336, 339
    Lorenzo de', 336, 351
    Piero de', 347
Médicis, Catherine de, 410, 411–412, 415, 428, 464
Médicis, Marie de, 460, 461
Medina, 208
Medina-Sidonia, duke of, 433
Mediterranean Sea, 10, 42, 42–43, 355, 470, 988
Megalopolis, 115
Megara, 70–71, 78
Mein Kampf (Hitler), 921, 968
Melanchthon, Philip, 380, 398
Méline Tariff, 809
Melun Act of 1851, 803
Memnon, 96
Memphis, 14, 16

Nantes, 647
  Edict of, 415–417, 458, 466–468, 518
Naples, 110, 273, 331, 334, 341, 347, 349, 515, 557, 697, 769
Napoleon I. *See* Bonaparte, Napoleon
Napoleon III, of France, 749–751, 754, 762, 765, 768–769, 772, 775–776, 800, 822
Napoleonic Code, 661, 666, 706, 817
Napoleonic Concordat, 847
Narbonese Gaul, 142
Narva, battle of, 512, 525
Naseby, battle of, 453
Nassau, 772
Nassau, Louis of, 425
Nasser, Gamal Abdel, 1008, 1038, 1039
Nathan the Wise (Lessing), 605
Nation-states, 763–793
  Crimean War and, 763–765
  France and, 775–780
  German unification, 770–775
  Great Britain and, 788–791
  Habsburg Empire and, 780–783
  Italian unification, 765–770
  Russia and, 783–787
National Assembly, 629–631, 633, 749, 750, 777, 778–779, 1034
National Constituent Assembly, 631, 632, 633–634, 636, 637, 638, 640
National Council of French Women (CNFF), 820
National Front, of France, 1034
National Government, of Great Britain, 644–645
National Guard, of Paris, 632, 776, 777
National Insurance Act of 1911, 826
National Liberation Front, 1018
National Socialist German Workers Party. *See* Nazi Party
National Union of Women's Suffrage Societies, 819
National Wheat Board, 948
Nationalism
  decolonization since World War II and, 1015–1020
  in early nineteenth century, 705–706
  in 1848, 747
  Germany and, 666–667
    Hitler and, 920
  Habsburgs and, 751–752
  in late nineteenth century, 861–862
  Napoleon and, 666
  Romantic movement and, 684–685
Nationalist Society, 768
Nations, battle of the, 670–671
Natural selection, principle of, 843, 844
Natural Theology (Paley), 846
Naturalism, in literature, 852–854
Nausea (Sartre), 1059
Navarino, battle of, 699
Navarre, 331, 384, 502
Navigation Acts, 456
Naxos, 60, 61
Nazi Party, 916, 919–921, 922, 923, 950–956, 982–986, 1037
  in France, 945
  see also Hitler, Adolf
Nazi–Soviet Pact, 975–976, 977, 981, 1061
Nearchus, 102
Nebuchadnezzar II, 24
Necker, Jacques, 626, 627, 631, 632

Nefertiti, 21
Neimöller, Martin, 1062
Nelson, Horatio, 657
Nemea, 44, 57
Neo-Babylonians, 23
Neo-Hittites, 21
Neo-orthodoxy, of twentieth century, 1062
Neolithic Age, 6–7
Neoplatonism, 192–193, 340
Nero, 160, 161, 163, 177, 178
Nerva, 161, 163, 165
Netherlands, 315, 367, 418, 432, 460, 502, 514
  Austria and, 643, 714
  Calvinism in, 424, 425
  Congress of Vienna and, 673
  democracy in, 822
  in eighteenth century, 502, 503
  England and, 314, 432
  France and, 469–470
  independence of, 427–429
  Indonesia and, 1014
  Japan and, 986
  literacy in late nineteenth century and, 839
  Spain and, 412, 413, 423–429
  Sweden and, 440
  World War II and, 978
  see also Holland
Neustria, 218
New Carthage, 124
New Comedy, 88, 89
New Economic Policy (NEP), of Soviet Union, 932–933, 958
New England, 574
New Granada, 571, 701
New Grub Street (Gissing), 840
New Guinea, Japan and, 986
New Harmony, Indiana, 743
New Imperialism, 865–873
New Kingdom, of Ancient Egypt, 16–21
New Lanark, 742–743
New Model Army, 453, 491
New Spain, 358, 362, 570, 702
  see also Mexico
New Testament, 364, 366, 373–374, 392, 846
New Zealand, 903, 915, 1034
Newburn, battle of, 452
Newcomen, Thomas, 551
Newfoundland, 568
Newspapers, in late nineteenth century, 840
Newton, Isaac, Sir, 484–486, 598–599, 604
Newton (Blake), 676
Nicaea, Council of, 193, 194, 204
  Second, 221
Nicene Christians, 214
Nicene Creed, 193, 194, 216, 218–219, 221
Nicholas I, Pope, 216, 230
Nicholas I of Russia, 706–709, 752, 765
Nicholas II, Pope, 240
Nicholas II of Russia, 786, 829, 831, 833, 834, 882, 894
Nicholas V, Pope, 341
Nicholas of Cusa, 328, 367
Nicias, 77
  Peace of, 78
Nicomedia, 184
Niemen River, 663

Nietzsche, Friedrich, 846, 854–855, 1058, 1059
Nigeria, 1014
Nijmegen, Peace of, 467
Nikon, Patriarch, 524
Nile Delta, 36
Nile River, 1, 7, 14
Nimwegen, Peace of, 470
Nine Years' War, 470
Nineteenth Dynasty, of Ancient Egypt, 21
Ninety-five theses, 371, 693
Nineveh, 22, 23, 42, 97
Nixon, Richard, 1012, 1019, 1046
Nkrumah, Kwame, 1014
Noah, 29
Nobiles, 116–117
Nobility, in Russia, 620
Nobles, of Middle Ages, 263
Nogaret, Guillaume de, 321
Nomarchs, 16
Nomes, 16
Nonconformist denominations, in Great Britain, 848
Nonsuch, Treaty of, 432
Norman Conquest, 292, 308
Normandy, 230, 310, 312
  D-Day and, 989–990
  duke of, 292
Normans. *See* Vikings
North, Lord, 586, 589, 591
North America, 568, 569
  American Revolution, 583–592
  French and Indian War, 581–582
  War of the Austrian Succession, 579
  see also Canada; United States
North Atlantic Treaty Organization (NATO), 1004–1005, 1008, 1020, 1021, 1029, 1032, 1036
North Briton, The, 589
North German Confederation, 772–773
North Korea, 1014–1015
North Sea, 439, 877, 888
North Vietnam, 1018, 1019
Northern Ireland, 915, 1027–1028
Northern Society, 706
Northern Star, The, 728
Northumberland, duke of, 395
Norway, 820, 1004
  democracy in, 822
  World War II and, 978
Notre Dame, cathedral school of, 255, 646
Nova Scotia, 568
Novalis (Friedrich von Hardenberg), 680
Novara, battle of, 349, 753
Novum Organum (Bacon), 481, 482
Novus homo, 134
Noyes, Charles, 723
Nubia, 17
Nuclear Test Ban Treaty, 1011, 1032
Nuclear weapons, 1012
  Chernobyl disaster, 1012
  France and, 1034
  Nuclear Test Ban Treaty, 1011, 1032
  Strategic Arms Defense initiative, 1012
  Strategic Arms Limitation Treaty, 1012, 1045
Numantia, 125
Numidia, 134, 135
Nuns and nunneries, 267, 277, 279, 399
Nuremberg, 399, 936, 966
Nuremberg Laws, 954
Nystad, Peace of, 525

Paris Opera, 800
Parker, Matthew, 430
Parlement of Paris, 460, 462, 626, 627, 628
Parlements, of France, 460, 461, 504, 555, 609, 626, 627, 636
Parliament
    Frankfurt, 754–755, 757
    of France, 1034
    of Italy, 926, 927
    of Prussia, 754, 770, 771, 772–773
    see also England; Great Britain
Parliament Act of 1911, 826
Parma, 769
Parmenides of Elea, 84–85
Parnell, Charles Stewart, 791
Parr, Catherine, 394
Parthia and Parthians, 143, 145, 167, 180
Pascal, Blaise, 466, 492–494
Passau, Peace of, 382
Past and Present (Carlyle), 726
Pasternak, Boris, 1041
Pasteur, Louis, 803
Patel, Pierre the Elder, 464
Patriarcha, or the Natural Power of Kings (Filmer), 498
Patricians, 113, 116
Patricius Romanorum, 219
Patroclus, 40
Paul IV, Pope, 387, 389
Paul VI, Pope, 1063–1064
Paul of Russia, 690
Paul of Tarsus, 176, 177, 179
Paulus, Aemilius, 125, 126
Pausanias, 70, 81
Pavia, 219
    battle of, 409
Pazzi, 336
Peace of God, 240, 241
Peace treaties. *See under names of specific treaties, e.g.,* Bretigny, Peace of
Peaceful coexistence, 1010, 1042
Pearl Harbor, 986, 987
Peasants
    in Austria, 616, 618
    in eighteenth century, 539–542
    in France, 651
    in Germany, 374–376
    in Middle Ages, 268–273
    in Prussia, 667
    Revolt of 1381, 317, 325
    see also Serfs and serfdom
Pedro, Dom, 702
Peel, Robert, Sir, 715, 717, 725, 737, 741
Pella, 97
Pelopidas, 81
Peloponnesian League, 52, 70, 77, 81, 82
Peloponnesian War, 69–71, 74, 75–76
Peloponnesian War, The (Thucydides), 73, 78
Peloponnesus, 36, 38, 49, 51, 52, 67, 70
Pencz, Georg, 397
Peninsulares, 359, 360, 573
Pensées [Thoughts] (Pascal), 492
Pentathlon, 48
Pentonville Prison, 739
People's Will, 786
Pepin, son of Charlemagne, 222
Pepin I of Aquitaine, son of Louis the Pious, 228, 229
Pepin I of Austrasia, 218
Pepin II of Austrasia, 218

Pepin III (the Short), 216, 218, 219
Peres, Shimon, 1040
Pergamum, 103, 132, 134
Pericles, 70, 71, 72, 74, 77, 84, 89, 94
Perinthus, 95
Peripatetics, 91
Peripatos, 91
Perpetual Edict, 427
Perrenot, Antoine, 423
Persepolis, 97–98
Perseus, King, 125, 126
Persia, 2, 21, 23, 96, 120, 180, 186
    Greece and, 67, 69, 81
    Muslims in, 208
    Persian Wars, 59–65, 69, 70, 88
Persian Gulf, 9, 22, 99, 1008
Persian Letters, The (Montesquieu), 601
Persian Wars, 59–65, 69, 70, 88
Peru, 359, 360, 361, 570, 701
    Incas of, 357, 358–359
Peruzzi, banking house of, 362
Pétain, Henri Philippe, 892, 978
Peter, Saint, 179–180, 214, 216, 404
    indulgence of, 368
Peter I (the Great) of Russia, 522–526, 541, 555, 560, 709
Peter II of Russia, 619
Peter III of Russia, 555, 580, 619
Peterloo Massacre, 694, 695, 737
Peter's pence, 293
Petit Journal, Le, 840
Petition of Right, 450, 451
Petrarch, Francesco, 332, 337, 338–339
Petrograd, 894, 896, 897, 962
Petroleum, late nineteenth century and, 807–808
Pfefferkorn, 365
Phaestus, 34
Phalanxes, 743
Pharaoh, 14, 21
Pharisees, 176
Phenomenology of Mind, The (Hegel), 686
Philadelphia system, 739
Philip, Archduke, 331
Philip II Augustus, 247, 248, 255, 292, 298, 302
Philip II of Macedon, 82, 91, 93–95, 96
Philip II of Spain, 393, 406, 410, 412, 413, 415, 418–429, 431, 433
Philip III of Spain, 433
Philip IV (the Fair) of France, 244, 308, 320–321
Philip IV of Spain, 433, 469
Philip V of Macedon, 123, 124, 125
Philip V of Spain, 472, 473, 502, 571
Philip VI of Valois, 308, 309
Philip of Anjou, 471, 472
    see also Philip V of Spain
Philip, Archduke, 331
Philip the Good, 312, 314
Philip of Hesse, 376, 377, 380, 381, 382, 424
Philip of Swabia, 298
Philippi, battle of, 144, 147
Philippine Islands
    Japan and, 986
    United States and, 870, 891
Philosophes, 597–598, 599, 600–601, 602, 603, 605, 606, 607, 609–613, 620, 621, 622, 675, 676, 742, 846, 1054
Philosophia Christi (Erasmus), 364

Philosophic Manuscripts of 1844, 1062
Philosophical Dictionary (Voltaire), 601, 605
Philosophy, 2
    in late nineteenth century, 854–855
    scholasticism concerned with, 257–259
Phocians, 94
Phocylides, 42
Phoenicia and Phoenicians, 1, 17, 24, 42–43, 120
    see also Carthage
Photius, Patriarch, 216
Phratries, 40
Phrygia, 54, 127
Physiocrats, of Enlightenment, 607
Pico della Mirandola, Giovanni, 339, 340, 486
Piedmont, 673, 752, 753, 766, 767, 768, 769
Pilgrim's Progress, The (Bunyan), 491
Pilsudski, Josef, 916
Piombo, Sebastiano del, 356
Piraeus, 63, 77
Pisa, 249, 251, 314, 333
    Council of, 326
Pisistratus, 54–55, 56
Pitt, "Diamond," 580–581
Pitt, William, the Elder, 566, 580, 581, 582, 588–589
Pitt, William, the Younger, 591, 643, 662, 716
Pius V, Pope, 432
Pius VII, Pope, 659, 660
Pius IX, Pope, 753, 754, 766, 848
Pius X, Pope, 850
Pizarro, Francisco, 358–359
Place Louis XV, 560
Plague. *See* Black Death
Plague, The (Camus), 1058, 1059
Plains of Abraham, battle of, 581
Planck, Max, 850–851
Plantagenet dynasty, 283
Plantation, in West Indies, 359
Plassey, Battle of, 582
Plataea, battle at, 65
Plato, 51, 57, 87, 90, 91, 92, 104, 339–340
    Florentine Academy and, 339–340
Platonism, 339–340
Plebeians, 113, 116
Plekhanov, Gregory, 831
Pliny the Younger, 169, 178
Plombières, 769
Plotinus, 192, 193, 340
Plutarch, 70, 104, 126, 128, 133, 138
Plymouth Colony, 450
Pnyx, 83
Po River, 120
Po valley, 110, 119, 142
Poaching, 556–557
Podesta, 336
Poincaré, Henri, 850
Poincaré, Raymond, 911
Poison gas, World War I and, 888, 889
Poissy, 411
Poitiers, 284, 310, 311
    battle of, 210, 218
    Edict of, 415
Poitiers, Diane de (Clouet), 410
Poitou, 311
Poland, 512, 519, 910
    agriculture in 1920s and, 939
    Austria and, 616

I-24

Rovere, Giuliano della, cardinal, 349; *see also* Julius II, Pope
Roxane, 100
Royal Air Force (RAF), 980
Royal Dutch, 808
Rubeanus, Crotus, 365
Rubens, Peter Paul, 406
Rubicon River, 142, 144, 146
Rudolf II, 438
Ruhr, 722, 911, 917, 918, 921, 922, 923, 924
Rule for Monasteries (St. Benedict), 211, 212, 226, 239
Rule of Saint Augustine, 267
Rural Solidarity, 1048
Rusk, Dean, 1011
Russell, John, Lord, 788
Russia, 509, 512, 810, 839, 900
  Alexander I, 690–691, 697, 706, 707
  Alexander II, 783–785, 786
  Alexander III, 786, 787
  Bolshevism in, 831–836, 896–898, 908, 925, 929
  Catherine II (the Great), 541, 613, 619–621, 622–623, 643, 690
  Decembrist Revolt of 1825, 707–708
  Duma, 834, 835, 894
  expansion of, 620, 621
  foreign relations
    Concert of Europe, 697
    Congress of Berlin, 873–874
    Congress of Vienna, 674
    Germany, 874–875, 876–878
    Great Britain, 878
    Holy Alliance, 674, 697
    Manchuria, 870
    Middle East, 698–699
    Ottoman Empire, 512
    Poland, 621–622, 709, 785
    Quadruple Alliance, 671, 674
    Spain, 698
    Sweden, 512
    Three Emperors' League, 873, 874, 875
    Triple Entente, 876–878
    Turkey, 699
  French Revolution and, 643
  illiteracy in, in late nineteenth century, 840
  industrialization, 829–831
  Lenin, 744, 831–833, 866, 896–898, 931, 932, 933, 934, 958, 961, 962, 1060
  medieval, 301
  middle classes in, 725
  Nicholas I, 706–709, 752, 765
  nobility in, 555
  Peter I (the Great), 522–526, 541, 555, 560, 709
  political parties
    Constitutional Democratic Party, 831, 834, 835
    Social Democratic Party, 831–832, 834, 835
    Social Revolutionary Party, 831, 834
  religion
    Jews, 799
    Russian Orthodox Church, 524, 709
  Revolution of 1905, 833–835, 878
  Revolution of 1917, 833, 894–898
  revolutionaries in, 785–786
  rise of, 382–383

serfs in, 532–533, 539–542, 706, 708, 723, 784–785
war and warfare
  Crimean War, 690, 763–765
  France, 656, 657, 662, 663, 665, 691
  Great Northern War, 512, 525
  Ottoman Turks, 525, 621
  Russo–Japanese War, 878
  Russo–Turkish War, 873
  Sweden, 525
  World War I, 879–894, 896, 900
  see also Soviet Union
Russian Orthodox Church, 524, 709
Russo–Japanese War, 878
Russo–Turkish War, 873
Ruthenians
  Habsburg Empire and, 782
  World War I and, 903
Rutherford, Ernest, 850
Ryswick, Peace of, 470

S

Saar, 722, 903
Sabbats, 443
Sabines, 109
Sadat, Anwar el-, 1039, 1040
Saeculum, 239, 266
Saguntum, 122
Saigon, 1018, 1019
Saint Bartholomew's Day Massacre, 412–413, 414, 415
Saint Denis, abbey church of, 287
Saint Domingue, 568
Saint Germain-en-Laye, Peace of, 411
Saint Helena, island of, 674
Saint Lawrence River, 568, 569, 581, 584
Saint Michael, Chapel of, 252–253
Saint Paul's Cathedral, 408
Saint Peter's Fields, 695
Saint Peter's indulgence, 368
Saint Petersburg, 525, 526, 558, 560, 707, 770, 786, 831, 833, 834, 894, 962; *see also* Leningrad
Saint-Simon, count of, 742, 744, 745
Saint-Simon, duke of, 470, 505
Saint Stephen, Crown of, 616
Saisset, Bernard, 320
Sakhalin, 996
Sakharov, Andrei, 1044
Saladin, 247
Salamis, 64
  battle of, 88
Salazar, Antonio, 1035
Saleph River, 247
Salic law, 228
Salisbury, Lord, 791
Salisbury cathedral, 290, 291
Sallust, 135, 155
Salutati, Calluccio, 341
Salvian, 203
Samarkand, 98, 99
Samnites, 109, 119–120
Samoa, United States and, 870
Samos, 65, 71
Samson Agonistes (Milton), 491
San Martín, José de, 701
San Stefano, Treaty of, 873, 874
Sand, Karl, 693
Sanitation, in cities of late nineteenth century, 802–804
Sanitation Act of 1848, 741

Sans-culottes, 639–641, 643, 645–646, 647, 649, 650, 651
Sanskrit, 21
Santiago, 701
Saône River, 460
Sappho of Lesbos, 58
Sarajevo, 882
Sardinia, 120, 121, 122, 643, 656, 766, 767
Sardinia-Corsica, 127
Sardis, 61
Sargon, 10
Sartre, Jean-Paul, 1059, 1060, 1061
Sassanians, 180, 186
Satanism, 444
Satires (Horace), 157
Satires (Juvenal), 129, 159
Satyr play, 84
Saudi Arabia, 208
Saul. *See* Paul of Tarsus
Savonarola, Girolamo, 347–348
Savoy, House of, 384, 409
Saxe, Maurice de, 578, 579
Saxons, 203, 218, 220
Saxony, 238, 371, 381, 382, 384, 440, 514, 674, 754
Schacht, Hjalmar, 922
Schamhorst, Gerhard von, 667
Schaufelein, Hans, 397
Scheidemann, Philipp, 904
Scheldt River, 643
Schiller, Friedrich von, 667
Schism, Great, 318, 326–327, 328
Schlegel, August Wilhelm von, 678, 680
Schlegel, Friedrich, 680, 681
Schleicher, Kurt von, 951, 953
Schleiermacher, Friedrich, 683–684
Schleitheim Confession, 379
Schleswig, 772
Schlieffen, Alfred von, 887, 888
Schlieffen Plan, 885, 886, 888
Schmalkaldic Articles, 380
Schmalkaldic League, 380, 381, 382
Schmidt, Helmut, 1030
Scholasticism, 256–260, 337, 398
Schönbrunn, 516
  Peace of, 668
School of Athens, The (Raphael), 306, 344
Schubert, Franz, 675
Schumann, Robert, 1021, 1022
Schuschnigg, Kurt von, 916, 972
Schutzmannschaft, 737
Schutzstaffel (SS), 953
Schwarzenberg, Felix, Prince, 752
Schwenckfeld, Caspar, 380
Schwenckfeldian Church, 380
Science, 2
  Christianity and, 846
  in mid-nineteenth century, 842–845
  Revolution, 475–486
  in twentieth century, 850–852
Science of Mechanics, The (Mach), 850
Scientific Revolution, 475–486
Scipio Aemilianus, 125, 127, 128
Scipio, Publius Cornelius, 123–124
Scotland, 284, 320
  Bruces of, 308
  England and, 451–452, 453
  Mary Stuart, Queen of Scots, and, 410, 431, 449
Scratch plow, 226
Screwtape Letters, The (Lewis), 1063

Scutage, 233
Scythians, 99
Sea Beggars, 425–426, 432
Second Act of Uniformity, 395
Second Athenian Confederation, 82
Second Balkan War, 880, 882
Second Coalition, 656, 657
Second Continental Congress, 586–587
Second Crusade, 246–247, 249
Second Empire, 776, 800
Second Estate
    of the Estates General, 628
    of the National Assembly, 631
Second Indochina War, 1019
Second Industrial Revolution, 805–808,
    810, 811, 844
Second Intermediate Period, of Ancient
    Egypt, 17
Second Isaiah, 26
Second Messenian War, 48
Second Republic, in France, 747–750
Second Treatise of Government (Locke),
    460
Second Triumvirate, 144, 148
Second World War. See World War II
Secondat, Charles Louis de. See Mon-
    tesquieu, baron de
Secret ballot, in Great Britain, 510
Secular clergy, in Middle Ages, 266–267
Security Council, of United Nations, 1001
Sedan, battle of, 775, 776
Seine River, 460, 800
Sejm, 513–514
Sekhmet, 28
Selassie, Haile, 969
Seleucid kingdom, 124
Seleucus I, 100
Seljuk Turks, 209, 247
Semicircular arch, of Roman architecture,
    169–170
Semites, 9–10
Semitic language, 22
Senate
    of ancient Rome, 111–112, 113, 114,
        120, 127, 132, 134, 135, 139, 140,
        141, 142, 143–144, 144, 151, 152,
        154, 160, 161, 182, 184
    of France, 820
    of Italy, 769
Seneca, Lucius Annaeus, 171, 173, 384
Sentences (Lombard), 369, 398
Sentinum, 119
September Massacres of 1792, 639, 647
Septimius Severus, 181, 182
Serbia, 873, 874, 879, 880, 882, 883, 900
    See also Balkans
Serbo-Croatia, Habsburg Empire and, 782
Serbs, 752, 903, 916
    See also Yugoslavia
Serfs and serfdom, 317
    in Austria, 616, 618, 751
    emancipation of, 723
    in Middle Ages, 210, 226–227, 270, 275
    in Prussia, 667
    in Russia, 532–533, 539–542, 706, 708,
        784–785
Sergents, 737
Sermon on the Mount, 175
Sertorius, 138
Servetus, Michael, 380, 386, 406
Servile manors, 270
Settlement, Act of, 460, 506

Sevastopol, battle of, 765
Seven Weeks' War, 772
Seven Years' War, 580–583, 625
Seville, 418, 573
Sewer systems, in late nineteenth century,
    803
Sextus, son of Pompey, 145
Seymour, Edward, 395
Seymour, Jane, 394
Sforza family, 336
Shaftesbury, earl of, 457
Shakespeare, William, 332, 488–490, 680
"Shaking off of burdens," 53
Shaw, George Bernard, 824, 853
Shcharansky, Anatoly, 1044
Sheffield, 728
Shelley, Mary, 818
Shelley, Percy Bysshe, 495, 678, 679–680,
    694, 698
Ship money, 451
Siberia, 559, 708, 787, 831, 870, 934, 982
Sic et Non (Abelard), 256
Sicily, 35, 42, 91, 120, 122, 123, 145, 216,
    240, 297, 314, 319, 348, 769
    ancient Rome and, 127
    Hohenstaufens and, 298
    World War II and, 987–988
Sieyès, Abbé, 628, 657
Sigismund, Emperor, 325, 326
Signoria, 336
Silesia, 514, 522, 576, 577, 579, 580, 582,
    614, 643, 903
Simon, Jules, 804
Simonides of Cos, 58
Simons, Menno, 380
Sinai Peninsula, 1038–1039
Sinn Fein Party, 914–915
Sistine Chapel, 344–345, 346
Sitte, Camillo, 801
Six Acts, 695, 715
Six Articles of 1539, 394, 395
Six Days' War, 1038, 1039
Six Points, 728, 729
Sixtus IV, Pope, 370
Sixtus V, Pope, 433
Sixty-Seven Articles, 378
Skepticism, 101
Slavery
    from Africa, 359
    in ancient Greece, 40
    forced labor, 359–362
    in Mesopotamia, 12–13
    in the New World, 362
    in the West Indies, 574
Slavonia, 512
Slavs, 752, 879
    Hitler and, 982–983
    World War I and, 892, 903
    see also Balkans
Slepak, Vladimir, 1044
Slovaks, 892, 903, 916, 973
Slovenes, 903, 916
    see also Yugoslavia
Slovenia, 879
Smallpox, inoculations against, 598
Smith, Adam, 602, 607–609, 704, 739
Smith, W. H., 797
Smith, William Robertson, 846
Snow, C. P., 852
Soares, Mario, 1035
Social Contract, The (Rousseau), 611, 612,
    677

Social Darwinism, 845
Social Democratic Federation, 824
Social Democratic Party (SDP)
    of Austria, 916
    of Germany, 822, 823, 826–829, 831,
        885, 889, 904, 917, 923, 949–950,
        952, 1029–1030
    of Great Britain, 1026
    of Russia, 831–832, 834, 894, 896
Social Revolutionary Party, of Russia, 831,
    834, 894, 897
Socialism, 742–744, 795, 822
    Fabianism, 824–825
    in France, 826
    in Germany, 822, 823, 826–829, 920–
        921
    Hitler and Nazis and, 920–921
    in Italy, 926
    see also Communism; Marxism; Russia;
        Social Democratic Party entries; So-
        viet Union
Socialist Party, 826
    in France, 946, 947–949, 1033, 1034
    in Italy, 926
    in Portugal, 1035
Society of Jesus. See Jesuits
Socinianism, 380
Sociology, Comte and, 844
Socrates, 87, 89, 90, 91, 102, 854
Sodom, 29
Solemn League and Covenant, 453
Solferino, battle of, 769
Solidarity Committee, 1048, 1049, 1050
Solomon, King, 24, 25
Solomon Islands, 986, 991
Solon, 53–54, 55, 56
Solvay process, 807
Solzhenitsyn, Aleksandr, 1041, 1044
Somaschi, 387
Somme River, 892
Songs of Experience (Blake), 678
Songs of Innocence (Blake), 678
"Sonnet: England in 1819," (Shelley),
    694, 695
Sophia of Russia, 522
Sophists, 85, 87
Sophocles, 88
Sophrosynē, 57
Soranus of Ephesus, 281
Sorbon, Robert de, 256
Sorbonne, 256, 466, 1056
Sorel, Georges, 826, 859
Sorrows of Young Werther, The (Goethe),
    681
Soubirous, Bernadette, 847
South Africa, 877, 878
South America. See Latin America
South Korea, 1015
South Sea Company, 507
South Tyrol, 891
South Vietnam, 1018, 1019
Southeast Asia. See Indochina; Vietnam
Southeast Asia Treaty Organization
    (SEATO), 1018
Southern Society, 706
Southwest Africa, 868
Soviet Union, 902
    Brezhnev and after, 1044–1045
    collectivization, 958–959
    Comintern, 930, 931
    Communist Party of, 930, 931, 933, 934
    Eastern Europe and, 978, 1046–1050

World War II, 915
  background, 967–976
  Holocaust, 982–986
  Indochina and, 1016
  peace settlement, 995–997
  territorial changes, 999, 1001
  war, course of, 976–995
Worms, 242
  Concordat of, 243, 245
  Diet of, 332, 333
  Edict of, 374
Wren, Christopher, 406, 408, 559
Writing, 1, 7
  ancient Greek, 42
  cuneiform, 11
  development of, 7, 8
  hieroglyphics, 15–16
Württemberg, 693, 754
Wycliffe, John, 324–325, 392
Wyvil, Christopher, 591

Xenophanes of Colophon, 29
Xenophon, 49, 82, 90

Xerxes, 63, 84, 88
X rays, 850, 851

Yalta, 996, 997
Yellow River, 7
Yishuv, 1037, 1038
Yom Kippur War, 1039
York, duke of, 332
York, House of, 332
Yorkshire, 591
Yorkshire Association Movement, 591
Yorktown, battle of, 587
Young, Arthur, 544
Young, Owen D., 925
Young Italy Society, 765
Young plan, 925, 939
Young Turks, 879
Yugoslavia, 1001
  France and, 910
  Soviet Union and, 1046
  World War I and, 903, 916
  World War II and, 980

see also Balkans
Yugoslavs, 879

Zacatecas, 418
Zacharias, Pope, 219
Zaire, 1014
Zama, battle of, 124
Zara, 250
Zasulich, Vera, 786
Zeeland, 425, 426, 428
Zemstvos, 831
Zeno of Citium, 84–85, 102, 203
Zeus, 57, 89–90
Ziggurat, 11
Zionist movement, 861, 900, 1037
Ziska, John, 325
Zola, Émile, 780, 845, 852, 853
Zollverein, 740, 770
Zoroastrianism, 190
Zurich, 379
  Protestant Reformation in, 376
Zurich Disputation, 378
Zwingli, Ulrich, 376–378, 379, 395, 398
Zwolle, 367